PLUNKETT'S ENTERTAINMENT, MOVIE, PUBLISHING & MEDIA INDUSTRY ALMANAC 2019

The only comprehensive guide to the entertainment & media industry

Jack W. Plunkett

Published by:
Plunkett Research®, Ltd., Houston, Texas
www.plunkettresearch.com

PLUNKETT'S ENTERTAINMENT, MOVIE, PUBLISHING & MEDIA INDUSTRY ALMANAC 2019

Editor and Publisher:
Jack W. Plunkett

Executive Editor and Database Manager:
Martha Burgher Plunkett

Senior Editor and Researchers:
Isaac Snider
Shuang Zhou

Editors, Researchers and Assistants:
Michael Cappelli
Annie Paynter
Anoosh Saidi
Jorden Smith
Gina Sprenkel

Information Technology Manager:
Rebeca Tijiboy

Special Thanks to:
American Gaming Association
Association of America Publishers
CTIA, The Wireless Association
International Federation of the Phonographic Industries (IFPI)
International Telecommunications Union
InternetWorldStats.com
Magna Global
National Association of Theatre Owners
Nielsen Media Research
Newspaper Association of America
NPD Group
PriceWaterhouseCoopers
Publishers Information Bureau
U.S. Bureau of Labor Statistics
U.S. Census Bureau
U.S. Federal Communications Commission (FCC)
Veronis Suhler Stevenson

Plunkett Research®, Ltd.
P. O. Drawer 541737, Houston, Texas 77254 USA
Phone: 713.932.0000   Fax: 713.932.7080
www.plunkettresearch.com

Copyright © 2019, Plunkett Research®, Ltd. All rights reserved. Except as provided for below, you may not copy, resell, reproduce, distribute, republish, download, display, post, or transmit any portion of this book in any form or by any means, including, but not limited to, electronic, mechanical, photocopying, recording, or otherwise, without the express prior written permission of Plunkett Research, Ltd. Additional copyrights are held by other content providers, including, in certain cases, Morningstar, Inc. The information contained herein is proprietary to its owners and it is not warranted to be accurate, complete or timely. Neither Plunkett Research, Ltd. nor its content providers are responsible for any damages or losses arising from any use of this information. Market and industry statistics, company revenues, profits and other details may be estimates. Financial information, company plans or status, and other data can change quickly and may vary from those stated here. **Past performance is no guarantee of future results**.

Plunkett Research®, Ltd.
P. O. Drawer 541737
Houston, Texas 77254-1737
Phone: 713.932.0000, Fax: 713.932.7080 www.plunkettresearch.com

ISBN13 # 978-1-62831-481-6 (eBook Edition # 978-1-62831-805-0)

Limited Warranty and Terms of Use:

Users' publications in static electronic format containing any portion of the content of this book (and/or the content of any related Plunkett Research, Ltd. online service to which you are granted access, hereinafter collectively referred to as the "Data") or Derived Data (that is, a set of data that is a derivation made by a User from the Data, resulting from the applications of formulas, analytics or any other method) may be resold by the User only for the purpose of providing third-party analysis within an established research platform under the following conditions: (However, Users may not extract or integrate any portion of the Data or Derived Data for any other purpose.)

a) Users may utilize the Data only as described herein. b) User may not export more than an insubstantial portion of the Data or Derived Data, c) Any Data exported by the User may only be distributed if the following conditions are met:

i) Data must be incorporated in added-value reports or presentations, either of which are part of the regular services offered by the User and not as stand-alone products.
ii) Data may not be used as part of a general mailing or included in external websites or other mass communication vehicles or formats, including, but not limited to, advertisements.
iii) Except as provided herein, Data may not be resold by User.

"Insubstantial Portions" shall mean an amount of the Data that (1) has no independent commercial value, (2) could not be used by User, its clients, Authorized Users and/or its agents as a substitute for the Data or any part of it, (3) is not separately marketed by the User, an affiliate of the User or any third-party source (either alone or with other data), and (4) is not retrieved by User, its clients, Authorized Users and/or its Agents via regularly scheduled, systematic batch jobs.

LIMITED WARRANTY; DISCLAIMER OF LIABILITY: While Plunkett Research, Ltd. ("PRL") has made an effort to obtain the Data from sources deemed reliable, PRL makes no warranties, expressed or implied, regarding the Data contained herein. This book and its Data are provided to the End-User "AS IS" without warranty of any kind. No oral or written information or advice given by PRL, its employees, distributors or representatives will create a warranty or in any way increase the scope of this Limited Warranty, and the Customer or End-User may not rely on any such information or advice. Customer Remedies: PRL's entire liability and your exclusive remedy shall be, at PRL's sole discretion, either (a) return of the price paid, if any, or (b) repair or replacement of a book that does not meet PRL's Limited Warranty and that is returned to PRL with sufficient evidence of or receipt for your original purchase.

NO OTHER WARRANTIES: TO THE MAXIMUM EXTENT PERMITTED BY APPLICABLE LAW, PRL AND ITS DISTRIBUTORS DISCLAIM ALL OTHER WARRANTIES AND CONDITIONS, EITHER EXPRESSED OR IMPLIED, INCLUDING, BUT NOT LIMITED TO, IMPLIED WARRANTIES OR CONDITIONS OF MERCHANTABILITY, FITNESS FOR A PARTICULAR PURPOSE, TITLE AND NON-INFRINGEMENT WITH REGARD TO THE BOOK AND ITS DATA, AND THE PROVISION OF OR FAILURE TO PROVIDE SUPPORT SERVICES. LIMITATION OF LIABILITY: TO THE MAXIMUM EXTENT PERMITTED BY APPLICABLE LAW, IN NO EVENT SHALL PRL BE LIABLE FOR ANY SPECIAL, INCIDENTAL OR CONSEQUENTIAL DAMAGES WHATSOEVER (INCLUDING, WITHOUT LIMITATION, DAMAGES FOR LOSS OF BUSINESS PROFITS, BUSINESS INTERRUPTION, ABILITY TO OBTAIN OR RETAIN EMPLOYMENT OR REMUNERATION, ABILITY TO PROFITABLY MAKE AN INVESTMENT, OR ANY OTHER PECUNIARY LOSS) ARISING OUT OF THE USE OF, OR RELIANCE UPON, THE BOOK OR DATA, OR THE INABILITY TO USE THIS DATA OR THE FAILURE OF PRL TO PROVIDE SUPPORT SERVICES, EVEN IF PRL HAS BEEN ADVISED OF THE POSSIBILITY OF SUCH DAMAGES. IN ANY CASE, PRL'S ENTIRE LIABILITY SHALL BE LIMITED TO THE AMOUNT ACTUALLY PAID BY YOU FOR THE BOOK.

PLUNKETT'S ENTERTAINMENT, MOVIE, PUBLISHING & MEDIA INDUSTRY ALMANAC 2019

CONTENTS

Introduction	1
How to Use This Book	3
Chapter 1: Major Trends Affecting the Entertainment, Movie, Publishing & Media Industry	7
1) Introduction to the Entertainment, Movie, Publishing & Media Industry	7
2) TVs are Internet Ready/Game Consoles and Set Top Accessories Like Roku and Chromecast Stream Content	10
3) DVR Market Evolves/Time-Shifting Hurts Advertisers	11
4) Apple's iTunes Set the Standard in the Music Industry, but Digital Sales Slow	12
5) Pandora and Spotify Lead in Streaming Music Via Internet Radio but Face Challenge from Apple Music/SiriusXM Tops 33 Million Subscribers	12
6) New Video Game Console Technologies and Features Boost Sales	14
7) Cable and Satellite TV Struggle with Cord-Cutting/Cheaper Streaming Options Proliferate, Including Netflix	16
8) Telecom Companies, Including AT&T and Verizon, Compete Fiercely Against Cable in the TV, Internet and Telephone Market	18
9) Television Ads Evolve to Face New Challenges, Formats and Online Competitors	19
10) Movie Attendance Rises/Film Companies Innovate with Digital Projection and Enhanced Cinema Experiences	20
11) China and India Expand Film and TV Production Activity	22
12) Global Internet Market Tops 4.2 Billion Users/Ultrafast Broadband Expands, both Fixed and Wireless	23
13) Entertainment-Based Retailing, including Power Towns	23
14) Newspapers and Magazines Rely on Digital Editions and Apps	24
15) Virtual Worlds Provide Revenue for Games Publishers	25
16) Virtual Reality/Augmented Reality and 3-D Games Create Opportunities for the Tech Industry/Immersion Games to Grow	26
17) Global Mobile Apps Revenues Hit $92.1 Billion Yearly	27
18) Embedded LTE Wi-Fi and Onboard Apps Incorporated by Auto Makers in New Car Infotainment Systems	28
19) Global Media Giants Acquire both Content and Distribution	29
20) Digital Assistants Include Amazon's Echo and Google's Home/Alexa and Similar Software Power Third-Party Developers	30
21) Overview of the Electronic Games Industry	31
22) The Future of Entertainment, Media and Publishing: Disruption, Portability and Consumer Control	31
Chapter 2: Entertainment, Movie, Publishing & Media Industry Statistics	33
Entertainment, Movie, Publishing & Media Industry Statistics and Market Size Overview	34

Continued on next page

Continued from previous page

Estimated U.S. Information & Entertainment Sector Revenues by NAICS Code: 2013-2018	**35**
Estimated U.S. Arts, Entertainment & Recreation Services Sector Revenues by NAICS Code: 2013-2018	**36**
Personal Consumption Expenditures for Recreation, U.S.: Selected Years, 2010-2017	**37**
Newspaper Publishers: Estimated Sources of Revenue & Expenses, U.S.: 2013-2018	**38**
Periodical Publishers: Estimated Sources of Revenue & Expenses, U.S.: 2013-2018	**39**
Book Publishers: Estimated Sources of Revenue, Inventories & Expenses, U.S.: 2013-2018	**40**
Motion Picture & Video Industries: Estimated Sources of Revenue, U.S.: 2013-2018	**41**
Sound Recording Industries: Estimated Sources of Revenue, U.S.: 2013-2018	**42**
Radio Networks & Radio Stations: Estimated Sources of Revenue & Expenses, U.S.: 2013-2018	**43**
Television Broadcasting: Estimated Sources of Revenue & Expenses, U.S.: 2013-2018	**44**
Cable & Other Subscription Programming: Estimated Sources of Revenue & Expenses, U.S.: 2013-2018	**45**
Internet Publishing & Broadcasting & Web Search Portals: Estimated Revenue & Expenses, U.S.: 2013-2018	**46**
Number of Business & Residential High Speed Internet Lines, U.S.: 2013-2018	**47**
Estimated Export Revenue for Information Sector Firms, U.S.: 2013-2017	**48**
Employment & Earnings in Selected Entertainment & Media Occupations, U.S.: May 2017	**49**
Employment in Selected Information & Entertainment Industries, U.S.: 2013-October 2018	**50**
Chapter 3: **Important Entertainment, Movie, Publishing & Media Industry Contacts**	**51**
(Addresses, Phone Numbers and Internet Sites)	
Chapter 4: THE ENTERTAINMENT 400:	
Who They Are and How They Were Chosen	**93**
Index of Companies Within Industry Groups	**94**
Alphabetical Index	**105**
Index of Headquarters Location by U.S. State	**108**
Index of Non-U.S. Headquarters Location by Country	**112**
Individual Data Profiles on Each of THE ENTERTAINMENT 400	**115**
Additional Indexes	
Index of Hot Spots for Advancement for Women/Minorities	**520**
Index by Subsidiaries, Brand Names and Selected Affiliations	**522**
A Short Entertainment, Movie, Publishing & Media Industry Glossary	**547**

INTRODUCTION

PLUNKETT'S ENTERTAINMENT, MOVIE, PUBLISHING & MEDIA INDUSTRY ALMANAC is designed to be used as a general source for researchers of all types.

The data and areas of interest covered are intentionally broad, ranging from the most important trends in the entertainment and media industry, to emerging technologies, to an in-depth look at the major firms (which we call THE ENTERTAINMENT 400) within the many industry sectors that make up the entertainment and media industry, such as book, newspaper and magazine publishing; electronic games; gambling and casinos; bookstores and retailers of entertainment and media products; radio; television, including broadcast, satellite and cable; movie production and distribution; movie theaters, and much more, including related services, hardware and software.

This reference book is designed to be a general source for researchers. It is especially intended to assist with market research, strategic planning, employment searches, contact or prospect list creation and financial research, and as a data resource for executives and students of all types.

PLUNKETT'S ENTERTAINMENT, MOVIE, PUBLISHING & MEDIA INDUSTRY ALMANAC takes a rounded approach for the general reader. This book presents a complete overview of the entertainment and media field (see "How To Use This Book"). For example, entertainment statistics are provided in exacting detail, along with easy-to-use charts and tables on all facets of the industry in general.

THE ENTERTAINMENT 400 is our unique grouping of the biggest, most successful corporations in all segments of the entertainment and media industry. Tens of thousands of pieces of information, gathered from a wide variety of sources, have been researched and are presented in a unique form that can be easily understood. This section includes thorough indexes to THE ENTERTAINMENT 400, by geography, industry, sales, brand names, subsidiary names and many other topics. (See Chapter 4.)

Especially helpful is the way in which PLUNKETT'S ENTERTAINMENT, MOVIE, PUBLISHING & MEDIA INDUSTRY ALMANAC enables readers who have no business background to readily compare the financial records and growth plans of media and entertainment companies and major industry groups. You'll see the mid-term financial record of each firm, along with the impact of earnings, sales and strategic plans on each company's potential to fuel growth, to serve new markets and to provide investment and employment opportunities.

No other source provides this book's easy-to-understand comparisons of growth, expenditures, technologies, corporations and many other items of great importance to people of all types who may be studying this, one of the largest and most complex industries in the world today.

By scanning the data groups and the unique indexes, you can find the best information to fit your personal research needs. The major companies in entertainment and media are profiled and then ranked using several different groups of specific criteria. Which firms are the biggest employers? Which companies earn the most profits? These things and much more are easy to find.

In addition to individual company profiles, an overview of entertainment and media technology and its trends is provided. This book's job is to help you sort through easy-to-understand summaries of today's trends in a quick and effective manner.

Whatever your purpose for researching the entertainment and media field, you'll find this book to be a valuable guide. Nonetheless, as is true with all resources, this volume has limitations that the reader should be aware of:

- Financial data and other corporate information can change quickly. A book of this type can be no more current than the data that was available as of the time of editing. Consequently, the financial picture, management and ownership of the firm(s) you are studying may have changed since the date of this book. For example, this almanac includes the most up-to-date sales figures and profits available to the editors as of late-2018. That means that we have typically used corporate financial data as of the end of 2017.

- Corporate mergers, acquisitions and downsizing are occurring at a very rapid rate. Such events may have created significant change, subsequent to the publishing of this book, within a company you are studying.

- Some of the companies in THE ENTERTAINMENT 400 are so large in scope and in variety of business endeavors conducted within a parent organization, that we have been unable to completely list all subsidiaries, affiliations, divisions and activities within a firm's corporate structure.

- This volume is intended to be a general guide to a vast industry. That means that researchers should look to this book for an overview and, when conducting in-depth research, should contact the specific corporations or industry associations in question for the very latest changes and data. Where possible, we have listed contact names, toll-free telephone numbers and Internet site addresses for the companies, government agencies and industry associations involved so that the reader may get further details without unnecessary delay.

- Tables of industry data and statistics used in this book include the latest numbers available at the time of printing, generally through the end of 2017. In a few cases, the only complete data available was for earlier years.

- We have used exhaustive efforts to locate and fairly present accurate and complete data. However, when using this book or any other source for business and industry information, the reader should use caution and diligence by conducting further research where it seems appropriate. We wish you success in your endeavors, and we trust that your experience with this book will be both satisfactory and productive.

Jack W. Plunkett
Houston, Texas
January 2019

HOW TO USE THIS BOOK

The two primary sections of this book are devoted first to the entertainment industry as a whole and then to the "Individual Data Listings" for THE ENTERTAINMENT 400. If time permits, you should begin your research in the front chapters of this book. Also, you will find lengthy indexes in Chapter 4 and in the back of the book.

> **Video Tip**
> For our brief video introduction to the Entertainment industry, see
> www.plunkettresearch.com/video/entertainment.

THE ENTERTAINMENT, MOVIE, PUBLISHING & MEDIA INDUSTRY

Chapter 1: Major Trends Affecting the Entertainment, Movie, Publishing & Media Industry. This chapter presents an encapsulated view of the major trends that are creating rapid changes in the entertainment, movie, publishing and media industry today.

Chapter 2: Entertainment, Movie, Publishing & Media Industry Statistics. This chapter presents in-depth statistics ranging from an industry overview to of markets, subsidiaries and much more.

Chapter 3: Important Entertainment, Movie, Publishing & Media Industry Contacts – Addresses, Telephone Numbers and Internet Sites. This chapter covers contacts for important government agencies, entertainment and media organizations and trade groups. Included are numerous important Internet sites.

THE ENTERTAINMENT 400

Chapter 4: THE ENTERTAINMENT 400: Who They Are and How They Were Chosen. The companies compared in this book were carefully selected from the entertainment and media industry, largely in the United States. Many of the firms are based outside the U.S. For a complete description, see THE ENTERTAINMENT 400 indexes in this chapter.

Individual Data Listings:
Look at one of the companies in THE ENTERTAINMENT 400's Individual Data Listings. You'll find the following information fields:

Company Name:
The company profiles are in alphabetical order by company name. If you don't find the company you are seeking, it may be a subsidiary or division of one of the firms covered in this book. Try looking it up in the Index by Subsidiaries, Brand Names and Selected Affiliations in the back of the book.

Industry Code:
Industry Group Code: An NAIC code used to group companies within like segments.

Types of Business:
A listing of the primary types of business specialties conducted by the firm.

Brands/Divisions/Affiliations:
Major brand names, operating divisions or subsidiaries of the firm, as well as major corporate affiliations—such as another firm that owns a significant portion of the company's stock. A complete Index by Subsidiaries, Brand Names and Selected Affiliations is in the back of the book.

Contacts:
The names and titles up to 27 top officers of the company are listed, including human resources contacts.

Growth Plans/ Special Features:
Listed here are observations regarding the firm's strategy, hiring plans, plans for growth and product development, along with general information regarding a company's business and prospects.

Financial Data:
Revenue (2017 or the latest fiscal year available to the editors, plus up to five previous years): This figure represents consolidated worldwide sales from all operations. These numbers may be estimates.

R&D Expense (2017 or the latest fiscal year available to the editors, plus up to five previous years): This figure represents expenses associated with the research and development of a company's goods or services. These numbers may be estimates.

Operating Income (2017 or the latest fiscal year available to the editors, plus up to five previous years): This figure represents the amount of profit realized from annual operations after deducting operating expenses including costs of goods sold, wages and depreciation. These numbers may be estimates.

Operating Margin % (2017 or the latest fiscal year available to the editors, plus up to five previous years): This figure is a ratio derived by dividing operating income by net revenues. It is a measurement of a firm's pricing strategy and operating efficiency. These numbers may be estimates.

SGA Expense (2017 or the latest fiscal year available to the editors, plus up to five previous years): This figure represents the sum of selling, general and administrative expenses of a company, including costs such as warranty, advertising, interest, personnel, utilities, office space rent, etc. These numbers may be estimates.

Net Income (2017 or the latest fiscal year available to the editors, plus up to five previous years): This figure represents consolidated, after-tax net profit from all operations. These numbers may be estimates.

Operating Cash Flow (2017 or the latest fiscal year available to the editors, plus up to five previous years): This figure is a measure of the amount of cash generated by a firm's normal business operations. It is calculated as net income before depreciation and after income taxes, adjusted for working capital. It is a prime indicator of a company's ability to generate enough cash to pay its bills. These numbers may be estimates.

Capital Expenditure (2017 or the latest fiscal year available to the editors, plus up to five previous years): This figure represents funds used for investment in or improvement of physical assets such as offices, equipment or factories and the purchase or creation of new facilities and/or equipment. These numbers may be estimates.

EBITDA (2017 or the latest fiscal year available to the editors, plus up to five previous years): This figure is an acronym for earnings before interest, taxes, depreciation and amortization. It represents a company's financial performance calculated as revenue minus expenses (excluding taxes, depreciation and interest), and is a prime indicator of profitability. These numbers may be estimates.

Return on Assets % (2017 or the latest fiscal year available to the editors, plus up to five previous years): This figure is an indicator of the profitability of a company relative to its total assets. It is calculated by dividing annual net earnings by total assets. These numbers may be estimates.

Return on Equity % (2017 or the latest fiscal year available to the editors, plus up to five previous years): This figure is a measurement of net income as a percentage of shareholders' equity. It is also called the rate of return on the ownership interest. It is a vital indicator of the quality of a company's operations. These numbers may be estimates.

Debt to Equity (2017 or the latest fiscal year available to the editors, plus up to five previous years): A ratio of the company's long-term debt to its shareholders' equity. This is an indicator of the overall financial leverage of the firm. These numbers may be estimates.

Address:

Address: The firm's full headquarters address, the headquarters telephone, plus toll-free and fax numbers where available. Also provided is the internet address.

Stock Ticker, Exchange: When available, the unique stock market symbol used to identify this firm's common stock for trading and tracking purposes is indicated. Where appropriate, this field may contain "private" or "subsidiary" rather than a ticker symbol. If the firm is a publicly-held company headquartered outside of the U.S., its international ticker and exchange are given.

Total Number of Employees: The approximate total number of employees, worldwide, as of the end of 2017 (or the latest data available to the editors).

Parent Company: If the firm is a subsidiary, its parent company is listed.

Salaries/Bonuses:

(The following descriptions generally apply to U.S. employers only.)

Highest Executive Salary: The highest executive salary paid, typically a 2017 amount (or the latest year available to the editors) and typically paid to the Chief Executive Officer.

Highest Executive Bonus: The apparent bonus, if any, paid to the above person.

Second Highest Executive Salary: The next-highest executive salary paid, typically a 2017 amount (or the latest year available to the editors) and typically paid to the President or Chief Operating Officer.

Second Highest Executive Bonus: The apparent bonus, if any, paid to the above person.

Other Thoughts:

Estimated Female Officers or Directors: It is difficult to obtain this information on an exact basis, and employers generally do not disclose the data in a public way. However, we have indicated what our best efforts reveal to be the apparent number of women who either are in the posts of corporate officers or sit on the board of directors. There is a wide variance from company to company.

Hot Spot for Advancement for Women/Minorities: A "Y" in appropriate fields indicates "Yes." These are firms that appear either to have posted a substantial number of women and/or minorities to high posts or that appear to have a good record of going out of their way to recruit, train, promote and retain women or minorities. (See the Index of Hot Spots For Women and Minorities in the back of the book.) This information may change frequently and can be difficult to obtain and verify. Consequently, the reader should use caution and conduct further investigation where appropriate.

Glossary: A short list of entertainment and media industry terms.

Chapter 1

MAJOR TRENDS AFFECTING THE ENTERTAINMENT, MOVIE, PUBLISHING & MEDIA INDUSTRY

Major Trends Affecting the Entertainment, Movie, Publishing & Media Industry:

1) Introduction to the Entertainment, Movie, Publishing & Media Industry
2) TVs are Internet Ready/Game Consoles and Set Top Accessories Like Roku and Chromecast Stream Content
3) DVR Market Evolves/Time-Shifting Hurts Advertisers
4) Apple's iTunes Set the Standard in the Music Industry, but Digital Sales Slow
5) Pandora and Spotify Lead in Streaming Music Via Internet Radio but Face Challenge from Apple Music/SiriusXM Tops 33 Million Subscribers
6) New Video Game Console Technologies and Features Boost Sales
7) Cable and Satellite TV Struggle with Cord-Cutting/Cheaper Streaming Options Proliferate, Including Netflix
8) Telecom Companies, Including AT&T and Verizon, Compete Fiercely Against Cable in the TV, Internet and Telephone Market
9) Television Ads Evolve to Face New Challenges, Formats and Online Competitors
10) Movie Attendance Rises/Film Companies Innovate with Digital Projection and Enhanced Cinema Experiences
11) China and India Expand Film and TV Production Activity
12) Global Internet Market Tops 4.2 Billion Users/Ultrafast Broadband Expands, both Fixed and Wireless
13) Entertainment-Based Retailing, including Power Towns
14) Newspapers and Magazines Rely on Digital Editions and Apps
15) Virtual Worlds Provide Revenue for Games Publishers
16) Virtual Reality/Augmented Reality and 3-D Games Create Opportunities in the Tech Industry/Immersion Games to Grow
17) Global Mobile Apps Revenues Hit $92.1 Billion Yearly
18) Embedded LTE Wi-Fi and Onboard Apps Incorporated by Auto Makers in New Car Infotainment Systems
19) Global Media Giants Acquire both Content and Distribution
20) Digital Assistants Include Amazon's Echo and Google's Home/Alexa and Similar Software Power Third-Party Developers
21) Overview of the Electronic Games Industry
22) The Future of Entertainment, Media and Publishing: Disruption, Portability and Consumer Control

1) Introduction to the Entertainment, Movie, Publishing & Media Industry

Video Tip
For our brief video introduction to the Entertainment industry, see www.plunkettresearch.com/video/entertainment.

With astonishing speed, entertainment, media and publishing have digitized, evolving into a highly dynamic industry, interconnected by global digital platforms in a manner that few people could even have conceived of a few decades ago. We've gone from static and flat (that is: books and media printed on paper, music on CDs, movies rented on DVD at the local Blockbuster and TV networks that forced the viewer to be in front of the screen at a given hour in order to watch a given show) to always-on, user-controlled, portable and always-with-you. Now, the industry is driven by the needs, habits and desires of individual consumers: delivering content that is accessible as customized digital streams; serving up news, entertainment, movies, ebooks and music on-demand. If you don't know what you want to watch, listen to or read, the best digital platforms push suggestions to you.

Entertainment and media, as a broad sector, are somewhat unique in that revenues are generated by multiple methods. Primarily, these methods are: 1) outright purchase, such as the download of an ebook or the purchase of a magazine or a movie theater ticket; 2) subscription, such as cable TV fees, Netflix fees or subscriptions to magazines or to music on Pandora; and 3) advertising fees. Many media rely on a combination of subscription fees plus advertising revenues. For example, most magazines have a cover price, but they also contain paid advertising. Elsewhere, subscribers pay for cable TV service, but then are subjected to seemingly endless commercials on cable channels.

Advertising revenues remain of vast importance to this industry, and the internet has created a multitude of new outlets for such advertising. Global advertising media revenues were estimated to be $551 billion in 2018, according to Magna Global, a unit of advertising agency leader Interpublic Group. Much of this revenue is made in online media, and the fastest growing markets are in developing nations such as China, Indonesia and India.

America continues to be the world's largest media market. Plunkett Research estimates that, broadly measured, total U.S. communications and media spending was $1.6 trillion in 2018. The U.S. entertainment and media industry spans multiple sectors, from America's 10,909 FM radio stations, to the 1.3 billion movie tickets sold yearly in American theaters. Also, the gambling sector is often included when considering entertainment as a whole. In America, legal gambling is estimated to be a $100 billion industry, and recent legal decisions are likely to make online gambling grow rapidly.

Today, digital media of all types must be included when considering the scope of the entertainment and media industry. As of the end of 2018, according to Plunkett Research estimates, broadband internet connections in U.S. homes and businesses totaled 111.3 million, plus 322.4 million wireless subscribers with access to smartphones and tablets. This means there is a vast market for online entertainment and media, and this segment represents one of the most important advertising revenue markets. Comcast (the cable TV provider) alone had more than 26.9 million high speed internet customers as of the third quarter of 2018. Digital advertising (including the internet and ads on wireless devices) grew to $111.1 billion in the U.S. in 2018, according to eMarketer, a 20% increase over the previous year. The firm forecasts this number will grow to $125.8 billion in 2019, including soaring growth in advertising on mobile devices. eMarketer estimates that digital advertising totaled $273.3 billion worldwide in 2018.

What some people refer to as "the third screen" (smartphone- and tablet-based viewing) has become a vital factor in entertainment and media. By the end of 2018, there were 699 million smartphone users in China alone.

Newspapers have been dramatically hurt by online alternatives. With an approximately 31 million paid daily circulation in the U.S. as of 2018 (down from nearly 60 million in 2000), newspapers are finding it increasingly difficult to compete against online news and advertising rivals. Many of America's leading newspapers have gone bankrupt, while others have downsized or become electronic only. The most successful newspapers have evolved into powerful online and print combinations, offering subscribers and advertisers a choice of digital, print or both. Both newspapers and magazines have adopted formats and new technologies with the goal of making themselves highly relevant and readable for internet users on PCs, and for mobile users on smartphones, tablets, ebook readers and other digital devices.

Recorded music sales are facing powerful competition from Pandora, Spotify and similar internet-based music subscription services. Traditional radio broadcasting is hurting, finding it challenging to gather listeners for advertising-based radio programming due to such alternatives as satellite radio. The satellite-based radio service, SiriusXM, had 32.7 million paid subscribers by the second quarter of 2018. During the fall of 2018, SiriusXM announced its intended acquisition of Pandora.

In the film industry, gross U.S. box office receipts for 2018 were $10.2 billion. Meanwhile, film production companies are suffering from dwindling DVD sales, as more viewers download them from Amazon.com or Netflix instead of buying films. Both emerging and mature economies outside the U.S. are of prime importance to film revenues. For 2017, China's box office receipts rose to $9 billion, up from only $2.8 billion in 2012.

New television sets are internet-enabled, meaning viewers are able to connect directly to entertainment options online. This brings up an important question: where will TV viewers of the future get their programming? Cable and satellite subscriptions are expensive, and do not appeal to many consumers under 35 years of age. Consumers have been dropping their paid cable and satellite TV subscriptions in large numbers, opting to watch free or lower-cost programming that is streamed online via services such as Hulu.com.

While content providers such as Disney and ESPN have long earned vast revenues by distributing through cable systems such as Comcast and satellite systems such as DISH, they are now also offering their own, inexpensive monthly subscriptions services that stream online. These low-cost, monthly internet-based plans are viable alternatives to expensive cable or satellite subscriptions. They tend to be user-friendly, with no additional equipment to install, no credit check, and no long-term subscription contracts required. Another vital advantage is that they can be watched on smartphones.

Also, consumers are eagerly buying relatively inexpensive devices that make it simple to connect their internet-ready TVs to online content. Competitors in this field include Roku, Chromecast, Apple TV and Amazon Fire. Roku connectors, for example, can be purchased for less than $50, and deliver hundreds of popular content apps to the TV screen, enabling the user to easily click to watch HBOgo, Netflix, PBS, YouTube and myriad other content providers (some of which require separate subscription fees).

The burning issue affecting all sectors of the entertainment and media industry is maintaining control of content and audiences while taking advantage of myriad new electronic delivery venues. Competition in the entertainment sector is fierce. Gone are the days when television and radio programmers enjoyed captive audiences who happily sat through ad after ad, or planned their schedules around a favorite show. Consumers now demand near-total control over what they watch, read and listen to.

Issues Related to Control of Entertainment and News Content:

1) Pricing for content, including free-of-charge access versus paid subscriptions; illegal downloads versus authorized downloads; and full ownership of a paid download versus pay-per-view.

2) Portability, including the ability for a consumer to download once and then use a file on multiple platforms and devices, including tablets and smartphones, or the ability to share a download with friends or family.

3) Delayed viewing or listening, such as viewing TV programming at the consumer's convenience via TiVo and similar digital video recorders.

Source: Plunkett Research, Ltd.

The competition among entertainment delivery platforms has intensified; all sectors face daunting challenges from alternative delivery methods. For example, telecommunications companies such as AT&T and Verizon are now delivering television programming to the home via high-speed internet connections, battling cable and satellite TV firms for market share.

Meanwhile, platforms and delivery methods are evolving quickly. Smartphones are widely used for entertainment purposes, including games, videos, sports and TV-like programming. Game machines have become multipurpose, with the ability to connect to the internet. Broadband to the home has matured into a true mass-market medium, while wireless broadband systems such as Wi-Fi are enhancing the mobility of entertainment and media access. A serious evolution of access and delivery methods will continue at a rapid-fire pace, and media companies will be forced to be more nimble than ever. 5G ultrafast cellular telephone systems will be the next leap forward.

Recommendation software that learns the habits and tastes of consumers have evolved to do a better job of pushing appropriate entertainment content toward audiences. Amazon.com has long been a leader in the use of such software. Pandora and Spotify recommend music to users. Netflix has created an admirable technology of its own. Likewise, Apple's iTunes software is strong on recommending content to customers.

Count on continued, lightning-fast changes in the entertainment, media and publishing environment. As the revolution in new media continues, platforms will evolve quickly, consumers will obtain even greater control and competition will become even hotter. Meanwhile, the global audience is growing quickly, thanks to emerging middle classes in developing nations as well as the booming spread of smartphones and internet access.

2) TVs Are Internet Ready/Game Consoles and Set Top Accessories Like Roku and Chromecast Stream Content

Many cash-strapped consumers are dropping their costly cable and satellite TV subscriptions and relying heavily on internet-based programming instead. Consumers in the under-35 age group are especially likely to bypass expensive cable or satellite subscriptions. The fact that new TV sets are internet-ready is adding fuel to this trend.

Internet-connected TVs boost consumers' options in news and entertainment, and they enable quick access to games on TV screens. Researchers at eMarketer forecasted 182.6 million Americans would use internet-connected TVs in 2018, up from 168.1 million in 2017. The firm expected the number to rise to 204.1 million by 2022. Samsung Electronics, Vizio and LG Electronics, among others, are all offering smart, internet-connected TVs that feature tools similar to mobile apps.

Home entertainment clusters now include TVs, sound systems, cable or satellite set-top boxes, game consoles, smartphones, tablets and computers. On the fixed end, a home's network is tied to a router connected to the internet. The faster the download speed the better. In an increasing number of newly constructed neighborhoods, access is achieved by fiber to the home (FTTH) networks capable of delivery at blazing speeds, enabling such media as video-on-demand and interactive TV. Verizon, Comcast and AT&T are among the leaders in this field in the U.S. Meanwhile, Google and AT&T are setting a new standard in selected cities by offering 1,000 Mbps connections, roughly 100 times typical high-speed internet rates.

Home entertainment networks are likely to include Wi-Fi, enabling devices to be connected without cables. The Apple TV unit acts as an interface between a consumer's television and computer, while enhancing access to content that is streamed from the internet. Apple TV can send digital entertainment that is stored on, or downloaded through, your computer directly to your TV. This is becoming increasingly important since widescreen home TVs are now standard equipment in many living rooms, and these widescreens are vastly superior to computer monitors for watching videos. Apple TV features apps that enable users to organize and select content in a smartphone screen-like manner, as a direct internet interface.

Amazon offers its own set-top box called Fire. Users get a box that streams hundreds of thousands of Amazon Instant Video TV episodes and movies, and video sites such as Netflix and Hulu Plus. Amazon Prime customers have access to even more programming. With an optional game controller (equipped with a microphone for voice commands), Fire users can access a library of games as well. With products like Fire, Amazon is branching out into manufacturing and deepening its relationship with consumers to include proprietary content and hardware. Amazon's revenues from its massive base of Prime members (who pay an annual subscription fee for better services including free access to streaming movies) enable the firm to offer products like Fire at subsidized hardware prices when appropriate.

Google has its own set-top box called Chromecast. It enables users to enjoy Google Play's library of movies and TV shows, as well as Netflix, Hulu Plus, YouTube and HBO Go. It doesn't have a remote control, so users rely on their smartphones to interact with the unit. Another top competitor in TV to internet interfaces is Roku.

Big news in video hubs includes game consoles, such as Microsoft's Xbox, that take users far beyond game playing. Xbox Live Gold memberships are offered that include access to Netflix, Hulu, HBO Go and live programming from all ESPN channels in addition to multiplayer gaming. (This is a significant bargain compared to a cable TV subscription.) Users are catching on, with the company reporting that Xbox users were spending more time listening to music or watching streaming video than playing games. Microsoft also launched Xbox SmartGlass, which allows smartphones, tablets and PCs to control Xbox features. Nintendo's Wii U game console's GamePad touchscreen device also operates as a remote control. It utilizes a feature called Nintendo TVii to integrate programming from Netflix, Amazon.com and Hulu. TVii is also compatible with TiVo.

Another trend in TV watching is applications that can be installed by consumers. The same "apps" enjoyed by users on their smartphones for access to anything from weather reports to recipes to games to sites such as Netflix and Twitter are available for TVs. Meanwhile, viewers keep their smartphones close at hand while watching their TVs. The fact that voice-activated personal assistants, such as Amazon Echo and Google Home, can take verbal commands

3) DVR Market Evolves/Time-Shifting Hurts Advertisers

Digital Video Recorders (DVRs, also known as Personal Video Recorders or PVRs) allow viewers to download broadcast television, satellite television and cable programs for later viewing. Viewers are typically able to store between 80 and 2,550 hours of programming for playback at their discretion, depending on the sophistication of their equipment and the type of programming. (High definition, HDTV programs require much more storage space than normal programs.) Programming can also be viewed and manipulated to skip commercials almost in real-time. (Or, in some cases, viewers can fast-forward through commercials.) Viewers can also play back key moments or watch in slow motion. This is all accomplished via a hard drive connected to a television set. The fact that very large hard drives are available at modest prices is accelerating the use of DVRs.

TiVo was the first DVR to attract any serious market share. Simple, elegant and easy to use, TiVo has attracted a very loyal subscriber base, reporting 22 million global subscriptions as of mid-2018. TiVo has generated significant revenues by licensing its software available for use in set-top boxes used by Comcast. Its Roamio DVRs integrate live television, recorded video and online video content. Roamio can send video from the DVR to a wireless tablet or smartphone as well. TiVo's Roamio OTA affords TV watchers who don't have cable or satellite service (called "cord cutters") to use a high-definition antenna to receive and capture broadcast TV programming. The firm offers TiVo Bolt, a combination DVR and streaming media box that can stream content to iOS and Android devices and search across provider services. Tivo Bolt Vox is voice activated.

Within the television industry, recording and delayed viewing of programming is referred to as "time-shifting." The impact of these devices on the advertising industry, as well as ancillary businesses such as television networks and cable companies, is very great indeed. Television advertising has long been based on charging the most for ad time in and around the highest-rated shows. It's not surprising then, that advertisers cry foul over DVR viewers' ability to skip or fast-forward through their extremely expensive ads.

The ad-skipping phenomenon is forcing advertising agencies to become more creative. Branded, single-company-sponsored programming may become a dominant trend and can increase both viewership and ad retention.

Other alternative ad approaches such as "showcases" and "branded tags" are available to DVR users. TiVo offers a setup screen in which advertising videos as well as film and television program previews are "showcased." Viewers must choose to view the showcase. Branded tags are advertising icons that appear while fast-forwarding through commercials while watching TiVo. Viewers can select the icon with their remotes to learn more information about the product. Another attempt to get ads to stick in viewer's minds is to design relatively static ads that convey a message even as viewers fast forward through them.

The real future of DVR companies lies in expanded services and more sophisticated technology. Portability of recorded programming is standard. New services include the ability to watch recorded programming on portable devices, via internet connections or wi-fi, that communicate with the DVR.

Another convenience to viewers is the Video-on-Demand (VOD) programming offered by major cable companies. Subscribers can quickly call up popular programs and movies that are stored on a cable system's servers, and watch this programming at a time of greatest convenience to the subscriber. Some VOD programs are offered at an additional fee. "Dynamic ad insertion" allows cable channels to insert ads into their video on demand (VOD) services in as little at 24 hours. The practice allows advertisers to insert timely ads that viewers are unable to bypass using fast-forward. In the past, advertisers were not so keen on VOD ads because programs often contained spots that were time sensitive and of little or no interest when viewed at a later date.

> **SPOTLIGHT: TV Bingeing**
>
> The advent of DVRs and streaming video available from services such as Netflix, Amazon Instant Video and Hulu Plus has sparked a new viewing practice. TV "bingeing" finds viewers spending extended periods (which could be a few hours or entire weekends) watching episode after episode of a series and miniseries such as Netflix's *The Crown*, HBO's *Big Little Lies* or Showtime's *Twin Peaks, The Return*. While the providers of the streaming content are attracting and keeping subscribers in record numbers. (Netflix had more than 118 million global streaming subscribers by the end of 2018, and its own Netflix-produced movies are among the most popular of all streaming content.)

4) Apple's iTunes Set the Standard in the Music Industry, but Digital Sales Slow

The sale of legal, downloadable music via the internet and smartphones has grown into an immense business, but it is facing daunting competition from internet-based music services like Pandora and Spotify, as well as from satellite-based radio service SiriusXM. Nielsen reported that combined sales of recorded CDs and music downloads sold in the U.S. declined from 116.1 million units during 2015 to 100.3 million in 2016 and 81.9 million units in 2017 (with digital sales accounting for 43.7% in 2016). As of mid-2018, consumption was up year over year by 18.4%. On a global scale, total recorded music sales rose slightly, from $15.0 billion in 2015 to $17.3 billion in 2017, according to the International Federation of the Phonographic Industry (IFPI). Profit margins for record companies, once a healthy 15% to 20% during the 1980s, have fallen dramatically, although they are benefitting from the receipt of royalties from services like Pandora.

A big step forward for the music industry came in the form of the groundbreaking iTunes Music Store, a digital service provided by Apple Computer, Inc. This global service offers single track and album files for download from major music companies. The music-playing capabilities of the wildly popular iPhone added to the power of Apple's entertainment empire.

iTunes, Apple's online music store, set the standard for ease of use and broad selections of music. The music companies benefit, receiving about $0.65 in gross revenue per $0.99 retail-priced song. More importantly, the advent of iTunes was a watershed for the industry, enabling it for the first time to significantly limit music file piracy in a manner that is extremely popular with consumers.

However, as internet-based music subscription services become more popular, iTunes music sales are slowing. Apple acquired Beats, which included Beats Audio hardware and the streaming service Beats Music for $3 billion. The acquisition fueled the launch of the Apple Music subscription service, a streaming app. Apple Music is a direct attempt to compete with subscription sites such as Pandora and Spotify.

5) Pandora and Spotify Lead in Streaming Music Via Internet Radio but Face Challenge from Apple Music/SiriusXM Tops 33 Million Subscribers

More and more people are shifting to streaming music services, accessed via online subscriptions or ad-supported plans. This is hurting recorded music sales, as consumers who subscribe to Pandora and similar services see little need to buy their own copies of their favorite songs. However, music publishers offset this revenue loss by licensing music to Pandora, Spotify and similar subscription services. In fact, streaming music over the internet means that more people are accessing more music than ever before.

BuzzAngle Music reported, for the U.S. market, 534.6 billion audio streams for all of 2018, up 41.8% from 2017's 376.9 billion. By the fourth quarter of 2018, 85% of all audio streams were subscription-based, up 50% from 2017. Physical album sales fell 15.3% from 2017 to 2018. The Recording Industry Association of America reported that industry revenue rose 10% during the first six months of 2018 to $4.6 billion, largely due to strong growth at subscription services like Spotify and Apple Music. Industry analysts estimate that subscription access results in roughly 70% of subscriber fees being paid to the music companies.

Streaming Music: A number of services offer ad-supported free streaming music services including Spotify, Pandora, Amazon Prime Music, Google Play music, and the recently launched Apple Music. Most also offer premium subscription access for a few dollars per month that is ad free.

Pandora's web-based platform allows its 68.8 million active users to build unique virtual radio stations based on their personal music preferences. Pandora allows up to 100 personalized stations to be created per account. The firm's technology is based in part on the Music Genome Project, which analyzes and catalogues thousands of songs from multiple genres to create a comprehensive database that breaks down songs by 480 individual musical attributes. In September 2018, Pandora announced that it had agreed to be acquired by SiriusXM Holdings, Inc., the satellite radio service provider, for $3.5 billion, potentially creating one of the largest audio entertainment companies in the world.

Pandora offers free accounts, which are ad-supported but restrict the ability to skip songs, as well as premium subscriptions through Pandora One, which give listeners the ability to skip an unlimited amount of songs, has no limit on monthly listening hours, delivers higher quality audio and removes advertisements. The firm branched out into mobile listening by releasing software for internet-enabled smartphones and tablets. It has also established partnerships with consumer electronics manufacturers, including Panasonic, Pioneer, Samsung and Sony, to integrate its software into new devices, as well as automakers like Honda, Ford, Lexus and Mercedes to include its software pre-installed on certain new model vehicles.

Competitor Spotify, Ltd. also offers a wide range of listening options. Spotify is a web-based subscription music service offering streaming music to registered users in Sweden, Norway, Finland, the Netherlands, the U.K., France, Spain and the U.S., with roughly 100 million listeners to the free service, plus more than 83 million paying subscribers by mid-2018. The firm's library of music is accessed via its proprietary Spotify streaming music player program, which users can download and install on a variety of platforms, offering them access to Spotify's entire music library and the ability to listen to chosen tracks at any time and in any order.

Spotify users can create personalized playlists and have the option to share these playlists with other Spotify users who can then edit the playlists and make their own updates, enabling a collaborative approach to online, peer-to-peer music sharing. The company offers two main access tiers. Spotify Free, allows free access to the online music library and is supported through advertisements, while the fee-based subscription service, Spotify Premium, offer a variety of upgraded features and does not include advertising. Subscribers to Spotify Premium can access Spotify on a variety of mobile platforms, including the iPhone, the iPod Touch, Android-based phones and Windows Mobile-based phones. Spotify also connects users to a range of music sellers, providing links to online music stores where customers can purchase albums and individual songs for download. Additionally, it introduced Spotify Platform, which allows third-party developers to create music-based apps.

Apple Music has been attempting to catch up with pioneers Spotify and Pandora. Paid subscribers are charged a modest fee per month for ad-free service. In addition to on-demand streaming service, Apple Music offers a 24-hour global internet radio station and a portal in which artists connect with listeners.

A major competitor is Tencent Music Entertainment Group, founded in 2016 in China. The firm's apps include QQ Music, Kugou and Kuwo, and have more than 700 million active users and 120 million paying subscribers. Parent Tencent Holdings Limited acquired China Music Corporation in 2016 to strengthen its music offerings, and subsequently changed China Music's name to Tencent Music Entertainment Group. In mid-2018, Sony/ATV Music Publishing acquired an equity stake in Tencent Music, and in October 2018, the firm filed for an initial public offering (IPO) of around $2 billion in the U.S.

Satellite Radio: While Spotify and Pandora have gained tremendous audiences in internet radio, they have not benefited financially as much as the world leader in delivering radio via satellite: SiriusXM.

Sirius XM Holdings, Inc., operating as Sirius XM Radio, is a U.S.-based satellite radio provider. (It also owns an interest in a related company Canada, where broadcasts are made in French and English.) It offers hundreds of channels to its more than 33.6 million subscribers, consisting of dozens of channels of commercial-free music; as well as popular channels of sports, news and talk that may include advertising in some cases, traffic and weather; and Latino channels.

The company's primary source of revenue is subscription fees, with most of its customers subscribing to Sirius on an annual basis. Sirius radios for the car, truck, home, RV, boat, office and store are distributed through automakers and retail locations nationwide as well as online through SiriusXM.com. Sirius also has agreements with every major automaker to offer its radios as factory or dealer-installed options in their vehicles. In addition, satellite radio services are offered to customers of certain rental car companies.

Sirius Internet Radio is an internet-only version of the firm's service that delivers a simulcast of select music and non-music channels. Additional services provided by the firm include Travel Link, a collection of data services that provides users with information on weather, fuel prices, movie listing and sports scores and scheduling; and both real-time weather and traffic services. The fact that voice-activated personal assistants, such as Amazon Echo and Google Home, can take verbal commands to find play music (by artist, genre or specific title), will add to the subscription music trend.

6) New Video Game Console Technologies and Features Boost Sales

New releases of Sony's PlayStation 4 and Microsoft's Xbox One in 2013 heralded a revival in game console sales. DFC Intelligence reported that both had stronger sales during their first two weeks on the market (more than 2 million each) than any earlier console. More recently, the March 2017 launch of the Nintendo Switch saw 2.74 million units sold in its first month.

Game Console History: Sony's PlayStation 2, released in the fall of 2001, was the first unit to play DVDs and audio CDs while offering top-of-the-line high-tech gaming. By mid-2007, PlayStation 2 had sold 115 million units worldwide, and the company dropped its retail price from $179 to $129, thereby extending the sales life of the unit.

Microsoft was hoping to break Sony's dominance in the market with its Xbox, which was released in November 2001 (with a $500 million marketing budget). Xbox was a major step in the company's attempt to revolutionize home entertainment in the same way that PCs revolutionized the office. The unit is a combination of some of the functions of a high-end PC, complete with high-speed internet port and a powerful graphics chip. Xbox Live, Microsoft's online gaming subscription service, was launched in November 2003 and had 52 million members by mid-2017. It provides gamers anywhere in the world with the ability to play against each other using the internet, and it has evolved into a key component to the video gaming experience.

Sony's PlayStation 3 (PS3) went on sale with great fanfare in November 2006. Sony saw sales surge when prices were reduced in 2009 and again in late 2011. PS3 includes a high-definition DVD player using the Sony standard called Blu-ray. This was a bold move since, in 2006, the entertainment industry was still undecided as to which DVD technology would be embraced by the buying public. Sony was actually taking a loss on the DVD player included in PS3 in order to market Blu-ray technology and soften the blow for movie watchers who would have to buy high-definition versions of their favorite DVDs. The gamble paid off since Blu-ray became a high-definition format of choice.

The debut of Microsoft's $4-billion enhanced game console, the Xbox 360, was a major milestone in video gaming. Released for sale at midnight, November 22, 2005, Xbox 360 was a completely redesigned product. The high-end model has a wireless controller, cables for TV connection, a DVD player, a removable hard drive and a complimentary pass to Xbox Live. The console includes ports for attaching digital cameras or portable music players. The Xbox 360, with its three-core 3.2-gigahertz custom chip from IBM, has been a big hit. The software giant hopes that the popularity of its game systems will spur sales of its other consumer products.

Nintendo, the third key player in video game sets, has been a powerful competitor. Its hand-held game player Nintendo DS (first released in 2004) was the best-selling game machine in the U.S. at the end of 2007. By the end of 2009, total DS units sold worldwide had reached 125.1 million. Meanwhile, in a vigorous attempt to hold on to its top spot and to compete with Sony's PSP, Nintendo launched a small player in 2005, the Game Boy Micro. Modestly priced, it is barely four inches wide and two inches tall. It had a leg up over other portable devices because it is compatible with more than 700 games designed for earlier Game Boy models.

Next, Nintendo released its revolutionary game system, Wii (pronounced "wee"), in 2006, which has been an immense success. Equipped with a state of the art wireless controller and moderately priced, the system provides gamers with sensory-enhanced playing. The controller communicates with sensors (mounted near a television) that respond to the player's body movements. A fishing game, for example, causes the controller to "tug" on the player's hand when a fish is hooked, and the player can then "jerk" on the controller like a fishing pole to reel the catch in. While many new games have been developed for Wii, the new technology also works with long-time game favorites including *Pokémon*, *Mario Bros.* and *The Legend of Zelda*.

For 2010, the big news in electronic games was the November launch of Microsoft's Kinect add-on for Xbox 360. Kinect is a sensory-enhanced system that reacts to body gestures, designed to compete head-on with Wii. Kinect also reacts to users' voice commands. It is revolutionary because, unlike Wii, it does not require the use of a handheld controller. Instead, Kinect incorporates a motion-sensing camera. This device definitely raises consumers' expectations for future machines. Through Kinect, Xbox Live users enjoy YouTube functionality, DVR and TV capability plus the ability to use voice controls. Microsoft acquired Canesta, a manufacturer specializing in semiconductors used in 3-D technology, in late 2010 to further enhance Kinect's three-dimensional experience. Most of the world's major game developers created new games for Kinect. Microsoft sold 8 million units in Kinect's first 60 days on the market, far exceeding its expectations.

Microsoft announced an upgrade to the Xbox 360 console in late 2011 that allows subscribers to watch a variety of mainstream TV programming from providers such as HBO, Verizon FiOS and Comcast Xfinity. Perhaps more importantly, users with Kinect will have the ability to search for programming with voice commands and hand signals. The technology is one step closer to freeing consumers from TV set-top boxes. Microsoft reports that Xbox Live users spent more time watching videos or listening to music than playing games in 2012, and it has released dozens of apps or upgrades to Xbox specifically targeting non-gamers.

Microsoft launched the Xbox One, in November 2013. Xbox One integrates gaming with cable or satellite television and Skype-based voice chatting. (Microsoft owns Skype.) It offers voice control in addition to a motion-sensing camera that works with the Kinect operating system to respond to user gestures. The console is not backwards-compatible with Xbox 360 games. Microsoft, like all console makers, has made continuous improvements to the Xbox One's software since the initial launch, including better chat and social functions, improved media player functionality and changes to its DVR features. Another console, the Xbox One S debuted in early 2017, and is 40% smaller than the Xbox One.

Nintendo earned headlines with the launch of a 3-D version of its DS game player. Unveiled at the 2011 Electronic Entertainment Expo in Los Angeles, California, the device comes with two screens, one capable of 3-D viewing and the other a standard 2-D. The Nintendo 3DS creates the illusion of depth by placing a parallax barrier in front of a liquid-crystal display which makes a 3-D effect possible without the game player having to wear special glasses.

Sony's response to Nintendo's new 3DS was the late 2011 release of a new hand-held unit called PlayStation Vita (formerly codenamed Next Generation Portable, or NGP). The unit has a five-inch, organic light-emitting diode (OLED) touch-screen display, a rear touch panel and wireless network connectivity. The buzz about Vita is its ability to offer gamers full-scale playing that's portable, as well as mobile access to Sony's full line of entertainment products (including movies, music and games). In addition, Sony is offering PlayStation games on a variety of portable devices such as smartphones and tablet computers running Google's Android operating system.

Nintendo released the first of the so-called "eighth generation consoles" in November 2012 with the Wii U. The system builds on the Wii's motion control innovations with high definition graphics and a controller that features touch screen capabilities. The controller also has the ability to play some games after the connected television has been turned off. The Wii U is backwards-compatible with Wii games.

Later Game Console Releases: Microsoft launched the Xbox One X in November 2017. The unit offers 4K graphics and high fidelity virtual reality, through eight CPU cores and six teraflops of GPU power, making it the most powerful console built to date. A new version of the Xbox was planned to be revealed in 2019.

In March 2017, Nintendo released Switch, which acts as both a mobile and home console game. Switch, which retails for about $300, sold 2.74 million units in its first month on the market. At the same time, the well-reviewed *The Legend of Zelda: Breath of the Wild* game for Switch was released which sold more copies on retailer GameStop in early 2017 than units of the Switch player.

Meanwhile, Sony's PlayStation 4 (PS4) also launched in time for the Christmas season of 2013. Its new features include the ability to play games streamed over the internet in a practice called "cloud streaming." Sony acquired cloud server developer Gaikai, Inc. in July 2012 for $380 million to enable the new technology on its devices. Games (including games from PlayStation 3) can be played from the cloud, but also from optional discs. In late 2016, Sony released the PlayStation 4 Pro console, with 4K display resolution and more processing power than PS4, just in time for the holiday season. The console's latest update, version 6.20, was released in late 2018. The next version of the PlayStation was planned to be revealed in 2019.

A relative newcomer to gaming consoles is the Steam Box. Steam Boxes are manufactured by third party hardware companies under their own brand names, but are powered by the SteamOS operating system, based on Linux and created by Valve Corporation. The operating system is an adjunct to Steam's downloadable gaming service. Valve has partnerships with more than a dozen game hardware manufacturers to build Steam Boxes with Valve-designed operating systems, game controllers and other equipment, including Taiwanese manufacturer HTC. Valve has partnered with HTC to develop a virtual reality headset. The real asset to Steam systems is the affordable, customizable controller which affords gamers motion controls that can be used for racing games in addition to game-specific configurations. Available machines as of 2018 were the Syber Steam Machine, Zotac NEN Steam Machine, and Maingear Drift, among a few others. Sales have been slow, but Steam technology may spur new releases from the big gaming manufacturers who want to keep pace.

An upstart in gaming consoles is called OUYA. This is a potentially disruptive product in many ways. To begin with, its basic price is only $99, and it was funded through "crowd-sourcing" on a site called Kickstarter that enables individuals to provide funds for products that are still under development. OUYA runs on the Google Android operating system which is also the most popular system used to power smartphones.

The console features an Nvidia Tegra 3 processor, 1 GB of RAM and 8 GB of internal memory that is expandable via a USB drive. It bills itself as the "first totally open video game console." Developer tools are free of charge and available to anyone who wants to write code for new game software. Meanwhile, OUYA console owners may try out any OUYA game free of charge, and will not be required to make a payment until they decide that they like a game and want to keep it.

OUYA also bills its consoles as tools for game developers. No license is required to use its platform, since it is Android-based. By late 2018, OUYA had a library of 1,249 games and its OUYA Developer Kit had been downloaded by over 40,000 game creators. It also provides AIDE for OUYA, which is an integrated developer environment with interactive coding tutorials. OUYA is owned by Razer, Inc., a maker of gaming devices.

Game playing on smartphones is creating intense competition to dedicated game consoles. The incredibly popular iPhone and Android-based phones are fueling the market. Many of the most popular apps downloaded for use on smartphones are games.

Typically, mobile video games are introduced as "freemium" titles which are free of charge to users, but are supported by virtual goods sales relating to the games. NPD reported that 40% of gamers who downloaded an upgradable freemium game made an in-game purchase.

7) **Cable and Satellite TV Struggle with Cord-Cutting/Cheaper Streaming Options Proliferate, Including Netflix**

Cord-Cutting: In the race for media consumers, cable companies and satellite firms are losing subscribers, as viewers increasingly turn to the internet for video programming, a practice that is being to as "cord cutting." There are millions of "Zero-TV" households, in which video watchers see content on devices other than traditional TV, according to Nielsen. In particular, people aged 25 or younger often do not own televisions, but watch programs solely on devices such as smartphones and tablets. More than 10 million U.S. homes have cut the cord or skipped over pay-TV distributors since 2010 according to MoffettNathanson LLC.

A significant challenge facing cable and satellite companies is programming costs. Historically, they increased their subscription fees year after year in order to boost profits while covering increased costs. Some programming is extremely expensive to produce, especially sports programming (due to immense licensing fees paid to the sports leagues), and the cable and satellite firms have been passing those higher costs on to their customers.

Cable and satellite firms, along with telecom companies, are fighting back with innovations such as Comcast's xfinitytv.com, which includes the ability for subscribers to watch recent episodes online, on-demand. AT&T U-Verse has a web site similar to Comcast's xfinitytv.com, as well as an app that acts as a remote control and a digital video recorder. In addition, it can download programming onto mobile devices for later viewing. DirecTV's remote-control app streams live TV programming and enables wireless devices to act as remote controls for TV viewing. DISH Network offers an automatic ad-skipping feature called AutoHop.

Competition from Netflix: Netflix.com is the largest movie and TV show rental site in the world, with more than 130 million subscribers in over 190 countries. For a monthly subscription fee, users can enjoy streaming an unlimited number of movies. Netflix's business model initially was based on mailing DVD copies of movies to its subscribers. This was a costly business, involving multiple warehouses and massive postage and handling expenses. Eventually, however, the firm invested in state of the art technology to enable it to focus on streaming via the internet. While Netflix still supported DVD subscribers as of 2019, this is not where its future lies.

Playback of a Netflix streaming movie starts a few seconds after download begins. Subscribers instantly watch movies and TV episodes streamed over the internet to PCs, Macs, game consoles, tablets, smartphones and TVs. Among the devices streaming from Netflix are Microsoft's Xbox 360, Nintendo's Wii and Sony's PS3 consoles; an array of Blu-ray disc players, internet-connected TVs, home theater systems, digital video recorders and internet video players; Apple's iPhone, iPad and iPod touch, as well as Apple TV and Google TV.

The Netflix streaming content library includes media acquired through deals with corporations such as: ABC, Nickelodeon, Disney, Twentieth Century Fox, Paramount, Miramax, Lionsgate, MGM and CBS, among others. Additionally, through its Netflix Originals division, the company produces content available exclusively on Netflix, which continues to rack up growing numbers of Emmy nominations. The company spent between $12 billion and $13 billion on content in 2018. An estimated $10 billion of that amount was for the production of its own unique films (far exceeding production budgets of any television company or film studio on non-sports content). Netflix produced 82 feature films in 2018 while Warner Brothers produced 23 and Disney 10.

Netflix's efforts to shift to streaming video not only is cost effective, it is also positioning the company to take on cable channels such as HBO and Showtime. Operating on a business model dramatically different from those of cable TV channels, Netflix has become a true web-based entertainment platform, highly competitive with traditional cable networks and systems.

Development of Lower-Cost Subscriptions and Online Video Streaming Platforms: In an effort to attract consumers who are not willing to pay for traditional cable and satellite subscriptions, many companies are offering stripped-down packages with limited programing. Some of these services are cable- or satellite-based, but many are delivered only via the internet. These services are offered by top cable, satellite and media firms including: CBS, DIRECTV, Hulu, Netflix, DISH and HBO. The competition is already intense, and others may jump into the fray. Watch for business models and offerings to evolve, as providers attempt to establish market share and attain profitability on these platforms.

Comcast's Digital Economy Service, a cable-based offering, includes only local broadcast channels and a limited selection of cable channels. Time Warner Cable offers a basic package that offers up to 200 digital channels and 100 HD channels, with on demand programs at no extra cost. Satellite provider DirecTV offers its own version, calling it a family package.

In early 2015, DISH Network introduced Sling TV, a moderately priced streaming internet-based service targeting young, mobile-intense viewers who refuse to subscribe to cable TV. Sling TV offers up to 180 of the most popular cable networks including ESPN, the Disney Channel, the Food Network, HGTV, TNT, TBS and CNN (but broadcast networks ABC, CBS, NBC and Fox are not included). Users select from basic Sling Orange or Sling Blue packages, which offer about 30 channels each (for about $25 per month), or can opt for a combination of the two ($40 per month). In addition, viewers can buy ad-on channels at modest cost. Vital differences from cable TV subscriptions include no long-term contract, a vastly lower monthly fee (in exchange for a much smaller selection of channels), no credit check and no need for additional hardware.

CBS All Access is a streaming service that offers subscribers limited commercial or commercial free access to its programming, and is available in more than 90% of the U.S. CBS holds back certain key content from other streaming providers.

Meanwhile, AT&T, after its $50 billion acquisition of satellite provider DirecTV in 2015, launched DirecTV Now. It offers streaming bundles of live channels and on-demand content at lower prices than its full DirecTV service. In addition to DirecTV, AT&T planned to launch an additional streaming service in late 2019, which will feature content from its June 2018 acquisition of Time Warner.

Sony's launch of its cloud-based TV service, called PlayStation Vue, is another competitor. Sony is relying on its base of millions of PlayStation video game users to help grow this new service. Vue includes content from CBS, Fox, Viacom and NBCUniversal. Vue offers a package of live TV channels, TV episodes on-demand and DVR capabilities with content streamed from existing internet connections. Users are not asked to sign a long-term contract.

Apple's iTunes offers films and TV shows from most major U.S. studios. Feature length films can download quickly if the customer has very high-speed broadband access, and may be purchased or rented online.

Amazon Instant Video offers its Prime premium service with the ability to watch a vast selection of titles instantly. In April 2014, Amazon entered the TV hardware arena with the launch of Fire, an inexpensive device for streaming video and games. The company has expanded Amazon Prime Video services to more than 200 countries and territories, and offered live NFL Thursday Night Football games in the U.S. Amazon's budget for production of unique content was estimated at $5 billion for 2018, and it is likely to continue to escalate its production spending in an effort to compete with Netflix.

Streaming one hour of a standard movie via Netflix can use 1 gigabit of bandwidth at standard settings. However, Netflix offers a reduced bandwidth setting that can reduce this by 70% to 300 megabits. High definition movies can require up to 3 gigabits of bandwidth per hour. These requirements create both headaches and revenue opportunities for internet service providers of all types, from cable to DSL to smartphone service. Simply put, downloading or streaming a movie uses up vast amounts of bandwidth and places great strain on internet providers' infrastructure, whether wired or wireless.

Disney launched an ESPN streaming service in 2018 called ESPN+ and planned another family-friendly service for 2019. This is the first time the entertainment empire will sell TV content directly to consumers instead of going through cable or satellite companies. In its first six months, ESPN+ signed up more than 1 million paying subscribers. Apple also planned to spend $1 billion per year to produce TV programming by 2018, and its budget is likely to grow quickly.

In November 2017, Philo was launched. The $16 per month service offers 43 channels, including AMC, A&E, Comedy Central, Food Network and TLC, and is backed by five companies that supply the programming: Discovery Communications, Inc., Viacom, Inc., Scripps Networks Interactive, A+E Networks and AMC Networks, Inc.

8) Telecom Companies, Including AT&T and Verizon, Compete Fiercely Against Cable in the TV, Internet and Telephone Market

Telecommunications companies like AT&T and Verizon are competing fiercely to take television viewers away from their cable and satellite competitors. Telecom companies are competing directly against cable companies by offering television programming in addition to telephone service and high-speed internet access.

Broadcast, cable and satellite TV providers are competing by positioning themselves with value-added content and services, such as enhanced interactive TV, video on demand and expensive programming such as made-for-TV movies and exclusive major league sports coverage.

AT&T launched an ambitious service called U-verse in 2006, which provides digital TV via the internet (IPTV) over its own proprietary high-speed DSL network. U-verse had 6 million TV customers by early 2015. However, U-verse was suffering subscriber losses in 2016 and into 2018, losing 60,000 subscribers in the fourth quarter of 2017 alone.

AT&T took a significant strategic step in mid-2015 by completing its acquisition of satellite TV firm DIRECTV for $48.5 billion. This made AT&T into America's largest TV distributor, with a combined subscribership of nearly 25 million at the end of 2017 when counting both DIRECTV's satellite customers and AT&T's U-verse TV via internet customers. AT&T clearly has the opportunity to offer bundles, including wireless subscriptions, to its new satellite customers. AT&T's June 2018 acquisition of Time Warner, including such entertainment assets as HBO, will give it significant competitive advantage.

In April 2016, the U.S. Federal Communications Commission and the Justice Departments approved Charter Communications' $65.5 billion acquisition of Time Warner Cable and Bright House Networks, which was completed in May of that year. However, a number of restrictions were set to protect streaming video providers and ensure the availability of relatively inexpensive broadband services to low income consumers (broadband is considered a utility in the U.S.). The new combined Charter entity became the second-largest broadband provider in the U.S.

Verizon is also investing heavily in the delivery of TV over its internet connections. The firm offers a full menu of hundreds of TV channels (including HD channels) plus an on-demand library of thousands of movies. The service, called FiOS, also provides premium channel packages for additional fees, as well as single or multi-room DVR. It provides subscribers with a very high-speed internet access service for speedy downloads.

The prospect of selling television subscriptions is a boon to telephone companies, since it gives them a highly coveted entertainment service to add to their phone service offerings. They have the ability to bundle services that might include any or all of the following: internet access, landline telephone, long-distance, VOIP telephony, cellular telephone and television—all on one discounted bill. The major telephone service providers have been in a tough spot in the past few years, with revenues from landline customers declining as more consumers switch to cellular phones and VOIP as their standard methods of communication. Delivering entertainment via the internet lines gives them a way to develop significant new revenues.

9) Television Ads Evolve to Face New Challenges, Formats and Online Competitors

An advance estimate of U.S. TV-owning households for 2018 was 119.9 million, up slightly from 2017's 119.6 million and 2016's 118.4 million, according to Nielsen Media Research. Nielsen also reported that the number of households with TV sets (TV penetration) fell slightly to 95.2%.

Many consumers are dropping their costly cable and satellite TV subscriptions and relying heavily on internet-based programming instead, particularly in the U.S. These consumers are called "cord cutters." This trend creates significant challenges for cable/satellite firms and broadcast television, along with the advertisers that pay for ads on these traditional TV platforms. The fact that new TV sets are internet-ready is adding fuel to this trend.

More and more, consumers are relying on non-TV sources for entertainment, such as Netflix and Amazon Prime. Both services deliver instant online access to movies and archived TV programming. Amazon shows some video content to non-subscribers, but includes ads. All internet-based entertainment platforms may come under some pressure to sell advertising, regardless of whether or not they also receive subscription payments. As content owners, such as TV show producers and movie producers, see the online audiences grow, they will have additional leverage to ask for ever-larger payments for their content. This could create situations where the online platforms have to weigh the pros and cons of selling ads, increasing subscription fees, or both.

The world's largest advertisers are reallocating a major portion of spending from TV ads to online ads. Concerns about audience size, the amount of time spent viewing TV, as well as the amount of attention paid to commercials continue to nag the television industry. Viewing-on-demand is another issue. Many television viewers skip at least some ads by channel surfing during commercial breaks. The network television business model is facing a need for radical change. Network scheduling, once an all-important strategy for attracting and keeping viewers, has lost its power since people are recording their favorite shows to watch whenever they want via DVRs such as TiVo.

Advertisers are increasingly making use of audience measurement to determine which ads are being watched and which are skipped. Nielsen Media Research has been providing formal ratings for commercial breaks since 2007. Today's set-top monitors measure average viewership for all the national commercial minutes that run during a televised program (individual ads or specific commercial time slots are not tracked). Audience ratings giant Nielsen has evolved its system to include TV viewership on smartphones, tablets and other wireless devices, on personal computers and time-shifted viewing via DVRs, as well as traditional TV viewing. Measurement also includes whether viewers channel surf during commercials or fast-forward through them using a DVR.

Millions of set-top boxes for satellite and cable TV subscribers are deemed "household accessible" or "household addressable," meaning that advertisers can use them to target ads based on viewing habits. Starcom MediaVest recently aired an addressable media campaign for Honda's luxury Acura TLX sedan, specially choosing 1.7 million households to show the ads. These targeted households' rate of buying Acuras was 60% higher than a demographically similar control group that did not see the ads.

Early findings point to higher viewership of ads that are perceived to be high in quality or entertainment value, and also of ads that are not shown over and over. Moreover, these measures are finding that viewers of top-rated television programs (which have the highest advertising costs) are not necessarily the most likely to watch ads.

Another challenge to traditional 30-second television ads on network TV is the proliferation of cable channels. There are hundreds of nationally delivered cable channels in the U.S. alone. Although many of these channels are limited in scope, budget and audience, many advertisers are starting to see the appeal of niche cable as a targeted advertising medium. Channels with very specific content can be a real marketing opportunity for certain kinds of advertising. Their audiences tend to be consistent, representing particular interests and spending habits.

A marketer targeting a niche market may simply look through a cable channel guide and find an appropriate channel. If you want to sell historic memorabilia, advertise on a history channel, and so on. Cable's ability to deliver highly-targeted audiences has appeal for many advertisers, and this appeal has translated into cable's increasing share in the market for television ad placements. Excellent examples are the huge successes scored by food channels and home remodeling channels.

In an effort to get more viewers to stay put during ads, Fox Sports began offering six-second television commercial slots during sporting events in 2017. The ads are similar to video ads on platforms such as Facebook and YouTube. Nielsen reported that in 2017, the average amount of ad time per hour of broadcast TV totaled just over 13 minutes.

New data analysis tools from firms including Nielsen Holdings NV, TiVo, Inc. and Simulmedia, Inc. can help advertisers target audiences and save costs in the process. As more data is collected and thoroughly analyzed, media companies can isolate very specific buying groups such as high-income business travelers or female gamers and pinpoint the shows that they have watched in the past. For example, big data links high-income business travelers with programming such as The Weather Channel's *Freaks of Nature*, a cable program that sells ads for far less than prime time, broadcast television shows. Likewise, female gamers have been shown to have watched reruns of *Roseanne* on WE TV, another lower-cost advertising buy.

Advertisers and networks alike are creating new ways to present advertisements and keep viewers engaged. Among the panoply of interesting strategies are new takes on product placement and sponsorship, mini-movies and situational commercials.

Advertisers are experimenting with different types of product placement on television, ranging from the visual placement used in the example above, in which the product merely appears on a show, to more complex (and expensive) types of product placement, such as spoken/verbal product placement, in which an actor mentions the product by name, or usage product placement, in which the actor directly engages with it.

To a growing extent, many viewers, particularly those in younger demographics, watch video that is "over the top," meaning it is broadcast via the internet. A surge in digital video advertising is occurring on sites such as YouTube, Facebook and Hulu.

10) Movie Attendance Rises/Film Companies Innovate with Digital Projection and Enhanced Cinema Experiences

Box office receipts are a vital part of total film industry revenues. Additional revenue streams come from pay television, cable and broadcast TV, while the rest comes from video rentals, DVD sales and video-on-demand. According to Box Office Mojo, 1.30 billion movie theater tickets were sold in 2018, up from 1.24 billion movie theater tickets in 2017 in the U.S. and Canada, compared to 1.32 billion in 2016 (the highest annual U.S. ticket sale total was 1.61 billion in 2002). Gross U.S. box office receipts for 2018 were $11.89 billion, up from 2017's $11.06 billion and 2016's $11.37 billion.

The top three grossing films in the U.S. in 2018 were produced at the Buena Vista studio. They were *Black Panther,* with a U.S. gross of $700.1 million, *Avengers: Infinity War* with $678.8 million and *Incredibles 2,* with $608.6 million. They were followed by Universal's *Jurassic World: Fallen Kingdom*, with a gross of $417.7 million, Fox's *Deadpool 2* with $318.5 million and Warner Brothers' *Aquaman,* $287.9 million. These figures are as of December 31, 2018 and reported by Box Office Mojo.

<u>Digital Projectors</u>: The movie industry is looking for ways to cut costs while attracting more customers. A landmark effort is replacing existing movie projectors in theaters with digital cinema equipment. The initiative will eventually save millions for the studios because they will produce fewer expensive film prints for distribution. Instead, movies are being distributed efficiently as digital files, at least in nations where theaters adopt advanced new digital technology. Theater owners have an easier time displaying films as well. A critical perk of digital projection is that it opens the door for new three-dimensional efforts such as the wildly successful *Avatar*.

A consortium called Digital Cinema Implementation Partners (DCIP), made up of Regal Entertainment Group, Cinemark Holdings and AMC Entertainment Holdings, had deployed 18,022 digital projection systems in the U.S. by early 2016. DCIP also actively manages the deployment digital systems in Canada (as part of the Canadian Digital Cinema Partnership which is a joint venture between Cineplex, Inc. and Empire Theatres Limited), and projection systems throughout Latin America for Cinemark. The cost for conversion is roughly $70,000 per screen. Lions Gate Entertainment Corp.,

Paramount Pictures, Twentieth Century Fox, Universal Pictures, Sony Pictures and Disney Studios are also supporting the deal, pledging to pay the cinema companies $850 per film booking. This is a boon to the studios that otherwise must spend $1,000 to $1,500 per screen for celluloid (film) prints, and then replace prints every six weeks of a film's engagement.

A possible alternative is the use of laser-illuminated projectors which deliver brilliant, bright images, excellent contrast and more natural colors in either 2-D or 3-D. The lasers generate little excess light or heat and last for tens of thousands of hours. However, laser projectors are extremely expensive, costing as much as $500,000 each. The first system was installed at a Cinerama theater in Seattle, Washington in late 2014 (Cinerama's parent company is Paul Allen-backed Vulcan, which is known to invest heavily in leading edge entertainment technologies). Another roadblock to the technology is that it requires a special license from the FDA and places additional requirements on theater staff.

Luxury Seating and Dining Concepts: Movie theater companies are investing heavily in another high-end new concept called Cinema De Lux (CDL) which outfits theaters with features such as martini bars, Starbucks coffee counters, concierge desks, private party rooms, and theaters that boast luxurious leather reclining seats which are assigned (as opposed to open seating), live performances before showings and escorted seating service. National Amusements, a Massachusetts-based theater business with more than 950 screens, already has several CDLs in multiple states, including New York, Ohio and Massachusetts. The concept is also in several locations in the UK.

Another new concept in a growing number of theaters around the U.S. is restaurant service meals to enjoy during films. Theaters are being refitted with room for dining tables for each seat and food selections such as Caesar salads, steak sandwiches, pizza, burgers and desserts, and in some locations, beer and wine. While the trend began with independent theaters, Regal Entertainment Group and AMC are getting into the act. Regal had eight Cinebarre locations as of early 2018.

One of the most innovative theater companies is Alamo Drafthouse (www.drafthouse.com), which originated in Austin, Texas and as of early 2018 had theaters in 24 U.S. cities, including Austin, Charlottesville, Denver, Kansas City, Los Angeles and New York The firm's founders are extremely innovative and aggressive marketers. Alamo Drafthouse shows new releases, but also brings back widely followed recent classics, such as *Pulp Fiction* and *Rocky III*, presented in their original 35mm format. The firm has also been known to show vintage movie trailers and music videos during these classic showings. Made-to-order food, drinks and beer are served directly to patrons' seats, which feature tables in front of each seat. Celebrity guests and live musical appearances are frequent perks for customers. A "Sommelier Cinema" event featured fine wines carefully paired with classic films.

Another twist on movie theater experiences is iPic, a luxury chain of theaters with 16 locations around the U.S (www.ipictheaters.com). Each iPic multiplex has about eight theaters with between 50 and 90 seats only. Premium seats are semi-private, reclining pods with push-button food and drink service. Tickets run between $18 and $25.

AMC Theaters offers a subscription service called Stubs A-List. For a monthly fee, users can see unlimited numbers of movies (there are also 2-movie and 3-movie per month packages). The service targets young audiences aged 18 to 34. By late 2018, Stubs A-List has more than 600,000 members. AMC is also spending $600 million through 2020 to outfit its theaters with oversize reclining seats at a cost of between $350,000 and $500,000 per auditorium.

IMAX Giant Screen Theaters: The popularity of the giant screen IMAX technology has spurred a significant expansion in the U.S. and promoted the growth of theaters with enhanced viewing experiences. Cinemark Holdings introduced Cinemark XD—Extreme Digital Cinema in 2009 with custom sound and giant screens. Likewise, AMC opened ETX (Enhanced Theater Experience) in such locales as Toronto and Quebec, Canada, and in California, Texas, Florida and Missouri in the U.S. Some theaters chains such as Regal are going so far as to equip theaters with undulating seats, scent machines and 270-degree screens to enhance movie experiences. Its 4DX Regal LA Live Stadium 14 in Los Angeles charges a premium for the experience which can also include rain, fog, wind and mist.

The fact that IMAX can be distributed digitally is a big help, since the cost of one celluloid print of an IMAX film is about $25,000 compared to the few hundred dollars necessary to deliver a film digitally. IMAX also has a huge following in China, where 400 theaters were expected to be open for business by 2018. IMAX is also expanding aggressively in the Middle East and Brazil.

IMAX also offers its larger-than-life experience to home theaters. For $2 million, wealthy households can enjoy IMAX entertainment at their home with systems built in Ontario in Canada. IMAX has a joint venture with China's TCL Multimedia Technology Holdings Limited to develop smaller, $250,000 systems for the Chinese home market.

Virtual Reality in Theaters: Yet another technology on the horizon from Hollywood studios is virtual reality (VR). In 2014, Facebook acquired VR startup Oculus for $2 billion. More recently, Lions Gate Entertainment and 21st Century Fox agreed to sell films through Oculus' online store, and Netflix plans to make its streaming service available on VR headsets. Popular headsets include the Oculus Rift, HTC Vive and Lenovo Explorer. There is even an inexpensive cardboard viewer called DodoCase P2 Popup. A VR experience was embedded into the 2015 film *The Martian*, while director Steven Spielberg completed filming *Ready Player One* with Virtual Reality Co. released in March 2018. IMAX is working with Google and a Swedish VR developer called Starbreeze AB to collaborate on a camera that captures 360-degree images. Production costs for VR content are exorbitantly high, as are the individual viewer units. It remains to be seen whether or not the concept will become popular enough to justify the costs.

11) China and India Expand Film and TV Production Activity

Global movie ticket and TV advertising sales have been rising dramatically. ComScore reported that global box office revenue increased by $1.16 billion to reach $41.66 billion in 2018.

The growth of the middle class in India and China particularly is fueling the construction of new cinemas. In 2018, China's box office reached $8.61 billion, up from 2017's $8.06 billion (if calculated at the same rate of currency exchange), according to the Hollywood Reporter.

In the past, U.S.-produced films have accounted for much of China's box office. China's sales of tickets to films produced in Hollywood fell about 10% in 2018 over 2017. Without the Chinese market, U.S. movie studios could face financial challenges. While many of 2018 highest-grossing films in China were American productions, seven of the top 10 were filmed and distributed by Chinese companies. The Chinese-made *Operation Red Sea*, for example, grossed $575.8 million.

Domestic audiences are on the rise along with the middle classes in both China and India. At the end of 2018, China had 59,009 movie screens, up substantially from 2017's 50,776. Although new theaters continue to open, the growth rate slowed, from a 30.2% rate of expansion in 2017 to 23.3% in 2018.

The government limits the number of foreign films allowed to be shown each year, but with Chinese investors involved, some projects with international casts, crews and shooting locales can be exhibited as domestic films. Wang Jianlin, the richest man in China, was building what promised to be the largest film studio complex in the world in Qingdao, China for an estimated $7.3 billion. However, Wang sold all but 9% of his stake in the project to Sunac China in mid-2017.

Studios whose movies play in China collect about 25% of the box-office proceeds, after costs, up from the previous 13.5% to 17.5%. Chinese distributors keep the rest of the proceeds. (In the U.S., box proceeds are split roughly evenly between exhibitors and studios.)

Hollywood studios are scrambling to make production deals with Chinese partners. China Media Capital, a private equity firm, has signed agreements with Warner Brothers, DreamWorks Animation and IMAX, while Shanghai Media Group has a deal with Walt Disney among others.

Chinese television production is also growing. However, government censors are known to stop programs abruptly if they do not approve of the message. A small number of nationally broadcast provincial channels are emerging. Popular shows have included western-style reality series and game shows in addition to programs devoted to the arts. However, the government has prohibited many types of highly popular shows from continuing, or has significantly censored what can be said or acted out on shows that are allowed to go on. All Chinese television is subject to rigorous government standards for morality. In addition to TV, many Chinese find their programming of choice on the internet, especially urban young adults, ages 18 to 34.

In recent years, a growing number of films have been produced annually in India. Major film studios include Zee, UTV, Suresh Productions, Reliance MediaWorks and Sun Pictures. One of the best known genres of Indian cinema is Bollywood, the term used for the Hindi-language film industry based in Mumbai. Bollywood musicals have become famous the world over.

12) Global Internet Market Tops 4.2 Billion Users/Ultrafast Broadband Expands, both Fixed and Wireless

By the end of 2018, fixed broadband connections in the U.S. totaled 111 million homes and businesses by wireline (DSL), direct fiber, satellite or cable, up from 102.2 million in 2015, according to Plunkett Research estimates. Fueling this growth has been intense price competition between cable and DSL providers. The internet is now reaching a vast U.S. market.

In addition, there were more than 322 million wireless internet subscriptions in America as of the end of 2018. The majority of American cellphones are now smartphones. Big improvements in the devices, such as the latest iPhones and Android-based units, along with enhanced high-speed access via 4G networks, are fueling this growth. In addition, most major e-commerce, news and entertainment sites have carefully designed their web pages to perform reasonably well on the "third screen," that is, cellphones (with TV being the first screen and desktop or laptop computers being the second screen). Globally, the International the number of internet users was more than 4.2 billion as of mid-2018, (including wireless), according to Plunkett Research estimates.

Internet access speeds continue to increase dramatically. Google launched its "Google Fiber" ultra-high-speed internet service in Kansas City, Kansas in 2012, and soon expanded into Austin, Texas; Provo, Utah; and Atlanta, Georgia. This system allows homes and businesses to have 1 gigabit per second access, roughly 100 to 200 times the speed of typical DSL or mobile broadband. More than 1,000 U.S. towns and cities applied for the service when it was first announced, but Google is gauging the results of this initial effort before making any decisions about rolling it out.

AT&T initially launched a similar 1 gigabit service in competition with Google in the Austin area called AT&T FIBER. The firm offers this fast service in dozens of cities across the U.S.

What will widespread use of fast internet access mean to consumers? The opportunities for new or enhanced products and services are endless, and the amount of entertainment, news, commerce and personal services designed to take advantage of broadband will continue to grow rapidly. For example, education support and classes via broadband is rapidly growing into a major industry.

Broadband in the home is essential for everyday activities ranging from children's homework to shopping to managing financial accounts. Online entertainment and information options, already vast, will grow daily. Some online services are becoming indispensable, and always-on is the new accepted standard. The quality of streaming video and audio is becoming clear and reliable, making music and movie downloads extremely fast, and allowing internet telephone users to see their parties on the other end as if they were in the same room. Compression and caching techniques are evolving, and distribution and storage costs are expected to plummet. Consumers are accepting pay-per-view or pay-per-use service offerings because of their convenience and moderate cost. A very significant portion of today's radio, television and movie entertainment is migrating to the web.

13) Entertainment-Based Retailing, including Power Towns

Since the earliest days of the marketplace, merchants have realized that entertainment draws crowds of people who linger and shop. Even during the Dark Ages, jugglers, storytellers and other entertainers were an integral part of public markets, helping to draw throngs of people who might purchase goods.

For the foreseeable future, entertainment's value as a drawing card for retail customers will be of growing importance, especially for the retailing of goods beyond everyday staple items. In fact, the explosive growth of retailing over the internet means that brick and mortar retailers must offer more than the mere availability of merchandise in order to lure shoppers out of their homes, away from their computer screens and web browsers and into the retail store. New shopping centers, especially those in urban areas, are devoting up to 40% of gross leasable area (GLA) to entertainment, restaurants and movie theaters. Developers say that shoppers stay on average more than six hours per visit when significant entertainment venues are available.

Yet consumers still want the convenience found in neighborhood centers. Consequently, many new shopping center developments are including the most desirable elements of both power centers and lifestyle centers, including dominant anchor tenants in large formats, dotted with smaller specialty retailers and a plethora of entertainment and dining facilities, all set in a pleasant outdoor environment with sidewalks, trees, lawns and ponds. In many ways, they are the shopping center equivalent of the super-merchandiser stores.

Developers are planning centers that not only provide entertainment but are also designed to be communities, with space for offices and residential areas. These projects may even include areas for post offices, day-care centers and community centers for performance theatres and galleries. An early form of this idea is found in the Easton Town Center, in Columbus, Ohio. Built for pedestrians instead of cars, the 1.7-million-square-foot retail center contains anchors such as Nordstrom, Barnes & Noble, a Trader Joe's and an AMC theatre, mixed in with a spa and fitness center, a comedy club and a mammography center. The retail center sits within a 1,300 acre, 12-million-square-foot mixed-use development overseen by The Georgetown Company and Limited Brands.

Destiny USA in Syracuse, New York offers go-kart racing, a WonderWorks interactive amusement park with laser tag, a 5 Wits immersive special effects and physical interaction attraction and a glow in the dark Glow Golf miniature golf course.

Canadian developer Triple Five Group (which owns the massive Mall of America in Minnesota) made headlines in early 2015 when it announced plans to build the largest enclosed mall in the U.S., to be located in Miami, Florida. The $4 billion American Dream Miami will feature a ski slope, a water park, a sea lion show, miniature golf, a bowling alley, a submarine ride, restaurants, a performing arts theater, a cinema, Ferris wheel, an ice rink and a roller coaster in addition to hotels and condominiums. Triple Five is hoping to capitalize on Miami's massive number of annual tourists, as well as explosive downtown population growth, which doubled from 40,466 in 2000 to 80,750 in 2014, and is expected to reach 92,519 by 2019.

Another ambitious project from the Triple Five Group is again on the drawing board in New Jersey. Originally called Xanadu, the rechristened American Dream Meadowlands was under construction on 21 acres as of late 2015. Anchor stores include Toys R Us (which is closing its Times Square flagship in 2016), Saks Fifth Avenue and Lord & Taylor. The complex will hold North America's largest indoor amusement park and the largest indoor water park, in addition to a ski slope, roller coaster and twin-body water slides. Completion was expected in 2017, but has been delayed until April of 2019.

Malls that have embraced entertainment tend to be the most successful. The Forum Shops at Caesars in Las Vegas, Nevada, which employs strolling musicians as well as performance artists, and lights the ceilings in common areas to look like brilliant day or night skies, averages $1,615 in sales per square foot. The Grove in Los Angeles, California transports shoppers with a refurbished 1950s Boston streetcar and hosts Summer Concert Series; it averages $2,200 per square foot.

14) Newspapers and Magazines Rely on Digital Editions and Apps

The printed publishing industry is undergoing drastic changes, including the sectors of books, magazines and newspapers. The internet has largely changed the way that people seek daily news, reading material and entertainment. Many publications have been struggling to maintain their subscription and advertiser bases, often without much success. For many publishing firms, plummeting advertising revenues and shrinking readerships have wreaked financial havoc.

Savvy newspaper publishers are evolving into hybrid business models based on both printed editions and powerful online sites. Others have completely dropped their costly print runs and gone to online only. For example, the *Christian Science Monitor*, once considered to be among the finest newspapers in America, stopped printing a daily newspaper and went to online delivery only in 2009.

As for magazines, most have suffered significant drops in ad pages. In April 2014, *Ladies Home Journal* shut down regular print publication after 130 years when ad sales fell 14% during 2013. Like newspapers, magazines are earning a rapidly growing portion of their revenues online, and virtually all major magazines have created apps to provide digital versions of their publications. Magazine publishing giant Condé Nast folded its long-lived cooking magazine called *Gourmet* in recent years, focusing instead on its *Bon Appetit* magazine, which appeals to a similar audience. *Bon Appetit* has been modernized to appeal to a broader, younger audience, and all printed edition subscribers now have free access to the digital app version.

The Newspaper Association of America reports that daily newspaper circulation peaked in 1993 at 62.5 million, and by 2008 was only 49.1 million. For 2017, U.S. total daily newspaper circulation was down to about 31 million, according to Pew Research Center estimates. The internet isn't the only problem faced by newspapers. Changing demographics and intense competition are also in play. While older generations of Americans were hooked on daily newspapers as their primary source of news, newer generations have enjoyed much greater choices of news media and have developed their own, more modern habits. For example, the extreme popularity of cable TV news coverage from CNN and weather coverage from The Weather Channel make newspapers much less dominant. Smartphone apps deliver instant, mobile access to a vast variety of news, weather and entertainment content.

Publishers have been cutting costs wherever they can, including sizeable layoffs. Gannett, one of the most successful newspaper companies, is insulated from the newspaper industry's woes to some extent by the success of its unique national newspaper, *USA Today*, the nation's second-largest newspaper by circulation after *The Wall Street Journal*. However, both *USA Today* and *The Wall Street Journal* are among the most sophisticated and successful publishers of online sites and digital editions. In 2016, *The Wall Street Journal* dramatically cut the number of pages and sections in its printed edition.

The rapidly growing use of specialty internet sites like Craigslist, eBay, Monster.com and Autotrader.com is slicing market share from classified ads. Craigslist, an extremely popular, localized news and classified ads site with a grassroots feeling, has already expanded to more than 700 cities in 70 nations. Craigslist users around the world post more than 100 million new classified ads monthly.

Newspapers are fighting back by putting more and more emphasis on their own local web sites. For example, most newspapers enable advertisers to write their own classified ads in an online form, and then preview and purchase the ad online. That classified ad is typically shown both in the printed newspaper and in the online edition. Other newspapers are improving online search at their web sites, so that consumers can easily find local services, stores and restaurants with a simple search. Many newspapers, including *The Wall Street Journal, The Financial Times* and *The New York Times* are successfully generating very substantial revenues by charging subscriptions for full online access.

Some of the largest newspaper organizations have entered the weekly newspaper business in a huge way, to better appeal to audience segments that include non-English speakers, young people and consumers in affluent suburbs or revitalized downtown areas. These weeklies tend to be smaller, more fun to read, and given away to consumers for free. Staff costs are minimal. Advertising in them appeals to smaller businesses, because the cost of an ad may be one-fourth the rate of advertising in a higher-circulation daily paper. Some of these papers are aimed at Spanish-language speakers and other ethnic groups. Other weekly newspapers are called "shoppers," that is, they are filled with discount coupons and shopping tips.

While the number of printed ad pages has fallen, ads in digital form have been on the rise. Some major magazine publishers, such as Condé Nast have acquired advertising-technology firms to help bolster revenue.

Another trend in magazine advertising is for periodicals to create and customize ads that relate to editorial content in new ways. Hearst worked with electronics manufacturer LG to place ads near the tables of contents in *House Beautiful* and *Cosmopolitan*. The *House Beautiful* ad read "Is this simply a home magazine? Or a recipe for living?" and had an internet link to an LG-backed microsite that discussed kitchen appliances. The *Cosmopolitan* ad was about using LG cellphones to send text messages to friends.

The big challenge for all magazine and newspaper publishers is remaining competitive and innovative in an increasingly digital entertainment and media landscape. A multi-step strategy has been adopted by many publishers:

1) Operate their own robust web sites, where they provide multiple features such as blogs and reader-generated commentary, along with videos and advertising.

2) Use new technology and the latest software to create mobile app editions specifically designed to be highly interactive on smartphones and tablets. The growing popularity of smartphones as well as mobile platforms with large color screens, such as the iPad and newer Kindles, means that advertisers have the potential to create enticing ads with multiple features such as video and music, along with links to further information.

3) Continue to maintain print operations and publications alongside new digital formats. In these cases, publishers must properly train and incentivize their advertising sales teams to sell advertising on all available platforms, printed and digital.

15) Virtual Worlds Provide Revenue for Games Publishers

Gaming has created entirely new ways of making money. Multi-player games (known as massively multiplayer online role-playing games or MMORPGs) have sparked a market in which players broker deals to buy and sell game currency, point-building online items and even players' online personas, which are called avatars. Gamers looking to cash in on the booming popularity of these games are finding ways to buy and sell virtual assets for real currency. It is not uncommon for an avid game player to spend $200 or $300 monthly on game avatars and accessories.

For a time, winning players' avatars and other assets were traded on eBay (the auction site has since ceased to allow these kinds of items on its site), and numerous private buying and selling sites have sprung up to handle the demand. Some game companies are setting up real money trade (RMT) services of their own. Facebook has its own selection of virtual world games such as *Clash of Clans* (developed by Supercell), in which players spend real money for virtual goods.

SwapMob, a social trading network for free games based in Michigan, offers an item-trading platform that crosses a wide variety of different games. Users can sell an item to another user in one game and have the proceeds sent to the seller in a different game, automatically converted into the correct game currency. SwapMob inserts a marketplace tab in games that users click on to list, bid and sell virtual goods without disrupting game play.

The practice of virtual world commerce raises some sticky questions, however, about the true ownership of cyber-assets. Some game companies maintain that all currency, points, avatars and other assets are their property and not that of its players. Others disagree. As greater and greater sums are being made from virtual asset brokerage, the question becomes more important. Is a game company liable to its players for their cyber-assets, should it discontinue the game or alter its rules?

16) Virtual Reality/Augmented Reality and 3-D Games Create Opportunities for the Tech Industry/Immersion Games to Grow

One of the most closely watched developments in the technology sector, especially in electronic games, is virtual reality, or "VR." Analysts at TrendForce reported global shipments of VR devices reached 3.7 million units in 2017, and expected shipments to rise to 5 million in 2018. Sony was the top producer in 2017, shipping 1.7 million units, followed by Oculus with 700,000, HTC with 500,000 and Microsoft with 300,000. SuperData Research reported VR revenue from consumer software and services combined with hardware reached $1.8 billion in 2016, and rose to $3.7 billion in 2017. By 2020, revenue is expected to reach $28.3 billion. In addition to gaming, potential major uses for VR include training/education as well as entertainment in general.

California-based Oculus VR launched a virtual reality headset in March 2016 that makes virtual reality seem startlingly lifelike. Its Oculus Rift headset makes stereoscopic 3-D gaming players feel immersed in the game, using some components that are commonly found in smartphones and tablets. This is sometimes referred to as "immersion" gaming.

Oculus followed a popular money-raising method used by other revolutionary consumer electronics firms by using crowdfunding site Kickstarter to collect $2.4 million in early funding. Facebook acquired Oculus VR for $2 billion in March 2014, and it created the Rift headsets to bring a realistic feeling to virtual meetings and entertainment, in addition to the obvious advantages for games. Rift is compatible with Microsoft Windows and the Xbox. Samsung has partnered with Oculus to launch the Gear VR, powered by an Android-based Galaxy device.

Sony's virtual reality headset, the PlayStation VR, was released in October 2016. It must be paired with a PS4 game player, which means an additional expenditure for gamers who don't already have the console. In addition, VR users must purchase a PlayStation Camera. Yet another (optional) add-on is a motion-based controller called Move.

Another virtual reality headset is HTC Corporation's Vive. Its price tag includes two wireless controllers and two base stations for 360-degree room-scale motion-tracking.

Google has had a major focus on the potential of VR since 2014. It was the lead investor in a $542 million funding round for Magic Leap, Inc., the developer of an eyeglass-based device that will project computer generated images over real settings (a twist on VR called augmented reality). The Magic Leap One device was released in early 2019.

In 2016, Google introduced Daydream, which it hopes will be a leading platform for high quality mobile VR. As part of this effort, Google's Android mobile operating system has been enhanced to support the sensors, software and other components that create VR experiences. Google is developing an advanced VR headset for Daydream. Of course, Google, as an advertising-driven technology company, will be alert to any opportunities to develop unique revenue streams in VR, such as embedded ads or links in VR games or other VR views.

Microsoft's 3D offering, HoloLens, made its debut in 2015. Another device that promises augmented reality, HoloLens imposes holograms over real views. The headset is designed to allow users to play electronic games, build 3D models and conduct immersive videoconferencing. Microsoft offers a HoloLens Commercial Suite for organizations and a Development Edition for individual developers. Microsoft's Windows 10 operating system supports VR headsets from a variety of manufacturers including Acer, Dell, HP, Lenovo Group and Samsung. Samsung's HMD Odyssey headset, for example, features OLED displays and includes headphones and a built-in microphone.

Augmented Reality (AR) is a technology that superimposes computer-generated, digital images on a real-time view, creating a composite view. For example, health technicians may use smart glasses, with AR installed, to see the location of a patient's veins before drawing blood, or technicians may wear smart glasses to see schematics and instructions relating to nearby equipment that needs fixing. The Daqri Smart Helmet enables factory workers to do just that in addition to providing protection. Analysts expect rapid growth among major corporations in adopting this technology. Forrester Research forecasted that 14.4 million U.S. workers will use AR related smart glasses such as Google Glass and HoloLens in 2025, up from 400,000 in 2016. Goldman Sachs Group, Inc. projected that AR and VR combined would generate $80 billion in hardware sales by 2025.

Apple, Inc. is investing heavily in both VR and AR technology. Its headset, codenamed T288, is expected to offer an 8K display for each eye, and could be ready for release by 2020. The company is also focusing on AR features for iPhones and iPads which, as of mid-2018, were already equipped with cameras that enable composite images.

VR uses are stretching far beyond gaming. Surgeons can practice complicated techniques before cutting into patients. Corporate training is another area where VR is coming into play. Wal-Mart, Inc., for example, now utilizes VR training in all 200 of its training centers, which serve 140,000 new hires per year.

Safety is a concern in 3D gaming and VR. Some people suffer eyestrain or other symptoms after looking at 3-D content. The 3DS comes with a warning for young children regarding possible side effects. Some ophthalmologists believe prolonged exposure to 3-D images may retard eye development in children younger than six. Developers can minimize these effects by softening sudden changes in viewing angles. Both Sony and Nintendo provide adjustment features that alter 3-D effects based on the size of the screen (Nintendo's 3DS has a sliding bar on the unit that allows the gamer to control the level of effects).

SPOTLIGHT: NextVR
NextVR, Inc. has developed and patented a technology platform capable of delivering live events in virtual reality. Its NextVR platform captures, compresses, transmits and displays immersive virtual reality content over the internet, primarily delivering live sports and music to fans globally. The NextVR experience requires either a Google Daydream View, Samsung Gear VR, Oculus Go, PlayStation VR Windows Mixed Reality or Mirage Solo headset and compatible phone. Users then download the free NextVR App, put the VR headset on and become engaged and immersed in the content. Inside the app is a range of regularly-scheduled content via partners. NextVR partners include the NBA, FOX Sports, Live Nation, International Champions Cup and more. NextVR was founded in 2009, and is headquartered in Newport Beach, California, USA.

17) Global Mobile Apps Revenues Hit $92.1 Billion Yearly

Short for applications, "apps" are small programs originally designed to run on mobile devices such as smartphones and tablets. Many can be downloaded to desktop PCs and laptops as well, and Apple operates an app store just for Mac computer users. An app may contain a considerable amount of software code and data in the app itself, or it may simply be a very convenient way to link directly to a specific web site. Want to check the weather forecast on your iPhone? Use a weather-related app. Get a recipe for pot roast? Use a cooking app. Watch a video? Use YouTube's app. A vast number are free of charge, published by companies such as airlines that are hoping to extend their relationships with customers, but growing numbers require a fee.

Health care is a field in which apps are proliferating. Examples include MyFitnessPal for tracking daily diet and exercise and Runkeeper, another fitness tracker. It is hoped that lifestyle apps such as these will lower the risk of heart disease, diabetes and other problems associated with obesity.

For purchased apps, developers receive most of the revenue, but the platforms also get a cut. Apple, for example, gets about 30% of the revenue for apps sold through its apps store. It also generates revenues from purchases made within certain apps.

Apps didn't really exist before the introduction of the iconic iPhone smartphone a few years ago (although "widgets," which offer similar features, had been around for quite some time). Today, Apple has more than 2 million apps for sale in the iTunes App Store. Newzoo estimated that mobile users spent $92.1 billion on apps and games in 2018 on a global basis, up from $74.0 billion in 2017 and $54.5 billion in 2016.

Meanwhile, vast numbers of apps are available for the Android mobile phone operating system (the world's leading smartphone platform). Android is the mobile operating system developed by Google, which makes apps available through its "Google Play" site. On all platforms, the most popular apps include games, tools such as Google Maps, the Facebook app, and entertainment and media related apps, such as those for Pandora internet-based radio and for leading newspapers. At the same time, important apps provide tools for business people, travelers, students, hobbyists, wine drinkers, people who like to cook, job seekers, students, children, sports fan, shoppers, car enthusiasts and myriad other special interest niches.

One problem for app developers is marketing their products. Aside from "Top 10" lists on app store web sites, it is difficult to reach potential consumers with new releases among millions of others available. Developers are hiring "pay for install" companies that know how to influence and market to consumers and promise set numbers of installations (helping new apps to rise from obscurity to best seller lists). Analysts at venture capital firm Kleiner Perkins Caufield & Byers estimate that developers are spending between 60% and 70% of their gross income on marketing.

Since the development of apps requires extensive programming and creative services, the app industry encompasses revenues and fees far beyond app store revenues. For example, corporate spending on app development has been soaring. Also, a large number of software companies have achieved success in selling app development tools and platforms to software coders. A study published in January 2016 called *Unleashing Innovation and Growth* by the Progressive Policy Institute estimated that mobile apps had spawned 1.66 million current U.S. jobs, including jobs that could be described as direct, indirect and spillover employment.

Competition is fierce. One study found that the average app loses 77% of its users within three days of download. In the U.S., 30% of apps downloaded are used just two times and then abandoned.

18) Embedded LTE Wi-Fi and Onboard Apps Incorporated by Auto Makers in New Car Infotainment Systems

Advanced information systems in automobiles, such as the Ford Sync system, utilize Wi-Fi to receive their initial software customization at the factory. For example, Wi-Fi may be used at the plant to load one type of emergency response package for cars intended for sale in the U.S., and another for cars that will be sold in other nations. Now, Tesla and other makers use Wi-Fi to install software updates to their vehicles.

As a next step, several car makers, including Ford, GM, Chrysler and Volkswagen are turning their vehicles into Wi-Fi hotspots, so that passengers can use their laptops, tablet computers and other devices on the road.

As advanced wireless broadband systems, such as LTE, are ultrafast, such systems can offer passengers access to conduct business, watch videos, listen to music of their choice and send emails. The GENIVI Alliance (www.genivi.org) has been formed by several auto industry leaders in order to create an open standard for "In-Vehicle Infotainment" or IVI. Members include GM, BMW, Volvo, Honda, Nissan and parts maker Visteon.

One way to enable onboard internet hotspots is to create a system whereby an owner's smartphone becomes a single internet connection for all passengers and all of their devices. However, auto makers are now embedding independent wireless receivers into their cars—systems that require their own wireless service contracts. GM is offering embedded 4G broadband provided by AT&T for onboard Wi-Fi. (GM's popular OnStar telematics system has long featured built-in wireless communications for directions and emergency phone calls.)

Meanwhile, car makers are rushing to develop sophisticated smartphone apps and onboard apps that enable owners to customize and communicate with their cars. Ford's AppLink service is available on most Ford models, including the Mustang, Fusion Hybrid, Focus, F-150 pickup and the E-Series van. Ford's SYNC already offers real-time traffic information, turn-by-turn directions and personalized sports and weather reports, in addition to hands-free operation of cellphones and sound systems.

Under new developments in AppLink, car owners will be able to download entertainment of their choice to SYNC for listening while they drive. The wildly popular Pandora music service was among the first offerings. But this is just the beginning of the services apps will bring to onboard SYNC infotainment systems. Owners will be able to download travel and time management apps, such as systems that will alert them to changes in the status of flights while in route to the airport. Voice-activated apps may even enable drivers to update their social media such as Facebook or Twitter.

Meanwhile, Ford wants apps to enable owners to better manage their cars remotely. Such apps will include systems to diagnose car performance and maintenance. SYNC Destination enables owners to enter a destination into a smartphone at their convenience, and then beam it to the car for turn-by-turn guidance later. A car maker's ability to offer the maximum synchronization with a consumer's smartphone in a safe and entertaining manner is rapidly becoming one of the most hotly contested fields in the automobile market.

Toyota, GM, Tesla and Mercedes-Benz, among others, are also jumping on the app access wagon in varying degrees. At Tesla, for example, new models sport 17-inch video monitors in the dashboard with USB plugs for internet access. At GM, the touch screen measures eight inches and can be activated by voice, touch or controls mounted on the steering wheel. Mercedes has developed an app called DriveStyle, and BMW offers an app program called ConnectedDrive.

Google's Android Auto as well as Apple's CarPlay stream phone data through a car's USB port to a monitor set into the dashboard. Proponents say the displays keep drivers from looking down at their smartphones or dashboards. Detractors are concerned that the displays are simply more distractions from the road.

An advanced system is installed in the new BMW 7-series sedan which includes the ability for the car to park itself when a driver exits the vehicle and presses a button on a remote control. The 7-series also has a color heads-up display that projects information on the windshield with 75% more display area than previous models, and the infotainment center offers its own app store. In addition, the vehicle has gesture control, allowing drivers to accept or reject phone calls and adjust sound system volume by waving their hands.

Apple has agreements with a number of auto manufacturers including Audi, BMW, GM, Honda and Toyota to install its Siri voice command service in new vehicles. The service utilizes "eyes free" buttons that engage Siri so that the driver can request information from the internet on everything from weather to navigation to nearby restaurant reviews.

The use of digital assistants such as Amazon's Alexa is expanding into vehicles. BMW announced in late 2016 that its "Connected" services would enable Alexa users to lock car doors or check tire pressures remotely. Ford is also integrating Alexa into its Fusion and Escape models. While driving, users can receive alerts regarding shopping lists and nearby stores that offer the necessary items. Mercedes-Benz offers a similar feature called In Car Office, which integrates Microsoft Exchange calendars into vehicles.

Samsung Electronics, with its subsidiary Harman International Industries (which Samsung acquired in 2016 for $2 billion), is working on a fully digital vehicle cockpit design featuring a bank of screens stretching from one side of the car to the other. Drivers will be able to adjust controls in the vehicle or use smart apps to command changes via digital assistants at home or at the office. Passengers will be able to watch streaming video or surf the internet. Samsung hopes to have the system installed in vehicles by the 2021-2022 model year.

There is some concern that connectivity opens the door for hackers who might take control of crucial systems such as braking, steering or engine startup and shutdown. Hackers also might be able to unlock doors and drive off using cellular, Bluetooth or other wireless connections. Manufacturers are working on ways to secure automotive computer systems. Toyota, for example, programs its onboard computers to recognize outside commands and reject them.

19) Global Media Giants Acquire both Content and Distribution

Large entertainment and media companies commonly use two strategies for long-term growth. Companies that control massive distribution systems (such as internet sites, cable TV channels or magazine publishing companies) often want to control more content. Conversely, companies that control large amounts of content often want to control more distribution. Such content-owning firms include those in film production, television production and publishing. In the long haul, the greatest profits in the global entertainment and media industries may come from distribution. Nonetheless, distribution companies often have good reason to diversify into content.

In 2011, Comcast acquired 51% of NBC Universal (General Electric (GE) held the remaining 49%) for $13.8 billion. In 2013, Comcast bought out GE's 49% to take full ownership of NBC Universal for $16.7 billion. Comcast's full ownership affords it control of the NBC network, NBC News, MSNBC, CNBC, Universal Pictures, Universal theme parks and resorts and a number of popular cable channels such as Bravo. In other words, it is now a giant in both content and distribution on a very wide scale. In 2018, Comcast agreed to acquire UK-based Sky, a massive broadband and TV delivery system that also produces a large amount of its own content.

During 2013, U.S. cable company Liberty Global acquired British cable titan Virgin Media for $16 billion, creating one of the largest cable TV and broadband companies in the world.

Many companies, such as Viacom, have acquired cable channels, not only because cable has proven to be profitable, but also because these channels give companies like Viacom (owner of BET, MTV and Nickelodeon, among many other networks) additional leverage with advertisers when combined with their existing ownership of broadcast networks.

In fact, most of the top cable channels are owned by a small number of media companies that also own cable or broadcast networks, including Viacom, Disney, News Corp. and Time Warner. Although a media company's ownership of both cable and broadcast channels is clearly to its benefit, this ownership strategy may offer advertisers an advantage as well. By aligning with these companies, advertisers can often secure cheaper package deals, in which their commercials air on both broadcast and cable networks for a single price.

In June 2018, telecommunications and internet service giant AT&T completed its acquisition of content leader Time Warner for $85 billion. This merges Time Warner's television and film assets, including HBO, Warner Brothers and Turner, into AT&T's massive business that delivers wireless smartphone connections and internet connections, as well as landlines and other services, to millions of homes and businesses. Earlier, AT&T had also acquired satellite delivery network DirecTV.

Disney's businesses include the ABC Television Network, ESPN, the History Channel and A&E on the distribution side. Its content-generating businesses include film studios such as Touchstone Pictures and Pixar. It also owns the Marvel comics business. Disney parks, resorts and cruise lines provide additional opportunities to convert content (such as Mickey Mouse) into revenue through distribution (such as the sale of Mickey-logoed apparel at theme parks). Meanwhile, the Disney Interactive Studios generate video games and Disney Online runs web sites.

In July 2018, in one of the largest media industry mergers of all time, Disney acquired Twenty-First Century Fox's movie and TV studios, in additional to other assets including Fox's 30% state in streaming service Hulu, for $84 billion.

20) Digital Assistants Include Amazon's Echo and Google's Home/Alexa and Similar Software Power Third-Party Developers

Apple, Google, Amazon and Microsoft are competing to offer the best voice-activated systems that can do anything from reporting the time and weather, to playing music on request, to performing web searches, to telling jokes, to making purchases from internet sites. These platforms utilize the latest in artificial intelligence in order to become more useful over time. Apple's Siri is available on iPhones, iPads, Apple Watches and through an app in some vehicles. Google Now is an app available on a variety of mobile devices as is Microsoft's Cortana app. Amazon's Alexa web app is installed on a gadget called Amazon Echo that sits on a countertop, desk or shelf. Alexa software can be installed on other devices as well. RBC Capital Markets predicts 128 million households will be using Alexa by 2020. Google offers a similar device called Google Home. All of these apps and platforms are voice-activated, and use connections to other apps and systems to find information such as directions, time, date, weather and trivia, or make purchases, which are reported audibly (users can choose their device's voice gender and language). The next step for these handy assistants is the ability to connect with apps relating to climate control, lighting and/or security enabling users to simply say, for example, "Set home temperature to 72 degrees," or "Activate alarm system," and have the action performed, even from remote locations.

Importantly, most systems are open to third-party developers. For example, Amazon has opened "Lex" to developers, which is the artificial intelligence engine behind the Alexa and Echo platforms. Lex is tied into Amazon's AWS cloud computing system. Software and product developers can incorporate Lex, enabling voice-activated or click-activated responsiveness (often in the form of specific task-oriented icons or apps known as "bots"). This gives these developers instant access to extremely powerful cloud computing, artificial intelligence and voice-activation in one easy-to-launch package. Amazon charges a modest fee per thousand uses or data accesses. This ease-of-use has spurred a tidal wave of new product development worldwide, with the potential to revolutionize the manner in which consumers interface with their digital devices and the internet.

> **Top Voice-Activated Technology Platforms and their Unique Advantages:**
> **Alexa**: Owned by Amazon. Connects to Amazon AWS Cloud services, making it easy to embed Alexa software in third-party products.
> **Siri**: Owned by Apple. Siri, already familiar to hundreds of millions of iPhone users worldwide, has evolved into a very sophisticated digital assistant.
> **Cortana**: Owned by Microsoft. Microsoft had deep partnerships and experience with third-party corporate software and technology firms, making this an easy platform for others to embed.
> **Google Assistant**: Owned by Google. Assistant capitalizes on Google's constantly evolving expertise in search and artificial intelligence.
> *Source: Plunkett Research, Ltd.*

21) Overview of the Electronic Games Industry

The global video games industry is so vast that it far surpasses the categories of adult and children's books in terms of total revenues. Estimates of the total size of the global electronic games market (including hardware, software and subscriptions) vary from one analyst to another, but it is likely that the market will grow to $150 billion or more by 2019. (Games tracking firm Newzoo forecast that the 2019 market will be $151.9 billion.)

The advertising industry has jumped into the GASM field in a massive way, as the number of hours spent by consumers accessing GASM daily has become much too large to ignore. Likewise, media, professional sports and entertainment corporations have entered the field with great enthusiasm. The fastest-growing advertising media in the world include the largest social media site: Facebook.

Historically, gaming was largely an industry driven by players on dedicated consoles, such as the PlayStation and Xbox. Manufacturers of consoles continue to compete fiercely to introduce the best new features and garner market share. Game console makers have been able to develop massive numbers of fans who pay monthly subscription fees. Sony's PlayStation network has more than 80 million members worldwide. Once logged in, subscribers can both play their favorite games and control their favorite media and entertainment. For example, they can log into Netflix to watch streaming movies on their consoles. However, retail sales of game software designed for specific consoles are slowly becoming of less importance. Game consoles offer exciting features but may become less relevant to the overall market as many gamers rely on their smartphones and the cloud for play.

The popularity of mobile games played on smartphones has been soaring. Newzoo forecasted this market would reach $63.2 billion in 2018. Mobile gaming has, to a large extent, become an industry of its own, with startup firms such as Ubisoft and GungHo showing stunning growth in this field.

22) The Future of Entertainment, Media and Publishing: Disruption, Portability and Consumer Control

Some products and platforms within the entertainment and media sector are accustomed to rapid change and disruption. Movies, for example, evolved fairly rapidly from silent to recorded sound; from black and white to color; from color to technicolor; from in-the-theater, to on-the-disc, to on-the-internet and your smartphone screen.

Newspapers still look largely as they did two centuries ago, although they have added internet sites to their portfolios. Printed books really haven't changed that much through the years, but consumers now have the option of reading the same title in ebook form, and audio versions are available for their smartphones and earbuds.

Over the mid-term, the evolution of media and entertainment technology is going to leap ahead dramatically. This is due to looming technology enhancements that include much-faster 5G service for smartphones, virtual reality, HTML5 for web sites and 1 gigabyte download speeds for fixed internet service.

The end result will be that consumers will be able to access their selected content much faster, such as downloading a full-length movie in a few minutes, while internet-based content pages will load much faster while having richer features.

Also, over the mid-term, another billion consumers around the globe will get their first smartphones. For example, in India, innovative hardware firms such as Xiaomi and Lenovo have launched well-equipped smartphones at incredibly low prices, aimed at consumers who, until now, simply could not afford the equipment. Meanwhile,

Reliance Jiu has launched incredibly inexpensive and capable 4G service within India, ready to serve hundreds of millions of new smartphone owners.

As it becomes incredibly fast and easy to stream movies, theaters will be forced to continue to innovate. That means more features within the theaters, such as the rapidly advancing trend of high quality food and cocktails available to patrons while they enjoy luxurious seating and plush surroundings.

Consumers have become accustomed to greater control over when, where and how they enjoy their media. For example, a few short years ago television viewers were at the mercy of a very small number of TV channels. Each program was available only on specified days in specified time slots. By the beginning of the 21st Century, that had altered dramatically, thanks to hundreds of unique cable and satellite TV channels and video-on-demand technologies. The next step is already underway, with dozens of services enabling consumers to subscribe to internet-based TV access that allows them to pick and choose the channels they want, rather than being forced to pay very high monthly subscription fees for huge packages of hundreds of channels in typical cable and satellite deals. If all you want to watch is Disney programming, then simply subscribe to Disney. If all you want to watch is Major League Baseball, then there's an internet-based offering that will suit you.

The changes discussed above are merely evolutionary. That is, they are improvements on legacy platforms. What comes next will be disruptive and revolutionary, in the form of immersive entertainment and media. This will largely utilize virtual reality hardware and software, which are very rapidly improving capabilities while prices drop. There is every reason to think that some of the best-known brands in entertainment and media today will be forced to evolve or fail as future technologies open up listening, viewing, reading and participating options that will change habits and tastes, and in many cases lower costs and improve efficiencies.

Chapter 2

ENTERTAINMENT, MOVIE, PUBLISHING & MEDIA INDUSTRY STATISTICS

Contents:	
Entertainment, Movie, Publishing & Media Industry Statistics and Market Size Overview	34
Estimated U.S. Information & Entertainment Sector Revenues by NAICS Code: 2013-2018	35
Estimated U.S. Arts, Entertainment & Recreation Services Sector Revenues by NAICS Code: 2013-2018	36
Personal Consumption Expenditures for Recreation, U.S.: Selected Years, 2010-2017	37
Newspaper Publishers: Estimated Sources of Revenue & Expenses, U.S.: 2013-2018	38
Periodical Publishers: Estimated Sources of Revenue & Expenses, U.S.: 2013-2018	39
Book Publishers: Estimated Sources of Revenue, Inventories & Expenses, U.S.: 2013-2018	40
Motion Picture & Video Industries: Estimated Sources of Revenue, U.S.: 2013-2018	41
Sound Recording Industries: Estimated Sources of Revenue, U.S.: 2013-2018	42
Radio Networks & Radio Stations: Estimated Sources of Revenue & Expenses, U.S.: 2013-2018	43
Television Broadcasting: Estimated Sources of Revenue & Expenses, U.S.: 2013-2018	44
Cable & Other Subscription Programming: Estimated Sources of Revenue & Expenses, U.S.: 2013-2018	45
Internet Publishing & Broadcasting & Web Search Portals: Estimated Revenue & Expenses, U.S.: 2013-2018	46
Number of Business & Residential High Speed Internet Lines, U.S.: 2013-2018	47
Estimated Export Revenue for Information Sector Firms, U.S.: 2013-2017	48
Employment & Earnings in Selected Entertainment & Media Occupations, U.S.: May 2017	49
Employment in Selected Information & Entertainment Industries, U.S.: 2013-October 2018	50

Entertainment, Movie, Publishing & Media Industry Statistics and Market Size Overview

	Amount	Unit	Date	Source
Total U.S. Communications & Media Spending	1.6	Tril. US$	2018	PRE
U.S. Advertising Revenues	207	Bil. US$	2018	Magna
Global Net Media Owners Advertising Revenues	551	Bil. US$	2018	Magna
Global Digital Advertising Sales	250	Bil. US$	2018	Magna
PRINT MEDIA				
U.S. Consumer Magazine Advertising Market	16.4	Bil. US$	2018	PWC
U.S. Trade Magazine Advertising Market	4.2	Bil. US$	2018	PWC
Estimated Total Daily Newspaper Circulation, U.S. (Weekday)	31	Mil.	2017	Pew
Estimated Total Daily Newspaper Circulation, U.S. (Sunday)	34	Mil.	2017	Pew
U.S. Print Advertising Sales (Newspaper and Magazines)	14.9	Bil. US$	2018	Magna
Net Revenues of U.S. Book Publishers	28.3	Bil. US$	2018	PRE
E-books as a percent of Trade Book Sales, U.S.	16	%	2017	AAP
TELEVISION				
Licensed TV Stations U.S. (Including Digital Class A)	1,162		Dec-18	FCC
Percent of TV Households with Traditional Cable	77.4	%	Q2-18	Nielsen
RADIO & MUSIC				
Full Service Licensed FM Radio Stations, Including Educational, U.S.	10,909		Dec-18	FCC
Licensed AM Radio Stations, U.S. (Daytime/Unlimited)	8,205		Dec-18	FCC
Total Album Equivalent Consumption, U.S.*	360.1	Mil. Units	Q2-18	Nielsen
Global Recorded Music Revenues	17.3	Bil. US$	2017	IFPI
Digital Music as a Percent of Global Music Sales	54	%	2017	IFPI
Satellite Radio Subscribers, U.S.	32.7	Mil.	Q2-18	Sirius XM
FILM				
U.S. Box Office Revenues	10.2	Bil. US$	2018	BOM
Global Box Office Revenues	40.6	Bil. US$	2017	MPAA
Number of Cinema Locations, U.S. (Including Indoor & Drive-in)	5,803		Jul-18	NATO
Number of Movie Screens, U.S. (Including Indoor & Drive-in)	40,837		Jul-18	NATO
U.S. Home Entertainment Spending	20.5	Bil. US$	2017	DEG
ELECTRONIC GAMES				
Global Computer & Video Game Sales	137.9	Bil. US$	2018	Newzoo
Computer & Video Game Sales, U.S.	30.4	Bil. US$	2018	Newzoo
OTHER				
Number of Wireless Connections, U.S.	400.2	Mil.	Dec-17	CTIA
Wireless Penetration, U.S.	120.7	%	Dec-17	CTIA
Number of Smartphones Sold, Worldwide	1.9	Bil. Units	2018	Gartner
Worldwide Shipments of PCs, Tablets and Mobile Phones	2.32	Bil. Units	2018	Gartner
Mobile Cellular Subscriptions, Worldwide (estimate)	8.1	Bil.	2018	PRE
Internet Users, Worldwide (estimate)	4.2	Bil.	Jun-18	IWS
Consumer Spending on Commercial Gaming, U.S.	40.3	Bil. US$	2017	AGA
High Speed Internet Subscribers, U.S., Fixed, Home & Business	111.3	Mil.	Dec-18	PRE
High Speed Internet Subscribers, U.S., Mobile	322.4	Mil.	Dec-18	PRE

* Includes album, TEA, and on-demand audio/video SEA. Track Equivalent Albums (TEA) ratio of 10 tracks to 1 album and Streaming Equivalent Albums ratio of 1,500 streams to 1 album. Data figure represent 12/29/2017 - 6/28/2018.

PRE = Plunkett Research Estimate; Magna = Magna Global (an Interpublic Group company); Pew = Pew Research Center; AAP = Association of American Publishers; FCC = Federal Communications Commission; IFPI = International Federation of the Phonographic Industry; BOM = Boxofficemojo.com; MPAA = Motion Picture Association of America; NATO = National Association of Theatre Owners; DEG = Digital Entertainment Group; ; CTIA = CTIA, The Wireless Association; ICI = IC Insights; IWS = Internetworldstats.com; AGA = American Gaming Association.

Plunkett Research, ® Ltd.   Copyright © 2019, All Rights Reserved
www.plunkettresearch.com

Estimated U.S. Information & Entertainment Sector Revenues by NAICS Code: 2013-2018

(In Millions of US$; Latest Year Available)

NAICS Code[1]	Kind of business	2018[2]	2017	2016	2015	2014	2013
51	Information	1,255,630	1,533,690	1,493,592	1,405,882	1,351,616	1,284,064
511	Publishing Industries (except Internet)	264,820	317,850	308,489	293,771	291,575	279,253
51111	Newspaper Publishers	NA	25,204	25,264	26,550	28,112	28,512
51112	Periodical Publishers	NA	28,258	28,237	28,314	29,378	29,185
51113	Book Publishers	NA	27,478	27,744	27,676	26,891	26,720
5112	Software Publishers	197,169	224,362	214,798	198,341	193,822	181,734
512	Motion Picture and Sound Recording Industries	84,772	103,886	103,120	98,982	94,745	95,084
5121x	Motion Picture and Video Production and Distribution[3]	NA	64,941	66,761	64,434	62,831	64,504
51213	Motion Picture and Video Exhibition	NA	17,526	16,536	15,787	14,563	14,144
512191	Teleproduction and Other Postproduction Services	NA	6,001	5,885	5,500	5,212	4,922
512199	Other Motion Picture and Video Industries	NA	425	407	398	448	379
51221	Record Production	NA	385	387	392	338	297
51222	Integrated Record Production/Distribution	NA	7,207	6,229	5,765	5,077	5,032
51223	Music Publishers	NA	5,754	5,250	5,054	4,732	4,314
51224	Sound Recording Studios	NA	1,073	1,097	1,086	1,002	951
51229	Other Sound Recording Industries	NA	574	568	566	542	541
515	Broadcasting (except Internet)	NA	160,879	159,227	148,462	140,792	131,413
515111	Radio Networks	NA	7,641	7,089	6,509	6,011	5,703
515112	Radio Stations	NA	12,360	12,807	12,445	12,397	12,523
51512	Television Broadcasting	NA	57,551	57,823	50,577	49,911	44,782
5152	Cable and Other Subscription Programming	NA	83,327	81,508	78,931	72,473	68,405
517	Telecommunications	486,608	617,160	628,045	601,970	588,172	558,935
5171	Wired Telecommunications Carriers	247,532	315,343	326,119	306,384	296,792	288,647
5172	Wireless Telecommunications Carriers (except Satellite)	201,372	257,845	259,321	254,406	251,766	233,123
5174	Satellite Telecommunications	NA	6,947	7,208	6,926	6,729	6,920
518	Data Processing, Hosting, and Related Services	137,997	155,934	139,715	129,957	120,450	116,040
519	Other Information Services	154,563	177,981	154,996	132,740	115,882	103,339

Notes: Estimates are based on data from the 2017 Service Annual Survey and administrative data. Dollar volume estimates are published in millions of dollars; consequently, results may not be additive. Estimates have been adjusted using results of the 2012 Economic Census where applicable.

[1] For a full description of the NAICS codes used in this table, see www.census.gov/eos/www/naics/index.html

[2] Year to date through 3rd quarter 2018. Preliminary estimate.

[3] Includes NAICS 51211 (Motion Picture and Video Production) and NAICS 51212 (Motion Picture and Video Distribution).

NA = Not Available

Source: U.S. Census Bureau
Plunkett Research, ® Ltd.   Copyright © 2019, All Rights Reserved
www.plunkettresearch.com

Estimated U.S. Arts, Entertainment & Recreation Services Sector Revenues by NAICS Code: 2013-2018

(In Millions of US$; Latest Year Available)

NAICS Code[1]	Kind of business	2018[2]	2017	2016	2015	2014	2013
71	Arts, entertainment & recreation	208,653	265,506	249,608	237,482	223,154	211,292
711	Performing arts, spectator sports & related industries	91,061	118,366	110,564	104,698	96,483	90,200
7111	Performing arts companies	NA	16,955	15,988	15,263	14,332	13,769
7112	Spectator sports	NA	45,466	42,415	40,095	37,264	34,977
711211	Sports teams & clubs	NA	33,977	31,192	28,979	26,668	24,145
711212	Racetracks	NA	7,788	7,560	7,596	7,238	7,421
711219	Other spectator sports	NA	3,701	3,663	3,520	3,358	3,411
7113	Promoters of performing arts, sports & similar events	NA	28,331	26,473	24,538	22,020	19,916
7114	Agents & managers for artists, athletes, entertainers & other public figures	NA	8,193	7,883	7,322	6,674	6,208
7115	Independent artists, writers & performers	NA	19,421	17,805	17,480	16,193	15,330
712	Museums, historical sites & similar institutions	11,050	17,175	15,210	15,168	15,900	15,080
713	Amusement, gambling & recreation industries	106,542	129,965	123,834	117,616	110,771	106,012
7131	Amusement parks & arcades	NA	20,250	19,145	18,075	16,374	15,168
71311	Amusement & theme parks	NA	17,945	17,144	16,252	14,694	13,524
71312	Amusement arcades	NA	2,305	2,001	1,823	1,680	1,644
7132	Gambling industries	NA	30,310	29,257	27,923	26,607	25,698
71321	Casinos (except casino hotels)	NA	19,460	18,965	18,323	17,094	16,617
71329	Other gambling industries	NA	10,850	10,292	9,600	9,513	9,081
7139	Other amusement & recreation industries	NA	79,405	75,432	71,618	67,790	65,146
71391	Golf courses & country clubs	NA	22,902	22,445	21,821	21,224	20,918
71392	Skiing facilities	NA	3,262	2,823	2,571	2,530	2,433
71393	Marinas	NA	4,608	4,382	4,291	4,203	3,999
71394	Fitness & recreational sports centers	NA	32,315	30,162	28,319	26,673	25,649
71395	Bowling centers	NA	3,894	3,787	3,629	3,403	3,224
71399	All other amusement & recreation industries	NA	12,424	11,833	10,987	9,757	8,923

Notes: Estimates are based on data from the 2017 Service Annual Survey and administrative data. Dollar volume estimates are published in millions of dollars; consequently, results may not be additive. Estimates have been adjusted using results of the 2012 Economic Census where applicable.

[1] For a full description of the NAICS codes used in this table, see www.census.gov/eos/www/naics/index.html
[2] Year-to-date through 3rd quarter. Preliminary estimate.
NA = Not Available.

Source: U.S. Census Bureau
Plunkett Research, ® Ltd.   Copyright © 2019, All Rights Reserved
www.plunkettresearch.com

Personal Consumption Expenditures for Recreation, U.S.: Selected Years, 2010-2017

(In Billions of US$; Latest Year Available)

Type of product or service	2010	2011	2012	2013	2014	2015	2016	2017
Total recreation expenditures	884.4	901.6	934.4	967.4	1,004.9	1,055.1	1,102.2	1,160.6
Percent of total personal consumption	8.7%	8.5%	8.5%	8.5%	8.5%	8.6%	8.6%	8.7%
Video & audio equipment, computers & related services	275.5	282.8	293.7	300.9	308.5	322.7	331.4	344.1
Video & audio equipment	83.2	81.5	77.8	77.5	77.9	77.9	78.6	80.9
Information processing equipment	95.0	101.8	107.9	111.0	114.6	119.2	123.8	131.6
Services related to video & audio goods & computers	97.3	99.5	108.0	112.4	115.9	125.6	129.1	131.5
Sports & recreational goods & related services	177.4	183.7	193.1	202.9	211.6	222.2	233.4	248.0
Sports & recreational vehicles	35.8	37.3	40.7	45.0	48.3	52.0	56.4	64.8
Other sporting & recreational goods	137.2	141.7	147.4	152.7	157.9	164.6	171.3	177.2
Maintenance & repair of recreational vehicles & sports equipment	4.4	4.8	5.0	5.2	5.4	5.6	5.7	6.0
Membership clubs, sports centers, parks, theaters & museums	146.1	147.2	153.7	160.1	168.1	178.5	189.2	201.8
Membership clubs & participant sports centers	40.9	41.7	43.8	45.6	47.2	49.6	52.1	54.8
Amusement parks, campgrounds & related recreational services	40.1	41.4	44.3	46.8	49.8	54.2	58.0	62.3
Admissions to specified spectator amusements	58.7	57.0	58.1	59.7	62.7	66.2	70.4	75.1
Motion picture theaters	12.3	11.4	12.4	12.7	12.9	13.3	13.9	14.7
Live entertainment, excluding sports	26.7	25.1	24.9	24.8	26.5	28.9	30.8	33.6
Spectator sports	19.7	20.5	20.9	22.1	23.2	24.0	25.6	26.9
Museums & libraries	6.5	7.1	7.5	8.1	8.4	8.4	8.7	9.6
Magazines, newspapers, books & stationery	74.8	72.9	70.0	72.0	75.9	80.8	86.5	92.2
Gambling	109.4	111.5	115.5	119.0	121.9	125.8	130.1	136.0
Pets, pet products & related services	76.2	80.0	84.3	88.1	93.2	98.4	104.5	110.5
Photographic goods & services	15.2	14.4	14.4	14.6	15.4	15.9	15.8	16.1
Package tours[1]	9.8	9.1	9.7	9.9	10.4	10.9	11.3	11.9

[1] Consists of tour operators' and travel agents' margins. Purchases of travel and accommodations included in tours are accounted for separately in other personal consumption expenditures categories.

Source: Bureau of Economic Analysis
Plunkett Research, ® Ltd.   Copyright © 2019, All Rights Reserved
www.plunkettresearch.com

Newspaper Publishers:
Estimated Sources of Revenue & Expenses, U.S.: 2013-2018

(In Millions of US$; Latest Year Available)

NAICS Code: 51111	2018*	2017	2016	2015	2014	2013
Total Operating Revenue	24,776	25,204	25,264	26,550	28,112	28,512
Subscriptions and sales		8,852	8,848	8,873	8,040	7,953
Advertising space		13,438	13,648	14,734	15,667	16,081
Printing services for others		1,067	1,081	1,109	1,454	1,452
Distribution services (e.g. flyers, inserts, samples)		533	547	614	1,052	1,078
All other operating revenue		1,314	1,140	1,220	1,899	1,948
Breakdown of Revenue by Media Type						
Print newspapers		17,270	17,775	19,033	20,421	21,389
Online newspapers		4,961	4,680	4,534	2,901	2,277
Other media newspapers		59	S	S	385	368
Breakdown of Revenue by Advertising Revenue						
Classified advertising		3,100	3,152	3,465	3,288	3,627
All other advertising		10,338	10,496	11,269	12,379	12,454
Operating Expenses						
Total		23,611	24,022	23,650	24,950	26,633	27,249

Notes: Estimates are based on data from the 2017 Service Annual Survey and administrative data. Dollar volume estimates are published in millions of dollars; consequently, results may not be additive. Estimates have been adjusted using results of the 2012 Economic Census where applicable

* Plunkett Research Estimate.

S = Estimate does not meet publication standards because of high sampling variability (coefficient of variation is greater than 30%) or poor response quality (total quantity response rate is less than 50%). Unpublished estimates derived from this table by subtraction are subject to these same limitations and should not be attributed to the U.S. Census Bureau.

Source: U.S. Census Bureau

Plunkett Research, ® Ltd.   Copyright © 2019, All Rights Reserved
www.plunkettresearch.com

Periodical Publishers:
Estimated Sources of Revenue & Expenses, U.S.: 2013-2018

(In Millions of US$; Latest Year Available)

NAICS Code: 51112	2018*	2017	2016	2015	2014	2013
Total Operating Revenue	27,128	28,258	28,237	28,314	29,378	29,185
Periodicals - subscriptions & sales		S	9,861	10,108	10,435	10,691
Periodicals - advertising space		S	14,425	14,496	12,475	12,617
Printing services for others			609	637	651	966	924
Sale or licensing of rights to content		S	483	486	497	432
All other operating revenue			2,601	2,831	2,573	5,005	4,521
Breakdown of Revenue by Media Type						
Print periodicals		S	16,550	16,818	17,790	18,499
Online periodicals			6,886	6,582	6,569	4,433	4,046
Other media periodicals		S	S	S	687	763
Operating Expenses						
Total	22,245	23,390	23,123	23,026	23,966	23,621

Notes: Estimates are based on data from the 2017 Service Annual Survey and administrative data. Dollar volume estimates are published in millions of dollars; consequently, results may not be additive. Estimates have been adjusted using results of the 2017 Economic Census where applicable.

S = Estimate does not meet publication standards because of high sampling variability (coefficient of variation is greater than 30%) or poor response quality (total quantity response rate is less than 50%) or other concerns about the estimate's quality.

* Plunkett Research Estimate.

Source: U.S. Census Bureau
Plunkett Research, ® Ltd.   Copyright © 2019, All Rights Reserved
www.plunkettresearch.com

Book Publishers: Estimated Sources of Revenue, Inventories & Expenses, U.S.: 2013-2018

(In Millions of US$; Latest Year Available)

NAICS Code: 51113	2018*	2017	2016	2015	2014	2013
Total Operating Revenue	**28,302**	**27,478**	**27,744**	**27,676**	**26,891**	**26,720**
Books		18,228	25,464	25,209	22,395	23,077
Textbooks		10,869	11,121	11,707	8,616	8,581
Children's books		1,981	1,911	1,900	3,234	3,223
General reference books		S	S	S	625	548
Professional, technical & scholarly books		S	7,007	6,426	4,369	4,414
Adult trade books		5,378	5,425	5,176	5,551	6,311
All other operating revenue		1,841	1,984	2,138	4,496	3,643
Breakdown of Revenue by Media Type						
Print books		16,109	16,569	16,636	17,127	17,690
Online books		S	7,760	7,513	4,274	4,630
Other media books		S	1,431	1,389	994	757
Inventories at End of the Year						
Total		4,638	4,748	4,272	3,021	2,840
Finished goods		4,360	4,209	3,716	2,724	2,594
Work-in-process		147	219	228	141	111
Materials, supplies, fuel, etc.		S	320	328	156	135
Operating Expenses						
Total	17,830	17,578	17,267	17,587	17,799	16,700

Notes: Estimates are based on data from the 2017 Service Annual Survey and administrative data. Dollar volume estimates are published in millions of dollars; consequently, results may not be additive. Estimates have been adjusted using results of the 2017 Economic Census where applicable

S = Estimate does not meet publication standards because of high sampling variability (coefficient of variation is greater than 30%) or poor response quality (total quantity response rate is less than 50%) or other concerns about the estimate's quality.

* Plunkett Research Estimate

Source: U.S. Census Bureau

Plunkett Research, ® Ltd.   Copyright © 2019, All Rights Reserved
www.plunkettresearch.com

Motion Picture & Video Industries:
Estimated Sources of Revenue, U.S.: 2013-2018

(In Millions of US$; Latest Year Available)

Industry	2018*	2017	2016	2015	2014	2013
Motion Picture & Video Production & Distribution[1] (NAICS Code 5121x)						
Total Operating Revenue	70,767	64,941	66,761	64,434	62,831	64,504
Domestic licensing of rights to films		13,973	14,403	15,235	12,156	13,282
Domestic licensing of rights to TV programs		13,347	13,971	13,093	13,225	12,974
International licensing of rights to films		6,705	7,814	7,958	6,897	8,125
International licensing of rights to TV programs		3,435	3,795	3,647	4,828	4,196
Audiovisual works speculatively produced for outright sale		302	323	321	347	289
Contract production of audiovisual works		5,660	5,493	5,612	6,921	6,355
Domestic licensing of rights to others to distribute audiovisual works		943	1,010	898	1,000	1,184
International licensing of rights to others to distribute audiovisual works		427	435	342	352	366
Sale of audiovisual works for the wholesale, retail & rental markets		5,810	6,983	7,474	6,395	8,164
Other production services		3,638	3,159	3,176	4,249	3,829
Merchandise licensing		809	930	877	370	429
All other operating revenue		9,892	8,445	5,801	6,091	5,311
Motion Picture & Video Exhibition (NAICS Code 51213)						
Total Operating Revenue	17,528	17,526	16,536	15,787	14,563	14,144
Admissions to feature film exhibitions		10,621	10,026	9,597	9,316	9,191
Food & beverage sales		5,652	5,306	4,940	4,388	4,140
Rental of retail space (concessionaire space in movie theaters)		69	65	61	53	41
Advertising services		240	193	173	177	170
Coin-operated games & rides		S	33	29	29	24
All other operating revenue		898	913	987	600	578
Postproduction Services & Other Motion Picture & Video Industries (NAICS Code 51219)						
Total Operating Revenue	6,670	6,426	6,292	5,898	5,660	5,301
Audiovisual postproduction services		3,707	3,713	3,410	3,674	3,572
Motion picture film laboratory services		86	S	S	166	140
Duplication & copying services		S	247	235	1,050	1,020
All other operating revenue		2,383	2,218	2,138	770	569

Notes: Estimates are based on data from the 2017 Service Annual Survey and administrative data. Dollar volume estimates are published in millions of dollars; consequently, results may not be additive. Estimates have been adjusted using results of the 2012 Economic Census where applicable.

* Plunkett Research Estimate.

S = Estimate does not meet publication standards because of high sampling variability (coefficient of variation is greater than 30%) or poor response quality (total quantity response rate is less than 50%) or other concerns about the estimate's quality.

Source: U.S. Census Bureau

Plunkett Research,® Ltd.   Copyright © 2019, All Rights Reserved

www.plunkettresearch.com

Sound Recording Industries:
Estimated Sources of Revenue, U.S.: 2013-2018

(In Millions of US$; Latest Year Available)

Industry	2018*	2017	2016	2015	2014	2013
Integrated Record Production/Distribution (NAICS Code 51222)						
Total Operating Revenue	7,495	7,207	6,229	5,765	5,077	5,032
Licensing revenue - Licensing of rights to use musical compositions		650	561	499	446	288
Licensing revenue - Licensing of rights to use musical recordings		148	131	143	113	100
Sale of recordings		5,522	4,778	4,457	3,890	3,982
All other operating revenue		887	759	666	628	662
Music Publishers (NAICS Code 51223)						
Total Operating Revenue	5,984	5,754	5,250	5,054	4,732	4,314
Licensing revenue - Licensing of rights to use musical compositions		4,756	4,420	4,274	3,753	3,496
Licensing revenue - Licensing of rights to use musical recordings		108	86	70	36	30
Administration of copyrights for others		230	165	168	237	205
Sale of recordings		61	S	38	266	173
Print music		303	263	268	242	272
All other operating revenue		296	269	236	198	138
Sound Recording Studios (NAICS Code 51224)						
Total Operating Revenue	1,116	1,073	1,097	1,086	1,002	951
Studio recording		659	742	765	644	647
Sound recording studio rental & leasing		75	62	60	47	46
All other operating revenue		339	293	261	311	258

Notes: Estimates are based on data from the 2017 Service Annual Survey and administrative data. Dollar volume estimates are published in millions of dollars; consequently, results may not be additive. Estimates have been adjusted using results of the 2012 Economic Census where applicable.

S = Estimate does not meet publication standards because of high sampling variability (coefficient of variation is greater than 30%) or poor response quality (total quantity response rate is less than 50%) or other concerns about the estimate's quality.

* Plunkett Research Estimate.

Source: U.S. Census Bureau

Plunkett Research, ® Ltd. Copyright © 2019, All Rights Reserved
www.plunkettresearch.com

Radio Networks & Radio Stations:
Estimated Sources of Revenue & Expenses, U.S.: 2013-2018

(In Millions of US$; Latest Year Available)

Radio Networks (NAICS 515111)	2018*	2017	2016	2015	2014	2013
Total Operating Revenue	8,023	7,641	7,089	6,509	6,011	5,703
National/regional/local air time		1,801	1,596	1,467	1,005	961
Public & non-commercial programming services		415	395	367	427	421
All other operating revenue		5,425	5,098	4,675	4,579	4,321
Total Operating Expenses	5,857	5,623	5,296	5,017	4,581	4,371
Radio Stations (NAICS 515112)						
Total Operating Revenue	12,978	12,360	12,807	12,445	12,397	12,523
National/regional/local air time		10,553	11,001	10,611	10,437	10,558
Public & non-commercial programming services		749	660	711	685	689
All other operating revenue		1,058	1,146	1,123	1,275	1276
Total Operating Expenses	10,642	10,236	10,343	10,034	9,473	9,842

Notes: Estimates are based on data from the 2017 Service Annual Survey and administrative data. Dollar volume estimates are published in millions of dollars; consequently, results may not be additive.

* Plunkett Research Estimate.

Source: U.S. Census Bureau
Plunkett Research, ® Ltd.   Copyright © 2019, All Rights Reserved
www.plunkettresearch.com

Television Broadcasting:
Estimated Sources of Revenue & Expenses, U.S.: 2013-2018

(In Millions of US$; Latest Year Available)

NAICS Code: 51512	2018*	2017	2016	2015	2014	2013
Total Operating Revenue	60,136	57,551	57,823	50,577	49,911	44,782
National/regional/local air time		37,105	39,435	35,706	37,274	34,240
Public & non-commercial programming services		2,004	2,175	2,117	2,246	2,121
All other operating revenue		18,442	16,213	12,754	10,391	8,421
Operating Expenses						
Total	48,109	46,103	47,131	42,448	40,160	36,484

Notes: Estimates are based on data from the 2017 Service Annual Survey and administrative data. Dollar volume estimates are published in millions of dollars; consequently, results may not be additive.

* Plunkett Research Estimate.

Source: U.S. Census Bureau

Plunkett Research, ® Ltd.   Copyright © 2019, All Rights Reserved
www.plunkettresearch.com

Cable & Other Subscription Programming: Estimated Sources of Revenue & Expenses, U.S.: 2013-2018

(In Millions of US$; Latest Year Available)

NAICS Code: 5152	2018*	2017	2016	2015	2014	2013
Total Operating Revenue	87,493	83,327	81,508	78,931	72,473	68,405
Advertising and program revenue - Licensing of rights to broadcast specialty programming protected by copyright		52,160	50,715	48,811	42,266	39,273
Air time (advertising and program content)		26,907	26,745	26,264	26,039	24,734
All other operating revenue		4,260	4,048	3,856	4,168	4,398
Operating Expenses						
Total Operating Expenses	51,621	49,669	48,351	46,359	44,080	40,731
Gross annual payroll		7,566	7,265	6,979	6,151	5,966
Health insurance		616	537	528	504	387
Defined benefit pension plans		S	127	141	91	136
Defined contribution plans		317	251	223	249	230
Payroll taxes, employer paid insurance premiums (except health), and other employer benefits		616	519	503	464	447
Temporary staff and leased employee expense		306	272	238	277	225
Expensed equipment		94	76	82	80	80
Expensed purchases of other materials, parts, and supplies		83	69	63	72	63
Expensed purchases of software		220	178	153	126	109
Purchased electricity		43	60	63	65	64
Purchased fuels (except motor fuels)		1	ZZ	ZZ	1	1
Lease and rental payments for machinery, equipment, and other tangible items		180	185	211	184	191
Lease and rental payments for land, buildings, structures, store spaces, and offices		540	526	502	525	481
Purchased repairs and maintenance to machinery and equipment		105	140	132	107	111
Purchased repairs and maintenance to buildings, structures, and offices		46	36	35	22	19
Purchased advertising and promotional services		3,350	3,228	3,143	2,828	2,632
Program and production costs		24,348	24,493	23,100	21,778	20,799
Depreciation and amortization charges		5,667	4,983	4,957	4,911	4,445
Governmental taxes and license fees		921	861	853	106	92
Data processing and other purchased computer services		59	52	40	53	54
Purchased communication services		116	106	102	102	96
Water, sewer, refuse removal, and other utility payments		27	16	13	11	11
Purchased professional and technical services		701	661	613	642	597
All other operating expenses		S	3,710	3,685	4,731	3,495

Notes: Estimates are based on data from the 2017 Service Annual Survey and administrative data. Dollar volume estimates are published in millions of dollars; consequently, results may not be additive.

ZZ = Absolute value is less than 0.5.

S = Estimate does not meet publication standards because of high sampling variability (coefficient of variation is greater than 30%) or poor response quality (total quantity response rate is less than 50%) or other concerns about the estimate's quality.

* Plunkett Research Estimate.

Source: U.S. Census Bureau
Plunkett Research, ® Ltd.   Copyright © 2019, All Rights Reserved
www.plunkettresearch.com

Internet Publishing & Broadcasting & Web Search Portals: Estimated Revenue & Expenses, U.S.: 2013-2018

(In Millions of US$; Latest Year Available)

NAICS Code 51913	2018*	2017	2016	2015	2014	2013
Total Operating Revenue	198,106	170,781	148,039	125,868	109,414	96,951
Publishing & broadcasting of content on the Internet		42,806	37,948	33,763	34,079	30,765
Licensing of rights to use intellectual property		4,317	4,125	3,590	4,133	3,782
Online advertising space		105,190	90,288	75,266	54,670	49,805
All other operating revenue		18,468	15,678	13,249	16,532	12,599
Total Operating Expenses	158,485	136,426	117,929	109,619	94,306	76,765

Notes: Estimates are based on data from the 2017 Service Annual Survey and administrative data. Dollar volume estimates are published in millions of dollars; consequently, results may not be additive.

* Plunkett Research Estimate.

Source: U.S. Census Bureau

Plunkett Research, ® Ltd.   Copyright © 2019, All Rights Reserved
www.plunkettresearch.com

Number of Business & Residential High Speed Internet Lines, U.S.: 2013-2018

(In Thousands)

Types of Technology	Dec-13	Dec-14	Dec-15	Dec-16	Dec-17*	Dec-18*
ADSL	30,690	29,533	28,134	26,527	24,614	22,839
SDSL	108	72	60	42	34	27
Other Wireline[1]	772	773	694	655	649	643
Cable Modem	54,009	55,785	59,706	63,325	66,007	68,803
FTTP[2]	7,745	9,077	10,498	12,053	13,960	16,169
Satellite	1,849	2,006	2,071	1,864	1,637	1,438
Fixed Wireless	858	999	1,054	1,238	1,293	1,351
Total Fixed	**96,032**	**98,245**	**102,216**	**105,704**	**108,194**	**111,270**
Mobile Wireless (Smartphone)	197,365	239,957	273,679	299,256	310,595	322,364
Total Lines	**293,397**	**338,202**	**375,895**	**404,960**	**418,790**	**433,634**

Notes: High-speed lines are connections to end-user locations that deliver services at speeds exceeding 200 kbps in at least one direction. Advanced services lines, which are a subset of high-speed lines, are connections that deliver services at speeds exceeding 200 kbps in both directions. Line counts presented in this report are not adjusted for the number of persons at a single end-user location who have access to, or who use, the Internet-access services that are delivered over the high-speed connection to that location.

[1] Power Line and Other are summarized with Other Wireline to maintain firm confidentiality.

[2] Fiber to the premises.

* Plunkett Research Estimate.

Source: U.S. Federal Communications Bureau (FCC), Plunkett Research Estimates
Plunkett Research, ® Ltd.   Copyright © 2019, All Rights Reserved
www.plunkettresearch.com

Estimated Export Revenue for Information Sector Firms, U.S.: 2013-2017

(In Millions of US$; Latest Year Available)

NAICS Code	Kind of business	2017	2016	2015	2014	2013
51111	Newspaper Publishers	S	157	133	115	133
51112	Periodical Publishers	S	934	981	S	S
51113	Book Publishers	S	955	883	1,300	1,250
51114	Directory & Mailing List Publishers	364	S	340	144	114
511191	Greeting Card Publishers	S	11	15	37	36
511199	All Other Publishers	81	65	52	68	60
5112	Software Publishers	36,580	33,911	31,778	30,359	27,735
5121x	Motion Picture & Video Production & Distribution[1]	3,323	4,038	4,468	S	S
512191	Teleproduction & Other Postproduction Services	222	D	96	55	60
512199	Other Motion Picture & Video Industries	S	S	S	S	S

Notes: Estimates are based on data from the 2017 Service Annual Survey and administrative data. Dollar volume estimates are published in millions of dollars; consequently, results may not be additive.

S = Estimate does not meet publication standards because of high sampling variability (coefficient of variation is greater than 30%) or poor response quality (total quantity response rate is less than 50%). Unpublished estimates derived from this table by subtraction are subject to these same limitations and should not be attributed to the U.S. Census Bureau.

D = Estimate in table is withheld to avoid disclosing data of individual companies; data are included in higher level totals.

[1] Includes NAICS 51211 (Motion Picture and Video Production) and NAICS 51212 (Motion Picture and Video Distribution).

Source: U.S. Census Bureau

Plunkett Research,® Ltd.   Copyright © 2019, All Rights Reserved
www.plunkettresearch.com

Employment & Earnings in Selected Entertainment & Media Occupations, U.S.: May 2017

(Latest Year Available)

Occupation Title	Number Employed[1]	Median Hourly Wage	Mean Hourly Wage	Annual Mean Wage[2]	Mean Wage RSE[3]
Art Directors	38,110	$44.47	$49.76	$103,510	0.7%
Multi-Media Artists & Animators	29,860	$33.91	$36.81	$76,560	1.4%
Fashion Designers	18,940	$32.41	$37.92	$78,870	1.5%
Graphic Designers	217,170	$23.41	$25.62	$53,280	0.4%
Set & Exhibit Designers	11,490	$25.52	$28.65	$59,590	1.5%
Actors	43,470	$17.49	$32.89	(4)	3.8%
Producers & Directors	117,520	$34.43	$43.64	$90,770	1.3%
Dancers	9,930	$14.25	$17.70	(4)	3.2%
Choreographers	5,310	$23.28	$25.47	$52,970	3.4%
Music Directors & Composers	15,400	$24.32	$29.56	61490	2.8%
Musicians & Singers	40,170	$26.96	$35.86	(4)	2.4%
Radio & TV Announcers	28,580	$15.60	$22.90	$47,630	1.7%
Broadcast News Analysts	5,700	$30.24	$42.43	$88,250	3.1%
Reporters & Correspondents	38,790	$18.93	$24.79	$51,550	1.6%
Editors	96,890	$28.25	$32.80	$68,230	0.8%
Technical Writers	49,960	$34.10	$35.79	$74,440	0.6%
Writers & Authors	45,300	$29.72	$34.67	$72,120	1.2%
Interpreters & Translators	53,150	$22.69	$24.90	$51,790	1.4%
Audio & Video Equipment Technicians	72,740	$20.28	$22.85	$47,530	0.8%
Broadcast Technicians	30,390	$18.78	$22.47	$46,730	1.5%
Radio Operators	770	$21.31	$21.39	$44,490	2.7%
Sound Engineering Technicians	13,370	$26.83	$32.78	$68,180	2.4%
Photographers	49,320	$15.62	$20.17	$41,940	1.9%
Camera Operators, TV, Video & Motion Picture	20,860	$25.74	$29.58	$61,530	2.0%
Film & Video Editors	30,770	$29.41	$40.36	$83,950	3.7%

[1] Estimates do not include self-employed workers.

[2] Annual wages have been calculated by multiplying the hourly mean wage by a "year-round, full-time" hours figure of 2,080 hours; for those occupations where there is not an hourly mean wage published, the annual wage has been directly calculated from the reported survey data.

[3] The relative standard error (RSE) is a measure of the reliability of a survey statistic. The smaller the relative standard error, the more precise the estimate.

[4] Wages for some occupations that do not generally work year-round, full time, are reported either as hourly wages or annual salaries depending on how they are typically paid.

Source: U.S. Bureau of Labor Statistics
Plunkett Research, ® Ltd.   Copyright © 2019, All Rights Reserved
www.plunkettresearch.com

Employment in Selected Information & Entertainment Industries, U.S.: 2013-October 2018

(Annual Estimates in Thousands of Employed Workers; Not Seasonally Adjusted)

NAICS Code[1]	Industry Sector	2013	2014	2015	2016	2017	Oct-18*
51	**Information**	**2,706.0**	**2,726.0**	**2,750.0**	**2,794.0**	**2,795.0**	**2,773.0**
511	Publishing industries, except Internet	732.7	726.9	726.5	730.3	723.0	714.3
5111	Newspaper, book & directory publishers	433.0	411.4	392.0	371.5	348.5	324.1
51111	Newspaper publishers	213.3	202.1	190.7	176.6	160.6	140.8
51112	Periodical publishers	107.4	103.1	99.8	97.3	92.9	89.5
51113	Book publishers	68.2	65.1	64.1	62.3	60.8	61.0
51114,9	Directory, mailing list, and other publishers	44.1	41.1	37.5	35.3	34.3	32.8
5112	Software publishers	299.6	315.5	334.4	358.8	374.5	390.2
512	Motion picture & sound recording industries	370.5	379.3	397.9	426.1	425.4	421.2
51211	Motion picture & video production	200.8	206.9	219.2	241.2	234.6	237.2
51213	Motion picture & video exhibition	129.5	129.6	135.6	142.6	146.1	142.2
515	Broadcasting, except Internet	283.7	282.8	276.7	270.5	265.7	263.6
5151	Radio & television broadcasting	214.6	220.0	217.3	216.7	214.2	213.9
51511	Radio broadcasting	90.4	89.7	86.9	84.9	83.5	82.1
51512	Television broadcasting	124.2	130.3	130.4	131.7	130.7	131.8
5152	Cable & other subscription programming	69.1	62.8	59.3	53.8	51.5	49.7
519	Other information services	196.2	219.0	241.4	262.3	281.3	298.9
51913	Internet publishing & broadcasting & web search portals	142.3	163.3	184.3	203.5	219.4	235.9

[1] For a full description of the NAICS codes used in this table, see www.census.gov/eos/www/naics/index.html
* Preliminary estimates as of October 2018.

Source: U.S. Bureau of Labor Statistics
Plunkett Research, ® Ltd.   Copyright © 2019, All Rights Reserved
www.plunkettresearch.com

Chapter 3

IMPORTANT ENTERTAINMENT, MOVIE, PUBLISHING & MEDIA INDUSTRY CONTACTS

Addresses, Telephone Numbers and Internet Sites

Contents:

1) Advertising Resources
2) Advertising/Marketing Associations
3) Audience & Circulation Research
4) Booksellers Associations
5) Broadcasting, Cable, Radio & TV Associations
6) Canadian Government Agencies-Communications
7) Canadian Government Agencies-General
8) Careers-First Time Jobs/New Grads
9) Careers-General Job Listings
10) Careers-Job Reference Tools
11) Communications Professional Associations
12) Computer & Electronics Industry Associations
13) Corporate Information Resources
14) Economic Data & Research
15) Electronic Publishing Associations
16) Engineering, Research & Scientific Associations
17) Entertainment & Amusement Associations-General
18) Entertainment and Video Statistics in Europe
19) Film & Television Resources
20) Film & Theater Associations
21) Gambling Industry Associations
22) Games Industry Associations
23) Games Industry Resources
24) Graphic Artists Associations
25) Hotel/Lodging Associations
26) Industry Research/Market Research
27) Internet Industry Associations
28) Internet Usage Statistics
29) MBA Resources
30) Media Associations-Educational
31) Media Industry Information
32) News Organizations & Resources
33) Printers & Publishers Associations
34) Public Relations Associations
35) Publishing Industry Resources
36) Recording & Music Associations
37) Restaurant Industry Associations
38) Retail Industry Associations
39) Satellite Industry Associations
40) Software Industry Associations
41) Sports Industry Resources
42) Sports Leagues-Electronic Games
43) Stocks & Financial Markets Data
44) Technology Transfer Associations
45) Toy Industry Associations
46) Trade Associations-General
47) Trade Associations-Global
48) Trade Resources
49) U.S. Government Agencies
50) Writers, Photographers & Editors Associations

1) Advertising Resources

AdAsia
c/o BluePrint Media Pte Ltd.
102F Pasir Panjang Rd., 07-02 Citilink Complex
118530 Singapore
Phone: 65-6276-9935
Fax: 65-6276-8831
E-mail Address: *info@adasia.com.sg*
Web Address: www.adasiaonline.com

The AdAsia is a online magazine for the advertising, marketing and media community in Singapore and the Asia-Pacific region. The website includes news articles, events, jobs and general industry links and information.

Interactive Advertising Bureau (IAB)
116 E. 27th St., Fl. 7
New York, NY 10016 USA
Phone: 212-380-4700
Web Address: www.iab.net
The Interactive Advertising Bureau (IAB) is dedicated to helping online, email, wireless and interactive advertisers increase their revenues. The organization publishes numerous research reports and articles regarding the Internet advertising industry.

2) Advertising/Marketing Associations

4A's (American Association of Advertising Agencies)
1065 Ave. of the Americas, Fl. 16
New York, NY 10018 USA
Phone: 212-682-2500
Web Address: www.aaaa.org
The 4A's (American Association of Advertising Agencies) is the national trade association representing the advertising agency industry in the U.S.

Advertising Club of New York (The)
989 Ave. of the Americas, Fl. 7
New York, NY 10018 USA
Phone: 212-533-8080
Web Address: www.theadvertisingclub.org
The Advertising Club of New York strives to elevate the understanding of marketing and advertising communications in New York by providing a forum for members of the industry to address common interests.

Advertising Research Foundation (ARF)
432 Park Ave. S., Fl. 6
New York, NY 10016-8013 USA
Phone: 212-751-5656
E-mail Address: Member-info@thearf.org
Web Address: www.thearf.org
The Advertising Research Foundation (ARF), a nonprofit corporate-membership association, is a leading professional organization in the fields of advertising, marketing and media research.

Advertising Self-Regulatory Council (ASRC)
112 Madison Ave., Fl. 3
New York, NY 10016 USA
Phone: 212-705-0104
Fax: 212-705-0134
E-mail Address: csasena@asrc.bbb.org
Web Address: www.asrcreviews.org
The Advertising Self-Regulatory Council (ASRC), formerly the National Advertising Division of the Council of Better Business Bureaus, Inc., provides the advertising community with a system of self-regulation, minimizes government intervention and fosters public confidence in the credibility of advertising.

Advertising Standards Canada (ASC)
175 Bloor St. E., S. Twr., Ste. 1801
Toronto, ON M4W 3R8 Canada
Phone: 416-961-6311
Fax: 416-961-7904
Web Address: www.adstandards.com
Advertising Standards Canada (ASC) is a nonprofit association that provides quality standards for the Canadian advertising industry.

Advertising Women of New York (AWNY)
28 W. 44th St., Ste. 912
New York, NY 10036 USA
Phone: 212-221-7969
E-mail Address: lynn.branigan@awny.org
Web Address: www.awny.org
Advertising Women of New York (AWNY) provides a forum for personal and professional growth, serves as a catalyst for the advancement of women in the communications field and promotes and supports philanthropic endeavors through the AWNY Foundation. The web site also provides content from Women Executives in Public Relations (WERP), such as its a dynamic job board.

American Advertising Federation, Inc. (AAF)
1101 Vermont Ave. NW, Ste. 500
Washington, DC 20005-6306 USA
Phone: 202-898-0089
E-mail Address: addyinfo@aaf.org
Web Address: www.aaf.org
The American Advertising Federation, Inc. (AAF) protects and promotes the well-being of advertising through a nationally coordinated network of advertisers, agencies, media companies, local advertising clubs and college chapters.

American Institute of Graphic Arts (AIGA)
233 Broadway, Fl. 17
New York, NY 10279 USA
Phone: 212-807-1990
Web Address: www.aiga.org
The American Institute of Graphic Arts (AIGA) strives to further excellence in communication design, both as a strategic tool for business and as a cultural force.

American Marketing Association (AMA)
130 E. Randolph St., Fl. 22
Chicago, IL 60601 USA
Phone: 312-542-9000
Fax: 312-542-9001
Toll Free: 800-262-1150
Web Address: www.ama.org

The American Marketing Association (AMA) serves marketing professionals in both business and education and serves all levels of marketing practitioners, educators and students.

Art Directors Club, Inc. (ADC)
106 W. 29th St.
New York, NY 10001 USA
Phone: 212-643-1440
Fax: 212-643-4266
E-mail Address: info@adcglobal.org
Web Address: www.adcglobal.org
The Art Directors Club (ADC) is an international not-for-profit organization of creative leaders in advertising, graphic design, interactive media, broadcast design, typography, packaging, environmental design, photography, illustration and related disciplines.

Association for Leaders in Print, Mail, Fulfillment and Marketing Services (EPICOMM)
1800 Diagonal Rd., Ste. 320
Alexandria, VA 22314-2806 USA
Phone: 703-836-9200
Web Address: www.mfsanet.org
Association for Leaders in Print, Mail, Fulfillment and Marketing Services (EPICOMM) is a nonprofit organization representing graphic communications industry in North America. It was formed through the merger of Association of Marketing Service Providers (AMSP) and the National Association for Printing Leadership (NAPL)/National Association of Quick Printers (NAQP).

Association of Accredited Advertising Agents, Singapore
38A N. Canal Rd.
Singapore, 059294 Singapore
Phone: 65-6836-0600
Fax: 65-6836-0700
E-mail Address: events@4as.org.sg
Web Address: www.4as.org.sg
The Association of Accredited Advertising Agents Singapore, better known as the 4As, represents advertising and marketing communications practitioners, agencies and related businesses in Singapore. It works in close co-operation with other related trade associations, schools and government bodies.

Association of Canadian Advertisers, Inc. (ACA)
95 St. Clair Ave. W., Ste. 1103
Toronto, ON M4V 1N6 Canada
Phone: 416-964-3805
Fax: 416-964-0771
Toll Free: 800-565-0109
E-mail Address: rlund@acaweb.ca
Web Address: www.acaweb.ca
The Association of Canadian Advertisers (ACA) is an organization that is expressly dedicated to representing the interests of companies that market and advertise their products in Canada.

Association of Independent Commercial Producers (AICP)
3 W. 18th St., Fl. 5
New York, NY 10011 USA
Phone: 212-929-3000
Fax: 212-929-3359
E-mail Address: mattm@aicp.com
Web Address: www.aicp.com
The Association of Independent Commercial Producers (AICP) represents the interests of U.S. companies that specialize in producing commercials in various media for advertisers and agencies.

Association of National Advertisers (ANA)
708 Third Ave., Fl. 33
New York, NY 10017-4270 USA
Phone: 212-697-5950
Fax: 212-687-7310
E-mail Address: info@ana.net
Web Address: www.ana.net
The Association of National Advertisers (ANA) is a leading industry association that is devoted to marketing and brand building. The agency represents 680 of the largest advertisers, who collectively spend $250 billion on advertising a year.

Business Marketing Association (BMA)
708 Third Ave.
New York, NY 10017 USA
Phone: 212-697-5950
Fax: 212-687-7310
E-mail Address: info@marketing.org
Web Address: www.marketing.org
The Business Marketing Association (BMA), a division of Association of National Advertisers (ANA) serves the professional, educational and career development needs of business-to-business marketers and their partner suppliers.

Cable & Telecommunications Association for Marketing (CTAM)
120 Waterfront St., Ste. 200
National Harbor, MD 20745 USA
Phone: 301-485-8900
Fax: 301-560-4964
E-mail Address: info@ctam.com
Web Address: www.ctam.com
The Cable & Telecommunications Association for Marketing (CTAM) is dedicated to the discipline and development of consumer marketing excellence in cable television, new media and telecommunications services.

Cinema Advertising Council (CAC)
Phone: 212-986-7080
Fax: 212-986-2354
E-mail Address: matt@lippingroup.com

Web Address: www.cinemaadcouncil.org
The Cinema Advertising Council (CAC) was formed to address the unique consumer research needs of the cinema media industry. CAC's goals are to: promote a positive image for the industry and its members while successfully positioning cinema advertising as an effective, independent consumer research media option, streamline the cinema media buying process by standardizing industry practices, and provide uniform data for measurement and evaluation of the cinema media research landscape.

Direct Marketing Association (DMA)
1120 Ave. of the Americas
New York, NY 10036-6700 USA
Phone: 212-768-7277
Web Address: thedma.org
The Direct Marketing Association (DMA) is the oldest and largest trade association for users and suppliers in the direct, database and interactive marketing fields.

Institute of Advertising, Singapore (IAS)
60 Paya Lebar Rd.
#05-15 Paya Lebar Square
Singapore, 409501 Singapore
Phone: 65-6220-8382
Fax: 65-6221-1106
E-mail Address: enquiry@ias.org.sg
Web Address: www.ias.org.sg
The Institute of Advertising (IAS) is a professional organization catering to the interests of individual advertising and marketing communications practitioners in Singapore.

Intermarket Agency Network (IAN)
Web Address: www.intermarketnetwork.com
The Intermarket Agency Network (IAN) is a network of independent, full-service advertising agencies established to exchange knowledge in a collaborative setting.

International Advertising Association (IAA)
747 Third Ave., Fl. 2
New York, NY 10017 USA
Phone: 646-722-2612
Fax: 646-722-2501
E-mail Address: iaa@iaaglobal.org
Web Address: www.iaaglobal.org
The International Advertising Association (IAA) is a strategic partnership that champions the common interests of disciplines across the full spectrum of the marketing communications industry.

Marketing Agencies Association Worldwide (MAA)
60 Peachcroft Dr.
Bernardsville, NJ 07924 USA
Phone: 908-428-4300
Fax: 908-766-1277
Web Address: www.maaw.org
Marketing Agencies Association Worldwide (MAA) is a global organization dedicated exclusively to the CEOs, presidents, managing directors and principals of top marketing services agencies.

Mobile Marketing Association (MMA)
41 E 11 St., Fl. 11
New York, NY 10003 USA
Phone: 646-257-4515
E-mail Address: mma@mmaglobal.com
Web Address: www.mmaglobal.com
MMA is a global organization with offices in many cities, including a New York headquarters, a Bellevue, Washington correspondence office, and chapters throughout Europe, Asia-Pacific, the Middle East and Latin America. MMA members include agencies, advertisers, hand held device manufacturers, carriers and operators, retailers, software providers and service providers, as well as companies focused on the potential of marketing via mobile devices.

New York American Marketing Association (NYAMA)
116 E. 27th St., Fl. 6
New York, NY 10016 USA
Phone: 212-687-3280
E-mail Address: amcmaster@nyama.org
Web Address: www.nyama.org
The New York American Marketing Association (NYAMA) is an organization of marketing professionals from a wide range of industries who seek the knowledge to make themselves more effective marketers.

Outdoor Advertising Association of America, Inc. (OAAA)
1850 M St. NW, Ste. 1040
Washington, DC 20036 USA
Phone: 202-833-5566
Fax: 202-833-1522
Web Address: www.oaaa.org
The Outdoor Advertising Association of America, Inc. (OAAA) is a leading trade association representing the outdoor advertising industry.

Point-of-Purchase Advertising International (POPAI)
440 N. Wells St., Ste. 740
Chicago, IL 60654 USA
Phone: 312-863-2900
Fax: 312-229-1152
Web Address: www.popai.com
Point-of-Purchase Advertising International (POPAI), formerly known as the Point-of-Purchase Advertising Institute is an international nonprofit trade association dedicated to serving the interests of advertisers, retailers, producers and suppliers of point-of-purchase products and services. POPAI has over 1,400 member companies.

3) Audience & Circulation Research

Alliance for Audited Media (AAM)
48 W. Seegers Rd.
Arlington Heights, IL 60005-3913 USA
Phone: 224-366-6939
Fax: 224-366-6949
Web Address: www.auditedmedia.com
The Alliance for Audited Media (AAM), formerly the Audit Bureau of Circulations, is the leading magazine circulation auditing organization for newspaper and magazine publishers in the U.S. and Canada, as well as advertising agencies and advertisers. It aims to conduct audits that set the industry standard for integrity, objectivity and accuracy.

Arbitron, Inc.
9705 Patuxent Woods Dr.
Columbia, MD 21046-1572 USA
Phone: 410-312-8000
E-mail Address: radioquestions@arbitron.com
Web Address: www.arbitron.com
Arbitron, Inc., an international media and marketing research firm, serves the radio, online radio, cable and television industries, as well as advertising agencies and advertisers in Europe and the U.S.

BPA Worldwide
100 Beard Sawmill Rd., Fl. 6
Shelton, CT 06484 USA
Phone: 203-447-2800
Fax: 203-447-2900
Web Address: www.bpaww.com
BPA Worldwide is a global provider of audited data to the marketing, media and information industries. Worldwide it serves over 3,800 media properties in more than 20 countries.

Media Rating Council (MRC)
420 Lexington Ave., Ste. 343
New York, NY 10170 USA
Phone: 212-972-0300
Fax: 212-972-2786
E-mail Address: staff@mediaratingcouncil.org
Web Address: www.mediaratingcouncil.org
The Media Rating Council (MRC) is a nonprofit regulatory agency that promotes valid, accurate audience measurement services for the media industry.

Television Bureau of Advertising (TVB)
120 Wall St., Fl. 15
New York, NY 10005-3908 USA
Phone: 212-486-1111
Fax: 212-935-5631
E-mail Address: info@tvb.org
Web Address: www.tvb.org
The Television Bureau of Advertising (TVB) is the not-for-profit trade association of America's broadcast television industry, providing resources that enable advertisers to make the best use of local television. It provides extensive TV audience studies, by market.

Television Bureau of Canada (TVB)
160 Bloor St. E., Ste. 1005
Toronto, ON M4W 1B9 Canada
Phone: 416-923-8813
Fax: 416-413-3879
E-mail Address: tvb@tvb.ca
Web Address: www.tvb.ca
The Television Bureau of Canada (TVB) is a resource center for television stations, networks and their sales representatives.

Video Advertising Bureau (The) (VAB)
830 3rd Ave., Fl. 2
New York, NY 10022 USA
Phone: 212-508-1200
Fax: 212-832-3268
E-mail Address: JoleenM@cabletvadbureau.com
Web Address: www.thevab.com
The Video Advertising Bureau (VAB) provides information and resources to the advertising community to support marketing and media planning; assists its industry members in maximizing advertising revenues; and promotes the use of professionally-produced, premium, multi-screen TV and video content for multi-screen advertising locally, regionally and nationally.

4) Booksellers Associations

American Booksellers Association, Inc.
333 Westchester Ave., Ste. S202
White Plains, NY 10604 USA
Phone: 914-406-7500
Fax: 914-417-4013
Toll Free: 800-637-0037
E-mail Address: info@bookweb.org
Web Address: www.bookweb.org
The American Booksellers Association is a nonprofit association representing independent bookstores in the United States.

Midwest Booksellers Association (MBA)
2355 Louisiana Ave. N., Ste. A
Golden Valley, MN 55427 USA
Phone: 763-544-2993
Fax: 612-354-5728
E-mail Address: info@midwestbooksellers.org
Web Address: www.midwestbooksellers.org
Midwest Booksellers Association (MBA) is a regional nonprofit organization that promotes retail bookselling and supports professional independent booksellers throughout the Midwest.

National Association of College Stores (NACS)
500 E. Lorain St.

Oberlin, OH 44074 USA
Fax: 440-775-4769
Toll Free: 800-622-7498
E-mail Address: webteam@nacs.org
Web Address: www.nacs.org
The National Association of College Stores (NACS) is the professional trade association representing college retailers and associate members who supply books and other products to college stores.

5) Broadcasting, Cable, Radio & TV Associations

Academy of Television Arts and Sciences
5220 Lankershim Blvd.
North Hollywood, CA 91601-3109 USA
Phone: 818-754-2800
Web Address: www.emmys.tv
The Academy of Television Arts and Sciences is a nonprofit corporation devoted to the advancement of telecommunications arts and sciences and to fostering creative leadership in the telecommunications industry. It is one of three organizations that administer the Emmy Awards. It is responsible for prime-time Emmys.

Advanced Television Systems Committee (ATSC)
1776 K St. NW, Ste. 200
Washington, DC 20006-2304 USA
Phone: 202-872-9160
Fax: 202-872-9161
E-mail Address: atsc@atsc.org
Web Address: www.atsc.org
The Advanced Television Systems Committee (ATSC) is an international nonprofit membership organization that develops voluntary standards for the entire spectrum of advanced television systems.

Alliance for Community Media (ACM)
4248 Park Glen Rd.
Minneapolis, MN 55416 USA
E-mail Address: info@allcommunitymedia.org
Web Address: www.allcommunitymedia.org/
The Alliance for Community Media (ACM) is a group committed to assuring universal access to electronic media.

Alliance for Women in Media
1760 Old Meadow Rd., Ste. 500
McLean, VA 22102 USA
Phone: 703-506-3290
Fax: 703-506-3266
E-mail Address: info@allwomeninmedia.org
Web Address: www.allwomeninmedia.org/
The Alliance for Women in Media, formerly the American Women in Radio and Television (AWRT), founded in 1951, is a national nonprofit organization dedicated to advancing the role of women in electronic media and related fields.

American Sportscasters Association (ASA)
225 Broadway, Ste. 2030
New York, NY 10007 USA
Phone: 212-227-8080
Fax: 212-571-0556
E-mail Address: inquiry@americansportscastersonline.com
Web Address: www.americansportscastersonline.com
The American Sportscasters Association (ASA) is a professional organization for the promotion and support of sports broadcasters. The ASA is also a resource for those interested in becoming sportscasters.

Association for International Broadcasting (AIB)
P.O. Box 141
Cranbrook, TN17 9AJ UK
Phone: 44-20-7993-2557
Fax: 44-20-7993-8043
E-mail Address: contactaib@aib.org.uk
Web Address: www.aib.org.uk
The Association for International Broadcasting (AIB) aims to increase the scope and effectiveness of international broadcasting, working on a global, co-operative basis.

Association of America's Public Television Stations (APTS)
2100 Crystal Dr., Ste. 700
Arlington, VA 22202 USA
Phone: 202-654-4200
Fax: 202-654-4236
E-mail Address: skarp@apts.org
Web Address: www.apts.org
The Association of America's Public Television Stations (APTS) is a nonprofit membership organization formed to support the continued growth and development of strong and financially sound noncommercial television service for the American public.

Association of Cable Communicators (ACC)
9259 Old Keene Mill Rd., Ste. 202
Burke, VA 22015 USA
Phone: 703-372-2215
Fax: 703-782-0153
Toll Free: 800-210-3396
E-mail Address: services@cablecommunicators.org
Web Address: www.cablecommunicators.org
Association of Cable Communicators (ACC) is the only national professional organization specifically addressing the issues, needs and interests of the cable industry's public affairs professionals.

Broadcast Cable Credit Association, Inc. (BCCA)
550 W. Frontage Rd.
Ste. 3600
Northfield, IL 60093 USA
Phone: 847-881-8757
Fax: 847-784-8059
E-mail Address: info@bccacredit.com

Web Address: www.bccacredit.com
The Broadcast Cable Credit Association, Inc., a subsidiary of Media Financial Management Association (formerly BCFM: Broadcast Cable Financial Management Association), represents credit and collection professionals from more than 600 TV, radio, cable, system operators, newspaper, and magazine organizations in the U.S. and Canada. BCCA functions as a central clearinghouse for credit information on advertisers, agencies and buying services, both locally and nationally.

Broadcast Education Association (BEA)
1771 N St. NW
Washington, DC 20036-2891 USA
Phone: 202-429-3935
Fax: 202-775-2981
E-mail Address: tbailey@nab.org
Web Address: www.beaweb.org
The Broadcast Education Association (BEA) is the professional association for professors, industry professionals and graduate students interested in teaching and research related to electronic media and multimedia enterprises.

Broadcast Pioneers Library of American Broadcasting (LAB)
Hornbake Library
University of Maryland
College Park, MD 20742 USA
Phone: 301-405-9212
E-mail Address: askhornbake@umd.edu
Web Address: http://www.lib.umd.edu/special/collections/massmedia/about-us
The Broadcast Pioneers Library of American Broadcasting (LAB) holds a wide-ranging collection of audio and video recordings, books, pamphlets, periodicals, personal collections, oral histories, photographs, scripts and vertical files devoted exclusively to the history of broadcasting.

Broadcasters' Foundation, Inc.
125 W 55th St., Fl. 3
New York, NY 10019-5366 USA
Phone: 212-373-8250
Fax: 212-373-8254
E-mail Address: info@thebfoa.org
Web Address: www.broadcastersfoundation.org
Broadcasters' Foundation, Inc. is the only organization in radio and television that provides anonymous financial assistance to fellow broadcasters in acute need.

Cable & Satellite Broadcasting Association of Asia (CASBAA)
802 Wilson House
19-27 Wyndham St.
Hong Kong, Hong Kong Hong Kong
Phone: 852-2854-9913
Fax: 852-2854-9530
E-mail Address: casbaa@casbaa.com
Web Address: www.casbaa.com
The Cable & Satellite Broadcasting Association of Asia (CASBAA) is an industry-based advocacy group dedicated to the promotion of multi-channel television via cable, satellite, broadband and wireless video networks across the Asia-Pacific. CASBAA represents some 135 corporations, which in turn serve more than 3 billion people.

Cable Center (The)
2000 Buchtel Blvd.
Denver, CO 80210 USA
Phone: 720-502-7500
E-mail Address: webmaster@cablecenter.org
Web Address: www.cablecenter.org
The Cable Center supports communication in the business, technology and programming of cable telecommunications and provides education, training and research for all aspects of the industry.

Cable in the Classroom (CIC)
25 Massachusetts Ave. NW, Ste. 100
Washington, DC 20001 USA
Phone: 202-222-2335
Fax: 202-222-2336
E-mail Address: help@ciconline.org
Web Address: www.ciconline.org
The Cable in the Classroom (CIC) program provides schools across the U.S. with free cable service and over 540 hours per month of commercial-free educational programming.

Cable Television Laboratories, Inc. (CableLabs)
858 Coal Creek Cir.
Louisville, CO 80027-9750 USA
Phone: 303-661-9100
Fax: 303-661-9199
E-mail Address: info@cablelabs.com
Web Address: www.cablelabs.com
Cable Television Laboratories (CableLabs) is a nonprofit research and development consortium dedicated to pursuing new cable telecommunications technologies and to helping its cable operator members integrate those technical advancements into their business objectives.

Canadian Association of Broadcasters (CAB)
700-45 O'Connor St.
Ottawa, ON K1P 1A4 Canada
Phone: 613-233-4035
Fax: 613-233-6961
E-mail Address: sbissonnette@cab-acr.ca
Web Address: www.cab-acr.ca
The Canadian Association of Broadcasters (CAB) is the collective voice of the majority of Canada's private radio and television stations, networks and specialty services.

Country Radio Broadcasters, Inc. (CRB)
1009 16th Ave. S.

Nashville, TN 37203 USA
Phone: 615-327-4487
Fax: 615-329-4492
Web Address: countryradioseminar.com
Country Radio Broadcasters (CRB) brings together country radio broadcasters from around the world for the purpose of assuring the continued vitality of the country radio format.

Hollywood Radio & Television Society (HRTS)
16530 Ventura Blvd., Ste. 411
Encino, CA 91436 USA
Phone: 818-789-1182
Fax: 818-789-1210
E-mail Address: info@hrts.org
Web Address: www.hrts.org
The Hollywood Radio & Television (HRTS) is an organization of executives from west coast networks, stations, studios, production companies, advertisers, ad agencies, cable companies, media companies, legal firms, publicity agencies, talent and management agencies, performers, services, suppliers and allied fields.

International Federation of Television Archives (IFTA)
DR - Emil Holms Kanal 20
Att.: Tobias Golodnoff, DR Medier
Copenhagen, C 0999 Denmark
E-mail Address: office@fiatifta.org
Web Address: www.fiatifta.org
International Federation of Television Archives (IFTA) is an association of broadcast and national audiovisual archives and libraries involved in the collection and preservation of film and television images.

Jones/NCTI, Inc.
9697 E. Mineral Ave. Centennial
Centennial, CO 80112 USA
Toll Free: 866-575-7206
Web Address: www.ncti.com
Jones/NCTI, Inc. provides workforce performance products, services and education to the broadband and cable television industry.

Media Development Authority (MDA)
3 Fusionopolis Way
16-22 Symbiosis
Singapore, 138633 Singapore
Phone: 65-6377-3800
Fax: 65-6577-3888
Web Address: www.mda.gov.sg
The Media Development Authority (MDA) has been created to develop the media industry in Singapore and respond to the convergence of different media that requires a consistent approach in developing and managing these different forms of media. The MDA was formed by the merger of the Singapore Broadcasting Authority, the Films and Publications Department, and the Singapore Film Commission.

Media Financial Management Association (MFM)
550 W. Frontage Rd., Ste. 3600
Northfield, IL 60093 USA
Phone: 847-716-7000
Fax: 847-716-7004
E-mail Address: info@mediafinance.org
Web Address: www.bcfm.com
The Media Financial Management Association (MFM) formerly Broadcast Cable Financial Management Association (BCFM) is a not-for profit professional association dedicated to the unique interests and needs of business and finance executives in the media industry. Founded in 1961, MFM membership is open to all industry business professionals. In addition, MFM welcomes associate members from allied fields including: accounting; auditing; brokerage; law; tax; and other related disciplines.

National Academy of Television Arts and Sciences
1697 Broadway, Ste. 404
New York, NY 10019 USA
Phone: 212-586-8424
Fax: 212-246-8129
E-mail Address: ppillitteri@emmyonline.tv
Web Address: www.emmyonline.org
The National Academy of Television Arts and Sciences is dedicated to the advancement of the arts and sciences of television and the promotion of creative leadership for artistic, educational and technical achievements within the television industry. It is responsible for awarding the Emmy Awards.

National Association of Black Owned Broadcasters, Inc. (NABOB)
1201 Connecticut Ave. NW, Ste. 200
Washington, DC 20036 USA
Phone: 202-463-8970
Fax: 202-429-0657
E-mail Address: nabobinfo@nabob.org
Web Address: www.nabob.org
National Association of Black Owned Broadcasters, Inc. (NABOB) is a trade organization representing the interests of black and minority owners of radio and television stations in the U.S.

National Association of Broadcasters (NAB)
1771 N St. NW
Washington, DC 20036 USA
Phone: 202-429-5300
Toll Free: 800-622-3976
E-mail Address: nab@nab.org
Web Address: www.nab.org
The National Association of Broadcasters (NAB) represents broadcasters for radio and television. The organization also provides benefits to employees of member companies and to individuals and companies that provide products and services to the electronic media industries.

National Association of Television Program Executives (NATPE)
5757 Wilshire Blvd., Penthouse 10
Los Angeles, CA 90036-3681 USA
Phone: 310-857-1601
E-mail Address: jpbommel@natpe.org
Web Address: www.natpe.org
The National Association of Television Program Executives (NATPE) is the leading association for content professionals in the global television industry. It is dedicated to the growth of video content development, creations, production, financing and distribution across various platforms by providing education and networking opportunities to its members.

National Broadcasting Society - Alpha Epsilon Rho (NBS-AERho)
P.O. Box 4206
Chesterfield, MO 63006 USA
Phone: 636-536-1943
Fax: 636-898-6920
E-mail Address: nbsaerho@swbell.net
Web Address: www.nbs-aerho.org
The National Broadcasting Society - Alpha Epsilon Rho (NBS-AERho) is a student and professional society of more than 85 chapters on college, university, community college and high school campuses.

National Cable and Telecommunications Association (NCTA)
25 Massachusetts Ave. NW, Ste. 100
Washington, DC 20001-1413 USA
Phone: 202-222-2300
Fax: 202-222-2514
E-mail Address: info@ncta.com
Web Address: www.ncta.com
The National Cable and Telecommunications Association (NCTA) is the principal trade association of the cable television industry in the United States. It represents cable operators as well as over 200 cable program networks that produce TV shows.

National Captioning Institute (NCI)
3725 Concorde Pkwy., Ste.100
Chantilly, VA 20151 USA
Phone: 703-917-7600
Fax: 703-917-9853
E-mail Address: mail@ncicap.org
Web Address: www.ncicap.org
The National Captioning Institute (NCI) is a nonprofit organization that provides domestic and international captioning, subtitling and described video for broadcast and cablecast television programs, TV commercials, home video programs, government agencies and corporations.

National Religious Broadcasters (NRB)
9510 Technology Dr.
Manassas, VA 20110 USA
Phone: 703-330-7000
Fax: 703-330-7100
E-mail Address: info@nrbtv.org
Web Address: www.nrb.org
National Religious Broadcasters (NRB) is an international association of Christian communicators whose mission is to advance Biblical truth, promote excellence in media and defend free speech.

New York State Broadcasters Association (NYSBA)
1805 Western Ave.
Albany, NY 12203 USA
Phone: 518-456-8888
Fax: 518-456-8943
E-mail Address: cjung@nysbroadcasters.org
Web Address: www.nysbroadcasters.org
New York State Broadcasters Association (NYSBA) serves as the primary advocate and active representative for New York State's broadcast industry in state and national issues.

Parents Television Council (PTC)
707 Wilshire Blvd., Ste. 2075
Los Angeles, CA 90017 USA
Phone: 213-403-1300
Fax: 213-403-1301
Toll Free: 800-882-6868
E-mail Address: kelly@kellyoliverpr.com
Web Address: www.parentstv.org
The Parents Television Council (PTC) provides reviews of television shows, screening for violence, sexuality and language.

PromaxBDA
5700 Wilshire Blvd.
Los Angeles, CA 90036 USA
Phone: 310-788-7600
Fax: 310-788-7616
E-mail Address: lucian@promaxbda.org
Web Address: www.promaxbda.org
Promax and Broadcast Designers' Association (BDA) together form PromaxBDA, an organization working on behalf of those involved in the promotion, marketing and design of all electronic media.

Public Radio News Directors, Inc. (PRNDI)
Christine Paige, Bus. Mgr.
P.O. Box 838
Sturgis, SD 57785-0838 USA
Phone: 605-490-3033
E-mail Address: gbodarky@wfuv.org
Web Address: www.prndi.org
Public Radio News Directors (PRNDI) is a nonprofit national service organization that encourages the professional development and training of public radio journalists.

Radio Advertising Bureau (RAB)
125 W. 55th St., Fl. 5
New York, NY 10019 USA
Phone: 212-681-7200
Toll Free: 800-232-3131
Web Address: www.rab.com
The mission of the Radio Advertising Bureau (RAB) is to increase the awareness, credibility and salability of radio by designing, developing and implementing appropriate programs, research, tools and activities for member stations.

Radio Television Digital News Association (RTDNA)
529 14th St. NW, Ste. 1240
Washington, DC 20045 USA
Fax: 202-223-4007
E-mail Address: mikec@rtdna.org
Web Address: www.rtdna.org
The Radio Television Digital News Association (RTDNA), formerly the Radio-Television News Directors Association (RTNDA), is the world's largest professional organization exclusively committed to professionals in electronic journalism.

Radio Television Digital News Association-Canada (RTDNA Canada)
439 University Ave., Fl. 5
Toronto, ON M5G 1Y8 Canada
Phone: 437-836-3088
E-mail Address: rtdna@icsevents.com
Web Address: www.rtndacanada.com
Radio Television Digital News Association-Canada (RTDNA Canada) offers a forum for open discussion and action in the broadcast news industry in Canada. It acts as a voice of electronic and digital journalists and news managers in Canada.

Screen Actor's Guild, American Federation of Television and Radio Artists (SAG-AFTRA)
5757 Wilshire Blvd., Fl. 7
Los Angeles, CA 90036-3600 USA
Phone: 323-634-8100
Fax: 323-549-6792
Toll Free: 855-724-2387
E-mail Address: sagaftrainfo@sagaftra.org
Web Address: www.sagaftra.org
The Screen Actor's Guild, American Federation of Television and Radio Artists (SAG-AFTRA), a product of the merger of the Screen Actors Guild (SAG) and the American Federation of Television and Radio Artists (AFTRA), is a national labor union representing actors and other professional performers and broadcasters in television, radio, sound recordings, non-broadcast/industrial programming and new technologies such as interactive programming and CD-ROMs.

Women in Cable & Telecommunications (WICT)
14555 Avion Pkwy., Ste. 250
Chantilly, VA 20151 USA
Phone: 703-234-9810
Fax: 703-817-1595
E-mail Address: tgibson@wict.org
Web Address: www.wict.org
Women in Cable & Telecommunications (WICT) exists to advance the position and influence of women in media through leadership programs and services at both the national and local level.

6) Canadian Government Agencies-Communications

Canadian Radio-Television and Telecommunications Commission (CRTC)
Les Terrasses de la Chaudiere, Central Bldg.
1 Promenade du Portage
Gatineau, QC J8X 4B1 Canada
Phone: 819-997-0313
Fax: 819-994-0218
Toll Free: 877-249-2782
Web Address: www.crtc.gc.ca
The Canadian Radio-Television and Telecommunications Commission (CRTC) is the government agency responsible for the regulation of the Canadian broadcasting and telecommunications industries.

7) Canadian Government Agencies-General

Canadian Intellectual Property Office (CIPO)
Place du Portage, 50 Victoria St., Rm. C-229
Gatineau, QC K1A 0C9 Canada
Phone: 819-934-0544
Fax: 819-953-2476
Toll Free: 866-997-1936
Web Address: www.cipo.ic.gc.ca
The Canadian Intellectual Property Office (CIPO) is the agency responsible for the administration and processing of intellectual property in Canada, including patents, trademarks, copyrights, industrial designs and integrated circuit topographies.

8) Careers-First Time Jobs/New Grads

CollegeGrad.com, Inc.
950 Tower Ln., Fl. 6
Foster City, CA 94404 USA
E-mail Address: info@quinstreet.com
Web Address: www.collegegrad.com
CollegeGrad.com, Inc. offers in-depth resources for college students and recent grads seeking entry-level jobs.

MonsterCollege
444 N. Michigan Ave., Ste. 600
Chicago, IL 60611 USA
E-mail Address: info@college.monster.com

Web Address: www.college.monster.com
MonsterCollege provides information about internships and entry-level jobs, as well as career advice and resume tips, to recent college graduates.

National Association of Colleges and Employers (NACE)
62 Highland Ave.
Bethlehem, PA 18017-9085 USA
Phone: 610-868-1421
E-mail Address: customer_service@naceweb.org
Web Address: www.naceweb.org
The National Association of Colleges and Employers (NACE) is a premier U.S. organization representing college placement offices and corporate recruiters who focus on hiring new grads.

9) Careers-General Job Listings

CareerBuilder, Inc.
200 N La Salle St., Ste. 1100
Chicago, IL 60601 USA
Phone: 773-527-3600
Fax: 773-353-2452
Toll Free: 800-891-8880
Web Address: www.careerbuilder.com
CareerBuilder, Inc. focuses on the needs of companies and also provides a database of job openings. The site has over 1 million jobs posted by 300,000 employers, and receives an average 23 million unique visitors monthly. The company also operates online career centers for 140 newspapers and 9,000 online partners. Resumes are sent directly to the company, and applicants can set up a special e-mail account for job-seeking purposes. CareerBuilder is primarily a joint venture between three newspaper giants: The McClatchy Company, Gannett Co., Inc. and Tribune Company.

CareerOneStop
Toll Free: 877-872-5627
E-mail Address: info@careeronestop.org
Web Address: www.careeronestop.org
CareerOneStop is operated by the employment commissions of various state agencies. It contains job listings in both the private and government sectors, as well as a wide variety of useful career resources and workforce information. CareerOneStop is sponsored by the U.S. Department of Labor.

LaborMarketInfo (LMI)
Employment Development Dept.
P.O. Box 826880, MIC 57
Sacramento, CA 94280-0001 USA
Phone: 916-262-2162
Fax: 916-262-2352
Web Address: www.labormarketinfo.edd.ca.gov
LaborMarketInfo (LMI) provides job seekers and employers a wide range of resources, namely the ability to find, access and use labor market information and services. It provides statistics for employment demographics on both a local and regional level, as well as career searching tools for California residents. The web site is sponsored by California's Employment Development Office.

MediaBistro.com
825 Eighth Ave., Fl. 29
New York, NY 10019 USA
E-mail Address: support@mediabistro.com
Web Address: www.mediabistro.com
MediaBistro.com provides news and information on current events relating to the media industry. It also offers an array of employment resources, including job listings within the industry.

Recruiters Online Network
E-mail Address: rossi.tony@comcast.net
Web Address: www.recruitersonline.com
The Recruiters Online Network provides job postings from thousands of recruiters, Careers Online Magazine, a resume database, as well as other career resources.

USAJOBS
USAJOBS Program Office
1900 E St. NW, Ste. 6500
Washington, DC 20415-0001 USA
Phone: 818-934-6600
Web Address: www.usajobs.gov
USAJOBS, a program of the U.S. Office of Personnel Management, is the official job site for the U.S. Federal Government. It provides a comprehensive list of U.S. government jobs, allowing users to search for employment by location; agency; type of work; or by senior executive positions. It also has special employment sections for individuals with disabilities, veterans and recent college graduates; an information center, offering resume and interview tips and other information; and allows users to create a profile and post a resume.

10) Careers-Job Reference Tools

Vault.com, Inc.
132 W. 31st St., Fl. 17
New York, NY 10001 USA
Fax: 212-366-6117
Toll Free: 800-535-2074
E-mail Address: customerservice@vault.com
Web Address: www.vault.com
Vault.com, Inc. is a comprehensive career web site for employers and employees, with job postings and valuable information on a wide variety of industries. Its features and content are largely geared toward MBA degree holders.

11) Communications Professional Associations

Association for Women In Communications (AWC)
1717 E Republic Rd., Ste. A
Springfield, MO 65804 USA
Phone: 417-886-8606
Fax: 417-886-3685
E-mail Address: members@womcom.org
Web Address: www.womcom.org
The Association for Women In Communications (AWC) is a professional organization that works for the advancement of women across all communications disciplines by recognizing excellence, promoting leadership and positioning its members at the forefront of the communications industry.

International Association of Business Communicators (IABC)
155 Montgomery St., Ste. 1210
San Francisco, CA 94111 USA
Phone: 415-544-4700
Fax: 415-544-4747
Toll Free: 800-776-4222
Web Address: www.iabc.com
The International Association of Business Communicators (IABC) is the leading resource for effective business communication practices.

12) Computer & Electronics Industry Associations

HomePlug Powerline Alliance
8305 SW Creekside Pl., Ste. C
Beaverton, OR 97008 USA
Phone: 503-766-2516
Fax: 503-863-3881
E-mail Address: help@homeplug.org
Web Address: www.homeplug.org
The HomePlug Powerline Alliance's goal is to promote standards-based home networks that utilize existing electrical wiring to carry signals between personal computers, entertainment systems and other home devices.

Multimedia Over Coax Alliance (MoCA)
Phone: 408-838-7458
E-mail Address: robgelphman@mocalliance.org
Web Address: www.mocalliance.org
Multimedia Over Coax Alliance (MoCA) is the standard for home networking of multiple streams of high definition video and entertainment using existing coaxial cable already in the home.

13) Corporate Information Resources

bizjournals.com
120 W. Morehead St., Ste. 400
Charlotte, NC 28202 USA
Toll Free: 866-853-3661
E-mail Address: gmurchison@bizjournals.com
Web Address: www.bizjournals.com
Bizjournals.com is the online media division of American City Business Journals, the publisher of dozens of leading city business journals nationwide. It provides access to research into the latest news regarding companies both small and large. The organization maintains 42 websites and 64 print publications and sponsors over 700 annual industry events.

Business Wire
101 California St., Fl. 20
San Francisco, CA 94111 USA
Phone: 415-986-4422
Fax: 415-788-5335
Toll Free: 800-227-0845
E-mail Address: info@businesswire.com
Web Address: www.businesswire.com
Business Wire offers news releases, industry- and company-specific news, top headlines, conference calls, IPOs on the Internet, media services and access to tradeshownews.com and BW Connect On-line through its informative and continuously updated web site.

Edgar Online, Inc.
11200 Rockville Pike, Ste. 310
Rockville, MD 20852 USA
Phone: 301-287-0300
Fax: 301-287-0390
Toll Free: 888-870-2316
Web Address: www.edgar-online.com
Edgar Online, Inc. is a gateway and search tool for viewing corporate documents, such as annual reports on Form 10-K, filed with the U.S. Securities and Exchange Commission.

PR Newswire Association LLC
350 Hudson St., Ste. 300
New York, NY 10014-4504 USA
Fax: 800-793-9313
Toll Free: 800-776-8090
E-mail Address: MediaInquiries@prnewswire.com
Web Address: www.prnewswire.com
PR Newswire Association LLC provides comprehensive communications services for public relations and investor relations professionals, ranging from information distribution and market intelligence to the creation of online multimedia content and investor relations web sites. Users can also view recent corporate press releases from companies across the globe. The Association is owned by United Business Media plc.

Silicon Investor
E-mail Address: si.admin@siliconinvestor.com
Web Address: www.siliconinvestor.com

Silicon Investor is focused on providing information about technology companies. Its web site serves as a financial discussion forum and offers quotes, profiles and charts.

14) Economic Data & Research

Centre for European Economic Research (The, ZEW)
L 7, 1
Mannheim, 68161 Germany
Phone: 49-621-1235-01
Fax: 49-621-1235-224
E-mail Address: empfang@zew.de
Web Address: www.zew.de/en
Zentrum fur Europaische Wirtschaftsforschung, The Centre for European Economic Research (ZEW), distinguishes itself in the analysis of internationally comparative data in a European context and in the creation of databases that serve as a basis for scientific research. The institute maintains a special library relevant to economic research and provides external parties with selected data for the purpose of scientific research. ZEW also offers public events and seminars concentrating on banking, business and other economic-political topics.

Economic and Social Research Council (ESRC)
Polaris House
North Star Ave.
Swindon, SN2 1UJ UK
Phone: 44-01793 413000
E-mail Address: esrcenquiries@esrc.ac.uk
Web Address: www.esrc.ac.uk
The Economic and Social Research Council (ESRC) funds research and training in social and economic issues. It is an independent organization, established by Royal Charter. Current research areas include the global economy; social diversity; environment and energy; human behavior; and health and well-being.

Eurostat
5 Rue Alphonse Weicker
Joseph Bech Bldg.
Luxembourg, L-2721 Luxembourg
Phone: 352-4301-1
E-mail Address: eurostat-pressoffice@ec.europa.eu
Web Address: ec.europa.eu/eurostat
Eurostat is the European Union's service that publishes a wide variety of comprehensive statistics on European industries, populations, trade, agriculture, technology, environment and other matters.

Federal Statistical Office of Germany
Gustav-Stresemann-Ring 11
Wiesbaden, D-65189 Germany
Phone: 49-611-75-2405
Fax: 49-611-72-4000
Web Address: www.destatis.de
Federal Statistical Office of Germany publishes a wide variety of nation and regional economic data of interest to anyone who is studying Germany, one of the world's leading economies. Data available includes population, consumer prices, labor markets, health care, industries and output.

India Brand Equity Foundation (IBEF)
Fl. 20, Jawahar Vyapar Bhawan
Tolstoy Marg
New Deli, 110001 India
Phone: 91-11-43845500
Fax: 91-11-23701235
E-mail Address: info.brandindia@ibef.org
Web Address: www.ibef.org
India Brand Equity Foundation (IBEF) is a public-private partnership between the Ministry of Commerce and Industry, the Government of India and the Confederation of Indian Industry. The foundation's primary objective is to build positive economic perceptions of India globally. It aims to effectively present the India business perspective and leverage business partnerships in a globalizing marketplace.

National Bureau of Statistics (China)
57, Yuetan Nanjie, Sanlihe
Xicheng District
Beijing, 100826 China
Fax: 86-10-6878-2000
E-mail Address: info@gj.stats.cn
Web Address: www.stats.gov.cn/english
The National Bureau of Statistics (China) provides statistics and economic data regarding China's economy and society.

Organization for Economic Co-operation and Development (OECD)
2 rue Andre Pascal, Cedex 16
Paris, 75775 France
Phone: 33-1-45-24-82-00
Fax: 33-1-45-24-85-00
E-mail Address: webmaster@oecd.org
Web Address: www.oecd.org
The Organization for Economic Co-operation and Development (OECD) publishes detailed economic, government, population, social and trade statistics on a country-by-country basis for over 30 nations representing the world's largest economies. Sectors covered range from industry, labor, technology and patents, to health care, environment and globalization.

Statistics Bureau, Director-General for Policy Planning (Japan)
19-1 Wakamatsu-cho, Shinjuku-ku
Tokyo, 162-8668 Japan
Phone: 81-3-5273-2020
E-mail Address: toukeisoudan@soumu.go.jp
Web Address: www.stat.go.jp/english
The Statistics Bureau, Director-General for Policy Planning (Japan) and Statistical Research and Training

Institute, a part of the Japanese Ministry of Internal Affairs and Communications, plays the central role of producing and disseminating basic official statistics and coordinating statistical work under the Statistics Act and other legislation.

Statistics Canada
150 Tunney's Pasture Driveway
Ottawa, ON K1A 0T6 Canada
Phone: 514-283-8300
Fax: 514-283-9350
Toll Free: 800-263-1136
E-mail Address: STATCAN.infostats-infostats.STATCAN@canada.ca
Web Address: www.statcan.gc.ca
Statistics Canada provides a complete portal to Canadian economic data and statistics. Its conducts Canada's official census every five years, as well as hundreds of surveys covering numerous aspects of Canadian life.

15) Electronic Publishing Associations

International Digital Enterprise Alliance (IDEAlliance)
1600 Duke St., Ste. 420
Alexandria, VA 22314 USA
Phone: 703-837-1070
Fax: 703-837-1072
Web Address: www.idealliance.org
IDEAlliance (International Digital Enterprise Alliance) is a non-profit membership organization supporting the digital media industry. It seeks to advance core technologies and develop standards and best practices that enhance the flow of information across the digital media supply chain, from creation and production to management and delivery, both in print and digital formats.

International Digital Publishing Forum (IDPF)
113 Cherry St., Ste. 70-719
Seattle, WA 98104 USA
Phone: 206-451-7250
E-mail Address: membership@idpf.org
Web Address: www.idpf.org
The International Digital Publishing Forum (IDPF) is a trade and standards organization dedicated to the development and promotion of electronic publishing, including electronic newspapers, books and other types of media. Members include software developers, authors and publishers of many types. The organization developed the ePub (electronic publication) open standard for the publication of eBooks.

16) Engineering, Research & Scientific Associations

Association of Federal Communications Consulting Engineers (AFCCE)
P.O. Box 19333
Washington, DC 20036 USA
Web Address: www.afcce.org
The Association of Federal Communications Consulting Engineers (AFCCE) is a professional organization of individuals who regularly assist clients on technical issues before the Federal Communications Commission (FCC).

Audio Engineering Society, Inc. (AES)
551 Fifth Ave., Ste. 1225
New York, NY 10176 USA
Phone: 212-661-8528
Web Address: www.aes.org
The Audio Engineering Society (AES) provides information on educational and career opportunities in audio technology and engineering.

Broadcast Engineering Society (India)
912 Surya Kiran Bldg., 19, K.G. Marg
New Delhi, Delhi 110 001 India
Phone: 91-11-23316709
Fax: 91-11-23316710
E-mail Address: rksi2906@gmail.com
Web Address: www.besindia.com
The Broadcast Engineering Society (India) aims to promote the interests of the broadcast engineering profession at the national and international levels.

IEEE Broadcast Technological Society (IEEE BTS)
445 Hoes Ln.
Piscataway, NJ 08854 USA
Phone: 732-562-5407
Fax: 732-981-1769
E-mail Address: a.temple@ieee.org
Web Address: bts.ieee.org
The IEEE Broadcast Technological Society (IEEE BTS) is the arm of the Institute of Electrical & Electronics Engineers (IEEE) devoted to devices, equipment, techniques and systems related to broadcast technology.

Institute of Electrical and Electronics Engineers (IEEE)
3 Park Ave., Fl. 17
New York, NY 10016-5997 USA
Phone: 212-419-7900
Fax: 212-752-4929
Toll Free: 800-678-4333
E-mail Address: society-info@ieee.org
Web Address: www.ieee.org
The Institute of Electrical and Electronics Engineers (IEEE) is a nonprofit, technical professional association of more than 430,000 individual members in approximately 160 countries. The IEEE sets global technical standards and acts as an authority in technical areas ranging from computer engineering, biomedical technology and telecommunications, to electric power, aerospace and consumer electronics.

Society of Broadcast Engineers, Inc. (SBE)
9102 N. Meridian St., Ste. 150
Indianapolis, IN 46260 USA
Phone: 317-846-9000
E-mail Address: jporay@sbe.org
Web Address: www.sbe.org
The Society of Broadcast Engineers (SBE) exists to increase knowledge of broadcast engineering and promote its interests, as well as to continue the education of professionals in the industry.

Society of Cable Telecommunications Engineers (SCTE)
140 Philips Rd.
Exton, PA 19341-1318 USA
Fax: 610-884-7237
Toll Free: 800-542-5040
E-mail Address: scte@scte.org
Web Address: www.scte.org
The Society of Cable Telecommunications Engineers (SCTE) is a nonprofit professional association dedicated to advancing the careers and serving the industry of telecommunications professionals by providing technical training, certification and information resources.

Society of Motion Picture and Television Engineers (SMPTE)
3 Barker Ave., Fl. 5
White Plains, NY 10601 USA
Phone: 914-761-1100
Fax: 914-761-3115
E-mail Address: marketing@smpte.org
Web Address: www.smpte.org
The Society of Motion Picture and Television Engineers (SMPTE) is the leading technical society for the motion imaging industry. The firm publishes recommended practice and engineering guidelines, as well the SMPTE Journal.

17) Entertainment & Amusement Associations-General

Airline Passenger Experience Association (APEX)
355 Lexington Ave., Fl. 15
New York, NY 10017-6603 USA
Phone: 212-297-2177
Fax: 212-370-9047
E-mail Address: info@apex.aero
Web Address: apex.aero
The Airline Passenger Experience Association (APEX), formerly the World Airline Entertainment Association (WAEA), is a worldwide network representing airlines, airline suppliers and related companies committed to excellence in inflight entertainment (IFE), communications and services.

American Amusement Machine Association (AAMA)
450 E. Higgins Rd., Ste. 201
Elk Grove Village, IL 60007 USA
Phone: 847-290-9088
E-mail Address: tschwartz@coin-op.org
Web Address: www.coin-op.org
The American Amusement Machine Association (AAMA) is an international nonprofit trade organization representing the manufacturers, distributors and suppliers of the coin-operated amusement industry.

Amusement and Music Operators Association (AMOA)
600 Spring Hill Ring Rd., Ste. 111
West Dundee, IL 60118 USA
Phone: 847-428-7699
Web Address: www.amoa.com
The Amusement and Music Operators Association (AMOA) serves the currency-activated amusement, vending, music and family entertainment center equipment companies and businesses. It offers continuing education programs, advocacy, member discount programs, research and industry information, annual membership directory and leadership and network opportunities to its members.

Amusement Industry Manufacturers and Suppliers, International (AIMS)
3026 S. Orange
Santa Ana, CA 92707 USA
Phone: 714-425-5747
Fax: 714-276-9666
E-mail Address: info@aimsintl.org
Web Address: www.aimsintl.org
Amusement Industry Manufacturers and Suppliers International (AIMS) is a nonprofit organization that represents amusement industry manufacturers and suppliers worldwide.

Entertainment Merchants Association
16530 Ventura Blvd., Ste. 400
Encino, CA 91436-4551 USA
Phone: 818-385-1500
Fax: 818-933-0911
Web Address: www.entmerch.org
The Entertainment Merchants Association (EMA) is the not-for-profit international trade association dedicated to advancing the interests of the $35 billion home entertainment industry. EMA was established in April 2006 through the merger of the Video Software Dealers Association (VSDA) and the Interactive Entertainment Merchants Association (IEMA).

Entertainment Technology Center (ETC)
2823 S. Flower St.
Los Angeles, CA 90089 USA
Phone: 949-502-7750
E-mail Address: info@etcenter.org
Web Address: www.etcenter.org
The Entertainment Technology Center at the University of Southern California (ETC@USC) exists to discover, research, develop and accelerate entertainment, consumer

electronics, technology and services industries. This research center brings together senior executives, thought leaders and innovators to explore issues related to creation, distribution and consumption of creative content. It provides research and publications, as well as conducts events, collaborative projects, shared exploratory labs and demonstrations.

Information Display and Entertainment Association (IDEA)
2001 E. Lohman Ave., Ste. 110-165
Las Cruces, NM 88001-3116 USA
Phone: 575-405-1977
E-mail Address: info@ideaontheweb.org
Web Address: www.ideaontheweb.org
The Information Display and Entertainment Association (IDEA) is a worldwide association of electronic display system and scoreboard operators.

International Association of Amusement Parks and Attractions (IAAPA)
1448 Duke St.
Alexandria, VA 22314 USA
Phone: 703-836-4800
Fax: 703-836-4801
E-mail Address: iaapa@iaapa.org
Web Address: www.iaapa.org
The International Association of Amusement Parks and Attractions (IAAPA) is dedicated to the preservation and prosperity of the amusement industry.

International Association of Venue Managers (IAVM)
635 Fritz Dr., Ste. 100
Coppell, TX 75019-4442 USA
Phone: 972-906-7441
Fax: 972-906-7418
E-mail Address: vicki.hawarden@iavm.org
Web Address: www.iavm.org
The International Association of Venue Managers (IAVM), formerly the International Association of Assembly Managers (IAAM), is an international trade organization representing managers and suppliers of public assembly facilities, such as arenas, amphitheaters, auditoriums, convention centers/exhibit halls, performing arts venues, stadiums and university complexes.

International Laser Display Association (ILDA)
7062 Edgeworth Dr.
Orlando, FL 32819 USA
Phone: 407-797-7654
E-mail Address: mail@laserist.org
Web Address: www.laserist.org
The International Laser Display Association (ILDA) is a nonprofit organization dedicated to advancing the use of laser displays in art, entertainment and education.

International Special Events Society (ISES)
330 N. Wabash Ave., Ste. 2000
Chicago, IL 60611-4267 USA
Phone: 312-321-6853
Fax: 312-673-6953
Toll Free: 800-688-4737
E-mail Address: info@ises.com
Web Address: www.ises.com
The International Special Events Society (ISES) is comprised of over 7,200 professionals in over 38 countries representing special event planners and producers (from festivals to trade shows), caterers, decorators, florists, destination management companies, rental companies, special effects experts, tent suppliers, audio-visual technicians, event and convention coordinators, balloon artists, educators, journalists, hotel sales managers, specialty entertainers, convention center managers, and many more professional disciplines.

International Ticketing Association (INTIX)
Two Meridian Plaza
10401 N. Meridian St., Ste. 300
Indianapolis, IN 46290 USA
Phone: 212-629-4036
Fax: 212-629-8532
E-mail Address: info@intix.org
Web Address: www.intix.org
International Ticketing Association (INTIX) is a nonprofit professional and trade organization for the admission services industry, representing professionals in the performing arts, theater, entertainment, professional sports and college and university athletics.

National Association of Theater Owners (NATO)
750 First St. NE, Ste. 1130
Washington, DC 20002 USA
Phone: 202-962-0054
E-mail Address: nato@natodc.com
Web Address: www.natoonline.org
The National Association of Theater Owners (NATO) is an exhibition trade organization represents 30,000 movie screens in the U.S., and additional cinemas in over 50 countries worldwide.

National Association of Ticket Brokers (NATB)
214 N. Hale St.
Wheaton, IL 60187 USA
Phone: 630-510-4594
Fax: 630-510-4501
E-mail Address: jason@allshows.com
Web Address: www.natb.org
The National Association of Ticket Brokers (NATB) is a nonprofit trade organization representing the ticket broker industry. The association promotes consumer protection and the education of the public concerning the ticket brokers industry.

World Waterpark Association (WWA)
8826 Santa Fe Dr., Ste. 310
Overland Park, KS 66212 USA

Phone: 913-599-0300
Fax: 913-599-0520
E-mail Address: wwamemberinfo@waterparks.org
Web Address: www.waterparks.org
The World Waterpark Association (WWA) is an international nonprofit partnership of private and public water leisure facility owners, managers, suppliers and developers.

18) Entertainment and Video Statistics in Europe

European Audiovisual Observatory
76 Allee de la Robertsau
Strasbourg, 67000 France
Phone: 33-0-3-9021-6000
Fax: 33-0-3-9021-6019
Web Address: www.obs.coe.int
The European Audiovisual Observatory is part of the Council of Europe in Strasbourg, France. It is a public service organization. The Observatory was created in 1992 in order to collect and distribute information about the audiovisual industries in Europe. The group publishes statistics and research on film, broadcasting (including TV and radio), video, satellite, cable and DVD markets. The Observatory provides information on the various audiovisual markets in Europe and their financing. It also analyses and reports on the legal issues affecting the different sectors of the audiovisual industry.

19) Film & Television Resources

Baseline, Inc.
3415 S. Sepulveda Blvd., Ste. 200
Los Angeles, CA 90034 USA
Phone: 310-482-3414
E-mail Address: contact@blssi.com
Web Address: www.blssi.com
Baseline, Inc., which does business as Baseline StudioSystems, Baseline/FilmTracker and associated names and web sites, offers subscription database with information regarding the film and television industries. The Studio System is its flagship service. Baseline is a division of The New York Times Company.

Independent Filmmaker Project (IFP, The)
68 Jay St., Ste. 425
Brooklyn, NY 11201 USA
Phone: 212-465-8200
Fax: 212-465-8525
Web Address: www.ifp.org
The Independent Filmmaker Project (IFP), formerly the Independent Feature Project, exists to facilitate the professional development and exhibition of new work from a diverse community of independent American filmmakers. It has chapters in New York, Seattle, Phoenix, Chicago and Minnesota.

Internet Movie Database (IMDB)
Web Address: www.imdb.com
Internet Movie Database (IMDB), a unit of Amazon.com, is a movie database that provides information on such topics as box office revenues and new DVD releases, in addition to production and cast details on thousands of movies and television shows.

Movieweb
E-mail Address: webmaster@watchrmedia.com
Web Address: www.movieweb.com
Movieweb is an Internet movie site featuring information on movies coming soon to theaters and available on home video.

Museum of Broadcast Communications (MBC)
360 N. State St.
Chicago, IL 60654-5411 USA
Phone: 312-245-8200
Fax: 312-245-8207
Toll Free: 888-698-9783
E-mail Address: jgieger@museum.tv
Web Address: www.museum.tv
Museum of Broadcast Communications (MBC) is a nonprofit broadcast museum and home to the only National Radio Hall of Fame. It seeks to collect, preserve and present historic and contemporary radio and television content, as well as to inform, educate and entertain through its archives, public programs, exhibits, screenings, online access and publications.

Palley Center for Media (The)
25 W. 52nd St.
New York, NY 10019-6129 USA
Phone: 212-621-6600
Fax: 212-621-6737
E-mail Address: coman@paleycenter.org
Web Address: www.paleycenter.org
The Palley Center for Media, formerly The Museum of Television & Radio, leads the discussion about the cultural, creative and social significance of television, radio and emerging platforms for the professional community and media-interested public.

Samuel French Theater and Film Bookshops
2335 Park Ave. S, Fl. 5
New York, NY 10003 USA
Phone: 212-206-8990
Fax: 212-206-1429
Toll Free: 866-598-8449
E-mail Address: info@samuelfrench.com
Web Address: www.samuelfrench.com
Samuel French seeks out the world's best plays and makes them available to a wide range of producing groups.

SCREENSite
Phone: 205-348-6350
E-mail Address: jbutler@ua.edu

Web Address: www.screensite.org
SCREENSite is a resource center for film and TV scholarship with an archive of course syllabi, e-mail listings of media scholars, conference information, school listings and job list.

Screenwriters Online
1314 Avenida De Cortez
Pacific Palisades, CA 90272 USA
Phone: 310-459-5278
E-mail Address: insider@screenwriter.com
Web Address: www.screenwriter.com
Screenwriters Online is a web site offering information on screenwriting, scriptwriting and creative writing software, books, supplies and contests.

Sundance Institute
5900 Wilshire Blvd., Ste. 800
Los Angeles, CA 90036 USA
Phone: 310-360-1981
Fax: 310-360-1969
E-mail Address: ideas@sundance.org
Web Address: www.sundance.org
The Sundance Institute is dedicated to the development of artists involved in independent film and the exhibition of their work.

20) Film & Theater Associations

Academy of Interactive Arts & Sciences (AIAS)
11175 Santa Monica Blvd., Fl. 4
Los Angeles, CA 90025 USA
Phone: 310-484-2560
E-mail Address: claudio@interactive.org
Web Address: www.interactive.org
The Academy of Interactive Arts & Sciences (AIAS) is a nonprofit membership organization serving the interactive entertainment development community. AIAS currently serves over 20,000 members.

Academy of Motion Picture Arts and Sciences (AMPAS)
8949 Wilshire Blvd.
Beverly Hills, CA 90211-1972 USA
Phone: 310-247-3000
Fax: 310-859-9619
Web Address: www.oscars.org
The Academy of Motion Picture Arts and Sciences (AMPAS) is a professional honorary organization, founded to advance the arts and sciences of motion pictures. Besides hosting the Academy Awards and selecting the winners of the Oscars, AMPAS organizes smaller events highlighting the art of filmmaking, including lectures and seminars, and is currently building the Academy Museum of Motion Pictures.

Alliance of Motion Picture and Television Producers (AMPTP)
15301 Ventura Blvd., Bldg. E
Sherman Oaks, CA 91403 USA
Phone: 818-995-3600
Web Address: www.amptp.org
The Alliance of Motion Picture and Television Producers (AMPTP) is the primary trade association with respect to labor issues in the motion picture and television industry.

American Cinema Editors, Inc. (ACE)
100 Universal City Plz.
Verna Fields Bldg. 2282, Rm. 190
Universal City, CA 91608 USA
Phone: 818-777-2900
E-mail Address: amercinema@earthlink.net
Web Address: www.ace-filmeditors.org
American Cinema Editors (ACE) is an honorary society of motion picture editors that seeks to advance the art and science of the editing profession.

American Society of Cinematographers (ASC)
1782 N. Orange Dr.
Hollywood, CA 90028 USA
Phone: 323-969-4333
Fax: 323-882-6391
Toll Free: 800-448-0145
E-mail Address: office@theasc.com
Web Address: www.theasc.com
The American Society of Cinematographers (ASC) is a trade association for cinematographers in the motion picture industry.

American Theatre Wing
570 Seventh Ave., Ste. 501
New York, NY 10018 USA
Phone: 212-765-0606
Fax: 212-307-1910
E-mail Address: mailbox@americantheatrewing.org
Web Address: www.americantheatrewing.org
The American Theatre Wing is a non-profit organization dedicated to supporting the theater. It is the creator of the annual Tony Awards, now presented in conjunction with The Broadway League.

Art Directors Guild (ADG)
11969 Ventura Blvd., Fl. 2
Studio City, CA 91604 USA
Phone: 818-762-9995
Fax: 818-760-4847
E-mail Address: nick@artdirectors.org
Web Address: www.artdirectors.org
The Art Directors Guild (ADG) represents the creative talents that conceive and manage the background and settings for most films and television projects.

Association of Cinema and Video Laboratories (ACVL)
Phone: 805-427-2620

E-mail Address: peterbulcke@hotmail.com
Web Address: www.acvl.org
The Association of Cinema and Video Laboratories (ACVL) is an international organization whose members are pledged to the highest possible standards of service to the film and video industries.

Association of Film Commissioners International (AFCI)
9595 Wilshire Blvd., Ste. 900
Beverly Hills, CA 90212 USA
Phone: 323-461-2324
Fax: 413-375-2903
E-mail Address: info@afci.org
Web Address: www.afci.org
The Association of Film Commissioners International (AFCI) is an association of government film contacts worldwide supporting video, television and film production.

Broadway League (The)
729 Seventh Ave., Fl. 5
New York, NY 10019 USA
Phone: 212-764-1122
Fax: 212-944-2136
Web Address: www.broadwayleague.com
The Broadway League is the national trade association for the Broadway industry. Its 700-plus members include theatre owners and operators, producers, presenters, and general managers in North American cities, as well as suppliers of goods and services to the commercial theatre industry. In conjunction with American Theatre Wing, it is the producer of the annual Tony Awards.

Canadian Media Production Association (CMPA)
601 Bank St., Fl. 2
Ottawa, ON K1S 3T4 Canada
Phone: 613-233-1444
Fax: 613-233-0073
Toll Free: 800-656-7440
E-mail Address: ottawa@cmpa.ca
Web Address: www.cmpa.ca
The mission of the Canadian Media Production Association (CMPA), formerly the Canadian Film and Television Production Association, is to create a favorable national and international environment for the film industry and culture to prosper.

Casting Society of America (CSA)
606 N. Larchmont Blvd., Ste. 4-B
Los Angeles, CA 90004-1309 USA
Phone: 323-463-1925
E-mail Address: info@castingsociety.com
Web Address: www.castingsociety.com
Casting Society of America (CSA) is an association of casting professionals in film, television and theater.

Directors Guild of America, Inc. (Los Angeles DGA)
7920 Sunset Blvd.
Los Angeles, CA 90046 USA
Phone: 310-289-2000
Toll Free: 800-421-4173
E-mail Address: morganr@dga.org
Web Address: www.dga.org
The Directors Guild of America, Inc. (Los Angeles DGA) seeks to protect directorial teams' legal and artistic rights, contend for their creative freedom and strengthen their ability to develop meaningful and credible careers.

Directors Guild of America, Inc. (New York DGA)
110 W. 57th St.
New York, NY 10019 USA
Phone: 212-581-0370
Fax: 212-581-1441
Toll Free: 800-356-3754
Web Address: www.dga.org
The Directors Guild of America, Inc. (New York DGA) seeks to protect directorial teams' legal and artistic rights, contend for their creative freedom and strengthen their ability to develop meaningful and credible careers.

Hollywood Post Alliance (HPA)
846 S. Broadway, Ste. 601
Los Angeles, CA 90014 USA
Phone: 213-614-0860
Fax: 213-614-0890
E-mail Address: arock@hpaonline.com
Web Address: www.hpaonline.com
The Hollywood Post Alliance (HPA) is an organization dedicated to serving the entertainment technology industry by bringing together the post-production community.

Independent Film & Television Alliance (IFTA)
10850 Wilshire Blvd., Fl. 9
Los Angeles, CA 90024-4311 USA
Phone: 310-446-1000
Fax: 310-446-1600
E-mail Address: info@ifta-online.org
Web Address: www.ifta-online.org
The Independent Film & Television Alliance (IFTA), formerly the American Film Marketing Association (AFMA), is a trade association whose mission is to provide the independent film and television industry with high-quality, market-oriented services and worldwide representation.

International Alliance of Theatrical Stage Employees (IATSE)
207 W. 25th St., Fl. 4
New York, NY 10001 USA
Phone: 212-730-1770
Fax: 212-730-7809
E-mail Address: webmaster@iatse-intl.org
Web Address: www.iatse-intl.org

The International Alliance of Theatrical Stage Employees (IATSE) is the labor union representing technicians, artisans and crafts workers in the entertainment industry, including live theater, film and television production and trade shows.

International Animated Film Society (ASIFA-Hollywood)
2114 W. Burbank Blvd.
Burbank, CA 91506 USA
Phone: 818-842-8330
E-mail Address: info@asifa-hollywood.org
Web Address: www.asifa-hollywood.org
International Animated Film Society (ASIFA-Hollywood) is a nonprofit organization dedicated to the advancement of the art of animation.

International Documentary Association (IDA)
3470 Wilshire Blvd., Ste. 980
Los Angeles, CA 90010 USA
Phone: 213-232-1660
Fax: 213-232-1669
E-mail Address: michael@documentary.org
Web Address: www.documentary.org
The International Documentary Association (IDA) is a nonprofit member service organization, providing publications, benefits and a public forum to its members for issues regarding nonfiction film, video and multimedia.

International Quorum of Motion Picture Producers
810 Dominican Dr.
Nashville, TN 37228-1906 USA
Phone: 615-255-4000
Fax: 615-255-4111
E-mail Address: andycohen@iqfilm.org
Web Address: www.iqfilm.org
International Quorum of Motion Picture Producers is a select group of filmmakers and video producers, limited to hand-picked members. The organization has representatives in 45 nations and hosts an annual conference.

Motion Picture Association of America (MPAA)
15301 Ventura Blvd., Bldg. E
Sherman Oaks, CA 91403 USA
Phone: 818-995-6600
Fax: 818-285-4403
E-mail Address: ContactUs@mpaa.org
Web Address: www.mpaa.org
The Motion Picture Association of America (MPAA) serves as the voice and advocate of the U.S. motion picture, home video and television industries.

Motion Picture Editors Guild (MPEG)
7715 Sunset Blvd., Ste. 200
Hollywood, CA 90046 USA
Phone: 323-876-4770
Fax: 323-876-0861
Toll Free: 800-705-8700
E-mail Address: social@editorsguild.com
Web Address: www.editorsguild.com
The Motion Picture Editors Guild's (MPEG) web site provides an online directory of editors, a discussion forum and links to related magazines and other organizations that serve the motion picture industry.

National Film Board of Canada (NFB)
P.O. Box 6100
Station Centre-ville
Montreal, Quebec H3C 3H5 Canada
Phone: 514-283-9000
Toll Free: 800-267-7710
Web Address: www.nfb.ca
The National Film Board of Canada (NFB) produces and distributes socially engaged documentaries, auteur animations, alternative dramas and more.

National Film Preservation Board (NFPB)
101 Independence Ave. SE
Library of Congress (4690)
Washington, DC 20540 USA
E-mail Address: sleg@loc.gov
Web Address: www.loc.gov/film
The National Film Preservation Board (NFPB) is a federally-chartered organization that seeks to preserve national film treasures.

National Film Preservation Foundation (NFPF)
870 Market St., Ste. 1113
San Francisco, CA 94102 USA
Phone: 415-392-7291
Fax: 415-392-7293
E-mail Address: info@filmpreservation.org
Web Address: www.filmpreservation.org
The National Film Preservation Foundation (NFPF), a nonprofit organization created by the U.S. Congress, supports activities that preserve American films and improves film access for study education and exhibition.

Producers Guild of America, Inc. (PGA)
8530 Wilshire Blvd., Ste. 400
Beverly Hills, CA 90211 USA
Phone: 310-358-9020
Fax: 310-358-9520
E-mail Address: info@producersguild.org
Web Address: www.producersguild.org
The Producers Guild of America, Inc. (PGA) is a nonprofit organization for career professionals who initiate, create, coordinate, supervise and control all aspects of the motion picture and television production processes.

SAG-AFTRA (New York)
360 Madison Ave., Fl. 12
New York, NY 10017 USA
Phone: 212-944-1030
E-mail Address: sagaftrainfo@sagaftra.org

Web Address: www.sagaftra.org
SAG-AFTRA (New York), a product of the merger between the Screen Actors Guild and American Federation of Television and Radio Artists, represents guild members in New York and serves as the east coast national headquarters.

Stuntmen's Association of Motion Pictures (SAMP)
5200 Lankershim Blvd., Ste. 190
N. Hollywood, CA 91601 USA
Phone: 818-766-4334
Fax: 818-766-5943
E-mail Address: hq@stuntmen.com
Web Address: www.stuntmen.com
The Stuntmen's Association of Motion Pictures (SAMP) is a nonprofit organization of top stuntmen in the motion picture and television industries.

Women In Film (WIF)
6100 Wilshire Blvd., Ste. 710
Los Angeles, CA 90048 USA
Phone: 323-935-2211
Fax: 323-935-2212
E-mail Address: info@wif.org
Web Address: www.wif.org
Women In Film (WIF) strives to empower, promote and mentor women in the entertainment, communication and media industries through a network of contacts, educational programs and events.

21) Gambling Industry Associations

American Gaming Association (AGA)
799 9th St. NW, Ste. 700
Washington, DC 20004 USA
Phone: 202-552-2675
Fax: 202-637-2676
Web Address: www.americangaming.org
The American Gaming Association (AGA) seeks to create a better understanding of the gaming entertainment industry by bringing facts about the industry to the general public, elected officials, other decision-makers and the media through education and advocacy. Its members consist of commercial and tribal casino operators, suppliers and other related entities.

Interactive Gaming Council (IGC)
175-2906 W. Broadway
Vancouver, BC V6K 2G8 Canada
Phone: 604-732-3833
Fax: 604-677-5785
E-mail Address: janetv@igcouncil.org
Web Address: www.igcouncil.org
The Interactive Gaming Council (IGC) provides a forum to address issues and advance common interests in the global interactive gaming industry. Additionally, the IGC serves as the industries public policy advocate and information clearinghouse. The council draws on a global membership, with members from the U.S., Canada, U.K., South Africa, Australia and Denmark, to name a few.

National Indian Gaming Association (NIGA)
224 2nd St. SE
Washington, DC 20003 USA
Phone: 202-546-7711
Fax: 202-546-1755
Web Address: www.indiangaming.org
The National Indian Gaming Association (NIGA) is a nonprofit organization of 168 Indian nations and other non-voting associate members, representing organizations, tribes and businesses engaged in tribal gaming enterprises across the country.

22) Games Industry Associations

Association for UK Interactive Entertainment (UKIE)
21-27 Lamb's Conduit St.
London, WC1N 3NL UK
Phone: 44-20-7534-0580
E-mail Address: info@ukie.org.uk
Web Address: www.ukie.info
The Association for UK Interactive Entertainment (UKIE) is the UK's leading trade body for games and wider interactive entertainment industry. Membership includes almost all major companies involved with the publishing and development of videogames in the UK.

Entertainment Consumers Association
64 Danbury Rd., Ste. 700
Wilton, CT 06897-4406 USA
Phone: 203-761-6180
E-mail Address: feedback@theeca.com
Web Address: www.theeca.com
The ECA is a non-profit membership organization that represents consumers of interactive entertainment in the US and Canada. The organization is committed to a host of public policy efforts, empowering and enabling the membership to effect change. Additionally, the association provides members substantial affinity benefits including discounts on games-related purchases, rentals and subscription services, as well as community and educational initiatives. The primary mission of the ECA is to give gaming consumers a voice and ensure that state and local politicians hear their concerns and appreciate their demographic power. The association focuses its advocacy efforts on consumer rights and anti-games legislation.

Entertainment Software Association (ESA)
575 7th St. NW, Ste. 300
Washington, DC 20004 USA
Phone: 202-223-2400
E-mail Address: esa@theesa.com
Web Address: www.theesa.com
The Entertainment Software Association (ESA) is a U.S. trade association for companies that publish video and computer games for consoles, personal computers and the

Internet. The ESA owns the E3 Media & Business Summit, a major invitation-only annual trade show for the video game industry.

Fantasy Sports Trade Association (FSTA)
600 N. Lake Shore Dr.
Chicago, IL 60611 USA
Phone: 312-771-7019
E-mail Address: megan@fsta.org
Web Address: www.fsta.org
The Fantasy Sports Trade Association (FSTA) was founded in 1997 to provide a forum for interaction between companies in a unique and growing fantasy sports industry. FSTA represents more than 300 member companies.

Game Manufacturers Association (GAMA)
240 N. Fifth St., Ste. 340
Columbus, OH 43215 USA
Phone: 614-255-4500
Fax: 614-255-4499
E-mail Address: ed@gama.org
Web Address: www.gama.org
The Game Manufacturers Association (GAMA) is an international non-profit trade association serving the hobby games industry. It hosts two annual events, the GAMA Trade Show and Origins Game Fair, and publishes a quarterly information newsletter, GAMATimes.

Hong Kong Digital Entertainment Industry Support Centre
78 Tat Chee Ave., HKPC Building
Kowloon, Hong Kong Hong Kong
Phone: 852-2788-5678
Fax: 852-2788-5900
E-mail Address: hkpcenq@hkpc.org
Web Address: www.hkpc.org/en/industry-support-services/support-centres/hong-kong-software-industry-information-centre
The Hong Kong Digital Entertainment Industry Support Centre comprises three major sectors in Hong Kong, namely entertainment software, computer animation and digital effects in the production of videos and films. The center supports the development of professionals in the field of animation, design and programming, as well as promotes traditional industries through business development, marketing and branding.

Independent Game Developers Association Limited (The, TIGA)
One London Wall, Fl. 6
London, EC2Y 5EB UK
Phone: 44-845-468-2330
E-mail Address: info@tiga.org
Web Address: www.tiga.org
The Independent Game Developers Association (TIGA) is the trade association representing the UK's games industry. Its members include independent games developers, in-house publisher owned developers, outsourcing companies, technology businesses and universities.

International Game Developers Association (IGDA)
19 Mantua Rd.
Mt. Royal, NJ 08061 USA
Phone: 856-423-2990
Web Address: www.igda.org
The International Game Developers Association (IGDA) represents members involved in the video game production industry. The firm aims to promote professional development within the gaming industry and advocates for issues that affect the game developer community, including anti-censorship issues.

23) Games Industry Resources

Entertainment Software Rating Board (ESRB)
420 Lexington Ave., Ste. 2024
New York, NY 10170 USA
E-mail Address: privacy@esrb.org
Web Address: www.esrb.org
The Entertainment Software Rating Board (ESRB) is a non-profit, self-regulatory body established in 1994 by the Entertainment Software Association (ESA), formerly known as the Interactive Digital Software Association (IDSA). ESRB assigns computer and video game content ratings, enforces industry-adopted advertising guidelines and helps ensure responsible online privacy practices for the interactive entertainment software industry.

GamesIndustry.biz (GI)
E-mail Address: james.brightman@gamesindustry.biz
Web Address: www.gamesindustry.biz
GamesIndustry.biz is a news and information site about the global videogames industry, covering all aspects of the interactive entertainment business from development through to retail.

24) Graphic Artists Associations

Society of Illustrators (SI)
128 E. 63rd St.
New York, NY 10065 USA
Phone: 212-838-2560
Fax: 212-838-2561
E-mail Address: info@societyillustrators.org
Web Address: www.societyillustrators.org
The Society of Illustrators (SI) promotes the appreciation of illustration through exhibitions, lectures, education and open discussion.

25) Hotel/Lodging Associations

Hotel Technology Next Generation
650 E. Algonquin Rd., Ste. 207
Schaumburg, IL 60173 USA

Phone: 847-303-5560
Web Address: www.htng.org
Hotel Technology Next Generation is a non-profit trade association that facilitates the development of next-generation, customer-centric technologies to better meet the needs of the global hotel community.

26) Industry Research/Market Research

ClickZ
Phone: 44-208-0806-489
E-mail Address: info@clickz.com
Web Address: www.clickz.com
ClickZ, is an online publication that offers news, information and e-commerce statistics.

Forrester Research
60 Acorn Park Dr.
Cambridge, MA 02140 USA
Phone: 617-613-5730
Toll Free: 866-367-7378
E-mail Address: press@forrester.com
Web Address: www.forrester.com
Forrester Research is a publicly traded company that identifies and analyzes emerging trends in technology and their impact on business. Among the firm's specialties are the financial services, retail, health care, entertainment, automotive and information technology industries.

Gartner, Inc.
56 Top Gallant Rd.
Stamford, CT 06902 USA
Phone: 203-964-0096
E-mail Address: info@gartner.com
Web Address: www.gartner.com
Gartner, Inc. is a publicly traded IT company that provides competitive intelligence and strategic consulting and advisory services to numerous clients worldwide.

Leichtman Research Group
567 Bay Rd.
Durham, NH 03824 USA
Phone: 603-397-5400
E-mail Address: info@leichtmanresearch.com
Web Address: www.leichtmanresearch.com
Leichtman Research conducts consumer research in the fields of broadband, media and entertainment. They publish very useful newsletters on their web site.

MarketResearch.com
11200 Rockville Pike, Ste. 504
Rockville, MD 20852 USA
Phone: 240-747-3093
Fax: 240-747-3004
Toll Free: 800-298-5699
E-mail Address: customerservice@marketresearch.com
Web Address: www.marketresearch.com
MarketResearch.com is a leading broker for professional market research and industry analysis. Users are able to search the company's database of research publications including data on global industries, companies, products and trends.

NPD Group (The)
900 W. Shore Rd.
Port Washington, NY 11050 USA
Phone: 516-625-0700
Toll Free: 866-444-1411
Web Address: www.npd.com
The NPD Group is one of the world's leading market research firms covering the retailing and related sectors. NPD covers industries including automotive, beauty, technology, entertainment, fashion, food & beverage, home, software, toys and wireless.

Plunkett Research, Ltd.
P.O. Drawer 541737
Houston, TX 77254-1737 USA
Phone: 713-932-0000
Fax: 713-932-7080
E-mail Address: customersupport@plunkettresearch.com
Web Address: www.plunkettresearch.com
Plunkett Research, Ltd. is a leading provider of market research, industry trends analysis and business statistics. Since 1985, it has served clients worldwide, including corporations, universities, libraries, consultants and government agencies. At the firm's web site, visitors can view product information and pricing and access a large amount of basic market information on industries such as financial services, InfoTech, e-commerce, health care and biotech.

Simba Information
11200 Rockville Pike, Ste. 504
Rockville, MD 20852 USA
Phone: 240-747-3096
Fax: 240-747-3004
Toll Free: 888-297-4622
E-mail Address: customerservice@simbainformation.com
Web Address: www.simbainformation.com
Simba Information is a leading authority for market intelligence and forecasts in all aspects of the media industry.

27) Internet Industry Associations

International Academy of Digital Arts and Sciences (IADAS)
22 W. 21st St., Fl. 7
New York, NY 10010 USA
Phone: 212-675-4890
E-mail Address: dmdavies@iadas.net
Web Address: www.iadas.net
The International Academy of Digital Arts and Sciences (IADAS) is dedicated to the progress of new media

worldwide. It runs The Webby Awards, honoring web sites for technological and creative achievements, as well as The Lovie Awards, honoring individuals involved in managing, designing, marketing online web sites, advertising, mobile apps and social content for European market.

28) Internet Usage Statistics

comScore, Inc.
11950 Democracy Dr., Ste. 600
Reston, VA 20190 USA
Phone: 703-438-2000
Fax: 703-438-2051
Toll Free: 866-276-6972
Web Address: www.comscore.com
comScore, Inc. provides excellent data on consumer behavior and audiences, particularly in terms of how consumers access and use online sites and digital data and entertainment. They are global leaders in Internet usage data.

eMarketer
11 Times Square
New York, NY 10036 USA
Toll Free: 800-405-0844
Web Address: www.emarketer.com
eMarketer is a comprehensive, objective and easy-to-use resource for any person or business interested in online marketing and emerging media. The firm offers news articles, market projections and analytical commentaries.

Nielsen
85 Broad St.
New York, NY 10004 USA
Toll Free: 800-864-1224
Web Address: www.nielsen.com
Nielsen offers detailed, real-time Internet, retail and media research and analysis.

Pew Internet & American Life Project
1615 L St. NW, Ste. 800
Washington, DC 20036 USA
Phone: 202-419-4300
Fax: 202-419-4349
E-mail Address: info@pewinternet.org
Web Address: www.pewinternet.org
The Pew Internet & American Life Project, an initiative of the Pew Research Center, produces reports that explore the impact of the Internet on families, communities, work and home, daily life, education, health care and civic and political life.

29) MBA Resources

MBA Depot
Web Address: www.mbadepot.com
MBA Depot is an online community and information portal for MBAs, potential MBA program applicants and business professionals.

30) Media Associations-Educational

Center for Communication, Inc.
110 E. 23rd St., Ste. 900
New York, NY 10010 USA
Phone: 212-686-5005
Fax: 212-504-2632
E-mail Address: info@cencom.org
Web Address: www.cencom.org
The Center for Communication Inc. is a nonprofit organization that encourages university students to meet professionals in communications industries.

31) Media Industry Information

BIA Financial Network, Inc.
15120 Enterprise Ct., Ste. 100
Chantilly, VA 20151 USA
Toll Free: 800-331-5086
E-mail Address: info@biakelsey.com
Web Address: www.bia.com
The BIA Financial Network, Inc., through BIA/Kelsey, offers law firms, government agencies and investment companies strategic advisory services for the media, telecommunications, mobile advertising, Yellow Pages and electronic markets.

Caslon Analytics Pty Ltd.
P.O. Box 132
Braddon, ACT 2612 Australia
E-mail Address: info@caslon.com.au
Web Address: www.caslon.com.au
Caslon Analytics Pty Ltd. is a research firm with a web site that offers a wealth of information on such sectors as publishing, intellectual property and media regulatory issues.

Ketupa.net
Web Address: www.ketupa.net
Ketupa.net offers resources for those interested in the media industries and the information economy in Australia, New Zealand, Asia, Europe and the Americas.

SRDS Media Solutions
1700 Higgins Rd., Fl. 5
Des Plaines, IL 60018-5605 USA
Phone: 847-375-5000
Toll Free: 800-851-7737 ext. 2
E-mail Address: next@srds.com
Web Address: www.srds.com
SRDS Media Solutions creates publications and directories that unite the buyers and sellers of media coverage throughout the nation.

Veronis Suhler Stevenson (VSS)
55 E. 52nd St., Fl. 33
New York, NY 10055 USA
Phone: 212-935-4990
Fax: 212-381-8168
E-mail Address: stevensonj@vss.com
Web Address: www.vss.com
Veronis Suhler Stevenson (VSS) is a private equity firm solely dedicated to the media, communications and information industries. Its web site offers a wealth of information about the media industry.

32) News Organizations & Resources

Associated Press (AP)
450 W. 33rd St., Fl. 14
New York, NY 10001 USA
Phone: 212-621-1500
E-mail Address: info@ap.org
Web Address: www.ap.org
The Associated Press (AP), a not-for-profit organization owned by its 1,500 U.S. daily newspaper members, is the leading provider of news, video, graphics, photo and audio services to newspaper, radio, television and online customers.

China Digital Times (CDT)
Graduate School of Journalism
121 North Gate Hall 5860
Berkeley, CA 94720-5860 USA
E-mail Address: cdt@chinadigitaltimes.net
Web Address: chinadigitaltimes.net
China Digital Times (CDT) is a bilingual news web site covering China's social and political transition and its emerging role in the world and includes news on the economy and various industries. This site is affiliated with the Berkeley China Internet Project hosted by the Berkeley Graduate School of Journalism and contains information gathered from translations of Chinese cyberspace and includes links to many Chinese websites.

Indian Times
I-World Tower, DLF Golf Course Rd.
DLF City Phase V
Gurgaon, Haryana 122 002 India
E-mail Address: editor.indiatimes@indiatimes.co.in
Web Address: www.indiatimes.com
The Indian Times is a leading news organization in India. The portal site includes news stories under subject headings and links to other information sources.

United Press International (UPI)
1133 19th St. NW
Washington, DC 20036 USA
Phone: 202-898-8000
Fax: 202-898-8048
Web Address: www.upi.com
Since 1907, United Press International (UPI) has been a leading provider of critical information to media outlets, businesses, governments and researchers worldwide. UPI is a global operation with offices in Beirut, Hong Kong, London, Santiago, Seoul and Tokyo.

33) Printers & Publishers Associations

American Book Producers Association (ABPA)
31 W 8th St., Fl. 2
New York, NY 10011 USA
E-mail Address: office@abpaonline.org
Web Address: www.abpaonline.org
The American Book Producers Association (ABPA) is the trade association for independent book producers in the U.S. and Canada.

Associated Collegiate Press (ACP)
2221 University Ave. SE, Ste. 121
Minneapolis, MN 55414 USA
Phone: 612-625-8335
E-mail Address: info@studentpress.org
Web Address: www.studentpress.org/acp
The Associated Collegiate Press (ACP), a member of the National Scholastic Press Association, is an organization of college media outlets, offering a forum for discussion, networking and awards for publications through different categories.

Association for Suppliers of Printing, Publishing and Converting Technologies (NPES)
1899 Preston White Dr.
Reston, VA 20191-4367 USA
Phone: 703-264-7200
Fax: 703-620-0994
E-mail Address: npes@npes.org
Web Address: www.npes.org
The Association for Suppliers of Printing, Publishing and Converting Technologies (NPES) is a trade association for companies that manufacture and distribute equipment, systems, software and supplies used in printing, publishing and converting printed material.

Association of Alternative Newsweeklies (AAN)
1156 15th St. NW, Ste. 1005
Washington, DC 20005 USA
Phone: 202-289-8484
Fax: 202-289-2004
E-mail Address: web@aan.org
Web Address: www.altweeklies.com
The Association of Alternative Newsweeklies (AAN) is the trade organization for the alternative newspaper industry.

Association of American Publishers, Inc. (AAP)
455 Massachusetts Ave. NW, Ste. 700
Washington, DC 20001-2777 USA
Phone: 202-347-3375

Fax: 202-347-3690
E-mail Address: info@publishers.org
Web Address: www.publishers.org
The Association of American Publishers (AAP) is the principal trade association of the book publishing industry.

Association of American University Presses, Inc. (AAUP)
28 W. 36th St., Ste. 602
New York, NY 10018 USA
Phone: 212-989-1010
Fax: 212-989-0975
E-mail Address: info@aaupnet.org
Web Address: www.aaupnet.org
The Association of American University Presses (AAUP) is a nonprofit group of scholarly publishers.

Association of Canadian Publishers (ACP)
174 Spadina Ave., Ste. 306
Toronto, ON M5T 2C2 Canada
Phone: 416-487-6116
Fax: 416-487-8815
E-mail Address: admin@canbook.org
Web Address: www.publishers.ca
The Association of Canadian Publishers (ACP) is the national trade organization for English-language Canadian book publishers.

Association of Educational Publishers (AEP)
325 Chestnut St., Ste. 1110
Philadelphia, PA 19106 USA
Phone: 267-351-4310
Fax: 267-351-4317
E-mail Address: prek12learning@publishers.org
Web Address: www.aepweb.org
The Association of Education Publishers (AEP) supports the growth of educational publishing and its positive impact on learning and teaching. It tracks education and industry information and trends, provides professional development and promotes quality supplemental materials as essential learning resources.

Association of Free Community Papers (AFCP)
7445 Morgan Rd., Ste. 203
Liverpool, NY 13090 USA
Fax: 781-459-7770
Toll Free: 877-203-2327
E-mail Address: afcp@afcp.org
Web Address: www.afcp.org
The Association of Free Community Papers (AFCP) represents publishers of more than 3,000 free-circulation community papers, reaching nearly 40 million homes weekly.

Audio Publishers Association
191 Clarksville Rd.
Princeton Junction, NJ 08550 USA
Phone: 609-799-6327
Web Address: www.audiopub.org
Formed in 1987, the Audio Publishers Association (APA) is a not-for-profit trade association that advocates the common, collective business interests of audio publishers. The APA consists of audio publishing companies and allied suppliers, distributors, and retailers of spoken word products and allied fields related to the production, distribution and sale of audiobooks.

Book & Periodical Council (BPC)
192 Spadina Ave., Ste. 107
Toronto, ON M5T 2C2 Canada
Phone: 416-975-9366
Fax: 416-975-1839
E-mail Address: info@thebpc.ca
Web Address: www.bookandperiodicalcouncil.ca
The Book & Periodical Council (BPC) is the umbrella organization for associations involved in the writing, editing, publishing manufacturing, distribution, selling and lending of books and periodicals in Canada.

Book Industry Study Group, Inc. (BISG)
145 W. 45th St., Ste. 601
New York, NY 10036 USA
Phone: 646-336-7141
Fax: 646-336-6214
E-mail Address: info@bisg.org
Web Address: www.bisg.org
Book Industry Study Group (BISG) is a nonprofit corporation examining the business of print and electronic media.

Book Manufacturers' Institute, Inc. (BMI)
2 Armand Beach Dr., Ste. 1B
Palm Coast, FL 32137-2612 USA
Phone: 386-986-4552
Fax: 386-986-4553
E-mail Address: info@bmibook.com
Web Address: www.bmibook.com
The Book Manufacturers' Institute (BMI) is the leading nationally recognized trade association of the book manufacturing industry.

Center for Book Arts, Inc.
28 W. 27th St., Fl. 3
New York, NY 10001 USA
Phone: 212-481-0295
E-mail Address: info@centerforbookarts.org
Web Address: www.centerforbookarts.org
The Center for Book Arts, Inc. is dedicated to preserving the traditional crafts of book-making, as well as exploring and encouraging contemporary interpretations of the book as an art object.

City & Regional Magazine Association (CRMA)
1970 E. Grand Ave., Ste. 330
El Segundo, CA 90245 USA
Phone: 310-364-0193

Fax: 310-364-0196
E-mail Address: admin@citymag.org
Web Address: www.citymag.org
The City & Regional Magazine Association (CRMA) is dedicated exclusively to the interests and concerns of city and regional magazines.

Council of Literary Magazines & Presses (CLMP)
154 Christopher St., Ste. 3C
New York, NY 10014-9110 USA
Phone: 212-741-9110
Fax: 212-741-9112
E-mail Address: info@clmp.org
Web Address: www.clmp.org
The Council of Literary Magazines & Presses (CLMP) serves the independent publishers of fiction, poetry and prose.

Epicomm
1800 Diagonal Rd., Ste. 320
Alexandria, VA 22314-2862 USA
Phone: 703-836-9200
Web Address: http://epicomm.org
Epicomm is a non-profit business management association formed in 2014, through the merger of the National Association of Printers & Lithographers (NAPL), National Association of Quick Printers (NAQP) and the Association of Marketing Service Providers (AMSP). It represents the interests of graphic communications industry in the U.S.

Evangelical Christian Publishers Association (ECPA)
9633 S. 48th St., Ste. 140
Phoenix, AZ 85044 USA
Phone: 480-966-3998
Fax: 480-966-1944
E-mail Address: info@ecpa.org
Web Address: www.ecpa.org
The Evangelical Christian Publishers Association (ECPA) is an international, nonprofit trade organization serving the Christian publishing industry.

Evangelical Press Association (EPA)
P.O. Box 80962
Colorado Springs, CO 80962 USA
Phone: 719-358-2322
Toll Free: 888-311-1731
E-mail Address: director@epassoc.org
Web Address: www.epassoc.org
The Evangelical Press Association (EPA) is a religious and educational nonprofit corporation that seeks to promote the cause of evangelical Christianity and enhance the influence of Christian journalism.

Independent Book Publishers Association (IBPA)
1020 Manhattan Beach Blvd., Ste. 204
Manhattan Beach, CA 90266 USA
Phone: 310-546-1818
Fax: 310-546-3939
E-mail Address: info@IBPA-online.org
Web Address: www.ibpa-online.org
The Independent Book Publishers Association (IBPA), formerly the Publishers Marketing Association (PMA), is a trade association for independent publishers. It offers education, professional advice, promotional opportunities and relevant tools to more than 3000 members.

In-Plant Printing and Mailing Association (IPMA)
105 S. Jefferson, Ste. B-4
Kearney, MO 64060 USA
Phone: 816-903-4762
Fax: 816-902-4766
E-mail Address: ipmainfo@ipma.org
Web Address: www.ipma.org
The In-Plant Printing and Mailing Association (IPMA), formerly the International Publishing Management Association, is an exclusive not-for-profit organization dedicated to assisting in-house corporate publishing and distribution professionals.

International Newspaper Marketing Association (INMA)
P.O. Box 740186
Dallas, TX 75374 USA
Phone: 214-373-9111
Fax: 214-373-9112
Web Address: www.inma.org
The International Newspaper Marketing Association (INMA) is dedicated to sharing of global best practices, spotting trends, identifying new business opportunities and strengthening the marketing of newspaper companies' products and brands.

International Publishers Association (IPA)
23 Ave. de France
Geneva, 1202 Switzerland
Phone: 41-22-704-18-20
Fax: 41-22-704-18-21
E-mail Address: secretariat@internationalpublishers.org
Web Address: www.internationalpublishers.org
The International Publishers Association (IPA) is a non-governmental global group representing all aspects of journal and book publishing worldwide through more than 60 organizations from over 50 countries.

International Regional Magazine Association, Inc. (IRMA)
38 Burgess Ave.
Toronto, ON M4E 1W7 Canada
Phone: 416-705-6884
Fax: 888-806-1533
E-mail Address: irma@regionalmagazines.org
Web Address: www.regionalmagazines.org
International Regional Magazine Association, Inc. (IRMA) exists to provide free and open communication among the publishers of magazines in North America and internationally.

Jewish Book Council (JBC)
520 8th Ave., Fl. 4
New York, NY 10018 USA
Phone: 212-201-2920
Fax: 212-532-4952
E-mail Address: jbc@jewishbooks.org
Web Address: www.jewishbookcouncil.org
The Jewish Book Council (JBC) is a nonprofit organization dedicated solely to promoting Jewish-interest literature. It serves as a catalyst for the writing, publication, distribution, reading and public awareness of books that reflect the Jewish experience.

Local Search Association
820 Kirts Blvd., Ste. 100
Troy, MI 48084-4836 USA
Phone: 248-244-6200
E-mail Address: communications@localsearchassociation.org
Web Address: www.localsearchassociation.org/
The Local Search Association, formerly the Yellow Pages Association, is a trade organization that leads, serves and helps to foster the global print, digital and social media industry focused on Yellow Pages publishers and other associated professionals.

Media Coalition, Inc.
19 Fulton St., Ste. 407
New York, NY 10038 USA
Phone: 212-587-4025
E-mail Address: info@mediacoalition.org
Web Address: www.mediacoalition.org
Media Coalition, Inc., founded in 1973, is an association that defends the U.S. Constitution's First Amendment right to produce and sell books, magazines, movies, recordings, videotapes, DVDs and video games. Members include booksellers, publishers, librarians, home video and game retailers and film, recording and video game producers.

MPA-The Association of Magazine Media
810 7th Ave., Fl. 24
New York, NY 10019 USA
Phone: 212-872-3700
E-mail Address: mpa@magazine.org
Web Address: www.magazine.org
MPA-The Association of Magazine Media (formerly the Magazine Publishers of America, Inc.) is the industry association for consumer magazines in all formats, including printed, mobile and online.

National Association of Independent Publishers Representatives (NAIPR)
111 E. 14th St., Ste. 157
New York, NY 10003 USA
Phone: 267-546-6561
Toll Free: 888-624-7779
E-mail Address: robert.rooney@naipr.org
Web Address: www.naipr.org
The National Association of Independent Publishers Representatives (NAIPR) is a trade association of book publishers' commission representatives, book publishers and other associate members.

National Newspaper Association (NNA)
309 S. Providence Rd.
Columbia, MO 65203 USA
Phone: 573-777-4980
Fax: 573-777-4985
Toll Free: 800-829-4662
E-mail Address: stan@nna.org
Web Address: www.nnaweb.org/
The National Newspaper Association (NNA) represents the owners, publishers and editors of America's community newspapers.

National Press Foundation (NPF)
1211 Connecticut Ave. NW, Ste. 310
Washington, DC 20036 USA
Phone: 202-663-7280
Fax: 202-530-2855
E-mail Address: npf@nationalpress.org
Web Address: nationalpress.org
The National Press Foundation (NPF) seeks to increase journalists' knowledge of complex issues in order to improve public understanding.

National Scholastic Press Association (NSPA)
2221 University Ave. SE, Ste. 121
Minneapolis, MN 55414 USA
Phone: 612-625-8335
Fax: 612-626-0720
E-mail Address: info@studentpress.org
Web Address: www.studentpress.org/nspa
The National Scholastic Press Association (NSPA) is a nonprofit educational association that provides journalism education services to students, teachers, media advisers and others worldwide.

Newspaper Association of America (NAA)
4401 Wilson Blvd., Ste. 900
Arlington, VA 22203-1867 USA
Phone: 571-366-1000
Fax: 571-366-1195
E-mail Address: membsvc@naa.org
Web Address: www.naa.org
The Newspaper Association of America (NAA) is a nonprofit organization representing the newspaper industry.

Newspaper Guild (The)
501 3rd St. NW, Fl. 6
Washington, DC 20001-2797 USA
Phone: 202-434-7177
Fax: 202-434-1472
E-mail Address: guild@cwa-union.org
Web Address: www.newsguild.org

The Newspaper Guild exists to advance the economic interests and improve the working conditions of its members, raise the standards of journalism and ethics in the industry and promote industrial unity.

Periodical & Book Association of America, Inc. (PBAA)
481 8th Ave., Ste. 526
New York, NY 10001 USA
Phone: 212-563-6502
Fax: 212-563-4098
E-mail Address: JCancio@pbaa.net
Web Address: www.pbaa.net
The Periodical & Book Association of America (PBAA) is an organization that represents newsstand publications to the retail community.

Printing Industries of America
301 Brush Creek Rd.
Warrendale, PA 15086 USA
Phone: 412-741-6860
Fax: 412-741-2311
Toll Free: 800-910-4283
E-mail Address: printing@printing.org
Web Address: www.printing.org/
The Printing Industries of America, formerly the Printing Industries of America/Graphic Arts Technical Foundation (PIA/GATF), is a graphic arts trade association serving the interests of thousands of member companies which seeks to reposition print media as an integral part of the information technology sector.

Protestant Church-Owned Publishers Association (PCPA)
6631 Westbury Oaks Ct.
Springfield, VA 22152 USA
Phone: 703-220-5989
E-mail Address: mulder@pcpaonline.org
Web Address: www.pcpaonline.org
The Protestant Church-Owned Publishers Association (PCPA) is an association of publishers directly connected to their respective church denominations and is devoted to the welfare of official church-owned publishing houses.

Society for Scholarly Publishing (SSP)
10200 W. 44th Ave., Ste. 304
Wheat Ridge, CO 80033-2840 USA
Phone: 303-422-3914
Fax: 303-422-8894
E-mail Address: info@sspnet.org
Web Address: www.sspnet.org
The mission of the Society for Scholarly Publishing (SSP) is to facilitate learning, communication and the advancement of appropriate technologies among those involved in scholarly communication.

Southern Newspaper Publishers Association (SNPA)
3680 N. Peachtree Rd., Ste. 300
Atlanta, GA 30341 USA
Phone: 404-256-0444
Fax: 404-252-9135
E-mail Address: edward@snpa.org
Web Address: www.snpa.org
The Southern Newspaper Publishers Association (SNPA) is a regional trade association representing daily newspaper owners and publishers.

Women's National Book Association, Inc. (WNBA)
P.O. Box 237
FDR Station
New York, NY 10150-0231 USA
Phone: 212-208-4629
Fax: 212-208-4629
E-mail Address: info@wna-books.org
Web Address: www.wnba-books.org
The Women's National Book Association (WNBA) is the oldest organization open to women and men in all occupations allied to the publishing industry.

World Association of Newspapers and News Publishers (WAN-IFRA)
Washingtonplatz 1
Darmstadt, 64287 Germany
Phone: 49-6151-733-6
Fax: 49-6151-733-800
E-mail Address: info@wan-ifra.org
Web Address: www.wan-ifra.org
The World Association of Newspapers and News Publishers (WAN-IFRA), created by the 2009 merger of the World Association of Newspapers and the IFRA, represents over 18,000 publications, 3,000 companies and 15,000 online sites in over 120 countries, including 79 national newspaper associations, in its mission to defend and promote the freedom of the press, quality journalism and editorial integrity.

34) Public Relations Associations

Arthur W. Page Society
230 Park Ave., Ste. 455
New York, NY 10169 USA
Phone: 212-400-7959
Fax: 347-474-7399
Web Address: www.awpagesociety.com
The Arthur W. Page Society is devoted to improving business skills among public relations professionals and corporate communications executives. Its members include chief communication officers of Fortune 500 companies and leading non-profit organizations, chief executives of leading public relations agencies, as well as distinguished academics from top business and communication schools.

Canadian Public Relations Society (CPRS)
4195 Dundas St. W., Ste. 346
Toronto, ON M8X 1Y4 Canada
Phone: 416-239-7034

Fax: 416-239-1076
E-mail Address: admin@cprs.ca
Web Address: www.cprs.ca
The Canadian Public Relations Society (CPRS) is a professional society dedicated to serving the needs of the Canadian public relations industry. It consists of 14 member societies located in major cities or organized province-wide.

Chartered Institute of Public Relations (CIPR)
52-53 Russell Sq.
London, WC1B 4HP UK
Phone: 44-20-7631-6900
Web Address: www.cipr.co.uk
The Chartered Institute of Public Relations (CIPR) promotes professional development in the public relations industry in the U.K. The organization offers six grades of membership, fellow, member, associate, affiliate, global affiliate and student.

International Public Relations Association (IPRA)
P.O. Box 6945
London, W1A 6US UK
Phone: 44-1634-818308
E-mail Address: info@ipra.org
Web Address: www.ipra.org
The International Public Relations Association (IPRA) is an international group of public relations practitioners that promotes the exchange of information and cooperation in the profession and creates development opportunities aimed at enhancing the role of public relations in management and international affairs.

National Black Public Relations Society (NBPRS)
14636 Runnymede St.
Van Nuys, CA 91405 USA
Fax: 888-976-0005
Toll Free: 888-976-0005
Web Address: www.nbprs.org
The National Black Public Relations Society (NBPRS) is a professional organization representing blacks in public relations with over 500 members comprised of public relations administrators, government relations directors, media specialists and communications professionals.

Public Affairs Council (PAC)
2121 K St. NW, Ste. 900
Washington, DC 20037 USA
Phone: 202-787-5950
Fax: 202-787-5942
E-mail Address: pac@pac.org
Web Address: www.pac.org
The Public Affairs Council (PAC) is the leading nonpartisan, nonpolitical association dedicated to the advancement of public affairs field and professionals through executive education and networking opportunities.

Public Relations Society of America-National Capital Chapter
10378 Democracy Ln., Ste. A
Fairfax, VA 22030 USA
Phone: 703-691-9212
Fax: 703-691-0866
E-mail Address: info@prsa-ncc.org
Web Address: www.prsa-ncc.org
Public Relations Society of America-National Capital Chapter is the DC-area chapter of the leading professional organization devoted to advancing public relations.

Public Relations Student Society of America (PRSSA)
33 Maiden Ln., Fl. 11
New York, NY 10038-5150 USA
Phone: 212-460-1474
Fax: 212-995-0757
E-mail Address: prssa@prsa.org
Web Address: www.prssa.org
The Public Relations Student Society of America (PRSSA) is an organization devoted to the advancement of students and public relations professionals. Currently, it has 11,000 college student members.

35) Publishing Industry Resources

BookWire
630 Central Ave.
c/o R.R. Bowker
New Providence, NJ 07974 USA
E-mail Address: isbn-san@bowker.com
Web Address: www.bookwire.com
BookWire, a service provided by R.R. Bowker LLC, provides information on thousands of titles, authors and publishers, as well as offering news, reviews and bestseller lists.

R.R. Bowker LLC
630 Central Ave.
New Providence, NJ 07974 USA
Phone: 908-286-1090
Fax: 908-219-0191
Toll Free: 888-269-5372
E-mail Address: sales@bowker.co.uk
Web Address: www.bowker.com
R.R. Bowker LLC is a leading source for book, serial and publishing data serving library, publishing and bookselling professionals and their patrons worldwide. The company is also the steward of the U.S. International Standard Book Numbering (ISBN) Agency.

36) Recording & Music Associations

American Composers Alliance (ACA)
P.O. Box 1108
New York, NY 10040 USA
Phone: 212-568-0036
E-mail Address: info@composers.com

Web Address: composers.com
The American Composers Alliance (ACA) is a membership organization serving professional composers of concert music in America. It serves as publisher, distributor and archivist for the music of its member composers. ACA currently has over 200 active members.

American Federation of Musicians (AFM)
1501 Broadway, Ste. 600
New York, NY 10036 USA
Phone: 212-869-1330
Fax: 212-764-6134
Web Address: www.afm.org
The American Federation of Musicians (AFM) is the largest union in the world for music professionals, serving musicians throughout the U.S. and Canada.

American Society of Composers, Authors & Publishers (ASCAP)
1900 Broadway
New York, NY 10023-7142 USA
Phone: 212-621-6000
Fax: 212-621-8453
Web Address: www.ascap.com
American Society of Composers, Authors & Publishers (ASCAP) is a membership association of U.S. composers, songwriters and publishers of every kind of music, with hundreds of thousands of members worldwide.

Brazilian Association of Record Producers
Phone: 55-21-3511-9908
Fax: 55-21-3511-9907
E-mail Address: abpd@abpd.org.br
Web Address: www.abpd.org.br
The Brazilian Association of Record Producers (Associacao Brasileira dos Produtores de Discos, or ABPD), founded in 1958, represents the interests of musicians, songwriters, producers and music publishers through a range of market research, statistical surveys and anti-piracy activities. ABPD is also responsible for tracking Brazilian record sales to certify albums as Gold, Platinum, etc., based on units sold. The group is affiliated with the International Federation of the Phonographic Industry, which oversees similar efforts in some 76 countries worldwide.

Broadcast Music, Inc. (BMI)
7 World Trade Ct., 250 Greenwich St.
New York, NY 10007-0030 USA
Phone: 212-220-3000
Toll Free: 800-925-8451
E-mail Address: newyork@bmi.com
Web Address: www.bmi.com
Broadcast Music, Inc. (BMI) is an American performing rights organization that represents songwriters, composers and music publishers in all genres of music.

Content Delivery & Storage Association (CDSA)
39 N. Bayles Ave.
Port Washington, NY 11050 USA
Phone: 516-767-6720
Fax: 516-883-5793
E-mail Address: mporter@CDSAonline.org
Web Address: www.cdsaonline.org
The Content Delivery & Storage Association (CDSA), formerly the International Recording Media Association, is a worldwide trade association for organizations involved in every facet of recording media, including entertainment, information and software content storage. CDSA is under the management of the Media & Entertainment Services Alliance (MESA).

Country Music Association, Inc. (CMA)
1 Music Cir. S.
Nashville, TN 37203 USA
Phone: 615-244-2840
Fax: 615-242-4783
E-mail Address: lklausing@cmaworld.com
Web Address: www.cmaworld.com
The Country Music Association (CMA) is a trade association dedicated to promoting and guiding the development of country music throughout the world.

International Association of Audio Information Services (IAAIS)
Toll Free: 800-280-5325
E-mail Address: Stuart.Holland@state.mn.us
Web Address: www.iaais.org
International Association of Audio Information Services (IAAIS) is an organization that provides audio access to information for people who are print-disabled.

International Federation of the Phonographic Industry (IFPI)
Utoquai 37
Postfach 581
Zurich, CH-8024 Switzerland
Phone: 41-1-254-6161
Fax: 41-1-254-6171
E-mail Address: info@ifpi.org
Web Address: www.ifpi.org
The International Federation of the Phonographic Industry (IFPI) represents the recording industry worldwide with 1400 members in 66 countries. Its goals include the fight against music piracy and the promotion of fair market access and adequate copyright laws. The IFPI publishes extensive studies yearly regarding its industry.

Music Canada
85 Mowat Ave.
Toronto, ON M6K 3E3 Canada
Phone: 416-967-7272
Fax: 416-967-9415
E-mail Address: info@musiccanada.com
Web Address: www.musiccanada.com

Music Canada, formerly the Canadian Recording Industry Association, is the trade organization for the sound recording manufacturing and marketing sector in Canada. The organizations primary members are the four big Canadian record labels: EMI Music Canada, Sony Music Entertainment Canada Inc., Universal Music Canada Inc. and Warner Music Canada Co.

Music Publisher's Association of the United States (MPA)
243 5th Ave., Ste. 236
New York, NY 10016 USA
Phone: 212-327-4044
E-mail Address: admin@mpa.org
Web Address: mpa.org
The Music Publisher's Association of the United States (MPA) serves as a forum for publishers to deal with the music industry's vital issues and is actively involved in supporting and advancing compliance with copyright law, combating copyright infringement and exploring the need for further reform.

National Music Publisher's Association (NMPA)
975 F St., NW, Ste. 375
Washington, DC 20004 USA
Phone: 202-393-6672
Fax: 202-393-6673
Web Address: www.nmpa.org
The National Music Publisher's Association (NMPA) seeks to protect, promote and advance the interests of music publishers and songwriters.

Recording Academy (The)
3030 Olympic Blvd.
Santa Monica, CA 90404 USA
Phone: 310-392-3777
Fax: 310-399-3090
E-mail Address: memservices@grammy.com
Web Address: www.grammy365.com
Once known as the National Academy of Recording Arts and Sciences, The Recording Academy is the producer of the GRAMMY music awards. It operates in 12 chapters throughout the U.S. Members include singers, songwriters, recording engineers, producers and other music industry professionals.

Recording Industry Association of America (RIAA)
1025 F St. NW, Fl. 10
Washington, DC 20004 USA
Phone: 202-775-0101
Web Address: www.riaa.com
The Recording Industry Association of America (RIAA) is the trade group that represents the U.S. recording industry.

Society of Professional Audio Recording Services (SPARS)
Fax: 214-722-1442
Toll Free: 800-771-7727
E-mail Address: info@spars.com
Web Address: www.spars.com
The Society of Professional Audio Recording Services (SPARS) is an organization for members of the recording industry to share practical business information about audio and multimedia facility ownership, management and operations.

Songwriters Guild of America
5120 Virginia Way, Ste. C22
Brentwood, TN 37027 USA
Phone: 615-742-9945
Fax: 615-630-7501
Toll Free: 800-524-6742
Web Address: www.songwritersguild.com
The Songwriters Guild of America is the nation's largest and oldest songwriters' organization, providing its members with information and programs to further their careers and understanding of the music industry.

37) Restaurant Industry Associations

National Association of Concessionaires (NAC)
180 N. Michigan Ave., Ste. 2215
Chicago, IL 60601 USA
Phone: 312-236-3858
Fax: 312-236-7809
E-mail Address: info@NAConline.org
Web Address: www.naconline.org
The National Association of Concessionaires (NAC) is the trade association for owners and operators of businesses in the recreation and leisure-time food and beverage concessions industry.

38) Retail Industry Associations

Music Business Association (Music Biz)
1 Eves Dr., Ste. 138
Marlton, NJ 08053 USA
Phone: 856-596-2221
Fax: 856-596-3268
Web Address: musicbiz.org
The Music Business Association (Music Biz), formerly the National Association of Recording Merchandisers (NARM) and digitalmusic.org, is a non-profit trade association that serves the music retailing community in the areas of networking, advocacy, education, information and promotion.

39) Satellite Industry Associations

Satellite Broadcasting & Communications Association (SBCA)
1100 17th St. NW, Ste. 1150
Washington, DC 20036 USA
Phone: 202-349-3620
Fax: 202-349-3621

Toll Free: 800-541-5981
E-mail Address: info@sbca.org
Web Address: www.sbca.com
The Satellite Broadcasting & Communications Association (SBCA) is the national trade organization representing all segments of the satellite consumer services industry in America.

40) Software Industry Associations

European Software Institute (ESI)
Parque Tecnologico de Bizkaia
Edificio 202
Zamudio, Bizkaia E-48170 Spain
Phone: 34-946-430-850
Fax: 34-901-706-009
Web Address: www.esi.es
The European Software Institute (ESI) is a nonprofit foundation launched as an initiative of the European Commission, with the support of leading European companies working in the information technology field.

Software & Information Industry Association (SIIA)
1090 Vermont Ave. NW, Fl. 6
Washington, DC 20005-4095 USA
Phone: 202-289-7442
Fax: 202-289-7097
Web Address: www.siia.net
The Software & Information Industry Association (SIIA) is a principal trade association for the software and digital content industry.

41) Sports Industry Resources

American Bar Association (ABA) Forum on the Entertainment & Sports Industries
321 N. Clark St.
Chicago, IL 60654-7598 USA
Phone: 312-988-5580
Fax: 312-988-5677
E-mail Address: Teresa.Ucok@americanbar.org
Web Address: www.abanet.org/groups/entertainment_sports.html
The American Bar Association (ABA) Forum on the Entertainment & Sports Industries, formed in 1977, seeks to educate attorneys in the transactional and legal principles of sports and entertainment law. The forum's quarterly newsletter is directed toward lawyers practicing entertainment, sports, arts and intellectual property law.

42) Sports Leagues-Electronic Games

Eleague
Web Address: www.e-league.com
Eleague was formed to promote electronic games competition to large scale audiences on such videos as TBS television and Twitch online.

43) Stocks & Financial Markets Data

SiliconValley.com
Phone: 408-920-5615
E-mail Address: svfeedback@mercurynews.com
Web Address: www.siliconvalley.com
SiliconValley.com, run by San Jose Mercury News and owned by MediaNews Group, offers a summary of current financial news and information regarding the field of technology.

44) Technology Transfer Associations

Licensing Executives Society (USA and Canada), Inc.
11130 Sunrise Valley Dr., Ste. 350
Reston, VA 20191 USA
Phone: 703-234-4058
Fax: 703-435-4390
E-mail Address: info@les.org
Web Address: www.lesusacanada.org
Licensing Executives Society (USA and Canada), Inc., established in 1965, is a professional association composed of about 3,000 members who work in fields related to the development, use, transfer, manufacture and marketing of intellectual property. Members include executives, lawyers, licensing consultants, engineers, academic researchers, scientists and government officials. The society is part of the larger Licensing Executives Society International, Inc. (same headquarters address), with a worldwide membership of some 12,000 members from approximately 80 countries.

45) Toy Industry Associations

British Toy & Hobby Association (BTHA)
80 Camberwell Rd.
London, SE5 0EG UK
Phone: 44-20-7701-7271
Fax: 44-20-7708-2437
E-mail Address: admin@btha.co.uk
Web Address: www.btha.co.uk
British Toy & Hobby Association (BTHA) represents the interests of British toy manufacturers and has roughly 144 members that represent the toy, hobby and game market.

Hong Kong Toys Council (HKTC)
8 Cheung Yue St.
Fl. 31, Billion Plz., Cheung Sha Wan
Kowloon, Hong Kong Hong Kong
Phone: 852-2732-3188
Fax: 852-2721-3494
E-mail Address: hktc@fhki.org.hk
Web Address: www.toyshk.org
The Hong Kong Toys Council is an independent trade organization intended to promote the interests of the toy industry, both within Hong Kong's borders and internationally.

International Council of Toy Industries (ICTI)
1115 Broadway, Ste. 400
New York, NY 10010 USA
Phone: 212-675-1141
E-mail Address: info@toy-icti.org
Web Address: www.toy-icti.org
International Council of Toy Industries (ICTI) represents the interests of the worldwide toy industry and promotes international toy safety standards and responsible marketing. Its membership consists of trade associations from 20 countries.

Toy Industry Association, Inc. (TIA)
1115 Broadway, Ste. 400
New York, NY 10010 USA
Phone: 212-675-1141
E-mail Address: info@toyassociation.org
Web Address: www.toyassociation.org
The Toy Industry Association, Inc. (TIA) is a leading organization for North American manufacturers, importers, designers, inventors and retailers of toys and games. It is the owner and manager of the annual PlayCon toy industry conference.

46) Trade Associations-General

Associated Chambers of Commerce and Industry of India (ASSOCHAM)
5, Sardar Patel Marg
Chanakyapuri
New Delhi, 110 021 India
Phone: 91-11-4655-0555
Fax: 91-11-2301-7008
E-mail Address: assocham@nic.in
Web Address: www.assocham.org
The Associated Chambers of Commerce and Industry of India (ASSOCHAM) has a membership of more than 300 chambers and trade associations and serves members from all over India. It works with domestic and international government agencies to advocate for India's industry and trade activities.

Brazilian Trade & Investment Promotion Agency (Apex-Brasil)
SBN, Quadra 02, Lote 11
Edificio Apex-Brasil
Brasilia, DF 70040-020 Brazil
Phone: 55-61-3426-0200
Web Address: www.apexbrasil.com.br
Apex-Brasil works to promote exports of Brazilian products and services, supporting some 70 industry sectors such as agribusiness, technology, civil engineering, entertainment, apparel and industrial equipment.

BUSINESSEUROPE
168 Ave. de Cortenbergh 168
Brussels, 1000 Belgium
Phone: 32-2-237-65-11
Fax: 32-2-231-14-45
E-mail Address: main@businesseurope.eu
Web Address: www.businesseurope.eu
BUSINESSEUROPE is a major European trade federation that operates in a manner similar to a chamber of commerce. Its members are the central national business federations of the 34 countries throughout Europe from which they come. Companies cannot become direct members of BUSINESSEUROPE, though there is a support group which offers the opportunity for firms to encourage BUSINESSEUROPE objectives in various ways.

United States Council for International Business (USCIB)
1212 Ave. of the Americas
New York, NY 10036 USA
Phone: 212-354-4480
Fax: 212-575-0327
E-mail Address: azhang@uscib.org
Web Address: www.uscib.org
The United States Council for International Business (USCIB) promotes an open system of world trade and investment through its global network. Standard USCIB members include corporations, law firms, consulting firms and industry associations. Limited membership options are available for chambers of commerce and sole legal practitioners.

47) Trade Associations-Global

World Trade Organization (WTO)
Centre William Rappard
Rue de Lausanne 154
Geneva 21, CH-1211 Switzerland
Phone: 41-22-739-51-11
Fax: 41-22-731-42-06
E-mail Address: enquiries@wto.og
Web Address: www.wto.org
The World Trade Organization (WTO) is a global organization dealing with the rules of trade between nations. To become a member, nations must agree to abide by certain guidelines. Membership increases a nation's ability to import and export efficiently.

48) Trade Resources

OneIndia
Elephant Rock Rd., Sanjana Plz., #74/2, Fl.2
Bangalore, 560 011 India
Phone: 91-80-6715-0800
Fax: 91-80-6715-0801
Web Address: www.oneindia.in
OneIndia provides information relating to national and international business, as well as general news, travel and entertainment information. The site includes an online directory of web links and an Indian language portal.

49) U.S. Government Agencies

Bureau of Economic Analysis (BEA)
4600 Silver Hill Rd.
Washington, DC 20233 USA
Phone: 301-278-9004
E-mail Address: customerservice@bea.gov
Web Address: www.bea.gov
The Bureau of Economic Analysis (BEA), an agency of the U.S. Department of Commerce, is the nation's economic accountant, preparing estimates that illuminate key national, international and regional aspects of the U.S. economy.

Bureau of Labor Statistics (BLS)
2 Massachusetts Ave. NE
Washington, DC 20212-0001 USA
Phone: 202-691-5200
Fax: 202-691-7890
Toll Free: 800-877-8339
E-mail Address: blsdata_staff@bls.gov
Web Address: stats.bls.gov
The Bureau of Labor Statistics (BLS) is the principal fact-finding agency for the Federal Government in the field of labor economics and statistics. It is an independent national statistical agency that collects, processes, analyzes and disseminates statistical data to the American public, U.S. Congress, other federal agencies, state and local governments, business and labor. The BLS also serves as a statistical resource to the Department of Labor.

FCC-Mass Media Bureau
445 12th St. SW
Washington, DC 20554 USA
Fax: 866-418-0232
Toll Free: 888-225-5322
E-mail Address: PRA@fcc.gov
Web Address: www.fcc.gov/mb
The Mass Media Bureau of the Federal Communications Commission (FCC) regulates broadcast television and radio stations in the U.S. for the FCC.

FCC-Office of Engineering & Technology (OET)
Office of Engineering and Technology
445 12th St. SW
Washington, DC 20554 USA
Phone: 202-418-2470
Fax: 202-418-1944
E-mail Address: oetinfo@fcc.gov
Web Address: www.fcc.gov/engineering-%26-technology
The Office of Engineering & Technology (OET) unit of the Federal Communications Commission (FCC) acts as a consultant to the FCC regarding matters of engineering and technology. It also provides evaluations of emerging technologies and equipment.

FCC-Wireline Competition Bureau (WCB)
445 12th St. SW
Washington, DC 20554 USA
Phone: 202-418-1500
Fax: 202-418-2825
Toll Free: 888-225-5322
E-mail Address: FOIA@fcc.gov
Web Address: www.fcc.gov/wcb
The FCC-Wireline Competition Bureau (WCB), formerly the Common Carrier Bureau, is a unit of the Federal Communications Commission (FCC). It is responsible for administering the FCC's policies concerning companies that provide wireline telecommunications.

Federal Communications Commission (FCC)
445 12th St. SW
Washington, DC 20554 USA
Fax: 866-418-0232
Toll Free: 888-225-5322
E-mail Address: PRA@fcc.gov
Web Address: www.fcc.gov
The Federal Communications Commission (FCC) is an independent U.S. government agency established by the Communications Act of 1934 responsible for regulating interstate and international communications by radio, television, wire, satellite and cable.

Federal Communications Commission (FCC)-International Bureau
445 12th St. SW
Washington, DC 20554 USA
Fax: 866-418-0232
Toll Free: 888-225-5322
E-mail Address: PRA@fcc.gov
Web Address: www.fcc.gov/international
The Federal Communications Commission (FCC)-International Bureau exists to administer the FCC's international telecommunications and satellite policies and obligations, such as licensing and regulatory functions, as well as promotes U.S. interests in international communications arena.

Federal Communications Commission (FCC)-Wireless Telecommunications Bureau
445 12th St. SW
Washington, DC 20554 USA
Phone: 202-418-0600
Fax: 202-418-0787
Toll Free: 888-225-5322
E-mail Address: PRA@fcc.gov
Web Address: www.fcc.gov/wireless-telecommunications#block-menu-block-4
The Federal Communications Commission (FCC)-Wireless Telecommunications Bureau handles nearly all FCC domestic wireless telecommunications programs and policies, including cellular and smarftphones, pagers and two-way radios. The bureau also regulates the use of radio spectrum for businesses, aircraft/ship operators and individuals.

U.S. Census Bureau
4600 Silver Hill Rd.
Washington, DC 20233-8800 USA
Phone: 301-763-4636
Toll Free: 800-923-8282
E-mail Address: pio@census.gov
Web Address: www.census.gov
The U.S. Census Bureau is the official collector of data about the people and economy of the U.S. Founded in 1790, it provides official social, demographic and economic information. In addition to the Population & Housing Census, which it conducts every 10 years, the U.S. Census Bureau numerous other surveys annually.

U.S. Copyright Office
101 Independence Ave. SE
Washington, DC 20559-6000 USA
Phone: 202-707-3000
Toll Free: 877-476-0778
Web Address: www.copyright.gov
Located within the Library of Congress, The U.S. Copyright Office is the official copyright administration body within the U.S. Its web site contains information regarding copyright laws and issues and allows users to register their work for copyright protection online.

U.S. Department of Commerce (DOC)
1401 Constitution Ave. NW
Washington, DC 20230 USA
Phone: 202-482-2000
E-mail Address: TheSec@doc.gov
Web Address: www.commerce.gov
The U.S. Department of Commerce (DOC) regulates trade and provides valuable economic analysis of the economy.

U.S. Department of Labor (DOL)
200 Constitution Ave. NW
Washington, DC 20210 USA
Phone: 202-693-4676
Toll Free: 866-487-2365
Web Address: www.dol.gov
The U.S. Department of Labor (DOL) is the government agency responsible for labor regulations.

U.S. Securities and Exchange Commission (SEC)
100 F St. NE
Washington, DC 20549 USA
Phone: 202-942-8088
Toll Free: 800-732-0330
E-mail Address: help@sec.gov
Web Address: www.sec.gov
The U.S. Securities and Exchange Commission (SEC) is a nonpartisan, quasi-judicial regulatory agency responsible for administering federal securities laws. These laws are designed to protect investors in securities markets and ensure that they have access to disclosure of all material information concerning publicly traded securities. Visitors to the web site can access the EDGAR database of corporate financial and business information.

50) Writers, Photographers & Editors Associations

American Medical Writers Association (AMWA)
30 W. Gude Dr., Ste. 525
Rockville, MD 20850-4347 USA
Phone: 240-238-0940
Fax: 301-294-9006
E-mail Address: amwa@amwa.org
Web Address: www.amwa.org
The American Medical Writers Association (AMWA) seeks to promote excellence in writing, editing and producing printed and electronic biomedical communications.

American Society of Journalists and Authors, Inc. (ASJA)
355 Lexington Ave., Fl. 15
New York, NY 10017 USA
Phone: 212-997-0947
Web Address: www.asja.org
The American Society of Journalists and Authors (ASJA) is one of the nation's leading organizations of independent nonfiction writers.

American Society of Magazine Editors (ASME)
757 Third Ave., Fl. 11
New York, NY 10017 USA
Phone: 212-872-3700
E-mail Address: mpa@magazine.org
Web Address: www.magazine.org/asme
The American Society of Magazine Editors (ASME) is a professional organization for editors of print and online magazines. ASME is part of the Magazine Publishers of America (MPA).

American Society of Media Photographers (ASMP)
150 N. 2nd St.
Philadelphia, PA 19106 USA
Phone: 215-451-2767
E-mail Address: info@asmp.org
Web Address: www.asmp.org
The American Society of Media Photographers (ASMP) is a trade organization that promotes photographers' rights, educates photographers in better business practices and produces business publications for photographers.

American Society of News Editors (ASNE)
209 Reynolds Journalism Institute
Missouri School of Journalism
Columbia, MO 65211 USA
Phone: 573-884-2405
Fax: 573-884-3824
Web Address: www.asne.org

The American Society of News Editors (ASNE) is an association that brings together editors of daily newspapers and people directly involved with developing content for daily newspapers.

Associated Press Sports Editors (APSE)
E-mail Address: byrne@usatoday.com
Web Address: apsportseditors.org
Associated Press Sports Editors (APSE) is a trade organization for professional sports reporters, editors, copy editors and designers.

Association for Women in Sports Media (AWSM)
7742 Spalding Dr., Ste. 377
Norcross, GA 30092 USA
E-mail Address: info@awsmonline.org
Web Address: www.awsmonline.org
The Association for Women in Sports Media (AWSM) is a global organization of over 600 people employed in sports writing, editing, broadcasting and production, public relations and sports information. Its mission is to support diversity in sports media through programs that aid females involved in the industry.

Association of Independent Creative Editors (AICE)
3 West 18th St., Fl. 5
New York, NY 10011 USA
Phone: 212-665-2679
E-mail Address: info@aice.org
Web Address: www.aice.org
The Association of Independent Creative Editors (AICE) is a national association serving the needs and interests of independent creative editorial companies.

Association of Opinion Journalists
801 Third St. South
c/o The Poynter Institute
St. Petersburg, FL 33701 USA
Phone: 518-454-5472
E-mail Address: AOJ@poynter.org
Web Address: https://aoj.wildapricot.org/
The Association of Opinion Journalists, formerly known as The National Conference of Editorial Writers (NCEW) strives to stimulate the conscience and improve the quality of opinion writing.

Association of Writers & Writing Programs (AWP)
4400 University Dr.
George Mason University
Fairfax, VA 22030 USA
Phone: 703-993-4301
Fax: 703-993-4302
E-mail Address: awp@awpwriter.org
Web Address: www.awpwriter.org
The Association of Writers & Writing Programs (AWP) exists to foster literary talent and achievement, to advance the art of writing as essential to a good education and to serve the makers, teachers, students and readers of contemporary writing.

Authors Guild
31 E. 32th St., Fl. 7
New York, NY 10016 USA
Phone: 212-563-5904
Fax: 212-564-5363
E-mail Address: staff@authorsguild.org
Web Address: www.authorsguild.org
The Authors Guild is a society of published authors and a leading advocate for fair compensation, free speech and copyright protection.

Authors Registry, Inc.
Phone: 212-563-6920
E-mail Address: staff@authorsregistry.org
Web Address: www.authorsregistry.org
The Authors Registry, Inc. is a nonprofit organization formed to help expedite the flow of royalty payments and small re-use fees to authors, particularly for new-media uses. It was founded by a consortium of organizations: the Authors Guild, the Dramatists Guild, the Association of Authors' Representatives and The American Society of Journalists & Authors.

Editorial Freelancers Association (EFA)
71 W. 23rd St., Fl. 4
New York, NY 10010-4102 USA
Phone: 212-929-5400
Fax: 212-929-5439
Toll Free: 866-929-5425
E-mail Address: office@the-efa.org
Web Address: www.the-efa.org
The Editorial Freelancers Association (EFA) is a national, nonprofit, professional organization of self-employed workers in the publishing and communications industries.

Education Writers Association (EWA)
3516 Connecticut Ave. NW
Washington, DC 20008 USA
Phone: 202-452-9830
Web Address: www.ewa.org
The Education Writers Association (EWA) is the national professional organization of education reporters.

Football Writers Association of America (FWAA)
18652 Vista del Sol
Dallas, TX 75287 USA
Phone: 972-713-6198
E-mail Address: tiger@fwaa.com
Web Address: www.sportswriters.net/fwaa
The Football Writers Association of America (FWAA) consists of North American journalists, broadcasters and publishers that cover college football. The FWAA also includes executives involved in various aspects of the game.

Garden Writers Association of America (GWAA)
7809 FM 179
Shallowater, TX 79363 USA
Phone: 806-832-1870
Fax: 806-832-5244
E-mail Address: info@gardenwriters.org
Web Address: www.gwaa.org
The Garden Writers Association of America (GWAA) is an organization of over 1,800 professional communicators in the lawn and garden industry.

Horror Writers Association (HWA)
P.O. Box 56687
Sherman Oaks, CA 91413 USA
Phone: 818-220-3965
E-mail Address: hwa@horror.org
Web Address: www.horror.org
The Horror Writers Association (HWA) is a worldwide organization of writers and publishing professionals dedicated to promoting the interests of writers of horror and dark fantasy.

International Journalists' Network (IJNet)
2000 M St. NW, Ste. 250
Washington, DC 20036 USA
Phone: 202-737-3700
Fax: 202-737-0530
Web Address: www.ijnet.org
International Journalists' Network (IJNet) is an online source for media news and journalism training opportunities. It reports on the state of media around the world and compiles media directories.

International Women's Writing Guild (IWWG)
274 Madison Ave., Ste. 1202
New York, NY 10016 USA
Phone: 917-720-6959
E-mail Address: iwwgquestions@gmail.com
Web Address: www.iwwg.com
The International Women's Writing Guild (IWWG) is a network for the personal and professional empowerment of women through writing.

Investigative Reporters & Editors, Inc. (IRE)
141 Neff Annex
Missouri School of Journalism
Columbia, MO 65211 USA
Phone: 573-882-2042
E-mail Address: info@ire.org
Web Address: www.ire.org
Investigative Reporters & Editors, Inc. (IRE) is a nonprofit organization that provides educational services to reporters, editors and others interested in investigative journalism.

Media Communications Association International (MCAI)
c/o MCA-I Chapter
P.O. Box 5135
Madison, WI 53705-0135 USA
Phone: 888-899-6224
E-mail Address: m_k_schaefer@yahoo.com
Web Address: www.mca-i.org
The Media Communications Association International (MCAI) is the leading global community for media communications professionals seeking to drive the convergence of communications and technology for the growth of the profession.

Mystery Writers of America (MWA)
1140 Broadway, Ste. 1507
New York, NY 10001 USA
Phone: 212-888-8171
Fax: 212-888-8107
Web Address: www.mysterywriters.org
Mystery Writers of America (MWA) is a nonprofit organization for mystery writers and other professionals in the mystery field.

National Association of Black Journalists (NABJ)
1100 Knight Hall, Ste. 3100
College Park, MD 20742 USA
Phone: 301-405-0248
Fax: 301-314-1714
Web Address: www.nabj.org
The National Association of Black Journalists (NABJ) is an organization of journalists, students and media-related professionals that provides programs and services to and advocates on behalf of black journalists worldwide.

National Association of Hispanic Journalists (NAHJ)
1050 Connecticut Ave. NW, Fl. 10
Washington, DC 20036 USA
Phone: 202-662-7145
E-mail Address: nahj@nahj.org
Web Address: www.nahj.org
The National Association of Hispanic Journalists (NAHJ) is dedicated to the recognition and professional advancement of Hispanics in the news industry.

National Association of Science Writers, Inc. (NASW)
P.O. Box 7905
Berkley, CA 94707 USA
Phone: 510-647-9500
Web Address: www.nasw.org
The National Association of Science Writers (NASW) exists to foster the dissemination of accurate information regarding science through all media devoted to informing the public.

National Collegiate Baseball Writers Association (NCBWA)
5201 N. O'Connor Blvd., Ste. 300
Irving, TX 75039 USA
Phone: 214-909-9314
E-mail Address: webmaster@sportswriters.net

Web Address: www.sportswriters.net/ncbwa
The National Collegiate Baseball Writers Association (NCBWA) consists of writers, broadcasters and publicists of college baseball in the U.S.

National Federation of Abstracting & Information Services (NFAIS)
801 Compass Way S., Ste. 201
Annapolis, MD 21401 USA
Phone: 443-221-2980
Fax: 443-221-2981
E-mail Address: nfais@nfais.org
Web Address: www.nfais.org
The National Federation of Abstracting & Information Services (NFAIS) serves groups that aggregate, organize and facilitate access to information and provides a forum for its members to address common interests through education and advocacy.

National Federation of Press Women (NFPW)
200 Little Falls St., Ste. 405
Falls Church, VA 22046 USA
Phone: 703-237-9804
Fax: 703-237-9808
E-mail Address: presswomen@aol.com
Web Address: www.nfpw.org
The National Federation of Press Women (NFPW) is an organization of professional journalists and communicators.

National Press Club (NPC)
529 14th St. NW, Fl. 13
Washington, DC 20045 USA
Phone: 202-662-7500
Web Address: press.org/
The National Press Club (NPC) provides people who gather and disseminate news with a center for the advancement of their professional standards and skills, the promotion of free expression, mutual support and social fellowship.

National Press Club Foundation of Canada
17 York St., Ste. 201
Ottawa, Ontario K1N 9J6 Canada
Phone: 613-567-9900
E-mail Address: info@pressclubcanada.ca
Web Address: pressclubcanada.ca/
The National Press Club Foundation of Canada provides a platform for discussion of public issues along with opportunities for social interaction for reporters, editors and others involved in the news industry.

National Press Photographers Association, Inc. (NPPA)
120 Hooper St.
Athens, GA 30602 USA
Phone: 919-383-7246
Toll Free: 702-542-2506
E-mail Address: info@nppa.org
Web Address: www.nppa.org
National Press Photographers Association, Inc. (NPPA) seeks to advance, create, edit and distribute photojournalism in all news media.

National Society of Newspaper Columnists (NSNC)
P.O. Box 411532
San Francisco, CA 94141 USA
Phone: 415-488-6762
Fax: 484-297-0336
E-mail Address: director@columnists.com
Web Address: www.columnists.com
The National Society of Newspaper Columnists (NSNC) provides a forum for newspaper columnists to discuss the industry and common interests.

National Writers Union (NWU)
256 W. 38th St., Ste. 703
New York, NY 10018 USA
Phone: 212-254-0279
Fax: 212-254-0673
E-mail Address: nwu@nwu.org
Web Address: www.nwu.org
The National Writers Union (NWU) is a labor union that represents freelance writers in all genres, formats and media. It is committed to improving the economic and working conditions of freelance writers.

Outdoor Writers Association of America (OWAA)
615 Oak St., Ste. 201
Missoula, MT 59801 USA
Phone: 406-728-7434
Fax: 406-728-7445
Toll Free: 800-692-2477
E-mail Address: info@owaa.org
Web Address: www.owaa.org
The Outdoor Writers Association of America (OWAA) exists to improve the professional skills of its members, set the highest ethical and communications standards, encourage public enjoyment and conservation of natural resources and be mentors for the next generation of professional outdoor communicators.

Overseas Press Club of America (OPCA)
40 W. 45th St.
New York, NY 10036 USA
Phone: 212-626-9220
Fax: 212-626-9210
Web Address: www.opcofamerica.org
The Overseas Press Club of America (OPCA) is an international association of journalists working in the United States and abroad.

Poetry Society of America
15 Gramercy Pk.
New York, NY 10003 USA
Phone: 212-254-9628
Fax: 212-673-2352

Web Address: www.poetrysociety.org
The Poetry Society of America provides a local meeting place for poets and information regarding readings, seminars, competitions, and other resources.

Reporters Committee for Freedom of the Press (RCFP)
1156 15th St., Ste. 1250
Washington, DC 20005 USA
Phone: 202-795-9300
Toll Free: 800-336-4243
E-mail Address: info@rcfp.org
Web Address: www.rcfp.org
The Reporters Committee for Freedom of the Press (RCFP) is a nonprofit organization dedicated to providing free legal help to journalists and news organizations.

Romance Writers of America (RWA)
14615 Benfer Rd.
Houston, TX 77069 USA
Phone: 832-717-5200
E-mail Address: info@rwa.org
Web Address: www.rwa.org
Romance Writers of America (RWA) is the professional association for published and aspiring romance writers.

Science Fiction & Fantasy Writers of America, Inc. (SFWA)
P.O. Box 3238
Enfield, CT 06083-3238 USA
Web Address: www.sfwa.org
Science Fiction & Fantasy Writers of America (SFWA) is an organization for writers in the science fiction and fantasy genres, promoting dialogue and furthering the rights of its members.

Society for Features Journalism
1100 Knight Hall
Philip Merrill College of Journalism
College Park, MD 20742-7111 USA
Phone: 301-314-2631
Fax: 301-314-9166
E-mail Address: anynka@umd.edu
Web Address: http://featuresjournalism.org/
The Society for Features Journalism, formerly the American Association of Sunday and Feature Editors, is an organization that promotes the writing craft as well as innovation in arts, entertainment and lifestyle journalism.

Society for Technical Communication (STC)
9401 Lee Highway, Ste. 300
Fairfax, VA 22031 USA
Phone: 703-522-4114
Fax: 703-522-2075
Web Address: www.stc.org
Society for Technical Communication (STC) is a membership organization dedicated to advancing the art and science of technical writing.

Society of American Business Editors & Writers (SABEW)
555 N. Central Ave., Ste. 406e
Phoenix, AZ 85004-1248 USA
Phone: 602-496-7862
Fax: 602-496-7041
E-mail Address: sabew@sabew.org
Web Address: www.sabew.org
The Society of American Business Editors & Writers (SABEW) is a not-for-profit organization of business journalists in North America that promotes business journalism through education.

Society of American Travel Writers (SATW)
1 Parkview Plaza, Ste. 800
Oakbrook Terrace, IL 60181 USA
Phone: 312-420-6846
E-mail Address: info@satw.org
Web Address: www.satw.org
The Society of American Travel Writers (SATW) promotes responsible journalism, provides professional support and development for members and encourages the conservation and preservation of travel resources worldwide.

Society of Children's Book Writers and Illustrators (SCBWI)
4727 Wilshire Blvd., Ste. 301
Los Angeles, CA 90010 USA
Phone: 323-782-1010
Fax: 323-782-1892
E-mail Address: scbwi@scbwi.org
Web Address: www.scbwi.org
The Society of Children's Book Writers and Illustrators (SCBWI) serves people who write, illustrate or share a vital interest in children's literature, including publishers, librarians, booksellers and agents.

Society of Environmental Journalists (SEJ)
P.O. Box 2492
Jenkintown, PA 19046 USA
Phone: 215-884-8174
Fax: 215-884-8175
E-mail Address: sej@sej.org
Web Address: www.sej.org
The Society of Environmental Journalists (SEJ) seeks to advance public understanding of environmental issues by improving the quality, accuracy and visibility of environmental reporting.

Society of Professional Journalists (SPJ)
3909 N. Meridian St.
Eugene S. Pulliam National Journalism Ctr.
Indianapolis, IN 46208 USA
Phone: 317-927-8000
Fax: 317-920-4789
E-mail Address: jskeel@spj.org
Web Address: www.spj.org

The Society of Professional Journalists (SPJ) is dedicated to the perpetuation of a free press.

United States Basketball Writers Association (USBWA)
Phone: 314-444-4325
E-mail Address: webmaster@sportswriters.net
Web Address: www.sportswriters.net/usbwa
The United States Basketball Writers Association (USBWA) is an organization representing college and high school basketball writers in the U.S.

Western Writers of America, Inc. (WWA)
500 Beaver Rd.
Encampment, WY 82325 USA
Phone: 307-329-8942
E-mail Address: wwa.moulton@gmail.com
Web Address: www.westernwriters.org
Western Writers of America, Inc. (WWA) exists to promote the literature of the American West.

Writers Guild of America East, Inc. (WGAE)
250 Hudson St., Ste. 700
New York, NY 10013 USA
Phone: 212-767-7800
Fax: 212-582-1909
E-mail Address: vgomez@wgaeast.org
Web Address: www.wgaeast.org
The Writers Guild of America East (WGAE) is the east coast branch of WGA, a labor union that protects and defends the rights of television, radio and film writers.

Writers Guild of America West, Inc. (WGAW)
7000 W. 3rd St.
Los Angeles, CA 90048 USA
Phone: 323-951-4000
Fax: 323-782-4800
Toll Free: 800-548-4532
Web Address: www.wga.org
The Writers Guild of America West (WGAW) is the west coast branch of the WGA, a labor union that protects and defends the rights of television and film writers.

Chapter 4

THE ENTERTAINMENT 400: WHO THEY ARE AND HOW THEY WERE CHOSEN

Includes Indexes by Company Name, Industry & Location

The companies chosen to be listed in PLUNKETT'S ENTERTAINMENT, MOVIE, PUBLISHING & MEDIA INDUSTRY ALMANAC comprise a unique list. THE ENTERTAINMENT 400 were chosen specifically for their dominance in the many facets of the entertainment and media industry in which they operate. Complete information about each firm can be found in the "Individual Profiles," beginning at the end of this chapter. These profiles are in alphabetical order by company name.

THE ENTERTAINMENT 400 companies are from all parts of the United States, Canada, Europe and Asia. THE ENTERTAINMENT 400 includes companies that are deeply involved in the technologies, services and products that keep the entire industry forging ahead.

Simply stated, THE ENTERTAINMENT 400 contains the largest, most successful, fastest growing firms in entertainment and related industries in the world. To be included in our list, the firms had to meet the following criteria:

1) Generally, these are corporations based in the U.S., however, the headquarters of many firms are located in other nations.
2) Prominence, or a significant presence, in entertainment, media services and supporting fields. (See the following Industry Codes section for a complete list of types of businesses that are covered).
3) The companies in THE ENTERTAINMENT 400 do not have to be exclusively in the entertainment and media field.
4) Financial data and vital statistics must have been available to the editors of this book, either directly from the company being written about or from outside sources deemed reliable and accurate by the editors. A small number of companies that we would like to have included are not listed because of a lack of sufficient, objective data.

INDEXES TO THE ENTERTAINMENT 400, AS FOUND IN THIS CHAPTER AND IN THE BACK OF THE BOOK:	
Index of Rankings Within Industry Groups	p. 94
Alphabetical Index	p. 105
Index of Headquarters Location by U.S. State	p. 108
Index of Non-U.S. Headquarters Location by Country	p. 112
Index of Firms Noted as "Hot Spots for Advancement" for Women/Minorities	p. 520
Index by Subsidiaries, Brand Names and Selected Affiliations	p. 522

INDEX OF COMPANIES WITHIN INDUSTRY GROUPS

The industry codes shown below are based on the 2012 NAIC code system (NAIC is used by many analysts as a replacement for older SIC codes because NAIC is more specific to today's industry sectors, see www.census.gov/NAICS). Companies are given a primary NAIC code, reflecting the main line of business of each firm.

Industry Group/Company	Industry Code	2017 Sales	2017 Profits
Advertising Agencies and Marketing Services			
DexYP	541810	2,309,000,000	
Advertising, Public Relations and Marketing Services			
MDI Entertainment LLC	541800		
Amusement and Theme Parks			
Ardent Leisure Group	713110	348,937,856	-43,828,908
Cedar Fair LP	713110	1,321,966,976	215,476,000
Euro Disney SCA	713110	1,500,000,000	
Merlin Entertainments Group Plc	713110	2,013,032,960	263,942,208
Oriental Land Co Ltd	713110	4,431,470,592	764,080,576
Palace Entertainment Holdings LLC	713110		
SeaWorld Entertainment Inc	713110	1,263,324,032	-202,386,000
Shenzhen Overseas Chinese Town Co Ltd (OCT Limited)	713110	6,501,360,000	1,430,820,000
Six Flags Entertainment Corporation	713110	1,359,074,048	273,816,000
Village Roadshow Limited	713110	698,141,952	-46,744,204
Amusement Arcades			
Dave & Buster's Entertainment Inc	713120	1,005,158,016	90,795,000
Sega Sammy Holdings Inc	713120	3,403,634,176	256,075,600
Book Publishing			
American Educational Products LLC	511130		
Educational Development Corporation	511130	106,628,096	2,860,900
Hachette Book Group Inc	511130	610,000,000	
HarperCollins Publishers LLC	511130	1,670,000,000	
Houghton Mifflin Harcourt Company	511130	1,407,511,040	-103,187,000
John Wiley & Sons Inc	511130	1,718,530,048	113,643,000
Lerner Publishing Group	511130		
McGraw-Hill Education Inc	511130	1,719,072,000	-65,930,000
Pearson North America	511130	3,951,580,000	531,555,000
Pearson PLC	511130	5,699,383,808	512,729,856
Penguin Group USA	511130	850,000,000	
Penguin Random House	511130	3,600,000,000	
Scholastic Corporation	511130	1,741,600,000	52,300,000
Simon & Schuster Inc	511130	829,000,000	
Thomas Nelson Inc	511130		
Book Stores			
Barnes & Noble Inc	451211	3,894,557,952	22,023,000
Books A Million Inc	451211	461,000,000	
Bowling Centers			
Bowlero Corporation	713950	600,000,000	
Cable TV Programming, Cable Networks and Subscription Video			
A&E Television Networks LLC	515210	4,050,000,000	
AMC Networks Inc	515210	2,805,690,880	471,316,000

Industry Group/Company	Industry Code	2017 Sales	2017 Profits
Cable News Network Inc (CNN)	515210	1,400,000,000	
Crown Media Family Networks	515210	505,000,000	
CW Network LLC (The)	515210	418,000,000	
Discovery Inc	515210	6,872,999,936	-337,000,000
ESPN Inc	515210	10,750,000,000	
Hearst Corporation (The)	515210	11,000,000,000	
Home Box Office Inc (HBO)	515210	5,810,000,000	
Hulu LLC	515210	2,870,000,000	
Netflix Inc	515210	11,692,712,960	558,929,024
Oprah Winfrey Network (OWN)	515210		
Sky Deutschland AG	515210		
SKY Perfect JSAT Corporation	515210	1,789,060,224	161,537,168
Turner Broadcasting System Inc	515210	12,081,000,000	4,489,000,000
Viacom Inc	515210	13,262,999,552	1,874,000,000
Walt Disney Company (The)	515210	55,137,001,472	8,979,999,744
Warner Media LLC	515210	31,271,000,064	5,247,000,064
Candy and Chocolate Manufacturing (From Cocao Beans)			
Hershey Company (The)	311351	7,515,425,792	782,980,992
Casino Hotels and Casino Resorts			
Affinity Gaming LLC	721120	380,000,000	
Ameristar Casinos Inc	721120	1,100,000,000	
Boyd Gaming Corp	721120	2,383,706,880	189,192,992
Caesars Entertainment Corporation	721120	4,851,999,744	-375,000,000
Century Casinos Inc	721120	154,068,992	6,259,000
Dover Downs Gaming & Entertainment Inc	721120	176,924,000	-1,068,000
Eldorado Resorts Inc	721120	1,473,504,000	73,940,000
Galaxy Entertainment Group Limited	721120	7,974,875,648	1,341,398,912
Genting Singapore PLC	721120	1,753,947,008	502,569,472
Golden Entertainment Inc	721120	509,808,000	2,171,000
Kangwon Land Inc	721120	1,502,440,000	409,717,000
Kerzner International Limited	721120	420,000,000	
Las Vegas Sands Corp (The Venetian)	721120	12,881,999,872	2,806,000,128
MGM Resorts International	721120	10,773,904,384	1,960,285,952
Pinnacle Entertainment Inc	721120	2,561,848,064	63,104,000
Station Casinos LLC	721120	980,000,000	
Trans World Corporation	721120	54,108,000	1,885,000
Wynn Resorts Limited	721120	6,306,368,000	747,180,992
Casinos (Except Casino Hotels)			
Canterbury Park Holding Corporation	713210	56,952,776	4,090,781
Churchill Downs Incorporated	713210	882,600,000	140,500,000
Codere SA	713210	1,842,863,872	3,096,879
Evergreen Gaming Corporation	713210	35,609,460	3,032,901
Full House Resorts Inc	713210	161,267,008	-5,028,000
Great Canadian Gaming Corporation	713210	455,752,768	62,542,660
Greek Organisation of Football Prognostics SA (OPAP)	713210	1,194,446,848	142,857,136
Melco International Development Limited	713210	5,258,665,984	60,546,808
Nevada Gold & Casinos Inc	713210	74,626,952	563,964
Penn National Gaming Inc	713210	3,147,970,048	473,463,008

Industry Group/Company	Industry Code	2017 Sales	2017 Profits
Rank Group plc (The)	713210	901,960,320	80,222,432
Tabcorp Holdings Limited	713210	1,565,263,104	-14,572,970
Tatts Group Limited	713210	1,935,809,664	154,498,016
William Hill plc	713210	2,160,916,480	-105,071,736
Computer Manufacturing, Including PCs, Laptops, Mainframes and Tablets			
Aristocrat Leisure Limited	334111	1,719,190,016	346,878,720
Concurrent Computer Corporation	334111	27,647,000	28,381,000
Nintendo Co Ltd	334111	4,536,722,432	951,450,688
Computer Software, Content & Document Management			
TiVo Corporation	511210L	826,456,000	-37,956,000
Computer Software, Educational & Training			
Rosetta Stone Inc	511210P	184,592,992	-1,546,000
Computer Software, Electronic Games, Apps & Entertainment			
Activision Blizzard Inc	511210G	7,016,999,936	273,000,000
Atari Interactive Inc	511210G	17,542,260	8,771,130
BioWare Corp	511210G		
Changyou.com Limited	511210G	580,260,992	108,834,000
Concrete Software Inc	511210G		
Electronic Arts Inc (EA)	511210G	4,845,000,192	967,000,000
FishBowl Worldwide Media LLC	511210G		
GigaMedia Limited	511210G	11,596,000	1,086,000
Glu Mobile Inc	511210G	286,827,008	-97,570,000
International Game Technology PLC	511210G	4,938,958,848	-1,068,576,000
Intralot SA	511210G	1,257,799,424	-60,812,412
IPlay	511210G		
King Digital Entertainment plc	511210G	2,100,000,000	
Koch Media GmbH	511210G		
LucasArts Entertainment Company LLC	511210G		
Magic Leap Inc	511210G		
Musical.ly	511210G		
NCsoft Corporation	511210G	1,646,880,000	415,806,000
NTN Buzztime Inc	511210G	21,274,000	-1,077,000
Scientific Games Corporation	511210G	3,083,599,872	-242,300,000
Storm8	511210G		
Take-Two Interactive Software Inc	511210G	1,779,747,968	67,303,000
Webzen Inc	511210G	148,652,112	27,060,642
Zynga Inc	511210G	861,390,016	26,639,000
Computer Software, Multimedia, Graphics & Publishing			
Avid Technology Inc	511210F	419,003,008	-13,555,000
RealNetworks Inc	511210F	78,718,000	-16,305,000
Shazam Entertainment Limited	511210F	55,100,200	-23,930,900
Computer Software, Operating Systems, Languages & Development Tools			
Microsoft Corporation	511210I	89,950,003,200	21,204,000,768
Consulting Services, Administrative and General Management			
Oak View Group	541611		

Industry Group/Company	Industry Code	2017 Sales	2017 Profits
Consumer Electronics Manufacturing, Including Audio and Video Equipment, Stereos, TVs and Radios			
Bose Corporation	334310	3,850,000,000	
Clarion Co Ltd	334310	2,050,000,000	
Dolby Laboratories Inc	334310	1,081,453,952	201,802,000
DTS Inc	334310	191,000,000	
LOUD Audio LLC	334310		
Panasonic Corporation	334310	68,118,388,736	1,385,425,920
Pioneer Corporation	334310	3,586,765,312	-46,879,640
Samsung Electronics Co Ltd	334310	213,122,596,864	36,779,499,520
Sharp Corporation	334310	19,021,213,696	-230,752,816
Sony Corporation	334310	70,525,837,312	679,810,368
Trans-Lux Corporation	334310	24,443,000	-2,849,000
Crafts, Toys, Hobbies and Games (including Electronic Games) Stores			
GameStop Corp	451120	8,607,899,648	353,200,000
Credit Card Processing, Online Payment Processing, EFT, ACH and Clearinghouses			
American Express Company	522320	24,423,999,488	2,736,000,000
Directory and Mailing List Publishers			
RELX PLC	511140	9,288,492,032	2,095,120,384
Yellow Pages Limited	511140	553,351,936	-437,225,120
Zagat Survey LLC	511140		
Financial Data Publishing - Print & Online			
Bloomberg LP	511120A	9,658,000,000	
Forbes Media LLC	511120A	180,000,000	
Thomson Reuters Corporation	511120A	11,333,000,192	1,395,000,064
Value Line Inc	511120A	42,697,000	10,367,000
Food Service Contractors			
Delaware North Companies Inc	722310	3,310,000,000	
Furniture Manufacturing, Laboratory, School and Gaming			
Gaming Partners International Corporation	337127	80,602,000	3,626,000
Golf Courses and Country Clubs			
American Golf Corp	713910	290,000,000	
ClubCorp Holdings Inc	713910	1,100,000,000	
Drive Shack Inc	713910	289,872,000	-42,201,000
Greeting Card Publishers			
American Greetings Corporation LLC	511191	1,900,000,000	
Hallmark Cards Inc	511191	3,912,000,000	
Hotels, Motels, Inns and Resorts (Lodging and Hospitality)			
Ryman Hospitality Properties Inc	721110	1,184,718,976	176,100,000
Sands China Ltd	721110	7,714,999,808	1,603,000,064
Shun Tak Holdings Limited	721110	815,807,232	185,184,336
Ice Skating, Magic, Circus and Carnival Performing Arts Companies			
Cirque du Soleil Inc	711190	900,000,000	
Feld Entertainment Inc	711190	1,320,000,000	

Industry Group/Company	Industry Code	2017 Sales	2017 Profits
Internet Search Engines, Online Publishing, Sharing, Gig and Consumer Services, Online Radio, TV and Entertainment Sites and Social Media			
Alphabet Inc (Google)	519130	110,854,995,968	12,661,999,616
Axios Media Inc (AXIOS)	519130		
Brightcove Inc	519130	155,912,992	-19,519,000
CBS Interactive Inc	519130		
Cengage Learning Holdings II Inc	519130	1,678,000,000	-43,100,000
China Literature Limited	519130	595,984,064	80,937,408
Crackle Inc (dba SonyCrackle)	519130		
Dotdash	519130	210,000,000	
EBSCO Industries Inc	519130	2,889,000,000	
Facebook Inc	519130	40,653,000,704	15,934,000,128
Hoover's Inc	519130		
IAC/InterActiveCorp	519130	3,307,238,912	304,924,000
IGN Entertainment Inc	519130		
iQiyi Inc	519130	2,529,194,752	-543,862,272
Leaf Group Ltd	519130	128,990,000	-31,133,000
Major League Baseball Advanced Media LP (MLBAM)	519130	110,000,000	
MarketWatch Inc	519130		
MobiTV Inc	519130	132,000,000	
MyHeritage Ltd	519130	133,000,000	18,100,000
Myspace LLC	519130		
NeuLion Inc	519130	95,570,000	-31,315,000
Patch Media Corporation	519130		
Pro Publica Inc	519130	13,300,000	
ProQuest LLC	519130	572,000,000	
Salon Media Group Inc	519130	4,570,000	-9,570,000
Scribd Inc	519130		
SoundCloud Limited	519130	100,000,000	
Texas Tribune Inc (The)	519130	7,508,251	-791,845
Verizon Media Group	519130	2,050,000,000	
Vox Media Inc	519130	158,500,000	
Youku Tudou Inc	519130	1,050,000,000	
YouTube LLC	519130	6,250,000,000	
Life Insurance and Annuity Underwriters (Direct Carriers)			
Sahara India Pariwar Ltd	524113		
Magazine Publishing and Financial Information Publishing			
Advance Publications Inc	511120	2,700,000,000	
Ascential plc	511120	507,001,000	24,284,200
Beat Holdings Limited	511120	10,109,500	1,260,360
Conde Nast Publications Inc	511120	240,000,000	
Dennis Publishing Ltd	511120	145,318,000	-5,855,200
Elsevier BV	511120	8,810,290,000	1,996,840,000
Hightimes Holding Corp	511120		
Ink Publishing Inc	511120		
International Data Group Inc	511120	3,940,000,000	
Lagardere Active Media	511120	1,044,540,000	83,850,400

Industry Group/Company	Industry Code	2017 Sales	2017 Profits
Martha Stewart Living Omnimedia Inc	511120	70,000,000	
Marvel Entertainment LLC	511120		
Meredith Corporation	511120	1,713,361,024	188,928,000
Playboy Enterprises Inc	511120	90,000,000	
RentPath LLC	511120	288,000,000	
Rolling Stone LLC	511120		
Sanoma Oyj	511120	1,632,797,184	-183,965,920
Trusted Media Brands Inc	511120	1,105,000,000	
UBM plc	511120	1,332,545,024	193,989,008
US News and World Report LP	511120		
VICE Media Inc	511120	608,000,000	-105,000,000
Ziff Davis LLC	511120	190,000,000	
Mail Order, Catalogs and Other Direct Marketing, and TV Shopping			
EVINE Live Inc	454113	666,212,992	-8,745,000
HSN Inc (Home Shopping Network)	454113	3,101,358,000	
Market Research, Business Intelligence and Opinion Polling			
Nielsen Holdings plc	541910	6,572,000,256	429,000,000
TNS UK Ltd	541910		
Motion Picture and Video Distribution			
Alliance Entertainment LLC	512120	770,000,000	
RLJ Entertainment Inc	512120	86,304,000	-6,126,000
Motion Picture, Movies, Films, Television (TV) Programming and Video Production			
2929 Entertainment	512110		
ABC Inc (Disney-ABC)	512110		
Central European Media Enterprises Ltd	512110	574,211,968	49,768,000
Dick Clark Productions Inc	512110		
DreamWorks Animation SKG Inc	512110	1,055,000,000	
DreamWorks II Holding Co LLC	512110		
Legendary Entertainment	512110	625,000,000	
Lions Gate Entertainment Corp	512110	3,201,499,904	14,800,000
Lucasfilm Ltd LLC	512110		
MGM Holdings Inc	512110	1,100,000,000	
Miramax LLC	512110		
Paramount Pictures Corporation	512110	2,700,000,000	
Pixar Animation Studios	512110	3,000,000,000	
Reliance Entertainment Pvt Ltd	512110		
Sony Pictures Entertainment Inc	512110	9,000,000,000	
Sony Pictures Motion Picture Group	512110		
Twentieth Century Fox Film Corporation	512110	9,000,000,000	
Twenty-First Century Fox Inc (21st Century Fox)	512110	28,500,000,768	2,952,000,000
Universal Pictures	512110	6,500,000,000	
Walt Disney Studios (The)	512110	8,379,000,000	2,355,000,000
Warner Bros Entertainment Inc	512110	14,000,000,000	
World Wrestling Entertainment Inc	512110	800,958,976	32,640,000
Movie (Motion Pictures) Theaters			
AMC Entertainment Holdings Inc	512131	5,079,199,744	-487,200,000

Industry Group/Company	Industry Code	2017 Sales	2017 Profits
Cinemark Inc	512131	2,991,546,880	264,180,000
Cineplex Inc	512131	1,153,713,280	52,499,480
Cineworld Group plc	512131	1,203,697,408	135,951,456
Dalian Wanda Group Co Ltd	512131	35,540,000,000	
IMAX Corporation	512131	380,767,008	2,344,000
National Amusements Inc	512131		
Reading International Inc	512131	279,734,016	30,999,000
Regal Entertainment Group	512131	3,163,000,064	112,300,000
SimEx-Iwerks	512131		
Music Publishers			
GMM Grammy PCL	512230	271,334,000	-11,767,300
Integrity Music	512230		
Nippon Columbia Co Ltd	512230	125,990,000	16,948,500
Sony Music Entertainment Inc	512230	6,000,000,000	
Universal Music Group Inc	512230	5,600,000,000	
Vivendi SA	512230	14,085,367,808	1,389,973,632
Warner Music Group Corp	512230	3,576,000,000	143,000,000
Newspaper Publishing			
A H Belo Corporation	511110	248,626,000	10,161,000
Axel Springer SE	511110	4,058,185,472	393,561,760
CNHI LLC	511110		
Daily Journal Corporation	511110	41,384,000	-918,000
Dow Jones & Company Inc	511110	2,950,000,000	
Gannett Co Inc	511110	3,146,480,128	6,887,000
GateHouse Media LLC	511110	318,000,000	
Harte-Hanks Inc	511110	383,905,984	-41,860,000
Hurriyet Gazetecilik ve Matbaacilik AS	511110	98,359,216	-48,336,204
Lagardere SCA	511110	8,001,403,392	202,610,160
Lee Enterprises Incorporated	511110	566,942,976	27,481,000
McClatchy Company (The)	511110	903,592,000	-332,358,000
Metro International SA	511110	280,000,000	
Morris Communications Company LLC	511110	300,000,000	
New Media Investment Group Inc	511110	1,342,003,968	-915,000
New York Times Company (The)	511110	1,675,639,040	4,296,000
News Corporation	511110	8,138,999,808	-738,000,000
Schibsted ASA	511110	1,949,681,536	245,090,992
Singapore Press Holdings Limited	511110	756,920,320	256,641,728
Torstar Corporation	511110	456,780,256	-21,642,134
Tribune Publishing Company	511110	1,524,018,000	5,535,000
Washington Times LLC (The)	511110		
Online Sales, B2C Ecommerce			
Amazon.com Inc	454111	177,865,998,336	3,032,999,936
Audible Inc	454111		
Qurate Retail Inc	454111	10,380,999,680	1,208,000,000
Rakuten Commerce LLC	454111		
Outdoor and Billboard Advertising			
Clear Channel Outdoor Holdings Inc	541850	2,591,265,024	-639,715,968
Lamar Advertising Company	541850	1,541,260,032	317,676,000

Industry Group/Company	Industry Code	2017 Sales	2017 Profits
Personal Care Services (excluding Weight Loss Centers)			
Steiner Leisure Limited	812199	924,000,000	
Photographic and Photocopying Equipment Manufacturing			
RealD Inc	333316	176,000,000	
Prerecorded Audio & Video Tapes & Discs, Musical Instruments & Accessories, Wood Products (except Lumber) and General Merchandise Wholesale Distribution			
Ingram Entertainment Holdings Inc	423990	455,000,000	
Printing, Commercial			
CSS Industries Inc	323111	322,431,008	28,504,000
Professional Sports Teams and Clubs			
Anschutz Entertainment Group Inc	711211		
Promoters and Producers of Performing Arts, Sports and Other Entertainment Events			
Live Nation Entertainment Inc	711300	10,337,447,936	-6,015,000
Renaissance Entertainment Corporation	711300		
Promoters of Performing Arts, Sports, and Similar Events without Facilities			
Entertainment Resources Inc	711320		
NightCulture Inc	711320	6,423,988	
Premier Exhibitions Inc	711320		
Property and Casualty (P&C) Insurance Underwriters (Direct Carriers)			
Berkshire Hathaway Inc	524126	242,137,006,080	44,940,001,280
Radio Networks, Including Commercial Networks Supporting Radio Broadcasting, and Public Radio Networks			
iHeartMedia Inc	515111	5,900,000,000	
MP3.com Inc	515111		
NPR (National Public Radio)	515111	232,753,133	2,378,953
Pandora Media Inc	515111	1,466,812,032	-518,395,008
Sirius XM Holdings Inc	515111	5,425,128,960	647,907,968
Spotify Technology SA	515111	4,658,950,656	-1,406,798,208
Tencent Music Entertainment Group	515111	1,598,142,976	192,982,208
Westwood One Inc	515111	346,165,000	25,635,000
Radio Stations (Satellite, Broadcast and Internet)			
Beasley Broadcast Group Inc	515112	232,179,456	87,131,168
Corus Entertainment Inc	515112	1,245,665,792	142,197,376
Cumulus Media Inc	515112	1,135,661,952	-206,564,992
Emmis Communications Corporation	515112	214,568,000	13,119,000
Entercom Communications Corp	515112	592,883,968	233,848,992
Grupo Radio Centro SAB de CV	515112		
Liberty Media Corporation	515112	7,594,000,000	1,354,000,000
Salem Media Group Inc	515112	263,736,000	24,644,000
Spanish Broadcasting System Inc	515112	134,708,992	19,621,000
Townsquare Media Inc	515112	507,433,984	-11,185,000
Urban One Inc	515112	460,000,000	

Industry Group/Company	Industry Code	2017 Sales	2017 Profits
Radio, Television and Other Electronics Stores			
Best Buy Co Inc	443142	39,402,999,808	1,228,000,000
Trans World Entertainment Corporation	443142	353,470,016	3,211,000
REITS (Real Estate Investment Trusts) - Nonresidential			
EPR Properties	531120A	575,990,976	264,516,992
Restaurants, Full-Service, Sit Down			
Fertitta Entertainment Inc.	722511	3,800,000,000	
Satellite Telecommunications			
Global Eagle Entertainment Inc	517410	619,468,992	-357,113,984
Snow Ski Resorts and Skiing Related Facilities			
Booth Creek Ski Holdings Inc	713920	130,000,000	
Boyne Resorts	713920	83,000,000	
Peak Resorts Inc	713920	123,249,000	1,241,000
Vail Resorts Inc	713920	1,907,218,048	210,552,992
Talent Agencies, Agents and Managers for Athletes and Entertainers			
Creative Artists Agency Inc (CAA)	711410	333,000,000	
Endeavor LLC	711410	2,700,000,000	
Ford Models Inc	711410	31,000,000	
ICM Partners	711410	23,000,000	
United Talent Agency Inc	711410	225,000,000	
Wasserman Media Group LLC	711410	114,000,000	
Telephone, Internet Access, Broadband, Data Networks, Server Facilities and Telecommunications Services Industry			
Altice USA Inc	517110	9,326,570,496	1,520,030,976
AT&T Inc	517110	160,545,996,800	29,450,000,384
Cequel Communications Holdings I LLC	517110	2,824,320,000	
Charter Communications Inc	517110	41,580,998,656	9,895,000,064
Cogeco Inc	517110	1,741,755,904	80,856,608
Comcast Corporation	517110	84,525,998,080	22,713,999,360
Cox Communications Inc	517110	11,550,000,000	
DirecTV LLC (DIRECTV)	517110	35,584,900,000	4,305,000,000
DISH Network Corporation	517110	14,391,374,848	2,098,689,024
EchoStar Corporation	517110	1,885,507,968	392,560,992
I-Cable Communications Limited	517110	160,700,544	-46,332,732
ITV plc	517110	3,994,541,312	521,637,120
Liberty Global plc	517110	3,590,000,128	-778,099,968
Mediacom Communications Corporation	517110	1,810,255,000	
Naspers Limited	517110	6,097,999,872	2,920,999,936
Net Servicos de Comunicacao SA	517110	4,252,500,000	
RCN Telecom Services LLC	517110	547,468,623	
Rogers Communications Inc	517110	10,492,773,376	1,269,400,832
Shaw Communications Inc	517110	3,621,984,000	631,361,856
SKY Network Television Limited	517110	597,608,832	77,604,168
Sky plc	517110	16,473,019,392	886,400,448
SONIFI Solutions	517110	370,000,000	
Tele Columbus AG	517110	510,000,000	
United Online Inc	517110	191,000,000	

Industry Group/Company	Industry Code	2017 Sales	2017 Profits
Verizon Communications Inc	517110	126,034,001,920	30,101,000,192
Virgin Media Business Ltd	517110	1,030,000,000	
Vodafone Kabel Deutschland GmbH	517110	2,585,830,400	301,663,072
Television Broadcasting			
Bertelsmann SE & Co KGaA	515120	20,591,300,000	1,435,040,000
British Broadcasting Corporation (BBC)	515120	4,954,000,000	-160,773,000
CBS Corporation	515120	13,692,000,256	357,000,000
Cogeco Communications Inc	515120	1,652,113,792	221,996,752
Cox Enterprises Inc	515120	20,500,000,000	
Cox Media Group Inc	515120	2,050,000,000	
Disney Media Networks	515120	23,510,000,000	6,902,000,000
E W Scripps Company (The)	515120	864,833,984	-13,106,000
Entravision Communications Corporation	515120	536,033,984	176,292,992
Fox Broadcasting Company	515120	7,065,000,000	
Fox Entertainment Group Inc	515120	16,800,000,000	
Fox Sports Interactive Media LLC	515120	8,850,000,000	
Globo Comunicacao e Participacoes SA (Grupo Globo)	515120		
Graham Holdings Company	515120	2,591,845,888	302,044,000
Gray Television Inc	515120	882,728,000	261,952,000
Grupo Televisa SAB	515120	4,808,805,888	230,788,640
Hearst Television Inc	515120		
ION Media Networks	515120	522,000,000	
Izzi Telecom SAB de CV	515120	606,900,000	
Korean Broadcasting System	515120	1,341,500,000	52,813,500
Mediaset SpA	515120	4,136,100,608	103,089,256
Modern Times Group MTG AB	515120	1,929,020,000	149,596,000
MX1 Ltd	515120	154,730,354	
National Geographic Society	515120	405,000,000	
NBCUniversal Media LLC	515120	32,997,000,000	5,218,000,000
Nexstar Media Group Inc	515120	2,431,965,952	474,996,992
Nine Entertainment Co Holdings Ltd	515120	974,968,448	-160,592,032
Promotora de Informaciones SA	515120	4,646,420,992	536,519,776
ProSiebenSat.1 Media SE	515120	1,304,085,888	-117,231,280
Raycom Media Inc	515120	2,000,000,000	
RTL Group SA	515120	7,259,534,336	841,800,704
Saga Communications Inc	515120	118,149,000	54,717,000
SBS (Seoul Broadcasting)	515120	724,060,000	14,074,200
Seven Group Holdings Limited	515120	1,599,033,088	31,177,748
Seven West Media Limited	515120	1,148,295,424	-521,961,728
Shanghai Media Group (SMG)	515120	593,250,000	
Sinclair Broadcast Group Inc	515120	2,734,117,888	576,012,992
Societe d'Edition de Canal Plus	515120		
Southern Cross Media Group Limited	515120	498,706,560	79,469,296
TEGNA Inc	515120	1,903,026,048	273,744,000
Television Francaise 1 SA	515120	2,405,175,040	154,051,632
Tribune Media Company	515120	1,848,958,976	197,496,992
TV Azteca SAB de CV	515120	705,419,584	59,345,200
TV Tokyo Holdings Corporation	515120	1,314,090,000	39,461,000
TVA Group Inc	515120	437,507,040	-11,834,140

Industry Group/Company	Industry Code	2017 Sales	2017 Profits
Univision Communications Inc	515120	3,000,000,000	
Vending Machine Operators			
Outerwall Inc	454210	2,000,000,000	
Venture Capital, Private Equity Investment and Hedge Funds			
Vulcan Inc	523910		
Video Rental			
Redbox Automated Retail LLC	532230	1,200,000,000	
Wireless Communications and Radio and TV Broadcasting Equipment Manufacturing, including Cellphones (Handsets)			
Apple Inc	334220	229,233,999,872	48,350,998,528
Roku Inc	334220	512,763,008	-63,509,000
Wireless Telecommunications Carriers (except Satellite)			
Altice NV	517210	26,768,805,888	-621,952,896
Zoos and Botanical Gardens			
Wildlife Reserves Singapore Group	712130	110,386,000	

ALPHABETICAL INDEX

2929 Entertainment
A H Belo Corporation
A&E Television Networks LLC
ABC Inc (Disney-ABC)
Activision Blizzard Inc
Advance Publications Inc
Affinity Gaming LLC
Alliance Entertainment LLC
Alphabet Inc (Google)
Altice NV
Altice USA Inc
Amazon.com Inc
AMC Entertainment Holdings Inc
AMC Networks Inc
American Educational Products LLC
American Express Company
American Golf Corp
American Greetings Corporation LLC
Ameristar Casinos Inc
Anschutz Entertainment Group Inc
Apple Inc
Ardent Leisure Group
Aristocrat Leisure Limited
Ascential plc
AT&T Inc
Atari Interactive Inc
Audible Inc
Avid Technology Inc
Axel Springer SE
Axios Media Inc (AXIOS)
Barnes & Noble Inc
Beasley Broadcast Group Inc
Beat Holdings Limited
Berkshire Hathaway Inc
Bertelsmann SE & Co KGaA
Best Buy Co Inc
BioWare Corp
Bloomberg LP
Books A Million Inc
Booth Creek Ski Holdings Inc
Bose Corporation
Bowlero Corporation
Boyd Gaming Corp
Boyne Resorts
Brightcove Inc
British Broadcasting Corporation (BBC)
Cable News Network Inc (CNN)
Caesars Entertainment Corporation
Canterbury Park Holding Corporation
CBS Corporation
CBS Interactive Inc
Cedar Fair LP
Cengage Learning Holdings II Inc
Central European Media Enterprises Ltd
Century Casinos Inc
Cequel Communications Holdings I LLC

Changyou.com Limited
Charter Communications Inc
China Literature Limited
Churchill Downs Incorporated
Cinemark Inc
Cineplex Inc
Cineworld Group plc
Cirque du Soleil Inc
Clarion Co Ltd
Clear Channel Outdoor Holdings Inc
ClubCorp Holdings Inc
CNHI LLC
Codere SA
Cogeco Communications Inc
Cogeco Inc
Comcast Corporation
Concrete Software Inc
Concurrent Computer Corporation
Conde Nast Publications Inc
Corus Entertainment Inc
Cox Communications Inc
Cox Enterprises Inc
Cox Media Group Inc
Crackle Inc (dba SonyCrackle)
Creative Artists Agency Inc (CAA)
Crown Media Family Networks
CSS Industries Inc
Cumulus Media Inc
CW Network LLC (The)
Daily Journal Corporation
Dalian Wanda Group Co Ltd
Dave & Buster's Entertainment Inc
Delaware North Companies Inc
Dennis Publishing Ltd
DexYP
Dick Clark Productions Inc
DirecTV LLC (DIRECTV)
Discovery Inc
DISH Network Corporation
Disney Media Networks
Dolby Laboratories Inc
Dotdash
Dover Downs Gaming & Entertainment Inc
Dow Jones & Company Inc
DreamWorks Animation SKG Inc
DreamWorks II Holding Co LLC
Drive Shack Inc
DTS Inc
E W Scripps Company (The)
EBSCO Industries Inc
EchoStar Corporation
Educational Development Corporation
Eldorado Resorts Inc
Electronic Arts Inc (EA)
Elsevier BV
Emmis Communications Corporation
Endeavor LLC
Entercom Communications Corp

Entertainment Resources Inc
Entravision Communications Corporation
EPR Properties
ESPN Inc
Euro Disney SCA
Evergreen Gaming Corporation
EVINE Live Inc
Facebook Inc
Feld Entertainment Inc
Fertitta Entertainment Inc.
FishBowl Worldwide Media LLC
Forbes Media LLC
Ford Models Inc
Fox Broadcasting Company
Fox Entertainment Group Inc
Fox Sports Interactive Media LLC
Full House Resorts Inc
Galaxy Entertainment Group Limited
GameStop Corp
Gaming Partners International Corporation
Gannett Co Inc
GateHouse Media LLC
Genting Singapore PLC
GigaMedia Limited
Global Eagle Entertainment Inc
Globo Comunicacao e Participacoes SA (Grupo Globo)
Glu Mobile Inc
GMM Grammy PCL
Golden Entertainment Inc
Graham Holdings Company
Gray Television Inc
Great Canadian Gaming Corporation
Greek Organisation of Football Prognostics SA (OPAP)
Grupo Radio Centro SAB de CV
Grupo Televisa SAB
Hachette Book Group Inc
Hallmark Cards Inc
HarperCollins Publishers LLC
Harte-Hanks Inc
Hearst Corporation (The)
Hearst Television Inc
Hershey Company (The)
Hightimes Holding Corp
Home Box Office Inc (HBO)
Hoover's Inc
Houghton Mifflin Harcourt Company
HSN Inc (Home Shopping Network)
Hulu LLC
Hurriyet Gazetecilik ve Matbaacilik AS
IAC/InterActiveCorp
I-Cable Communications Limited
ICM Partners
IGN Entertainment Inc
iHeartMedia Inc
IMAX Corporation
Ingram Entertainment Holdings Inc
Ink Publishing Inc
Integrity Music

International Data Group Inc
International Game Technology PLC
Intralot SA
ION Media Networks
IPlay
iQiyi Inc
ITV plc
Izzi Telecom SAB de CV
John Wiley & Sons Inc
Kangwon Land Inc
Kerzner International Limited
King Digital Entertainment plc
Koch Media GmbH
Korean Broadcasting System
Lagardere Active Media
Lagardere SCA
Lamar Advertising Company
Las Vegas Sands Corp (The Venetian)
Leaf Group Ltd
Lee Enterprises Incorporated
Legendary Entertainment
Lerner Publishing Group
Liberty Global plc
Liberty Media Corporation
Lions Gate Entertainment Corp
Live Nation Entertainment Inc
LOUD Audio LLC
LucasArts Entertainment Company LLC
Lucasfilm Ltd LLC
Magic Leap Inc
Major League Baseball Advanced Media LP (MLBAM)
MarketWatch Inc
Martha Stewart Living Omnimedia Inc
Marvel Entertainment LLC
McClatchy Company (The)
McGraw-Hill Education Inc
MDI Entertainment LLC
Mediacom Communications Corporation
Mediaset SpA
Melco International Development Limited
Meredith Corporation
Merlin Entertainments Group Plc
Metro International SA
MGM Holdings Inc
MGM Resorts International
Microsoft Corporation
Miramax LLC
MobiTV Inc
Modern Times Group MTG AB
Morris Communications Company LLC
MP3.com Inc
Musical.ly
MX1 Ltd
MyHeritage Ltd
Myspace LLC
Naspers Limited
National Amusements Inc
National Geographic Society

NBCUniversal Media LLC
NCsoft Corporation
Net Servicos de Comunicacao SA
Netflix Inc
NeuLion Inc
Nevada Gold & Casinos Inc
New Media Investment Group Inc
New York Times Company (The)
News Corporation
Nexstar Media Group Inc
Nielsen Holdings plc
NightCulture Inc
Nine Entertainment Co Holdings Ltd
Nintendo Co Ltd
Nippon Columbia Co Ltd
NPR (National Public Radio)
NTN Buzztime Inc
Oak View Group
Oprah Winfrey Network (OWN)
Oriental Land Co Ltd
Outerwall Inc
Palace Entertainment Holdings LLC
Panasonic Corporation
Pandora Media Inc
Paramount Pictures Corporation
Patch Media Corporation
Peak Resorts Inc
Pearson North America
Pearson PLC
Penguin Group USA
Penguin Random House
Penn National Gaming Inc
Pinnacle Entertainment Inc
Pioneer Corporation
Pixar Animation Studios
Playboy Enterprises Inc
Premier Exhibitions Inc
Pro Publica Inc
Promotora de Informaciones SA
ProQuest LLC
ProSiebenSat.1 Media SE
Qurate Retail Inc
Rakuten Commerce LLC
Rank Group plc (The)
Raycom Media Inc
RCN Telecom Services LLC
Reading International Inc
RealD Inc
RealNetworks Inc
Redbox Automated Retail LLC
Regal Entertainment Group
Reliance Entertainment Pvt Ltd
RELX PLC
Renaissance Entertainment Corporation
RentPath LLC
RLJ Entertainment Inc
Rogers Communications Inc
Roku Inc
Rolling Stone LLC
Rosetta Stone Inc
RTL Group SA
Ryman Hospitality Properties Inc
Saga Communications Inc
Sahara India Pariwar Ltd
Salem Media Group Inc
Salon Media Group Inc
Samsung Electronics Co Ltd
Sands China Ltd
Sanoma Oyj
SBS (Seoul Broadcasting)
Schibsted ASA
Scholastic Corporation
Scientific Games Corporation
Scribd Inc
SeaWorld Entertainment Inc
Sega Sammy Holdings Inc
Seven Group Holdings Limited
Seven West Media Limited
Shanghai Media Group (SMG)
Sharp Corporation
Shaw Communications Inc
Shazam Entertainment Limited
Shenzhen Overseas Chinese Town Co Ltd (OCT Limited)
Shun Tak Holdings Limited
SimEx-Iwerks
Simon & Schuster Inc
Sinclair Broadcast Group Inc
Singapore Press Holdings Limited
Sirius XM Holdings Inc
Six Flags Entertainment Corporation
Sky Deutschland AG
SKY Network Television Limited
SKY Perfect JSAT Corporation
Sky plc
Societe d'Edition de Canal Plus
SONIFI Solutions
Sony Corporation
Sony Music Entertainment Inc
Sony Pictures Entertainment Inc
Sony Pictures Motion Picture Group
SoundCloud Limited
Southern Cross Media Group Limited
Spanish Broadcasting System Inc
Spotify Technology SA
Station Casinos LLC
Steiner Leisure Limited
Storm8
Tabcorp Holdings Limited
Take-Two Interactive Software Inc
Tatts Group Limited
TEGNA Inc
Tele Columbus AG
Television Francaise 1 SA
Tencent Music Entertainment Group
Texas Tribune Inc (The)
Thomas Nelson Inc

Thomson Reuters Corporation
TiVo Corporation
TNS UK Ltd
Torstar Corporation
Townsquare Media Inc
Trans World Corporation
Trans World Entertainment Corporation
Trans-Lux Corporation
Tribune Media Company
Tribune Publishing Company
Trusted Media Brands Inc
Turner Broadcasting System Inc
TV Azteca SAB de CV
TV Tokyo Holdings Corporation
TVA Group Inc
Twentieth Century Fox Film Corporation
Twenty-First Century Fox Inc (21st Century Fox)
UBM plc
United Online Inc
United Talent Agency Inc
Universal Music Group Inc
Universal Pictures
Univision Communications Inc
Urban One Inc
US News and World Report LP
Vail Resorts Inc
Value Line Inc
Verizon Communications Inc
Verizon Media Group
Viacom Inc
VICE Media Inc
Village Roadshow Limited
Virgin Media Business Ltd
Vivendi SA
Vodafone Kabel Deutschland GmbH
Vox Media Inc
Vulcan Inc
Walt Disney Company (The)
Walt Disney Studios (The)
Warner Bros Entertainment Inc
Warner Media LLC
Warner Music Group Corp
Washington Times LLC (The)
Wasserman Media Group LLC
Webzen Inc
Westwood One Inc
Wildlife Reserves Singapore Group
William Hill plc
World Wrestling Entertainment Inc
Wynn Resorts Limited
Yellow Pages Limited
Youku Tudou Inc
YouTube LLC
Zagat Survey LLC
Ziff Davis LLC
Zynga Inc

INDEX OF U.S. HEADQUARTERS LOCATION BY STATE

To help you locate firms geographically, the city and state of the headquarters of each company are in the following index.

ALABAMA
Books A Million Inc; Birmingham
CNHI LLC; Montgomery
EBSCO Industries Inc; Birmingham
Raycom Media Inc; Montgomery

CALIFORNIA
2929 Entertainment; Santa Monica
ABC Inc (Disney-ABC); Burbank
Activision Blizzard Inc; Santa Monica
Alphabet Inc (Google); Mountain View
American Golf Corp; Los Angeles
Anschutz Entertainment Group Inc; Los Angeles
Apple Inc; Cupertino
CBS Interactive Inc; San Francisco
Crackle Inc (dba SonyCrackle); Culver City
Creative Artists Agency Inc (CAA); Los Angeles
Crown Media Family Networks; Studio City
CW Network LLC (The); Burbank
Daily Journal Corporation; Los Angeles
Dick Clark Productions Inc; Santa Monica
DirecTV LLC (DIRECTV); El Segundo
Disney Media Networks; Burbank
Dolby Laboratories Inc; San Francisco
DreamWorks Animation SKG Inc; Glendale
DreamWorks II Holding Co LLC; Glendale
DTS Inc; Calabasas
Electronic Arts Inc (EA); Redwood City
Endeavor LLC; Beverly Hills
Entertainment Resources Inc; Huntington Beach
Entravision Communications Corporation; Santa Monica
Facebook Inc; Menlo Park
FishBowl Worldwide Media LLC; Los Angeles
Fox Broadcasting Company; Los Angeles
Fox Sports Interactive Media LLC; Los Angeles
Global Eagle Entertainment Inc; Los Angeles
Glu Mobile Inc; San Francisco
Hightimes Holding Corp; Los Angeles
Hulu LLC; Santa Monica
ICM Partners; Los Angeles
IGN Entertainment Inc; San Francisco
IPlay; San Francisco
Leaf Group Ltd; Santa Monica
Legendary Entertainment; Burbank
Lions Gate Entertainment Corp; Santa Monica
Live Nation Entertainment Inc; Beverly Hills
LucasArts Entertainment Company LLC; San Francisco
Lucasfilm Ltd LLC; San Francisco
MarketWatch Inc; San Francisco
McClatchy Company (The); Sacramento

MGM Holdings Inc; Beverly Hills
Miramax LLC; Santa Monica
MobiTV Inc; Emeryville
MP3.com Inc; San Francisco
Musical.ly; Santa Monica
Myspace LLC; Beverly Hills
Netflix Inc; Los Gatos
NTN Buzztime Inc; Carlsbad
Oak View Group; Los Angeles
Oprah Winfrey Network (OWN); Los Angeles
Palace Entertainment Holdings LLC; Newport Beach
Pandora Media Inc; Oakland
Paramount Pictures Corporation; Hollywood
Pixar Animation Studios; Emeryville
Playboy Enterprises Inc; Beverly Hills
Rakuten Commerce LLC; Aliso Viejo
Reading International Inc; Los Angeles
RealD Inc; Beverly Hills
Roku Inc; Los Gatos
Salem Media Group Inc; Camarillo
Salon Media Group Inc; San Francisco
Scribd Inc; San Francisco
Sony Pictures Entertainment Inc; Culver City
Sony Pictures Motion Picture Group; Culver City
Storm8; Redwood City
TiVo Corporation; San Jose
Twentieth Century Fox Film Corporation; Los Angeles
United Online Inc; Woodland Hills
United Talent Agency Inc; Beverly Hills
Universal Music Group Inc; Santa Monica
Universal Pictures; Universal City
Walt Disney Company (The); Burbank
Walt Disney Studios (The); Burbank
Warner Bros Entertainment Inc; Burbank
Wasserman Media Group LLC; Los Angeles
YouTube LLC; San Bruno
Zynga Inc; San Francisco

COLORADO
American Educational Products LLC; Fort Collins
Booth Creek Ski Holdings Inc; Vail
Century Casinos Inc; Colorado Springs
DISH Network Corporation; Englewood
EchoStar Corporation; Englewood
Liberty Media Corporation; Englewood
Qurate Retail Inc; Englewood
Renaissance Entertainment Corporation; Lafayette
Vail Resorts Inc; Broomfield

CONNECTICUT
Charter Communications Inc; Stamford
ESPN Inc; Bristol
Townsquare Media Inc; Greenwich
World Wrestling Entertainment Inc; Stamford

DELAWARE
Dover Downs Gaming & Entertainment Inc; Dover

DISTRICT OF COLUMBIA
National Geographic Society; Washington
NPR (National Public Radio); Washington
US News and World Report LP; Washington
Vox Media Inc; Washington
Washington Times LLC (The); Washington

FLORIDA
Alliance Entertainment LLC; Sunrise
Beasley Broadcast Group Inc; Naples
Feld Entertainment Inc; Palmetto
HSN Inc (Home Shopping Network); St. Petersburg
ION Media Networks; West Palm Beach
Magic Leap Inc; Plantation
SeaWorld Entertainment Inc; Orlando
Spanish Broadcasting System Inc; Miami

GEORGIA
Cable News Network Inc (CNN); Atlanta
Concurrent Computer Corporation; Duluth
Cox Communications Inc; Atlanta
Cox Enterprises Inc; Atlanta
Cox Media Group Inc; Atlanta
Cumulus Media Inc; Atlanta
Gray Television Inc; Atlanta
MDI Entertainment LLC; Alpharetta
Morris Communications Company LLC; Augusta
Premier Exhibitions Inc; Peachtree Corners
RentPath LLC; Atlanta
Turner Broadcasting System Inc; Atlanta

ILLINOIS
Redbox Automated Retail LLC; Oakbrook Terrace
Tribune Media Company; Chicago
Tribune Publishing Company; Chicago

INDIANA
Emmis Communications Corporation; Indianapolis

IOWA
Lee Enterprises Incorporated; Davenport
Meredith Corporation; Des Moines

KANSAS
AMC Entertainment Holdings Inc; Leawood

KENTUCKY
Churchill Downs Incorporated; Louisville

LOUISIANA
Lamar Advertising Company; Baton Rouge

MARYLAND
Discovery Inc; Silver Spring
RLJ Entertainment Inc; Silver Spring
Sinclair Broadcast Group Inc; Hunt Valley

Urban One Inc; Silver Spring

MASSACHUSETTS
Avid Technology Inc; Burlington
Bose Corporation; Framingham
Brightcove Inc; Cambridge
Cengage Learning Holdings II Inc; Boston
Houghton Mifflin Harcourt Company; Boston
International Data Group Inc; Boston
National Amusements Inc; Norwood

MICHIGAN
Boyne Resorts; Petoskey
ProQuest LLC; Ann Arbor
Saga Communications Inc; Grosse Pointe Farm

MINNESOTA
Best Buy Co Inc; Richfield
Canterbury Park Holding Corporation; Shakopee
Concrete Software Inc; Eden Prairie
EVINE Live Inc; Eden Prairie
Lerner Publishing Group; Minneapolis

MISSOURI
EPR Properties; Kansas City
Hallmark Cards Inc; Kansas City
Peak Resorts Inc; Wildwood

NEBRASKA
Berkshire Hathaway Inc; Omaha

NEVADA
Affinity Gaming LLC; Las Vegas
Ameristar Casinos Inc; Las Vegas
Boyd Gaming Corp; Las Vegas
Caesars Entertainment Corporation; Las Vegas
Eldorado Resorts Inc; Reno
Full House Resorts Inc; Las Vegas
Gaming Partners International Corporation; North Las Vegas
Golden Entertainment Inc; Las Vegas
Las Vegas Sands Corp (The Venetian); Las Vegas
MGM Resorts International; Las Vegas
Nevada Gold & Casinos Inc; Las Vegas
Pinnacle Entertainment Inc; Las Vegas
Station Casinos LLC; Las Vegas
Wynn Resorts Limited; Las Vegas

NEW JERSEY
Audible Inc; Newark
Forbes Media LLC; Jersey City
Hoover's Inc; Short Hills
John Wiley & Sons Inc; Hoboken
RCN Telecom Services LLC; Princeton

NEW YORK
A&E Television Networks LLC; New York
Advance Publications Inc; New York
Altice USA Inc; Bethpage
AMC Networks Inc; New York
American Express Company; New York
Atari Interactive Inc; New York
Barnes & Noble Inc; New York
Bloomberg LP; New York
Bowlero Corporation; New York
CBS Corporation; New York
Cequel Communications Holdings I LLC; Bethpage
Conde Nast Publications Inc; New York
Delaware North Companies Inc; Buffalo
Dotdash; New York
Dow Jones & Company Inc; New York
Drive Shack Inc; New York
Ford Models Inc; New York
Fox Entertainment Group Inc; New York
GateHouse Media LLC; Pittsford
Hachette Book Group Inc; New York
HarperCollins Publishers LLC; New York
Hearst Corporation (The); New York
Hearst Television Inc; New York
Home Box Office Inc (HBO); New York
IAC/InterActiveCorp; New York
Major League Baseball Advanced Media LP (MLBAM); New York
Martha Stewart Living Omnimedia Inc; New York
Marvel Entertainment LLC; New York
McGraw-Hill Education Inc; New York
Mediacom Communications Corporation; Mediacom Park
NBCUniversal Media LLC; New York
NeuLion Inc; Plainview
New Media Investment Group Inc; New York
New York Times Company (The); New York
News Corporation; New York
Nielsen Holdings plc; New York
Patch Media Corporation; New York
Pearson North America; New York
Penguin Group USA; New York
Penguin Random House; New York
Pro Publica Inc; New York
Rolling Stone LLC; New York
Scholastic Corporation; New York
Scientific Games Corporation; New York
Simon & Schuster Inc; New York
Sirius XM Holdings Inc; New York
Sony Music Entertainment Inc; New York
Take-Two Interactive Software Inc; New York
Thomson Reuters Corporation; New York
Trans World Corporation; New York
Trans World Entertainment Corporation; Albany
Trans-Lux Corporation; New York
Trusted Media Brands Inc; Pleasantville
Twenty-First Century Fox Inc (21st Century Fox); New York
Univision Communications Inc; New York
Value Line Inc; New York
Verizon Communications Inc; New York

Verizon Media Group; New York
Viacom Inc; New York
VICE Media Inc; Brooklyn
Warner Media LLC; New York
Warner Music Group Corp; New York
Westwood One Inc; New York
Zagat Survey LLC; New York
Ziff Davis LLC; New York

OHIO
American Greetings Corporation LLC; Cleveland
Cedar Fair LP; Sandusky
E W Scripps Company (The); Cincinnati

OKLAHOMA
Educational Development Corporation; Tulsa

PENNSYLVANIA
Comcast Corporation; Philadelphia
CSS Industries Inc; Plymouth Meeting
Entercom Communications Corp; Bala Cynwyd
Hershey Company (The); Hershey
Penn National Gaming Inc; Wyomissing

SOUTH DAKOTA
SONIFI Solutions; Sioux Falls

TENNESSEE
Ingram Entertainment Holdings Inc; La Vergne
Integrity Music; Brentwood
Regal Entertainment Group; Knoxville
Ryman Hospitality Properties Inc; Nashville
Thomas Nelson Inc; Nashville

TEXAS
A H Belo Corporation; Dallas
AT&T Inc; Dallas
Cinemark Inc; Plano
Clear Channel Outdoor Holdings Inc; San Antonio
ClubCorp Holdings Inc; Dallas
Dave & Buster's Entertainment Inc; Dallas
DexYP; Dallas
Fertitta Entertainment Inc.; Houston
GameStop Corp; Grapevine
Harte-Hanks Inc; San Antonio
iHeartMedia Inc; San Antonio
Nexstar Media Group Inc; Irving
NightCulture Inc; Houston
Six Flags Entertainment Corporation; Grand Prairie
Texas Tribune Inc (The); Austin

VIRGINIA
Axios Media Inc (AXIOS); Arlington
Gannett Co Inc; McLean
Graham Holdings Company; Arlington
Rosetta Stone Inc; Arlington
TEGNA Inc; McLean

WASHINGTON
Amazon.com Inc; Seattle
Evergreen Gaming Corporation; Lakewood
LOUD Audio LLC; Woodinville
Microsoft Corporation; Redmond
Outerwall Inc; Bellevue
RealNetworks Inc; Seattle
Vulcan Inc; Seattle

INDEX OF NON-U.S. HEADQUARTERS LOCATION BY COUNTRY

AUSTRALIA
Ardent Leisure Group; Milsons Point
Aristocrat Leisure Limited; North Ryde
Nine Entertainment Co Holdings Ltd; Paddington
Seven Group Holdings Limited; Sydney
Seven West Media Limited; Osborne Park
Southern Cross Media Group Limited; Sydney
Tabcorp Holdings Limited; Melbourne
Tatts Group Limited; Brisbane
Village Roadshow Limited; South Yarra

BAHAMAS
Steiner Leisure Limited; Nassau

BERMUDA
Central European Media Enterprises Ltd; Hamilton

BRAZIL
Globo Comunicacao e Participacoes SA (Grupo Globo); Rio de Janeiro
Net Servicos de Comunicacao SA; Sao Paulo

CANADA
BioWare Corp; Edmonton
Cineplex Inc; Toronto
Cirque du Soleil Inc; Montreal
Cogeco Communications Inc; Montreal
Cogeco Inc; Montreal
Corus Entertainment Inc; Toronto
Great Canadian Gaming Corporation; Coquitlam
IMAX Corporation; Mississauga
Rogers Communications Inc; Toronto
Shaw Communications Inc; Calgary
SimEx-Iwerks; Toronto
Torstar Corporation; Toronto
TVA Group Inc; Montreal
Yellow Pages Limited; Verdun

CHINA
Changyou.com Limited; Beijing
China Literature Limited; Shanghai
Dalian Wanda Group Co Ltd; Beijing
iQiyi Inc; Beijing
Shanghai Media Group (SMG); Shanghai
Shenzhen Overseas Chinese Town Co Ltd (OCT Limited); Shenzhen
Tencent Music Entertainment Group; Shenzhen
Youku Tudou Inc; Beijing

FINLAND
Sanoma Oyj; Helsinki

FRANCE
Euro Disney SCA; Paris
Lagardere Active Media; Levallois-Perret
Lagardere SCA; Paris
Societe d'Edition de Canal Plus; Issy-les-Moulineaux
Television Francaise 1 SA; Boulogne-Billancourt
Vivendi SA; Paris

GERMANY
Axel Springer SE; Berlin
Bertelsmann SE & Co KGaA; Gutersloh
Koch Media GmbH; Munich
ProSiebenSat.1 Media SE; Madrid
Sky Deutschland AG; Unterföehring
SoundCloud Limited; Berlin
Tele Columbus AG; Berlin
Vodafone Kabel Deutschland GmbH; Unterfoehring

GREECE
Greek Organisation of Football Prognostics SA (OPAP); Athens
Intralot SA; Athens

HONG KONG
Beat Holdings Limited; Hong Kong
Galaxy Entertainment Group Limited; Hong Kong
I-Cable Communications Limited; Hong Kong
Melco International Development Limited; Hong Kong
Shun Tak Holdings Limited; Hong Kong

INDIA
Reliance Entertainment Pvt Ltd; Mumbai
Sahara India Pariwar Ltd; Aliganj, Lucknow

IRELAND
King Digital Entertainment plc; Dublin

ISRAEL
MX1 Ltd; Airport City
MyHeritage Ltd; Or Yehuda

ITALY
Mediaset SpA; Milano

JAPAN
Clarion Co Ltd; Saitama
Nintendo Co Ltd; Kyoto
Nippon Columbia Co Ltd; Tokyo
Oriental Land Co Ltd; Chiba
Panasonic Corporation; Osaka
Pioneer Corporation; Tokyo
Sega Sammy Holdings Inc; Tokyo
Sharp Corporation; Sakai City, Osaka
SKY Perfect JSAT Corporation; Tokyo
Sony Corporation; Tokyo
TV Tokyo Holdings Corporation; Tokyo

KOREA
Kangwon Land Inc; Kangwon-do
Korean Broadcasting System; Seoul
NCsoft Corporation; Seongnam
Samsung Electronics Co Ltd; Suwon-si
SBS (Seoul Broadcasting); Seoul
Webzen Inc; Seongnam-si, Gyeonggi-do

LUXEMBOURG
Metro International SA; Luxembourg
RTL Group SA; Luxembourg
Spotify Technology SA; Luxembourg City

MACAO
Sands China Ltd; Senhora da Esparanc

MEXICO
Grupo Radio Centro SAB de CV; Col Lomas Altas
Grupo Televisa SAB; Mexico City
Izzi Telecom SAB de CV; Mexico DF
TV Azteca SAB de CV; Mexico City

NEW ZEALAND
SKY Network Television Limited; Auckland

NORWAY
Schibsted ASA; Oslo

SINGAPORE
Genting Singapore PLC; Singapore
Singapore Press Holdings Limited; Singapore
Wildlife Reserves Singapore Group; Singapore

SOUTH AFRICA
Naspers Limited; Cape Town

SPAIN
Codere SA; Alcobendas
Promotora de Informaciones SA; Madrid

SWEDEN
Modern Times Group MTG AB; Stockholm

TAIWAN
GigaMedia Limited; Taipei

THAILAND
GMM Grammy PCL; Bangkok

THE NETHERLANDS
Altice NV; Amsterdam
Elsevier BV; Amsterdam

TURKEY
Hurriyet Gazetecilik ve Matbaacilik AS; Istanbul

UNITED ARAB EMIRATES
Kerzner International Limited; Dubai

UNITED KINGDOM
Ascential plc; London
British Broadcasting Corporation (BBC); London
Cineworld Group plc; Brentford
Dennis Publishing Ltd; London
Ink Publishing Inc; London
International Game Technology PLC; London
ITV plc; London
Liberty Global plc; London
Merlin Entertainments Group Plc; Poole, Dorset
Pearson PLC; London
Rank Group plc (The); Maidenhead
RELX PLC; London
Shazam Entertainment Limited; London
Sky plc; Isleworth
TNS UK Ltd; London
UBM plc; London
Virgin Media Business Ltd; Hook
William Hill plc; London

Individual Profiles
On Each Of
THE ENTERTAINMENT 400

2929 Entertainment

NAIC Code: 512110

www.2929entertainment.com

TYPES OF BUSINESS:
Movie & TV Production & Distribution
Movie Theaters
Cable Television Networks

BRANDS/DIVISIONS/AFFILIATES:
2929 Productions
Magnolia Pictures
ASX TV
Good Night and Good Luck
I Am Not Your Negro
Lucky
Big Interview With Dan Rather (The)
Real Money

CONTACTS:
Note: Officers with more than one job title may be intentionally listed here more than once.

Todd R. Wagner, CEO
Mark Cuban, Co-Owner

GROWTH PLANS/SPECIAL FEATURES:
2929 Entertainment has ownership stakes in movie and TV distribution and exhibition companies. 2929 Productions develops, finances and produces independent feature films outside of the Hollywood studio system, with a focus on producing interesting and thought-provoking films for both specialized and mainstream audiences. Good Night and Good Luck is among 2929 Productions' award-winning favorites. Magnolia Pictures is the theatrical and home entertainment distribution arm of 2929 Entertainment, with a library of more than 500 titles. Releases by Magnolia Pictures include I Am Not Your Negro, Lucky, The Square, and many others. AXS TV is a network offering classic rock content, including original series such as The Big Interview With Dan Rather, Rock & Roll Road Trip With Sammy Hagar, and Real Money, as well as music festival coverage, mixed martial arts events, documentaries and concerts. 2929 Entertainment is owned by partners Mark Cuban and Todd Wagner. In December 2018, 2929 Entertainment sold Landmark Theatres to Cohen Media Group.

FINANCIAL DATA:
Note: Data for latest year may not have been available at press time.

In U.S. $	2018	2017	2016	2015	2014	2013
Revenue						
R&D Expense						
Operating Income						
Operating Margin %						
SGA Expense						
Net Income						
Operating Cash Flow						
Capital Expenditure						
EBITDA						
Return on Assets %						
Return on Equity %						
Debt to Equity						

CONTACT INFORMATION:
Phone: 310-309-5701   Fax: 310-309-5716
Toll-Free:
Address: 2425 Olympic Blvd., Ste. 6040 W., Santa Monica, CA 90404 United States

STOCK TICKER/OTHER:
Stock Ticker: Private
Employees: 8
Parent Company:

Exchange:
Fiscal Year Ends: 12/31

SALARIES/BONUSES:
Top Exec. Salary: $ Bonus: $
Second Exec. Salary: $ Bonus: $

OTHER THOUGHTS:
Estimated Female Officers or Directors:
Hot Spot for Advancement for Women/Minorities:

Sales, profits and employees may be estimates. Financial information, benefits and other data can change quickly and may vary from those stated here.

A H Belo Corporation

NAIC Code: 511110

www.ahbelo.com

TYPES OF BUSINESS:
Newspaper Publishers and Printing Combined

BRANDS/DIVISIONS/AFFILIATES:
Dallas Morning News (The)
Denton Record-Chronicle (The)
Your Speakeasy LLC
DMV Digital Holdings Company Inc
AHC Proven Performance Media LLC
DMN CrowdSource LLC
Distribion Inc
Vertical Nerve Inc

CONTACTS:
Note: Officers with more than one job title may be intentionally listed here more than once.

Mary Murray, Assistant Secretary
Robert Decherd, Chairman of the Board
Michael Ohara, Chief Information Officer
Grant Moise, Executive VP
Christine Larkin, General Counsel
Michael Wilson, Other Corporate Officer
Julie Hoagland, Other Executive Officer
Timothy Storer, President, Subsidiary

GROWTH PLANS/SPECIAL FEATURES:

A. H. Belo Corporation is a newspaper publishing and local news and information company that owns and operates two metropolitan daily newspapers and several associated websites. It publishes The Dallas Morning News, which is a leading metropolitan newspaper, emphasizing local news and information and community service and has won nine Pulitzer Prizes. The paper is distributed in Dallas County and 10 surrounding counties. The Dallas Morning News also publishes Briefing, a condensed newspaper distributed four days a week at no charge to nonsubscribers in select coverage areas; as well as Al Dia, a Spanish-language newspaper published on Wednesdays and Sundays and distributed at no charge in select coverage areas. Additional news products are also published targeting other communities in North Texas. A. H. Belo also provides marketing, event marketing and other services to businesses through the following subsidiaries: Your Speakeasy, LLC; DMV Digital Holdings Company, Inc.; and AHC Proven Performance Media, LLC. DMN CrowdSource, LLC provides event marketing services such as event management consulting and sponsorship for large-scale community events, seminars and festivals. CrowdSource serves customers in the North Texas region, as well as in major Texas cities. In addition, 80%-owned Distribion Inc., Vertical Nerve, Inc. and CDFX LLC are located in Dallas, Texas and specialize in local marketing automation, search engine marketing, direct mail and promotional products.

Employee benefits include health and dental coverage, vision care, life insurance, accident insurance, long-term disability, a 401(k), adoption assistance, tuition assistance and an employee assistance program.

FINANCIAL DATA:
Note: Data for latest year may not have been available at press time.

In U.S. $	2018	2017	2016	2015	2014	2013
Revenue		248,626,000	259,984,000	272,108,000	272,788,000	366,250,000
R&D Expense						
Operating Income		-6,709,000	-1,064,000	-18,295,000	-7,686,000	6,331,000
Operating Margin %		-2.69%	-.40%	-6.72%	-2.81%	1.72%
SGA Expense		105,966,000	104,009,000	120,818,000	111,710,000	146,307,000
Net Income		10,161,000	-19,310,000	-17,842,000	92,929,000	16,119,000
Operating Cash Flow		-12,095,000	7,616,000	-4,803,000	-26,462,000	14,238,000
Capital Expenditure		12,005,000	6,597,000	7,572,000	7,844,000	6,362,000
EBITDA		4,505,000	10,555,000	-5,431,000	106,003,000	31,624,000
Return on Assets %		5.64%	-9.32%	-6.85%	32.15%	5.64%
Return on Equity %		10.81%	-18.77%	-14.65%	63.13%	11.91%
Debt to Equity						

CONTACT INFORMATION:
Phone: 214-977-8200 Fax: 214-977-8201
Toll-Free:
Address: 508 Young St., Dallas, TX 75202-4808 United States

SALARIES/BONUSES:
Top Exec. Salary: $600,000 Bonus: $487,500
Second Exec. Salary: $469,231 Bonus: $125,000

STOCK TICKER/OTHER:
Stock Ticker: AHC Exchange: NYS
Employees: 1,221 Fiscal Year Ends: 12/31
Parent Company:

OTHER THOUGHTS:
Estimated Female Officers or Directors: 4
Hot Spot for Advancement for Women/Minorities: Y

Sales, profits and employees may be estimates. Financial information, benefits and other data can change quickly and may vary from those stated here.

A&E Television Networks LLC

www.aenetworks.com

NAIC Code: 515210

TYPES OF BUSINESS:
Television Broadcasting
Cable Television
Magazine Publishing
Web Sites
CDs, DVDs & Videos

BRANDS/DIVISIONS/AFFILIATES:
Hearst Communications Inc
Walt Disney Company (The)
A&E
Lifetime
History Channel (The)
VICELAND
FYI
Lifetime Movies

CONTACTS:
Note: Officers with more than one job title may be intentionally listed here more than once.

Paul Buccieri, Pres.
David Granville-Smith, CFO
Amanda Hill, CMO
Kamilah Thomas, Sr. VP-Human Resources
Pete Sgro, Sr. VP-Prod.
Pete Sgro, Sr. VP-Eng.
Douglas P. Jacobs, General Counsel
Pete Sgro, Sr. VP-Oper.
Robert DeBitetto, Pres., Bus. Dev.
Michael Feeney, Sr. VP-Corp. Comm.
Abbe Raven, Chmn.
Melvin Berning, Pres., Ad Sales
Sean Cohan, Exec. VP-Int'l
David Zagin, Pres., Dist.

GROWTH PLANS/SPECIAL FEATURES:

A&E Television Networks is an international media company with operations in television programming, magazine publishing, websites, soundtrack CDs, and home videos and DVDs of its television programs. The company, a joint venture between Hearst Communications, Inc. and The Walt Disney Company, is primarily a cable television group that focuses its programming on history, the arts, current events, popular culture, reality and nature. A&E Television reaches 335 million people worldwide, and has 500+ million digital users. The firm's primary networks include: A&E, Lifetime, The History Channel, VICELAND, FYI and Lifetime Movies. A&E provides original content that inspires and challenges audiences to be original. Its entertainment ranges from original-scripted series such as Bates Motel and The Returned to signature non-fiction franchises such as Wahlburgers and Storage Wars. The A&E website is located at AETV.com. Lifetime is an American cable and satellite television channel offering programming geared toward women or features women in lead roles. The History Channel is an American digital cable and satellite television network airs historical dramas and documentaries covering a range of historical periods and topics. VICELAND is a multi-national brand of television with a focus on lifestyle-oriented documentaries and reality series aimed toward millennials. FYI (for your inspiration) is an American digital cable and satellite channel that features lifestyle programming, with a mixture of reality, culinary, home renovation and makeover series. Last, Lifetime Movies is an American digital cable and satellite television network that features movies and exclusive shows geared toward women. Other networks include Crime & Investigation, Military History, Lifetime Real Women, History En Espanol and Bio. In November 2018, the European Commission approved Disney's proposed acquisition of 21st Century Fox assets, but ordered A&E Networks U.K. to divest certain television European networks that overlap with Fox, including Blaze, Crime & Investigation, and more.

FINANCIAL DATA:
Note: Data for latest year may not have been available at press time.

In U.S. $	2018	2017	2016	2015	2014	2013
Revenue		4,050,000,000	3,950,000,000	3,800,000,000	3,500,000,000	3,300,000,000
R&D Expense						
Operating Income						
Operating Margin %						
SGA Expense						
Net Income						
Operating Cash Flow						
Capital Expenditure						
EBITDA						
Return on Assets %						
Return on Equity %						
Debt to Equity						

CONTACT INFORMATION:
Phone: 212-210-1400 Fax: 212-850-9370
Toll-Free:
Address: 235 E. 45th St., New York, NY 10017 United States

SALARIES/BONUSES:
Top Exec. Salary: $ Bonus: $
Second Exec. Salary: $ Bonus: $

STOCK TICKER/OTHER:
Stock Ticker: Joint Venture Exchange:
Employees: 1,050 Fiscal Year Ends: 10/03
Parent Company: Hearst Communications Inc

OTHER THOUGHTS:
Estimated Female Officers or Directors: 3
Hot Spot for Advancement for Women/Minorities: Y

Sales, profits and employees may be estimates. Financial information, benefits and other data can change quickly and may vary from those stated here.

ABC Inc (Disney-ABC)

NAIC Code: 512110

www.disneyabcpress.com/disneyabctv/

TYPES OF BUSINESS:
Television Show Production

BRANDS/DIVISIONS/AFFILIATES:
Walt Disney Company (The)
Disney Media Networks
Disney-ABC Television Group
ABC Entertainment
ABC Studios
ABC Owned Television Stations Group
Disney Channels Worldwide
Disney XD

CONTACTS:
Note: Officers with more than one job title may be intentionally listed here more than once.

Ben Sherwood, Pres., Disney Media
Tom Ascheim, Pres., Freeform
Robert Langer, CFO
Gary Marsh, Pres., Disney Channels Worldwide
Sonia Coleman, Sr. VP-Global Human Resources
James Goldston, Pres., ABC News
Channing Dungey, Pres., ABC Entertainment

GROWTH PLANS/SPECIAL FEATURES:

ABC, Inc., doing business as Disney/ABC Television Group (Disney-ABC), manages all the Disney- and ABC-branded broadcast content. The firm is a subsidiary of Disney Media Networks, a business segment of The Walt Disney Company (Disney). Disney-ABC units include: ABC, Disney channels, distribution and equity holdings. The ABC unit is comprised of ABC Entertainment, which airs programming including dramas, game shows, comedies, reality phenomenon and late-night talk shows; ABC Entertainment Group, overseeing ABC Entertainment and ABC Studios, which develop and produce day-time programming for national and international broadcast and digital platforms; ABC Signature Studios, offering premium and basic cable, as well as streaming platforms; ABC News, which is responsible for all ABC Television Network news programming; and ABC Owned Television Stations Group for the New York, Los Angeles, Chicago, Philadelphia, San Francisco, Houston, Raleigh-Durham and Fresno markets. Freeform distributes coming of age programming, from first kiss to first child, to millions of homes. The Disney channels unit offers: Disney Channels Worldwide, with a global portfolio of 116 kid-focused, family-inclusive entertainment channels; Disney Channel, a 24-hour television network offering channels for children and families; Disney XD, a basic cable channel and multi-platform brand showcasing a mix of live-action and animated programming for kids aged 6-11; Disney Junior, for kids aged 2-7; Radio Disney, a 24-hour radio network for families; and Disney TV Animation, a studio that creates animated TV product for preschoolers, kids and tweens. The distribution unit comprises: Disney-ABC Home Entertainment and Television Distribution, the in-home content distribution arm for Disney within North America; and Walt Disney Direct-to-Consumer and International, responsible for the international distribution of Disney's branded and non-branded content to all platforms. The equity holdings unit controls Disney-ABC's 50% interest in A+E Networks, and its 30% interest in Hulu.

FINANCIAL DATA:
Note: Data for latest year may not have been available at press time.

In U.S. $	2018	2017	2016	2015	2014	2013
Revenue						
R&D Expense						
Operating Income						
Operating Margin %						
SGA Expense						
Net Income						
Operating Cash Flow						
Capital Expenditure						
EBITDA						
Return on Assets %						
Return on Equity %						
Debt to Equity						

CONTACT INFORMATION:
Phone: 818-560-1000 Fax: 818-560-1930
Toll-Free:
Address: 500 S. Buena Vista St., Burbank, CA 91521-4581 United States

STOCK TICKER/OTHER:
Stock Ticker: Subsidiary
Employees:
Parent Company: Walt Disney Company (The)

Exchange:
Fiscal Year Ends: 09/30

SALARIES/BONUSES:
Top Exec. Salary: $ Bonus: $
Second Exec. Salary: $ Bonus: $

OTHER THOUGHTS:
Estimated Female Officers or Directors:
Hot Spot for Advancement for Women/Minorities:

Activision Blizzard Inc

NAIC Code: 511210G

www.activisionblizzard.com

TYPES OF BUSINESS:
Electronic Games, Apps & Entertainment
League-Based, Live Gaming Competition
Apps
TV Distribution of Gaming Events
Merchandising
Licensing Game Content for Movies
Licensing Content to Comic Books

BRANDS/DIVISIONS/AFFILIATES:
Activision Publishing Inc
Blizzard Entertainment Inc
King Digital Entertainment
Call of Duty
World of Warcraft
Overwatch
Activision Blizzard Studios
Activision Blizzard Distribution

CONTACTS:
Note: Officers with more than one job title may be intentionally listed here more than once.

Riccardo Zacconi, CEO, Subsidiary
Eric Hirshberg, CEO, Subsidiary
Robert Kotick, CEO
Spencer Neumann, CFO
Brian Kelly, Chairman of the Board
Stephen Wereb, Chief Accounting Officer
Christopher Walther, Chief Legal Officer
Collister Johnson, COO
Dennis Durkin, Other Executive Officer
Brian Stolz, Other Executive Officer

GROWTH PLANS/SPECIAL FEATURES:

Activision Blizzard, Inc. is a leading international publisher and developer of subscription-based massively multiplayer online role-playing games (MMORPGs) and other PC-based, console, handheld and mobile games. The firm develops and distributes content and services across all major gaming platforms, including video game consoles, personal computers (PCs) and mobile devices. Activision operates through four business segments: Activision Publishing, Inc.; Blizzard Entertainment, Inc.; King Digital Entertainment; and other. Activision Publishing is a developer and publisher of interactive software products and entertainment content, particularly in console gaming. Key product franchises include: Call of Duty and Destiney. Blizzard Entertainment develops and publishes interactive software products and entertainment content, particularly in PC gaming. Its content is primarily delivered through retail channels or digital downloads, including subscriptions, full-game sales and in-game purchases. This division's key product franchises include World of Warcraft, a subscription-based MMORPG; StarCraft, a real-time strategy PC franchise; Diablo, an action-role-playing franchise; Hearthstone, an online collectible card franchise; Heroes of the Storm, a free-to-play team brawler; and Overwatch, a team-based, first-person shooter. In addition, Overwatch League sells tickets to fans who watch teams competing at live events or via TV broadcasting. King Digital develops and publishes interactive entertainment content and services, particularly on mobile platforms such as Android and iOS, but distributes its content and services on online social platforms as well. King's games are free. Its product franchises include Candy Crush, Farm Heroes and Bubble Witch. Last, the other segment includes: Activision Blizzard Studios, which creates original film and television content based on the company's library of globally-recognized intellectual properties, including the animated TV series Skylanders Academy; and Activision Blizzard Distribution, consisting of operations in Europe that provide warehousing, logistics and sales distribution services to third-party publishers of interactive entertainment software.

FINANCIAL DATA:
Note: Data for latest year may not have been available at press time.

In U.S. $	2018	2017	2016	2015	2014	2013
Revenue		7,017,000,000	6,608,000,000	4,664,000,000	4,408,000,000	4,583,000,000
R&D Expense		1,069,000,000	958,000,000	646,000,000	571,000,000	584,000,000
Operating Income		1,309,000,000	1,412,000,000	1,319,000,000	1,183,000,000	1,372,000,000
Operating Margin %		18.65%	21.36%	28.28%	26.83%	29.93%
SGA Expense		2,138,000,000	1,844,000,000	1,114,000,000	1,129,000,000	1,096,000,000
Net Income		273,000,000	966,000,000	892,000,000	835,000,000	1,010,000,000
Operating Cash Flow		2,213,000,000	2,155,000,000	1,192,000,000	1,292,000,000	1,264,000,000
Capital Expenditure		155,000,000	136,000,000	111,000,000	107,000,000	74,000,000
EBITDA		2,508,000,000	2,562,000,000	1,813,000,000	1,535,000,000	1,692,000,000
Return on Assets %		1.51%	5.88%	5.87%	5.80%	7.16%
Return on Equity %		2.93%	11.19%	11.51%	12.05%	11.26%
Debt to Equity		0.46	0.53	0.50	0.59	0.70

CONTACT INFORMATION:
Phone: 310 255-2000
Fax: 310 255-2100
Toll-Free:
Address: 3100 Ocean Park Blvd., Santa Monica, CA 90405 United States

STOCK TICKER/OTHER:
Stock Ticker: ATVI
Employees: 9,600
Parent Company:

Exchange: NAS
Fiscal Year Ends: 12/31

SALARIES/BONUSES:
Top Exec. Salary: $1,750,000   Bonus: $
Second Exec. Salary: $675,000   Bonus: $1,000,000

OTHER THOUGHTS:
Estimated Female Officers or Directors:
Hot Spot for Advancement for Women/Minorities:

Sales, profits and employees may be estimates. Financial information, benefits and other data can change quickly and may vary from those stated here.

Advance Publications Inc

NAIC Code: 511120

www.advance.net

TYPES OF BUSINESS:
Magazine Publishing
Online Publications
Newspaper Publishing
Newspaper Industry Consulting & Technology
Internet Service Provider
Cable Television

BRANDS/DIVISIONS/AFFILIATES:
Conde Nast
Advance Local
American City Business Journals
1010data
POP
Charter Communications
Discover
Reddit

CONTACTS: Note: Officers with more than one job title may be intentionally listed here more than once.
Donald E. Newhouse, CEO
Donald E. Newhouse, Pres.
Oren Klein, CFO
Peter Weinberger, Pres., Advance Digital, Inc.
Robert A. Sauerberg, Jr., Pres., Conde Nast
Charles H. Townsend, CEO-Conde Nast
Steven O. Newhouse, Chmn.

GROWTH PLANS/SPECIAL FEATURES:
Advance Publications, Inc. is a diversified, family-owned company that operates and invests in a range of media, communications and technology businesses globally. The firm operates through five divisions: Conde Nast, Advance Local, American City Business Journals, 1010data and POP. Conde Nast and Conde Nast International are premium content companies with a global portfolio of magazine and digital brands, including Vogue, Vanity Fair, Gentlemen's Quarterly (GQ), Architectural Digest (AD), The New Yorker, Conde Nast Traveler and Wired. Advanced Local is a leading media group in the U.S., offering news and information in more than 25 cities. American City Business Journals is a business information and events company that comprises 40 metro business journals and vertical global brands such as Sports Business Journal and Leaders. 1010data provides cloud-based analytical intelligence and consumer insights solutions. POP is a digital marketing agency. In addition, Advance Publications is among the largest shareholders in: Charter Communications, an American broadband communications company and cable operator; Discovery, which comprises a portfolio of premium non-fiction, lifestyle, sports and kids video programming brands; and Reddit, a social news and interest forum.

FINANCIAL DATA: Note: Data for latest year may not have been available at press time.

In U.S. $	2018	2017	2016	2015	2014	2013
Revenue	2,800,000,000	2,700,000,000	2,600,000,000			
R&D Expense						
Operating Income						
Operating Margin %						
SGA Expense						
Net Income						
Operating Cash Flow						
Capital Expenditure						
EBITDA						
Return on Assets %						
Return on Equity %						
Debt to Equity						

CONTACT INFORMATION:
Phone: 718-981-1234 Fax: 718-981-1456
Toll-Free:
Address: 1 World Trade Center, 43/Fl, New York, NY 10007 United States

STOCK TICKER/OTHER:
Stock Ticker: Private
Employees: 9,000
Parent Company:

Exchange:
Fiscal Year Ends: 12/31

SALARIES/BONUSES:
Top Exec. Salary: $ Bonus: $
Second Exec. Salary: $ Bonus: $

OTHER THOUGHTS:
Estimated Female Officers or Directors:
Hot Spot for Advancement for Women/Minorities:

Sales, profits and employees may be estimates. Financial information, benefits and other data can change quickly and may vary from those stated here.

Affinity Gaming LLC

NAIC Code: 721120

www.affinitygamingllc.com

TYPES OF BUSINESS:
Casino Hotels
Slot Machine Operation
Slot Machine Installation

BRANDS/DIVISIONS/AFFILIATES:
Z Capital Group LLC
Z Capital Partners LLC
Silver Sevens Hotel & Casino
Rail City Casino
Primm Valley Resort and Casino
Golden Mardi Gras Casino
St Jo Frontier Casino
Lakeside Hotel and Casino

CONTACTS:
Note: Officers with more than one job title may be intentionally listed here more than once.

Tony Rodio, CEO
Eric Fiocco, CMO
Stana Subaric, Sr. VP-Human Resources
Paige Lion, CIO
Marc H. Rubinstein, General Counsel
William Schmitt, Head-Comm.
William Schmitt, Head-Investor Rel.
Donna Lehmann, Treas.
James J. Zenni, Jr., Chmn.

GROWTH PLANS/SPECIAL FEATURES:
Affinity Gaming, LLC is a diversified gaming company with slot route operations and casino operations. The firm operates 11 wholly-owned casinos, five of which are in Nevada, three in Colorado, two in Missouri, and one in Iowa. Silver Sevens Hotel & Casino in Las Vegas has more than 300 rooms, a buffet and a Sperling Spoon Cafe. Rail City Casino in Sparks has roughly 24,000 square feet of gaming space, a 24-hour-a-day restaurant and a bar. Affinity's other Nevada properties consist of three casino operations: Primm Valley Resort and Casino, Buffalo Bill's Resort and Casino, and Whiskey Pete's Hotel and Casino. Outside of Nevada, Affinity owns and operates Golden Mardi Gras Casino, Golden Gates Casino and Golden Gulch Casino all in Black Hawk, Colorado; St. Jo Frontier Casino in St. Joseph, Missouri, and Mark Twain Casino in LaGrange, Missouri; and Lakeside Hotel and Casino in Osceola, Iowa. Together, these properties outside of Nevada contain approximately 3,305 slot machines and 55 table games. Affinity Gaming is wholly-owned by Z Capital Partners, LLC, the private equity management arm of Z Capital Group, LLC. In late-2018, Affinity Capital proposed to acquire Full House Resorts, owner, developer and operator of gaming facilities.

FINANCIAL DATA:
Note: Data for latest year may not have been available at press time.

In U.S. $	2018	2017	2016	2015	2014	2013
Revenue	400,000,000	380,000,000	375,500,000	393,300,000	385,902,000	389,774,000
R&D Expense						
Operating Income						
Operating Margin %						
SGA Expense						
Net Income				-13,096,000	-23,677,000	-1,227,000
Operating Cash Flow						
Capital Expenditure						
EBITDA						
Return on Assets %						
Return on Equity %						
Debt to Equity						

CONTACT INFORMATION:
Phone: 702-341-2400   Fax:
Toll-Free:
Address: 3755 Breakthrough Way, Ste. 300, Las Vegas, NV 89135 United States

STOCK TICKER/OTHER:
Stock Ticker: Private
Employees: 3,400
Parent Company:

Exchange:
Fiscal Year Ends: 12/31

SALARIES/BONUSES:
Top Exec. Salary: $ Bonus: $
Second Exec. Salary: $ Bonus: $

OTHER THOUGHTS:
Estimated Female Officers or Directors: 1
Hot Spot for Advancement for Women/Minorities:

Sales, profits and employees may be estimates. Financial information, benefits and other data can change quickly and may vary from those stated here.

Alliance Entertainment LLC

www.aent.com

NAIC Code: 512120

TYPES OF BUSINESS:
Audio Equipment Distributors
E-Commerce Software
Online Entertainment Portal

BRANDS/DIVISIONS/AFFILIATES:
Super D Inc
AMPED Distribution
NCircle Entertainment
Vinyl Styl

CONTACTS: Note: Officers with more than one job title may be intentionally listed here more than once.
Jeff Walker, CEO
Peter Blei, COO
Mike Davis, Pres.
George Campagna, CFO

GROWTH PLANS/SPECIAL FEATURES:
Alliance Entertainment, LLC, a subsidiary of Super D, Inc., distributes entertainment products such as music, movies and consumer electronics. The company offers thousands of compact discs, vinyl LP records, DVDs, Blu-rays, video games and a full line of complementary consumer electronics accessories. Alliance services small and large business customers, providing a suite of services to resellers and retailers around the globe. The firm helps businesses reduce costs by streamlining purchasing efforts and providing seller tools/web content. Alliance streamlines the overall purchasing experience, which reduces the costs associated with administrating multiple vendor relationships. The company's three brands include: AMPED Distribution, NCircle Entertainment and Vinyl Styl. AMPED distributes vinyl long-playing (LP) records, compact discs (CDs), digital versatile discs (DVDs) and Blu-rays, as well as state-of-the-art digital distribution for audio and video. NCircle is a content distributor specializing in the sales, marketing and distribution of children and family programming content. Vinyl Styl offers LP solutions, including portable turntables for playing vinyl records of the past on modern, portable, 3-speed turntables. Available LP accessories include a record brush, cleaning products, replacement needles, carrying case, sleeves and a turntable/LP crate. Based in Florida, the firm has sales offices in California, Illinois and Texas. Its 660,000-square-foot warehouse distribution center is in Shepherdsville, Kentucky.

FINANCIAL DATA: Note: Data for latest year may not have been available at press time.

In U.S. $	2018	2017	2016	2015	2014	2013
Revenue	790,000,000	770,000,000	780,000,000			
R&D Expense						
Operating Income						
Operating Margin %						
SGA Expense						
Net Income						
Operating Cash Flow						
Capital Expenditure						
EBITDA						
Return on Assets %						
Return on Equity %						
Debt to Equity						

CONTACT INFORMATION:
Phone: 954-255-4000 Fax: 954-255-4078
Toll-Free: 800-329-7664
Address: 1401 NW 136th Ave., Sunrise, FL 33323 United States

STOCK TICKER/OTHER:
Stock Ticker: Subsidiary
Employees: 22,000
Parent Company: Super D Inc

Exchange:
Fiscal Year Ends: 12/31

SALARIES/BONUSES:
Top Exec. Salary: $ Bonus: $
Second Exec. Salary: $ Bonus: $

OTHER THOUGHTS:
Estimated Female Officers or Directors:
Hot Spot for Advancement for Women/Minorities:

Alphabet Inc (Google)

NAIC Code: 519130

www.google.com

TYPES OF BUSINESS:
Search Engine-Internet
Paid Search Listing Advertising Services
Online Software and Productivity Tools
Online Video and Photo Services
Travel Booking
Analytical Tools
Venture Capital
Online Maps

BRANDS/DIVISIONS/AFFILIATES:
Google LLC
Search
Android
Maps
Chrome
YouTube
GooglePlay
Gmail

CONTACTS: Note: Officers with more than one job title may be intentionally listed here more than once.
Sundar Pichai, CEO, Subsidiary
Diane Greene, CEO, Subsidiary
Larry Page, CEO
Ruth Porat, CFO
John Hennessy, Chairman of the Board
Sergey Brin, Director
David Drummond, Other Executive Officer
James Campbell, Vice President

GROWTH PLANS/SPECIAL FEATURES:

Alphabet, Inc. owns a collection of businesses, the largest of which is Google, LLC, an information company offering a leading online search and advertising platform. Alphabet states that its primary job is to make the internet available to as many people as possible, and does this by tailoring hardware and software experiences that suit the needs of emerging markets, mainly through Android and Chrome. Google's core products include Search, Android, Maps, Chrome, YouTube, GooglePlay and Gmail, each of which have more than 1 billion monthly active users. Within Google, Alphabet's investments in machine learning are what enable the firm to continually innovate and build Google products, making them smarter and more useful over time. Machine learning also dramatically improves the energy efficiency of the company's data centers. Alphabet's other businesses include Access, Calico, CapitalG, GV, Nest, Verily, Waymo and X, all of which are not primarily engaged in the company's main internet offerings. Across these businesses, machine learning has the capability of doing things like helping self-driving cars better detect and respond to others on the road, or aiding clinicians in detecting diabetic retinopathy. Therefore, these firms utilize technology to try and solve big problems across many industries. They are early-stage businesses with the goal to become thriving ones in the medium- to long-term.

Employee perks at the main campus include on-site wellness, fitness, massage and health care facilities; along with free cafes, snacks and micro-kitchens. Other benefits for qualified employees include generous savings plans, training programs and flexibl

FINANCIAL DATA: Note: Data for latest year may not have been available at press time.

In U.S. $	2018	2017	2016	2015	2014	2013
Revenue		110,855,000,000	90,272,000,000	74,989,000,000	66,001,000,000	59,825,000,000
R&D Expense		16,625,000,000	13,948,000,000	12,282,000,000	9,831,999,000	7,952,000,000
Operating Income		28,882,000,000	23,716,000,000	19,360,000,000	16,496,000,000	13,966,000,000
Operating Margin %		26.05%	26.27%	25.81%	24.99%	23.34%
SGA Expense		19,765,000,000	17,470,000,000	15,183,000,000	13,982,000,000	12,049,000,000
Net Income		12,662,000,000	19,478,000,000	16,348,000,000	14,444,000,000	12,920,000,000
Operating Cash Flow		37,091,000,000	36,036,000,000	26,024,000,000	22,376,000,000	18,659,000,000
Capital Expenditure		13,471,000,000	11,198,000,000	10,151,000,000	15,847,000,000	8,806,000,000
EBITDA		34,217,000,000	30,418,000,000	24,818,000,000	22,339,000,000	18,518,000,000
Return on Assets %		6.94%	12.36%	11.36%	11.93%	12.62%
Return on Equity %		8.68%	15.01%	14.07%	15.06%	16.24%
Debt to Equity		0.02	0.02	0.01	0.03	0.02

CONTACT INFORMATION:
Phone: 650 253-0000   Fax: 650 253-0001
Toll-Free:
Address: 1600 Amphitheatre Pkwy., Mountain View, CA 94043 United States

STOCK TICKER/OTHER:
Stock Ticker: GOOG
Employees: 85,080
Parent Company:

Exchange: NAS
Fiscal Year Ends: 12/31

SALARIES/BONUSES:
Top Exec. Salary: $1,250,000   Bonus: $
Second Exec. Salary: $650,000   Bonus: $

OTHER THOUGHTS:
Estimated Female Officers or Directors: 3
Hot Spot for Advancement for Women/Minorities: Y

Sales, profits and employees may be estimates. Financial information, benefits and other data can change quickly and may vary from those stated here.

Altice NV

NAIC Code: 517210

www.altice.net

TYPES OF BUSINESS:
Wireless Telecommunications Carriers
Television Subscription Services

BRANDS/DIVISIONS/AFFILIATES:
Altice USA Inc

GROWTH PLANS/SPECIAL FEATURES:
Altice NV is a multinational cable, fiber, telecommunications, contents and media company. Its global presence covers the following regions: Western Europe (France, Belgium, Luxembourg, Portugal and Switzerland), the U.S., Israel, and overseas territories (the French Caribbean, the Indian Ocean region and the Dominican Republic). Altice provides original content, high-quality TV shows and international, national and local news channels. The firm delivers live broadcast premium sports events as well as well-known media and entertainment. Altice innovates with technology in its labs across the world; links leading brands to audiences through its premium advertising solutions; and provides enterprise digital solutions to businesses. All of the company's products are marketed under the Altice brand name. In May 2018, Altice NV approved the separation of Altice USA, Inc. into a stand-alone company.

CONTACTS:
Note: Officers with more than one job title may be intentionally listed here more than once.

Alain Weill, CEO
Francois Vauthier, CFO

FINANCIAL DATA:
Note: Data for latest year may not have been available at press time.

In U.S. $	2018	2017	2016	2015	2014	2013
Revenue		26,768,810,000	23,642,980,000	16,574,360,000	4,481,820,000	1,466,487,000
R&D Expense						
Operating Income		2,223,197,000	2,554,335,000	1,781,678,000	445,505,100	132,364,300
Operating Margin %		8.26%	10.80%	10.74%	9.94%	3.22%
SGA Expense		2,023,967,000	1,696,359,000	1,333,326,000	579,805,900	91,926,000
Net Income		-621,952,900	-1,774,274,000	-363,717,100	-470,565,400	81,787,940
Operating Cash Flow		9,187,360,000	7,977,286,000	5,281,360,000	2,091,174,000	500,182,200
Capital Expenditure		5,177,700,000	4,726,500,000	3,004,852,000	1,099,467,000	328,974,300
EBITDA		8,798,696,000	7,733,403,000	6,639,973,000	1,515,697,000	792,477,200
Return on Assets %		-.71%	-2.14%	-.63%	-2.00%	1.76%
Return on Equity %				-21.32%	-40.53%	38.74%
Debt to Equity				43.45	10.55	40.34

CONTACT INFORMATION:
Phone: 41-79946 4931 Fax:
Toll-Free:
Address: Prins Bernhardplein 200, Amsterdam, 1097JB Netherlands

STOCK TICKER/OTHER:
Stock Ticker: ALVVF
Employees: 47,143
Parent Company:

Exchange: PINX
Fiscal Year Ends:

SALARIES/BONUSES:
Top Exec. Salary: $ Bonus: $
Second Exec. Salary: $ Bonus: $

OTHER THOUGHTS:
Estimated Female Officers or Directors:
Hot Spot for Advancement for Women/Minorities:

Altice USA Inc

NAIC Code: 517110

www.alticeusa.com/

TYPES OF BUSINESS:
Cable Television Service
Professional Sports Teams
Television Programming
Communications Services
Movie Theatres
Voice Over Internet Protocol
High-Speed Internet

BRANDS/DIVISIONS/AFFILIATES:
Altice NV
Suddenlink Communications
Optimum
Lightpath
Altice Media Solutions
News 12 Networks
Altice Business
a4 Media & Data Solutions LLC

CONTACTS:
Note: Officers with more than one job title may be intentionally listed here more than once.

Dexter Goei, Chairman of the Board
Abdelhakim Boubazine, Co-President
Charles Stewart, Director
David Connolly, Executive VP
Lisa Rosenblum, Vice Chairman

GROWTH PLANS/SPECIAL FEATURES:

Altice USA, a subsidiary of Altice NV, is a leading media and telecommunications firm, offering telecommunication and digital voice, TV and high-speed internet services. The company serves more than 4.9 million customers across 21 states. The company is composed of several brands: Suddenlink Communications, Optimum, Lightpath, Altice Media Solutions, News 12 Networks and a4. Suddenlink provides digital cable television, voice services and high-speed internet to business and residential customers in the western, Midwestern and southern states. Optimum provides services in the New York tristate area, which include high-speed internet, digital cable services and voice services, as well as Optimum WiFi, its branded service that offers some of the fastest speeds in the nation. Lightpath, also marketed as Altice Business, develops customized, commercial telecommunications services and solutions for both medium and large-sized businesses, including schools and hospitals in the New York tristate area. Altice Media Solutions is the advertising and sales division of Altice USA and is driven by advanced technologies and exclusive census-level data of audiences. Its offerings include targeted advertising on digital, cable TV and other platforms to Fortune 500 brands, local businesses and programmers. News 12 Networks provide 24-hour, regional news programming services with seven individual news channels and five traffic and weather channels servicing to New Jersey, Connecticut, Long Island, Westchester, the Bronx, Hudson Valley and Brooklyn. A4 Media & Data Solutions, LLC provides data-driven, audience-based advertising solutions to the media industry, including AMS, programmers and multichannel video programming distributors. Total Audience Data, its flagship portfolio of products, consists of advanced analytics tools providing granular measurement of consumer groups, accurate hyper-local ratings and other insights into target audience behavior not available through traditional sample-based measurement services.

FINANCIAL DATA:
Note: Data for latest year may not have been available at press time.

In U.S. $	2018	2017	2016	2015	2014	2013
Revenue		9,326,570,000	6,017,212,000			
R&D Expense						
Operating Income		1,017,785,000	700,061,000			
Operating Margin %		10.91%	11.63%			
SGA Expense						
Net Income		1,520,031,000	-832,030,000			
Operating Cash Flow		2,001,743,000	1,184,455,000			
Capital Expenditure		993,071,000	625,647,000			
EBITDA		3,202,258,000	2,065,702,000			
Return on Assets %		4.26%	-2.28%			
Return on Equity %		40.40%	-40.99%			
Debt to Equity		3.88	10.72			

CONTACT INFORMATION:
Phone: 516 803-2300 Fax: 516 803-2273
Toll-Free:
Address: 1111 Stewart Ave., Bethpage, NY 11714 United States

STOCK TICKER/OTHER:
Stock Ticker: ATUS
Employees: 16,000
Parent Company: Altice NV

Exchange: NYS
Fiscal Year Ends: 12/31

SALARIES/BONUSES:
Top Exec. Salary: $ Bonus: $
Second Exec. Salary: $ Bonus: $

OTHER THOUGHTS:
Estimated Female Officers or Directors: 4
Hot Spot for Advancement for Women/Minorities: Y

Sales, profits and employees may be estimates. Financial information, benefits and other data can change quickly and may vary from those stated here.

Amazon.com Inc

www.amazon.com

NAIC Code: 454111

TYPES OF BUSINESS:
Online Retailing and Related Services
Robotics
Cloud Computing Services
Logistics Services
Retail Supermarkets & Grocery Delivery
Online Household Goods Retail
Online Auto & Industrial Retail
E-Commerce Support & Hosting

BRANDS/DIVISIONS/AFFILIATES:
Amazon Web Services (AWS)
Amazon Marketplace
Amazon Prime
Echo
Whole Foods Market
Amazon Go

CONTACTS:
Note: Officers with more than one job title may be intentionally listed here more than once.

Andrew Jassy, CEO, Divisional
Jeffrey Wilke, CEO, Divisional
Jeffrey Bezos, CEO
Brian Olsavsky, CFO
Shelley Reynolds, Chief Accounting Officer
David Zapolsky, General Counsel
Jeffrey Blackburn, Senior VP, Divisional

GROWTH PLANS/SPECIAL FEATURES:

Amazon.com, Inc. is an internet consumer-shopping site that offers millions of new, used, refurbished and collectible items in categories such as books, movies, music and games, electronics and computers, home and garden, toys, children's goods, grocery, apparel and jewelry, health and beauty, sports, outdoors, digital downloads, tools and auto and industrial. The company, which serves more than 50 million members, operates in three segments: North America (which generates about 60% of annual revenue), international (33%) and Amazon Web Services (AWS) (7%), which offers computing, storage, database and other service offerings globally for start-ups, enterprises, government agencies and academic institutions. The Amazon Marketplace and Merchants programs allow third parties to integrate their products on Amazon websites and provide related fulfillment and advertising services to third-party merchants; allow customers to shop for products owned by third parties using Amazon's features and technologies; and enable customers to complete transactions that include multiple sellers in a single checkout process. Amazon Prime memberships afford members a host of perks including free two-day shipping, streaming music and video, delivery from participating restaurants and much more. The company also sells proprietary electronic devices, including eReaders, tablets, TVs and phones; as well as the Echo personal digital assistant. The firm serves authors and independent publishers with Kindle Direct Publishing, an online platform that lets independent authors and publishers choose a 70% royalty option and make their books available in the Kindle Store. Subsidiary Whole Foods Market is a supermarket chain featuring foods without artificial preservatives, colors, flavors, sweeteners and hydrogenated fats, with stores throughout the U.S and internationally. During 2018, Amazon opened Amazon Go stores, the first in Seattle, which uses cameras and sensors to detect items that a shopper purchases. The firm plans to open as many as 3,000 Amazon Go locations throughout the U.S. by 2021.

FINANCIAL DATA:
Note: Data for latest year may not have been available at press time.

In U.S. $	2018	2017	2016	2015	2014	2013
Revenue		177,866,000,000	135,987,000,000	107,006,000,000	88,988,000,000	74,452,000,000
R&D Expense		22,620,000,000	16,085,000,000	12,540,000,000	9,275,000,000	6,565,000,000
Operating Income		4,106,000,000	4,186,000,000	2,233,000,000	178,000,000	745,000,000
Operating Margin %		2.30%	3.07%	2.08%	.20%	1.00%
SGA Expense		13,743,000,000	9,665,000,000	7,001,000,000	5,884,000,000	4,262,000,000
Net Income		3,033,000,000	2,371,000,000	596,000,000	-241,000,000	274,000,000
Operating Cash Flow		18,434,000,000	16,443,000,000	11,920,000,000	6,842,000,000	5,475,000,000
Capital Expenditure		11,955,000,000	6,737,000,000	4,589,000,000	4,893,000,000	3,444,000,000
EBITDA		16,132,000,000	12,492,000,000	8,308,000,000	4,845,000,000	3,900,000,000
Return on Assets %		2.82%	3.18%	.99%	-.50%	.75%
Return on Equity %		12.90%	14.51%	4.94%	-2.35%	3.05%
Debt to Equity		1.36	0.78	1.05	1.16	0.53

CONTACT INFORMATION:
Phone: 206 266-1000 Fax:
Toll-Free:
Address: 410 Terry Ave. N., Seattle, WA 98109 United States

SALARIES/BONUSES:
Top Exec. Salary: $175,000 Bonus: $
Second Exec. Salary: $175,000 Bonus: $

STOCK TICKER/OTHER:
Stock Ticker: AMZN
Employees: 613,300
Parent Company:

Exchange: NAS
Fiscal Year Ends: 12/31

OTHER THOUGHTS:
Estimated Female Officers or Directors: 3
Hot Spot for Advancement for Women/Minorities: Y

AMC Entertainment Holdings Inc

www.amctheatres.com

NAIC Code: 512131

TYPES OF BUSINESS:
Motion Picture Theaters (except Drive-Ins)

BRANDS/DIVISIONS/AFFILIATES:
Dalian Wanda Group Co Ltd
American Multi Cinema Inc
Nordic Cinema Group Holding AB
Carmike Cinemas Inc
Odeon and UCI Cinemas Holdings Limited
Dreamscape Immersive Inc
Central Services Studios Inc
Silver Lake

CONTACTS:
Note: Officers with more than one job title may be intentionally listed here more than once.

Craig Ramsey, CFO
Chris Cox, Chief Accounting Officer
Stephen Colanero, Chief Marketing Officer
Adam Aron, Director
Mao Jun Zeng, Director
John McDonald, Executive VP, Divisional
Mark McDonald, Executive VP, Divisional
Elizabeth Frank, Executive VP, Divisional
Kevin Connor, General Counsel
Carla Sanders, Senior VP, Divisional

GROWTH PLANS/SPECIAL FEATURES:
AMC Entertainment Holdings, Inc. owns, operates or has interests in theaters located throughout the U.S., Europe and the world. Through its subsidiaries, the company operates more than 1,000 theaters and 11,165+ screens globally, including approximately 650 theaters with over 8,200 screens in the U.S., and 365 theaters with approximately 3,000 screens in Europe. Subsidiaries of the firm include: American Multi Cinema, Inc. (which stands for the AMC abbreviation); Nordic Cinema Group Holding AB; Carmike Cinemas, Inc.; and Odeon and UCI Cinemas Holdings Limited. Approximately 350 million consumers attended AMC, Nordic and Odeon theater circuits in 2018. The theaters offer enhanced consumer experience via formats such as IMAX, Dolby Cinema and 3D, among others. IMAX is a world-leading entertainment technology company, specializing in motion picture technologies and presentations; Dolby Cinema offers state-of-the-art image and sound technologies; and 3D stands for three-dimensional stereoscopic films, offering an enhanced illusion of depth perception. During 2017, AMC Entertainment made investments in Dreamscape Immersive, Inc. as well as Central Services Studios, Inc., as part of its virtual reality technologies strategy. In mid-2018, the firm sold the entirety of its remaining interest in National CineMedia, LLC (NCM). A substantial portion of AMC Entertainment's shares is owned by Chinese entertainment conglomerate Dalian Wanda and private equity firm Silver Lake.

FINANCIAL DATA:
Note: Data for latest year may not have been available at press time.

In U.S. $	2018	2017	2016	2015	2014	2013
Revenue		5,079,200,000	3,235,846,000	2,946,900,000	2,695,390,000	2,749,428,000
R&D Expense						
Operating Income		208,400,000	266,297,000	242,157,000	179,382,000	191,897,000
Operating Margin %		4.10%	8.22%	8.21%	6.65%	6.97%
SGA Expense		927,800,000	596,182,000	526,034,000	520,112,000	549,116,000
Net Income		-487,200,000	111,667,000	103,856,000	64,080,000	364,400,000
Operating Cash Flow		558,700,000	431,655,000	467,557,000	297,302,000	357,342,000
Capital Expenditure		626,800,000	421,713,000	333,423,000	270,734,000	260,823,000
EBITDA		479,500,000	539,419,000	502,580,000	434,497,000	437,485,000
Return on Assets %		-5.28%	1.62%	2.10%	1.30%	7.22%
Return on Equity %		-23.62%	6.28%	6.80%	4.24%	24.17%
Debt to Equity		2.37	2.27	1.40	1.34	1.57

CONTACT INFORMATION:
Phone: 913 213-2000 Fax:
Toll-Free:
Address: One AMC Way, 11500 Ash St., Leawood, KS 66211 United States

STOCK TICKER/OTHER:
Stock Ticker: AMC
Employees: 39,000
Parent Company: Dalian Wanda Group

Exchange: NYS
Fiscal Year Ends: 12/31

SALARIES/BONUSES:
Top Exec. Salary: $1,100,000 Bonus: $
Second Exec. Salary: $650,000 Bonus: $

OTHER THOUGHTS:
Estimated Female Officers or Directors:
Hot Spot for Advancement for Women/Minorities:

AMC Networks Inc

www.amcnetworks.com

NAIC Code: 515210

TYPES OF BUSINESS:
Cable Television Broadcasting
Network Services
Advertisement Sales
Independent Film Distribution

BRANDS/DIVISIONS/AFFILIATES:
AMC
WE tv
BBC America
IFC
Sundance TV
ICF Films
AMC Networks Broadcasting & Technology
Levity Entertainment Group LLC

CONTACTS:
Note: Officers with more than one job title may be intentionally listed here more than once.

Frank Biondi,
Joshua Sapan, CEO
Sean Sullivan, CFO
Charles Dolan, Chairman of the Board
Christian Wymbs, Chief Accounting Officer
Edward Carroll, COO
James Gallagher, Executive VP

GROWTH PLANS/SPECIAL FEATURES:

AMC Networks, Inc. is a holding company that operates nearly all its business through majority-owned or -controlled subsidiaries. The firm's television brands deliver high-quality content to audiences, as well as a platform to distributors and advertisers. In the U.S., AMC Networks' programming channels include AMC, WE tv, BBC America, IFC and Sundance TV. Each of these channels have established themselves within their respective markets, and are also distributed through emerging virtual multi-channel video programming distributors. AMC Networks obtains programming through a combination of development, production and licensing; and distributes programming directly to consumers in the U.S. and the world through its programming networks, digital and other forms of distribution. It also distributes the theatrical releases of IFC Films' acquired content; and produces some of its own original programming. IFC Films is the company's independent film distribution business. AMC Networks Broadcasting & Technology unit primarily serves most of the programming networks included in the domestic division. Internationally, AMC Networks delivers programming to subscribers in more than 140 countries and territories, including Europe, Latin America, the Middle East and parts of Asia and Africa. AMC Networks International consists of global brands such as AMC and Sundance Channel in the movie and entertainment programming genres, as well as popular local channels in various other programming genres. AMCNI-DMC is the broadcast solutions unit of certain networks within AMC Networks International, third-party networks and various developing online content distribution initiatives. During 2018, AMC Networks acquired a majority stake (57%) in Levity Entertainment Group, LLC, a production services and comedy venues company.

FINANCIAL DATA:
Note: Data for latest year may not have been available at press time.

In U.S. $	2018	2017	2016	2015	2014	2013
Revenue		2,805,691,000	2,755,654,000	2,580,935,000	2,175,641,000	1,591,858,000
R&D Expense						
Operating Income		756,635,000	754,864,000	724,191,000	562,068,000	449,223,000
Operating Margin %		26.96%	27.39%	28.05%	25.83%	28.22%
SGA Expense		613,342,000	636,028,000	636,580,000	560,950,000	425,735,000
Net Income		471,316,000	270,510,000	366,788,000	260,797,000	290,738,000
Operating Cash Flow		385,729,000	514,325,000	370,039,000	372,807,000	-49,463,000
Capital Expenditure		80,049,000	79,220,000	68,321,000	39,739,000	24,303,000
EBITDA		1,823,255,000	1,525,537,000	1,542,505,000	1,226,184,000	1,137,136,000
Return on Assets %		9.90%	6.18%	8.90%	7.88%	11.06%
Return on Equity %		898.92%				
Debt to Equity		23.16				

CONTACT INFORMATION:
Phone: 212 324-8500 Fax:
Toll-Free:
Address: 11 Penn Plaza, New York, NY 10001 United States

SALARIES/BONUSES:
Top Exec. Salary: $2,000,000   Bonus: $
Second Exec. Salary: $1,734,000   Bonus: $

STOCK TICKER/OTHER:
Stock Ticker: AMCX
Employees: 2,343
Parent Company:

Exchange: NAS
Fiscal Year Ends: 12/31

OTHER THOUGHTS:
Estimated Female Officers or Directors: 2
Hot Spot for Advancement for Women/Minorities: Y

Sales, profits and employees may be estimates. Financial information, benefits and other data can change quickly and may vary from those stated here.

American Educational Products LLC

www.amep.com

NAIC Code: 511130

TYPES OF BUSINESS:
Manufacturing-Educational Products
Educational Video Production
Map Manufacturing

BRANDS/DIVISIONS/AFFILIATES:
Aristotle Corporation (The)
Scott Resources
Hubbard Scientific
National Teaching Aids
Ginsberg Scientific
Fraction Bars
Decimal Squares
Line-Master

CONTACTS:
Note: Officers with more than one job title may be intentionally listed here more than once.
Michael Warring, Pres.

GROWTH PLANS/SPECIAL FEATURES:
American Educational Products, LLC (AEP) develops, manufactures and distributes hands-on educational products for school and home to parents, teachers and public and private schools throughout the U.S. and international locations. The firm is an indirect subsidiary of The Aristotle Corporation, which manufactures medical teaching aids such as CPR mannequins and computer-based teaching aids. The company is an original equipment manufacturer (OEM) through the Scott Resources, Hubbard Scientific, Ginsberg Scientific and National Teaching Aids names. AEP's products are supplemental instructional aids for elementary to high school mathematics, history and science courses. The products present educational content in a format different than traditional textbooks. Scott Resources produces math manipulatives, videos and workbooks as well as teacher guides. It is the exclusive manufacturer of math products such as Fraction Bars, Decimal Squares, Line-Master, Clever Catch balls and the Math Chase series. Additionally, Scott Resources provides earth science educational materials, including bulk rock, minerals, fossil specimens and the Earth Science Videolabs series. Hubbard Scientific manufactures science educational materials in such areas as earth science, geology, astronomy, meteorology, oceanography, biology, zoology, botany, ecology, anatomy, physiology, chemistry, physical science, the environment, geography and health. It is also one of the world's largest manufacturers of raised relief maps, with a library of titles and custom map production capabilities. Ginsberg Scientific is a producer of secondary level lab equipment, glassware and measurement devices for chemistry, physics and earth science classes. National Teaching Aids produces the Microslide Viewer and over 100 titles of Microslide Slide Lesson Sets. AEP also markets products manufactured by Gonge USA and Match Learner that focus on physical education and early childhood development. In addition, AEP sells a line of sensory tools for kids with Autism.

FINANCIAL DATA:
Note: Data for latest year may not have been available at press time.

In U.S. $	2018	2017	2016	2015	2014	2013
Revenue						
R&D Expense						
Operating Income						
Operating Margin %						
SGA Expense						
Net Income						
Operating Cash Flow						
Capital Expenditure						
EBITDA						
Return on Assets %						
Return on Equity %						
Debt to Equity						

CONTACT INFORMATION:
Phone: 970-484-7445
Fax: 970-484-1198
Toll-Free: 800-289-9299
Address: 401 Hickory St., Fort Collins, CO 80522 United States

STOCK TICKER/OTHER:
Stock Ticker: Subsidiary
Employees: 95
Parent Company: Aristotle Corporation (The)
Exchange:
Fiscal Year Ends: 12/31

SALARIES/BONUSES:
Top Exec. Salary: $
Bonus: $
Second Exec. Salary: $
Bonus: $

OTHER THOUGHTS:
Estimated Female Officers or Directors: 6
Hot Spot for Advancement for Women/Minorities: Y

Sales, profits and employees may be estimates. Financial information, benefits and other data can change quickly and may vary from those stated here.

American Express Company

www.americanexpress.com

NAIC Code: 522320

TYPES OF BUSINESS:
Credit Card Processing and Issuing
Travel-Related Services
Lending & Financing
Transaction Services
Bank Holding Company
International Banking Services
Expense Management
Magazine Publishing

BRANDS/DIVISIONS/AFFILIATES:
American Express Travel Related Services Co Inc
American Express Bank FSB
American Express Centurion Bank
Mezi (www.mezi.com)

CONTACTS:
Note: Officers with more than one job title may be intentionally listed here more than once.

Stephen Squeri, CEO
Anre Williams, President, Divisional
Linda Zukauckas, CFO, Divisional
Jeffrey Campbell, CFO
David Fabricant, Chief Accounting Officer
Richard Petrino, Chief Accounting Officer
Marc Gordon, Chief Information Officer
Elizabeth Rutledge, Chief Marketing Officer
Denise Pickett, Chief Risk Officer
Michael ONeill, Executive VP, Divisional
Laureen Seeger, Executive VP
L. Cox, Other Executive Officer
Douglas Buckminster, President, Divisional
Paul Fabara, President, Divisional
Douglas Buckminster, President, Divisional

GROWTH PLANS/SPECIAL FEATURES:

American Express Company (AmEx), a bank holding company, is a leading global payments and travel firm. Its principal products are charge and credit payment card products and travel-related services. The firm primarily operates through subsidiary American Express Travel Related Services Company, Inc. AmEx's business is organized into four main segments: U.S. card services, international card services, global commercial services and global network & merchant services. The U.S. card services segment operates through AmEx's USA banking subsidiaries American Express Centurion Bank and American Express Bank, FSB. The division provides a wide array of card products and services to consumers and small businesses in the USA. The firm's international card services division offers these services in countries worldwide. The global commercial services segment offers expense management services to firms and organizations worldwide. Its products and services include corporate purchasing cards, corporate cards, corporate meeting cards, buyer-initiated payment programs and business travel accounts. The global network & merchant services division operates a global general-purpose charge and credit card network for both proprietary and issued cards; manages merchant services internationally, which includes signing merchants to accept cards and processing and settling card transactions for those merchants; and offers merchants point-of-sale (POS), servicing/settlement and marketing/information products and services. In January 2018, the firm announced that it had acquired Mezi (www.mezi.com), a personal travel assistant app that helps consumers plan and book trips.

FINANCIAL DATA:
Note: Data for latest year may not have been available at press time.

In U.S. $	2018	2017	2016	2015	2014	2013
Revenue		24,424,000,000	25,411,000,000	24,804,000,000	34,292,000,000	32,974,000,000
R&D Expense						
Operating Income						
Operating Margin %						
SGA Expense		8,751,000,000	9,211,000,000	8,430,000,000	17,551,000,000	16,837,000,000
Net Income		2,736,000,000	5,408,000,000	5,163,000,000	5,885,000,000	5,359,000,000
Operating Cash Flow		13,540,000,000	8,224,000,000	10,972,000,000	10,990,000,000	8,547,000,000
Capital Expenditure		1,062,000,000	1,375,000,000	1,341,000,000	1,195,000,000	1,006,000,000
EBITDA						
Return on Assets %		1.54%	3.30%	3.16%	3.73%	3.46%
Return on Equity %		13.60%	25.67%	24.49%	29.07%	27.67%
Debt to Equity		3.06	2.29	2.32	2.80	2.83

CONTACT INFORMATION:
Phone: 212 640-2000 Fax: 212 640-2458
Toll-Free: 800-528-4800
Address: 200 Vesey St., World Financial Ctr., New York, NY 10285 United States

STOCK TICKER/OTHER:
Stock Ticker: AXP
Employees: 55,000
Parent Company:

Exchange: NYS
Fiscal Year Ends: 12/31

SALARIES/BONUSES:
Top Exec. Salary: $1,375,962 Bonus: $7,000,000
Second Exec. Salary: $815,385 Bonus: $5,034,000

OTHER THOUGHTS:
Estimated Female Officers or Directors: 4
Hot Spot for Advancement for Women/Minorities: Y

American Golf Corp

NAIC Code: 713910

www.americangolf.com

TYPES OF BUSINESS:
Golf Courses
Resorts
Golf Promotion
Weddings & Events

BRANDS/DIVISIONS/AFFILIATES:
American Golf Foundation
Platinum Club
AmericanGolf.com
Heartwell Golf Course
Ko'olau Golf Club
Waterview Golf Club
The National Golf Club

CONTACTS:
Note: Officers with more than one job title may be intentionally listed here more than once.

Jim Hinckley, CEO
Craig Kniffen, Sr. VP-Maintenance
Jim Hinckley, Pres.
Rick Rosen, CFO
Christine Chong, Sr. VP-Legal Affairs
Christine Chong, Sr. VP-Real Property

GROWTH PLANS/SPECIAL FEATURES:

American Golf Corp. is a premier manager of golf courses and resorts, owning and operating more than 80 private, public and resort golf courses in the U.S. American Golf's portfolio includes courses for golfers of all skill levels. Its properties include Heartwell Golf Course in Long Beach, California; Ko'olau Golf Club in Oahu, Hawaii; and Waterview Golf Club in Rowlett, Texas. A majority of the firm's golf courses are located within New York, Georgia and California, with 49 courses found in California alone near popular locations such as Los Angeles and San Diego. Additionally, the company operates country clubs featuring spas, tennis, swimming, dining and golf facilities. American Golf offers junior rates for kids who enjoy golfing and has junior camps in operation year around. The firm offers regional golfers clubs throughout the country that provide discount green fees, early twilight access and merchandise discounts. The company also offers the Platinum Club, which enables members to golf at participating American Golf private clubs and public courses all over the country for only a cart fee. Membership also allows golfers to reserve tee times in advance and to bring guests to private clubs for the prevailing guest rate. In addition, the company offers The National Golf Club, which affords members unrestricted access to 30 private clubs and 120 resort and daily fee courses; a member does not have to pay any fees at the course. The firm's website, AmericanGolf.com, allows users to view the firm's portfolio of courses as well as providing the ability to make golf reservations, access course specials, research wedding and event locations and purchase golf lessons and golf merchandise. American Golf established the American Golf Foundation, a nonprofit organization devoted to promoting the sport of golf.

FINANCIAL DATA:
Note: Data for latest year may not have been available at press time.

In U.S. $	2018	2017	2016	2015	2014	2013
Revenue	280,000,000	290,000,000	280,000,000	296,008,000	261,684,000	
R&D Expense						
Operating Income						
Operating Margin %						
SGA Expense						
Net Income						
Operating Cash Flow						
Capital Expenditure						
EBITDA						
Return on Assets %						
Return on Equity %						
Debt to Equity						

CONTACT INFORMATION:
Phone: 310-664-4000 Fax: 310-664-4386
Toll-Free:
Address: 6080 Center Dr., Ste. 500, Los Angeles, CA 90045 United States

STOCK TICKER/OTHER:
Stock Ticker: Subsidiary
Employees: 16,000
Parent Company: Newcastle Investment Corp

Exchange:
Fiscal Year Ends: 12/31

SALARIES/BONUSES:
Top Exec. Salary: $ Bonus: $
Second Exec. Salary: $ Bonus: $

OTHER THOUGHTS:
Estimated Female Officers or Directors: 5
Hot Spot for Advancement for Women/Minorities: Y

Sales, profits and employees may be estimates. Financial information, benefits and other data can change quickly and may vary from those stated here.

American Greetings Corporation LLC

www.americangreetings.com

NAIC Code: 511191

TYPES OF BUSINESS:
Greeting Cards
Gift Wrap
Party Supplies
Stationery
Digital Media
Online Greetings Cards

BRANDS/DIVISIONS/AFFILIATES:
Clayton Dubilier & Rice LLC
AmericanGreetings.com
justWink.com
BlueMountain.com
CardStore.com
Recycled Paper Greetings
Papyrus
DesignWare

CONTACTS:
Note: Officers with more than one job title may be intentionally listed here more than once.

John W. Beeder, CEO
John W. Beeder, Pres.
Gregory M. Steinberg, CFO
Thomas H. Johnston, Sr. VP-Creative & Merch.
Christopher W. Haffke, General Counsel
Robert D. Tyler, Corp. Controller
Erwin Weiss, Sr. VP
Jeffrey Weiss, Co-CEO
Gregory Steinberg, Treas.
Morry Weiss, Chmn.

GROWTH PLANS/SPECIAL FEATURES:

American Greetings Corporation LLC designs, manufactures and sells everyday and seasonal greeting cards and other social expression products. The firm's products are sold across the U.S., as well as in countries all over the world, including Canada, the U.K., Australia and New Zealand. The company markets its products through AG Interactive, Inc. (AGI), a subsidiary that focuses on digital media marketing. American Greetings' major domestic greeting card brands are Recycled Paper Greetings, Papyrus, Carlton Cards, Just For You, Tender Thoughts, American Greetings and Gibson. Besides greeting cards, the firm's product lines also include Plus Mark gift wrap, stationery, DesignWare party goods and AGI in-store display fixtures. AGI also provides ringtones, avatars, emoticons and other digital content products. American Greetings operates through the following internet sites: AmericanGreetings.com, justWink.com, BlueMountain.com and CardStore.com. These sites offer services including email greetings, personalized printable greeting cards, photo sharing and design/verse content services for use in CD-ROM software products. American Greetings' largest customers include mass merchandisers, national supermarket chains and major drug stores. During 2018, after a 100+-year history of being majority-owned by the Sapirstein, Stone and Weiss family line, American Greetings became 60%-owned by private equity company Clayton, Dubilier & Rice LLC, with the Weiss family retaining a 40% share.

American Greetings employee discounts and other company perks, which vary per location.

FINANCIAL DATA:
Note: Data for latest year may not have been available at press time.

In U.S. $	2018	2017	2016	2015	2014	2013
Revenue	2,000,000,000	1,900,000,000	1,889,994,000	1,986,352,000	1,941,809,000	1,868,739,000
R&D Expense						
Operating Income						
Operating Margin %						
SGA Expense						
Net Income			129,842,000	65,107,000	50,522,000	49,918,000
Operating Cash Flow						
Capital Expenditure						
EBITDA						
Return on Assets %						
Return on Equity %						
Debt to Equity						

CONTACT INFORMATION:
Phone: 216 252-7300
Fax: 216 255-6777
Toll-Free:
Address: 1 American Rd., Cleveland, OH 44144 United States

STOCK TICKER/OTHER:
Stock Ticker: Joint Venture
Employees: 27,000
Parent Company: Clayton Dubilier & Rice LLC
Exchange:
Fiscal Year Ends: 02/28

SALARIES/BONUSES:
Top Exec. Salary: $ Bonus: $
Second Exec. Salary: $ Bonus: $

OTHER THOUGHTS:
Estimated Female Officers or Directors:
Hot Spot for Advancement for Women/Minorities: Y

Ameristar Casinos Inc

NAIC Code: 721120

www.ameristar.com

TYPES OF BUSINESS:
Casino Resorts
Casino Management

BRANDS/DIVISIONS/AFFILIATES:
Pinnacle Entertainment Inc
Ameristar Kansas City
Ameristar St Charles
Ameristar Council Bluffs
Ameristar Vicksburg
Cactus Pete's Resort Casino
Ameristar Black Hawk
Ameristar Casino Hotel East Chicago

CONTACTS:
Note: Officers with more than one job title may be intentionally listed here more than once.

Anthony Sanfilippo, CEO-Pinnacle Entertainment
Neil Walkoff, Exec. VP-Oper.-Pinnacle Entertainment
Carlos Ruisanchez, CFO
Christina Donelson, Sr. VP-Human Resources-Pinnacle Entertainment
Jim Frank, Sr. VP

GROWTH PLANS/SPECIAL FEATURES:

Ameristar Casinos, Inc., a subsidiary of Pinnacle Entertainment, Inc., is a gaming and entertainment company that develops, owns and operates seven casino facilities. Its properties include Ameristar St. Charles and Ameristar Kansas City in Missouri; Ameristar Vicksburg in Mississippi; Ameristar Council Bluffs in southwestern Iowa; Ameristar Black Hawk in Denver, Colorado; Ameristar Casino Hotel East Chicago in Indiana; and Cactus Pete's Resort Casino in Jackpot, Nevada. The casinos typically offer slot machines and a variety of table games, including blackjack, craps, roulette, baccarat and numerous live poker variations such as Texas Hold 'Em and Pai Gow. In addition, some locations offer sports book wagering. The casinos also offer a variety of casual dining and upscale restaurants, sports bars and private clubs for Star Awards members. Ameristar St. Charles offers two ballrooms for its guests, five meeting rooms and an executive board room. Ameristar Kansas City features an 18-screen movie theater, a 4,280-square-foot arcade and an activity center called Kids Quest. Ameristar Vicksburg is a permanently docked riverboat casino located on the Mississippi River, while Ameristar Council Bluffs offers a cruising riverboat casino that travels down the Missouri River. The East Chicago property is a 56,000-square-foot complex that features a 550-seat ballroom. Cactus Pete's features an outdoor amphitheater, arcades, an 18-hole golf course and tennis courts.

The firm offers employees medical, dental and vision insurance; prescription drug coverage; a 401(k); life & disability insurance; flexible spending accounts; an employee assistance program; and tuition reimbursement.

FINANCIAL DATA:
Note: Data for latest year may not have been available at press time.

In U.S. $	2018	2017	2016	2015	2014	2013
Revenue	1,110,000,000	1,100,000,000	1,064,013,000	1,275,000,000	775,381,800	
R&D Expense						
Operating Income						
Operating Margin %						
SGA Expense						
Net Income						
Operating Cash Flow						
Capital Expenditure						
EBITDA						
Return on Assets %						
Return on Equity %						
Debt to Equity						

CONTACT INFORMATION:
Phone: 702-567-7000 Fax:
Toll-Free:
Address: 3773 Howard Hughes Pkwy., Ste. 490S, Las Vegas, NV 89169 United States

STOCK TICKER/OTHER:
Stock Ticker: Subsidiary
Employees: 7,115
Parent Company: Pinnacle Entertainment Inc
Exchange:
Fiscal Year Ends: 12/31

SALARIES/BONUSES:
Top Exec. Salary: $ Bonus: $
Second Exec. Salary: $ Bonus: $

OTHER THOUGHTS:
Estimated Female Officers or Directors: 1
Hot Spot for Advancement for Women/Minorities: Y

Sales, profits and employees may be estimates. Financial information, benefits and other data can change quickly and may vary from those stated here.

Anschutz Entertainment Group Inc

www.aegworldwide.com

NAIC Code: 711211

TYPES OF BUSINESS:
Stadiums & Sports Teams
Sports Team Franchises
Sports Facilities Management & Development
Entertainment Complexes
Entertainment Investments
Concerts & Live Entertainment Events
Filmed Entertainment
Marketing & Consulting Services

BRANDS/DIVISIONS/AFFILIATES:
Anschutz Company (The)
AEG China
AEG Presents
AEG Merchandising
AEG Global Partnerships
AEG Digital Media
Ken Ehrlich Productions
STAPLES Center

CONTACTS:
Note: Officers with more than one job title may be intentionally listed here more than once.

Dan Beckerman, CEO
Kelly Cheeseman, COO
Dan Beckerman, Pres.
Denise Taylor, CIO

GROWTH PLANS/SPECIAL FEATURES:

Anschutz Entertainment Group, Inc. (AEG), a subsidiary of The Anschutz Company, is a leading sports and entertainment investment, development and management company, operating through more than 50 divisions. The firm, through AEG Facilities, owns several venues including STAPLES Center (Los Angeles), Sprint Center (Kansas City, Missouri), Oakland Almeda-County Coliseum (Oakland, California), T-Mobile Arena (Las Vegas, Nevada), Target Center (Minneapolis) and the AmericanAirlines Arena (Miami, Florida). It also owns facilities internationally, including Viedotron Centre (Quebec City), Cadillac Arena (Beijing), Barclaycard Arena (Hamburg), Ericsson Globe Arenas (Stockholm) and Mercedes-Benz Arena (London). Furthermore, the company operates the StubHub Center in California, an official U.S. Olympic training site. In addition, it designed The O2, a 28-acre entertainment development located in London, which includes a 20,000-seat arena. AEG Presents is the live-entertainment division of Los Angeles-based AEG and is comprised of touring, festival, exhibition, broadcast, merchandise and special event divisions, 15 regional offices and owns, operates or books 35 state-of-the-art venues. AEG Merchandising maintains e-commerce sites for sports teams and events. Additional divisions include AEG Global Partnerships (worldwide sales and servicing of sponsorships naming rights and other strategic partnerships), AEG China (development and management of arenas and venues in China), AEG Digital Media (media production services), Bounce AEG (event production, management and branding services) and Ken Ehrlich Productions (television programming production). In 2018 AEG acquired the Firefly Music Festival, a music festival in Dover, Delaware and PromoWest Productions, the largest independent promoter in Central Ohio and Western Pennsylvania. In September 2018 AEG announced a joint strategic partnership with The Mall Group, Thailand's leading retail and entertainment complex developer with a $305,000 investment by AEG.

FINANCIAL DATA:
Note: Data for latest year may not have been available at press time.

In U.S. $	2018	2017	2016	2015	2014	2013
Revenue						
R&D Expense						
Operating Income						
Operating Margin %						
SGA Expense						
Net Income						
Operating Cash Flow						
Capital Expenditure						
EBITDA						
Return on Assets %						
Return on Equity %						
Debt to Equity						

CONTACT INFORMATION:
Phone: 213-763-7700 Fax: 213-763-5406
Toll-Free:
Address: 800 W. Olympic Blvd., Ste. 305, Los Angeles, CA 90015 United States

STOCK TICKER/OTHER:
Stock Ticker: Subsidiary
Employees:
Parent Company: Anschutz Company (The)

Exchange:
Fiscal Year Ends: 12/31

SALARIES/BONUSES:
Top Exec. Salary: $ Bonus: $
Second Exec. Salary: $ Bonus: $

OTHER THOUGHTS:
Estimated Female Officers or Directors:
Hot Spot for Advancement for Women/Minorities:

Apple Inc

NAIC Code: 334220

www.apple.com

TYPES OF BUSINESS:
Electronics Design and Manufacturing
Software
Computers and Tablets
Retail Stores
Smartphones
Online Music Store
Apps Store
Home Entertainment Software & Systems

BRANDS/DIVISIONS/AFFILIATES:
iPhone
iPad
Apple Watch
Apple TV
iOS
watchOS
HomePod
AirPods

CONTACTS:
Note: Officers with more than one job title may be intentionally listed here more than once.

Timothy Cook, CEO
Luca Maestri, CFO
Arthur Levinson, Chairman of the Board
Chris Kondo, Chief Accounting Officer
Jeffery Williams, COO
Katherine Adams, General Counsel
Eduardo Cue, Senior VP, Divisional
Daniel Riccio, Senior VP, Divisional
Johny Srouji, Senior VP, Divisional
Craig Federighi, Senior VP, Divisional
Philip Schiller, Senior VP, Divisional
Angela Ahrendts, Senior VP, Divisional

GROWTH PLANS/SPECIAL FEATURES:

Apple, Inc. designs, manufactures and markets personal computers, portable digital music players and mobile communication devices and sells a variety of related software, services, peripherals and networking applications. The company's products and services include iPhone, iPad, Mac, Apple Watch, Apple TV; a portfolio of consumer and professional software applications; iOS, macOS, watchOS and tvOS operating systems; iCloud, Apple Pay and a variety of accessory, service and support offerings. iPhone is the company's line of smartphones based on its iOS operating system. iCloud stores music, photos, contacts, calendars, mail, documents and more, keeping them up-to-date and available across multiple iOS devices, Mac and Windows personal computers and Apple TV. Other products include apple-branded and third-party accessories; the HomePod wireless speaker; AirPods wireless headphone; and iPod touch, a flash memory-based digital music and medial player that works with the iTunes store, App Store, iBooks store and Apple Music (collectively referred to as digital content and services) for purchasing and playing digital content and apps. The firm has more than 500 brick and mortar stores in 24 countries, but also sells its products worldwide through online stores and direct sales force, as well as through third-party cellular network carriers, wholesalers, retailers and value-added resellers. During 2018, Apple agreed acquired Texture, a digital magazine subscription service by Next Issue Media, LLC, which gives users unlimited access to their favorite titles for a monthly subscription fee. That December, Apple announced a major expansion of its operations in Austin, including a $1 billion new campus, with plans to establish new sites in Seattle, San Diego and Culver City. Apple added 6,000 jobs in America in 2018, with plans to create 20,000 jobs in the U.S. by 2023. Apple offers employees comprehensive health benefits, retirement plans and various employee assistance programs.

FINANCIAL DATA:
Note: Data for latest year may not have been available at press time.

In U.S. $	2018	2017	2016	2015	2014	2013
Revenue	265,595,000,000	229,234,000,000	215,639,000,000	233,715,000,000	182,795,000,000	170,910,000,000
R&D Expense	14,236,000,000	11,581,000,000	10,045,000,000	8,067,000,000	6,041,000,000	4,475,000,000
Operating Income	70,898,000,000	61,344,000,000	60,024,000,000	71,230,000,000	52,503,000,000	48,999,000,000
Operating Margin %		26.76%	27.83%	30.47%	28.72%	28.66%
SGA Expense	16,705,000,000	15,261,000,000	14,194,000,000	14,329,000,000	11,993,000,000	10,830,000,000
Net Income	59,531,000,000	48,351,000,000	45,687,000,000	53,394,000,000	39,510,000,000	37,037,000,000
Operating Cash Flow	77,434,000,000	63,598,000,000	65,824,000,000	81,266,000,000	59,713,000,000	53,666,000,000
Capital Expenditure	13,313,000,000	12,795,000,000	13,548,000,000	11,488,000,000	9,813,000,000	9,076,000,000
EBITDA	87,046,000,000	76,569,000,000	73,333,000,000	84,505,000,000	61,813,000,000	57,048,000,000
Return on Assets %		13.87%	14.92%	20.44%	18.00%	19.33%
Return on Equity %		36.86%	36.90%	46.24%	33.61%	30.63%
Debt to Equity		0.72	0.58	0.44	0.25	0.13

CONTACT INFORMATION:
Phone: 408 996-1010   Fax: 408 974-2483
Toll-Free: 800-692-7753
Address: One Apple Park Way, Cupertino, CA 95014 United States

SALARIES/BONUSES:
Top Exec. Salary: $3,000,000   Bonus: $
Second Exec. Salary: $1,019,231   Bonus: $

STOCK TICKER/OTHER:
Stock Ticker: AAPL
Employees: 132,000
Parent Company:

Exchange: NAS
Fiscal Year Ends: 09/30

OTHER THOUGHTS:
Estimated Female Officers or Directors:
Hot Spot for Advancement for Women/Minorities:

Ardent Leisure Group

NAIC Code: 713110

www.ardentleisure.com.au

TYPES OF BUSINESS:
Amusement and Theme Parks
Bowling Centers
Amusement Arcades

BRANDS/DIVISIONS/AFFILIATES:
Dreamworld
Tiger Island
WhiteWater World
Main Event Entertainment
SkyPoint

CONTACTS:
Note: Officers with more than one job title may be intentionally listed here more than once.

Chris Morris, CEO
John Osborne, CEO-Theme Parks
Darin Harper, CFO

GROWTH PLANS/SPECIAL FEATURES:

Ardent Leisure Group is an owner and operator of leisure assets. It invests in and operates leisure and entertainment businesses in Australia, New Zealand and the U.S. The operations of the firm are divided into three segments: Theme Parks, Indoor Entertainment and Attractions. The Theme Park segment is composed of two theme parks. Dreamworld in Gold Coast, Australia is Australia's largest theme park consisting of 50 rides and attractions, as well as wild life in 10 different worlds, including the world's largest interactive tiger facility, Tiger Island. Next door to Dreamworld is Ardent's second theme park, the water park WhiteWater World. The Indoor Entertainment unit currently consists of the firm's 39 Main Event Entertainment family entertainment centers. Main Event is a bowling anchored, entertainment business that also offers laser tag, high ropes adventure courses, billiards, video games and dining options for everyone. The Attractions segment consists of the SkyPoint Observation Deck of the Q1 Building in Surfers Paradise and the SkyPoint Climb, an external climb atop the Q1 Building. In May 2018, to better focus on its theme parks and Main Event assets, Ardent Leisure Group sold its bowling and arcade assets to The Entertainment and Education Group for approximately $122.6 million.

FINANCIAL DATA:
Note: Data for latest year may not have been available at press time.

In U.S. $	2018	2017	2016	2015	2014	2013
Revenue	295,938,500	348,937,900	465,637,900	416,316,100	349,795,400	314,118,300
R&D Expense						
Operating Income	2,412,948	3,648,147	53,533,950	47,144,260	50,356,620	43,189,240
Operating Margin %		1.04%	11.49%	11.32%	14.39%	13.74%
SGA Expense	140,847,800	166,036,600	209,068,900	186,826,900	156,375,700	142,689,700
Net Income	-63,539,550	-43,828,910	29,697,330	22,505,430	34,331,960	24,954,110
Operating Cash Flow						
Capital Expenditure	85,700,980	148,647,100	108,207,100	93,859,040	60,489,740	43,985,150
EBITDA	-66,534,020	-42,733,130	85,197,930	73,761,650	73,741,330	62,034,610
Return on Assets %		-5.86%	3.93%	3.47%	5.92%	4.81%
Return on Equity %		-10.86%	7.06%	5.92%	9.87%	7.96%
Debt to Equity		0.33	0.50	0.48	0.51	0.46

CONTACT INFORMATION:
Phone: 61 294093670 Fax: 61 294093679
Toll-Free:
Address: Level 16, 61 Lavender St., Milsons Point, NSW 2061 Australia

STOCK TICKER/OTHER:
Stock Ticker: ANRRF
Employees:
Parent Company:

Exchange: PINX
Fiscal Year Ends: 06/30

SALARIES/BONUSES:
Top Exec. Salary: $ Bonus: $
Second Exec. Salary: $ Bonus: $

OTHER THOUGHTS:
Estimated Female Officers or Directors:
Hot Spot for Advancement for Women/Minorities:

Aristocrat Leisure Limited

NAIC Code: 334111

www.aristocrat.com.au

TYPES OF BUSINESS:
Gambling Devices and Casino Equipment Manufacturing
Gaming Services
Gaming Management Systems

BRANDS/DIVISIONS/AFFILIATES:
Aristocrat Technologies Inc
Reel Power
Xtreme Mystery
Hyperlink
OZ Games Studio
Secret Sauce Studio
HRG
Biggest Little Studio

CONTACTS:
Note: Officers with more than one job title may be intentionally listed here more than once.

Trvor Croker, CEO
Rich Schneider, Chief Product Officer
Julie Cameron-Doe, CFO
Rich Schneider, Chief Prod. Officer
Mark Dunn, General Counsel
Craig Billings, Managing Dir.-Strategy & Bus. Dev.
Victor Blanco, Sr. VP-Platform Architecture
Atul Bali, Pres., Americas
Ian D. Blackburne, Chmn.
Trevor Croker, Managing Dir. Australia, New Zealand & Asia Pacific
Jason Walbridge, Chief Supply Officer

GROWTH PLANS/SPECIAL FEATURES:

Aristocrat Leisure Limited is a major manufacturer of gaming machines and their components, including games, systems, electronic tables and equipment. The firm supplies casinos and other customers worldwide with electronic gaming machines, interactive video terminal systems and casino management systems. Aristocrat also provides gaming services, including technical support, onsite preventative maintenance and spare parts and logistics service. Its products include: multiline games, the most traditional form of video reel games, which use combinations across lines to award wins; Power Pay, a game line offering ante/bet-style games and extra features; Reel Power & Xtra Reel Power, which allows players to purchase reels rather than lines; Stand Alone Progressive (SAP) and Double Stand Alone Progressive (DSAP) products, which combine base games with independent jackpot meters; Player's Choice Multigame, which offers four games and multiple denominations in one system; and specialty games, including the Bonus Bank product line. The firm also markets cabinet games, such as Pachislo machines (manufactured specifically for the Japanese market); and multi-station games. Hyperlink is the company's patented bonusing product, which links all electronic gaming machines to its progressive gaming platform. Aristocrat studios include: OZ Games Studio, which is structured to drive performance and realize opportunities across the global market; Secret Sauce Studio, which creates eye-popping content; HRG, which specializes in content for high-growth premium jackpot segments; Studio 6, located in Australia and creator of award-winning content; Studio 9, based in India; and Biggest Little Studio, based in Reno, Nevada. Aristocrat is headquartered in Australia, and operates in more than 90 countries and 200 jurisdictions worldwide.

FINANCIAL DATA:
Note: Data for latest year may not have been available at press time.

In U.S. $	2018	2017	2016	2015	2014	2013
Revenue	2,487,074,000	1,719,190,000	1,491,417,000	1,104,226,000	593,816,300	566,581,600
R&D Expense	289,777,900	188,047,400	167,589,200	134,082,500	91,181,950	83,297,140
Operating Income	290,863,900	82,323,270	-18,286,280	-100,458,900	-96,260,070	-90,125,420
Operating Margin %		4.78%	-1.22%	-9.09%	-16.21%	-15.90%
SGA Expense	454,529,600	572,409,500	534,996,200	475,125,100	297,652,900	281,791,500
Net Income	380,158,300	346,878,700	245,568,600	130,617,300	-11,510,550	75,106,850
Operating Cash Flow						
Capital Expenditure	189,238,400	150,143,600	134,940,100	97,866,600	63,182,940	31,301,760
EBITDA	962,096,300	752,539,800	621,242,900	336,133,300	87,388,780	135,740,900
Return on Assets %		15.76%	11.29%	8.60%	-1.65%	12.27%
Return on Equity %		40.89%	35.17%	22.96%	-3.02%	28.25%
Debt to Equity		0.89	1.19	1.93		0.62

CONTACT INFORMATION:
Phone: 61 290136000   Fax: 61 290136200
Toll-Free:
Address: 85 Epping Rd., Pinnacle Office Park, Bldg. A, North Ryde, NSW 2113 Australia

STOCK TICKER/OTHER:
Stock Ticker: ARLUF   Exchange: PINX
Employees: 2,274   Fiscal Year Ends: 12/31
Parent Company:

SALARIES/BONUSES:
Top Exec. Salary: $ Bonus: $
Second Exec. Salary: $ Bonus: $

OTHER THOUGHTS:
Estimated Female Officers or Directors: 3
Hot Spot for Advancement for Women/Minorities: Y

Sales, profits and employees may be estimates. Financial information, benefits and other data can change quickly and may vary from those stated here.

Ascential plc

NAIC Code: 511120

www.ascential.com/

TYPES OF BUSINESS:
Trade and Business Magazines and Web Sites
Brand Advisory

BRANDS/DIVISIONS/AFFILIATES:
WGSN
Cannes Lions
MediaLink
WARC
Money 20/20
Retail Week
Flywheel
Groundsure

CONTACTS:
Note: Officers with more than one job title may be intentionally listed here more than once.

Duncan Painter, CEO
Mandy Gradden, CFO
Sarah Kemp, Head-Press & PR
Andy Baker, Managing Dir.-Public Sector & Environment
Scott Forbes, Chmn.

GROWTH PLANS/SPECIAL FEATURES:

Ascential plc is a U.K.-based information company whose solutions enable businesses to make informed decisions concerning the development, promotion and marketing of their own products. The company operates from nearly 40 offices worldwide, serving customers in over 150 countries. Ascential's products and solutions are grouped into the categories of product design, marketing, sales and sector-specific intelligence. Product design encompasses the WGSN brand, which combines high-end technology and data science with human expertise to forecast trends and provide insight to customers, enabling them to design for future consumers. The marketing category helps customers create, execute and measure the effectiveness of marketing campaigns, and includes: Cannes Lions, offering digital solutions that enable inspiration and measurement in relation to campaign effectiveness; MediaLink, an advisory firm with a focus on media, marketing, advertising, entertainment, technology and finance; and WARC, which offers advertising best practice, evidence and insights for leading brands. The sales category offers eCommerce data analytics and intelligence solutions for maximizing distribution opportunities. This division's solutions include: Edge by Ascential, offering actionable sales data, insights and advisory services for global eCommerce brands and retailers; Money 20/20, which enables payments and financial services at global events; World Retail Congress, a three-day event for global retailers to meet, share insight and form business connections; Retail Week, which explains digital transformation, benchmarking performance, connecting with the right partners and inspiring business leaders; and Flywheel, offering customers Amazon-specific software, tools and expertise to drive sales and brand performance across Amazon platforms by directly actioning solutions for clients. Last, the sector-specific intelligence category provides environmental, construction and political intelligence for enabling informed and accurate decisions through the Groundsure, Glenigan and DeHavilland brands. During 2018, Ascential sold its exhibitions business, and acquired WARC, Flywheel and Brand View Limited (offering price analytics).

FINANCIAL DATA:
Note: Data for latest year may not have been available at press time.

In U.S. $	2018	2017	2016	2015	2014	2013
Revenue		507,001,000	368,556,000	380,374,000	475,726,145	412,894,390
R&D Expense						
Operating Income						
Operating Margin %						
SGA Expense						
Net Income		24,284,200	19,190,500	-37,451,300	32,960,700	2,278,390
Operating Cash Flow						
Capital Expenditure						
EBITDA						
Return on Assets %						
Return on Equity %						
Debt to Equity						

CONTACT INFORMATION:
Phone: 44-0207-5165000   Fax:
Toll-Free:
Address: The Prow, 1 Wilder Walk, London, W1B 5AP United Kingdom

SALARIES/BONUSES:
Top Exec. Salary: $ Bonus: $
Second Exec. Salary: $ Bonus: $

STOCK TICKER/OTHER:
Stock Ticker: ASCL
Employees: 1,736
Parent Company:

Exchange: London
Fiscal Year Ends: 03/31

OTHER THOUGHTS:
Estimated Female Officers or Directors: 3
Hot Spot for Advancement for Women/Minorities: Y

Sales, profits and employees may be estimates. Financial information, benefits and other data can change quickly and may vary from those stated here.

AT&T Inc

NAIC Code: 517110

www.att.com

TYPES OF BUSINESS:
Local Telephone Service
Wireless Telecommunications
Long-Distance Telephone Service
Corporate Telecom, Backbone & Wholesale Services
Internet Access
Entertainment & Television via Internet
Satellite TV
VOIP

BRANDS/DIVISIONS/AFFILIATES:
Home Box Office Inc (HBO)
Turner Broadcasting System Inc
Warner Bros Entertainment Inc
FiberTower Corp
Time Warner Inc

CONTACTS: Note: Officers with more than one job title may be intentionally listed here more than once.
Brian Lesser, CEO, Divisional
John Stankey, CEO, Divisional
John Donovan, CEO, Subsidiary
Lori Lee, CEO, Subsidiary
Randall Stephenson, CEO
John Stephens, CFO
David McAtee, General Counsel
David Huntley, Other Executive Officer
Robert Quinn, Senior Executive VP, Divisional
William Blase, Senior Executive VP, Divisional

GROWTH PLANS/SPECIAL FEATURES:

AT&T, Inc. is one of the world's largest providers of diversified telecommunications services. The company and its subsidiaries offers communications, digital entertainment services and products to consumers in the U.S., Mexico and Latin America, as well as to businesses and other providers of telecommunications services worldwide. AT&T also owns and operates three regional sports networks. Services and products include wireless communications, data/broadband and internet services, digital video services, local and long-distance telephone services, telecommunications equipment, managed networking and wholesale services. The company operates through four business segments: communication, generating revenues greater than $150 billion in 2017; media business, $31 billion; international, $8 billion; and advertising & analytics business. The communications segment provides mobile, broadband, video and other communications services to over 100 million U.S.-based consumers and nearly 3.5 million companies, ranging from the smallest business to nearly all the Fortune 1000, with highly secure, smart solutions. The media business segment consists of the operations of Home Box Office, Inc. (HBO); Turner Broadcasting System, Inc. (Turner); and Warner Bros Entertainment, Inc. Together these firms create premium content, operate one of the largest TV and film studios and own a vast library of entertainment. The international business provides mobile service in Mexico to consumers and businesses, plus pay-tv services across 11 countries in South America and the Caribbean. The advertising & analytics business segment provides marketers with advanced solutions using valuable customer insights from AT&T's TV, mobile and broadband services, combined with extensive ad inventory from Turner and AT&T's pay-tv services. In February 2018, the firm acquired FiberTower Corp., giving it millimeter wave spectrum. That June, it acquired media company Time Warner, Inc. In August of the same year, AT&T, to create a cybersecurity solutions business division, acquired AlienVault, Inc., a developer of commercial and open source solutions to manage cyber-attacks.

FINANCIAL DATA: Note: Data for latest year may not have been available at press time.

In U.S. $	2018	2017	2016	2015	2014	2013
Revenue		160,546,000,000	163,786,000,000	146,801,000,000	132,447,000,000	128,752,000,000
R&D Expense						
Operating Income		23,863,000,000	24,708,000,000	24,785,000,000	13,866,000,000	30,479,000,000
Operating Margin %		14.86%	15.08%	16.88%	10.46%	23.67%
SGA Expense		34,917,000,000	36,347,000,000	32,954,000,000	39,697,000,000	28,414,000,000
Net Income		29,450,000,000	12,976,000,000	13,345,000,000	6,224,000,000	18,249,000,000
Operating Cash Flow		39,151,000,000	39,344,000,000	35,880,000,000	31,338,000,000	34,796,000,000
Capital Expenditure		20,647,000,000	21,516,000,000	19,218,000,000	21,199,000,000	20,944,000,000
EBITDA		45,826,000,000	50,569,000,000	46,828,000,000	31,846,000,000	50,112,000,000
Return on Assets %		6.94%	3.21%	3.83%	2.18%	6.63%
Return on Equity %		22.31%	10.55%	12.76%	7.01%	19.90%
Debt to Equity		0.89	0.92	0.96	0.88	0.76

CONTACT INFORMATION:
Phone: 210 821-4105 Fax:
Toll-Free:
Address: 208 S. Akard St., Dallas, TX 75202 United States

STOCK TICKER/OTHER:
Stock Ticker: T
Employees: 273,210
Parent Company:

Exchange: NYS
Fiscal Year Ends: 12/31

SALARIES/BONUSES:
Top Exec. Salary: $1,800,000 Bonus: $
Second Exec. Salary: $1,035,833 Bonus: $

OTHER THOUGHTS:
Estimated Female Officers or Directors: 4
Hot Spot for Advancement for Women/Minorities: Y

Atari Interactive Inc

www.atari.com

NAIC Code: 511210G

TYPES OF BUSINESS:
Computer Software, Electronic Games, Apps & Entertainment
Educational Software
Apps
Game Consoles

BRANDS/DIVISIONS/AFFILIATES:
Atari SA
Asteroids
Centipede
Missile Command
Pong
RollerCoaster Tycoon
Atari Studios
Atari Licensing

CONTACTS: Note: Officers with more than one job title may be intentionally listed here more than once.
Frederic Chesnais, Pres.
Kristin Keller, General Counsel

GROWTH PLANS/SPECIAL FEATURES:
Atari Interactive, Inc., a subsidiary of French software publisher Atari SA, is a publisher and distributor of interactive entertainment. It publishes and distributes video game software for most major gaming consoles as well as personal computer (PC) platforms, including Microsoft and Sony consoles. It also publishes and sublicenses games for online, mobile and other evolving platforms. Atari's products extend across most major video game genres, including action, adventure, strategy, role-playing and racing. The company's products are based on intellectual properties that it has created internally and owns, or that have been licensed to it by third parties. Atari's properties include popular franchises such as Asteroids, Centipede, Missile Command, Pong and RollerCoaster Tycoon. Atari Studios works with broadcasters and content creators to bring Atari's games to life via television and digital media formats worldwide. Atari Licensing is a business line of Atari Games, exploiting the catalog of more than 200 games with partners and licensees. In October 2018, Atari announced its official affiliation with Nasdaq International under the symbol PONGF on the U.S. OTC market, an over-the-counter platform designed for non-U.S. companies.

FINANCIAL DATA: Note: Data for latest year may not have been available at press time.

In U.S. $	2018	2017	2016	2015	2014	2013
Revenue		17,542,260	14,352,760	8,657,219	3,759,056	1,366,929
R&D Expense		4,328,610	3,759,056	2,847,770	1,366,929	
Operating Income		9,682,416	455,643	1,366,929	3,645,145	683,465
Operating Margin %						
SGA Expense		6,948,558	6,037,272	4,556,432	1,480,840	1,480,840
Net Income		8,771,130	341,732	1,366,929	-2,847,770	-40,780,060
Operating Cash Flow		3,531,234	-569,554	-227,822	2,619,948	-2,733,859
Capital Expenditure		4,442,521	4,442,521	3,189,502		
EBITDA		10,821,520	2,392,127	3,189,502	5,809,450	-2,961,680
Return on Assets %						
Return on Equity %						
Debt to Equity						

CONTACT INFORMATION:
Phone: 212-726-6500 Fax: 212-726-6590
Toll-Free:
Address: 475 Park Avenue S., New York, NY 10016 United States

STOCK TICKER/OTHER:
Stock Ticker: PONGF
Employees: 679
Parent Company: Atari SA

Exchange: GREY
Fiscal Year Ends: 03/31

SALARIES/BONUSES:
Top Exec. Salary: $ Bonus: $
Second Exec. Salary: $ Bonus: $

OTHER THOUGHTS:
Estimated Female Officers or Directors: 1
Hot Spot for Advancement for Women/Minorities:

Audible Inc

NAIC Code: 454111

www.audible.com

TYPES OF BUSINESS:
Audio Books-Online Sales
Audio Programming Software
Time-Shifted Radio Programming
Digital Audio Players
Educational Audio Materials

BRANDS/DIVISIONS/AFFILIATES:
Amazon.com Inc
Audible.com
AudibleListener

CONTACTS: Note: Officers with more than one job title may be intentionally listed here more than once.
Donald R. Katz, CEO
Anthony Nash, CFO
Guy A. Story, Jr., Chief Scientist
Guy A. Story Jr., CTO
Beth Anderson, Exec. VP
Foy C. Sperring, Jr., Exec. VP-Customer Experience

GROWTH PLANS/SPECIAL FEATURES:
Audible, Inc., a subsidiary of Amazon.com, Inc., provides internet-delivered premium spoken audio content for playback on personal computers and mobile devices. The company offers a variety of software systems and audio programming software designed to download, store and play between 2 and 24 hours of content from its online store, Audible.com. Audible sells a wide array of audio content, including educational materials, humor, periodicals, fiction, nonfiction and time-shifted radio programming comprised of 150,000 different programs and 2,700 content providers. For an annual membership fee, the company's AudibleListener membership plans provide up to one free audiobook per month, two Audible originals, a 30% discount on additional purchases, exposure to periodic sales and member-only free content offerings. It also has partnerships with leading audiobook, magazine and newspaper publishers as well as broadcasters, business information providers and educational and cultural institutions. Audible.com features daily selected audio content from The Wall Street Journal and The New York Times, both available on a subscription basis. Other publications offered include Fast Company, Forbes, Harvard Business Review and Scientific American. In addition, the site offers a large collection of audiobook bestsellers and classics by authors such as Stephen King, James Patterson, William Shakespeare and Jane Austen as well as speeches, lectures and on-demand radio programs. Around 425,000 titles are available for purchase on its U.S., U.K., German, Australian and French websites.

The firm offers employees health insurance, a 401(k) savings plan and a stock ownership program.

FINANCIAL DATA: Note: Data for latest year may not have been available at press time.

In U.S. $	2018	2017	2016	2015	2014	2013
Revenue						
R&D Expense						
Operating Income						
Operating Margin %						
SGA Expense						
Net Income						
Operating Cash Flow						
Capital Expenditure						
EBITDA						
Return on Assets %						
Return on Equity %						
Debt to Equity						

CONTACT INFORMATION:
Phone: 973-820-0400 Fax:
Toll-Free: 888-283-5051
Address: 1 Washington Park, Fl. 16, Newark, NJ 07102 United States

SALARIES/BONUSES:
Top Exec. Salary: $ Bonus: $
Second Exec. Salary: $ Bonus: $

STOCK TICKER/OTHER:
Stock Ticker: Subsidiary Exchange:
Employees: 172 Fiscal Year Ends: 12/31
Parent Company: Amazon.com Inc

OTHER THOUGHTS:
Estimated Female Officers or Directors: 1
Hot Spot for Advancement for Women/Minorities: Y

Avid Technology Inc

NAIC Code: 511210F

www.avid.com

TYPES OF BUSINESS:
Computer Software, Multimedia, Graphics & Publishing
Digital Audio Equipment
Network & Storage Products
Asset Management Products
Musical Score Electronic Publishing Products

BRANDS/DIVISIONS/AFFILIATES:
Media Composer
Pro Tools
Avid NEXIS
MediaCentral
iNEWS
AirSpeed
Avid VENU
FastServe

CONTACTS:
Note: Officers with more than one job title may be intentionally listed here more than once.

Jeff Rosica, CEO
Kenneth Gayron, CFO
Nancy Hawthorne, Chairman of the Board
Jason Duva, Chief Administrative Officer
Dana Ruzicka, Other Executive Officer
Ryan Murray, Vice President, Divisional

GROWTH PLANS/SPECIAL FEATURES:

Avid Technology, Inc. develops, markets, sells and supports software and hardware for digital media content production, management and distribution. The firm provides an open platform for digital media, along with tools and workflow solutions that enable the creation, distribution and optimization of audio and video content. Digital media are video, audio or graphic elements in which the image, sound or picture is recorded and stored as digital values. Avid's products are used in production and post-production facilities; film studios; network, affiliate, independent and cable television stations; recording studios; live-sound performance venues; advertising agencies; government and educational institutions; corporate communications departments; and by independent video and audio creative professionals. Projects utilizing Avid products include feature films, television programming, live events, news broadcasts, sports productions, commercials, music, video and other digital media content. Avid Technology markets and sells its products and solutions through a combination of direct, indirect and digital sales channels. The firm's solutions include Media Composer, Pro Tools, Avid NEXIS, MediaCentral, iNEWS, AirSpeed, Avid VENU, FastServe, Maestro and PlayMaker, each of which are either trademarks or registered trademarks of Avid Technology or its subsidiaries. Based in Massachusetts, USA, the firm has offices in 22 countries and the ability to reach over 170 countries through its direct sales force and resellers. Sales to customers outside the U.S account for 62% of total net revenues.

The company offers its employees health care and life insurance; short- and long-term disability coverage; flexible spending accounts; a 401(k) plan; a stock purchase plan; and education assistance, employee assistance programs and an employee equipment p

FINANCIAL DATA:
Note: Data for latest year may not have been available at press time.

In U.S. $	2018	2017	2016	2015	2014	2013
Revenue		419,003,000	511,930,000	505,595,000	530,251,000	563,412,000
R&D Expense		68,212,000	81,564,000	95,898,000	90,390,000	95,249,000
Operating Income		12,305,000	76,852,000	13,278,000	19,534,000	30,138,000
Operating Margin %		2.93%	15.01%	2.62%	3.68%	5.34%
SGA Expense		160,149,000	171,809,000	196,620,000	214,230,000	211,468,000
Net Income		-13,555,000	48,219,000	2,480,000	14,728,000	21,153,000
Operating Cash Flow		8,936,000	-49,195,000	-34,026,000	-9,897,000	-9,145,000
Capital Expenditure		7,877,000	11,003,000	15,330,000	13,292,000	11,625,000
EBITDA		28,879,000	89,726,000	26,999,000	36,641,000	48,433,000
Return on Assets %		-5.59%	19.38%	1.12%	6.90%	7.98%
Return on Equity %						
Debt to Equity						

CONTACT INFORMATION:
Phone: 978 640-6789 Fax: 978 640-3116
Toll-Free:
Address: 75 Network Dr., Burlington, MA 01803 United States

SALARIES/BONUSES:
Top Exec. Salary: $700,000 Bonus: $
Second Exec. Salary: $450,000 Bonus: $

STOCK TICKER/OTHER:
Stock Ticker: AVID
Employees: 1,945
Parent Company:

Exchange: NAS
Fiscal Year Ends: 12/31

OTHER THOUGHTS:
Estimated Female Officers or Directors: 4
Hot Spot for Advancement for Women/Minorities: Y

Axel Springer SE

NAIC Code: 511110

www.axel-springer.de

TYPES OF BUSINESS:
Newspaper Publishers

BRANDS/DIVISIONS/AFFILIATES:
Business Insider
Auto Bild
Computer Bild
Axel Springer Digital Classifieds
Group Nine Media
POLITICO.se
Purplebricks
Homeday GmbH

CONTACTS:
Note: Officers with more than one job title may be intentionally listed here more than once.

Mathias Dopfner, CEO
Jan Bayer, Pres.- News Media
Julian Deutz, CFO
Andreas Wiele, Pres.-Mktg.
Stephanie Caspar, Pres.-Technology and Data
Jan Bayer, Pres., WELT Group & Printing
Andreas Wiele, Pres., BILD Group & Magazines
Mathias Dopfner, Chmn.
Ralph Buchi, Pres., Intl Div.

GROWTH PLANS/SPECIAL FEATURES:

Axel Springer SE is a German integrated multimedia company producing a range of print and digital media. The firm's activities are divided into three primary segments: news media, marketing media and classified ads media. The news media segment targets paying readers that use digital media offerings, as well as printed newspapers and magazines. This division's content covers news, automobiles, sports, computers, consumer electronics and lifestyle. Just a few of Axel Springer's many publications include: Business Insider, covering business news in the U.S. and Germany; Auto Bild, an automobile magazine with a leading circulation in Europe; Computer Bild, published in nine European countries, is a best-selling computer magazine; and POLITICO.se, covers European politics and policymaking. The marketing media segment combines all the business models whose revenues are primarily generated by advertising clients in reach-based and performance-based marketing. Reach-based clients include MeinProspekt, idealo, kaufDA and Smarthouse; and performance clients include Awin. The classified ads media segment covers all the business models which generate revenue through job and real estate advertising clients. This includes the online classified ad portals bundled together in Axel Springer Digital Classifieds such as SeLoger, Immonet, Immoweb.be, StepStone, Totaljobs and meinestadt.de. In 2018, Axel Springer acquired a minority stake of 11.5% in Purplebricks, a digital real estate platform; Universum, a Swedish employee branding specialist, in April 2018; and 22% of Homeday GmbH, a digital real estate platform in Germany, in conjunction with Purplebricks. In April 2018, Axel Springer sold its 78% stake in aufeminin group to Television Francasise 1 S.A.

FINANCIAL DATA:
Note: Data for latest year may not have been available at press time.

In U.S. $	2018	2017	2016	2015	2014	2013
Revenue		4,058,185,000	3,748,006,000	3,753,246,000	3,460,496,000	3,191,210,000
R&D Expense						
Operating Income		374,880,400	355,743,400	357,907,700	345,491,400	274,638,900
Operating Margin %		7.89%	8.42%	6.45%	6.45%	10.67%
SGA Expense		364,628,400	336,036,800	340,137,600	198,546,500	184,535,500
Net Income		393,561,800	486,740,800	287,510,800	911,058,400	224,518,100
Operating Cash Flow		558,960,200	408,711,900	421,014,200	410,990,100	482,298,200
Capital Expenditure		228,846,800	178,612,100	149,678,800	109,582,200	112,088,200
EBITDA		882,125,100	954,116,700	771,859,500	693,261,000	534,469,400
Return on Assets %		5.35%	6.59%	4.18%	15.48%	4.11%
Return on Equity %		15.33%	19.96%	12.41%	41.28%	10.49%
Debt to Equity		0.46	0.56	0.57	0.52	0.38

CONTACT INFORMATION:
Phone: 49-30-25910 Fax:
Toll-Free:
Address: Axel-Springer-Strasse 65, Berlin, 10888 Germany

SALARIES/BONUSES:
Top Exec. Salary: $ Bonus: $
Second Exec. Salary: $ Bonus: $

STOCK TICKER/OTHER:
Stock Ticker: AXELF
Employees: 15,836
Parent Company:
Exchange: GREY
Fiscal Year Ends: 12/31

OTHER THOUGHTS:
Estimated Female Officers or Directors: 1
Hot Spot for Advancement for Women/Minorities:

Sales, profits and employees may be estimates. Financial information, benefits and other data can change quickly and may vary from those stated here.

Axios Media Inc (AXIOS)

www.axios.com

NAIC Code: 519130

TYPES OF BUSINESS:
News Website

BRANDS/DIVISIONS/AFFILIATES:

GROWTH PLANS/SPECIAL FEATURES:
Axios Media, Inc. is a media company delivering news and analysis in shareable ways. The firm offers a mix of original and narrated coverage of media trends, technology, business and politics via voice and smart capabilities on an innovative web and mobile platform called AXIOS. The company's social videos and live streams focus on brevity so that big executives can quickly learn everything they need to know about the news in just a few minutes. Articles feature easy-to-scan bullet points, and posts are typically shorter than 300 words. Axios also sends daily and weekly newsletters. Founded in 2016, Axios Media plans to have 150 employees by the end of 2018, and launch new verticals and a paywall. In November 2017, the firm announced that it had raised $20 million to fund an increase of both its staff and its operations, with the round being led by Greycroft Partners and Lerer Hippeau Ventures. NBCUniversal, Emerson Collective, Greg Penner and WndrCo also invested.

CONTACTS:
Note: Officers with more than one job title may be intentionally listed here more than once.

Jim Vandehei, CEO
Roy Schwartz, Pres.
Abby Clawson, VP-Finance & Acctg.

FINANCIAL DATA:
Note: Data for latest year may not have been available at press time.

In U.S. $	2018	2017	2016	2015	2014	2013
Revenue						
R&D Expense						
Operating Income						
Operating Margin %						
SGA Expense						
Net Income						
Operating Cash Flow						
Capital Expenditure						
EBITDA						
Return on Assets %						
Return on Equity %						
Debt to Equity						

CONTACT INFORMATION:
Phone: 703-291-3600 Fax:
Toll-Free:
Address: 3100 Clarendon Blvd., Ste. 200, Arlington, VA 22201 United States

SALARIES/BONUSES:
Top Exec. Salary: $ Bonus: $
Second Exec. Salary: $ Bonus: $

STOCK TICKER/OTHER:
Stock Ticker: Private
Employees: 150
Parent Company:

Exchange:
Fiscal Year Ends:

OTHER THOUGHTS:
Estimated Female Officers or Directors:
Hot Spot for Advancement for Women/Minorities:

Sales, profits and employees may be estimates. Financial information, benefits and other data can change quickly and may vary from those stated here.

Barnes & Noble Inc

NAIC Code: 451211

www.barnesandnobleinc.com

TYPES OF BUSINESS:
Book Stores
Music & Software Sales
In-Store Cafes
Online Sales
Book Publishing
Book Distribution
eBooks and eBook Readers
College Book Stores

BRANDS/DIVISIONS/AFFILIATES:
Barnes & Noble Booksellers
Sterling Publishing Co Inc
NOOK
www.barnesandnoble.com

CONTACTS:
Note: Officers with more than one job title may be intentionally listed here more than once.

Demos Parneros, CEO
Allen Lindstrom, CFO
Peter Herpich, Chief Accounting Officer
William Wood, Chief Information Officer
Leonard Riggio, Founder
Bradley Feuer, General Counsel
Frederic Argir, Other Executive Officer
Mary Keating, Senior VP, Divisional
Michelle Smith, Vice President, Divisional
Carl Hauch, Vice President, Divisional

GROWTH PLANS/SPECIAL FEATURES:

Barnes & Noble, Inc. (B&N) is one of the largest booksellers in the U.S. The company operates approximately 630 bookstores in 50 states, maintains a B&N eCommerce site, develops digital reading products and operates an immense digital bookstore. The firm's retail segment is comprised of its bookstores, which are branded under the Barnes & Noble Booksellers trade name. This segment also includes Sterling Publishing Co., Inc., a general trade book publishing firm. NOOK represents B&N's digital business, offering books and magazines for sale and consumption online; NOOK reading devices; and NOOK reading software for iOS, Android and Windows. B&N's principal business is the sale of trade books, generally hardcover and paperback consumer titles; mass market paperbacks, such as mystery, romance, science fiction and other popular fiction; children's books; eBooks/digital content; NOOK and related accessories; bargain books; magazines; gifts; cafe products and services; educational toys and games; music and movies; and the www.barnesandnoble.com website. The company also offers textbook options through its website, including new, used, digital and rental.

Employee benefits include medical and dental insurance, a flexible spending account, continuing education programs, merchandise discounts and a 401(k) savings plan.

FINANCIAL DATA:
Note: Data for latest year may not have been available at press time.

In U.S. $	2018	2017	2016	2015	2014	2013
Revenue	3,662,280,000	3,894,558,000	4,163,844,000	6,069,497,000	6,381,357,000	6,839,005,000
R&D Expense						
Operating Income	5,754,000	54,308,000	14,656,000	133,173,000	34,192,000	-220,004,000
Operating Margin %	0.15	1.39%	.35%	2.19%	.53%	-3.21%
SGA Expense	999,109,000	1,040,007,000	1,176,778,000	1,545,152,000	1,606,936,000	1,675,376,000
Net Income	-125,480,000	22,023,000	-24,446,000	36,596,000	-47,268,000	-157,806,000
Operating Cash Flow	37,106,000	145,243,000	114,044,000	55,908,000	319,956,000	117,391,000
Capital Expenditure	87,651,000	96,258,000	94,274,000	143,257,000	134,981,000	165,835,000
EBITDA	-19,565,000	174,145,000	153,794,000	332,825,000	256,956,000	12,600,000
Return on Assets %	-6.81%	1.11%	-1.34%	.37%	-1.30%	-4.20%
Return on Equity %	-25.46%	3.73%	-3.93%	1.37%	-6.88%	-21.59%
Debt to Equity	0.38	0.11	0.07			0.28

CONTACT INFORMATION:
Phone: 212 633-3300   Fax: 212 366-5186
Toll-Free:
Address: 122 Fifth Ave., New York, NY 10011 United States

SALARIES/BONUSES:
Top Exec. Salary: $398,077   Bonus: $1,050,000
Second Exec. Salary: $560,000   Bonus: $377,775

STOCK TICKER/OTHER:
Stock Ticker: BKS   Exchange: NYS
Employees: 20,000   Fiscal Year Ends: 04/30
Parent Company:

OTHER THOUGHTS:
Estimated Female Officers or Directors: 3
Hot Spot for Advancement for Women/Minorities: Y

Beasley Broadcast Group Inc

www.bbgi.com

NAIC Code: 515112

TYPES OF BUSINESS:
Radio Station Owner/Operator
Radio Broadcasting
Online Media
Web Development

BRANDS/DIVISIONS/AFFILIATES:
iRadioNow
Greater Media Inc
Beasley Media Group 2 Inc

CONTACTS:
Note: Officers with more than one job title may be intentionally listed here more than once.

Caroline Beasley, CEO
Marie Tedesco, CFO
Brian Beasley, Director
George Beasley, Founder
Bruce Beasley, President
Joyce Fitch, Secretary
Allen Shaw, Vice Chairman of the Board

GROWTH PLANS/SPECIAL FEATURES:

Beasley Broadcast Group, Inc. (BBG) is a radio broadcasting company that operates radio stations throughout the U.S. The company owns or operates 63 radio stations (45 FM and 18 AM) in 15 radio markets including Atlanta and Augusta, Georgia; Boston, Massachusetts; Charlotte and Fayetteville, North Carolina; Fort Myers-Naples, West Palm Beach-Boca Raton and Tampa-Saint Petersburg, Florida; Las Vegas, Nevada; Philadelphia, Pennsylvania; Middlesex, Monmouth and Morristown, New Jersey; Detroit, Michigan; and Wilmington, Delaware. The company's business strategy is to secure and maintain a leadership position in the markets it serves by developing market-leading clusters of radio stations in each individual market. The company's radio stations program a variety of formats, including rock, country, Hispanic, reggae, oldies, contemporary hit radio, sports and talk. A number of BBG stations transmit digital and analog broadcasts using HD Radio. BBG's iRadioNow app allows listeners to tune in to Beasley stations on mobile devices via mobile app stores. The company fully owns and operates its subsidiary, Beasley Media Group 2, Inc.

FINANCIAL DATA:
Note: Data for latest year may not have been available at press time.

In U.S. $	2018	2017	2016	2015	2014	2013
Revenue		232,179,500	136,665,300	105,946,700	58,705,900	104,905,700
R&D Expense						
Operating Income		34,422,480	23,423,280	17,518,670	7,279,579	26,830,630
Operating Margin %		15.60%	17.13%	16.53%	12.40%	25.57%
SGA Expense		15,832,410	10,303,500	8,983,860	8,923,117	8,624,395
Net Income		87,131,170	47,488,410	6,362,322	39,999,370	11,546,260
Operating Cash Flow		28,021,060	17,151,100	14,371,760	16,913,700	19,913,680
Capital Expenditure		5,326,717	3,435,832	2,520,259	3,202,388	2,901,631
EBITDA		63,466,760	68,616,530	17,805,900	8,381,340	27,880,240
Return on Assets %		13.23%	9.76%	2.02%	13.78%	4.41%
Return on Equity %		35.66%	28.26%	4.81%	35.68%	13.07%
Debt to Equity		0.74	1.22	0.64	0.72	1.09

CONTACT INFORMATION:
Phone: 239 263-5000 Fax: 941 263-8191
Toll-Free:
Address: 3033 Riviera Dr., Ste. 200, Naples, FL 34103 United States

STOCK TICKER/OTHER:
Stock Ticker: BBGI
Employees: 1,406
Parent Company:

Exchange: NAS
Fiscal Year Ends: 12/31

SALARIES/BONUSES:
Top Exec. Salary: $749,175 Bonus: $
Second Exec. Salary: $739,084 Bonus: $

OTHER THOUGHTS:
Estimated Female Officers or Directors: 6
Hot Spot for Advancement for Women/Minorities: Y

Beat Holdings Limited

NAIC Code: 511120

beatholdings.com

TYPES OF BUSINESS:
Financial Data Publishing
Education Programs
Agricultural Research & Information
Publishing

BRANDS/DIVISIONS/AFFILIATES:
Xinhua Mobile
GINSMS Inc

CONTACTS:
Note: Officers with more than one job title may be intentionally listed here more than once.
Lian Yih Hann, CEO
Lian Yih Hann, Chmn.

GROWTH PLANS/SPECIAL FEATURES:
Beat Holdings Limited is a multi-disciplinary group primarily invested in social-impact sectors throughout China. The firm's products and devices in the areas of developing and operating application software for smartphones, telecom software platforms, global messaging gateways and mobile advertising platforms, as well as health-related wearable devices. The firm's business services include the operations of Xinhua Mobile and GINSMS, Inc. Xinhua Mobile develops and distributes innovative software products and services for smartphones, telecom software platforms and mobile advertising platforms. It is engaged in licensing intellectual properties, investing in companies with undervalued IP assets. Xinhua Mobile also provides cloud-based applications in relation to short message service (SMS). GINSMS develops and distributes proprietary intelligent routing algorithm that assures reliable and cost-efficient delivery of SMS to mobile subscribers. Its application-to-peer SMS services are commonly used for customer relationship management, promotional campaigns, pushed content services, interactive services and other services such as inquiries and searches. GINSMS serves more than 200 mobile operators worldwide.

FINANCIAL DATA:
Note: Data for latest year may not have been available at press time.

In U.S. $	2018	2017	2016	2015	2014	2013
Revenue		10,109,500	7,231,370	4,806,670	3,294,240	4,869,080
R&D Expense						
Operating Income						
Operating Margin %						
SGA Expense						
Net Income		1,260,360	-3,565,780	-4,177,960	-2,802,580	-5,600,900
Operating Cash Flow						
Capital Expenditure						
EBITDA						
Return on Assets %						
Return on Equity %						
Debt to Equity						

CONTACT INFORMATION:
Phone: 852-3196-3939   Fax: 852-2541-8266
Toll-Free:
Address: 199 Des Voeux Rd. Central, Ste. 2103, Infinttus Plaza, Hong Kong, Hong Kong

STOCK TICKER/OTHER:
Stock Ticker: 9399
Employees: 51
Parent Company:

Exchange: Tokyo
Fiscal Year Ends: 12/31

SALARIES/BONUSES:
Top Exec. Salary: $ Bonus: $
Second Exec. Salary: $ Bonus: $

OTHER THOUGHTS:
Estimated Female Officers or Directors:
Hot Spot for Advancement for Women/Minorities:

Sales, profits and employees may be estimates. Financial information, benefits and other data can change quickly and may vary from those stated here.

Berkshire Hathaway Inc

www.berkshirehathaway.com

NAIC Code: 524126

TYPES OF BUSINESS:
Insurance--Property & Casualty, Specialty, Surety
Retail Operations
Foodservice Operations
Building Products & Services
Apparel & Footwear
Technology Training
Manufactured Housing & RVs
Business Jet Flexible Ownership Services

BRANDS/DIVISIONS/AFFILIATES:
General Re Corporation
GEICO Corporation
Berkshire Hathaway Reinsurance Group
Berkshire Hathaway Primary Group
Clayton Homes Inc
Acme Building Brands
FlightSafety International Inc
Borsheim Jewelry Company Inc

CONTACTS: Note: Officers with more than one job title may be intentionally listed here more than once.
Warren Buffett, CEO
Marc Hamburg, CFO
Daniel Jaksich, Chief Accounting Officer
Charles Munger, Director

GROWTH PLANS/SPECIAL FEATURES:
Berkshire Hathaway, Inc. is a holding company that owns subsidiaries engaged in diverse business activities, most importantly insurance and reinsurance. Berkshire provides property and casualty insurance and reinsurance, as well as life, accident and health reinsurance, through U.S. and foreign businesses. The company conducts its insurance underwriting business through three subsidiary divisions. First, GEICO Corporation mainly provides private passenger auto insurance to individuals in all 50 U.S. states and Washington, D.C. Second, Berkshire Hathaway Reinsurance Group underwrites excess-of-loss and quota-share reinsurance for insurers and reinsurers. Third, Berkshire Hathaway Primary Group offers insurance for property and casualty. The company's financial subsidiaries include Clayton Homes, Inc., a manufactured housing company; XTRA Corporation, a provider of transportation equipment leases; and CORT Business Services Corporation, a furniture rental company. Berkshire's apparel and footwear businesses include Fruit of the Loom, Russell, Vanity Fair, Garan, Fechheimer Brothers, H.H. Brown Shoe Company, Brooks Sports and Justin Brands. The firm manufactures and distributes building products through Acme Building Brands, Benjamin Moore & Co., Johns Manville, Shaw Industries, Duracell Company and MiTek Industries. Subsidiary FlightSafety International, Inc. provides training to aircraft and ship pilots, while NetJets, Inc. offers fractional ownership programs for aircraft. In addition, subsidiary International Dairy Queen services approximately 6,800 DQ Grill and Chill, Dairy Queen and Orange Julius stores. Borsheim Jewelry Company, Inc. is a retailer of fine jewelry, watches, crystal, china, stemware, flatware, gifts and collectibles. Other non-insurance operations include grocery and foodservice distribution, furniture retailing, carpet manufacturing, utilities and energy, newspapers, cleaning products, confectioneries, agricultural equipment, kitchen tools and recreational vehicles.

FINANCIAL DATA: Note: Data for latest year may not have been available at press time.

In U.S. $	2018	2017	2016	2015	2014	2013
Revenue		242,137,000,000	223,604,000,000	210,821,000,000	194,673,000,000	182,150,000,000
R&D Expense						
Operating Income						
Operating Margin %						
SGA Expense		18,181,000,000	18,217,000,000	15,309,000,000	13,721,000,000	11,917,000,000
Net Income		44,940,000,000	24,074,000,000	24,083,000,000	19,872,000,000	19,476,000,000
Operating Cash Flow		45,776,000,000	32,535,000,000	31,491,000,000	32,010,000,000	27,704,000,000
Capital Expenditure		11,708,000,000	12,954,000,000	16,082,000,000	15,185,000,000	11,087,000,000
EBITDA						
Return on Assets %		6.79%	4.10%	4.46%	3.93%	4.26%
Return on Equity %		14.23%	8.94%	9.71%	8.60%	9.51%
Debt to Equity		0.22	0.35	0.32	0.33	0.32

CONTACT INFORMATION:
Phone: 402 346-1400   Fax: 402 346-3375
Toll-Free:
Address: 3555 Farnam St., Omaha, NE 68131 United States

STOCK TICKER/OTHER:
Stock Ticker: BRK.A
Employees: 377,000
Parent Company:

Exchange: NYS
Fiscal Year Ends: 12/31

SALARIES/BONUSES:
Top Exec. Salary: $1,775,000   Bonus: $500,000
Second Exec. Salary: $100,000   Bonus: $

OTHER THOUGHTS:
Estimated Female Officers or Directors:
Hot Spot for Advancement for Women/Minorities:

Sales, profits and employees may be estimates. Financial information, benefits and other data can change quickly and may vary from those stated here.

Bertelsmann SE & Co KGaA

NAIC Code: 515120

www.bertelsmann.com

TYPES OF BUSINESS:
Television Broadcasting
Radio Broadcasting
Magazine & Newspaper Publishing
Book Publishing
e-Commerce
Music Publishing
Print & Media Services
Book & Music Clubs

BRANDS/DIVISIONS/AFFILIATES:
RTL Group
Arvato Bertelsmann
Gruner + Jahr
Penguin Random House
BMG

CONTACTS:
Note: Officers with more than one job title may be intentionally listed here more than once.

Thomas Rabe, CEO
Bernd Hirsch, CFO
Immanuel Hermreck, Chief Human Resources Officer
Thomas Hesse, Pres., Corp. Dev. & New Bus.
Karin Schlautmann, Dir.-Corp. Comm.
Henrik Pahis, Sr. VP-Investor Rel.
Roger Schweitzer, Exec. VP-Treasury & Finance
Julia Jakel, CEO-Gruner + Jahr AG
Anke Schaferkordt, CEO-RTL Group
Markus Dohle, CEO-Penguin Random House
Bertram Stausberg, CEO-Be Printers
Annabelle Yu Long, Dir.-Bertelsmann China & Asia Investment

GROWTH PLANS/SPECIAL FEATURES:

Bertelsmann SE & Co KGaA is a leading private media company operating in more than 50 countries worldwide. Its global reach encompasses television and radio, magazines and newspapers, book publishers, professional information, print and media services, book and music clubs and e-commerce media. Each of the firm's primary subsidiaries handles a different aspect of media. Subsidiaries include RTL Group, Arvato Bertelsmann, Gruner + Jahr, Penguin Random House and BMG. RTL Group is a broadcasting and production company that owns and operates 56 television channels and 31 radio stations, as well as production companies. The firm produces, licenses and distributes television content. Arvato is an internationally-networked outsourcing provider. It designs and implements custom-tailored solutions for all kinds of business processes along integrated service chains, including data management, customer care, customer relations management services, supply chain management, digital distribution, financial services and individualized IT services. Gruner + Jahr has approximately 500 media activities in over 20 countries; professional websites; and printing operations in the U.S., China and Europe. Penguin Random House, held in tandem with Pearson PLC (25% stake), is one of the world's largest book publishing groups and publishes authors such as Dan Brown, John Grisham and Danielle Steel. BMG is a music publishing company, representing 2.5 million songs and recordings. In addition to its subsidiaries, Bertelsmann operates three divisions: printing, a market leader in Europe, and converges offset and gravure printing technology; education, offering digital education and service offerings in the health and technology sectors; and investments, which bundles Bertelsmann's shares in startups worldwide, and is focused on the growth regions of Brazil, China and India, as well as the U.S. and Europe.

The company offers its employees medical, dental and vision coverage; an employee assistance program; an employee discount program; life insurance; an employee health program; and tuition assistance.

FINANCIAL DATA:
Note: Data for latest year may not have been available at press time.

In U.S. $	2018	2017	2016	2015	2014	2013
Revenue		20,591,300,000	17,860,700,000	17,857,402,800	18,024,299,025	22,599,660,000
R&D Expense						
Operating Income						
Operating Margin %						
SGA Expense						
Net Income		1,435,040,000	1,198,090,000	883,854,520	619,365,717	1,202,000,000
Operating Cash Flow						
Capital Expenditure						
EBITDA						
Return on Assets %						
Return on Equity %						
Debt to Equity						

CONTACT INFORMATION:
Phone: 49-5241-80-0
Fax: 49-5241-80-9662
Toll-Free:
Address: Carl-Bertelsmann-Strasse 270, Gutersloh, D-33311 Germany

STOCK TICKER/OTHER:
Stock Ticker: BTG4
Employees: 119,000
Parent Company:

Exchange: Frankfurt
Fiscal Year Ends: 12/31

SALARIES/BONUSES:
Top Exec. Salary: $
Bonus: $
Second Exec. Salary: $
Bonus: $

OTHER THOUGHTS:
Estimated Female Officers or Directors: 6
Hot Spot for Advancement for Women/Minorities: Y

Best Buy Co Inc

NAIC Code: 443142

www.bestbuy.com

TYPES OF BUSINESS:
Consumer Electronics Stores
Retail Music & Video Sales
Personal Computers
Office Supplies
Cell Phones and Accessories
Appliances
Cameras
Consumer Electronics Installation & Service

BRANDS/DIVISIONS/AFFILIATES:
bestbuy.com
Best Buy Direct
Best Buy Express
Geek Squad
Magnolia Home Theater
Pacific Kitchen and Home
bestbuy.ca
bestbuy.com.mx

CONTACTS:
Note: Officers with more than one job title may be intentionally listed here more than once.

Hubert Joly, CEO
Corie Barry, CFO
Mathew Watson, Chief Accounting Officer
Michael Mohan, Chief Marketing Officer
Keith Nelsen, General Counsel
Asheesh Saksena, Other Executive Officer
Kamy Scarlett, Other Executive Officer
Trish Walker, President, Divisional

GROWTH PLANS/SPECIAL FEATURES:
Best Buy Co., Inc. is a leading provider of technology products, services and solutions. The company offers these products and solutions through Best Buy stores, Geek Squad agents, eCommerce channels and mobile apps. Retail operations are located in the U.S., Canada and Mexico. Best Buy Co. operates its business through two segments: domestic and international. The domestic segment is comprised of the U.S. operations, including brand names such as Best Buy, bestbuy.com, Best Buy Mobile, Best Buy Direct, Best Buy Express, Geek Squad, Magnolia Home Theater and Pacific Kitchen and Home. In March 2018, the company announced plans to close all 257 Best Buy Mobile stand-alone stores in the U.S., with the majority being closed by the end of 2019. The international segment is comprised of all operations in Canada and Mexico, including brand names such as Best Buy, Best Buy Express, Best Buy Mobile, Geek Squad and the domain names bestbuy.ca and bestbuy.com.mx. Both segment's development of merchandise and service offerings, pricing and promotions, procurement and supply chain, online and mobile application operations, marketing and advertising and labor deployment across all channels are centrally managed. The company has field operations that support retail teams from corporate as well as regional office locations. Best Buy's merchandise and services consist of the following: consumer electronics, including digital imaging, health/fitness, home automation, home theater and portable audio devices; computing and mobile phones, including computers, laptops, tablets, eReaders, mobile phones, networking and wearables; entertainment, including drones, gaming hardware/software, movies, music, technology toys, virtual reality and other software; appliances, including dishwashers, laundry, ovens, refrigerators, blenders, coffee makers and much more; and services, including consultation, delivery, design, educational classes, installation, memberships, protection plans, repair, set-up and tech support. In August 2018, the firm acquired GreatCall, Inc., maker of senior-focused mobile phones, for $800 million.

Employee benefits include medical, dental, vision, life and disability insurance; 401(k); and various assistance programs.

FINANCIAL DATA:
Note: Data for latest year may not have been available at press time.

In U.S. $	2018	2017	2016	2015	2014	2013
Revenue	42,151,000,000	39,403,000,000	39,528,000,000	40,339,000,000	42,410,000,000	45,085,000,000
R&D Expense						
Operating Income	1,853,000,000	1,893,000,000	1,573,000,000	1,455,000,000	1,299,000,000	1,147,000,000
Operating Margin %	4.39	4.80%	3.97%	3.60%	3.06%	
SGA Expense	8,023,000,000	7,547,000,000	7,618,000,000	7,592,000,000	8,391,000,000	9,502,000,000
Net Income	1,000,000,000	1,228,000,000	897,000,000	1,233,000,000	532,000,000	-441,000,000
Operating Cash Flow	2,141,000,000	2,545,000,000	1,322,000,000	1,935,000,000	1,094,000,000	1,454,000,000
Capital Expenditure	688,000,000	582,000,000	649,000,000	561,000,000	547,000,000	705,000,000
EBITDA	2,575,000,000	2,542,000,000	2,047,000,000	2,133,000,000	1,903,000,000	758,000,000
Return on Assets %	7.43%	8.97%	6.23%	8.42%	3.79%	
Return on Equity %	24.03%	27.02%	19.14%	27.45%	13.34%	
Debt to Equity	0.22	0.28	0.30	0.31	0.40	

CONTACT INFORMATION:
Phone: 612 291-1000 Fax: 612 292-4001
Toll-Free:
Address: 7601 Penn Ave. S., Richfield, MN 55423 United States

SALARIES/BONUSES:
Top Exec. Salary: $1,286,058   Bonus: $
Second Exec. Salary: $866,346   Bonus: $

STOCK TICKER/OTHER:
Stock Ticker: BBY   Exchange: NYS
Employees: 125,000   Fiscal Year Ends: 02/28
Parent Company:

OTHER THOUGHTS:
Estimated Female Officers or Directors: 5
Hot Spot for Advancement for Women/Minorities: Y

Sales, profits and employees may be estimates. Financial information, benefits and other data can change quickly and may vary from those stated here.

BioWare Corp

www.bioware.com

NAIC Code: 511210G

TYPES OF BUSINESS:
Computer Software, Electronic Games, Apps & Entertainment
E-commerce
Apps

BRANDS/DIVISIONS/AFFILIATES:
Electronic Arts Inc
Baldur's Gate
Neverwinter Nights
Dragon Age
BioWare Odyssey Engine
StarWars: The Old Republic-Knights of the Eternal
Mass Effect: Andromeda
Anthem

CONTACTS:
Note: Officers with more than one job title may be intentionally listed here more than once.
Andrew Wilson, CEO-Electronic Arts
Greg Zeschuk, Pres.
Greg Zeschuk, Gen. Mgr.-BioWare Austin

GROWTH PLANS/SPECIAL FEATURES:

BioWare Corp., a division of Electronic Arts, Inc., is an international interactive entertainment software company. BioWare specializes in developing multiplatform, role-playing, massively multiplayer online (MMO) and strategy games for personal computers, online platforms and video game consoles. The firm's popular Baldur's Gate game was followed by Baldur's Gate: Tales of the Sword Coast, Baldur's Gate II: Shadows of Amn, Baldur's Gate II: Throne of Bhaal, Baldur's Gate: Dark Alliance, Baldur's Gate: Dark Alliance II, Baldur's Gate: Enhanced Edition, Baldur's Gate II: Enhanced Edition and Baldur's Gate: Siege of Dragonspear. Other titles the company has released include Neverwinter Nights, Jade Empire, Mass Effect and Star Wars: Knights of the Old Republic (KOTOR). The firm also produces the critically-acclaimed Dragon Age game series, Dragon Age: Origins, Dragon Age 2 and Dragon Age Inquisition as well as the science fiction role playing game (RPG) trilogy, Mass Effect. BioWare licenses its game engine technology. Games including Planescape: Torment and the Icewind Dale series were developed using BioWare's Infinity Engine. Neverwinter Nights 2 was powered by its Aurora Engine. Star Wars: Knights of the Old Republic 2: The Sith Lords was made with the BioWare Odyssey Engine. Mass Effect: Andromeda was released in 2017 as a RPG; and Anthem, an action role-playing video game (ARPG), is scheduled for an early-2019 release. BioWare operates its own eCommerce site, www.biowarestore.com.

Parent EA Games offers employees an employee stock purchase plan; an employee assistance program; spot stock awards; education assistance; life, health care and business travel accident coverage; onsite daycare; company car options; gym and sports facilit

FINANCIAL DATA:
Note: Data for latest year may not have been available at press time.

In U.S. $	2018	2017	2016	2015	2014	2013
Revenue						
R&D Expense						
Operating Income						
Operating Margin %						
SGA Expense						
Net Income						
Operating Cash Flow						
Capital Expenditure						
EBITDA						
Return on Assets %						
Return on Equity %						
Debt to Equity						

CONTACT INFORMATION:
Phone: 780-430-0164 Fax: 780-439-6374
Toll-Free:
Address: 200, 4445 Calgary Trail, Edmonton, AB T6H 5R7 Canada

SALARIES/BONUSES:
Top Exec. Salary: $ Bonus: $
Second Exec. Salary: $ Bonus: $

STOCK TICKER/OTHER:
Stock Ticker: Subsidiary
Employees: 659
Parent Company: Electronic Arts Inc

Exchange:
Fiscal Year Ends: 12/31

OTHER THOUGHTS:
Estimated Female Officers or Directors:
Hot Spot for Advancement for Women/Minorities:

Sales, profits and employees may be estimates. Financial information, benefits and other data can change quickly and may vary from those stated here.

Bloomberg LP

www.bloomberg.com

NAIC Code: 511120A

TYPES OF BUSINESS:
Financial Data and News Publishing
Magazine Publishing
Management Software
Multimedia Presentation Services
Broadcast Television
Radio Broadcasting
Electronic Exchange Systems
Economic Data

BRANDS/DIVISIONS/AFFILIATES:
Bloomberg Businessweek
Bloomberg Terminal
Bloomberg Tradebook
Bloomberg Vault
Bloomberg Government
Bloomberg New Energy Finance Limited
Bloomberg BNA
Bloomberg Intelligence

CONTACTS:
Note: Officers with more than one job title may be intentionally listed here more than once.

John Eastright, CEO
Daniel M. Fine, COO
Daniel L. Doctoroff, Pres.
Mike McCarty, CFO
Steve Crossman, VP, Sales
Christina Correira, Chief HR Officer
Rich Thompson, CTO
Jason Schechter, Chief Communications Officer
Matthew Winkler, Editor-in-Chief, Bloomberg News
Thomas Secunda, Vice Chmn.
Gregory C. McCaffery, Chmn.

GROWTH PLANS/SPECIAL FEATURES:

Bloomberg LP is an information services, news and media company, serving the financial services industry, government offices and agencies, corporations and news organizations. The company operates in six segments: communications, financial products, enterprise products, industry products, media and media services. Communications provides press announcements involving Bloomberg through its worldwide press contact centers, including the Americas, Europe/Middle East/Africa and Asia Pacific. Bloomberg's QuickTake franchise offers Q&A-style explainers to help readers quickly navigate breaking news and understand a story's fundamentals as news develops. Financial products is comprised of the Bloomberg Terminal, a platform for financial professionals who need real-time data, news and analytics to make fast and informed decisions; and the Bloomberg Tradebook, a global agency broker that provides anonymous direct market access and algorithmic trading to more than 125 global liquidity venues across 43 countries. This division also includes Bloomberg Briefs, Bloomberg Indexes, Bloomberg SEF (swap execution facility) and Bloomberg Institute. Enterprise provides solutions such as enterprise data, distribution and information; and trading solutions that address workflow with front-end portfolio, inventory, sales and trading, as well as middle and back office operations solutions for buy-side and sell-side firms. This division's Bloomberg Vault is a secure, managed service for information governance, data analytics and trade reconstruction across the enterprise. Industry products include Bloomberg Government, a web-based information service for professionals who interact with the federal government; Bloomberg Law/BNA and Bloomberg Big Law for legal, tax and regulatory professionals; and Bloomberg New Energy Finance Limited for decision-makers in the energy system. Media delivers business and political news through Bloomberg Business, Bloomberg Politics, Bloomberg View, Bloomberg Television, Bloomberg Radio, Bloomberg Mobile Apps and news bureaus. Media Services includes advertising, Bloomberg Content Service and Bloomberg Live Conferences.

The New York City headquarters features television and radio studios, open work areas (including open executive offices), dramatically modern architecture and an infinite variety of employee snacks.

FINANCIAL DATA:
Note: Data for latest year may not have been available at press time.

In U.S. $	2018	2017	2016	2015	2014	2013
Revenue	10,000,000,000	9,658,000,000	9,400,000,000	9,184,000,000	9,000,000,000	8,275,000,000
R&D Expense						
Operating Income						
Operating Margin %						
SGA Expense						
Net Income						
Operating Cash Flow						
Capital Expenditure						
EBITDA						
Return on Assets %						
Return on Equity %						
Debt to Equity						

CONTACT INFORMATION:
Phone: 212-318-2000   Fax: 917-369-5000
Toll-Free:
Address: 731 Lexington Ave., New York, NY 10022 United States

STOCK TICKER/OTHER:
Stock Ticker: Private
Employees: 19,000
Parent Company:

Exchange:
Fiscal Year Ends: 12/31

SALARIES/BONUSES:
Top Exec. Salary: $ Bonus: $
Second Exec. Salary: $ Bonus: $

OTHER THOUGHTS:
Estimated Female Officers or Directors: 8
Hot Spot for Advancement for Women/Minorities: Y

Sales, profits and employees may be estimates. Financial information, benefits and other data can change quickly and may vary from those stated here.

Books A Million Inc

NAIC Code: 451211

www.booksamillion.com/

TYPES OF BUSINESS:
Book Stores
Newsstands
Coffee Bars
Wholesale Distribution
Online Sales
Internet Development & Services

BRANDS/DIVISIONS/AFFILIATES:
Books-A-Million
Joe Muggs CafÃ©
American Wholesale Book Company
Book$mart Inc
booksamillion.com
NetCentral

CONTACTS: Note: Officers with more than one job title may be intentionally listed here more than once.
Terrance Finley, CEO
R. Todd Noden, CFO
James Turner, Executive VP, Divisional
Clyde Anderson, Chmn.

GROWTH PLANS/SPECIAL FEATURES:

Books-A-Million, Inc. (also referred to as BAM!) is a leading retailer of books, magazines and related items in the southeastern U.S. The currently operates more than 260 stores in 32 states and Washington, D.C. The company has three business operating segments: retail stores, wholesale distribution and eCommerce/internet services development. The retail stores segment is comprised of Books-A-Million stores, which range from 4,000 to 30,000 square feet and provide a selection of books, magazines, bargain books, collectible supplies, toys, technology and gifts. These stores also feature the Joe Muggs Cafe, which offers a line of coffee and espresso beverages, teas, desserts and brewing supplies. The wholesale distribution segment is comprised of American Wholesale Book Company, which is based in Florence, Alabama. This subsidiary and segment provides book and distribution services for retailers across the southeast; and provides internet fulfillment services for book products sold by various eCommerce companies. This division also is comprised of Book$mart, Inc., a full-service bargain book distributor, servicing retail and wholesale clients throughout the country. Its 200,000-square-foot distribution facility offers value-priced books, including specially published packages to publisher remainders of previous bestsellers. Last, the eCommerce/internet services development segment is comprised of booksamillion.com, the firm's website. This division also includes NetCentral, an internet development and services company which provides systems solutions and web development for all of the corporation's internet and networking initiatives.

FINANCIAL DATA: Note: Data for latest year may not have been available at press time.

In U.S. $	2018	2017	2016	2015	2014	2013
Revenue	440,000,000	461,000,000	470,000,000	474,084,000	470,300,992	503,787,008
R&D Expense						
Operating Income						
Operating Margin %						
SGA Expense						
Net Income				3,538,000	-7,584,000	2,545,000
Operating Cash Flow						
Capital Expenditure						
EBITDA						
Return on Assets %						
Return on Equity %						
Debt to Equity						

CONTACT INFORMATION:
Phone: 205 942-3737   Fax: 205 945-1772
Toll-Free: 800-201-3550
Address: 402 Industrial Ln., Birmingham, AL 35211 United States

STOCK TICKER/OTHER:
Stock Ticker: Private   Exchange:
Employees: 5,400   Fiscal Year Ends: 01/31
Parent Company:

SALARIES/BONUSES:
Top Exec. Salary: $ Bonus: $
Second Exec. Salary: $ Bonus: $

OTHER THOUGHTS:
Estimated Female Officers or Directors:
Hot Spot for Advancement for Women/Minorities:

Sales, profits and employees may be estimates. Financial information, benefits and other data can change quickly and may vary from those stated here.

Booth Creek Ski Holdings Inc

www.boothcreek.com

NAIC Code: 713920

TYPES OF BUSINESS:
Ski Resorts
Golf Courses
Event Hosting
Summer Recreation

BRANDS/DIVISIONS/AFFILIATES:
Booth Creek Ski Group Inc
Sierra-at-Tahoe Snowsports Resort

GROWTH PLANS/SPECIAL FEATURES:
Booth Creek Ski Holdings, Inc. is a business management company. The firm specializes in ski resort operations and administration as well as the advertising and marketing of those resorts. Booth Creek currently owns Sierra-at-Tahoe Snowsports Resort in Lake Tahoe, California, which operates under a long-term lease agreement with real estate investment trust (REIT), CNL Lifestyle Properties. Sierra-at-Tahoe comprises over 40 ski lifts across 200 acres, and provides a full range of services such as equipment rentals, skiing lessons and restaurants. In addition to alpine skiing and snowboarding, Booth Creek's resorts offer opportunities for cross-country skiing, tubing, snowmobiling and snowshoeing. Sierra-at-Tahoe Snowsports Resort receives approximately 500 inches of annual snowfall; its mountain has roughly 2,200 vertical feet on which to ski. Its most popular runs include West Bowl, Grandview and Huckleberry Canyon. Booth Creek is a wholly-owned subsidiary of Booth Creek Ski Group, Inc.

CONTACTS:
Note: Officers with more than one job title may be intentionally listed here more than once.

George N. Gillett, Jr., CEO
Jeffrey J. Joyce, VP-Finance
Christopher P. Ryman, Pres.
Brian Pope, VP-Accounting & Finance
Timothy H. Beck, Exec. VP-Planning
Brian Pope, Principal Acct. Officer

FINANCIAL DATA:
Note: Data for latest year may not have been available at press time.

In U.S. $	2018	2017	2016	2015	2014	2013
Revenue	131,000,000	130,000,000	125,400,000	120,000,000	110,000,000	116,000,000
R&D Expense						
Operating Income						
Operating Margin %						
SGA Expense						
Net Income						
Operating Cash Flow						
Capital Expenditure						
EBITDA						
Return on Assets %						
Return on Equity %						
Debt to Equity						

CONTACT INFORMATION:
Phone: 530-550-5100
Fax: 530-550-5116
Toll-Free:
Address: 950 Red Sand Stone Rd., #43, Vail, CO 81657 United States

STOCK TICKER/OTHER:
Stock Ticker: Subsidiary
Employees: 530
Parent Company: Booth Creek Ski Group Inc
Exchange:
Fiscal Year Ends: 10/31

SALARIES/BONUSES:
Top Exec. Salary: $ Bonus: $
Second Exec. Salary: $ Bonus: $

OTHER THOUGHTS:
Estimated Female Officers or Directors: 1
Hot Spot for Advancement for Women/Minorities:

Bose Corporation

NAIC Code: 334310

www.bose.com

TYPES OF BUSINESS:
Audio Equipment-Manufacturing & Retailing
Speaker Technology
Home & Automobile Sound Systems
Professional Sound Systems
Noise Reduction Headsets
Materials Testing Equipment

BRANDS/DIVISIONS/AFFILIATES:
Wave
SoundSport
A20 Aviation
Frames

CONTACTS:
Note: Officers with more than one job title may be intentionally listed here more than once.

John T. Coleman, Pres.
Daniel A. Grady, CFO
Bryan K. Fontaine, Exec. VP-Mfg.
Daniel A. Grady, VP-Finance
Nic Merks, VP-Europe
Bryan K. Fontaine, Exec. VP-Global Supply Chain

GROWTH PLANS/SPECIAL FEATURES:
Bose Corporation is a leading global manufacturer of audio products, with stores nationwide. Bose manufactures sound systems for homes and automobiles as well as professional audio products for large venues and stage performers. It is best known for the development of its acoustic waveguide speaker technology found in Wave systems. Speaker products include soundbars, smart home speakers, portable speakers, home theaters and wearable speakers. Headphone products include: over-the-ear and earbud wireless headphones, with noise cancelling capabilities; SoundSport headphones, designed to resist sweat and weather during workouts; wireless sleepbuds, delivering soothing sounds that mask noises like snoring, pets and loud neighbors, to help people fall asleep; conversation-enhancing headphones, which enable users to control the sound in noisy environments; and the A20 Aviation Headset, which is engineered to be lightweight, comfortable and provide more noise reduction than any headset offered by Bose. In December 2018, Bose announced Frames, a product that combines the protection and style of premium sunglasses, the functionality and performance of wireless headphones, and an audio augmented reality platform into a single wearable. Frames were due to be available in January 2019, with pre-orders beginning in early December 2018.

The firm offers employees medical, dental, long-term care and vision coverage; a 401(k) plan; an employee assistance program; employee discounts; adoption assistance; and tuition assistance.

FINANCIAL DATA:
Note: Data for latest year may not have been available at press time.

In U.S. $	2018	2017	2016	2015	2014	2013
Revenue	4,000,000,000	3,850,000,000	3,800,000,000	3,500,000,000	3,400,000,000	2,970,000,000
R&D Expense						
Operating Income						
Operating Margin %						
SGA Expense						
Net Income						
Operating Cash Flow						
Capital Expenditure						
EBITDA						
Return on Assets %						
Return on Equity %						
Debt to Equity						

CONTACT INFORMATION:
Phone: 508-879-7330
Fax: 508-820-3465
Toll-Free: 800-999-2673
Address: The Mountain, Framingham, MA 01701-9168 United States

STOCK TICKER/OTHER:
Stock Ticker: Private
Employees: 8,000
Parent Company:
Exchange:
Fiscal Year Ends: 03/31

SALARIES/BONUSES:
Top Exec. Salary: $
Bonus: $
Second Exec. Salary: $
Bonus: $

OTHER THOUGHTS:
Estimated Female Officers or Directors:
Hot Spot for Advancement for Women/Minorities:

Sales, profits and employees may be estimates. Financial information, benefits and other data can change quickly and may vary from those stated here.

Bowlero Corporation

www.bowlerocorp.com

NAIC Code: 713950

TYPES OF BUSINESS:
Bowling Centers
Bowling Equipment
Bowling Software
Bowling Apparel

BRANDS/DIVISIONS/AFFILIATES:
Bowlmor Lanes
Bowlero
AMF
Brunswick Zone
QubicaAMF Worldwide

CONTACTS:
Note: Officers with more than one job title may be intentionally listed here more than once.

Tom Shannon, CEO
Brett Parker, CFO
John Walker, Pres.

GROWTH PLANS/SPECIAL FEATURES:

Bowlero Corporation is one of the largest owners and operators of commercial bowling centers in the world. The company has more than 300 bowling centers throughout the U.S., as well as in Mexico and Canada. These centers operate under the Bowlmor Lanes, Bowlero, AMF and Brunswick Zone brand names. Bowlero's portfolio of brands include value-based, mid-range and high-end bowling entertainment experiences. The firm's bowling centers typically feature billiards, video games, food and beverage services and Xtreme Bowling with music and lights. Bowlero also organizes and sponsors various bowling leagues and clubs for adults and children, as well as corporate parties and birthday parties. Affiliate QubicaAMF Worldwide is one of the largest manufacturers and distributors of bowling products in the world, with 10 sales offices worldwide. Its bowling products include automatic scoring software, center management software, ten-pin pinsetters, lanes and lane care products, pins, ball returns and furniture.

The company offers its employees benefits including health care, dental, vision and prescription drug coverage; flexible spending accounts; incentive programs; a 401(k) plan; tuition assistance; scholarships; and employee discounts on bowling, bowling pro

FINANCIAL DATA:
Note: Data for latest year may not have been available at press time.

In U.S. $	2018	2017	2016	2015	2014	2013
Revenue	605,000,000	600,000,000	582,641,000	531,902,000	386,200,000	
R&D Expense						
Operating Income						
Operating Margin %						
SGA Expense						
Net Income			-1,503,000	-46,613,000	-33,234,000	
Operating Cash Flow						
Capital Expenditure						
EBITDA						
Return on Assets %						
Return on Equity %						
Debt to Equity						

CONTACT INFORMATION:
Phone: 212-777-2214 Fax:
Toll-Free: 800-342-5263
Address: 222 W. 44th St., New York, NY 10036 United States

STOCK TICKER/OTHER:
Stock Ticker: Private
Employees: 7,700
Parent Company:

Exchange:
Fiscal Year Ends: 06/30

SALARIES/BONUSES:
Top Exec. Salary: $ Bonus: $
Second Exec. Salary: $ Bonus: $

OTHER THOUGHTS:
Estimated Female Officers or Directors:
Hot Spot for Advancement for Women/Minorities:

Boyd Gaming Corp

NAIC Code: 721120

www.boydgaming.com

TYPES OF BUSINESS:
Casinos & Hotels
Casino Management

BRANDS/DIVISIONS/AFFILIATES:
Orleans Hotel and Casino (The)
Gold Coast Hotel and Casino
Eldorado Casino
Jokers Wild Casino
Suncoast Hotal and Casino
Aliante Casino + Hotel + Spa
California Hotel & Casino
Blue Chip Hotel and Casino

CONTACTS:
Note: Officers with more than one job title may be intentionally listed here more than once.

William Boyd, Chairman of the Board
Anthony McDuffie, Chief Accounting Officer
Marianne Johnson, Director
William Boyd, Director
Theodore Bogich, Executive VP, Divisional
Stephen Thompson, Executive VP, Divisional
Josh Hirsberg, Executive VP
Keith Smith, President
Brian Larson, Secretary

GROWTH PLANS/SPECIAL FEATURES:
Boyd Gaming Corp. is a multi-jurisdictional gaming company and one of the country's leading casino operators. It currently owns and operates 24 casinos totaling over 1.3 million square feet and housing 30,267 slot machines, 632 table games and 9,372 hotel rooms. The firm divides its properties into three segments: Las Vegas locals, downtown Las Vegas and Midwest & South. The Las Vegas local properties include The Orleans Hotel and Casino, Sam's Town Hotel & Gambling Hall, Gold Coast Hotel and Casino, Eldorado Casino, Jokers Wild Casino, Suncoast Hotel and Casino, Aliante Casino + Hotel + Spa and Cannery Casino Hotel. Downtown Las Vegas facilities consist of the Fremont Hotel & Casino; California Hotel & Casino; and Main Street Casino, Brewery and Hotel. The Midwest & South properties include IP Casino Resort Spa, Sam's Town Hotel and Gambling Hall, Delta Downs Racetrack and Casino & Hotel, Treasure Chest Casino, Par-a-Dice Hotel and Casino and Blue Chip Hotel and Casino. Additionally, Boyd owns and operates a travel agency and an insurance company that underwrites travel-related insurance, each located in Hawaii. In December 2017, the firm announced it had entered into a definitive agreement with Valley Forge Convention Center Partners, L.P., to acquire Valley Forge Casino Resort in King of Prussia, Pennsylvania, for $280.5 million; and with Penn National Gaming, Inc. to acquire the operations of Ameristar St. Charles (Missouri), Ameristar Kansas City (Missouri), Belterra Casino Resort (Indiana) and Belterra Park (Ohio) for $575 million.

Boyd Gaming offers its employees pharmacy, life, short-term disability, medical, dental and vision coverage; flexible spending accounts; and a 401(k).

FINANCIAL DATA:
Note: Data for latest year may not have been available at press time.

In U.S. $	2018	2017	2016	2015	2014	2013
Revenue		2,383,707,000	2,183,976,000	2,199,432,000	2,701,319,000	2,894,438,000
R&D Expense						
Operating Income		343,069,000	298,929,000	363,188,000	312,296,000	288,684,000
Operating Margin %		14.39%	13.68%	16.51%	11.56%	9.97%
SGA Expense		362,037,000	322,009,000	322,420,000	429,529,000	490,226,000
Net Income		189,193,000	418,003,000	47,234,000	-53,041,000	-80,264,000
Operating Cash Flow		414,350,000	275,085,000	339,846,000	322,859,000	274,891,000
Capital Expenditure		190,464,000	160,358,000	131,170,000	149,374,000	144,520,000
EBITDA		561,437,000	416,905,000	471,768,000	493,546,000	506,749,000
Return on Assets %		4.04%	9.26%	1.06%	-1.03%	-1.32%
Return on Equity %		18.59%	57.97%	9.98%	-11.68%	-20.74%
Debt to Equity		2.77	3.42	6.37	7.83	9.26

CONTACT INFORMATION:
Phone: 702 792-7200   Fax: 702 792-7266
Toll-Free:
Address: 3883 Howard Hughes Pkwy., 9th Fl., Las Vegas, NV 89169 United States

STOCK TICKER/OTHER:
Stock Ticker: BYD   Exchange: NYS
Employees: 19,932   Fiscal Year Ends: 12/31
Parent Company:

SALARIES/BONUSES:
Top Exec. Salary: $1,325,000   Bonus: $
Second Exec. Salary: $1,065,000   Bonus: $250,000

OTHER THOUGHTS:
Estimated Female Officers or Directors: 3
Hot Spot for Advancement for Women/Minorities: Y

Sales, profits and employees may be estimates. Financial information, benefits and other data can change quickly and may vary from those stated here.

Boyne Resorts

www.boyne.com

NAIC Code: 713920

TYPES OF BUSINESS:
Ski Resorts
Golf Courses
Real Estate Development
Retail Operations
Indoor Waterpark
Spas
Restaurants

BRANDS/DIVISIONS/AFFILIATES:
Boyne Highlands Resort
Boyne Mountain Resort
Inn at Bay Harbor (The)
Bay Harbor Golf Club
Country Club of Boyne
Avalanche Bay Indoor Waterpark
Boyne Realty
Brighton Resort

CONTACTS: Note: Officers with more than one job title may be intentionally listed here more than once.
Stephen Kircher, Pres.-Eastern Operations
John Kircher, Pres.-Western Operations
Ed Grice, Pres., Boyne Mountain Resort
Brad Keen, Pres., Boyne Highlands Resort
Kathrynn Kircher, Principal - Boyne Design Group
Amy Kircher Wright, Chmn.

GROWTH PLANS/SPECIAL FEATURES:
Boyne Resorts operates year-round Michigan-based mountain resorts known for skiing, golf and spas. The resorts include retail stores and real estate opportunities based in Lower Northern Michigan. Boyne's ski resorts include Boyne Highlands Resort in Harbor Springs, and Boyne Mountain Resort in Boyne Falls. In addition to its skiing operations there is: The Inn at Bay Harbor, a Renaissance Lake Michigan spa resort in Bay Harbor; Cottages at Bay Harbor, which are standalone cottage style accommodations near The Inn; Bay Harbor Golf Club and Boyne Golf, which are golf resorts; Country Club of Boyne, its exclusive golf, social and resort based membership club; Avalanche Bay Indoor Waterpark, which features water rides and slides, as well as lodging and party packages; Boyne Country Sports, retail stores offering backpacks, apparel, ski/snowboard/golf equipment, footwear and travel gear; and Boyne Realty, a real estate firm. The company has a rewards program, BoyneRewards, where guests can earn points through purchases such as new gear or lift tickets, with rewards such as gift certificates, zipline tours, spa admission and hotel lodging. In May 2018, Boyne Resorts acquired six mountain resorts and a scenic chairlift attraction currently leased by Boyne. The agreement was with Ski Resort Holdings, LLC, an affiliate of Och-Ziff Capital Management Group, LLC. The resorts include: Brighton Resort, in Utah; Gatlinburg Sky Lift, in Tennessee; Loon Mountain, in New Hampshire; Sugarloaf and Sunday River resorts, in Maine; The Summit at Snoqualmie, in Washington; and Cypress Mountain, in British Columbia, Canada.

FINANCIAL DATA: Note: Data for latest year may not have been available at press time.

In U.S. $	2018	2017	2016	2015	2014	2013
Revenue	88,000,000	83,000,000	82,250,000	82,000,000	80,000,000	82,000,000
R&D Expense						
Operating Income						
Operating Margin %						
SGA Expense						
Net Income						
Operating Cash Flow						
Capital Expenditure						
EBITDA						
Return on Assets %						
Return on Equity %						
Debt to Equity						

CONTACT INFORMATION:
Phone: 231-549-6000　Fax: 231-439-4786
Toll-Free:
Address: 3951 Charlevoix Ave, Petoskey, MI 49770 United States

STOCK TICKER/OTHER:
Stock Ticker: Private
Employees: 5,500
Parent Company:

Exchange:
Fiscal Year Ends: 12/31

SALARIES/BONUSES:
Top Exec. Salary: $　Bonus: $
Second Exec. Salary: $　Bonus: $

OTHER THOUGHTS:
Estimated Female Officers or Directors: 2
Hot Spot for Advancement for Women/Minorities:

Sales, profits and employees may be estimates. Financial information, benefits and other data can change quickly and may vary from those stated here.

Brightcove Inc

NAIC Code: 519130

www.brightcove.com

TYPES OF BUSINESS:
Internet TV Broadcasting

BRANDS/DIVISIONS/AFFILIATES:
Brightcove Video Cloud
Brightcove Zencoder
Brightcove SSAI
Brightcove Player
Brightcove OTT Flow
Brightcove Video Marketing Suite
Brightcove Enterprise Video Suite

CONTACTS:
Note: Officers with more than one job title may be intentionally listed here more than once.

Hugh Ray, CEO
Robert Noreck, CFO
Gary Haroian, Director
David Plotkin, Other Executive Officer

GROWTH PLANS/SPECIAL FEATURES:
Brightcove, Inc. is an internet television company that enables emerging media companies and independent producers to launch commercial broadband channels. The firm allows content owners to create, distribute and monetize internet TV channels through its Brightcove Video Cloud. This platform charges content publishers a usage fee, but it does allow them to keep all ad revenues. The Video Cloud platform features: advanced adaptive transcoding, which means it must only be uploaded to a computer once; content management; customized viewing; live and on-demand video delivery and streaming; mobile device (including iPhone and iPad) compatibility; and comprehensive audience analytics and reporting. Other products include the Brightcove Zencoder, a cloud-based video encoding service; Brightcove SSAI, a cloud-based ad insertion and video stitching service that addresses the limitations of traditional online video ad insertion technology; Brightcove Player, a cloud-based service for creating and managing video player experiences; Brightcove OTT Flow, a service for media companies and content owners to rapidly deploy high-quality, direct-to-consumer, live and on-demand video services across platforms; Brightcove Video Marketing Suite, a comprehensive suite of video technologies designed to address the needs of marketers to drive awareness, engagement and conversion; and Brightcove Enterprise Video Suite, an enterprise-class platform for internal communications, employee training, live streaming, marketing and ecommerce videos. The Brightcove professional services division provides consulting, strategy, design and development services in conjunction with cloud platform. Its service is currently used by more than 4,168 professional media customers in over 70 countries, ranging from media and technology enterprises to financial services firms and government, educational and nonprofit entities. The firm has offices in the U.S., the U.K., Australia, Spain, France, Singapore, Japan, South Korea and the UAE.

FINANCIAL DATA:
Note: Data for latest year may not have been available at press time.

In U.S. $	2018	2017	2016	2015	2014	2013
Revenue		155,913,000	150,266,000	134,706,000	125,017,000	109,895,000
R&D Expense		31,850,000	30,171,000	29,302,000	28,252,000	21,052,000
Operating Income		-19,696,000	-8,957,000	-6,730,000	-12,118,000	-7,425,000
Operating Margin %		-12.63%	-5.96%	-4.99%	-9.69%	-6.75%
SGA Expense		79,141,000	73,205,000	65,657,000	65,150,000	59,478,000
Net Income		-19,519,000	-9,986,000	-7,580,000	-16,893,000	-10,262,000
Operating Cash Flow		-6,441,000	11,077,000	9,081,000	1,485,000	7,318,000
Capital Expenditure		4,112,000	5,494,000	2,846,000	4,552,000	3,915,000
EBITDA		-11,866,000	-1,717,000	1,594,000	-7,950,000	-4,163,000
Return on Assets %		-14.78%	-7.56%	-5.93%	-14.64%	-10.25%
Return on Equity %		-26.93%	-12.77%	-9.54%	-23.93%	-16.68%
Debt to Equity						

CONTACT INFORMATION:
Phone: 617-500-4947 Fax: 617-261-4830
Toll-Free: 888-882-1880
Address: 290 Congress St., 4/Fl, Cambridge, MA 02210 United States

SALARIES/BONUSES:
Top Exec. Salary: $381,250   Bonus: $
Second Exec. Salary: $300,000   Bonus: $21,166

STOCK TICKER/OTHER:
Stock Ticker: BCOV
Employees: 490
Parent Company:

Exchange: NAS
Fiscal Year Ends: 12/31

OTHER THOUGHTS:
Estimated Female Officers or Directors: 1
Hot Spot for Advancement for Women/Minorities: Y

British Broadcasting Corporation (BBC)

NAIC Code: 515120

www.bbc.co.uk

TYPES OF BUSINESS:
Television Broadcasting
Television Production
News Agency
Radio Broadcasting
Online Publishing
Media Distribution & Services

BRANDS/DIVISIONS/AFFILIATES:
BBC One
BBC Two
BBC Three
BBC Radio 1
BBC Radio 5 live sports extra
BBC News
BBC Sounds
BBC Studios

CONTACTS: Note: Officers with more than one job title may be intentionally listed here more than once.

Tony Hall, General Dir.
Ralph Rivers, Dir.-Future Tech & Media
Anne Bulford, Managing Dir.-Oper.
James Purnell, Dir.-Strategy
James Purnell, Dir.-Digital
Anne Bulford, Managing Dir.-Finance
Danny Cohen, Dir.-Television
James Harding, Dir.-News & Current Affairs
Helen Boaden, Dir.-Radio
Ken MacQuarrie, Dir.-Scotland
David Clementi, Chmn.
Tim Davie, CEO-BBC Worldwide

GROWTH PLANS/SPECIAL FEATURES:

British Broadcasting Corporation (BBC) is a public service broadcaster funded by the license fees paid by U.K. households. The income from the license fees provides public service broadcasting services, including: nine national TV channels; 10 national radio stations in the U.K., as well as national radio stations for listeners in Wales, Scotland and Norther Ireland, plus local radio stations throughout England; and online. BBC One offers the broadest range of programming of any U.K. mainstream network, covering national and international sports events and issues. BBC Two is a mixed-genre channel that combines factual and specialist subjects with comedy and drama in an attempt to bring intelligent television to a wide audience. BBC Three, aimed primarily at younger viewers, combines news, current affairs, education, music, arts, science and coverage of international issues as well as offering drama, comedy and entertainment. Other TV channels include BBC Four, CBBC, CBeebies, BBC News, BBC Parliament and BBC Alba. BBC radio stations include: BBC Radio 1, which broadcasts a mix of new music and entertainment for 15-29 year olds, plus news, documentaries and advice for young adults; BBC Radio 3, featuring arts and cultural broadcasting, including classical music, jazz, speech programs, documentaries and drama; and BBC Radio 5 live sports extra, offering live coverage of various sporting events. Other radio stations include BBC Radio 1Xtra, BBC Radio 2, BBC Radio 4, BBC Radio 4 Extra, BBC Radio 5 live, BBC Radio 6 Music, BBC Asian Network and BBC Nations and Local Radio. Online service includes BBC News, Sport Weather, BBC, iPlayer and BBC Sounds, which together comprise a portfolio of websites offering news, sports info, weather updates, children's sites, knowledge/learning and access to radio and TV programs on-demand. BBC Studios is the firm's commercial subsidiary.

BBC offers employees comprehensive benefits.

FINANCIAL DATA: Note: Data for latest year may not have been available at press time.

In U.S. $	2018	2017	2016	2015	2014	2013
Revenue	7,103,630,000	4,954,000,000	6,054,495,151	6,026,047,216	6,354,605,588	6,287,450,092
R&D Expense						
Operating Income						
Operating Margin %						
SGA Expense						
Net Income	252,002,000	-160,773,000	74,007,447	-156,809,918	188,171,902	196,953,245
Operating Cash Flow						
Capital Expenditure						
EBITDA						
Return on Assets %						
Return on Equity %						
Debt to Equity						

CONTACT INFORMATION:
Phone: 44-370-901-1227   Fax:
Toll-Free:
Address: Portland Place, Broadcasting House, London, W1A 1AA United Kingdom

STOCK TICKER/OTHER:
Stock Ticker: Government-Owned
Employees: 21,459
Parent Company:

Exchange:
Fiscal Year Ends: 03/31

SALARIES/BONUSES:
Top Exec. Salary: $ Bonus: $
Second Exec. Salary: $ Bonus: $

OTHER THOUGHTS:
Estimated Female Officers or Directors: 3
Hot Spot for Advancement for Women/Minorities: Y

Cable News Network Inc (CNN)

NAIC Code: 515210

www.cnn.com

TYPES OF BUSINESS:
TV News Production
News Radio Broadcasting
Satellite Networks
Online News Information
Syndicated News Service

BRANDS/DIVISIONS/AFFILIATES:
AT&T Inc
Warner Media LLC
Turner Broadcasting System Inc
CNN
CNN.com
CNN Money
CNN International
CNN Aerial Imagery and Reporting (CNN AIR)

CONTACTS:
Note: Officers with more than one job title may be intentionally listed here more than once.
Jeffrey Adam Zucker, Pres.
Kenneth Estenson, Gen. Mgr.-CNN Digital
Parisa Khosravi, Sr. VP-Global Rel.
Cynthia Hudson, Sr. VP
Katherine Green, Sr. VP-Programming
Richard Davis, Exec. VP-News Standards & Practices
Ken Jautz, Exec. VP-U.S.
Tony Maddox, Exec. VP-Int'l

GROWTH PLANS/SPECIAL FEATURES:

Cable News Network, known as CNN, operates cable and satellite television networks. The firm is a unit of Turner Broadcasting System, Inc., which is owned by Warner Media LLC, itself a subsidiary of AT&T, Inc. The company is comprised of private, place-based networks; radio networks; network-affiliated websites, including CNN.com; CNN Mobile, which sends news reports and other information to members' wireless devices; CNN Newsource, one of the world's most extensively syndicated news services; and CNN Live Video, a free live streaming content and video on demand service. Other CNN operations include CNN Money, CNN Airport Network, CNN en Espanol, CNN Headline News, CNN Radio and CNN en Espanol Radio. The firm's TV news programs include Early Start, Anderson Cooper 360, CNN Newsroom, New Day Saturday, CNN Presents and The Situation Room. In addition, CNN Aerial Imagery and Reporting (CNN AIR) is the firm's drone-based news-collecting operation which reports across all CNN networks and platforms, along with Time Warner entities; and CNN Virtual Reality (CNNVR) produces 360-degree videos for Android and iOS apps within CNN's digital division. CNN International, a global 24-news network accessible in over 200 countries, operates through five regional channels: CNN International Europe/Middle East/Africa, CNN International Asia Pacific, CNN International South Asia, CNN International Latin America and CNN International North America. The company's other international affiliates include: CNNj, a Japanese news outlet; CNN Turk, a Turkish media outlet; and CNN-News18, an Indian news channel.

The firm offers its employees flexible medical, dental, vision, life and AD&D coverage; bonuses; 401(k); short and long-term disability; maternity, adoption and parental leave; transportation reimbursement; tuition reimbursement; business travel accident

FINANCIAL DATA: Note: Data for latest year may not have been available at press time.

In U.S. $	2018	2017	2016	2015	2014	2013
Revenue	1,450,000,000	1,400,000,000	1,500,000,000	1,250,000,000	1,230,000,000	1,110,000,000
R&D Expense						
Operating Income						
Operating Margin %						
SGA Expense						
Net Income						
Operating Cash Flow						
Capital Expenditure						
EBITDA						
Return on Assets %						
Return on Equity %						
Debt to Equity						

CONTACT INFORMATION:
Phone: 404-878-2276
Fax: 404-827-1995
Toll-Free:
Address: 1 CNN Center, Atlanta, GA 30303 United States

SALARIES/BONUSES:
Top Exec. Salary: $
Second Exec. Salary: $
Bonus: $
Bonus: $

STOCK TICKER/OTHER:
Stock Ticker: Subsidiary
Employees: 4,000
Parent Company: AT&T Inc
Exchange:
Fiscal Year Ends: 12/31

OTHER THOUGHTS:
Estimated Female Officers or Directors: 5
Hot Spot for Advancement for Women/Minorities: Y

Sales, profits and employees may be estimates. Financial information, benefits and other data can change quickly and may vary from those stated here.

Plunkett Research, Ltd.   163

Caesars Entertainment Corporation
www.caesars.com

NAIC Code: 721120

TYPES OF BUSINESS:
Casino Hotels
Dockside & Riverboat Casinos
Racing Venues
Casino Management
Online Games

BRANDS/DIVISIONS/AFFILIATES:
Caesars Interactive Entertainment Inc
World Series of Poker
LINQ Promenade (The)
Caesars Acquisition Company

CONTACTS: Note: Officers with more than one job title may be intentionally listed here more than once.
Mark Frissora, CEO
Steven Tight, Pres., Divisional
Eric Hession, CFO
Christopher Holdren, Chief Marketing Officer
James Hunt, Director
Christian Stuart, Executive VP, Divisional
Janis Jones, Executive VP, Divisional
Mary Thomas, Executive VP, Divisional
Richard Broome, Executive VP, Divisional
Janis Blackhurst, Executive VP, Divisional
Les Ottolenghi, Executive VP
Timothy Donovan, Executive VP
Scott Wiegand, Other Corporate Officer
Marco Roca, Other Executive Officer
Thomas Jenkin, President, Divisional
Keith Causey, Senior VP

GROWTH PLANS/SPECIAL FEATURES:
Caesars Entertainment Corporation is one of the largest gaming companies in the world. The firm owns or manages 47 casinos in 13 U.S. states and four countries outside of the U.S. Caesars' facilities have an aggregate of over 2.8 million square feet of gaming space and approximately 39,000 hotel rooms. Of the 47 casinos, 35 are in the U.S. and primarily consist of land-based and riverboat or dockside casinos. The 12 international casinos are land-based casinos, most of which are in the U.K. The firm's consolidated business is composed of five complementary businesses: casino entertainment, food and beverage, rooms and hotel, casino management services and entertainment and other business operations. The casino entertainment operations generate revenues from approximately 36,000 slot machines and 2,700 table games, as well as other games such as keno, poker, and race and sports books, all of which comprised approximately 52% of total net revenues in 2017. The food and beverage operations, 17%, generate revenues from over 150 buffets, restaurants, bars, nightclubs, and lounges located throughout our casinos, as well as banquets and room service. Rooms and hotel operations, 19%, generate revenues from hotel stays at our casino properties in our approximately 39,000 guest rooms and suites worldwide. Casino management services earns revenue from fees paid for the management of eight casinos. The entertainment and other business operations provides a variety of retail and entertainment offerings in its casinos and The LINQ Promenade, an open-air dining, entertainment and retail development. Through its subsidiary Caesars Interactive Entertainment, Inc., the company owns and operates the World Series of Poker tournament and develops online games, both real money wagered and play-for-fun games. In October 2017, Caesars Acquisition Company merged with and into Caesars.

FINANCIAL DATA: Note: Data for latest year may not have been available at press time.

In U.S. $	2018	2017	2016	2015	2014	2013
Revenue		4,852,000,000	3,877,000,000	4,654,000,000	8,516,000,000	8,559,700,000
R&D Expense						
Operating Income		532,000,000	257,000,000	574,000,000	778,000,000	987,600,000
Operating Margin %		10.96%	6.62%	12.33%	9.13%	11.53%
SGA Expense		1,181,000,000	1,166,000,000	1,319,000,000	2,558,000,000	2,436,700,000
Net Income		-375,000,000	-3,569,000,000	5,920,000,000	-2,783,000,000	-2,948,200,000
Operating Cash Flow		-2,323,000,000	476,000,000	113,000,000	-795,000,000	-118,800,000
Capital Expenditure		598,000,000	220,000,000	350,000,000	998,000,000	726,300,000
EBITDA		-975,000,000	-5,062,000,000	7,091,000,000	132,000,000	-1,464,100,000
Return on Assets %		-1.85%	-26.35%	33.13%	-11.54%	-11.19%
Return on Equity %		-1562.50%				
Debt to Equity		5.66		6.86		

CONTACT INFORMATION:
Phone: 702 407-6000   Fax: 702 407-6037
Toll-Free: 800-318-0047
Address: 1 Caesars Palace Dr., Las Vegas, NV 89109 United States

SALARIES/BONUSES:
Top Exec. Salary: $2,000,000   Bonus: $330,000
Second Exec. Salary: $1,236,927   Bonus: $164,999

STOCK TICKER/OTHER:
Stock Ticker: CZR
Employees: 65,000
Parent Company:

Exchange: NAS
Fiscal Year Ends: 12/31

OTHER THOUGHTS:
Estimated Female Officers or Directors: 2
Hot Spot for Advancement for Women/Minorities: Y

Sales, profits and employees may be estimates. Financial information, benefits and other data can change quickly and may vary from those stated here.

Canterbury Park Holding Corporation

NAIC Code: 713210

www.canterburypark.com

TYPES OF BUSINESS:
Gambling-Horse Races
Simulcasting
Card Club
Event Hosting

BRANDS/DIVISIONS/AFFILIATES:
Canterbury Park Racetrack and Card Casino

CONTACTS:
Note: Officers with more than one job title may be intentionally listed here more than once.
Randall Sampson, CEO
Robert Wolf, CFO
Curtis Sampson, Chairman of the Board
Dale Schenian, Co-Founder

GROWTH PLANS/SPECIAL FEATURES:
Canterbury Park Holding Corporation hosts seasonal pari-mutuel wagering on live thoroughbred and quarter horse racing and hosts unbanked card games at its Canterbury Park Racetrack and Card Casino facility in Shakopee, Minnesota. The company divides its business into three segments: horse racing, card casino and food and beverage. The horse racing segment includes live racing operations and simulcast. In pari-mutuel wagering, bettors wager against each other in a pool rather than against the facility operator or with preset odds. Live thoroughbred and quarter horse racing takes place at the racetrack from May to September. Simulcast racing is the process by which races are held at one facility and transmitted simultaneously to another, allowing patrons to place wagers on races transmitted from the host track. The company offers simulcast racing from 20 different racetracks per day, seven days a week, 364 days per year. The card casino segment represents the operations of the card club, open 24/7 and featuring several variations of poker, blackjack and other casino games. The food and beverage segment consists of concession stands, restaurant and buffet, bars and other food venues. This division also offers catering and events services. Its Twin Cities facility comprises more than 100,000 square feet of available space for events. The firm's revenues are principally derived from card casino operations (which generated approximately 56.2% of fiscal 2017-18 revenues) and wagering on horse races (29.3%), with the remainder from food and beverages. When not conducting horse races, the firm hosts events such as snowmobile racing, arts and crafts shows, community events, automobile shows and competitions and private parties.

FINANCIAL DATA:
Note: Data for latest year may not have been available at press time.

In U.S. $	2018	2017	2016	2015	2014	2013
Revenue		56,952,780	52,460,200	52,263,050	48,469,840	46,736,440
R&D Expense						
Operating Income		4,382,803	1,807,678	3,111,492	3,141,828	1,710,057
Operating Margin %		7.69%	3.44%	5.95%	6.48%	3.65%
SGA Expense		31,578,800	26,234,570	24,681,910	22,883,460	22,898,000
Net Income		4,090,781	4,195,980	2,727,022	2,411,155	1,016,712
Operating Cash Flow		7,086,121	4,941,485	4,429,432	4,590,111	3,543,919
Capital Expenditure		3,781,755	4,431,418	4,341,792	5,657,743	4,311,011
EBITDA		7,100,218	9,718,811	6,914,485	5,279,606	3,571,759
Return on Assets %		7.85%	8.83%	6.42%	6.29%	2.82%
Return on Equity %		10.58%	12.04%	8.50%	8.13%	3.68%
Debt to Equity				0.07		

CONTACT INFORMATION:
Phone: 952-445-7223   Fax:
Toll-Free: 800-340-6361
Address: 1100 Canterbury Rd., Shakopee, MN 55379 United States

SALARIES/BONUSES:
Top Exec. Salary: $256,687   Bonus: $
Second Exec. Salary: $129,231   Bonus: $

STOCK TICKER/OTHER:
Stock Ticker: CPHC   Exchange: NAS
Employees: 864   Fiscal Year Ends: 12/31
Parent Company:

OTHER THOUGHTS:
Estimated Female Officers or Directors:
Hot Spot for Advancement for Women/Minorities:

Sales, profits and employees may be estimates. Financial information, benefits and other data can change quickly and may vary from those stated here.

CBS Corporation

www.cbscorporation.com

NAIC Code: 515120

TYPES OF BUSINESS:
Television Broadcasting
News Organization
Outdoor Advertising
Radio Networks & Programming
Television Production
Cable TV Networks
Book Publishing

BRANDS/DIVISIONS/AFFILIATES:
National Amusements Inc
CBS Television Network
CBS Films
CBS All Access
Showtime Networks
CBS Television Stations
CBS Local Digital Media
Simon & Schuster

CONTACTS:
Note: Officers with more than one job title may be intentionally listed here more than once.

Jonathan Anschell, Assistant General Counsel
Joseph Ianniello, CEO
Christina Spade, CFO
Strauss Zelnick, Chairman of the Board
Lawrence Liding, Chief Accounting Officer
Lawrence Tu, Chief Legal Officer
Shari Redstone, Director
Richard Jones, Executive VP

GROWTH PLANS/SPECIAL FEATURES:

CBS Corporation is a leading mass media company in the U.S. National Amusements, Inc. owns approximately 80% of the voting stock of CBS. The firm operates through four segments: entertainment, accounting for 67% of annual revenues; cable networks, 18%; local media, 12%; and publishing 6%. The entertainment division is composed of the following: CBS Television Network, CBS Television Studios, CBS Studios International, CBS Television Distribution, CBS Interactive and CBS Films; and the digital streaming services of CBS All Access and CBSN. The cable networks segment is composed of Showtime Networks, which operates the firm's premium subscription program services: Showtime, The Movie Channel and Flix; CBS Sports Network, the company's cable network which focuses on college athletics and other sports; and Smithsonian Networks, a venture between Showtime Networks and Smithsonian Institution, which operates Smithsonian Channel, a basic cable program service. The local media segment is composed of CBS Television Stations, the company's 29 owned broadcast television stations; and CBS Local Digital Media, which operates local websites, including content from the company's television stations. The publishing segment is composed of Simon & Schuster, which publishes and distributes consumer books under imprints such as Simon & Schuster, Pocket Books, Scribner, Gallery Books, Touchstone and Atria Books. In late-2017, the firm disposed of its radio business, CBS Radio, Inc., along with radio-related subsidiaries, in a transaction that involved the split-off of CBS Radio through an exchange offer followed by the merger of CBS Radio with a subsidiary of Entercom Communications Corporation.

CBS offers its employees health, vision, dental & life insurance; a 401(k) plan; short & long term disability; flexible spending accounts; adoption assistance; eldercare programs; and paid leave to care for a terminally ill family member.

FINANCIAL DATA:
Note: Data for latest year may not have been available at press time.

In U.S. $	2018	2017	2016	2015	2014	2013
Revenue		13,692,000,000	13,166,000,000	13,886,000,000	13,806,000,000	15,284,000,000
R&D Expense						
Operating Income		2,486,000,000	2,659,000,000	2,843,000,000	2,974,000,000	3,279,000,000
Operating Margin %		18.15%	20.19%	20.47%	21.54%	21.45%
SGA Expense		2,564,000,000	2,335,000,000	2,455,000,000	2,462,000,000	2,735,000,000
Net Income		357,000,000	1,261,000,000	1,413,000,000	2,959,000,000	1,879,000,000
Operating Cash Flow		887,000,000	1,685,000,000	1,394,000,000	1,275,000,000	1,873,000,000
Capital Expenditure		185,000,000	196,000,000	193,000,000	206,000,000	270,000,000
EBITDA		2,659,000,000	2,866,000,000	2,679,000,000	2,808,000,000	3,730,000,000
Return on Assets %		1.58%	5.25%	5.90%	11.72%	7.11%
Return on Equity %		12.59%	27.25%	22.54%	34.94%	18.62%
Debt to Equity		4.78	2.41	1.47	0.93	0.59

CONTACT INFORMATION:
Phone: 212 975-4321   Fax: 212 975-4516
Toll-Free:
Address: 51 W. 52nd St., New York, NY 10019 United States

STOCK TICKER/OTHER:
Stock Ticker: CBS
Employees: 21,270
Parent Company:

Exchange: NYS
Fiscal Year Ends: 12/31

SALARIES/BONUSES:
Top Exec. Salary: $3,500,000   Bonus: $20,000,000
Second Exec. Salary: $2,500,000   Bonus: $12,000,000

OTHER THOUGHTS:
Estimated Female Officers or Directors: 3
Hot Spot for Advancement for Women/Minorities: Y

CBS Interactive Inc

NAIC Code: 519130

www.cbsinteractive.com

TYPES OF BUSINESS:
Online Content
Web Site Management
Music Downloads
Entertainment News
Recipes

BRANDS/DIVISIONS/AFFILIATES:
CBS Corporation
CBS All Access
CBSN
GameSpot
CBS.com
CBSNews.com
CBSSports.com
CNET

CONTACTS:
Note: Officers with more than one job title may be intentionally listed here more than once.

Jim Lanzone, CEO
Jim Lanzone, Pres.
Renee Budig, CFO
Steve Comstock, CIO
Rosabel Tao, Sr. VP-Comm.
David Rice, Sr. VP-CBS Interactive Games
Jason Kint, Sr. VP-Interactive

GROWTH PLANS/SPECIAL FEATURES:
CBS Interactive, Inc. handles the online content operations of its parent company, CBS Corporation. The firm delivers information and entertainment in the fields of technology, entertainment, sports, news, music and gaming. CBS Interactive's properties include the websites, apps and streaming services of the CBS Television Network, such as the CBS All Access digital subscription, video-on-demand and live streaming service; the 24/7 digital news network, CBSN; and CBS Sports' digital brands and properties, including GameSpot, an online sport destination for gamers, offering previews, reviews and information on video, digital and computer games. Websites and apps include, but are not limited to: CBS.com, an online television network; CBSNews.com, providing online worldwide news anytime; and CBSSports.com, providing the full spectrum of sports, from prep to pro, across all digital screens. CBS Interactive's additional sites include: CNET, which offers product reviews, technology news and downloads; TV.com, a television fan site offering forums, episode reviews and program ratings; Chowhound, enabling food enthusiasts to discover recipes and resources for cooking and eating food; Comic Vine, an online comic database featuring comic reviews, news, videos and forums; and last.fm, an online platform featuring music.

CBS Interactive offers its employees medical, dental and vision plans; wellness programs; an employee assistance program; life insurance; wellness programs; flexible spending accounts; and a 401(k) plan.

FINANCIAL DATA:
Note: Data for latest year may not have been available at press time.

In U.S. $	2018	2017	2016	2015	2014	2013
Revenue						
R&D Expense						
Operating Income						
Operating Margin %						
SGA Expense						
Net Income						
Operating Cash Flow						
Capital Expenditure						
EBITDA						
Return on Assets %						
Return on Equity %						
Debt to Equity						

CONTACT INFORMATION:
Phone: 415-344-2000 Fax:
Toll-Free:
Address: 235 2nd St., San Francisco, CA 94105 United States

STOCK TICKER/OTHER:
Stock Ticker: Subsidiary   Exchange:
Employees: 2,080   Fiscal Year Ends:
Parent Company: CBS Corporation

SALARIES/BONUSES:
Top Exec. Salary: $ Bonus: $
Second Exec. Salary: $ Bonus: $

OTHER THOUGHTS:
Estimated Female Officers or Directors: 2
Hot Spot for Advancement for Women/Minorities: Y

Sales, profits and employees may be estimates. Financial information, benefits and other data can change quickly and may vary from those stated here.

Cedar Fair LP

NAIC Code: 713110

www.cedarfair.com

TYPES OF BUSINESS:
Amusement Parks
Water Parks
Hotels
Camping
Marina

BRANDS/DIVISIONS/AFFILIATES:
Cedar Point
Knott's Berry Farm
Dorney Park & Wildwater Kingdom
Valleyfair
Kings Island
Kings Dominion
Carowinds
Castaway Bay Indoor Waterpark Resort

CONTACTS:
Note: Officers with more than one job title may be intentionally listed here more than once.

Brian Witherow, CFO
Matthew Ouimet, Chairman of the Board
David Hoffman, Chief Accounting Officer
Kelley Semmelroth, Chief Marketing Officer
Tim Fisher, COO
H. Bender, Executive VP, Divisional
Duffield Milkie, General Counsel
Richard Zimmerman, President
Craig Heckman, Senior VP, Divisional
Robert Decker, Senior VP, Divisional

GROWTH PLANS/SPECIAL FEATURES:
Cedar Fair LP owns and operates 11 amusement parks, two outdoor water parks, one indoor water park and four hotels. The amusement parks include Cedar Point, in Sandusky, Ohio; Knott's Berry Farm, in Buena Park, California; Canada's Wonderland near Toronto, Canada; Kings Island near Cincinnati, Ohio; Carowinds in Charlotte, North Carolina; Kings Dominion near Richmond, Virginia; California's Great America located in Santa Clara, California; Dorney Park & Wildwater Kingdom, in South Whitehall Township, Pennsylvania; Worlds of Fun, in Kansas City, Missouri; Valleyfair, in Shakopee, Minnesota; and Michigan's Adventure, near Muskegon, Michigan. The two outdoor water parks are located adjacent to Cedar Point and Knott's Berry Farm. Cedar Point's only year-round hotel is Castaway Bay Indoor Waterpark Resort, an indoor water park resort. Cedar also owns and operates the Cedar Point Causeway across Sandusky Bay, a major access route to Cedar Point; and owns dormitory facilities located near the park that house approximately 4,000 of the park's seasonal employees. Castaway Bay features a tropical Caribbean theme with 237 hotel rooms centered around a 38,000-square-foot indoor water park. The park's largest hotel, the Hotel Breakers, has more than 600 guest rooms. Located near the Causeway entrance to the park is Breakers Express, a 350-room, limited-service seasonal hotel. Cedar Fair also owns and operates the Cedar Point Marina, Castaway Bay Marina and Lighthouse Point. Additionally, the company has a management contract for Gilroy Gardens Family Theme Park in Gilroy, California.

FINANCIAL DATA:
Note: Data for latest year may not have been available at press time.

In U.S. $	2018	2017	2016	2015	2014	2013
Revenue		1,321,967,000	1,288,721,000	1,235,778,000	1,159,605,000	1,134,572,000
R&D Expense						
Operating Income		306,062,000	329,526,000	316,204,000	287,168,000	295,557,000
Operating Margin %		23.15%	25.56%	25.58%	24.76%	26.05%
SGA Expense		193,770,000	181,830,000	171,490,000	156,864,000	152,412,000
Net Income		215,476,000	177,688,000	112,222,000	104,215,000	108,204,000
Operating Cash Flow		331,179,000	357,427,000	342,217,000	337,103,000	324,457,000
Capital Expenditure		188,150,000	161,233,000	175,865,000	166,719,000	120,448,000
EBITDA		455,413,000	464,845,000	346,894,000	334,672,000	354,005,000
Return on Assets %		10.67%	8.95%	5.56%	5.14%	5.35%
Return on Equity %		300.38%	302.37%	146.47%	88.56%	72.52%
Debt to Equity		20.01	25.35	27.30	16.20	10.92

CONTACT INFORMATION:
Phone: 419 626-0830   Fax: 419 627-2234
Toll-Free:
Address: 1 Cedar Point Dr., Sandusky, OH 44870 United States

SALARIES/BONUSES:
Top Exec. Salary: $1,063,462   Bonus: $
Second Exec. Salary: $646,154   Bonus: $

STOCK TICKER/OTHER:
Stock Ticker: FUN   Exchange: NYS
Employees: 44,700   Fiscal Year Ends: 12/31
Parent Company:

OTHER THOUGHTS:
Estimated Female Officers or Directors: 3
Hot Spot for Advancement for Women/Minorities: Y

Cengage Learning Holdings II Inc

NAIC Code: 519130

www.cengage.com

TYPES OF BUSINESS:
Electronic Information Publishing
Reference Databases
eBook Platforms
e-Learning Solutions
Library Solutions
Reference Books
Humanities and Science Reference

BRANDS/DIVISIONS/AFFILIATES:
Academic OneFile
Business Collection
Analytics on Demand
Course360
MindTap
Gale Research
Cengage Gale

CONTACTS:
Note: Officers with more than one job title may be intentionally listed here more than once.

Michael E. Hansen, CEO
Alexander Broich, Pres.-International
John Leahy, CFO
Sharon Loeb, Chief Mktg. Officer
Gary Fortier, Chief People Officer
George Moore, CTO
Jim Donohue, Chief Product Officer
Ken Carson, General Counsel
James McCusker, VP-Public & Media Rel.
Kevin Stone, Chief Sales & Mktg. Officer
Fernando Bleichmar, Chief Product Officer
Alexander Broich, Pres., Int'l

GROWTH PLANS/SPECIAL FEATURES:

Cengage Learning Holdings II, Inc. provides textbooks, reference materials, technology and other educational resources for the higher education, K-12, professional and library markets worldwide. The company's purpose is to engage learners, both in the classroom and beyond. Cengage products include: WebAssign, CourseMate, Aplia, Course360 and MindTap. WebAssign is a flexible and fully customizable online instructional system that puts tools in the hands of teachers. It enables teachers to deploy assignments, instantly assess individual student performance and strategize their teaching goals; and enables students to submit answers to homework assignments, tests and assessments. CourseMate is an integrated web-based solution that includes an interactive e-Textbook, multimedia resources, flashcards and quizzes. Aplia provides interactive chapter assignments correlating to specific textbooks. Course360 is an online course solution that helps schools reach a broad spectrum of students. With MindTap, instructors can create and edit courses, manage assignments and grade tests and assignments. For students, it features a comprehensive guide to explaining course requirements, viewing rubrics, completing assignments, providing feedback, monitoring progress and accessing grades. MindTap is also available as a mobile app. Cengage is comprised of a team of student ambassadors whose mission is to help their peers reach new levels of confidence and exceed their learning and life goals. The company's Gale Researcher library reference resource offers students a way to access peer-viewed materials in order to search for the most popular undergraduate courses and research topics. Headquartered in Boston, Massachusetts, the firm also has an office hub located in San Francisco, California, and employees that reside in nearly 40 countries.

Cengage offers its employees tuition reimbursement; an employee assistance program; flexible spending accounts; a 401(k) plan; and medical, dental, vision, life and disability insurance.

FINANCIAL DATA:
Note: Data for latest year may not have been available at press time.

In U.S. $	2018	2017	2016	2015	2014	2013
Revenue			1,630,500,000	1,663,400,000	1,366,000,000	1,677,500,000
R&D Expense						
Operating Income			51,100,000	-98,300,000	200,300,000	180,600,000
Operating Margin %			3.13%	-5.90%		10.76%
SGA Expense			437,500,000	476,500,000	342,700,000	456,800,000
Net Income			-72,400,000	-153,600,000	1,723,400,000	-2,064,900,000
Operating Cash Flow			334,400,000	359,900,000	509,800,000	139,700,000
Capital Expenditure			55,200,000	80,800,000	68,700,000	63,700,000
EBITDA			210,400,000	69,600,000	2,221,100,000	-1,993,100,000
Return on Assets %			-1.76%	-3.60%		-33.23%
Return on Equity %			-5.30%	-10.41%		
Debt to Equity			1.56	1.32		

CONTACT INFORMATION:
Phone: 617-289-7700
Fax: 617-289-7844
Toll-Free: 800-354-9706
Address: 20 Channel Center St., Boston, MA 02210 United States

STOCK TICKER/OTHER:
Stock Ticker: CNGO
Employees: 5,000
Parent Company:
Exchange: GREY
Fiscal Year Ends: 03/31

SALARIES/BONUSES:
Top Exec. Salary: $
Bonus: $
Second Exec. Salary: $
Bonus: $

OTHER THOUGHTS:
Estimated Female Officers or Directors: 2
Hot Spot for Advancement for Women/Minorities:

Sales, profits and employees may be estimates. Financial information, benefits and other data can change quickly and may vary from those stated here.

Central European Media Enterprises Ltd

www.cetv-net.com

NAIC Code: 512110

TYPES OF BUSINESS:
Television Broadcasting
Television Production
Video-on-Demand Service

BRANDS/DIVISIONS/AFFILIATES:
AT&T Inc
BTV
TV NOVA
NOVA
PRO TV
TV Markiza
DOMA

CONTACTS:
Note: Officers with more than one job title may be intentionally listed here more than once.

Michael Del Nin, Co-CEO
Christoph Mainusch, Co-CEO
David Sturgeon, CFO
Daniel Penn, General Counsel
John K. Billock, Chmn.

GROWTH PLANS/SPECIAL FEATURES:

Central European Media Enterprises Ltd. (CME) is an international television broadcasting company. Founded on the idea that the newly democratized nations of the former Soviet Bloc could support independent television broadcasting, CME began operating in 1994 and quickly grew into a large and successful enterprise. The group invests in, develops and operates a collection of national and regional commercial television stations and networks across Central and Eastern Europe. Its operations consist of four geographically-based segments: Bulgaria, the Czech Republic, Romania, and the Slovak Republic. CME owns 94% of its Bulgaria operations and 100% of the rest. CME also has broadcast operations in Moldova. In Bulgaria, the firm operates BTV, a general entertainment channel; and five other channels: BTV Cinema, BTV Comedy, RING, BTV Action and BTV Lady. In the Czech Republic, it operates one general entertainment channel, TV NOVA (CR); and seven other channels: NOVA 2, NOVA Cinema, NOVA Sport 1, NOVA Sport 2, NOVA Action, NOVA Gold and NOVA International. In Romania, it operates one general entertainment channel, PRO TV; and seven other channels: PRO 2, PRO X, PRO GOLD, PRO CINEMA, PRO TV INTERNATIONAL, MTV ROMANIA and PRO TV CHISINAU. In the Slovak Republic, it operates one general entertainment channel, TV Markiza; and three other channels, DOMA, DAJTO and MARKIZA International. AT&T, Inc. holds an approximate 75% share in CME (as of September 2018). In mid-2018, CME sold its operations in Croatia to Slovenia Broadband Sarl, a subsidiary of United Group. That same year, it agreed to sell its operations in Slovenia to the United Group, subject to regulatory approval.

FINANCIAL DATA:
Note: Data for latest year may not have been available at press time.

In U.S. $	2018	2017	2016	2015	2014	2013
Revenue		574,212,000	638,013,000	605,841,000	680,793,000	691,034,000
R&D Expense						
Operating Income		129,949,000	111,589,000	96,297,000	48,136,000	-84,845,000
Operating Margin %		22.63%	17.49%	15.89%	7.07%	-12.27%
SGA Expense		104,755,000	112,598,000	107,001,000	143,616,000	150,220,000
Net Income		49,768,000	-180,291,000	-114,901,000	-227,428,000	-277,651,000
Operating Cash Flow		91,115,000	35,111,000	82,858,000	-66,184,000	-64,198,000
Capital Expenditure		24,905,000	29,567,000	33,517,000	28,685,000	30,449,000
EBITDA		435,813,000	303,417,000	401,460,000	421,620,000	291,888,000
Return on Assets %		3.29%	-13.63%	-8.60%	-12.70%	-13.42%
Return on Equity %				-74.03%	-63.18%	-52.08%
Debt to Equity				11.93	2.22	2.18

CONTACT INFORMATION:
Phone: 441 2961431 Fax:
Toll-Free:
Address: O'Hara House, 3 Bermudiana Rd., Hamilton, HM 08 Bermuda

SALARIES/BONUSES:
Top Exec. Salary: $910,000 Bonus: $
Second Exec. Salary: $910,000 Bonus: $

STOCK TICKER/OTHER:
Stock Ticker: CETV   Exchange: NAS
Employees: 2,950   Fiscal Year Ends: 12/31
Parent Company:

OTHER THOUGHTS:
Estimated Female Officers or Directors: 1
Hot Spot for Advancement for Women/Minorities: Y

Century Casinos Inc

www.cnty.com

NAIC Code: 721120

TYPES OF BUSINESS:
Casinos and Hotels
Cruise Ship Casinos

BRANDS/DIVISIONS/AFFILIATES:
Century Casino & Hotel
Century Casino Calgary
Century Downs Racetrack and Casino
Century Casino St. Alvert
Century Bets! Inc
Casinos Poland Ltd

CONTACTS:
Note: Officers with more than one job title may be intentionally listed here more than once.

Margaret Stapleton, CFO
Erwin Haitzmann, Chairman of the Board
Andreas Terler, Chief Information Officer
Peter Hoetzinger, Co-CEO
Nikolaus Strohriegel, Managing Director, Subsidiary

GROWTH PLANS/SPECIAL FEATURES:

Century Casinos, Inc. (CCI) is an international casino entertainment company involved in developing and operating mid-sized gaming establishments and related lodging and restaurant facilities. CCI's casinos within the U.S. include two Century Casino & Hotels in Colorado. The casino located in Central City, Colorado is comprised of nearly 496 ticket in/ticket out (TITO) slot machines, eight tables, 26 hotel rooms, a bar, two restaurants and a 500-space on-site covered parking garage. The casino in Cripple Creek is comprised of 442 TITO slot machines, six tables, 21 hotel rooms, two bars, a restaurant and 271 surface parking spaces. CCI's gets 21% of its revenue from its U.S. operations. Casinos located in Canada are all based in Alberta, and include: Century Casino & Hotel, with 800 TITO slot machines, 35 tables, 22 video lottery terminals, 26 hotel rooms and a 10,700-square-foot showroom; Century Casino Calgary, with 504 TITO slot machines, 18 tables, 25 video lottery terminals, a full-service off-track betting parlor, a restaurant, a lounge, and several showrooms; Century Downs Racetrack and Casino, with 590 TITO slot machines, 10 video lottery terminals, a racetrack, bar, lounge, restaurant and an off-track betting area; Century Casino St. Albert, with 407 TITO slot machines, 11 tables, 15 video lottery terminals, a restaurant, bar, lounge and banquet facility; and Century Bets!, Inc., which oversees the sourcing of common pool pari-mutuel wagering content for racetracks throughout North America and worldwide. Canadian casinos make up 37% of CCI's annual profits. In Poland, CCI owns a 66.6 % stake in Casinos Poland Ltd., which owns and operates six casinos in hotels in the country, with 375 slot machines and 69 tables. Moreover, CCI holds concession agreements to operate casinos on Windstar Cruises, TUI Cruises, Marella Cruises and Diamond Cruises.

FINANCIAL DATA:
Note: Data for latest year may not have been available at press time.

In U.S. $	2018	2017	2016	2015	2014	2013
Revenue		154,069,000	139,234,000	134,431,000	120,048,000	104,588,000
R&D Expense						
Operating Income		14,615,000	16,165,000	16,493,000	2,657,000	5,618,000
Operating Margin %		9.48%	11.60%	12.26%	2.21%	5.37%
SGA Expense		50,526,000	44,306,000	42,747,000	38,932,000	32,554,000
Net Income		6,259,000	9,215,000	11,907,000	1,232,000	6,181,000
Operating Cash Flow		19,446,000	22,257,000	19,674,000	7,322,000	7,443,000
Capital Expenditure		11,127,000	7,104,000	18,875,000	16,097,000	4,746,000
EBITDA		25,057,000	27,109,000	26,656,000	11,090,000	14,951,000
Return on Assets %		2.54%	4.55%	6.35%	.65%	3.76%
Return on Equity %		4.01%	7.23%	9.88%	1.02%	5.15%
Debt to Equity		0.28	0.37	0.26	0.27	0.24

CONTACT INFORMATION:
Phone: 719 527-8300   Fax: 719 689-9700
Toll-Free:
Address: 455 E. Pikes Peak Ave., Ste 210, Colorado Springs, CO 80903 United States

SALARIES/BONUSES:
Top Exec. Salary: $609,107   Bonus: $
Second Exec. Salary: $608,510   Bonus: $

STOCK TICKER/OTHER:
Stock Ticker: CNTY   Exchange: NAS
Employees: 1,791   Fiscal Year Ends: 12/31
Parent Company:

OTHER THOUGHTS:
Estimated Female Officers or Directors: 2
Hot Spot for Advancement for Women/Minorities: Y

Plunkett Research, Ltd.

Cequel Communications Holdings I LLC

www.suddenlink.com

NAIC Code: 517110

TYPES OF BUSINESS:

Cable TV Service
High-Speed Internet Services
Telephone Services

BRANDS/DIVISIONS/AFFILIATES:

Altice Europe NV
Altice USA
Cequel Corporation
suddenLink

GROWTH PLANS/SPECIAL FEATURES:

Cequel Communications Holdings I, LLC offers suddenLink-branded digital cable television, high-speed internet, voice and security services. The firm's products and services are provided to residential and business customers across the western, midwestern and southern U.S. states. SuddenLink's connected security offering is an interactive and automated platform that provides real-time personal text, email alerts and video monitoring from online, smartphone or tablet. Additional safety features such as smoke, carbon monoxide and water detection are available. For business customers, suddenLink also provides targeted television and online advertising services. Altice Europe NV, through subsidiary Altice USA, holds a 70% equity interest in Cequel Corporation, the parent of Cequel.

CONTACTS: Note: Officers with more than one job title may be intentionally listed here more than once.

Dexter Goei, CEO-Altice
Ivan Lamoureux Ivan Lamoureux, VP-Network Eng.
Craig Rosenthal, General Counsel
Dan Spoelman, VP-Oper.
Aaron Boyll, VP-Corp. Dev.
Pete M. Abel, Sr. VP-Corp. Comm.
James B. Fox, Chief Acct. Officer
Patricia L. McCaskill, Chief Programming Officer
Ralph G. Kelly, Sr. VP
Frederick Ricker, VP-Corp. Taxes
Gibbs Jones, Sr. VP-Customer Experience

FINANCIAL DATA: Note: Data for latest year may not have been available at press time.

In U.S. $	2018	2017	2016	2015	2014	2013
Revenue		2,824,320,000	2,573,160,000	2,420,312,000	2,330,697,000	2,183,301,000
R&D Expense						
Operating Income						
Operating Margin %						
SGA Expense						
Net Income			-228,436,000	-227,053,000	-17,116,000	-209,937,000
Operating Cash Flow						
Capital Expenditure						
EBITDA						
Return on Assets %						
Return on Equity %						
Debt to Equity						

CONTACT INFORMATION:

Phone: 516-803-2300   Fax:
Toll-Free:
Address: 1111 Stewart Ave., Bethpage, NY 11714 United States

STOCK TICKER/OTHER:

Stock Ticker: Subsidiary
Employees: 5,670
Parent Company: Altice Europe NV

Exchange:
Fiscal Year Ends: 12/31

SALARIES/BONUSES:

Top Exec. Salary: $ Bonus: $
Second Exec. Salary: $ Bonus: $

OTHER THOUGHTS:

Estimated Female Officers or Directors: 12
Hot Spot for Advancement for Women/Minorities: Y

Sales, profits and employees may be estimates. Financial information, benefits and other data can change quickly and may vary from those stated here.

Changyou.com Limited

NAIC Code: 511210G

www.changyou.com/en/index.shtml

TYPES OF BUSINESS:
Computer Software, Electronic Games, Apps & Entertainment Apps

BRANDS/DIVISIONS/AFFILIATES:
Tian Long Ba Bu
Steel Ocean
Blade Online
Dashfire
Feng Yun
Qin Shi Ming Yue 2
17173.com
Raidcall

CONTACTS:
Note: Officers with more than one job title may be intentionally listed here more than once.

Dewen Chen, CEO
Xiaojian Hong, COO
Dewen Chen, Pres.
Yaobin Wang, CFO
Angie Chang, Head-Investor Rel.
Charles Zhang, Chmn.

GROWTH PLANS/SPECIAL FEATURES:
Changyou.com Limited is a developer and operator of internet-based games in China. The firm primarily produces massively multiplayer online role-playing games (MMORPGs), which allow players logging on from any location to interact with one another. Its titles include both licensed and proprietary content in a variety of different genres. The firm's technology platform includes 2.5D and 3D graphics engines, proprietary cross-network technologies, a uniform game development platform and anti-cheating/anti-hacking data protection. Tian Long Ba Bu (TLBB), which translates as Novel of Eight Demigods, is a martial arts style fighting and community-building game that was developed in-house. Changyou also produces the TLBB mobile game, Legacy TLBB. Steel Ocean is an in-house developed MMORPG. Blade Online, an online action/fighting game set in a mythical Chinese universe, is licensed. Other games include the co-developed titles of Dashfire, an action role playing game (ARPG); Feng Yun, a 3D martial arts MMO based on a popular Hong Kong comic that was adapted for movies and a TV series; and Qin Shi Ming Yue 2, a 3D role playing game. Changyou's games are free to play, but users can purchase virtual items that appear within the game. Changyou.com also owns and operates the 17173.com website, a leading game information portal in China; Dolphin Browser, a gateway to a host of user activities on mobile devices, primarily used by gamers in Europe, Russia and Japan; Raidcall, a free social communication software that is used by professional and casual gamers; and subsidiary Jingmao, a theater cinema advertiser, advertising in 900 cinemas in 200 cities. The firm operates subsidiaries in the U.S., Europe and Malaysia.

FINANCIAL DATA:
Note: Data for latest year may not have been available at press time.

In U.S. $	2018	2017	2016	2015	2014	2013
Revenue		580,261,000	525,385,000	761,636,000	755,266,000	737,875,000
R&D Expense		131,032,000	121,619,000	170,605,000	194,113,000	119,909,000
Operating Income		177,363,000	130,853,000	201,646,000	10,533,000	305,508,000
Operating Margin %		30.56%	24.90%	26.47%	1.39%	41.40%
SGA Expense		108,080,000	107,103,000	172,624,000	348,758,000	186,021,000
Net Income		108,834,000	144,947,000	212,784,000	-3,381,000	268,642,000
Operating Cash Flow		198,775,000	205,662,000	213,344,000	50,316,000	358,643,000
Capital Expenditure		3,605,000	13,035,000	35,610,000	59,359,000	95,723,000
EBITDA		146,785,000	198,994,000	294,128,000	52,954,000	374,013,000
Return on Assets %		5.99%	8.31%	12.78%	-.21%	19.90%
Return on Equity %		8.95%	13.50%	22.16%	-.37%	35.71%
Debt to Equity					0.38	

CONTACT INFORMATION:
Phone: 86 1062727777 Fax: 86 1068873201
Toll-Free:
Address: No. 65 Bajiao East Rd., Shijingshan Distr., Beijing, 100043 China

STOCK TICKER/OTHER:
Stock Ticker: CYOU
Employees: 2,838
Parent Company:

Exchange: NAS
Fiscal Year Ends: 12/31

SALARIES/BONUSES:
Top Exec. Salary: $ Bonus: $
Second Exec. Salary: $ Bonus: $

OTHER THOUGHTS:
Estimated Female Officers or Directors: 2
Hot Spot for Advancement for Women/Minorities:

Sales, profits and employees may be estimates. Financial information, benefits and other data can change quickly and may vary from those stated here.

Charter Communications Inc

www.charter.com

NAIC Code: 517110

TYPES OF BUSINESS:
Cable TV Service
Internet Access
Advanced Broadband Cable Services
Telephony Services
Voice Over Internet Protocol

BRANDS/DIVISIONS/AFFILIATES:
Spectrum
Spectrum TV
Spectrum Internet
Spectrum Voice
Spectrum Business
Spectrum Enterprise Solutions
Spectrum Community Solutions
Spectrum Reach

CONTACTS: Note: Officers with more than one job title may be intentionally listed here more than once.
Thomas Rutledge, CEO
Michael Baird, Executive VP, Divisional
Christopher Winfrey, CFO
Kevin Howard, Chief Accounting Officer
Jonathan Hargis, Chief Marketing Officer
John Bickham, COO
John Malone, Director Emeritus
Kathleen Mayo, Executive VP, Divisional
Thomas Adams, Executive VP, Divisional
James Blackley, Executive VP, Divisional
Scott Weber, Executive VP, Divisional
Tom Montemagno, Executive VP, Divisional
Catherine Bohigian, Executive VP, Divisional
James Nuzzo, Executive VP, Divisional
Richard DiGeronimo, Executive VP, Divisional

GROWTH PLANS/SPECIAL FEATURES:
Charter Communications, Inc. operates broadband communications businesses in the U.S., offering traditional cable video programming, high-speed internet access and voice service as well as advanced broadband services. The company serves more than 27 million residential and business customers. In addition, Charter sells video and online advertising inventory to local, regional and national advertising customers, as well as fiber-delivered communications and managed information technology (IT) solutions to larger enterprise customers. The firm owns and operates regional sports networks and local sports, news and lifestyle channels; and sells security and home management services to the residential marketplace. Charter's products and services include subscription-based video services, including video on demand (VOD), high definition (HD) television, and digital video recorder (DVR), internet services and voice services. Video, internet and voice services are offered to residential and commercial customers on a subscription basis, sold as bundled or individually. The firm sells its products and services under the Spectrum brand name, including Spectrum TV, Spectrum Internet, Spectrum Voice, Spectrum Business, Spectrum Enterprise Solutions, Spectrum Community Solutions, Spectrum Reach and Spectrum Guide.

Employee benefits include medical, dental and vision coverage; a 401(k); flexible spending accounts; health savings accounts; life and AD&D insurance; short- and long-term disability; adoption reimbursement; tuition reimbursement; and employee discounts.

FINANCIAL DATA: Note: Data for latest year may not have been available at press time.

In U.S. $	2018	2017	2016	2015	2014	2013
Revenue		41,581,000,000	29,003,000,000	9,754,000,000	9,108,000,000	8,155,000,000
R&D Expense						
Operating Income		4,453,000,000	4,340,000,000	1,203,000,000	1,033,000,000	956,000,000
Operating Margin %		10.70%	22.64%	21.73%	21.02%	11.72%
SGA Expense		1,000,000	899,000,000			
Net Income		9,895,000,000	3,522,000,000	-271,000,000	-183,000,000	-169,000,000
Operating Cash Flow		11,954,000,000	8,041,000,000	2,359,000,000	2,359,000,000	2,158,000,000
Capital Expenditure		7,870,000,000	33,532,000,000	1,812,000,000	2,177,000,000	2,425,000,000
EBITDA		15,041,000,000	11,247,000,000	3,328,000,000	3,135,000,000	2,810,000,000
Return on Assets %		6.69%	3.73%	-.84%	-.87%	-1.02%
Return on Equity %		24.98%	17.56%	-542.00%	-123.23%	-112.66%
Debt to Equity		1.74	1.48		143.99	93.91

CONTACT INFORMATION:
Phone: 203-905-7801   Fax:
Toll-Free:
Address: 400 Atlantic St., Stamford, CT 06901 United States

SALARIES/BONUSES:
Top Exec. Salary: $2,000,000   Bonus: $
Second Exec. Salary: $1,500,000   Bonus: $

STOCK TICKER/OTHER:
Stock Ticker: CHTR
Employees: 94,800
Parent Company:

Exchange: NAS
Fiscal Year Ends: 12/31

OTHER THOUGHTS:
Estimated Female Officers or Directors: 1
Hot Spot for Advancement for Women/Minorities:

China Literature Limited

NAIC Code: 519130

ir.yuewen.com

TYPES OF BUSINESS:
Internet Publishing and Broadcasting and Web Search Portals
Online Literature

BRANDS/DIVISIONS/AFFILIATES:
Tencent Holdings Limited
QQ Reading

CONTACTS:
Note: Officers with more than one job title may be intentionally listed here more than once.

Wenhui Wu, Co-CEO
Xiaodong Liang, Co-CEO
Xuesong Shang, Pres.

GROWTH PLANS/SPECIAL FEATURES:

China Literature Limited operates an online literature market and platform in China. As of mid-2018, the company had 7.3 million writers and 10.7 million online literary works, covering over 200 genres. During the first half of 2018, China Literature had on average 213.5 monthly active users on its platform, along with its self-operated channels on partner distribution platforms. The firm owns nine major branded products, among which QQ Reading serves as a flagship product and is a unified mobile content aggregation and distribution platform, while the other products focus on individual genres and their respective fan bases. Parent Tencent Holdings Limited provides China Literature with exclusive content distribution access through its suite of mobile and internet products such as Mobile QQ, QQ Browser, Tencent News, Weixin Reading and Tencent Video. In addition, China Literature: licenses its content to third-parties such as Baidu, Sogou, JD.com and Xiaomi Duokan for distribution; and monetizes its proprietary content library through online paid reading and content adaptations into various entertainment formats.

FINANCIAL DATA:
Note: Data for latest year may not have been available at press time.

In U.S. $	2018	2017	2016	2015	2014	2013
Revenue		595,984,100	372,118,900	233,825,700	67,850,570	
R&D Expense						
Operating Income		62,964,740	-6,580,170	-36,766,170	597,866	
Operating Margin %		10.56%	-1.76%	-15.72%	.88%	
SGA Expense		243,831,000	106,995,800	75,219,110	19,085,590	
Net Income		80,937,410	5,338,738	-50,586,370	-3,075,199	
Operating Cash Flow		128,903,700	27,038,900	28,819,110	15,895,420	
Capital Expenditure		19,402,570	19,369,820	22,649,650	8,107,727	
EBITDA		123,975,500	39,036,400	-10,245,810	4,244,590	
Return on Assets %		4.99%	.54%	-5.44%	-.33%	
Return on Equity %		6.25%	.76%	-7.74%	-.45%	
Debt to Equity		0.03				

CONTACT INFORMATION:
Phone: 86 1059357051 Fax:
Toll-Free:
Address: No. 6 Bldg., 690 Bi Bo Rd., Pudong, Shanghai, 201203 China

SALARIES/BONUSES:
Top Exec. Salary: $ Bonus: $
Second Exec. Salary: $ Bonus: $

STOCK TICKER/OTHER:
Stock Ticker: CHLLF Exchange: PINX
Employees: 1,600 Fiscal Year Ends: 12/31
Parent Company: Tencent Holdings Limited

OTHER THOUGHTS:
Estimated Female Officers or Directors:
Hot Spot for Advancement for Women/Minorities:

Sales, profits and employees may be estimates. Financial information, benefits and other data can change quickly and may vary from those stated here.

Churchill Downs Incorporated

www.churchilldownsincorporated.com

NAIC Code: 713210

TYPES OF BUSINESS:
Horse Racing
Pari-mutuel Wagering
Simulcasting
Video Poker
Computer Graphics & Gambling Software
Online Retail

BRANDS/DIVISIONS/AFFILIATES:
Churchill Downs Racetrack
Arlington International Racecourse
Calder Race Course
Fair Grounds Race Course
Riverwalk Casino Hotel
TwinSpires
Ocean Downs

CONTACTS:
Note: Officers with more than one job title may be intentionally listed here more than once.

William Carstanjen, CEO
Marcia Dall, CFO
R. Rankin, Chairman of the Board
William Mudd, COO

GROWTH PLANS/SPECIAL FEATURES:

Churchill Downs Incorporated (CDI) is a diversified provider of pari-mutuel horseracing, entertainment, casino gaming and online horseracing wagering. The company operates four core segments: racing, casinos, TwinSpires, and other investments. Racing operations include Churchill Downs Racetrack in Louisville, Kentucky, an internationally known thoroughbred racing operation and home of the Kentucky Derby; Arlington International Racecourse, a thoroughbred racing operation in Arlington Heights along with 11 off-track betting facilities (OTBs) in Illinois; Calder Race Course, a thoroughbred racing operation in Miami Gardens, Florida; and Fair Grounds Race Course, a thoroughbred racing operation in New Orleans along with 12 OTBs in Louisiana. Casinos includes Oxford Casino in Oxford, Maine; Riverwalk Casino Hotel in Vicksburg, Mississippi; Harlow's Casino Resort & Spa in Greenville, Mississippi; Calder Casino in Miami Gardens, Florida; Fair Grounds Slots in Louisiana; Video Services, LLC, in southeast Louisiana; Ocean Downs in Ocean City, Maryland; 50%-owned Miami Valley Gaming, LLC in Lebanon, Ohio; and 25%-owned Saratoga Casino Holdings, LLC in New York. These casinos offer a range of facilities, which vary per location, including slot machines, table games, dining, event centers, pool, spa and lottery terminals. TwinSpires is an advanced deposit wagering unit that allows customers to wager on horse racing from computers, tablet devices and smart phones. Other investments include United Tote Company and United Tote Canada, which manufacture and operate pari-mutuel wagering systems. During 2018, CDI sold Big Fish Games to Aristocrat Leisure for $990 million; took full ownership of Ocean Downs; opened Derby City Gaming, an historical racing parlor in Louisville; and agreed to acquire a majority share in Rivers Casino Des Plaines.

FINANCIAL DATA:
Note: Data for latest year may not have been available at press time.

In U.S. $	2018	2017	2016	2015	2014	2013
Revenue		882,600,000	1,308,600,000	1,212,301,000	812,934,000	779,325,000
R&D Expense			39,000,000	39,399,000		
Operating Income		167,400,000	173,900,000	145,360,000	94,219,000	90,100,000
Operating Margin %		18.96%	13.28%	11.99%	11.59%	11.56%
SGA Expense		83,100,000	100,200,000	90,787,000	84,683,000	83,071,000
Net Income		140,500,000	108,100,000	65,197,000	46,357,000	54,900,000
Operating Cash Flow		218,200,000	226,800,000	264,526,000	141,619,000	144,915,000
Capital Expenditure		116,900,000	57,200,000	45,760,000	56,736,000	51,421,000
EBITDA		266,400,000	337,600,000	260,068,000	165,617,000	153,487,000
Return on Assets %		6.09%	4.77%	2.81%	2.49%	4.45%
Return on Equity %		21.20%	16.60%	9.89%	6.59%	8.13%
Debt to Equity		1.75	1.32	1.24	1.08	0.52

CONTACT INFORMATION:
Phone: 502 636-4400
Fax: 502 636-4560
Toll-Free:
Address: 600 N. Hurstbourne Pkwy., Ste. 400, Louisville, KY 40222 United States

STOCK TICKER/OTHER:
Stock Ticker: CHDN
Employees: 4,000
Parent Company:

Exchange: NAS
Fiscal Year Ends: 12/31

SALARIES/BONUSES:
Top Exec. Salary: $1,023,077   Bonus: $
Second Exec. Salary: $642,269   Bonus: $

OTHER THOUGHTS:
Estimated Female Officers or Directors: 1
Hot Spot for Advancement for Women/Minorities:

Cinemark Inc

NAIC Code: 512131

www.cinemark.com

TYPES OF BUSINESS:
Movie Theaters

BRANDS/DIVISIONS/AFFILIATES:
Cinemark Holdings Inc
National CineMedia LLC
XD Extreme Digital Cinema

CONTACTS: Note: Officers with more than one job title may be intentionally listed here more than once.
Mark Zoradi, CEO
Sean Gamble, CFO
Lee Mitchell, Chairman of the Board
Michael Cavalier, Executive VP
Valmir Fernandes, President, Subsidiary

GROWTH PLANS/SPECIAL FEATURES:
Cinemark, Inc. is a multinational theater corporation which conducts business under two primary operating segments: U.S. markets and international markets. The company operates 541 theaters with a total of 6,014 screens throughout 41 U.S. states and Latin America. Cinemark's theater circuit is the one of the largest in the U.S., with 340 theaters and 4,579 screens in 41 states, with the heaviest concentrations in Texas, California, Ohio, Utah and Nevada. Its international circuit has 201 theaters and 1,435 screens. Admissions are the firm's primary source of revenue, accounting for approximately 63.5% annually. Concession sales, with a much higher profit margin than admissions, are the firm's second largest income source, representing approximately 31.5% of total revenues. Other minor sources of income, accounting for 4.9% of revenues, include on-screen advertising sales and vendor marketing programs as well as pay phones, ATMs and video games located at some theaters. The firm has developed a new large screen digital format, XD Extreme Digital Cinema, which it has in place at over 225 theaters. It is currently in the process of converting the entirety of its theater chain to digital projection technology. Cinemark, Inc. operates as a wholly-owned subsidiary of Cinemark Holdings, Inc. In June 2018, Cinemark announced it had purchased the remaining units of National Cinemedia, LLC, which offers pre-feature programming as well as in-theater conference and event services.

FINANCIAL DATA: Note: Data for latest year may not have been available at press time.

In U.S. $	2018	2017	2016	2015	2014	2013
Revenue		2,991,547,000	2,918,765,000	2,852,609,000	2,626,990,000	2,682,894,000
R&D Expense						
Operating Income		430,178,000	446,230,000	440,096,000	385,432,000	415,440,000
Operating Margin %		14.37%	15.28%	15.42%	14.67%	15.48%
SGA Expense		507,788,000	469,120,000	457,835,000	425,324,000	434,704,000
Net Income		264,180,000	255,091,000	216,869,000	192,610,000	148,470,000
Operating Cash Flow		528,477,000	451,834,000	455,871,000	454,634,000	309,666,000
Capital Expenditure		380,862,000	326,908,000	331,726,000	244,705,000	259,670,000
EBITDA		688,808,000	678,030,000	649,614,000	579,417,000	552,548,000
Return on Assets %		6.01%	6.04%	5.23%	4.64%	3.70%
Return on Equity %		19.89%	21.60%	19.60%	17.46%	13.63%
Debt to Equity		1.45	1.59	1.80	1.81	1.85

CONTACT INFORMATION:
Phone: 972 665-1000 Fax: 972 665-1004
Toll-Free: 800-246-3627
Address: 3900 Dallas Pkwy., Ste. 500, Plano, TX 75093 United States

SALARIES/BONUSES:
Top Exec. Salary: $958,645 Bonus: $
Second Exec. Salary: $950,000 Bonus: $

STOCK TICKER/OTHER:
Stock Ticker: CNK
Employees: 19,200
Parent Company: Cinemark Holdings Inc
Exchange: NYS
Fiscal Year Ends: 12/31

OTHER THOUGHTS:
Estimated Female Officers or Directors:
Hot Spot for Advancement for Women/Minorities:

Cineplex Inc

NAIC Code: 512131

www.cineplex.com

TYPES OF BUSINESS:
Investments
Movie Theaters

BRANDS/DIVISIONS/AFFILIATES:
Cineplex Entertainment LP
Cineplex Starburst Inc
Cineplex Cinemas
Cineplex Odeon
UltraAVX
Xscape Entertainment Centre
OutTakes
Poptopia

CONTACTS:
Note: Officers with more than one job title may be intentionally listed here more than once.

Ellis Jacob, CEO
Gord Nelson, CFO
Jeffrey Kent, Chief Technology Officer
Dan McGrath, COO
Ian Greenberg, Director
Michael Kennedy, Executive VP, Divisional
Anne Fitzgerald, Executive VP, Divisional
Heather Briant, Senior VP, Divisional

GROWTH PLANS/SPECIAL FEATURES:
Cineplex, Inc. is an entertainment company that operates numerous businesses, including movie theaters, food services, gaming, alternative programming and the online sale of home entertainment content. Cineplex is also a joint venture partner in SCENE, a Canadian entertainment loyalty program. Through subsidiary Cineplex Entertainment LP, the firm operates 164 theatres with 1,677 screens in all 10 Canadian provinces. Cineplex Entertainment serves approximately 77 million guests annually through theatre brands such as Cineplex Cinemas, Cineplex Odeon, SilverCity, Galaxy Cinemas, Cinema City, Famous Players, Scotiabank Theatres, Cineplex VIP Cinemas and The Rec Room. The Rec Room is a recently-developed entertainment restaurant chain that features food and beverages, arcades, recreational games, bar areas and an auditorium used for live entertainment, sports events and more on its cinema-style display. Cineplex also owns and operates its own brands for entertainment, such as UltraAVX, Xscape Entertainment Centre and Cineplex Starburst; and for food and beverage, such as OutTakes movie meals and Poptopia gourmet popcorn. In addition, CineplexStore.com is the company's online e-commerce site which sells home entertainment content. Merchandise can also be obtained through mobile apps.

FINANCIAL DATA:
Note: Data for latest year may not have been available at press time.

In U.S. $	2018	2017	2016	2015	2014	2013
Revenue		1,153,713,000	1,096,779,000	1,017,111,000	916,043,000	868,969,700
R&D Expense						
Operating Income		85,864,470	94,069,210	116,169,100	88,709,680	94,587,060
Operating Margin %		8.65%	8.57%	12.35%	10.63%	12.73%
SGA Expense		373,100,000	347,177,800	320,613,100	294,201,300	274,174,200
Net Income		52,499,480	59,139,540	99,932,480	56,585,900	61,991,420
Operating Cash Flow		114,514,600	123,166,800	171,079,000	133,734,500	166,667,700
Capital Expenditure		130,772,800	78,731,050	71,722,260	81,532,480	46,302,340
EBITDA		178,418,000	173,661,600	209,922,300	146,016,700	147,021,200
Return on Assets %		3.94%	4.64%	8.13%	4.76%	5.72%
Return on Equity %		9.68%	10.51%	17.96%	10.30%	11.17%
Debt to Equity		0.66	0.54	0.43	0.46	0.44

CONTACT INFORMATION:
Phone: 416 323 6600 Fax: 416 323 6603
Toll-Free: 800-333-0061
Address: 1303 Yonge St., Toronto, ON M4T 2Y9 Canada

STOCK TICKER/OTHER:
Stock Ticker: CGX
Employees: 13,000
Parent Company:

Exchange: TSE
Fiscal Year Ends: 12/31

SALARIES/BONUSES:
Top Exec. Salary: $ Bonus: $
Second Exec. Salary: $ Bonus: $

OTHER THOUGHTS:
Estimated Female Officers or Directors: 4
Hot Spot for Advancement for Women/Minorities: Y

Cineworld Group plc

NAIC Code: 512131

www.cineworldplc.com

TYPES OF BUSINESS:
Motion Picture Theaters (except Drive-Ins)

BRANDS/DIVISIONS/AFFILIATES:
Cinema City International NV
Picturehouse Cinemas Ltd
Cineworld
Cinema City
Picture House
Yes Planet
Regal Entertainment Group

GROWTH PLANS/SPECIAL FEATURES:
Cineworld Group plc is the second largest cinema operator in the world, comprising five subsidiary brands: Cineworld, Cinema City International NV, Picture House, Yes Planet and Regal Entertainment Group. Cineworld theaters operate in the U.K., Ireland, Poland, the Czech Republic, Slovakia, Hungary, Bulgaria, Romania, Israel and the U.S. Cinema City is the largest cinema operator in Central Eastern Europe (CEE) as well as in Israel, with approximately 100 multiplexes. In the CEE countries, Cinema City operates under the Cinema City brand name, and in Israel under the Yes Planet brand name. Picture House cinemas is operated by subsidiary Picturehouse Cinemas Ltd., and comprises 21 locations within the U.K. Regal Entertainment Group operates more than 500 theaters in the U.S. In June 2018, Cineworld, in conjunction with Cinemark, agree to acquire the remaining units of National CineMedia, LLC, an in-theater advertising network, from AMC

CONTACTS:
Note: Officers with more than one job title may be intentionally listed here more than once.

Moshe (Mooky) Greidinger, CEO
Nisan Cohen, CFO
Renana Teperberg, Chief Commercial Officer
Anthony Herbert Bloom, Chmn.

FINANCIAL DATA:
Note: Data for latest year may not have been available at press time.

In U.S. $	2018	2017	2016	2015	2014	2013
Revenue		1,203,697,000	984,330,700	1,045,645,000	933,253,000	669,656,800
R&D Expense						
Operating Income		168,520,400	135,842,100	153,483,800	117,824,300	78,821,960
Operating Margin %		14.00%	13.80%	14.60%	12.26%	9.23%
SGA Expense		149,330,400	126,958,700	70,519,560	83,622,120	66,949,200
Net Income		135,951,500	101,172,100	120,446,200	82,115,420	34,628,890
Operating Cash Flow		233,523,000	185,194,300	245,781,400	129,727,300	91,684,120
Capital Expenditure		143,519,300	103,269,600	131,261,200	72,472,500	31,166,000
EBITDA		263,389,100	203,084,500	234,670,100	186,982,100	99,104,590
Return on Assets %		7.44%	6.86%	7.59%	7.10%	4.35%
Return on Equity %		13.98%	13.68%	15.61%	15.56%	10.98%
Debt to Equity		0.42	0.48	0.54	0.57	0.64

CONTACT INFORMATION:
Phone: 44-20-8987-5000 Fax:
Toll-Free:
Address: Vantage London, 8/Fl, Great West Rd., Brentford, TW8 9AG United Kingdom

STOCK TICKER/OTHER:
Stock Ticker: CNWGY
Employees: 10,244
Parent Company:

Exchange: GREY
Fiscal Year Ends: 12/31

SALARIES/BONUSES:
Top Exec. Salary: $703,425 Bonus: $551,879
Second Exec. Salary: $479,895 Bonus: $376,339

OTHER THOUGHTS:
Estimated Female Officers or Directors:
Hot Spot for Advancement for Women/Minorities:

Cirque du Soleil Inc

www.cirquedusoleil.com

NAIC Code: 711190

TYPES OF BUSINESS:
Circuses
Merchandising
Performing Arts Touring Groups
Resort & Casino Entertainment
Ticket Sales Services
Events Management

BRANDS/DIVISIONS/AFFILIATES:
Mystere
O
Zumanity
Beatles LOVE (The)
Michael Jackson ONE
Volta
Crystal
Blue Man Group

CONTACTS: *Note: Officers with more than one job title may be intentionally listed here more than once.*

Daniel Lamarre, CEO
Jonathan Tetrault, COO
Daniel Lamarre, Pres.
Guy Laliberte, Creative Guide
Jacque Paquin, Designer-Acrobatic Equipment & Rigging
Chantal Cote, Mgr.-Corp. Public Rel.
Aldo Giampaolo, Head-New Bus. Unit Theater Shows
Eric Fournier, Sr. VP-New Ventures
Gilles Ste-Croix, Sr. VP-Creative Content

GROWTH PLANS/SPECIAL FEATURES:

Cirque du Soleil, Inc. is a performing arts company that combines traditional circus elements, acrobatics, street entertainment, exotic costumes, cabaret, music and dance. Cirque du Soleil currently (December 2018) has 18 active shows: Mystere, O, Zumanity, KA, Corteo, The Beatles LOVE, KOOZA, OVO, TOTEM, Amaluna, Michael Jackson ONE, KURIOS: Cabinet of Curiosities, JOYA, TORUK-The First Flight, LUZIA, Volta, Crystal and Bazzar. In 2019, Alegria is be reformatted to Grand Chapiteau, Paramour is scheduled to reopen and X (The Land of Fantasy) is scheduled for release in Hangzhou, China. The company's active various shows can be attended at venues located in Las Vegas, New York and Orlando, in the U.S.; and at Riviera Maya, in Mexico. Cirque du Soleil also provides shows on tour. The duration of each touring show usually comprises a 55-minute first act followed by a 50-minute second act, with a 30-minute interval. Permanent shows are usually 90 minutes in length without intermission. JOYA, is an exception, being only 70 minutes in length. Both touring and permanent shows typically perform 10 shows a week. The firm sells merchandise including music, DVDs, books, apparel, collectables and souvenirs through its website and at live shows. Cirque du Soleil has partnered with Grupo Vidanta to construct and operate the world's first entertainment park animated by Cirque du Soleil, which will be located in Nuevo Vallarta, Mexico; with an estimated mid-2019 opening date, but delays could extend the opening into 2020. Subsidiary Blue Man Group is known for incorporating various categories of music and art into its stage performances, which are presented worldwide.

The firm offers employee benefits including retirement plans, an employee cafeteria, an employee assistance program, flexible insurance coverage, complimentary show tickets, discounts on merchandise and commute compensation.

FINANCIAL DATA: *Note: Data for latest year may not have been available at press time.*

In U.S. $	2018	2017	2016	2015	2014	2013
Revenue	950,000,000	900,000,000	872,000,000	839,000,000	825,000,000	800,000,000
R&D Expense						
Operating Income						
Operating Margin %						
SGA Expense						
Net Income						
Operating Cash Flow						
Capital Expenditure						
EBITDA						
Return on Assets %						
Return on Equity %						
Debt to Equity						

CONTACT INFORMATION:
Phone: 514-722-2324 Fax: 514-722-3692
Toll-Free: 800-678-2119
Address: 8400 2nd Ave., Montreal, QC H1Z 4M6 Canada

STOCK TICKER/OTHER:
Stock Ticker: Private
Employees: 5,000
Parent Company:

Exchange:
Fiscal Year Ends: 12/31

SALARIES/BONUSES:
Top Exec. Salary: $ Bonus: $
Second Exec. Salary: $ Bonus: $

OTHER THOUGHTS:
Estimated Female Officers or Directors: 1
Hot Spot for Advancement for Women/Minorities:

Sales, profits and employees may be estimates. Financial information, benefits and other data can change quickly and may vary from those stated here.

Clarion Co Ltd

NAIC Code: 334310

www.clarion.com

TYPES OF BUSINESS:
Audio & Video Equipment, Manufacturing
Navigation Systems
Security Systems

BRANDS/DIVISIONS/AFFILIATES:
Hitachi Ltd
Dynamic Beat Enhancer
Intelligent Tune App

CONTACTS:
Note: Officers with more than one job title may be intentionally listed here more than once.

Atsushi Kawabata, CEO
Toru Kaneko, Exec. Dir.
Hidetoshi Kawamoto, Exec. Dir.
Hidetoshi Kawamoto, Chmn.

GROWTH PLANS/SPECIAL FEATURES:
Clarion Co., Ltd., headquartered in Japan, develops safety, information and audio technology for automobiles and recreational vehicles. The safety and information systems division includes applications in automatic parking, safe driving support systems and autonomous driving technologies. Information systems comprise cloud information services that enhance connectivity for user information, vehicle operation and safety purposes. These cloud-based information networks include information management/control, cloud management, application management and policy management via onboard information devices that provide comfort and convenience in vehicles. The company's smart cockpit solutions integrate advanced connectivity technologies, safety, information, human machine interface and sound to create seamless connectivity within the vehicle. Clarion's proprietary map formats are used as a core source of information in its navigation systems. These formats comprise map readiness and map updates that cover the entire world, and provide data concerning road conditions in various regions, as well as a 3D locator that combines various sensor data with map data. The audio technology segment features Clarion's sound processing technology; fully-digital speakers; Dynamic Beat Enhancer for emphasizing the feel of the beat via bass sounds; and Intelligent Tune App, which allows users to tune audio settings based on the car model and speaker quality. Clarion continues to develop sound technologies that enable customers to enjoy better sound and sound options within their vehicles. The firm operates as a subsidiary of Hitachi Ltd.

FINANCIAL DATA:
Note: Data for latest year may not have been available at press time.

In U.S. $	2018	2017	2016	2015	2014	2013
Revenue		2,050,000,000	1,981,080,000	1,832,380,000	1,859,092,000	1,621,700,000
R&D Expense						
Operating Income						
Operating Margin %						
SGA Expense						
Net Income			70,539,300	70,500,000	32,476,000	12,432,000
Operating Cash Flow						
Capital Expenditure						
EBITDA						
Return on Assets %						
Return on Equity %						
Debt to Equity						

CONTACT INFORMATION:
Phone: 81 486013700   Fax: 81 486013701
Toll-Free:
Address: 7-2 Shintoshin, Chuo-ku, Saitama-Shi, Saitama, 330-0081 Japan

STOCK TICKER/OTHER:
Stock Ticker: 6796
Employees: 10,000
Parent Company: Hitachi Ltd

Exchange: Tokyo
Fiscal Year Ends: 03/31

SALARIES/BONUSES:
Top Exec. Salary: $ Bonus: $
Second Exec. Salary: $ Bonus: $

OTHER THOUGHTS:
Estimated Female Officers or Directors:
Hot Spot for Advancement for Women/Minorities:

Sales, profits and employees may be estimates. Financial information, benefits and other data can change quickly and may vary from those stated here.

Clear Channel Outdoor Holdings Inc

www.clearchanneloutdoor.com

NAIC Code: 541850

TYPES OF BUSINESS:
Outdoor Advertising
Mall Displays
Outdoor Furniture Advertising
Billboards & Wallscapes

BRANDS/DIVISIONS/AFFILIATES:
iHeartMedia Inc
iHeartCommunications Inc
Smartbike

CONTACTS:
Note: Officers with more than one job title may be intentionally listed here more than once.

Scott Hamilton, Assistant Secretary
Scott Wells, CEO, Divisional
Christopher Eccleshare, CEO, Divisional
Robert Walls, CEO, Subsidiary
Robert Pittman, CEO
Steven Macri, CFO, Subsidiary
Richard Bressler, CFO

GROWTH PLANS/SPECIAL FEATURES:

Clear Channel Outdoor Holdings, Inc. provides clients with advertising opportunities through billboards, street furniture displays, transit displays and other out-of-home advertising displays. It owns and operates over 450,000 advertising displays globally, with a digital platform including more than 1,200 digital billboards across 28 markets in the U.S. and more than 13,000 digital displays in international markets. The company operates in two segments: Americas and international, which represent 48% and 52% of annual revenue, respectively. The Americas business segment includes operations in the U.S., Canada and Latin America, with most revenue derived from operations in the U.S. The Americas segment has operations in 44 of the top 50 markets in the U.S. The international business segment includes operations in Asia and Europe, with 35% of revenue from operations in France and the U.K. Assets consist of billboards; street furniture and transmit displays; airport displays; mall displays; wallscapes; and spectaculars, or displays that incorporate video, 3D lettering or figures, mechanical devices and other embellishments to create special effects. The company also operates the SmartBike program, an urban bike-sharing service in Europe. Most of the structures used to support the billboards are produced at a facility in Illinois, USA. Clear Channel Outdoor Holdings is a publicly-traded subsidiary of iHeartCommunications, Inc., which is itself a subsidiary of iHeartMedia, Inc.

The firm provides its employees with medical, dental, vision, disability and life insurance plans; a flexible spending account; an employee assistance program; and a 401(k) plan.

FINANCIAL DATA:
Note: Data for latest year may not have been available at press time.

In U.S. $	2018	2017	2016	2015	2014	2013
Revenue		2,591,265,000	2,702,395,000	2,806,204,000	2,961,259,000	2,946,190,000
R&D Expense						
Operating Income		236,585,000	290,117,000	287,456,000	278,715,000	280,321,000
Operating Margin %		9.13%	10.73%	10.24%	9.41%	9.51%
SGA Expense		508,637,000	632,585,000	647,884,000	679,413,000	667,971,000
Net Income		-639,716,000	141,431,000	-96,072,000	-9,590,000	-48,460,000
Operating Cash Flow		147,588,000	310,293,000	298,933,000	348,423,000	414,640,000
Capital Expenditure		224,238,000	229,772,000	218,332,000	231,169,000	216,670,000
EBITDA		-200,595,000	960,124,000	710,500,000	767,840,000	746,436,000
Return on Assets %		-12.31%	2.34%	-1.51%	-.14%	-.69%
Return on Equity %						-62.21%
Debt to Equity						

CONTACT INFORMATION:
Phone: 210 832-3700   Fax:
Toll-Free:
Address: 20880 Stone Oak Pkwy., San Antonio, TX 78258 United States

STOCK TICKER/OTHER:
Stock Ticker: CCO
Employees: 1,400
Parent Company: iHeartMedia Inc

Exchange: NYS
Fiscal Year Ends: 12/31

SALARIES/BONUSES:
Top Exec. Salary: $964,948   Bonus: $1,350,000
Second Exec. Salary: $427,920   Bonus: $1,073,366

OTHER THOUGHTS:
Estimated Female Officers or Directors: 7
Hot Spot for Advancement for Women/Minorities: Y

ClubCorp Holdings Inc

NAIC Code: 713910

www.clubcorp.com

TYPES OF BUSINESS:
Golf Courses & Country Clubs
Business/Sports Clubs
Resorts

BRANDS/DIVISIONS/AFFILIATES:
Apollo Global Management LLC

CONTACTS: Note: Officers with more than one job title may be intentionally listed here more than once.
David Pillsbury, CEO
Chuck Feddersen, Exec. VP-Oper.
Curt D. McClellan, CFO/Treas.
Meg Tollison, CMO
John Beckert, Director
Patrick Droesch, Executive VP, Divisional
Charles Feddersen, Executive VP, Divisional
Andrew Miller, Executive VP, Divisional
Ingrid Keiser, Executive VP, Divisional

GROWTH PLANS/SPECIAL FEATURES:
ClubCorp Holdings, Inc. is an owner and operator of more than 200 golf and country clubs, business clubs, sports clubs and alumni clubs. With over 430,000 members, the company's properties are located in 28 states, Washington D.C., Mexico and China. ClubCorp has organized its operations into two principle business segments: golf and country clubs, and business, sports and alumni clubs (BSA). The golf and country clubs segment includes clubs designed to appeal to individuals and families who lead an active lifestyle and seek an outlet for golf, tennis, swimming and other activities. ClubCorp owns or operates more than 3,400 holes of golf, as well as tennis courts. These clubs consist of private country clubs, semi-private clubs and public courses and courts. The BSA segment provides members with private upscale locations where they can work, network and socialize. The firm owns or manages these clubs, which consist of business clubs, sports clubs, alumni clubs and a hybrid of business and sports clubs. Business clubs are generally located in office towers or business complexes and cater to professionals who entertain clients, are engaged in expanding their business networks, work and socialize. Sports clubs include a variety of fitness and racquet facilities. Alumni clubs are associated with universities with large alumni networks, and are designed to provide a connection between the university and its alumni. ClubCorp is priavetely-held by Apollo Global Management, LLC.

FINANCIAL DATA: Note: Data for latest year may not have been available at press time.

In U.S. $	2018	2017	2016	2015	2014	2013
Revenue	1,150,000,000	1,100,000,000	1,088,480,000	1,052,867,008	884,155,008	815,080,000
R&D Expense						
Operating Income						
Operating Margin %						
SGA Expense						
Net Income			3,577,000	-9,512,000	13,226,000	-40,892,000
Operating Cash Flow						
Capital Expenditure						
EBITDA						
Return on Assets %						
Return on Equity %						
Debt to Equity						

CONTACT INFORMATION:
Phone: 972-243-6191 Fax: 972-406-7856
Toll-Free:
Address: 3030 LBJ Freeway, Ste. 600, Dallas, TX 75234 United States

SALARIES/BONUSES:
Top Exec. Salary: $ Bonus: $
Second Exec. Salary: $ Bonus: $

STOCK TICKER/OTHER:
Stock Ticker: Private Exchange:
Employees: 20,000 Fiscal Year Ends: 12/27
Parent Company: Apollo Global Management LLC

OTHER THOUGHTS:
Estimated Female Officers or Directors: 1
Hot Spot for Advancement for Women/Minorities:

Sales, profits and employees may be estimates. Financial information, benefits and other data can change quickly and may vary from those stated here.

CNHI LLC

NAIC Code: 511110

www.cnhi.com

TYPES OF BUSINESS:
Newspaper Publishing
Marketing Agencies
Online Publishing

BRANDS/DIVISIONS/AFFILIATES:
Raycom Media Inc
Community Newspaper Holdings Inc
Eagle Marketing

GROWTH PLANS/SPECIAL FEATURES:
CNHI, LLC, formerly Community Newspaper Holdings, Inc., owns community newspapers, websites and niche publications across the U.S. The firm publishes daily and non-daily publications throughout the U.S. CNHI also has interests in a variety of ancillary publications and services that complement its newspapers. Additionally, the company operates the marketing agency Eagle Marketing, a full-service advertising agency based in Enid, Oklahoma that offers clients high-quality printed materials, design services, website design and multimedia development, special event marketing, sales and targeted marketing options. Raycom Media, Inc. is the parent company of CNHI. In June 2018, the firm announced it was exploring the sale of its newspaper properties in 22 states. The announcement was made after its parent company, Raycom Media, reported it has signed an agreement to be acquired by Gray Television group, a public company headquartered in Atlanta.

CONTACTS: Note: Officers with more than one job title may be intentionally listed here more than once.
Donna Barrett, CEO
Steve McPhaul, COO
Chris Cato, Dir.-Finance
Greg Maibach, Chief Revenue Officer
Terrence Alexander, Dir.-Human Resources
Michelle Talerico, CIO
Tom Shafer, VP-Prod.
Matthew Gray, General Counsel
Steve McPhaul, COO
Jennifer Pustaver, Sr. VP-Finance
Bill Ketter, VP-News
Linnie Pride, Sr. VP-Audience Dev.
David Joyner, VP-Content

FINANCIAL DATA: Note: Data for latest year may not have been available at press time.

In U.S. $	2018	2017	2016	2015	2014	2013
Revenue						
R&D Expense						
Operating Income						
Operating Margin %						
SGA Expense						
Net Income						
Operating Cash Flow						
Capital Expenditure						
EBITDA						
Return on Assets %						
Return on Equity %						
Debt to Equity						

CONTACT INFORMATION:
Phone: 334-293-5800
Fax: 334-293-5910
Toll-Free:
Address: 445 Dexter Ave., Ste. 7000, Montgomery, AL 36104 United States

STOCK TICKER/OTHER:
Stock Ticker: Subsidiary
Employees:
Parent Company: Raycom Media Inc

Exchange:
Fiscal Year Ends: 12/31

SALARIES/BONUSES:
Top Exec. Salary: $
Second Exec. Salary: $
Bonus: $
Bonus: $

OTHER THOUGHTS:
Estimated Female Officers or Directors: 6
Hot Spot for Advancement for Women/Minorities: Y

Codere SA

NAIC Code: 713210

www.codere.com

TYPES OF BUSINESS:
Gambling Device Concession Operators
Slot Machine Operations
Racetrack Management

BRANDS/DIVISIONS/AFFILIATES:
Codere
Turff Bet & Sports Bar
Hipodromo de las Americas
Hipodromo Presidente Remon
Hipodromo Nacional de Maronas
Hipodromo de las Pidras
The Game Yearbook in Spain

CONTACTS:
Note: Officers with more than one job title may be intentionally listed here more than once.
Jose Antonio Martinez Sampedro, CEO
Rafael Catala Polo, Chief Legal Officer
Javier Martinez Sampedro, Dir.-Codere America
Luis Arguello Alvarez, Sec.
Serafin Rafael Gomez Rodriguez, Chief Compliance Officer

GROWTH PLANS/SPECIAL FEATURES:
Codere SA is engaged in private gaming sector. Its core business is the management of slot machines, bingo halls, betting facilities, casinos and racetracks in Europe and the Americas. Countries of operation include Spain, Italy, Argentina, Mexico, Colombia, Panama, Uruguay and Brazil. The company manages 56,548 gaming machines, 149 gaming halls, 5,581 sports betting locations and four racetracks. The company's gaming machines can be found in Mexico, Spain, Colombia, Italy, Argentina, Panama and Uruguay and consist of slot machines found in such places as casinos, bingos and racetracks. The company acts as a reference operator in gaming halls, which may house within them not only betting and gambling games, but also entertainment services such as night clubs, theaters, restaurants, hotels, conference centers and more. Sports betting operations are located in Spain, Mexico, Panama, Uruguay and Brazil. Sports betting is defined as a type of game mode, with special rooms set up in such venues as casinos, bingo halls and sports venues. These sports betting rooms operate under both the Codere name as well as Turff Bet & Sports Bar. The company's four racetracks, located in Mexico, Panama and Uruguay, specialize in horse racing and may exist in combination with casinos (known as racinos). The race tracks are Hipodromo de las Americas, Hipodromo Presidente Remon, Hipodromo Nacional de Maronas and Hipodromo de las Pidras. In the online gaming market, the company operates online sports betting and online slots in Spain, via license agreements. This division seeks to expand its online gaming across Europe and abroad as new markets emerge. The company annually publishes the "Game Yearbook in Spain" through the Institute for Policy and Governance at Carlos III University of Madrid.

FINANCIAL DATA:
Note: Data for latest year may not have been available at press time.

In U.S. $	2018	2017	2016	2015	2014	2013
Revenue						
R&D Expense						
Operating Income						
Operating Margin %						
SGA Expense						
Net Income						
Operating Cash Flow						
Capital Expenditure						
EBITDA						
Return on Assets %						
Return on Equity %						
Debt to Equity						

CONTACT INFORMATION:
Phone: 34 913542800   Fax: 34 913542890
Toll-Free:
Address: Avda. de Bruselas 26, Alcobendas, 28108 Spain

SALARIES/BONUSES:
Top Exec. Salary: $ Bonus: $
Second Exec. Salary: $ Bonus: $

STOCK TICKER/OTHER:
Stock Ticker: CODEF   Exchange: PINX
Employees: 13,050   Fiscal Year Ends: 12/31
Parent Company:

OTHER THOUGHTS:
Estimated Female Officers or Directors:
Hot Spot for Advancement for Women/Minorities:

Sales, profits and employees may be estimates. Financial information, benefits and other data can change quickly and may vary from those stated here.

Cogeco Communications Inc

corpo.cogeco.com/cca/en/home/

NAIC Code: 515120

TYPES OF BUSINESS:
Cable Television
High Speed Internet
Telecommunications

BRANDS/DIVISIONS/AFFILIATES:
Cogeco Inc
Cogeco Connexion
Atlantic Broadband
Cogeco Peer 1

CONTACTS: Note: Officers with more than one job title may be intentionally listed here more than once.

Richard Shea, CEO, Subsidiary
Nathalie Dorval, VP, Divisional
Philippe Jette, CEO
Patrice Ouimet, CFO
Louis Audet, Chairman of the Board
Christian Jolivet, Chief Legal Officer
Luc Noiseux, Chief Strategy Officer
Pierre Maheux, Controller
David Isenberg, Other Executive Officer
Susan Bowen, President, Divisional
Ken Smithard, President, Subsidiary
Marie-Helene Labrie, Senior VP, Divisional
Diane Nyisztor, Senior VP, Divisional
Rene Guimond, Senior VP, Divisional
Andree Pinard, Treasurer
Philippe Bonin, Vice President, Divisional
Elizabeth Alves, Vice President, Divisional
Martin Grenier, Vice President, Divisional

GROWTH PLANS/SPECIAL FEATURES:

Cogeco Communications, Inc. is a communications corporation, and among the 10 largest hybrid fiber coaxial cable operators in North America. The company provides its residential and business customers with video, internet and telephone services through its two-way broadband fiber networks. Cogeco operates through three wholly-owned subsidiaries: Cogeco Connexion, Atlantic Broadband and Cogeco Peer 1. Cogeco Connexion serves customers in the provinces of Ontario and Quebec, offering internet with speeds of up to 1 gigabits per second (Gbps). Atlantic Broadband serves customers in western Pennsylvania, south Florida, Maryland/Delaware, South Carolina and eastern Connecticut. Cogeco Peer 1 provides global clients with a suite of information and communication technology solutions. Its business-to-business products and services include colocation, network connectivity, managed hosting, cloud services and managed IT services. With 16 data centers, an extensive fiber network and more than 50 points-of-presence in North America and Europe combined, Peer 1 provides small, medium and large businesses the ability to access, move, manage and store mission-critical data worldwide. Cogeco Communications is owned by Cogeco, Inc. During 2018, the firm acquired all of Harron Communications LP's cable systems operating under the MetroCast brand names; and acquired 10 spectrum licenses in the 2500 MHz paired spectrum band from Kian Telecom, enhancing its wireless services.

FINANCIAL DATA: Note: Data for latest year may not have been available at press time.

In U.S. $	2018	2017	2016	2015	2014	2013
Revenue	1,798,045,000	1,652,114,000	1,614,498,000	1,515,948,000	1,444,929,000	1,255,650,000
R&D Expense						
Operating Income	410,148,500	393,137,400	352,179,000	364,420,400	321,300,900	295,136,800
Operating Margin %	23.79%	22.30%	24.03%	22.23%	23.50%	
SGA Expense	174,268,500	151,489,700	149,701,800	131,800,300	127,299,200	110,684,900
Net Income	257,552,600	221,996,800	-140,686,100	191,226,200	155,385,500	137,314,200
Operating Cash Flow	514,956,800	709,749,400	552,844,500	511,116,700	562,637,600	404,346,100
Capital Expenditure	406,476,800	317,578,000	346,848,400	325,859,900	308,241,100	302,152,300
EBITDA	786,946,200	737,187,300	376,449,700	692,324,200	628,860,900	557,030,300
Return on Assets %		5.60%	-3.34%	4.60%	4.01%	4.53%
Return on Equity %		19.33%	-11.65%	15.77%	14.68%	14.61%
Debt to Equity		1.52	1.89	1.69	1.78	2.14

CONTACT INFORMATION:
Phone: 514 764-4754 Fax: 514 874-0776
Toll-Free:
Address: 5 Place Ville-Marie, Ste. 1700, Montreal, QC H3B 0B3 Canada

STOCK TICKER/OTHER:
Stock Ticker: CCA Exchange: TSE
Employees: 4,574 Fiscal Year Ends: 08/31
Parent Company: Cogeco Inc

SALARIES/BONUSES:
Top Exec. Salary: $ Bonus: $
Second Exec. Salary: $ Bonus: $

OTHER THOUGHTS:
Estimated Female Officers or Directors: 4
Hot Spot for Advancement for Women/Minorities: Y

Cogeco Inc

NAIC Code: 517110

www.cogeco.ca/en/

TYPES OF BUSINESS:
Cable TV
Internet Access

BRANDS/DIVISIONS/AFFILIATES:
Cogeco Communications Inc
Cogeco Media
Cogeco Connexion
Atlantic Broadband
Cogeco Peer 1
Cogeco News
Cogeco Force Radio
Cogeco Nouvelles

CONTACTS: *Note: Officers with more than one job title may be intentionally listed here more than once.*
Richard Shea, CEO, Subsidiary
Martin Grenier, VP-Divisional
Philippe Jette, CEO
Patrice Ouimet, CFO
Louis Audet, Chairman of the Board
Luc Noiseux, Chief Technology Officer
Pierre Maheux, Controller
Christian Jolivet, Other Executive Officer
Ken Smithard, President, Subsidiary
Susan Bowen, President, Subsidiary
Michel Lorrain, President, Subsidiary
Marie-Helene Labrie, Senior VP, Divisional
Diane Nyisztor, Senior VP, Divisional
Rene Guimond, Senior VP, Divisional
Andree Pinard, Treasurer
Nathalie Dorval, Vice President, Divisional
Elizabeth Alves, Vice President, Divisional
Philippe Bonin, Vice President, Divisional

GROWTH PLANS/SPECIAL FEATURES:
Cogeco, Inc. is a Canadian diversified telecommunications and media company, serving residential and commercial customers through its subsidiaries. The firm operates through two primary subsidiaries: Cogeco Communications, Inc. and Cogeco Media. Cogeco Communications provides Canadian broadband services through its two-way broadband fiber network. It operates as Cogeco Connexion in Quebec and Ontario; and as Atlantic Broadband in the U.S. This segment's Cogeco Peer 1 provides business customers with a suite of information technology services such as colocation, network connectivity, hosting, cloud and managed services through the firm's 16 data centers, fiber network and more than 50 points of presence in North America and Europe. Cogeco Media is one of Quebec's largest radio broadcasters, operating 22 radio stations, as well as news agency, Coegeco News. Rythme FV operates a flagship radio station in Montreal, which primarily targets women between 25 and 54 with a pop music format. Other stations include 98.5 FM, FM 93, 106.9 FM, 107.7 FM, 104.7 FM, 96.9 CKOI, Radio Circulation 730 (AM), MFM, CIME and Beat 92.5. Cogeco Media owns Cogeco Force Radio, which provides access to a network of top-performing radio stations; and owns Cogeco Nouvelles, which provides information to all of the stations operated by Cogeco Media. Cogeco Nouvelles has also established strategic relationships in order to provide many other radio stations with national and international news.

FINANCIAL DATA: *Note: Data for latest year may not have been available at press time.*

In U.S. $	2018	2017	2016	2015	2014	2013
Revenue	1,883,087,000	1,741,756,000	1,711,876,000	1,622,669,000	1,555,063,000	1,360,846,000
R&D Expense						
Operating Income	428,529,200	413,311,300	383,262,600	357,580,800	328,377,900	303,551,500
Operating Margin %		23.72%	22.38%	22.03%	21.11%	22.30%
SGA Expense						
Net Income	92,939,280	80,856,610	-21,775,680	66,494,790	50,212,180	47,547,260
Operating Cash Flow	528,035,900	724,902,100	563,128,800	515,105,200	567,387,300	409,676,700
Capital Expenditure	408,778,200	319,989,200	348,960,600	328,423,200	311,733,200	304,541,200
EBITDA	809,240,400	761,902,400	413,436,600	709,700,400	638,434,400	568,694,500
Return on Assets %		1.98%	-.50%	1.54%	1.25%	1.49%
Return on Equity %		19.34%	-5.09%	16.03%	13.93%	14.98%
Debt to Equity		4.28	5.33	5.10	5.41	6.52

CONTACT INFORMATION:
Phone: 514 874-2600 Fax: 514 874-2625
Toll-Free:
Address: 5, Place Ville-Marie, Office 1700, Montreal, QC H3B 0B3 Canada

STOCK TICKER/OTHER:
Stock Ticker: CGO
Employees: 5,199
Parent Company:

Exchange: TSE
Fiscal Year Ends: 08/31

SALARIES/BONUSES:
Top Exec. Salary: $ Bonus: $
Second Exec. Salary: $ Bonus: $

OTHER THOUGHTS:
Estimated Female Officers or Directors: 1
Hot Spot for Advancement for Women/Minorities:

Sales, profits and employees may be estimates. Financial information, benefits and other data can change quickly and may vary from those stated here.

Comcast Corporation

corporate.comcast.com

NAIC Code: 517110

TYPES OF BUSINESS:
Cable Television
VoIP Service
Cable Network Programming
High-Speed Internet Service
Video-on-Demand
Advertising Services
Interactive Program Schedules
Wireless Services

BRANDS/DIVISIONS/AFFILIATES:
XFINITY
NBC Universal
Telemundo
Sky plc
Comcast Spectator
Philadelphia Flyers
Wells Fargo Center
Amblin Partners

CONTACTS:
Note: Officers with more than one job title may be intentionally listed here more than once.

Stephen Burke, CEO, Subsidiary
Dave Watson, CEO, Subsidiary
Brian Roberts, CEO
Michael Cavanagh, CFO
Daniel Murdock, Chief Accounting Officer
Joseph Collins, Director Emeritus
Judith Rodin, Director Emeritus
Arthur Block, Executive VP
David Cohen, Senior Executive VP

GROWTH PLANS/SPECIAL FEATURES:

Comcast Corporation provides information, entertainment and communications products and services. Comcast operates through five segments: cable communications, cable networks, broadcast television, filmed entertainment and theme parks. The cable communications segment maintains the firm's video, high-speed internet and voice servicing operations, serving residential customers under the XFINITY brand. This division also sells advertising, as well as video, high-speed internet, voice and other services to small- and medium-sized businesses. The cable networks segment includes the firm's national cable networks, its regional sports and news networks, its international cable networks and its cable television production operations. The broadcast television segment consists primarily of the company's NBC and Telemundo broadcast networks, its 11 NBC- and 17 Telemundo-owned local broadcast television stations and its broadcast television production operations. Filmed entertainment is comprised of the studio operations of Universal Pictures, which produces, acquires, markets and distributes filmed entertainment worldwide. Theme parks is comprised of the Universal theme parks in Orlando, Florida; Hollywood, California; and Osaka, Japan. Additionally, subsidiary Comcast Spectator owns the Philadelphia Flyers and the Wells Fargo Center in Philadelphia, Pennsylvania, and operates arena management-related businesses. In October 2018, Comcast acquired control of UK/EU media and telecommunications giant Sky plc at a value of $38.8 billion. In December 2018, Comcast announced that, in conjunction with Amazon, its customers will be able to watch Amazon Prime Video on Comcast's Xfinity X1 at no additional cost.

FINANCIAL DATA:
Note: Data for latest year may not have been available at press time.

In U.S. $	2018	2017	2016	2015	2014	2013
Revenue		84,526,000,000	80,403,000,000	74,510,000,000	68,775,000,000	64,657,000,000
R&D Expense						
Operating Income		17,987,000,000	16,859,000,000	15,998,000,000	14,904,000,000	13,563,000,000
Operating Margin %		21.27%	20.96%	21.47%	21.67%	20.97%
SGA Expense		31,330,000,000	29,523,000,000	27,282,000,000	24,940,000,000	23,553,000,000
Net Income		22,714,000,000	8,695,000,000	8,163,000,000	8,380,000,000	6,816,000,000
Operating Cash Flow		21,403,000,000	19,240,000,000	18,778,000,000	16,945,000,000	14,160,000,000
Capital Expenditure		11,297,000,000	10,821,000,000	9,869,000,000	8,542,000,000	7,605,000,000
EBITDA		28,675,000,000	26,853,000,000	24,754,000,000	23,101,000,000	29,809,000,000
Return on Assets %		12.36%	5.01%	5.00%	5.26%	4.21%
Return on Equity %		37.06%	16.37%	15.55%	16.20%	13.62%
Debt to Equity		0.86	1.03	0.93	0.83	0.87

CONTACT INFORMATION:
Phone: 215 286-1700   Fax:
Toll-Free: 800-266-2278
Address: One Comcast Center, Philadelphia, PA 19103 United States

SALARIES/BONUSES:
Top Exec. Salary: $3,103,566   Bonus: $
Second Exec. Salary: $2,881,100   Bonus: $

STOCK TICKER/OTHER:
Stock Ticker: CMCSA   Exchange: NAS
Employees: 166,000   Fiscal Year Ends: 12/31
Parent Company:

OTHER THOUGHTS:
Estimated Female Officers or Directors: 16
Hot Spot for Advancement for Women/Minorities: Y

Sales, profits and employees may be estimates. Financial information, benefits and other data can change quickly and may vary from those stated here.

Concrete Software Inc

NAIC Code: 511210G

www.concretesoftware.com

TYPES OF BUSINESS:
Computer Software, Electronic Games, Apps & Entertainment Apps

BRANDS/DIVISIONS/AFFILIATES:
Aces Gin Rummy
Jellyflop
Aces Spades
Aces Hearts
PBA Bowling Challenge
Aces Cribbage 2
NHL Hockey Target Smash
Arctic Cat Extreme Snowmobile Racing

GROWTH PLANS/SPECIAL FEATURES:
Concrete Software, Inc., founded in 2003, designs and produces games for mobile devices. The company develops content for the Kindle, iPhone and iPad, Xbox, PlayStation and Android platforms. Concrete Software's product line includes games such as Aces Gin Rummy, Jellyflop, Aces Spades, Aces Hearts, PBA Bowling Challenge, Aces Cribbage 2, Rapala Fishing, Arctic Cat Extreme Snowmobile Racing and NHL Hockey Target Smash. Many of Concrete's games support Bluetooth communication, allowing users to play head-to-head against their friends over a wireless connection.

CONTACTS:
Note: Officers with more than one job title may be intentionally listed here more than once.

Keith Pichelman, CEO

FINANCIAL DATA:
Note: Data for latest year may not have been available at press time.

In U.S. $	2018	2017	2016	2015	2014	2013
Revenue						
R&D Expense						
Operating Income						
Operating Margin %						
SGA Expense						
Net Income						
Operating Cash Flow						
Capital Expenditure						
EBITDA						
Return on Assets %						
Return on Equity %						
Debt to Equity						

CONTACT INFORMATION:
Phone: 952-942-5206   Fax:
Toll-Free:
Address: 7500 Flying Cloud Dr., Ste 625, Eden Prairie, MN 55344 United States

STOCK TICKER/OTHER:
Stock Ticker: Private   Exchange:
Employees: 20   Fiscal Year Ends:
Parent Company:

SALARIES/BONUSES:
Top Exec. Salary: $ Bonus: $
Second Exec. Salary: $ Bonus: $

OTHER THOUGHTS:
Estimated Female Officers or Directors:
Hot Spot for Advancement for Women/Minorities:

Sales, profits and employees may be estimates. Financial information, benefits and other data can change quickly and may vary from those stated here.

Concurrent Computer Corporation

NAIC Code: 334111

www.ccur.com

TYPES OF BUSINESS:
Computer Manufacturing
Networking Systems Architecture
Operating Systems Software
Government Technology Services

BRANDS/DIVISIONS/AFFILIATES:
MediaScaleX
MediaScaleX Storage
MediaScaleX Transcode
MediaScaleX Origin
MediaScaleX Cache
Vecima Networks, Inc.

CONTACTS:
Note: Officers with more than one job title may be intentionally listed here more than once.

Warren Sutherland, CFO
Wayne Barr, Chairman of the Board

GROWTH PLANS/SPECIAL FEATURES:

Concurrent Computer Corporation develops and provides software and professional services for the video, media data and high-performance streaming media markets. Its solutions fall into two categories: content provider solutions and service provider solutions. Within the content provider solutions category, Concurrent builds scalable and high-performance systems to support every content owner's media operations, from ingest through delivery. Its solutions include: media operations storage, media archive storage, NAM (network analysis module) and transcode storage, and a private/public hybrid content delivery network (CDN). The service provider solutions category develops solutions for service providers to deliver advanced, revenue-generating video services. The firm works with customers to define, develop and support solutions that exceed their needs and longevity expectations. Both categories use the MediaScaleX hyperscale platform suite that rapidly deploys and scales videos across a variety of CDNs. MediaScaleX comes in four categories: Storage, Transcode, Origin and Cache. MediaScaleX Storage is a scalable software-defined application designed for content management. It is easily deployable on various hardware platforms and uses multiple forms of metadata capture to enable easy search-and-find functionality. MediaScaleX Transcode is a software platform providing audio and video content processing. Transcode allows service providers, broadcasters and content owners to operate live and file-based workflows over common infrastructures. MediaScaleX Origin is an origin solution that allows users to package over-the-top (OTT) programming using dynamic adaptive streaming over HTTP (DASH) and common media application format (CMAF). MediaScaleX Cache is a high-density, intelligent caching system that supports simultaneous delivery to mobile devices, smart TVs and set-top boxes. Concurrent is a subsidiary of Vecima Networks, Inc.

Concurrent offers employees medical, vision and dental insurance; disability coverage; a 401(k) plan; and paid holidays.

FINANCIAL DATA:
Note: Data for latest year may not have been available at press time.

In U.S. $	2018	2017	2016	2015	2014	2013
Revenue		27,647,000	61,149,000	64,459,000	71,171,000	63,444,000
R&D Expense						
Operating Income						
Operating Margin %						
SGA Expense						
Net Income		28,381,000	-11,113,000	-345,000	18,505,000	4,248,000
Operating Cash Flow						
Capital Expenditure						
EBITDA						
Return on Assets %						
Return on Equity %						
Debt to Equity						

CONTACT INFORMATION:
Phone: 678 258-4000   Fax: 678 258-4300
Toll-Free: 877-978-7363
Address: 4375 River Green Pkwy., Ste. 100, Duluth, GA 30096 United States

SALARIES/BONUSES:
Top Exec. Salary: $ Bonus: $
Second Exec. Salary: $ Bonus: $

STOCK TICKER/OTHER:
Stock Ticker: Private
Employees: 110
Parent Company: Vecima Networks Inc

Exchange:
Fiscal Year Ends: 06/30

OTHER THOUGHTS:
Estimated Female Officers or Directors: 1
Hot Spot for Advancement for Women/Minorities:

Conde Nast Publications Inc

NAIC Code: 511120

www.condenast.com

TYPES OF BUSINESS:
Magazine Publishing
Internet Publishing
Digital Media
Clothing Merchandising

BRANDS/DIVISIONS/AFFILIATES:
Advance Publications Inc
Vogue
Brides
GQ
Architectural Digest
Pitchfork Media Inc
Poetica
Conde Nast Entertainment

CONTACTS: Note: Officers with more than one job title may be intentionally listed here more than once.
Robert Sauerberg, CEO
David Geithner, CFO
Pamela Drucker Mann, Chief Revenue and Marketing Officer
JoAnn Murray, Chief Human Resources Officer
Joe Simon, CTO
Jill Bright, Chief Admin. Officer
Anna Wintour, Dir.-Artistic
Luis Cona, Chief Revenue Officer
Thomas J. Wallace, Dir.-Editorial
Charles H. Townsend, Chmn.

GROWTH PLANS/SPECIAL FEATURES:
Conde Nast Publications, Inc. is a media company, attracting more than 144 million consumers across its industry-leading print, digital and video brands. The firm's portfolio includes titles such as Vogue, Vanity Fair, Glamour, Brides, Self, GQ, GQ Style, The New Yorker, Conde Nast Traveler, Allure, Architectural Digest, Bon Apetit, Epicurious, Wired, W, Golf Digest, Teen Vogue, Ars Technica, Pitchfork, them and Iris. The company owns Pitchford Media, Inc, an American online magazine with a focus on independent music, but also covers independent and popular music content; and Poetica, a London-based startup that has developed a real-time content editing system. In addition, Conde Nast Entertainment is a division that develops film, television and premium digital video programming. Conde Nast operates as a subsidiary of Advance Publications, Inc. In January 2018, Conde Nast announced it had acquired Lighthouse Datalab, a data solutions firm with a focus on extracting actionable insights from client data. In 2018, Conde Nast launched Concierge.com, a guest management software platform; a reimagined WIRED.com; and an OTT (over the top) channel for WIRED.

The company offers employees medical and dental insurance, a prescription plan, a health and fitness allowance, a company funded pension plan, a 401(k) plan, short- and long-term disability insurance, flexible spending accounts, a commuter program, life i

FINANCIAL DATA: Note: Data for latest year may not have been available at press time.

In U.S. $	2018	2017	2016	2015	2014	2013
Revenue	250,000,000	240,000,000	234,000,000	210,000,000	200,000,000	197,629,092
R&D Expense						
Operating Income						
Operating Margin %						
SGA Expense						
Net Income						
Operating Cash Flow						
Capital Expenditure						
EBITDA						
Return on Assets %						
Return on Equity %						
Debt to Equity						

CONTACT INFORMATION:
Phone: 212-286-2860 Fax: 212-286-5960
Toll-Free:
Address: 1 World Trade Ctr., New York, NY 10007 United States

SALARIES/BONUSES:
Top Exec. Salary: $ Bonus: $
Second Exec. Salary: $ Bonus: $

STOCK TICKER/OTHER:
Stock Ticker: Subsidiary   Exchange:
Employees: 660   Fiscal Year Ends: 12/31
Parent Company: Advance Publications Inc

OTHER THOUGHTS:
Estimated Female Officers or Directors: 2
Hot Spot for Advancement for Women/Minorities: Y

Sales, profits and employees may be estimates. Financial information, benefits and other data can change quickly and may vary from those stated here.

Corus Entertainment Inc

www.corusent.com

NAIC Code: 515112

TYPES OF BUSINESS:
Radio Broadcasting
Television Broadcast & Cable
Animated Children's Programming
Children's Book Publishing
Digital Music Services
Radio Marketing Services
Online Media
Advertising Services

BRANDS/DIVISIONS/AFFILIATES:
Global Television
W Network
OWN: Oprah Winfrey Network Canada
HGTV Canada
Nelvana
Franklin
Toon Boom
Kids Can Press

CONTACTS: Note: Officers with more than one job title may be intentionally listed here more than once.
Douglas Murphy, CEO
John Gossling, CFO
Heather Shaw, Chairman of the Board
Julie Shaw, Director
Dale Hancocks, Executive VP
Gregory McLelland, Executive VP
Gary Maavara, Secretary
Judy Adam, Senior VP, Divisional

GROWTH PLANS/SPECIAL FEATURES:
Corus Entertainment, Inc. is a Canadian-based media entertainment company with interests in radio broadcasting, television broadcasting and the production and distribution of children's media content. These interests comprise Corus' operating segments of radio, television and content. The company's radio broadcasting business includes 39 radio stations in Canadian urban centers, such as Vancouver, Calgary, Edmonton, Toronto and Montreal. These stations offer a portfolio of news-talk radio stations, as well as classic rock, new country and contemporary music formats. The television segment provides interactive and informative content to millions of viewers every day. Corus' TV portfolio includes 44 specialty television channels and 15 conventional television stations. Its brands include Global Television, W Network, OWN: Oprah Winfrey Network Canada, HGTV Canada, Food Network Canada, History, Showcase, National Geographic, Disney Channel Canada, YTV and Nickelodeon Canada. The content segment sells its creations and content in more than 160 countries worldwide. This division's portfolio includes Nelvana, a creator, producer and distributor of children's animated content, as well as related consumer products. Products and content brands include Franklin, Little Charmers, Max & Ruby and Beyblade. Toon Boom is part of the Corus family, operating within the content division, and provides digital content and animation creation software. Kids Can Press operates as a children's publishing company. This segment's business also includes a growing portfolio of unscripted lifestyle content targeted to women and families.

FINANCIAL DATA: Note: Data for latest year may not have been available at press time.

In U.S. $	2018	2017	2016	2015	2014	2013
Revenue	1,222,176,000	1,245,666,000	869,004,700	604,886,900	618,019,400	596,151,700
R&D Expense						
Operating Income	378,345,200	378,587,900	267,499,300	208,461,400	209,248,600	199,474,700
Operating Margin %		28.96%	28.77%	31.04%	31.88%	30.25%
SGA Expense	154,335,700	158,574,200	125,587,600	99,851,620	103,018,800	93,877,790
Net Income	-582,031,800	142,197,400	93,428,940	-18,661,900	111,588,600	118,627,000
Operating Cash Flow	275,178,000	221,186,600	148,549,600	156,069,500	144,283,600	123,923,500
Capital Expenditure	19,604,860	24,690,630	31,258,720	30,789,090	17,411,790	17,730,070
EBITDA	44,805,920	789,110,300	505,366,900	221,225,200	362,145,000	346,631,000
Return on Assets %			3.15%	2.88%	-.92%	6.04%	7.50%
Return on Equity %			8.05%	7.15%	-2.01%	12.05%	13.79%
Debt to Equity			0.78	0.89	0.54	0.67	0.45

CONTACT INFORMATION:
Phone: 416 479-7000   Fax: 416 479-7006
Toll-Free:
Address: Corus Quay, 25 Dockside Dr., Toronto, ON M5A 0B5 Canada

STOCK TICKER/OTHER:
Stock Ticker: CJR.B
Employees: 1,523
Parent Company:

Exchange: TSE
Fiscal Year Ends: 08/31

SALARIES/BONUSES:
Top Exec. Salary: $ Bonus: $
Second Exec. Salary: $ Bonus: $

OTHER THOUGHTS:
Estimated Female Officers or Directors: 7
Hot Spot for Advancement for Women/Minorities: Y

Cox Communications Inc

NAIC Code: 517110

www.cox.com/residential/home.cox

TYPES OF BUSINESS:
Cable TV Service and Internet Access
Digital Cable TV Service
Cable-Based Internet Access
Local & Long-Distance Phone Service
Commercial Telecommunications Services
Data & Video Transport Services

BRANDS/DIVISIONS/AFFILIATES:
Cox Enterprises Inc
Cox Business Services
Managed IP PBX
Cox Media
Kudzu.com

CONTACTS: Note: Officers with more than one job title may be intentionally listed here more than once.
Patrick J. Esser, Pres.
Jill Campbell, COO
Mark Bowser, CFO
Mark Greatrex, CMO
Kevin Hart, CTO
Len Barlik, Exec. VP-Prod. Mgmt. & Dev.
Asheesh Saksena, Chief Strategy Officer
Joseph J. Rooney, Sr. VP-Social Media, Advertising & Brand Mktg.
William (Bill) J. Fitzsimmons, Chief Acct. Officer
Philip G. Meeks, Sr. VP-Cox Bus.
Jennifer W. Hightower, Sr. VP-Law & Policy
David Pugliese, Sr. VP-Product Mktg.
Mark A. Kaish, Sr. VP-Tech. Oper.
George Richter, VP-Supply Chain Mgmt.

GROWTH PLANS/SPECIAL FEATURES:
Cox Communications, Inc., owned by Cox Enterprises, Inc., is a broadband communications and entertainment company, serving millions of customers throughout the U.S. Cox offers advanced digital video, high speed internet, and local and long-distance telephone services over its own nationwide IP network in 18 states. Cox Business Services provides data, video and voice solutions to small and regional businesses such as schools and universities, government organizations and financial institutions. The firm's Managed IP PBX service provides small business customers that have limited internal information technology departments with telecommunication systems that are monitored and managed around the clock by Cox Business. Cox Media offers national and local cable advertising in traditional spot and new media formats, along with promotional opportunities and production services. The company also maintains Kudzu.com, an online directory that aggregates user reviews and ratings on local businesses, merchants and service providers.

FINANCIAL DATA: Note: Data for latest year may not have been available at press time.

In U.S. $	2018	2017	2016	2015	2014	2013
Revenue	12,000,000,000	11,550,000,000	11,000,000,000	10,650,000,000	10,400,000,000	9,900,000,000
R&D Expense						
Operating Income						
Operating Margin %						
SGA Expense						
Net Income						
Operating Cash Flow						
Capital Expenditure						
EBITDA						
Return on Assets %						
Return on Equity %						
Debt to Equity						

CONTACT INFORMATION:
Phone: 404-843-5000 Fax: 404-843-5939
Toll-Free: 888-566-7751
Address: 1400 Lake Hearn Dr., Atlanta, GA 30319 United States

SALARIES/BONUSES:
Top Exec. Salary: $ Bonus: $
Second Exec. Salary: $ Bonus: $

STOCK TICKER/OTHER:
Stock Ticker: Subsidiary
Employees: 23,000
Parent Company: Cox Enterprises Inc
Exchange:
Fiscal Year Ends: 12/31

OTHER THOUGHTS:
Estimated Female Officers or Directors: 3
Hot Spot for Advancement for Women/Minorities: Y

Sales, profits and employees may be estimates. Financial information, benefits and other data can change quickly and may vary from those stated here.

Plunkett Research, Ltd. 193

Cox Enterprises Inc

www.coxenterprises.com

NAIC Code: 515120

TYPES OF BUSINESS:
Cable Television and Internet Services
Television Broadcasting
Newspaper Publishing
Radio Stations
Online News, Information and Services Sites
Auctions
Automotive E-Commerce
Technology Products

BRANDS/DIVISIONS/AFFILIATES:
Cox Communications Inc
Cox Business Services
Cox Media Group
Cox Automotive
autotrader.com
Kelley Blue Book
Clutch
Flexdrive

CONTACTS:
Note: Officers with more than one job title may be intentionally listed here more than once.

Alex Taylor, CEO
Jill Campbell, Exec. VP
Jimmy W. Hayes, Pres.
Dallas S. Clement, CFO
Marybeth N. Leamer, Exec. VP-Admin.
Shauna Sullivan Muhl, VP-Legal
Roberto I. Jimenez, VP-Corp. Comm. & Public Affairs
J. Lacey Lewis, Sr. VP-Finance
Patrick J. Esser, Pres., Cox Comm.
Sanford Schwartz, Pres., Manheim
Bill Hoffman, Pres., Cox Media Group
Kathy Decker, Treas.
James Cox Kennedy, Chmn.

GROWTH PLANS/SPECIAL FEATURES:
Cox Enterprises, Inc., through subsidiary Cox Communications, Inc., is a broadband communications and entertainment company, serving millions of customers across the U.S. Cox offers advanced digital video, high-speed internet and local and long-distance telephone services over its own nationwide IP network. Cox Business Services provides data, video and voice solutions to small and regional businesses such as schools and universities, government organizations and financial institutions. The firm provides small business customers that have limited internal information technology departments with telecommunication systems that are monitored and managed around the clock by Cox Business. Cox Media Group offers national and local cable advertising in traditional spot and new media formats, along with promotional opportunities and production services. Cox Automotive owns significant automobile industry websites and marketing platforms, including autotrader.com, Kelley Blue Book and motors.co.uk. In late-2018, this division announced it was expanding its business model to include vehicle subscription services, namely Clutch and Flexdrive, in which customers pay a recurring fee for the right to use one or more automotive vehicles. This form of automobile ownership enables subscribers to use the kind of vehicles they need at the times they need them.

Cox offers employees medical, dental, vision, life and disability insurance coverage; and a 401(k) plan.

FINANCIAL DATA:
Note: Data for latest year may not have been available at press time.

In U.S. $	2018	2017	2016	2015	2014	2013
Revenue	20,750,000,000	20,500,000,000	20,250,000,000	18,885,000,000	17,450,000,000	15,920,000,000
R&D Expense						
Operating Income						
Operating Margin %						
SGA Expense						
Net Income						
Operating Cash Flow						
Capital Expenditure						
EBITDA						
Return on Assets %						
Return on Equity %						
Debt to Equity						

CONTACT INFORMATION:
Phone: 678-645-0000 Fax:
Toll-Free:
Address: 6205 Peachtree Dunwoody Rd. 1400 Lake Hearn Dr., Atlanta, GA 30328 United States

STOCK TICKER/OTHER:
Stock Ticker: Private
Employees: 60,000
Parent Company:

Exchange:
Fiscal Year Ends: 12/31

SALARIES/BONUSES:
Top Exec. Salary: $ Bonus: $
Second Exec. Salary: $ Bonus: $

OTHER THOUGHTS:
Estimated Female Officers or Directors: 7
Hot Spot for Advancement for Women/Minorities: Y

Sales, profits and employees may be estimates. Financial information, benefits and other data can change quickly and may vary from those stated here.

Cox Media Group Inc

NAIC Code: 515120

www.coxmediagroup.com

TYPES OF BUSINESS:
Television Broadcasting
Radio Broadcasting
Sales & Marketing Services
Newspaper Publishing

BRANDS/DIVISIONS/AFFILIATES:
Cox Enterprises Inc
Rare.us
Clark.com
Dawg Nation
SEC Country
Hookem.com
CoxReps
Gamut

CONTACTS: Note: Officers with more than one job title may be intentionally listed here more than once.
Kimberly A. Guthrie, Pres.
Kim Guthrie, Exec VP-Radio, Cox Media Group
Brett Fennell, CFO
Mary Ellen Marcilliat-Falkner, Sr. VP-Human Resources
Bill Hoffman, Pres., Cox Media Group

GROWTH PLANS/SPECIAL FEATURES:
Cox Media Group, Inc., a subsidiary of Cox Enterprises, Inc., is an integrated broadcasting, publishing direct marketing and digital media company. The firm's operations currently include 14 broadcast television stations and one local cable channel, 61 radio stations, four daily newspapers, 11 non-daily publications and 16 digital brands. Cox Television reaches 52 million weekly viewers in 20 markets, including more than 31 million TV viewers, more than two million newspaper readers and nearly 15 million radio listeners. Cox Media also operations more than 100 digital news outlets. These digital news outlets and services include Rare.us, Clark.com, Dawg Nation, SEC Country, Hookem.com, Mundo Hispanico, Southern Kitchen and All22. Additionally, Cox Media operates the National Advertising Platform businesses of CoxReps: Gamut and Videa. In July 2018, Cox Media Group sold the operations of Southern Kitchen, an Atlanta-based Southern food and lifestyle brand, to Gatehouse Media. In September of the same year, the firm sold Mundo Hispanico, Atlanta's largest Spanish-language newspaper, to Mundo Hispanico Digitial Network.

The company offers its employees health benefits, retirement health coverage, a 401(k) and a pension plan.

FINANCIAL DATA: Note: Data for latest year may not have been available at press time.

In U.S. $	2018	2017	2016	2015	2014	2013
Revenue	2,100,000,000	2,050,000,000	2,000,000,000	1,900,000,000	1,800,000,000	
R&D Expense						
Operating Income						
Operating Margin %						
SGA Expense						
Net Income						
Operating Cash Flow						
Capital Expenditure						
EBITDA						
Return on Assets %						
Return on Equity %						
Debt to Equity						

CONTACT INFORMATION:
Phone: 678-645-0000   Fax: 678-645-5002
Toll-Free:
Address: 6205 Peachtree Dunwoody Rd., Atlanta, GA 30328 United States

STOCK TICKER/OTHER:
Stock Ticker: Subsidiary
Employees: 7,300
Parent Company: Cox Enterprises Inc

Exchange:
Fiscal Year Ends: 12/31

SALARIES/BONUSES:
Top Exec. Salary: $ Bonus: $
Second Exec. Salary: $ Bonus: $

OTHER THOUGHTS:
Estimated Female Officers or Directors: 3
Hot Spot for Advancement for Women/Minorities: Y

Crackle Inc (dba SonyCrackle)

www.sonycrackle.com

NAIC Code: 519130

TYPES OF BUSINESS:
Internet Streaming Movies & Television Shows
Original Content
Advertising

BRANDS/DIVISIONS/AFFILIATES:
Sony Pictures Entertainment Inc
Sony Crackle
Always On

CONTACTS: Note: Officers with more than one job title may be intentionally listed here more than once.
David Samuel, Co-Pres.
Joshua M. Felser, Co-Pres.
Aviv Eyal, CTO
Eric Berger, Sr. VP-Digital Networks

GROWTH PLANS/SPECIAL FEATURES:

Crackle, Inc., doing business as Sony Crackle, is the multi-platform, online video entertainment subsidiary of Sony Pictures Entertainment, Inc.. The company distributes full-length digital content and original short-form series from Sony Pictures' library of television series and feature films through a streaming network that includes Sony devices, IPTV, leading social networks and viral web and app distribution. The firm maintains distribution partnerships with content providers for cable TV, set-top boxes, mobile phones, PCs, video game consoles and virtual worlds, including Aniplex, FOX Digital, Lionsgate Entertainment, Metro-Goldwyn-Mayer, Red Bull, Universal Studios, The Walt Disney Company, Miramax and many more. Digital content plays on its proprietary media player, the Sony Crackle, allowing partners to easily integrate the content into their online channels. Content includes: movies, films originally produced by Sony Pictures, Sony Pictures Classics, Columbia TriStar or Screen Gems; television, which offers content from Sony Pictures Television; minisodes, which are current and archived TV episodes that have been edited down to five minutes or less; and Sony Crackle originals, which are content from TV shows produced in-house before digital, TV and DVD distribution. Sony Crackle's Always On personalized feature automatically plays the user's favorites, and also allows them to search and stream on Roku, PlayStation, Xbox, Apple TV, iPhone, Android and more. The company's target audience is men from 18-34 years of age. Sony Crackle is available in 21 countries and English, Spanish and Portugese

FINANCIAL DATA: Note: Data for latest year may not have been available at press time.

In U.S. $	2018	2017	2016	2015	2014	2013
Revenue						
R&D Expense						
Operating Income						
Operating Margin %						
SGA Expense						
Net Income						
Operating Cash Flow						
Capital Expenditure						
EBITDA						
Return on Assets %						
Return on Equity %						
Debt to Equity						

CONTACT INFORMATION:
Phone: 415-877-4800 Fax: 415-331-5501
Toll-Free:
Address: 10202 West Washington Blvd, Ste. 2141, Culver City, CA 90232 United States

STOCK TICKER/OTHER:
Stock Ticker: Subsidiary Exchange:
Employees: 100 Fiscal Year Ends: 12/31
Parent Company: Sony Pictures Entertainment Inc

SALARIES/BONUSES:
Top Exec. Salary: $ Bonus: $
Second Exec. Salary: $ Bonus: $

OTHER THOUGHTS:
Estimated Female Officers or Directors:
Hot Spot for Advancement for Women/Minorities:

Sales, profits and employees may be estimates. Financial information, benefits and other data can change quickly and may vary from those stated here.

Creative Artists Agency Inc (CAA)

NAIC Code: 711410

www.caa.com

TYPES OF BUSINESS:
Talent Agency
Market Research

BRANDS/DIVISIONS/AFFILIATES:

GROWTH PLANS/SPECIAL FEATURES:
Creative Artists Agency, Inc. (CAA), headquartered in Los Angeles, is a leading talent agency in the U.S. The firm represents artists of all kinds, including actors, athletes, writers, directors and companies and their products. CAA's most famous division is the one working with Hollywood talent. Its roster includes George Clooney, Brad Pitt and Tom Cruise. The agency also represents many leading musicians and athletes. CAA also has a division dedicated to contemporary Christian music. Some of the artists represented by the division have included Amy Grant, Michael W. Smith, Third Day, Steven Curtis Chapman and TobyMac. Besides its Los Angeles headquarters, the company maintains offices throughout the U.S., as well as internationally in cities such as London, Beijing, Shanghai, Stockholm, Munich and Geneva.

CONTACTS:
Note: Officers with more than one job title may be intentionally listed here more than once.

Richard Lovett, Pres.
Michael Rubel, General Counsel

FINANCIAL DATA:
Note: Data for latest year may not have been available at press time.

In U.S. $	2018	2017	2016	2015	2014	2013
Revenue	348,000,000	333,000,000	312,000,000	290,600,000	260,000,000	250,000,000
R&D Expense						
Operating Income						
Operating Margin %						
SGA Expense						
Net Income						
Operating Cash Flow						
Capital Expenditure						
EBITDA						
Return on Assets %						
Return on Equity %						
Debt to Equity						

CONTACT INFORMATION:
Phone: 424-288-2000 Fax: 310-288-2900
Toll-Free:
Address: 2000 Avenue of the Stars, Los Angeles, CA 90067 United States

STOCK TICKER/OTHER:
Stock Ticker: Private
Employees: 1,500
Parent Company:

Exchange:
Fiscal Year Ends: 12/31

SALARIES/BONUSES:
Top Exec. Salary: $ Bonus: $
Second Exec. Salary: $ Bonus: $

OTHER THOUGHTS:
Estimated Female Officers or Directors:
Hot Spot for Advancement for Women/Minorities:

Sales, profits and employees may be estimates. Financial information, benefits and other data can change quickly and may vary from those stated here.

Crown Media Family Networks

www.hallmarkchannel.com/about-us

NAIC Code: 515210

TYPES OF BUSINESS:
Cable Television
Film Distribution
Television Production

BRANDS/DIVISIONS/AFFILIATES:
Hallmark Cards Inc
Hallmark Channel (The)
Hallmark Movies & Mysteries Channel (The)

CONTACTS:
Note: Officers with more than one job title may be intentionally listed here more than once.

Bill Abbott, CEO
William Abbott, CEO
James Shay, Director
Brian Gardner, Director
Dwight Arn, Director
Deanne Stedem, Director
Brad Moore, Director
Robert Bloss, Director
Molly Biwer, Director
Edward Georger, Executive VP, Divisional
Michelle Vicary, Executive VP, Divisional
Laura Lee, Executive VP, Divisional
Kristen Roberts, Executive VP, Divisional
Susanne McAvoy, Executive VP, Divisional
Charles Stanford, Executive VP, Divisional

GROWTH PLANS/SPECIAL FEATURES:
Crown Media Family Networks is the umbrella unit subsidiary of Hallmark Cards, Inc. that houses the Hallmark Channel and Hallmark Movies & Mysteries cable networks, as well as their digital website extensions. Crown Media operates and distributes both channels in high definition (HD) and standard definition. Hallmark Channel is a 24-hour cable network that reaches 86 million homes, featuring signature new and original movies, as well as original content such as scripted primetime series, annual specials and a lifestyle show (Home & Family). Hallmark Movies & Mysteries is a 24-hour linear channel distributed to homes throughout the U.S. The channel offers a lighter side into the suspense and mystery genres via dramatic and thought-provoking storytelling. Its programming features a mix of new, original movies and acquired series, as well as holiday and seasonal programming. In late-2018, Crown Media and the W Network signed a deal in which W Network would acquire Hallmark Media's original programming library's exclusive Canadian rights, and began offering Hallmark Channel programming that November. That same year, Crown Media's publishing division began selling its first set of printed novels.

FINANCIAL DATA:
Note: Data for latest year may not have been available at press time.

In U.S. $	2018	2017	2016	2015	2014	2013
Revenue	521,000,000	505,000,000	478,700,000	478,734,016	415,596,000	377,800,992
R&D Expense						
Operating Income						
Operating Margin %						
SGA Expense						
Net Income				86,083,000	94,497,000	67,715,000
Operating Cash Flow						
Capital Expenditure						
EBITDA						
Return on Assets %						
Return on Equity %						
Debt to Equity						

CONTACT INFORMATION:
Phone: 818 755-2400 Fax:
Toll-Free: 888-390-7474
Address: 12700 Ventura Blvd., Ste. 200, Studio City, CA 91604 United States

STOCK TICKER/OTHER:
Stock Ticker: Private
Employees: 240
Parent Company: Hallmark Cards Inc

Exchange:
Fiscal Year Ends: 12/31

SALARIES/BONUSES:
Top Exec. Salary: $ Bonus: $
Second Exec. Salary: $ Bonus: $

OTHER THOUGHTS:
Estimated Female Officers or Directors: 5
Hot Spot for Advancement for Women/Minorities: Y

Sales, profits and employees may be estimates. Financial information, benefits and other data can change quickly and may vary from those stated here.

CSS Industries Inc

NAIC Code: 323111

www.cssindustries.com

TYPES OF BUSINESS:
Commercial Printing
Educational Products

BRANDS/DIVISIONS/AFFILIATES:
Paper Magic Group Inc
Berwick Offray LLC
C R Gibson LLC
McCall Pattern Company Inc (The)
Butterick
Kwik Sew
Simplicity
Wrights

CONTACTS:
Note: Officers with more than one job title may be intentionally listed here more than once.

Christopher Munyan, CEO
Keith Pfeil, CFO
Steven Eck, Chief Accounting Officer
Rebecca Matthias, Director
Cara Farley, Executive VP, Divisional
Carey Edwards, Executive VP, Divisional
John White, Executive VP, Divisional
William Kiesling, Vice President, Divisional

GROWTH PLANS/SPECIAL FEATURES:

CSS Industries, Inc. is a consumer products company that specializes primarily in the design, manufacture and sale of occasional and non-seasonal merchandise to mass-market retailers. It manufactures gift bags, boxed greeting cards, gift tags, tissue paper, paper and vinyl decorations, calendars, classroom exchange valentines, decorative ribbons and bows. Approximately 66% of the company's sales are attributable to all gift and craft products with the remainder attributable to seasonal. Its products are manufactured, packaged, and warehoused in facilities across the U.S., as well as in the U.K. and Australia. CSS Industries operates four subsidiaries: Paper Magic Group, Inc.; Berwick Offray, LLC; C.R. Gibson, LLC; and The McCall Pattern Company, Inc. Paper Magic produces every day and seasonal products, including Christmas decor products, holiday cards and educational products. Berwick Offray specializes in the creation of woven ribbons, gift bags, wrapping paper and other gift wrapping accessories. C.R Gibson manufactures stationary, puzzles, casual dining products and products meant for scrapbooking and memory archiving. The firm maintains permanent showrooms in Pennsylvania, Texas, Georgia and Hong Kong, where buyers for major retail customers can visit for a presentation and review new lines of products. Direct customers are generally mass-market retailers; discount department stores; specialty chains; warehouse clubs; drug and food chains; dollar stores; office supply stores; independent card, gift and floral shops; and retail teachers' stores. McCall provides home sewing patterns, selling to mass-market retailers, specialty fabric and craft chains, as well as to wholesale distributors. Its patterns are marketed under the McCall's, Butterick, Kwik Sew and Vogue Patterns brand names. Other related brands include Simplicity, Wrights, Boye, Dimensions and Perler, offering home sewing patterns, decorative trims, knitting and crocheting tools, needle arts and more.

CSS offers medical, prescription, dental, vision and disability insurance; and 401(k) and employee stock purchase plans.

FINANCIAL DATA:
Note: Data for latest year may not have been available at press time.

In U.S. $	2018	2017	2016	2015	2014	2013
Revenue	361,896,000	322,431,000	317,017,000	313,044,000	320,459,000	364,193,000
R&D Expense						
Operating Income	-12,372,000	9,714,000	26,224,000	26,640,000	27,952,000	28,472,000
Operating Margin %	-3.41	3.01%	8.27%	8.51%	8.72%	7.81%
SGA Expense	105,201,000	83,375,000	76,047,000	75,062,000	75,204,000	80,619,000
Net Income	-36,520,000	28,504,000	17,236,000	16,954,000	18,769,000	15,227,000
Operating Cash Flow	31,368,000	14,871,000	15,123,000	32,991,000	27,830,000	29,863,000
Capital Expenditure	7,291,000	5,057,000	6,411,000	3,924,000	5,024,000	4,494,000
EBITDA	-1,885,000	18,191,000	34,532,000	34,518,000	35,495,000	36,066,000
Return on Assets %	-10.36%	8.78%	5.56%	5.62%	6.44%	5.28%
Return on Equity %	-13.33%	10.07%	6.36%	6.42%	7.41%	6.18%
Debt to Equity	0.15					

CONTACT INFORMATION:
Phone: 610-729-3959   Fax:
Toll-Free:
Address: 450 Plymouth Rd., Ste. 300, Plymouth Meeting, PA 19462 United States

STOCK TICKER/OTHER:
Stock Ticker: CSS
Employees: 1,540
Parent Company:

Exchange: NYS
Fiscal Year Ends: 03/31

SALARIES/BONUSES:
Top Exec. Salary: $654,491   Bonus: $186,530
Second Exec. Salary: $437,750   Bonus: $73,542

OTHER THOUGHTS:
Estimated Female Officers or Directors: 4
Hot Spot for Advancement for Women/Minorities: Y

Sales, profits and employees may be estimates. Financial information, benefits and other data can change quickly and may vary from those stated here.

Cumulus Media Inc

NAIC Code: 515112

www.cumulus.com

TYPES OF BUSINESS:
Radio Station Operator
Sales & Marketing Services
Media Operations Software

BRANDS/DIVISIONS/AFFILIATES:
NASH
Westwood One

CONTACTS:
Note: Officers with more than one job title may be intentionally listed here more than once.

Mary Berner, CEO/Pres.
John Abbot, CFO/Treas./Exec. VP
Richard Denning, General Counsel/Sec./Exec. VP
Andy Hobson, Chmn.

GROWTH PLANS/SPECIAL FEATURES:
Cumulus Media, Inc. primarily owns, operates, acquires and develops radio stations and clusters serving regional mid-size markets throughout the U.S. With approximately 434 owned-and-operated radio stations in 89 cities nationally, the company is the largest pure-play radio company in the U.S. The firm also operates a fully distributed programming network serving 8,000 broadcast radio stations affiliated with its Westwood One network and numerous digital channels. The Cumulus/Westwood One partnership broadcasts some of the largest brands in sports, entertainment, news and talk, including the NFL, the NCAA, the Masters, the Olympics, the GRAMMYs, the Academy of Country Music Awards and many more. In addition, Cumulus Media provides country music and lifestyle content through its NASH brand, which serves fans nationwide through radio programming, exclusive digital content and live events. On June 4, 2018, Cumulus Media completed its financial restricting and emerged from Chapter 11 bankruptcy; in July the company announced it would relist on the NASDAQ stock market.

FINANCIAL DATA:
Note: Data for latest year may not have been available at press time.

In U.S. $	2018	2017	2016	2015	2014	2013
Revenue		1,135,662,000	1,141,400,000	1,168,679,000	1,263,423,000	1,026,138,000
R&D Expense						
Operating Income		122,964,000	100,481,000	109,289,000	160,488,000	181,829,000
Operating Margin %						
SGA Expense		547,481,000	525,872,000	560,859,000	83,623,000	63,546,000
Net Income		-206,565,000	-510,720,000	-546,494,000	11,769,000	176,083,000
Operating Cash Flow		86,596,000	35,745,000	82,432,000	136,796,000	121,141,000
Capital Expenditure		31,932,000	23,037,000	19,236,000	19,006,000	11,081,000
EBITDA		-192,355,000	-310,973,000	-348,550,000	282,831,000	270,374,000
Return on Assets %						
Return on Equity %						
Debt to Equity						

CONTACT INFORMATION:
Phone: 404 949-0700
Fax: 404 949-0740
Toll-Free:
Address: 3280 Peachtree Rd. NW, Ste. 2300, Atlanta, GA 30305 United States

STOCK TICKER/OTHER:
Stock Ticker: CMLS
Employees: 5,479
Parent Company:

Exchange: NAS
Fiscal Year Ends: 12/31

SALARIES/BONUSES:
Top Exec. Salary: $1,450,000
Bonus: $1,087,500
Second Exec. Salary: $600,000
Bonus: $360,000

OTHER THOUGHTS:
Estimated Female Officers or Directors: 1
Hot Spot for Advancement for Women/Minorities:

Sales, profits and employees may be estimates. Financial information, benefits and other data can change quickly and may vary from those stated here.

CW Network LLC (The)

NAIC Code: 515210

www.cwtv.com

TYPES OF BUSINESS:
Television Broadcasting
Television Production
Soundtrack Recordings
DVD Distribution

BRANDS/DIVISIONS/AFFILIATES:
CBS Corporation
AT&T Inc
WarnerMedia
CW (The)
CW SEED

CONTACTS: Note: Officers with more than one job title may be intentionally listed here more than once.
Mark Pedowitz, Pres.
John Maatta, General Counsel
Paul Hewitt, Sr. VP-Network Comm.
Russell Myerson, Exec. VP

GROWTH PLANS/SPECIAL FEATURES:
The CW Network, LLC operates an English-language broadcast television network commonly referred to as The CW. The firm is a 50/50 joint venture between CBS Corporation and AT&T, Inc. The CW airs its prime-time programming for two hours on Monday through Friday evenings to its owned-and-operated and affiliated stations. Currently (October 2018), the network provides 20 hours of regularly-scheduled programming each week, over the course of seven days. Outside of prime time, an hour of daytime programming is also offered Monday through Fridays, from 3-4pm in all time zones, in the form of a talk show, The Jerry Springer Show; and weekend programming consists of a three-hour educational programming block called One Magnificent Morning, aired on Saturdays from 8-11am in all time zones. CW SEED is the firm's digital-only network that enables viewers to watch episodes for free, at any time. The CW does not produce any national news content; it has eight affiliates that produce their own local news programming, most of which were carry-ons from previous affiliations. These news operations include WPIX in New York City, KTLA in Los Angeles, WCCB in Charlotte, and WISH-TV in Indianapolis. In mid-2018, AT&T acquired Time Warner, parent of WarnerMedia, making AT&T a co-owner of The CW with CBS.

FINANCIAL DATA: Note: Data for latest year may not have been available at press time.

In U.S. $	2018	2017	2016	2015	2014	2013
Revenue		418,000,000	410,000,000	390,000,000	404,000,000	464,000,000
R&D Expense						
Operating Income						
Operating Margin %						
SGA Expense						
Net Income				17,000,000	16,000,000	8,000,000
Operating Cash Flow						
Capital Expenditure						
EBITDA						
Return on Assets %						
Return on Equity %						
Debt to Equity						

CONTACT INFORMATION:
Phone: 818-977-2500 Fax: 818-977-2595
Toll-Free:
Address: 3300 W. Olive Ave., 3/Fl, Burbank, CA 91505-4640 United States

STOCK TICKER/OTHER:
Stock Ticker: Joint Venture
Employees:
Parent Company:

Exchange:
Fiscal Year Ends: 12/31

SALARIES/BONUSES:
Top Exec. Salary: $ Bonus: $
Second Exec. Salary: $ Bonus: $

OTHER THOUGHTS:
Estimated Female Officers or Directors:
Hot Spot for Advancement for Women/Minorities:

Sales, profits and employees may be estimates. Financial information, benefits and other data can change quickly and may vary from those stated here.

ns, Ltd.

Daily Journal Corporation
NAIC Code: 511110

www.dailyjournal.com

TYPES OF BUSINESS:
Newspaper Publishing
Online Publishing
Information Services
Judicial Publishing Technology

BRANDS/DIVISIONS/AFFILIATES:
Los Angeles Daily Journal
San Francisco Daily Journal
Daily Commerce
Daily Transcript (The)
Riverside Business Journal
Orange County Reporter
Record Reporter (The)
REDLOC Online

CONTACTS: Note: Officers with more than one job title may be intentionally listed here more than once.
Gerald Salzman, Assistant Secretary
Charles Munger, Chairman of the Board
J.P. Guerin, Director

GROWTH PLANS/SPECIAL FEATURES:
Daily Journal Corporation publishes newspapers and news websites covering California and Arizona, as well as the California Lawyer online magazine. The company also serves as a newspaper representative, specializing in public notice advertising. It publishes newspapers in general circulation, each of which offer news of interest to the general public along with a particular area of in-depth focus with regard to its coverage. Publications include the Los Angeles Daily Journal, San Francisco Daily Journal, Daily Commerce (Los Angeles), The Daily Transcript (San Diego), Riverside Business Journal, Orange County Reporter, San Jose Post-Record, The Inter-City Express (Oakland), The Daily Recorder (Sacramento), The Record Reporter (Phoenix) and REDLOC Online. These publications operate predominately on a subscription basis, and many of them cover issues concerning business, legal and real estate matters. Additionally, the company produces various informational publications, including court rules and judicial profiles. Daily Journal's wholly-owned subsidiary, Journal Technologies, Inc., provides case management software systems and related products to courts and other justice agencies, including district attorney offices and administrative law organizations. These products enable agencies to automate their operations, file cases electronically and publish information online. Daily Journal supplements service to subscribers and advertisers with an increasing internet-based online information service. Some of these services come as part of a newspaper subscription or advertising placement, while others can only be obtained when customers pay additional fees. The company's publications carry commercial advertising and most also contain public notice advertising, which consists of various types of legal notices required by law to be published in an adjudicated newspaper of general circulation.

FINANCIAL DATA: Note: Data for latest year may not have been available at press time.

In U.S. $	2018	2017	2016	2015	2014	2013
Revenue	40,703,000	41,384,000	41,612,000	43,978,000	43,423,000	37,676,000
R&D Expense						
Operating Income	-14,060,000	-13,167,000	-6,640,000	-3,512,000	-2,190,000	3,843,000
Operating Margin %		-31.81%	-15.95%	-7.98%	-5.04%	10.20%
SGA Expense	45,161,000	42,424,000	36,761,000	35,892,000	34,383,000	25,671,000
Net Income	8,201,000	-918,000	-1,043,000	810,000	631,000	3,779,000
Operating Cash Flow	-1,881,000	-2,651,000	1,224,000	7,755,000	4,507,000	5,672,000
Capital Expenditure	212,000	253,000	3,779,000	565,000	435,000	280,000
EBITDA	-6,915,000	-2,261,000	3,215,000	5,541,000	6,424,000	7,107,000
Return on Assets %		-.36%	-.45%	.34%	.28%	2.33%
Return on Equity %		-.64%	-.82%	.61%	.50%	3.76%
Debt to Equity			0.19	0.25	0.22	0.21

CONTACT INFORMATION:
Phone: 213 229-5300 Fax: 213 229-5481
Toll-Free:
Address: 915 E. First St., Los Angeles, CA 90012 United States

STOCK TICKER/OTHER:
Stock Ticker: DJCO
Employees: 355
Parent Company:

Exchange: NAS
Fiscal Year Ends: 09/30

SALARIES/BONUSES:
Top Exec. Salary: $250,000 Bonus: $400,000
Second Exec. Salary: $ Bonus: $

OTHER THOUGHTS:
Estimated Female Officers or Directors: 1
Hot Spot for Advancement for Women/Minorities:

Sales, profits and employees may be estimates. Financial information, benefits and other data can change quickly and may vary from those stated here.

Dalian Wanda Group Co Ltd

NAIC Code: 512131

www.wanda-group.com

TYPES OF BUSINESS:
Motion Picture Theaters (except Drive-Ins)
Motion Picture Production
Motion Picture Distribution
Performing Arts Companies
Amusement and Theme Parks
Hotels
Department Stores
Internet Publishing and Broadcasting and Web Search Portals

BRANDS/DIVISIONS/AFFILIATES:
Wanda Plaza
Kidsplace Parks
Kidsplace Early Education Club
Wanda Cities
Wanda Sports
Wanda Investment Company
Aeon Insurance Asset Management Company
Guangzhou Wanda Puhui Microcredit Co Ltd

CONTACTS: Note: Officers with more than one job title may be intentionally listed here more than once.
Wang Jianlin, Chmn.

GROWTH PLANS/SPECIAL FEATURES:

Dalian Wanda Group Co., Ltd. is a private property developer with assets totaling $101.71 billion (700 billion yuan) in 2017. The company operates in four major industries: commercial properties, cultural industry, real estate and financial. Dalian Wanda's commercial properties division comprises 268 Wanda Plazas, each of which have shopping malls, hotels, food and beverage locations, culture and entertainment destinations and residential apartments. Each plaza forms an independent business district and represents the center of a city. The cultural industry division is comprised of cinemas, film production, film industry parks, performing arts, film technology entertainment, theme parks, entertainment franchises, print media, art investment and travel. This segment owns and operates: AMC, Odeon-UCI, Wanda and other cinema chains, totaling more than 1,550 cinemas globally; six ultra-large themed entertainment parks; 182 Kidsplace Parks and 51 Kidsplace Early Education Clubs, which are children's entertainment franchises that integrate education, entertainment, food/beverage and retail operations; six Wanda Cities, which include theme parks, cultural tourist activities, hotels and resorts; and Wanda Sports, which operates 20 sports events worldwide, including football, hockey, cycling, basketball and triathlons. The real estate division develops the company's urban complexes and apartment buildings, including Wanda's plazas, hotels, cities and other properties. Last, the financial division comprises investment, asset management, insurance and financial services companies, including Wanda Investment Company, Aeon Insurance Asset Management Company, Aeon Life Insurance, and Guangzhou Wanda Puhui Microcredit Co., Ltd. During 2018, Wanda Group (51%) announced plans to establish an internet technology joint venture with Tencent Holdings Ltd. (42.48%) and Gaopeng (6.52%) to build a world-class new consumption model that will integrate both online and offline businesses.

FINANCIAL DATA:
Note: Data for latest year may not have been available at press time.

In U.S. $	2018	2017	2016	2015	2014	2013
Revenue		35,540,000,000	37,030,806,050	45,279,800,000	22,197,644,000	16,803,616,508
R&D Expense						
Operating Income						
Operating Margin %						
SGA Expense						
Net Income				2,431,000,000	2,235,113,672	2,203,732,677
Operating Cash Flow						
Capital Expenditure						
EBITDA						
Return on Assets %						
Return on Equity %						
Debt to Equity						

CONTACT INFORMATION:
Phone: 86-10-85853888   Fax: 86-10-85853222
Toll-Free:
Address: Tower B, Wanda Plaza, No. 93, Jianguo Rd., Chaoyang District, Beijing, 100022 China

STOCK TICKER/OTHER:
Stock Ticker: Private
Employees: 130,000
Parent Company:

Exchange:
Fiscal Year Ends: 12/31

SALARIES/BONUSES:
Top Exec. Salary: $ Bonus: $
Second Exec. Salary: $ Bonus: $

OTHER THOUGHTS:
Estimated Female Officers or Directors:
Hot Spot for Advancement for Women/Minorities:

Dave & Buster's Entertainment Inc

www.daveandbusters.com

NAIC Code: 713120

TYPES OF BUSINESS:
Amusement Arcades
Casual Dining Restaurants

BRANDS/DIVISIONS/AFFILIATES:

GROWTH PLANS/SPECIAL FEATURES:

Dave & Buster's Entertainment, Inc. (D&B) owns and operates entertainment and dining venues in the U.S. and Canada. The firm's locations offer casual dining food items and a full selection of non-alcoholic and alcoholic beverage items together with an array of entertainment options, including skill- and sports-oriented redemption games, video games, interactive simulators and other traditional games. Each location also contains multiple large screen televisions and high-quality audio systems, providing guests with a venue for watching live sports and other televised events. D&B currently owns and operates 103 stores in 35 states, two in Canada and one in Puerto Rico. On average, the company's stores are 44,000 square-feet, ranging in size between 16,000 and 66,000 square feet and typically feature over 150 redemption and simulation games.

Dave & Buster's offers some of its employees medical, dental and vision insurance and a 401(k).

CONTACTS: Note: Officers with more than one job title may be intentionally listed here more than once.

Brian Jenkins, CEO
Stephen King, Chairman of the Board
John Mulleady, Senior VP, Divisional
Kevin Bachus, Senior VP, Divisional
Angelia Pelham, Senior VP, Divisional
J. Plunkett, Senior VP, Divisional
Sean Gleason, Senior VP
Margo Manning, Senior VP
Joe DeProspero, Vice President, Divisional
Michael Metzinger, Vice President, Divisional

FINANCIAL DATA: Note: Data for latest year may not have been available at press time.

In U.S. $	2018	2017	2016	2015	2014	2013
Revenue	1,139,791,000	1,005,158,000	866,982,000	746,751,000	635,579,000	608,067,000
R&D Expense						
Operating Income	165,772,000	150,516,000	110,036,000	73,861,000	51,039,000	43,714,000
Operating Margin %	14.54	14.97%	12.69%	9.89%	8.03%	7.18%
SGA Expense	59,565,000	54,474,000	53,600,000	44,574,000	36,440,000	40,356,000
Net Income	120,949,000	90,795,000	59,619,000	7,636,000	2,169,000	8,782,000
Operating Cash Flow	264,672,000	231,329,000	186,983,000	86,715,000	109,878,000	82,796,000
Capital Expenditure	219,901,000	180,577,000	162,892,000	129,688,000	105,894,000	78,689,000
EBITDA	267,066,000	238,270,000	180,840,000	115,185,000	114,521,000	104,561,000
Return on Assets %	10.75%	8.82%	6.09%	.84%	.25%	1.09%
Return on Equity %	28.09%	23.10%	19.70%	3.73%	1.45%	6.16%
Debt to Equity	0.83	0.58	0.95	1.65	3.21	3.18

CONTACT INFORMATION:
Phone: 214 357-9588 Fax:
Toll-Free:
Address: 2481 Manana Dr., Dallas, TX 75220 United States

STOCK TICKER/OTHER:
Stock Ticker: PLAY
Employees: 13,983
Parent Company:

Exchange: NAS
Fiscal Year Ends: 02/02

SALARIES/BONUSES:
Top Exec. Salary: $802,884 Bonus: $
Second Exec. Salary: $463,846 Bonus: $4,616

OTHER THOUGHTS:
Estimated Female Officers or Directors: 1
Hot Spot for Advancement for Women/Minorities:

Sales, profits and employees may be estimates. Financial information, benefits and other data can change quickly and may vary from those stated here.

Delaware North Companies Inc

NAIC Code: 722310

www.delawarenorth.com

TYPES OF BUSINESS:
Food Service Contractors
Catering & Food Services
Park & Resort Visitor Services
Professional Hockey Team
Event Centers
Casinos

BRANDS/DIVISIONS/AFFILIATES:

CONTACTS: Note: Officers with more than one job title may be intentionally listed here more than once.
Jerry Jacobs, Co-CEO
Lou Jacobs, Co-CEO
Charles E. Moran, Pres.
Christopher J. Feeney, CFO
Todd Merry, CMO
Eileen Morgan, Chief Human Resources Officer
Bernard Gay, CIO
Rajat Shah, General Counsel
Nate Brunner, VP-Financial Planning & Analysis
Wendy A. Watkins, VP-Corp. Comm.
Scott Socha, Treas.
John Wentzell, Pres., DNC Sportservice
Paula Halligan, VP-Retail
Simon Dobson, Managing Dir.-U.K.
William J. Bissett, Pres., DNC Gaming & Entertainment
Jeremy M. Jacobs, Chmn.
Gary Brown, Managing Dir.-Australia & New Zealand
Michael Reinert, VP-Supply Mgmt. Svcs.

GROWTH PLANS/SPECIAL FEATURES:
Delaware North Companies, Inc. is a global provider of food services and hospitality management serving 500 million guests a year. The firm manages and provides food & beverage concessions, premium dining, entertainment, lodging and retail at many large venues (sports stadiums, entertainment complexes, national & state parks, airports and casinos). Delaware North is a major player in several sectors of sports, including stadiums, arenas and ballparks, with more than 60 venues worldwide at which it operates premium dining, restaurants and food/beverage concession stands. Serving the national and state parks, the firm delivers lodging, retail, food service, recreational and transportation services across the U.S. Delaware North also has a portfolio of distinct luxury resorts in Australia and the U.S., including resorts on Australia's Great Barrier Reef: Lizard Island, Wilson Island and Heron Island, as well as the U.S.' Tenaya Lodge at Yosemite and Gideon Putnam Resort in New York. The company is a world-leading airport food service and retail company, operating at over 300 restaurants and retail stores at more than 30 airports and travel centers in the U.S., Great Britain and Australia. The company operates gaming casinos in the U.S., including video gaming machines, table games, poker rooms, racing simulcast centers, restaurants, lounges, nightclubs, sports bars, event centers, retail shops and hotels. The firm's restaurants are located at venues such as the Kennedy Space Center, Wheeling Island, Yellowstone, Niagara Falls and the Grand Canyon.

FINANCIAL DATA: Note: Data for latest year may not have been available at press time.

In U.S. $	2018	2017	2016	2015	2014	2013
Revenue	3,320,000,000	3,310,000,000	3,300,000,000	3,210,000,000	2,940,000,000	3,000,000,000
R&D Expense						
Operating Income						
Operating Margin %						
SGA Expense						
Net Income						
Operating Cash Flow						
Capital Expenditure						
EBITDA						
Return on Assets %						
Return on Equity %						
Debt to Equity						

CONTACT INFORMATION:
Phone: 716-858-5000 Fax: 716-858-5479
Toll-Free:
Address: 40 Fountain Plz., Buffalo, NY 14202 United States

STOCK TICKER/OTHER:
Stock Ticker: Private
Employees: 55,000
Parent Company:

Exchange:
Fiscal Year Ends: 12/31

SALARIES/BONUSES:
Top Exec. Salary: $ Bonus: $
Second Exec. Salary: $ Bonus: $

OTHER THOUGHTS:
Estimated Female Officers or Directors: 5
Hot Spot for Advancement for Women/Minorities: Y

Sales, profits and employees may be estimates. Financial information, benefits and other data can change quickly and may vary from those stated here.

Dennis Publishing Ltd

NAIC Code: 511120

www.dennis.co.uk

TYPES OF BUSINESS:
Magazine Publishing
Mailing Lists
Interactive Media
Mail Order & Fulfillment Services
Video Production
Digital Advertising Services

BRANDS/DIVISIONS/AFFILIATES:
Exponent Private Equity LLP
Exponent Private Equity Partners IV LP
Week (The)
Men's Fitness
Cyclist
Carbuyer
AutoExpress
PC Pro

GROWTH PLANS/SPECIAL FEATURES:
Dennis Publishing, Ltd., based in London, is an independent publisher of magazines and digital media. Operating through multiple subsidiaries in the U.K. and the U.S., it is one of the world's fastest-growing independently owned media companies. Dennis publishes over 30 magazines, websites, digital magazines and mobile sites in the U.K. It publishes magazines in six categories: current affairs, including The Week, the company's most profitable U.K. magazine; automotive, which includes Auto Express and Carbuyer; technology, which publishes PC Pro and Expert Review, among others; and lifestyle, which includes Cyclist and Men's Fitness; The company offers online and mobile versions of several of its subscription-based magazines as well as free digital magazines such as iMotor. In August 2018, Dennis announced that it had been acquired by Exponent Private Equity LLP's fourth fund, Exponent Private Equity Partners IV, LP.

CONTACTS:
Note: Officers with more than one job title may be intentionally listed here more than once.

James Tye, CEO
Luke Walker, Head-Project Mgmt.
Jerina Hardy, Dir.-Public Rel. & Comm.
Pete Wootton, Managing Dir.-Dennis Interactive

FINANCIAL DATA:
Note: Data for latest year may not have been available at press time.

In U.S. $	2018	2017	2016	2015	2014	2013
Revenue	155,000,000	145,318,000	115,821,000	131,832,000	126,604,000	134,280,000
R&D Expense						
Operating Income						
Operating Margin %						
SGA Expense						
Net Income		-5,855,200	-1,440,520	3,741,480	5,178,370	4,146,730
Operating Cash Flow						
Capital Expenditure						
EBITDA						
Return on Assets %						
Return on Equity %						
Debt to Equity						

CONTACT INFORMATION:
Phone: 44-20-3890-3890 Fax:
Toll-Free:
Address: 31-32 Alfred Place, London, WC1E 7DP United Kingdom

SALARIES/BONUSES:
Top Exec. Salary: $ Bonus: $
Second Exec. Salary: $ Bonus: $

STOCK TICKER/OTHER:
Stock Ticker: Private   Exchange:
Employees: 1,100   Fiscal Year Ends: 12/31
Parent Company: Exponent Private Equity LLP

OTHER THOUGHTS:
Estimated Female Officers or Directors: 3
Hot Spot for Advancement for Women/Minorities: Y

Sales, profits and employees may be estimates. Financial information, benefits and other data can change quickly and may vary from those stated here.

DexYP

NAIC Code: 541810

www.thryv.com

TYPES OF BUSINESS:
Publishing of Telephone Directories
Business Management

BRANDS/DIVISIONS/AFFILIATES:
Thryv
Dex Media Inc
YP Holdings

CONTACTS:
Note: Officers with more than one job title may be intentionally listed here more than once.

Joe Walsh, CEO
Alan Schultz, Chairman of the Board
Mark Cairns, Executive VP, Divisional
John Wholey, Executive VP, Divisional
Raymond Ferrell, Executive VP
Debra Ryan, Executive VP
Andrew Hede, Other Executive Officer
Joseph Walsh, President

GROWTH PLANS/SPECIAL FEATURES:

DexYP (formerly Dex Media, Inc.) provides business management services and solutions to local businesses throughout the U.S. The company helps these firms win and retain customers via customer relationship management, an online presence, bookings, analytics and more from a single mobile platform called Thryv. Thryv's estimating, invoicing, online payment and mobile QuickPay features informs business owners how much money they have, when it is coming and where it is going, 24/7 from any device. The platform enables ongoing connection and communication with customers via detailed customer profiles, social media postings, texts, emails, websites and more. Thryv turns a business' online presence into profits by creating a website that stands out, being listed on more than 70 important websites, keeping tabs on online ratings and reviews, and getting noticed on search sites such as Google, Yahoo! and Bing. Thryv's starter plan costs $59 per month, with no setup fee; its basic plan costs $99 per month, with no setup fee; and the plus plan is $199 per month, along with a $149 setup fee. All plans include individual support; invoices, estimates and QuickPay; a place to manage all contact information; consistent listings on more than 70 sites; 24/7 online booking capability; and a place where consumers can request a call back. Extras include text and email promotions, custom coupons, social media, a website and a video.

FINANCIAL DATA:
Note: Data for latest year may not have been available at press time.

In U.S. $	2018	2017	2016	2015	2014	2013
Revenue	2,450,000,000	2,309,000,000	2,803,300,000	1,500,300,000	1,815,000,064	1,444,000,000
R&D Expense						
Operating Income						
Operating Margin %						
SGA Expense						
Net Income				-262,100,000	-371,000,000	-819,000,000
Operating Cash Flow						
Capital Expenditure						
EBITDA						
Return on Assets %						
Return on Equity %						
Debt to Equity						

CONTACT INFORMATION:
Phone: 972-453-7000   Fax: 919 297-1285
Toll-Free:
Address: 2200 W. Airfield Dr., Dallas, TX 75261 United States

SALARIES/BONUSES:
Top Exec. Salary: $ Bonus: $
Second Exec. Salary: $ Bonus: $

STOCK TICKER/OTHER:
Stock Ticker: Private   Exchange:
Employees: 3,500   Fiscal Year Ends: 12/31
Parent Company:

OTHER THOUGHTS:
Estimated Female Officers or Directors: 1
Hot Spot for Advancement for Women/Minorities:

Sales, profits and employees may be estimates. Financial information, benefits and other data can change quickly and may vary from those stated here.

Dick Clark Productions Inc

www.dickclarkproductions.com

NAIC Code: 512110

TYPES OF BUSINESS:
Television Production
Film Production
Restaurants
Publicity Services

BRANDS/DIVISIONS/AFFILIATES:
Dick Clark's American Bandstand Grill
Countryville
American Bandstand Express
Dick Clark's American Bandstand Theater

CONTACTS: Note: Officers with more than one job title may be intentionally listed here more than once.
Mike Mahan, CEO
Amy Thurlow, CFO
Ariel Elazar, Exec. VP-Brand, Mktg. & Digital Strategy
Michael Kohn, General Counsel
Michael Kohn, Sr. VP-Bus. Oper.
Greg Economou, Chief Revenue Officer
Michael Mahan, Pres., DC Media
Barry Adelman, Exec. VP-Television
Michael Antinoro, Exec. VP-Programming
Allen Shapiro, Chmn.
Mark Rafalowski, Exec. VP-Int'l Distributions

GROWTH PLANS/SPECIAL FEATURES:
Dick Clark Productions, Inc. (DCPI) is a diversified entertainment company made up of television, communications and restaurant businesses. The firm develops and produces television programming for television networks, first-run domestic syndicators, cable networks and advertisers. DCPI has been a significant supplier of television programming for over 55 years and has produced shows such as American Dreams, the Golden Globe Awards, the American Music Awards, the Academy of Country Music Awards, the Family Television Awards, the Daytime Emmy Awards, Bloopers and Beyond Belief: Fact or Fiction. Programming includes awards shows, comedy specials, children's programming, talk and game show series and dramatic series. The market for this programming is mainly composed of ABC, CBS, NBC, Fox and The CW network. DCPI also licenses the rebroadcast rights to some of its programs, licenses certain segments of its programming to third parties, produces home videos and develops and produces theatrical motion pictures, generally in conjunction with third parties who provide the financing. DCPI operates a chain of entertainment-themed restaurants named Dick Clark's American Bandstand Grill, located in Branson, Missouri, offering burgers, sandwiches, salads, steaks, pasta and desserts; Countryville, located in Devol, Oklahoma, a place where patrons can listen to country music and order food and beverages; and American Bandstand Express, located in Chandler, Arizona, offering burgers, sandwiches, salads and hand-dipped milkshakes. In addition, Dick Clark's American Bandstand Theater, located in Branson, Missouri, presents Legends in Concert live tribute shows, which cover the Bandstand era and the history of its music.

FINANCIAL DATA: Note: Data for latest year may not have been available at press time.

In U.S. $	2018	2017	2016	2015	2014	2013
Revenue	600,000,000					
R&D Expense						
Operating Income						
Operating Margin %						
SGA Expense						
Net Income						
Operating Cash Flow						
Capital Expenditure						
EBITDA						
Return on Assets %						
Return on Equity %						
Debt to Equity						

CONTACT INFORMATION:
Phone: 310-255-4600 Fax: 310-255-4601
Toll-Free:
Address: 2900 Olympic Blvd., Santa Monica, CA 90404 United States

SALARIES/BONUSES:
Top Exec. Salary: $ Bonus: $
Second Exec. Salary: $ Bonus: $

STOCK TICKER/OTHER:
Stock Ticker: Private Exchange:
Employees: 600 Fiscal Year Ends: 06/30
Parent Company:

OTHER THOUGHTS:
Estimated Female Officers or Directors:
Hot Spot for Advancement for Women/Minorities:

Sales, profits and employees may be estimates. Financial information, benefits and other data can change quickly and may vary from those stated here.

DirecTV LLC (DIRECTV)

NAIC Code: 517110

www.directv.com

TYPES OF BUSINESS:
Satellite Broadcasting
Commercial Satellite Fleet
Satellite-Based Internet Services
Digital Television

BRANDS/DIVISIONS/AFFILIATES:
AT&T Inc
DirectNOW
Genie HD DVR

CONTACTS: Note: Officers with more than one job title may be intentionally listed here more than once.
Michael White, CEO
Patrick Doyle, CFO
Romulo Pontual, Chief Technology Officer
Larry Hunter, Executive VP
Joseph Bosch, Executive VP
Bruce Churchill, Executive VP
Steven Adams, Senior VP
Fazal Merchant, Senior VP

GROWTH PLANS/SPECIAL FEATURES:
DirecTV, LLC (DIRECTV), a wholly-owned subsidiary of AT&T, Inc., is a leading provider of digital television entertainment throughout the U.S. and Latin America. The company manages a fleet of satellites in geostationary orbit to ensure strong coverage of the North American continent. DIRECTV's current (as of June 2018) packages include: Select, offering 155 channels for a monthly fee; Entertainment, offering 160 channels; Choice, offering 185 channels; XTRA, offering 235 channels; Ultimate, offering more than 250 channels; and Premier, offering more than 330 channels. Choice through Premier options receive the firm's NFL Sunday season package for free. DirectNOW offers streaming services of more than 60 live channels, as well as 25,000 titles on demand, with no annual contract, installation or equipment needed. DirectNOW packages start at $35 per month. DIRECTV's Genie HD DVR enables customers to seamlessly swap what they are watching from one TV to another, or from tablet to TV, anywhere in the home. Genie HD can record up to five shows at once and store up to 200 hours of HD entertainment. In addition, shows that have aired within the last 72 hours can be rewound and watched as live shows with Genie's DIRECTV 72 Hour Rewind feature. DIRECTV packages can be bundled with AT&T services, and the firm offers DIRECTV services for businesses.

Employees receive medical, dental and vision coverage; flexible spending accounts; wellness plans; employee assistance programs; and a 401(k) savings plan with a matching contribution opportunity.

FINANCIAL DATA: Note: Data for latest year may not have been available at press time.

In U.S. $	2018	2017	2016	2015	2014	2013
Revenue		35,584,900,000	33,703,000,000	34,000,000,000	33,260,000,000	31,754,000,000
R&D Expense						
Operating Income						
Operating Margin %						
SGA Expense						
Net Income		4,305,000,000	32,000,000	-100,000	3,102,000,000	2,995,000,000
Operating Cash Flow						
Capital Expenditure						
EBITDA						
Return on Assets %						
Return on Equity %						
Debt to Equity						

CONTACT INFORMATION:
Phone: 310-964-5000 Fax:
Toll-Free:
Address: 2260 E. Imperial Hwy., El Segundo, CA 90245 United States

SALARIES/BONUSES:
Top Exec. Salary: $ Bonus: $
Second Exec. Salary: $ Bonus: $

STOCK TICKER/OTHER:
Stock Ticker: Subsidiary Exchange:
Employees: 32,150 Fiscal Year Ends: 12/31
Parent Company: AT&T Inc

OTHER THOUGHTS:
Estimated Female Officers or Directors: 3
Hot Spot for Advancement for Women/Minorities: Y

Discovery Inc

corporate.discovery.com

NAIC Code: 515210

TYPES OF BUSINESS:
Cable TV Networks
Digital Media
Catalog & Online Sales
Educational Products
E-commerce
Merchandising

BRANDS/DIVISIONS/AFFILIATES:
Discovery Channel
TLC
Eurosport
Oprah Winfrey Network (OWN, The)
DMAX
Investigation Discovery
Velocity

CONTACTS: Note: Officers with more than one job title may be intentionally listed here more than once.
Jean-Briac Perrette, CEO, Divisional
David Zaslav, CEO
Gunnar Wiedenfels, CFO
Robert Miron, Chairman of the Board
Kurt Wehner, Chief Accounting Officer
Savalle Sims, Executive VP
Adria Romm, Other Corporate Officer
David Leavy, Other Executive Officer
Bruce Campbell, Other Executive Officer

GROWTH PLANS/SPECIAL FEATURES:
Discovery, Inc, formerly Discovery Communications, is a global media and entertainment company that produces and distributes original and purchased programming across multiple platforms to 3 billion cumulative subscribers. Discovery spans a variety of diverse genres, including exploration, survival, natural history, environment, technology, docu-series, health and wellness and space. The firm operates in four segments: U.S. networks, international networks, education and other. The U.S. networks segment operates and owns ten national TV networks: Discovery Channel, TLC, Animal Planet, Investigation Discovery, Science and Velocity. The division also includes the firm's interests in The Oprah Winfrey Network (OWN) and Discovery Family. The firm's international networks reach more than 220 countries and territories around the world and are distributed in over 50 languages. Networks include Discovery Channel, Animal Planet, Eurosport, Turbo, Real Time, DMAX and Discovery Kids. Education offers a suite of curriculum-based tools and educator enhancement resources that promote the integration of media and technology in the classroom. Other is largely comprised of production studios that develop television content for our networks and television service providers throughout the world. The company's portfolio also includes websites, retail, merchandising and various digital media products and services. In March 2018, Discovery announced it had acquired Scripps Networks Interactive, a lifestyle programming firm that specializes in comfort-food television.

FINANCIAL DATA: Note: Data for latest year may not have been available at press time.

In U.S. $	2018	2017	2016	2015	2014	2013
Revenue		6,873,000,000	6,497,000,000	6,394,000,000	6,265,000,000	5,535,000,000
R&D Expense						
Operating Income		2,119,000,000	2,053,000,000	2,052,000,000	2,120,000,000	1,995,000,000
Operating Margin %		30.83%	31.59%	32.09%	33.83%	36.04%
SGA Expense		1,768,000,000	1,690,000,000	1,669,000,000	1,692,000,000	1,575,000,000
Net Income		-337,000,000	1,194,000,000	1,034,000,000	1,139,000,000	1,075,000,000
Operating Cash Flow		1,629,000,000	1,373,000,000	1,277,000,000	1,318,000,000	1,285,000,000
Capital Expenditure		135,000,000	88,000,000	103,000,000	120,000,000	115,000,000
EBITDA		2,578,000,000	4,119,000,000	3,928,000,000	3,961,000,000	3,508,000,000
Return on Assets %		-1.75%	7.55%	6.48%	7.34%	7.70%
Return on Equity %		-6.89%	22.49%	18.71%	19.31%	17.22%
Debt to Equity		3.20	1.51	1.39	1.07	1.04

CONTACT INFORMATION:
Phone: 240 662-2000   Fax: 240 662-1868
Toll-Free:
Address: 1 Discovery Pl., Silver Spring, MD 20910 United States

SALARIES/BONUSES:
Top Exec. Salary: $3,000,000   Bonus: $
Second Exec. Salary: $1,591,910   Bonus: $

STOCK TICKER/OTHER:
Stock Ticker: DISCA
Employees: 7,000
Parent Company:

Exchange: NAS
Fiscal Year Ends: 12/31

OTHER THOUGHTS:
Estimated Female Officers or Directors: 1
Hot Spot for Advancement for Women/Minorities: Y

Sales, profits and employees may be estimates. Financial information, benefits and other data can change quickly and may vary from those stated here.

DISH Network Corporation

NAIC Code: 517110

www.dishnetwork.com

TYPES OF BUSINESS:
Satellite Broadcasting

BRANDS/DIVISIONS/AFFILIATES:
DISH
DISH On Demand
Sling TV
Sling Orange
Sling Blue
Sling International
dishNET
Parkifi

CONTACTS:
Note: Officers with more than one job title may be intentionally listed here more than once.

Paul Orban, CFO
Charles Ergen, Chairman of the Board
Cantey Ergen, Co-Founder
James Defranco, Co-Founder
Thomas Cullen, Executive VP, Divisional
Jeffrey McSchooler, Executive VP, Divisional
John Swieringa, Executive VP
Timothy Messner, Executive VP
Brian Neylon, Executive VP
Warren Schlichting, Executive VP
David Scott, Other Executive Officer
W. Carlson, President

GROWTH PLANS/SPECIAL FEATURES:
DISH Network Corporation is a leading pay-TV provider with more than 13 million customers throughout the U.S. Products and services offered by DISH Network include pay-TV programming and broadband. Within pay-TV programming, the firm offers a wide selection of video services under the DISH brand, with access to hundreds of channels depending on the level of subscription. The standard package includes programming provided by national broadcast networks, local broadcast networks and national and regional cable networks. Other packages include regional and specialty sports channels, premium movie channels and Latino and international programming. The Latino and international programming packages allow subscribers to choose from over 270 channels in 28 languages. In addition, DISH branded pay-TV subscribers have access through DISH On Demand to more than 10,000 movies and TV shows via their TV or internet-connected tablets, smartphones and computers. Sling branded pay-TV services markets Sling TV services primarily to consumers who do not subscribe to traditional satellite and cable pay-TV services. Sling TV services require an internet connection, and offer the following services: Sling Orange, a single-stream domestic service; Sling Blue, a multi-stream domestic service; Sling international; Sling Latino; and add-on extras, pay-per-view events and a cloud-based DVR service. Broadband products offered by DISH Network are marketed under the dishNET brand. This service leverages advanced technology and high-powered satellites launched by Hughes and ViaSat to provide broadband coverage nationwide. DishNET primarily targets rural residents that are underserved, or unserved, by wireline broadband. In early-2018, DISH acquired Parkifi, which builds and sells patent-pending internet of things (IoT)-enabled parking sensors with cloud-based analytics.

FINANCIAL DATA:
Note: Data for latest year may not have been available at press time.

In U.S. $	2018	2017	2016	2015	2014	2013
Revenue		14,391,370,000	15,094,560,000	15,068,900,000	14,643,390,000	13,904,870,000
R&D Expense						
Operating Income		2,009,378,000	2,211,109,000	1,971,303,000	1,824,451,000	1,785,754,000
Operating Margin %		13.96%	14.64%	13.08%	12.45%	12.84%
SGA Expense		687,054,000	783,224,000	777,507,000	815,745,000	776,711,000
Net Income		2,098,689,000	1,449,853,000	747,092,000	944,693,000	807,492,000
Operating Cash Flow		2,779,507,000	2,802,152,000	2,436,080,000	2,378,124,000	2,272,465,000
Capital Expenditure		6,096,447,000	1,327,350,000	10,084,770,000	3,879,233,000	1,253,499,000
EBITDA		2,530,823,000	3,312,601,000	2,630,010,000	2,894,887,000	2,935,926,000
Return on Assets %		7.25%	5.68%	3.32%	4.44%	4.27%
Return on Equity %		36.26%	39.25%	31.37%	63.18%	159.27%
Debt to Equity		2.18	3.35	4.44	6.84	12.91

CONTACT INFORMATION:
Phone: 303 723-1000 Fax: 303 723-1499
Toll-Free: 800-823-4929
Address: 9601 S. Meridian Blvd., Englewood, CO 80112 United States

SALARIES/BONUSES:
Top Exec. Salary: $1,000,000 Bonus: $
Second Exec. Salary: $519,231 Bonus: $

STOCK TICKER/OTHER:
Stock Ticker: DISH
Employees: 16,000
Parent Company:

Exchange: NAS
Fiscal Year Ends: 12/31

OTHER THOUGHTS:
Estimated Female Officers or Directors:
Hot Spot for Advancement for Women/Minorities:

Sales, profits and employees may be estimates. Financial information, benefits and other data can change quickly and may vary from those stated here.

Disney Media Networks

thewaltdisneycompany.com/disney-companies/media-networks

NAIC Code: 515120

TYPES OF BUSINESS:
Broadcast TV
Cable Networks
Television Production
Online Television
Radio Broadcasting

BRANDS/DIVISIONS/AFFILIATES:
Walt Disney Company (The)
ABC Television Network
ABC Family Worldwide
ABC Owned Television Stations Group
A+E Networks
Disney XD
Hulu
ESPN Inc

CONTACTS:
Note: Officers with more than one job title may be intentionally listed here more than once.

Bob Iger, CEO
James Pitar, Pres.-ESPN
Vince Roberts, CTO
Peter DiCecco, Sr. VP-Bus. & Legal Affairs, Music
Vince Roberts, Exec. VP-Global Oper.
Albert Cheng, Exec. VP
Kevin Brockman, Exec. VP-Global Comm.
Ben Sherwood, Co-Pres., Disney
James Goldston, Pres., ABC News
Paul Lee, Pres., ABC Entertainment Group
Gary Marsh, Pres.

GROWTH PLANS/SPECIAL FEATURES:

The Disney Media Networks is a diverse media holding company that contains the company's various television networks, cable channels, associated production and distribution companies and owned/operated television stations. Disney Media is organized into two divisions: Disney-ABC Television Group and ESPN, Inc. The Disney-ABC Television Group division is comprised of the ABC Television Network, an American commercial broadcast television network which owns and operates eight television stations, as well as more than 244 affiliated television stations throughout the U.S. and Canada; ABC Family Worldwide, which is responsible for the operations of the U.S. cable network Freeform; ABC Owned Television Stations Group, which oversees the owned and operated stations of ABC; A+E Networks (a 50/50 joint venture), an American media company that owns a group of television channels available via cable and satellite in the U.S. and abroad; Disney Channels Worldwide, which operates various children and family television channels worldwide, including Disney Channel, Disney Junior, Disney XD and Radio Disney; and Hulu (30%owned), an American online company and partially ad-supported streaming service offering a variety of television shows, clips, movies and other media. ESPN is an American sports media conglomerate which owns various sports broadcasting operations, including cable channels, a sports radio network, an accompanying website and other assets. ESPN operates eight domestic channels and 19 international channels in 64 countries. Disney Media Networks is a subsidiary of The Walt Disney Company. In December 2018, Disney announced that it planned to launch the ACC Network, a sports channel dedicated to the Atlantic Coast Conference, under ESPN, Inc. in 2019.

FINANCIAL DATA:
Note: Data for latest year may not have been available at press time.

In U.S. $	2018	2017	2016	2015	2014	2013
Revenue	23,800,000,000	23,510,000,000	23,689,000,000	23,264,000,000	21,152,000,000	20,356,000,000
R&D Expense						
Operating Income						
Operating Margin %						
SGA Expense						
Net Income		6,902,000,000	7,755,000,000	7,793,000,000	7,321,000,000	6,818,000,000
Operating Cash Flow						
Capital Expenditure						
EBITDA						
Return on Assets %						
Return on Equity %						
Debt to Equity						

CONTACT INFORMATION:
Phone: 818-560-1000   Fax:
Toll-Free:
Address: 500 S. Buena Vista St., Burbank, CA 91521 United States

STOCK TICKER/OTHER:
Stock Ticker: Subsidiary   Exchange:
Employees: 21,000   Fiscal Year Ends: 09/30
Parent Company: Walt Disney Company (The)

SALARIES/BONUSES:
Top Exec. Salary: $ Bonus: $
Second Exec. Salary: $ Bonus: $

OTHER THOUGHTS:
Estimated Female Officers or Directors: 3
Hot Spot for Advancement for Women/Minorities: Y

Dolby Laboratories Inc

NAIC Code: 334310

www.dolby.com

TYPES OF BUSINESS:
Audio Technology

BRANDS/DIVISIONS/AFFILIATES:
Dolby Digital
Dolby Digital Plus
Dolby TrueHD
Dolby Atmos
Dolby Voice

CONTACTS:
Note: Officers with more than one job title may be intentionally listed here more than once.

Kevin Yeaman, CEO
Lewis Chew, CFO
Peter Gotcher, Chairman of the Board
Todd Pendleton, Chief Marketing Officer
Andy Sherman, Executive VP
Giles Baker, Senior VP, Divisional
Steve Forshay, Senior VP, Divisional

GROWTH PLANS/SPECIAL FEATURES:

Dolby Laboratories, Inc. is an audio technology provider that designs, manufactures and sells products for the motion picture, broadcast and music industries and home entertainment systems. The company's products are used in content creation, distribution and playback to provide surround sound, improve sound quality and increase the efficiency of sound storage and distribution. The firm produces only professional audio products and licenses its technologies, such as Dolby Digital, Dolby Digital Plus, Dolby TrueHD, Dolby Atmos and Dolby Voice, to manufacturers of consumer electronics products and media software vendors. Licensing accounts for approximately 90% of Dolby's revenues. Its technologies are used in virtually all at-home entertainment platforms, including DVD players, computer software, digital televisions, set top boxes, portable media devices and in a wide array of consumer electronic products such as gaming systems and audio/video receivers. Dolby's product sales are derived from digital cinema processors and media adapters, which decode digital cinema soundtracks, and digital cinema accessories, which interface its digital cinema servers with theaters' existing automation systems. It also derives product sales from traditional cinema processors, which movie theaters use to process film soundtracks, and, to a lesser extent, broadcast products used to encode and distribute content to viewers. The company works with a growing number of online content streaming and download service providers, offering high-efficiency audio coding, which helps reduce strains on streaming bandwidth and limited storage capacity. Dolby also offers a variety of audio engineering services to support production of motion picture, broadcast, music and video game content. The company's Dolby Atmos audio system contains up to 64 speakers, allowing control over the movement of sound over the audience to create dynamic and realistic acoustics; and Dolby Voice provides audio conference technology with superior spatial perception. The company has 9,300 issued patents and approximately 4,100 pending patents.

FINANCIAL DATA:
Note: Data for latest year may not have been available at press time.

In U.S. $	2018	2017	2016	2015	2014	2013
Revenue	1,171,924,000	1,081,454,000	1,025,738,000	970,638,000	960,176,000	909,674,000
R&D Expense	236,794,000	233,312,000	219,607,000	201,324,000	183,128,000	168,746,000
Operating Income	299,552,000	261,488,000	233,028,000	213,148,000	276,121,000	251,136,000
Operating Margin %		24.17%	22.71%	21.95%	28.75%	27.60%
SGA Expense	507,318,000	468,347,000	464,121,000	461,350,000	430,751,000	393,073,000
Net Income	122,246,000	201,802,000	185,860,000	181,390,000	206,103,000	189,271,000
Operating Cash Flow	352,202,000	371,051,000	356,839,000	309,377,000	361,547,000	274,661,000
Capital Expenditure	85,357,000	104,867,000	221,782,000	194,968,000	116,668,000	30,761,000
EBITDA	394,348,000	341,079,000	321,181,000	315,098,000	329,560,000	304,466,000
Return on Assets %		8.33%	8.36%	8.81%	11.07%	10.23%
Return on Equity %		9.79%	9.79%	10.22%	12.75%	11.67%
Debt to Equity						

CONTACT INFORMATION:
Phone: 415 558-0200 Fax: 415 863-1373
Toll-Free:
Address: 1275 Market St., San Francisco, CA 94103-1410 United States

SALARIES/BONUSES:
Top Exec. Salary: $783,250 Bonus: $
Second Exec. Salary: $111,923 Bonus: $536,438

STOCK TICKER/OTHER:
Stock Ticker: DLB
Employees: 2,030
Parent Company:

Exchange: NYS
Fiscal Year Ends: 09/24

OTHER THOUGHTS:
Estimated Female Officers or Directors:
Hot Spot for Advancement for Women/Minorities:

Sales, profits and employees may be estimates. Financial information, benefits and other data can change quickly and may vary from those stated here.

Dotdash

www.about.com

NAIC Code: 519130

TYPES OF BUSINESS:
Online Information
Niche Online Communities
Human-Filtered Online Directories

BRANDS/DIVISIONS/AFFILIATES:
IAC/InterActiveCorp
Very Well
Spruce (The)
Lifewire
Balance (The)
Trip Savvy
ThoughtCo

CONTACTS: Note: Officers with more than one job title may be intentionally listed here more than once.
Neil Vogel, CEO
Alex Ellerson, COO
Tim Quinn, CFO
Sandy Pinos-Chin, Sr. Dir.-Human Resources
Nabil Ahmad, CTO
Nabil Ahmad, Sr. VP-Tech.
Tricia Han, Sr. VP-Product
Brad Simon, General Counsel
Chris Coluzzi, Sr. VP-Oper.
Igor Lebovic, Sr. VP-Growth
Alex Ellerson, Sr. VP-Content
Brian Colbert, Chief Revenue Officer

GROWTH PLANS/SPECIAL FEATURES:
Dotdash, formerly About.com, is an internet directory that operates topic-specific web guide sites that offer expert solutions to a variety of daily needs, including healthcare, technology, cooking, travel and parenting. The firm is a subsidiary of IAC/InterActiveCorp. Dotdash has more than 100 million unique visitors every month. The sites are grouped into six brand categories: Very Well, The Spruce, Lifewire, The Balance, Trip Savvy and ThoughtCo. Very Well takes a human approach to health and well-being, delivering accessible solutions and an alternative to clinical sites. Verywell.com has more than 16 million monthly unique users, with its writers comprising doctors, pharmacists, dietitians, trainers and other professionals. The Spruce is a home and food website for people looking for information on home improvements or upgrading cooking and baking skills. Thespruce.com has 3.3 million millennial users, 30 million monthly unique users and 5 million homeowners. Lifewire helps people get the most out of technology, and shows them how to fix, choose what to buy and get the best out of what they have. Lifewire.com has 10 million monthly unique visitors. The Balance is a financial site to help people gain better control of their money or career plans. It helps them earn more, spend smarter, invest well and build a more secure future at its www.thebalance.com website. The Balance has 24 million monthly unique visitors, with 57% of them being female. Trip Savvy is a travel site written by local experts to offer vacationers guidance and confidence before traveling. Tripsavvy.com has 6.3 million monthly unique visitors. Last, ThoughtCo. provides in-depth articles on many subjects, including science, history, math and religion. Thoughtco.com has 74,000 pieces of content and 13 million monthly unique visitors. Headquartered in New York, the firm has offices in Chicago and San Francisco.

FINANCIAL DATA: Note: Data for latest year may not have been available at press time.

In U.S. $	2018	2017	2016	2015	2014	2013
Revenue	215,000,000	210,000,000	200,588,940	185,000,000	160,000,000	150,000,000
R&D Expense						
Operating Income						
Operating Margin %						
SGA Expense						
Net Income						
Operating Cash Flow						
Capital Expenditure						
EBITDA						
Return on Assets %						
Return on Equity %						
Debt to Equity						

CONTACT INFORMATION:
Phone: 212-204-4000   Fax:
Toll-Free:
Address: 1500 Broadway, Fl. 6, New York, NY 10036 United States

STOCK TICKER/OTHER:
Stock Ticker: Subsidiary   Exchange:
Employees: Fiscal Year Ends: 12/31
Parent Company: IAC/InterActiveCorp

SALARIES/BONUSES:
Top Exec. Salary: $ Bonus: $
Second Exec. Salary: $ Bonus: $

OTHER THOUGHTS:
Estimated Female Officers or Directors: 1
Hot Spot for Advancement for Women/Minorities: Y

Sales, profits and employees may be estimates. Financial information, benefits and other data can change quickly and may vary from those stated here.

Dover Downs Gaming & Entertainment Inc

www.doverdowns.com

NAIC Code: 721120

TYPES OF BUSINESS:
Casino Hotels, Casinos & Gaming Facilities
Slot Machine Casino
Hotel & Conference Center
Horse Racing
Live Events

BRANDS/DIVISIONS/AFFILIATES:
Dover Downs Gaming Management Corp
Dover Downs Inc
Dover Downs Casino
Dover Downs Hotel and Conference Center
Dover Downs Raceway
Capital Club

CONTACTS:
Note: Officers with more than one job title may be intentionally listed here more than once.
Denis Mcglynn, CEO
Henry Tippie, Chairman of the Board
Timothy Horne, Director
Edward Sutor, Executive VP
Klaus Belohoubek, General Counsel

GROWTH PLANS/SPECIAL FEATURES:
Dover Downs Gaming & Entertainment, Inc. (Dover) is a gaming and entertainment resort firm. It is a holding company which operates through wholly-owned subsidiaries Dover Downs Gaming Management Corp. and Dover Downs, Inc. Dover's operations are located entirely in Delaware, consisting of: Dover Downs Casino, a 165,000-square-foot casino complex; the Dover Downs Hotel and Conference Center, comprised of a 6,000-square-foot spa and 35,000-square-feet of conference space; and Dover Downs Raceway, comprised of a 5/8-mile harness racing track located on Dover property. The Dover Downs Casino features approximately 2,200 slot machines and multi-player electronic table games such as blackjack and poker. The casino operates blackjack, craps and roulette tables. Through its Capital Club program, the company rewards playing members through various marketing programs. The Dover Downs Hotel is a 500-room hotel with conference, banquet, fine dining, ballroom, concert, swimming and spa facilities. In addition to casino activities, the hotel offers entertainment to its guests, such as music concerts and boxing. Dover Downs Raceway, which is adjacent to the hotel and casino, conducts live harness races between November and April, all of which are simulcast to more than 300 tracks and other off-track betting locations across North America on each of the company's 106 scheduled live race dates. The racing track has presented pari-mutuel harness racing events for nearly 50 consecutive years. In mid-2018, Dover Downs agreed to be acquired by and merged into Twin River Worldwide Holdings, Inc. The transaction was expected to close in early 2019, subject to regulatory approvals and customary closing conditions.

Employees receive medical, dental, vision, prescription and disability coverage; 401(k) with company contribution; and a variety of employee assistance programs.

FINANCIAL DATA:
Note: Data for latest year may not have been available at press time.

In U.S. $	2018	2017	2016	2015	2014	2013
Revenue		176,924,000	182,292,000	182,946,000	185,382,000	197,231,000
R&D Expense						
Operating Income		233,000	2,281,000	3,875,000	1,301,000	2,148,000
Operating Margin %		.13%	1.25%	2.11%	.70%	1.08%
SGA Expense		5,174,000	5,375,000	5,499,000	5,711,000	5,645,000
Net Income		-1,068,000	786,000	1,873,000	-706,000	13,000
Operating Cash Flow		6,700,000	10,355,000	9,719,000	6,280,000	11,137,000
Capital Expenditure		2,193,000	2,812,000	1,651,000	900,000	1,574,000
EBITDA		8,401,000	10,024,000	12,250,000	10,071,000	11,874,000
Return on Assets %		-.64%	.44%	1.03%	-.37%	
Return on Equity %		-.92%	.66%	1.60%	-.61%	.01%
Debt to Equity						

CONTACT INFORMATION:
Phone: 302 674-4600 Fax: 302 857-3253
Toll-Free: 800-711-5882
Address: 1131 N. DuPont Hwy., Dover, DE 19901 United States

SALARIES/BONUSES:
Top Exec. Salary: $300,000 Bonus: $
Second Exec. Salary: $285,000 Bonus: $

STOCK TICKER/OTHER:
Stock Ticker: DDE
Employees: 1,401
Parent Company:

Exchange: NYS
Fiscal Year Ends: 12/31

OTHER THOUGHTS:
Estimated Female Officers or Directors:
Hot Spot for Advancement for Women/Minorities:

Plunkett Research, Ltd.   215

Dow Jones & Company Inc

www.dowjones.com

NAIC Code: 511110

TYPES OF BUSINESS:
Newspaper Publishing-Financial News
Business Publishing
Community Newspapers
Electronic & Online Publishing
Financial Indices
Financial Information Services

BRANDS/DIVISIONS/AFFILIATES:
Dow Jones Curation Services
Dow Jones Risk & Compliance
Dow Jones Newswires
WSJ Pro
Wall Street Journal (The)
Barrons
MarketWatch
News Corporation

CONTACTS:
Note: Officers with more than one job title may be intentionally listed here more than once.

William Lewis, CEO
Anna Sedgley, COO
Edwin A. Finn, Jr., Pres.
Christina Van Tassell, CFO
Mark Musgrave, Chief People Officer
Ramin Beheshti, Chief Product & Technology Officer
Stephen Orban, Head-Tech.
Dean Del Vecchio, Chief Admin. Officer
Mark H. Jackson, General Counsel
Joseph Vincent, Head-Oper.
Ingrid Verschuren, Head-Data Strategy
Michael Rolnick, Head-Digital
Paula Keve, Chief Comm. Officer
Christina Komporlis, Head-Print Circulation
Daniel Hayter, Head-Institutional Sales
Georgene Huang, Head-Institutional Products
Daniel Hayter, Head-Institutional Sales, Americas
Rupert Murdoch, Chmn.
Kelly E. Leach, Managing Dir.-EMEA

GROWTH PLANS/SPECIAL FEATURES:

Dow Jones & Company, Inc., a subsidiary of News Corporation, is a global provider of business and financial news information. With millions of readers worldwide, the firm distributes information through newspapers, newswires, magazines, television, radio stations and the internet. Its products include: Dow Jones Curation Services, a curation offering providing relevant world news content grouped by subject matter according to personal business needs; Dow Jones Factiva, a global news database featuring nearly 33,000 sources; Dow Jones Risk & Compliance, a provider of third-party risk management and regulatory compliance solutions; and Dow Jones Newswires, delivering comprehensive global business insights, rolling market commentary and expert analysis. Other products include WSJ Pro, a global, industry-specific membership offering reporting, insight and data; Dow Jones Private Equity & Venture Capital, a suite of news and data on companies backed by venture capital and private equity in every region, industry and stage of development; and The Wall Street Journal, which includes coverage of U.S. and world news, politics, arts, culture, lifestyle, sports, health and more. Barron's is a source of market ideas and insights to help self-directed investors grow their portfolios; MarketWatch provides financial news and market data; Financial News provides news, analysis and commentary on wholesale financial and European securities industries across the sectors of investment banking, asset management, private equity, trading and technology and Fintech; and Dow Jones DJX unites Factiva, Risk and Compliance, Private Equity/Venture Capital and Dow Jones Newswires in one place. In addition, Dow Jones Integrated Solutions integrates premium data into client and third-party products via feeds and APIs; and Dow Jones Reprints provides transaction-based services for the licensing of Dow Jones' branded content. In March 2018, subsidiary Dow Jones Risk & Compliance acquired Cerico, a digital compliance tool company for international business.

FINANCIAL DATA:
Note: Data for latest year may not have been available at press time.

In U.S. $	2018	2017	2016	2015	2014	2013
Revenue	3,000,000,000	2,950,000,000	2,810,000,000	2,650,000,000	2,500,000,000	2,350,000,000
R&D Expense						
Operating Income						
Operating Margin %						
SGA Expense						
Net Income						
Operating Cash Flow						
Capital Expenditure						
EBITDA						
Return on Assets %						
Return on Equity %						
Debt to Equity						

CONTACT INFORMATION:
Phone: 212-416-2000 Fax: 212-416-4348
Toll-Free: 800-223-2274
Address: 200 Liberty St., 1 World Financial Ctr., New York, NY 10281 United States

STOCK TICKER/OTHER:
Stock Ticker: Subsidiary
Employees: 7,100
Parent Company: News Corporation

Exchange:
Fiscal Year Ends: 12/31

SALARIES/BONUSES:
Top Exec. Salary: $ Bonus: $
Second Exec. Salary: $ Bonus: $

OTHER THOUGHTS:
Estimated Female Officers or Directors: 10
Hot Spot for Advancement for Women/Minorities: Y

Sales, profits and employees may be estimates. Financial information, benefits and other data can change quickly and may vary from those stated here.

DreamWorks Animation SKG Inc

www.dreamworksanimation.com

NAIC Code: 512110

TYPES OF BUSINESS:
Animated Film Production
Animation Software

BRANDS/DIVISIONS/AFFILIATES:
Comcast Corporation
NBCUniversal Inc
Shrek
Kung Fu Panda
How to Train Your Dragon
Madagascar
Awesomeness TV
DreamWorks Animation Publishing LLC

CONTACTS:
Note: Officers with more than one job title may be intentionally listed here more than once.

Christopher DeFaria, CEO
Abhijay Prakash, COO
Mellody Hobson, Chairman of the Board
Andrew Chang, General Counsel
Daniel Satterthwaite, Other Corporate Officer
Jim Fielding, Other Corporate Officer
Ann Daly, President

GROWTH PLANS/SPECIAL FEATURES:

DreamWorks Animation SKG, Inc. (DW Animation) creates animated feature films, television programs, online virtual content, imprints and gaming platforms. The firm is part of NBCUniversal, Inc's entertainment division, and NBCUniversal itself is owned by Comcast Corporation. DW Animation's film division has released approximately 35 feature films, including the franchises Shrek, Madagascar, Kung Fu Panda, How to Train Your Dragon, The Croods, Trolls, Captain Underpants and The Boss Baby. Upcoming releases (as of December 2018) include: How to Train Your Dragon: The Hidden World (2019), Trolls World Tour (2020), The Croods 2 (2020) and Spooky Jack (2021). The TV division consists of three networks: DreamWorks Animation and Netflix, which created and delivered 12 original series streaming between 2013 and 2018, including DreamWorks Dragons and Madagascar; AwesomenessTV, offering content such as beauty gurus, advice for teens, celebrity gossip, teen pop stars, performance sports, comedy sketches, pranks and YouTube Stars; and DreamWorksTV, which offers lovable characters, life hacks, music, gaming, pranks and more. DW Animation's films and shows can be viewed on television, web and mobile devices. The firm's animation technology is created through digital design and a computer-generated (CG) media platform, deployed through the studio's cloud architecture. DreamWorks Press is an imprint of DreamWorks Animation Publishing, LLC, focused on extending the storytelling for DreamWorks franchises through digital storytelling and printed books. Last, the games division expands the firm's CG movies into interactive entertainment, including Shrek, How To Train Your Dragon and Madagascar. Recently, DW Animation started a shorts program called DreamWorks Shorts, to show original animated short films before its feature films. The first short film, Bird Karma, premiered in 2018.

FINANCIAL DATA:
Note: Data for latest year may not have been available at press time.

In U.S. $	2018	2017	2016	2015	2014	2013
Revenue	1,070,000,000	1,055,000,000	1,000,000,000	915,862,976	684,622,976	706,915,968
R&D Expense						
Operating Income						
Operating Margin %						
SGA Expense						
Net Income				-54,806,000	-309,614,016	55,084,000
Operating Cash Flow						
Capital Expenditure						
EBITDA						
Return on Assets %						
Return on Equity %						
Debt to Equity						

CONTACT INFORMATION:
Phone: 818 695-5000   Fax: 818 695-9944
Toll-Free:
Address: 1000 Flower St., Glendale, CA 91201 United States

SALARIES/BONUSES:
Top Exec. Salary: $ Bonus: $
Second Exec. Salary: $ Bonus: $

STOCK TICKER/OTHER:
Stock Ticker: Subsidiary
Employees: 2,550
Parent Company: Comcast Corporation
Exchange:
Fiscal Year Ends: 12/31

OTHER THOUGHTS:
Estimated Female Officers or Directors: 3
Hot Spot for Advancement for Women/Minorities: Y

Sales, profits and employees may be estimates. Financial information, benefits and other data can change quickly and may vary from those stated here.

DreamWorks II Holding Co LLC

www.dreamworksstudios.com

NAIC Code: 512110

TYPES OF BUSINESS:
Film Production & Distribution
Television Production
Foreign Film Distribution

BRANDS/DIVISIONS/AFFILIATES:
Amblin Partners
DreamWorks Pictures
Light Between Oceans (The)
BFG (The)
Girl on the Train (The)
Ghost in the Shell
Ready Player One
Thank You for Your Service

CONTACTS: Note: Officers with more than one job title may be intentionally listed here more than once.
Steven Speilberg, CEO
Jeffrey Small, Pres.
Chris Leotis, CFO
Steven Spielberg, Co-Chmn.
Holly Bario, Pres., Prod.
Steven Speilberg, Chmn.

GROWTH PLANS/SPECIAL FEATURES:
DreamWorks II Holding Co., LLC, also known as DreamWorks Pictures, is an American film production label and division of Amblin Partners, which was formerly known as Storyteller Holding Co., LLC. The company's films are marketed and distributed by Universal Pictures, and the firm operates out of offices at Universal Studios. The distribution deal between DreamWorks and Disney expired August 2016, with The Light Between Oceans being released in September as the final DreamWorks film distributed by Disney under their original distribution agreement. Films released and to be released by DreamWorks Studios under Amblin Partners include: The BFG, The Light Between Oceans, The Girl on the Train and Office Christmas Party (all in 2016); Ghost in the Shell (2017); Thank You for Your Service (2017); and Ready Player One (2018). Other films DreamWorks has produced include American Beauty, A Beautiful Mind, Gladiator, The Hundred-Foot Journey and Lincoln.

FINANCIAL DATA: Note: Data for latest year may not have been available at press time.

In U.S. $	2018	2017	2016	2015	2014	2013
Revenue						
R&D Expense						
Operating Income						
Operating Margin %						
SGA Expense						
Net Income						
Operating Cash Flow						
Capital Expenditure						
EBITDA						
Return on Assets %						
Return on Equity %						
Debt to Equity						

CONTACT INFORMATION:
Phone: 818-733-9300 Fax: 818-695-7574
Toll-Free:
Address: 1000 Flower St., Glendale, CA 91201 United States

STOCK TICKER/OTHER:
Stock Ticker: Private
Employees:
Parent Company: Amblin Partners

Exchange:
Fiscal Year Ends: 12/31

SALARIES/BONUSES:
Top Exec. Salary: $ Bonus: $
Second Exec. Salary: $ Bonus: $

OTHER THOUGHTS:
Estimated Female Officers or Directors: 1
Hot Spot for Advancement for Women/Minorities:

Sales, profits and employees may be estimates. Financial information, benefits and other data can change quickly and may vary from those stated here.

Drive Shack Inc

NAIC Code: 713910

ir.driveshack.com

TYPES OF BUSINESS:
Golf Courses (Except Miniature, Pitch-n-Putt)
Driving Ranges, Golf

BRANDS/DIVISIONS/AFFILIATES:
Randall's Island Golf Center

CONTACTS: Note: Officers with more than one job title may be intentionally listed here more than once.
Lawrence Goodfield, CFO
Wesley Edens, Chairman of the Board
Sara Yakin, COO
Sarah Watterson, Director

GROWTH PLANS/SPECIAL FEATURES:
Drive Shack, Inc. owns and operates golf-related leisure and entertainment businesses. The firm operates through two segments: traditional golf properties and entertainment golf venues. The traditional golf properties segment owns, leases or manages 75 properties across 13 U.S. states, and operates in three segments: public properties, private properties and managed properties. Drive Shack owns 48 public properties which generate revenue through daily green fees, The Players Club membership program, food and beverage sales and golf cart rentals; 18 private properties that are open to members only, with amenities such as practice facilities, clubhouses, pro shop, locker rooms, multiple food and beverage outlets, and banquet facilities; and nine managed properties, each pursuant to a management agreement with the property owners. The entertainment golf venues segment combines golf, competition, dining and fun via a chain of next-generation entertainment golf venues across the U.S. and internationally. Each venue features multiple stories of hitting suites where players can compete in technologically-enhanced golf games, designed for individuals or groups. The first of the entertainment golf venues opened in early April 2018 in Orlando, Florida and features 90 hitting bays and a 220-yard range. In November 2018, Drive Shack was awarded the contract to renovate and remodel the Randall's Island Golf Center in Long Island, New York by the New York City Department of Parks and Recreation; it will reopen in 2019 as a Drive Shack subsidiary.

FINANCIAL DATA: Note: Data for latest year may not have been available at press time.

In U.S. $	2018	2017	2016	2015	2014	2013
Revenue		289,872,000	415,674,000	334,412,000	416,023,000	302,411,000
R&D Expense						
Operating Income						
Operating Margin %						
SGA Expense		58,993,000	46,139,000	299,540,000	284,375,000	176,533,000
Net Income		-42,201,000	71,499,000	21,847,000	33,246,000	151,413,000
Operating Cash Flow		-11,155,000	3,378,000	-2,641,000	40,380,000	106,186,000
Capital Expenditure		33,451,000				
EBITDA						
Return on Assets %		-5.59%	4.99%	1.00%	.83%	3.31%
Return on Equity %		-35.93%	43.18%	9.41%	4.25%	13.79%
Debt to Equity		1.49	1.06	3.71	4.44	2.39

CONTACT INFORMATION:
Phone: 212 798-6100 Fax: 212 798-6133
Toll-Free:
Address: 1345 Avenue of the Americas, New York, NY 10105 United States

SALARIES/BONUSES:
Top Exec. Salary: $200,000 Bonus: $275,000
Second Exec. Salary: $ Bonus: $

STOCK TICKER/OTHER:
Stock Ticker: DS Exchange: NYS
Employees: 4,700 Fiscal Year Ends: 12/31
Parent Company:

OTHER THOUGHTS:
Estimated Female Officers or Directors:
Hot Spot for Advancement for Women/Minorities:

DTS Inc

www.dts.com

NAIC Code: 334310

TYPES OF BUSINESS:
Audio & Video Equipment, Manufacturing
Digital Multi-Channel (Surround Sound) Audio Technology
Digital Remastering
Video Restoration & Enhancement

BRANDS/DIVISIONS/AFFILIATES:
Xperi Corporation
DTS:X
DTS Headphone:X
DTS Play-Fi
DTS Virtual:X

CONTACTS:
Note: Officers with more than one job title may be intentionally listed here more than once.

Brian Towne, COO
Melvin Flanigan, CFO
Melvin Flanigan, CFO
Kris Graves, Executive VP, Divisional
Patrick Watson, Executive VP, Divisional
Blake Welcher, Executive VP, Divisional
Brian Towne, Executive VP
Geir Skaaden, Senior VP, Divisional

GROWTH PLANS/SPECIAL FEATURES:
DTS, Inc. is a leading global provider of branded entertainment technologies and products. The firm is a wholly-owned subsidiary of Xperi Corporation. Its core digital multi-channel audio technology enables the delivery and playback of surround sound. DTS develops, markets, licenses and sells its proprietary technology and services for home theater and consumer electronics, car audio and video devices, game consoles, PCs, professional audio products for encoding and decoding digital multi-channel content, audio signal processing for satellite digital audio radio services and audio encoding and enhancement tools for live sports broadcasting in North America. The company also provides products for emerging markets for digital multi-channel audio, such as digital home networks, portable electronic devices and digital satellite and cable broadcast products. As a result of the company's quality and reputation, the consumer electronics industry mandated that DTS technology be standard in all Blu-ray devices. The firm also provides products and services to studios, radio and television broadcasters, game developers and other content creators to facilitate the inclusion of DTS-encoded soundtracks in movies, music and broadcast entertainment content. In addition, the firm integrates its services into consumer products such as mobile devices and personal computers. Audio-related brands of the firm include the DTS:X home theater, the DTS Headphone:X, the DTS Play-Fi and the DTS Virtual:X.

FINANCIAL DATA:
Note: Data for latest year may not have been available at press time.

In U.S. $	2018	2017	2016	2015	2014	2013
Revenue	199,000,000	191,000,000	187,500,000	138,208,992	143,912,992	125,148,000
R&D Expense						
Operating Income						
Operating Margin %						
SGA Expense						
Net Income				-12,301,000	27,143,000	15,755,000
Operating Cash Flow						
Capital Expenditure						
EBITDA						
Return on Assets %						
Return on Equity %						
Debt to Equity						

CONTACT INFORMATION:
Phone: 818 436-1000 Fax: 818 706-1868
Toll-Free:
Address: 5220 Las Virgenes Rd., Calabasas, CA 91302 United States

STOCK TICKER/OTHER:
Stock Ticker: Subsidiary
Employees: 600
Parent Company: Xperi Corporation

Exchange:
Fiscal Year Ends: 12/31

SALARIES/BONUSES:
Top Exec. Salary: $ Bonus: $
Second Exec. Salary: $ Bonus: $

OTHER THOUGHTS:
Estimated Female Officers or Directors:
Hot Spot for Advancement for Women/Minorities:

E W Scripps Company (The)
NAIC Code: 515120

www.scripps.com

TYPES OF BUSINESS:
Broadcast Television Stations
Newspaper Publishing
Television & Online Retail
Online Media
Newswire Service
Video News Service

BRANDS/DIVISIONS/AFFILIATES:
Newsy
Midroll Media
Bounce
Grit
Escape
Laff
Scripps National Spelling Bee
Triton

GROWTH PLANS/SPECIAL FEATURES:
The E.W. Scripps Company serves audiences and businesses through a growing portfolio of local and national media brands. The firm has 33 television stations, making Scripps one of the nation's largest independent TV station owners. The company also runs a collection of national journalism and content businesses, including: Newsy, a next-generation national news network; the Midroll Media podcast; and broadcast networks Bounce, Grit, Escape and Laff. Scripps produces original programming such as Pickler & Ben, an award-winning investigative reporting newsroom in Washington, D.C., and the Scripps National Spelling Bee. During 2018, Scripps divested its radio assets, including all of the radio stations. In December 2018, the firm acquired Triton, a provider of digital audio technology and measurement services.

CONTACTS:
Note: Officers with more than one job title may be intentionally listed here more than once.

Adam Symson, CEO
Lisa Knutson, CFO
Richard Boehne, Chairman of the Board
Douglas Lyons, Chief Accounting Officer
William Appleton, Executive VP
Brian Lawlor, President, Divisional
Laura Tomlin, Senior VP, Divisional

FINANCIAL DATA:
Note: Data for latest year may not have been available at press time.

In U.S. $	2018	2017	2016	2015	2014	2013
Revenue		864,834,000	943,047,000	715,656,000	869,068,000	816,871,000
R&D Expense						
Operating Income		24,308,000	127,771,000	-19,788,000	40,851,000	18,695,000
Operating Margin %		2.81%	13.54%	-2.76%	4.70%	2.28%
SGA Expense		14,112,000	27,963,000	70,771,000	24,022,000	25,175,000
Net Income		-13,106,000	67,235,000	-82,477,000	10,529,000	-474,000
Operating Cash Flow		40,852,000	146,493,000	8,870,000	102,055,000	33,505,000
Capital Expenditure		27,677,000	27,948,000	23,105,000	19,008,000	20,522,000
EBITDA		50,964,000	182,585,000	-32,341,000	69,818,000	49,638,000
Return on Assets %		-.67%	3.94%	-6.07%	1.05%	-.04%
Return on Equity %		-1.39%	7.28%	-11.62%	1.97%	-.08%
Debt to Equity		0.73	0.40	0.43	0.37	0.36

CONTACT INFORMATION:
Phone: 513 977-3000 Fax: 513 977-3721
Toll-Free:
Address: 312 Walnut St., Cincinnati, OH 45202 United States

SALARIES/BONUSES:
Top Exec. Salary: $975,000 Bonus: $
Second Exec. Salary: $533,000 Bonus: $

STOCK TICKER/OTHER:
Stock Ticker: SSP
Employees: 4,100
Parent Company:
Exchange: NAS
Fiscal Year Ends: 12/31

OTHER THOUGHTS:
Estimated Female Officers or Directors: 8
Hot Spot for Advancement for Women/Minorities: Y

EBSCO Industries Inc

www.ebscoind.com

NAIC Code: 519130

TYPES OF BUSINESS:
Information Services & Databases
Subscription Management
Insurance
eBook Platforms
Electrical Parts Distribution
Manufacturing-Sporting Goods & Firearms
Manufacturing-Furniture and Signage
Real Estate

BRANDS/DIVISIONS/AFFILIATES:
EBSCO Information Services
Vulcan Industries
EBSCO Health
All Current
IMAGEN Brands
Valley Joist
Grand View Media Group
152 Media

CONTACTS:
Note: Officers with more than one job title may be intentionally listed here more than once.

David Walker, CEO
Nathan R. Bouknight, Pres.
Heather Moore, VP-Acct.
Tim Collins, CEO-EBSCO Info Services
Brian Wilson, Sr. VP-Corporate Human Resources
Ryan Loy, CIO
Becky Caldarello, VP
Carol M. Johnson, Chief Acct. Officer
Matt Carrington, Dir.-Acquisitions
Mark Williams, Pres.
Bryson Stephens, Chmn.

GROWTH PLANS/SPECIAL FEATURES:

EBSCO Industries, Inc., founded in 1944, competes in a wide variety of markets. However, the publishing and distribution of data, including electronic databases, ebooks and magazines, is EBSCO's main focus. The firm operates through five divisions: information services, insurance services, manufacturing & distribution, publishing & digital media and real estate. The information services segment provides research solutions based on databases, e-books and e-journals through EBSCO Information Services (the firm's largest business unit), CINAHL, GOBI Library Solutions from EBSCO, LearningExpress and NoveList. The insurance services segment provides risk management services through S.S. Nesbitt. The firm's manufacturing & distribution division includes companies that develop a variety of products, including electrical components, signage and specialty furniture. Companies in this segment include: All Current Electrical Sales, EBSCO Sign Group, IMAGEN Brands, Luxor, PRADCO Outdoor brands, Vulcan Industries and Valley Joist. The publishing & digital media services division provides magazine subscription management, through Consumer Subscription Services; advertising services, through 152 Media, Publisher Promotion & Fulfillment and EBSCO Professional Partnership Group; and research publishing services, through EBSCO Research and Grand View Media Group. The real estate division has interests in two planned communities, Mt. Laurel, near Birmingham, Alabama, and Alys Beach, in the Florida Panhandle. Additionally, this segment, through EBSCO Income Properties, invests in multi-home properties for short-term and long-term timeframes.

The firm offers employees medical, dental, vision, life and disability insurance; college scholarships; a savings and profit sharing trust that receives 15% of all pre-tax profits; credit union access; and employee discounts.

FINANCIAL DATA:
Note: Data for latest year may not have been available at press time.

In U.S. $	2018	2017	2016	2015	2014	2013
Revenue	2,900,000,000	2,889,000,000	2,750,000,000	2,700,000,000	2,500,000,000	2,325,000,000
R&D Expense						
Operating Income						
Operating Margin %						
SGA Expense						
Net Income						
Operating Cash Flow						
Capital Expenditure						
EBITDA						
Return on Assets %						
Return on Equity %						
Debt to Equity						

CONTACT INFORMATION:
Phone: 205-991-6600 Fax:
Toll-Free:
Address: 5724 Hwy. 280 E., Birmingham, AL 35242 United States

STOCK TICKER/OTHER:
Stock Ticker: Private
Employees: 5,800
Parent Company:

Exchange:
Fiscal Year Ends: 06/30

SALARIES/BONUSES:
Top Exec. Salary: $ Bonus: $
Second Exec. Salary: $ Bonus: $

OTHER THOUGHTS:
Estimated Female Officers or Directors: 3
Hot Spot for Advancement for Women/Minorities: Y

Sales, profits and employees may be estimates. Financial information, benefits and other data can change quickly and may vary from those stated here.

EchoStar Corporation

NAIC Code: 517110

www.echostar.com

TYPES OF BUSINESS:
Digital Set-Top Boxes & Related Products
Fixed Satellite Services

BRANDS/DIVISIONS/AFFILIATES:
Hughes Communications Inc
Echostar Satellite Services
EchoStar Mobile Limited
EchoStar XXI
EchoStar XXIII
EchoStar 105/SES-11

CONTACTS:
Note: Officers with more than one job title may be intentionally listed here more than once.

Michael Dugan, CEO
David Rayner, CFO
Charles Ergen, Chairman of the Board
Pradman Kaul, Director
Kranti Kilaru, Executive VP
Dean Manson, Executive VP
Anders Johnson, Other Executive Officer

GROWTH PLANS/SPECIAL FEATURES:

EchoStar Corporation is a global provider of satellite operations, video delivery solutions and broadband satellite technologies and services for home and office, delivering innovative network technologies, managed services and solutions for enterprises and governments. The company operates in two business segments: Hughes Communications, Inc. and EchoStar Satellite Services. Hughes Communications provides satellite broadband internet to North American consumers and broadband network services and equipment to domestic and international enterprise markets. The Hughes segment also offers managed services to large enterprises, as well as solutions to customers for mobile satellite systems. EchoStar Satellite Services provides satellite services on a full-time and occasional-use basis primarily to DISH Network Corporation, Dish Mexico S de RI de CV, U.S. government service providers, internet service providers, broadcast news organizations, programmers and private enterprise customers. Subsidiary EchoStar Mobile Limited is based in Ireland and licensed by the European Union (EU) to provide mobile satellite service/complementary ground component (MSS/CGC) services covering the entire EU using S-band spectrum. During 2017, this division launched: EchoStar XXI, which provides broadband services over Europe; EchoStar XXIII, which provides direct-to-home broadcast services over Brazil; and EchoStar 105/SES-11, which provides Ku-Band coverage to the U.S., the Gulf of Mexico and the Caribbean, respectively.

EchoStar offers employees medical, dental, vision, life, AD&D and disability insurance; various assistance programs; 401(k) and other retirement/savings plans; paid vacation/holidays; tuition reimbursement and more.

FINANCIAL DATA:
Note: Data for latest year may not have been available at press time.

In U.S. $	2018	2017	2016	2015	2014	2013
Revenue		1,885,508,000	3,056,730,000	3,143,714,000	3,445,578,000	3,282,452,000
R&D Expense		31,745,000	76,024,000	78,287,000	60,886,000	67,942,000
Operating Income		207,069,000	364,398,000	358,433,000	328,090,000	142,002,000
Operating Margin %		10.98%	11.92%	11.40%	9.52%	4.32%
SGA Expense		366,007,000	385,634,000	374,116,000	372,010,000	358,499,000
Net Income		392,561,000	179,930,000	153,357,000	152,874,000	2,525,000
Operating Cash Flow		726,892,000	803,343,000	776,451,000	840,131,000	450,507,000
Capital Expenditure		610,231,000	721,506,000	729,275,000	680,026,000	433,621,000
EBITDA		851,783,000	905,542,000	871,796,000	906,358,000	665,629,000
Return on Assets %		4.43%	2.23%	2.25%	2.36%	.03%
Return on Equity %		9.74%	4.77%	4.52%	4.89%	.07%
Debt to Equity		0.86	0.92	0.59	0.65	0.73

CONTACT INFORMATION:
Phone: 303 706-4000 Fax:
Toll-Free:
Address: 100 Inverness Terrace E., Englewood, CO 80112 United States

STOCK TICKER/OTHER:
Stock Ticker: SATS
Employees: 4,000
Parent Company:

Exchange: NAS
Fiscal Year Ends: 12/31

SALARIES/BONUSES:
Top Exec. Salary: $936,545 Bonus: $
Second Exec. Salary: $787,153 Bonus: $

OTHER THOUGHTS:
Estimated Female Officers or Directors: 1
Hot Spot for Advancement for Women/Minorities:

Educational Development Corporation

www.edcpub.com

NAIC Code: 511130

TYPES OF BUSINESS:
Children's Book Publishing
Book Distribution

BRANDS/DIVISIONS/AFFILIATES:
Usborne Publishing Limited
Usborne Books & More
Kane Miller Book Publishers
Touchy-Feely

CONTACTS:
Note: Officers with more than one job title may be intentionally listed here more than once.

Randall White, CEO
Dan O'Keefe, CFO
Heather Cobb, Chief Marketing Officer
Craig White, COO

GROWTH PLANS/SPECIAL FEATURES:

Educational Development Corporation (EDC) is the sole U.S. trade publisher and distributor of a line of children's books produced in the U.K. by Usborne Publishing Limited. With over 2,000 titles available, many of the company's products are interactive in nature and include Touchy-Feely board books, jigsaw puzzles, activity and flashcards, adventure and search books, art books, sticker books and foreign language books. The company operates two divisions. The home business division (Usborne Books & More, or UBAM) is a multi-level direct selling organization that markets its products through independent sales representatives. The publishing division markets books to bookstores, toy stores, specialty stores, museums and other retail outlets throughout the country. UBAM generates 93% of the company's net revenue, and oversees approximately 35,500 consultants in 50 states. Publishing brings in the remaining 7% of net revenue, marketing books to bookstores, toy stores, specialty stores, museums and other retail outlets throughout the country. EDC also owns Kane Miller Book Publishers, a California-based children's book publisher and is the sole distributor. The company operates out of its 400,000-square-foot office and warehouse facilities in Tulsa, Oklahoma; the company also owns another 95,000-square-foot warehouse for overflow inventory in Tulsa, Oklahoma.

FINANCIAL DATA:
Note: Data for latest year may not have been available at press time.

In U.S. $	2018	2017	2016	2015	2014	2013
Revenue	111,966,100	106,628,100	63,618,300	32,548,300	26,097,000	25,487,500
R&D Expense						
Operating Income	7,368,300	5,028,500	3,313,400	1,386,400	1,251,700	1,228,100
Operating Margin %	6.58	4.71%	5.20%	4.25%	4.79%	4.81%
SGA Expense	73,666,500	72,986,100	39,810,700	18,398,000	14,321,800	13,765,200
Net Income	5,214,700	2,860,900	2,119,300	859,200	357,600	802,900
Operating Cash Flow	9,232,700	-1,572,400	6,650,600	-261,600	2,765,100	639,000
Capital Expenditure	1,437,700	2,485,400	24,911,600	325,000	77,500	29,300
EBITDA	10,203,200	6,719,900	4,065,300	1,515,800	1,367,100	1,342,300
Return on Assets %	8.15%	4.93%	6.26%	4.94%	2.06%	4.47%
Return on Equity %	29.28%	20.11%	16.58%	6.89%	2.74%	5.80%
Debt to Equity	0.97	1.35	1.33			

CONTACT INFORMATION:
Phone: 918 622-4522   Fax: 918 665-7919
Toll-Free: 800-743-5660
Address: 5402 S. 122nd E. Ave., Tulsa, OK 74146 United States

STOCK TICKER/OTHER:
Stock Ticker: EDUC
Employees: 193
Parent Company:

Exchange: NAS
Fiscal Year Ends: 02/28

SALARIES/BONUSES:
Top Exec. Salary: $218,200   Bonus: $50,400
Second Exec. Salary: $174,000   Bonus: $ 400

OTHER THOUGHTS:
Estimated Female Officers or Directors: 1
Hot Spot for Advancement for Women/Minorities:

Eldorado Resorts Inc

www.eldoradoresorts.com

NAIC Code: 721120

TYPES OF BUSINESS:
Casino Hotel Properties

BRANDS/DIVISIONS/AFFILIATES:
Eldorado Hotel and Casino Reno
Silver Legacy Resort Casino
Circus Circus Reno
Isle Casino Hotel-Black Hawk
Lady Luck Casino-Black Hawk
Pompano Park
RacelineBet Inc
Isle of Capri Casinos Inc

CONTACTS:
Note: Officers with more than one job title may be intentionally listed here more than once.

Gary Carano, CEO
Stephanie Lepori, Chief Accounting Officer
Anthony Carano, COO
Thomas Reeg, Director
Edmund Quatmann, Executive VP

GROWTH PLANS/SPECIAL FEATURES:

Eldorado Resorts, Inc. is a gaming and hospitality company established in 1973 that owns and operates gaming facilities located in Louisiana, Nevada, Ohio, Pennsylvania and West Virginia. The firm's primary source of revenue is gaming, but its hotels, restaurants, bars, shops and other venues are used to attract customers to its properties. As of 2017, the firm owned and operated approximately 950,000 square feet of casino space with approximately 21,000 slot machines and VLTs, approximately 600 table and poker games and over 7,000 hotel rooms. Eldorado's properties and divided by region and consist of Eldorado Hotel and Casino Reno, Silver Legacy Resort Casino, Circus Circus Reno, Isle Casino Hotel-Black Hawk and Lady Luck Casino-Black Hawk in the west region. The Midwest segment consists of six properties, four of which are dockside casinos and two land-based casinos, located in Iowa and Missouri. The South segment consists of five properties, four of which are dockside casinos in Louisiana and Mississippi and Pompano Park, a racino in Florida. The East segment consists of four properties, three of which are racinos, located in Pennsylvania, Ohio and West Virginia. Through subsidiary RacelineBet, Inc., Eldorado operates Racelinebet.com, a national account wagering service that offers online and telephone wagering on horse races. In May 2017, the firm completed its acquisition of Isle of Capri Casinos, Inc. In February 2018, Eldorado Resorts agreed to sell all of the assets and liabilities of Presque Isle Downs & Casino in Erie, Pennsylvania, and Lady Luck Casino Vicksburg in Vicksburg, Mississippi, to Churchill Downs, Inc.

FINANCIAL DATA:
Note: Data for latest year may not have been available at press time.

In U.S. $	2018	2017	2016	2015	2014	2013
Revenue		1,473,504,000	892,896,000	719,784,000	361,823,000	247,186,000
R&D Expense						
Operating Income		206,348,000	99,138,000	71,514,000	22,345,000	22,626,000
Operating Margin %		14.00%	11.10%	9.93%	6.17%	9.15%
SGA Expense		354,359,000	190,652,000	144,566,000	85,337,000	61,453,000
Net Income		73,940,000	24,802,000	114,183,000	-14,425,000	18,897,000
Operating Cash Flow		130,241,000	97,570,000	56,715,000	33,879,000	23,536,000
Capital Expenditure		83,522,000	47,380,000	36,762,000	10,564,000	7,413,000
EBITDA		162,330,000	152,412,000	163,082,000	46,841,000	51,609,000
Return on Assets %		3.05%	1.89%	9.13%	-1.99%	6.99%
Return on Equity %		11.89%	8.71%	54.09%	-12.70%	25.00%
Debt to Equity		2.31	2.66	3.18	5.14	2.22

CONTACT INFORMATION:
Phone: 775 328-0100 Fax:
Toll-Free:
Address: 100 W. Liberty St., Reno, NV 89501 United States

STOCK TICKER/OTHER:
Stock Ticker: ERI
Employees: 7,400
Parent Company:

Exchange: NAS
Fiscal Year Ends: 12/31

SALARIES/BONUSES:
Top Exec. Salary: $850,000 Bonus: $3,000,000
Second Exec. Salary: $950,000 Bonus: $

OTHER THOUGHTS:
Estimated Female Officers or Directors:
Hot Spot for Advancement for Women/Minorities:

Electronic Arts Inc (EA)

www.ea.com

NAIC Code: 511210G

TYPES OF BUSINESS:
Computer Software, Electronic Games, Apps & Entertainment
Online Interactive Games
E-Commerce Sales
Mobile Games
Apps

BRANDS/DIVISIONS/AFFILIATES:
Battlefield
Mass Effect
Need for Speed
Sims vs Zombies (The)
Origin
Respawn Entertainment LLC
Titanfall

CONTACTS: Note: Officers with more than one job title may be intentionally listed here more than once.

Andrew Wilson, CEO
Blake Jorgensen, CFO
Lawrence Probst, Chairman of the Board
Kenneth Barker, Chief Accounting Officer
Christopher Bruzzo, Chief Marketing Officer
Kenneth Moss, Chief Technology Officer
Joel Linzner, Executive VP, Divisional
Matt Bilbey, Executive VP, Divisional
Matthew Bilbey, Executive VP, Divisional
Jacob Schatz, Executive VP
Laura Miele, Other Executive Officer
Patrick Soderlund, Other Executive Officer
Vijayanthimala Singh, Other Executive Officer

GROWTH PLANS/SPECIAL FEATURES:
Electronic Arts, Inc. (EA) develops, markets, publishes and distributes games, content and services that can be played by consumers on a variety of platforms. These platforms include consoles such as PlayStation and Xbox, personal computers (PCs), mobile phones and tablets. Some of the company's games are based on its wholly-owned intellectual property, including Battlefield, Mass Effect, Need for Speed, The Sims vs. Zombies; and some games leverage content that EA licenses from others, such as FIFA, Madden NFL and Star Wars. EA also publishes and distributes games developed by third parties. The company's products and services can be purchased through multiple distribution channels, including physical and online retailers, platform providers (console manufacturers, providers of free-to-download PC games and mobile carriers) and through EA's own digital distribution platform, Origin. In December 2017, the firm acquired Respawn Entertainment, LLC, a leading independent game development studio and creators of AAA shooter and action games including the critically-acclaimed Titanfall franchise

EA offers its employees health care coverage, employee assistance programs, onsite childcare, employee discount programs, business travel accident insurance, retirement savings/pension and free EA games.

FINANCIAL DATA: Note: Data for latest year may not have been available at press time.

In U.S. $	2018	2017	2016	2015	2014	2013
Revenue	5,150,000,000	4,845,000,000	4,396,000,000	4,515,000,000	3,575,000,000	3,797,000,000
R&D Expense	1,320,000,000	1,205,000,000	1,109,000,000	1,094,000,000	1,125,000,000	1,153,000,000
Operating Income	1,434,000,000	1,224,000,000	898,000,000	945,000,000	-3,000,000	84,000,000
Operating Margin %	27.84	25.26%	20.42%	20.93%	-.08%	2.21%
SGA Expense	1,110,000,000	1,112,000,000	1,028,000,000	1,033,000,000	1,090,000,000	1,142,000,000
Net Income	1,043,000,000	967,000,000	1,156,000,000	875,000,000	8,000,000	98,000,000
Operating Cash Flow	1,692,000,000	1,383,000,000	1,223,000,000	1,067,000,000	712,000,000	324,000,000
Capital Expenditure	107,000,000	123,000,000	93,000,000	95,000,000	97,000,000	106,000,000
EBITDA	1,627,000,000	1,427,000,000	1,102,000,000	1,176,000,000	264,000,000	432,000,000
Return on Assets %	12.79%	13.09%	17.51%	14.75%	.14%	1.85%
Return on Equity %	24.10%	25.93%	35.94%	32.06%	.34%	4.14%
Debt to Equity	0.21	0.24	0.29	0.01	0.23	0.24

CONTACT INFORMATION:
Phone: 650 628-1500   Fax: 650 628-1414
Toll-Free:
Address: 209 Redwood Shores Parkway, Redwood City, CA 94065 United States

STOCK TICKER/OTHER:
Stock Ticker: EA
Employees: 9,300
Parent Company:

Exchange: NAS
Fiscal Year Ends: 03/31

SALARIES/BONUSES:
Top Exec. Salary: $1,141,731   Bonus: $
Second Exec. Salary: $821,539   Bonus: $

OTHER THOUGHTS:
Estimated Female Officers or Directors: 2
Hot Spot for Advancement for Women/Minorities:

Sales, profits and employees may be estimates. Financial information, benefits and other data can change quickly and may vary from those stated here.

Elsevier BV

NAIC Code: 511120

www.elsevier.com

TYPES OF BUSINESS:
Scientific, Medical and Technical Journal Publishing
Software
Online Publishing

BRANDS/DIVISIONS/AFFILIATES:
Reed Elsevier Group plc
ScienceDiet
Scopus
ClinicalKey
Reaxys
Mendeley
Knovel
Evolve

CONTACTS:
Note: Officers with more than one job title may be intentionally listed here more than once.

Ron Mobed, CEO
Anita Chandraprakash, Exec. VP-Oper.
Stuart Whayman, CFO
Simon Helliwell, Exec. VP-Human Resources
Dan Olley, CIO
Bill Godfrey, Head-Global Electronic Prod. Dev.
Mark Seeley, General Counsel
Adriaan Roosen, Exec. VP-Oper.
Eser Keskiner, Dir.-Strategy
David Ruth, Sr. VP-Global. Comm.
Youngsuk Chi, Chmn.

GROWTH PLANS/SPECIAL FEATURES:

Elsevier BV is a publishing and communications business that serves over 30 million scientists, health and information professionals and students throughout the world. Elsevier also serves authors, editors, reviewers and librarians. The firm is a subsidiary of U.K.-based publisher Reed Elsevier Group plc. Elsevier BV consists of three main divisions: products and solutions, services, and book and journals. The firm's search and discovery segment includes ScienceDirect, a leading full-text scientific database offering journal articles and book chapters from over 3,800 journals representing more than 612,000 issues and 37,000 books; Scopus, a database and intuitive tool for navigating research; ClinicalKey, a medical and surgical database for clinicians; Reaxys, which offers chemistry literature and data; Mendeley, a free reference manager and academic social network that helps with organizing research, collaborating with others online and discovering recent researches; and Knovel, a cloud-based application integrating technical information with analytical and search tools for engineers. The planning and performance segment consists of the Evolve learning system, an interactive classroom environment for nursing and health professions students. Through books and journals, the firm provides an online marketplace for books, journals and more, which are categorized by subject within the four categories of health; life sciences; physical sciences and engineering; and social sciences and humanities. Elsevier announced in September 2018 that it had acquired Aries Solutions, a workflow solutions company focusing on scientific publications.

Elsevier offers employees benefits including disability, life and vision plans; flexible spending accounts; a retirement plan; a stock purchase plan; and tuition reimbursement.

FINANCIAL DATA:
Note: Data for latest year may not have been available at press time.

In U.S. $	2018	2017	2016	2015	2014	2013
Revenue	9,000,000,000	8,810,290,000	8,250,000,000	8,196,037,450	8,868,973,305	8,133,144,416
R&D Expense						
Operating Income						
Operating Margin %						
SGA Expense						
Net Income		1,996,840,000	1,758,390,000	1,101,280,000	1,863,513,705	1,283,864,020
Operating Cash Flow						
Capital Expenditure						
EBITDA						
Return on Assets %						
Return on Equity %						
Debt to Equity						

CONTACT INFORMATION:
Phone: 31-20-485-3911 Fax: 31-20-485-2457
Toll-Free:
Address: Radarweg 29, Amsterdam, 1043 NX Netherlands

SALARIES/BONUSES:
Top Exec. Salary: $ Bonus: $
Second Exec. Salary: $ Bonus: $

STOCK TICKER/OTHER:
Stock Ticker: Subsidiary Exchange:
Employees: 30,000 Fiscal Year Ends: 12/31
Parent Company: Reed Elsevier Group plc

OTHER THOUGHTS:
Estimated Female Officers or Directors:
Hot Spot for Advancement for Women/Minorities:

Sales, profits and employees may be estimates. Financial information, benefits and other data can change quickly and may vary from those stated here.

Emmis Communications Corporation

www.emmis.com

NAIC Code: 515112

TYPES OF BUSINESS:
Radio Broadcasting
Magazine Publishing

BRANDS/DIVISIONS/AFFILIATES:
Indianapolis Monthly
Emmis Digital
Incite
NextRadio
TagStation
Digonex Technologies

CONTACTS:
Note: Officers with more than one job title may be intentionally listed here more than once.

Ryan Hornaday, CFO
Patrick Walsh, COO
J. Enright, Executive VP
Jeffrey Smulyan, Founder
Gregory Loewen, Other Executive Officer
Paul Brenner, President, Subsidiary

GROWTH PLANS/SPECIAL FEATURES:
Emmis Communications Corporation is a diversified communications company principally focused on radio broadcasting. Emmis owns and operates 14 radio stations, 11 FM and 3 AM, which are located in New York, Indianapolis and Austin. The company's publishing operation comprises the Indianapolis Monthly. Emmis Digital integrates the firm's radio properties via online, mobile and social media platforms, and engages in digital technologies and solutions. Incite is the company's social marketing platform with a strategy of engaging and immersing audiences for promotional purposes. Incite offers innovative promotional tools and resources, as well as access to celebrity and talent influencers for shaping public opinion. Emmis' Incite team works in collaboration with corporations, government entities and non-profit organizations to confront social challenges and engage audiences via marketing and influence. NextRadio is a smartphone app that combines the device's built-in FM tuner and the internet to provide users an enhanced radio listening experience. The app features album art and program information as well as station feedback and other interactive components. TagStation is a cloud-based data service that enables radio stations to synchronize their broadcasts with images, interactive touch points and other related data for display in the NextRadio app, HD Radio Artist Experience and connected car dashboards. Last, Digonex Technologies, Inc. is a pricing and pricing analytics provider that operates in the sports, live entertainment, attraction and retail markets. Its data insights enable control of every aspect of pricing strategy; and creates solutions that help businesses learn from their historical data. During 2018, the firm sold its four St. Louis radio stations.

FINANCIAL DATA:
Note: Data for latest year may not have been available at press time.

In U.S. $	2018	2017	2016	2015	2014	2013
Revenue	148,487,000	214,568,000	231,433,000	237,938,000	205,146,000	196,084,000
R&D Expense						
Operating Income	14,389,000	18,318,000	29,219,000	34,373,000	24,247,000	19,472,000
Operating Margin %	9.69	8.53%	12.62%	13.39%	11.81%	9.93%
SGA Expense						
Net Income	82,129,000	13,119,000	2,114,000	-99,259,000	43,481,000	43,772,000
Operating Cash Flow	241,000	19,052,000	25,114,000	18,456,000	24,695,000	1,845,000
Capital Expenditure	1,809,000	2,850,000	3,388,000	3,514,000	3,057,000	3,364,000
EBITDA	91,798,000	35,934,000	26,518,000	-36,010,000	26,526,000	17,706,000
Return on Assets %	29.30%	4.33%	.59%	-33.08%	16.62%	13.93%
Return on Equity %	1542.90%				340.26%	
Debt to Equity	2.58				3.21	

CONTACT INFORMATION:
Phone: 317 266-0100 Fax: 317 631-3750
Toll-Free:
Address: 40 Monument Cir., Ste. 700, 1 Emmis Plz., Indianapolis, IN 46204 United States

STOCK TICKER/OTHER:
Stock Ticker: EMMS
Employees: 865
Parent Company:

Exchange: NAS
Fiscal Year Ends: 02/28

SALARIES/BONUSES:
Top Exec. Salary: $1,001,648 Bonus: $
Second Exec. Salary: $619,464 Bonus: $

OTHER THOUGHTS:
Estimated Female Officers or Directors: 8
Hot Spot for Advancement for Women/Minorities: Y

Endeavor LLC

NAIC Code: 711410

www.endeavorco.com

TYPES OF BUSINESS:
Talent Agency
Literary Agency
Sports Marketing & Agents
Media Consulting
Book Publishing

BRANDS/DIVISIONS/AFFILIATES:
WME
IMG Worldwide
William Morris Agency Inc
Endeavor Talent Agency
IMG Live
Kovert Creative
MADE
Wall Group (The)

CONTACTS:
Note: Officers with more than one job title may be intentionally listed here more than once.

Ariel Emanuel, Co-CEO
Patrick Whitesell, Co-CEO
David Wirtschafter, Pres.
David Wirtschafter, Co-CEO

GROWTH PLANS/SPECIAL FEATURES:

Endeavor LLC, first formed by the 2009 merger of the William Morris Agency (which had earlier acquired IMG Worldwide, Inc.) and the Endeavor Talent Agency, is one of the largest talent and literary agencies in the world. The firm offers its clients and partners with global access and insights into every facet of entertainment, sports and fashion. It represents artists across all media platforms, specifically movies, television, music, theater, comedy, culinary, sports, public speaking, voiceover, digital and book publishing. Integrated network companies William Morris either owns, partners with in a joint venture, or has created includes: art+commerce, an agency that represents image makers that work in photography, film, set design, illustration, styling and more; IMG College Licensing, a collegiate trademark licensing company that has served nearly 200 institutions; and dixon talent, inc., which represents comedic artists and personalities. Other units include droga, a creative agency; ELEAGUE, a televised e-Sports league created by Endeavor and Turner Broadcasting; Turkish Airlines EuroLeague, a joint venture that provides a platform for the development of European basketball; and Fusion, an experiential marketing agency. Additionally, the firm owns or has interests in frieze, an arts media and events company; HEAD, a joint venture that leverages Internet of Things technology to enhance live event experience for consumers; IMG Live, an experiential marketing agency; and Kovert Creative, offering digital services, personal representation, brand marketing and communications. In October 2017, William Morris Agency, Inc. transitioned itself into a new holding company under the name Endeavor.

FINANCIAL DATA:
Note: Data for latest year may not have been available at press time.

In U.S. $	2018	2017	2016	2015	2014	2013
Revenue	2,900,000,000	2,700,000,000	2,500,000,000	2,200,000,000	2,100,000,000	
R&D Expense						
Operating Income						
Operating Margin %						
SGA Expense						
Net Income						
Operating Cash Flow						
Capital Expenditure						
EBITDA						
Return on Assets %						
Return on Equity %						
Debt to Equity						

CONTACT INFORMATION:
Phone: 310-859-4000 Fax: 310-859-4440
Toll-Free:
Address: 9601 Wilshire Blvd., Beverly Hills, CA 90210 United States

STOCK TICKER/OTHER:
Stock Ticker: Private
Employees: 4,700
Parent Company:
Exchange:
Fiscal Year Ends: 12/31

SALARIES/BONUSES:
Top Exec. Salary: $ Bonus: $
Second Exec. Salary: $ Bonus: $

OTHER THOUGHTS:
Estimated Female Officers or Directors:
Hot Spot for Advancement for Women/Minorities:

Sales, profits and employees may be estimates. Financial information, benefits and other data can change quickly and may vary from those stated here.

Entercom Communications Corp

www.entercom.com

NAIC Code: 515112

TYPES OF BUSINESS:
Radio Broadcasting
Radio Advertising
Digital Radio

BRANDS/DIVISIONS/AFFILIATES:
CBS Corporation
CBS Radio Inc
Radio.com
Eventful

CONTACTS: Note: Officers with more than one job title may be intentionally listed here more than once.
James Hamill, Assistant Controller
David Field, Chairman of the board
Eugene Levin, Chief Accounting Officer
Louise Kramer, COO
Richard Schmaeling, Executive VP
Andrew Sutor, Executive VP
Joseph Field, Founder
Robert Philips, Other Executive Officer

GROWTH PLANS/SPECIAL FEATURES:
Entercom Communications Corp. is an American broadcasting company and radio network. The firm owns and runs over 235 stations in the top 50 markets throughout the nation. These radio stations offer the following broadcast formats: adult contemporary, active rock, adult hits, alternative, business news, classic hip hop, classic hits, classis R&B, classic rock, comedy, country, gospel, hot adult contemporary, Indian, mainstream rock, mainstream urban, news, news/talk, oldies, regional Mexican, rhythmic adult contemporary, rhythmic CHR (crossover), rhythmic hot adult contemporary, rhythmic Top 40, soft rock, Spanish, sports, talk, Top 40, urban and urban adult contemporary. Entercom's media offerings reach and engage over 100 million people every week through broadcast, audio and digital platforms, as well as live events. Its Radio.com site offers 24/7 streaming access to the company's stations anytime, anywhere. Its Eventful local events offering provides online and mobile access to ticketing options, exclusive screenings, sporting events, concert presales and personalized email notifications on favorite artists and activities. Entercom is majority-owned (72%) by CBS Radio, Inc., which itself is a subsidiary of CBS Corporation. In mid-2018, Entercom announced that Radio.com would become the exclusive streaming provider for all of its stations, and all Entercom properties would be branded on-air as a Radio.com station. That same year, Entercom agreed to acquire 101.1 MORE FM from Jerry Lee Radio, LLC; in return, the company agreed to divest 92.5 XTU to Beasely Broadcast Group, Inc., to comply with ownership limits.

FINANCIAL DATA: Note: Data for latest year may not have been available at press time.

In U.S. $	2018	2017	2016	2015	2014	2013
Revenue		592,884,000	460,245,000	411,378,000	379,789,000	377,618,000
R&D Expense						
Operating Income		85,967,000	98,380,000	88,769,000	86,239,000	92,096,000
Operating Margin %		14.49%	21.37%	21.57%	22.70%	24.38%
SGA Expense		47,859,000	33,328,000	26,479,000	26,572,000	24,381,000
Net Income		233,849,000	38,065,000	29,184,000	26,823,000	26,024,000
Operating Cash Flow		29,112,000	72,030,000	64,790,000	65,296,000	63,349,000
Capital Expenditure		21,193,000	7,689,000	7,043,000	8,408,000	4,800,000
EBITDA		25,073,000	99,348,000	94,007,000	93,349,000	97,136,000
Return on Assets %		8.25%	3.44%	2.91%	2.91%	2.84%
Return on Equity %		21.76%	9.94%	8.23%	8.55%	9.24%
Debt to Equity		1.05	1.27	1.25	1.44	1.72

CONTACT INFORMATION:
Phone: 610 660-5610   Fax: 610 660-5620
Toll-Free:
Address: 401 E. City Ave., Ste. 809, Bala Cynwyd, PA 19004 United States

STOCK TICKER/OTHER:
Stock Ticker: ETM
Employees: 2,828
Parent Company: CBS Corporation

Exchange: NYS
Fiscal Year Ends: 12/31

SALARIES/BONUSES:
Top Exec. Salary: $439,541   Bonus: $650,000
Second Exec. Salary: $1,034,792   Bonus: $

OTHER THOUGHTS:
Estimated Female Officers or Directors: 2
Hot Spot for Advancement for Women/Minorities:

Sales, profits and employees may be estimates. Financial information, benefits and other data can change quickly and may vary from those stated here.

Entertainment Resources Inc

NAIC Code: 711320

www.entertainmentresources.com

TYPES OF BUSINESS:
Promoters of Performing Arts, Sports, and Similar Events without Facilities

BRANDS/DIVISIONS/AFFILIATES:

CONTACTS:
Note: Officers with more than one job title may be intentionally listed here more than once.

Kristie Beck, Pres.

GROWTH PLANS/SPECIAL FEATURES:
Entertainment Resources, Inc. is a sponsorship company which develops partnerships between corporate communities and entertainment/lifestyle properties. The company assists in designing sponsorship programs which attract sponsorship investment. These services include representation, development, consultation, evaluation, design, sales, implementation, sales promotion and ethnic marketing. Additionally, it is also involved in event and property representation, interfacing with advertising and PR agencies and connecting clients with traditional advertising mediums. The company has provided services in such environments as professional sports teams and events, concerts, fairs and festivals, theme parks, motion picture and television programming, charity or cause-related events, celebrity endorsements or appearances, ethnic events and live theater. Clients have included DirecTV, True Value Hardware, Ford, Pepsi, Lexus, Nordstrom, Shell, Farmers Insurance Group, the United States Post Service and more

FINANCIAL DATA:
Note: Data for latest year may not have been available at press time.

In U.S. $	2018	2017	2016	2015	2014	2013
Revenue						
R&D Expense						
Operating Income						
Operating Margin %						
SGA Expense						
Net Income						
Operating Cash Flow						
Capital Expenditure						
EBITDA						
Return on Assets %						
Return on Equity %						
Debt to Equity						

CONTACT INFORMATION:
Phone: 714 847-5658 Fax:
Toll-Free:
Address: 409 20th St., Huntington Beach, CA 92648 United States

STOCK TICKER/OTHER:
Stock Ticker: Private Exchange:
Employees: Fiscal Year Ends:
Parent Company:

SALARIES/BONUSES:
Top Exec. Salary: $ Bonus: $
Second Exec. Salary: $ Bonus: $

OTHER THOUGHTS:
Estimated Female Officers or Directors: 1
Hot Spot for Advancement for Women/Minorities:

Sales, profits and employees may be estimates. Financial information, benefits and other data can change quickly and may vary from those stated here.

Entravision Communications Corporation

www.entravision.com

NAIC Code: 515120

TYPES OF BUSINESS:
Television Broadcasting
Spanish-Language Broadcasting
Radio Broadcasting

BRANDS/DIVISIONS/AFFILIATES:
Univision
UniMas
Smadex

CONTACTS: Note: Officers with more than one job title may be intentionally listed here more than once.
Walter Ulloa, CEO
Christopher Young, CFO
Jeffery Liberman, COO
Mario Carrera, Other Executive Officer

GROWTH PLANS/SPECIAL FEATURES:

Entravision Communications Corporation, along with its subsidiaries, is a diversified Spanish-language media company utilizing its television and radio operations to reach Hispanic consumers across the U.S. as well as the border markets of Mexico. Entravision owns and operates 55 television stations, primarily located in California, Colorado, Connecticut, Florida, Kansas, Massachusetts, Nevada, New Mexico, Texas and Washington, D.C. The firm owns and operates 49 radio stations in 18 U.S. markets, consisting of 38 FM and 11 AM stations located in Arizona, California, Colorado, Florida, Nevada, New Mexico and Texas. Entravision generates revenue from sales of national and local advertising time. The firm's television operations are one of the largest affiliate groups of the Univision networks, with Univision-affiliated stations in 19 markets reaching approximately 60% of all U.S. Hispanic households. Its television programming consists of: Univision primary network programming, targeting a young, family-oriented audience; UniMas network programming, a 24-hour general interest Spanish language broadcasting station that offers sports, movies and novelas; local programming; and network affiliation agreements with Fox Broadcasting Company, Telemundo Network Group LLC, MyNetworkTV, The CW Network and LATV Networks. Entravision's radio stations broadcast into markets with an aggregate of approximately 40% of the Hispanic population in the U.S. Its radio operations combine network and local programming with local time slots available for advertising, news, traffic, weather, promotions and community events. Revenue generated by the television segment accounts for 77% of annual sales, radio accounts for 12% and digital media accounts for the remainder. During 2018, Entravision acquired: television station KMCC-TV; and Smadex, a digital advertising technology company based in Barcelona, Spain.

FINANCIAL DATA: Note: Data for latest year may not have been available at press time.

In U.S. $	2018	2017	2016	2015	2014	2013
Revenue		536,034,000	258,514,000	254,134,000	242,038,000	223,916,000
R&D Expense						
Operating Income		278,741,000	48,856,000	55,245,000	60,401,000	53,950,000
Operating Margin %		52.00%	18.89%	21.73%	24.95%	24.09%
SGA Expense		49,116,000	46,798,000	42,815,000	35,399,000	31,556,000
Net Income		176,293,000	20,405,000	25,625,000	27,122,000	133,825,000
Operating Cash Flow		301,520,000	57,296,000	62,283,000	54,412,000	32,755,000
Capital Expenditure		44,666,000	9,053,000	13,696,000	8,609,000	10,174,000
EBITDA		292,532,000	64,337,000	71,075,000	74,133,000	39,272,000
Return on Assets %		27.46%	3.90%	4.85%	5.08%	27.41%
Return on Equity %		66.23%	11.63%	16.38%	19.26%	189.25%
Debt to Equity		0.83	1.56	1.87	2.31	2.64

CONTACT INFORMATION:
Phone: 310 447-3870   Fax: 310 447-3899
Toll-Free:
Address: 2425 Olympic Blvd., Ste. 6000 W., Santa Monica, CA 90404 United States

STOCK TICKER/OTHER:
Stock Ticker: EVC
Employees: 1,111
Parent Company:

Exchange: NYS
Fiscal Year Ends: 12/31

SALARIES/BONUSES:
Top Exec. Salary: $1,250,000   Bonus: $320,000
Second Exec. Salary: $627,500   Bonus: $290,000

OTHER THOUGHTS:
Estimated Female Officers or Directors:
Hot Spot for Advancement for Women/Minorities:

EPR Properties

www.eprkc.com

NAIC Code: 531120A

TYPES OF BUSINESS:
REIT-Entertainment Properties
Megaplex Movie Theaters
Entertainment Retail Centers
Ski Resorts
Vineyards & Wineries
Public Charter Schools

BRANDS/DIVISIONS/AFFILIATES:

CONTACTS:
Note: Officers with more than one job title may be intentionally listed here more than once.

Mark Peterson, CFO
Robert Druten, Chairman of the Board
Tonya Mater, Chief Accounting Officer
Gregory Silvers, President
Michael Hirons, Senior VP, Divisional
Craig Evans, Senior VP
Barrett Brady, Trustee
Peter Brown, Trustee
Robin Sterneck, Trustee
Jack Newman, Trustee
Thomas Bloch, Trustee

GROWTH PLANS/SPECIAL FEATURES:

EPR Properties is a self-administered, specialty REIT (real estate investment trust) that invests in select market segments. The firm's operations are conducted through three segments: entertainment, education and recreation. The entertainment segment accounts for 44% of the firm's revenue and consists of 147 megaplex movie theaters, seven entertainment retail centers, 11 family entertainment centers, land parcels leased to restaurant and retail operators adjacent to several theatre properties, several retail redevelopment projects totaling approximately $101.3 million and over $4.5 million in undeveloped land inventory. EPR's owned real estate portfolio of megaplex theatre properties consist of approximately 11 million square feet (msf), and its remaining owned entertainment real estate portfolio consists of 2 msf. The company's megaplex theaters usually have at least 10 screens with elevated, stadium-style seating and amenities such as digital projection, which allow greater enhancement to audio and visual experiences for theater patrons. EPR's theaters are leased to operators such as American Multi-Cinema, Inc. (AMC); Alamo Draft House Cinemas; AmStar Cinemas, LLC; Southern Theatres; and Cinemark USA, Inc. The education segment includes 65 public charter school properties, 65 early childhood centers, 15 private schools and properties under construction totaling approximately $1.4 billion. The firm's owned education real estate consists of approximately 4.2 million square feet. The recreation segment comprises 26 ski properties located in 6 states, 20 attractions located in 12 states, 30 golf entertainment complexes in 17 states and eight other recreation properties in 6 states, with $125.2 million in construction in progress for golf entertainment complexes and waterpark hotel projects. At December 31, 2017, EPR's owned recreation real estate portfolio was 100% leased.

FINANCIAL DATA:
Note: Data for latest year may not have been available at press time.

In U.S. $	2018	2017	2016	2015	2014	2013
Revenue		575,991,000	493,242,000	421,017,000	385,051,000	343,064,000
R&D Expense						
Operating Income		367,767,000	325,519,000	257,720,000	261,301,000	236,831,000
Operating Margin %		63.80%				
SGA Expense		43,383,000	37,543,000	49,599,000	27,566,000	25,613,000
Net Income		264,517,000	225,887,000	194,802,000	179,934,000	186,392,000
Operating Cash Flow		391,100,000	306,202,000	278,460,000	250,295,000	234,120,000
Capital Expenditure						
EBITDA		527,011,000	426,553,000	360,246,000	324,261,000	298,660,000
Return on Assets %		4.23%	4.43%	4.31%	4.46%	5.03%
Return on Equity %		9.16%	9.44%	8.53%	8.62%	9.94%
Debt to Equity		1.03	1.13	0.95	0.85	0.87

CONTACT INFORMATION:
Phone: 816-472-1700   Fax:
Toll-Free: 888-377-7348
Address: 909 Walnut St., Ste. 200, Kansas City, MO 64106 United States

STOCK TICKER/OTHER:
Stock Ticker: EPR
Employees: 57
Parent Company:

Exchange: NYS
Fiscal Year Ends: 12/31

SALARIES/BONUSES:
Top Exec. Salary: $725,000   Bonus: $877,250
Second Exec. Salary: $437,000   Bonus: $475,893

OTHER THOUGHTS:
Estimated Female Officers or Directors: 2
Hot Spot for Advancement for Women/Minorities:

Sales, profits and employees may be estimates. Financial information, benefits and other data can change quickly and may vary from those stated here.

Plunkett Research, Ltd.

ESPN Inc
NAIC Code: 515210

espn.go.com

TYPES OF BUSINESS:
Sports Television-Cable
Sports Radio Broadcasting
Online Sports Information
Magazine & Book Publishing
Sports Websites

BRANDS/DIVISIONS/AFFILIATES:
Walt Disney Company (The)
ABC Inc
Hearst Corporation (The)
ESPN
SportsCenter
ESPN+
ESPNEWS
WatchESPN

CONTACTS: Note: Officers with more than one job title may be intentionally listed here more than once.
James Pitaro, Pres.
Christine Driessen, CFO
Aaron LaBerge, Exec. VP-IT
Patrick Stiegman, Editor-in-Chief

GROWTH PLANS/SPECIAL FEATURES:
ESPN, Inc. is a multi-faceted media conglomerate that offers global cable and satellite sports content to approximately 90 million homes. The company broadcasts live sports, and also airs a variety of sports-related news, highlights, talk and documentary-styled shows. ESPN's flagship program, SportsCenter, has aired since 1979. The firm has nine domestic television networks, including ESPN, SEC Network, ESPN2, ESPN+, ESPN Classic, ESPN Deportes, ESPNU, ESPNEWS and Longhorn Network. ESPN programs the sports schedule on the ABC Television Network, branded as ESPN on ABC. Internationally, ESPN either owns, whole or in part, television networks in four languages (English, French, Portuguese and Spanish), as well as additional businesses that allow ESPN to reach sports fans in more than 60 countries and territories across all continents. ESPN+ is a digital cable and satellite television network seen in various South American countries, including Colombia, Ecuador, Peru and Venezuela. ESPN Deportes is a 24-hour sports channel that provides Spanish language simulcasts. WatchESPN is a website for desktop computers as well as an application for smartphones and tablet computers that allows subscribers of participating cable and satellite providers to watch live streams of programming from ESPN and its sister networks (except for ESPN Classic) on PC, mobile devices, Apple TV, Roku and Xbox Live via TV Everywhere login. ESPN3 is an online streaming service that provides live streams and replays of global sports events. ESPN Regional Television is the network's syndication arm, which produces collegiate sporting events for broadcast television throughout the U.S. The company is 80%-owned by ABC, Inc., an indirect subsidiary of The Walt Disney Company; and 20%-owned by The Hearst Corporation. The ACC Network is scheduled for a 2019 launch, which will cover the Atlantic Coast Conference via cable and satellite television, as well as a digital platform for streaming ACC events.

FINANCIAL DATA: Note: Data for latest year may not have been available at press time.

In U.S. $	2018	2017	2016	2015	2014	2013
Revenue	10,820,000,000	10,750,000,000	10,810,000,000	11,000,000,000	11,200,000,000	11,000,000,000
R&D Expense						
Operating Income						
Operating Margin %						
SGA Expense						
Net Income						
Operating Cash Flow						
Capital Expenditure						
EBITDA						
Return on Assets %						
Return on Equity %						
Debt to Equity						

CONTACT INFORMATION:
Phone: 860-766-2000   Fax: 860-766-2213
Toll-Free:
Address: 545 Middle St., Bristol, CT 06010 United States

STOCK TICKER/OTHER:
Stock Ticker: Subsidiary   Exchange:
Employees: 8,000   Fiscal Year Ends: 09/30
Parent Company: Walt Disney Company (The)

SALARIES/BONUSES:
Top Exec. Salary: $ Bonus: $
Second Exec. Salary: $ Bonus: $

OTHER THOUGHTS:
Estimated Female Officers or Directors: 1
Hot Spot for Advancement for Women/Minorities: Y

Sales, profits and employees may be estimates. Financial information, benefits and other data can change quickly and may vary from those stated here.

Euro Disney SCA

NAIC Code: 713110

http://www.disneylandparis.com/en-us/

TYPES OF BUSINESS:
Theme Park
Resorts
Hotels
Golf
Property Developments

BRANDS/DIVISIONS/AFFILIATES:
Walt Disney Company (The)
Euro Disney Associes SCA
Disneyland Park
Golf Disneyland
Disney Village
Space Mountain Mission 2
EDL Hotels SCA
Disneyland Resort Paris

CONTACTS:
Note: Officers with more than one job title may be intentionally listed here more than once.

Catherine Powell, Pres.
Daniel Delcourt, COO
Natacha Rafalski, Sr. VP-Finance
Gregoire Champetier, Sr. VP-Commercial
Daniel Dreux, VP-Human Resources
Gilles Dobelle, General Counsel
Francois Banon, VP-Comm.
Olivier Lambert, Contact-Investor Rel.
Julien Kauffmann, VP-Revenue Mgmt. & Analytics
Francis Borezee, VP-Resort & Real Estate Dev.
Axel Duroux, Chmn.

GROWTH PLANS/SPECIAL FEATURES:

Euro Disney SCA operates Disneyland Resort Paris, a top European vacation destination, through subsidiary Euro Disney Associes SCA (EDA). Located east of Paris, Disneyland Resort Paris is comprised of Disneyland Park, Walt Disney Studios Park, seven themed hotels (with a total of 5,800 rooms), two convention centers (including one of France's largest conference centers), Golf Disneyland and Disney Village, a 322,917-square-foot dining, shopping and entertainment center. Combined, the resort's two theme parks, Disneyland Park and Walt Disney Studios Park, offer 58 attractions, including Space Mountain Mission 2, the Twilight Zone Tower of Terror, Big Thunder Mountain and the Cars Race Rally. Wholly-owned EDA-subsidiary EDL Hotels SCA operates Disney Village as well as six of the Disney themed hotels, including Disney's Newport Bay Club, Sequoia Lodge, Hotel Santa Fe, Hotel New York and Hotel Cheyenne. The other two hotels, Disneyland Hotel and the Davy Crockett Ranch, are operated by EDA itself. Located in Hotel New York and Newport Bay Club, the firm's convention centers, totaling almost 183,000 square feet, handle over 1,000 events per year. EDA also has a large stake in Val d'Europe, a 4,800-acre full-scale town near the park, featuring a shopping center, international business center, offices, apartments, homes and hotels. Euro Disney is 88%-owned by The Walt Disney Company.

FINANCIAL DATA:
Note: Data for latest year may not have been available at press time.

In U.S. $	2018	2017	2016	2015	2014	2013
Revenue		1,500,000,000	1,432,414,208	1,539,004,800	1,434,319,616	1,467,608,192
R&D Expense						
Operating Income						
Operating Margin %						
SGA Expense						
Net Income			-790,181,568	-94,373,456	-104,685,048	-72,181,128
Operating Cash Flow						
Capital Expenditure						
EBITDA						
Return on Assets %						
Return on Equity %						
Debt to Equity						

CONTACT INFORMATION:
Phone: 33 164744000   Fax: 33 164745636
Toll-Free:
Address: Route Nationale 34, Immeubles Administratifs, Paris, 77144 France

STOCK TICKER/OTHER:
Stock Ticker: EUDSF   Exchange: PINX
Employees: 15,000   Fiscal Year Ends: 09/30
Parent Company: Walt Disney Company (The)

SALARIES/BONUSES:
Top Exec. Salary: $ Bonus: $
Second Exec. Salary: $ Bonus: $

OTHER THOUGHTS:
Estimated Female Officers or Directors: 1
Hot Spot for Advancement for Women/Minorities:

Sales, profits and employees may be estimates. Financial information, benefits and other data can change quickly and may vary from those stated here.

Evergreen Gaming Corporation

www.evergreengaming.com

NAIC Code: 713210

TYPES OF BUSINESS:
Casinos
Gaming
Poker
Pull tabs
Casino

BRANDS/DIVISIONS/AFFILIATES:
Chips Casino
Goldies Shoreline Casino
Palace Casino
Riverside Casino

GROWTH PLANS/SPECIAL FEATURES:
Evergreen Gaming Corporation owns and operates four casino-type card rooms in Washington state. Each of these casinos operate on-site restaurants. Chips Casino is located in Lakewood, and comprises 15 gaming tables. Goldie's Shoreline Casino is located in Shoreline, and has 15 gaming tables and pull tabs. Pull tabs are tickets which are turned in for a monetary prize; other names for them include break-opens, Nevada Tickets, cherry bells, Lucky 7s, pickle cards, instant bingo, bowl games or popp-opens. The game manager operates the game by selling tickets and distributing cash prizes. Palace Casino is located in Lakewood, and comprises 15 gaming tables, 10 of which are poker, and pull tabs. Last, Riverside Casino is located in Tukwilla, and has 15 gaming tables and pull tabs.

CONTACTS:
Note: Officers with more than one job title may be intentionally listed here more than once.

Dawn Mangano, CEO
Dennis Wisner, CFO
Leonard Libin, Chairman of the Board

FINANCIAL DATA:
Note: Data for latest year may not have been available at press time.

In U.S. $	2018	2017	2016	2015	2014	2013
Revenue		35,609,460	33,326,620	33,338,540	30,555,760	28,341,630
R&D Expense						
Operating Income		4,324,935	3,229,778	4,316,691	3,286,111	1,852,376
Operating Margin %		12.14%	9.69%	12.94%	10.75%	6.53%
SGA Expense		20,796,520	3,514,110	4,377,786	4,021,414	3,585,435
Net Income		3,032,901	1,909,408	3,933,883	2,720,669	1,344,683
Operating Cash Flow		6,317,699	2,819,477	4,087,424	3,197,601	1,852,802
Capital Expenditure		194,495	4,722,441	26,847	303,609	131,370
EBITDA		5,017,450	3,548,115	4,752,544	3,775,612	2,325,383
Return on Assets %		11.89%	8.77%	20.84%	15.99%	8.50%
Return on Equity %		22.30%	17.15%	47.93%	55.75%	47.22%
Debt to Equity		0.36	0.64	0.59	1.33	2.27

CONTACT INFORMATION:
Phone: 425-282-4172   Fax: 425-572-6437
Toll-Free:
Address: 8200 Tacoma Mall Blvd., Lakewood, WA 98499 United States

STOCK TICKER/OTHER:
Stock Ticker: TNA
Employees: 1,600
Parent Company:

Exchange: TSX
Fiscal Year Ends: 12/31

SALARIES/BONUSES:
Top Exec. Salary: $ Bonus: $
Second Exec. Salary: $ Bonus: $

OTHER THOUGHTS:
Estimated Female Officers or Directors:
Hot Spot for Advancement for Women/Minorities:

EVINE Live Inc

NAIC Code: 454113

www.shophq.com

TYPES OF BUSINESS:
Television Shopping Programs
Online Sales

BRANDS/DIVISIONS/AFFILIATES:
Evine
Evine Too
evine.com

CONTACTS:
Note: Officers with more than one job title may be intentionally listed here more than once.
Diana Purcel, Chief Financial Officer
Nicole Ostoya, Chief Marketing Officer
Nicholas Vassallo, Controller
Robert Rosenblatt, Director
Landel Hobbs, Director
Andrea Fike, General Counsel
Michael Henry, Other Executive Officer

GROWTH PLANS/SPECIAL FEATURES:
EVINE Live, Inc. is a digital commerce company that markets, sells and distributes consumer products through multi-media channels, including TV, internet, mobile and social media. The company's principal electronic media activity is its television home shopping network, which markets brand-name merchandise as well as proprietary and private-label consumer products. EVINE's live, 24-hour-a-day home shopping programs, Evine and Evine Too, is broadcast through cable and satellite affiliations to more than 87 million homes throughout the U.S. Products sold on the network include jewelry, watches, computers and other electronics, housewares, apparel, cosmetics, seasonal items and other merchandise. The company complements its television home shopping business with the sale of merchandise through its eCommerce website, evine.com, which also includes a live webcast feed of the television program, an archive of recent past programming, videos of individual products and links to clearance and auction sites. Watches and jewelry generated 39% of the firm's 2017 sales. The home and electronics division, representing everything from bed and bath textiles to GPS devices, generates 27% of the company's sales. Beauty, health and fitness accounts for 16%, while the fashion (apparel, outerwear and accessories) category generates the remaining 18%. In December 2017, the firm sold its Boston television station, WWDP.

FINANCIAL DATA:
Note: Data for latest year may not have been available at press time.

In U.S. $	2018	2017	2016	2015	2014	2013
Revenue	648,220,000	666,213,000	693,312,000	674,618,000	640,489,000	586,820,000
R&D Expense						
Operating Income	2,671,000	-2,018,000	-8,738,000	1,003,000	77,000	-12,186,000
Operating Margin %	0.41	-.30%	-1.26%	.14%	.01%	-2.07%
SGA Expense	226,071,000	235,504,000	238,744,000	235,600,000	217,627,000	211,334,000
Net Income	143,000	-8,745,000	-12,284,000	-1,378,000	-2,515,000	-27,676,000
Operating Cash Flow	3,278,000	7,284,000	-9,411,000	-1,315,000	13,953,000	-8,482,000
Capital Expenditure	10,499,000	10,261,000	22,014,000	25,178,000	11,077,000	10,157,000
EBITDA	12,089,000	9,202,000	1,597,000	9,885,000	12,680,000	-10,262,000
Return on Assets %	.05%	-3.23%	-4.69%	-.56%	-1.12%	-12.85%
Return on Equity %	.17%	-11.02%	-15.21%	-1.69%	-3.23%	-30.94%
Debt to Equity	0.85	1.00	0.91	0.60	0.48	0.49

CONTACT INFORMATION:
Phone: 952 943-6000
Fax: 952 947-0188
Toll-Free: 800-676-5523
Address: 6740 Shady Oak Rd., Eden Prairie, MN 55344 United States

STOCK TICKER/OTHER:
Stock Ticker: EVLV
Employees: 1,300
Parent Company:
Exchange: NAS
Fiscal Year Ends: 01/31

SALARIES/BONUSES:
Top Exec. Salary: $778,846   Bonus: $
Second Exec. Salary: $389,923   Bonus: $

OTHER THOUGHTS:
Estimated Female Officers or Directors: 4
Hot Spot for Advancement for Women/Minorities: Y

Sales, profits and employees may be estimates. Financial information, benefits and other data can change quickly and may vary from those stated here.

Facebook Inc

NAIC Code: 519130

investor.fb.com/

TYPES OF BUSINESS:
Social Networking
Advertising Services
Developer Tools
Online Video
3-D Headset Manufacturing
Apps

BRANDS/DIVISIONS/AFFILIATES:
Facebook Platform
Instagram
Messenger
WhatsApp Messenger
Oculus
Portal
Portal+

CONTACTS: Note: Officers with more than one job title may be intentionally listed here more than once.
Mark Zuckerberg, CEO
David Wehner, CFO
Susan Taylor, Chief Accounting Officer
Michael Schroepfer, Chief Technology Officer
Sheryl Sandberg, COO
Christopher Cox, Other Executive Officer
David Fischer, Vice President, Divisional
Colin Stretch, Vice President

GROWTH PLANS/SPECIAL FEATURES:

Facebook, Inc. owns and operates a free social networking utility for communicating online with family, friends and acquaintances. As of September 2018, the company had 2.27 billion monthly active users in general, and 1.49 billion daily active users who specifically used the company's mobile products. Some of the site's core functions and applications include individual profiles and home pages; friend lists; group pages; and photos, videos, events and other shared items. Communication is enabled through means such as in-site instant messaging, personal messages, public posts and status updates. Third-party applications (such as games, quizzes and personality tests) can also be added to users' pages to further personalize the site. For privacy, the firm gives users the ability to limit, to some extent, who can view their profile, postings and other personal information. The company's Facebook Platform is a set of development tools and application programming interfaces that enable developers to integrate with Facebook to create social apps and websites. Millions of apps and websites have been integrated as part of the platform. Facebook generates the majority of its revenues from advertising, which can be customized to reach specifically targeted audiences by accessing information users provide the company on their individual profiles. Subsidiary Instagram is a mobile phone-based photo-sharing service that makes it simple for users to upload photos to their profiles; Messenger is a mobile-to-mobile messaging application; WhatsApp Messenger is a cross-platform mobile messaging app that allows people to exchange messages on mobile devices; and Oculus, a virtual reality technology and content platform that power products and enable users to immerse and interact in connected environments. In late-2018, Facebook launched a brand of smart displays called Portal and Portal+, comprising enhanced smart speakers for Amazon's Alexa and Facebook Messenger.

Facebook offers its employees comprehensive benefits.

FINANCIAL DATA: Note: Data for latest year may not have been available at press time.

In U.S. $	2018	2017	2016	2015	2014	2013
Revenue		40,653,000,000	27,638,000,000	17,928,000,000	12,466,000,000	7,872,000,000
R&D Expense		7,754,000,000	5,919,000,000	4,816,000,000	2,666,000,000	1,415,000,000
Operating Income		20,203,000,000	12,427,000,000	6,225,000,000	4,994,000,000	2,804,000,000
Operating Margin %		49.69%	44.96%	34.72%	40.06%	35.61%
SGA Expense		7,242,000,000	5,503,000,000	4,020,000,000	2,653,000,000	1,778,000,000
Net Income		15,934,000,000	10,217,000,000	3,688,000,000	2,940,000,000	1,500,000,000
Operating Cash Flow		24,216,000,000	16,108,000,000	8,599,000,000	5,457,000,000	4,222,000,000
Capital Expenditure		6,733,000,000	4,491,000,000	2,523,000,000	1,831,000,000	1,362,000,000
EBITDA		23,625,000,000	14,870,000,000	8,162,000,000	6,176,000,000	3,821,000,000
Return on Assets %		21.29%	17.81%	8.19%	10.07%	9.03%
Return on Equity %		23.84%	19.70%	9.13%	11.34%	10.95%
Debt to Equity						0.01

CONTACT INFORMATION:
Phone: 650 543-4800 Fax:
Toll-Free:
Address: 1601 Willow Rd., Menlo Park, CA 94025 United States

SALARIES/BONUSES:
Top Exec. Salary: $795,769 Bonus: $640,378
Second Exec. Salary: $711,539 Bonus: $633,317

STOCK TICKER/OTHER:
Stock Ticker: FB
Employees: 17,048
Parent Company:

Exchange: NAS
Fiscal Year Ends: 12/31

OTHER THOUGHTS:
Estimated Female Officers or Directors: 2
Hot Spot for Advancement for Women/Minorities: Y

Sales, profits and employees may be estimates. Financial information, benefits and other data can change quickly and may vary from those stated here.

Feld Entertainment Inc

NAIC Code: 711190

www.feldentertainment.com

TYPES OF BUSINESS:
Ice Skating Shows
Circuses
Monster Trucks
Motocross

BRANDS/DIVISIONS/AFFILIATES:
Disney on Ice
Disney Live
Monster Energy AMA Supercross
Monster Jam
Marvel Universe Live
Sesame Street Live
Trolls: The Experience
Feld Entertainment Studios

CONTACTS: Note: Officers with more than one job title may be intentionally listed here more than once.
Kenneth Feld, CEO

GROWTH PLANS/SPECIAL FEATURES:

Feld Entertainment, Inc. is a producer of branded live entertainment shows. The firm's shows, performed in 75 countries, include performances on ice, interactive shows and around the track by both people and characters. Disney on Ice is an ice skating show that combines professional ice skaters and the stories of Disney. They are performed in various languages, depending on the country and culture location of the show. Disney Live is an interactive theatrical experience where audience members can sing along with live performances of Disney's stories. Monster Energy AMA Supercross, an FIM World Championship, is an off-road motorcycle racing series held in U.S. and international stadiums. Monster Jam is the largest touring monster truck show in the world, with over 350 shows depicting 1,500-horsepower trucks such as Grave Digger, Max-D, Man of Steel, El Toro Loco and Batman. Marvel Universe Live is a live action arena experience with cutting edge special effects, featuring the characters of Marvel doing aerial stunts, martial arts and more. Sesame Street Live, an interactive show that unfolds the famous street along with its traditional characters. Trolls: The Experience, an interactive adventure that takes guests through the Trolls forest where they will encounter favorite Trolls, find gems inside the Caterbus and dance to popular Troll music. Feld Entertainment Studios is located on Florida's Gulf Coast and comprises more than 580,000 square feet under a single roof. The studio facility sets up tours, designs and builds sets, creates shows, has space for rehearsals and creates/packs everything needed for on-the-road performances. During 2018, Feld and Universal Brand Development partnered to develop multiple properties into pop-up attractions, with the first being DreamWorks' Trolls: The Experience starting its tour in late-2018 in New York.

FINANCIAL DATA: Note: Data for latest year may not have been available at press time.

In U.S. $	2018	2017	2016	2015	2014	2013
Revenue	1,330,000,000	1,320,000,000	1,300,000,000	1,000,000,000	1,100,000,000	1,000,000,000
R&D Expense						
Operating Income						
Operating Margin %						
SGA Expense						
Net Income						
Operating Cash Flow						
Capital Expenditure						
EBITDA						
Return on Assets %						
Return on Equity %						
Debt to Equity						

CONTACT INFORMATION:
Phone: 941-721-1200 Fax:
Toll-Free:
Address: 800 Feld Way, Palmetto, FL 34221 United States

SALARIES/BONUSES:
Top Exec. Salary: $ Bonus: $
Second Exec. Salary: $ Bonus: $

STOCK TICKER/OTHER:
Stock Ticker: Private   Exchange:
Employees: 3,150   Fiscal Year Ends:
Parent Company:

OTHER THOUGHTS:
Estimated Female Officers or Directors:
Hot Spot for Advancement for Women/Minorities:

Sales, profits and employees may be estimates. Financial information, benefits and other data can change quickly and may vary from those stated here.

Fertitta Entertainment Inc.

www.landrysinc.com

NAIC Code: 722511

TYPES OF BUSINESS:
Casual Dining Restaurants
Hotel & Casino Resorts
Fine dining Restaurants
Entertainment & Tourist Venues
Lusury Hotels

BRANDS/DIVISIONS/AFFILIATES:
Landrys
Chart House
Saltgrass Steak House
Bubba Gump Shrimp Co
Golden Nugget
Downtown Aquarium
San Luis Resort Hotel
Post Oak Hotel at Uptown Houston (The)

CONTACTS: Note: Officers with more than one job title may be intentionally listed here more than once.
Tilman J. Fertitta, CEO
Stephen L. Cavallaro, COO
Marc J. Falcone, CFO
Scott M. Nielson, Chief Devel. Off.
K. Kelly Roberts, Chief Admin. Officer-Hospitality & Gaming
Steven L. Scheinthal, General Counsel
Jeffrey L. Cantwell, Sr. VP-Dev.
Tilman J. Fertitta, Chmn.

GROWTH PLANS/SPECIAL FEATURES:
Fertita Entertainment, Inc., wholly-owned by CEO Tilman J. Fertitta, is a restaurant, hospitality, entertainment and retail company principally engaged in the ownership and operation of both casual and fine dining restaurants. The firm owns and operates more than 600 properties, including more than 60 unique brands. Restaurant brands include Landry's Seafood, Chart House, Saltgrass Steak House, Bubba Gump Shrimp Co., Claim Jumper, Morton's The Steakhouse, McCormick & Schmick's, Mastro's Restaurants and Rainforest Cafe. Fertitta also owns five Golden Nugget Hotel and Casino locations which are operated by affiliated entities, as well as numerous hotel properties and other entertainment destinations. Golden Nugget locations include Las Vegas, Lake Charles, Atlantic City, Biloxi and Laughlin. Entertainment properties include Downtown Aquarium, located in both Houston and the Kemah Boardwalk, Texas, as well as in Nashville, Tennessee and Denver, Colorado. The downtown Houston complex is comprised of a 20-acre complex with an aquarium exhibit, a restaurant built around a 100,000-gallon, floor-to-ceiling centerpiece aquarium, a bar, banquet facilities, amusement rides and midway games. A train carries guests into a tunnel running through a 200,000-gallon shark tank. In Galveston, Texas, Fertitta owns the 140,000-square-foot Galveston Island Convention Center at the San Luis Resort, as well as the Hilton Resort Galveston Island, the Holiday Inn Resort Galveston and The Villas (a set of five, high-end private suites within a secluded area of The San Luis Resort). The Post Oak Hotel at Uptown Houston, features a 700,000-square-foot vertical, multi-use residential, business and tourist property.

FINANCIAL DATA: Note: Data for latest year may not have been available at press time.

In U.S. $	2018	2017	2016	2015	2014	2013
Revenue	4,100,000,000	3,800,000,000	3,500,000,000	3,100,000,000	3,000,000,000	2,800,000,000
R&D Expense						
Operating Income						
Operating Margin %						
SGA Expense						
Net Income						
Operating Cash Flow						
Capital Expenditure						
EBITDA						
Return on Assets %						
Return on Equity %						
Debt to Equity						

CONTACT INFORMATION:
Phone: 713-850-1010 Fax:
Toll-Free: 800-552-6379
Address: 1510 W. Loop S., Houston, TX 77027 United States

STOCK TICKER/OTHER:
Stock Ticker: Private
Employees: 60,000
Parent Company:

Exchange:
Fiscal Year Ends: 12/31

SALARIES/BONUSES:
Top Exec. Salary: $ Bonus: $
Second Exec. Salary: $ Bonus: $

OTHER THOUGHTS:
Estimated Female Officers or Directors: 1
Hot Spot for Advancement for Women/Minorities:

Sales, profits and employees may be estimates. Financial information, benefits and other data can change quickly and may vary from those stated here.

FishBowl Worldwide Media LLC

NAIC Code: 511210G

www.fbwmedia.com/

TYPES OF BUSINESS:
Computer Software, Electronic Games, Apps & Entertainment
Social Networking App

BRANDS/DIVISIONS/AFFILIATES:

GROWTH PLANS/SPECIAL FEATURES:
FishBowl Worldwide Media, LLC is an independent production company founded in 2010, and focused on transmedia development and production. Transmedia refers to storytelling, portraying a single story or story experience across multiple platforms and formats using current digital technologies. Founder Vin Di Bona created and produced America's Funniest Home Videos, a successful television series and is leveraging the success of this flagship series to create and produce a variety of series for both TV and digital platforms, including reality shows, game shows, scripted series, animation and short-form. FishBowl clients range from the major broadcast networks to premium cable outlets and high-end digital platforms. The firm has produced several unscripted television series, including Upload with Shaquille O'Neal on truTV, I'm Married to A ... on VH1 and Toned Up on Bravo. On the scripted side, projects have been sold to NBC, Fox, ABC, CW, Comedy Central, MTV and Adult Swim.

CONTACTS:
Note: Officers with more than one job title may be intentionally listed here more than once.

Rob Katz, Exec. Producer
Vin Di Bona, Chmn.

FINANCIAL DATA:
Note: Data for latest year may not have been available at press time.

In U.S. $	2018	2017	2016	2015	2014	2013
Revenue						
R&D Expense						
Operating Income						
Operating Margin %						
SGA Expense						
Net Income						
Operating Cash Flow						
Capital Expenditure						
EBITDA						
Return on Assets %						
Return on Equity %						
Debt to Equity						

CONTACT INFORMATION:
Phone: 310-826-4912 Fax:
Toll-Free:
Address: 12233 W. Olympic Blvd., Ste. 170, Los Angeles, CA 90064 United States

STOCK TICKER/OTHER:
Stock Ticker: Private Exchange:
Employees: Fiscal Year Ends:
Parent Company:

SALARIES/BONUSES:
Top Exec. Salary: $ Bonus: $
Second Exec. Salary: $ Bonus: $

OTHER THOUGHTS:
Estimated Female Officers or Directors:
Hot Spot for Advancement for Women/Minorities:

Forbes Media LLC

NAIC Code: 511120A

www.forbesmedia.com

TYPES OF BUSINESS:
Business and Financial Magazine Publishing
Online Publishing & Forums
Television Production
Newsletters
Conferences

BRANDS/DIVISIONS/AFFILIATES:
Forbes Magazine
BrandVoice
Women@Forbes
Forbes.com

CONTACTS: Note: Officers with more than one job title may be intentionally listed here more than once.
Mike Perlis, CEO
Mike Federle, COO
Michael York, CFO
Margy Loftus, VP-Human Resources
Lewis D'Vorkin, Chief Prod. Officer
Mark Howard, Chief Revenue Officer
Robert Forbes, Pres., ForbesLife
Steve Forbes, Editor-in-Chief
Christopher Forbes, Vice Chmn.
Timothy C. Forbes, Chief Strategist
Steve Forbes, Editor-in-Chief

GROWTH PLANS/SPECIAL FEATURES:

Forbes Media, LLC is a publishing and new media company, primarily known as the publisher of Forbes Magazine (Forbes). The firm offers seven platforms: digital, mobile, magazines, video, live, BrandVoice and insight. Digital includes Forbes.com, which provides top stories, video and trending features through its social journalism platform, reaching 71 million unique visitors monthly. Its Women@Forbes channel aims to help women advance their careers through business-first content, podcasts, live mentoring and more. Mobile streams content via innovative smartphone and tablet applications and sites, with 75% of its digital audience on mobile. Magazines is comprised of a global readership of more than 7.4 million, offering online coverage of the world's most influential leaders. Video is comprised of more than 580,000 YouTube channel subscribers, 10,000 YouTube channel videos and 73 million YouTube channel video views. This division's pre-roll and in-banner ads enable advertisers to place their brands at the heart of editorial content. Forbes' branding solutions cross all video platforms. The live events division hosts 12 key events every year, bringing together the world's top leaders, policy makers, innovators, experts and change-makers in order to explore the ever-changing world. BrandVoice is a content-sharing channel and integrated platform that enables marketers to join conversations of thought with their own narrative and expertise. This division includes over 200 BrandVoice partners, 123 million BrandVoice page views, 22 million social actions & referrals and 11,000 BrandVoice posts. Insight is a research and thought leadership practice of Forbes Media, Forbes Magazine and Forbes.com, reaching nearly 75 million business decision makers worldwide on a monthly basis.

FINANCIAL DATA: Note: Data for latest year may not have been available at press time.

In U.S. $	2018	2017	2016	2015	2014	2013
Revenue	189,000,000	180,000,000	177,100,000	154,000,000	150,000,000	165,000,000
R&D Expense						
Operating Income						
Operating Margin %						
SGA Expense						
Net Income						
Operating Cash Flow						
Capital Expenditure						
EBITDA						
Return on Assets %						
Return on Equity %						
Debt to Equity						

CONTACT INFORMATION:
Phone: 212-620-2200   Fax: 212-620-5109
Toll-Free: 800-295-0893
Address: 499 Washington Blvd., Jersey City, NJ 07310 United States

SALARIES/BONUSES:
Top Exec. Salary: $ Bonus: $
Second Exec. Salary: $ Bonus: $

STOCK TICKER/OTHER:
Stock Ticker: Subsidiary   Exchange:
Employees: 400   Fiscal Year Ends: 12/31
Parent Company: Integrated Whale Media Investments

OTHER THOUGHTS:
Estimated Female Officers or Directors:
Hot Spot for Advancement for Women/Minorities:

Sales, profits and employees may be estimates. Financial information, benefits and other data can change quickly and may vary from those stated here.

Ford Models Inc

NAIC Code: 711410

www.fordmodels.com

TYPES OF BUSINESS:
Modeling Agency
Online Community
How to Video Production

BRANDS/DIVISIONS/AFFILIATES:
Alpoint Capital Partners LLC
Supermodel of the World

CONTACTS:
Note: Officers with more than one job title may be intentionally listed here more than once.

Gerald T. Banks, Managing Dir.-Altpoint

GROWTH PLANS/SPECIAL FEATURES:
Ford Models, Inc., owned by Altpoint Capital Partners, LLC, is one of the top fashion model representation agencies in the world. Based out of New York City, it has offices in Chicago, Los Angeles and Paris. The company was founded in 1947 by Eileen and Jerry Ford, and represents supermodels such as Rachel Hunter, Christie Brinkley, Stephanie Seymour and Veronica Webb. In the past, it has managed the careers of stars such as Lindsey Lohan, Jennifer Connelly, Tippi Hedron, Mischa Barton and Kirsten Dunst. The company operates through several divisions representing different categories of models. The children's division works with children aged six months and older that live within 100 miles of New York City, Chicago or Los Angeles. During the summer, the division also works with out-of-town child models staying temporarily in the area. Ford also has a men's division, a women's division and a plus-sized women's division. Additional divisions specialize in older/mature models and models who display specific body parts, such as hands or feet. The company holds open casting at many of its locations throughout the year. Ford hosts Supermodel of the World, an international competition for women ages 14-21, with the winner awarded a monetary contract, an editorial photo shoot and other prizes.

FINANCIAL DATA:
Note: Data for latest year may not have been available at press time.

In U.S. $	2018	2017	2016	2015	2014	2013
Revenue	31,500,000	31,000,000	30,000,000	27,000,000	26,500,000	26,000,000
R&D Expense						
Operating Income						
Operating Margin %						
SGA Expense						
Net Income						
Operating Cash Flow						
Capital Expenditure						
EBITDA						
Return on Assets %						
Return on Equity %						
Debt to Equity						

CONTACT INFORMATION:
Phone: 212-219-6500   Fax: 212-966-5028
Toll-Free:
Address: 11 E. 26th St., Fl. 14, New York, NY 10010 United States

STOCK TICKER/OTHER:
Stock Ticker: Private   Exchange:
Employees: 100   Fiscal Year Ends:
Parent Company: Altpoint Capital Partners LLC

SALARIES/BONUSES:
Top Exec. Salary: $ Bonus: $
Second Exec. Salary: $ Bonus: $

OTHER THOUGHTS:
Estimated Female Officers or Directors:
Hot Spot for Advancement for Women/Minorities:

Sales, profits and employees may be estimates. Financial information, benefits and other data can change quickly and may vary from those stated here.

Plunkett Research, Ltd.

Fox Broadcasting Company

www.fox.com

NAIC Code: 515120

TYPES OF BUSINESS:
Television Broadcasting
Television Stations

BRANDS/DIVISIONS/AFFILIATES:
Twenty-First Century Fox Inc
Fox Television Stations Inc
MyNetworkTV
FX
Twentieth Century Fox Television
Fox Television Studios
Fox News Channel
Fox Sports Networks

CONTACTS: Note: Officers with more than one job title may be intentionally listed here more than once.
Dana Walden, Co-Chmn.
Gary Newman, Co-Chmn.
Del Mayberry, CFO
Ira Kurgan, Chief-Network Bus. Oper.
Preston Beckman, Sr. Strategist
David Wertheimer, Pres., Digital
Shannon Ryan, Exec. VP-Mktg. & Comm.
Simon Andrae, Exec. VP-Alternative Entertainment
Jean Rossi, Exec. VP-Sales
Dan Harrison, Exec. VP-Scheduling
Laurel Bernard, Exec. VP-Mktg.
Jon Hookstratten, Exec. VP-Network Distribution

GROWTH PLANS/SPECIAL FEATURES:
Fox Broadcasting Company (FOX) operates as an American commercial broadcast television network within Twenty-First Century Fox, Inc.'s entertainment division. The network consists of 28 owned-and-operated, full-power stations, as well as affiliate agreements with 225 additional television stations through its Fox Television Stations, Inc. subsidiary. Of those 28 channels, 17 are affiliates of FOX. These stations reach approximately 99.9% of all households in the U.S. FOX also oversees the MyNetworkTV service. The company's target audience consists of adults aged 18-49, with the median age of the FOX viewer around 51. The firm broadcasts approximately 15 hours of primetime, sports events and a 60 minute, Sunday morning news television programming created by other Fox Entertainment subsidiaries, including Twentieth Century Fox Television, Fox Television Studios, Fox News Channel, Fox Sports Networks, FX Network and several foreign subsidiaries. The company principally derives its revenues from the sale of advertising time sold to national advertisers. FOX's most prominent primetime programs include The Simpsons, Hell's Kitchen, Family Guy, American Idol and New Girl. From the FOX website, Fox.com, viewers can stream full episodes of most of its aired programs. The firm licenses sports programming from organizations such as the NFL, MLB and NASCAR. In December 2017, Fox agreed to sell most of its businesses to Walt Disney Co in a deal valued at $52 billion. As of 2018 the transaction has received both Disney and Fox shareholder approval, but is still subject government approval from some international governments, including Mexico and Brazil.

FOX offers employees medical, dental and vision benefits; life insurance; long-term disability; hybrid vehicle purchase/lease program; child care discounts; counseling services; movie screenings; education reimbursement; and employee discounts.

FINANCIAL DATA: Note: Data for latest year may not have been available at press time.

In U.S. $	2018	2017	2016	2015	2014	2013
Revenue		7,065,000,000	7,010,000,000	6,460,000,000	6,030,000,000	
R&D Expense						
Operating Income						
Operating Margin %						
SGA Expense						
Net Income						
Operating Cash Flow						
Capital Expenditure						
EBITDA						
Return on Assets %						
Return on Equity %						
Debt to Equity						

CONTACT INFORMATION:
Phone: 310-369-3553   Fax: 310-369-1283
Toll-Free:
Address: 10201 W. Pico Blvd., Los Angeles, CA 90035 United States

SALARIES/BONUSES:
Top Exec. Salary: $ Bonus: $
Second Exec. Salary: $ Bonus: $

STOCK TICKER/OTHER:
Stock Ticker: Subsidiary   Exchange:
Employees: Fiscal Year Ends: 06/30
Parent Company: Twenty-First Century Fox Inc (21st Century Fox)

OTHER THOUGHTS:
Estimated Female Officers or Directors: 6
Hot Spot for Advancement for Women/Minorities: Y

Sales, profits and employees may be estimates. Financial information, benefits and other data can change quickly and may vary from those stated here.

Fox Entertainment Group Inc

www.fox.com

NAIC Code: 515120

TYPES OF BUSINESS:
Broadcast Television
Film Distribution and Production
Television Programming
Online Communities and Game Sites
Professional Sports
Electronic Games
Cable TV Programming
Online Entertainment

BRANDS/DIVISIONS/AFFILIATES:
Twenty-First Century Fox Inc
FX
National Geographic Channel
Fox News
Fox Sports
20th Century Fox
21st Century Fox

CONTACTS: *Note: Officers with more than one job title may be intentionally listed here more than once.*
Roger Ailes, CEO

GROWTH PLANS/SPECIAL FEATURES:
Fox Entertainment Group, Inc., a wholly-owned subsidiary of Twenty-First Century Fox, Inc., is a conglomerate focused on film and television entertainment. The company engages in feature film and television production and distribution principally through the following businesses: filmed entertainment, television stations, a television broadcast network and cable networks. The filmed entertainment business finances, develops, produces, distributes and markets motion pictures, as well as television and home entertainment programming. The television stations business owns and operates network broadcast groups, comprised of stations offering content throughout the U.S. The television broadcast network operates entertainment channels in the U.S. and internationally. The network provides regularly-scheduled network programming, prime-time programming, late-night programming and weekend programming. Programming includes, but is not limited to, adult animation, children's programming, news and sports. The cable networks business includes domestic programming services that together reach hundreds of millions of subscribing television homes. Fox networks include FX, National Geographic Channel, Fox News, Fox Sports, 20th Century Fox and 21st Century Fox. In December 2017, Fox agreed to sell most of its businesses to Walt Disney Co in a deal valued at $52 billion. The transaction received shareholder approval in mid-2018, but remained subject to regulatory approval.

FINANCIAL DATA: *Note: Data for latest year may not have been available at press time.*

In U.S. $	2018	2017	2016	2015	2014	2013
Revenue	16,900,000,000	16,800,000,000	16,500,000,000	14,500,000,000	13,300,000,000	
R&D Expense						
Operating Income						
Operating Margin %						
SGA Expense						
Net Income						
Operating Cash Flow						
Capital Expenditure						
EBITDA						
Return on Assets %						
Return on Equity %						
Debt to Equity						

CONTACT INFORMATION:
Phone: 212-852-7111   Fax: 212-852-7145
Toll-Free:
Address: 1211 Avenue of the Americas, New York, NY 10036 United States

STOCK TICKER/OTHER:
Stock Ticker: Subsidiary   Exchange:
Employees: 12,500   Fiscal Year Ends: 06/30
Parent Company: Twenty-First Century Fox Inc

SALARIES/BONUSES:
Top Exec. Salary: $ Bonus: $
Second Exec. Salary: $ Bonus: $

OTHER THOUGHTS:
Estimated Female Officers or Directors:
Hot Spot for Advancement for Women/Minorities:

Sales, profits and employees may be estimates. Financial information, benefits and other data can change quickly and may vary from those stated here.

Fox Sports Interactive Media LLC

www.foxsports.com

NAIC Code: 515120

TYPES OF BUSINESS:
Television Production-Sports
Film & TV Production & Distribution
Online Sports Broadcasting
Regional Sports Networks

BRANDS/DIVISIONS/AFFILIATES:
Twenty-First Century Fox, Inc. (21st Century Fox)
Fox Sports Network
Fox Sports 1
Fox Sports 2
Big Ten Network
Fox Soccer Plus
Fox College Sports
Fox Deportes

CONTACTS:
Note: Officers with more than one job title may be intentionally listed here more than once.

Eric Shanks, COO
George Greenberg, Exec. VP-Prod. & Programming
Pete Vlastelica, Sr. VP-Digital
Lou D'Ermilio, Sr. VP-Comm.
Robert Thompson, Pres., Fox National Cable Sports Networks
Randy Freer, Co-Pres., Fox Sports Media

GROWTH PLANS/SPECIAL FEATURES:
Fox Sports Interactive Media, LLC, owned by Twenty-First Century Fox, Inc., produces and distributes films and television programs. In addition to its broadcast division, Fox Sports owns many regional and national cable sports channels in the U.S., including Fox Sports Network, Fox Sports 1, Fox Sports 2, Big Ten Network, Fox Soccer Plus, Fox College Sports and Fox Deportes. These channels broadcast national general sports, school sporting events, domestic and international soccer matches, college sports and Spanish-language coverage of professional soccer and baseball sports. The company is the exclusive holder of national over-the-air television broadcasting rights of MLB, the NFL's NFC Package and NASCAR's Sprint Cup. The firm has various partnerships with Rainbow Media Sports, with the result that the two companies have owned different stakes in various regional Fox Sports Net operations. Fox Sports provides special programming through its partnerships with Fox News, FOX, Fox Sports Supports, FX, Speed TV, Fuel TV and What If Sports. Customers can access live streaming of breaking plays, headlines and score updates through the company's website and mobile applications. The firm has a 12-year deal to broadcast three major open championships of the U.S. Golf Association, including the U.S. Open, from 2015 to 2027. As of 2018, after the proposed merger of The Walt Disney Co. and Twenty-First Century Fox, Disney is actively looking to sale off Fox Sport's regional sports channels.

FINANCIAL DATA:
Note: Data for latest year may not have been available at press time.

In U.S. $	2018	2017	2016	2015	2014	2013
Revenue	8,900,000,000	8,850,000,000	8,750,000,000	8,250,000,000		
R&D Expense						
Operating Income						
Operating Margin %						
SGA Expense						
Net Income						
Operating Cash Flow						
Capital Expenditure						
EBITDA						
Return on Assets %						
Return on Equity %						
Debt to Equity						

CONTACT INFORMATION:
Phone: 310-369-7069   Fax: 310-969-5660
Toll-Free:
Address: 10201 W. Pico Blvd., Bldg. 103, Los Angeles, CA 90035 United States

STOCK TICKER/OTHER:
Stock Ticker: Subsidiary   Exchange:
Employees: 2,200   Fiscal Year Ends: 06/30
Parent Company: Twenty-First Century Fox Inc (21st Century Fox)

SALARIES/BONUSES:
Top Exec. Salary: $ Bonus: $
Second Exec. Salary: $ Bonus: $

OTHER THOUGHTS:
Estimated Female Officers or Directors:
Hot Spot for Advancement for Women/Minorities:

Sales, profits and employees may be estimates. Financial information, benefits and other data can change quickly and may vary from those stated here.

Full House Resorts Inc

NAIC Code: 713210

www.fullhouseresorts.com

TYPES OF BUSINESS:
Casinos

BRANDS/DIVISIONS/AFFILIATES:
Silver Slipper Casino and Hotel
Bronco Billy's Casino and Hotel
Risting Star Casino Resort
Stockman's Casino
Grand Lodge Casino
Buffalo Billy's Casino
Billy's Casino

CONTACTS: Note: Officers with more than one job title may be intentionally listed here more than once.
Daniel Lee, CEO
Bradley Tirpak, Director
Carl Braunlich, Director
Elaine Guidroz, General Counsel
Lewis Fanger, Senior VP

GROWTH PLANS/SPECIAL FEATURES:
Full House Resorts, Inc. develops, manages, operates and/or invests in gaming-related enterprises. The company currently owns four properties: Silver Slipper Casino and Hotel, located in Hancock County, Mississippi; Bronco Billy's Casino and Hotel, located in Cripple Creek, Colorado; Rising Star Casino Resort, located in Rising Sun, Indiana; and Stockman's Casino located in Fallon, Nevada. It leases Grand Lodge Casino, which is located in Incline Village, Nevada. The Silver Slipper is located along the far west end of the Mississippi Gulf Coast, approximately one hour from New Orleans, Louisiana. The property has over 37,000 square feet of gaming space containing slot and video poker machines, table games, a poker room and live keno. It includes a fine dining restaurant, buffet, quick service restaurant, two casino bars and a 129-room hotel. Silver Slipper draws heavily from the New Orleans metropolitan area and other communities in southern Louisiana and southwestern Mississippi. Bronco Billy's includes three adjoining licensed operations: Bronco Billy's Casino, Buffalo Billy's Casino and Billy's Casino. These casinos contain approximately 17,000 square feet of gaming space, 24 hotel rooms, a steakhouse and four casual dining outlets. Customers are primarily from the Colorado Springs metro area. Rising Star Casino Resort has 40,000 square feet of casino space and, includes slot and video poker machines, table games, a 190-room hotel, dining outlets and an 18-hole Scottish links golf course on 380 acres. Rising Star also has a 56-space RV park, and is currently developing a 10-car ferry boat service across the river to Kentucky. Stockman's Casino has approximately 8,400 square feet of gaming space with slot machines, table games, keno, as well as a fine-dining restaurant and coffee shop. Grand Lodge Casino has 18,900 square feet of gaming area, and is integrated into the Hyatt Lake Tahoe on the north shore of Lake Tahoe.

FINANCIAL DATA: Note: Data for latest year may not have been available at press time.

In U.S. $	2018	2017	2016	2015	2014	2013
Revenue		161,267,000	145,992,000	124,588,000	121,421,000	144,727,000
R&D Expense		284,000	1,314,000	891,000	296,000	67,000
Operating Income		7,069,000	6,533,000	5,047,000	-1,919,000	6,960,000
Operating Margin %		4.38%	4.47%	4.05%	-1.58%	4.80%
SGA Expense		53,472,000	49,756,000	42,040,000	46,683,000	46,974,000
Net Income		-5,028,000	-5,094,000	-1,317,000	-20,845,000	-3,962,000
Operating Cash Flow		7,143,000	7,920,000	7,509,000	7,561,000	12,279,000
Capital Expenditure		11,070,000	3,496,000	11,354,000	9,567,000	6,162,000
EBITDA		13,398,000	11,886,000	12,949,000	-6,378,000	12,333,000
Return on Assets %		-2.86%	-3.18%	-.92%	-14.12%	-2.49%
Return on Equity %		-9.26%	-9.01%	-2.31%	-30.81%	-4.98%
Debt to Equity		1.89	1.76	1.19	1.13	0.82

CONTACT INFORMATION:
Phone: 702 221-7800   Fax: 702 221-8101
Toll-Free:
Address: 4670 S. Fort Apache Rd., Ste. 190, Las Vegas, NV 89147 United States

STOCK TICKER/OTHER:
Stock Ticker: FLL
Employees: 1,692
Parent Company:

Exchange: NAS
Fiscal Year Ends: 12/31

SALARIES/BONUSES:
Top Exec. Salary: $450,000   Bonus: $8,333
Second Exec. Salary: $272,583   Bonus: $

OTHER THOUGHTS:
Estimated Female Officers or Directors: 3
Hot Spot for Advancement for Women/Minorities: Y

Plunkett Research, Ltd.

Galaxy Entertainment Group Limited
www.galaxyentertainment.com

NAIC Code: 721120

TYPES OF BUSINESS:
Casino Hotels
Construction Materials

BRANDS/DIVISIONS/AFFILIATES:
Galaxy Macau
Broadway Macau
StarWorld Macau
Societe Anonyme des Baines de Mer

CONTACTS:
Note: Officers with more than one job title may be intentionally listed here more than once.

Philip Cheng Yee Sing, Managing Dir.
Robert Drake, CFO
Kevin Clayton, CMO
Eileen Lui Wai Ling, Dir.-Human Resources & Admin
James Houghton, Dir.-Info. Systems
Ian Farnsworth, Dir.-Tech.
Eileen Lui Wai Ling, Dir.-Admin.
Raymond Kwok Mun Sang, Dir.-Legal
John Au Chung On, Dir.-Bus. Dev.
Charles So Chak Lum, Deputy COO-Starworld Macau
Baschar Hraki, Dir.-Project Dev
Gabriel Hunterton, COO-Starworld
Gillian Murphy, Sr. VP-Hospitality
Lui Che Woo, Chmn.
Raymond Yap Yin Min, Sr. VP-Intl Premium Market Dev.
Lisa Ng Lai Ming, Sr. VP-Procurement

GROWTH PLANS/SPECIAL FEATURES:
Galaxy Entertainment Group Limited is a resort, hospitality and gaming company, delivering innovative and award-winning properties, products and services. Galaxy Entertainment operates five flagship destinations in Macau: on Cotai, Galaxy Macau, an integrated destination resort with more than 2,200 rooms, suites and villas across three hotels as well as a skytop acquatic ride, pools, theater, themed tropical gardens, waterpark, waterslides, beach lagoons, restaurants and more; the adjoining Broadway Macau, a landmark entertainment and food street destination with a hotel, theater, markets, authentic foods/restaurants and performances; and StarWorld Macau, a premium property located on the Peninsula, consisting of a 39-storey hotel, entertainment, dining and other options. Galaxy Entertainment has additional undeveloped land in Macau that can be used for enhancing current resort properties and for adding off-site tourism and leisure spaces. Internationally, Galaxy Entertainment has an investment in Societe Anonyme des Bains de Mer et du Cercle des Etrangers a Monaco, which encompasses luxury hotels and resorts in the Principality of Monaco.

FINANCIAL DATA:
Note: Data for latest year may not have been available at press time.

In U.S. $	2018	2017	2016	2015	2014	2013
Revenue		7,974,876,000	6,745,855,000	6,511,488,000	9,162,736,000	8,432,300,000
R&D Expense						
Operating Income		1,257,898,000	780,262,700	540,990,800	1,289,529,000	1,294,665,000
Operating Margin %		15.81%	11.63%	8.30%	14.17%	15.35%
SGA Expense						
Net Income		1,341,399,000	802,385,000	531,362,900	1,320,386,000	1,283,603,000
Operating Cash Flow		2,364,954,000	1,625,855,000	846,078,600	1,534,894,000	1,701,180,000
Capital Expenditure		258,179,300	268,599,500	842,066,400	1,193,032,000	657,239,600
EBITDA		1,792,991,000	1,272,396,000	935,509,100	1,593,665,000	1,596,529,000
Return on Assets %		13.99%	10.33%	7.76%	21.08%	22.17%
Return on Equity %		20.63%	14.37%	10.47%	29.20%	37.02%
Debt to Equity		0.01	0.01	0.01		

CONTACT INFORMATION:
Phone: 852-3150-1111 Fax: 852-3150-1100
Toll-Free:
Address: 1606, 16/Fl Hutchison House, 10 Harcourt Rd., Hong Kong, Hong Kong

STOCK TICKER/OTHER:
Stock Ticker: GXYEF
Employees: 20,500
Parent Company:

Exchange: PINX
Fiscal Year Ends: 12/31

SALARIES/BONUSES:
Top Exec. Salary: $ Bonus: $
Second Exec. Salary: $ Bonus: $

OTHER THOUGHTS:
Estimated Female Officers or Directors: 5
Hot Spot for Advancement for Women/Minorities: Y

Sales, profits and employees may be estimates. Financial information, benefits and other data can change quickly and may vary from those stated here.

GameStop Corp

NAIC Code: 451120

www.gamestop.com

TYPES OF BUSINESS:
Video Games-Retail
PC Software Sales
Game Accessories
Online Sales
Magazine Publication
Cellphone and Game Machine Refurbishing

BRANDS/DIVISIONS/AFFILIATES:
Spring Mobile
Simply Mac
Cricket
GameStop
Micromania
EB Games

CONTACTS:
Note: Officers with more than one job title may be intentionally listed here more than once.
J. Raines, CEO
Robert Lloyd, CFO
Daniel Dematteo, Chairman of the Board
Troy Crawford, Chief Accounting Officer
Tony Bartel, COO
Michael Hogan, Executive VP, Divisional
Michael Buskey, Executive VP, Divisional
Michael Mauler, Executive VP

GROWTH PLANS/SPECIAL FEATURES:

GameStop Corp. is a retailer of video and PC games. GameStop operates more than 7,275 company-operated stores worldwide, primarily in the U.S., Australia, Canada and Europe (as of early-2018). Business is divided into two segments: video game brands and technology brands. Video game brands is comprised of nearly 6,000 stores (3,864 are in the U.S.) which engage in the sale of new and pre-owned video game systems, software and accessories. They sell various types of digital products, such as downloadable content, network point cards, prepaid digital/online timecards and digitally-downloadable software. The technology brands segment includes GameStop's Spring Mobile and Simply Mac businesses. Spring Mobile sells post-paid AT&T services and wireless products through its 1,329 AT&T-branded stores, as well as related products and accessories. Spring Mobile also sells pre-paid AT&T services, wireless devices and accessories through its 69 Cricket-branded stores. Simply Mac operates 50 stores which sell Apple products, including desktop computers, laptops, tablets and smart phones, as well as related products and accessories. Substantially all of GameStop's U.S. and European stores are operated under the GameStop name, except for Micromania in France. Canadian and Australian stores operate under the EB Games name. GameStop distributes its video game products to its U.S. stores through two distribution centers in Grapevine, Texas, (519,000 square feet and 182,000 sf) and a 631,000-sf distribution center in Shepherdsville, Kentucky; its Canadian products from a distribution center in Brampton, Ontario; its Australian products from its Queensland distribution center; and its European products from its Milan, Italy distribution center.

GameStop offers its employees medical, dental, vision and prescription drug coverage; paid holidays/vacation; flexible spending accounts; short- and long-term disability; 401(k); tuition reimbursement; and employee discounts.

FINANCIAL DATA:
Note: Data for latest year may not have been available at press time.

In U.S. $	2018	2017	2016	2015	2014	2013
Revenue	9,224,600,000	8,607,900,000	9,363,800,000	9,296,000,000	9,039,500,000	8,886,700,000
R&D Expense						
Operating Income	526,400,000	591,500,000	652,800,000	620,500,000	602,200,000	639,100,000
Operating Margin %	5.7	6.87%	6.97%	6.67%	6.66%	7.19%
SGA Expense	2,363,000,000	2,252,600,000	2,108,900,000	2,001,000,000	1,892,400,000	1,835,900,000
Net Income	34,700,000	353,200,000	402,800,000	393,100,000	354,200,000	-269,700,000
Operating Cash Flow	434,900,000	537,100,000	656,800,000	480,500,000	762,700,000	632,400,000
Capital Expenditure	113,400,000	142,700,000	173,200,000	159,600,000	125,600,000	139,600,000
EBITDA	289,000,000	725,200,000	806,800,000	775,500,000	743,600,000	138,200,000
Return on Assets %	.69%	7.58%	9.38%	9.42%	8.61%	-6.00%
Return on Equity %	1.55%	16.29%	19.41%	18.20%	15.61%	-10.12%
Debt to Equity	0.36	0.36	0.16			

CONTACT INFORMATION:
Phone: 817 424-2000 Fax: 817 424-2062
Toll-Free: 800-883-8895
Address: 625 Westport Pkwy., Grapevine, TX 76051 United States

SALARIES/BONUSES:
Top Exec. Salary: $1,285,077 Bonus: $
Second Exec. Salary: $924,923 Bonus: $

STOCK TICKER/OTHER:
Stock Ticker: GME
Employees: 23,000
Parent Company:

Exchange: NYS
Fiscal Year Ends: 01/31

OTHER THOUGHTS:
Estimated Female Officers or Directors: 1
Hot Spot for Advancement for Women/Minorities:

Gaming Partners International Corporation

www.gpigaming.com

NAIC Code: 337127

TYPES OF BUSINESS:
Gaming Furniture and Accessories for Casinos
Gaming Furniture
Cards, Dice, Chips & Roulette Wheels
RFID-Equipped Devices
Gaming Table Accessories

BRANDS/DIVISIONS/AFFILIATES:
Gaming Partners International USA Inc
Gaming Partners International SAS
Gaming Partners International Asia Limited
GPI Mexicana SA de CV
Paulson
Bud Jones
Dolphin
Bourgogne et Grasset

CONTACTS: *Note: Officers with more than one job title may be intentionally listed here more than once.*
Alain Thieffry, CEO

GROWTH PLANS/SPECIAL FEATURES:
Gaming Partners International Corporation (GPI) manufactures gambling equipment, focusing on the manufacture and supply of gaming chips, table layouts, playing cards, gaming furniture, dice, radio frequency identification device (RFID) readers and software, roulette wheels and miscellaneous accessories to casinos worldwide. GPI, with its headquarters in Las Vegas, currently operates through three primary subsidiaries: Gaming Partners International USA, Inc. (GPI USA); Gaming Partners International SAS (GPI SAS); and Gaming Partners International Asia Limited (GPI Asia). GPI USA sells in the U.S., Canada, the Caribbean and Latin America. It sells GPI's full product line, with most of the products manufactured in either San Luis Rio Colorado, Mexico, or in Blue Springs, Missouri. Some products are manufactured in France or purchased from U.S. vendors. GPI Mexicana SA de CV is this segment's manufacturing operation in Mexico. GPI SAS sells primarily in Europe and Africa out of its office in Beaune, France. This division primarily sells casino currencies, including both American-style (chips) and European-style (plaques and jetons). GPI Asia, located in Macau, China, distributes all of GPI's currencies, radio frequency identification (RFID) product solutions, playing cards and other table accessories in the Asia-Pacific region. This division also sells layouts and upholstery manufactured in Macau. Brands and trademarks of the firm include Paulson, Bud Jones, Blue Chip, BC, Dolphin and Bourgogne et Grasset. In November 2018, GPI agreed to be acquired by Angel Holdings Godo Kaisha, and is subject to regulatory approval.

FINANCIAL DATA: *Note: Data for latest year may not have been available at press time.*

In U.S. $	2018	2017	2016	2015	2014	2013
Revenue		80,602,000	82,139,000	78,238,000	60,972,000	56,173,000
R&D Expense		1,517,000	1,188,000	1,215,000	1,521,000	1,959,000
Operating Income		5,526,000	7,560,000	9,909,000	2,188,000	619,000
Operating Margin %		6.85%	9.20%	12.66%	3.58%	1.10%
SGA Expense		15,635,000	16,588,000	15,711,000	14,606,000	15,011,000
Net Income		3,626,000	5,183,000	6,931,000	2,676,000	1,166,000
Operating Cash Flow		10,140,000	3,547,000	10,586,000	5,406,000	-4,008,000
Capital Expenditure		4,474,000	11,875,000	4,264,000	2,033,000	1,772,000
EBITDA		10,291,000	11,360,000	12,660,000	5,357,000	3,058,000
Return on Assets %		4.43%	6.59%	9.51%	4.32%	1.96%
Return on Equity %		6.10%	9.31%	13.58%	5.59%	2.47%
Debt to Equity		0.08	0.11	0.14		

CONTACT INFORMATION:
Phone: 702 384-2425 Fax: 702 384-1965
Toll-Free:
Address: 3945 West Cheyenne Ave., North Las Vegas, NV 89032 United States

STOCK TICKER/OTHER:
Stock Ticker: GPIC
Employees: 730
Parent Company:

Exchange: NAS
Fiscal Year Ends: 12/31

SALARIES/BONUSES:
Top Exec. Salary: $350,000   Bonus: $200,000
Second Exec. Salary: $ Bonus: $

OTHER THOUGHTS:
Estimated Female Officers or Directors: 1
Hot Spot for Advancement for Women/Minorities: Y

Sales, profits and employees may be estimates. Financial information, benefits and other data can change quickly and may vary from those stated here.

Gannett Co Inc

NAIC Code: 511110

www.gannett.com

TYPES OF BUSINESS:
Newspaper Publishing
Direct Marketing
Online Publishing
Electronic Information Services
Magazine Publishing

BRANDS/DIVISIONS/AFFILIATES:
USA TODAY NETWORK
Newsquest
ReachLocal Inc
ReachSearch
ReachDisplay
ReachSite+ReachEdge
ReachSEO
Kickserv

CONTACTS: Note: Officers with more than one job title may be intentionally listed here more than once.
Henry Faure Walker, CEO, Subsidiary
Robert Dickey, CEO
Alison Engel, CFO
John Louis, Chairman of the Board
Lori Locke, Chief Accounting Officer
Andrew Yost, Chief Marketing Officer
Jamshid Khazenie, Chief Technology Officer
David Harmon, Other Executive Officer
Barbara Wall, Other Executive Officer
Maribel Wadsworth, President, Divisional
Sharon Rowlands, President, Divisional

GROWTH PLANS/SPECIAL FEATURES:

Gannett Co., Inc. is an international media and marketing solutions company that delivers content to consumers through multiple platforms, including digital, mobile, print and broadcast media. Gannett publishes one of the nation's largest-selling daily print newspapers, USA TODAY NETWORK; 109 local media organizations in 34 states and Guam; and with more than 170 local news brands in the U.K. The firm reports in two operating segments, publishing and ReachLocal, Inc. The publishing segment is comprised of the USA TODAY NETWORK and Newsquest. USA TODAY is the largest newspaper in consolidated print and digital circulation on the U.S., with a total daily circulation of 5 million and Sunday circulation of 11 million. The wholly-owned subsidiary of Newsquest controls Gannett's U.K. based local media assets. Newsquest has a total average weekly readership of 5.7 million. Revenue in this segment is generated through both print and digital advertising, as well as through subscriptions to the various publications. The ReachLocal segment provides more customers to local businesses by helping these local businesses advertise online. The digital marketing firm groups its products into three categories: digital advertising, which includes such products as ReachSearch, ReachDisplay, ReachSocial Ads and ReachRetargeting; web presence, which includes such products as ReachSite+ReachEdge, ReachSEO, ReachCast, ReachListings and TotalLiveChat; and software-as-a-service, which includes such products as ReachEdge and Kickserv. ReachLocal conducts sales operations in the U.S., Canada, Australia, New Zealand, Japan, Germany, the Netherlands, Austria, Brazil and Mexico. In May 2018, Gannett agreed to acquire WordStream, Inc a provider of cloud-based software-as-a-service (SaaS) solutions for local and regional businesses and agencies to optimize their digital marketing services campaign, for $130 million.

The firm offers employees medical, dental and vision insurance; mental health and substance abuse coverage; an employee assistance program; a 401(k) plan; life insurance; an employee stock purchase plan; flexible spending accounts; and adoption assistance

FINANCIAL DATA: Note: Data for latest year may not have been available at press time.

In U.S. $	2018	2017	2016	2015	2014	2013
Revenue		3,146,480,000	3,047,474,000	2,885,012,000	3,171,878,000	3,324,939,000
R&D Expense						
Operating Income		158,651,000	137,259,000	203,709,000	297,547,000	351,684,000
Operating Margin %		5.04%	4.50%	7.06%	9.38%	10.57%
SGA Expense		836,306,000	807,398,000	707,022,000	765,465,000	773,409,000
Net Income		6,887,000	52,710,000	146,091,000	210,705,000	274,461,000
Operating Cash Flow		236,468,000	165,555,000	231,020,000	346,138,000	254,535,000
Capital Expenditure		72,325,000	60,048,000	53,979,000	72,307,000	53,619,000
EBITDA		249,768,000	212,183,000	311,261,000	408,610,000	461,782,000
Return on Assets %		.25%	1.99%	6.07%	8.63%	11.00%
Return on Equity %		.73%	5.50%	14.63%	19.13%	21.69%
Debt to Equity		0.34	0.46			

CONTACT INFORMATION:
Phone: 703 854-6000 Fax: 703 364-0855
Toll-Free:
Address: 7950 Jones Branch Dr., McLean, VA 22107 United States

STOCK TICKER/OTHER:
Stock Ticker: GCI
Employees: 17,100
Parent Company:

Exchange: NYS
Fiscal Year Ends: 12/31

SALARIES/BONUSES:
Top Exec. Salary: $967,308 Bonus: $
Second Exec. Salary: $231,346 Bonus: $621,720

OTHER THOUGHTS:
Estimated Female Officers or Directors: 5
Hot Spot for Advancement for Women/Minorities: Y

Sales, profits and employees may be estimates. Financial information, benefits and other data can change quickly and may vary from those stated here.

GateHouse Media LLC

www.gatehousemedia.com

NAIC Code: 511110

TYPES OF BUSINESS:
Newspaper Publishing
Community & Small Town Newspapers
Printing Services
Niche Publications

BRANDS/DIVISIONS/AFFILIATES:
New Media Investment Group Inc
UpCurve
Creative Solutions
Center for News & Design
ThriveHive
GateHouse Live
UpCurve Cloud
Southern Kitchen

CONTACTS:
Note: Officers with more than one job title may be intentionally listed here more than once.

Kirk Davis, CEO
Kirk A. Davis, Pres.
Keri Curtis, Chief Accounting Officer
Paul Ameden, CIO
Polly G. Sack, General Counsel
Mark Maring, VP-Investor Rel.
Mark Maring, Treas.
Brad Dennison, VP-Publishing, Large Daily Div.
David Arkin, VP-Content & Audience
Jay Fogarty, VP-New Revenue Platforms
Nick Monico, VP-Publishing, Community Div.

GROWTH PLANS/SPECIAL FEATURES:
GateHouse Media, LLC is a publisher of locally-based print and online media in the U.S. The company's portfolio of products includes 145 daily newspapers, more than 325 community publications and over 555 local market websites and 37 states. The firm's local content comprises various community publications, related websites, as well as directories for business advertising accounts. Its publications focus on hyper-local news, and offer useful information, depth, analysis and multimedia content. GateHouse Media reaches over 23 million people on a weekly basis through its community publications and local websites. The company's UpCurve division provides marketing, digital solutions and cloud services to small- and mid-sized businesses. UpCurve Cloud offers businesses tools to integrate business-related technologies onto one platform. GateHouse's ThriveHive helps businesses grow their companies via easy-to-use technology used for marketing purposes. The firm's Creative Solutions platform offers full creative services to businesses of all sizes, whether it be creating graphics, full-page ads, annual campaigns or newsletters. Its Center for News & Design, based in Austin, Texas, serves 93 daily and 203 weekly GateHouse newspapers, and 8 newspaper partners. GateHouse Live is an event production company specializing in delivering world-class events for the media industry. GateHouse Media operates as a wholly-owned subsidiary of New Media Investment Group, Inc. In 2018, the firm acquired Online Automotive Solutions, a video, data, and auto-focused inventory solutions provider; the Austin American-Statesman in Austin, Texas; The Palm Beach Post and Palm Beach Daily News in Palm Beach, Florida; the Akron Beacon Journal in Akron, Ohio; and Southern Kitchen, an Atlanta-based Southern food and lifestyle brand. Gatehouse Media sold GateHouse Media Alaska Holdings, Inc. to Black Press Ltd. in May 2018.

FINANCIAL DATA:
Note: Data for latest year may not have been available at press time.

In U.S. $	2018	2017	2016	2015	2014	2013
Revenue	328,000,000	318,000,000	315,000,000	310,000,000	300,000,000	314,929,984
R&D Expense						
Operating Income						
Operating Margin %						
SGA Expense						
Net Income						
Operating Cash Flow						
Capital Expenditure						
EBITDA						
Return on Assets %						
Return on Equity %						
Debt to Equity						

CONTACT INFORMATION:
Phone: 585 598-0030   Fax: 585 248-2631
Toll-Free:
Address: 175 Sully's Trail, 3/Fl, Corporate Crossing Office Park, Pittsford, NY 14534 United States

SALARIES/BONUSES:
Top Exec. Salary: $ Bonus: $
Second Exec. Salary: $ Bonus: $

STOCK TICKER/OTHER:
Stock Ticker: Private   Exchange:
Employees: 5,720   Fiscal Year Ends: 12/31
Parent Company: New Media Investment Group Inc

OTHER THOUGHTS:
Estimated Female Officers or Directors: 2
Hot Spot for Advancement for Women/Minorities: Y

Genting Singapore PLC

NAIC Code: 721120

www.gentingsingapore.com

TYPES OF BUSINESS:
Casinos & Resorts Development & Operation

BRANDS/DIVISIONS/AFFILIATES:
Genting Group
Resort World Sentosa
SEA Aquarium
Adventure Cove Waterpark
Universal Studios Singapore
ESPA

CONTACTS:
Note: Officers with more than one job title may be intentionally listed here more than once.

Tan Hee Teck, COO
Tan Hee Teck, Pres.
Tay Wei Heng Terence, General Counsel
Yap Chee Yuen, Head-Mgmt. Oper.
Krist Boo, Head-Comm.
Roger Lienhard, Head-Hospitality Dev. & Projects
Tan Sri Lim Kok Thay, Chmn.

GROWTH PLANS/SPECIAL FEATURES:
Genting Singapore PLC, a member of the Genting Group, is a global developer, operator and marketer of casinos and integrated resorts in Australia, the Bahamas, the U.K., Malaysia, Singapore and the Philippines. The principle activities of the company include resort development, casino operations, international sales and marketing services and IT application related services. The firm's property portfolio includes: Resort World Sentosa, located on Singapore's resort island Sentosa, one of the largest fully-integrated resorts in South East Asia, with six hotels comprising different themes and approximately 1,600 rooms total; S.E.A. Aquarium, an aquatic park integrated with marine life; Adventure Cove Waterpark, a Universal Studios theme park in Southeast Asia; Universal Studios Singapore, a spa destination in Singapore; and ESPA, a major destination spa with a wide selection of indoor and outdoor MICE (meetings, incentives, conferencing and exhibitions) venues, as well as dining, retail and entertainment options. In addition, the Resort World's casino comprises more than 550 gaming tables and over 2,400 slots and electronic table games, as well as exclusive and private club rooms. Genting Singapore's locations offer more than 60 restaurants, cafes and bars.

FINANCIAL DATA:
Note: Data for latest year may not have been available at press time.

In U.S. $	2018	2017	2016	2015	2014	2013
Revenue		1,753,947,000	1,633,348,000	1,760,060,000	2,098,442,000	2,087,321,000
R&D Expense						
Operating Income		654,122,900	401,294,600	422,957,300	712,881,000	555,750,300
Operating Margin %		37.29%	24.56%	24.03%	33.97%	26.62%
SGA Expense		160,925,900	158,603,500	184,686,600	214,295,100	248,204,000
Net Income		502,569,500	281,905,300	141,529,900	465,659,400	518,516,300
Operating Cash Flow		920,662,700	853,919,800	925,098,600	700,536,600	601,511,600
Capital Expenditure		57,399,020	101,271,200	129,311,600	143,010,800	329,014,700
EBITDA		854,643,300	604,073,000	486,833,100	918,515,500	956,486,300
Return on Assets %		5.70%	2.26%	.60%	4.01%	4.52%
Return on Equity %		7.08%	2.78%	.77%	6.24%	7.46%
Debt to Equity		0.13	0.10	0.15	0.12	

CONTACT INFORMATION:
Phone: 65-6577-8888 Fax: 65-6577-8890
Toll-Free:
Address: 10 Sentosa Gateway, Resorts World Sentosa, Singapore, 098270 Singapore

STOCK TICKER/OTHER:
Stock Ticker: GIGNF
Employees: 9,935
Parent Company: Genting Group
Exchange: PINX
Fiscal Year Ends: 12/31

SALARIES/BONUSES:
Top Exec. Salary: $ Bonus: $
Second Exec. Salary: $ Bonus: $

OTHER THOUGHTS:
Estimated Female Officers or Directors: 1
Hot Spot for Advancement for Women/Minorities:

Sales, profits and employees may be estimates. Financial information, benefits and other data can change quickly and may vary from those stated here.

GigaMedia Limited

www.gigamedia.com

NAIC Code: 511210G

TYPES OF BUSINESS:
Computer Software, Electronic Games, Apps & Entertainment
Online Gaming Services
Apps

BRANDS/DIVISIONS/AFFILIATES:
FunTown World Limited
GigaCloud Media

CONTACTS:
Note: Officers with more than one job title may be intentionally listed here more than once.
James Cheng Ming Huang, CEO

GROWTH PLANS/SPECIAL FEATURES:
GigaMedia Limited is a diversified provider of digital entertainment services in Taiwan, Hong Kong and Macau. The firm operates through two business segments: digital entertainment and cloud computing. The digital entertainment segment consists of wholly-owned FunTown World Limited, a digital entertainment portal in Taiwan and Hong Kong, which is focused on the mobile and online casual games market in Asia. FunTown develops and monetizes PC-based casual games, most of which are operated under the item-billing revenue model, where users can access the basic functions of the company's casual online games free of charge. Players have the option to purchase in-game value-added services as well as in-game virtual items and premium features to enhance the game experience. Digital entertainment products include MahJong, a Chinese tile game, as well as various card and table games. FunTown offers more than 40 PC-based casual games and one sports game, one web-based roll-playing game and several mobile games. The firm also offers eight massively multiplayer online role-playing games (MMORPGs) and three massively multiplayer online games (MMOs) of other sub-genres through FunTown. The cloud computing segment consists of wholly-owned GigaCloud Media, a provider of computing solutions and related services, with a focus on serving the company-wide, internal business of GigaMedia. This division (cloud computing) is in wind-down status, as of 2018.

FINANCIAL DATA:
Note: Data for latest year may not have been available at press time.

In U.S. $	2018	2017	2016	2015	2014	2013
Revenue		11,596,000	8,971,000	10,251,000	9,779,000	15,032,000
R&D Expense		1,072,000	1,045,000	688,000	892,000	1,698,000
Operating Income		-2,222,000	-5,181,000	-13,740,000	-12,071,000	-5,426,000
Operating Margin %		-19.16%	-57.75%	-134.03%	-123.43%	-36.09%
SGA Expense		7,521,000	8,969,000	14,414,000	13,086,000	11,139,000
Net Income		1,086,000	-6,066,000	-2,243,000	-5,155,000	-34,780,000
Operating Cash Flow		-1,110,000	-5,688,000	-16,845,000	-10,838,000	-4,305,000
Capital Expenditure		203,000	582,000	270,000	530,000	1,452,000
EBITDA		-496,000	-6,861,000	-1,981,000	-3,303,000	-32,318,000
Return on Assets %		1.58%	-8.00%	-2.36%	-4.87%	-28.54%
Return on Equity %		1.79%	-9.65%	-3.09%	-6.15%	-33.65%
Debt to Equity						

CONTACT INFORMATION:
Phone: 886 226568016   Fax: 886 226568003
Toll-Free:
Address: 8/Fl, No. 22, Lane 407, Section 2 Tiding Blvd., Taipei, 114 Taiwan

STOCK TICKER/OTHER:
Stock Ticker: GIGM
Employees: 150
Parent Company:

Exchange: NAS
Fiscal Year Ends: 12/31

SALARIES/BONUSES:
Top Exec. Salary: $ Bonus: $
Second Exec. Salary: $ Bonus: $

OTHER THOUGHTS:
Estimated Female Officers or Directors:
Hot Spot for Advancement for Women/Minorities:

Global Eagle Entertainment Inc

www.geemedia.com

NAIC Code: 517410

TYPES OF BUSINESS:
Satellite Telecommunications

BRANDS/DIVISIONS/AFFILIATES:

CONTACTS: *Note: Officers with more than one job title may be intentionally listed here more than once.*
Joshua Marks, CEO
Jeffrey Leddy, Chairman of the Board
Sarlina See, Chief Accounting Officer
Paul Rainey, Executive VP
Stephen Ballas, Executive VP
Per Noren, Executive VP
Wale Adepoju, Executive VP

GROWTH PLANS/SPECIAL FEATURES:
Global Eagle Entertainment, Inc. provides satellite-based connectivity and media to fast-growing, global enterprise, consumer and government markets across aviation, maritime and land. Through the firm's proprietary and other technologies, Global Eagle entertains, informs and connects travelers and crew with its integrated suite of rich media content and seamless connectivity solutions that cover the globe. The company operates through two business segments: connectivity and media and content. The connectivity segment provides satellite-based connectivity services to enterprise and government customers in the aviation, maritime and land vertical markets. These services include: Wi-Fi connectivity that enables access to the internet, live television, texting services, eCommerce, on-demand content and travel-related information; and connectivity-enabled solutions for advertising, operational performance management and analytics that enable customers to increase profitability through the generation of new revenue streams and efficient operations. This segment connects aircraft, vessels and fixed ground stations to orbiting satellites which link data to ground earth stations. Global Eagle develops, integrates and sells, leases and/or provides a right to use provides a right to use proprietary third-party manufactured antenna systems for connectivity customers. The media and content segment buys, produces, manages, distributes and provides post-production services and wholly-owned and licensed media content, video and music programming, advertising, applications and video games for and to the airline, maritime and other away-from-home, non-theatrical markets.

FINANCIAL DATA: *Note: Data for latest year may not have been available at press time.*

In U.S. $	2018	2017	2016	2015	2014	2013
Revenue		619,469,000	529,755,000	426,030,000	387,735,000	259,722,000
R&D Expense		35,608,000	37,718,000	28,610,000	23,010,000	9,068,000
Operating Income		-112,808,000	-98,663,000	-8,400,000	-32,760,000	-45,524,000
Operating Margin %		-18.21%	-18.62%	-1.97%	-8.44%	-17.52%
SGA Expense		189,159,000	146,136,000	99,670,000	91,060,000	80,959,000
Net Income		-357,114,000	-112,932,000	-2,126,000	-57,388,000	-115,031,000
Operating Cash Flow		-53,707,000	-36,600,000	21,575,000	-23,395,000	-54,145,000
Capital Expenditure		74,994,000	54,173,000	20,653,000	9,074,000	11,477,000
EBITDA		-22,954,000	-26,573,000	28,192,000	1,662,000	-14,674,000
Return on Assets %		-36.43%	-12.98%	-.36%	-10.31%	-29.92%
Return on Equity %		-261.12%	-34.60%	-.63%	-17.43%	-65.58%
Debt to Equity			1.56	0.20		

CONTACT INFORMATION:
Phone: 310-437-6000   Fax:
Toll-Free:
Address: 6100 Center Dr., Ste. 1020, Los Angeles, CA 90045 United States

STOCK TICKER/OTHER:
Stock Ticker: ENT   Exchange: NAS
Employees: 781   Fiscal Year Ends: 12/31
Parent Company:

SALARIES/BONUSES:
Top Exec. Salary: $425,893   Bonus: $185,000
Second Exec. Salary: $372,500   Bonus: $175,000

OTHER THOUGHTS:
Estimated Female Officers or Directors:
Hot Spot for Advancement for Women/Minorities:

Sales, profits and employees may be estimates. Financial information, benefits and other data can change quickly and may vary from those stated here.

Globo Comunicacao e Participacoes SA (Grupo Globo)

grupoglobo.globo.com
NAIC Code: 515120

TYPES OF BUSINESS:
Television Broadcasting
Radio Stations
Internet Services
Satellite Television
Newspapers
Magazines

BRANDS/DIVISIONS/AFFILIATES:
Globo
Rede Globo
TV Globo
Globo Filmes
Globosat
Infoglobo
Editora Globo
Som Livre

CONTACTS: Note: Officers with more than one job title may be intentionally listed here more than once.
Jorge Nobrega, Pres.
Sergio Marques, Dir. Of Finance and Investor Relations
Claudia Falcao, Corporate Dir. Of Human Resources

GROWTH PLANS/SPECIAL FEATURES:

Globo Comunicacao e Participacoes SA (Globo) is the largest media group in Brazil. Globo Comunicacao controls the leading broadcast television network, the leading pay-TV programmer in Brazil and a diversified group of publishing, Internet content and music label companies. TV Globo (Rede Globo), founded in 1965, is a free-to-air commercial television network. TV Globo's programming is distributed throughout Brazil, on five stations, and in 100 countries through affiliates. Globo Filmes produces and co-produces films in Brazil for a wide audience. Globosat is a pay-TV programmer with a diversified portfolio of more than 30 channels and 24-hour daily television programming. Infoglobo brings together newspapers O Globo, Extra, Expresso and Valor Economico. Editora Globo edits classic books and contemporary books through Globo Books, a book seller in Brazil. Som Livre focuses on music, producing and commercializing Brazilian artists though physical sales, digital sales and live events. The ZAP is an online classified portal of national action with a focus on the real estate market. Globo.com is the company's technology services provider and supports digital planning. The Global Radio System brings together Globo's broadcasters and offers programming for multiple platforms in talk, news and musical segments. Globo is part of Organizacoes Globo Participacoes SA, a diversified media group.

FINANCIAL DATA: Note: Data for latest year may not have been available at press time.

In U.S. $	2018	2017	2016	2015	2014	2013
Revenue						
R&D Expense						
Operating Income						
Operating Margin %						
SGA Expense						
Net Income						
Operating Cash Flow						
Capital Expenditure						
EBITDA						
Return on Assets %						
Return on Equity %						
Debt to Equity						

CONTACT INFORMATION:
Phone: 55-21-2129-0009 Fax:
Toll-Free:
Address: R. Lopes Quintas, 303 - Jardim Botanico, Rio de Janeiro, RJ 22460-000 Brazil

STOCK TICKER/OTHER:
Stock Ticker: Private
Employees:
Parent Company: Organizacoes Globo Participacoes SA
Exchange:
Fiscal Year Ends:

SALARIES/BONUSES:
Top Exec. Salary: $ Bonus: $
Second Exec. Salary: $ Bonus: $

OTHER THOUGHTS:
Estimated Female Officers or Directors:
Hot Spot for Advancement for Women/Minorities:

Glu Mobile Inc

NAIC Code: 511210G

www.glu.com

TYPES OF BUSINESS:
Computer Software, Electronic Games, Apps & Entertainment
Mobile Phone Games
Apps

BRANDS/DIVISIONS/AFFILIATES:
Blood & Glory
Contract Killer
Cooking Dash
Deer Hunter
Racing Rivals
Kim Kardashian: Hollywood
Gordon Ramsay DASH
Tencent Holdings Limited

CONTACTS:
Note: Officers with more than one job title may be intentionally listed here more than once.

Eric Ludwig, CFO
Niccolo de Masi, Chairman of the Board
Gordon Lee, Chief Accounting Officer
Nicholas Earl, Director
Scott Leichtner, General Counsel
Chris Akhavan, Other Executive Officer

GROWTH PLANS/SPECIAL FEATURES:
Glu Mobile, Inc. is a global developer and publisher of free-to-play mobile games for smartphones, tablet devices and social networking websites. The company designs games for a large swath of users who make in-game purchases. The company has developed and published an extensive portfolio of casual and traditional games across a number of genres, including action, board game, card/casino, puzzle, sports, strategy/role playing and television/movie. The firm creates games and related applications based on third-party licensed brands and other intellectual property as well as on its own original brands and intellectual property. Glu Mobile's business leverages the marketing resources and distribution infrastructure of wireless carriers and the brands and other intellectual property of third-party content owners, in order to focus on developing and publishing mobile games. Original Glu Mobile games include Space Monkey, Bonsai Blast, Super K.O. Boxing, Brain Genius, Hero Project, Magic Life, Zombie Isle and Beat It! Its current games based on its own brands include Blood & Glory, Contract Killer, Cooking Dash, Deer Hunter, Diner Dash, Eternity Warriors, Frontline Commando, Gun Bros, Heroes of Destiny, QuizUp, Racing Rivals and Tap Sports. The company's marketed third-party licensed games include Kim Kardashian: Hollywood, Kendall & Kylie, Gordon Ramsay DASH and MLB Tap Sports Baseball 2018. Its most recent third-party celebrity game features global music star Taylor Swift. Glu Mobile has 3.8 million daily active users, 28.6 million monthly active users and approximately 1.7 billion cumulative game installs on primary distribution platforms. Glu Mobile has offices in the U.S, Canada and India. In February 2018, Glu announced it was working with Disney Consumer Products and Interactive Media to develop upcoming games based on character and stories from Disney and Pixar franchises.

FINANCIAL DATA:
Note: Data for latest year may not have been available at press time.

In U.S. $	2018	2017	2016	2015	2014	2013
Revenue		286,827,000	200,581,000	249,900,000	223,146,000	105,613,000
R&D Expense		92,420,000	81,879,000	72,856,000	64,284,000	46,877,000
Operating Income		-85,527,000	-79,711,000	-5,226,000	2,500,000	-21,314,000
Operating Margin %		-29.81%	-39.74%	-2.09%	1.12%	-20.18%
SGA Expense		138,781,000	78,275,000	74,332,000	70,095,000	41,670,000
Net Income		-97,570,000	-87,440,000	-7,185,000	8,148,000	-19,909,000
Operating Cash Flow		-28,236,000	-19,784,000	-11,465,000	30,574,000	-9,578,000
Capital Expenditure		11,344,000	5,570,000	5,251,000	3,292,000	2,975,000
EBITDA		-82,332,000	-61,972,000	7,389,000	10,288,000	-13,033,000
Return on Assets %		-30.54%	-23.55%	-2.19%	4.81%	-24.99%
Return on Equity %		-50.46%	-32.43%	-3.00%	7.46%	-46.52%
Debt to Equity						

CONTACT INFORMATION:
Phone: 415-800-6100 Fax: 415-800-6087
Toll-Free:
Address: 500 Howard St., Ste. 300, San Francisco, CA 94105 United States

STOCK TICKER/OTHER:
Stock Ticker: GLUU
Employees: 754
Parent Company:

Exchange: NAS
Fiscal Year Ends: 12/31

SALARIES/BONUSES:
Top Exec. Salary: $450,000 Bonus: $
Second Exec. Salary: $375,000 Bonus: $

OTHER THOUGHTS:
Estimated Female Officers or Directors: 3
Hot Spot for Advancement for Women/Minorities: Y

Sales, profits and employees may be estimates. Financial information, benefits and other data can change quickly and may vary from those stated here.

GMM Grammy PCL

NAIC Code: 512230

www.gmmgrammy.com

TYPES OF BUSINESS:
Music & Entertainment Media Production & Publishing
Marketing Services
Media
Music

BRANDS/DIVISIONS/AFFILIATES:
GMM 25
ONE31
GDH 559 Co Ltd
GMM CJ O Shopping Co Ltd
Chill Online
Bad Genius
GMM Z Satellite TV
Satellite TV Media

CONTACTS:
Note: Officers with more than one job title may be intentionally listed here more than once.

Boosaba Daorueng, CEO
Karnsuda Sansuthi, CFO
Jiraporn Rungsrithong, Interim Chief Admin. Officer
Saithip Montrikul Na Audhaya, CEO-Media Bus.
Jiraporn Rungsrithong, Chief Investment Officer
Kanchit Kawachat, CEO-Digital TV Bus.
Krij Thomas, CEO-Music Bus.
Paiboon Damrongchaitham, Chmn.

GROWTH PLANS/SPECIAL FEATURES:
GMM Grammy PCL is a Thailand-based holding company engaged in the entertainment and multimedia industry. The company consolidates its business model and operating structure into two groups: core business and other business. The core business group is comprised of GMM's music and digital terrestrial TV businesses. The music business includes the sale and distribution of physical products, digital content, copyright management, show business and artist management. The digital terrestrial TV business includes two channels: GMM 25, which is under standard definition; and One31, which is under high definition. The other business group is comprised of GMM's radio, movie, home shopping and satellite TV businesses. The radio business includes three radio stations: Chill Online, a 24-hour/day online station for urban society, covering dining/travel/shopping and music; EFM 104.5, a 24-hour business radio station; and FM 106.5, a 24-hour easy listening music station. The movie business operates under subsidiary GDH 559 Co. Ltd., which released two films in fiscal 2017-18, namely Bad Genius and The Promise. The home shopping business is a 24-hour distribution of goods through program channel O-Shopping, where customers can choose products and shop from home or online. This business is managed by GMM CJ O Shopping Co. Ltd., a joint venture between GMM and CJ O Shopping Co. Ltd. The satellite TV business is divided into two components: GMM Z Satellite TV and Satellite TV Media. GMM Z is responsible for the sale of satellite TV set-top-box to consumers. Satellite TV Media is the production of TV shows to be aired on satellite TV channels. This group has produced free-to-air television programs for audiences of every platform transmitted via Thai-Com. These programs provide pop, rock, dance, and local folk music and songs, as well as financial and investment information.

FINANCIAL DATA:
Note: Data for latest year may not have been available at press time.

In U.S. $	2018	2017	2016	2015	2014	2013
Revenue		271,334,000	204,280,000	274,054,351	282,297,216	333,842,596
R&D Expense						
Operating Income						
Operating Margin %						
SGA Expense						
Net Income		-11,767,300	-14,561,400	-33,314,071	-65,121,698	-37,050,041
Operating Cash Flow						
Capital Expenditure						
EBITDA						
Return on Assets %						
Return on Equity %						
Debt to Equity						

CONTACT INFORMATION:
Phone: 66-2-669-9000   Fax: 66-2-666-8137
Toll-Free:
Address: 50 GMM Grammy Place, 21 Sukhumvit Rd., Bangkok, 10110 Thailand

STOCK TICKER/OTHER:
Stock Ticker: GRAMMY
Employees: 2,632
Parent Company:

Exchange: Bangkok
Fiscal Year Ends: 12/31

SALARIES/BONUSES:
Top Exec. Salary: $ Bonus: $
Second Exec. Salary: $ Bonus: $

OTHER THOUGHTS:
Estimated Female Officers or Directors: 3
Hot Spot for Advancement for Women/Minorities: Y

Sales, profits and employees may be estimates. Financial information, benefits and other data can change quickly and may vary from those stated here.

Golden Entertainment Inc

NAIC Code: 721120

www.goldenent.com

TYPES OF BUSINESS:
Casino Hotels
Racetracks

BRANDS/DIVISIONS/AFFILIATES:
PT's Pub
PT's Gold
Sierra Gold
PT's Brewing Company
Rocky Gap Casino Resort
Pahrump Nugget Hotel Casino
Gold Town Casino
T-Bird Lounge & Restaurant

CONTACTS:
Note: Officers with more than one job title may be intentionally listed here more than once.

Charles Protell, CFO
Blake Sartini, Chairman of the Board
Stephen Arcana, COO
Sean Higgins, Executive VP, Divisional
Edward Martin, Executive VP
Blake Sartini, Senior VP, Divisional
Gary Vecchiarelli, Senior VP, Divisional
Thomas Haas, Senior VP, Divisional

GROWTH PLANS/SPECIAL FEATURES:

Golden Entertainment, Inc. is a diverse gaming company that operates through two segments: distributed gaming and casinos. The distributed gaming segment is comprised of the installation, maintenance and operation of gaming devices in certain strategic, high-traffic, non-casino locations (such as grocery stores, convenience stores, restaurants and bars); and the operation of traditional, branded taverns targeting local patrons primarily in the Las Vegas, Nevada metropolitan area. This division has more than 10,900 game slot devices in over 1,000 locations. The taverns offer a casually-upscale environment and serve food and alcoholic beverages, and typically include 15 onsite gaming devices. This segment operates 57 taverns under PT's Pub, PT's Gold, PT's Place, PT's Ranch, Sierra Gold, SG Bar and Sean Patrick's brand names. It also owns and operates PT's Brewing Company, located in Las Vegas, which produces craft beer for the company's taverns and casinos, as well as for other establishments. The casinos segment owns and operates Rocky Gap Casino Resort in Flintstone, Maryland; and three casinos in Pahrump, Nevada: Pahrump Nugget Hotel Casino, Gold Town Casino and Lakeside Casino & RV Park. Rocky Gap offers 665 gaming devices, 17 table games, two casino bars, three restaurants, a spa and a Jack Nicklaus golf course. It has a four-diamond hotel with 200 rooms, as well as an event and conference center. Pahrump Nugget offers 419 gaming devices, eight table games, a race and sports book, a 200-seat bingo facility and a bowling center. Its three-diamond hotel is comprised of 70 rooms. Gold Town Casino offers 226 gaming devices and a 100-seat bingo facility. Lakeside is located on approximately 35 acres, and offers 188 gaming devices, as well as 160 RV hook-up sites. During 2018, the firm acquired T-Bird Lounge & Restaurant; and agreed to acquire the Colorado Belle and Edgewater in Laughlin, Nevada.

FINANCIAL DATA:
Note: Data for latest year may not have been available at press time.

In U.S. $	2018	2017	2016	2015	2014	2013
Revenue		509,808,000	403,204,000	177,042,000	55,172,000	38,790,000
R&D Expense						
Operating Income		20,126,000	14,740,000	6,667,000	-2,822,000	-4,226,000
Operating Margin %		3.94%	3.65%	3.76%	-5.11%	-10.89%
SGA Expense		105,155,000	70,626,000	38,708,000	22,566,000	20,516,000
Net Income		2,171,000	16,300,000	24,520,000	-24,845,000	18,651,000
Operating Cash Flow		22,102,000	37,395,000	9,342,000	1,285,000	3,530,000
Capital Expenditure		29,463,000	30,634,000	7,946,000	4,516,000	20,695,000
EBITDA		60,912,000	42,246,000	28,159,000	-20,123,000	22,884,000
Return on Assets %		.24%	4.08%	9.79%	-18.45%	13.97%
Return on Equity %		.81%	7.76%	15.41%	-20.73%	15.27%
Debt to Equity		3.00	0.80	0.66	0.08	0.07

CONTACT INFORMATION:
Phone: 702-893-7777   Fax:
Toll-Free:
Address: 6595 S. Jones Blvd., Las Vegas, NV 89118 United States

SALARIES/BONUSES:
Top Exec. Salary: $500,000   Bonus: $1,700,000
Second Exec. Salary: $1,000,000   Bonus: $

STOCK TICKER/OTHER:
Stock Ticker: GDEN   Exchange: NAS
Employees: 2,802   Fiscal Year Ends: 11/30
Parent Company:

OTHER THOUGHTS:
Estimated Female Officers or Directors:
Hot Spot for Advancement for Women/Minorities:

Sales, profits and employees may be estimates. Financial information, benefits and other data can change quickly and may vary from those stated here.

Graham Holdings Company

www.ghco.com

NAIC Code: 515120

TYPES OF BUSINESS:
Television Broadcasting
Internet Publishing
Cable Television Systems
Magazine Publishing
Educational Services
Printing/Distribution Services

BRANDS/DIVISIONS/AFFILIATES:
Kaplan Inc
Slate Group LLC (The)
Foreign Policy
Panoply
Kaplan University
Graham Media Group Inc
Social Code LLC
Graham Healthcare Group

CONTACTS:
Note: Officers with more than one job title may be intentionally listed here more than once.

Andrew Rosen, CEO, Subsidiary
Timothy O'Shaughnessy, CEO
Wallace Cooney, CFO
Donald Graham, Chairman of the Board
Nicole Maddrey, General Counsel
Denise Demeter, Other Executive Officer
Jacob Maas, Senior VP, Divisional
Marcel Snyman, Vice President

GROWTH PLANS/SPECIAL FEATURES:

Graham Holdings Company is a diversified education and media company. The firm's Kaplan, Inc. subsidiary provides educational services, both domestically and outside the U.S. Graham Holdings' media operations comprise the ownership and operation of television broadcasting, as well as two magazines, Slate and Foreign Policy, and a podcast network, Panoply. The company also owns home health and hospice providers, industrial companies, a marketing solutions provider and more. Kaplan offers an extensive range of education and related services worldwide for students and professionals. It conducts its operations through the three segments of: Kaplan higher education (Kaplan University), Kaplan test preparation and Kaplan international. Subsidiary Graham Media Group, Inc. owns seven television stations located in Houston and San Antonio, Texas; Detroit, Michigan; Orlando and Jacksonville (2), Florida; and Roanoke, Virginia. Graham Media also owns SocialNewsDesk, a provider of social media management tools designed to connect newsrooms with their users. The Slate Group, LLC publishes Slate, a left-leaning online magazine featuring articles and podcasts analyzing news, politics and contemporary culture. The FP Group produces the Foreign Policy magazine and the ForeignPolicy.com website, which cover developments in national security, international politics, global economics and related issues. Panoply is an ad-supported podcast network that creates original audio programming in partnership with leading publishers and thinkers. Panoply also licenses a proprietary SAAS platform, Megaphone, that provides content management services to podcasters. Social Code, LLC is a marketing and insights company that manages digital advertising for leading brands. The Graham Healthcare Group provides home health and hospice services in three states. Other subsidiaries include Forney Corporation; Joyce/Dayton Corp.; Group Dekko, Inc.; CyberVista, LLC; and Hoover Treated Wood Products, Inc.

FINANCIAL DATA:
Note: Data for latest year may not have been available at press time.

In U.S. $	2018	2017	2016	2015	2014	2013
Revenue		2,591,846,000	2,481,890,000	2,586,114,000	3,535,166,000	3,487,864,000
R&D Expense						
Operating Income		218,716,000	305,137,000	178,875,000	425,234,000	348,815,000
Operating Margin %		8.43%	12.29%	6.91%	12.02%	10.00%
SGA Expense		909,592,000	904,517,000	1,104,163,000	1,325,558,000	1,327,322,000
Net Income		302,044,000	168,590,000	-100,655,000	1,293,843,000	236,865,000
Operating Cash Flow		268,055,000	261,256,000	74,804,000	372,370,000	327,864,000
Capital Expenditure		60,358,000	66,612,000	136,859,000	237,292,000	224,093,000
EBITDA		329,985,000	378,942,000	80,501,000	1,588,078,000	602,153,000
Return on Assets %		6.44%	3.83%	-2.00%	22.36%	4.32%
Return on Equity %		11.25%	6.82%	-3.59%	40.15%	8.01%
Debt to Equity		0.16	0.19	0.16	0.12	0.13

CONTACT INFORMATION:
Phone: 703-345-6300 Fax:
Toll-Free:
Address: 1300 N. 17th St., 17/Fl, Arlington, VA 22209 United States

SALARIES/BONUSES:
Top Exec. Salary: $1,625,000 Bonus: $
Second Exec. Salary: $750,000 Bonus: $

STOCK TICKER/OTHER:
Stock Ticker: GHC
Employees: 11,300
Parent Company:

Exchange: NYS
Fiscal Year Ends: 12/31

OTHER THOUGHTS:
Estimated Female Officers or Directors: 12
Hot Spot for Advancement for Women/Minorities: Y

Gray Television Inc

NAIC Code: 515120

www.gray.tv

TYPES OF BUSINESS:
Television Broadcasting

BRANDS/DIVISIONS/AFFILIATES:
Raycom Media, Inc.

CONTACTS: Note: Officers with more than one job title may be intentionally listed here more than once.
James Ryan, CFO
Hilton Howell, Chairman of the Board
Jackson Cowart, Chief Accounting Officer
Donald LaPlatney, Co-CEO
Kevin Latek, Executive VP

GROWTH PLANS/SPECIAL FEATURES:
Gray Television, Inc. is a television broadcasting company that provides news and entertainment services to the local markets in which it operates. The firm owns and/or operates more than 100 television stations across 57 television markets that collectively broadcast over 200 program streams within the CBS Network, the NBC Network and the FOX Network. Gray broadcasts and operates secondary channels affiliated with networks different from the primary channels, and broadcasts local news/weather channels in certain areas of its existing markets. The combined TV station group reaches approximately 10.6% of total U.S. households. Gray's stations affiliated with the primary networks receive the majority of each day's programming from their respective networks, which in turn retains ownership of a majority of the available advertising time during the network programming. Its stations affiliated with other networks receive less of their content from their respective affiliates and must purchase or produce a greater amount of their programming. This results in generally higher programming costs but allows these stations to retain the majority of their advertising revenues. Overall operating revenues of Gray's television stations are derived primarily from broadcast advertising revenues and internet advertising revenues, as well as from ancillary services. In January 2019, Gray Television acquired Raycom Media, Inc. in a transformation transaction that creates the single largest owner of top-rated local television stations and digital assets in the U.S. As part of the merger process, Gray sold eight television stations in eight markets (August 2018) in which both it and Raycom owned stations to ensure that competition in those markets would not be reduced, per regulatory requirements.

FINANCIAL DATA: Note: Data for latest year may not have been available at press time.

In U.S. $	2018	2017	2016	2015	2014	2013
Revenue		882,728,000	812,465,000	597,356,000	508,134,000	346,298,000
R&D Expense						
Operating Income		217,026,000	234,468,000	140,137,000	154,396,000	84,645,000
Operating Margin %		24.58%	28.85%	23.45%	30.38%	24.44%
SGA Expense		31,541,000	40,347,000	34,343,000	29,203,000	19,810,000
Net Income		261,952,000	62,273,000	39,301,000	48,061,000	18,288,000
Operating Cash Flow		180,015,000	206,633,000	105,614,000	134,219,000	60,239,000
Capital Expenditure		34,516,000	43,604,000	24,222,000	32,215,000	60,676,000
EBITDA		386,615,000	284,447,000	203,814,000	200,126,000	119,679,000
Return on Assets %		8.66%	2.52%	1.95%	2.99%	1.41%
Return on Equity %		35.26%	13.50%	12.17%	24.63%	11.50%
Debt to Equity		1.84	3.56	2.87	5.71	4.84

CONTACT INFORMATION:
Phone: 404 504-9828 Fax: 912 888-9374
Toll-Free:
Address: 4370 Peachtree Rd. NE, Atlanta, GA 30319 United States

SALARIES/BONUSES:
Top Exec. Salary: $1,050,566 Bonus: $
Second Exec. Salary: $679,778 Bonus: $

STOCK TICKER/OTHER:
Stock Ticker: GTN
Employees: 3,996
Parent Company:

Exchange: NYS
Fiscal Year Ends: 12/31

OTHER THOUGHTS:
Estimated Female Officers or Directors: 5
Hot Spot for Advancement for Women/Minorities: Y

Sales, profits and employees may be estimates. Financial information, benefits and other data can change quickly and may vary from those stated here.

Great Canadian Gaming Corporation

www.greatcanadiancasinos.com

NAIC Code: 713210

TYPES OF BUSINESS:
Gaming
Hospitality
Casinos
Horse Racing
Off-track Betting
Food & Beverage

BRANDS/DIVISIONS/AFFILIATES:
River Rock Casino Resort
Hard Rock Casino Vancouver
Casino New/Nouveau Brunswick
Casino Nova Scotia Halifax
Casino Woodbine
Casino Ajax
Great American Casino Everett
Shorelines Casino Peterborough

CONTACTS:
Note: Officers with more than one job title may be intentionally listed here more than once.

Rod Baker, CEO
Matthew Newsome, CFO
Radek Kielar, Controller
Terrance Doyle, COO
Peter Meredith, Director
Walter Soo, Executive VP, Divisional
Raj Mutti, Senior VP, Divisional

GROWTH PLANS/SPECIAL FEATURES:

Great Canadian Gaming Corporation provides gaming, entertainment and hospitality services. It owns 28 entertainment destinations that include casinos, thoroughbred racetracks with slot machines, standardbred racetracks with slot machines, a standardbred racetrack with both slot machines and table games; a four-diamond casino resort with a conference center, two hotel towers, two show theaters with more than 1,000 seats each, one bingo hall; and various associated hospitality facilities. Great Canadian offers its entertainment and hospitality services throughout British Columbia, Ontario, New Brunswick and Nova Scotia, Canada, as well as in Washington state, USA. The firm's properties include, but are not limited to, River Rock Casino Resort, Hard Rock Casino Vancouver, Casino New/Nouveau, Brunswick, Casino Nova Scotia Halifax, Casino Nova Scotia Sydney, Casino Woodbine, Casino Ajax, Great Blue Heron Casino, Great American Casino Everett, Great American Casino Lakewood and Great American Casino Tukwila. In October 2018, Great Canadian Gaming opened Shorelines Casino Peterborough, a 50,000-square-foot full-service casino featuring an array of updated slot machines, live dealer table games, a Racebook, a live entertainment area and dining options.

The firm offers its employees benefits including health coverage and employee and family assistance programs.

FINANCIAL DATA:
Note: Data for latest year may not have been available at press time.

In U.S. $	2018	2017	2016	2015	2014	2013
Revenue		455,752,800	420,215,500	336,676,900	331,260,900	302,178,200
R&D Expense						
Operating Income		114,105,100	107,502,200	101,047,600	96,447,750	68,255,340
Operating Margin %		25.03%	25.58%	30.01%	29.11%	22.68%
SGA Expense		136,436,500	121,969,300	83,464,400	78,938,780	78,567,820
Net Income		62,542,660	56,162,270	55,346,170	58,165,420	46,814,260
Operating Cash Flow		142,668,500	131,688,300	100,973,400	121,004,800	100,454,000
Capital Expenditure		38,950,060	28,785,950	11,128,590	10,980,210	18,399,260
EBITDA		159,361,400	145,487,700	130,649,600	136,213,900	125,530,500
Return on Assets %		7.47%	7.27%	7.41%	8.12%	7.09%
Return on Equity %		19.82%	19.80%	19.14%	22.15%	21.46%
Debt to Equity		1.03	1.24	1.16	1.10	1.43

CONTACT INFORMATION:
Phone: 604-303-1000 Fax: 604-516-7155
Toll-Free:
Address: 95 Schooner St., Coquitlam, BC V3K 7A8 Canada

STOCK TICKER/OTHER:
Stock Ticker: GC
Employees: 5,700
Parent Company:

Exchange: TSE
Fiscal Year Ends: 12/31

SALARIES/BONUSES:
Top Exec. Salary: $ Bonus: $
Second Exec. Salary: $ Bonus: $

OTHER THOUGHTS:
Estimated Female Officers or Directors:
Hot Spot for Advancement for Women/Minorities:

Sales, profits and employees may be estimates. Financial information, benefits and other data can change quickly and may vary from those stated here.

Greek Organisation of Football Prognostics SA (OPAP)

www.opap.gr
NAIC Code: 713210

TYPES OF BUSINESS:
Lottery Operations
Digital Media
Telecommunications

BRANDS/DIVISIONS/AFFILIATES:
EMMA Delta Investment Fund
Baupost Group
OPAP Sports Ltd
OPAP Cyprus Ltd
OPAP Services SA
OPAP International Ltd
OPAP Investments Ltd

CONTACTS:
Note: Officers with more than one job title may be intentionally listed here more than once.
Damian Cope, CEO
Kamil Ziegler, Chmn.

GROWTH PLANS/SPECIAL FEATURES:
Greek Organisation of Football Prognostics SA (OPAP) is engaged in the ownership, operation and advertising of lottery games. The company operates the largest lottery gaming retail network in Greece, and owns the majority of the gaming market in the country as well. OPAP offers a large portfolio of games with a focus on sports betting and numerical lottery games. Sports betting includes various football and soccer games. Popular numerical lottery games include LOTTO, PROTO, TZOKER, SUPER 3, EXTRA 5 and KINO. KINO is the most-played lottery game in Greece. Other lottery-based games include bowling, scratch, draw, races and PowerSpin. While many of the games were developed internally, the firm has also had success re-launching existing games such as Monitor Games. Products are distributed from point-of-sale (POS) agents and for online play, with the exception of the Video Lottery Terminals, which are only distributed in gaming halls. OPAP is a member of international and European lottery associations and organizes seminars and conferences in cooperation with organizations worldwide. OPAP's group of companies include OPAP Sports Ltd., OPAP Cyprus Ltd., OPAP Services SA, OPAP International Ltd. and OPAP Investments Ltd. OPAP's largest shareholders include EMMA Delta Investment Fund (33%), Baupost Group (5.19%) and others (27.81% combined).

FINANCIAL DATA:
Note: Data for latest year may not have been available at press time.

In U.S. $	2018	2017	2016	2015	2014	2013
Revenue						
R&D Expense						
Operating Income						
Operating Margin %						
SGA Expense						
Net Income						
Operating Cash Flow						
Capital Expenditure						
EBITDA						
Return on Assets %						
Return on Equity %						
Debt to Equity						

CONTACT INFORMATION:
Phone: 30 2105798800   Fax: 30 2105798931
Toll-Free:
Address: 112 Athinon Ave, Athens, 104 42 Greece

SALARIES/BONUSES:
Top Exec. Salary: $ Bonus: $
Second Exec. Salary: $ Bonus: $

STOCK TICKER/OTHER:
Stock Ticker: GOFPY   Exchange: PINX
Employees: 1,422   Fiscal Year Ends: 12/31
Parent Company: EMMA Delta Investment Fund

OTHER THOUGHTS:
Estimated Female Officers or Directors:
Hot Spot for Advancement for Women/Minorities:

Sales, profits and employees may be estimates. Financial information, benefits and other data can change quickly and may vary from those stated here.

Plunkett Research, Ltd.

Grupo Radio Centro SAB de CV

www.radiocentro.com.mx

NAIC Code: 515112

TYPES OF BUSINESS:
Radio Broadcasting
Radio Programming

BRANDS/DIVISIONS/AFFILIATES:
Organization Impulsora de Radio

CONTACTS: Note: Officers with more than one job title may be intentionally listed here more than once.
Francisco A. Gomez, CEO
Arturo Yanez, CFO
Gonzalo Yanez, Dir.-Mktg. and Operations
Luis Cepero, Dir.-Audio Eng.
Pedro Beltran, Dir.-Admin.
Alvaro F. De la Mora, Legal Counsel
Maria Barona, Contact-Corp. Comm.
Alfredo Azpeitia Mera, Investor Rel. Officer
Pedro N. Beltran, Dir.-Finance
Arturo Yanez, Dir.-Auditing
Rodolfo C. Nava, Treas.
Luis M. Carrasco, Dir.-Commercial
Francisco A. Gomez, Chmn.

GROWTH PLANS/SPECIAL FEATURES:
Grupo Radio Centro SAB de CV is a leading radio broadcasting company in Mexico, and the number one broadcaster in Mexico City. The firm produces and transmits music, talk shows, special events programs, entertainment programs and news. Grupo owns and/or operates 15 radio stations, most of which are based in Mexico City and one in Los Angeles, California. Of the total stations, 12 are FM and located in Mexico City, one AM station is located in Guadalajara and another in Monterrey. Outside of Mexico, the Los Angeles station is an FM. In relation to sound quality, FM stands for the frequency per second that the current/carrier signal is varied, and AM stands for the amplitude (overall strength) of the signal. Grupo Radio also operates Organization Impulsora de Radio (OIR), which provides programming and acts as a national sales representative for more than 100 radio stations affiliated with Grupo Radio throughout the Mexican Republic. The firm's main source of revenues is derived from the sale of commercial airtime at its stations.

FINANCIAL DATA: Note: Data for latest year may not have been available at press time.

In U.S. $	2018	2017	2016	2015	2014	2013
Revenue			78,526,660	66,395,620	50,319,930	49,304,190
R&D Expense						
Operating Income			36,553,800	5,633,503	9,188,656	3,040,272
Operating Margin %			46.54%	8.48%	18.26%	6.16%
SGA Expense			4,952,792	19,637,480	1,904,359	7,174,730
Net Income			10,010,360	-2,691,729	4,352,674	-6,267,796
Operating Cash Flow			6,409,855	13,188,660	10,073,610	6,285,802
Capital Expenditure			352,368	421,995	171,389	834,859
EBITDA			16,523,810	11,253,790	15,228,650	8,833,533
Return on Assets %			2.83%	-1.22%	3.52%	-6.77%
Return on Equity %			5.31%	-2.49%	5.96%	-8.51%
Debt to Equity			0.45	0.52	0.69	

CONTACT INFORMATION:
Phone: 52 5557284800 Fax: 52 5557284875
Toll-Free:
Address: Constituyentes 1154, 7 Piso, Colonia Lomas Altas, Col Lomas Altas, 11950 Mexico

STOCK TICKER/OTHER:
Stock Ticker: RCENTROA
Employees: 484
Parent Company:

Exchange: MEX
Fiscal Year Ends: 12/31

SALARIES/BONUSES:
Top Exec. Salary: $ Bonus: $
Second Exec. Salary: $ Bonus: $

OTHER THOUGHTS:
Estimated Female Officers or Directors: 3
Hot Spot for Advancement for Women/Minorities: Y

Sales, profits and employees may be estimates. Financial information, benefits and other data can change quickly and may vary from those stated here.

Grupo Televisa SAB

NAIC Code: 515120

www.televisa.com

TYPES OF BUSINESS:
Television Broadcasting
Cable Services
Satellite Services
Internet Services
Paging Services
Film & Music Production
Radio Broadcasting
Magazine Publishing

BRANDS/DIVISIONS/AFFILIATES:
SKY
Ocesa Entretenimiento SA de CV
Univision Communication Inc

CONTACTS:
Note: Officers with more than one job title may be intentionally listed here more than once.

Alfonso de Angoitia Noriega, Co-CEO
Bernardo Gomez Martinez, Co-CEO
Emilio Azcarraga Jean, Pres.
Carlos Ferreiro Rivas, VP-Finance
Ricardo Perez Teuffer, VP-Sales and Marketing
Bernardo Gomez Martinez, Exec. VP-Bus. Dev., Strategy & Expansion
Manuel Gilardi, VP-Digital & New Media
Adolfo Lagos, Corp. VP-Telecommunications
Carlos Madrazo, Investor Rel. Officer
Alfonso de Angoitia Noriega, Exec. VP-Finance
Alexandre Penna, CEO-SKY
Jean Paul Broc Haro, CEO-Cablevision
Emilio Azcarraga Jean, Chmn.
Martha Elena Diaz Llanos, Intl VP-Televisa Publishing

GROWTH PLANS/SPECIAL FEATURES:

Grupo Televisa SAB, based in Mexico, is one of the largest Spanish-speaking media companies in the world and a major participant in the international entertainment industry. The firm has interests in television broadcasting and production, print publishing, radio broadcasting and production, cinema production, sports and an internet portal. Televisa broadcasts programs through its networks, cable system and its own satellite services. The company holds approximately 70% of the television audience share in Mexico through its 62 television stations and affiliated stations. It also distributes programming throughout Latin America, the U.S., Canada, Europe and Asia. The firm owns 58.7% of SKY, a direct-to-home satellite television provider. In relation to cable, Televisa's network consists of approximately 53,000 miles of coaxial cable and 22,00 miles of fiber-optic cables. The company's multiple system operators division offers video, high-speed data and voice services to residential and commercial customers, including small- and medium-sized businesses and hotels. Its enterprise division provides telecommunications services such as voice, data and managed services, to domestic and international carriers as well as to enterprise, corporate and government customers in Mexico and the U.S. Other businesses of Televisa include: publishing, comprising approximately 110 magazine titles written in Spanish; gaming, owning 17 casino sites throughout Mexico, with 6,500 gaming machines, as well as an online lottery business; soccer, owning a first division soccer team of the Mexican league as well as the Azteca stadium; radio, owning 58 stations; and feature film distribution, distributing movies in Mexico and Latin America. Unconsolidated businesses include: 10%-owned Univision Communication Inc., a Spanish-language media company in the U.S., and 40%-owned in Ocesa Entretenimiento SA de CV, a live entertainment company in Mexico, Central America and Colombia. In June 2018, Grupo Televisa sold its 19% stake in Imagina, a Spanish media group.

FINANCIAL DATA:
Note: Data for latest year may not have been available at press time.

In U.S. $	2018	2017	2016	2015	2014	2013
Revenue		4,808,806,000	4,911,493,000	4,491,409,000	4,086,733,000	3,763,968,000
R&D Expense						
Operating Income		810,591,000	944,847,500	950,259,600	958,494,000	948,619,600
Operating Margin %		16.85%	19.23%	21.15%	23.45%	25.20%
SGA Expense		1,259,014,000	1,292,964,000	1,142,661,000	930,231,900	792,404,400
Net Income		230,788,600	189,824,100	555,950,700	274,779,000	395,229,600
Operating Cash Flow		1,280,305,000	1,869,820,000	1,595,836,000	1,451,857,000	1,214,324,000
Capital Expenditure		945,556,200	1,551,364,000	1,381,211,000	907,895,400	800,568,400
EBITDA		1,970,649,000	1,718,143,000	2,017,801,000	1,364,748,000	1,459,492,000
Return on Assets %		1.49%	1.26%	4.21%	2.50%	4.31%
Return on Equity %		5.34%	4.34%	13.27%	7.42%	12.01%
Debt to Equity		1.51	1.61	1.29	1.11	0.94

CONTACT INFORMATION:
Phone: 52 5552612433   Fax: 52 5552612465
Toll-Free:
Address: Ave. Vasco De Quiroga #2000, Bldg. A, 4/Fl, Alvaro Obregon, Mexico City, 01210 Mexico

STOCK TICKER/OTHER:
Stock Ticker: TV
Employees: 43,964
Parent Company:

Exchange: NYS
Fiscal Year Ends: 12/31

SALARIES/BONUSES:
Top Exec. Salary: $ Bonus: $
Second Exec. Salary: $ Bonus: $

OTHER THOUGHTS:
Estimated Female Officers or Directors: 1
Hot Spot for Advancement for Women/Minorities:

Hachette Book Group Inc

NAIC Code: 511130

www.hachettebookgroup.com

TYPES OF BUSINESS:
Book Publishing

BRANDS/DIVISIONS/AFFILIATES:
Legardere SCA
Hachette Livre
Hachette Book Group Canada Inc
Grand Central Publishing
Little Brown and Company
Orbit
Persius Books

CONTACTS: Note: Officers with more than one job title may be intentionally listed here more than once.
Michael Pietsch, CEO
Joe Mangan, COO
Stephen Mubarek, CFO
Alison Lazarus, Exec. VP-Sales
Andrea Weinzimer, Sr. VP-Human Resources
Sophie Cottrell, Sr. VP-Corp. Comm.

GROWTH PLANS/SPECIAL FEATURES:
Hachette Book Group, Inc., a subsidiary of Legardere SCA, is a trade publisher based in New York and a division of Hachette Livre, one of the largest trade and educational publishers in the world. Every year, Hachette Book publishes: more than 1,400 adult books, including 50-100 digital-only titles; 300 books for young readers; and 450 audio book titles, including physical and downloadable-only titles. The company's best-selling authors include Sherman Alexi, David Baldacci, Sandra Brown, Stephen Colbert, Joel Osteen, James Patterson, J.K. Rowling and many more. Genre categories include children's books, cooking, fiction, mind/body/spirit, mystery/thriller, non-fiction, romance, sci-fi/fantasy, teen/young adult and travel. In addition to selling and distributing its own imprints, Hachette Book provides a wide range of custom services to third-party publishers, such as distribution, fulfillment, digital and sales services. The firm has additional offices in Massachusetts, Indiana, Tennessee, Colorado, Pennsylvania and California. In addition, wholly-owned Hachette Book Group Canada, Inc. is a marketing and publicity company based in Toronto, Ontario, Canada. Other publishing groups and companies within the group's structure include: Grand Central Publishing; Hachette Audio; Hachette Books; Little, Brown and Company; Hachette Nashville; Orbit and Perseus Books.

FINANCIAL DATA: Note: Data for latest year may not have been available at press time.

In U.S. $	2018	2017	2016	2015	2014	2013
Revenue	625,000,000	610,000,000	596,250,000	582,886,000	584,640,000	613,287,000
R&D Expense						
Operating Income						
Operating Margin %						
SGA Expense						
Net Income						
Operating Cash Flow						
Capital Expenditure						
EBITDA						
Return on Assets %						
Return on Equity %						
Debt to Equity						

CONTACT INFORMATION:
Phone: 212-364-1200   Fax: 212-364-0628
Toll-Free: 800-759-0190
Address: 1290 Ave. of the Americas, New York, NY 10104 United States

STOCK TICKER/OTHER:
Stock Ticker: Subsidiary
Employees: 1,200
Parent Company: Legardere SCA

Exchange:
Fiscal Year Ends:

SALARIES/BONUSES:
Top Exec. Salary: $ Bonus: $
Second Exec. Salary: $ Bonus: $

OTHER THOUGHTS:
Estimated Female Officers or Directors:
Hot Spot for Advancement for Women/Minorities:

Hallmark Cards Inc

NAIC Code: 511191

www.hallmark.com

TYPES OF BUSINESS:
Greeting Cards Publishing
Cable Television Broadcasting
Crayons & Art Products
Television Production & Distribution
Stationery

BRANDS/DIVISIONS/AFFILIATES:
Hallmark Gold Crown
Crayola LLC
Crown Media Holdings Inc
DaySpring Cards Inc
Mary & Martha
Hallmark Business Connections
Hallmark Baby
Hallmark Marketing Corporation

CONTACTS: Note: Officers with more than one job title may be intentionally listed here more than once.

Donald J. Hall, Jr., CEO
David E. Hall, Pres.
Jim Shay, CFO
David E. Hall, Pres., North America Div.
Donald J. Hall, Chmn.

GROWTH PLANS/SPECIAL FEATURES:

Hallmark Cards, Inc. markets greeting cards and related products. The company operates wholesale and retail businesses for the sale of greeting and holiday cards, gifts, gift wrap, ornaments, memory-keeping products and stationery, with over 49,000 products available at any one time. The wholesale business distributes products to over 40,000 U.S. retailers and more than 100 countries, with products in approximately 30 languages. As a retailer, Hallmark distributes products in over 2,000 Hallmark Gold Crown stores, of which most are independently-owned. Its Hallmark Home division offers seasonal and holiday home collections as well as everyday items such as pillows, wall art and kitchen entertaining items. The firm also operates through several subsidiaries. Crayola, LLC produces Crayola crayons, art supplies and Silly Putty. Crown Media Holdings, Inc. operates various cable television channels, including Hallmark Channel, which is viewed by 67 million subscribers worldwide. Crown Center Redevelopment Corporation is a commercial and residential complex near Hallmark's headquarters in Kansas City, Missouri. DaySpring Cards, Inc. produces Christian greeting cards and gifts available in Christian retail stores in the U.S., and in over 60 countries. Mary & Martha is a direct sales company in which consultants sell products in the host's home or other place. Hallmark Business Connections, the firm's business-to-business (B2B) division, supplies business greeting cards and operates employee recognition programs, sales programs and corporate health and wellness programs. Hallmark Baby, a wholly-owned subsidiary of Hallmark Marketing Corporation is a digital store offering baby and children's clothing online.

The company offers its employees medical, dental and vision coverage; flexible spending plans; a 401(k) plan and profit sharing plan; child and elder care benefits; a fitness center; tuition reimbursement; and product discounts.

FINANCIAL DATA: Note: Data for latest year may not have been available at press time.

In U.S. $	2018	2017	2016	2015	2014	2013
Revenue	4,000,000,000	3,912,000,000	3,700,000,000	3,650,000,000	3,400,000,000	3,900,000,000
R&D Expense						
Operating Income						
Operating Margin %						
SGA Expense						
Net Income						
Operating Cash Flow						
Capital Expenditure						
EBITDA						
Return on Assets %						
Return on Equity %						
Debt to Equity						

CONTACT INFORMATION:
Phone: 816-274-5111 Fax:
Toll-Free: 800-425-5627
Address: 2501 McGee Trafficway, Kansas City, MO 64108 United States

STOCK TICKER/OTHER:
Stock Ticker: Private
Employees: 30,000
Parent Company:

Exchange:
Fiscal Year Ends: 12/31

SALARIES/BONUSES:
Top Exec. Salary: $ Bonus: $
Second Exec. Salary: $ Bonus: $

OTHER THOUGHTS:
Estimated Female Officers or Directors:
Hot Spot for Advancement for Women/Minorities:

Sales, profits and employees may be estimates. Financial information, benefits and other data can change quickly and may vary from those stated here.

HarperCollins Publishers LLC

NAIC Code: 511130

www.harpercollins.com

TYPES OF BUSINESS:
Book Publishing
Online Publishing & E-Books
Audio Books

BRANDS/DIVISIONS/AFFILIATES:
News Corporation
Harlequin

CONTACTS:
Note: Officers with more than one job title may be intentionally listed here more than once.

Brian Murray, CEO
Larry Nevins, Exec. VP-Oper.
Janet Gervasio, CFO
Diane Bailey, Human Resources
Chantal Restivo-Alessi, Chief Digital Officer
Rick Schwartz, CTO
Christopher Goff, General Counsel
Josh Marwell, Pres., Sales
Susan Katz, Pres.
Chantal Restivo Alessi, Chief Digital Officer

GROWTH PLANS/SPECIAL FEATURES:

HarperCollins Publishers, LLC, a subsidiary of News Corporation, publishes books that cover a wide range of interests. HarperCollins has publishing operations in 18 countries, with more than 120 branded imprints worldwide. The company publishes about 10,000 new books every year in 17 languages, and has a print and digital catalog of more than 200,000 titles. Popular authors the firm houses include Mark Twain, the Bronte sisters, Thackeray, Dickens, John F. Kennedy, Martin Luther King Jr., Maurice Sendak, Shel Silverstein and Margaret Wise Brown. HarperCollins has also published a range of Bibles, atlases, dictionaries and reissued classics from authors such as H. G. Wells, Agatha Christie, J. R. R. Tolkien and C. S. Lewis. Currently, HarperCollins is comprised of several company divisions: general books, children's books, Christian publishing, HarperCollins U.K., HarperCollins Canada, HarperCollins Australia/New Zealand, HarperCollins India, HarperCollins Germany, HarperCollins Espanol, HarperCollins Iberica, HarperCollins Japan, HarperCollins Holland, HarperCollins Nordic, HarperCollins Polska and Harlequin. Harlequin is a world-leading publisher of books for women. The Toronto-based Harlequin company publishes more than 110 titles each month in over 30 languages in as many as 150 international markets on six continents. These books are written by authors worldwide, with content including fiction, romance, young adult novels, non-fiction, African-American novels, inspirational romance and more.

FINANCIAL DATA:
Note: Data for latest year may not have been available at press time.

In U.S. $	2018	2017	2016	2015	2014	2013
Revenue	1,685,000,000	1,670,000,000	1,646,000,000	1,667,000,000	1,434,000,000	1,369,000,000
R&D Expense						
Operating Income						
Operating Margin %						
SGA Expense						
Net Income				194,000,000	198,000,000	122,760,000
Operating Cash Flow						
Capital Expenditure						
EBITDA						
Return on Assets %						
Return on Equity %						
Debt to Equity						

CONTACT INFORMATION:
Phone: 212-207-7000
Fax: 212-207-7909
Toll-Free:
Address: 195 Broadway, New York, NY 10007 United States

SALARIES/BONUSES:
Top Exec. Salary: $ Bonus: $
Second Exec. Salary: $ Bonus: $

STOCK TICKER/OTHER:
Stock Ticker: Subsidiary
Employees: 700
Parent Company: News Corporation
Exchange:
Fiscal Year Ends: 06/30

OTHER THOUGHTS:
Estimated Female Officers or Directors: 4
Hot Spot for Advancement for Women/Minorities: Y

Harte-Hanks Inc

NAIC Code: 511110

www.harte-hanks.com

TYPES OF BUSINESS:
Shopper Newspaper Publishing
Direct Mail Services
Direct & Interactive Marketing Services
Customer Relationship Management Software
Marketing Material Printing

BRANDS/DIVISIONS/AFFILIATES:

CONTACTS:
Note: Officers with more than one job title may be intentionally listed here more than once.

Jon Biro, CFO
Alfred Tobia, Chairman of the Board
Laurilee Kearnes, Chief Accounting Officer
Martin Reidy, Director
John Griffin, Director
Andrew Harrison, Executive VP, Divisional
Keith Sedlak, Senior VP, Divisional

GROWTH PLANS/SPECIAL FEATURES:

Harte-Hanks, Inc. is a global marketing firm specializing in helping brands to deliver relevant, connected and quality customer interactions. The company offers a variety of integrated, multi-channel, data-driven solutions so that clients can gain insight into their customer's behaviors and then create marketing programs that will drive sales and productivity. Harte-Hanks' marketing services include: agency and digital services such as direct and digital communications for both consumer and business-to-business (B2B) markets; and contact centers, operating teleservice workstations worldwide to provide advanced contact center solutions such as speech, voice, video chat, integrated voice response, analytics, social cloud monitoring and web self-service. The firm provides both inbound and outbound contact center services, and supports many languages. Harte Hanks fulfillment services include fulfillment services technology, to keep clients up-to-date on their customer needs; custom kitting and assembly, for complex packages; and digital printing, to maximize client inventory quickly. Harte-Hanks services the B2B, consumer, technology, travel and leisure, insurance, entertainment, pharmaceuticals, automotive, finance and retail industries. The company has offices located throughout North America, Asia-Pacific, Europe and Latin America.

FINANCIAL DATA:
Note: Data for latest year may not have been available at press time.

In U.S. $	2018	2017	2016	2015	2014	2013
Revenue		383,906,000	404,412,000	495,301,000	553,676,000	559,609,000
R&D Expense						
Operating Income		-6,355,000	-17,111,000	22,363,000	40,762,000	45,411,000
Operating Margin %		-1.65%	-4.23%	4.51%	7.36%	8.11%
SGA Expense		40,384,000	44,804,000	54,530,000	51,900,000	54,937,000
Net Income		-41,860,000	-130,937,000	-170,928,000	23,991,000	13,370,000
Operating Cash Flow		-30,800,000	14,590,000	30,943,000	25,561,000	59,572,000
Capital Expenditure		5,684,000	6,691,000	11,277,000	11,096,000	12,150,000
EBITDA		4,152,000	-4,759,000	36,608,000	55,682,000	61,148,000
Return on Assets %		-24.31%	-41.69%	-32.19%	3.60%	1.92%
Return on Equity %			-183.16%	-73.20%	7.10%	3.94%
Debt to Equity				0.52	0.19	0.23

CONTACT INFORMATION:
Phone: 210 829-9000   Fax: 210 829-9403
Toll-Free: 800-456-9748
Address: 9601 McAllister Fwy., Ste. 610, San Antonio, TX 78216 United States

STOCK TICKER/OTHER:
Stock Ticker: HHS
Employees: 5,652
Parent Company:

Exchange: NYS
Fiscal Year Ends: 12/31

SALARIES/BONUSES:
Top Exec. Salary: $694,261   Bonus: $
Second Exec. Salary: $374,635   Bonus: $125,000

OTHER THOUGHTS:
Estimated Female Officers or Directors: 3
Hot Spot for Advancement for Women/Minorities: Y

Sales, profits and employees may be estimates. Financial information, benefits and other data can change quickly and may vary from those stated here.

Hearst Corporation (The)

www.hearst.com

NAIC Code: 515210

TYPES OF BUSINESS:
Cable Television Networks
Magazine Publishing
Television & Radio Broadcasting & Production
Advertising Services
Internet Businesses
Syndicated Media Content
Newspaper Publishing
Health Care Software and Data Analytics

BRANDS/DIVISIONS/AFFILIATES:
Houston Chronicle
San Francisco Chronicle
LocalEdge
Hearst News Service
Oprah Magazine (The)
A&E Networks
ESPN
Black Book

CONTACTS:
Note: Officers with more than one job title may be intentionally listed here more than once.

Steven R. Swartz, CEO
Mark Aldam, Exec. VP
Mitchell Scherzer, CFO
James M. Asher, Chief Legal Officer
James M. Asher, Chief Dev. Officer
David Carey, Pres., Hearst Magazines
David J. Barrett, CEO
Richard P. Malloch, Pres., Hearst Business Media
Mark E. Aldam, Pres., Hearst Newspapers
William R. Hearst III, Chmn.

GROWTH PLANS/SPECIAL FEATURES:

The Hearst Corporation is engaged in the businesses of newspapers, magazines, broadcasting, cable television, entertainment and syndication, interactive media, business media and real estate. The firm publishes 24 daily newspapers, including the Houston Chronicle and the San Francisco Chronicle; and publishes 64 weeklies across the nation. The newspaper segment also owns LocalEdge, a publisher of yellow page print directories; and Hearst News Service, which syndicates Hearst newspaper stories. Hearst Magazines publishes approximately 20 U.S. titles and nearly 300 international editions. Its publications include Redbook, Road & Track and The Oprah Magazine. Through Hearst Digital Media, it operates the digital media businesses of its magazines. Moreover, through its subsidiary Hearst Magazines U.K., the company publishes an additional 19 magazines. Broadcasting subsidiary Hearst Television, Inc. owns more than 32 local television stations as well as two radio stations. Hearst Entertainment & Syndication operates the A&E Networks and ESPN networks as well as King Features Syndicate, a distributor of newspaper comics, puzzles and columns; and Reed Brennan Media Associates, which provides pagination and editing services for 400 newspapers. The firm's business media unit has interests in over 20 business-to-business (B2B) information services companies, including Black Book, FitchRatings and MedHOK. Black Book publishes reports to help shoppers find used cars; FitchRatings is one of three nationally-recognized statistical rating organizations designated by the U.S. Securities and Exchange Commission; and MedHOK enables health plans and other payers to comply with all state and federal regulations and deliver quality care across medical and pharmaceutical disciplines. In 2018, Hearst acquired Rodale, Inc. Magazine Media Brands, Fitch Group, Fulcrum Financial Data, Slickdeals and assets from Hersam Acorn Newspapers, LLC.

Hearst offers its employees medical, dental, vision and life insurance; flexible spending accounts; a 401(k) plan; and adoption and tuition assistance.

FINANCIAL DATA:
Note: Data for latest year may not have been available at press time.

In U.S. $	2018	2017	2016	2015	2014	2013
Revenue	11,150,000,000	11,000,000,000	10,800,000,000	10,700,000,000	10,300,000,000	9,870,000,000
R&D Expense						
Operating Income						
Operating Margin %						
SGA Expense						
Net Income						
Operating Cash Flow						
Capital Expenditure						
EBITDA						
Return on Assets %						
Return on Equity %						
Debt to Equity						

CONTACT INFORMATION:
Phone: 212-649-2000 Fax: 212-649-2108
Toll-Free:
Address: 300 W. 57th St., New York, NY 10019 United States

STOCK TICKER/OTHER:
Stock Ticker: Private
Employees: 20,250
Parent Company:

Exchange:
Fiscal Year Ends: 12/31

SALARIES/BONUSES:
Top Exec. Salary: $ Bonus: $
Second Exec. Salary: $ Bonus: $

OTHER THOUGHTS:
Estimated Female Officers or Directors: 5
Hot Spot for Advancement for Women/Minorities: Y

Sales, profits and employees may be estimates. Financial information, benefits and other data can change quickly and may vary from those stated here.

Hearst Television Inc

NAIC Code: 515120

www.hearsttelevision.com

TYPES OF BUSINESS:
Broadcast Television
Radio Stations
Web Sites
Television Production

BRANDS/DIVISIONS/AFFILIATES:
Hearst Corporation (The)
Matter of Fact

CONTACTS:
Note: Officers with more than one job title may be intentionally listed here more than once.

Jordan Wertlieb, Pres.
John Drain, CFO
Ashley Gold, VP-Sales
Katherine Barnett, VP-Human Resources
Andrew Fitzgerald, VP-Chief Digital Content Officer.
Martin Faubell, VP-Eng.
Jonathan Mintzer, General Counsel
Barbara Maushard, VP-News
Frank Biancuzzo, Sr. VP
Jeana Stanley, VP-Financial Planning

GROWTH PLANS/SPECIAL FEATURES:

Hearst Television, Inc., a wholly-owned subsidiary of The Hearst Corporation, owns and operates local television and radio stations serving 29 media markets across 39 U.S. states. Through its partnership with nearly all of the major networks, Hearst Television distributes national content over nearly 70 video channels, including programming from ABC, NBC, CBS, CW, My Net, MeTV, This TV, Estrella and more. Hearst Television produces the weekly public-affairs program Matter of Fact with Soledad O'Brien, which entered its fourth season in Fall 2018. Stations Hearst owns include, but are not limited to, WVTM in Alabama, KCRA in California, WESH in Florida, WLKY in Kentucky, and WPXT in Maine (acquired in 2018). Also in 2018, the firm acquired WCWG, a CW-affiliated television station licensed to North Carolina's Winston-Salem, Greensboro and High Point regions. Hearst Television's wholly-owned and operated radio stations include WBAL-1090 AM and WIYY-97.9 FM, each of which are broadcasted to the Baltimore area, offering news, talk and music content. The company has interests in many other radio stations via partnerships.

FINANCIAL DATA:
Note: Data for latest year may not have been available at press time.

In U.S. $	2018	2017	2016	2015	2014	2013
Revenue						
R&D Expense						
Operating Income						
Operating Margin %						
SGA Expense						
Net Income						
Operating Cash Flow						
Capital Expenditure						
EBITDA						
Return on Assets %						
Return on Equity %						
Debt to Equity						

CONTACT INFORMATION:
Phone: 212-887-6800   Fax: 212-887-6855
Toll-Free:
Address: 300 West 57th St., New York, NY 10019 United States

SALARIES/BONUSES:
Top Exec. Salary: $ Bonus: $
Second Exec. Salary: $ Bonus: $

STOCK TICKER/OTHER:
Stock Ticker: Subsidiary   Exchange:
Employees: 2,890   Fiscal Year Ends: 12/31
Parent Company: Hearst Corporation (The)

OTHER THOUGHTS:
Estimated Female Officers or Directors: 5
Hot Spot for Advancement for Women/Minorities: Y

Hershey Company (The)

www.hersheys.com

NAIC Code: 311351

TYPES OF BUSINESS:
Candy Manufacturing
Baking Supplies
Chocolate Products
Confectionaries & Snacks
Amusement Parks
Resorts/Hotels

BRANDS/DIVISIONS/AFFILIATES:
Reese's
Kit Kat
Hershey Bars
Hershey Kisses
Hershey's Chocolate World
Amplify Snack Brands Inc
SkinnyPop
Pirate Brands

CONTACTS:
Note: Officers with more than one job title may be intentionally listed here more than once.

Michele Buck, CEO
Javier Idrovo, Chief Accounting Officer
Terence ODay, Chief Technology Officer
Kevin Walling, Other Executive Officer
Mary Stone West, Other Executive Officer
Todd Tillemans, President, Divisional
Patricia Little, Senior VP

GROWTH PLANS/SPECIAL FEATURES:

The Hershey Company is an industry-leading snacks company known for its iconic brands. The company's more than 80 branded products are marketed in approximately 70 countries worldwide. Hershey's principal product groups include confectionery products such as Reese's, Kit Kat, Hershey Bars and Hershey Kisses; packaged items; and grocery products, such as baking ingredients, chocolate drink mixes, peanut butter, dessert toppings and beverages. Its products are sold primarily to wholesale distributors, chain grocery stores, mass merchandisers, chain drug stores, vending companies, wholesale clubs, convenience stores, dollar stores, concessionaires, department stores and natural food stores. Its direct retail operations include Hershey's Chocolate World in Hershey, Pennsylvania, and Hershey's retail stores in New York City, Las Vegas, Shanghai, Niagara Falls (Ontario), Dubai and Singapore. The firm's operations are therefore divided into geographical segments: North America and international and other. The North America segment is responsible for Hershey's traditional chocolate and non-chocolate confectionery market position, as well as its grocery and snacks market positions in the U.S. and Canada. The international and other segment is a combination of all other Hershey business. This includes operations and product manufacturing facilities in China, Mexico, Brazil, India and Malaysia, which also distribute and sell confectionery products in the export markets of Asia, Latin America, the Middle East, Europe, Africa and other regions. This segment also includes the Hershey's Chocolate World stores (even the ones in the U.S.); and is responsible for licensing the use of certain of the company's trademarks and products to third parties worldwide. During 2018, the firm acquired Amplify Snack Brands, Inc., which owns better-for-you snack brands such as SkinnyPop, Oatmega, Pagui and Tyrrells; and acquired Pirate Brands from B&G Foods, Inc., including the Pirate's Booty, Smart Puffs and Original Tings brands.

The firm offers employees comprehensive health benefits and retirement plans.

FINANCIAL DATA:
Note: Data for latest year may not have been available at press time.

In U.S. $	2018	2017	2016	2015	2014	2013
Revenue		7,515,426,000	7,440,181,000	7,386,626,000	7,421,768,000	7,146,079,000
R&D Expense						
Operating Income		1,531,116,000	1,242,513,000	1,413,367,000	1,435,196,000	1,358,340,000
Operating Margin %		20.37%	16.69%	19.13%	19.33%	19.00%
SGA Expense		1,913,403,000	1,915,378,000	1,969,308,000	1,900,970,000	1,922,508,000
Net Income		782,981,000	720,044,000	512,951,000	846,912,000	820,470,000
Operating Cash Flow		1,249,515,000	983,475,000	1,214,456,000	838,221,000	1,188,405,000
Capital Expenditure		257,675,000	269,476,000	356,810,000	370,789,000	350,911,000
EBITDA		1,472,587,000	1,493,266,000	1,227,758,000	1,605,173,000	1,543,866,000
Return on Assets %		14.13%	13.24%	9.34%	15.41%	16.22%
Return on Equity %		92.05%	80.72%	41.82%	55.35%	62.11%
Debt to Equity		2.25	2.98	1.56	1.06	1.11

CONTACT INFORMATION:
Phone: 717 534-4200 Fax: 717 531-6161
Toll-Free: 800-468-1714
Address: 100 Crystal A Dr., Hershey, PA 17033 United States

SALARIES/BONUSES:
Top Exec. Salary: $437,500 Bonus: $1,350,000
Second Exec. Salary: $1,043,462 Bonus: $

STOCK TICKER/OTHER:
Stock Ticker: HSY
Employees: 17,980
Parent Company:

Exchange: NYS
Fiscal Year Ends: 12/31

OTHER THOUGHTS:
Estimated Female Officers or Directors: 4
Hot Spot for Advancement for Women/Minorities: Y

Hightimes Holding Corp

NAIC Code: 511120

hightimesinvestor.com

TYPES OF BUSINESS:
Periodical Publishers
Online Magazine Publishers
Event/Festival Organizers

BRANDS/DIVISIONS/AFFILIATES:
THC Group
High Times
Cannabis Cup (The)
High Times Magazine
Green Rush Daily
Culture Magazine
Dope Magazine

CONTACTS:
Note: Officers with more than one job title may be intentionally listed here more than once.

Adam Levin, CEO
David Newberg, Principal Financial & Accounting Officer

GROWTH PLANS/SPECIAL FEATURES:
Hightimes Holding Corp., founded in 2014, was originally formed to acquire 100% of the capital stock of Trans-High Corporation and the THC Group. Trans-High was renamed as Hightimes Holding and the THC Group was already engaged in the publication of a monthly print and online magazine under the High Times brand. THC also sponsored and produced cannabis-related trade shows and events. Therefore, Hightimes' ultimate goal was to monetize the intellectual property and High Times brand. High Times is currently fueled by two things: the belief that the cannabis movement should focus on its community (loyal High Times fans, cannabis enthusiasts and early investors), so, in addition to its media offerings and festival events, has created an eCommerce store that offers clothing and other products associated with cannabis; and owning stock through the purchase of High Times shares for as little as $99 using a credit card or automated clearing house (ACH) account prior to its expected listing on an exchange. Hightimes' three business segments include: media, which provides cannabis information via magazines (printed and online) ranging from cultivation to legalization, and entertainment to culture; cannabis-focused festival events, which connect enthusiasts, advocates, businesses and policymakers; and licensing, whether it be cannabis-related apparel, merchandise, media or other, all under the High Times brand. As marijuana becomes legal across the U.S. and internationally, Hightimes is seizing the opportunity to spread its High Times brand, especially in the segments of media/magazines, brand licensing and eCommerce. Hightimes' family of brands include The Cannabis Cup, High Times Magazine, Green Rush Daily, Culture Magazine and Dope Magazine.

FINANCIAL DATA:
Note: Data for latest year may not have been available at press time.

In U.S. $	2018	2017	2016	2015	2014	2013
Revenue						
R&D Expense						
Operating Income						
Operating Margin %						
SGA Expense						
Net Income						
Operating Cash Flow						
Capital Expenditure						
EBITDA						
Return on Assets %						
Return on Equity %						
Debt to Equity						

CONTACT INFORMATION:
Phone: 844-933-3287 Fax:
Toll-Free:
Address: 10990 Wilshire Blvd., Penthouse, Los Angeles, CA 90024 United States

STOCK TICKER/OTHER:
Stock Ticker: HITM
Employees: 23
Parent Company:

Exchange: NAS
Fiscal Year Ends: 12/31

SALARIES/BONUSES:
Top Exec. Salary: $ Bonus: $
Second Exec. Salary: $ Bonus: $

OTHER THOUGHTS:
Estimated Female Officers or Directors:
Hot Spot for Advancement for Women/Minorities:

Sales, profits and employees may be estimates. Financial information, benefits and other data can change quickly and may vary from those stated here.

Home Box Office Inc (HBO)

NAIC Code: 515210

www.hbo.com

TYPES OF BUSINESS:
Cable Television Network
Television Production
Movie Production

BRANDS/DIVISIONS/AFFILIATES:
AT&T In
Warner Media LLC
HBO Comedy
HBO Latino
HBO on Demand
HBO Go
HBO NOW
Cinemax

CONTACTS:
Note: Officers with more than one job title may be intentionally listed here more than once.

Richard Plepler, CEO
Scott McElhone, Exec. VP-Admin.
Tom Woodbury, General Counsel
Susan Ennis, Exec. VP-Program Planning & Strategy
Quentin Schaffer, Exec. VP-Corp. Comm.
Len Amato, Pres., HBO Films
Kary Antholis, Pres., HBO Miniseries
Michael Ellenberg, Exec. VP-HBO Programming
Bruce Grivetti, Exec. VP-Bus. Affairs
Simon Sutton, Pres., HBO Int'l
Simon Sutton, Pres., Content Dist.

GROWTH PLANS/SPECIAL FEATURES:

Home Box Office, Inc. (HBO) is a premium cable and satellite television network. The firm is a subsidiary of Warner Media LLC, itself a subsidiary of AT&T, Inc. HBO's pay television (TV) division operates seven 24-hour networks, including HBO Family, HBO Comedy and HBO Latino. Pay TV subscribers can also watch over 150 hours of HBO's programming any time via HBO on Demand through set-top boxes. A major portion of the programming on the firm's channels consist of theatrically-released motion pictures and original television series, but also includes made-for-cable movies and documentaries, and stand-up comedy and concert specials. HBO GO enables subscribers to access over 1,000 of the channels' programming titles online. HBO NOW is a standalone streaming service from HBO, of which subscribers can watch HBO offerings anywhere, any time, on any device without a TV package required. HBO NOW has over 2 million subscribers in the U.S. alone. HBO's Cinemax division offers several channels, broadcasting movies, softcore adult films and series, original action series, thrillers, Spanish-language feeds and more. While HBO's content is primarily distributed via cable and satellite television providers, it is also distributed online through the iTunes store and various mobile platforms. The company's eCommerce site, Shop.HBO.com, offers for purchase its merchandise and DVDs related to its programming. In total, HBO has more than 140 million subscribers worldwide. In late-2018, HBO announced plans to discontinue its boxing telecasts after 45 years.

FINANCIAL DATA:
Note: Data for latest year may not have been available at press time.

In U.S. $	2018	2017	2016	2015	2014	2013
Revenue	5,850,000,000	5,810,000,000	5,820,000,000	5,615,000,000	5,398,000,000	4,890,000,000
R&D Expense						
Operating Income						
Operating Margin %						
SGA Expense						
Net Income						
Operating Cash Flow						
Capital Expenditure						
EBITDA						
Return on Assets %						
Return on Equity %						
Debt to Equity						

CONTACT INFORMATION:
Phone: 212-512-1000 Fax: 212-512-1182
Toll-Free:
Address: 1100 Avenue of the Americas, New York, NY 10036 United States

STOCK TICKER/OTHER:
Stock Ticker: Subsidiary
Employees: 2,000
Parent Company: AT&T Inc

Exchange:
Fiscal Year Ends: 12/31

SALARIES/BONUSES:
Top Exec. Salary: $ Bonus: $
Second Exec. Salary: $ Bonus: $

OTHER THOUGHTS:
Estimated Female Officers or Directors: 6
Hot Spot for Advancement for Women/Minorities: Y

Hoover's Inc

NAIC Code: 519130

www.hoovers.com

TYPES OF BUSINESS:
Online Corporate Intelligence
Reference Books
E-Commerce
Advertising Services
Sales & Marketing Lists

BRANDS/DIVISIONS/AFFILIATES:
Dun & Bradstreet Corporation (D&B)
IPO Scorecard
Hoover's Handbooks
Jobseeker Report

CONTACTS:
Note: Officers with more than one job title may be intentionally listed here more than once.

Gary Hoover, Co-Founder
Patrick Spain, Co-Founder
Hyune Hand, Pres.

GROWTH PLANS/SPECIAL FEATURES:
Hoover's, Inc., a subsidiary of Dun & Bradstreet (D&B), is an online provider of company and industry information, designed to meet the diverse needs of business organizations, sales executives, investors and researchers of many types. Through its website, customers can access information for their professional endeavors, including financial and competitive research as well as marketing and job search activities. Hoover's core asset is its proprietary editorial content, which includes a database of more than 85 million companies and 100 million people, with coverage written and edited in-house. Hoover's also provides data on initial public offerings (through the IPO Scorecard pages), corporate news, executive biographical information, corporate financial data, Jobseeker Reports and access to items such as credit reports by D&B. While the firm's primary focus is the delivery of company intelligence via the internet, it also publishes reference books including Hoover's Handbooks. The company generates most of its revenue from the sale of annual subscriptions to its premium-level data services. Significant revenue is also generated from licensing fees, e-commerce and the sale of advertising.

FINANCIAL DATA:
Note: Data for latest year may not have been available at press time.

In U.S. $	2018	2017	2016	2015	2014	2013
Revenue						
R&D Expense						
Operating Income						
Operating Margin %						
SGA Expense						
Net Income						
Operating Cash Flow						
Capital Expenditure						
EBITDA						
Return on Assets %						
Return on Equity %						
Debt to Equity						

CONTACT INFORMATION:
Phone: 512-374-4500   Fax: 512-374-4501
Toll-Free: 866-473-3932
Address: 103 John F Kennedy Parkway, Short Hills, NJ 07078 United States

STOCK TICKER/OTHER:
Stock Ticker: Subsidiary   Exchange:
Employees: 200   Fiscal Year Ends: 12/31
Parent Company: Dun & Bradstreet Corporation (D&B)

SALARIES/BONUSES:
Top Exec. Salary: $ Bonus: $
Second Exec. Salary: $ Bonus: $

OTHER THOUGHTS:
Estimated Female Officers or Directors:
Hot Spot for Advancement for Women/Minorities: Y

Sales, profits and employees may be estimates. Financial information, benefits and other data can change quickly and may vary from those stated here.

Houghton Mifflin Harcourt Company

www.hmhco.com

NAIC Code: 511130

TYPES OF BUSINESS:
Book Publishing
Educational Materials
Software, CD-ROMs & Mixed Media
Textbooks
Electronic & Multimedia Publishing
Test Design & Consulting
Reference Materials

BRANDS/DIVISIONS/AFFILIATES:

CONTACTS: Note: Officers with more than one job title may be intentionally listed here more than once.
John Lynch, CEO
Joseph Abbott, CFO
Lawrence Fish, Chairman of the Board
Amy Dunkin, Chief Marketing Officer
Lee Ramsayer, Executive VP, Divisional
William Bayers, Executive VP
Matthew Fields, Executive VP
James ONeill, Executive VP
Rosamund Else-Mitchell, Executive VP
Alejandro Reyes, Other Executive Officer
Ellen Archer, President, Divisional

GROWTH PLANS/SPECIAL FEATURES:

Houghton Mifflin Harcourt Company (HMHC) publishes textbooks and other educational materials as well as fiction, nonfiction, children's books, dictionaries and reference materials. HMHC delivers interactive education solutions to more than 50 million students in over 150 countries. The firm operates through two segments: education and trade publishing. The education segment accounts for 88% of total revenue and offers educational products and technology platforms in form of textbooks, digital courseware, instructional aids, educational assessment and intervention solutions. The principal markets for this division's products are K-12 school systems, which purchase core curriculum materials, intervention and supplemental materials, professional development and school turnaround services and various assessment products. The trade publishing segment develops, markets and sells consumer books in print and digital formats and licenses book rights to other publishers and electronic businesses in the U.S. and abroad. The books are offered in a variety of general interest topics as well as reference works, and include well-known characters and brands, such as J.R.R. Tolkien titles, The Best American Series, CliffsNotes series of test prep and study guides, Curious George and Martha Speaks early learning books and Webster's New World Dictionary. While the firm has traditionally published printed materials, it now publishes in other formats, including computer software, laser discs, CD-ROM and other electronic and multimedia products. In 2018, Houghton Mifflin ended its Channel One newscast, a news show created for students.

FINANCIAL DATA: Note: Data for latest year may not have been available at press time.

In U.S. $	2018	2017	2016	2015	2014	2013
Revenue		1,407,511,000	1,372,685,000	1,416,059,000	1,372,316,000	1,378,612,000
R&D Expense						
Operating Income		-68,175,000	-155,918,000	-111,284,000	-76,432,000	-67,605,000
Operating Margin %		-4.84%	-11.35%	-7.85%	-5.56%	-4.90%
SGA Expense		654,860,000	699,544,000	681,124,000	612,535,000	580,887,000
Net Income		-103,187,000	-284,558,000	-133,869,000	-111,491,000	-111,186,000
Operating Cash Flow		135,130,000	143,751,000	348,359,000	491,043,000	157,203,000
Capital Expenditure		60,294,000	105,553,000	82,987,000	67,145,000	59,803,000
EBITDA		167,701,000	-13,218,000	175,145,000	232,773,000	254,484,000
Return on Assets %		-3.89%	-9.69%	-4.35%	-3.76%	-3.74%
Return on Equity %		-12.31%	-27.38%	-9.05%	-6.17%	-5.86%
Debt to Equity		0.95	0.86	0.65	0.09	0.13

CONTACT INFORMATION:
Phone: 617-351-5000 Fax: 617-351-1125
Toll-Free:
Address: 125 High St., Boston, MA 02110 United States

STOCK TICKER/OTHER:
Stock Ticker: HMHC
Employees: 4,500
Parent Company:

Exchange: NAS
Fiscal Year Ends: 12/31

SALARIES/BONUSES:
Top Exec. Salary: $520,000 Bonus: $250,000
Second Exec. Salary: $500,000 Bonus: $250,000

OTHER THOUGHTS:
Estimated Female Officers or Directors: 6
Hot Spot for Advancement for Women/Minorities: Y

Sales, profits and employees may be estimates. Financial information, benefits and other data can change quickly and may vary from those stated here.

HSN Inc (Home Shopping Network)

NAIC Code: 454113

www.hsn.com

TYPES OF BUSINESS:
Television Shopping
Direct Marketing
Online Sales
Cable & Broadcast Television
Catalog Sales
Retail Stores
Outlet Stores

BRANDS/DIVISIONS/AFFILIATES:
Qurate Retail Group
HSN
Cornerstone Brands Inc
Ballard Designs
Frontgate
Garnet Hill
Grandin Road
Improvements

CONTACTS:
Note: Officers with more than one job title may be intentionally listed here more than once.
Mike Fitzharris, Pres.
Arthur Martinez, Chairman of the Board
Maria Martinez, Other Executive Officer
Gregory Henchel, Other Executive Officer

GROWTH PLANS/SPECIAL FEATURES:
HSN, Inc. (Home Shopping Network) is a multi-channel retailer offering shopping alternatives to U.S. consumers through its two operational segments, HSN and Cornerstone Brands, Inc. HSN offers home shopping experiences via: television; online through HSN.com and joymangano.com; in catalogs; and at retail stores and outlets. The Home Shopping Network television program offers items ranging from 14-karat jewelry to cosmetics, home goods and apparel. HSN broadcasts reach approximately 90 million households through its live television, video and website formats. Cornerstone Brands distributes around 300 million catalogs annually, operates eCommerce websites and runs retail and outlet stores. The segment is comprised of home and apparel lifestyle brands, including Ballard Designs, Frontgate, Garnet Hill, Grandin Road and Improvements. Its websites correspond with each brand. In January 2018, QVC, through its parent company Liberty Interactive, concluded the acquisition of competitor HSN, Inc., a leading competitor in home shopping. This merger made QVC the world's leading TV shopping firm by far, as well as one of the top ecommerce companies. Later that year, Liberty Interactive changed its corporate name to Qurate Retail Group.

HSN offers employees medical, dental and vision insurance; life insurance; short- and long-term disability coverage; pet insurance; a retirement savings plan; wellness screenings; onsite car washing; dry cleaning services; and discounted home insurance, c

FINANCIAL DATA:
Note: Data for latest year may not have been available at press time.

In U.S. $	2018	2017	2016	2015	2014	2013
Revenue		3,101,358,000	3,567,484,928	3,690,575,104	3,587,994,880	3,403,983,104
R&D Expense						
Operating Income						
Operating Margin %						
SGA Expense						
Net Income			118,708,000	169,239,008	172,984,000	178,448,992
Operating Cash Flow						
Capital Expenditure						
EBITDA						
Return on Assets %						
Return on Equity %						
Debt to Equity						

CONTACT INFORMATION:
Phone: 727 872-1000 Fax:
Toll-Free: 800-284-3100
Address: 1 HSN Dr., St. Petersburg, FL 33729 United States

STOCK TICKER/OTHER:
Stock Ticker: Subsidiary
Employees: 6,500
Parent Company: Qurate Retail Group

Exchange:
Fiscal Year Ends: 12/31

SALARIES/BONUSES:
Top Exec. Salary: $ Bonus: $
Second Exec. Salary: $ Bonus: $

OTHER THOUGHTS:
Estimated Female Officers or Directors: 9
Hot Spot for Advancement for Women/Minorities: Y

Sales, profits and employees may be estimates. Financial information, benefits and other data can change quickly and may vary from those stated here.

Hulu LLC

NAIC Code: 515210

www.hulu.com

TYPES OF BUSINESS:
Streaming Entertainment Online, Including Movies and TV Shows
Advertising

BRANDS/DIVISIONS/AFFILIATES:
Walt Disney Company (The)
21st Century Fox
Comcast
AT&T
Hulu with Live TV

CONTACTS:
Note: Officers with more than one job title may be intentionally listed here more than once.

Randy Freer, CEO
Craig Erwich, Sr. VP-Operations
Elaine Paul, CFO
Kelly Campbell, CMO
Dan Phillips, Chief Technology Officer
Chadwick Ho, General Counsel
Jean-Paul Colaco, Sr. VP-Advertising

GROWTH PLANS/SPECIAL FEATURES:
Hulu, LLC provides a subscription streaming service that offers instant access to live and on-demand channels, original series and films, and a premium library of TV and movies. Hulu is primarily oriented toward television series, carrying both current and past episodes from its owners' television networks and other content partners. The service also streams anime titles from many distributors, including Funimation, TMS Entertainment, Bandai Visual and Viz Media. Hulu has more than 20 million subscribers in the U.S., with nearly 70% of viewing taking place on regular televisions via connected devices. Hulu is free for the first 30 days at startup, and then $5.99 per month for a year, then $7.99/month thereafter. This subscription service enables customers to stream on preferred devices, and have unlimited access to the Hulu streaming library with limited or no commercials. Add-ons are offered. Hulu with Live TV combines live TV offerings with Hulu's existing library of television series and films, in beta (meaning that some features or parts of the plug-in is still in testing mode and can cause issues of not used properly). The $39.99-per-month Hulu with Live TV service provides support for Xbox One, Apple TV, Chromecast, iOS and Android devices, and offers live streams of more than 50 broadcast and cable-originated channels. The Walt Disney Company, having acquired 21st Century Fox, holds 60% of Hulu; Comcast holds a 30% share; and AT&T holds the remaining 10%.

FINANCIAL DATA:
Note: Data for latest year may not have been available at press time.

In U.S. $	2018	2017	2016	2015	2014	2013
Revenue		2,870,000,000	2,375,000,000	1,577,800,000	1,285,000,000	1,000,000,000
R&D Expense						
Operating Income						
Operating Margin %						
SGA Expense						
Net Income			-560,000,000	-321,000,000	-61,000,000	
Operating Cash Flow						
Capital Expenditure						
EBITDA						
Return on Assets %						
Return on Equity %						
Debt to Equity						

CONTACT INFORMATION:
Phone: 310-571-4700　　Fax: 310-571-4701
Toll-Free:
Address: 2500 Broadway, 2/Fl, Santa Monica, CA 90404 United States

STOCK TICKER/OTHER:
Stock Ticker: Joint Venture
Employees: 725
Parent Company:

Exchange:
Fiscal Year Ends: 12/31

SALARIES/BONUSES:
Top Exec. Salary: $　　Bonus: $
Second Exec. Salary: $　　Bonus: $

OTHER THOUGHTS:
Estimated Female Officers or Directors:
Hot Spot for Advancement for Women/Minorities:

Hurriyet Gazetecilik ve Matbaacilik AS

www.hurriyetkurumsal.com

NAIC Code: 511110

TYPES OF BUSINESS:
Newspaper Publishing
Internet Publication
Advertising

BRANDS/DIVISIONS/AFFILIATES:
Dogan Sirketler Grubu Holding AS
Hurriyet.comtr
Hurriyet TV
Bigpara.com
Hurrietaile.com
Mahmure.com
Hurriyetoto.com
Yenibiris.com

CONTACTS:
Note: Officers with more than one job title may be intentionally listed here more than once.

Mehmet Soysal, CEO
Huseyin Emrah Kuroglu, COO
Hilmi Erkal, CFO
Cenk Okan Ozpay, Dir.-IT
Kadri Enis Berberoglu, Editor-in-Chief
Ayfle Sozeri Cemal, Head-Advertising
Yildirim Demiroren, Chmn.

GROWTH PLANS/SPECIAL FEATURES:
Hurriyet Gazetecilik ve Matbaacilik AS, a subsidiary of Dogan Sirketler Grubu Holding AS, is involved in the publication of online and print newspapers and advertising sales in Turkey and abroad. The firm's print media includes newspapers via print, web and mobile platforms, offering a variety of content such as news, human resources, economy, art/literature, fashion, television, entertainment, culture, shopping, music, humor, food, nature, lifestyle, life events, travel, local information/activities, periodicals, sports and much more. Hurriyet's digital media division includes the Hurriyet.com.tr flagship website, the Hurriyet TV video platform, Bigpara.com, Hurriyetaile.com, Mahmure.com, Hurriyetoto.com, Yenibiris.com and yakaia.co. Printing services offered by the company include journalism, printing, advertisement, publicity and internet publishing. This division has seven printing facilities in locations such as Istanbul, Ankara, Izmir, Adana, Antalya, Trabzon and Germany. Hurriyet Gazetecilik's foreign operations consist of Hurriyet Germany, a publishing center and printing facility based in Morfelden-Walldorf, and offers a Turkish newspaper to Turkish citizens and Turkish-based people living in Europe. Hurriyet Germany sells about 8,000 copies in Germany and 10,000 in other European countries. This division also provides newspaper print, folding, distribution and other services to third-party newspaper entities, including Japanese newspaper Nikkei and English newspaper The Financial Times. Recently (2017), this segment began to print regional prints of Germany's daily soccer newspaper, Fussball Bild.

FINANCIAL DATA:
Note: Data for latest year may not have been available at press time.

In U.S. $	2018	2017	2016	2015	2014	2013
Revenue		98,359,220	103,085,000	108,929,400	131,497,800	147,212,200
R&D Expense						
Operating Income		871,256	-468,562	4,118,493	7,153,659	7,141,141
Operating Margin %		.88%	-.45%	3.78%	5.44%	4.85%
SGA Expense		13,517,850	41,653,580	46,435,560	50,299,200	52,921,300
Net Income		-48,336,200	-13,242,180	-5,573,465	-30,823,540	-11,164,430
Operating Cash Flow		3,483,639	1,160,039	1,002,492	2,065,202	26,143,940
Capital Expenditure		4,335,346	3,584,580	2,971,104	2,940,526	3,602,767
EBITDA		61,872,550	12,572,430	4,193,977	19,900,410	21,476,600
Return on Assets %		-31.06%	-8.02%	-3.37%	-14.21%	-4.08%
Return on Equity %		-74.13%	-18.48%	-7.73%	-31.01%	-9.02%
Debt to Equity		0.49	0.33	0.16	0.22	0.39

CONTACT INFORMATION:
Phone: 90-212-677-00-00   Fax: 90-212-677-01-82
Toll-Free:
Address: Hurriyet Medya Towers Gunesli, Istanbul, 34212 Turkey

SALARIES/BONUSES:
Top Exec. Salary: $ Bonus: $
Second Exec. Salary: $ Bonus: $

STOCK TICKER/OTHER:
Stock Ticker: HURRY   Exchange: GREY
Employees: 1,521   Fiscal Year Ends: 12/31
Parent Company: Dogan Sirketler Grubu Holding AS

OTHER THOUGHTS:
Estimated Female Officers or Directors: 3
Hot Spot for Advancement for Women/Minorities: Y

Sales, profits and employees may be estimates. Financial information, benefits and other data can change quickly and may vary from those stated here.

IAC/InterActiveCorp

www.iac.com

NAIC Code: 519130

TYPES OF BUSINESS:
E-Commerce, Online Advertising & Search Engines
Online Personals & Dating Services
Online Entertainment & Shopping Directories
Service Provider Listings Online

BRANDS/DIVISIONS/AFFILIATES:
Match Group Inc
ANGI Homeservices Inc
Angie's List
Vimeo
IAC Films
Apalon
SlimWare
Dotdash

CONTACTS:
Note: Officers with more than one job title may be intentionally listed here more than once.

Barry Diller, Chairman of the Board
Joseph Levin, Director
Victor Kaufman, Director
Glenn Schiffman, Executive VP
Mark Stein, Executive VP
Gregg Winiarski, General Counsel
Michael Schwerdtman, Senior VP

GROWTH PLANS/SPECIAL FEATURES:
IAC/InterActiveCorp is a leading media and internet company organized into five segments: Match Group, ANGI Homeservices, video, applications and publishing. The Match Group consists of Match Group, Inc., which operates a dating business available in 42 languages across more than 190 countries. It offers subscription dating products via websites and mobile applications, which enable users to establish a profile and review the profiles of other users without charge. Additional features are either free or obtained by purchase. Access to premium features require a subscription. The ANGI Homeservices segment consists of ANGI Homeservices, Inc., which owns and operates HomeAdvisor, Angie's List, mHelpDesk, CraftJack and Felix, which are digital marketplaces for home services. The video segment consists of Vimeo, Electus, IAC Films and Daily Burn. Vimeo operates a global video sharing platform for creators and their audiences; Electus provides production and producer services for both unscripted and scripted television and digital content, primarily for initial sale and distribution in the U.S.; IAC Films provides production and producer services for feature films, primarily for initial sale and distribution in the U.S. and internationally; and Daily Burn is a health and fitness property that provides streaming fitness and workout videos across a variety of platforms. The applications segment consists of two divisions: consumer and partnerships. The consumers division develops and distributes downloadable desktop and mobile apps, and includes: Apalon, which houses the firm's mobile apps; and SlimWare, a community-powered software that cleans, repairs, updates, secures and optimizes computers, mobile phones and digital devices. The partnership division designs and develops browser-based search applications to be bundled and distributed with the partners' products and services. Last, the publishing segment consists of: Dotdash, Dictionary.com, The Daily Beast, Ask.com and CityGrid, which publish digital content and/or provide search services to users.

FINANCIAL DATA:
Note: Data for latest year may not have been available at press time.

In U.S. $	2018	2017	2016	2015	2014	2013
Revenue		3,307,239,000	3,139,882,000	3,230,933,000	3,109,547,000	3,022,987,000
R&D Expense		250,879,000	197,885,000	185,766,000	160,515,000	141,330,000
Operating Income		188,466,000	242,742,000	193,644,000	378,727,000	426,203,000
Operating Margin %		5.69%	7.73%	5.99%	12.17%	14.09%
SGA Expense		2,100,478,000	1,792,423,000	1,871,205,000	1,568,047,000	1,336,601,000
Net Income		304,924,000	-41,280,000	119,472,000	414,873,000	285,784,000
Operating Cash Flow		416,690,000	292,377,000	349,405,000	424,048,000	410,961,000
Capital Expenditure		75,523,000	78,039,000	62,049,000	57,233,000	80,311,000
EBITDA		288,661,000	178,938,000	418,666,000	445,325,000	568,649,000
Return on Assets %		5.80%	-.83%	2.51%	9.75%	7.10%
Return on Equity %		14.18%	-2.24%	6.29%	22.55%	17.10%
Debt to Equity		0.81	0.84	0.96	0.54	0.64

CONTACT INFORMATION:
Phone: 212 314-7300 Fax: 212 314-7399
Toll-Free:
Address: 555 W. 18th St., New York, NY 10011 United States

SALARIES/BONUSES:
Top Exec. Salary: $1,000,000 Bonus: $4,000,000
Second Exec. Salary: $600,000 Bonus: $2,500,000

STOCK TICKER/OTHER:
Stock Ticker: IAC
Employees: 9,100
Parent Company:

Exchange: NAS
Fiscal Year Ends: 12/31

OTHER THOUGHTS:
Estimated Female Officers or Directors: 6
Hot Spot for Advancement for Women/Minorities: Y

I-Cable Communications Limited

NAIC Code: 517110

www.i-cablecomm.com

TYPES OF BUSINESS:
Cable TV Service
Internet Service Provider
VoIP Telephony Services
Film Production
Advertising

BRANDS/DIVISIONS/AFFILIATES:
Forever Top (Asia) Limited
Hong Kong Cable Enterprises Limited
Hong Kong Cable Television Limited
Cable Guide
i-Cable.com

CONTACTS: Note: Officers with more than one job title may be intentionally listed here more than once.
Leung Shuk Yee Irene, COO
Kwok Chi Kin, CFO
Simon K. K. Yu, Sr. VP-iCable Network Oper. Limited
S.Y. Wai, VP-External Affairs & Svcs. Oper.
Ronald Y. C. Chiu, Exec. Dir.-i-CABLE News & i-CABLE Sports Limited
Samuel C.C. Tsang, Gen. Mgr.-Hong Kong Cable Enterprises Limited
David Chiu, Chmn.

GROWTH PLANS/SPECIAL FEATURES:
i-Cable Communications Limited is a leading Hong Kong-based provider of pay-TV services, original media content, broadband internet access and telecommunications services. The company divides its business into four segments: pay-TV, internet and multimedia services, network and Hong Kong Cable Enterprises Limited. Pay-TV is multi-channel pay-television service operated through wholly-owned subsidiary, Hong Kong Cable Television Limited, which produces over 10,000 hours of programming each year. This segment also offers high definition (HD) television channels and includes channels like FOX, the Discovery Channel, Animal Planet and beIN Sports. The internet and multimedia segment provides broadband services through its internet protocol (IP) overlay network, deploying cable-modem based technology. The firm also provides residential markets VoIP service, allowing users to use traditional headsets connect to a voice-enabled cable modem to make and receive calls. The network segment operates universal coverage telecommunications network in Hong Kong, which consists of fiber optic trunk transmission and in-building coaxial networks providing services to over 2 million households. The Hong Kong Cable Enterprises Limited is the commercial airtime sales distributor of i-CABLE Channels and serves as advertising sales distributor for Cable Guide, i-Cable.com and other media. This segment also runs the Hong Kong News Express Limited, a commercial airtime sales distributor and content provider of MTR in-train TV. Forever Top (Asia) Limited is the controlling shareholder of i-Cable Communications with a 43.2% stake.

FINANCIAL DATA: Note: Data for latest year may not have been available at press time.

In U.S. $	2018	2017	2016	2015	2014	2013
Revenue		160,700,500	179,592,100	192,784,700	212,703,300	246,683,500
R&D Expense						
Operating Income		-56,690,930	-39,824,670	-30,937,950	-17,722,480	-11,216,850
Operating Margin %		-35.27%	-22.17%	-16.04%	-8.33%	-4.54%
SGA Expense		39,566,840	43,401,010	43,730,860	42,592,800	47,460,320
Net Income		-46,332,730	-39,943,050	-29,766,440	-17,812,770	-11,864,540
Operating Cash Flow		-26,371,550	10,748,830	17,470,530	14,577,510	32,687,050
Capital Expenditure		37,530,680	45,086,390	40,482,960	42,818,960	33,653,730
EBITDA		-3,010,127	1,471,606	13,141,150	11,203,570	30,802,840
Return on Assets %		-19.66%	-19.39%	-14.26%	-8.10%	-4.96%
Return on Equity %		-44.37%	-47.23%	-24.91%	-12.42%	-7.50%
Debt to Equity		0.08				

CONTACT INFORMATION:
Phone: 852-2112-8118   Fax: 852-2112-7878
Toll-Free:
Address: 9 Hoi Shing Rd, Tsuen Wan, Hong Kong, Hong Kong

SALARIES/BONUSES:
Top Exec. Salary: $ Bonus: $
Second Exec. Salary: $ Bonus: $

STOCK TICKER/OTHER:
Stock Ticker: ICABF   Exchange: GREY
Employees: 1,876   Fiscal Year Ends: 12/31
Parent Company: Forever Top (Asia) Limited

OTHER THOUGHTS:
Estimated Female Officers or Directors: 1
Hot Spot for Advancement for Women/Minorities:

Sales, profits and employees may be estimates. Financial information, benefits and other data can change quickly and may vary from those stated here.

Plunkett Research, Ltd. 281

ICM Partners
NAIC Code: 711410

www.icmtalent.com

TYPES OF BUSINESS:
Talent Agency
Agents-Writers & Musicians
Agents-Literary
Agents-Lecture

BRANDS/DIVISIONS/AFFILIATES:
ICM Community Partners Foundation

CONTACTS: Note: Officers with more than one job title may be intentionally listed here more than once.
Chris Silberman, Managing Dir.
Richard Joe Levy, General Counsel
Joe Friedman, Controller

GROWTH PLANS/SPECIAL FEATURES:
ICM Partners, an employee-owned company, is one of the world's largest talent and literary agencies, with offices in Los Angeles, New York and London. The company represents actors, directors, musicians and writers as well as creative talent in theater, commercials, public speaking and new media. ICM's clients have included actors Christopher Walken, Alan Alda, Al Pacino, Sigourney Weaver, Ellen DeGeneres, Robert Duvall and Samuel L. Jackson; musicians Courtney Love, Beyonce and Nadia Turner; authors E. L. Doctorow, Tom Bodett and Toni Morrison; and film director Woody Allen. The firm's branded entertainment division uses its assets to form alliances with major corporations for a range of activities, including celebrity endorsements, product integrations and tour sponsorships. ICM also provides services to writers, actors, composers, directors, choreographers and designers in theater. ICM's television department represents on-air and creative talent in all segments of the industry, including network, cable and first-run syndication. Its publishing department represents recipients of the Nobel Prize, Pulitzer Prize, National Book Award and many other prestigious literary honors. Its music and comedy department includes concerts and live appearances and represents artists in all musical genres. Its motion pictures department represents film actors, directors and writers ranging from Hollywood's best-known names to the next generation of emerging stars. The philanthropic arm of the firm, ICM Community Partners Foundation, provides guidance and financial resources to arts and social services organizations.

FINANCIAL DATA: Note: Data for latest year may not have been available at press time.

In U.S. $	2018	2017	2016	2015	2014	2013
Revenue	233,000,000	23,000,000	22,500,000	22,000,000	21,500,000	20,000,000
R&D Expense						
Operating Income						
Operating Margin %						
SGA Expense						
Net Income						
Operating Cash Flow						
Capital Expenditure						
EBITDA						
Return on Assets %						
Return on Equity %						
Debt to Equity						

CONTACT INFORMATION:
Phone: 310-550-4000   Fax: 310-550-4100
Toll-Free:
Address: 10250 Constellation Blvd., Los Angeles, CA 90067 United States

STOCK TICKER/OTHER:
Stock Ticker: Private
Employees: 400
Parent Company:

Exchange:
Fiscal Year Ends: 06/30

SALARIES/BONUSES:
Top Exec. Salary: $ Bonus: $
Second Exec. Salary: $ Bonus: $

OTHER THOUGHTS:
Estimated Female Officers or Directors: 1
Hot Spot for Advancement for Women/Minorities:

Sales, profits and employees may be estimates. Financial information, benefits and other data can change quickly and may vary from those stated here.

IGN Entertainment Inc

NAIC Code: 519130

www.ign.com

TYPES OF BUSINESS:
Online Video Game Information
Online Software Retail & Distribution
Video Game Development Services
Online Movie Reviews
Video Game Market Statistics
Lifestyle Web Site

BRANDS/DIVISIONS/AFFILIATES:
j2 Global Inc
Ziff Davis Inc
IGN.com
FilePlanet.com
GameSpy
GamerMetrics
AskMen.com

GROWTH PLANS/SPECIAL FEATURES:
IGN Entertainment, Inc. is a provider of web-based video game information, software and services. The firm is a subsidiary of Ziff Davis, Inc., itself a subsidiary of j2 Global, Inc. The company operates in three business segments: media properties, digital distribution and game technology. With one of the highest visitation rates on the internet for the 18-to-34-year-old male demographic, the media properties segment develops IGN's gaming and entertainment content. Users can access videogame reviews, news, trailers and videos from the company's premier website IGN.com. The digital distribution segment also provides software through the digital distribution site FilePlanet.com, featuring demos and trials of upcoming games. Its game technology services include Powered by GameSpy, offering technological services to game developers and GamerMetrics, which analyzes the traffic and buying patterns of IGN's visitors. Non-video game site, AskMen.com, is a leading male lifestyle website owned and operated by IGN Entertainment.

CONTACTS:
Note: Officers with more than one job title may be intentionally listed here more than once.

Peer Schneider, Managing Dir.
Adam Doree, Head-Int'l Bus. Dev.
Will Guyatt, Head-Global Comm.
Peer Schneider, Sr. VP-Content
Christopher Law, VP-Canadian Ad Sales

FINANCIAL DATA: *Note: Data for latest year may not have been available at press time.*

In U.S. $	2018	2017	2016	2015	2014	2013
Revenue						
R&D Expense						
Operating Income						
Operating Margin %						
SGA Expense						
Net Income						
Operating Cash Flow						
Capital Expenditure						
EBITDA						
Return on Assets %						
Return on Equity %						
Debt to Equity						

CONTACT INFORMATION:
Phone: 415-696-5453   Fax:
Toll-Free: 877-531-5597
Address: 625 2nd St., 4/Fl, San Francisco, CA 94107 United States

STOCK TICKER/OTHER:
Stock Ticker: Subsidiary   Exchange:
Employees: 469   Fiscal Year Ends: 06/30
Parent Company: j2 Global Inc

SALARIES/BONUSES:
Top Exec. Salary: $ Bonus: $
Second Exec. Salary: $ Bonus: $

OTHER THOUGHTS:
Estimated Female Officers or Directors:
Hot Spot for Advancement for Women/Minorities: Y

Sales, profits and employees may be estimates. Financial information, benefits and other data can change quickly and may vary from those stated here.

iHeartMedia Inc

NAIC Code: 515111

www.clearchannel.com

TYPES OF BUSINESS:
Radio Networks

BRANDS/DIVISIONS/AFFILIATES:
Katz Media Group
Clear Channel Outdoor Holdings Inc
iHeartRadio
Total Traffic & Weather Network

CONTACTS:
Note: Officers with more than one job title may be intentionally listed here more than once.

Bob Pittman, CEO
Richard J. Bressler, CFO
Gayle Troberman, CMO
Bob Pittman, Chmn.

GROWTH PLANS/SPECIAL FEATURES:

iHeartMedia, Inc. is a diversified media and entertainment company. The firm specializes in radio, digital, out-of-home, mobile and on-demand entertainment and information services for national audiences and local communities. It operates through three business segments: iHeartMedia, Americas outdoor advertising and international outdoor advertising. iHeartMedia (54% of revenue) delivers media and entertainment content via broadcast and digital delivery, and also includes the company's national syndication business. This segment owns 858 domestic radio stations servicing more than 150 U.S. markets; is the beneficiary of Aloha Station Trust, LLC, which owns and operates 14 radio stations; and operates Premiere Networks, a national radio network that produces, distributes or represents approximately 100 syndicated radio programs. The Americas outdoor and international outdoor advertising segments provide outdoor advertising services in their respective geographic regions using various digital and traditional display types. Americas outdoor consists of operations primarily in the U.S. and Canada, and international outdoor generally operates in Europe and Asia. Americas outdoor owns or operates approximately 85,000 display structures. International outdoor owns or operates more than 490,000 displays across 19 countries. In addition, iHeartMedia is comprised of a full-service media representation business, Katz Media Group, as well as other general support services and initiatives, which are ancillary to its other businesses. Publicly-traded subsidiary, Clear Channel Outdoor Holdings, Inc. (CCO), focuses on new technologies, operates displays and expands upon traditional billboard advertising by packaging unique combinations of displays in airports, rails and malls. iHeartRadio is the firm's free digital music service, providing users access to live radio stations; and Total Traffic & Weather Network, a leading provider of traffic, transit and weather information in the U.S. In March 2018, iHeartMedia filed for Chapter 11 bankruptcy protection in order to restructure its balance-sheet. In 2018, iHeartMedia acquired Stuff Media and Jelli, Inc.

FINANCIAL DATA:
Note: Data for latest year may not have been available at press time.

In U.S. $	2018	2017	2016	2015	2014	2013
Revenue		5,900,000,000	6,273,572,864	6,241,516,032	6,318,533,120	6,243,043,840
R&D Expense						
Operating Income						
Operating Margin %						
SGA Expense						
Net Income			-296,318,016	-754,620,992	-793,761,024	-606,883,008
Operating Cash Flow						
Capital Expenditure						
EBITDA						
Return on Assets %						
Return on Equity %						
Debt to Equity						

CONTACT INFORMATION:
Phone: 210-822-2828 Fax:
Toll-Free:
Address: 200 E. Basse Rd., Ste. 100, San Antonio, TX 78209 United States

STOCK TICKER/OTHER:
Stock Ticker: IHRT
Employees: 18,700
Parent Company:

Exchange: PINX
Fiscal Year Ends: 12/31

SALARIES/BONUSES:
Top Exec. Salary: $ Bonus: $
Second Exec. Salary: $ Bonus: $

OTHER THOUGHTS:
Estimated Female Officers or Directors:
Hot Spot for Advancement for Women/Minorities:

Sales, profits and employees may be estimates. Financial information, benefits and other data can change quickly and may vary from those stated here.

IMAX Corporation

NAIC Code: 512131

www.imax.com

TYPES OF BUSINESS:
Movie Theaters-Giant Screen Format
Giant-Screen Film Production & Distribution
Feature Film Reformatting
Audio & Video Technology

BRANDS/DIVISIONS/AFFILIATES:
IMAX DMR

CONTACTS:
Note: Officers with more than one job title may be intentionally listed here more than once.
Greg Foster, CEO, Divisional
Jiande Chen, CEO, Subsidiary
Richard Gelfond, CEO
Patrick McClymont, CFO
Bradley Wechsler, Chairman of the Board
Jeffrey Vance, Chief Accounting Officer
JL Pomeroy, Chief Marketing Officer
Brian Bonnick, Chief Technology Officer
Carrie Lindzon-Jacobs, Executive VP
Robert Lister, Other Executive Officer
Mark Welton, President, Divisional
Don Savant, President, Divisional
Kenneth Weissman, Secretary

GROWTH PLANS/SPECIAL FEATURES:
IMAX Corporation is a leading global entertainment technology company, specializing in digital and film-based motion picture technologies and large-format 2D and 3D film presentations. IMAX's principal business is the design, manufacture, sale and lease of its proprietary large-format theaters. There are currently 1,370 IMAX theaters located in 75 countries, including 1,272 commercial multiplex theaters and 86 institutional theaters located in museums and science centers. IMAX's laser-based digital projection system incorporates Kodak technology, allowing theaters to present greater brightness and clarity. More than 32 laser-based digital theater systems have been installed. The company generally does not own IMAX theaters, but licenses the use of its trademarks along with the sale or lease of its equipment. The firm is also engaged in the production, digital re-mastering, post-production and distribution of large-format films. IMAX theater systems combine advanced, high-resolution projectors with film handling equipment and automated theater control systems; sound system components; and screen components as large as eight stories high to create immersive audio-visual experiences. To increase the demand for its theater systems, the company has positioned its theater network as a new distribution platform for Hollywood blockbuster films. To this end, IMAX has developed IMAX DMR (Digital Re-Mastering) technology, which allows conventional 35 millimeter movies to be digitally converted to its large format; has introduced lower cost theater systems designed for multiplex owners; and is continuing to build relationships with Hollywood studios and commercial exhibition companies. In addition, the company produces adventure, science and nature films specifically for IMAX theaters. The company also maintains research and development efforts to continually improve digital and film-based projection and sound system component design, engineering and imaging technology, particularly in 3D. In May 2018, IMAX announced that it had partnered with Vox cinemas to bring IMAX to Saudi Arabia.

FINANCIAL DATA:
Note: Data for latest year may not have been available at press time.

In U.S. $	2018	2017	2016	2015	2014	2013
Revenue		380,767,000	377,334,000	373,805,000	290,541,000	287,937,000
R&D Expense		20,855,000	16,315,000	12,730,000	16,096,000	14,771,000
Operating Income		48,325,000	58,585,000	88,601,000	61,390,000	65,100,000
Operating Margin %		12.69%	15.52%	23.70%	21.12%	22.60%
SGA Expense		110,400,000	124,745,000	115,345,000	93,260,000	82,669,000
Net Income		2,344,000	28,788,000	55,844,000	39,736,000	44,115,000
Operating Cash Flow		85,366,000	77,872,000	83,685,000	86,605,000	55,033,000
Capital Expenditure		29,357,000	20,065,000	48,322,000	43,022,000	15,502,000
EBITDA		98,760,000	106,143,000	131,542,000	92,031,000	102,327,000
Return on Assets %		.27%	3.21%	7.09%	7.12%	9.77%
Return on Equity %		.43%	4.85%	10.94%	11.19%	15.40%
Debt to Equity		0.04	0.04	0.04	0.01	

CONTACT INFORMATION:
Phone: 905 403-6500 Fax: 905 403-6450
Toll-Free:
Address: 2525 Speakman Dr., Mississauga, ON L5K 1B1 Canada

STOCK TICKER/OTHER:
Stock Ticker: IMAX Exchange: NYS
Employees: 703 Fiscal Year Ends: 12/31
Parent Company:

SALARIES/BONUSES:
Top Exec. Salary: $1,198,077 Bonus: $850,000
Second Exec. Salary: $1,024,039 Bonus: $250,000

OTHER THOUGHTS:
Estimated Female Officers or Directors: 3
Hot Spot for Advancement for Women/Minorities: Y

Ingram Entertainment Holdings Inc

www.ingramentertainment.com

NAIC Code: 423990

TYPES OF BUSINESS:
Video Tapes, Prerecorded, Distributors
Entertainment Product Distribution
Internet Services
Business-to-Business Sales
Marketing Services
Magazine Publishing
Graphic Design

BRANDS/DIVISIONS/AFFILIATES:
AccessIngram.com
MyVideoStore.com
Monarch Home Entertainment
DBI Beverage Inc

CONTACTS:
Note: Officers with more than one job title may be intentionally listed here more than once.

Robert W. Webb, CEO
William D. Daniel, Vice-Chmn.
David B. Ingram, Chmn.

GROWTH PLANS/SPECIAL FEATURES:
Ingram Entertainment Holdings, Inc. (IEI) is a leading national distributor of home entertainment products including DVD hardware and software, video games, music players, electronics and accessories and audiobooks. The company provides support services for internet retailers, business-to-business (B2B) sales through AccessIngram.com, and creation and maintenance of customer websites under the MyVideoStore.com program. Services include ad placement; promotional premiums; catalog sell-through promotion programs; electronic trading; merchandising and marketing tools; weekly and monthly publications; and creative services, such as print and collateral, editorial, illustration, slide presentation, product photography, print buying and media placement solutions. Additionally, IEI releases direct-to-video and smaller titles to the home video market under the Monarch Home Entertainment label. DBI Beverage, Inc., another company affiliated with IEI, is a leading beverage distributor in the U.S., supplying domestic, craft and import beers; specialty waters; energy drinks; and soft drinks to select markets in California. The firm offers its services to retail locations including video specialty stores, electronics and video game stores, internet retailers, drugstores and supermarkets. IEI processes an average of 5 million units per month through 10 sales and distribution facilities comprising 500,000 square feet of warehouse space.

IEI offers its employees medical, dental and vision coverage; a 401(k) plan; short- and long-term disability; life insurance; tuition reimbursement; and employee discounts.

FINANCIAL DATA:
Note: Data for latest year may not have been available at press time.

In U.S. $	2018	2017	2016	2015	2014	2013
Revenue	450,000,000	455,000,000	445,000,000	500,000,000	485,000,000	480,000,000
R&D Expense						
Operating Income						
Operating Margin %						
SGA Expense						
Net Income						
Operating Cash Flow						
Capital Expenditure						
EBITDA						
Return on Assets %						
Return on Equity %						
Debt to Equity						

CONTACT INFORMATION:
Phone: 615-287-4000 Fax:
Toll-Free: 800-621-1333
Address: Two Ingram Blvd., La Vergne, TN 37089 United States

STOCK TICKER/OTHER:
Stock Ticker: Private
Employees: 500
Parent Company:

Exchange:
Fiscal Year Ends: 12/31

SALARIES/BONUSES:
Top Exec. Salary: $ Bonus: $
Second Exec. Salary: $ Bonus: $

OTHER THOUGHTS:
Estimated Female Officers or Directors:
Hot Spot for Advancement for Women/Minorities:

Ink Publishing Inc

NAIC Code: 511120

ink-global.com

TYPES OF BUSINESS:
Inflight Magazine Publishing
Digital Magazine Publishing
Advertising Space Retail

BRANDS/DIVISIONS/AFFILIATES:

CONTACTS:
Note: Officers with more than one job title may be intentionally listed here more than once.
Michael Keating, Co-CEO
Simon Leslie, Co-CEO
Jim Campbell, Chief Operational & Financial Officer
Chris Deacon, Dir.-Design-London
Carole Bellars, Group Dir.-Financial
Simon Leslie, Dir.-Publishing
Michael Keating, Exec. Dir.-Creative
James Malone, Group Dir.-Credit
Kevin Rolfe, Dir.-Commercial
Gerry Ricketts, Managing Dir.-Singapore

GROWTH PLANS/SPECIAL FEATURES:
Ink Publishing, Inc. is a publisher of specialized inflight print and digital publications, including onboard magazines, retail catalogues, targeted consumer magazines, entertainment guides and pre-pay wall onboard websites. The firm is a media partner to more than 20 airlines and global travel groups worldwide, publishing 28 magazines in multiple languages and creating and distributing dozens of digital products to passengers throughout Europe, Africa, the Middle East, North America, South America and Asia. Ink's operations encompass media strategy development, content design and origination, advertising space retail and the management of media printing, programming, production and delivery. Its advertising retail services include the sale of space inside its magazines as well as on headrest covers, tray tables, menus, timetables, seatbacks and inflight entertainment systems. The firm also designs and maintains online versions of its onboard magazines, including websites and content optimized for social networking, smartphone and iPad applications. Ink sells digital media space for KLM, easyJet, Cebu Pacific and many more. The firm serves many airlines internationally, including American Airlines, United, Qatar Airways, airberlin, Norwegian, Etihad and Scoot.

FINANCIAL DATA:
Note: Data for latest year may not have been available at press time.

In U.S. $	2018	2017	2016	2015	2014	2013
Revenue						
R&D Expense						
Operating Income						
Operating Margin %						
SGA Expense						
Net Income						
Operating Cash Flow						
Capital Expenditure						
EBITDA						
Return on Assets %						
Return on Equity %						
Debt to Equity						

CONTACT INFORMATION:
Phone: 44-20-76250700　　Fax: 44-845-2809898
Toll-Free:
Address: Blackburn House, Blackburn Rd., London, NW6 1RZ United Kingdom

STOCK TICKER/OTHER:
Stock Ticker: Private　　Exchange:
Employees: 300　　Fiscal Year Ends:
Parent Company:

SALARIES/BONUSES:
Top Exec. Salary: $　　Bonus: $
Second Exec. Salary: $　　Bonus: $

OTHER THOUGHTS:
Estimated Female Officers or Directors: 1
Hot Spot for Advancement for Women/Minorities: Y

Integrity Music

NAIC Code: 512230

www.integritymusic.com

TYPES OF BUSINESS:
Christian Music Publishing
Mobile Phone Media
Music Production
Videos
Songbooks & Sheet Music
Music Club

BRANDS/DIVISIONS/AFFILIATES:
David C. Cook
iWorship

GROWTH PLANS/SPECIAL FEATURES:
Integrity Music, a division of nonprofit Christian publisher David C. Cook, produces and publishes Christian music. The firm's product formats include compact discs, software, videos and songbooks. It produces products in English, Spanish, Mandarin, Cantonese, Dutch, French, Portuguese and Hindi. Integrity's resources are distributed in more than 200 countries and sold worldwide. Integrity offers iWorship, a line of CDs, DVDs, songbooks and books for worship enhancement. The firm has international offices in the U.K. and Canada.

CONTACTS:
Note: Officers with more than one job title may be intentionally listed here more than once.

C. Ryan Dunham, Pres.
Donald S. Ellington, Sr. VP-Admin.
Donald S. Ellington, Sr. VP-Finance
Samuel Chappell, Pres., Integrity Music

FINANCIAL DATA:
Note: Data for latest year may not have been available at press time.

In U.S. $	2018	2017	2016	2015	2014	2013
Revenue						
R&D Expense						
Operating Income						
Operating Margin %						
SGA Expense						
Net Income						
Operating Cash Flow						
Capital Expenditure						
EBITDA						
Return on Assets %						
Return on Equity %						
Debt to Equity						

CONTACT INFORMATION:
Phone:
Fax:
Toll-Free: 888-888-4726
Address: 1646 Westgate Cir., Ste. 106, Brentwood, TN 37027 United States

STOCK TICKER/OTHER:
Stock Ticker: Subsidiary
Employees: 220
Parent Company: David C Cook

Exchange:
Fiscal Year Ends: 12/31

SALARIES/BONUSES:
Top Exec. Salary: $
Bonus: $
Second Exec. Salary: $
Bonus: $

OTHER THOUGHTS:
Estimated Female Officers or Directors:
Hot Spot for Advancement for Women/Minorities:

International Data Group Inc

NAIC Code: 511120

www.idg.com

TYPES OF BUSINESS:
Publishing-Magazines
Research
Online
Events
Global Solutions

BRANDS/DIVISIONS/AFFILIATES:
China Oceanwide Holdings Group Co Ltd
IDG Connect
Macworld
Computerworld
IDG Amplify
International Data Corporation
Network World
TechHive

CONTACTS:
Note: Officers with more than one job title may be intentionally listed here more than once.

Michael Friedenberg, CEO
Ted Bloom, Pres.
Ted Bloom, CFO
David Hill, Pres., IDG Comm.
Patrick J. McGovern, Chmn.
Michael Friedenberg, CEO-IDG Comm. Worldwide

GROWTH PLANS/SPECIAL FEATURES:

International Data Group, Inc. (IDG), owned by China Oceanwide Holdings Group Co., Ltd., is a technology media, research and events company. The company's primary global digital media brands include CIO, CSO, Computerworld, ChannelWorld, GamePro, InfoWorld, Macworld, Network World, PCWorld and TechHive. The firm's marketing and research services operate through IDG Connect, a custom publisher; IDG Enterprise LeadAccel, which connects consumers with IT decision-makers to determine next stages in communication or sales engagement; IDG List and Brokerage Services, a full-service list management and brokerage group; and IDG Direct, a provider of multi-lingual business-to-business (B2B) telemarketing, event booking and market research services. IDG's TechNetwork operates in conjunction with the firm's media brands by representing independent websites in an ad network that produces over 700 globally branded technology events, including the E3 Expo and the Macworld Conference & Expo. In addition, the company provides subscription services, custom consulting and reports. The IDG News Service is a daily publisher of global IT news, editorials and commentary. International Data Corporation (IDC), an IDG subsidiary, is a research provider of technology intelligence, market data, industry analysis and strategic guidance to the IT industry. IDG Knowledge Hub manages audience insight operations by providing technology buyers with a range of data, research, events and insights from industry experts. IDG also offers IDG Amplify, a social media marketing service that provide clients with community and content platform management as well as social web integration services.

The firm offers employees flexible spending accounts, disability benefits, an employee assistance program, a 401(k) and paid time off.

FINANCIAL DATA:
Note: Data for latest year may not have been available at press time.

In U.S. $	2018	2017	2016	2015	2014	2013
Revenue	3,980,000,000	3,940,000,000	3,925,000,000	3,800,000,000	3,750,000,000	3,550,000,000
R&D Expense						
Operating Income						
Operating Margin %						
SGA Expense						
Net Income						
Operating Cash Flow						
Capital Expenditure						
EBITDA						
Return on Assets %						
Return on Equity %						
Debt to Equity						

CONTACT INFORMATION:
Phone: 617-534-1200 Fax:
Toll-Free:
Address: 1 Exeter Plz., Fl. 15, Boston, MA 02116 United States

STOCK TICKER/OTHER:
Stock Ticker: Subsidiary Exchange:
Employees: 13,200 Fiscal Year Ends: 09/30
Parent Company: China Oceanwide Holdings Group Co Ltd

SALARIES/BONUSES:
Top Exec. Salary: $ Bonus: $
Second Exec. Salary: $ Bonus: $

OTHER THOUGHTS:
Estimated Female Officers or Directors:
Hot Spot for Advancement for Women/Minorities: Y

Sales, profits and employees may be estimates. Financial information, benefits and other data can change quickly and may vary from those stated here.

International Game Technology PLC

www.igt.com

NAIC Code: 511210G

TYPES OF BUSINESS:
Computer Software, Electronic Games, Apps & Entertainment
Computerized Gambling Devices
Gaming Services
Gambling Software
Consulting
Online Gaming

BRANDS/DIVISIONS/AFFILIATES:

CONTACTS: Note: Officers with more than one job title may be intentionally listed here more than once.
Marco Sala, CEO
John Vandemore, CFO
Alberto Fornaro, CFO
Eric Tom, Executive VP, Divisional
Paul Gracey, General Counsel
Cindy Klimstra, Other Corporate Officer
Kate Pearlman, Vice President, Divisional

GROWTH PLANS/SPECIAL FEATURES:

International Game Technology PLC (IGT) is a global end-to-end gaming company. The firm operates and provides an integrated portfolio of technology products and services across all gaming markets, including lottery management services, online and instant lotteries, electronic gaming machines, sports betting, interactive gaming and commercial services to customers in 100 countries. The company operates through four business segments: North America gaming and interactive, North America lottery, international and Italy. The North America gaming and interactive segment develops and delivers games, systems and solutions for land-based casinos; interactive for-wager online play; and the DoubleDown Casino free-to-play social casino app. This division is headquartered in Las Vegas, Nevada, and provides its products and solutions to commercial, government and tribal customers in the U.S. and Canada. The North America lottery segment develops and delivers innovative and future-focused lottery solutions. This division's revenue is derived from the sale or lease of lottery central system hardware and software, as well as the sale or lease of lottery and gaming terminals to government entities. The international segment delivers end-to-end products across all channels and regulated gaming segments. It is responsible for development and operation management for all markets in Europe, the Middle East, Central/Latin America, the Caribbean, Asia Pacific and Oceania, across IGT's entire product portfolio. Last, the Italy segment operates and provides business-to-consumer gaming products, including lotteries, machine gaming, sports betting, commercial services and interactive gaming. In November 2018, IGT entered the electronic bingo market in Canada by launching electronic bingo content in Canada.

IGT offers its employees medical, dental and vision coverage; a prescription drug plan; short- and long-term disability; life insurance; and business travel insurance.

FINANCIAL DATA: Note: Data for latest year may not have been available at press time.

In U.S. $	2018	2017	2016	2015	2014	2013
Revenue		4,938,959,000	5,153,896,000	4,689,056,000	3,732,736,000	4,229,382,000
R&D Expense		313,088,000	343,531,000	277,401,000		
Operating Income		704,004,000	726,114,000	629,349,000	722,403,800	780,455,100
Operating Margin %		14.25%	14.08%	13.42%	19.35%	18.45%
SGA Expense		816,093,000	945,824,000	795,252,000		
Net Income		-1,068,576,000	211,337,000	-75,574,000	101,304,800	242,251,900
Operating Cash Flow		685,928,000	961,887,000	785,997,000	1,192,435,000	961,430,800
Capital Expenditure		698,010,000	557,238,000	402,634,000	272,965,600	454,537,500
EBITDA		284,414,000	1,675,150,000	1,220,781,000	1,152,408,000	1,371,923,000
Return on Assets %		-7.07%	1.40%	-.63%	1.09%	2.48%
Return on Equity %		-42.12%	6.94%	-2.57%	3.44%	8.02%
Debt to Equity		3.90	2.58	2.78	0.76	1.20

CONTACT INFORMATION:
Phone: 44-03-131-0300 Fax:
Toll-Free:
Address: 66 Seymour St., 2/Fl, London, W1H 5BT United Kingdom

SALARIES/BONUSES:
Top Exec. Salary: $905,293   Bonus: $2,457,750
Second Exec. Salary: $ Bonus: $

STOCK TICKER/OTHER:
Stock Ticker: IGT
Employees: 12,613
Parent Company:

Exchange: NYS
Fiscal Year Ends: 09/30

OTHER THOUGHTS:
Estimated Female Officers or Directors: 3
Hot Spot for Advancement for Women/Minorities: Y

Sales, profits and employees may be estimates. Financial information, benefits and other data can change quickly and may vary from those stated here.

Intralot SA

NAIC Code: 511210G

www.intralot.com

TYPES OF BUSINESS:
Computer Software, Electronic Games, Apps & Entertainment

BRANDS/DIVISIONS/AFFILIATES:
Lotos X
Intralot Orion
Player Pulse
Retailer Pulse
Intralot Canvas
Horizon
RGS

CONTACTS:
Note: Officers with more than one job title may be intentionally listed here more than once.

Antonios I. Kerastaris, CEO
Michael Kogeler, COO
George Koliastasis, CFO
Nikos Nikolakopoulos, Chief Commercial Officer
Alina Papgeorgiou, Dir.-Human Resources
Argirios Diamantis, CTO
Persa Kartsoli, Head-Corp. & Public Rel.
Socrates Kokkalis, Chmn.

GROWTH PLANS/SPECIAL FEATURES:
Intralot SA is a supplier of integrated gaming and transaction processing systems, innovative game content and sports betting management as well as interactive gaming services to state-licensed gaming organizations. The firm is active in 52 regulated jurisdictions worldwide, having installed and operates more than 300,000 proprietary terminals. Intralot's business portfolio is divided into four segments: verticals, channels, platforms and services. The verticals segment develops, produces and services strategies that drives operational success across the lottery, betting and interactive games verticals. The channels segment offers a vast range of products and services that help operators build a cohesive land-based and digital ecosystem, from retail terminals and platforms to web and mobile portals and to native applications. The platforms segment provides gaming solutions and services, including content management, loyalty schemes, network incentivization, trading, analytics, monitoring and reporting. These platforms are created for operators who wish to optimally market their offerings and meet operational needs. Products within this segment include: Lotos X, a fully modular, fully paramertical ecosystem; Intralot Orion, a next-generation sports betting platform; Player Pulse, offering player management across all channels; Retailer Pulse, offering retailer management; Intralot Canvas, unifying gaming content across touchpoints; Horizon, a retail digital signage for all verticals; RGS, a remote gaming server; connected retail device management; and a monitoring system that manages gaming venues and video lottery terminals (VLTs). Last, the services segment addresses the entire spectrum of lottery and betting organizations' needs, whether it be technical support, system administration, marketing, risk management, online services, media and/or broadcasting.

FINANCIAL DATA:
Note: Data for latest year may not have been available at press time.

In U.S. $	2018	2017	2016	2015	2014	2013
Revenue		1,257,799,000	1,507,714,000	2,181,261,000	2,110,954,000	1,753,577,000
R&D Expense		7,002,096	5,372,033	6,906,411	8,227,776	7,947,556
Operating Income		104,273,900	85,728,110	62,170,230	77,069,760	94,463,940
Operating Margin %		8.71%	8.18%	4.15%	4.69%	6.51%
SGA Expense		156,407,500	163,654,500	218,012,700	205,324,200	183,348,500
Net Income		-60,812,410	1,059,370	-74,210,600	-56,438,240	-5,202,306
Operating Cash Flow		175,457,900	191,486,300	129,612,200	108,624,200	92,579,850
Capital Expenditure		84,614,070	74,520,430	80,632,890	76,673,340	66,261,900
EBITDA		164,309,500	201,868,100	219,291,900	220,683,900	222,322,000
Return on Assets %		-5.12%	.08%	-5.16%	-3.97%	-.40%
Return on Equity %		-57.60%	.72%	-37.54%	-20.43%	-1.60%
Debt to Equity		12.61	5.05	5.54	2.60	1.38

CONTACT INFORMATION:
Phone: 30-210-615-6000 Fax: 30-210-610-6800
Toll-Free:
Address: 64, Kifissias Ave. & 3, Premetis St., Athens, 15125 Greece

STOCK TICKER/OTHER:
Stock Ticker: IRLTY
Employees: 5,149
Parent Company:

Exchange: PINX
Fiscal Year Ends: 12/30

SALARIES/BONUSES:
Top Exec. Salary: $ Bonus: $
Second Exec. Salary: $ Bonus: $

OTHER THOUGHTS:
Estimated Female Officers or Directors: 1
Hot Spot for Advancement for Women/Minorities:

Sales, profits and employees may be estimates. Financial information, benefits and other data can change quickly and may vary from those stated here.

ION Media Networks

www.ionmedianetworks.com

NAIC Code: 515120

TYPES OF BUSINESS:
Television Broadcasting
Television Production

BRANDS/DIVISIONS/AFFILIATES:
ION Television
Qubo
ION Life

CONTACTS: Note: Officers with more than one job title may be intentionally listed here more than once.
Brandon Burgess, CEO
Tim Clyne, Dir.-Finance
David A. Glenn, Pres., Eng.
Terri Santisi, Chief Admin. Officer
Chris Addeo, Head-Mktg.
Russell Frederickson, Head-On-Air Svcs.
Joseph Koker, Head-Stations
Marc Zand, Head-Programming Acquisitions
Brandon Burgess, Chmn.
Douglas Holloway, Head-Dist.

GROWTH PLANS/SPECIAL FEATURES:

ION Media Networks owns one of the largest broadcast television groups in the U.S., broadcasting its television, cable and satellite stations seven-days-a-week, 24-hours-a-day to more than 100 million households. The company's flagship station, ION Television, offers a varied mix of popular television series, made-for-TV movies, sports and special programming. During the network entertainment hours, which are between 1:00 pm to 1:00 am, the station airs shows with little or no violence, sexual content or questionable language. This focus on family-oriented programming is one of the firm's primary business strategies. Current hit series and originals (as of December 2018) include Blue Bloods, Chicago P.D., Criminal Minds, CSI: Crime Scene Investigation, Law & Order, Leverage, NCIS: Los Angeles, Private Eyes, Saving Hope and Qubo Kids Corner. The firm's Qubo channel airs bilingual programs targeting children ages five to eight years old and focuses on education. Shows include Madeline, Miss Spider's Sunny Patch Friends, Monster Math Squad, The Adventures of Paddington Bear, Babar, Doki, Pet Alien and many more. Its ION Life subsidiary focuses on health and wellness, diet and nutrition, competitive and lifestyle sports, travel, design and decor, shopping, family activities and personal achievement. The company's revenue comes from selling network long form paid programming (infomercials), network spot advertising (nationwide advertising) and station advertising (local or regional advertising). Network long form paid programming is the firm's strongest source of revenue, and its sales team is divided into three categories: national long form sales, local long form sales and direct response. In September 2018, ION Media expanded its television station group with the purchase of five full-power UHF stations: KILM-TV (Los Angeles), WDLI-TV (Cleveland), WCLJ-TV (Indianapolis), WSFJ-TV (Columbus) and WKOI-TV (Dayton).

FINANCIAL DATA: Note: Data for latest year may not have been available at press time.

In U.S. $	2018	2017	2016	2015	2014	2013
Revenue	530,000,000	522,000,000	515,000,000	502,000,000	415,000,000	
R&D Expense						
Operating Income						
Operating Margin %						
SGA Expense						
Net Income						
Operating Cash Flow						
Capital Expenditure						
EBITDA						
Return on Assets %						
Return on Equity %						
Debt to Equity						

CONTACT INFORMATION:
Phone: 561-659-4122 Fax: 561-659-4252
Toll-Free:
Address: 601 Clearwater Park Rd., West Palm Beach, FL 33401 United States

STOCK TICKER/OTHER:
Stock Ticker: Private
Employees: 450
Parent Company:

Exchange:
Fiscal Year Ends: 12/31

SALARIES/BONUSES:
Top Exec. Salary: $ Bonus: $
Second Exec. Salary: $ Bonus: $

OTHER THOUGHTS:
Estimated Female Officers or Directors: 1
Hot Spot for Advancement for Women/Minorities:

IPlay

NAIC Code: 511210G

www.iplay.com

TYPES OF BUSINESS:
Computer Software, Electronic Games, Apps & Entertainment Apps

BRANDS/DIVISIONS/AFFILIATES:
iWin Inc
iWin.com
Iplay.com
Download-Free-Games.com
JenkatGames.com

CONTACTS:
Note: Officers with more than one job title may be intentionally listed here more than once.

C.J. Wolf, CEO-iWin

GROWTH PLANS/SPECIAL FEATURES:
IPlay publishes and distributes downloadable and built-in entertainment software and video games across multiple devices. The firm is a subsidiary of iWin, Inc. As a game publisher, the firm has produced more than 100 titles for mobile, personal computer (PC) and social platforms. Its games include Jewel Quest, Jojo's Fashion Show and Jewel Quest Mysteries. Licensed properties include Family Feud, Deal or No Deal and $100,000 Pyramid video games. Jewel Quest is one of the most widely-played match 3 game, enjoyed by more than 75 million players worldwide across all devices. In all, IPlay offers more than 3,000 games through its website, either as free-to-play (with advertising interruptions) or with no ad interruptions for $9.99 per month. As a distributor, IPlay provides casual games solutions via more than 500 developers worldwide and distributes that content through its own websites, as well as third-party partner sites. Parent iWin-owned and operated sites include iWin.com, Iplay.com, Download-Free-Games.com and JenkatGames.com.

FINANCIAL DATA:
Note: Data for latest year may not have been available at press time.

In U.S. $	2018	2017	2016	2015	2014	2013
Revenue						
R&D Expense						
Operating Income						
Operating Margin %						
SGA Expense						
Net Income						
Operating Cash Flow						
Capital Expenditure						
EBITDA						
Return on Assets %						
Return on Equity %						
Debt to Equity						

CONTACT INFORMATION:
Phone: 415-351-1016   Fax:
Toll-Free:
Address: 180 Sansome St., Fl. 2, San Francisco, CA 94104 United States

STOCK TICKER/OTHER:
Stock Ticker: Subsidiary   Exchange:
Employees: Fiscal Year Ends: 12/31
Parent Company: iWin Inc

SALARIES/BONUSES:
Top Exec. Salary: $ Bonus: $
Second Exec. Salary: $ Bonus: $

OTHER THOUGHTS:
Estimated Female Officers or Directors:
Hot Spot for Advancement for Women/Minorities:

Sales, profits and employees may be estimates. Financial information, benefits and other data can change quickly and may vary from those stated here.

iQiyi Inc

NAIC Code: 519130

www.iqiyi.com

TYPES OF BUSINESS:
Online Video Streaming Service
Online Video

BRANDS/DIVISIONS/AFFILIATES:
Baidu Inc
iQiyi Motion Pictures

CONTACTS: Note: Officers with more than one job title may be intentionally listed here more than once.
Ma Dong, COO
Tang Xing, CTO

GROWTH PLANS/SPECIAL FEATURES:
iQiyi, Inc. is an online video platform based in Beijing, China. As one of the largest online video sites in the country, iQiyi has more than 500 million monthly active users with nearly 6 billion hours spent on its service each month. The company issued its initial public offering in the U.S. during 2018, raising $2.25 billion. iQiyi's film production division, iQiyi Motion Pictures, expands the firm's existing cooperative projects with overseas partners, including purchasing releases and co-producing movies. As a result, iQiyi Motion Pictures has streamed Venice Film Festivals' movies online, generating over 6.95 billion hours of viewing on its website; and participated in the Busan Film Festival, signing exclusive rights to nearly 100 South Korean titles. iQiyi also owns online copyrights of eight top entertainment shows in mainland China, and several entertainment shows in Taiwan and South Korea, including the Running Man. This acquisition enabled iQiyi to launch in Taiwan, and has more than 20 million subscribers. During 2017, Netflix announced a licensing deal with iQiyi, under which some Netflix original productions would be available on iQiyi. iQiyi operates as a subsidiary of Baidu, Inc., a Chinese multinational technology company specializing in internet-related services and products, as well as artificial intelligence (AI).

FINANCIAL DATA: Note: Data for latest year may not have been available at press time.

In U.S. $	2018	2017	2016	2015	2014	2013
Revenue		2,529,195,000	1,635,460,000	774,051,300		
R&D Expense		184,803,900	119,992,700	72,762,300		
Operating Income		-575,309,500	-405,974,900	-353,306,000		
Operating Margin %		-22.74%	-24.82%	-45.64%		
SGA Expense		389,310,300	256,992,900	175,294,200		
Net Income		-543,862,300	-447,384,300	-374,774,300		
Operating Cash Flow		583,863,400	380,160,500	155,836,800		
Capital Expenditure		1,487,396,000	834,341,400	423,824,900		
EBITDA		652,998,200	217,490,800	26,235,100		
Return on Assets %		-22.09%	-22.55%			
Return on Equity %						
Debt to Equity		0.03				

CONTACT INFORMATION:
Phone: 86-10-6267-7171 Fax:
Toll-Free:
Address: Fl. 9, iQIYI Innovation Bldg., 2 Haidian N. First St., Haidian Dist., Beijing, Beijing 100080 China

STOCK TICKER/OTHER:
Stock Ticker: IQ
Employees: 6,014
Parent Company: Baidu Inc

Exchange: NAS
Fiscal Year Ends: 12/31

SALARIES/BONUSES:
Top Exec. Salary: $ Bonus: $
Second Exec. Salary: $ Bonus: $

OTHER THOUGHTS:
Estimated Female Officers or Directors:
Hot Spot for Advancement for Women/Minorities:

Sales, profits and employees may be estimates. Financial information, benefits and other data can change quickly and may vary from those stated here.

ITV plc

NAIC Code: 517110

www.itvplc.com

TYPES OF BUSINESS:
Cable TV Channel
Satellite Channels
Broadcast TV
TV Production

BRANDS/DIVISIONS/AFFILIATES:
ITV
CITV
ITV2
ITV3
ITV4
ITVBe
ITV Encore
ITV Studios

CONTACTS:
Note: Officers with more than one job title may be intentionally listed here more than once.

Julian Bellamy, Managing Dir.-ITV Studios
Ian Griffiths, COO
Kelly Williams, Managing Dir.-Commercial
David Osborn, Dir.-Group Human Resources
Mark Smith, Group Chief Technology Officer
Andrew Garard, Dir.-Group Legal
Simon Pitts, Dir.-Strategy & Transformation
Fru Hazlitt, Head-Online & Commercial
Mary Fagan, Dir.-Group Comm. & Corp. Affairs
Pippa Foulds, Head-Investor Rel.
Charles van der Welle, Dir.-Treasury
Ian Griffiths, Group Dir.-Finance
Kevin Lygo, Managing Dir.-ITV Studios
Peter Bazalgette, Chmn.

GROWTH PLANS/SPECIAL FEATURES:

ITV plc is a leading television broadcasting company in the U.K. It operates in two segments: broadcasting and online and ITV Studios. The broadcasting and online segment includes ITV, one of the largest U.K. commercial television channels, and its digital channels, including ITV2, ITV3, ITV4, ITV Encore, ITVBe and CITV. ITV accounts for almost half of the U.K.'s television advertising market and broadcasts popular programs. ITV2 features a mix of entertainment, mainstream movies and live events programming available free-to-air on satellite, cable and digital terrestrial platforms. ITV3 shows proprietary contemporary dramas, including Inspector Morse, Agatha Christie's Poirot and Taggart and Lewis. ITV4 primarily showcases male-focused shows and sports content. ITV Encore airs dramas. ITV Be is an entertainment, lifestyle and reality television channel. CITV features children's programming. Online operations are delivered across various platforms that include ITV.com, video on demand cable, game consoles and mobile devices. The company's primary revenues come from the U.K. advertising market. Through ITV Studios, the company produces drama, soap operas, entertainment, factual, daytime, arts, current affairs and game show programming for its in-house channels as well as other U.K. and international broadcasters. In addition, ITV Studios consists of ITV's U.K. operations and its international production operations. ITV Studios currently has offices and a presence in the U.K., the U.S., the Netherlands, Germany, France, Italy, the Nordics and Australia. This segment also runs Global Entertainment, ITV's distribution business, distributing ITV content and acquired third-party content to other broadcasters and platforms in the U.K. and internationally.

FINANCIAL DATA:
Note: Data for latest year may not have been available at press time.

In U.S. $	2018	2017	2016	2015	2014	2013
Revenue						
R&D Expense						
Operating Income						
Operating Margin %						
SGA Expense						
Net Income						
Operating Cash Flow						
Capital Expenditure						
EBITDA						
Return on Assets %						
Return on Equity %						
Debt to Equity						

CONTACT INFORMATION:
Phone: 44-344-881-4150   Fax:
Toll-Free:
Address: The London Television Centre, Upper Ground, London, SE1 9LT United Kingdom

STOCK TICKER/OTHER:
Stock Ticker: ITVPF
Employees: 6,055
Parent Company:

Exchange: PINX
Fiscal Year Ends: 12/31

SALARIES/BONUSES:
Top Exec. Salary: $767,832   Bonus: $1,236,361
Second Exec. Salary: $593,554   Bonus: $1,046,929

OTHER THOUGHTS:
Estimated Female Officers or Directors: 3
Hot Spot for Advancement for Women/Minorities: Y

Izzi Telecom SAB de CV

NAIC Code: 515120

www.izzi.mx

TYPES OF BUSINESS:
Television Broadcasting
High Speed Internet
Digital Telephony

BRANDS/DIVISIONS/AFFILIATES:
Grupo Televisa SAB
VEO Revenue
VEO Play
Dr WiFi

CONTACTS: Note: Officers with more than one job title may be intentionally listed here more than once.
Alfonso de Angoitia, Co-CEO-Grupo Televisa
Bernardo Gomez Martinez, Co-CEO-Grupo Televisa
Emilio Fernando Azcarraga Jean, Pres.
Juan Carlos Salazar Cerda, Exec. Dir.-Oper.
Heriberto Lopez Mejia, Exec. Dir.-Signal Reception

GROWTH PLANS/SPECIAL FEATURES:
Izzi Telecom SAB de CV is a major provider of cable and digital communications services in Mexico, serving more than 60 cities in 29 states. The company's product offerings include digital cable TV, video-on-demand (VOD), high-speed internet and digital telephony services. The firm's cable TV services include channels in standard definition (SD) and high definition (HD), along with thousands of titles via On Demand. Izzi also offers premium channels, as well as an over-the-top platform and mobile app. Through VEO Revenue, customers can rent movies for the TV and supported devices connected to the internet. VEO Play provides unlimited access to movies and series for a monthly fee. The company's internet and telephone services can be purchased together and includes unlimited calls through Mexico, the Americas and Europe as well as 30-megabyte (MB) internet download speeds. Faster speeds can also be purchased. In addition, Izzi offers 24/7 assistance under the name Dr. WiFi. The firm is part of Grupo Televisa SAB, one of the largest media companies in the Spanish-speaking world.

FINANCIAL DATA: Note: Data for latest year may not have been available at press time.

In U.S. $	2018	2017	2016	2015	2014	2013
Revenue	610,000,000	606,900,000	578,000,000	550,000,000	580,782,241	593,371,712
R&D Expense						
Operating Income						
Operating Margin %						
SGA Expense						
Net Income						
Operating Cash Flow						
Capital Expenditure						
EBITDA						
Return on Assets %						
Return on Equity %						
Debt to Equity						

CONTACT INFORMATION:
Phone: Fax:
Toll-Free: 800-120-5000
Address: Dr. Rio de la Loza 182, Mexico DF, 06720 Mexico

STOCK TICKER/OTHER:
Stock Ticker: Subsidiary   Exchange:
Employees: 4,039   Fiscal Year Ends: 12/31
Parent Company: Grupo Televisa SAB

SALARIES/BONUSES:
Top Exec. Salary: $ Bonus: $
Second Exec. Salary: $ Bonus: $

OTHER THOUGHTS:
Estimated Female Officers or Directors:
Hot Spot for Advancement for Women/Minorities:

John Wiley & Sons Inc

NAIC Code: 511130

www.wiley.com

TYPES OF BUSINESS:
Reference Book Publishing
Trade Books
Business Books
Scientific & Technical Books
Textbooks & Educational Materials
Professional Journals
Consumer Guides
Online Information

BRANDS/DIVISIONS/AFFILIATES:
Workplace Learning Solutions
Wiley Online Library
Atypon Systems Inc
Literatum

CONTACTS:
Note: Officers with more than one job title may be intentionally listed here more than once.

John Kritzmacher, CFO
Christopher Caridi, Chief Accounting Officer
Clay Stobaugh, Chief Marketing Officer
Matthew Kissner, Director
Brian Napack, Director
Ella Balagula, Executive VP, Divisional
Judy Verses, Executive VP, Divisional
Aref Matin, Executive VP
Gary Rinck, Executive VP
Archana Singh, Executive VP
Vincent Marzano, Senior VP

GROWTH PLANS/SPECIAL FEATURES:

John Wiley & Sons, Inc. (Wiley) publishes print and electronic products primarily for the scientific, technical, medical and scholarly (STMS) markets. Wiley operates publishing, marketing and distribution centers in the U.S., Canada, Europe, Asia and Australia. The firm produces STMS journals, encyclopedias, books, online products and services; professional and consumer books, subscription products, training materials, online applications and websites; and educational materials. The firm's STMS publications cover the physical science, engineering, medical, social science, humanities, life science and technology disciplines. Other publishing services and solutions include test preparation services and course workflow tools, which are primarily offered to libraries, corporations, students, professionals and researchers. Wiley's professional products segment acquires, develops and publishes books and subscription products in the areas of business, technology, architecture, culinary arts, psychology, education, travel, consumer reference and general interest. Its Workplace Learning Solutions business creates products and assessment services for organizational and professional development. The company's educational materials are largely targeted to the business and accounting, sciences, engineering, computer science, mathematics, social sciences and professional technology fields. The firm's other imprints include the For Dummies reference books. Wiley Online Library offers searchable access to more than 1,700 journals and 19,000 books. Wholly-owned Atypon Systems, Inc. is a publishing software and service provider. Its Literatum platform hosts nearly 9,000 journals, 13 million journal articles and more than 1,800 publication websites for over 1,500 societies and publishers. John Wiley completed the acquisition of Learning House, online program management for online schooling courses and other skill training, in November 2018 from Weld North Holdings.

Wiley offers its employees medical, dental, life, disability and vision coverage; flexible spending accounts; 401(k); a discount stock purchase plan; a work/life assistance program; tuition reimbursement; adoption assistance; discounts; and discounted aut

FINANCIAL DATA:
Note: Data for latest year may not have been available at press time.

In U.S. $	2018	2017	2016	2015	2014	2013
Revenue	1,796,103,000	1,718,530,000	1,727,037,000	1,822,440,000	1,775,195,000	1,760,778,000
R&D Expense						
Operating Income	268,101,000	219,508,000	216,724,000	266,543,000	254,181,000	253,416,000
Operating Margin %	14.92	12.77%	12.54%	14.62%	14.31%	14.39%
SGA Expense	994,552,000	988,597,000	994,632,000	1,005,000,000	969,456,000	933,148,000
Net Income	192,186,000	113,643,000	145,782,000	176,868,000	160,510,000	144,225,000
Operating Cash Flow	381,838,000	314,501,000	349,957,000	355,122,000	348,224,000	337,037,000
Capital Expenditure	140,908,000	110,700,000	93,705,000	69,121,000	57,564,000	58,704,000
EBITDA	339,762,000	324,406,000	307,691,000	355,824,000	312,450,000	297,999,000
Return on Assets %	7.05%	4.11%	4.92%	5.81%	5.45%	5.40%
Return on Equity %	17.52%	11.14%	13.93%	15.81%	14.78%	14.37%
Debt to Equity	0.30	0.36	0.58	0.61	0.59	0.68

CONTACT INFORMATION:
Phone: 201 748-6000   Fax: 201 748-6088
Toll-Free:
Address: 111 River St., Hoboken, NJ 07030 United States

STOCK TICKER/OTHER:
Stock Ticker: JW.A
Employees: 5,100
Parent Company:

Exchange: NYS
Fiscal Year Ends: 04/30

SALARIES/BONUSES:
Top Exec. Salary: $681,667   Bonus: $
Second Exec. Salary: $550,000   Bonus: $

OTHER THOUGHTS:
Estimated Female Officers or Directors: 2
Hot Spot for Advancement for Women/Minorities: Y

Sales, profits and employees may be estimates. Financial information, benefits and other data can change quickly and may vary from those stated here.

Kangwon Land Inc

NAIC Code: 721120

www.kangwonland.com

TYPES OF BUSINESS:
Casino
Hotels
Ski Resort
Country Club

BRANDS/DIVISIONS/AFFILIATES:
Kangwon Land Casino
Kangwon Land Hotel
High1 Ski Resort
High1 C.C
High1 Hotel
Kangwon Land Convention Hotel
High1 Condominium

CONTACTS:
Note: Officers with more than one job title may be intentionally listed here more than once.

Ham Seung-Huie, CEO
Baek Myeong-Ying, Head-Construction & Mgmt. Div.
Choi Dong-Yeol, Head-Planning & Coordination
Lee Dong-Hwa, Head-Safety & Mgmt. Div.
Jeon In-Hyeok, Head-Resort Div.
Kim Sung-Won, Head-Int'l Affairs

GROWTH PLANS/SPECIAL FEATURES:
Kangwon Land, Inc. owns and operates the Kangwon Land Casino, Kangwon Land Hotel, High1 Ski Resort, High1 C.C and High1 Hotel, all located in Korea. The Kangwon Land Casino, the first Korean casino to allow the admission of both Koreans and foreigners, contains 200 game tables, 1360 machine games, a bar and a VIP lounge. Table games at Kangwon Land Casino include black jack, baccarat, roulette, big wheel, tai-sai and Poker. Machine games include slot machines and video games. It also offers a VIP lounge and a restaurant serving Korean, Chinese and Japanese cuisine as well as Western dishes. The Kangwon Land Hotel, with 24 floors, features four different types of rooms; a restaurant and lounge; banquet hall; and swimming pool, sauna and business center. Kangwon's High1 Ski Resort includes a mountain condo, hotel, Hanulsam (open-air spa) and ski school as well as beginner to advanced mountain runs. Kangwon's High1 C.C features Korea's longest 18-hole golf course. The High1 Hotel is a mountain resort featuring a European villa design. Kangwon Land also operates the Kangwon Land Convention Hotel and High1 Condominium, which operates Valley Condominium, Hill Condominium and Mountain Condominium.

FINANCIAL DATA:
Note: Data for latest year may not have been available at press time.

In U.S. $	2018	2017	2016	2015	2014	2013
Revenue		1,502,440,000	1,492,156,509	1,408,642,215	1,296,842,568	1,237,100,000
R&D Expense						
Operating Income						
Operating Margin %						
SGA Expense						
Net Income		409,717,000	399,716,862	371,779,692	311,410,467	270,500,000
Operating Cash Flow						
Capital Expenditure						
EBITDA						
Return on Assets %						
Return on Equity %						
Debt to Equity						

CONTACT INFORMATION:
Phone: 82-1588-7789   Fax: 82-33-590-7930
Toll-Free:
Address: 424 Sabuk-ri Sabuk-eup Jeongseon-gun, Kangwon-do, 233-901 South Korea

STOCK TICKER/OTHER:
Stock Ticker: 35250
Employees: 3,600
Parent Company:

Exchange: Seoul
Fiscal Year Ends: 12/31

SALARIES/BONUSES:
Top Exec. Salary: $ Bonus: $
Second Exec. Salary: $ Bonus: $

OTHER THOUGHTS:
Estimated Female Officers or Directors:
Hot Spot for Advancement for Women/Minorities:

Sales, profits and employees may be estimates. Financial information, benefits and other data can change quickly and may vary from those stated here.

Kerzner International Limited

NAIC Code: 721120

www.kerzner.com

TYPES OF BUSINESS:
Casino Hotels
Luxury Resort Hotels
Resort Development

BRANDS/DIVISIONS/AFFILIATES:
Atlantis
One & Only
Mazagan

CONTACTS: Note: Officers with more than one job title may be intentionally listed here more than once.
Michael Wale, CEO
Bonnie S. Biumi, Pres.
Saif Al Yaarubi, CFO
Stuart Thomson, Exec. VP-Human Resources
John Shamon, CTO
Monica Digilio, Exec. VP-Admin.
Tim Brown, Sr. VP-Project Planning & Dev.
George Markantonis, Pres., Kerzner Int'l Bahamas
Serge Zaalof, Pres., Atlantis & The Palm

GROWTH PLANS/SPECIAL FEATURES:

Kerzner International Limited is a resort and gaming company that develops, operates and manages premier resorts, casinos and luxury hotels under the Atlantis, One & Only and Mazagan brands. Kerzner's flagship property is Atlantis Paradise Island in the Bahamas. The over 2,300-room ocean themed Atlantis resort features three interconnected hotel towers built around 100 acres of pools and marine environments, home to over 50,000 marine animals. Atlantis, The Palm, located in Dubai, is an ocean-themed hotel and resort, featuring restaurants, a water park, spa & fitness centers and night life entertainment, as well as rooms for meetings and events. Atlantis Sanya, located in China, is an artifacts-themed resort encompassing more than 62 acres, restaurants, bars and lounges, spas, a water park, fresh and saltwater pools, marine exhibits and a dolphin interaction center alongside a beach. Kerzner's One & Only brand of resort properties are located in Mexico, the Bahamas, South Africa, Dubai, Mauritius, Maldives, the Great Barrier Reef and Australia. One & Only resorts are designed to reflect the uniqueness of their surroundings, each ultra-luxurious, with an authentic sense of place, and include beach resorts, nature resorts, urban resorts and private homes. The company's Mazagan Beach & Golf Resort in Morocco, features an 18-hole Gary Player golf course, the largest casino in Morocco, five-star hotel accommodations and a wide range of family activities. Mazagan is a year-round destination for the entire family. Properties currently under development by Kerzner (as of April 2018) include: Atlantis Ko Olina in Hawaii and the Royal Atlantis Resort & Residences in Dubai; and One & Only resorts in Montenegro, Greece, Mexico and Rwanda.

FINANCIAL DATA: Note: Data for latest year may not have been available at press time.

In U.S. $	2018	2017	2016	2015	2014	2013
Revenue	430,000,000	420,000,000	410,000,000	400,000,000	380,000,000	395,000,000
R&D Expense						
Operating Income						
Operating Margin %						
SGA Expense						
Net Income						
Operating Cash Flow						
Capital Expenditure						
EBITDA						
Return on Assets %						
Return on Equity %						
Debt to Equity						

CONTACT INFORMATION:
Phone: 242-363-6000   Fax: 242-363-5401
Toll-Free:
Address: One Central, Bldg. 2, Fl. 9, World Trade Center, Dubai, United Arab Emirates

STOCK TICKER/OTHER:
Stock Ticker: Private
Employees: 8,574
Parent Company:

Exchange:
Fiscal Year Ends: 12/31

SALARIES/BONUSES:
Top Exec. Salary: $ Bonus: $
Second Exec. Salary: $ Bonus: $

OTHER THOUGHTS:
Estimated Female Officers or Directors: 2
Hot Spot for Advancement for Women/Minorities:

Sales, profits and employees may be estimates. Financial information, benefits and other data can change quickly and may vary from those stated here.

King Digital Entertainment plc

www.king.com

NAIC Code: 511210G

TYPES OF BUSINESS:
Computer Software, Electronic Games, Apps & Entertainment Apps

BRANDS/DIVISIONS/AFFILIATES:
Activision Blizzard Inc
Bubble Witch Saga
Candy Crush Saga
Farm Heroes Saga
Alpha Betty Saga
Scrubby Dubby Saga
Legend of Solgard
Diamond Diaries Saga

CONTACTS:
Note: Officers with more than one job title may be intentionally listed here more than once.

Riccardo Zacconi, CEO
Stefane Kurgan, COO
Humam Saknini, CFO
Colin Daly, Chief People Officer
Thomas Hartwing, CTO
Rob Miller, Chief Legal Officer
Susannah Clark, Sr. Dir.-Global Comm.
Alice Ryder, VP-Investor Rel.
Sebastian Knutsson, Chief Creative Officer
Martin Bunge-Meyer, Mgr.-Public Rel., Sweden

GROWTH PLANS/SPECIAL FEATURES:

King Digital Entertainment plc is a developer of online social games. The company has a back catalog of 200+ titles in as many countries through its King.com and Royalgames.com websites, social network sites and mobile distribution platforms such as Apple App Store, Google Play Store and Amazon Appstore. Games include Bubble Witch Saga, Pyramid Solitaire Saga, Candy Crush Saga, Pet Rescue Saga, Papa Pear Saga, Farm Heroes Saga, Pepper Panic Saga, Diamond Digger Saga, Candy Crush Soda Saga, Alpha Betty Saga, Scrubby Dubby Saga, Paradise Bay and Blossom Blast Saga. Games released in 2017 and 2018 include Bubble Witch 3 Saga, Royal Charm Slots, Legend of Solgard, Candy Crush Friends Saga and Diamond Diaries Saga. Revenue is generated through display, video and game integration ad sales. King maintains game studios in London, Stockholm, Bucharest, Malmo, Barcelona, Berlin and Singapore, along with offices in San Francisco, Malta, Seoul, Tokyo and Shanghai. King Digital operates as a subsidiary of Activision Blizzard, Inc.

King employees enjoy benefits including flexible hours, health and life insurance, a pension plan, gym membership and personal travel concierge service. All new hires attend a three day company induction program in Sweden.

FINANCIAL DATA:
Note: Data for latest year may not have been available at press time.

In U.S. $	2018	2017	2016	2015	2014	2013
Revenue	2,150,000,000	2,100,000,000	2,000,000,000	1,999,000,000	2,269,403,904	1,884,301,056
R&D Expense						
Operating Income						
Operating Margin %						
SGA Expense						
Net Income				517,000,000	574,851,008	567,593,984
Operating Cash Flow						
Capital Expenditure						
EBITDA						
Return on Assets %						
Return on Equity %						
Debt to Equity						

CONTACT INFORMATION:
Phone: 4420-3451-5464   Fax:
Toll-Free:
Address: Fitzwilton House, Wilton Place, Dublin, 2 Ireland

STOCK TICKER/OTHER:
Stock Ticker: Subsidiary
Employees: 1,200
Parent Company: Activision Blizzard Inc

Exchange:
Fiscal Year Ends:

SALARIES/BONUSES:
Top Exec. Salary: $ Bonus: $
Second Exec. Salary: $ Bonus: $

OTHER THOUGHTS:
Estimated Female Officers or Directors: 4
Hot Spot for Advancement for Women/Minorities: Y

Koch Media GmbH

NAIC Code: 511210G

www.kochmedia.com

TYPES OF BUSINESS:
Computer Software, Electronic Games, Apps & Entertainment
Video Games
Software Development
Apps

BRANDS/DIVISIONS/AFFILIATES:
THQ Nordic AB
Deep Silver
Ravenscourt
Saints Row
Deep Silver Volition
Deep Silver Fishlabs
Deep Silver Dambuster Studios
Home Entertainment

CONTACTS:
Note: Officers with more than one job title may be intentionally listed here more than once.
Klemens Kundratitz, CEO
Stefan Kapelari, COO
Reinhard Gratl, CFO

GROWTH PLANS/SPECIAL FEATURES:
Koch Media GmbH is a German company that publishes, markets and distributes digital entertainment products, such as computer software, video games and films. The company has subsidiaries located in the Netherlands, Sweden, the U.K., Italy, Switzerland, Austria, France, Spain, Benelux (Belgium, the Netherlands and Luxembourg) and the U.S. The software division is a leading retail distributor of digital media products. Its distribution network and catalogue of products are united in the entire distribution portfolio of Koch Media. In local markets, this division works with distribution partners for the creation, manufacture, sale and distribution of digital entertainment products. The games division develops, produces and markets video games, which are self-published under the Deep Silver and Ravenscourt labels. Deep Silver has released more than 200 games, including brands such as Saints Row and Metro. Additionally, Deep Silver also possesses three development studios of its own: Deep Silver Volition in Champaign, Illinois, USA; Deep Silver Fishlabs (Mobile Games) in Hamburg, Germany; and Deep Silver Dambuster Studios in Nottingham, England. Last, the films division is an independent all rights distributor and co-producer for German-speaking Europe, with a sister company in Italy. This business segment releases up to 10 international feature productions theatrically every year and is known as a leading video distributor. Its portfolio of more than 1,000 products includes arthouse, crossover and commercial feature films, as well as straight-to-video products, TV series and special interest titles released by Koch Media's Home Entertainment label on DVD, Blu-ray and as video-on-demand. In February 2018, Koch Media was acquired by the publicly listed Swedish firm THQ Nordic AB. The two firms will continue to operate as two separate entities under the publicly listed entity. In August of the same year, the firm acquired the video game series Timesplitters.

FINANCIAL DATA:
Note: Data for latest year may not have been available at press time.

In U.S. $	2018	2017	2016	2015	2014	2013
Revenue						
R&D Expense						
Operating Income						
Operating Margin %						
SGA Expense						
Net Income						
Operating Cash Flow						
Capital Expenditure						
EBITDA						
Return on Assets %						
Return on Equity %						
Debt to Equity						

CONTACT INFORMATION:
Phone: 49-89-24245-0   Fax: 49-89-24245-100
Toll-Free:
Address: Lochhamer Strasse 9, Munich, D-82152 Germany

STOCK TICKER/OTHER:
Stock Ticker: Subsidiary   Exchange:
Employees: 800   Fiscal Year Ends:
Parent Company: THQ Nordic AB

SALARIES/BONUSES:
Top Exec. Salary: $ Bonus: $
Second Exec. Salary: $ Bonus: $

OTHER THOUGHTS:
Estimated Female Officers or Directors:
Hot Spot for Advancement for Women/Minorities:

Sales, profits and employees may be estimates. Financial information, benefits and other data can change quickly and may vary from those stated here.

Plunkett Research, Ltd.

Korean Broadcasting System

NAIC Code: 515120

english.kbs.co.kr

TYPES OF BUSINESS:
Broadcasting, Television & Radio
Art Production

BRANDS/DIVISIONS/AFFILIATES:
KBS Arts Vision
Global Korean Network
Happy FM
KBS Business
KBS Media
KBS N
KBS America
KBS Japan

CONTACTS: Note: Officers with more than one job title may be intentionally listed here more than once.
Sung-dong Yang, Pres.
Jeon Hong-Gu, Sr. Researcher-Broadcast Research Institute
Lee Jong-Ok, Exec. Dir.-Broadcast Facility Mgmt.
Ryu Hyun-Soon, Executive Managing Dir.-Planning & Policy
Jun Jin-Kuk, Exec. Dir.-Entertainment
Lim Chang-Keun, Exec. Dir.-News & Sports
Kim Seung-Jong, Executive Managing Dir.-Programming Division
Kwon Soon-Beom, Exec. Dir.-Current Affairs

GROWTH PLANS/SPECIAL FEATURES:

Korean Broadcasting System (KBS) is a public service broadcaster offering terrestrial and satellite TV as well as radio programming. KBS operates eight TV stations, seven radio stations, five digital multimedia broadcasting (DMB) stations and two international stations. All programs are produced and broadcast in high-definition. In addition, KBS operates 18 regional stations, 11 overseas bureaus and eight subsidiary companies. KBS radio media channels include news channel Radio1; Radio2 (Happy FM); and Radio3 (The Voice of Love), which offers programming directed to disabled and elderly listeners. Other radio channels include traditional and classical music channel FM1 (Classic FM); pop music channel FM2 (Cool FM); and Global Korean Network channel, which broadcasts programming specifically tailored for Koreans in other countries. The firm has two terrestrial TV media channels, both of which can be accessed via satellite. These two channels include 1TV, a national service channel offering news, current affairs and cultural programming; and 2TV, a family cultural entertainment channel. Its six cable TV channels are KBS Sports, KBS Prime (culture), KBS Drama, KBS Joy (quiz and variety), KBS W and KBS Kids. Finally, the company runs two international channels: KBS World TV, an International satellite channel; and KBS World Radio, a channel for international exchange. Subsidiaries include KBS Business, which maintains KBS' Korean facilities and does philanthropic work; KBS N, which operates multiple formats of specialized channels; KBS Media, which conducts the firm's licensing, global sales and production operations; KBS Art Vision, which provides support services including sets, props, special effects, computer graphics and costuming; KBS America, which is based in Los Angeles; and KBS Japan, which is based in Tokyo.

FINANCIAL DATA: Note: Data for latest year may not have been available at press time.

In U.S. $	2018	2017	2016	2015	2014	2013
Revenue		1,341,500,000	1,232,240,000	13,268,116,874	12,979,890,720	13,619,594,060
R&D Expense						
Operating Income						
Operating Margin %						
SGA Expense						
Net Income		52,813,500	28,016,800	64,358,347	1,162,396	3,906,794
Operating Cash Flow						
Capital Expenditure						
EBITDA						
Return on Assets %						
Return on Equity %						
Debt to Equity						

CONTACT INFORMATION:
Phone: 82-2-781-1464   Fax:
Toll-Free:
Address: 13 Yeouigongwon-ro, Yeongdeungpo-gu, Seoul, 07235 South Korea

STOCK TICKER/OTHER:
Stock Ticker: Government-Owned
Employees: 4,591
Parent Company:

Exchange:
Fiscal Year Ends: 12/31

SALARIES/BONUSES:
Top Exec. Salary: $ Bonus: $
Second Exec. Salary: $ Bonus: $

OTHER THOUGHTS:
Estimated Female Officers or Directors: 1
Hot Spot for Advancement for Women/Minorities:

Sales, profits and employees may be estimates. Financial information, benefits and other data can change quickly and may vary from those stated here.

Lagardere Active Media

www.lagardere.com/businesses/lagardere-active-2615.html

NAIC Code: 511120

TYPES OF BUSINESS:
Magazine Publishing
Radio Broadcasting
Audiovisual Production
Digital Media
Advertising Services
Television Broadcasting & Production

BRANDS/DIVISIONS/AFFILIATES:
Lagardere SCA
Elle
Paris Match
Europe 1
Gulli
Doctissimo

GROWTH PLANS/SPECIAL FEATURES:
Lagardere Active Media is a division of the international publisher of multimedia content, Lagardere SCA. Lagardere Active plays a central role in the French media, with iconic brands such as Elle, Paris Match, Europe 1, Gulli and Doctissimo. It is also a major player in television and radio, with 26 radio stations worldwide, 17 TV channels and France's number one production company (studio shows and drama). In addition, Lagardere Active is France's premier magazine publishing group, with 13 press titles in France and 80 under license worldwide. In mid-2018, the firm announced plans to sell its eHealth business, including Doctissimo. It sold online medical appoint platform, MonDocteur, to Doctolib, consolidating its eHealth business in Europe.

CONTACTS:
Note: Officers with more than one job title may be intentionally listed here more than once.

Denis Olivennes, Chmn.

FINANCIAL DATA:
Note: Data for latest year may not have been available at press time.

In U.S. $	2018	2017	2016	2015	2014	2013
Revenue	1,100,000,000	1,044,540,000	972,398,000	1,017,580,000	1,192,390,000	1,353,490,000
R&D Expense						
Operating Income						
Operating Margin %						
SGA Expense						
Net Income		83,850,400	82,892,900	83,564,600	69,701,500	-419,909,000
Operating Cash Flow						
Capital Expenditure						
EBITDA						
Return on Assets %						
Return on Equity %						
Debt to Equity						

CONTACT INFORMATION:
Phone: 33-1-41-34-94-37   Fax: 33-1-41-34-94-42
Toll-Free:
Address: 149-151 rue Anatole France, Levallois-Perret, 92300 France

STOCK TICKER/OTHER:
Stock Ticker: Subsidiary
Employees: 3,700
Parent Company: Lagardere SCA

Exchange:
Fiscal Year Ends: 12/31

SALARIES/BONUSES:
Top Exec. Salary: $ Bonus: $
Second Exec. Salary: $ Bonus: $

OTHER THOUGHTS:
Estimated Female Officers or Directors:
Hot Spot for Advancement for Women/Minorities:

Sales, profits and employees may be estimates. Financial information, benefits and other data can change quickly and may vary from those stated here.

Lagardere SCA

NAIC Code: 511110

www.lagardere.com

TYPES OF BUSINESS:
Newspaper, Periodical, Book, and Directory Publishers
Duty Free Retail

BRANDS/DIVISIONS/AFFILIATES:
Lagardere Publishing
Lagardere Travel Retail
Lagardere Active
Lagadere Sports & Entertainment
Elle
Paris Match
Relay
Gulli

CONTACTS:
Note: Officers with more than one job title may be intentionally listed here more than once.

Arnaud Legardere, CEO

GROWTH PLANS/SPECIAL FEATURES:
Lagardere SCA is a diversified media group operating in 30 countries. The firm is structured around four divisions: Lagardere Publishing, Lagardere Travel Retail, Lagardere Active and Lagardere Sports & Entertainment. Lagardere Publishing is a trade book publisher for the general public and education markets. This division is a federation of publishing companies with a large degree of editorial independence, united by common management rules and expands its books into the digital marketshare. Lagardere Travel Retail is a leading travel retail company, present in more than 30 countries, primarily located in travel retail locations such as travel essentials, duty-free, fashion and foodservice stores. This division's international brands include Relay and Aelia Duty Free, and has numerous restaurant and distribution brands either under license or directly operated. Lagardere Active is engaged in providing French media under brands such as Elle, Paris Match, Europe 1, Gulli and Doctissimo. It is one of France's premier mainstream magazine publishers, with 13 press titles on the domestic market, as well as several under license worldwide. This division is also a major player in television and radio, with 17 TV channels and 26 radio stations worldwide. Lagardere Sports & Entertainment is an agency with a global network of local experts dedicated to delivering innovative sports and entertainment media and solutions to clients. In July 2018, Lagardere announced that it had agreed to sell Doctissimo SAS to Television Francaise 1 SA.

FINANCIAL DATA:
Note: Data for latest year may not have been available at press time.

In U.S. $	2018	2017	2016	2015	2014	2013
Revenue						
R&D Expense						
Operating Income						
Operating Margin %						
SGA Expense						
Net Income						
Operating Cash Flow						
Capital Expenditure						
EBITDA						
Return on Assets %						
Return on Equity %						
Debt to Equity						

CONTACT INFORMATION:
Phone: 33-140-6916-00   Fax: 33-140-691854
Toll-Free:
Address: 4 rue de Presbourg, Paris, 75016 France

STOCK TICKER/OTHER:
Stock Ticker: LGDDF
Employees: 28,543
Parent Company:

Exchange: PINX
Fiscal Year Ends:

SALARIES/BONUSES:
Top Exec. Salary: $ Bonus: $
Second Exec. Salary: $ Bonus: $

OTHER THOUGHTS:
Estimated Female Officers or Directors:
Hot Spot for Advancement for Women/Minorities:

Sales, profits and employees may be estimates. Financial information, benefits and other data can change quickly and may vary from those stated here.

Lamar Advertising Company

NAIC Code: 541850

www.lamar.com

TYPES OF BUSINESS:
Billboards
Highway Logo Signs
Graphic Design Services
Transit Advertising

BRANDS/DIVISIONS/AFFILIATES:

CONTACTS: Note: Officers with more than one job title may be intentionally listed here more than once.
Sean Reilly, CEO
Keith Istre, CFO
Kevin Reilly, Chairman of the Board

GROWTH PLANS/SPECIAL FEATURES:

Lamar Advertising Company is a leading outdoor advertising company, owning and operating nearly 150,000 billboard advertising displays in 45 U.S. states, Canada and Puerto Rico. Lamar leases space for advertising on billboards, buses, shelters, benches, logo plats and in airport terminals. The firm offers customers a fully-integrated advertising service, from ad copy production to placement and maintenance. Lamar owns and operates more than 2,800 digital billboard advertising displays in 43 states, Canada and Puerto Rico; and approximately 53,300 transit advertising displays in 21 states and Canada. Transit ads are placed on transportation vehicles, in airport terminals and on transit shelters and benches. The company aids in the strategic placement of advertisements throughout an advertiser's market by using software that allows it to analyze the target audience and its demographics. Lamar is also a real estate investment trust, owning 127 local operating facilities with front office administration and sales office space connected to back-shop poster and bulletin production space. Lamar owns approximately 7,600 parcels of property beneath its advertising displays. It also leases an additional 138 operating facilities at an aggregate lease expense of approximately $8.3 million, as well as nearly 70,000 outdoor sites for an annualized lease expense of approximately $258.9 million.

FINANCIAL DATA: Note: Data for latest year may not have been available at press time.

In U.S. $	2018	2017	2016	2015	2014	2013
Revenue		1,541,260,000	1,500,294,000	1,353,396,000	1,287,060,000	1,245,842,000
R&D Expense						
Operating Income		450,703,000	423,950,000	374,262,000	275,478,000	219,633,000
Operating Margin %		29.24%	28.25%	27.65%	21.40%	17.62%
SGA Expense		276,229,000	269,423,000	242,182,000	230,800,000	231,574,000
Net Income		317,676,000	298,809,000	262,570,000	253,518,000	40,139,000
Operating Cash Flow		507,016,000	521,823,000	477,650,000	452,529,000	394,705,000
Capital Expenditure		109,329,000	107,612,000	110,425,000	107,573,000	105,650,000
EBITDA		666,406,000	640,811,000	574,494,000	507,115,000	509,836,000
Return on Assets %		7.82%	8.18%	7.81%	7.53%	1.15%
Return on Equity %		29.20%	28.55%	26.18%	26.44%	4.40%
Debt to Equity		2.30	2.16	1.85	1.91	2.01

CONTACT INFORMATION:
Phone: 225 926-1000   Fax: 225 926-1005
Toll-Free: 800-235-2627
Address: 5321 Corporate Blvd., Baton Rouge, LA 70808 United States

SALARIES/BONUSES:
Top Exec. Salary: $700,000   Bonus: $
Second Exec. Salary: $500,000   Bonus: $

STOCK TICKER/OTHER:
Stock Ticker: LAMR
Employees: 3,300
Parent Company:

Exchange: NAS
Fiscal Year Ends: 12/31

OTHER THOUGHTS:
Estimated Female Officers or Directors: 2
Hot Spot for Advancement for Women/Minorities:

Sales, profits and employees may be estimates. Financial information, benefits and other data can change quickly and may vary from those stated here.

Las Vegas Sands Corp (The Venetian)

www.sands.com

NAIC Code: 721120

TYPES OF BUSINESS:
Hotel Casinos
Convention & Conference Centers
Shopping Center Development
Casino Property Development

BRANDS/DIVISIONS/AFFILIATES:
Venetian Resort Hotel Casino (The)
Sands Expo and Convention Center (The)
Sands China Ltd
Sands Macao Casino (The)
Palazzo Resort Hotel Casino (The)
Venetian Macao Resort Hotel (The)
Marina Bay Sands Pte Ltd
Parisian Macao

CONTACTS:
Note: Officers with more than one job title may be intentionally listed here more than once.

Sheldon Adelson, CEO
Patrick Dumont, CFO
Randy Hyzak, Chief Accounting Officer
Robert Goldstein, COO
Lawrence Jacobs, Executive VP

GROWTH PLANS/SPECIAL FEATURES:

Las Vegas Sands Corp. (LVSC) is an international hotel, resort and casino firm. Its flagship property is The Venetian Resort Hotel Casino, which is connected to The Palazzo Resort Hotel Casino. Together, The Venetian and The Palazzo offer 225,000 square feet of gaming space, with 245 table games and 1,790 slot machines, as well as 7,092 hotel suites. LVSC also runs the 1.2 million square foot convention and trade show facility, The Sands Expo and Convention Center, and a supplemental event and conference center. Additionally, the firm operates the Sands Casino Resort Bethlehem in eastern Pennsylvania, which features 146,000 square feet of gaming space, a 282-room hotel, 150,000 square feet of retail space and other amenities. Outside the U.S., LVSC has operations in Macao, through majority-owned subsidiary Sands China Ltd., and Singapore, through Marina Bay Sands Pte. Ltd. The company's largest development project, the multi-billion dollar Cotai Strip, is a collection of hotel properties, casinos and entertainment venues in Macao. Sands China runs The Sands Macao and The Venetian Macao Resort Hotel, the anchor property on the Cotai Strip. Other properties on the Cotai Strip include the Four Seasons Macao, the Plaza Casino and Parisian Macao. Its Singapore property, Marina Bay Sands features three 55-story hotel towers, gaming space, convention space, two state-of-the-art theaters and The Shoppes at Marina Bay Sands. Recently, LVSC celebrated the opening of the Parisian Macao on the Cotai Strip. The Parisian Macao features approximately 253,000 square feet of gaming space with approximately 385 table games and 1,560 slot machines, as well as approximately 3,000 rooms and suites and the Shoppes at Parisian, approximately 300,000 square feet of unique retail shopping. In March 2018, the firm agreed to sell the Sands Bethlehem property in Pennsylvania for $1.3 billion.

FINANCIAL DATA:
Note: Data for latest year may not have been available at press time.

In U.S. $	2018	2017	2016	2015	2014	2013
Revenue		12,882,000,000	11,410,000,000	11,688,460,000	14,583,850,000	13,769,880,000
R&D Expense		13,000,000	9,000,000	10,372,000	14,325,000	15,809,000
Operating Income		3,482,000,000	2,572,000,000	2,876,707,000	4,106,082,000	3,419,399,000
Operating Margin %		27.03%	22.54%	24.61%	28.15%	24.83%
SGA Expense		1,415,000,000	1,284,000,000	1,267,415,000	1,258,133,000	1,329,740,000
Net Income		2,806,000,000	1,670,000,000	1,966,236,000	2,840,629,000	2,305,997,000
Operating Cash Flow		4,543,000,000	4,043,000,000	3,449,971,000	4,832,844,000	4,439,412,000
Capital Expenditure		837,000,000	1,445,000,000	1,528,642,000	1,178,656,000	943,982,000
EBITDA		4,587,000,000	3,678,000,000	3,924,666,000	5,179,079,000	4,462,543,000
Return on Assets %		13.63%	8.05%	9.07%	12.60%	10.27%
Return on Equity %		44.29%	25.70%	28.02%	38.18%	31.31%
Debt to Equity		1.43	1.52	1.37	1.37	1.22

CONTACT INFORMATION:
Phone: 702 414-1000 Fax: 702 414-4884
Toll-Free:
Address: 3355 Las Vegas Blvd. S., Las Vegas, NV 89109 United States

SALARIES/BONUSES:
Top Exec. Salary: $5,000,000 Bonus: $
Second Exec. Salary: $3,400,000 Bonus: $

STOCK TICKER/OTHER:
Stock Ticker: LVS
Employees: 50,500
Parent Company:

Exchange: NYS
Fiscal Year Ends: 12/31

OTHER THOUGHTS:
Estimated Female Officers or Directors:
Hot Spot for Advancement for Women/Minorities:

Sales, profits and employees may be estimates. Financial information, benefits and other data can change quickly and may vary from those stated here.

Leaf Group Ltd

NAIC Code: 519130

www.demandmedia.com

TYPES OF BUSINESS:
Internet Portals
Online Video Publishing
Online Leisure Activities Information
How-to Internet Sites
Advertising Services
Domain Name Registration Services
Social Media Tools

BRANDS/DIVISIONS/AFFILIATES:
LIVESTRONG.COM
eHow
Socitey 6
Saatchi Art
Other Art Fair (The)
Deny Designs
Well+Good

CONTACTS: Note: Officers with more than one job title may be intentionally listed here more than once.
Jantoon Reigersman, CFO
James Quandt, Chairman of the Board
Wendy Voong, Chief Accounting Officer
Brian Pike, Chief Technology Officer
Sean Moriarty, Director
Dion Sanders, Executive VP, Divisional
Adam Wergeles, Executive VP, Divisional
Daniel Weinrot, Executive VP, Divisional

GROWTH PLANS/SPECIAL FEATURES:
Leaf Group Ltd. is a diversified internet company which owns and operates consumer media and marketplace businesses. The firm builds platforms across its media and marketplace properties in an effort to enable communities of creators to reach audiences in large and growing lifestyle categories, as well as to help advertisers find innovative ways to engage with their customers. Leaf Group's media brands include LIVESTRONG.COM and eHow, as well as more than 40 other media properties focused on specific categories or interests. The firm's marketplace brands include: Society 6, which provides artists with an eCommerce platform to feature and sell their original designs in the home decor and apparel categories; Saatchi Art, an online art gallery featuring a selection of original paintings, drawings, sculptures and photography; The Other Art Fair, an art fair for discovering emerging artists; and Deny Designs, which offers a collection of statement pieces for the home, created by artists, with designs printed on an assortment of premium decor products, including proprietary furniture products manufactured in-house at Deny Designs' Denver, Colorado facility. In mid-2018, Leaf Group acquired wellness site, Well+Good, enhancing its fitness and wellness category.

FINANCIAL DATA: Note: Data for latest year may not have been available at press time.

In U.S. $	2018	2017	2016	2015	2014	2013
Revenue		128,990,000	113,452,000	125,969,000	172,428,992	394,598,016
R&D Expense						
Operating Income						
Operating Margin %						
SGA Expense						
Net Income		-31,133,000	-2,011,000	-43,501,000	-267,356,992	-20,174,000
Operating Cash Flow						
Capital Expenditure						
EBITDA						
Return on Assets %						
Return on Equity %						
Debt to Equity						

CONTACT INFORMATION:
Phone: 310-656-6253 Fax:
Toll-Free:
Address: 1655 26th St., Santa Monica, CA 90404 United States

SALARIES/BONUSES:
Top Exec. Salary: $ Bonus: $
Second Exec. Salary: $ Bonus: $

STOCK TICKER/OTHER:
Stock Ticker: LFGR Exchange: NYS
Employees: 265 Fiscal Year Ends: 12/31
Parent Company:

OTHER THOUGHTS:
Estimated Female Officers or Directors: 2
Hot Spot for Advancement for Women/Minorities: Y

Lee Enterprises Incorporated

NAIC Code: 511110

www.lee.net

TYPES OF BUSINESS:
Newspaper Publishing
Specialty Publications
Advertising Services
Internet Publishing & Services
Commercial Printing

BRANDS/DIVISIONS/AFFILIATES:
Madison Newspapers Inc
TNI Partners
INN Partners LC
St Louis Post-Dispatch LLC
TownNews.com
Central Illinois Newspaper Group
River Valley Newspaper Group
Magic Valley Group

CONTACTS:
Note: Officers with more than one job title may be intentionally listed here more than once.

Timothy Millage, CFO
Mary Junck, Chairman of the Board
Michele White, Chief Information Officer
Kevin Mowbray, President
Suzanna Frank, Vice President, Divisional
Paul Farrell, Vice President, Divisional
James Green, Vice President, Divisional
Astrid Garcia, Vice President, Divisional
Nathan Bekke, Vice President, Divisional
John Humenik, Vice President, Divisional
Ray Farris, Vice President, Divisional

GROWTH PLANS/SPECIAL FEATURES:

Lee Enterprises, Incorporated is a provider of local news and information, with a major platform for advertising. The company publishes 46 daily newspapers, a joint interest in two others, and nearly 300 weekly, classified and specialty publications across 21 states. Lee's platform also includes websites and mobile and tablet products in all of its markets that complement its newspapers and attract up to 25 million unique visitors per month. The firm focuses mainly on mid-sized and smaller markets located in the Midwest, Mountain West and West regions of the U.S. with the exception of St. Louis, Missouri. Lee Enterprises owns and operates its newspapers (with a combined circulation of 0.9 million daily and 1.4 million on Sunday) through several publishing subsidiaries, including St. Louis Post-Dispatch LLC, Lincoln Group, Central Illinois Newspaper Group, River Valley Newspaper Group, Missoula Group, and Magic Valley Group. Lee also operates through 50%-owned joint ventures Madison Newspapers, Inc. and TNI Partners. The firm's internet activities consist of websites supporting its newspapers as well as its 82.5%-owned subsidiary, INN Partners LC (which does business as TownNews.com), a provider of web infrastructure for over 1,600 small daily and weekly newspapers and shoppers. In late-2017, the firm acquired the assets of the Dispatch-Argus, including QCOnline.com and related publications serving Moline, Rock Island and other communities in western Illinois. In mid-2018, Lee Enterprises agreed to manage Berkshire Hathaway's newspaper and digital operations in 30 markets beginning July 2018.

The firm offers employees benefits including medical, dental, vision and life insurance; a retirement plan; disability benefits; vacation time; and flexible spending accounts.

FINANCIAL DATA:
Note: Data for latest year may not have been available at press time.

In U.S. $	2018	2017	2016	2015	2014	2013
Revenue	543,955,000	566,943,000	614,364,000	648,543,000	656,697,000	674,740,000
R&D Expense						
Operating Income	91,253,000	83,788,000	125,156,000	101,220,000	106,544,000	105,090,000
Operating Margin %		16.10%	15.68%	16.11%	16.41%	15.57%
SGA Expense			30,646,000			
Net Income	45,766,000	27,481,000	34,961,000	23,316,000	6,795,000	-78,317,000
Operating Cash Flow	59,296,000	72,281,000	79,190,000	74,476,000	82,075,000	89,515,000
Capital Expenditure	6,025,000	4,078,000	7,091,000	9,707,000	13,661,000	9,740,000
EBITDA	115,428,000	139,071,000	165,869,000	155,884,000	142,196,000	5,861,000
Return on Assets %		4.19%	4.81%	2.96%	.82%	-8.29%
Return on Equity %						
Debt to Equity						

CONTACT INFORMATION:
Phone: 563 383-2100　　Fax: 563 326-2972
Toll-Free:
Address: 201 N. Harrison St., Ste. 600, Davenport, IA 52801 United States

STOCK TICKER/OTHER:
Stock Ticker: LEE
Employees: 3,976
Parent Company:

Exchange: NYS
Fiscal Year Ends: 09/30

SALARIES/BONUSES:
Top Exec. Salary: $737,500　　Bonus: $
Second Exec. Salary: $575,000　　Bonus: $

OTHER THOUGHTS:
Estimated Female Officers or Directors: 5
Hot Spot for Advancement for Women/Minorities: Y

Legendary Entertainment

NAIC Code: 512110

www.legendary.com

TYPES OF BUSINESS:
Motion Picture and Video Production

BRANDS/DIVISIONS/AFFILIATES:
Wanda Group
Legendary Television & Digital Media
Pacific Rim
Hangover (The)
Dark Knight Trilogy (The)
Dead Rising:Endgame
Kong: Skull Island
Nerdist.com

CONTACTS:
Note: Officers with more than one job title may be intentionally listed here more than once.

Josh Grode, CEO

GROWTH PLANS/SPECIAL FEATURES:
Legendary Entertainment is a California-based media firm which owns, produces and distributes content in film, television, digital and comic formats. The company's films include Pacific Rim, Man of Steel, Sucker Punch, The Town, Inception, The Hangover franchise, The Dark Knight Trilogy, Watchmen, Superman Returns and 300. Recently-released films include Pacific Rim: Uprising, Skyscraper, Jurassic World: Fallen Kingdom, Mamma Mia! Here We Go Again, Kong: Skull Island, The Great Wall and BlacKkKlansman. Upcoming features include Godzilla: King of the Monsters and Pokemon Detective Pikachu. Legendary's television and digital operations take place through Legendary Television and Legendary Distribution. Series to air on cable and digital platforms include: The Expanse, a science fiction series based on the novels by Daniel Abraham and Ty Franck; LOVE, an unromantic half-hour comedy; COLONY, a one-hour drama series; Electra Woman & Dyna Girl, an action-comedy reboot released on all major digital platforms; and Downward Dog, a comedy television series broadcast on ABC. The firm's other comic titles include Frank Miller's Epochalypse, A Town Called Dragon, The Tower Chronicles series, The Harvester and Annihilator. This division also brings big-screen adventure from comic books, including Godzilla: Awakening and Pacific Rim: Tales From Year Zero. Legendary Digital Networks (LDN) gives content creators a network home that fosters audience engagement and participation. Networks include Nerdist Industries, which operates the nerd culture website Nerdist.com; Geek and Sundry, which operates nerd-culture website Geekandsundry.com; Smart Girls, actress and comedian Amy Poehler's website focused on cultivating young people's authentic selves; and The Players' Tribune, a platform for athletes to connect with fans through athlete-written articles. Legendary Entertainment is owned by Wanda Group.

FINANCIAL DATA:
Note: Data for latest year may not have been available at press time.

In U.S. $	2018	2017	2016	2015	2014	2013
Revenue	677,000,000	625,000,000	612,000,000			
R&D Expense						
Operating Income						
Operating Margin %						
SGA Expense						
Net Income						
Operating Cash Flow						
Capital Expenditure						
EBITDA						
Return on Assets %						
Return on Equity %						
Debt to Equity						

CONTACT INFORMATION:
Phone: 818-861-1800 Fax: 818-954-3884
Toll-Free:
Address: 2900 West Alameda Ave., 15/Fl, Burbank, CA 91505 United States

STOCK TICKER/OTHER:
Stock Ticker: Private
Employees:
Parent Company: Wanda Group

Exchange:
Fiscal Year Ends:

SALARIES/BONUSES:
Top Exec. Salary: $ Bonus: $
Second Exec. Salary: $ Bonus: $

OTHER THOUGHTS:
Estimated Female Officers or Directors:
Hot Spot for Advancement for Women/Minorities:

Sales, profits and employees may be estimates. Financial information, benefits and other data can change quickly and may vary from those stated here.

Lerner Publishing Group

www.lernerbooks.com

NAIC Code: 511130

TYPES OF BUSINESS:
Book Publishing
Educational Books
Children's Books
Online Information

BRANDS/DIVISIONS/AFFILIATES:
Andersen Press USA
LernerClassroom
Lerner Digital
Lerner Publications
Millbrook Press
Muscle Bound
VGSbooks.com
Lerner eSource

CONTACTS:
Note: Officers with more than one job title may be intentionally listed here more than once.

Harry Lerner, CEO
Adam Lerner, Pres.
Margaret Wunderlich, CFO
David Wexler, Exec. VP-Sales
Harry Lerner, Chmn.

GROWTH PLANS/SPECIAL FEATURES:

Lerner Publishing Group is a publisher of both hardcover and paperback K-12 children's books for the retail, school and library markets. The company currently has more than 5,000 titles in print on a variety of subjects, most of which fall into the nonfiction category, including biographies, social studies, language arts, science, geography, sports, picture books, activity books and multicultural issues. Books range from information-intensive school and library books to graphic, colorful general-interest titles. The firm publishes through the following divisions and imprints: Andersen Press USA, Big & Small, Carolrhoda Books, Darby Creek, Full Tilt Press, Gecko Press USA, Graphic Universe, Hungry Tomato, JR Comics, Kane Press, Kar-Ben Publishing, Lantana Publishing, LernerClassroom, Lerner Digital, Lerner Publications, Live Oak Media, Lorimer Children & Teens, Millbrook Press, Quarto Publishing Group USA, Red Chair Press, Twenty-First Century Books and We Do Listen Foundation. The firm uses its proprietary Muscle Bound hardcover library binding, guaranteeing its books to last a lifetime in the classroom and library. Lerner also maintains a free educational website, Visual Geography Series Online, which offers country-specific information, links and downloadable photos and maps at VGSbooks.com. In addition, Lerner has an online portal, Lerner eSource, which provides content and further learning experiences to complement the content of its books. In addition to libraries, schools and other educational organizations, the company's books are purchased by traditional book stores such as Barnes & Noble; educational stores such as the Discovery Store; and non-traditional channels such as direct sales, catalogs, book clubs and fairs and non-book retail stores, including museums, gift shops and toy stores. In November 2018, Lerner acquired Zest books, a publisher of young adult and nonfiction books; Zest will operate as an imprint of Lerner Publishing.

FINANCIAL DATA:
Note: Data for latest year may not have been available at press time.

In U.S. $	2018	2017	2016	2015	2014	2013
Revenue						
R&D Expense						
Operating Income						
Operating Margin %						
SGA Expense						
Net Income						
Operating Cash Flow						
Capital Expenditure						
EBITDA						
Return on Assets %						
Return on Equity %						
Debt to Equity						

CONTACT INFORMATION:
Phone: 612-332-3344 Fax: 800-332-1132
Toll-Free: 800-328-4929
Address: 1251 Washington Ave. N, Minneapolis, MN 55401 United States

STOCK TICKER/OTHER:
Stock Ticker: Private
Employees:
Parent Company:

Exchange:
Fiscal Year Ends: 12/31

SALARIES/BONUSES:
Top Exec. Salary: $ Bonus: $
Second Exec. Salary: $ Bonus: $

OTHER THOUGHTS:
Estimated Female Officers or Directors: 2
Hot Spot for Advancement for Women/Minorities:

Sales, profits and employees may be estimates. Financial information, benefits and other data can change quickly and may vary from those stated here.

Liberty Global plc

NAIC Code: 517110

www.libertyglobal.com

TYPES OF BUSINESS:
Video, Voice & Broadband Internet Access Services
Telephony Services
VoIP Services
Mobile Telephony Services
Video on Demand Services

BRANDS/DIVISIONS/AFFILIATES:
Virgin Media
Unitymedia
Telenet
UPC
Vodafone Ziggo
ITV
All3Media
LionsGate

CONTACTS: *Note: Officers with more than one job title may be intentionally listed here more than once.*
Michael Fries, CEO
John Malone, Chairman of the Board
Charlie Bracken, CFO
Diederik Karsten, Exec. VP
Baptiest Coopmans, Exec. VP-IT
Bryan Hall, Executive VP
Diederik Karsten, Executive VP
Leonard Stegman, Managing Director
John Malone, Chmn.

GROWTH PLANS/SPECIAL FEATURES:
Liberty Global plc is an international provider of TV and broadband services, with operations in 10 European countries under the Virgin Media, Unitymedia, Telenet and UPC brand names. The company invests in the infrastructure and digital platforms that enable Liberty Global customers to utilize and enjoy video, internet and communications services. Liberty Global has developed market-leading products delivered through next-generation networks that connect these more than 21 million customers who subscribe to 45 million TV, broadband internet and telephone services. The firm also serves 6 million mobile subscribers and offers WiFi services across 12 million access points. In addition, Liberty Global owns 50% of VodafoneZiggo, a joint venture in the Netherlands with 4 million customers subscribing to 10 million fixed-line and 5 million mobile services. The firm has significant content investments in ITV, All3Media, ITI Neovision, Casa Systems, LionsGate, the Formula E racing series and several regional sports networks. During 2018, Liberty Global spun off Liberty Latin America into a new publicly-traded company, operating independently throughout parts of the Caribbean and South America; sold UPC Austria to T-Mobile Austria for $2.2 billion; and agreed to sell its operations in Germany, Hungary, Romania and the Czech Republic to Vodafone Group plc for approximately $22.7 billion.

FINANCIAL DATA: *Note: Data for latest year may not have been available at press time.*

In U.S. $	2018	2017	2016	2015	2014	2013
Revenue		3,590,000,000	2,723,800,000	1,217,300,000	1,204,600,000	1,288,800,000
R&D Expense						
Operating Income		559,200,000	481,400,000	272,200,000	248,500,000	110,200,000
Operating Margin %		15.57%	17.67%	22.36%	20.62%	8.55%
SGA Expense		688,400,000	539,200,000	193,400,000	224,000,000	225,100,000
Net Income		-778,100,000	-235,800,000	43,900,000	12,000,000	-39,100,000
Operating Cash Flow		573,900,000	468,200,000	306,500,000	289,000,000	292,200,000
Capital Expenditure		639,300,000	490,400,000	227,200,000	223,100,000	262,100,000
EBITDA		524,300,000	803,600,000	466,600,000	381,200,000	357,300,000
Return on Assets %		-5.59%	-2.70%	1.45%	.43%	
Return on Equity %		-20.52%	-10.57%	38.74%	59.40%	
Debt to Equity		1.83	1.38	11.30	102.61	

CONTACT INFORMATION:
Phone: 44-208-483-6300   Fax:
Toll-Free:
Address: Griffin House, 161 Hammersmith Rd., London, W6 8BS United Kingdom

STOCK TICKER/OTHER:
Stock Ticker: LILA
Employees: 26,700
Parent Company:

Exchange: NAS
Fiscal Year Ends: 12/31

SALARIES/BONUSES:
Top Exec. Salary: $ Bonus: $
Second Exec. Salary: $ Bonus: $

OTHER THOUGHTS:
Estimated Female Officers or Directors: 3
Hot Spot for Advancement for Women/Minorities: Y

Liberty Media Corporation

www.libertymedia.com

NAIC Code: 515112

TYPES OF BUSINESS:
Media and Communications Investments
TV Broadcasting
Satellite Radio
Professional Sports Teams
Video Production & Distribution
Wireless Location Technology

BRANDS/DIVISIONS/AFFILIATES:
Sirius XM Holdings Inc
Braves Holdings LLC
Formula 1
Live Nation Entertainment
Liberty Israel Venture Fund LLC
Associated Partners LP
ideiasnet
Kroenke Sports & Entertainment

CONTACTS:
Note: Officers with more than one job title may be intentionally listed here more than once.
Gregory Maffei, CEO
Mark Carleton, CFO
John Malone, Director
Pamela Coe, Other Corporate Officer
Richard Baer, Other Executive Officer
Albert Rosenthaler, Other Executive Officer

GROWTH PLANS/SPECIAL FEATURES:
Liberty Media Corporation is a holding company with interests in entertainment, media and communications operations primarily in North America. The firm's subsidiaries include: Sirius XM Holdings, Inc.; Braves Holdings, LLC; and the Formula One Group. Sirius XM is 71%-owned by Liberty Media, and is a satellite radio company that delivers commercial-free music as well as sports, entertainment, comedy, talk, news, traffic and weather content. Wholly-owned Braves Holdings indirectly owns the Atlanta Braves major league baseball club, as well as the Braves' stadium and associated real estate projects. The Formula One Group consists of: wholly-owned Formula 1, a global motorsports business; 34%-owned Live Nation Entertainment, which offers concert promotion, venue management, concert sponsorship, advertising, ticketing and artist management services; 7%-owned Kroenke Sports & Entertainment, which owns the Pepsi Center, a sports and entertainment facility in Colorado; and 3%-owned DRL, a premier drone racing league. Other investments include: 80%-owned Liberty Israel Venture Fund, LLC, an investment fund focused on Israeli technology companies; 33%-owned Associated Partners, LP, offering long-term investment solutions; 25%-owned ideiasnet, a Brazil-based project developer that acquires stakes in companies engaged in technology, media and telecommunications; 6%-owned Tastemade, a creator of food and lifestyle content for digital platforms; 6%-owned saavn, an Indian music streaming service focused on Bollywood music; 4%-owned INRIX, a provider of data and analytics to auto OEMs (original equipment manufacturers), governments, businesses and consumers; and less-than-1%-owned viacom, a global entertainment content company.

FINANCIAL DATA:
Note: Data for latest year may not have been available at press time.

In U.S. $	2018	2017	2016	2015	2014	2013
Revenue		7,594,000,000	5,276,000,000	4,794,999,808	4,449,999,872	4,001,999,872
R&D Expense						
Operating Income						
Operating Margin %						
SGA Expense						
Net Income		1,354,000,000	377,000,000	64,000,000	178,000,000	8,780,000,256
Operating Cash Flow						
Capital Expenditure						
EBITDA						
Return on Assets %						
Return on Equity %						
Debt to Equity						

CONTACT INFORMATION:
Phone: 720 875-5400 Fax: 720 875-7469
Toll-Free:
Address: 12300 Liberty Blvd., Englewood, CO 80112 United States

STOCK TICKER/OTHER:
Stock Ticker: LMCA
Employees: 4,393
Parent Company:

Exchange: NAS
Fiscal Year Ends: 12/31

SALARIES/BONUSES:
Top Exec. Salary: $ Bonus: $
Second Exec. Salary: $ Bonus: $

OTHER THOUGHTS:
Estimated Female Officers or Directors: 1
Hot Spot for Advancement for Women/Minorities:

Lions Gate Entertainment Corp

www.lionsgate.com

NAIC Code: 512110

TYPES OF BUSINESS:
Film Production
TV Production & Distribution
Film Distribution
Video-on-Demand Services

BRANDS/DIVISIONS/AFFILIATES:
Lionsgate Television Group
STARZ
Power
Outlander
Pop
Celestial Tiger
PANTAYA
Atom Tickets

CONTACTS:
Note: Officers with more than one job title may be intentionally listed here more than once.

Jon Feltheimer, CEO
James Barge, CFO
Brian Goldsmith, COO
Mark Rachesky, Director
Michael Burns, Director
Corii Berg, General Counsel

GROWTH PLANS/SPECIAL FEATURES:

Lions Gate Entertainment Corp. (Lionsgate) is a producer and distributor of motion pictures, television programming, home entertainment, video-on-demand, digitally-delivered content and linear and over-the-top (OTT) platforms. In addition, Lionsgate in gaining a presence in interactive games and location-based entertainment, virtual reality and other entertainment technologies. The firm's content initiatives are backed by its nearly 16,000-title film and television library and delivered through a global licensing infrastructure. Lionsgate's motion picture division comprises eight film labels and more than 40 feature film releases each year. Television-wise, the company operates one of the largest independent television businesses in the world, with approximately 90 television shows on 40 different networks. The Lionsgate Television Group supplies premium quality programming to streaming platforms, cable, broadcast, and streaming. This division's STARZ offers premium programming such as the flagship series Power and Outlander, as well as other successes such as American Gods, The White Princess and Vida. Lionsgate's home entertainment division offers film TV and digital content, including its own content as well as third-party titles. The firm's linear and digital channel offerings include: STARZ, a premium pay television network with a growing OTT subscriber base; the Pop joint venture channel with CBS; and a minority interest in the Celestial Tiger platform in Asia. This division also connects its content directly with consumers via the Laugh Out Loud comedy platform, a partnership with comedian Kevin Hart, and PANTAYA, a Spanish-language streaming service for audiences in the U.S. Last, Lionsgate's consumer-facing businesses include location-based entertainment such as theme parks, interactive ventures, video and mobile games, and a moviegoer app (Atom Tickets). During 2018, Lionsgate acquired a majority stake in 3 Arts Entertainment. In October 2018, Lionsgate agreed to a partnership with BBC Studios Los Angeles to identify, develop and fund scripted formats and originals for the U.S. market.

FINANCIAL DATA:
Note: Data for latest year may not have been available at press time.

In U.S. $	2018	2017	2016	2015	2014	2013
Revenue	4,129,100,000	3,201,500,000	2,347,419,000	2,399,640,000	2,630,254,000	2,708,141,000
R&D Expense						
Operating Income	308,500,000	72,400,000	-25,030,000	222,281,000	259,948,000	273,079,000
Operating Margin %	7.47	2.26%	-1.06%	9.26%	9.80%	10.16%
SGA Expense	1,352,000,000	1,162,200,000	944,021,000	854,998,000	994,386,000	1,036,203,000
Net Income	473,600,000	14,800,000	50,209,000	181,781,000	152,037,000	232,127,000
Operating Cash Flow	389,200,000	558,600,000	-19,006,000	96,509,000	252,512,000	276,119,000
Capital Expenditure	45,900,000	25,200,000	18,433,000	17,013,000	8,799,000	2,581,000
EBITDA	2,128,800,000	1,445,000,000	1,054,029,000	1,159,602,000	1,161,748,000	1,224,268,000
Return on Assets %	5.21%	.22%	1.40%	5.91%	5.41%	8.36%
Return on Equity %	16.70%	.87%	5.93%	25.48%	32.31%	104.02%
Debt to Equity	0.83	1.25	1.88	1.62	2.01	4.00

CONTACT INFORMATION:
Phone: 310-449-9200 Fax:
Toll-Free:
Address: 2700 Colorado Ave., Ste. 200, Santa Monica, CA 90404 United States

STOCK TICKER/OTHER:
Stock Ticker: LGF.B
Employees: 1,427
Parent Company:

Exchange: NYS
Fiscal Year Ends: 02/28

SALARIES/BONUSES:
Top Exec. Salary: $1,500,000   Bonus: $3,000,000
Second Exec. Salary: $1,000,000   Bonus: $2,000,000

OTHER THOUGHTS:
Estimated Female Officers or Directors: 1
Hot Spot for Advancement for Women/Minorities: Y

Sales, profits and employees may be estimates. Financial information, benefits and other data can change quickly and may vary from those stated here.

Live Nation Entertainment Inc

www.livenationentertainment.com

NAIC Code: 711300

TYPES OF BUSINESS:
Concerts & Events Production
Artist Management
Entertainment Marketing Solutions

BRANDS/DIVISIONS/AFFILIATES:
House of Blues
Fillmore (The)
Hollywood Palladium
Ziggo Dome
3 Arena
Royal Arena
Spark Arena

CONTACTS: Note: Officers with more than one job title may be intentionally listed here more than once.
Michael Rapino, CEO
Russell Wallach, President, Divisional
Kathy Willard, CFO
Arthur Fogel, Chairman, Divisional
Brian Capo, Chief Accounting Officer
Joe Berchtold, Co-President
Gregory Maffei, Director
John Hopmans, Executive VP, Divisional
Michael Rowles, General Counsel
Jordan Zachary, Other Executive Officer
Alan Ridgeway, President, Divisional
Ron Bension, President, Divisional
Bob Roux, President, Divisional
John Reid, President, Divisional
Mark Yovich, President, Divisional
Jared Smith, President, Divisional

GROWTH PLANS/SPECIAL FEATURES:
Live Nation Entertainment, Inc. is one of the world's largest live entertainment companies. The company annually promotes and/or produces tours for more than 29,500 events featuring over 4,000 artists. Globally, the firm owns, operates, has booking rights for or has an equity interest in 22 venues, including House of Blues, The Fillmore in San Francisco, the Hollywood Palladium, the Ziggo Dome in Amsterdam, 3 Arena in Ireland, Royal Arena in Copenhagen and Spark Arena in New Zealand. Live Nation operates in three segments: concerts, ticketing and sponsorship & advertising. The concerts segment principally involves the promotion of live music shows in the company's owned and/or operated venues and in rented third-party venues throughout the world. The ticketing segment is primarily an agency business that sells tickets for events on behalf of clients and retains a service charge for these services. The firm sells tickets for its own events and for third-party clients across multiple live event categories, providing ticketing services for leading arenas, stadiums, amphitheaters, music clubs, concert promoters, professional sports franchises and leagues, college sports teams, performing arts venues, museums and theaters. The segment sells tickets through websites, mobile apps, ticket outlets and telephone call centers. The sponsorship & advertisement segment establishes and maintains relationships with sponsors on the local, national and international levels.

FINANCIAL DATA: Note: Data for latest year may not have been available at press time.

In U.S. $	2018	2017	2016	2015	2014	2013
Revenue		10,337,450,000	8,354,934,000	7,245,731,000	6,866,964,000	6,478,547,000
R&D Expense						
Operating Income		90,428,000	195,064,000	146,315,000	147,692,000	107,840,000
Operating Margin %		.87%	2.33%	2.01%	2.15%	1.66%
SGA Expense		1,907,723,000	1,548,450,000	1,397,908,000	1,330,160,000	1,226,892,000
Net Income		-6,015,000	2,942,000	-32,508,000	-90,807,000	-43,378,000
Operating Cash Flow		623,006,000	597,490,000	300,202,000	269,409,000	417,472,000
Capital Expenditure		249,412,000	180,061,000	142,491,000	142,937,000	135,390,000
EBITDA		552,876,000	558,483,000	506,475,000	374,635,000	475,445,000
Return on Assets %		-1.36%	-.72%	-1.08%	-1.65%	-.79%
Return on Equity %		-8.46%	-3.97%	-5.18%	-7.12%	-3.13%
Debt to Equity		1.65	2.00	1.61	1.55	1.08

CONTACT INFORMATION:
Phone: 310 867-7000
Fax: 310 867-7001
Toll-Free: 800-431-3462
Address: 9348 Civic Center Dr., Beverly Hills, CA 90210 United States

SALARIES/BONUSES:
Top Exec. Salary: $2,416,667
Bonus: $1,000,000
Second Exec. Salary: $1,100,000
Bonus: $

STOCK TICKER/OTHER:
Stock Ticker: LYV
Employees: 8,300
Parent Company:

Exchange: NYS
Fiscal Year Ends: 12/31

OTHER THOUGHTS:
Estimated Female Officers or Directors: 1
Hot Spot for Advancement for Women/Minorities:

Sales, profits and employees may be estimates. Financial information, benefits and other data can change quickly and may vary from those stated here.

LOUD Audio LLC

NAIC Code: 334310

loudaudio.com

TYPES OF BUSINESS:
Audio Equipment
Recording Equipment
Audio Software
Audio & Music Accessories

BRANDS/DIVISIONS/AFFILIATES:
Transom Capital Group
Blackheart
Crate
Mackie
TAPCO

CONTACTS: Note: Officers with more than one job title may be intentionally listed here more than once.
Mark Graham, CEO
Brian McClain, CFO
Tony Del Gianni, VP-Oper.
Adrian Bell, VP-Corp. Comm. & Market Dev.
Alex Nelson, Pres.
Clifford Nathan, Gen. Mgr.-China
Davwinder Sheena, Managing Dir.-Asia Pacific
Paul Yue, Dir.-Procurement

GROWTH PLANS/SPECIAL FEATURES:
LOUD Audio, LLC develops, manufactures, sells and supports professional audio and recording equipment under the Crate, Mackie, TAPCO and Blackheart brand names. LOUD's primary product lines include sound reinforcement speakers, analog mixers, guitar and bass amplifiers, professional loudspeaker systems and branded musical instruments. The firm's products can be found in professional and project recording studios, video and broadcast suites, post-production facilities, television events, sound reinforcement applications including churches and nightclubs and on major musical concert tours. LOUD distributes its products primarily through retail dealers, mail order outlets and installed sound contractors. Its primary operations are in the U.S., with other operations in the U.K., Canada and Japan., which are sold in musical instrument stores, professional audio outlets and several mail order outlets. For Crate and Mackie, the company uses a dedicated, domestic employee sales force that sells to musical instrument stores, retail locations, professional audio outlets and several mail order outlets. Internationally, products are offered direct to dealers in the U.K., Canada, France, Germany, Belgium, the Netherlands, Luxembourg and Denmark through its subsidiaries in the U.K. and Canada. It also sells direct to dealers in Japan. In 2018, LOUD sold its Ampeg brand in May 2018; sold its Martin Audio London brand to LDC, a U.K.-based mid-market private equity investor, in July 2018; and sold its EAW brand to RCF Group, an Italy-based Pro-audio company, in September 2018.

FINANCIAL DATA: Note: Data for latest year may not have been available at press time.

In U.S. $	2018	2017	2016	2015	2014	2013
Revenue						
R&D Expense						
Operating Income						
Operating Margin %						
SGA Expense						
Net Income						
Operating Cash Flow						
Capital Expenditure						
EBITDA						
Return on Assets %						
Return on Equity %						
Debt to Equity						

CONTACT INFORMATION:
Phone: 425-892-6500 Fax: 425-487-4337
Toll-Free: 866-858-5832
Address: 16220 Wood-Red Rd. NE, Woodinville, WA 98072 United States

STOCK TICKER/OTHER:
Stock Ticker: Private
Employees: 533
Parent Company: Transom Capital Group
Exchange:
Fiscal Year Ends: 12/31

SALARIES/BONUSES:
Top Exec. Salary: $ Bonus: $
Second Exec. Salary: $ Bonus: $

OTHER THOUGHTS:
Estimated Female Officers or Directors:
Hot Spot for Advancement for Women/Minorities:

Sales, profits and employees may be estimates. Financial information, benefits and other data can change quickly and may vary from those stated here.

LucasArts Entertainment Company LLC

www.starwars.com/games-apps

NAIC Code: 511210G

TYPES OF BUSINESS:
Computer Software, Electronic Games, Apps & Entertainment
Online Retail

BRANDS/DIVISIONS/AFFILIATES:
Walt Disney Company (The)
Lucasfilm Ltd
Starwars.com
Star Wars Battlefront
Star Wars Pinball
Lego Star Wars
Angry Birds

GROWTH PLANS/SPECIAL FEATURES:
LucasArts Entertainment Company, LLC is a video game publisher and licensor. The firm is a subsidiary of Lucasfilm Ltd., LLC, which is itself a subsidiary of The Walt Disney Company. The most recently-released games offered on the Starwars.com website include Star Wars Battlefront, Star Wars Battlefront II, Star Wars Pinball, Lego Star Wars: The Force Awakens, Star Wars Pinball: The Force Awakens, Lego Star Wars III: The Clone Wars., and Star Wars: The Force Unleashed II. Other games and apps include a variety of Angry Birds, Disney, Star Wars and Lego Star Wars series.

Employees of Lucasfilm companies are offered benefits including vision, medical, dental, life and disability coverage; flexible spending accounts; commuter benefits; 401(k); and adoption assistance.

CONTACTS:
Note: Officers with more than one job title may be intentionally listed here more than once.

Kathleen Kennedy, Pres., Lucasfilm
Darrell Rodriguez, Pres.
Mary Bihr, VP-Global Publishing

FINANCIAL DATA:
Note: Data for latest year may not have been available at press time.

In U.S. $	2018	2017	2016	2015	2014	2013
Revenue						
R&D Expense						
Operating Income						
Operating Margin %						
SGA Expense						
Net Income						
Operating Cash Flow						
Capital Expenditure						
EBITDA						
Return on Assets %						
Return on Equity %						
Debt to Equity						

CONTACT INFORMATION:
Phone: 415-746-8000   Fax:
Toll-Free:
Address: 1110 Gorgas Ave., San Francisco, CA 94129 United States

STOCK TICKER/OTHER:
Stock Ticker: Subsidiary   Exchange:
Employees: 10   Fiscal Year Ends: 04/30
Parent Company: Walt Disney Company (The)

SALARIES/BONUSES:
Top Exec. Salary: $ Bonus: $
Second Exec. Salary: $ Bonus: $

OTHER THOUGHTS:
Estimated Female Officers or Directors: 2
Hot Spot for Advancement for Women/Minorities: Y

Lucasfilm Ltd LLC

NAIC Code: 512110

www.lucasfilm.com

TYPES OF BUSINESS:
Film Production
Special Effects
Sound Effects
Digital Animation
Software & Video Games
Online Publishing
Merchandising

BRANDS/DIVISIONS/AFFILIATES:
Walt Disney Company (The)
Industrial Light & Magic
Skywalker Sound
LucasArts
Lucasfilm Animation

CONTACTS:
Note: Officers with more than one job title may be intentionally listed here more than once.

Kathleen Kennedy, Pres.
Steve Condiotti, VP-Finance
Lynwen Brennan, Pres., Industrial Light & Magic
Josh Lowden, Gen. Mgr.-Skywalker Sound
Howard Roffman, Sr. Advisor
Paul Southern, VP-Licensing & Consumer Products Mktg.

GROWTH PLANS/SPECIAL FEATURES:

Lucasfilm Ltd., LLC is a leading independent film production company created by filmmaker George Lucas in 1971, and is a subsidiary of The Walt Disney Company. The firm has produced some of the most popular films in history, including the original Star Wars franchise and the Indiana Jones films. It operates through eight divisions. Lucasfilm is responsible for production, promotion and strategic management of theatrical, television and entertainment properties. Industrial Light & Magic (ILM) creates digital and visual special effects for the entertainment industry and has received several Academy Award nominations and Scientific and Technical Achievement Awards; ILM also runs LucasFilm's Immersive Entertainment division. Skywalker Sound produces post-production digital sound effects, for which it has won 15 Academy Awards and received 62 nominations. LucasFilm Games develops video games for PC, mobile and console based on Lucas' movies, especially the Star Wars franchise. The firm's licensing division is responsible for licensing and merchandising Lucasfilm properties. Animation and Lucasfilm Animation Singapore are the firm's digital animation studios, producing cartoon series for children. Lucasfilm Singapore consists of all the firm's overseas operations, including ILM Singapore, Lucasfilm Animation Singapore and LucasArts Singapore. Finally, Lucasfilm's online division produces entertainment, education, reference and e-commerce sites for Lucasfilm properties. The company is headquartered at the Letterman Digital Arts Center in San Francisco, California and maintains two other offices in Marin County, California and one in Singapore. The Letterman Digital Arts Center brings the entire organization together and enables units producing games and films to collaborate more closely and share technologies. In 2018, the firm released Solo: A Star Wars Story, with upcoming releases including: Star Wars: Episode IX in 2019 and Indiana Jones 5 in 2020. U.S.

Lucasfilm offers 401(k); medical, dental, life, disability and vision coverage; flexible spending accounts; commuter benefits; and adoption assistance.

FINANCIAL DATA:
Note: Data for latest year may not have been available at press time.

In U.S. $	2018	2017	2016	2015	2014	2013
Revenue						
R&D Expense						
Operating Income						
Operating Margin %						
SGA Expense						
Net Income						
Operating Cash Flow						
Capital Expenditure						
EBITDA						
Return on Assets %						
Return on Equity %						
Debt to Equity						

CONTACT INFORMATION:
Phone: 415-662-1800 Fax:
Toll-Free:
Address: 1110 Gorgas Ave., San Francisco, CA 94129 United States

SALARIES/BONUSES:
Top Exec. Salary: $ Bonus: $
Second Exec. Salary: $ Bonus: $

STOCK TICKER/OTHER:
Stock Ticker: Subsidiary   Exchange:
Employees: 1,000   Fiscal Year Ends: 03/31
Parent Company: Walt Disney Company (The)

OTHER THOUGHTS:
Estimated Female Officers or Directors: 2
Hot Spot for Advancement for Women/Minorities: Y

Sales, profits and employees may be estimates. Financial information, benefits and other data can change quickly and may vary from those stated here.

Magic Leap Inc

www.magicleap.com

NAIC Code: 511210G

TYPES OF BUSINESS:
Computer Software, Electronic Games, Apps & Entertainment
Virtual Reality Software
Augmented Reality Technology

BRANDS/DIVISIONS/AFFILIATES:
Dynamic Digitized Lightfield Signal
Digital Lightfield
Magic Leap One
Lightwear
Lightpack
Magic Leap Control
Lumin OS

CONTACTS:
Note: Officers with more than one job title may be intentionally listed here more than once.

Rony Abovitz, CEO

GROWTH PLANS/SPECIAL FEATURES:

Magic Leap, Inc. is engaged in the development of human computing interfaces, mobile wearable systems, and gaming and software products that cater to the entertainment, computing, education and communication markets. The company is the creator of Dynamic Digitized Lightfield Signal, popularly known as Digital Lightfield technology, which can be used to generate images that look like real objects. The firm has developed Magic Leap One, a mixed reality computing platform, such as the head-mounted virtual retinal display which superimposes 3D computer-generated imagery over real world objects, by projecting light field into the user's eye. The headset is Magic Leap One can be equipped with a lens insert based on the wearer's personalized prescription for eyeglasses. Lightwear is another headset comprised of cameras, sensors, speakers and optical relay, which work together with the Lightpack processor to provide unique input to the wearer's visual system. Lightpack comprises an integrated GPU and CPU that generates high-fidelity, gaming-quality graphics to create experiences, such as dodging jellyfish while walking. Magic Leap Control, which is similar to a hand-held remote-control device, enables headset wearers to create and control the types of special effects they can visualize and experience. Magic Leap's operating system, Lumin OS, is fully optimized for environment recognition, persistent digital content and the performance to power high-fidelity visual experiences that turns one's imagination into reality. Lumin OS' social features support sharing experiences in mixed reality; its screens enable users to create multiple screens of any size; and its gallery enables organization and share-ability of favorite photos, videos or 3D models that have been created or captured with Magic Leap One. In addition, Magic Leap is creating a product for web developers, enabling them to quickly design and develop spatial websites while working with familiar platforms like CSS and javascript.

FINANCIAL DATA:
Note: Data for latest year may not have been available at press time.

In U.S. $	2018	2017	2016	2015	2014	2013
Revenue						
R&D Expense						
Operating Income						
Operating Margin %						
SGA Expense						
Net Income						
Operating Cash Flow						
Capital Expenditure						
EBITDA						
Return on Assets %						
Return on Equity %						
Debt to Equity						

CONTACT INFORMATION:
Phone: 954-889-7010 Fax:
Toll-Free:
Address: 7500 W. Sunrise Blvd., Plantation, FL 33322 United States

SALARIES/BONUSES:
Top Exec. Salary: $ Bonus: $
Second Exec. Salary: $ Bonus: $

STOCK TICKER/OTHER:
Stock Ticker: Private Exchange:
Employees: 850 Fiscal Year Ends:
Parent Company:

OTHER THOUGHTS:
Estimated Female Officers or Directors:
Hot Spot for Advancement for Women/Minorities:

Sales, profits and employees may be estimates. Financial information, benefits and other data can change quickly and may vary from those stated here.

Major League Baseball Advanced Media LP (MLBAM)

www.mlbam.com
NAIC Code: 519130

TYPES OF BUSINESS:
Online Delivery of Sporting Events
Streaming Sports Media

BRANDS/DIVISIONS/AFFILIATES:
At Bat

CONTACTS:
Note: Officers with more than one job title may be intentionally listed here more than once.
Bob Starkey, CFO

GROWTH PLANS/SPECIAL FEATURES:

Major League Baseball Advanced Media LP (MLBAM) is a full-service solutions provider that delivers digital content through all forms of interactive media. Its capabilities are designed for web, mobile applications and connected devices while integrating live and on-demand multimedia. MLBAM's services include business & content strategy, delivering back-end infrastructure, as well as development and operational management of custom multi-platform applications; UX (user experience) & product design, providing solutions for all forms of digital presence such as websites, mobile web applications, connected devices, marketing campaigns and social media; social media & marketing, a suite of marketing solutions that are fully customizable and able to develop, integrate and manage initiatives; ticketing, which supports digital ticketing strategies such as print-at-home, mobile, season & package plans, secondary market, dynamic pricing and interactive seating; sponsorship & advertising; ecommerce & paid content, a subscription platform that supports digital products such as live and on-demand multimedia, fantasy games, gamecast applications and fan clubs with password-protected login; multimedia & live streaming, which operates and distributes live events and daily streams; mobile web & applications; and statistics & data applications, which deploys proprietary software to chronicle every pitch of every game throughout the season, in-game highlights, box scores and player stats. The firm's At Bat offering is a subscription-based application that provides live scores, statistics, pitch tracking, player cards, notifications and news via online and mobile devices.

FINANCIAL DATA:
Note: Data for latest year may not have been available at press time.

In U.S. $	2018	2017	2016	2015	2014	2013
Revenue	130,000,000	110,000,000	900,000,000	850,000,000	800,000,000	
R&D Expense						
Operating Income						
Operating Margin %						
SGA Expense						
Net Income						
Operating Cash Flow						
Capital Expenditure						
EBITDA						
Return on Assets %						
Return on Equity %						
Debt to Equity						

CONTACT INFORMATION:
Phone: 212-485-6142 Fax: 212-485-8111
Toll-Free:
Address: 75 Ninth Ave., New York, NY 10011 United States

STOCK TICKER/OTHER:
Stock Ticker: Private
Employees:
Parent Company:

Exchange:
Fiscal Year Ends:

SALARIES/BONUSES:
Top Exec. Salary: $ Bonus: $
Second Exec. Salary: $ Bonus: $

OTHER THOUGHTS:
Estimated Female Officers or Directors:
Hot Spot for Advancement for Women/Minorities:

Sales, profits and employees may be estimates. Financial information, benefits and other data can change quickly and may vary from those stated here.

Plunkett Research, Ltd.

MarketWatch Inc

www.marketwatch.com

NAIC Code: 519130

TYPES OF BUSINESS:
Online Financial Information
Television & Radio Programming

BRANDS/DIVISIONS/AFFILIATES:
Dow Jones & Company Inc
Barrons.com
Financial News London
Moneyish
Mansion Global
MarketWatch Weekend
MarketWatch.com Radio Network

CONTACTS:
Note: Officers with more than one job title may be intentionally listed here more than once.

Jim Bernard, Managing Dir.
Paul Mattison, CFO
Raju Narisetti, Managing Editor-WSJ.com

GROWTH PLANS/SPECIAL FEATURES:

MarketWatch, Inc., a wholly-owned subsidiary of Dow Jones & Company, Inc., is a financial media company providing web-based, real-time business news, financial programming and analytic tools. The firm is a member of Dow Jones Media Group, which also includes: Barrons.com, a financial information website; Financial News London, a financial newspaper and news website published in London; Moneyish, offering features, essays, videos and news about money; and Mansion Global, offering digital content about the global real estate market, featuring luxury listings for sale around the world. These free, advertising-supported websites serve the business and financial communities with timely market news and information, provided by bureaus in the U.S., Europe and Asia. In addition to business and financial news, MarketWatch sites offer in-depth commentary on trends and events, personal finance commentary and data, community features and other services designed to provide a one-stop-shop for audiences. Other features include a mutual fund center, a seasonal tax guide, market advisors and research columns. Customers have the ability to create personal user settings including portfolio trackers, news and quotes, custom views, allocation analysis, financials and charting. MarketWatch also delivers relevant financial news to user e-mail accounts, hosts investment discussion communities, offers personalized automatic alerts and provides customers with wireless capabilities. In addition, the firm sells subscription-based content for individual investors under the Hulbert Financial Digest, Retirement Weekly and ETF Trader brand names. MarketWatch produces the syndicated MarketWatch Weekend television program and provides business and financial news updates every 30 minutes on the MarketWatch.com Radio Network. MarketWatch's website has approximately 19 million visitors per month (as of October 2018).

MarketWatch offers employees health care coverage, fitness programs, a retirement savings program and tuition assistance.

FINANCIAL DATA:
Note: Data for latest year may not have been available at press time.

In U.S. $	2018	2017	2016	2015	2014	2013
Revenue						
R&D Expense						
Operating Income						
Operating Margin %						
SGA Expense						
Net Income						
Operating Cash Flow						
Capital Expenditure						
EBITDA						
Return on Assets %						
Return on Equity %						
Debt to Equity						

CONTACT INFORMATION:
Phone: 415-439-6400   Fax: 415-439-6485
Toll-Free:
Address: 201 California St., Ste. 1300, San Francisco, CA 94111 United States

STOCK TICKER/OTHER:
Stock Ticker: Subsidiary
Employees: 206
Parent Company: Dow Jones & Company Inc

Exchange:
Fiscal Year Ends: 12/31

SALARIES/BONUSES:
Top Exec. Salary: $ Bonus: $
Second Exec. Salary: $ Bonus: $

OTHER THOUGHTS:
Estimated Female Officers or Directors:
Hot Spot for Advancement for Women/Minorities: Y

Sales, profits and employees may be estimates. Financial information, benefits and other data can change quickly and may vary from those stated here.

Martha Stewart Living Omnimedia Inc

www.marthastewart.com

NAIC Code: 511120

TYPES OF BUSINESS:
Magazine Publishing
Television & Video Production
Book Publishing
Home & Garden Products
Web Sites
Satellite Radio
Merchandising

BRANDS/DIVISIONS/AFFILIATES:
Sequential Brands Group Inc
Martha Stewart Living
Martha Stewart Weddings
MarthaStewart.com
MarthaStewartWeddings.com
Emerils.com
Martha Stewart Crafts
Martha Stewart Home Office

CONTACTS:
Note: Officers with more than one job title may be intentionally listed here more than once.
Kenneth West, CFO
Gary Klein, CFO
Allison Hoffman, Executive VP
Patricia Pollack, Senior Executive VP, Divisional

GROWTH PLANS/SPECIAL FEATURES:
Martha Stewart Living Omnimedia, Inc. (MSL) is an integrated media and merchandising firm that provides lifestyle content and products. The company is comprised of three business segments: publishing, merchandising and broadcasting. This combination of segments enables the company to cross-promote its content and products, which generally span eight core areas: home; cooking & entertaining; gardening; crafts; holidays; organizing; weddings; and whole living, which focuses on healthy living and sustainable practices. The publishing segment publishes both print and digital editions of Martha Stewart Living and Martha Stewart Weddings magazines; publishes several website properties including MarthaStewart.com, MarthaStewartWeddings.com and Emerils.com; and maintains multi-year agreements with The Crown Publishing Group and HarperCollins Publishers to publish Martha Stewart and Emeril Lagasse branded books. The merchandising segment consists of operations related to the design of merchandise and related packaging, collateral and advertising materials and the licensing of various proprietary trademarks in connection with retail programs conducted through a number of retailers and manufacturers. Select manufacturing licensees include Martha Stewart Crafts and Martha Stewart Home Office; and select Emeril Lagasse Manufacturing Licensees include Emerilware, Emeril's Original, Emeril Cutlery and Emeril's Gourmet Coffee. The broadcasting segment consists of operations relating to the production of television programming, the domestic and international distribution of library of programming in existing and repurposed formats and the operations of the company's satellite radio channel. MSL operates as a subsidiary of Sequential Brands Group, Inc.

FINANCIAL DATA:
Note: Data for latest year may not have been available at press time.

In U.S. $	2018	2017	2016	2015	2014	2013
Revenue	71,000,000	70,000,000	68,000,000	72,756,000	141,916,000	160,675,008
R&D Expense						
Operating Income						
Operating Margin %						
SGA Expense						
Net Income				-6,798,000	-5,058,000	-1,772,000
Operating Cash Flow						
Capital Expenditure						
EBITDA						
Return on Assets %						
Return on Equity %						
Debt to Equity						

CONTACT INFORMATION:
Phone: 212 827-8000   Fax: 212 827-8204
Toll-Free:
Address: 601 W. 26th St., New York, NY 10001 United States

SALARIES/BONUSES:
Top Exec. Salary: $ Bonus: $
Second Exec. Salary: $ Bonus: $

STOCK TICKER/OTHER:
Stock Ticker: Subsidiary   Exchange:
Employees: 270   Fiscal Year Ends: 12/31
Parent Company: Sequential Brands Group Inc

OTHER THOUGHTS:
Estimated Female Officers or Directors: 5
Hot Spot for Advancement for Women/Minorities: Y

Sales, profits and employees may be estimates. Financial information, benefits and other data can change quickly and may vary from those stated here.

Marvel Entertainment LLC

www.marvel.com

NAIC Code: 511120

TYPES OF BUSINESS:
Comic Book Publishing
Toys
Licensing & Merchandising
Movie Production
Online Services

BRANDS/DIVISIONS/AFFILIATES:
Walt Disney Company (The)
Spider-Man
Iron Man
Incredible Hulk (The)
Captain America
X-Men
Iron Man Experience
Marvel Stadium

CONTACTS:
Note: Officers with more than one job title may be intentionally listed here more than once.

Dan Buckley, Pres.
Jeff Klein, Exec. VP-Comm.
Kevin Feige, Pres., Production -Marvel Studios
Isaac Perlmutter, Chmn.

GROWTH PLANS/SPECIAL FEATURES:
Marvel Entertainment, LLC, a subsidiary of The Walt Disney Company, is one of the world's most prominent character-based entertainment companies, with a proprietary library of over 8,000 characters. Some of its most recognizable properties include Spider-Man, Iron Man, The Incredible Hulk, Captain America, X-Men, The Punisher, The Avengers and Silver Surfer. The company's business is divided into three divisions: licensing, publishing and film production. The licensing division licenses the company's characters for use in a wide variety of products and media, including toys, games, apparel, accessories and collectibles. This segment also receives fees from the sale of licenses to a variety of media, including feature films, television and video games. The publishing division creates and publishes comic books and trade paperbacks principally in North America. Aside from traditional printed retail sales and subscriptions, Marvel Entertainment also sells subscription virtual access through Marvel Unlimited, which allows users to browse through over 15,000 classic and new titles in the firm's online catalog, with more continuously being added. The film production division develops, produces and distributes films based on its character properties, which are financed by a company-owned film facility. Marvel Entertainment also operates a kids' website, MarvelKids.com, featuring Marvel characters and content for children ages 6-11. During 2018, The Walt Disney Company Australia purchased eight-year naming rights to Docklands Stadium from Melbourne Stadiums Limited, and selected the Marvel brand as part of the name; therefore, since September 2018, the stadium has been commercially represented as Marvel Stadium, with related retail space at the stadium.

Marvel employees receive benefits including medical, dental and life insurance; sick days; a 401(k); a 529 College savings plan; bonus plans; and credit union access.

FINANCIAL DATA:
Note: Data for latest year may not have been available at press time.

In U.S. $	2018	2017	2016	2015	2014	2013
Revenue						
R&D Expense						
Operating Income						
Operating Margin %						
SGA Expense						
Net Income						
Operating Cash Flow						
Capital Expenditure						
EBITDA						
Return on Assets %						
Return on Equity %						
Debt to Equity						

CONTACT INFORMATION:
Phone: 212-576-4000   Fax:
Toll-Free: 888-511-5480
Address: 135 W. 50th St., 7/Fl, New York, NY 10016 United States

STOCK TICKER/OTHER:
Stock Ticker: Subsidiary   Exchange:
Employees: 910   Fiscal Year Ends: 12/31
Parent Company: Walt Disney Company (The)

SALARIES/BONUSES:
Top Exec. Salary: $ Bonus: $
Second Exec. Salary: $ Bonus: $

OTHER THOUGHTS:
Estimated Female Officers or Directors:
Hot Spot for Advancement for Women/Minorities:

Sales, profits and employees may be estimates. Financial information, benefits and other data can change quickly and may vary from those stated here.

McClatchy Company (The)

NAIC Code: 511110

www.mcclatchy.com

TYPES OF BUSINESS:
Newspaper Publishing
Online Publishing
Direct Marketing
Paper Manufacturing

BRANDS/DIVISIONS/AFFILIATES:
Star-Telegram
Sacramento Bee (The)
Kansas City Star
Miami Herald
Charlotte Observer (The)
McClatchy Interactive

CONTACTS:
Note: Officers with more than one job title may be intentionally listed here more than once.

Craig Forman, CEO
Billie McConkey, General Counsel
Christian Hendricks, Vice President, Divisional

GROWTH PLANS/SPECIAL FEATURES:

The McClatchy Company is a news firm and local media company that connects with communities via print, online, digital and mobile app formats. McClatchy produces daily newspapers as well as several non-daily publications across multiple U.S. markets. These newspapers have a total average paid daily circulation of more than 1 million and average Sunday circulation of over 1.6 million. The firm's portfolio of publications includes Star-Telegram (Fort Worth), The Sacramento Bee, The Kansas City Star, the Miami Herald and The Charlotte Observer. Over the decades, McClatchy's newspapers have been awarded 54 Pulitzer Prizes, some of which were gold medals for public service; the Robert F. Kennedy Journalism Award for coverage of human rights and social justice; and the George Polk Award. The company's oldest and largest daily newspaper is The Sacramento Bee, originally published in 1857. McClatchy's core newspaper business is supplemented by a growing array of niche products and direct marketing initiatives. The company operates McClatchy Interactive, an online publishing business that provides newspapers with content publishing tools and software development.

The firm offers employees benefits including medical, dental, vision and life insurance; Healthworks, a health care assistance program; and a 401(k).

FINANCIAL DATA:
Note: Data for latest year may not have been available at press time.

In U.S. $	2018	2017	2016	2015	2014	2013
Revenue		903,592,000	977,092,992	1,056,574,016	1,146,552,064	1,242,237,056
R&D Expense						
Operating Income						
Operating Margin %						
SGA Expense						
Net Income		-332,358,000	-34,193,000	-300,161,984	373,988,992	18,803,000
Operating Cash Flow						
Capital Expenditure						
EBITDA						
Return on Assets %						
Return on Equity %						
Debt to Equity						

CONTACT INFORMATION:
Phone: 916-321-1844   Fax:
Toll-Free:
Address: 2100 Q St., Sacramento, CA 95816 United States

SALARIES/BONUSES:
Top Exec. Salary: $ Bonus: $
Second Exec. Salary: $ Bonus: $

STOCK TICKER/OTHER:
Stock Ticker: MNI   Exchange: NYS
Employees: 4,200   Fiscal Year Ends: 12/31
Parent Company:

OTHER THOUGHTS:
Estimated Female Officers or Directors: 5
Hot Spot for Advancement for Women/Minorities: Y

McGraw-Hill Education Inc

www.mheducation.com

NAIC Code: 511130

TYPES OF BUSINESS:
Book Publishing
Educational Books
Testing Services

BRANDS/DIVISIONS/AFFILIATES:
Apollo Global Management LLC

CONTACTS:
Note: Officers with more than one job title may be intentionally listed here more than once.

Nana Banerjee, CEO
Patrick Milano, CFO
Sheila O'Neil, Chief Culture and Talent Officer
Stephen Laster, Chief Digital Officer
Patrick Milano, Chief Admin. Officer
David Stafford, General Counsel
Daniel Sieger, VP-Comm.
Philip Ruppel, Pres., Professional
Peter Cohen, Pres., School Education
Ellen Haley, Pres., CTB
Brian Kibby, Pres., Higher Education
Mark Dorman, Pres., Int'l

GROWTH PLANS/SPECIAL FEATURES:
McGraw-Hill Education, Inc. provides educational materials and learning solutions for students, instructors, professionals and institutions around the world. The firm defines itself as a learning science company, combining research, data and practices to help educators. McGraw-Hill draws its research and data from cognitive neuroscience, learning analytics, data science, behavioral economics and education psychology to create education solutions that the firm integrates into its products. McGraw-Hill targets the pre-kindergarten through secondary school market (PreK-12), the 2- and 4-year college and university market and the professional learning and information market with content, tools and services delivered via print, digital and hybrid solutions. McGraw-Hill Education divides its operations into four segments, higher education, K-12, international and professional. The high education segment offers adaptive digital learning tools, digital platforms, custom publishing solutions and printed textbook solutions to two- and four-year non-profit college and university students, instructors and institutions. This segment makes up 42% of the firm's total revenue. The K-12 segment sells learning solutions and curriculum directly to K-12 school districts across the U.S. This segment makes up 35% of the firm's total revenue. The international segment serves 125 countries outside of the U.S. and offers an extensive product portfolio to higher education, K-12 and professional markets. This segment makes up about 16% of the firm's total revenue. The professional segment provides medical, technical, engineering and business content for the professional, education and test preparation communities. This segment makes up 7% of the firm's total revenue.

FINANCIAL DATA:
Note: Data for latest year may not have been available at press time.

In U.S. $	2018	2017	2016	2015	2014	2013
Revenue		1,719,072,000	1,740,027,000	1,828,592,000	1,832,833,000	1,823,868,000
R&D Expense						
Operating Income						
Operating Margin %						
SGA Expense						
Net Income		-65,930,000	-137,007,000	-179,131,000	-354,710,000	-167,423,000
Operating Cash Flow						
Capital Expenditure						
EBITDA						
Return on Assets %						
Return on Equity %						
Debt to Equity						

CONTACT INFORMATION:
Phone: 212-904-2588　Fax:
Toll-Free:
Address: 2 Penn Plaza, New York, NY 10121 United States

SALARIES/BONUSES:
Top Exec. Salary: $　Bonus: $
Second Exec. Salary: $　Bonus: $

STOCK TICKER/OTHER:
Stock Ticker: Subsidiary　Exchange:
Employees: 4,700　Fiscal Year Ends: 12/31
Parent Company: Apollo Global Management LLC

OTHER THOUGHTS:
Estimated Female Officers or Directors: 2
Hot Spot for Advancement for Women/Minorities:

MDI Entertainment LLC

NAIC Code: 541800

www.mdientertainment.com

TYPES OF BUSINESS:
Lottery-Focused Marketing
Events & Promotions
Web Design
Electronic Lottery Cards
Advertising
Game Development
Research

BRANDS/DIVISIONS/AFFILIATES:
Scientific Games Corporation

CONTACTS:
Note: Officers with more than one job title may be intentionally listed here more than once.
Barry Cottle, CEO-Scientific Games Corp
Steve Saferin, Pres.
Rob Arnold, Sr. VP-Oper.
Jim Acton, VP-Bus. Dev.
Bob Kowalczyk, Sr. VP-Internet Svcs.
Bryon Bonafede, Sr. Dir-Finance
Liz Johnson, Dir.-Creative & Client Svcs.
Debbie Amundson, Assistant Controller
Kyle Rogers, Exec. VP
Pam Lee, VP-Linked Games
Gary Holcroft, Dir.-European Sales
Ray Watson, Mgr.-Purchasing & Fulfillment

GROWTH PLANS/SPECIAL FEATURES:
MDI Entertainment, LLC, a wholly owned subsidiary of Scientific Games Corporation, specializes in creating, marketing and providing entertainment-based promotions for the worldwide lottery industry. Its strategic focus is to develop and market lottery ticket games based on well-known entertainment and pop cultural icon licensed properties. The company operates a licensed Lottery Product portfolio that includes brands such as 7-Up, Bally, Betty Boop, Chevrolet Camaro, Clue, Monopoly, Pac-Man, Scrabble and World Poker Tour. MDI's basic selling proposition to lotteries is that niche brand names will create appeal and loyalty among a segment of consumers much better than a generic lottery game. Revenue comes from two main sources: the sale of bonus prize products to lotteries using MDI-licensed games; and license/royalty fees paid by lotteries for the rights to market the games in their jurisdictions. The company has printed billions of its licensed pull-tab lottery tickets and scratch off games that have an aggregated value of nearly $13 billion. MDI purchases prize products resold to lotteries from other licensees of a particular brand. Products are sold to lotteries in bulk and then MDI fulfills prizes individually to lottery winners as designated by the lottery, which are packaged as elements of a full-service lottery promotion tied to licenses that the company acquires. The company also provides additional services such as website development, advertising support, game development, promotions and research for its lottery customers. The company's MDI interactive division enables lotteries to engage players by delivering content via the web and multiple digital platforms.

FINANCIAL DATA:
Note: Data for latest year may not have been available at press time.

In U.S. $	2018	2017	2016	2015	2014	2013
Revenue						
R&D Expense						
Operating Income						
Operating Margin %						
SGA Expense						
Net Income						
Operating Cash Flow						
Capital Expenditure						
EBITDA						
Return on Assets %						
Return on Equity %						
Debt to Equity						

CONTACT INFORMATION:
Phone: 770-664-3700   Fax: 770-343-8798
Toll-Free: 800-572-7082
Address: 1500 Bluegrass Lakes Pkwy., Alpharetta, GA 30004 United States

STOCK TICKER/OTHER:
Stock Ticker: Subsidiary   Exchange:
Employees: 20   Fiscal Year Ends: 12/31
Parent Company: Scientific Games Corporation

SALARIES/BONUSES:
Top Exec. Salary: $ Bonus: $
Second Exec. Salary: $ Bonus: $

OTHER THOUGHTS:
Estimated Female Officers or Directors: 27
Hot Spot for Advancement for Women/Minorities: Y

Mediacom Communications Corporation

www.mediacomcc.com

NAIC Code: 517110

TYPES OF BUSINESS:
Cable TV Service
Internet Service
Digital Cable
Telephone Service

BRANDS/DIVISIONS/AFFILIATES:
Xtream
Mediacom Digital Phone
Home Controller

CONTACTS: Note: Officers with more than one job title may be intentionally listed here more than once.
Rocco B. Commisso, CEO
John G. Pascarelli, VP-Operations
Mark E. Stephan, CFO
David M. McNaughton, Sr. VP-Mktg.
Italia Commisso Weinand, Sr. VP-Human Resources & Programming
Peter Lyons, Sr. VP-IT
Joseph E. Young, General Counsel
John G. Pascarelli, Exec. VP-Oper.
Jack Griffin, Dir.-Corp. Finance
Edward S. Pardini, Sr. VP-Divisional Oper.-North Central Division
Brian M. Walsh, Sr. VP
Tapan Dandnaik, Sr. VP-Customer Service & Financial Oper.
Steve Litwer, Sr. VP-Advertising Sales, OnMedia Div.
Rocco B. Commisso, Chmn.

GROWTH PLANS/SPECIAL FEATURES:

Mediacom Communications Corporation, a leading cable company, supplies an array of broadband products and services to more than 1,500 communities throughout the U.S., reaching over 1.4 million homes. The firm offers its customers a full array of traditional video services, which includes basic service, digital video service, pay-per-view service, high definition television, digital video recorders and video-on-demand. Xtream is the company's all-in-one integrated platform where TV and internet work together to deliver TV, Wi-Fi, caller ID (without interrupting the show), TiVo, On-Demand and apps. In addition, the company offers five types of high-speed internet access: Internet 60, allows for download speeds up to 60 Mbps (megabits per second); Internet 100, speeds up to 100 Mbps; Internet 200, up to 200 Mbps; Internet 500, caps at 500 Mbps; and 1GIG, which allows for up to 1,000 Mbps of download speeds. The firm's Mediacom Digital Phone offers customers unlimited local, regional and long-distance calling within the U.S., Puerto Rico, U.S. Virgin Islands and Canada. It is delivered over voice over internet protocol (VoIP) that digitizes voice signals and routes them as data packets through Mediacom's controlled broadband cable systems. It includes features such as Caller ID with name and number, call waiting, three-way calling and enhanced Emergency 911 dialing. Mediacom also offers video, HSD (high speed data), phone, network and transport services to commercial and large enterprise customers. It offers large enterprise customers who require high-bandwidth connections solutions such as the point-to-point circuits required by wireless communications providers. Additionally, Mediacom offers a home security product, Home Controller, which provides 24-hour-a-day monitoring from a UL-approved facility.

FINANCIAL DATA: Note: Data for latest year may not have been available at press time.

In U.S. $	2018	2017	2016	2015	2014	2013
Revenue	1,877,551,000	1,810,255,000				
R&D Expense						
Operating Income						
Operating Margin %						
SGA Expense						
Net Income						
Operating Cash Flow						
Capital Expenditure						
EBITDA						
Return on Assets %						
Return on Equity %						
Debt to Equity						

CONTACT INFORMATION:
Phone: 855-633-4226   Fax: 845-698-4069
Toll-Free: 800-479-2082
Address: 1 Mediacom Way, Mediacom Park, NY 10918 United States

STOCK TICKER/OTHER:
Stock Ticker: Private   Exchange:
Employees: 7,000   Fiscal Year Ends: 12/31
Parent Company:

SALARIES/BONUSES:
Top Exec. Salary: $ Bonus: $
Second Exec. Salary: $ Bonus: $

OTHER THOUGHTS:
Estimated Female Officers or Directors: 1
Hot Spot for Advancement for Women/Minorities:

Sales, profits and employees may be estimates. Financial information, benefits and other data can change quickly and may vary from those stated here.

Mediaset SpA

NAIC Code: 515120

www.mediaset.it

TYPES OF BUSINESS:
Media Svcs. & Broadcasting
Cable Television Networks
Film & TV Production

BRANDS/DIVISIONS/AFFILIATES:
Fingruppo Holding SpA
Rete 4
Venti
La 5
Mediaset Extra
Boing
Radio 101
Radio Subasio

CONTACTS: *Note: Officers with more than one job title may be intentionally listed here more than once.*
D. Paolo Vasile, CEO
Marco Giordani, CFO
Gina Nieri, Head-Legal Affairs
Simone Sole, Head-Investor Rel.
Pier Silvio Berlusconi, Vice Chmn.
Gina Nieri, Head-Institutional Affairs & Strategic Analysis
D. Alejandro Echevarria Busquet, Chmn.

GROWTH PLANS/SPECIAL FEATURES:

Mediaset SpA is a media sector holding company based in Italy. Mediaset's holdings are comprised of television channels and radio channels, with all of its television channels provided as free-to-view. The firm's TV channels include: Rete4, Canale 5 and Italia 1, offering general programming; Venti and Iris, offering series TV and movies; La 5, offering female-oriented programming; Mediaset Extra, offering series TV and shows; Italia 2, offering male-oriented programming; Top Crime, offering crime series TV and movies; Boing, offering child-oriented programming; Cartoonito, which is baby-oriented; and Mediaset TGCOM 24, an all news channel. Radio channels include: R101, Radio 105 Network, Virgin Radio Italia and Radio Subasio. The Venti channel was launched in December 2017. Foreign channels include the 25%-owned Nessma TV in northern Africa; and Mediaset Italia also offers broadcasting services outside of Italy. Mediaset SpA operates as a subsidiary of Fingruppo Holding SpA. In November 2018, Mediaset launched LOVEStv, a free television platform jointly promoted by Atresmedia, Mediaset Espana and RTVE; LOVEStv is based on HbbTV (hybrid broadcast broadband television) technology.

FINANCIAL DATA: *Note: Data for latest year may not have been available at press time.*

In U.S. $	2018	2017	2016	2015	2014	2013
Revenue		4,136,101,000	4,176,881,000	4,015,355,000	3,889,256,000	3,889,825,000
R&D Expense						
Operating Income		375,108,200	-44,311,300	281,587,500	314,735,500	308,584,300
Operating Margin %		9.06%	-1.06%	7.01%	8.09%	7.93%
SGA Expense						
Net Income		103,089,300	-335,467,300	4,556,432	26,996,860	10,138,060
Operating Cash Flow		1,510,001,000	1,625,507,000	1,751,948,000	1,548,617,000	1,451,223,000
Capital Expenditure		752,039,000	825,967,100	845,104,100	1,942,293,000	625,939,800
EBITDA		1,632,797,000	1,294,026,000	1,573,677,000	1,455,438,000	1,377,523,000
Return on Assets %		1.46%	-4.32%	.05%	.33%	.12%
Return on Equity %		4.68%	-13.88%	.17%	1.06%	.41%
Debt to Equity		0.69	0.51	0.48	0.47	0.62

CONTACT INFORMATION:
Phone: 39 02251419588 Fax: 39 0225149590
Toll-Free:
Address: Via Paleocapa, 3, Milano, MI 20121 Italy

STOCK TICKER/OTHER:
Stock Ticker: MDIUY Exchange: PINX
Employees: 5,470 Fiscal Year Ends: 12/31
Parent Company: Fingruppo Holding SpA

SALARIES/BONUSES:
Top Exec. Salary: $ Bonus: $
Second Exec. Salary: $ Bonus: $

OTHER THOUGHTS:
Estimated Female Officers or Directors: 2
Hot Spot for Advancement for Women/Minorities:

Sales, profits and employees may be estimates. Financial information, benefits and other data can change quickly and may vary from those stated here.

Melco International Development Limited

www.melco-group.com

NAIC Code: 713210

TYPES OF BUSINESS:
Casinos (except Casino Hotels)
Resorts
Gaming
Entertainment
Attractions
Restaurants

BRANDS/DIVISIONS/AFFILIATES:
Melco Resorts & Entertainment
Aberdeen Restaurant Enterprises Limited
Entertainment Gaming Asia Inc
Altira Macau
City of Dreams
Studio City
Jumbo
Tai-Pak

CONTACTS: Note: Officers with more than one job title may be intentionally listed here more than once.
Lawrence Yau Lung Ho, Managing Dir.

GROWTH PLANS/SPECIAL FEATURES:

Melco International Development Limited is engaged in the leisure and entertainment sector. The firm's group companies include: Melco Resorts & Entertainment, Aberdeen Restaurant Enterprises Limited and Entertainment Gaming Asia, Inc. Melco Resorts & Entertainment is one of the world's largest integrated resort operators and an owner/developer of casino gaming and entertainment facilities. Its resort and entertainment properties include: Altira Macau, a 38-storey, five-star hotel and spa featuring both contemporary and luxury guest rooms, suites, villas and services; City of Dreams, an integrated resort in Macau, combining entertainment, accommodations, dining and shopping; City of Dreams Manila, a casino, hotel, retail and entertainment resort in the Philippines; Studio City, a cinematically-themed resort in Macau, offering entertainment, rides, indoor play center, 5,000-seat multipurpose entertainment center, plug-in and play facilities, production capabilities, guest rooms, restaurants, lounges/bars, retail and nightclubs; and Mocha Clubs, a brand of electronic gaming facilities in Macau. Aberdeen Restaurant Enterprises operates restaurants in Hong Kong, including the Jumbo and Tai-Pak floating restaurants located in Aberdeen, Hong Kong. Entertainment Gaming Asia provides gaming technology solutions for slot machine operations in gamine venues in the Philippines. The company retains ownership of the gaming machines and systems, and received recurring daily fees based on an agreed-upon percentage of the net gaming win per machine and provides on-site maintenance services. Entertainment Gaming has also developed a social gaming platform with a focus on the Asian markets; the platform is currently in the market testing phase. In mid-2018, Melco announced that it broke ground for a City of Dreams resort in the Mediterranean, set to open in Limassol, Cyprus in 2021. The resort will feature a casino, a range of attractions and entertainment beyond gaming.

FINANCIAL DATA: Note: Data for latest year may not have been available at press time.

In U.S. $	2018	2017	2016	2015	2014	2013
Revenue		5,258,666,000	3,045,986,000	54,577,250	25,761,410	23,403,950
R&D Expense						
Operating Income		468,662,100	140,133,300	-1,996,833	-22,089,540	-10,725,080
Operating Margin %		8.90%	4.59%	-3.65%	-46.50%	-33.46%
SGA Expense		140,603,900	220,482,700			
Net Income		60,546,810	1,323,723,000	12,887,920	189,910,700	203,899,300
Operating Cash Flow		1,342,557,000	1,046,199,000	2,784,227	-7,009,028	-13,954,340
Capital Expenditure		169,329,600	74,550,300	2,506,992	993,245	218,621
EBITDA		1,027,262,000	1,846,764,000	22,532,530	189,988,000	211,591,300
Return on Assets %		.46%	17.57%	.71%	10.99%	13.96%
Return on Equity %		2.29%	59.68%	.81%	12.38%	15.16%
Debt to Equity		1.81	1.43	0.10	0.06	0.10

CONTACT INFORMATION:
Phone: 852 31513777   Fax: 852 31623579
Toll-Free:
Address: 36/Fl, 60 Wyndham St., Central, Hong Kong, K3 00000 Hong Kong

STOCK TICKER/OTHER:
Stock Ticker: MDEVF
Employees: 19,844
Parent Company:

Exchange: GREY
Fiscal Year Ends: 12/31

SALARIES/BONUSES:
Top Exec. Salary: $ Bonus: $
Second Exec. Salary: $ Bonus: $

OTHER THOUGHTS:
Estimated Female Officers or Directors:
Hot Spot for Advancement for Women/Minorities:

Sales, profits and employees may be estimates. Financial information, benefits and other data can change quickly and may vary from those stated here.

Meredith Corporation

NAIC Code: 511120

www.meredith.com

TYPES OF BUSINESS:
Magazine Publishing
Television Broadcasting
Marketing Services
Book Publishing
Interactive Media
Advertising Agencies
Video Production

BRANDS/DIVISIONS/AFFILIATES:
People
Better Homes & Gardens
InStyle
Allrecipes
Shape
Southern Living
Martha Stewart Living
Time Inc

CONTACTS: *Note: Officers with more than one job title may be intentionally listed here more than once.*
Thomas Harty, CEO
Joseph Ceryanec, CFO
Stephen Lacy, Chairman of the Board
D. Mell Frazier, Director
John Zieser, General Counsel
Jonathan Werther, President, Divisional
Patrick McCreery, President, Divisional

GROWTH PLANS/SPECIAL FEATURES:

Meredith Corporation, a U.S. media and marketing company, engages in magazine and book publishing, television broadcasting, integrated marketing and interactive media, with a primary focus on women and the home and family market. It operates in two segments: national media and local media. The national media segment consists of national consumer media brands that are delivered through multiple media platforms, including print magazines, digital and mobile media, brand licensing activities, database-related activities, affinity marketing, and business-to-business marketing products and services. Its focus is on the entertainment, food, lifestyle, parenting and home categories, which include titles such as People, Better Homes & Gardens, InStyle, Allrecipes, Shape, Southern Living and Martha Stewart Living, among others. During 2018, in addition to subscription magazines, this division published nearly 275 special interest publications. Most brands within this segment are also available as digital editions, with a presence of more than 60 websites, nearly 60 mobile-optimized websites and 14 apps. The local media segment consists of 17 television stations located throughout the U.S., as well as related digital and mobile media assets. The television stations include seven CBS affiliates, five FOX affiliates, two MyNetworkTV affiliates, one NBC affiliate and two independent stations. Local media's digital presence includes 12 websites, 12 mobile-optimized websites and approximately 30 apps focused on news, sports and weather information. This division also sells geographic and demographic advertising programs (print and digital), which are sold to third parties. In early-2018, Meredith acquired Time, Inc., which operates as a wholly-owned subsidiary. During 2018, Meredith subsequently sold the Golf brand, Time Inc. (UK) Limited and the TIME media brand; and agreed to sell the Fortune magazine that November.

Meredith offers employees medical, dental and disability coverage; 401(k) and pension plans; and a variety of assistance programs.

FINANCIAL DATA: *Note: Data for latest year may not have been available at press time.*

In U.S. $	2018	2017	2016	2015	2014	2013
Revenue	2,247,400,000	1,713,361,000	1,649,628,000	1,594,176,000	1,468,708,000	1,471,340,000
R&D Expense						
Operating Income	295,100,000	315,296,000	248,530,000	242,112,000	186,515,000	210,834,000
Operating Margin %		18.40%	15.06%	15.18%	12.69%	14.32%
SGA Expense	962,700,000	741,188,000	730,074,000	695,319,000	655,241,000	654,098,000
Net Income	99,400,000	188,928,000	33,937,000	136,791,000	113,541,000	123,650,000
Operating Cash Flow	151,400,000	219,346,000	226,597,000	192,347,000	178,090,000	189,087,000
Capital Expenditure	53,200,000	34,785,000	25,035,000	33,245,000	24,822,000	25,969,000
EBITDA	443,300,000	386,768,000	324,417,000	315,234,000	246,453,000	265,861,000
Return on Assets %		7.05%	1.24%	5.07%	4.84%	5.94%
Return on Equity %		20.04%	3.68%	14.84%	13.00%	14.97%
Debt to Equity		0.63	0.69	0.76	0.70	0.35

CONTACT INFORMATION:
Phone: 515 284-3000 Fax: 515 284-2700
Toll-Free:
Address: 1716 Locust St., Des Moines, IA 50309-3023 United States

SALARIES/BONUSES:
Top Exec. Salary: $938,270 Bonus: $
Second Exec. Salary: $841,154 Bonus: $

STOCK TICKER/OTHER:
Stock Ticker: MDP
Employees: 7,915
Parent Company:

Exchange: NYS
Fiscal Year Ends: 06/30

OTHER THOUGHTS:
Estimated Female Officers or Directors: 3
Hot Spot for Advancement for Women/Minorities: Y

Merlin Entertainments Group Plc

www.merlinentertainments.biz

NAIC Code: 713110

TYPES OF BUSINESS:
Location-Based Visitor Attractions
Theme Parks & Hotels

BRANDS/DIVISIONS/AFFILIATES:
Blackstone Group LP (The)
Warwick Castle
Gardaland Resort
Heide Park Resort
LEGOLAND
Madame Tussauds
SEA LIFE
Shrek's Adventure

CONTACTS: Note: Officers with more than one job title may be intentionally listed here more than once.
Nick Varney, CEO
Anne-Francoise Nesmes, CFO
Natalie Bickford, Dir.-Human Resources
Mark Allsop, CIO
Grant Stenhouse, Dir.-Project Dev.

GROWTH PLANS/SPECIAL FEATURES:
Merlin Entertainments Group Plc., majority-owned by The Blackstone Group LP, operates 124 location-based visitor attractions in 25 countries. Merlin maintains three operating groups: resort theme parks, midway attractions and LEGOLAND parks. Resort theme parks include six resorts, mostly located in the U.K. Warwick Castle recreates Medieval England for visitors, including jousting shows and hawking demonstrations. Gardaland Resort in Italy comprises an amusement park, a themed aquarium and two hotels. Heide Park Resort, an 8.5-million-square-foot resort in North Germany, offers more than 50 attractions and shows, an adventure hotel and a holiday camp. Chessington World of Adventures & Zoo offers various rides and animal attractions. Family-themed Alton Towers Resort offers two hotels with their own water park and other rides and events. Thorpe Park features over 30 rides and attractions, including Stealth, one of Europe's fastest rollercoasters. Midway attractions consist of 13 brands: Madame Tussauds worldwide attractions, Little BIG City miniature-scale attraction, The Eye Brand 360-degree views, Sea Life aquariums, The Dungeons horror attractions, LEGOLAND Discovery Center for small children, Seal Sanctuaries marine life, Shrek's Adventure attraction in London, The Blackpool Tower ballroom, Wildlife park in Australia, Australian Treetop Adventures rainforest experience, Hotham Alpine Resort for skiing in the Australian Alps National Park, and Falls Creek ski resort in Victoria, Australia. Last, the firm operates eight LEGOLAND parks and resorts located in Billund (Denmark), Windsor (U.K.), California (U.S.), Deutschland (Germany), Florida (U.S.), Malaysia, Dubai and Japan. Merlin offers annual passes in the U.K., Germany, the U.S and Australia, providing access to attractions within a 12-month time period. In June 2018, Merlin announced plans for the world's first Peppa Pig World of Play attraction, due to open in Shanghai later that year.

FINANCIAL DATA: Note: Data for latest year may not have been available at press time.

In U.S. $	2018	2017	2016	2015	2014	2013
Revenue		2,013,033,000	1,840,018,000	1,613,962,000	1,577,339,000	1,505,355,000
R&D Expense						
Operating Income		407,910,700	404,122,000	367,498,500	392,756,100	366,235,600
Operating Margin %		20.26%	21.96%	22.76%	24.89%	21.81%
SGA Expense		107,344,900	94,716,100	85,875,940	78,298,650	
Net Income		263,942,200	266,468,000	214,689,800	204,586,800	183,117,800
Operating Cash Flow		521,570,000	546,827,600	410,436,400	450,848,700	460,951,700
Capital Expenditure		424,328,200	327,086,300	271,519,500	242,473,200	191,958,000
EBITDA		594,817,200	573,348,200	497,575,300	492,523,700	473,580,500
Return on Assets %		6.00%	6.99%	6.15%	5.90%	5.56%
Return on Equity %		13.99%	16.42%	15.42%	16.20%	18.67%
Debt to Equity		0.93	0.86	0.94	1.14	1.34

CONTACT INFORMATION:
Phone: 44-1202-666900 Fax: 44-1202-661303
Toll-Free:
Address: 3 Market Close, Poole, Dorset, BH15 1NQ United Kingdom

STOCK TICKER/OTHER:
Stock Ticker: MIINF
Employees: 19,863
Parent Company:

Exchange: PINX
Fiscal Year Ends: 12/31

SALARIES/BONUSES:
Top Exec. Salary: $753,940 Bonus: $
Second Exec. Salary: $488,735 Bonus: $

OTHER THOUGHTS:
Estimated Female Officers or Directors:
Hot Spot for Advancement for Women/Minorities:

Sales, profits and employees may be estimates. Financial information, benefits and other data can change quickly and may vary from those stated here.

Metro International SA

NAIC Code: 511110

www.metro.lu

TYPES OF BUSINESS:
Newspaper Publishing
Free Daily Newspapers

BRANDS/DIVISIONS/AFFILIATES:
ReadMetro.com
Kinnevik Media Holding AB
Investment AB Kinnevik

CONTACTS: *Note: Officers with more than one job title may be intentionally listed here more than once.*
Juan Manuel Romero, CEO
Per Mikael Jensen, Pres.
David Trads, Exec. VP
Maggie Samways, Global Editor-in-Chief
Pablo Mazzei, Exec. VP-Latin America Oper.
Jeremy Bryant, VP-Logistics

GROWTH PLANS/SPECIAL FEATURES:
Metro International SA is a Swedish international newspaper company based in Luxembourg. The firm publishes free daily newspapers in major cities across Europe, North and South America and Asia, attracting 17.6 million daily readers. Metro publishes newspapers on weekday mornings for distribution in high-traffic commuter zones or on public transportation networks. Weekend editions are published on Saturdays in select cities. All Metro editions carry headline local, national and international news in a standardized format. The newspapers are distributed at over 30,000 points through self-service racks or by hand distributors located in or around public transport networks (such as subways, train and bus stations and airports), office buildings and retail outlets; at key distribution points on busy streets; or in other high-density population areas, universities, high schools and hotels. The company derives revenue solely from selling space for display or classified advertisements in its newspapers. The timing and method of Metro's distribution allows it to target a high proportion of young and professional readers. Readers can access all of Metro's editions online at ReadMetro.com. Investment AB Kinnevik, held 100% by private limited liability company Kinnevik Media Holding AB, holds over a 98% stake in the firm.

FINANCIAL DATA: *Note: Data for latest year may not have been available at press time.*

In U.S. $	2018	2017	2016	2015	2014	2013
Revenue	288,000,000	280,000,000	278,000,000	284,000,000	282,000,000	280,000,000
R&D Expense						
Operating Income						
Operating Margin %						
SGA Expense						
Net Income						
Operating Cash Flow						
Capital Expenditure						
EBITDA						
Return on Assets %						
Return on Equity %						
Debt to Equity						

CONTACT INFORMATION:
Phone: 352-27-751-350   Fax: 352-27-751-312
Toll-Free:
Address: 2-4 Avenue Marie-Thérèse, Luxembourg, 2132 Luxembourg

STOCK TICKER/OTHER:
Stock Ticker: Private   Exchange:
Employees: 855   Fiscal Year Ends: 12/31
Parent Company: Kinnevik Media Holding AB

SALARIES/BONUSES:
Top Exec. Salary: $ Bonus: $
Second Exec. Salary: $ Bonus: $

OTHER THOUGHTS:
Estimated Female Officers or Directors: 2
Hot Spot for Advancement for Women/Minorities: Y

Sales, profits and employees may be estimates. Financial information, benefits and other data can change quickly and may vary from those stated here.

MGM Holdings Inc

www.mgm.com

NAIC Code: 512110

TYPES OF BUSINESS:
Film Production & Distribution
Television, Video & Music Production & Distribution
Broadcast & Cable Television

BRANDS/DIVISIONS/AFFILIATES:
James Bond
Fighting with My Family
Hustle (The)
Sun Is Also a Star (The)
Child's Play
Stargate Origins
TKO: Total Knock Out
Condor

CONTACTS:
Note: Officers with more than one job title may be intentionally listed here more than once.

Christopher Bearton, COO
Jonathan Glickman, Pres., Motion Picture Group
Roma Khanna, Pres., Television Group & Digital
Mark Burnett, Chmn.

GROWTH PLANS/SPECIAL FEATURES:

MGM Holdings, Inc. is an entertainment company that produces and globally distributes film and television content across all platforms. These platforms include theatrics, home entertainment and television, with an increasing contribution from global distribution platforms. MGM also generates revenue from the licensing of its content and intellectual property rights for use in consumer products and interactive games, among other licensing activities. The company's operations include the development, production and financing of feature films and television content, and the worldwide distribution of entertainment content. Feature films currently in various stages of development, production and post-production include: the 25th installment of the James Bond franchise, Fighting with My Family, The Hustle, The Sun Is Also a Star, Child's Play, The Addams Family and more. Current and upcoming television shows include Stargate Origins, TKO: Total Knock Out, Condor, The Contender, The Awesome Show, The World's Best and Our Lady, LTD. In addition, MGM owns or holds interests in MGM-branded channels in the U.S., as well as in pay-TV networks in the U.S. and Brazil.

FINANCIAL DATA:
Note: Data for latest year may not have been available at press time.

In U.S. $	2018	2017	2016	2015	2014	2013
Revenue		1,100,000,000	1,184,214,000	1,558,364,000	1,444,691,000	1,527,216,000
R&D Expense						
Operating Income						
Operating Margin %						
SGA Expense						
Net Income			155,224,000	252,454,000	155,657,000	122,161,000
Operating Cash Flow						
Capital Expenditure						
EBITDA						
Return on Assets %						
Return on Equity %						
Debt to Equity						

CONTACT INFORMATION:
Phone: 310-449-3000 Fax: 310-449-8857
Toll-Free:
Address: 245 N. Beverly Dr., Beverly Hills, CA 90210 United States

STOCK TICKER/OTHER:
Stock Ticker: Joint Venture
Employees: 1,300
Parent Company:

Exchange: GREY
Fiscal Year Ends: 12/31

SALARIES/BONUSES:
Top Exec. Salary: $ Bonus: $
Second Exec. Salary: $ Bonus: $

OTHER THOUGHTS:
Estimated Female Officers or Directors: 1
Hot Spot for Advancement for Women/Minorities:

MGM Resorts International

www.mgmresorts.com

NAIC Code: 721120

TYPES OF BUSINESS:
Casino Hotels & Resorts
Casino & Resort Management

BRANDS/DIVISIONS/AFFILIATES:
Bellagio
MGM Grand Las Vegas
Mandalay Bay
Mirage (The)
Luxor
Excalibur
New York-New York
Circus Circus Las Vegas

CONTACTS:
Note: Officers with more than one job title may be intentionally listed here more than once.

James Murren, CEO
Daniel DArrigo, CFO
Robert Selwood, Chief Accounting Officer
Corey Sanders, COO
Phyllis James, Executive VP, Divisional
John McManus, Executive VP
Robert Baldwin, Other Executive Officer
William Hornbuckle, President

GROWTH PLANS/SPECIAL FEATURES:

MGM Resorts International (MGM) is a holding company that, through its subsidiaries, owns and operates integrated casino, hotel and entertainment resorts throughout the U.S. and in Macau. MGM's wholly-owned domestic resorts include nine properties located in Las Vegas, as well as five within Michigan, Mississippi (2), New Jersey and Maryland. These resorts include the following brand lines: Bellagio, MGM Grand Las Vegas, Mandalay Bay, The Mirage, Luxor, Excalibur, New York-New York, Monte Carlo, Circus Circus Las Vegas, MGM Grand Detroit, Beau Rivage, Gold Strike, Borgata and MGM National Harbor. In China, MGM has a 55.95% stake in MGM Macau (with Macau SAR) via MGM China Holdings Ltd. Other operations include 50%-owned CityCenter, located in Las Vegas; and 50%-owned Grand Victoria, located in Elgin, Illinois. In all, MGM Resort's resorts comprise more than 47,800 guest rooms and suites, 2 million square feet of casino gaming space, over 27,000 slot machines and 1,860+ gaming tables. MGM Springfield is a casino-hotel establishment located in Springfield, Massachusetts, expected to open in late-2018. The MGM Springfield resort will include approximately 2,550 slots and 120 table games (including poker), a 250-room hotel, 100,000 square feet of retail/restaurant space, 44,000 square feet of meeting and event space, and more.

The firm offers employees health insurance, savings plans, employee assistance & wellness programs, child development center, life & disability insurance, auto/home/renter/pet insurance and adoption assistance.

FINANCIAL DATA:
Note: Data for latest year may not have been available at press time.

In U.S. $	2018	2017	2016	2015	2014	2013
Revenue		10,773,900,000	9,455,123,000	9,190,068,000	10,081,980,000	9,809,663,000
R&D Expense						
Operating Income		1,647,349,000	1,401,463,000	1,119,251,000	1,327,748,000	1,183,237,000
Operating Margin %		14.19%	13.34%	11.40%	12.78%	11.92%
SGA Expense		1,559,915,000	1,378,617,000	1,309,104,000	1,318,749,000	1,278,450,000
Net Income		1,960,286,000	1,101,440,000	-447,720,000	-149,873,000	-156,606,000
Operating Cash Flow		2,206,411,000	1,533,972,000	1,005,079,000	1,130,670,000	1,310,448,000
Capital Expenditure		1,864,082,000	2,262,473,000	1,466,819,000	957,041,000	562,124,000
EBITDA		2,625,980,000	2,803,477,000	571,219,000	2,043,712,000	1,794,337,000
Return on Assets %		6.77%	4.12%	-1.72%	-.56%	-.59%
Return on Equity %		28.07%	19.42%	-9.72%	-3.60%	-3.64%
Debt to Equity		1.67	2.08	2.41	3.15	3.17

CONTACT INFORMATION:
Phone: 702 693-7120   Fax: 702 693-8626
Toll-Free:
Address: 3600 Las Vegas Blvd. South, Las Vegas, NV 89109 United States

STOCK TICKER/OTHER:
Stock Ticker: MGM
Employees: 68,000
Parent Company:

Exchange: NYS
Fiscal Year Ends: 12/31

SALARIES/BONUSES:
Top Exec. Salary: $2,000,000   Bonus: $833,000
Second Exec. Salary: $1,650,000   Bonus: $333,000

OTHER THOUGHTS:
Estimated Female Officers or Directors: 5
Hot Spot for Advancement for Women/Minorities: Y

Sales, profits and employees may be estimates. Financial information, benefits and other data can change quickly and may vary from those stated here.

Plunkett Research, Ltd.

Microsoft Corporation

www.microsoft.com

NAIC Code: 511210I

TYPES OF BUSINESS:
Computer Software, Operating Systems, Languages & Development Tools
Enterprise Software
Game Consoles
Operating Systems
Software as a Service (SAAS)
Search Engine and Advertising
E-Mail Services
Instant Messaging

BRANDS/DIVISIONS/AFFILIATES:
Office 365
Dynamics
SQL
Windows
Visual Studio
Azure
Xbox
GitHub

CONTACTS: Note: Officers with more than one job title may be intentionally listed here more than once.
Satya Nadella, CEO
Amy Hood, CFO
John Thompson, Chairman of the Board
Frank Brod, Chief Accounting Officer
Christopher Capossela, Chief Marketing Officer
William Gates, Co-Founder
Kathleen Hogan, Executive VP, Divisional
Margaret Johnson, Executive VP, Divisional
Jean-Philippe Courtois, Executive VP
Bradford Smith, Other Executive Officer

GROWTH PLANS/SPECIAL FEATURES:

Microsoft Corporation develops, license and supports software products, services and devices. It is a technology company that builds best-in-class platforms and productivity services for a mobile-first, cloud-first world. The firm's products include operating systems; cross-device productivity applications; server applications; business solution applications; desktop and server management tools; software development tools; video games; and training and certification of computer system integrators and developers. Microsoft also designs, manufactures and sells devices such as personal computers (PCs), tablets, gaming and entertainment consoles, phones, other intelligent devices and related accessories that integrate with its cloud-based offerings. The company operates its business in two segments: productivity and business processes, which consists of products in its portfolio of productivity, communication and information services through its devices and platforms; intelligent cloud, which consists of the company's public, private and hybrid server products and cloud services; and more personal computing, which consists of products geared towards harmonizing the interests of end users, developers and IT professionals across all devices. Products offered through the productivity and business processes segment include Office 365 and Dynamics. Products offered through the intelligent cloud segment include SQL servers, Windows servers, Visual Studio, system centers and Azure, as well as enterprise and consulting services. The more personal computing segment primarily consists of Windows, including Windows OEM licensing and other non-volume licensing of the Windows operating system; Devices, including Microsoft Surface, PC accessories, and other intelligent devices; Gaming, including Xbox hardware, software and services, comprising Xbox Live transactions, subscriptions and advertising, video games and third-party video game royalties; and search advertising. In October 2018, Microsoft Corporation completed its acquisition of GitHub, Inc., a web-based version control repository (Git) and internet hosting service, for $7.5 billion.

Microsoft offers its employees health, dental and vision coverage; onsite health screenings; adoption assistance; childcare service discounts; a 401(k) plan; an employee stock purchase plan; and tuition assistance.

FINANCIAL DATA: Note: Data for latest year may not have been available at press time.

In U.S. $	2018	2017	2016	2015	2014	2013
Revenue	110,360,000,000	89,950,000,000	85,320,000,000	93,580,000,000	86,833,000,000	77,849,000,000
R&D Expense	14,726,000,000	13,037,000,000	11,988,000,000	12,046,000,000	11,381,000,000	10,411,000,000
Operating Income	35,058,000,000	22,632,000,000	21,292,000,000	28,172,000,000	27,886,000,000	26,764,000,000
Operating Margin %		25.16%	24.95%	30.10%	32.11%	34.37%
SGA Expense	22,223,000,000	20,020,000,000	19,260,000,000	20,324,000,000	20,632,000,000	20,425,000,000
Net Income	16,571,000,000	21,204,000,000	16,798,000,000	12,193,000,000	22,074,000,000	21,863,000,000
Operating Cash Flow	43,884,000,000	39,507,000,000	33,325,000,000	29,080,000,000	32,231,000,000	28,833,000,000
Capital Expenditure	11,632,000,000	8,129,000,000	8,343,000,000	5,944,000,000	5,485,000,000	4,257,000,000
EBITDA	49,468,000,000	34,149,000,000	27,616,000,000	25,245,000,000	33,629,000,000	31,236,000,000
Return on Assets %		9.75%	9.08%	6.99%	14.02%	16.58%
Return on Equity %		29.37%	22.09%	14.35%	26.16%	30.09%
Debt to Equity		1.05	0.56	0.34	0.22	0.15

CONTACT INFORMATION:
Phone: 425 882-8080 Fax: 425 936-7329
Toll-Free: 800-642-7676
Address: One Microsoft Way, Redmond, WA 98052 United States

SALARIES/BONUSES:
Top Exec. Salary: $1,500,000 Bonus: $
Second Exec. Salary: $875,000 Bonus: $

STOCK TICKER/OTHER:
Stock Ticker: MSFT Exchange: NAS
Employees: 131,000 Fiscal Year Ends: 06/30
Parent Company:

OTHER THOUGHTS:
Estimated Female Officers or Directors: 4
Hot Spot for Advancement for Women/Minorities: Y

Miramax LLC

NAIC Code: 512110

www.miramax.com

TYPES OF BUSINESS:
Movie Production & Distribution
Online Merchandise Retail

BRANDS/DIVISIONS/AFFILIATES:
beIN Media Group LLC
Chicago
English Patient (The)
No Country for Old Men
Aviator (The)
Crow's Blood
Spy Kids: Mission Critical
TOFF GUYS

CONTACTS: Note: Officers with more than one job title may be intentionally listed here more than once.
Bill Block, CEO
Adrienne Gary, Sr. VP-Admin.
Beth Minehart, Exec. VP-Global Digital
Nasser Al-Khelaifi, Chmn.

GROWTH PLANS/SPECIAL FEATURES:
Miramax, LLC is a producer and distributor of motion pictures. Founded in 1979 by brothers Bob and Harvey Weinstein, Miramax was originally known for producing small, quirky art-house pictures. It has since expanded to develop bigger-budget movies in recent years, such as Chicago, The English Patient, Shakespeare in Love and No Country for Old Men. To date, Miramax has more than 700 titles in its library, has received 278 Academy Award nominations and 68 Oscars. Iconic titles within the company's library include Pulp Fiction, Good Will Hunting, Bridget Jones's Diary, the Scream film franchise, Kill Bill Vol. 1&2 and The Aviator. Miramax Television is the firm's television production division that launched Crow's Blood in 2017, in connection with the El Rey Network. This division launched Spy Kids: Mission Critical on Netflix in 2018. Miramax content and information can be obtained on its website, as well as social and mobile platforms. Apparel, art, collectibles, novelty items and content on discs can be purchased from the website and mobile app as well. Miramax is owned by beIN Media Group, LLC. In late-2018, Miramax began production on a new Guy Ritchie film, TOFF GUYS, which will star Matthew McConaughey as Henry Golding.

FINANCIAL DATA: Note: Data for latest year may not have been available at press time.

In U.S. $	2018	2017	2016	2015	2014	2013
Revenue						
R&D Expense						
Operating Income						
Operating Margin %						
SGA Expense						
Net Income						
Operating Cash Flow						
Capital Expenditure						
EBITDA						
Return on Assets %						
Return on Equity %						
Debt to Equity						

CONTACT INFORMATION:
Phone: 310-409-4321   Fax:
Toll-Free:
Address: 1601 Cloverfield Blvd., Ste. 2000, Santa Monica, CA 90404 United States

STOCK TICKER/OTHER:
Stock Ticker: Subsidiary
Employees:
Parent Company: beIN Media Group LLC

Exchange:
Fiscal Year Ends: 09/30

SALARIES/BONUSES:
Top Exec. Salary: $ Bonus: $
Second Exec. Salary: $ Bonus: $

OTHER THOUGHTS:
Estimated Female Officers or Directors: 2
Hot Spot for Advancement for Women/Minorities: Y

Sales, profits and employees may be estimates. Financial information, benefits and other data can change quickly and may vary from those stated here.

Plunkett Research, Ltd.

MobiTV Inc

NAIC Code: 519130

www.mobitv.com

TYPES OF BUSINESS:
Mobile Phone Media Service

BRANDS/DIVISIONS/AFFILIATES:

CONTACTS: Note: Officers with more than one job title may be intentionally listed here more than once.

Charlie Nooney, CEO
Bill Routt, COO
Terri Stevens, CFO
Lauren Johnson, VP-Sales
Kerry Travilla, VP-IT
Ellen McDonald, General Counsel
Rick Herman, Chief Strategy Officer
Charlie Nooney, Chmn.

GROWTH PLANS/SPECIAL FEATURES:

MobiTV, Inc. provides managed services to deliver live and on-demand television and related media content. The company provides its customers with a video platform that constantly adapts, is cost-effective and is a complete end-to-end solution. MobiTV delivers its streaming video experience to subscribers in-home, in-hand and other electronic devices. The firm's core technologies focus on content management, media distribution, access control, multi-tenancy, network DVR (digital video recording), digital rights management, application services and cloud-based analytics. During 2018, MobiTV announced it had secured hosted streaming delivery rights from another 90 networks, including Bloomberg Television, Discovery, MGM HD, Newsmax, Outside TV, Smithsonian Channel, Stingray Music, Univision and others, bringing its total to more than 350 networks. That November, the firm announced a partnership with Distributel to bring customers and businesses in Canada TV experiences from any device, at any time.

FINANCIAL DATA: Note: Data for latest year may not have been available at press time.

In U.S. $	2018	2017	2016	2015	2014	2013
Revenue	140,000,000	132,000,000	130,000,000	127,000,000	113,000,000	112,000,000
R&D Expense						
Operating Income						
Operating Margin %						
SGA Expense						
Net Income						
Operating Cash Flow						
Capital Expenditure						
EBITDA						
Return on Assets %						
Return on Equity %						
Debt to Equity						

CONTACT INFORMATION:
Phone: 510-450-5000 Fax: 510-450-5001
Toll-Free: 877-795-5300
Address: 1900 Powell St., 9/Fl, Emeryville, CA 94608 United States

SALARIES/BONUSES:
Top Exec. Salary: $ Bonus: $
Second Exec. Salary: $ Bonus: $

STOCK TICKER/OTHER:
Stock Ticker: Private   Exchange:
Employees: 275   Fiscal Year Ends:
Parent Company:

OTHER THOUGHTS:
Estimated Female Officers or Directors: 2
Hot Spot for Advancement for Women/Minorities: Y

Sales, profits and employees may be estimates. Financial information, benefits and other data can change quickly and may vary from those stated here.

Modern Times Group MTG AB

NAIC Code: 515120

www.mtg.se

TYPES OF BUSINESS:
Television Broadcasting & Cable
Radio Broadcasting
Television & Film Production
Internet Businesses
Home Shopping Network
Gambling Operations
Magazine Publishing
Video Games

BRANDS/DIVISIONS/AFFILIATES:
Nordic Entertainment Group
MTG
Viafree
Viaplay
Kinnevik AB

CONTACTS:
Note: Officers with more than one job title may be intentionally listed here more than once.

Jorgen Madson Lindemann, CEO
Jorgen Madson Lindemann, Pres.
Maria Redfin, CFO
Rikard Steiber, Chief Digital Officer
Matthew Hooper, Exec. VP-Corp. Comm.
Matthew Hooper, Investor Rel.
Marc Zagar, Exec. VP-Finance
Joseph Hundah, Exec. VP-African Oper.
Patrick Svensk, Exec. VP-Content
Jette Nygaard-Andersen, Exec. VP-Nordic Pay-TV Broadcasting Oper.
Marek Singer, Exec. VP-Central Europe Broadcasting Oper.
David Chance, Chmn.
Irina Gofman, CEO-MTG Russia & CIS

GROWTH PLANS/SPECIAL FEATURES:
Modern Times Group MTG AB is an international digital entertainment group. The firm's brands and products are categorized into two groups: the Nordic Entertainment Group and MTG. The Nordic Entertainment Group offers: Viafree, a free video streaming service offering recent TV episodes and exclusive online content across the Nordic region; Viaplay, a subscription on-demand service that provides multi-screen and multi-channel through any device; Viasat, a satellite internet-protocol TV and broadband provider; radio operations, with stations available online and via mobile apps; advertisement-funded television channels offering a variety of international and original scripted and non-scripted content; and production and commission of original content. MTG offers: eSports, including live, online and televised eSport entertainment; online games, a division that develops and publishes online and mobile games internationally; digital video content, creating and distributing online video content worldwide; and investment, which invests in and supports global gaming, eSports and interactive entertainment entrepreneurs. Modern Times Group is majority-owned by Swedish investment company, Kinnevik AB. During 2018, Modern Times sold its 95% share in Nova Broadcasting Group Jsc to PPF Group; sold a 75% shareholding in TRACE PARTNERS SAS to TPG Growth; and announced plans to split Modern Times Group into two companies, which is subject to regulatory and shareholder approvals.

FINANCIAL DATA:
Note: Data for latest year may not have been available at press time.

In U.S. $	2018	2017	2016	2015	2014	2013
Revenue		1,929,020,000	1,881,890,000	1,857,740,000	2,110,400,000	2,151,580,000
R&D Expense						
Operating Income						
Operating Margin %						
SGA Expense						
Net Income		149,596,000	-11,999,200	28,751,500	157,081,000	177,864,000
Operating Cash Flow						
Capital Expenditure						
EBITDA						
Return on Assets %						
Return on Equity %						
Debt to Equity						

CONTACT INFORMATION:
Phone: 46 856200050   Fax: 46 8205074
Toll-Free:
Address: Skeppsbron 18 Box 2094, Stockholm, SE-103 13 Sweden

SALARIES/BONUSES:
Top Exec. Salary: $ Bonus: $
Second Exec. Salary: $ Bonus: $

STOCK TICKER/OTHER:
Stock Ticker: MTG   Exchange: Stockholm
Employees: 3,280   Fiscal Year Ends: 12/31
Parent Company:

OTHER THOUGHTS:
Estimated Female Officers or Directors: 5
Hot Spot for Advancement for Women/Minorities: Y

Morris Communications Company LLC

www.morris.com

NAIC Code: 511110

TYPES OF BUSINESS:
Newspaper Publishing
Radio Broadcasting
Magazine Publishing
Book Publishing
Printing Services
Online Publishing

BRANDS/DIVISIONS/AFFILIATES:
Morris Media Network
Milepost (The)
American Angler
Charlotte Wedding
CitySpin
National Barrel Horse Association
Hippodrome
Main Street Digital

CONTACTS:
Note: Officers with more than one job title may be intentionally listed here more than once.

William S. Morris, IV, CEO
Craig S. Mitchell, Sr. VP
Craig S. Mitchell, Sec.
Craig S. Mitchell, Sr. VP-Finance
Susie Morris Baker, VP-Morris Communications Company
William S. Morris, IV, CEO-Morris Venture Capital
Derek May, Exec. VP-Newspapers
J. Tyler Morris, VP-Cowboy Publishing Group (The)
William S. Morris, III, Chmn.

GROWTH PLANS/SPECIAL FEATURES:

Morris Communications Company, LLC is a progressive media company offering community news, information, advertising, entertainment and related content through diverse digital channels and distribution outlets. Morris Communications operates through six business divisions. The magazine division comprises a collection of magazines and books, which are provided through the Morris Media Network, the firm's print-digital publishing group. Magazines cover the genres of travel, cities and lifestyle, with brands including The Milepost, Where, Alaska, Orlando, American Angler, BarrelHorse News and Charlotte Wedding, among many others. The broadband division provides digital cable television, internet and telephone services to the Hendersonville, Franklin, Sylva, Nebo and West Jefferson communities of North Carolina. The event marketing division consists of CitySpin, a box office and event management solution with fully-customizable event software that provides businesses and their customers a user-friendly, secure way to create events and sell tickets. The associations and facilities division consists of two units: the National Barrel Horse Association, which has an international database of more than 55,000 members and horse owners throughout the U.S., Canada, Europe, Central America and South America, and provides money-earning barrel racing events for riders of all skill levels; and Hippodrome, a facility in South Carolina for the stabling and care of horses, as well as serving as an evacuation center, sheltering people and animals during hurricanes, floods and other disasters. The property and services division consists of property holdings across the U.S., which are primarily locations in downtown business districts for lease, sale and/or redevelopment purposes. Last, the business ventures division is operated by Main Street Digital, a Morris publishing services company that helps local businesses use digital marketing for their communities. Main Street Digital has a presence in 55 U.S. cities, with hubs in Myrtle Beach and Columbia, South Carolina; Jacksonville and Orlando, Florida; and Augusta, Georgia.

FINANCIAL DATA:
Note: Data for latest year may not have been available at press time.

In U.S. $	2018	2017	2016	2015	2014	2013
Revenue	308,000,000	300,000,000	288,000,000	275,000,000	270,000,000	265,000,000
R&D Expense						
Operating Income						
Operating Margin %						
SGA Expense						
Net Income						
Operating Cash Flow						
Capital Expenditure						
EBITDA						
Return on Assets %						
Return on Equity %						
Debt to Equity						

CONTACT INFORMATION:
Phone: 706-724-0851 Fax:
Toll-Free: 800-622-6358
Address: 725 Broad St., Augusta, GA 30901 United States

SALARIES/BONUSES:
Top Exec. Salary: $ Bonus: $
Second Exec. Salary: $ Bonus: $

STOCK TICKER/OTHER:
Stock Ticker: Private
Employees: 6,000
Parent Company:

Exchange:
Fiscal Year Ends: 12/31

OTHER THOUGHTS:
Estimated Female Officers or Directors: 1
Hot Spot for Advancement for Women/Minorities:

Sales, profits and employees may be estimates. Financial information, benefits and other data can change quickly and may vary from those stated here.

MP3.com Inc

NAIC Code: 515111

www.mp3.com

TYPES OF BUSINESS:
Radio Networks, Traditional, Satellite and Online
Audio Hosting
Digital Music Information Portal

BRANDS/DIVISIONS/AFFILIATES:
CBS Corporation
CBS Interactive Inc
CNET

CONTACTS: Note: Officers with more than one job title may be intentionally listed here more than once.
Joseph Ianniello, Interim CEO-CBS Corporation
Jim Lanzone, Pres., CBS Interactive

GROWTH PLANS/SPECIAL FEATURES:
MP3.com, Inc. provides an online platform that offers a collection of millions of digital music tracks from a wide range of genres. Customers purchase and listen to the music, and both tracks and albums can be played on computers and digital music players. The website also offers a wide selection of articles, reviews, free streaming music, forums and information about mp3 players. MP3.com specializes in promoting lesser-known artists, accessible through bios, discographies, reviews, videos, photos and news. Over 6 million 30-second song clips are available on the site with links to digital-music providers where legal downloads are available. In addition, the site allows musicians to view zip codes where their music is being downloaded. MP3.com is operated by CNET, a tech media firm owned by CBS Interactive, Inc., which itself is a division of CBS Corporation.

The company offers its employees medical, dental and vision insurance; wellness programs; an employee assistance plan; short- and long-term disability insurance; and tuition reimbursement.

FINANCIAL DATA: Note: Data for latest year may not have been available at press time.

In U.S. $	2018	2017	2016	2015	2014	2013
Revenue						
R&D Expense						
Operating Income						
Operating Margin %						
SGA Expense						
Net Income						
Operating Cash Flow						
Capital Expenditure						
EBITDA						
Return on Assets %						
Return on Equity %						
Debt to Equity						

CONTACT INFORMATION:
Phone: 415-344-2000 Fax:
Toll-Free:
Address: 235 2nd St., San Francisco, CA 94105 United States

STOCK TICKER/OTHER:
Stock Ticker: Subsidiary Exchange:
Employees: 308 Fiscal Year Ends: 12/31
Parent Company: CBS Corporation

SALARIES/BONUSES:
Top Exec. Salary: $ Bonus: $
Second Exec. Salary: $ Bonus: $

OTHER THOUGHTS:
Estimated Female Officers or Directors:
Hot Spot for Advancement for Women/Minorities:

Sales, profits and employees may be estimates. Financial information, benefits and other data can change quickly and may vary from those stated here.

Musical.ly

NAIC Code: 511210G

www.musical.ly

TYPES OF BUSINESS:
Computer Software, Electronic Games, Apps & Entertainment

GROWTH PLANS/SPECIAL FEATURES:
Musical.ly, Inc., a subsidiary of Beijing Byte Dance Telecommunications Co., Ltd., offers the video social network app Musical.ly. The app is used for video creation, messaging and live broadcasting. Users access and edit licensed audio tracks and videos on both the iPhone and Android platforms. In November 2017, Musical.ly was acquired by Beijing Byte Dance Telecommunications.

BRANDS/DIVISIONS/AFFILIATES:
Beijing Byte Dance Telecommunications Co Ltd

CONTACTS:
Note: Officers with more than one job title may be intentionally listed here more than once.

Zhu June, CEO

FINANCIAL DATA:
Note: Data for latest year may not have been available at press time.

In U.S. $	2018	2017	2016	2015	2014	2013
Revenue						
R&D Expense						
Operating Income						
Operating Margin %						
SGA Expense						
Net Income						
Operating Cash Flow						
Capital Expenditure						
EBITDA						
Return on Assets %						
Return on Equity %						
Debt to Equity						

CONTACT INFORMATION:
Phone: 415-520-0640 Fax: 415-520-0640
Toll-Free:
Address: 1920 Olympic Blvd., Santa Monica, CA 90404 United States

STOCK TICKER/OTHER:
Stock Ticker: Subsidiary Exchange:
Employees: Fiscal Year Ends:
Parent Company: Beijing Byte Dance Telecommunications Co Ltd

SALARIES/BONUSES:
Top Exec. Salary: $ Bonus: $
Second Exec. Salary: $ Bonus: $

OTHER THOUGHTS:
Estimated Female Officers or Directors:
Hot Spot for Advancement for Women/Minorities:

MX1 Ltd

NAIC Code: 515120

www.mx1.com

TYPES OF BUSINESS:
Television Broadcasting

BRANDS/DIVISIONS/AFFILIATES:
SES SA
MX1 360

CONTACTS: Note: Officers with more than one job title may be intentionally listed here more than once.
Wilfred Urner, CEO
Oz Peleg, COO
Martin Oberfrank, CFO
Elad Manishviz, CMO
Katharina Baumgart, Dir.-Human Resources
Ziv Mor, Chief Technology Officer

GROWTH PLANS/SPECIAL FEATURES:
MX1 Ltd., a wholly-owned subsidiary of SES SA, is a global media services provider. The company works with leading businesses to transform content into ultimate view experiences for a global audience, shaping the content for any device, anytime, anywhere. Every day MX1: distributes 3,200 television channels, manages the playout of more than 500 channels, manages over 5 million media assets, delivers 8,400+ hours of streaming video and delivers 560+ hours of premium sports and live events. Clients of the firm include Dish, Premier League, DreamWorks, IMG, VuBiquity, Arsenal, NFL, PGA, HSE24, Universal and many more. The company's MX1 360 solution offers an end-to-end open media service platform for broadcasters, TV channels, content and rights holders, sports organizations, TV service providers and distributors. The platform serves all content requirements in a single place, from preparing, packaging, managing and validating high-quality content, to playout and delivery for multi-screen viewing. MX1 360 is highly scalable, flexible and agile, and can be easily integrated with any third-party application and service via an open application programming interface (API). Its user-friendly dashboard is fully transparent and automated, providing a window to content for full monitoring, insight and workflow management. MX1's technical team is available 24/7, providing customer service and support. The firm has more than 15 offices worldwide, including media centers in the U.K., the U.S., Israel, Romania and Germany.

FINANCIAL DATA: Note: Data for latest year may not have been available at press time.

In U.S. $	2018	2017	2016	2015	2014	2013
Revenue	160,000,000	154,730,354	147,362,242	140,344,992	131,226,000	121,795,000
R&D Expense						
Operating Income						
Operating Margin %						
SGA Expense						
Net Income				7,808,000	5,150,000	6,522,000
Operating Cash Flow						
Capital Expenditure						
EBITDA						
Return on Assets %						
Return on Equity %						
Debt to Equity						

CONTACT INFORMATION:
Phone: 972 39280808   Fax: 972 38280809
Toll-Free:
Address: 4 Hagoren St., Airport City, 7019900 Israel

STOCK TICKER/OTHER:
Stock Ticker: Subsidiary
Employees: 335
Parent Company: SES SA

Exchange:
Fiscal Year Ends: 12/31

SALARIES/BONUSES:
Top Exec. Salary: $ Bonus: $
Second Exec. Salary: $ Bonus: $

OTHER THOUGHTS:
Estimated Female Officers or Directors:
Hot Spot for Advancement for Women/Minorities:

Sales, profits and employees may be estimates. Financial information, benefits and other data can change quickly and may vary from those stated here.

MyHeritage Ltd

www.myheritage.com

NAIC Code: 519130

TYPES OF BUSINESS:
Online Genealogy

BRANDS/DIVISIONS/AFFILIATES:
MyHeritage.com
Family Tree Builder

CONTACTS:
Note: Officers with more than one job title may be intentionally listed here more than once.

Gilad Japhet, CEO
Russ Wilding, Chief Content Officer
Smadar Levi, CFO
Sagi Bashari, CTO
Uri Gonen, Sr. VP-Prod. Mgmt.
Russ Wilding, Chief Content Officer
Roger Bell, VP-Prod.
Noah Tutak, Gen. Mgr.-USA
Ran Peled, Chief Architect

GROWTH PLANS/SPECIAL FEATURES:

MyHeritage Ltd. owns and manages MyHeritage.com, a private social networking site which allows family members to connect with one another and upload and share family trees, events, videos and messages. The firm offers a series of tools and software which allow its 100 million members across 196 countries to update and maintain their family profiles. Family Tree Builder, a free windows software, provides tools for building geographical maps of family members' and ancestors' locations, photo albums, family charts, a report generator, tools for building family member profiles and making timelines, a digital scrapbook, a family statistic compiler and an automatic historical record search and match from WorldVitalRecords. Family Tree Builder is available in 42 languages and allows users to choose from Gregorian, Hebrew and French Revolutionary calendars. Users can upload files created in Family Tree Builder directly onto their MyHeritage.com profile for other family members to see. The genealogy tools offered by the firm allow users to cross compare their family trees with the other users on MyHeritage.com for matches using the firm's proprietary smart match technology. Users are able to confirm or reject matches pulled up by the matching technology and connect with possible family members through their MyHeritage.com accounts. The company comprises a global search engine that retrieves and delivers historical records of births, deaths, marriages, immigration, census and original documents. The search engine utilizes semantics analysis to find matches for family trees in newspapers, books and other free text documents. MyHeritage offers DNA testing through the maternal and paternal lines to find family matches using autosomal DNA.

FINANCIAL DATA:
Note: Data for latest year may not have been available at press time.

In U.S. $	2018	2017	2016	2015	2014	2013
Revenue	165,000,000	133,000,000	60,000,000			
R&D Expense						
Operating Income						
Operating Margin %						
SGA Expense						
Net Income		18,100,000				
Operating Cash Flow						
Capital Expenditure						
EBITDA						
Return on Assets %						
Return on Equity %						
Debt to Equity						

CONTACT INFORMATION:
Phone: 972-3-6280000 Fax: 972-3-6280003
Toll-Free:
Address: 3 Ariel Sharon St., 4/Fl, Or Yehuda, 60250 Israel

STOCK TICKER/OTHER:
Stock Ticker: Private
Employees: 450
Parent Company:

Exchange:
Fiscal Year Ends:

SALARIES/BONUSES:
Top Exec. Salary: $ Bonus: $
Second Exec. Salary: $ Bonus: $

OTHER THOUGHTS:
Estimated Female Officers or Directors: 1
Hot Spot for Advancement for Women/Minorities:

Sales, profits and employees may be estimates. Financial information, benefits and other data can change quickly and may vary from those stated here.

Myspace LLC

NAIC Code: 519130

www.myspace.com

TYPES OF BUSINESS:
Social Networking
Online Content Distribution-Audio & Video

BRANDS/DIVISIONS/AFFILIATES:
Meredith Corporation

CONTACTS: *Note: Officers with more than one job title may be intentionally listed here more than once.*
Tim Vanderhook, CEO
Roger Mincheff, Pres.
Tim Vanderhook, CEO-Specific Media

GROWTH PLANS/SPECIAL FEATURES:
Myspace, LLC is an internet-based music social networking website with access to millions of songs, photos, personal profiles, blogs and videos. Its site enables users, such as individuals, bands, comedians and filmmakers, to create and customize content-rich internet profile pages, share user-generated video, participate in user groups and communicate with each other using various technologies, including instant messaging. In addition, Myspace provides a way for artists to connect with their fan base, and allows users to discover new music, films and other media. The website has approximately 50 million unique users. The Myspace mobile app features a tool for users to create and edit gif images and post them to their Myspace stream. It also allows users to stream available live streams of concerts. The app is available from the App Store and Google Play. Myspace app offers filters that can be added when a user has just taken a photo or just created a gif. The app allows users to play Myspace radio channels from the device. Myspace's niche no longer operates as a network of targeted video ads, but has expanded into an interactive media platform focused on brand marketing using integrated digital media messaging tools that engages users and produces loyalty. Myspace is owned by Meredith Corporation.

FINANCIAL DATA: *Note: Data for latest year may not have been available at press time.*

In U.S. $	2018	2017	2016	2015	2014	2013
Revenue						
R&D Expense						
Operating Income						
Operating Margin %						
SGA Expense						
Net Income						
Operating Cash Flow						
Capital Expenditure						
EBITDA						
Return on Assets %						
Return on Equity %						
Debt to Equity						

CONTACT INFORMATION:
Phone: 310-969-7400 Fax:
Toll-Free:
Address: 407 N. Maple Dr., Beverly Hills, CA 90210 United States

SALARIES/BONUSES:
Top Exec. Salary: $ Bonus: $
Second Exec. Salary: $ Bonus: $

STOCK TICKER/OTHER:
Stock Ticker: Subsidiary Exchange:
Employees: 150 Fiscal Year Ends: 12/31
Parent Company: Meredith Corporation

OTHER THOUGHTS:
Estimated Female Officers or Directors:
Hot Spot for Advancement for Women/Minorities: Y

Sales, profits and employees may be estimates. Financial information, benefits and other data can change quickly and may vary from those stated here.

Naspers Limited

www.naspers.com

NAIC Code: 517110

TYPES OF BUSINESS:
Cable Television
Internet Subscriber Platforms
Printing & Distribution Services
Content Protection Technology
Magazine & Book Publishing
e-Commerce
Online Games & Social Networking

BRANDS/DIVISIONS/AFFILIATES:
MIH Holdings Ltd
AutoTrader.co.za
Swiggy
WeBuyCars.co.za
inlocomedia
MultiChoice
Showmax
Tencent

CONTACTS:
Note: Officers with more than one job title may be intentionally listed here more than once.

Bob van Dijk, CEO
Pat Kolek, COO
Basil (Vasili) Sgourdos, CFO
Aileen O'Toole, Chief People Officer
Andre Coetzee, General Counsel
Mark Sorour, Head-Mergers & Acquisitions
Melody Horn, Head-Investor Rel.
Mark Sorour, Head-Corp. Finance
Craig Opperman, Chief Intellectual Property Officer
Basil (Vasili) Sgourdos, CFO-MIH Holdings Ltd.
Koos Bekker, Chmn.

GROWTH PLANS/SPECIAL FEATURES:
Naspers Limited is a multinational media company. The firm is the sole holding company for MIH Holdings Ltd., through which the company maintains interests in media and internet ventures and technology services. Naspers also maintains direct interests in various print media businesses in South Africa and internationally. The company's operations are divided into three business segments: internet, media and video entertainment. The internet segment consists of businesses that cover food, education, big data, health, agriculture, blockchain, classifieds, E-retail, listed, marketplaces, online comparison shopping, payments and other sectors, and include: AutoTrader.co.za, Avito, eMag, FarmLogs, ibibo Group, Kreditech, MakeMyTrip, Swiggy, Takealot.com and WeBuyCars.co.za, among many others. The media segment is engaged in the publishing sector and includes two businesses: inlocomedia and Media24. Last, the video entertainment segment develops, produces and distributes content, direct-to-home digital satellite service (DTH), digital terrestrial television (DTT), online content and more, with businesses including MultiChoice Africa, ShowMax and SuperSport-World of Champions. During 2018, Naspers reduced its shares in Tencent from 33.2% to 31.2%; and sold its stake in Flipkart to Walmart for $2.2 billion. That same year, Naspers announced plans to list video entertainment business, MultiChoice on the Johannesburg Stock Exchange (JSE) as MultiChoice Group.

FINANCIAL DATA:
Note: Data for latest year may not have been available at press time.

In U.S. $	2018	2017	2016	2015	2014	2013
Revenue	6,660,000,000	6,098,000,000	5,930,000,000	6,018,393,000	5,915,253,000	5,437,444,000
R&D Expense						
Operating Income	-153,000,000	-303,000,000	116,000,000	187,982,100	314,773,500	499,172,700
Operating Margin %		-4.96%	1.95%	3.12%	5.32%	9.18%
SGA Expense	2,786,000,000	2,827,000,000	2,423,000,000	2,309,636,000	2,260,749,000	1,920,836,000
Net Income	11,357,000,000	2,921,000,000	994,000,000	1,154,653,000	542,319,500	654,345,900
Operating Cash Flow	-158,000,000	-40,000,000	78,000,000	137,590,100	308,738,300	1,065,327,000
Capital Expenditure	159,000,000	173,000,000	228,000,000	282,343,700	437,457,900	
EBITDA	12,277,000,000	3,330,000,000	1,553,000,000	1,952,610,000	1,389,039,000	1,168,776,000
Return on Assets %		15.11%	6.70%	9.21%	4.64%	6.00%
Return on Equity %		23.17%	11.76%	17.92%	8.99%	10.89%
Debt to Equity		0.22	0.36	0.55	0.52	0.49

CONTACT INFORMATION:
Phone: 27-21-406-2121   Fax: 27-21-406-3753
Toll-Free:
Address: 40 Heerengrarcht, Cape Town, 8001 South Africa

STOCK TICKER/OTHER:
Stock Ticker: NPSNY
Employees: 24,482
Parent Company:

Exchange: PINX
Fiscal Year Ends: 03/31

SALARIES/BONUSES:
Top Exec. Salary: $ Bonus: $
Second Exec. Salary: $ Bonus: $

OTHER THOUGHTS:
Estimated Female Officers or Directors: 1
Hot Spot for Advancement for Women/Minorities: Y

National Amusements Inc

www.showcasecinemas.com

NAIC Code: 512131

TYPES OF BUSINESS:
Movie Theaters

BRANDS/DIVISIONS/AFFILIATES:
Showcase SuperLux
Cinema De Lux
Showcase Cinemas
Multiple Cinemas
Viacom
CBS Corporation
Sensory Sensitive Screenings

GROWTH PLANS/SPECIAL FEATURES:
National Amusements, Inc. (NAI) is involved in the international motion picture exhibition industry. The firm operates under the Showcase SuperLux, Cinema De Lux, Showcase Cinemas and Multiple Cinemas brands, which together maintain theaters across the Northeastern U.S. as well as internationally in Argentina, Brazil and the U.K. NAI offers theater rentals for meetings, sales conferences, product launches and private events. The company's facilities include restaurants, cocktail lounges, food courts and concession stands. All locations are handicapped accessible and offer assistance devices for the hearing and sight impaired. NAI is the parent company of both Viacom and CBS Corporation. In mid-2018, NAI announced the launch of Sensory Sensitive Screenings, a new monthly program that offers reduced sensory input accommodations for movie-goers who find regular showings overly-loud or overly-stimulating, making it more comfortable for them to enjoy a movie. Sensory Sensitive Screenings are offered at select locations.

CONTACTS:
Note: Officers with more than one job title may be intentionally listed here more than once.

Sumner M. Redstone, CEO
Shari Redstone, Pres.
Sumner M. Redstone, Chmn.

FINANCIAL DATA:
Note: Data for latest year may not have been available at press time.

In U.S. $	2018	2017	2016	2015	2014	2013
Revenue						
R&D Expense						
Operating Income						
Operating Margin %						
SGA Expense						
Net Income						
Operating Cash Flow						
Capital Expenditure						
EBITDA						
Return on Assets %						
Return on Equity %						
Debt to Equity						

CONTACT INFORMATION:
Phone: 781-461-1600 Fax:
Toll-Free:
Address: 846 University Ave., Norwood, MA 02062 United States

STOCK TICKER/OTHER:
Stock Ticker: Private Exchange:
Employees: Fiscal Year Ends: 12/31
Parent Company:

SALARIES/BONUSES:
Top Exec. Salary: $ Bonus: $
Second Exec. Salary: $ Bonus: $

OTHER THOUGHTS:
Estimated Female Officers or Directors: 1
Hot Spot for Advancement for Women/Minorities:

Sales, profits and employees may be estimates. Financial information, benefits and other data can change quickly and may vary from those stated here.

National Geographic Society

www.nationalgeographic.com

NAIC Code: 515120

TYPES OF BUSINESS:
Television Broadcasting
Television Show Production
Motion Picture Production
Book Publishers
Periodical Publishers

BRANDS/DIVISIONS/AFFILIATES:
Twenty-First Century Fox Inc
Big Cats
Beyond Yellowstone
Okavango Wilderness Project
Out of Eden Walk
Photo Ark
Pristine Seas
Space Archaeology

CONTACTS: Note: Officers with more than one job title may be intentionally listed here more than once.
Tracy R. Wolstencroft, CEO
Lina Gomez, VP-Oper. & Strategy
Michael Ulica, CFO
Emma Carrasco, Chief Mktg.. & Engagement Officer
Yvonne Perry, Exec. Dir.-Human Resources
Melina Gerosa Bellows, Chief Creative Officer-Books, Kids & Family
Jonathan Young, CTO
William H. Lively, Sr. VP-Dev.
Declan Moore, Exec. VP-Publishing & Digital Media
Betty Hudson, Exec. VP-Comm.
Brooke Runnette, Pres., Television
Chris Johns, Editor in Chief-Nat'l Geographic Magazine
Lisa Truitt, Pres., Cinema Ventures
Jean M. Case, Chmn.
Claudia Malley, Exec. VP
Mark Katz, Pres., Distribution-Cinema Ventures

GROWTH PLANS/SPECIAL FEATURES:
National Geographic Society (NGS) is a nonprofit organization dedicated to global scientific research, increasing cultural and public awareness and conservation of natural resources. The firm has funded thousands of scientific research conservation and exploration projects worldwide. NGS provides more than 450 grants every year to scientists, educators and storytellers worldwide. To date, NGS has given out more than 13,000 grants to those whose work is making a significant difference in the world. The firm's operations are categorized in four divisions: exploration and protection, education, grant programs and events and exhibitions. Exploration and protection projects currently include: the Big Cats Initiative, a project to protect seven big cat species in 27 countries; Beyond Yellowstone, preserving the park's ecosystems and animal species; Okavango Wilderness Project, comprising the largest freshwater wetland in southern Africa and the main source of water a 1 million people, which is unprotected in relation to water and animal species outside of Botswana; and Out of Eden Walk, a 21-mile walkway of the first humans who migrated out of Africa in the Stone Age, creating a global record of human life as told by people. Other projects include Photo Ark, Photo Camp, Pristine Seas, Space Archaeology and more. The education division provides resources, reference materials, maps and programs. NGS' grant program enables the exploration of planet earth in order to understand it and empower the global community to generate solutions for a healthier and more sustainable future. Last, the exhibition and events division hosts world-class exhibitions, exclusive events and inspiring explorers. Twenty-First Century Fox, Inc. owns 73% of Society's media operations. NGS magazines and cable networks are a for-profit venture owned by Twenty-First Century; and NGS is a non-profit with an enhanced endowment.

Employees of the firm receive health and dental coverage, tuition assistance and a 401(k).

FINANCIAL DATA: Note: Data for latest year may not have been available at press time.

In U.S. $	2018	2017	2016	2015	2014	2013
Revenue		405,000,000	400,000,000	470,000,000	500,000,000	504,774,000
R&D Expense						
Operating Income						
Operating Margin %						
SGA Expense						
Net Income						
Operating Cash Flow						
Capital Expenditure						
EBITDA						
Return on Assets %						
Return on Equity %						
Debt to Equity						

CONTACT INFORMATION:
Phone: 202-857-7000 Fax:
Toll-Free: 800-647-5463
Address: 1145 17th St. N.W., Washington, DC 20036-4688 United States

STOCK TICKER/OTHER:
Stock Ticker: Nonprofit
Employees:
Parent Company:

Exchange:
Fiscal Year Ends: 12/31

SALARIES/BONUSES:
Top Exec. Salary: $ Bonus: $
Second Exec. Salary: $ Bonus: $

OTHER THOUGHTS:
Estimated Female Officers or Directors: 7
Hot Spot for Advancement for Women/Minorities: Y

NBCUniversal Media LLC

NAIC Code: 515120

www.nbcuni.com

TYPES OF BUSINESS:
Television Broadcasting
Online News & Information
TV & Movie Production
Radio Broadcasting
Interactive Online Content
Cable Television Programming
Theme Parks
Film, TV & Home Video Distribution

BRANDS/DIVISIONS/AFFILIATES:
Comcast Corporation
Bravo Media
E! Entertainment
NBC Entertainment
NBC News
Hulu
Universal Pictures
Cozi

CONTACTS: Note: Officers with more than one job title may be intentionally listed here more than once.
Steve Burke, CEO
Anand Kini, CFO
Jeff Shell, Chmn.-Universal Filmed Entertainment
Kimberley D. Harris, General Counsel
Maggie McLean Suniewick, Sr. VP-Strategic Integration
Cameron Blanchard, Exec. VP-Comm.
Patricia Fili-Krushel, Chmn.-NBCUniversal News Group
Robert Greenblatt, Chmn., NBC Entertainment
Bonnie Hammer, Chmn., NBCUniversal Cable Entertainment Group
Ted Harbert, Chmn., NBC Broadcasting
Mark Hoffman, Chmn.
Kevin MacLellan, Chmn., NBCUniversal Int'l
Matt Bond, Exec. VP-Content Dist.

GROWTH PLANS/SPECIAL FEATURES:
NBCUniversal Media, LLC is a world-leading entertainment and media company engaged in the development, production and marketing of news, entertainment and information. NBCU is a product of a 2004 merger of Vivendi Universal Entertainment and National Broadcasting Company (NBC). The firm now operates as a wholly-owned subsidiary of Comcast Corporation. NBCU operates in eight divisions: cable, broadcast, digital, film, parks, local media, TV studios production and international. The cable division includes Bravo Media, CNBC, E! Entertainment, Golf Channel, MSNBC, NBC Sports Network, Oxygen Media, SYFY, The Olympic Channel: Home of Team USA, Universal Kids, UNIVERSO and USA Network. The broadcast division includes NBC Entertainment, NBC News, NBC Olympics, NBC Sports and Telemundo. The digital division consists of Bluprint, Fandango, GolfNow, Hulu and SportsEngine. The film division includes DreamWorks Animation, Focus Features, Universal Brand Development, Universal Pictures, Universal Pictures Home Entertainment and Universal Pictures International. The parks division includes Universal Orlando Resort, Universal Studios Hollywood, Universal Studios Japan and Universal Studios Singapore. The local media division consists of Cozi TV, NBC Sports Regional Networks, NBCUniversal-owned television stations and TeleXitos. The international division includes CNBC International, hayu and global distribution. The TV studios production division consists of Telemundo Studios, Universal Cable Productions and Universal Television.

NBC Universal offers its employees medical, dental, vision and prescription drug coverage; a 401(k) plan; health club discounts; same-sex domestic partner benefits; life insurance; and flexible spending accounts.

FINANCIAL DATA: Note: Data for latest year may not have been available at press time.

In U.S. $	2018	2017	2016	2015	2014	2013
Revenue		32,997,000,000	31,593,000,000	28,462,000,000	25,428,000,000	23,650,000,000
R&D Expense						
Operating Income						
Operating Margin %						
SGA Expense						
Net Income		5,218,000,000	4,546,000,000	3,624,000,000	3,297,000,000	2,122,000,000
Operating Cash Flow						
Capital Expenditure						
EBITDA						
Return on Assets %						
Return on Equity %						
Debt to Equity						

CONTACT INFORMATION:
Phone: 212-664-4444   Fax: 212-664-4085
Toll-Free:
Address: 30 Rockefeller Plaza, New York, NY 10112 United States

SALARIES/BONUSES:
Top Exec. Salary: $ Bonus: $
Second Exec. Salary: $ Bonus: $

STOCK TICKER/OTHER:
Stock Ticker: Subsidiary   Exchange:
Employees: 62,500   Fiscal Year Ends: 12/31
Parent Company: Comcast Corporation

OTHER THOUGHTS:
Estimated Female Officers or Directors: 12
Hot Spot for Advancement for Women/Minorities: Y

NCsoft Corporation

us.ncsoft.com

NAIC Code: 511210G

TYPES OF BUSINESS:
Computer Software, Electronic Games, Apps & Entertainment
Massively Multiplayer Online Role-Playing Games
Apps
MMORPG

BRANDS/DIVISIONS/AFFILIATES:
NCsoft West
NC Interactive Inc
Carbine Studios
ArenaNet
Lineage
ArenaNet
Lineage
AION

CONTACTS: Note: Officers with more than one job title may be intentionally listed here more than once.
Songyee Yoon, CEO
Richard Zinser, Sr. VP-IT & Online Operations
Jae Hyun Bae, Chief Product Officer
Jin Soo Jung, Chief Legal Officer

GROWTH PLANS/SPECIAL FEATURES:
NCsoft Corporation is a Korean publisher of online multiplayer games in a range of genres, including sports, fighting action, shooter, rhythm/dance and side-scrolling action. The company is dedicated to research and development and manages a portfolio that contains a vast amount of games and game optimization tools. The firm has offices in Taiwan, China, Japan, the U.K. and the U.S., in addition to a publishing network that spans major markets throughout the world. NCsoft's portfolio of game franchises includes several massively multiplayer online role-playing games (MMORPGs) such as Lineage, AION, Guild Wars, Blade & Soul, Punch Monster (Korean only) and WildStar. In October 2018, the firm released Lineage II Classic, and an updated AION: Awakened Legacy. NCsoft also produces games aimed at a broader demographic of casual online gamers, including titles such as Love Beat and FreeRic; and mobile games such as Lineage RED NIGHTS and Lineage M. PlayNC is an online gaming portal developed by NCsoft. Subsidiary NCsoft West oversees the firm's operations in North America, Europe, South America and Australia and New Zealand. NC Interactive, Inc., based in Seattle, focuses on operations and administration, publishing, marketing, customer services, public relations, third-party publishing, localization and the development of next-generation online games. NCsoft maintains several U.S.-based development studios, including Carbine Studios, located in Aliso Viejo, California; and ArenaNet in Bellevue, Washington, which has been responsible for the ongoing development of the Guild Wars franchise.

FINANCIAL DATA: Note: Data for latest year may not have been available at press time.

In U.S. $	2018	2017	2016	2015	2014	2013
Revenue		1,646,880,000	838,286,000	723,140,661	559,657,322	501,787,520
R&D Expense						
Operating Income						
Operating Margin %						
SGA Expense						
Net Income		415,806,000	232,055,000	143,522,171	188,894,791	134,867,888
Operating Cash Flow						
Capital Expenditure						
EBITDA						
Return on Assets %						
Return on Equity %						
Debt to Equity						

CONTACT INFORMATION:
Phone: 82-2-2186-3330 Fax: 82-2-2186-3550
Toll-Free:
Address: 12, Daewangpangyo-ro 644beon-gil, Bundang-gu, Seongnam, 13494 South Korea

STOCK TICKER/OTHER:
Stock Ticker: 36570 Exchange: Seoul
Employees: 2,203 Fiscal Year Ends: 12/31
Parent Company:

SALARIES/BONUSES:
Top Exec. Salary: $ Bonus: $
Second Exec. Salary: $ Bonus: $

OTHER THOUGHTS:
Estimated Female Officers or Directors:
Hot Spot for Advancement for Women/Minorities:

Net Servicos de Comunicacao SA

NAIC Code: 517110

www.netcombo.com.br

TYPES OF BUSINESS:
Cable Television & Broadband Internet
Fixed-Line Telephony

BRANDS/DIVISIONS/AFFILIATES:
Claro SA
NET
NET Digital
NET Digital HD MAX
NET Virtua
NET Fone Via Embratel

CONTACTS: *Note: Officers with more than one job title may be intentionally listed here more than once.*
Jose Antonio Felix, CEO
Daniel Feldmann Barros, COO
Roberto Catalao Cardoso, CFO
Andre Muller Borges, Chief Legal Counsel
Renato Vergas Saibro, Chief Organizational Dev. Officer
Jose Antonio Guaraldi Felix, Investor Rel. Officer

GROWTH PLANS/SPECIAL FEATURES:

Net Servicos de Comunicacao SA, branded as NET, is a leading multimedia company in Brazil, offering pay television, broadband internet and phone services. The firm has more than 10 million connected pay TV subscribers throughout the country. NET provides high-speed broadband internet services, ranging from 15 to 120 megabytes. Its network of coaxial and fiber-optic cable covers over 61,000 miles and passes approximately 17 million homes, most of which belong to high- and middle-income classes. Approximately 80% of the network has two-way communication capability. NET's digital cable network is marketed under the NET Digital brand; high-definition cable television combined with digital video recorder (DVR) under the NET Digital HD MAX brand; broadband internet service under the NET Virtua brand; and fixed line telephone service under the NET Fone Via Embratel brand. Cell phone solutions and coverage is also provided by NET. The firm's web products and solutions serve both individuals and businesses, and include cloud server, customized email, website creation within one week's time and online backup via the cloud. The firm is owned by Claro SA.

FINANCIAL DATA: *Note: Data for latest year may not have been available at press time.*

In U.S. $	2018	2017	2016	2015	2014	2013
Revenue	4,300,000,000	4,252,500,000	4,050,000,000	4,000,000,000	4,210,550,765	3,667,121,012
R&D Expense						
Operating Income						
Operating Margin %						
SGA Expense						
Net Income						
Operating Cash Flow						
Capital Expenditure						
EBITDA						
Return on Assets %						
Return on Equity %						
Debt to Equity						

CONTACT INFORMATION:
Phone: 55-11-2111-2809 Fax: 55-11-2111-2780
Toll-Free:
Address: Rua Verbo Divino, 1356, Fl. 1, Sao Paulo, SP 04719 Brazil

STOCK TICKER/OTHER:
Stock Ticker: Subsidiary
Employees: 11,000
Parent Company: Claro SA

Exchange:
Fiscal Year Ends: 12/31

SALARIES/BONUSES:
Top Exec. Salary: $ Bonus: $
Second Exec. Salary: $ Bonus: $

OTHER THOUGHTS:
Estimated Female Officers or Directors:
Hot Spot for Advancement for Women/Minorities:

Sales, profits and employees may be estimates. Financial information, benefits and other data can change quickly and may vary from those stated here.

Netflix Inc

www.netflix.com

NAIC Code: 515210

TYPES OF BUSINESS:
Streaming Movies and TV Shows
DVD Rentals by Mail
Motion Picture Production

BRANDS/DIVISIONS/AFFILIATES:

CONTACTS: Note: Officers with more than one job title may be intentionally listed here more than once.
Reed Hastings, CEO
David Wells, CFO
Kelly Bennett, Chief Marketing Officer
David Hyman, General Counsel
Jonathan Friedland, Other Executive Officer
Jessica Neal, Other Executive Officer
Greg Peters, Other Executive Officer
Ted Sarandos, Other Executive Officer

GROWTH PLANS/SPECIAL FEATURES:
Netflix, Inc. is one of the largest online movie rental subscription services, providing access to a library of movie, television and other filmed entertainment titles to nearly 130 million subscribers in over 190 countries. The company has three operating segments: domestic streaming, international streaming and domestic DVD. The domestic and international streaming segments derive revenues from monthly membership fees for services consisting solely of streaming content. Domestic streaming membership plans are priced at $7.99 per month (basic), $10.99 per month (standard) of which can be watched on two screens at the same time, and $13.99 per month (premium) of which can be watched on up to four devices concurrently. International streaming membership is priced at the equivalent of USD $7 to $14 per month. The domestic DVD segment derives revenues from monthly membership fees for services consisting solely of DVD-by-mail. The price per plan for DVD-by-mail varies from $7.99 to $14.99 per month according to the plan chosen by the member. DVD-by-mail plans differ by the number of DVDs a member may have out at any given point and the type of DVD, either a standard DVD or an HD Blu-ray disc. Netflix's streaming service allows subscribers to view a growing library of movies and television episodes over the internet or on Netflix-ready devices such as Blu-ray players, internet-connected TVs, digital video players, smartphones and game consoles. The Netflix streaming content library includes media acquired through deals with corporations. Additionally, through its Netflix Studios division, the company produces original content available exclusively on Netflix.

FINANCIAL DATA: Note: Data for latest year may not have been available at press time.

In U.S. $	2018	2017	2016	2015	2014	2013
Revenue		11,692,710,000	8,830,669,000	6,779,511,000	5,504,656,000	4,374,562,000
R&D Expense		1,052,778,000	852,098,000	650,788,000	472,321,000	378,769,000
Operating Income		838,679,000	379,793,000	305,826,000	402,648,000	228,347,000
Operating Margin %		7.17%	4.30%	4.51%	7.31%	5.21%
SGA Expense		2,141,590,000	1,568,877,000	1,231,421,000	876,927,000	684,190,000
Net Income		558,929,000	186,678,000	122,641,000	266,799,000	112,403,000
Operating Cash Flow		-1,785,948,000	-1,473,984,000	-749,439,000	16,483,000	97,831,000
Capital Expenditure		173,302,000	107,653,000	91,248,000	69,726,000	54,143,000
EBITDA		795,436,000	468,149,000	336,884,000	453,616,000	248,590,000
Return on Assets %		3.42%	1.56%	1.42%	4.27%	2.39%
Return on Equity %		17.85%	7.61%	6.01%	16.72%	10.81%
Debt to Equity		1.81	1.25	1.06	0.48	0.37

CONTACT INFORMATION:
Phone: 408 540-3700   Fax: 408 540-3737
Toll-Free: 1-877-742-1480
Address: 100 Winchester Cir., Los Gatos, CA 95032 United States

STOCK TICKER/OTHER:
Stock Ticker: NFLX
Employees: 4,700
Parent Company:

Exchange: NAS
Fiscal Year Ends: 12/31

SALARIES/BONUSES:
Top Exec. Salary: $2,500,000   Bonus: $
Second Exec. Salary: $1,761,538   Bonus: $

OTHER THOUGHTS:
Estimated Female Officers or Directors: 3
Hot Spot for Advancement for Women/Minorities: Y

Sales, profits and employees may be estimates. Financial information, benefits and other data can change quickly and may vary from those stated here.

NeuLion Inc

NAIC Code: 519130

www.neulion.com

TYPES OF BUSINESS:
Internet Protocol Television
Television, web, sports media, mobile solutions and services.

BRANDS/DIVISIONS/AFFILIATES:
William Morris Endeavor Entertainment LLC
NeuLion Digital Platform
NeuLion CE SDK
MainConcept

CONTACTS:
Note: Officers with more than one job title may be intentionally listed here more than once.

Charles Wang, Chairman of the Board
Tim Alavathil, CFO
Michael Her, CTO
Roy Reichbach, Director
J. Wagner, Executive VP, Divisional
Ronald Nunn, Executive VP, Divisional
Horngwei Her, Executive VP, Divisional
Alexander Arato, General Counsel
Nancy Li, Vice Chairman of the Board

GROWTH PLANS/SPECIAL FEATURES:

NeuLion, Inc. is a technology product and service provider that specializes in the digital video broadcasting, distribution and monetization of live and on-demand content to internet-enabled devices. The firm's flagship solution, the NeuLion Digital Platform, is a complete end-to-end, cloud-based, fully integrated video solution that simplifies the digital video workflow and provides all the tools necessary for NeuLion's customers to monetize their digital video content. The NeuLion Digital Platform offers content owners and rights holders a highly configurable and scalable suite of digital technologies, together with services for back-end content preparation, management, marketing, monetization, secure delivery, real time analytics and end user application development, in an end-to-end solution that addresses the complexities associated with successfully streaming and marketing their content. Other solutions include the NeuLion consumer electronics (CE) software development kit (the CE SDK), which allows CE manufacturers to provide a secure, high quality video experience with premium screen resolution, up to Ultra HD/4K, across virtually all content formats, for a wide range of connected devices. Additionally, NeuLion offers a library of high quality video and audio compression-decompression programs, or codecs, that are licensed under the MainConcept brand. In May 2018, NeuLion was acquired by William Morris Endeavor Entertainment LLC, a privately-held holding company, for $250 million.

FINANCIAL DATA:
Note: Data for latest year may not have been available at press time.

In U.S. $	2018	2017	2016	2015	2014	2013
Revenue		95,570,000	99,788,000	94,043,000	55,519,740	47,107,176
R&D Expense						
Operating Income						
Operating Margin %						
SGA Expense						
Net Income		-31,315,000	-1,753,000	25,916,000	3,567,230	-2,278,345
Operating Cash Flow						
Capital Expenditure						
EBITDA						
Return on Assets %						
Return on Equity %						
Debt to Equity						

CONTACT INFORMATION:
Phone: 516 622-830 Fax:
Toll-Free:
Address: 1600 Old Country Rd., Plainview, NY 11803 United States

SALARIES/BONUSES:
Top Exec. Salary: $ Bonus: $
Second Exec. Salary: $ Bonus: $

STOCK TICKER/OTHER:
Stock Ticker: Subsidairy Exchange: TSE
Employees: 767 Fiscal Year Ends: 12/31
Parent Company: William Morris Endeavor Entertainment LLC

OTHER THOUGHTS:
Estimated Female Officers or Directors: 2
Hot Spot for Advancement for Women/Minorities: Y

Sales, profits and employees may be estimates. Financial information, benefits and other data can change quickly and may vary from those stated here.

Nevada Gold & Casinos Inc

www.nevadagold.com

NAIC Code: 713210

TYPES OF BUSINESS:
Casinos (except Casino Hotels)

BRANDS/DIVISIONS/AFFILIATES:
AG Trucano Son and Grandsons Inc
Gold Mountain Development LLC
Club Fortune Casino
Red Dragon
Dakota Players Club
Crazy Moose
Coyote Bob's Roadhouse
Silver Dollar

CONTACTS:
Note: Officers with more than one job title may be intentionally listed here more than once.

James Meier, CFO
William Sherlock, Chairman of the Board
Michael Shaunnessy, President
Victor Mena, Vice President, Divisional

GROWTH PLANS/SPECIAL FEATURES:
Nevada Gold & Casinos, Inc. is mainly a gaming company involved in financing, developing, owning and operating gaming projects. The firm operates: nine mini casinos in the state of Washington; A.G. Trucano, Son and Grandsons, Inc. located in South Dakota; and Club Fortune Casino located in Nevada. The company's mini-casinos include restaurants, bars and approximately 125 table games. A. G. Trucano is a slot machine route operation, consisting of more than 655 slot machines in 16 locations. Club Fortune has about 405 slot machines, seven table games and a poker room, as well as bars, an entertainment lounge, cafe, snack bar and gift shop. Nevada Gold's other casinos are branded under the Red Dragon, Dakota Players Club, Crazy Moose, Coyote Bob's Roadhouse, Silver Dollar, Club Hollywood and Royal names. In addition, Nevada Gold's wholly-owned subsidiary, Gold Mountain Development, LLC, owns approximately 268 acres of undeveloped land in Colorado. The firm agreed to sell this land in 2016, receiving a $75,000 down payment and a balloon payment due April 30, 2019. In September 2018, Nevada Gold & Casinos agreed to be acquired by Maverick Casinos, LLC, which would result with the company becoming private.

FINANCIAL DATA:
Note: Data for latest year may not have been available at press time.

In U.S. $	2018	2017	2016	2015	2014	2013
Revenue	74,552,530	74,626,950	70,341,010	64,349,550	62,807,390	65,923,920
R&D Expense						
Operating Income	2,963,649	2,949,606	4,395,227	3,606,782	2,643,161	2,656,403
Operating Margin %		3.95%	6.24%	5.60%	4.20%	4.02%
SGA Expense	25,733,360	25,765,260	23,695,250	21,392,160	20,705,420	22,975,490
Net Income	1,323,425	563,964	1,301,046	1,807,077	447,981	36,907
Operating Cash Flow	5,464,944	4,754,488	6,371,227	5,951,452	3,343,316	3,019,206
Capital Expenditure	983,568	1,019,351	778,119	682,863	346,590	685,699
EBITDA	5,184,990	5,123,627	5,854,062	5,566,410	4,091,243	4,310,439
Return on Assets %		1.02%	2.57%	4.10%	.98%	.07%
Return on Equity %		1.63%	4.01%	6.15%	1.59%	.13%
Debt to Equity		0.34	0.48	0.24	0.37	0.46

CONTACT INFORMATION:
Phone: 702-685-1000   Fax: 702-685-1265
Toll-Free:
Address: 133 E. Warm Springs Rd., Ste. 102, Las Vegas, NV 89119 United States

STOCK TICKER/OTHER:
Stock Ticker: UWN
Employees: 1,260
Parent Company:

Exchange: ASE
Fiscal Year Ends: 04/30

SALARIES/BONUSES:
Top Exec. Salary: $300,000   Bonus: $21,500
Second Exec. Salary: $215,000   Bonus: $21,500

OTHER THOUGHTS:
Estimated Female Officers or Directors:
Hot Spot for Advancement for Women/Minorities:

New Media Investment Group Inc

NAIC Code: 511110

www.newmediainv.com

TYPES OF BUSINESS:
Newspaper Publishers

BRANDS/DIVISIONS/AFFILIATES:
Online Automotive Solutions
GateHouse Media Alaska Holdings Inc
Rugged Events Holding LLC
Rugged Maniac Obstacle Race

CONTACTS:
Note: Officers with more than one job title may be intentionally listed here more than once.
Michael Reed, CEO
Gregory Freiberg, CFO
Wesley Edens, Chairman of the Board
Kirk Davis, COO

GROWTH PLANS/SPECIAL FEATURES:
New Media Investment Group Inc. is a company that owns, operates and invests in high quality local media assets. The firm focuses on owning and acquiring strong local media assets in small- to mid-size markets. New Media's 325 weekly newspapers have a weekly reach of 2.4 million, spanning 35+ U.S. states, via print, directory and web format. These channels reach millions of individual customers each week, as well as 5 million business customers. Print and online products of New Media focus on local communities from a content, advertising and digital marketing perspective. Because of this focus on small- and mid-size markets, the firm's assets are usually the primary, and sometimes, the sole provider of comprehensive and in-depth local market news and information in the communities served. Of New Media's 145 daily newspapers, 85% have been published for more than 100 years and 100% of them have been published for over 50 years. During 2018, New Media acquired Online Automotive Solutions, a tech-enabled video, data and auto-focused inventory solutions provider; swapped the publishing and related assets of its GateHouse Media Alaska Holdings, Inc. subsidiary for Black Press Ltd.'s publishing and related assets in Akron Beacon Journal; and acquired a majority interest in Rugged Events Holding, LLC, a production company featuring the Rugged Maniac Obstacle Race series, as well as 90+ endurance events held in the U.S. and Canada.

FINANCIAL DATA:
Note: Data for latest year may not have been available at press time.

In U.S. $	2018	2017	2016	2015	2014	2013
Revenue		1,342,004,000	1,255,356,000	1,195,815,000	652,323,000	
R&D Expense						
Operating Income		67,554,000	73,287,000	65,226,000	27,828,000	
Operating Margin %		5.03%	5.83%	5.45%	4.26%	
SGA Expense		457,234,000	414,983,000	406,282,000	214,625,000	
Net Income		-915,000	31,641,000	67,614,000	-3,205,000	
Operating Cash Flow		110,806,000	98,361,000	115,319,000	41,446,000	
Capital Expenditure		11,090,000	10,631,000	10,155,000	5,012,000	
EBITDA		104,436,000	126,731,000	168,115,000	57,594,000	
Return on Assets %		-.06%	2.49%	6.67%	-.42%	
Return on Equity %		-.12%	4.51%	11.95%	-.72%	
Debt to Equity		0.52	0.44	0.54	0.45	

CONTACT INFORMATION:
Phone: 212-479-3160 Fax:
Toll-Free:
Address: 1345 Ave. of the Americas, New York, NY 10105 United States

STOCK TICKER/OTHER:
Stock Ticker: NEWM
Employees: 10,092
Parent Company:

Exchange: NYS
Fiscal Year Ends: 12/31

SALARIES/BONUSES:
Top Exec. Salary: $550,000   Bonus: $750,000
Second Exec. Salary: $ Bonus: $

OTHER THOUGHTS:
Estimated Female Officers or Directors:
Hot Spot for Advancement for Women/Minorities:

New York Times Company (The)

NAIC Code: 511110

www.nytco.com

TYPES OF BUSINESS:
Newspaper Publishing
Newspaper Distribution
Newsprint & Paper Manufacturing
Online Publishing

BRANDS/DIVISIONS/AFFILIATES:
New York Times (The)
NYTimes.com
Times (The)
Wirecutter (The)
NYT Live
Madison Paper Industries

CONTACTS: Note: Officers with more than one job title may be intentionally listed here more than once.
Mark Thompson, CEO
Roland Caputo, CFO
Arthur Sulzberger, Chairman of the Board
R. Benten, Chief Accounting Officer
Meredith Kopit Levien, COO
A. Sulzberger, Director
Michael Golden, Director
Diane Brayton, Executive VP

GROWTH PLANS/SPECIAL FEATURES:
The New York Times Company (NYT) is a diversified media company with operations that include newspapers, digital media and paper mill investments. NYT's businesses consist of The New York Times; website NYTimes.com; mobile applications, including The Time's core news applications, as well as interest-specific apps such as NYT Cooking, Crossword and others; and related businesses such as The Times news services division, product review and recommendation website The Wirecutter, digital archive distribution, live events business NYT Live, as well as other products and services under The Times brand. The firm generates revenues principally from circulation and advertising, delivering breaking news and multimedia on local, national and world business and occurrences. The Times is currently printed at the company's production and distribution facility in New York, as well as under contract at 26 remote print sites throughout the U.S. The Time's award-winning content is available in print, web and mobile platforms. The Time's print edition is a daily newspaper in the U.S., with average circulation on a weekday being 540,000 and 1,066,000 for Sunday (as of December 2017). Internationally, average circulation for the international edition of the firm's newspaper is approximately 173,000, respectively. Additionally, NYT owns a 40% interest in a Maine paper mill, Madison Paper Industries. During 2017, NYT sold its 49% equity interest in Donohue Malbaie, Inc., and its 30% ownership in Women in the World Media, LLC.

The firm offers employees medical, dental and health insurance; a 401(k) plan; health and wellness programs; an employee stock purchase plan; tuition assistance; and a bonus plan.

FINANCIAL DATA: Note: Data for latest year may not have been available at press time.

In U.S. $	2018	2017	2016	2015	2014	2013
Revenue		1,675,639,000	1,555,342,000	1,579,215,000	1,588,528,000	1,577,230,000
R&D Expense						
Operating Income		122,456,000	116,408,000	136,585,000	94,498,000	156,087,000
Operating Margin %		7.30%	7.48%	8.64%	5.94%	9.89%
SGA Expense		875,906,000	749,107,000	763,221,000	770,580,000	715,753,000
Net Income		4,296,000	29,068,000	63,246,000	33,307,000	65,105,000
Operating Cash Flow		86,712,000	94,247,000	175,326,000	80,491,000	34,855,000
Capital Expenditure		84,753,000	30,095,000	26,965,000	35,350,000	16,942,000
EBITDA		202,775,000	136,074,000	204,740,000	165,681,000	239,864,000
Return on Assets %		.20%	1.26%	2.53%	1.29%	2.42%
Return on Equity %		.49%	3.47%	8.14%	4.24%	8.82%
Debt to Equity		0.27	0.29	0.29	0.58	0.81

CONTACT INFORMATION:
Phone: 212 556-1234 Fax:
Toll-Free:
Address: 620 Eighth Ave., New York, NY 10018 United States

SALARIES/BONUSES:
Top Exec. Salary: $1,107,904 Bonus: $
Second Exec. Salary: $1,019,231 Bonus: $

STOCK TICKER/OTHER:
Stock Ticker: NYT
Employees: 3,710
Parent Company:

Exchange: NYS
Fiscal Year Ends: 12/31

OTHER THOUGHTS:
Estimated Female Officers or Directors: 6
Hot Spot for Advancement for Women/Minorities: Y

Sales, profits and employees may be estimates. Financial information, benefits and other data can change quickly and may vary from those stated here.

News Corporation

www.newscorp.com

NAIC Code: 511110

TYPES OF BUSINESS:
Newspaper Publishing
Magazine & Book Publishing
Advertising Services
Online Media
Sports Broadcasting
Business Information
Financial Information

BRANDS/DIVISIONS/AFFILIATES:
Wall Street Journal
News Corp Australia
News UK
New York Post (The)
New Foxtel
REA Group Limited
Move Inc
News IQ

CONTACTS: *Note: Officers with more than one job title may be intentionally listed here more than once.*
Robert Thomson, CEO
Susan Panuccio, CFO
Keith Murdoch, Chairman of the Board
Kevin Halpin, Chief Accounting Officer
Lachlan Murdoch, Co-Chairman
David Pitofsky, Executive VP

GROWTH PLANS/SPECIAL FEATURES:
News Corporation, doing business as News Corp, is a global media and entertainment company. The firm operates in five segments: news and information services, subscription video services, digital real estate services, book publishing and other. The news and information services segments consists of Dow Jones (which publishes The Wall Street Journal newspaper), News Corp Australia, News UK, The New York Post and News America Marketing. The subscription video services segment provides video sports, entertainment and news services to pay-TV subscribers and other commercial licensees. This happens primarily through cable, satellite and IP distribution. This segment includes New Foxtel, a video subscription service in Australia with over 200 channels, and Australian News Channel. The digital real estate services segment consists of the company's 61.6% interest in REA Group Limited, a digital advertising business specializing in real estate services. Operations in this segment include those of Move, Inc., which News Corp has an 80% interest in, providing online real estate services in the U.S. through realtor.com. The book publishing segment consists of HarperCollins Publishers, which publishes and distributes consumer books globally through print, digital and audio formats. The other segment includes general corporate overhead expenses; Strategy Group, which identifies new products and services to increase profitability; News IQ, New Corp's advertising platform; and costs related to U.K. Newspaper Matters. The company owns a 65% stake in New Foxtel, an Australian pay-TV provider. In March 2018, News Corp and Telstra, the other 35% stake holder in New Foxtel, signed an agreement to combine Foxtel and FOX SPORTS Australia. News Corp acquired Opcity, a real estate technology platform, in October 2018.

FINANCIAL DATA: *Note: Data for latest year may not have been available at press time.*

In U.S. $	2018	2017	2016	2015	2014	2013
Revenue	9,024,000,000	8,139,000,000	8,292,000,000	8,633,000,000	8,574,000,000	8,891,000,000
R&D Expense						
Operating Income	600,000,000	436,000,000	337,000,000	322,000,000	-529,000,000	140,000,000
Operating Margin %		5.35%	4.06%	3.72%	2.23%	1.57%
SGA Expense	3,049,000,000	2,725,000,000	2,722,000,000	2,756,000,000	2,665,000,000	2,783,000,000
Net Income	-1,514,000,000	-738,000,000	179,000,000	-147,000,000	239,000,000	506,000,000
Operating Cash Flow	757,000,000	494,000,000	952,000,000	831,000,000	854,000,000	501,000,000
Capital Expenditure	364,000,000	256,000,000	256,000,000	378,000,000	379,000,000	332,000,000
EBITDA	1,072,000,000	885,000,000	842,000,000	852,000,000	49,000,000	688,000,000
Return on Assets %		-4.92%	1.15%	-.94%	1.48%	3.52%
Return on Equity %		-6.62%	1.50%	-1.18%	1.85%	4.71%
Debt to Equity		0.02	0.03			

CONTACT INFORMATION:
Phone: 212 852-7000   Fax:
Toll-Free:
Address: 1211 Avenue of the Americas, New York, NY 10036 United States

SALARIES/BONUSES:
Top Exec. Salary: $2,000,000   Bonus: $
Second Exec. Salary: $1,100,000   Bonus: $

STOCK TICKER/OTHER:
Stock Ticker: NWS
Employees: 26,000
Parent Company:

Exchange: NAS
Fiscal Year Ends: 06/30

OTHER THOUGHTS:
Estimated Female Officers or Directors: 6
Hot Spot for Advancement for Women/Minorities: Y

Nexstar Media Group Inc

www.nexstar.tv

NAIC Code: 515120

TYPES OF BUSINESS:
Television Broadcasting
Online Content

BRANDS/DIVISIONS/AFFILIATES:

CONTACTS: Note: Officers with more than one job title may be intentionally listed here more than once.
Perry Sook, CEO
Keith Hopkins, Sr. VP, Divisional
Thomas Carter, CFO
Brett Jenkins, Chief Technology Officer
Brian Jones, COO, Subsidiary
Elizabeth Ryder, Executive VP
Andrew Alford, Other Corporate Officer
Diane Kniowski, Other Corporate Officer
Douglas Davis, Other Corporate Officer
Mike Vaughn, Other Corporate Officer
Julie Pruett, Other Corporate Officer
William Sally, Other Corporate Officer
Theresa Underwood, Other Corporate Officer
Timothy Busch, President, Subsidiary
Gregory Raifman, President, Subsidiary
Blake Russell, Senior VP, Divisional
Rajesh Ramanan, Senior VP, Subsidiary
Anthony Katsur, Senior VP, Subsidiary
Daniel Street, Senior VP, Subsidiary

GROWTH PLANS/SPECIAL FEATURES:

Nexstar Media Group, Inc. is a television broadcasting company focused exclusively on the acquisition, development and operation of television stations in medium-sized markets in the U.S. The company owns, operates, programs or provides sales and other services to 171 full-power television stations and their related low-power and digital multicast signals, reaching 100 markets. These television stations reach roughly 38.7% of U.S. households. Its portfolio includes primary affiliates of NBC, CBS, ABC, FOX and The CW, as well as 20 multicast affiliates, including Telemundo, MyNetworkTV, Bounce TV, MeTV, LATV and more. Stations belonging to the company provide free-to-air programming to its television viewing audiences, including programs produced by networks with which the stations are affiliates, programs that the stations produce and first-run and re-run syndicated programs that the stations acquire. In addition, the firm operates community portal websites that publish local news and other local interest content. Nexstar's primary source of revenue is the sale of commercial air time to local and national advertisers. In October 2017, the firm acquired the non-spectrum operating assets of WLWC-TV, the CW affiliate serving Providence, Rhode Island, from OTA Broadcasting (PVD), LLC for $4.1 million. In December 2018, Nexstar agreed to acquire Tribune Media Company for $4.1 billion. The combined companies would create the largest local TV company in the U.S.

FINANCIAL DATA: Note: Data for latest year may not have been available at press time.

In U.S. $	2018	2017	2016	2015	2014	2013
Revenue		2,431,966,000	1,103,190,000	896,377,000	631,311,000	502,330,000
R&D Expense						
Operating Income		481,014,000	302,570,000	206,107,000	173,875,000	104,521,000
Operating Margin %		19.77%	27.42%	22.99%	27.54%	20.80%
SGA Expense		591,986,000	263,606,000	232,480,000	174,791,000	150,933,000
Net Income		474,997,000	91,537,000	77,684,000	64,550,000	-1,785,000
Operating Cash Flow		136,721,000	247,757,000	197,266,000	166,527,000	27,339,000
Capital Expenditure		72,461,000	31,870,000	29,021,000	20,389,000	18,955,000
EBITDA		848,140,000	442,852,000	361,123,000	267,823,000	166,223,000
Return on Assets %		9.09%	3.81%	4.71%	4.91%	-.16%
Return on Equity %		54.60%	73.28%	116.63%	328.44%	
Debt to Equity		2.71	13.68	18.02	23.22	

CONTACT INFORMATION:
Phone: 972 373-8800 Fax:
Toll-Free:
Address: 545 E. John Carpenter Fwy., Ste. 700, Irving, TX 75062 United States

STOCK TICKER/OTHER:
Stock Ticker: NXST
Employees: 4,527
Parent Company:

Exchange: NAS
Fiscal Year Ends: 12/31

SALARIES/BONUSES:
Top Exec. Salary: $1,500,000   Bonus: $9,000,000
Second Exec. Salary: $747,115   Bonus: $2,562,500

OTHER THOUGHTS:
Estimated Female Officers or Directors: 2
Hot Spot for Advancement for Women/Minorities: Y

Sales, profits and employees may be estimates. Financial information, benefits and other data can change quickly and may vary from those stated here.

Nielsen Holdings plc

NAIC Code: 541910

www.nielsen.com

TYPES OF BUSINESS:
Market Research
Magazine Publishing
Media/Entertainment Audience Research
Trade Publications
Directories
Business Consulting
Internet Audience Research

BRANDS/DIVISIONS/AFFILIATES:
SuperData Research

CONTACTS:
Note: Officers with more than one job title may be intentionally listed here more than once.

David Kenny, CEO
David Anderson, CFO
Jeffrey Charlton, Chief Accounting Officer
Giovanni Tavolieri, Chief Technology Officer
James Attwood, Director
Nancy Phillips, Other Executive Officer
Eric Dale, Other Executive Officer

GROWTH PLANS/SPECIAL FEATURES:

Nielsen Holdings plc is a leading global provider of marketing information, audience measurement and business media products and services with operations in over 100 countries and data measurements of millions of consumers worldwide. The firm has two major segments: what consumers watch (watch) and what consumers buy (buy). Accounting for about half (51% in 2017) of Nielsen's annual revenues, the watch segment provides viewership data and analytics primarily to the media industry, and advertising across three primary platforms that include mobile screens, online and television. Clients of this segment use Nielsen's data to plan and optimize their advertising spending and to better ensure that their advertisements reach the intended audience. The buy segment provides consumer behavior information and analytics primarily to businesses in the consumer packaged goods industry. Clients use the data to manage their brands, find new sources of demand, launch and grow new products, improve their marketing mix and establish more effective consumer relationships. In September 2018, Nielsen acquired SuperData Research, a provider of market intelligence on digital games, gaming video content and virtual/augmented reality across mobile, PC online, console and other digital platforms.

FINANCIAL DATA:
Note: Data for latest year may not have been available at press time.

In U.S. $	2018	2017	2016	2015	2014	2013
Revenue		6,572,000,000	6,309,000,000	6,172,000,000	6,288,000,000	5,703,000,000
R&D Expense						
Operating Income		1,305,000,000	1,248,000,000	1,144,000,000	1,178,000,000	980,000,000
Operating Margin %		19.85%	19.78%	18.53%	18.73%	17.18%
SGA Expense		1,862,000,000	1,851,000,000	1,915,000,000	1,917,000,000	1,815,000,000
Net Income		429,000,000	502,000,000	570,000,000	384,000,000	740,000,000
Operating Cash Flow		1,310,000,000	1,296,000,000	1,179,000,000	1,093,000,000	901,000,000
Capital Expenditure		489,000,000	433,000,000	408,000,000	412,000,000	374,000,000
EBITDA		1,842,000,000	1,752,000,000	1,846,000,000	1,494,000,000	1,350,000,000
Return on Assets %		2.63%	3.23%	3.71%	2.48%	4.91%
Return on Equity %		10.27%	11.76%	12.01%	7.12%	13.88%
Debt to Equity		1.96	1.88	1.58	1.27	1.13

CONTACT INFORMATION:
Phone: 646 654-5000   Fax:
Toll-Free: 800-864-1224
Address: 85 Broad St., New York, NY 10004 United States

SALARIES/BONUSES:
Top Exec. Salary: $750,000   Bonus: $325,000
Second Exec. Salary: $1,000,000   Bonus: $

STOCK TICKER/OTHER:
Stock Ticker: NLSN   Exchange: NYS
Employees: 46,000   Fiscal Year Ends: 12/31
Parent Company:

OTHER THOUGHTS:
Estimated Female Officers or Directors: 4
Hot Spot for Advancement for Women/Minorities: Y

NightCulture Inc

nightculture.com

NAIC Code: 711320

TYPES OF BUSINESS:
Promoters of Performing Arts, Sports, and Similar Events without Facilities

BRANDS/DIVISIONS/AFFILIATES:
Stereo Live LLC
Stereo Live Dallas LLC
Stereo Live

GROWTH PLANS/SPECIAL FEATURES:
NightCulture Inc. is a promoter and producer of live concerts, events and festivals, primarily featuring the electronic dance music genre. The firm operates out of Houston, Dallas and San Antonio, Texas. Within Houston, the company's wholly-owned Stereo Live, LLC operates Stereo Live, a 25,000-square-foot music and live events venue located on two and one-half acres of land; and within Dallas, Stereo Live Dallas, LLC operates branded concert venues. The primary target market of the firm is those in the age group of 18-35 years old. In San Antonio, the company has promotional operations, and is looking to expand its venue operations not only in that market, but in all of its markets.

CONTACTS: Note: Officers with more than one job title may be intentionally listed here more than once.
Michael Long, CEO

FINANCIAL DATA: Note: Data for latest year may not have been available at press time.

In U.S. $	2018	2017	2016	2015	2014	2013
Revenue	66,000,000	6,423,988	6,118,083	5,826,746	6,501,353	5,653,776
R&D Expense						
Operating Income						
Operating Margin %						
SGA Expense						
Net Income				-1,665,760	-673,311	2,992,781
Operating Cash Flow						
Capital Expenditure						
EBITDA						
Return on Assets %						
Return on Equity %						
Debt to Equity						

CONTACT INFORMATION:
Phone: 832 535-9070 Fax:
Toll-Free:
Address: 6400 Richmond Ave., Houston, TX 77057 United States

STOCK TICKER/OTHER:
Stock Ticker: Private
Employees: 44
Parent Company:

Exchange:
Fiscal Year Ends: 12/31

SALARIES/BONUSES:
Top Exec. Salary: $ Bonus: $
Second Exec. Salary: $ Bonus: $

OTHER THOUGHTS:
Estimated Female Officers or Directors:
Hot Spot for Advancement for Women/Minorities:

Sales, profits and employees may be estimates. Financial information, benefits and other data can change quickly and may vary from those stated here.

Nine Entertainment Co Holdings Ltd   www.nineentertainment.com.au

NAIC Code: 515120

TYPES OF BUSINESS:
Television Broadcasting
News Publishing

BRANDS/DIVISIONS/AFFILIATES:
Fairfax Media Limited

GROWTH PLANS/SPECIAL FEATURES:
Nine Entertainment is a leading Australian broadcaster that creates and distributes content for the purpose of engaging audiences and advertisers. Nine's content spans news, sport, lifestyle and entertainment, and its digital and broadcast solutions are created for entertainment, innovation and performance purposes. Nine utilizes imagination to develop impactful ad formats, creative and branded content, and combines this with data, insight and technology to meet advertising goals and objectives. The company's solutions span mobile, television, performance, programmatic and publishing segments. In late-2018, Nine Entertainment acquired Fairfax Media Limited and merged it into the Nine brand, with Nine shareholders owning a 51.1% stake in the combined entity and Fairfax shareholders holding 48.9%.

CONTACTS:
Note: Officers with more than one job title may be intentionally listed here more than once.

Hugh Marks, Managing Dir.
Peter Costello, Chmn.

FINANCIAL DATA:
Note: Data for latest year may not have been available at press time.

In U.S. $	2018	2017	2016	2015	2014	2013
Revenue		974,968,448	1,010,310,976	1,082,542,592	1,217,083,904	
R&D Expense						
Operating Income						
Operating Margin %						
SGA Expense						
Net Income		-160,592,032	256,358,544	-467,438,400	45,683,612	
Operating Cash Flow						
Capital Expenditure						
EBITDA						
Return on Assets %						
Return on Equity %						
Debt to Equity						

CONTACT INFORMATION:
Phone: 61-2-9383-6000   Fax: 61-2-9383-6100
Toll-Free:
Address: 120B Underwood St., Locked Bag 2000, Paddington, NSW 2021 Australia

STOCK TICKER/OTHER:
Stock Ticker: NEC
Employees:
Parent Company:

Exchange: ASX
Fiscal Year Ends:

SALARIES/BONUSES:
Top Exec. Salary: $ Bonus: $
Second Exec. Salary: $ Bonus: $

OTHER THOUGHTS:
Estimated Female Officers or Directors:
Hot Spot for Advancement for Women/Minorities:

Sales, profits and employees may be estimates. Financial information, benefits and other data can change quickly and may vary from those stated here.

Nintendo Co Ltd

NAIC Code: 334111

www.nintendo.com

TYPES OF BUSINESS:
Video Game Hardware & Software
Electronic Games
Online Games

BRANDS/DIVISIONS/AFFILIATES:
Nintendo DS
Nintendo DSi
Nintendo 3DS
Wii
Wii U
Legend of Zelda (The)
Donkey Kong
Pokemon

CONTACTS:
Note: Officers with more than one job title may be intentionally listed here more than once.

Tatsumi Kimishima, Managing Dir.
Satoru Iwata, Pres.
Genyo Takeda, Gen. Manager-Integrated R&D Div.
Genyo Takeda, Chief Dir.-Total Dev.
Tatsumi Kimishima, Managing Dir.-Nintendo of America
Genyo Takeda, Head-European PR

GROWTH PLANS/SPECIAL FEATURES:
Nintendo Co., Ltd. develops, manufactures and sells home entertainment products globally. Based in Kyoto, Japan, Nintendo is comprised of 27 subsidiaries and five associated companies located in the U.S., Canada, Korea, Australia and several European countries. Its main products are the video game systems and related software and merchandise for the Nintendo DS (dual screen), Nintendo DSi, Nintendo 3DS and Nintendo Switch. Nintendo currently focuses on selling the Nintendo Switch. The Switch is a home console that can transition to a portable handheld that can be taken anywhere. The included controllers attach to the console while in handheld mode, and can be removed and used separately with compatible games in TV or tabletop modes. The system's features include built-in amiibo support, motion controls and HD Rumble to makes games more immersive, and the Nintendo Switch Online service. The firm's home game station product was the Wii, a motion sensitive game station that picks up user movements with the controller. The Wii's successor, Wii U features a touch screen, camera and microphone in addition to motion sensors on its controller. Well-known video game titles from the company include Mario Brothers, Donkey Kong, Pokemon, Animal Crossing, Splatoon and The Legend of Zelda. Other operations of the company include the manufacture and sale of poker and Japanese-style playing cards (Karuta) and Pokemon animation products in addition to the management of services for electronic registration of in-home console machines and intellectual property rights.

FINANCIAL DATA:
Note: Data for latest year may not have been available at press time.

In U.S. $	2018	2017	2016	2015	2014	2013
Revenue	9,792,242,000	4,536,722,000	4,679,235,000	5,099,621,000	5,303,187,000	5,894,015,000
R&D Expense						
Operating Income	1,646,974,000	272,363,800	305,005,200	229,760,300	-430,635,900	-337,730,000
Operating Margin %	16.81	6.00%	6.51%	4.50%	-8.12%	-5.73%
SGA Expense						
Net Income	1,294,802,000	951,450,700	153,096,200	388,125,200	-215,401,400	65,848,540
Operating Cash Flow	1,411,843,000	177,176,100	511,928,600	559,262,800	-214,399,700	-374,647,500
Capital Expenditure	89,130,670	97,005,790	43,317,750	42,501,480	181,248,100	53,688,040
EBITDA	1,731,050,000	349,964,800	389,776,300	313,344,100	-338,639,100	-220,512,400
Return on Assets %	8.99%	7.41%	1.24%	3.14%	-1.68%	.50%
Return on Equity %	10.86%	8.50%	1.41%	3.66%	-1.97%	.58%
Debt to Equity						

CONTACT INFORMATION:
Phone: 81 756629614 Fax: 81 756629540
Toll-Free: 1-800-255-3700
Address: 11-1 Kamitoba, Hokotate-cho, Minami-ku, Kyoto, 601-8116 Japan

STOCK TICKER/OTHER:
Stock Ticker: NTDOF
Employees: 6,030
Parent Company:

Exchange: PINX
Fiscal Year Ends: 03/31

SALARIES/BONUSES:
Top Exec. Salary: $ Bonus: $
Second Exec. Salary: $ Bonus: $

OTHER THOUGHTS:
Estimated Female Officers or Directors:
Hot Spot for Advancement for Women/Minorities:

Nippon Columbia Co Ltd

NAIC Code: 512230

columbia.jp/company/en/index.html

TYPES OF BUSINESS:
Music Production
Software Manufacturing
Software Sales
Software Advertising
Musician Management

BRANDS/DIVISIONS/AFFILIATES:
Faith Inc
Columbia Songs Inc
Columbia Marketing Co Ltd
C2 Design
CME Inc
Omagatoko Co Ltd

CONTACTS:
Note: Officers with more than one job title may be intentionally listed here more than once.

Miyomatsu Abe, Pres.
Toshinori Abe, General Manager-Admin.
Miyomatsu Abe, Exec. Officer
Hajime Hirasawa, Chmn.

GROWTH PLANS/SPECIAL FEATURES:
Nippon Columbia Co., Ltd. is a Japanese music production company, with additional operations in artist management, advertising and sales of audio, gaming and video software. Among its operating subsidiaries are Columbia Songs, Inc.; Columbia Marketing Co., Ltd; C2 Design; CME, Inc.; and Omagatoki Co.,Ltd. Columbia Songs is a copyright management company for music and TV programs, with approximately 30,000 songs under management. Columbia Marketing is in the business of pressing and distributing CDs and DVDs, and also manages the firm's mail order division. C2 Design designs and develops audio-visual software, posters, flyers and other promotional materials; provides editing and planning services for the publication of books, magazines and other publications; and provides merchandising, trademark and design rights and distribution management services. CME is a U.S. holding company for SLG. Omagatoki is responsible for the sale and production of multimedia products and audio. Nippon Columbia operates as a wholly-owned subsidiary of Faith, Inc.

FINANCIAL DATA:
Note: Data for latest year may not have been available at press time.

In U.S. $	2018	2017	2016	2015	2014	2013
Revenue	127,000,000	125,990,000	125,443,000	127,946,759	102,524,747	144,921,655
R&D Expense						
Operating Income						
Operating Margin %						
SGA Expense						
Net Income		16,948,500	16,874,900	9,373,388	-13,362,557	3,635,451
Operating Cash Flow						
Capital Expenditure						
EBITDA						
Return on Assets %						
Return on Equity %						
Debt to Equity						

CONTACT INFORMATION:
Phone: 81-3-6895-9001 Fax: 81-3-3598-5382
Toll-Free:
Address: Toranomon Mori Bldg., 4-1-40 Toranomon, Minato-ku, Tokyo, 105-8482 Japan

STOCK TICKER/OTHER:
Stock Ticker: Subsidiary
Employees: 330
Parent Company: Faith Inc
Exchange:
Fiscal Year Ends: 03/31

SALARIES/BONUSES:
Top Exec. Salary: $ Bonus: $
Second Exec. Salary: $ Bonus: $

OTHER THOUGHTS:
Estimated Female Officers or Directors:
Hot Spot for Advancement for Women/Minorities:

Sales, profits and employees may be estimates. Financial information, benefits and other data can change quickly and may vary from those stated here.

NPR (National Public Radio)

www.npr.org

NAIC Code: 515111

TYPES OF BUSINESS:
Radio Networks, Traditional, Satellite and Online

BRANDS/DIVISIONS/AFFILIATES:
Corporation for Public Broadcasting
Morning Edition
All Things Considered
Planet Money
NPR Fresh Air
Best of Car Talk
NPR Generation Listen
NPR.Org

CONTACTS: Note: Officers with more than one job title may be intentionally listed here more than once.
Jarl Mohn, CEO
Loren Mayor, COO
Deborah A. Cowan, CFO
Meg Goldthwaite, CMO
Mike Starling, Exec. Dir.-Tech. Research Center & Labs
Marty Garrison, VP-IT
Marty Garrison, VP-Tech. Oper.
Marty Garrison, VP-Broadcast Eng.
Joyce Slocum, Chief Admin. Officer
Terri Minatra, General Counsel
Sarah Lumbard, VP-Oper. & Content Strategy
Monique Hanson, Chief Development Officer
Zach Brand, VP-NPR Digital Media
Deborah A. Cowan, VP-Finance
Kinsey Wilson, Chief Content Officer
Stephen Moss, CEO/Pres., National Public Media
Joyce MacDonald, Chief of Staff
Eric Nuzum, VP-Programming
Marty Garrison, VP-Distribution

GROWTH PLANS/SPECIAL FEATURES:
NPR (National Public Radio), owned by the Corporation for Public Broadcasting, is a nonprofit network of over 1,074 independent radio stations with an average of 36.6 million weekly listeners. The firm has 17 domestic bureaus, with an additional 17 bureaus internationally, and its programs reach over 150 countries. NPR aims to deliver informative journalism and cultural programming to listeners through its network of stations which have both local and national content. The firm has news and conversation programs, including Morning Edition, All Things Considered, TED Radio Hour, Weekend Edition, Planet Money, StoryCorps and NPR Shots; arts and culture programs, including NPR Fresh Air, Wait Wait-Don't Tell Me!, Ask Me Another, Best of Car Talk, All Songs Considered, World Cafe, Alt.Latino, First Listen and Bullseye; and special series, including NPR Generation Listen and NPR Books. The firm's digital services include its website NPR.Org, which offers additional news, media and entertainment content including blogs, multimedia downloads, streaming audio and free access to over 10 years of archived coverage. The firm also offers NPR Podcasts, which are delivered to 5.6 million unique users every week. The firm invests and researches broadcast radio technology through NPR Labs.

FINANCIAL DATA: Note: Data for latest year may not have been available at press time.

In U.S. $	2018	2017	2016	2015	2014	2013
Revenue		232,753,133	213,129,508	203,693,585	204,723,265	197,187,079
R&D Expense						
Operating Income						
Operating Margin %						
SGA Expense						
Net Income		2,378,953				
Operating Cash Flow						
Capital Expenditure						
EBITDA						
Return on Assets %						
Return on Equity %						
Debt to Equity						

CONTACT INFORMATION:
Phone: 202-513-3232   Fax:
Toll-Free:
Address: 1111 N. Capitol St., NE, Washington, DC 20002 United States

STOCK TICKER/OTHER:
Stock Ticker: Nonprofit   Exchange:
Employees: 710   Fiscal Year Ends: 12/31
Parent Company: Corporation for Public Broadcasting

SALARIES/BONUSES:
Top Exec. Salary: $ Bonus: $
Second Exec. Salary: $ Bonus: $

OTHER THOUGHTS:
Estimated Female Officers or Directors: 17
Hot Spot for Advancement for Women/Minorities: Y

Sales, profits and employees may be estimates. Financial information, benefits and other data can change quickly and may vary from those stated here.

NTN Buzztime Inc

NAIC Code: 511210G

www.buzztime.com

TYPES OF BUSINESS:
Computer Software, Electronic Games, Apps & Entertainment
On-Site Wireless Communications Products

BRANDS/DIVISIONS/AFFILIATES:

CONTACTS:
Note: Officers with more than one job title may be intentionally listed here more than once.
Allen Wolff, CFO
Sandra Gurrola, Chief Accounting Officer
Ram Krishnan, Director
Jeff Berg, Director

GROWTH PLANS/SPECIAL FEATURES:

NTN Buzztime, Inc. provides marketing services through interactive game content for hospitality venues that offer the games free to their customers. The company has evolved from a developer and distributor of content to an interactive entertainment network provider that helps the company's network subscribers acquire, engage and retain their patrons. Built on an extended network platform, this entertainment system has historically allowed multiple players to interact at the venue, but also enables competition between different venues, referred to as massively multiplayer gaming. The company is now embarking on a complete change of network architecture, technology platform and player engagement paradigm, otherwise known as the next generation product line or Next-Gen. NTN charges subscription fees for its service to network subscribers and sells advertising airs on in-venue screens as well as in conjunction with customized games. These games are available in locations in the U.S. and Canada, with over 115 million games played per year. Approximately 56% of the company's network subscriber venues are related to national and regional restaurants, including Buffalo Wild Wings, Buffalo Wings & Rings, Old Chicago, Native Grill & Wings, Houlihans, Beef O'Brady's, Boston Pizza and Arooga's. The majority of NTN Buzztime's annual revenue is derived from the the U.S. (approximately 97%), with the remaining 3% from Canada.

Employees of NTN Buzztime receive medical and dental insurance, annual performance reviews, wellness programs, flexible scheduling and holiday pay.

FINANCIAL DATA:
Note: Data for latest year may not have been available at press time.

In U.S. $	2018	2017	2016	2015	2014	2013
Revenue		21,274,000	22,312,000	24,519,000	26,046,000	23,749,000
R&D Expense						
Operating Income		-1,402,000	-2,278,000	-6,600,000	-4,074,000	-1,119,000
Operating Margin %		-6.59%	-10.20%	-26.91%	-15.64%	-4.71%
SGA Expense		15,587,000	16,458,000	18,060,000	18,367,000	16,449,000
Net Income		-1,077,000	-2,923,000	-7,226,000	-5,030,000	-1,053,000
Operating Cash Flow		549,000	23,000	-4,180,000	-6,385,000	1,493,000
Capital Expenditure		1,452,000	840,000	1,632,000	1,901,000	2,449,000
EBITDA		1,804,000	578,000	-3,626,000	-1,978,000	1,868,000
Return on Assets %		-6.47%	-17.65%	-37.36%	-26.66%	-7.49%
Return on Equity %		-22.43%	-73.86%	-97.84%	-49.99%	-12.32%
Debt to Equity		0.03	1.32	1.69	0.29	0.11

CONTACT INFORMATION:
Phone: 760 438-7400 Fax: 760 438-7470
Toll-Free:
Address: 2231 Rutherford Rd., Ste. 200, Carlsbad, CA 92008 United States

STOCK TICKER/OTHER:
Stock Ticker: NTN
Employees: 109
Parent Company:

Exchange: ASE
Fiscal Year Ends: 12/31

SALARIES/BONUSES:
Top Exec. Salary: $350,000 Bonus: $
Second Exec. Salary: $265,000 Bonus: $

OTHER THOUGHTS:
Estimated Female Officers or Directors: 2
Hot Spot for Advancement for Women/Minorities:

Oak View Group

www.oakviewgroup.com

NAIC Code: 541611

TYPES OF BUSINESS:
Administrative Management and General Management Consulting Services

BRANDS/DIVISIONS/AFFILIATES:
OVG Business Development
OVG Global Partnership
OVG Media & Conferences
OVG Arena Alliance
OVG Facilities
Prevent Advisors
PollStar

CONTACTS:
Note: Officers with more than one job title may be intentionally listed here more than once.

Tim Leiweke, CEO

GROWTH PLANS/SPECIAL FEATURES:
Oak View Group is a family of companies engaged in alliance, consulting, sponsorship, partnership, venture capital and facilities businesses within the sports and live entertainment industry. OVG Business Development offers services and solutions for venue design, venue construction, brand strategy, premium seating strategy/execution, ticketing, security/terrorism prevention, team operations, marketing, social media campaign analysis, event bids and media rights. OVG Global Partnership creates and connects people with sports and entertainment brands via storytelling, sponsorship sales and partnership consulting. OVG Media & Conferences communicates relevant industry information and builds innovative experiences. Its partners include VenuesNow, PollStar and SportTechie. OVG Arena Alliance provides consulting services to each venue member, including business review, negotiations, ticketing strategy, pricing, sales, inventory optimization, evaluation of current processes, operating expenses, database management/utilization, evaluation of event scheduling, venue security, media rights and labor negotiations (unions). This company also offers provision services such as establishing artist residencies at the venue, packaging Alliance members together for entertainment tours, activating reality television and social media brands and providing member access. OVG Facilities provides venue management and event programming services. It also provides venue assessments, and security and emergency preparedness services. Last, Prevent Advisors combines the knowledge and expertise of counterterrorism experts, leaders in safety and security, and venue operators to deliver safe and secure environments. In mid-2017, Oak View Group acquired PollStar, which offers print and online publications.

FINANCIAL DATA:
Note: Data for latest year may not have been available at press time.

In U.S. $	2018	2017	2016	2015	2014	2013
Revenue						
R&D Expense						
Operating Income						
Operating Margin %						
SGA Expense						
Net Income						
Operating Cash Flow						
Capital Expenditure						
EBITDA						
Return on Assets %						
Return on Equity %						
Debt to Equity						

CONTACT INFORMATION:
Phone: 310-954-4800 Fax:
Toll-Free:
Address: 1100 Glendon Ave., Ste. 2100, Los Angeles, CA 90024 United States

STOCK TICKER/OTHER:
Stock Ticker: Private
Employees:
Parent Company:

Exchange:
Fiscal Year Ends:

SALARIES/BONUSES:
Top Exec. Salary: $ Bonus: $
Second Exec. Salary: $ Bonus: $

OTHER THOUGHTS:
Estimated Female Officers or Directors:
Hot Spot for Advancement for Women/Minorities:

Oprah Winfrey Network (OWN)

NAIC Code: 515210

www.oprah.com/own

TYPES OF BUSINESS:
Cable TV Network
Online News and Entertainment
Film Production

BRANDS/DIVISIONS/AFFILIATES:
Discovery Inc
Harpo Productions Inc
Greenleaf
Black Love
Book of John Gray (The)
Checked Inn
Oprah.com
WatchOWN.tv

CONTACTS: Note: Officers with more than one job title may be intentionally listed here more than once.
Oprah Winfrey, CEO
Neal Kirsch, Pres.
Joe Klopp, CFO
Harriet Seitler, CMO
David Gleason, Sr. VP-Research
Rita Mullin, Exec. VP-Programming & Dev.
Peggy Panosh, Sr. VP-Consumer Mktg.
Tina Perry, Sr. VP
Nicole Nichols, Sr. VP-Strategy
Glenn Kaino, Sr. VP-Digital
Nicole Nichols, Sr. VP-Comm.
Erik Logan, Co-Pres.
Kathy Kayse, Exec. VP-Advertising Sales
Scott Garner, Sr. VP-Scheduling & Acquisitions
Mashawn Nix, Sr. VP-Programming
Oprah Winfrey, Chmn.
Meg Lowe, Sr. VP-Dist. & Strategy

GROWTH PLANS/SPECIAL FEATURES:
The Oprah Winfrey Network (OWN) is a 24-hour-a-day cable network that provides premium scripted and unscripted, inspiring programming. OWN is a joint venture between Discovery Communications, Inc. (majority share), and Oprah Winfrey's Harpo Productions, Inc. (minority share). OWN's current programming include: Greenleaf, a television drama series featuring a family with secrets and lies, but have a megachurch in Memphis; Black Love, a docuseries that features love stories from the Black community, in an effort to show the various ways they make a marriage work; The Book of John Gray, a drama docuseries featuring an associate pastor at Joel Osteen's Lakewood Church in Houston, Texas; and Checked Inn, a docuseries featuring Essence magazine editor-in-chief Monique Greenwood as she pursues her dream of running her own bed and breakfast. OWN also includes the Oprah.com digital platform. OWN can be accessed anytime, anywhere via WatchOWN.tv or mobile devices and connected TVs.

FINANCIAL DATA: Note: Data for latest year may not have been available at press time.

In U.S. $	2018	2017	2016	2015	2014	2013
Revenue						
R&D Expense						
Operating Income						
Operating Margin %						
SGA Expense						
Net Income						
Operating Cash Flow						
Capital Expenditure						
EBITDA						
Return on Assets %						
Return on Equity %						
Debt to Equity						

CONTACT INFORMATION:
Phone: 323-602-5500 Fax: 323-602-5680
Toll-Free:
Address: 5700 Wilshire Blvd., Ste. 120, Los Angeles, CA 90036 United States

STOCK TICKER/OTHER:
Stock Ticker: Joint Venture
Employees: 530
Parent Company: Discovery Inc

Exchange:
Fiscal Year Ends:

SALARIES/BONUSES:
Top Exec. Salary: $ Bonus: $
Second Exec. Salary: $ Bonus: $

OTHER THOUGHTS:
Estimated Female Officers or Directors: 9
Hot Spot for Advancement for Women/Minorities: Y

Sales, profits and employees may be estimates. Financial information, benefits and other data can change quickly and may vary from those stated here.

Oriental Land Co Ltd

NAIC Code: 713110

www.olc.co.jp

TYPES OF BUSINESS:
Amusement and Theme Parks
Theme Parks
Resorts
Monorail

BRANDS/DIVISIONS/AFFILIATES:
Maihama Corporation Co Ltd
Photo Works Co Ltd
Design Factory Co Ltd
Milial Resort Hotels Co Ltd
Ikspiari Co Ltd
Maihama Resort Line Co Ltd
Green and Arts Co Ltd
Bay Food Service Co Ltd

CONTACTS: *Note: Officers with more than one job title may be intentionally listed here more than once.*

Toshio Kagami, CEO
Kyoichiro Uenishi, Pres.
Toshio Kagami, Chmn.

GROWTH PLANS/SPECIAL FEATURES:

Oriental Land Co., Ltd. develops, operates and manages theme parks, hotels and other properties. The theme park business division includes two parks: Tokyo Disneyland and Tokyo DisneySea, which have a combined annual attendance of more than 25 million. Tokyo Disneyland is composed of seven areas themed to adventure, the future and more; and Tokyo DisneySea features myths and legends of the sea, with seven distinct themed ports. Subsidiaries within this segment include: Maihama Corporation Co. Ltd., Photo Works Co. Ltd., Design Factory Co. Ltd., Resort Costuming Service Co. Ltd., MBN Co. Ltd. and M Tech Co. Ltd. The hotel business division is comprised of eight facilities, including Disney Ambassador Hotel, Tokyo DisneySea Hotel MiraCosta, Palm & Fountain Terrace Hotel, Urayasu Brighton Hotel and Kyoto Brighton Hotel. Milial Resort Hotels Co., Ltd. is Oriental Land's subsidiary within this segment. The other business division includes: a shopping, dining and entertainment complex called Ikspiari; and a monorail service running within the Tokyo Disney Resort. Subsidiaries within this segment include Ikspiari Co. Ltd., Maihama Resort Line Co. Ltd., Green and Arts Co. Ltd. and Bay Food Service Co. Ltd.

FINANCIAL DATA: *Note: Data for latest year may not have been available at press time.*

In U.S. $	2018	2017	2016	2015	2014	2013
Revenue	4,445,681,000	4,431,471,000	4,316,498,000	4,325,198,000	4,392,735,000	3,668,800,000
R&D Expense						
Operating Income	1,022,976,000	1,049,570,000	995,816,600	1,025,944,000	1,061,999,000	755,667,500
Operating Margin %	23.01	23.68%	23.07%	23.72%	24.17%	20.59%
SGA Expense						
Net Income	753,107,400	764,080,600	685,737,600	668,438,300	654,598,900	477,552,700
Operating Cash Flow	1,139,619,000	1,090,930,000	1,028,773,000	978,712,100	1,119,342,000	853,201,900
Capital Expenditure	536,017,700	466,625,800	313,882,100	259,470,500	172,473,300	216,217,700
EBITDA	1,398,700,000	1,422,418,000	1,350,373,000	1,352,924,000	1,400,759,000	1,100,762,000
Return on Assets %	9.19%	9.92%	9.49%	10.21%	10.69%	8.07%
Return on Equity %	11.66%	12.72%	12.43%	13.62%	15.24%	12.62%
Debt to Equity	0.07	0.08	0.08	0.09	0.10	0.24

CONTACT INFORMATION:
Phone: 81 473052045   Fax:
Toll-Free:
Address: 1-1 Maihama, Urayasu-City, Chiba, Chiba, 279-8511 Japan

SALARIES/BONUSES:
Top Exec. Salary: $ Bonus: $
Second Exec. Salary: $ Bonus: $

STOCK TICKER/OTHER:
Stock Ticker: OLCLF   Exchange: PINX
Employees: 4,348   Fiscal Year Ends:
Parent Company:

OTHER THOUGHTS:
Estimated Female Officers or Directors:
Hot Spot for Advancement for Women/Minorities:

Sales, profits and employees may be estimates. Financial information, benefits and other data can change quickly and may vary from those stated here.

Outerwall Inc

NAIC Code: 454210

www.outerwall.com

TYPES OF BUSINESS:
DVD Rental Vending Machines
Coin Exchange Machines
Wireless Device Refurbishing and Reselling

BRANDS/DIVISIONS/AFFILIATES:
Apollo Global Management LLC
Coinstar
Redbox
ecoATM

GROWTH PLANS/SPECIAL FEATURES:
Outerwall, Inc. is a leading provider of automated retail solutions. The company's core offering consists of Coinstar kiosks, where consumers convert coins either into cash, a no-fee eGift card or a charity donation. There is no need to sort or count the coins; instead, by pressing the Start button on the kiosk and pouring the coins into the Coinstar tray, the machine issues a voucher that can be used in that store, or exchanged for cash. Coinstar kiosks can be found in grocery stores and other types of retail stores such as hypermarkets and discount department stores throughout the U.S., the U.K., Ireland and Canada. Outerwall is privately-owned by Apollo Global Management, LLC, a global alternative investment manager that also owns and operates Redbox and ecoATM kiosks.

CONTACTS:
Note: Officers with more than one job title may be intentionally listed here more than once.

Erik E. Prusch, CEO
Galen Smith, CFO
Donald Rench, General Counsel
David Maquera, President, Divisional
James Gaherity, President, Subsidiary
Susan Johnston, Vice President, Divisional

FINANCIAL DATA:
Note: Data for latest year may not have been available at press time.

In U.S. $	2018	2017	2016	2015	2014	2013
Revenue	1,900,000,000	2,000,000,000	2,100,000,000	2,193,210,880	2,303,002,880	2,306,600,960
R&D Expense						
Operating Income						
Operating Margin %						
SGA Expense						
Net Income				44,337,000	106,618,000	174,792,000
Operating Cash Flow						
Capital Expenditure						
EBITDA						
Return on Assets %						
Return on Equity %						
Debt to Equity						

CONTACT INFORMATION:
Phone: 425 943-8000   Fax: 425 943-8030
Toll-Free: 800-928-2274
Address: 1800 114th Ave. S.E., Bellevue, WA 98004 United States

SALARIES/BONUSES:
Top Exec. Salary: $ Bonus: $
Second Exec. Salary: $ Bonus: $

STOCK TICKER/OTHER:
Stock Ticker: Subsidiary   Exchange:
Employees: 2,670   Fiscal Year Ends: 12/31
Parent Company: Apollo Global Management LLC

OTHER THOUGHTS:
Estimated Female Officers or Directors: 4
Hot Spot for Advancement for Women/Minorities: Y

Sales, profits and employees may be estimates. Financial information, benefits and other data can change quickly and may vary from those stated here.

Palace Entertainment Holdings LLC

www.palaceentertainment.com

NAIC Code: 713110

TYPES OF BUSINESS:
Amusement Parks
Auto Racetracks
Water Parks

BRANDS/DIVISIONS/AFFILIATES:
Parques Reunidos SA
Castle Park
Dutch Wonderland
Noah's Ark
Raging Waters
WetnWild
Boomers
Malubu Grand Prix

CONTACTS:
Note: Officers with more than one job title may be intentionally listed here more than once.

Rolf Paegert, COO
Fernando Eiroa, Pres.
Meghan Gardner, Dir.-Mktg.
Sam Sutton, Exec. VP-Human Resources
Dan Vogt, Exec. Dir.-IT

GROWTH PLANS/SPECIAL FEATURES:
Palace Entertainment Holdings, LLC, a subsidiary of Parques Reunidos SA, owns and operates multiple-attraction entertainment and amusement parks designed for families. The company's parks are located in 10 U.S. states, namely California, Connecticut, Florida, Georgia, Hawaii, New Hampshire, New York, North Carolina, Pennsylvania and Washington. Palace Entertainment hosts millions of visitors annually at its 21 locations, which are divided into three groups: theme parks, water parks and family entertainment centers. Theme parks include: Castle Park, Dutch Wonderland, Idlewilde & Soak Zone, Kennywood, Lake Compounce, Miami Seaquarium, Sea Life Park Hawaii and Story Land. Water parks include: Noah's Ark, Raging Waters, Sandcastle, Splish Splash, Water Country and Wet-n-Wild. Family entertainment centers include Boomers, Malibu Grand Prix and Mountasia. Together these attractions provide family-oriented activities such as roller coasters, Ferris wheels, live shows, variable depth pools, water slides, animal shows, miniature golf courses, arcade games and more. Parent Parques Reunidos operates a diversified portfolio of more than 60 attraction parks, animal parks, water parks, family entertainment centers and other attractions.

FINANCIAL DATA:
Note: Data for latest year may not have been available at press time.

In U.S. $	2018	2017	2016	2015	2014	2013
Revenue						
R&D Expense						
Operating Income						
Operating Margin %						
SGA Expense						
Net Income						
Operating Cash Flow						
Capital Expenditure						
EBITDA						
Return on Assets %						
Return on Equity %						
Debt to Equity						

CONTACT INFORMATION:
Phone: 949-261-0404
Fax: 949-261-1414
Toll-Free:
Address: 4590 MacArthur Blvd., Ste. 400, Newport Beach, CA 92660 United States

STOCK TICKER/OTHER:
Stock Ticker: Subsidiary
Employees: 740
Parent Company: Parques Reunidos SA

Exchange:
Fiscal Year Ends: 12/31

SALARIES/BONUSES:
Top Exec. Salary: $
Second Exec. Salary: $
Bonus: $
Bonus: $

OTHER THOUGHTS:
Estimated Female Officers or Directors:
Hot Spot for Advancement for Women/Minorities:

Panasonic Corporation

NAIC Code: 334310

www.panasonic.com

TYPES OF BUSINESS:
Audio & Video Equipment, Manufacturing
Lithium Rechargeable Batteries
Home Appliances
Electronic Components
Cellular Phones
Medical Equipment
Photovoltaic Equipment
Telecommunications Equipment

BRANDS/DIVISIONS/AFFILIATES:
PanaHome
Technics
Panasonic System Solutions Co North America
Connected Solutions Company of North America
Panasonic System Communications Co North America
Panasonic Media Entertainment Company
Panasonic Factory Solutions Company of America

CONTACTS: Note: Officers with more than one job title may be intentionally listed here more than once.
Kazuhiro Tsuga, CEO
Shusaku Nagae, Chmn.

GROWTH PLANS/SPECIAL FEATURES:
Panasonic Corporation produces consumer, professional and industrial electronics products under brand names such as Panasonic, Technics and PanaHome. The company owns 592 consolidated companies around the world and operates in four business segments: Appliances Company, Eco Solutions Company, Connected Solutions Company and Automotive & Industrial Systems Company. The Appliances Company develops and manufactures home appliances, personal-care products, consumer electronics as well as commercial-use heating/refrigeration/air-conditioning equipment. The Eco Solutions Company develops, manufactures and sells lighting fixtures, lamps, lighting devices, wiring devices, distribution panelboards, housing-related materials and equipment, solar photovoltaic power generation systems, storage batteries, ventilation fans, and nursing care equipment and services as well as the provision of business solutions in various areas. The Connected Solutions Company focuses on the development, manufacturing and sales of products as well as system integration, installation, support and maintenance in the areas of aviation, manufacturing, entertainment, retail and logistics. The Automotive & Industrial Systems Company is engaged in the development, manufacture and sales of automotive infotainment and electronics products (such as car-use-multimedia-related equipment and electrical components), energy products (such as lithium-ion batteries and primary batteries) and industrial devices (such as electronic components, electromechanical control components, electronic materials, semiconductors, display and electric motors). In January 2018, Panasonic announced the establishment of Panasonic System Solutions Company of North America, which will consolidate four existing divisions of Panasonic Corporation of North America: Connected Solutions Company North America; Panasonic System Communications Company of North America, a provider of security camera systems, ruggedized personal computers and POS systems; Panasonic Media Entertainment Company, which provides projectors, broadcast-use cameras and other products to the entertainment industry; and Panasonic Factory Solutions Company of America, whose products include surface mounted machines for circuit board manufacturing, welding robots and factory systems management software.

FINANCIAL DATA: Note: Data for latest year may not have been available at press time.

In U.S. $	2018	2017	2016	2015	2014	2013
Revenue	74,040,560,000	68,118,390,000	70,066,390,000	71,562,750,000	71,762,210,000	67,741,220,000
R&D Expense						
Operating Income	3,436,340,000	2,489,667,000	3,856,013,000	3,542,529,000	5,088,694,000	2,344,381,000
Operating Margin %	4.64	4.67%	5.50%	4.95%	3.94%	2.20%
SGA Expense	17,976,490,000	17,094,540,000	16,677,880,000	16,751,180,000	16,627,320,000	15,974,890,000
Net Income	2,189,448,000	1,385,426,000	1,792,594,000	1,664,858,000	1,117,190,000	-6,996,234,000
Operating Cash Flow	3,925,330,000	3,574,967,000	3,698,056,000	4,558,687,000	5,398,022,000	3,142,160,000
Capital Expenditure	4,411,574,000	3,170,581,000	2,243,210,000	2,079,271,000	1,871,243,000	2,969,798,000
EBITDA	6,410,146,000	5,281,454,000	4,719,650,000	4,513,116,000	5,187,175,000	-309,977,000
Return on Assets %	3.84%	2.57%	3.34%	3.21%	2.27%	-12.57%
Return on Equity %	14.39%	9.11%	10.95%	10.64%	8.56%	-47.23%
Debt to Equity	0.50	0.60	0.41	0.39	0.36	0.52

CONTACT INFORMATION:
Phone: 81 669081121 Fax:
Toll-Free:
Address: 1006 Oaza Kadoma, Kadoma City, Osaka, 571-8501 Japan

SALARIES/BONUSES:
Top Exec. Salary: $ Bonus: $
Second Exec. Salary: $ Bonus: $

STOCK TICKER/OTHER:
Stock Ticker: PCRFF
Employees: 274,143
Parent Company:

Exchange: PINX
Fiscal Year Ends: 03/31

OTHER THOUGHTS:
Estimated Female Officers or Directors:
Hot Spot for Advancement for Women/Minorities:

Sales, profits and employees may be estimates. Financial information, benefits and other data can change quickly and may vary from those stated here.

ň
Pandora Media Inc

www.pandora.com

NAIC Code: 515111

TYPES OF BUSINESS:
Radio Networks, Traditional, Satellite and Online

BRANDS/DIVISIONS/AFFILIATES:
Music Genome Project
Pandora Plus
Pandora Premium
Pandor API

CONTACTS: Note: Officers with more than one job title may be intentionally listed here more than once.
Naveen Chopra, CFO
Karen Walker, Chief Accounting Officer
Aimee Lapic, Chief Marketing Officer
David Gerbitz, COO
Gregory Maffei, Director
Roger Lynch, Director
Stephen Bene, General Counsel
Kristen Robinson, Other Executive Officer
John Trimble, Other Executive Officer
Christopher Phillips, Other Executive Officer

GROWTH PLANS/SPECIAL FEATURES:
Pandora Media, Inc. is an internet-based music streaming service. Available in the U.S., Australia and New Zealand, and annually streams 21.96 billion hours of internet radio by 68.8 million active users. The company's website enables users to build unique virtual radio stations based on music preferences. The firm's technology is based in part on the Music Genome Project, which analyzes and catalogues thousands of songs from multiple genres to create a comprehensive database that breaks down songs by hundreds of individual musical attributes. Pandora's catalog contains over 1.5 million songs from more than 250,000 artists in 600 genres and sub-genres. The company offers free accounts, which are currently ad-supported but restrict the ability to skip songs; and premium subscriptions through Pandora Plus, which give listeners the ability to skip an unlimited amount of songs, has no limit on monthly listening hours, delivers higher quality audio and removes advertisements. The firm also operates Pandora Premium, its paid subscription service. Pandora Premium offers a unique, on-demand experience, providing users with the ability to search, play and collect songs and albums, build playlists on their own or with the tap of a button and automatically generate playlists based on the user's listening activity. The firm also offers mobile listening via smartphones and tablets. Pandora has established partnerships with consumer electronics manufacturers to integrate its Pandora API software into new devices, as well as automakers like Honda, Ford, Lexus and Mercedes. Pandora is now available on more than 1,000 partner integrations, including consumer electronic devices and various car models. In September 2018, Pandora announced that it had agreed to be acquired by SiriusXM Holdings, Inc., the satellite radio service provider, for $3.5 billion, potentially creating one of the largest audio entertainment companies in the world.

Pandora offers employees different insurance and savings plans.

FINANCIAL DATA: Note: Data for latest year may not have been available at press time.

In U.S. $	2018	2017	2016	2015	2014	2013
Revenue		1,466,812,000	1,384,826,000	1,164,043,000	920,802,000	427,145,000
R&D Expense		154,325,000	141,636,000	84,581,000	53,153,000	18,118,000
Operating Income		1,492,364,000	-318,759,000	-169,991,000	-30,128,000	-37,702,000
Operating Margin %		101.74%	-23.01%	-14.60%	-3.27%	-8.82%
SGA Expense			667,027,000	552,112,000	389,773,000	155,962,000
Net Income		-518,395,000	-342,978,000	-169,661,000	-30,406,000	-38,148,000
Operating Cash Flow		-210,709,000	-181,691,000	-42,082,000	21,029,000	-250,000
Capital Expenditure		35,813,000	89,979,000	32,074,000	30,039,000	7,580,000
EBITDA		-426,902,000	-256,305,000	-145,533,000	-14,697,000	-30,532,000
Return on Assets %		-47.51%	-28.28%	-17.05%	-4.27%	-19.22%
Return on Equity %		-158.02%	-52.86%	-25.57%	-5.57%	-37.48%
Debt to Equity		1.78	0.61	0.31		

CONTACT INFORMATION:
Phone: 510 451-4100 Fax:
Toll-Free:
Address: 2101 Webster St., Ste. 1650, Oakland, CA 94612 United States

STOCK TICKER/OTHER:
Stock Ticker: P
Employees: 2,488
Parent Company:

Exchange: NYS
Fiscal Year Ends: 12/31

SALARIES/BONUSES:
Top Exec. Salary: $493,927 Bonus: $300,000
Second Exec. Salary: $448,750 Bonus: $100,000

OTHER THOUGHTS:
Estimated Female Officers or Directors: 5
Hot Spot for Advancement for Women/Minorities: Y

Paramount Pictures Corporation

NAIC Code: 512110

www.paramount.com

TYPES OF BUSINESS:
Film Production & Distribution
Television Production
Post-Production Services
Home Video & DVD Production & Distribution

BRANDS/DIVISIONS/AFFILIATES:
Viacom Inc
Paramount Pictures
Paramount Classics
MTV Films
Nickelodeon Movies
Paramount Television
Paramount Network

CONTACTS:
Note: Officers with more than one job title may be intentionally listed here more than once.

James N. Gianopulos, CEO
Nicole Clemens, Pres.
Mark Badagliacca, CFO
Marc Evans, Pres., Prod.
Amy Powell, Pres., Insurge Pictures & Digital Entertainment
Randall Baumberger, Pres., Paramount Studio Group
Dennis Maguire, Pres., Paramount Worldwide Home Media Dist.
Adam Goodman, Pres., Paramount Film Group
LeeAnne Stables, Pres., Consumer Prod.
Andrew Gumpert, COO
Anthony Marcoly, Pres., Paramount Pictures Int'l
Hal Richardson, Pres., Home Media Distribution

GROWTH PLANS/SPECIAL FEATURES:

Paramount Pictures Corporation, a subsidiary of Viacom, Inc., produces and distributes feature films and television programs. The firm distributes products under brands such as Paramount Pictures, Paramount Classics, MTV Films and Nickelodeon Movies. Its global operations are managed through business divisions such as entertainment, distribution, international, licensing, production and parks/resorts, among others. The firm's studio assets include sound stages, interior/exterior sets, production offices and related built-in amenities. Paramount releases about a dozen films annually and is also engaged in producing television shows. As of December 2018, Paramount Pictures' movie showcases included Instant Family, Nobody's Fool, Overlord, Bumblebee, Wonder Park, Mission Impossible: Fallout, Rocketman, Pet Sematary, Scrooged 30th, What Men Want, A Quiet Place, Book Club, Action Point, Sherlock Gnomes, Downsizing and many more. The television department is divided into two groups: Paramount Television and Paramount Network. Paramount Television is a studio and develops and finances a wide range of cutting-edge and entertaining TV content across all media platforms for distribution worldwide. Its shows include Jack Ryan, Berlin Station, The Haunting, The Alienist, First Wives Club, Maniac and more. Paramount Network is a premium entertainment destination that offers story-telling with original scripted and non-scripted series. Its shows include American Woman, Yellowstone, Lip Sync Battle, Ink Master, Bar Rescue, Bellator MMA and more.

The company offers its employees accident, life, disability, medical, dental and vision insurance; a 401(k) plan; flexible spending accounts; same sex domestic partner benefits; and an employee assistance program.

FINANCIAL DATA:
Note: Data for latest year may not have been available at press time.

In U.S. $	2018	2017	2016	2015	2014	2013
Revenue	2,812,000,000	2,700,000,000	2,662,000,000	2,883,000,000	3,725,000,000	4,282,000,000
R&D Expense						
Operating Income						
Operating Margin %						
SGA Expense						
Net Income						
Operating Cash Flow						
Capital Expenditure						
EBITDA						
Return on Assets %						
Return on Equity %						
Debt to Equity						

CONTACT INFORMATION:
Phone: 323-956-5000   Fax: 323-956-1388
Toll-Free:
Address: 5555 Melrose Ave., Hollywood, CA 90038 United States

SALARIES/BONUSES:
Top Exec. Salary: $ Bonus: $
Second Exec. Salary: $ Bonus: $

STOCK TICKER/OTHER:
Stock Ticker: Subsidiary   Exchange:
Employees: Fiscal Year Ends: 12/31
Parent Company: Viacom Inc

OTHER THOUGHTS:
Estimated Female Officers or Directors: 4
Hot Spot for Advancement for Women/Minorities: Y

Sales, profits and employees may be estimates. Financial information, benefits and other data can change quickly and may vary from those stated here.

Patch Media Corporation

www.patch.com

NAIC Code: 519130

TYPES OF BUSINESS:
Online Publishing
Interactive News Media Service

BRANDS/DIVISIONS/AFFILIATES:
Hale Global
Patch.com
Give 5

CONTACTS:
Note: Officers with more than one job title may be intentionally listed here more than once.

Warren St. John, CEO
Andreas Turanski, CTO
Melanie Pereira, VP-Finance
Jim Lipuma, Sr. VP-Revenue
Charles C. Hale, Chmn.

GROWTH PLANS/SPECIAL FEATURES:
Patch Media Corporation operates Patch.com, a website devoted to covering local news for individual towns and communities. The firm typically targets areas it believes would benefit from having access to information and news regarding local schools, businesses and government. These can include anything from inner-city neighborhoods to semi-rural districts and towns. Residents in each neighborhood or town, which the site refers to as patches, post information regarding news, events, automotive, athletics, health, dining, education, businesses, shopping, travel, nightlife and other local facts. The company seeks to fill in gaps for markets that are underserved by traditional media outlets. Each patch is presided over by writers, photographers, editors and videographers, but most content is supplied by members who contribute articles, reviews, photographs or classified items for sale. Members can then offer comments or suggestions on posted items and submit personal stories about their specific communities. A central team of editors at the company's headquarters offers advice and direction when needed. In addition to providing a media platform where individuals can obtain local information, Patch supports local charities through a program called Give 5 that donates free advertising space to help charities and organizations recruit local volunteers. The company is primarily supported by advertisements and enhanced company directories on each individual patch. Patch Media is majority-owned by Hale Global, a holding company that specializes in turnarounds mostly with technology firms.

FINANCIAL DATA:
Note: Data for latest year may not have been available at press time.

In U.S. $	2018	2017	2016	2015	2014	2013
Revenue						
R&D Expense						
Operating Income						
Operating Margin %						
SGA Expense						
Net Income						
Operating Cash Flow						
Capital Expenditure						
EBITDA						
Return on Assets %						
Return on Equity %						
Debt to Equity						

CONTACT INFORMATION:
Phone: 212-625-0331   Fax:
Toll-Free:
Address: 584 Broadway, Ste. 1206, New York, NY 10012 United States

STOCK TICKER/OTHER:
Stock Ticker: Subsidiary   Exchange:
Employees: Fiscal Year Ends:
Parent Company: Hale Global

SALARIES/BONUSES:
Top Exec. Salary: $ Bonus: $
Second Exec. Salary: $ Bonus: $

OTHER THOUGHTS:
Estimated Female Officers or Directors: 3
Hot Spot for Advancement for Women/Minorities: Y

Peak Resorts Inc

NAIC Code: 713920

www.peakresorts.com

TYPES OF BUSINESS:
Skiing Facilities

BRANDS/DIVISIONS/AFFILIATES:
Alpine Valley
Boston Mills
Hidden Valley
Jack Frost
Big Boulder
Liberty Mountain Resort
Mount Snow
Roundtop Mountain

CONTACTS:
Note: Officers with more than one job title may be intentionally listed here more than once.

Christopher Bub, CFO
Timothy Boyd, Chairman of the Board
Stephen Mueller, Director
Richard Deutsch, Vice President, Divisional

GROWTH PLANS/SPECIAL FEATURES:

Peak Resorts, Inc. operates individually-branded ski resorts in the U.S. As of December 2018, the firm operates 17 ski resorts primarily located in the Northeast and Midwest, 15 of which are company-owned. Most of the resorts are within 100 miles of major metropolitan markets, including New York City, Boston, Philadelphia, Baltimore, Washington D.C., Cleveland and St. Louis. They offer an array of activities, services and amenities, including snow skiing, snowboarding, terrain parks, tubing, dining, lodging, equipment rentals/sales and ski/snowboard instruction, as well as mountain biking, golf, zip line tours, music festivals and other summer activities. Park Resorts' properties include Alpine Valley in Ohio, Attitash in New Hampshire, Boston Mills in Ohio, Brandy Wine in Ohio, Crotched Mountain in New Hampshire, Hidden Valley in Missouri, Hunter Mountain in New York, Jack Frost in Pennsylvania, Big Boulder in Pennsylvania, Liberty Mountain Resort in Pennsylvania, Mad River in Ohio, Mount Snow in Vermont, Paoli Peaks in Indiana, Roundtop Mountain in Pennsylvania, Snow Creek in Missouri, Whitetail Mountain in Pennsylvania and Wildcat in New Hampshire. The Mad River resort is leased. In November 2018, Peak Resorts acquired Snow Time, Inc. adding three ski areas to its portfolio, including Liberty Mountain Resort, Whitetail Resort and Roundtop Mountain Resort.

FINANCIAL DATA:
Note: Data for latest year may not have been available at press time.

In U.S. $	2018	2017	2016	2015	2014	2013
Revenue	131,662,000	123,249,000	95,729,000	104,858,000	105,205,100	99,688,000
R&D Expense						
Operating Income	12,354,000	14,069,000	4,974,000	15,382,000	15,701,000	16,973,000
Operating Margin %		11.41%	5.19%	14.66%	14.92%	17.02%
SGA Expense	7,198,000	6,826,000	5,899,000	5,528,000	4,704,100	3,957,000
Net Income	1,352,000	1,241,000	-3,226,000	-1,854,000	-1,501,400	2,707,000
Operating Cash Flow	-210,000	12,663,000	10,193,000	6,872,000	9,762,200	14,125,000
Capital Expenditure	31,070,000	11,454,000	12,407,000	12,225,000	6,281,000	6,004,000
EBITDA	23,943,000	27,176,000	16,219,000	22,276,000	24,551,500	26,165,000
Return on Assets %		.13%	-1.16%	-.82%	-.73%	1.33%
Return on Equity %		.68%	-4.24%	-4.41%	-35.41%	54.25%
Debt to Equity		3.12	1.71	1.23	50.12	34.24

CONTACT INFORMATION:
Phone: 636 938-7474 Fax: 636 549-0064
Toll-Free:
Address: 17409 Hidden Valley Dr., Wildwood, MO 63025 United States

SALARIES/BONUSES:
Top Exec. Salary: $442,000   Bonus: $
Second Exec. Salary: $416,000   Bonus: $

STOCK TICKER/OTHER:
Stock Ticker: SKIS
Employees: 600
Parent Company:

Exchange: NAS
Fiscal Year Ends: 04/30

OTHER THOUGHTS:
Estimated Female Officers or Directors:
Hot Spot for Advancement for Women/Minorities:

Sales, profits and employees may be estimates. Financial information, benefits and other data can change quickly and may vary from those stated here.

Plunkett Research, Ltd.

Pearson North America
NAIC Code: 511130

www.pearsoned.com

TYPES OF BUSINESS:
Book Publishing
Education Services and Tests
Adult Learning
Higher Education Services
K-12 Curriculum and Services

BRANDS/DIVISIONS/AFFILIATES:
Pearson plc

CONTACTS:
Note: Officers with more than one job title may be intentionally listed here more than once.
John Fallon, CEO-Pearson PLC
Sidney Taurel, Chmn.-Pearson PLC

GROWTH PLANS/SPECIAL FEATURES:
Pearson North America is an education company providing courseware, assessment and digital services to teachers and students of all ages. Pearson North America is the largest market within its U.K.-based parent, Pearson plc, representing 65% of sales in 2017. The firm provides a range of products and services to institutions, governments and directly to individual learners. Pearson North America divides its products and services into three segments: PreK-12 education, higher education and professional. PreK-12 education offers assessment services, curriculum resources, online and blended learning solutions, professional development and consulting services, and grants and funding location services. Higher education services offer course content and digital resources, online program management, consulting services, curriculum services, grant help, online tutoring, interactive learning, interactive assessment, online courses, learning applications, alternative credentials, competency-based education and personalized help desk support. The professional segment offers professional development and skills training, including: assessment solutions designed to help organizations measure and make improvements to ensure the success of employees and learners, custom content, curriculum development, custom training courseware, informal learning programs, knowledge capture and transfer system solutions that facilitate the documentation of employees' expertise, managed education strategies, online mentoring, talent/leadership development and workforce education. Professional categories include non-profit, clinician, corporation, creative professional, government, healthcare professional, human resources professional, IT professional and youth organization.

FINANCIAL DATA:
Note: Data for latest year may not have been available at press time.

In U.S. $	2018	2017	2016	2015	2014	2013
Revenue	4,000,000,000	3,951,580,000	3,845,489,990	4,246,977,000	4,685,820,000	4,200,736,400
R&D Expense						
Operating Income						
Operating Margin %						
SGA Expense						
Net Income		531,555,000	-315,793,666	163,239,800	485,415,840	
Operating Cash Flow						
Capital Expenditure						
EBITDA						
Return on Assets %						
Return on Equity %						
Debt to Equity						

CONTACT INFORMATION:
Phone: 212-641-2400 Fax:
Toll-Free: 800-745-8489
Address: 330 Hudson St., New York, NY 10013 United States

SALARIES/BONUSES:
Top Exec. Salary: $ Bonus: $
Second Exec. Salary: $ Bonus: $

STOCK TICKER/OTHER:
Stock Ticker: Subsidiary
Employees: 16,295
Parent Company: Pearson plc

Exchange:
Fiscal Year Ends: 12/31

OTHER THOUGHTS:
Estimated Female Officers or Directors:
Hot Spot for Advancement for Women/Minorities:

Sales, profits and employees may be estimates. Financial information, benefits and other data can change quickly and may vary from those stated here.

Pearson PLC

NAIC Code: 511130

www.pearson.com

TYPES OF BUSINESS:
Book Publishing
Educational Products
Financial Newspapers
Online Publishing
Testing Services
Language Training Centers

BRANDS/DIVISIONS/AFFILIATES:
REVEL
MyLab and Mastering
Bug Club
Wall Street English

CONTACTS: Note: Officers with more than one job title may be intentionally listed here more than once.
John Fallon, CEO
Coram Williams, CFO
Anna Vikstrom Persson, Chief Human Resources Officer
Albert Hitchcock, Chief Technology and Operations Officer
Philip J. Hoffman, Corp. Sec.
John Makinson, CEO
Will Ethridge, CEO-North American Education
Kate James, Chief Corp. Affairs Officer
Sidney Taurel, Chmn.
David Shanks, CEO-Penguin Group USA, Inc.

GROWTH PLANS/SPECIAL FEATURES:

Pearson PLC is an international education company, with expertise in educational courseware and assessment, as well as a range of teaching and learning services powered by technology. The firm's products cover every stage of the education journey. REVEL is an interactive learning environment that enables students to read, practice and study in one continuous experience. It replaces the textbook and gives students everything they need for each course they take. The interactive learning environment seamlessly blends authors' narrative, media and assessment tools. Pearson's trademarked MyLab and Mastering offering enables educators to personalize/customize teaching and learning tools for individual students, since one approach to learning does not suit everyone. Bug Club is an independent reading solution for schools, encouraging reluctant readers to read online at home. Wall Street English is a global English language school for adults. It offers a flexible and entertaining approach to help learners stay motivated to achieve language goals. Pearson's online program management and U.K. qualifications platforms help people understand and manage the qualifications, requirements and education necessary for particular courses, schools and/or vocations. In February 2018, Pearson announced a three year strategic partnership in China with Microsoft Research Asia to integrate artificial intelligence into English language learning curriculum.

Pearson offers its employees health benefits, a profit-sharing scheme, retirement and savings plans and stock purchase plans.

FINANCIAL DATA: Note: Data for latest year may not have been available at press time.

In U.S. $	2018	2017	2016	2015	2014	2013
Revenue		5,699,384,000	5,748,636,000	5,642,554,000	6,155,284,000	6,401,546,000
R&D Expense		17,680,340				
Operating Income		570,822,400	357,395,400	540,513,200	544,301,900	732,471,200
Operating Margin %		10.01%	6.21%	7.09%	6.29%	7.97%
SGA Expense		2,744,241,000	2,823,803,000	2,740,452,000	2,986,714,000	2,878,107,000
Net Income		512,729,900	-2,951,354,000	1,039,351,000	594,817,200	679,430,200
Operating Cash Flow		376,338,700	517,781,400	266,468,000	574,611,000	449,585,800
Capital Expenditure		292,988,500	309,406,000	311,931,700	229,844,400	229,844,400
EBITDA		1,051,980,000	541,776,100	1,045,666,000	995,150,500	976,207,300
Return on Assets %		4.52%	-21.53%	7.14%	4.21%	4.82%
Return on Equity %		9.71%	-43.44%	13.28%	8.06%	9.45%
Debt to Equity		0.26	0.55	0.31	0.31	0.29

CONTACT INFORMATION:
Phone: 44 2070102000 Fax: 44 2070106060
Toll-Free:
Address: 80 Strand, London, WC2R ORL United Kingdom

STOCK TICKER/OTHER:
Stock Ticker: PSO Exchange: NYS
Employees: 30,339 Fiscal Year Ends: 12/31
Parent Company:

SALARIES/BONUSES:
Top Exec. Salary: $985,048 Bonus: $
Second Exec. Salary: $650,384 Bonus: $

OTHER THOUGHTS:
Estimated Female Officers or Directors: 4
Hot Spot for Advancement for Women/Minorities: Y

Sales, profits and employees may be estimates. Financial information, benefits and other data can change quickly and may vary from those stated here.

Penguin Group USA

www.penguin.com

NAIC Code: 511130

TYPES OF BUSINESS:
Book Publishing

GROWTH PLANS/SPECIAL FEATURES:
Penguin Group USA, the largest division of Penguin Random House, Inc., is one of the leading U.S. adult trade book publishers with a wide range of imprints and trademarks. Penguin Group's imprints include: Avery, Berkley, Blue Rider Press, Dutton, Penguin Books, Penguin Classics, The Penguin Press, Plume, Portfolio, G. P. Putnam's Sons, Riverhead, Sentinel, TarcherPerigee and Viking Books. In addition to its adult trade books, Penguin Young Readers Group is a global leader in children's publishing with preeminent imprints such as Dial Books, Dutton, Grosset & Dunlap, Kathy Dawson Books, Nancy Paulsen Books, Philomel, Puffin, G. P. Putnam's Sons, Razorbill, Viking and Frederick Warne.

BRANDS/DIVISIONS/AFFILIATES:
Penguin Random House Inc
Avery
Penguin Books
Penguin Classics
Penguin Press (The)
Dial Books
Dutton
Viking

CONTACTS: Note: Officers with more than one job title may be intentionally listed here more than once.
Madeline McIntosh, Pres.

FINANCIAL DATA: Note: Data for latest year may not have been available at press time.

In U.S. $	2018	2017	2016	2015	2014	2013
Revenue	860,000,000	850,000,000	833,693,000	972,804,000	876,400,000	700,000,000
R&D Expense						
Operating Income						
Operating Margin %						
SGA Expense						
Net Income						
Operating Cash Flow						
Capital Expenditure						
EBITDA						
Return on Assets %						
Return on Equity %						
Debt to Equity						

CONTACT INFORMATION:
Phone: 212-366-2000 Fax:
Toll-Free:
Address: 375 Hudson St., New York, NY 10014 United States

STOCK TICKER/OTHER:
Stock Ticker: Subsidiary Exchange:
Employees: Fiscal Year Ends:
Parent Company: Penguin Random House Inc

SALARIES/BONUSES:
Top Exec. Salary: $ Bonus: $
Second Exec. Salary: $ Bonus: $

OTHER THOUGHTS:
Estimated Female Officers or Directors:
Hot Spot for Advancement for Women/Minorities:

Sales, profits and employees may be estimates. Financial information, benefits and other data can change quickly and may vary from those stated here.

Penguin Random House

NAIC Code: 511130

www.penguinrandomhouse.com

TYPES OF BUSINESS:
Book Publishing

BRANDS/DIVISIONS/AFFILIATES:
Bertelsmann SE & Co KGaA
Pearson plc
DK
Penguin
Random House
Knopf Doubleday

CONTACTS:
Note: Officers with more than one job title may be intentionally listed here more than once.

Madeline McIntosh, CEO
Nihar Malaviya, COO
Jim Jonston, CFO
Sanyu Dillon, Exec. VP-Mktg.
Frank Steinnert, Chief Human Resources Officer
Jaci Updike, Pres.-Sales
Frank Sambeth, Chmn.
Gina Centrello, Pres., Random House Publishing Group
Maya Mavjee, Pres.
Gail Rebuck, Chmn.

GROWTH PLANS/SPECIAL FEATURES:
Penguin Random House is one of the world's largest English-language general trade book publishers. The company's publishing brands include DK (Dorling Kindersley), Penguin, Random House and Knopf Doubleday. Each publishing house has complete editorial freedom, meaning that each house has the freedom to publish what it wants without having to go through its parent company. Publishing under the Random House name, the company releases a broad variety of titles, including fiction, non-fiction and reference books, such as the widely popular Random House Webster's Collegiate Dictionary. Other divisions of the publishing house devote themselves to children's books, discount books, large print and audio books. The firm partners with nearly 250 independent publishing imprints. Together with its own imprints, Penguin Random House publishes over 70,000 digital and 15,000 print titles every year, with more than 100,000 eBooks available worldwide. The company's operations are located in the U.S., as well as in 20 countries worldwide. Bertelsmann SE & Co. KGaA holds a 75% stake in the firm, with Pearson plc holding the remaining 25%. In October 2018, Penguin Random House announced the merging/consolidation of its Random House and Crown publishing lines, but each will retain their distinct editorial identities.

The company offers its employees medical, dental, life and vision insurance; back-up child care; a 401(k); sabbatical programs; tuition reimbursement; and flexible spending accounts.

FINANCIAL DATA:
Note: Data for latest year may not have been available at press time.

In U.S. $	2018	2017	2016	2015	2014	2013
Revenue	3,620,000,000	3,600,000,000	3,541,000,000	4,130,000,000	3,572,385,900	2,852,320,150
R&D Expense						
Operating Income						
Operating Margin %						
SGA Expense						
Net Income			565,760,000	621,580,000	485,775,700	390,125,175
Operating Cash Flow						
Capital Expenditure						
EBITDA						
Return on Assets %						
Return on Equity %						
Debt to Equity						

CONTACT INFORMATION:
Phone: 212-782-9000 Fax: 212-940-7381
Toll-Free:
Address: 1745 Broadway, New York, NY 10019 United States

STOCK TICKER/OTHER:
Stock Ticker: Subsidiary
Employees: 12,000
Parent Company: Bertelsmann AG

Exchange:
Fiscal Year Ends: 12/31

SALARIES/BONUSES:
Top Exec. Salary: $ Bonus: $
Second Exec. Salary: $ Bonus: $

OTHER THOUGHTS:
Estimated Female Officers or Directors: 7
Hot Spot for Advancement for Women/Minorities: Y

Sales, profits and employees may be estimates. Financial information, benefits and other data can change quickly and may vary from those stated here.

Plunkett Research, Ltd.

Penn National Gaming Inc

www.pngaming.com

NAIC Code: 713210

TYPES OF BUSINESS:
Horse Racetracks
Casinos
Online Wagering

BRANDS/DIVISIONS/AFFILIATES:
Hollywood Casino
Meadows Casino (The)
L'Auberge Lake Charles
Boomtown Casino Biloxi
Argosy Casino Riverside
Tropicana Las Vegas
Zia Park Casino
Pinnacle Entertainment Inc

CONTACTS: Note: Officers with more than one job title may be intentionally listed here more than once.
Timothy Wilmott, CEO
William Fair, CFO
Peter Carlino, Chairman of the Board
Jay Snowden, COO
Carl Sottosanti, General Counsel

GROWTH PLANS/SPECIAL FEATURES:

Penn National Gaming, Inc. owns, operates or has ownership interests in gaming properties and racing facilities, primarily concentrating on slot machine entertainment. The company operates 40 facilities located throughout the U.S., which may include thoroughbred racetracks or greyhound racetracks as well as either land-based or dockside casinos. As of October 15, 2018, the company's facilities feature 49,400 gaming machines, 1,200 table games, 8,800 hotel rooms, 377 video game terminals and 193 food outlets. Just a few of Penn National's assets include: Hollywood Casino at Charles Town Races and The Meadows Casino, which are located in the northeastern portion of the country; L'Auberge Lake Charles and Boomtown Casino Biloxi, which are located in the southern region; Argosy Casino Riverside and River City Casino and Hotel, located in the midwest; and Tropicana Las Vegas and Zia Park Casino, located in the west. Racetracks and off-track wagering facilities (OTWs) provide areas for viewing import simulcast races of thoroughbred and standardbred horse racing, televised sporting events, placing pari-mutuel wagers and dining. Penn National operates two OTWs in Pennsylvania, and owns 50% of a leased OTW in New Jersey through joint venture Pennwood Racing, Inc. Racetracks and OTWs include, but are not limited to, Sam Houston Race Park, Freehold Raceway, Off-Track Wagering Lancaster and Off-Track Wagering York. In October 2018, Penn National acquired Pinnacle Entertainment, Inc. for $2.8 billion. For regulatory approval purposes, Pinnacle sold four properties to Boyd Gaming, and Penn National sold the real estate of Plainridge Park Casino to affiliate Faming and Leisure Properties, Inc., a real estate investment trust.

Penn National employees receive medical, dental, vision and prescription drug coverage; an employee assistance plan; life insurance; a 401(k); and flexible spending accounts for health and dependent care expenses.

FINANCIAL DATA: Note: Data for latest year may not have been available at press time.

In U.S. $	2018	2017	2016	2015	2014	2013
Revenue		3,147,970,000	3,034,380,000	2,838,358,000	2,590,527,000	2,918,754,000
R&D Expense						
Operating Income		553,524,000	543,016,000	507,888,000	80,667,000	360,445,000
Operating Margin %		17.57%	17.87%	17.89%	2.89%	12.35%
SGA Expense		514,487,000	462,302,000	449,433,000	862,119,000	596,092,000
Net Income		473,463,000	109,310,000	686,000	-233,195,000	-794,339,000
Operating Cash Flow		459,079,000	404,823,000	398,982,000	220,001,000	440,802,000
Capital Expenditure		100,761,000	100,310,000	249,845,000	228,145,000	199,913,000
EBITDA		708,779,000	851,074,000	759,198,000	-46,818,000	-520,459,000
Return on Assets %		9.27%	2.16%	.01%	-10.55%	-20.29%
Return on Equity %					-35.52%	-52.79%
Debt to Equity					2.21	1.34

CONTACT INFORMATION:
Phone: 610 373-2400 Fax: 610 376-4966
Toll-Free:
Address: 825 Berkshire Blvd., Ste. 200, Wyomissing, PA 19610 United States

SALARIES/BONUSES:
Top Exec. Salary: $1,496,731 Bonus: $
Second Exec. Salary: $897,642 Bonus: $

STOCK TICKER/OTHER:
Stock Ticker: PENN
Employees: 18,808
Parent Company:

Exchange: NAS
Fiscal Year Ends: 12/31

OTHER THOUGHTS:
Estimated Female Officers or Directors: 1
Hot Spot for Advancement for Women/Minorities:

Sales, profits and employees may be estimates. Financial information, benefits and other data can change quickly and may vary from those stated here.

Pinnacle Entertainment Inc

NAIC Code: 721120

www.pnkinc.com

TYPES OF BUSINESS:
Casinos
Hospitality & Entertainment Facilities
Racetrack Facilities

BRANDS/DIVISIONS/AFFILIATES:
Gaming and Leisure Properties Inc
L'Auberge Casino Resort
L'Auberge Baton Rouge
River City Casino & Hotel
Belterra Casino Resort
Boomtown Casino Hotel
Cactus Petes and The Horseshu Jackpot
Heartland Poker Tour

CONTACTS: Note: Officers with more than one job title may be intentionally listed here more than once.
Anthony Sanfilippo, CEO
Carlos Ruisanchez, CFO
Virginia Shanks, Chief Administrative Officer
Neil Walkoff, Executive VP, Divisional
Troy Stremming, Executive VP, Divisional
Donna Negrotto, Executive VP

GROWTH PLANS/SPECIAL FEATURES:
Pinnacle Entertainment, Inc. is a developer, owner and operator of casinos and other hospitality facilities. The company owns and operates 16 gaming entertainment properties, located in Colorado, Indiana, Iowa, Louisiana, Mississippi, Missouri, Nevada and Texas. The company's largest casino resort, L'Auberge Casino Resort located in Lake Charles, Louisiana, offers 995 guestrooms, suites and villas, as well as 1,518 slot machines, 75 table games, a golf course and a full-service spa. L'Auberge Casino Hotel in Baton Rouge, Louisiana, features 1,440 slot machines, 49 table games, a hotel with 205 guestrooms and a rooftop pool, nine dining outlets, an amphitheater style event lawn feature and a multi-purpose event center. The River City Casino & Hotel in St. Louis, Missouri includes 200 hotel rooms, 1.925 slot machines and 53 table games. Other properties include Belterra Casino Resort located near Florence, Indiana; six Ameristar Casino Hotels in Iowa, Indiana, Missouri, Mississippi and Colorado; two Boomtown Casino Hotels featuring dockside riverboat casinos in New Orleans and Bossier City, Louisiana; and Cactus Petes and The Horseshu Jackpot, featuring a hotel, gaming, dining, golf course and showroom entertainment. The company also owns the Heartland Poker Tour, a live and televised poker tournament series; and owns a majority interest in Retama Park Racetrack outside of San Antonio, Texas. In December 2017, Pinnacle Entertainment entered into a definitive agreement with Penn National Gaming, Inc. in which Penn National would acquire Pinnacle Entertainment in a transaction valued at $2.8 billion.

FINANCIAL DATA: Note: Data for latest year may not have been available at press time.

In U.S. $	2018	2017	2016	2015	2014	2013
Revenue		2,561,848,064	2,378,854,912	2,291,847,936	2,210,543,104	1,487,836,032
R&D Expense						
Operating Income						
Operating Margin %						
SGA Expense						
Net Income		63,104,000	-457,409,984	48,887,000	43,843,000	-255,870,000
Operating Cash Flow						
Capital Expenditure						
EBITDA						
Return on Assets %						
Return on Equity %						
Debt to Equity						

CONTACT INFORMATION:
Phone: 702 541-7777 Fax:
Toll-Free:
Address: 3980 Howard Hughes Pkwy, Las Vegas, NV 89169 United States

STOCK TICKER/OTHER:
Stock Ticker: PNK Exchange: NAS
Employees: 16,092 Fiscal Year Ends: 12/31
Parent Company: Gaming and Leisure Properties Inc

SALARIES/BONUSES:
Top Exec. Salary: $ Bonus: $
Second Exec. Salary: $ Bonus: $

OTHER THOUGHTS:
Estimated Female Officers or Directors: 3
Hot Spot for Advancement for Women/Minorities: Y

Sales, profits and employees may be estimates. Financial information, benefits and other data can change quickly and may vary from those stated here.

Pioneer Corporation

NAIC Code: 334310

global.pioneer/en/

TYPES OF BUSINESS:
Consumer Electronics
Audio/Video Equipment
CD/DVD Players
Automotive Electronics
Telecommunications Equipment
Research & Development
Software Development

BRANDS/DIVISIONS/AFFILIATES:
Pioneer Digital Design and Manufacturing Corp
Anyo Pioneer Motor Info Tech Co Ltd

CONTACTS: Note: Officers with more than one job title may be intentionally listed here more than once.
Koichi Moriya, CEO
Susumu Kotani, Pres.
Masanori Koshoubu, Gen. Mgr.-R&D
Hideki Okayasu, Sr. Mgr. Dir.-Gen. Admin. Div.
Masanori Koshoubu, Mgr. Dir.-Legal & Intellectual Property Div.
Mikio Ono, Gen. Mgr.-Corp. Planning Div.
Hideki Okayasu, Sr. Mgr. Dir.-Corp. Comm.
Hideki Okayasu, Sr. Mgr. Dir.-Finance & Acct. Div.
Satoshi Matsumoto, Mgr. Dir.-Quality Assurance Div.
Mikio Ono, Gen. Mgr.-Home Audiovisual Bus.
Tatsuo Takeuchi, Gen. Mgr.-Intl Bus. Div.

GROWTH PLANS/SPECIAL FEATURES:
Pioneer Corporation, headquartered in Japan, is a leading manufacturer of consumer electronics. The firm operates primarily in two segments: car electronics business and others. The car electronics business is divided into four subsections: consumer, OEM, Map and Autonomous Driving Field. The Consumer subsection provides a lineup of in-vehicle hardware for car entertainment, such as car navigation, car Audio/Visual and car speakers. The OEM subsection sells high-quality in-vehicle hardware for automakers. For next-generation vehicles, Pioneer also provides proposals for comfort and safety in vehicles using Pioneer's advanced technologies. The Map business creates and sells maps for navigation systems, smartphones and PCs. This business also sells maps in the corporate and GIS markets, as well as creating maps for autonomous driving. The Autonomous Driving Field consists of firms telematic services and its 3D-LiDAR sensors that measure distances to objects accurately and capture information on distances and surroundings in real time and in three dimensions. The other segment manufactures home theater components, such as Blu-ray disc players, surround sound systems, audiovisual components, Blu-ray and DVD drives for computers, professional disc jockey equipment and professional speakers. Additionally, the segment produces bicycle GPS systems; organic electroluminescent lighting, electronics manufacturing services and components; medical and healthcare equipment; electric and autonomous vehicle products; and horizontal vertical transforming (HVT) speakers. The firm is part of two joint ventures: optical disk developer Pioneer Digital Design and Manufacturing Corporation (with Sharp Corporation); and Anyo Pioneer Motor Information Technology Co., Ltd., a Chinese car navigation systems developer (with Shanghai Automotive Industry Corporation Group).

FINANCIAL DATA: Note: Data for latest year may not have been available at press time.

In U.S. $	2018	2017	2016	2015	2014	2013
Revenue	3,389,517,000	3,586,765,000	4,170,655,000	4,653,421,000	4,619,796,000	4,191,164,000
R&D Expense						
Operating Income	11,075,250	38,652,050	67,750,070	72,146,780	103,600,800	55,626,670
Operating Margin %	0.32	1.07%	1.62%	1.55%	2.24%	1.32%
SGA Expense						
Net Income	-66,071,160	-46,879,640	6,780,573	135,722,800	4,925,423	-181,359,500
Operating Cash Flow	147,883,300	181,934,500	178,947,800	320,607,000	317,620,200	10,936,110
Capital Expenditure						
EBITDA	153,977,400	216,087,900	307,797,200	479,880,900	311,804,300	163,754,100
Return on Assets %	-2.50%	-1.74%	.23%	4.45%	.16%	-6.17%
Return on Equity %	-8.73%	-6.00%	.78%	16.79%	.71%	-24.36%
Debt to Equity	0.19	0.21	0.29	0.09		0.17

CONTACT INFORMATION:
Phone: 81-3-6634-8777 Fax:
Toll-Free:
Address: 28-8, Honkomagome 2-chome, Bunkyo-ku, Tokyo, 113-0021 Japan

STOCK TICKER/OTHER:
Stock Ticker: PNCOF
Employees: 16,798
Parent Company:

Exchange: PINX
Fiscal Year Ends: 03/31

SALARIES/BONUSES:
Top Exec. Salary: $ Bonus: $
Second Exec. Salary: $ Bonus: $

OTHER THOUGHTS:
Estimated Female Officers or Directors:
Hot Spot for Advancement for Women/Minorities:

Pixar Animation Studios

NAIC Code: 512110

www.pixar.com

TYPES OF BUSINESS:
Computer-Animated Film Production
Special Effects Software
Children's Merchandise

BRANDS/DIVISIONS/AFFILIATES:
Walt Disney Company (The)
Toy Story
Monsters Inc
Finding Nemo
Cars
Coco
Piper
RenderMan

CONTACTS:
Note: Officers with more than one job title may be intentionally listed here more than once.

Edwin Catmull, Pres.
John Lasseter, Chief Creative Officer

GROWTH PLANS/SPECIAL FEATURES:

Pixar Animation Studios, a wholly-owned subsidiary of The Walt Disney Company, is a pioneer in computer-animated feature films through its combination of creative, technical and production capabilities. Pixar, which had its beginning as the computer graphics division of Lucasfilm, Ltd., began its own feature film productions through an agreement with Disney to develop up to three computer-animated feature films to be marketed and distributed by Disney, an agreement which was later extended. The first film produced was Toy Story, which met with wide success and established Pixar as an early leader in computer-animated films. Pixar has released 20 feature films: Toy Story; A Bug's Life; Toy Story 2; Monsters, Inc.; Finding Nemo; The Incredibles; Cars; Cars 2; Ratatouille; Toy Story 3; Wall-E; Up; Brave; Monster's University, Insideout, The Good Dianosaur, Finding Dory; Cars 3; Coco; and Incredibles 2. Many of these films have been very successful at the box office. The studio has earned 19 Academy Awards, eight Golden Globe Awards and 11 Grammy Awards, among others. The company also makes short films, such as the Academy Award-winning Tin Toy, For the Birds and Piper. The firm's proprietary RenderMan software incorporates texture mapping, programmable shading and procedural modeling technologies. In addition to Pixar's own projects, the software has helped create visual special effects for films including Terminator 2, The Matrix, Gladiator, King Kong, The Lord of the Rings trilogy, Indiana Jones and the Kingdom of the Crystal Skull and the Harry Potter film series. Toy Story 4 is scheduled to be released in mid-2019, and Onward is scheduled for a 2020 release.

Pixar offers paid technical and non-technical internships to college students, as well as residency for recent graduates.

FINANCIAL DATA:
Note: Data for latest year may not have been available at press time.

In U.S. $	2018	2017	2016	2015	2014	2013
Revenue	3,000,000,000	3,000,000,000	2,850,000,000	2,800,000,000		
R&D Expense						
Operating Income						
Operating Margin %						
SGA Expense						
Net Income						
Operating Cash Flow						
Capital Expenditure						
EBITDA						
Return on Assets %						
Return on Equity %						
Debt to Equity						

CONTACT INFORMATION:
Phone: 510-922-3000 Fax: 510-922-3151
Toll-Free:
Address: 1200 Park Ave., Emeryville, CA 94608 United States

SALARIES/BONUSES:
Top Exec. Salary: $ Bonus: $
Second Exec. Salary: $ Bonus: $

STOCK TICKER/OTHER:
Stock Ticker: Subsidiary Exchange:
Employees: 1,500 Fiscal Year Ends: 12/31
Parent Company: Walt Disney Company (The)

OTHER THOUGHTS:
Estimated Female Officers or Directors:
Hot Spot for Advancement for Women/Minorities:

Sales, profits and employees may be estimates. Financial information, benefits and other data can change quickly and may vary from those stated here.

Playboy Enterprises Inc

NAIC Code: 511120

www.playboyenterprises.com

TYPES OF BUSINESS:
Magazine Publishing
Adult Entertainment
Movie, Video & Game Production
Internet Gaming
Online Sales & Subscriptions
Cable TV & Radio Networks
Licensing

BRANDS/DIVISIONS/AFFILIATES:
Playboy Magazine
PlayboyShop.com
Playboy.com
Playboy TV
Playboy Radio

CONTACTS: Note: Officers with more than one job title may be intentionally listed here more than once.
Ben Kohn, CEO
David Israel, COO
Jared Doughterty, CMO
Kendice Briggs, Sr. VP-Human Resources
Reena Patel, Chief Commercial Officer
Rachel Sagan, General Counsel
Rachel Sagan, Exec. VP-Bus. Affairs
Jimmy Jellinek, Chief Content Officer
David Israel, COO
Matthew A. Nordby, Pres., Global Licensing
Cooper Hefner, Chief Creative Officer

GROWTH PLANS/SPECIAL FEATURES:
Playboy Enterprises, Inc. (PEI) is a multimedia entertainment company operating in three segments: print/digital, entertainment and licensing. The print/digital segment is responsible for the domestic and international editions of Playboy Magazine, free and pay websites and the firm's mobile business division. Playboy products are sold in over 180 countries. A general-interest magazine targeting men, Playboy generally includes pictorials of women; articles on current issues and trends; interviews with high-profile political, business, entertainment and sports figures; and cartoons. PEI operates e-commerce sites, such as PlayboyShop.com; provides various subscription sites featuring Playboy content; and offers online gaming, entertainment and advice through Playboy.com. PEI also offers content for the mobile market such as ring tones, video clips, images and games. The entertainment segment operates television and radio entertainment venues. Playboy TV is available on a subscription basis via satellite and cable networks. In addition to producing shows for its own networks, the segment also co-produces programming for third party networks. Playboy Radio is an internet radio station that offers adult programming. The licensing segment is responsible for licensing the Playboy brand; trademarks and images for consumer products; third-party owned and operated retail stores; location-based entertainment, such as casinos; and other revenue-generating marketing activities.

FINANCIAL DATA: Note: Data for latest year may not have been available at press time.

In U.S. $	2018	2017	2016	2015	2014	2013
Revenue	90,000,000	90,000,000	80,000,000	88,000,000	100,000,000	125,000,000
R&D Expense						
Operating Income						
Operating Margin %						
SGA Expense						
Net Income						
Operating Cash Flow						
Capital Expenditure						
EBITDA						
Return on Assets %						
Return on Equity %						
Debt to Equity						

CONTACT INFORMATION:
Phone: 312-751-8000 Fax: 312-751-2818
Toll-Free:
Address: 9346 Civic Center Dr. #200, Beverly Hills, CA 90210 United States

STOCK TICKER/OTHER:
Stock Ticker: Private
Employees: 170
Parent Company:

Exchange:
Fiscal Year Ends: 12/31

SALARIES/BONUSES:
Top Exec. Salary: $ Bonus: $
Second Exec. Salary: $ Bonus: $

OTHER THOUGHTS:
Estimated Female Officers or Directors: 2
Hot Spot for Advancement for Women/Minorities: Y

Sales, profits and employees may be estimates. Financial information, benefits and other data can change quickly and may vary from those stated here.

Premier Exhibitions Inc
NAIC Code: 711320

www.premierexhibitions.com

TYPES OF BUSINESS:
Exhibition Tours
Exhibition & Installation Design & Management

BRANDS/DIVISIONS/AFFILIATES:
RMS Titanic Inc
Premier Exhibition Management LLC
Arts and Exhibitions International LLC
Titanic: The Artifact Exhibition
Titanic: The Experience
Bodies Revealed
Bodies: The Exhibition

CONTACTS:
Note: Officers with more than one job title may be intentionally listed here more than once.
Daoping Bao, CEO
Michael Little, CFO
John Norman, President, Subsidiary

GROWTH PLANS/SPECIAL FEATURES:
Premier Exhibitions, Inc., established in 1993, develops and exhibits museum-quality installations worldwide. Its operations consist of two divisions: content management and exhibition management. Content management, through wholly-owned subsidiary RMS Titanic, Inc., is the sole salvor-in-possession of the Titanic wreck and wreck site. As such, the firm has exclusive rights to recover objects from the site. It currently owns approximately 5,500 items related to the Titanic. The exhibition management division, through Premier Exhibition Management, LLC, operates and manages the company's touring and permanent exhibitions, which include Titanic, Bodies, Real Pirates and King Tut exhibitions. The Titanic exhibitions, which include Titanic: The Artifact Exhibition and Titanic: The Experience, features historically correct re-creations of significant rooms aboard the ship with stories and artifacts placed throughout. The Bodies exhibits, Bodies Revealed and Bodies: The Exhibition, contain collections of intact human bodies as well as organs and body parts, which are preserved through the process of polymer preservation. Premier has been under chapter 11 bankruptcy protection since mid-2016.

FINANCIAL DATA:
Note: Data for latest year may not have been available at press time.

In U.S. $	2018	2017	2016	2015	2014	2013
Revenue				29,390,000	29,348,000	39,465,000
R&D Expense						
Operating Income						
Operating Margin %						
SGA Expense						
Net Income				-10,475,000	-714,000	1,950,000
Operating Cash Flow						
Capital Expenditure						
EBITDA						
Return on Assets %						
Return on Equity %						
Debt to Equity						

CONTACT INFORMATION:
Phone: 404 842-2600 Fax: 404 842-2626
Toll-Free:
Address: 3045 Kingston Ct., Ste. I, Peachtree Corners, GA 30071 United States

STOCK TICKER/OTHER:
Stock Ticker: PRXIQ
Employees: 46
Parent Company:

Exchange: NAS
Fiscal Year Ends: 02/28

SALARIES/BONUSES:
Top Exec. Salary: $ Bonus: $
Second Exec. Salary: $ Bonus: $

OTHER THOUGHTS:
Estimated Female Officers or Directors:
Hot Spot for Advancement for Women/Minorities:

Sales, profits and employees may be estimates. Financial information, benefits and other data can change quickly and may vary from those stated here.

Plunkett Research, Ltd.

Pro Publica Inc
NAIC Code: 519130

www.proPublica.org

TYPES OF BUSINESS:
Online Publishing

BRANDS/DIVISIONS/AFFILIATES:
ProPublica

CONTACTS: Note: Officers with more than one job title may be intentionally listed here more than once.
Stephen Engelberg, CEO
Richard Tofel, Pres.
Robin Fields, Managing Editor
Cynthia Gordy, Dir.-Mktg.
Liz Sharp, Dir.-Human Resources
Liz Day, Dir.-Research
Nicholas Lanese, Dir.-IT
Heather Troup, Associate Dir.-Admin.
Barbara Zinkant, Dir.-Oper.
Debby Goldberg, VP-Dev.
Nicole Collins Bronzan, Dir.-Comm.
Barbara Zinkant, Dir.-Finance
Robin Fields, Managing Editor
Mark Schoofs, Sr. Editor
Tom Detzel, Sr. Editor
Paul Sagan, Chmn.

GROWTH PLANS/SPECIAL FEATURES:
Pro Publica, Inc. is an independent, nonprofit news organization that focuses on public interest journalism. The company's format includes investigative journalism and analyses of issues that affect the public good. The firm offers the results of its investigative inquiries to traditional media organizations to be republished free of charge. Completed stories are also made available on its website, under the ProPublica banner (combining the company's name into one word). Its topics include government and politics, business, criminal justice, the environment, education, healthcare, immigration and technology, among many others. Pro Publica primarily targets large businesses and government in an attempt to uncover misdeeds and abuses of power, but also examines unions, hospitals, universities, foundations and media institutions. Notable topics for investigation include the beneficiaries of government funding, Wall Street firms and oil spills. Pro Publica is mostly funded by a multi-year commitment from the Sandler Foundation as well as donations from other philanthropic organizations and private donors. Approximately 85% of Pro Publica's funding is utilized to produce news stories.

FINANCIAL DATA: Note: Data for latest year may not have been available at press time.

In U.S. $	2018	2017	2016	2015	2014	2013
Revenue		13,300,000	14,545,521	17,046,930	10,324,275	13,765,467
R&D Expense						
Operating Income						
Operating Margin %						
SGA Expense						
Net Income			778,640	4,585,781	-1,162,177	3,432,658
Operating Cash Flow						
Capital Expenditure						
EBITDA						
Return on Assets %						
Return on Equity %						
Debt to Equity						

CONTACT INFORMATION:
Phone: 212-514-5250 Fax: 212-785-2634
Toll-Free:
Address: 155 Ave. of the Americas, 13/Fl, New York, NY 10013 United States

STOCK TICKER/OTHER:
Stock Ticker: Nonprofit
Employees: 50
Parent Company:

Exchange:
Fiscal Year Ends: 12/31

SALARIES/BONUSES:
Top Exec. Salary: $ Bonus: $
Second Exec. Salary: $ Bonus: $

OTHER THOUGHTS:
Estimated Female Officers or Directors: 7
Hot Spot for Advancement for Women/Minorities: Y

Sales, profits and employees may be estimates. Financial information, benefits and other data can change quickly and may vary from those stated here.

Promotora de Informaciones SA

NAIC Code: 515120

www.prisa.com/en

TYPES OF BUSINESS:
Television Broadcasting

BRANDS/DIVISIONS/AFFILIATES:
PRISA
Santillana
Prisa Radio
El Pais
AS
Cinco Dia
El Huffpost
Market Place

CONTACTS: Note: Officers with more than one job title may be intentionally listed here more than once.
Manuel Mirat Santiago, CEO
Antonio Garcia-Mon, Sec.
Fernando Martinez, Dir.-Strategic Planning, Mgmt. Control & Budgeting
Barbara Manrique de Lara, Dir.-Corp Comm, Mktg & External Rel.
Manuel Polanco Moreno, Deputy Chmn.
Andres Cardo, Intl Managing Dir.-Prisa Radio
Miguel Angel Cayuela, CEO-Santillana
Pedro Garcia Guillen, CEO-Prisa TV

GROWTH PLANS/SPECIAL FEATURES:
Promotora de Informaciones SA, operating as PRISA, is a leading multimedia group in Spain and Portugal, which operates in over 23 countries, including Brazil, Mexico, Argentina, the U.S. and other Latin American countries. It divides its operations into five segments: audiovisual, education, radio, news and brand solutions. The audiovisual segment consists of pay television, free-to-air television and television and film production. The company is a leading producer and distributor of Spanish and Portuguese audiovisual content, and the largest in the Iberian market, with operations mainly in Spain and Portugal, with some presence in Brazil and Portuguese-speaking African countries. The education segment includes the sale of general publishing and educational books and education systems. Its publishing arm, Santillana, offers a range of products and services, including school textbooks, language teaching books, general publishing and distribution. The radio segment sells advertising to the company's networks and, in addition, organizes and manages events and provides other supplementary services in 22 countries. Prisa Radio has 23 million listeners in more than 1, 250 broadcasting stations, distributed in 13 countries. The news segment includes the publishing of newspapers and magazines, distribution and the sale of advertising in such publications. Publication includes El Pais in Spain, sports newspaper AS, financial newspaper Cinco Dia, Spanish news site El Huffpost, as well as a number of corporate magazines. Last, the brand solutions segment sells group advertising, boasting a portfolio of 28 media outlets to reach all kinds of targets. In October 2018, PRISA announced the creation of a programmatic and sales platform with Vocento, Spain's number one press group. The goal of the new platform, Market Place, will be to leverage qualitative audience aggregation for the sale of programmatic advertising.

FINANCIAL DATA: Note: Data for latest year may not have been available at press time.

In U.S. $	2018	2017	2016	2015	2014	2013
Revenue		4,646,421,000	4,327,471,000	3,714,289,000	3,275,732,000	2,967,718,000
R&D Expense						
Operating Income		606,005,400	882,808,600	822,663,700	783,250,600	768,670,000
Operating Margin %		20.07%	20.40%	22.15%	23.91%	25.67%
SGA Expense		711,942,400	609,422,700	485,715,600	391,397,400	318,380,600
Net Income		536,519,800	457,921,300	445,277,200	394,473,000	355,515,600
Operating Cash Flow		1,846,494,000	1,796,373,000	1,730,077,000	1,645,213,000	1,602,497,000
Capital Expenditure		1,371,486,000	1,312,252,000	1,214,745,000	1,126,464,000	1,086,709,000
EBITDA		1,132,273,000	1,085,570,000	966,077,300	894,655,300	855,242,200
Return on Assets %		7.15%	6.74%	8.48%	9.28%	6.95%
Return on Equity %		35.77%	34.51%	47.09%	52.77%	30.15%
Debt to Equity		2.63	2.29	2.97	2.77	3.35

CONTACT INFORMATION:
Phone: 34 913301000 Fax:
Toll-Free:
Address: Gran Via 32, Madrid, 28013 Spain

STOCK TICKER/OTHER:
Stock Ticker: PBSFY
Employees: 6,483
Parent Company:
Exchange: PINX
Fiscal Year Ends: 12/31

SALARIES/BONUSES:
Top Exec. Salary: $ Bonus: $
Second Exec. Salary: $ Bonus: $

OTHER THOUGHTS:
Estimated Female Officers or Directors: 1
Hot Spot for Advancement for Women/Minorities:

Sales, profits and employees may be estimates. Financial information, benefits and other data can change quickly and may vary from those stated here.

… (Plunkett Research, Ltd.)

ProQuest LLC

NAIC Code: 519130

www.proquest.com

TYPES OF BUSINESS:
Online Database of News and Information
Dissertation Publishing
Streaming Videos
eBook Platforms
Content Discovery Systems
Library Tools
Primary Research Collections
News Collections

BRANDS/DIVISIONS/AFFILIATES:
360 Link
iFound
OASIS
Ex Libris
PsycEXTRA
ProQuest Dialog
Alexander Street Press
Intota

CONTACTS:
Note: Officers with more than one job title may be intentionally listed here more than once.

Matti Shem-Tov, CEO
Robert VanHees, CFO, Sr. VP
James Holmes, CMO
Kevin A. Norris, Chief People Officer
Roger Valade, CTO
Kevin A. Norris, General Counsel
Tim Wahlberg, Sr. VP
Simon Beale, Sr. VP
Kevin Sayar, Sr. VP
Rafael Sidi, Sr. VP
Andy Snyder, Chmn.

GROWTH PLANS/SPECIAL FEATURES:

ProQuest, LLC, a unit of Cambridge Information Group, is primarily a publisher of electronic research databases and related services, including deep archives of news and other types of information. The company's services are focused on subscriptions to ProQuest's vast databases, utilized by the world's top libraries, institutions of higher learning, research organizations and government agencies. Its management solutions include iFound integrated out-of-print and hard-to-find service that allows libraries to search and purchase second-hand books via the company's web-based search system, OASIS. Data services include the Bookwire App, which allows users to evaluate, order and purchase books via smartphones; and PsycEXTRA, a database of book reviews, bibliographic records and lay audience literature in relation to the field of psychology. Research tools such as ProQuest Research Companion, its flagship information literacy product, helps students research effectively and supports educators as they teach core information literacy principles of finding, evaluating and using information. The databases service includes access to scholarly journals, newspapers, reports, working papers and datasets, as well as digitized historical primary sources. Ebook platforms enable libraries and other clients to access hundreds of thousands of books online. News and newspapers provides access to approximately 5,000 journals, magazines and newspapers, as well as information by ProQuest Dialog and others for global news on trading. Primary sources offer access into The British Library and the U.S. Library of Congress for retrieval of historical documents. University student dissertation and theses dissemination and ordering services archive more than 90,000 new graduate works every year. The company also offers data on microfilm and provides online access to Safari, a collection of O'Reilly technical books.

FINANCIAL DATA:
Note: Data for latest year may not have been available at press time.

In U.S. $	2018	2017	2016	2015	2014	2013
Revenue	590,000,000	572,000,000	560,000,000	550,000,000		
R&D Expense						
Operating Income						
Operating Margin %						
SGA Expense						
Net Income						
Operating Cash Flow						
Capital Expenditure						
EBITDA						
Return on Assets %						
Return on Equity %						
Debt to Equity						

CONTACT INFORMATION:
Phone: 734-761-4700 Fax:
Toll-Free: 800-521-0600
Address: 789 E. Eisenhower Pkwy, Ann Arbor, MI 48106-1346 United States

STOCK TICKER/OTHER:
Stock Ticker: Private Exchange:
Employees: 2,450 Fiscal Year Ends:
Parent Company: Cambridge Information Group Inc (CIG)

SALARIES/BONUSES:
Top Exec. Salary: $ Bonus: $
Second Exec. Salary: $ Bonus: $

OTHER THOUGHTS:
Estimated Female Officers or Directors: 1
Hot Spot for Advancement for Women/Minorities:

Sales, profits and employees may be estimates. Financial information, benefits and other data can change quickly and may vary from those stated here.

ProSiebenSat.1 Media SE

NAIC Code: 515120

www.prosiebensat1.com/en/

TYPES OF BUSINESS:
Television Broadcasting

BRANDS/DIVISIONS/AFFILIATES:
maxdome
Studio71
Red Arrow Entertainment Group
eharmony
NuCom Group

CONTACTS:
Note: Officers with more than one job title may be intentionally listed here more than once.

Mox Conze, CEO
Jan Kemper, CFO
Sabine Eckhardt, Exec. Board Member Sales and Marketing
Conrad Albert, Chief Legal, Distribution & Reg. Affairs Officer
Christian Wegner, Head-Digital & Adjacent
Werner Brandt, Chmn.

GROWTH PLANS/SPECIAL FEATURES:
ProSiebenSat.1 Media SE is a media company specializing in TV broadcasting throughout Germany, Austria and Switzerland. The firm is officially abbreviated as P7S1. The company operates through three business segments: entertainment, content production and global sales and commerce. The entertainment segment operates 14 free and pay TV channels in Germany, Austria and Switzerland. This division also encompasses the firm's digital presence, which comprises two units: the online video business unit, including pay video-on-demand portal maxdome, multi-channel network Studio71, and the fields of advertising technology and data; and the adjacent business unit, which operates ProSiebenSat.1's own record label, is actively-engaged in music and live entertainment, and provides artist management. The content production and global sales segment includes the Red Arrow Entertainment Group, which is responsible for ProSiebenSat.1's international program production and distribution business. This business includes a group of more than 20 international television production companies across eight countries, and the distribution of over 500 productions. This segment's program catalog includes nearly 1,000 titles overall; and is currently expanding its portfolio via acquisitions, with a focus on English-speaking regions, with 70% of revenue coming from the United States. The commerce segment exchanges advertising time for a share in revenues and/or an equity interest, and also acquires related companies and platforms. It is also responsible for the company's e-commerce business. The company bundles all its commerce subsidiaries into one subsidiary, NuCom Group (NCG). In 2018, ProSiebenSat.1 sold Tropo, a tour operator with more than 200 million vacation options; and 7NXT, a provider of online fitness programs. The firm announced in October 2018 that it had acquired eharmony, an online dating site based in the U.S.

FINANCIAL DATA:
Note: Data for latest year may not have been available at press time.

In U.S. $	2018	2017	2016	2015	2014	2013
Revenue		1,304,086,000	1,514,969,000	1,535,524,000	1,604,109,000	3,053,128,000
R&D Expense						
Operating Income		91,685,650	120,550,600	108,399,800	-12,241,990	21,027,930
Operating Margin %		10.10%	9.73%	8.54%	.76%	1.55%
SGA Expense		180,275,200	204,371,900	206,568,100	219,778,300	296,017,700
Net Income		-117,231,300	-77,298,720	6,030,437	-2,547,993,000	-738,945,000
Operating Cash Flow		119,999,300	219,096,000	191,449,900	120,633,800	163,880,000
Capital Expenditure		72,208,050	82,133,090	91,662,860	84,420,420	173,922,400
EBITDA		222,349,300	254,756,900	257,036,300	336,081,200	252,534,500
Return on Assets %		-5.08%	-3.02%	.17%	-43.45%	-9.03%
Return on Equity %					-395.86%	-34.21%
Debt to Equity						2.01

CONTACT INFORMATION:
Phone: 49-89-95-07-10   Fax: 49-89-95-07-91199
Toll-Free:
Address: Medianallee 7, Unterfohring, Madrid, 2801385774 Germany

SALARIES/BONUSES:
Top Exec. Salary: $1,366,929   Bonus: $1,161,890
Second Exec. Salary: $1,139,108   Bonus: $774,593

STOCK TICKER/OTHER:
Stock Ticker: PRISY   Exchange: PINX
Employees: 8,785   Fiscal Year Ends: 12/31
Parent Company:

OTHER THOUGHTS:
Estimated Female Officers or Directors: 1
Hot Spot for Advancement for Women/Minorities:

Qurate Retail Inc

www.qurateretailgroup.com

NAIC Code: 454111

TYPES OF BUSINESS:
Online and Internet Businesses
e-Commerce

BRANDS/DIVISIONS/AFFILIATES:
QVC Inc
Zulily LLC
HSN Inc
HSN
Cornerstone
Liberty Interactive Corporation

CONTACTS:
Note: Officers with more than one job title may be intentionally listed here more than once.

Michael George, CEO
Mark Carleton, CFO
Gregory Maffei, Chairman of the Board
Richard Baer, Other Executive Officer
Albert Rosenthaler, Other Executive Officer

GROWTH PLANS/SPECIAL FEATURES:

Qurate Retail, Inc. (formerly Liberty Interactive Corporation) is primarily engaged in selling consumer products through video and eCommerce channels throughout North America, Europe and Asia. The firm's wholly-owned subsidiaries include: QVC, Inc.; Zulily LLC; and HSN, Inc., along with its catalog retail business called Cornerstone. QVC serves 13 million customers in the U.S. alone, with 93% of sales deriving from repeat/reactivate customers. Existing customers usually order 25 items per year, on average. Internationally, its video commerce, eCommerce (website) and social commerce channels earned $8.8 billion in 2017 revenue, and reached 370 million homes worldwide, including the U.S., the U.K., Europe and Asia. QVC has 14 television networks, more than 220 active social pages, and more than 1 billion visit its websites annually. Zulily is an American eCommerce company based in Washington. Through its website and mobile app, consumers can shop new sales daily beginning at 6am Pacific Time, which feature prices of up to 70% off regular prices. How Zulily works is once sales have ended, the firm places one large order to the brands presented that day. The brands ship the items to Zulily in about 8-10 days, and then Zulily ships them individually from its warehouse to its consumers. This process keeps prices low and selections fresh. HSN stands for Home Shopping Network, and is an American broadcast, basic cable and satellite television network based in Florida. HSN broadcasts reach approximately 90 million households via live programming 364 days per year, as well as through its website HSN.com. Mobile apps are offered through iPad, iPhone and Android devices. In March 2018, Liberty Interactive Corporation reorganized its business, reattributing certain assets and liabilities to QVC and selling others, and subsequently changed its corporate name to Qurate Retail, Inc.

FINANCIAL DATA: Note: Data for latest year may not have been available at press time.

In U.S. $	2018	2017	2016	2015	2014	2013
Revenue		10,381,000,000	10,219,000,000	9,169,000,000	10,028,000,000	10,307,000,000
R&D Expense						
Operating Income		1,135,000,000	1,011,000,000	1,170,000,000	1,213,000,000	1,164,000,000
Operating Margin %		10.93%	9.89%	12.76%	12.09%	11.29%
SGA Expense		1,088,000,000	1,063,000,000	875,000,000	940,000,000	1,033,000,000
Net Income		1,208,000,000	473,000,000	640,000,000	520,000,000	438,000,000
Operating Cash Flow		1,222,000,000	1,273,000,000	981,000,000	1,204,000,000	972,000,000
Capital Expenditure		201,000,000	206,000,000	218,000,000	226,000,000	295,000,000
EBITDA		2,265,000,000	1,947,000,000	1,918,000,000	1,835,000,000	1,745,000,000
Return on Assets %		7.64%	3.20%	4.54%	3.73%	2.92%
Return on Equity %		20.68%	9.40%	13.50%	9.75%	6.54%
Debt to Equity		0.98	1.30	1.18	1.36	0.79

CONTACT INFORMATION:
Phone: 720 875-5300   Fax:
Toll-Free:
Address: 12300 Liberty Blvd, Englewood, CO 80112 United States

SALARIES/BONUSES:
Top Exec. Salary: $1,250,000   Bonus: $
Second Exec. Salary: $1,059,227   Bonus: $

STOCK TICKER/OTHER:
Stock Ticker: QRTEA
Employees: 21,080
Parent Company:

Exchange: NAS
Fiscal Year Ends: 12/31

OTHER THOUGHTS:
Estimated Female Officers or Directors: 1
Hot Spot for Advancement for Women/Minorities:

Sales, profits and employees may be estimates. Financial information, benefits and other data can change quickly and may vary from those stated here.

Rakuten Commerce LLC

NAIC Code: 454111

www.rakuten.com

TYPES OF BUSINESS:
Consumer Electronics, Online Retail
Book, Game, DVD, VHS & Music Sales
Software & Accessories Sales
Music Downloads
Social Networking
Jewelry and Watches
Household Items

BRANDS/DIVISIONS/AFFILIATES:
Rakuten Inc
Rakuten.com
Rakuten Super Points

CONTACTS:
Note: Officers with more than one job title may be intentionally listed here more than once.
Hiroshi Mikitani, CEO
Hiroshi Mikitani, Chmn. & CEO-Rakuten, Inc.
Fumio Kobayashi, Chief Marketplace Officer

GROWTH PLANS/SPECIAL FEATURES:
Rakuten Commerce, LLC does business as Rakuten.com, an online retailer. The firm offers over 18 million products, both directly and through third-party retailers that utilize the eCommerce marketplace. The wide variety of items sold include: computer hardware, accessories and software; electronics; jewelry and fragrances; wine; sporting goods; apparel; cellular products; books; bags; games and toys; and DVDs, CDs and music downloads. Rakuten's computer products include computers, printers, monitors, modems and peripherals as well as software from manufacturers including Microsoft, Norton and Adobe. The firm also offers hardback, paperback and audio book titles, enabling customers to read the first chapter of many books, submit book reviews and read professional/customer reviews. Rakuten's rewards program, Rakuten Super Points, enables users to earn points every time they purchase from its site. The points can be used to pay for a current purchase or be saved for future purchases. In addition to its U.S. site, Rakuten Commerce maintains eCommerce sites for Japan, France, Germany, the U.K. Austria, Brazil, Indonesia, Malaysia, Spain, Taiwan, Singapore and Thailand. Rakuten is a wholly-owned subsidiary of Rakuten, Inc. During 2018, Rakuten joined with Ebates to offer up to 40% cash back at more than 2,500 stores, including Macy's, Nike, Amazon and Walmart.

FINANCIAL DATA:
Note: Data for latest year may not have been available at press time.

In U.S. $	2018	2017	2016	2015	2014	2013
Revenue						
R&D Expense						
Operating Income						
Operating Margin %						
SGA Expense						
Net Income						
Operating Cash Flow						
Capital Expenditure						
EBITDA						
Return on Assets %						
Return on Equity %						
Debt to Equity						

CONTACT INFORMATION:
Phone: 949-389-2000　Fax:
Toll-Free:
Address: 85 Enterprise, Ste. 100, Aliso Viejo, CA 92656 United States

STOCK TICKER/OTHER:
Stock Ticker: Subsidiary
Employees: 115
Parent Company: Rakuten Inc
Exchange:
Fiscal Year Ends: 12/31

SALARIES/BONUSES:
Top Exec. Salary: $　Bonus: $
Second Exec. Salary: $　Bonus: $

OTHER THOUGHTS:
Estimated Female Officers or Directors: 1
Hot Spot for Advancement for Women/Minorities:

Sales, profits and employees may be estimates. Financial information, benefits and other data can change quickly and may vary from those stated here.

Rank Group plc (The)

NAIC Code: 713210

www.rank.com

TYPES OF BUSINESS:
Gambling Resorts & Casinos
Gambling Equipment

BRANDS/DIVISIONS/AFFILIATES:
Mecca Bingo
Grosvenor Casinos
Enracha
Hong Leong Company (Malaysia) Berhad

CONTACTS:
Note: Officers with more than one job title may be intentionally listed here more than once.

John O'Reilly, CEO
Bill Floydd, CFO
Olly Raeburn, CMO
David Balls, Dir.-Human Resources
Jonathan Greensted, CIO
Frances Bingham, Corp. Sec.
Daniel Waugh, Dir.-Group Strategy
Sarah Powell, Head-Investor Rel.
Sarah Powell, Head-Treasury
Mark V. Jones, Managing Dir.-Mecca Bingo
Phil Urban, Managing Dir.-Grosvenor Casinos
Ian Burke, Chmn.
Jorge Ibanez, Gen. Dir.-Top Rank Espana

GROWTH PLANS/SPECIAL FEATURES:

The Rank Group plc is a U.K.-based holding company with interests in a variety of gaming and leisure businesses. The firm operates through three main segments: Mecca Bingo, Grosvenor Casinos and Enracha. Mecca Bingo is a leading bingo club operator in the U.K., with 85 clubs marketed under the Mecca Bingo banner. These locations offer a variety of games of chance, including traditional bingo, and many sites also include gaming arcades, restaurants and bars. Grosvenor Casinos is one of the largest casino operators in the U.K., with 54 casinos operating under the Grosvenor brand in England and one in Belgium. These locations feature a variety of traditional table games, electronic games and card room games as well as onsite restaurants and bars. Enracha operates nine bingo clubs in major cities across Spain. The business is headquartered in Barcelona, with clubs in the provinces of Madrid, Catalonia, Andalucia and Galicia. Hong Leong Company (Malaysia) Berhad holds a 56.16% ownership stake in the company.

The company offers employees medical insurance, a pension scheme and company discounts.

FINANCIAL DATA:
Note: Data for latest year may not have been available at press time.

In U.S. $	2018	2017	2016	2015	2014	2013
Revenue						
R&D Expense						
Operating Income						
Operating Margin %						
SGA Expense						
Net Income						
Operating Cash Flow						
Capital Expenditure						
EBITDA						
Return on Assets %						
Return on Equity %						
Debt to Equity						

CONTACT INFORMATION:
Phone: 44 1628504000　　Fax: 44 1628504042
Toll-Free:
Address: TOR, Saint-Cloud Way, Maidenhead, Berkshire SL6 1AY United Kingdom

STOCK TICKER/OTHER:
Stock Ticker: RANKF
Employees: 10,378
Parent Company:

Exchange: PINX
Fiscal Year Ends: 06/30

SALARIES/BONUSES:
Top Exec. Salary: $625,126　　Bonus: $394,787
Second Exec. Salary: $397,808　　Bonus: $133,234

OTHER THOUGHTS:
Estimated Female Officers or Directors: 3
Hot Spot for Advancement for Women/Minorities: Y

Sales, profits and employees may be estimates. Financial information, benefits and other data can change quickly and may vary from those stated here.

Raycom Media Inc

NAIC Code: 515120

www.raycommedia.com

TYPES OF BUSINESS:
Television Broadcasting
Telecommunications
Event Management
Postproduction Services

BRANDS/DIVISIONS/AFFILIATES:
KAIT
KCBD
PureCars
Raycom Sports
Tupelo Raycom
RTM Productions
Broadview Media
CNHI LLC

CONTACTS: Note: Officers with more than one job title may be intentionally listed here more than once.
Pat LaPlatney, CEO
Susana Schuler, Exec. VP-Oper.
Paul McTear, Pres.
Wayne Freedman, VP-Sales
Dianne Wilson, VP-Human Resources
Billy McDowell, VP-Research
David Burke, VP-IT
David Folsom, CTO
Rebecca Bryan, General Counsel
Pat LaPlatney, VP-Bus. Dev.
Pat LaPlatney, VP-Digital Media
Don Richards, VP-Television

GROWTH PLANS/SPECIAL FEATURES:
Raycom Media, Inc., an employee-owned company, is one of the largest broadcasters in the U.S. The firm owns and/or operates 65 television stations and two radio stations in 44 markets in 20 states. Raycom Media owns or provides services for stations covering more than 16% of U.S. television households. Just a few television stations owned by the firm include KAIT, KCBD, KNIN, KRHD, KSWX, KTRE, WECT, WLOX and WXTX. Raycom Media also owns PureCars, a digital ad platform for the automotive industry; Raycom Sports, a marketing, production and events management and distribution firm; Tupelo Raycom, a sports and entertainment production company; RTM Productions, a Tennessee-based automotive programming production and marketing solutions firm; and Broadview Media, a post-production/digital signage company based in Alabama. In addition, Raycom is responsible for the design and hosting of Alabama's Robert Trent Jones Golf Trail website. Subsidiary CNHI, LLC (formerly Community Newspaper Holdings, Inc.) is an American publisher of newspapers and advertising-related publications. In January 2019, Raycom Media was acquired by Gray Television, Inc., which owns and/or operates over 100 television stations across 57 television markets that collectively broadcast over 200 program streams. At closing, Raycom merged into Gray, creating the single largest owner of top-rated local television stations and digital assets in the U.S. CNHI was not included in the sale to Gray.

FINANCIAL DATA: Note: Data for latest year may not have been available at press time.

In U.S. $	2018	2017	2016	2015	2014	2013
Revenue	2,050,000,000	2,000,000,000	1,800,000,000	1,600,000,000		
R&D Expense						
Operating Income						
Operating Margin %						
SGA Expense						
Net Income						
Operating Cash Flow						
Capital Expenditure						
EBITDA						
Return on Assets %						
Return on Equity %						
Debt to Equity						

CONTACT INFORMATION:
Phone: 334-206-1400 Fax: 334-206-1555
Toll-Free:
Address: 201 Monroa St., RSA Tower, 20/Fl, Montgomery, AL 36104 United States

STOCK TICKER/OTHER:
Stock Ticker: Subsidiary
Employees: 8,300
Parent Company: Gray Television

Exchange:
Fiscal Year Ends: 12/31

SALARIES/BONUSES:
Top Exec. Salary: $ Bonus: $
Second Exec. Salary: $ Bonus: $

OTHER THOUGHTS:
Estimated Female Officers or Directors: 4
Hot Spot for Advancement for Women/Minorities: Y

Sales, profits and employees may be estimates. Financial information, benefits and other data can change quickly and may vary from those stated here.

RCN Telecom Services LLC

NAIC Code: 517110

www.rcn.com

TYPES OF BUSINESS:
Local & Long-Distance Telephone Service
High-Speed Internet Access
Cable Television Service

GROWTH PLANS/SPECIAL FEATURES:
RCN Telecom Services, LLC provides advanced high-speed internet, digital TV and phone services to residential and small, medium and enterprise businesses. RCN's offerings include 100% digital programming, a fiber-optic network and free video on demand. For businesses, the company's communications products and services include internet, voice, video and network solutions. RCN also offers bundled package deals. RCN Telecom is privately-owned by TPG Capital.

BRANDS/DIVISIONS/AFFILIATES:
TPG Capital

CONTACTS:
Note: Officers with more than one job title may be intentionally listed here more than once.

Jim Holanda, CEO
Douglas Bradbury, Exec. VP
James Holanda, CEO-Video High-Speed Internet & Premium Voice Svcs
Felipe Alvarez, Pres.-RCN Metro Optical Networks

FINANCIAL DATA:
Note: Data for latest year may not have been available at press time.

In U.S. $	2018	2017	2016	2015	2014	2013
Revenue		547,468,623	521,398,689	550,000,000	530,000,000	520,000,000
R&D Expense						
Operating Income						
Operating Margin %						
SGA Expense						
Net Income						
Operating Cash Flow						
Capital Expenditure						
EBITDA						
Return on Assets %						
Return on Equity %						
Debt to Equity						

CONTACT INFORMATION:
Phone: 703-434-8200 Fax:
Toll-Free: 800-746-4726
Address: 650 College Road, Ste 3100, Princeton, NJ 20170 United States

STOCK TICKER/OTHER:
Stock Ticker: Private
Employees: 1,500
Parent Company: TPC Capital

Exchange:
Fiscal Year Ends: 12/31

SALARIES/BONUSES:
Top Exec. Salary: $ Bonus: $
Second Exec. Salary: $ Bonus: $

OTHER THOUGHTS:
Estimated Female Officers or Directors:
Hot Spot for Advancement for Women/Minorities:

Reading International Inc

www.readingrdi.com

NAIC Code: 512131

TYPES OF BUSINESS:
Movie Theaters

BRANDS/DIVISIONS/AFFILIATES:

CONTACTS:
Note: Officers with more than one job title may be intentionally listed here more than once.

Ellen Cotter, CEO
Devasis Ghose, CFO
Steve Lucas, Chief Accounting Officer
Margaret Cotter, Director
Andrzej Matyczynski, Executive VP, Divisional
S. Tompkins, Executive VP
Wayne Smith, Managing Director, Geographical
Robert Smerling, President, Divisional

GROWTH PLANS/SPECIAL FEATURES:

Reading International, Inc. is an internationally diversified company mainly focused on the development, ownership and operation of entertainment and real property assets in the U.S., Australia and New Zealand. Currently, the firm operates in two business segments: theatrical motion picture exhibition, which is comprised of 59 multiplex theaters; and real estate, which includes real estate development, as well as the rental or licensing of retail, commercial and live theater assets. Within the cinema theatrical motion picture exhibition, Reading International focuses on the ownership and operation of three variations of cinema: modern stadium seating multiplex cinemas featuring conventional film products; specialty and art cinemas; and in some markets, conventional sloped-floor cinemas. Cinema assets include 58 operational cinemas comprised of 473 screens; and three live theaters located in New York City and Chicago. The company's real estate activities have historically consisted of the ownership of fee or long-term leasehold interests in properties used in its cinema exhibition activities, or which were acquired for the development of cinemas or cinema-based real estate development projects, the acquisition of fee interests for general real estate development, the leasing to shows of its live theaters, and the redevelopment of existing cinema sites to their highest and best use. Current real estate assets include interests in the company's cinemas, live theaters, a fee interest in one cinema in New York City, a fee interest in a Union Square property, shopping centers located worldwide, and an additional 20.7 million square feet of developed and undeveloped property worldwide. In June 2018, Reading announced that it had launched Spotlight, a cinema with seat-side waiter services at Reading Cinemas at Cal Oaks Plaza in Murrieta, California.

FINANCIAL DATA:
Note: Data for latest year may not have been available at press time.

In U.S. $	2018	2017	2016	2015	2014	2013
Revenue		279,734,000	270,473,000	257,323,000	254,748,000	258,221,000
R&D Expense						
Operating Income		20,561,000	20,311,000	23,154,000	22,173,000	20,935,000
Operating Margin %		7.35%	7.50%	8.99%	8.70%	8.10%
SGA Expense		25,347,000	26,906,000	18,652,000	18,902,000	18,053,000
Net Income		30,999,000	9,403,000	22,773,000	25,701,000	9,041,000
Operating Cash Flow		23,851,000	30,188,000	28,574,000	28,343,000	25,183,000
Capital Expenditure		65,903,000	49,166,000	53,119,000	14,914,000	20,082,000
EBITDA		57,483,000	37,791,000	50,486,000	39,974,000	38,359,000
Return on Assets %		7.48%	2.40%	5.86%	6.51%	2.21%
Return on Equity %		19.42%	6.83%	17.48%	20.99%	7.41%
Debt to Equity		0.69	1.00	0.87	0.98	0.79

CONTACT INFORMATION:
Phone: 213 235-2240 Fax: 213 235-2229
Toll-Free:
Address: 6100 Center Dr., Ste. 900, Los Angeles, CA 90045 United States

STOCK TICKER/OTHER:
Stock Ticker: RDI
Employees: 88
Parent Company:

Exchange: NAS
Fiscal Year Ends: 12/31

SALARIES/BONUSES:
Top Exec. Salary: $463,800 Bonus: $
Second Exec. Salary: $412,000 Bonus: $

OTHER THOUGHTS:
Estimated Female Officers or Directors: 2
Hot Spot for Advancement for Women/Minorities:

Sales, profits and employees may be estimates. Financial information, benefits and other data can change quickly and may vary from those stated here.

Plunkett Research, Ltd. 393

RealD Inc
NAIC Code: 333316

www.reald.com

TYPES OF BUSINESS:
3D Movie Projection Technologies

BRANDS/DIVISIONS/AFFILIATES:
Rizvi Traverse Management LLC
RealD Ultimate Screen
RealD XL Cinema
RealD TrueMotion

CONTACTS:
Note: Officers with more than one job title may be intentionally listed here more than once.

John Batter, CEO
Jeff Spain, CFO
Leo Bannon, Exec VP, Divisional
Vivian Yang, Executive VP
Anthony Marcoly, President, Divisional
Michael V. Lewis, Chmn.

GROWTH PLANS/SPECIAL FEATURES:

RealD, Inc. develops and licenses 3D viewing technology for use in movies and other formats. The company operates in three segments: cinema, consumer electronics and professional. The cinema segment primarily licenses its 3D technology to movie theaters. This technology consists of cinema systems and both passive and active eyewear needed to view the movies. The company conducts operations through partnerships with major theater operators like AMC, Cinemark and Regal, and accrues revenue by licensing its technology and selling products necessary to view the movies in 3D. The firm's RealD Ultimate Screen is a scientifically-engineered matte-white screen that delivers incredible images in both 2D and 3D formats. Images are 85% brighter and the stereo contrast is 10 times better than on traditional silver screens. Because there is minimal surface texture, images are sharper, clearer and truer in color. The RealD XL Cinema system is a solution for digital light processing (DLP) cinema projectors, maximizing user viewing experiences in larger-than-life formats. RealD TrueMotion software creates a synthetic shutter, allowing creative control of the look of motion. The software enables the adjustment of sharpness, judder and motion blur. Currently (late-2018), the firm's RealD Cinema systems are deployed on over 26,500 theater screens in 72 countries. The consumer-electronics segment develops and sells technology for consumers to view 3D content on televisions and laptops. It maintains licensing agreements with a number of leading consumer electronics manufacturers. The professional segment licenses its technology to product developers, the military and research organizations. RealD's technology was used to give NASA's Mars Rover the ability to record footage in 3D. RealD is owned by Rizvi Traverse Management, LLC, an affiliate of founder and Chairman Michael V. Lewis.

FINANCIAL DATA:
Note: Data for latest year may not have been available at press time.

In U.S. $	2018	2017	2016	2015	2014	2013
Revenue	180,000,000	176,000,000	174,000,000	163,463,008	199,234,000	215,552,000
R&D Expense						
Operating Income						
Operating Margin %						
SGA Expense						
Net Income				-23,822,000	-11,406,000	-9,690,000
Operating Cash Flow						
Capital Expenditure						
EBITDA						
Return on Assets %						
Return on Equity %						
Debt to Equity						

CONTACT INFORMATION:
Phone: 310 385-4000 Fax: 310 385-4001
Toll-Free:
Address: 100 N. Crescent Dr., Ste. 120, Beverly Hills, CA 90210 United States

SALARIES/BONUSES:
Top Exec. Salary: $ Bonus: $
Second Exec. Salary: $ Bonus: $

STOCK TICKER/OTHER:
Stock Ticker: Subsidiary
Employees: 162
Parent Company: Rizvi Traverse Management llc

Exchange:
Fiscal Year Ends: 03/31

OTHER THOUGHTS:
Estimated Female Officers or Directors: 1
Hot Spot for Advancement for Women/Minorities:

Sales, profits and employees may be estimates. Financial information, benefits and other data can change quickly and may vary from those stated here.

RealNetworks Inc

www.realnetworks.com

NAIC Code: 511210F

TYPES OF BUSINESS:
Computer Software, Multimedia, Graphics & Publishing
Computer Software-Streaming Audio & Video
Online Retail-Digital Media
Mobile Games
Mobile Music
Mobile Video

BRANDS/DIVISIONS/AFFILIATES:
RealPlayer
GameHouse
Zylom
Rhapsody International Inc
Napster

CONTACTS: Note: Officers with more than one job title may be intentionally listed here more than once.
Robert Glaser, CEO
Cary Baker, CFO
Michael Parham, General Counsel
Massimiliano Pellegrini, President

GROWTH PLANS/SPECIAL FEATURES:
RealNetworks, Inc. is a creator of digital media services and software. The company operates in three segments: consumer entertainment, mobile services and games. The consumer entertainment business consists of RealPlayer and related products and services. Nearly all this segments revenue is derived from legacy products and services related to the RealPlayer, and these revenues are primarily generated in the U.S. and Canada. The mobile services segment consists of digital media services to network service providers as software as a service (SaaS) offerings. Revenues from this segment are primarily in North America and Asia. Within the games business segment, the firm owns and operates a large casual game service, offering games via digital downloads, online subscription play, third-party portals, social networks and mobile devices. Casual games typically have simple graphics, rules and controls and are quick to learn; they include board, card, puzzle, word and hidden-object games. Games are primarily distributed in North America, Europe and Latin America through GameHouse and Zylom websites, as well as through websites owned or managed by third parties. This segment monetizes social and mobile games largely through sales of games licenses, advertising and microtransactions from mobile and social games. Additionally, the firm owns approximately 42% in Rhapsody International, Inc., which does business as Napster. Napster provides music products and services that enable consumers to have access to digital music content from a variety of devices.

FINANCIAL DATA: Note: Data for latest year may not have been available at press time.

In U.S. $	2018	2017	2016	2015	2014	2013
Revenue		78,718,000	120,468,000	125,296,000	156,212,000	206,196,000
R&D Expense		29,710,000	29,923,000	43,626,000	52,765,000	60,880,000
Operating Income		-18,105,000	-35,685,000	-63,908,000	-64,161,000	-53,518,000
Operating Margin %		-22.99%	-27.76%	-49.00%	-37.94%	-24.45%
SGA Expense		43,949,000	59,023,000	72,780,000	100,927,000	116,654,000
Net Income		-16,305,000	-36,550,000	-81,847,000	-71,815,000	-58,990,000
Operating Cash Flow		-21,350,000	-24,328,000	-68,982,000	-60,244,000	-49,879,000
Capital Expenditure		734,000	2,438,000	1,319,000	2,460,000	7,727,000
EBITDA		-15,169,000	-28,628,000	-53,498,000	-52,202,000	-34,770,000
Return on Assets %		-12.94%	-25.05%	-39.76%	-24.21%	-15.19%
Return on Equity %		-19.43%	-34.93%	-51.49%	-30.81%	-19.28%
Debt to Equity						

CONTACT INFORMATION:
Phone: 206 674-2700   Fax: 206 674-2699
Toll-Free:
Address: 1501 First Avenue South, Ste. 600, Seattle, WA 98134 United States

STOCK TICKER/OTHER:
Stock Ticker: RNWK
Employees: 534
Parent Company:

Exchange: NAS
Fiscal Year Ends: 12/31

SALARIES/BONUSES:
Top Exec. Salary: $450,000   Bonus: $
Second Exec. Salary: $400,000   Bonus: $

OTHER THOUGHTS:
Estimated Female Officers or Directors: 4
Hot Spot for Advancement for Women/Minorities: Y

Sales, profits and employees may be estimates. Financial information, benefits and other data can change quickly and may vary from those stated here.

Redbox Automated Retail LLC

www.redbox.com

NAIC Code: 532230

TYPES OF BUSINESS:
DVD Rentals

BRANDS/DIVISIONS/AFFILIATES:
Apollo Global Management LLC
Redbox

CONTACTS:
Note: Officers with more than one job title may be intentionally listed here more than once.

Galen C. Smith, CEO
Pamela Smith, Sr. VP-Finance
J. Scott Di Valerio, CEO-Outerwall Inc

GROWTH PLANS/SPECIAL FEATURES:
Redbox Automated Retail, LLC is one of the largest DVD and video game rental firms in the U.S. The company vends DVDs, Blu-rays and video games through 12-square-foot kiosks in locations such as grocery stores, drugstores, fast food stores and more. Redbox has more than 41,500 units throughout every U.S state. Nearly 70% of Americans live within a five-minute drive from a Redbox kiosk and approximately 1 million discs are rented from them on a daily basis. Redbox kiosks can even be found at national landmarks such as the Empire State Building and Willis Tower in Chicago. Movies are priced at roughly $1.75 per day for DVDs, $2 per day for Blu-ray discs and $3 a day for video games. The kiosks offer up to 200 titles and hold 630 DVDs. Movies can also be rented online and picked up at Redbox locations. Customers can return the movies to any Redbox location. The company has distribution agreements with several major studios, including Universal Studios, Paramount Home Entertainment, Warner Home Video, 20th Century Fox, Lionsgate and Sony Pictures Home Entertainment. Since its inception, Redbox has rented more than 5 billion discs. Redbox operates as a subsidiary of Apollo Global Management, LLC.

FINANCIAL DATA:
Note: Data for latest year may not have been available at press time.

In U.S. $	2018	2017	2016	2015	2014	2013
Revenue	1,000,000,000	1,200,000,000	1,410,000,000	1,760,899,000	1,893,135,000	1,974,531,000
R&D Expense						
Operating Income						
Operating Margin %						
SGA Expense						
Net Income						
Operating Cash Flow						
Capital Expenditure						
EBITDA						
Return on Assets %						
Return on Equity %						
Debt to Equity						

CONTACT INFORMATION:
Phone: 630-756-8000 Fax: 630-756-8888
Toll-Free:
Address: One Tower Ln., Ste. 900, Oakbrook Terrace, IL 60181 United States

STOCK TICKER/OTHER:
Stock Ticker: Subsidiary
Employees: 2,470
Parent Company: Apollo Global Management LLC
Exchange:
Fiscal Year Ends: 01/31

SALARIES/BONUSES:
Top Exec. Salary: $ Bonus: $
Second Exec. Salary: $ Bonus: $

OTHER THOUGHTS:
Estimated Female Officers or Directors: 1
Hot Spot for Advancement for Women/Minorities:

Sales, profits and employees may be estimates. Financial information, benefits and other data can change quickly and may vary from those stated here.

Regal Entertainment Group

NAIC Code: 512131

www.regmovies.com

TYPES OF BUSINESS:
Movie Theaters
In-Theater Advertising
Theater Rental & Special Events
Film Distribution

BRANDS/DIVISIONS/AFFILIATES:
Cineworld Group PLC
Regal Cinemas
Edwards
Great Escape
Hollywood
Regal Crown Club
National CineMedia Inc
Digital Cinema Implementation Partners LLC

CONTACTS: *Note: Officers with more than one job title may be intentionally listed here more than once.*
David Ownby, CFO
Anthony Bloom, Chmn.-Cineworld Group PLC

GROWTH PLANS/SPECIAL FEATURES:
Regal, a subsidiary of Cineworld Group PLC, operates one of the largest and most geographically-diverse motion picture theater circuits in the U.S. The firm's nationwide network of theaters include the Regal Cinemas, United Artists, Edwards, Great Escape and Hollywood brands, which operate 7,322 screens in 560 theaters in 43 states, Guam, Saipan, American Samoa and Washington, D.C. The company develops, acquires and operates theaters primarily in mid-sized metropolitan markets and suburban growth areas, with theaters present in 48 of the top 50 U.S. designated market areas and drawing over 197 million annual attendees. On average, Regal's theaters feature 13 screens per location. Typically, the firm's theater complexes contain 10 to 18 screens, each with auditoriums ranging from 100 to 500 seats. The firm continues to install additional IMAX digital projection and RPX (Regal Premium Experience) screens in selected theatres across the U.S. The firm offers a loyalty program, the Regal Crown Club, which currently has nearly 12 million active members. Regal holds minority interests in National CineMedia, Inc., which offers ancillary services such as in-theater advertising; Digital Cinema Implementation Partners, LLC, which focuses on implementing digital projection systems in theaters nationwide; and Open Road Films, an acquisition-based domestic film distribution company. In February 2018, Cineworld Group completed its $3.6 billion acquisition of Regal Entertainment Group, creating the second-largest movie chain based on number of screens.

FINANCIAL DATA: *Note: Data for latest year may not have been available at press time.*

In U.S. $	2018	2017	2016	2015	2014	2013
Revenue	3,200,000,000	3,163,000,064	3,197,100,032	3,127,300,096	2,990,099,968	3,038,099,968
R&D Expense						
Operating Income						
Operating Margin %						
SGA Expense						
Net Income		112,300,000	170,400,000	153,400,000	105,600,000	157,700,000
Operating Cash Flow						
Capital Expenditure						
EBITDA						
Return on Assets %						
Return on Equity %						
Debt to Equity						

CONTACT INFORMATION:
Phone: 865 922-1123
Fax: 865 922-3188
Toll-Free: 866-734-2534
Address: 7132 Regal Lane, Knoxville, TN 37918 United States

SALARIES/BONUSES:
Top Exec. Salary: $
Bonus: $
Second Exec. Salary: $
Bonus: $

STOCK TICKER/OTHER:
Stock Ticker: Subsidiary
Employees: 25,500
Parent Company: Cineworld Group PLC
Exchange:
Fiscal Year Ends: 12/31

OTHER THOUGHTS:
Estimated Female Officers or Directors: 1
Hot Spot for Advancement for Women/Minorities:

Reliance Entertainment Pvt Ltd

www.relianceentertainment.net

NAIC Code: 512110

TYPES OF BUSINESS:
Media & Entertainment Products
Movie Production
Film Restoration & Conversion Services
Cinemas
TV & Radio Broadcasting
Advertising Services
Online DVD Rental
Online Gaming & Social Networking

BRANDS/DIVISIONS/AFFILIATES:
Reliance Anil Dhirubhai Ambani Group
Phantoms
Rohit Shetty Picturez
Big Synergy
Reliance Animation
Reliance Education
Talent House
Reliance Games

CONTACTS: Note: Officers with more than one job title may be intentionally listed here more than once.
Anil Dhirubhai Ambani, Chmn.-Reliance Anil Dhirubhai Ambani Group
Anil Ambani, Chmn.

GROWTH PLANS/SPECIAL FEATURES:
Reliance Entertainment Pvt. Ltd. is the media and entertainment arm of Indian conglomerate Reliance Anil Dhirubhai Ambani Group. The firm's offerings are grouped into five divisions: film, web series & TV, animation, digital and gaming. The film division produces, distributes and exhibits motion pictures under the Reliance Entertainment brand; and other film content under the Phantoms, Planc, Rohit Shetty Picturez, Ynot, Global Cinemas, World Wide Open, SelectFlix, Entropy and Reliance labels. The web series & TV division produces, distributes and exhibits TV and web series programming for Reliance Entertainment through the Big Synergy, Phantom and Rohit Shetty labels. Shows in division include the TV shows 10 Ka Dum and India's Got Talent and the web series Bose: Dead/Alive. The animation division is operated through Reliance Animation. Working in conjuncture with Rohit Shetty and Reliance Education, the division creates entertaining animated content such as Little Singham, which brings the iconic character of Bajirao Singham to life. The digital division includes Big Fix, which provides home entertainment across many languages, as well as devices, and Talent House, an open source platform that aims to help professional creative people to be seen, heard and compensated. The games division includes Reliance Games, comprising more than 20 game titles based on films, including RealSteel, Duck Dynasty, BFG, Super Pixel Heroes and Hotel Transylvania; and Zapak, offering a variety of free games at zapak.com. Reliance Entertainment has also firm formed a 50-50 JV with Friday Filmworks, called Plan C Studios, which produced its first movie, Rustom, in 2016.

FINANCIAL DATA: Note: Data for latest year may not have been available at press time.

In U.S. $	2018	2017	2016	2015	2014	2013
Revenue						
R&D Expense						
Operating Income						
Operating Margin %						
SGA Expense						
Net Income						
Operating Cash Flow						
Capital Expenditure						
EBITDA						
Return on Assets %						
Return on Equity %						
Debt to Equity						

CONTACT INFORMATION:
Phone: 91-22-4955-4000 Fax:
Toll-Free:
Address: Fl. 8, 'Grandeur', Veera Desai, Rd. Extension, Andheri (W), Mumbai, 400 053 India

STOCK TICKER/OTHER:
Stock Ticker: Subsidiary   Exchange:
Employees: Fiscal Year Ends:
Parent Company: Reliance Anil Dhirubhai Ambani Group

SALARIES/BONUSES:
Top Exec. Salary: $ Bonus: $
Second Exec. Salary: $ Bonus: $

OTHER THOUGHTS:
Estimated Female Officers or Directors:
Hot Spot for Advancement for Women/Minorities:

RELX PLC

NAIC Code: 511140

www.relx.com

TYPES OF BUSINESS:
Online Information Publishing
Textbooks
Scientific and Medical Journals
Business and Trade Magazines
Legal Databases
Marketing Support, Lists and Research
Exhibitions and Trade Shows
Consulting and Technical Services

BRANDS/DIVISIONS/AFFILIATES:
RELX Group
RELX NV

CONTACTS:
Note: Officers with more than one job title may be intentionally listed here more than once.

Erik Engstrom, CEO
Nick Luff, CFO
Anthony Habgood, Chmn.

GROWTH PLANS/SPECIAL FEATURES:

RELX PLC is the parent company of the RELX Group. The RELX Group provides students, business executives and professionals with information in the fields of science, medicine, law, education and business. Operating segments include: scientific, technical and medical, which provides information and tools to help customers improve scientific and health care outcomes; risk and business information, which offers data services and tools that combine proprietary, public and third-party information with technology and analytics to business and government customers; legal, which provides legal, tax, regulatory news and business information to legal, corporate, government and academic markets; and exhibitions, with information about organizing exhibitions and conferences. The firm's principal operations are in North America and Europe, with North America representing 50% of total revenues. Revenue is derived primarily from subscriptions, transactional and advertising sales. The RELX Group announced in January 2018 that it had acquired ThreatMatrix, a data security firm specializing in risk-based authentication. In September 2018, the RELX Group announced the completion of the simplification of its corporate structure by which its previous dual parent company structure, with RELX PLC headquartered in London and RELX NV headquartered in Amsterdam, has been simplified to a single parent company, RELX PLC.

FINANCIAL DATA:
Note: Data for latest year may not have been available at press time.

In U.S. $	2018	2017	2016	2015	2014	2013
Revenue		9,288,492,000	8,707,568,000	7,540,665,000	7,290,615,000	7,621,489,000
R&D Expense						
Operating Income		2,359,063,000	2,110,275,000	1,809,709,000	1,725,096,000	1,701,101,000
Operating Margin %		25.19%	24.03%	23.99%	23.66%	22.31%
SGA Expense		3,606,789,000	3,455,244,000	3,042,281,000	3,032,178,000	3,245,605,000
Net Income		2,095,120,000	1,466,205,000	1,272,984,000	1,206,052,000	1,401,798,000
Operating Cash Flow		2,333,805,000	2,124,167,000	1,776,874,000	1,738,988,000	1,750,354,000
Capital Expenditure		447,060,000	420,539,500	387,704,600	340,978,000	388,967,500
EBITDA		3,152,152,000	2,855,375,000	2,532,077,000	2,412,103,000	2,476,510,000
Return on Assets %		12.95%	9.47%	9.05%	8.85%	10.32%
Return on Equity %		71.00%	52.01%	47.43%	42.48%	47.53%
Debt to Equity		1.78	1.58	1.52	1.49	1.10

CONTACT INFORMATION:
Phone: 44-20-7166-5500   Fax: 44-20-7166-5799
Toll-Free:
Address: 1-3 Strand, London, WC2N 5JR United Kingdom

SALARIES/BONUSES:
Top Exec. Salary: $1,501,566   Bonus: $1,563,447
Second Exec. Salary: $884,017   Bonus: $916,852

STOCK TICKER/OTHER:
Stock Ticker: RELX   Exchange: NYS
Employees: 31,000   Fiscal Year Ends: 12/31
Parent Company:

OTHER THOUGHTS:
Estimated Female Officers or Directors: 3
Hot Spot for Advancement for Women/Minorities: Y

Renaissance Entertainment Corporation

www.renfair.com

NAIC Code: 711300

TYPES OF BUSINESS:
Renaissance Entertainment Parks
Food & Beverages
Halloween Events
Skiing Facilities

BRANDS/DIVISIONS/AFFILIATES:
Bristol Renaissance Faire
Original Renaissance Pleasure Faire (The)
New York Renaissance Faire
Forest of Fear

CONTACTS:
Note: Officers with more than one job title may be intentionally listed here more than once.

J. Stanley Gilbert, Pres.

GROWTH PLANS/SPECIAL FEATURES:
Renaissance Entertainment Corporation (REC) owns and operates Renaissance fairs in the U.S. The company's fairs include the New York Renaissance Faire; the Bristol Renaissance Faire in Illinois and Wisconsin; and The Original Renaissance Pleasure Faire in California. All of the company's Renaissance fairs are outdoor family entertainment events that romanticize the ambiance of a Renaissance-era marketplace. These marketplaces include craft shops, dancers, jousters, musicians and historical characters from Elizabethan England. The fairs run from 6-9 weekends, all day long, with comedies and dramas enacted on multiple stages and minstrels and troubadours that walk about singing and dancing. More than 100 foods and desserts are offered, including shepherd's pie, roasted turkey legs, crepes and strawberries and cream. Each year, the fairs bring in more than 500,000 people. For Halloween, the New York fair site is turned into the Forest of Fear, a haunted house with various Halloween-inspired games, such as an axe toss, as well as various attractions such as Circus of the Damned and the Slaughter House.

FINANCIAL DATA:
Note: Data for latest year may not have been available at press time.

In U.S. $	2018	2017	2016	2015	2014	2013
Revenue						
R&D Expense						
Operating Income						
Operating Margin %						
SGA Expense						
Net Income						
Operating Cash Flow						
Capital Expenditure						
EBITDA						
Return on Assets %						
Return on Equity %						
Debt to Equity						

CONTACT INFORMATION:
Phone: 303-664-0300 Fax:
Toll-Free:
Address: 2687 Northpark Dr. 101, Lafayette, CO 80026 United States

STOCK TICKER/OTHER:
Stock Ticker: Private Exchange:
Employees: 36 Fiscal Year Ends: 12/31
Parent Company:

SALARIES/BONUSES:
Top Exec. Salary: $ Bonus: $
Second Exec. Salary: $ Bonus: $

OTHER THOUGHTS:
Estimated Female Officers or Directors:
Hot Spot for Advancement for Women/Minorities:

Sales, profits and employees may be estimates. Financial information, benefits and other data can change quickly and may vary from those stated here.

RentPath LLC

NAIC Code: 511120

rentpath.com

TYPES OF BUSINESS:
Magazine Publishing
Housing Guides
Magazine Distribution
Online Media

BRANDS/DIVISIONS/AFFILIATES:
TPG Capital
Apartment Guide (The)
ApartmentGuide.com
Rentals.com
Rent.com
Livelovely.com

CONTACTS:
Note: Officers with more than one job title may be intentionally listed here more than once.

Marc Lefar, CEO
Kim Payne, CFO
Juliet Johansson, Sr. VP-Sales
Jackson Lynch, Sr. VP
Mike Child, CTO
Marlon Starr, General Counsel
Scott Asher, VP-Oper.
Rob Sternot, VP-Corp. Dev. & Strategy
Arlene Mayfield, Sr. VP
Amit Jain, Pres., Rent.com

GROWTH PLANS/SPECIAL FEATURES:
RentPath LLC, owned by TPG Capital, is a targeted media company that publishes and distributes advertising-supported print and online consumer guides primarily for the apartment and other rental property sectors of the residential real estate industry. Its guides are provided free of charge to end users. The Apartment Guide delivers apartment and apartment community rental information to consumers via print, internet and mobile devices. Additional brands include: ApartmentGuide.com, which offers, in addition to rental listings, virtual tours, flexible search functionality, detailed photos and floorplans; Rentals.com, a residential real estate rental website offering listings, as well as rental insurance and other related services; Rent.com, a rental listing website; and Livelovely.com, a real-time rental marketplace that displays available rentals, instantly notifies customers of new listings and directly connects them with the landlords.

FINANCIAL DATA:
Note: Data for latest year may not have been available at press time.

In U.S. $	2018	2017	2016	2015	2014	2013
Revenue	291,000,000	288,000,000	281,000,000	265,000,000	260,000,000	265,000,000
R&D Expense						
Operating Income						
Operating Margin %						
SGA Expense						
Net Income						
Operating Cash Flow						
Capital Expenditure						
EBITDA						
Return on Assets %						
Return on Equity %						
Debt to Equity						

CONTACT INFORMATION:
Phone: 678-421-3000   Fax:
Toll-Free: 800-216-1423
Address: 950 E. Paces Ferry Rd., Ste. 2600, Atlanta, GA 30326 United States

STOCK TICKER/OTHER:
Stock Ticker: Private
Employees: 750
Parent Company: TPG Capital

Exchange:
Fiscal Year Ends: 12/31

SALARIES/BONUSES:
Top Exec. Salary: $ Bonus: $
Second Exec. Salary: $ Bonus: $

OTHER THOUGHTS:
Estimated Female Officers or Directors: 3
Hot Spot for Advancement for Women/Minorities: Y

Sales, profits and employees may be estimates. Financial information, benefits and other data can change quickly and may vary from those stated here.

RLJ Entertainment Inc

www.rljentertainment.com

NAIC Code: 512120

TYPES OF BUSINESS:
Motion Picture and Video Distribution

BRANDS/DIVISIONS/AFFILIATES:
AMC Networks Inc
Digital Entertainment Holdings LLC
Acorn TV
UMC (Urban Movie Channel)
Acorn Media Enterprises
Agatha Christie Limited

GROWTH PLANS/SPECIAL FEATURES:
RLJ Entertainment, Inc. is a digital channel company serving distinct audiences primarily through its over-the-top (OTT) branded channels, Acorn TV (British TV) and UMC (Urban Movie Channel). These channels comprise a large library of international and British dramas, independent feature films and urban content. RLJ's titles are also distributed in multiple formats, including broadcast and pay television, theatrical and non-theatrical, digital video disk (DVD), Blu-ray and a variety of digital distribution models (including EST, VOD, SVOD and AVOD) in North America, the U.K. and Australia. In addition, Acorn Media Enterprises is RLJ's U.K. development arm and co-produces and develops new programs. Acorn Medial also owns 64% of Agatha Christie Limited. Agatha Christie Limited manages the literary and media rights to Agatha Christie's works worldwide. In late-2018, RLJ Entertainment was taken private by Digital Entertainment Holdings, LLC, itself a subsidiary of AMC Networks, Inc.

CONTACTS:
Note: Officers with more than one job title may be intentionally listed here more than once.

Miguel Penella, CEO
Nazir Rostom, CFO
Mark Nunis, Dir.-Finance & Acctg.
Sylvia George, CMO
Titus Bicknell, Chief Digital Officer
Robert Johnson, Chmn.

FINANCIAL DATA:
Note: Data for latest year may not have been available at press time.

In U.S. $	2018	2017	2016	2015	2014	2013
Revenue	88,000,000	86,304,000	80,238,000	124,917,000	137,688,992	164,830,000
R&D Expense						
Operating Income						
Operating Margin %						
SGA Expense						
Net Income		-6,126,000	-21,874,000	-54,980,000	-21,200,000	-31,077,000
Operating Cash Flow						
Capital Expenditure						
EBITDA						
Return on Assets %						
Return on Equity %						
Debt to Equity						

CONTACT INFORMATION:
Phone: 301-608-2115 Fax:
Toll-Free:
Address: 8515 Georgia Ave., Ste 650, Silver Spring, MD 20910 United States

STOCK TICKER/OTHER:
Stock Ticker: Private
Employees: 92
Parent Company: AMC Networks INc

Exchange:
Fiscal Year Ends: 03/31

SALARIES/BONUSES:
Top Exec. Salary: $ Bonus: $
Second Exec. Salary: $ Bonus: $

OTHER THOUGHTS:
Estimated Female Officers or Directors:
Hot Spot for Advancement for Women/Minorities:

Sales, profits and employees may be estimates. Financial information, benefits and other data can change quickly and may vary from those stated here.

Rogers Communications Inc

NAIC Code: 517110

www.rogers.com

TYPES OF BUSINESS:
Cable TV Service
Internet Service Provider
Wireless Phone Service
Telephone Service
Television Broadcasting
Magazine Publishing
Radio Stations
Professional Sports Teams

BRANDS/DIVISIONS/AFFILIATES:
Rogers Unison
Rogers 4K TV
LTE-M
5G

CONTACTS: Note: Officers with more than one job title may be intentionally listed here more than once.
Alan Horn, CEO, Subsidiary
Deepak Khandelwal, Other Executive Officer
Joseph Natale, CEO
Anthony Staffieri, CFO
Edward Rogers, Chairman of the Board, Subsidiary
John Hill, Chief Information Officer
Jorge Fernandes, Chief Technology Officer
Philip Lind, Director
Melinda Rogers, Director
James Reid, Other Executive Officer
Frank Boulben, Other Executive Officer
Dale Hooper, Other Executive Officer
Lisa Durocher, Other Executive Officer
David Miller, Other Executive Officer
Dean Prevost, President, Divisional

GROWTH PLANS/SPECIAL FEATURES:
Rogers Communications, Inc. (RCI) is a Canadian company engaged in providing communications and media. The firm operates in four divisions: consumer services, media brands, business services and innovations. The consumer services division helps Canadians connect via communication channels, including wireless devices, home telephones, television, internet and home monitoring systems. This division is comprised of more than 10.1 million wireless subscribers, six customer service touch points, 6,058 cell towers, and 4.2 million homes utilizing RCI's cable services. The media brands division is comprised of 53 radio stations, 64 television networks, 9 magazine brands, four shop-at-home/digital services networks and three sports entertainment networks, providing a mix of television shows, sports, music, information and shopping across the entire country. The business services division delivers communications services and information technology solutions that help customers operate more efficiently, reduce costs and improve productivity and collaboration. These services and solutions include security, cloud and data centers, internet of Things, business collaboration via wireless-driven technology, and business network connectivity. This division's Rogers Unison offering enables Canadian businesses to offer their employees a way to communicate across multiple devices, via its fully-managed, truly mobile communications system. Last, the innovations division works to bring customers the fastest speeds and latest innovations. This division currently provides an LTE network, Rogers 4K TV and Gigabit internet. In April 2018, Rogers announced a partnership with Ericsson, a North American 5G developer, to bring 5G to Canada. Rogers announced a plan in October 2018 to launch a national LTE-M network to help businesses connect and track their assets in real time.

FINANCIAL DATA: Note: Data for latest year may not have been available at press time.

In U.S. $	2018	2017	2016	2015	2014	2013
Revenue		10,492,770,000	10,165,590,000	9,951,924,000	9,533,489,000	9,426,655,000
R&D Expense						
Operating Income		2,356,293,000	2,043,951,000	2,003,146,000	2,105,529,000	2,233,879,000
Operating Margin %		22.45%	20.10%	20.12%	22.08%	23.69%
SGA Expense						
Net Income		1,269,401,000	619,491,300	1,024,572,000	994,895,600	1,238,241,000
Operating Cash Flow		2,921,625,000	2,935,721,000	2,779,921,000	2,743,568,000	2,960,204,000
Capital Expenditure		1,770,187,000	1,855,506,000	1,943,793,000	1,813,218,000	1,797,638,000
EBITDA		3,921,714,000	3,156,809,000	3,675,401,000	3,575,986,000	3,663,531,000
Return on Assets %		5.98%	2.90%	4.95%	5.35%	7.72%
Return on Equity %		29.45%	15.16%	24.60%	26.42%	39.56%
Debt to Equity		1.99	2.90	2.76	2.52	2.60

CONTACT INFORMATION:
Phone: 416 935-2303　　Fax: 416 935-3548
Toll-Free:
Address: 333 Bloor St. E., 10/Fl, Toronto, ON M4W 1G9 Canada

STOCK TICKER/OTHER:
Stock Ticker: RCI　　Exchange: NYS
Employees: 24,500　　Fiscal Year Ends: 12/31
Parent Company:

SALARIES/BONUSES:
Top Exec. Salary: $1,029,711　　Bonus: $
Second Exec. Salary: $712,635　　Bonus: $

OTHER THOUGHTS:
Estimated Female Officers or Directors: 6
Hot Spot for Advancement for Women/Minorities: Y

Roku Inc

NAIC Code: 334220

www.roku.com

TYPES OF BUSINESS:
Radio and Television Broadcasting and Wireless Communications Equipment Manufacturing

BRANDS/DIVISIONS/AFFILIATES:
Roku
Roku Channel Store

CONTACTS:
Note: Officers with more than one job title may be intentionally listed here more than once.

Steve Louden, CFO
Stephen Kay, General Counsel
Chas Smith, General Manager
Scott Rosenberg, General Manager
Anthony Wood, President

GROWTH PLANS/SPECIAL FEATURES:

Roku, Inc. manufactures home digital media products. The company's digital media players connect users to streaming content, enable content publishers to build and monetize large audiences, and provide advertisers with unique capabilities to engage consumers. As of early-2018, Roku had approximately 20 million active accounts, with users streaming more than 15 billion hours on the Roku platform during the fiscal year. Roku's home screen helps users find the content they want to watch, and offers the ability to search, discover and access over 500,000 movies and TV episodes in the U.S., as well as live sports, music, news and more. Users can also compare the price of content from various channels available on the Roku platform, and choose from ad-supported, subscriptions and transactional video on-demand content. For content publishers, Roku's platform offers direct-to-consumer distribution, ease of publishing and monetization, and enables drive tune in through a range of advertising capabilities. In addition, developers can create non-certified streaming channels that can only be installed on a Roku device, and therefore are not found in the Roku Channel Store. Through these channels, developers can test their channel offerings before releasing them to the general public. For advertisers, Roku offers access to hard-to-reach audiences, TV and digital advertising delivery and large-scale advertising access to over-the-top audiences. Roku branded streaming players and television models are available worldwide through direct retail sales and licensing arrangements through TV original equipment manufacturers (OEMs) and service operators.

FINANCIAL DATA:
Note: Data for latest year may not have been available at press time.

In U.S. $	2018	2017	2016	2015	2014	2013
Revenue		512,763,000	398,649,000	319,857,000		
R&D Expense		107,945,000	76,177,000	50,469,000		
Operating Income		-19,616,000	-43,361,000	-37,552,000		
Operating Margin %		-3.82%	-10.87%	-11.74%		
SGA Expense		111,504,000	88,229,000	76,861,000		
Net Income		-63,509,000	-42,758,000	-40,611,000		
Operating Cash Flow		37,292,000	-32,463,000	-32,604,000		
Capital Expenditure		9,229,000	8,596,000	5,019,000		
EBITDA		-56,246,000	-37,245,000	-37,213,000		
Return on Assets %		-23.05%	-24.54%	-23.00%		
Return on Equity %						
Debt to Equity						

CONTACT INFORMATION:
Phone: 408-556-9040 Fax:
Toll-Free:
Address: 150 Winchester Cir., Los Gatos, CA 95032 United States

SALARIES/BONUSES:
Top Exec. Salary: $835,577   Bonus: $
Second Exec. Salary: $575,000   Bonus: $

STOCK TICKER/OTHER:
Stock Ticker: ROKU
Employees: 696
Parent Company:

Exchange: NAS
Fiscal Year Ends: 12/31

OTHER THOUGHTS:
Estimated Female Officers or Directors:
Hot Spot for Advancement for Women/Minorities:

Rolling Stone LLC

NAIC Code: 511120

www.rollingstone.com

TYPES OF BUSINESS:
Magazine Publishing

BRANDS/DIVISIONS/AFFILIATES:
Penske Media Corporation

GROWTH PLANS/SPECIAL FEATURES:
Rolling Stone, LLC publishes an American monthly magazine, Rolling Stone, which focuses on pop culture. The magazine was founded by Jann Wenner in 1967 and music critic Ralph J. Gleason. At first, it was known for covering music and politics, but began adding content in relation to television shows, film actors, pop artists and more during the 1990s. In December 2017, Penske Media Corporation acquired Wenner Media, LLC's remaining majority stake (51%) in Rolling Stone, causing the firm to become a Penske Media subsidiary.

CONTACTS:
Note: Officers with more than one job title may be intentionally listed here more than once.

Dana Rosen, General Counsel
Timothy Walsh, VP-Finance & Tax
Edward Gross, Mgr.-Ad Svcs., Men's Journal
Mary Parente, Mgr.-Ad Svcs., Us Weekly
Jann S. Wenner, Chmn.

FINANCIAL DATA:
Note: Data for latest year may not have been available at press time.

In U.S. $	2018	2017	2016	2015	2014	2013
Revenue						
R&D Expense						
Operating Income						
Operating Margin %						
SGA Expense						
Net Income						
Operating Cash Flow						
Capital Expenditure						
EBITDA						
Return on Assets %						
Return on Equity %						
Debt to Equity						

CONTACT INFORMATION:
Phone: 212-484-1616 Fax: 212-484-3435
Toll-Free:
Address: 1290 Ave. of the Americas, New York, NY 10104-0298 United States

STOCK TICKER/OTHER:
Stock Ticker: Subsidiary Exchange:
Employees: 450 Fiscal Year Ends: 12/31
Parent Company: Penske Media Corporation

SALARIES/BONUSES:
Top Exec. Salary: $ Bonus: $
Second Exec. Salary: $ Bonus: $

OTHER THOUGHTS:
Estimated Female Officers or Directors: 2
Hot Spot for Advancement for Women/Minorities: Y

Sales, profits and employees may be estimates. Financial information, benefits and other data can change quickly and may vary from those stated here.

Rosetta Stone Inc

www.rosettastone.com

NAIC Code: 511210P

TYPES OF BUSINESS:
Language Learning Software

BRANDS/DIVISIONS/AFFILIATES:
Rosetta Stone
Rosetta Stone Kids Reading
Dynamic Immersion
Lexia Learning

CONTACTS:
Note: Officers with more than one job title may be intentionally listed here more than once.

Thomas Pierno, CFO
M. Hartford, Chief Accounting Officer
Arthur Hass, Director
Sonia Galindo, General Counsel
Matt Hulett, President, Divisional
Nicholas Gaehde, President, Subsidiary

GROWTH PLANS/SPECIAL FEATURES:
Rosetta Stone, Inc. is a leading provider of cloud-based language learning programs. The company develops, markets and sells learning systems consisting of software, online services and audio practice tools primarily under its Rosetta Stone brand. The company's teaching method, known as Dynamic Immersion, is designed to leverage the natural language learning ability that children use to learn their native language. Its interactive courses are based on proprietary technology and pedagogical content and utilize sequences of images, texts and sounds to teach a new language without translation or grammar explanation, which also makes Rosetta Stone programs more easily deployable across many languages. The firm's courses cover 30 languages, and its customers include individuals, educational institutions, armed forces, government agencies and corporations. Rosetta Stone's digital literacy product, Rosetta Stone Kids Reading, is designed to help young children learn to read and to reinforce core reading skills. The kid's reading product also comes as an app. The firm also operates Lexia Learning, a literary solutions and education division within Rosetta Stone. Lexia Learning has many subscription-based English literacy-learning and assessment solutions, while providing research and proven educational skills for students and teachers. The company's programs are also distributed through retailers such as Amazon.com, Target, Books-a-Million, Staples, Best Buy, Barnes & Noble, Borders, and others in and outside of the U.S.

FINANCIAL DATA:
Note: Data for latest year may not have been available at press time.

In U.S. $	2018	2017	2016	2015	2014	2013
Revenue		184,593,000	194,089,000	217,670,000	261,853,000	264,645,000
R&D Expense		24,747,000	26,273,000	29,939,000	33,176,000	33,995,000
Operating Income		-4,501,000	-21,346,000	-37,004,000	-54,705,000	-17,600,000
Operating Margin %		-2.43%	-10.99%	-17.00%	-20.89%	-6.65%
SGA Expense		130,726,000	154,841,000	186,208,000	230,328,000	202,536,000
Net Income		-1,546,000	-27,550,000	-46,796,000	-73,706,000	-16,134,000
Operating Cash Flow		19,302,000	1,240,000	-5,645,000	6,673,000	8,068,000
Capital Expenditure		12,944,000	12,514,000	8,856,000	9,736,000	8,941,000
EBITDA		8,455,000	-11,255,000	-31,599,000	-66,058,000	-8,322,000
Return on Assets %		-.79%	-13.03%	-18.10%	-25.45%	-5.69%
Return on Equity %		-404.71%	-265.52%	-109.01%	-75.71%	-11.69%
Debt to Equity		0.76		0.11	0.04	

CONTACT INFORMATION:
Phone: 800 788-0822   Fax:
Toll-Free: 800-811-2755
Address: 1621 N. Kent St., Ste. 1200, Arlington, VA 22209 United States

SALARIES/BONUSES:
Top Exec. Salary: $340,000   Bonus: $
Second Exec. Salary: $312,500   Bonus: $

STOCK TICKER/OTHER:
Stock Ticker: RST
Employees: 1,012
Parent Company:

Exchange: NYS
Fiscal Year Ends: 12/31

OTHER THOUGHTS:
Estimated Female Officers or Directors: 5
Hot Spot for Advancement for Women/Minorities: Y

RTL Group SA

NAIC Code: 515120

www.rtlgroup.com

TYPES OF BUSINESS:
Television Broadcasting
Television Production
Radio Broadcasting

BRANDS/DIVISIONS/AFFILIATES:
Bertelsmann AG
RTL
M6
VOX
SpotX
StyleHaul
BroadbandTV
UFA Film & TV Produktion

CONTACTS:
Note: Officers with more than one job title may be intentionally listed here more than once.

Bert Habets, CEO
Elmar Heggen, CFO
Andreas Rudas, Exec. VP-Regional Oper.
Andrew Buckhurst, Sr. VP-Investor Rel.
Anke Schaferkordt, Co-CEO
Andreas Rudas, Exec. VP-Bus. Dev., Asia
Thomas Rabe, Chmn.
Andreas Rudas, Exec. VP-Bus. Dev., Central & Eastern Europe

GROWTH PLANS/SPECIAL FEATURES:
RTL Group SA, based in Luxembourg, is one of the largest television and radio broadcasters in Europe, with more than 61 television stations and 30 radio stations. The company's television segment includes: three stations in Asia under the RTL label; three RTL stations in Belgium; seven stations in Croatia; eleven stations in France under the M6, RTL, Serie Club, Teva, 6ter and W9 labels; 12 stations in Germany under the RTL, VOX, Nitro, Toggo Plus, n-tv and Geo Television labels; nine stations in Hungary under the RTL, Cool TV, Film+, Sorozat+ and Muzsika TV labels; four in Luxembourg under the RTL label; and nine in the Netherlands under the RTL label. In Spain, RTL owns a 19.17%-stake in six stations under the Antena 3, laSexta, Neox, Nova, Mega and Atreseries labels. The firm's radio operations are headed by its wholly-owned flagship RTL, RTL 2 and Fun Radio stations in France. The majority of RTL's radio stations are in Germany, comprising three wholly-owned stations, and more than 20 joint venture stations. Other radio stations either wholly- or jointly-owned by the company are located in Luxembourg, Belgium and Spain. Digital programs include SpotX in Denver, Colorado; StyleHaul in Los Angeles, California; BroadbandTV in Vancouver, Canada; and Divimove in Berlin, Germany. RTL's production and rights trading entities include FremantleMedia, UFA Film & TV Produktion, Grundy Television and CLT-UFA International, located in London, Los Angeles, Potsdam, Sydney and Luxembourg, respectively. Through these production subsidiaries, RTL has more than 400 programs on air or in production throughout the world. RTL Group is 75.1%-owned by Bertelsmann AG, and 24.1%-owned by the public. In January 2018, the firm acquired United Screens, the leading multi-platform network in the Nordic countries.

FINANCIAL DATA:
Note: Data for latest year may not have been available at press time.

In U.S. $	2018	2017	2016	2015	2014	2013
Revenue		7,259,534,000	7,104,616,000	6,867,681,000	6,615,938,000	6,708,206,000
R&D Expense						
Operating Income		1,343,008,000	1,297,444,000	1,275,801,000	1,257,575,000	1,263,271,000
Operating Margin %		18.49%	18.26%	18.57%	19.00%	18.83%
SGA Expense		448,808,500	443,112,900	440,834,700	434,000,100	
Net Income		841,800,700	820,157,600	898,756,100	743,837,400	991,023,800
Operating Cash Flow		1,165,307,000	1,259,853,000	1,119,743,000	1,063,927,000	1,276,940,000
Capital Expenditure		272,246,800	292,750,700	256,299,300	209,595,800	190,231,000
EBITDA		1,683,601,000	1,622,090,000	1,590,195,000	1,435,276,000	1,692,714,000
Return on Assets %		9.12%	8.72%	9.90%	8.53%	11.25%
Return on Equity %		24.49%	23.87%	27.28%	21.81%	23.12%
Debt to Equity		0.19	0.16	0.17	0.18	0.16

CONTACT INFORMATION:
Phone: 352 24861   Fax: 352 24862760
Toll-Free:
Address: 45, boulevard Pierre Frieden, Luxembourg, L-1543 Luxembourg

STOCK TICKER/OTHER:
Stock Ticker: RGLXY
Employees: 11,011
Parent Company:

Exchange: PINX
Fiscal Year Ends: 12/31

SALARIES/BONUSES:
Top Exec. Salary: $ Bonus: $
Second Exec. Salary: $ Bonus: $

OTHER THOUGHTS:
Estimated Female Officers or Directors: 1
Hot Spot for Advancement for Women/Minorities:

Ryman Hospitality Properties Inc

rymanhp.com

NAIC Code: 721110

TYPES OF BUSINESS:
Hotels & Convention Centers
Vacation Property Management
Live Entertainment Venues
Golf Courses
Radio Station Operation

BRANDS/DIVISIONS/AFFILIATES:
Gaylord Opryland Resort & Convention Center
Gaylord Palms Resort & Convention Center
Gaylord Texan Resort & Convention Center
Gaylord National Resort & Convention Center
Grand Ole Opry (The)
General Jackson Showboat
Gaylord Springs Golf Links
Opry City Stage

CONTACTS:
Note: Officers with more than one job title may be intentionally listed here more than once.

Colin Reed, CEO
Mark Fioravanti, CFO
Jennifer Hutcheson, Controller
Bennett Westbrook, Executive VP, Divisional
Scott Lynn, General Counsel
Patrick Chaffin, Senior VP, Divisional

GROWTH PLANS/SPECIAL FEATURES:

Ryman Hospitality Properties, Inc. is a real estate investment trust (REIT) that owns hospitality assets focused on the large group meetings and conventions sector of the lodging market. The firm's hospitality assets include four upscale, meetings-focused resorts totaling 7,811 rooms and 2 million square feet of meeting and exhibit space that are managed by Marriott International, Inc. under the Gaylord Hotels brand. These four hotels consist of the Gaylord Opryland Resort & Convention Center in Nashville, Tennessee; the Gaylord Palms Resort & Convention Center near Orlando, Florida; the Gaylord Texan Resort & Convention Center near Dallas, Texas; and the Gaylord National Resort & Convention Center near Washington, D.C. Other assets managed by Marriott include the General Jackson Showboat; the Gaylord Springs Golf Links, a championship golf course; the Wildhorse Saloon; and the Inn at Opryland, a 303-room overflow hotel adjacent to Gaylord Opryland. Additionally, the firm owns The Grand Ole Opry, a live country music variety show and one of the longest-running radio shows in the U.S.; the Ryman Auditorium; and the country radio station WSM-AM radio. Joint venture Opry City Stage is a four-level entertainment complex on Broadway in Times Square, featuring live entertainment, simulcast performances from the Grand Ole Opry House, a listening room private event space and two-story bar/restaurant space. Ryman transformed Black Shelton's hit song, Ol Red, into a multi-level entertainment venue brand called Ole Red Nashville, which opened in 2018. Currently (as of April 2018), the firm is constructing a luxury indoor/outdoor waterpark adjacent to Gaylord Opryland Resort & Convention Center in Nashville, with over 200,000 square feet of water attractions and amenities. The waterpark is scheduled to open later that year.

FINANCIAL DATA:
Note: Data for latest year may not have been available at press time.

In U.S. $	2018	2017	2016	2015	2014	2013
Revenue		1,184,719,000	1,149,207,000	1,092,124,000	1,040,991,000	954,562,000
R&D Expense						
Operating Income		221,996,000	213,805,000	182,171,000	153,116,000	79,218,000
Operating Margin %		18.57%	18.60%	16.59%	14.70%	8.29%
SGA Expense						
Net Income		176,100,000	159,366,000	111,511,000	126,452,000	118,352,000
Operating Cash Flow		295,830,000	293,601,000	234,362,000	247,004,000	137,699,000
Capital Expenditure		182,565,000	117,977,000	79,815,000	58,377,000	36,959,000
EBITDA		304,955,000	336,488,000	277,940,000	298,725,000	203,259,000
Return on Assets %		7.14%	6.72%	4.70%	5.00%	4.56%
Return on Equity %		47.20%	42.63%	28.55%	20.88%	14.08%
Debt to Equity		4.20	4.08	3.77	3.34	1.52

CONTACT INFORMATION:
Phone: 615-316-6000   Fax: 615-316-6555
Toll-Free:
Address: One Gaylord Dr., Nashville, TN 37214 United States

STOCK TICKER/OTHER:
Stock Ticker: RHP
Employees: 807
Parent Company:

Exchange: NYS
Fiscal Year Ends: 12/31

SALARIES/BONUSES:
Top Exec. Salary: $907,830   Bonus: $250,000
Second Exec. Salary: $511,676   Bonus: $

OTHER THOUGHTS:
Estimated Female Officers or Directors: 1
Hot Spot for Advancement for Women/Minorities:

Saga Communications Inc

NAIC Code: 515120

www.sagacommunications.com

TYPES OF BUSINESS:
Television Broadcasting
Radio Broadcasting
Local News Coverage
Television Broadcasting

BRANDS/DIVISIONS/AFFILIATES:
Lazer 103.3
Sunny95/94.7FM
Star 102.5
102.9FM-The Hog
Everything That Rocks

GROWTH PLANS/SPECIAL FEATURES:
Saga Communications, Inc. is a broadcast company engaged in acquiring, developing and operating broadcast properties. As of early-2018, the firm owned 75 FM and 33 AM radio stations, serving 26 markets, including Bellingham, Washington; Columbus, Ohio; Norfolk, Virginia; Milwaukee, Wisconsin; Manchester, New Hampshire; and Des Moines Iowa. Saga comprises more than 100 brands, but its featured brands include Lazer 103.3/Everything That Rocks, Sunny95/94.7FM, Star 102.5 and 102.9FM/The Hog/Everything That Rocks!. The company builds and maintains products for brands and clients, including websites, mobile apps, content streaming, podcasts, eCommerce and more. In October 2018, Saga agreed to acquire the assets of WOGK (FM), WNDT (FM), WNDD (FM) and WNDN (FM) from Ocala Broadcasting Corporation, LLC, each of which serve the Gainesville-Ocala, Florida radio market.

CONTACTS:
Note: Officers with more than one job title may be intentionally listed here more than once.

Edward Christian, CEO
Samuel Bush, CFO
Catherine Bobinski, Chief Accounting Officer
Warren Lada, COO
Chris Forgy, Senior VP, Divisional
Marcia Lobaito, Senior VP

FINANCIAL DATA:
Note: Data for latest year may not have been available at press time.

In U.S. $	2018	2017	2016	2015	2014	2013
Revenue		118,149,000	142,591,008	132,856,000	133,998,000	129,478,000
R&D Expense						
Operating Income						
Operating Margin %						
SGA Expense						
Net Income		54,717,000	18,186,000	13,414,000	14,904,000	15,273,000
Operating Cash Flow						
Capital Expenditure						
EBITDA						
Return on Assets %						
Return on Equity %						
Debt to Equity						

CONTACT INFORMATION:
Phone: 313 886-7070   Fax: 313 886-7150
Toll-Free:
Address: 73 Kercheval Ave., Grosse Pointe Farm, MI 48236 United States

STOCK TICKER/OTHER:
Stock Ticker: SGA
Employees: 1,146
Parent Company:

Exchange: ASE
Fiscal Year Ends: 12/31

SALARIES/BONUSES:
Top Exec. Salary: $ Bonus: $
Second Exec. Salary: $ Bonus: $

OTHER THOUGHTS:
Estimated Female Officers or Directors: 2
Hot Spot for Advancement for Women/Minorities:

Sahara India Pariwar Ltd

NAIC Code: 524113

www.sahara.in

TYPES OF BUSINESS:
Life Insurance
Financial Services
Hospitality
Cinema Production
Newspapers
Manufacturing
Information Technology
Retail

BRANDS/DIVISIONS/AFFILIATES:
Sahara Life Insurance Company Limited
Sahara Asset Management Co Pvt Ltd
Sahara Housingfina Corporation Limited
Sahara City Homes
Sahara Grace
Sahara Star
Sahara Hospital
Sahara Q Shop

CONTACTS:
Note: Officers with more than one job title may be intentionally listed here more than once.

Subrata Roy Sahara, Managing Dir.
Subrata Roy Sahara, Chmn.

GROWTH PLANS/SPECIAL FEATURES:

Sahara India Pariwar Ltd. (SIP) is a diversified India-based holding company involved in finance, infrastructure, media, retail, manufacturing and information technology, among other interests. The firm's financial businesses offer residuary non-banking services, life insurance, mutual fund investment management and housing financing. These services are conducted through Sahara India Life Insurance Company Limited.; Sahara Asset Management Private Limited; and Sahara Housingfina Corporation Limited. SIP's infrastructure activities include: residential communities Aamby Vallet City, Sahara City Homes and Sahara Grace; Sahara Star, a five-star hotel; and Sahara Hospital, a multi-specialty health complex. The company's media businesses include filmed entertainment, such as Sahara Motion Pictures; Geon Studios, a cinema visual effects firm; Film City, a fully-featured movie studio; FIRANGI, a 24-hour movie channel broadcasting cinema dubbed in Hindi; and Cinema Halls, a chain of multiplexes. It is also active in broadcasting through Sahara One, Filmy, the National News channel and Sahara Samay; and print publishing through Rashtriya Sahara, a daily newspaper; Sahara Time, a weekly English news magazine; Roznama Rashtriya Sahara, an Urdu-language daily newspaper; Aalmi Sahara, an Urdu-language weekly newsmagazine; and Bazm-E-Sahara, an Urdu-language monthly magazine. Its retail segment is in the process of launching Sahara Q Shop, a chain of mega marts featuring the firm's branded products as well as groceries, consumer durables, IT products, jewelry and more. The firm's manufacturing operations, conducted by Araria Jute Project, create consumer products like blankets, carpets, textiles and other similar products. SIP's information technology business, Sahara Next, provides standard information technology services, outsourcing services, web design and software. The company is also engaged in the consumer merchandise, luxury real estate, dairy and power generation industries, among others.

FINANCIAL DATA:
Note: Data for latest year may not have been available at press time.

In U.S. $	2018	2017	2016	2015	2014	2013
Revenue						
R&D Expense						
Operating Income						
Operating Margin %						
SGA Expense						
Net Income						
Operating Cash Flow						
Capital Expenditure						
EBITDA						
Return on Assets %						
Return on Equity %						
Debt to Equity						

CONTACT INFORMATION:
Phone: 91-522-32577921   Fax: 91-522-23244632
Toll-Free:
Address: Sahara India Ctr., 2, Kapoorthala Complex, Aliganj, Lucknow, 226024 India

STOCK TICKER/OTHER:
Stock Ticker: Private
Employees: 13,000
Parent Company:

Exchange:
Fiscal Year Ends:

SALARIES/BONUSES:
Top Exec. Salary: $ Bonus: $
Second Exec. Salary: $ Bonus: $

OTHER THOUGHTS:
Estimated Female Officers or Directors:
Hot Spot for Advancement for Women/Minorities:

Salem Media Group Inc

salemmedia.com

NAIC Code: 515112

TYPES OF BUSINESS:
Radio Broadcasting
Religious & Family Radio
Online Christian Content & Streaming Radio
Magazine Publishing
Internet Content Provider

BRANDS/DIVISIONS/AFFILIATES:
Salem Radio Network
Salem Media Representatives
Salem Web Network
Salem Publishing
TownHall.com
OnePlace.com
Faith Talk
Youthworker Journal

CONTACTS:
Note: Officers with more than one job title may be intentionally listed here more than once.

Edward Atsinger, CEO
Evan Masyr, CFO
Stuart Epperson, Chairman of the Board
Christopher Henderson, Executive VP, Divisional
David Santrella, President, Divisional
David Evans, President, Divisional

GROWTH PLANS/SPECIAL FEATURES:

Salem Media Group, Inc., formerly known as Salem Communications Corp., is a multi-media company with integrated business operations covering radio broadcasting, publishing and the internet, geared towards audiences interested in Christian and conservative opinion content. The company operates in three segments: broadcast, digital media and publishing. Salem is among the largest religious-and family-themed radio broadcasting companies in the U.S., operating 115 radio stations, including 73 stations in the top 25 markets nationwide. The stations are divided into five formats: Christian teaching and talk; news talk; contemporary Christian music; Spanish language Christian teaching and talk; and business. Of its stations, 40 are in the Christian teaching and talk format. Its 13 contemporary Christian music stations are branded The FISH and are targeted to all ages. Eight stations are Spanish language Christian teaching and talk. The 13 business format stations feature financial experts, business talk and Bloomberg programming. The firm also owns a Christian teaching and talk channel on SiriusXM Satellite Radio. It owns Salem Radio Network, SRN News Network, Today's Christian Music, Singing News Network (formerly Solid Gospel Network) and Salem Media Representatives. The firm's digital media segment operates Salem Web Network, a leading internet provider of Christian content and online streaming radio. It also operates radio station websites, including Townhall.com, BearingArms.com, OnePlace.com and GodTube.com. Salem Publishing owns and operates several magazine titles, such as Youthworker Journal, Faith Talk and Homecoming. The publishing segment includes Regnery Publishing, a publisher of leading conservative authors; Salem Author Services, a self-publishing service for authors through Xulon Press, Mill City Press andBookprinting.com; and Singing News, a magazine for readers interested in southern gospel music. In 2018, Salem acquired ChildrenMinistryDeals.com, a platform for Bible-based curriculum for children, and Hilary Kramer's investment products and newsletters. In November 2018, Salem launched Salem Surround, a multimedia advertising agency.

FINANCIAL DATA:
Note: Data for latest year may not have been available at press time.

In U.S. $	2018	2017	2016	2015	2014	2013
Revenue		263,736,000	274,321,000	265,787,000	266,536,000	236,934,000
R&D Expense						
Operating Income		26,875,000	33,269,000	31,927,000	29,680,000	35,713,000
Operating Margin %		10.19%	12.12%	12.01%	11.13%	15.07%
SGA Expense		16,255,000	14,994,000	15,146,000	17,092,000	21,430,000
Net Income		24,644,000	8,873,000	11,150,000	5,475,000	-2,736,000
Operating Cash Flow		27,330,000	38,866,000	36,130,000	41,925,000	28,698,000
Capital Expenditure		10,866,000	11,792,000	24,278,000	16,269,000	16,139,000
EBITDA		37,442,000	45,659,000	51,015,000	45,058,000	25,263,000
Return on Assets %		4.23%	1.49%	1.88%	.94%	-.48%
Return on Equity %		11.07%	4.18%	5.38%	2.69%	-1.34%
Debt to Equity		1.07	1.22	1.29	1.35	1.42

CONTACT INFORMATION:
Phone: 805 987-0400   Fax: 805 384-4520
Toll-Free:
Address: 4880 Santa Rosa Rd., Ste. 300, Camarillo, CA 93012 United States

STOCK TICKER/OTHER:
Stock Ticker: SALM
Employees: 1,590
Parent Company:

Exchange: NAS
Fiscal Year Ends: 12/31

SALARIES/BONUSES:
Top Exec. Salary: $982,404   Bonus: $
Second Exec. Salary: $522,731   Bonus: $10,000

OTHER THOUGHTS:
Estimated Female Officers or Directors:
Hot Spot for Advancement for Women/Minorities:

Sales, profits and employees may be estimates. Financial information, benefits and other data can change quickly and may vary from those stated here.

Salon Media Group Inc

NAIC Code: 519130

www.salon.com

TYPES OF BUSINESS:
Online News & Media
Online Communities

BRANDS/DIVISIONS/AFFILIATES:
Salon.com

GROWTH PLANS/SPECIAL FEATURES:
Salon Media Group, Inc. is a technology-based advertising media business that wholly-owns and operates Salon.com, a news website. Its writing style combines investigative journalism with personal essays, as well as quick-take commentary, articles, podcasts and original video. News topics include politics, culture, entertainment, race, religion, sustainability, innovation, technology and business. Salon targets educated, culturally-engaged audiences interested in original thoughts and reporting of the day's big stories. Advertising is the company's primary source of revenue, with internet advertising accounting for 78% of Salon's annual revenue; and revenue from referring users to third party websites accounting for the remaining 22%. Salon averages approximately 20 million unique viewers a month.

CONTACTS:
Note: Officers with more than one job title may be intentionally listed here more than once.

Richard Gingras, CEO
Norman Blashka, CFO
John Warnock, Chairman of the Board
David Talbot, Founder
Joan Walsh, Other Corporate Officer
Benjamin Zagorski, Vice President, Divisional

FINANCIAL DATA:
Note: Data for latest year may not have been available at press time.

In U.S. $	2018	2017	2016	2015	2014	2013
Revenue						
R&D Expense						
Operating Income						
Operating Margin %						
SGA Expense						
Net Income						
Operating Cash Flow						
Capital Expenditure						
EBITDA						
Return on Assets %						
Return on Equity %						
Debt to Equity						

CONTACT INFORMATION:
Phone: 415-870-7566
Fax: 415 645-9206
Toll-Free:
Address: 870 Market St., San Francisco, CA 94102 United States

STOCK TICKER/OTHER:
Stock Ticker: SLNM
Employees: 44
Parent Company:

Exchange: PINX
Fiscal Year Ends: 03/31

SALARIES/BONUSES:
Top Exec. Salary: $172,370   Bonus: $74,166
Second Exec. Salary: $194,925   Bonus: $46,875

OTHER THOUGHTS:
Estimated Female Officers or Directors: 3
Hot Spot for Advancement for Women/Minorities: Y

Samsung Electronics Co Ltd

NAIC Code: 334310

www.samsung.com

TYPES OF BUSINESS:
Consumer Electronics
Semiconductors and Memory Products
Smartphones
Computers & Accessories
Digital Cameras
Fuel-Cell Technology
LCD Displays
Solar Energy Panels

BRANDS/DIVISIONS/AFFILIATES:
Samsung Group

CONTACTS:
Note: Officers with more than one job title may be intentionally listed here more than once.
Hyun Suk Kim, Pres.
Oh-Hyun Kwon, Vice Chmn.
Gregory Lee, CEO

GROWTH PLANS/SPECIAL FEATURES:
Samsung Electronics Co., Ltd., the flagship company of Samsung Group, is a global leader in innovative electronic technologies and products. The company operates through three business areas, including: consumer electronics, information technology (IT) & mobile communications, and device solutions. The consumer electronics business develops and expands strategic products in regards to consumer electronics, including flat panel televisions and monitors as well as home appliances and health/medical equipment. The IT & mobile communications business sells more than 400 million mobile devices on a global scale every year. This division's telecommunications equipment and solutions power the global expansion of 4G, and its digital technology not only captures special moments but enables them to be shared in real-time. The device solutions business designs and manufactures memory technology and products for mobile devices. These solutions include memory semiconductor chips, large-scale integration (LSI) on a single silicon semiconductor microchip for virtual/augmented reality devices, dynamic random access memory (DRAM) and NAND technologies, solid state drive (SSD) components and more. Samsung Electronics also has a foundry business to mass produce 2nd-generation 14-nanometer (nm) and 10 nm FinFET mobile System-on-Chips (SoCs), as well as to develop future technologies beyond 8nm and 18nm fully-depleted silicon on insulator (FD-SOI) nodes. As of 2018, Samsung no longer makes printers after selling that business to HP.

FINANCIAL DATA:
Note: Data for latest year may not have been available at press time.

In U.S. $	2018	2017	2016	2015	2014	2013
Revenue		213,122,600,000	179,577,600,000	178,498,300,000	183,437,700,000	203,441,500,000
R&D Expense		14,549,700,000	12,553,270,000	12,192,380,000	12,797,130,000	12,738,320,000
Operating Income		47,721,810,000	26,012,060,000	23,497,000,000	22,261,920,000	32,723,390,000
Operating Margin %		22.39%	14.48%	13.16%	12.13%	16.08%
SGA Expense		21,277,860,000	20,326,900,000	20,306,740,000	21,142,270,000	22,451,940,000
Net Income		36,779,500,000	19,940,620,000	16,630,460,000	20,533,840,000	26,528,500,000
Operating Cash Flow		55,298,400,000	42,153,550,000	35,638,330,000	32,892,740,000	41,550,230,000
Capital Expenditure		38,942,440,000	22,409,210,000	24,358,700,000	20,787,150,000	21,432,170,000
EBITDA		70,249,410,000	46,271,260,000	42,405,050,000	41,384,730,000	49,211,250,000
Return on Assets %		14.66%	8.88%	7.91%	10.38%	15.09%
Return on Equity %		21.01%	12.48%	11.16%	15.06%	22.82%
Debt to Equity		0.01				0.01

CONTACT INFORMATION:
Phone: 82-31-200-1114   Fax: 82-31-200-7538
Toll-Free:
Address: 129 Samsung-ro, Yeongtong-gu, Suwon-si, 443-742 South Korea

STOCK TICKER/OTHER:
Stock Ticker: SSNLF
Employees: 321,000
Parent Company: Samsung Group

Exchange: GREY
Fiscal Year Ends: 12/31

SALARIES/BONUSES:
Top Exec. Salary: $ Bonus: $
Second Exec. Salary: $ Bonus: $

OTHER THOUGHTS:
Estimated Female Officers or Directors:
Hot Spot for Advancement for Women/Minorities:

Sales, profits and employees may be estimates. Financial information, benefits and other data can change quickly and may vary from those stated here.

Sands China Ltd

NAIC Code: 721110

www.sandschinaltd.com

TYPES OF BUSINESS:
Resorts & Casinos
Ferry & Limo Services
Travel Agency

BRANDS/DIVISIONS/AFFILIATES:
Las Vegas Sands Corporation
Venetian Macao
Sands Macao
Plaza Macao
Sands Cotai Central
Parisian Macao (The)
Cotai Expo
Parisian Theatre

CONTACTS:
Note: Officers with more than one job title may be intentionally listed here more than once.

Sheldom Gary Adelson, CEO
Ying Wai Wong, COO
Edward Matthew Tracy, Pres.
Sun Minqi, CFO
David Alec Andrew Fleming, General Counsel

GROWTH PLANS/SPECIAL FEATURES:

Sands China Ltd., a subsidiary of Las Vegas Sands Corporation, is a developer, owner and operator of resorts in Macao, China's hub of tourism and gaming. Its properties include the Venetian Macao, the Sands Macao, the Plaza Macao, Sands Cotai Central and The Parisian Macao. The Venetian Macao features a 39-floor luxury hotel with 3,000 suites, 376,000 square feet of gaming and casino space, 1 million square feet of retail and dining space, as well as the Malo Clinic and Spa, one of Asia's largest medical and beauty spas. It also owns Macao's largest entertainment venue, The Cotai Arena. The Sands Macao offers 241,000-square-feet of gaming space and a 289-suite hotel tower, restaurants, VIP facilities, a theater and other high-end services and amenities. The Plaza Macao features 105,000-square-feet of gaming space; Paiza mansions which average 7,000 square feet each; retail space, which is connected to the mall at The Venetian Macao; several food and beverage offerings; and conference, banquet and other facilities. The Sands Cotai Central, located in the center of the Cotai Strip, consists of over 6,200 hotel rooms under the brand names St. Regis, Conrad, Sheraton Grand and Holiday Inn, and more than 150 boutiques and galleries. The Parisian Macao includes 3,000 guestrooms and suites, convention and meeting space, restaurants, spa, kids' club, health club, pool deck with themed water park and a 1,200-seat theater, among other amenities. In addition, Sands China owns the Cotai Expo, a convention and exhibition hall in Asia; the 1,800-seat luxury Venetian Theatre; the 1,200-seat Parisian Theatre; the Cotai Water Jet, a major high-speed ferry company; and the upcoming 1,700-seat Sands Cotai Theatre.

Sands China offers its employees full medical and dental insurance plans, 24-hour staff meals, staff shuttle buses and employee discounts.

FINANCIAL DATA:
Note: Data for latest year may not have been available at press time.

In U.S. $	2018	2017	2016	2015	2014	2013
Revenue		7,715,000,000	6,653,000,000	6,820,078,000	9,505,230,000	8,907,859,000
R&D Expense						
Operating Income		1,796,000,000	1,363,000,000	1,538,051,000	2,629,703,000	2,316,027,000
Operating Margin %		22.98%	20.48%	22.55%	29.20%	25.99%
SGA Expense		362,000,000	328,000,000	349,123,000	443,863,000	389,988,000
Net Income		1,603,000,000	1,224,000,000	1,459,442,000	2,547,704,000	2,214,882,000
Operating Cash Flow		2,626,000,000	2,346,000,000	1,967,522,000	3,223,849,000	3,078,706,000
Capital Expenditure		432,000,000	1,051,000,000	1,123,636,000	726,489,000	609,925,000
EBITDA		2,444,000,000	1,956,000,000	2,055,606,000	3,145,281,000	2,799,083,000
Return on Assets %		14.68%	11.15%	13.19%	22.33%	20.27%
Return on Equity %		33.58%	22.57%	23.79%	39.56%	36.80%
Debt to Equity		0.96	0.86	0.57	0.49	0.46

CONTACT INFORMATION:
Phone: 853 8118-2888 Fax: 853 2888-3382
Toll-Free:
Address: L2 Estrada da Baia de Nossa, Senhora da Esparanc, Taipa Macao

STOCK TICKER/OTHER:
Stock Ticker: SCHYY   Exchange: PINX
Employees: 28,504   Fiscal Year Ends: 12/31
Parent Company: Las Vegas Sands Corporation

SALARIES/BONUSES:
Top Exec. Salary: $ Bonus: $
Second Exec. Salary: $ Bonus: $

OTHER THOUGHTS:
Estimated Female Officers or Directors:
Hot Spot for Advancement for Women/Minorities:

Sales, profits and employees may be estimates. Financial information, benefits and other data can change quickly and may vary from those stated here.

Sanoma Oyj
NAIC Code: 511120

www.sanomawsoy.fi

TYPES OF BUSINESS:
Periodical Publishers

BRANDS/DIVISIONS/AFFILIATES:
Sanoma Magazines
Helsingin Sanomat
Hintaseuranta.fi
Ilta-Sanomat
Nelonen
Radio Aalto
Autotie.fi

CONTACTS: Note: Officers with more than one job title may be intentionally listed here more than once.
Susan Duinhoven, CEO
Markus Holm, CFO
John Martin, Chief Strategy & Digital Officer
Jacqueline Cuthbert, Chief Communications Officer
Jacques Eijkens, CEO-Sanoma Learning
Aime Van Hecke, CEO-Sanoma Media Belgium
Anu Nissinen, CEO-Sanome Media Finland
Heike Rosener, CEO-Sanoma Media Russia

GROWTH PLANS/SPECIAL FEATURES:
Sanoma Oyj is a European media group with operations in more than 10 European countries. The group consists of five business areas: magazines, newspapers, television and radio, learning solutions and online media. Sanoma Magazines publishes through operating firms in three countries. Magazines include women's titles, home and decoration, lifestyle, entertainment, cartoons, TV titles, youth publications, ICT consumer magazines, children's magazines and technical publications. Newspapers includes national and regional newspapers, local papers, free sheets as well as related online editions and services. This business area operates primarily in Finland, publishing Helsingin Sanomat, the leading daily newspaper in Scandinavia. Major online business news resources include Taloussanomat.fi, Hintaseuranta.fi and Ilta-Sanomat. Television and radio operates the Finnish TV channel Nelonen as well as free-to-air TV channels Jim and Liv. Additionally, this business area includes three commercial radio channels, Radio Aalto, Radio Rock and Radio Suomipop. Sanoma Learning is an educational publisher in Europe, which publishes pedagogical communication products in printed and online digital format. It also publishes Finnish fiction, translated fiction and non-fiction books in Finland, as well as operating a marketing company of multivolume non-fiction books and dictionaries. The division offers multilingual communications, including training, translation services and consulting services. Sanoma Learning provides its digital learning and online solutions across 40 countries. In addition, this business segment maintains an automotive comparison site, Autotie.fi. In 2018, Sanoma Oyj acquired N.C.D. Production Ltd., an event business, in April 2018; Scoupy, a marketing and cashback service driven by data, in June 2018; STT, a Finnish nationwide news service, in June 2018; and Iddink, a Dutch educational platform and service provider, in December 2018.

FINANCIAL DATA: Note: Data for latest year may not have been available at press time.

In U.S. $	2018	2017	2016	2015	2014	2013
Revenue		1,632,797,000	1,867,112,000	1,955,393,000	2,166,127,000	2,527,338,000
R&D Expense						
Operating Income		205,722,900	209,481,900	-68,802,110	7,176,380	-289,675,100
Operating Margin %		11.82%	10.49%	-4.28%	.32%	-11.47%
SGA Expense		243,199,500	280,448,400	330,227,400	247,072,500	276,575,400
Net Income		-183,965,900	126,213,100	-162,778,500	66,409,990	-364,286,700
Operating Cash Flow		160,842,000	174,853,100	28,705,520	83,952,250	141,363,300
Capital Expenditure		41,577,440	39,299,220	62,764,840	58,094,500	77,231,510
EBITDA		-43,400,010	562,719,300	317,811,100	517,838,400	449,264,100
Return on Assets %		-7.69%	4.12%	-4.94%	1.78%	-8.46%
Return on Equity %		-25.51%	15.21%	-17.36%	6.32%	-28.22%
Debt to Equity		0.35	0.32	0.68	0.57	0.81

CONTACT INFORMATION:
Phone: 358 1051999 Fax: 358 105195068
Toll-Free:
Address: Toolonlahdenkatu 2, Helsinki, 00101 Finland

SALARIES/BONUSES:
Top Exec. Salary: $ Bonus: $
Second Exec. Salary: $ Bonus: $

STOCK TICKER/OTHER:
Stock Ticker: SWYBF Exchange: GREY
Employees: 4,425 Fiscal Year Ends: 12/31
Parent Company:

OTHER THOUGHTS:
Estimated Female Officers or Directors: 7
Hot Spot for Advancement for Women/Minorities: Y

Sales, profits and employees may be estimates. Financial information, benefits and other data can change quickly and may vary from those stated here.

SBS (Seoul Broadcasting)

NAIC Code: 515120

global.sbs.co.kr

TYPES OF BUSINESS:
Broadcasting, Television & Radio

BRANDS/DIVISIONS/AFFILIATES:
SBS Channel 6
Power FM
Love AM
SBS Plus
SBS HD
SBS Viceland
SBS Food
SBSu

CONTACTS:
Note: Officers with more than one job title may be intentionally listed here more than once.

Jung Hoon Park, Managing Dir.
Jin-Won Kim, Dir.-News & Sports
Young Mook Yoon, Dir.-Programming & Contents

GROWTH PLANS/SPECIAL FEATURES:
SBS broadcasts terrestrial, cable and satellite TV as well as radio programming in South Korea. SBS Channel 6, its terrestrial TV service, offers general programming such as news, sports, films, TV dramas, documentaries and entertainment shows. Power FM offers programming that varies throughout the day, targeting commuters in the early morning, homemakers in the late morning, youth in the afternoon and general audiences in the evening. Love FM broadcasts simultaneously on AM and FM frequencies, offering inspirational stories; morning shows; news; popular and traditional music; and programming directed at children, commuters and homemakers. SBS Plus offers cable and satellite TV programming focusing on drama series and entertainment shows. Its television services include SBS HD (high definition), SBS Viceland (for young audiences), SBS Food and NITV (national indigenous television). SBS Sports offers domestic and international sports coverage, including American football, the World Cup, the Olympics and general sports shows, news and highlights. SBSu is a digital multimedia broadcasting (DMB) service broadcasting to DMB phones, offering retransmitted SBS TV programming, DMB-specific programming and late-night shows after midnight, when TV networks in Korea typically stop broadcasting. SBSu also offers radio and data channels, which are either company-operated or are leased out.

FINANCIAL DATA:
Note: Data for latest year may not have been available at press time.

In U.S. $	2018	2017	2016	2015	2014	2013
Revenue	740,000,000	724,060,000	687,216,000	679,812,931	710,787,524	676,500,000
R&D Expense						
Operating Income						
Operating Margin %						
SGA Expense						
Net Income		14,074,200	-433,780	42,905,564	-585,332	22,700,000
Operating Cash Flow						
Capital Expenditure						
EBITDA						
Return on Assets %						
Return on Equity %						
Debt to Equity						

CONTACT INFORMATION:
Phone: 82-2-2061-0006 Fax: 82-2-2113-4749
Toll-Free:
Address: SBS Broadcasting Ctr. 161, Mok-Dongseo-Ro, Yangcheon-Gu, Seoul, 158-725 South Korea

STOCK TICKER/OTHER:
Stock Ticker: Private
Employees: 1,144
Parent Company:

Exchange:
Fiscal Year Ends: 12/31

SALARIES/BONUSES:
Top Exec. Salary: $ Bonus: $
Second Exec. Salary: $ Bonus: $

OTHER THOUGHTS:
Estimated Female Officers or Directors:
Hot Spot for Advancement for Women/Minorities:

Sales, profits and employees may be estimates. Financial information, benefits and other data can change quickly and may vary from those stated here.

Schibsted ASA

NAIC Code: 511110

www.schibsted.no

TYPES OF BUSINESS:
Newspaper Publishers

BRANDS/DIVISIONS/AFFILIATES:
Affonbladet
Svenska Dagbladet
Aftenposten
VG
MPI

CONTACTS:
Note: Officers with more than one job title may be intentionally listed here more than once.

Kristin Skogen Lund, CEO
Trond Berger, CFO
Tina Stiegler, Exec. VP-Human Resources
Rian Liebenberg, Exec. VP-IT
Camilla Jarlsby, Head-Legal Affairs
Frode Eilertsen, Exec. VP-Strategy & Digital Transformation
Lena K. Samuelsson, Exec. VP-Comm. & Corp. Social Responsibility
Terje Seljeseth, CEO-Schibsted Classified Media

GROWTH PLANS/SPECIAL FEATURES:

Schibsted ASA is an international media company operating in 22 countries. It groups its business into three divisions: marketplaces, publishing and growth. The marketplaces division provides general classified ads online, reaching more than 200 million people worldwide, with established markets in Western Europe. This segment is engaged in emerging markets within Eastern Europe, Latin America and North America. The publishing division owns leading newspapers in: Sweden, the Affonbladet and the Svenska Dagbladet; and in Norway, the Aftenposten and the VG. The growth division invests in entrepreneurs to help scale their businesses locally and internationally by leveraging the Schibsted ecosystem. This segment's investments include, but are certainly not limited to, Style Time, Ahum, Yepstr, Hygglo, Bynk, GoodOnes, Compricer and Hypoteket. In addition, Schibsted's products and technology unit ensures that the firm is at the forefront of modern media and technology. It actively designs and creates tools, platforms and services to make that expectation a reality. The firm announced in September 2018 that it's international classifieds operations will become as an independent and listed company. The new firm, tentatively named MPI, will spun-off in a demerger and begin trading publicly in early 2019. Schibsted will retain a majority ownership in MPI and will continue to maintain classified operations in Norway, Sweden and Finland.

Schibsted provides its employees with pay and benefits specific to global location.

FINANCIAL DATA:
Note: Data for latest year may not have been available at press time.

In U.S. $	2018	2017	2016	2015	2014	2013
Revenue		1,949,682,000	1,824,259,000	1,739,456,000	1,723,116,000	1,752,688,000
R&D Expense						
Operating Income		239,798,000	190,664,700	171,333,600	181,229,300	119,668,800
Operating Margin %		12.29%	10.45%	9.84%	10.51%	6.82%
SGA Expense		461,875,700	429,887,300	376,151,400	366,831,000	422,523,100
Net Income		245,091,000	53,505,780	145,328,600	-20,711,910	176,741,700
Operating Cash Flow		148,435,400	173,289,700	114,260,700	141,531,400	73,067,030
Capital Expenditure		99,532,260	80,316,200	52,930,450	72,491,700	61,100,150
EBITDA		452,555,300	215,749,100	353,943,600	129,334,400	309,413,000
Return on Assets %		8.87%	2.21%	6.39%	-1.02%	9.44%
Return on Equity %		17.02%	4.42%	14.57%	-2.49%	23.02%
Debt to Equity		0.28	0.17	0.21	0.32	0.25

CONTACT INFORMATION:
Phone: 47 23106600 Fax:
Toll-Free:
Address: Postboks 490, Sentrium, Oslo, NO-0105 Norway

SALARIES/BONUSES:
Top Exec. Salary: $ Bonus: $
Second Exec. Salary: $ Bonus: $

STOCK TICKER/OTHER:
Stock Ticker: SBSNY   Exchange: PINX
Employees: 8,070   Fiscal Year Ends: 12/31
Parent Company:

OTHER THOUGHTS:
Estimated Female Officers or Directors: 2
Hot Spot for Advancement for Women/Minorities:

Plunkett Research, Ltd. 417

Scholastic Corporation

www.scholastic.com

NAIC Code: 511130

TYPES OF BUSINESS:

Children's Book Publishing
Children's TV Programming
Educational Software
Educational Magazines
Book Fairs & Clubs
Consumer Products
Movies

BRANDS/DIVISIONS/AFFILIATES:

Scholastic News
Scope
Storyworks
Let's Find Out
Junior Scholastic

CONTACTS: Note: Officers with more than one job title may be intentionally listed here more than once.

Richard Robinson, CEO
Kenneth Cleary, CFO
Paul Hukkanen, Chief Accounting Officer
Andrew Hedden, Director
Satbir Bedi, Executive VP
Iole Lucchese, Executive VP
Judith Newman, Executive VP
Alan Boyko, President, Subsidiary

GROWTH PLANS/SPECIAL FEATURES:

Scholastic Corporation, a global children's publishing and media company, is among the largest publishers and distributors of children's books in the world. The company operates in three segments: children's book publishing and distribution, education and international. Children's book publishing and distribution division derived 60.4% of the firm's 2017 revenue, and includes the publication and distribution of children's books, e-books, media and interactive products in the U.S. This division is also a leading publisher of children's print books, e-books and audiobooks distributed through a trade channel. Scholastic's original publications include Harry Potter, The Hunger Games, The 39 Clues, Spirit Animals, The Magic School Bus, I Spy, Captain Underpants, Goosebumps and Clifford The Big Red Dog, as well as licensed properties such as Star Wars, Lego, Pokemon and Geronimo Stilton. The education segment derived 18% of annual revenue, and includes the publications and distribution to schools and libraries of children's books, classroom magazines, supplemental classroom materials, custom curriculum and teaching guides, print and online reference products, as well as non-fiction products for grades PreK-12 in the U.S. This division is a leading provider of classroom libraries and paperback collections, including classroom books/reading products to schools, school districts and literacy organizations. Classroom magazines include Scholastic News, Scope, Storyworks, Let's Find Out and Junior Scholastic. The international segment accounted for 21.6% of annual revenue, and includes the publication and distribution of products and services outside the U.S., including Canada, the U.K., Australia, New Zealand and Asia.

FINANCIAL DATA: Note: Data for latest year may not have been available at press time.

In U.S. $	2018	2017	2016	2015	2014	2013
Revenue	1,628,400,000	1,741,600,000	1,672,800,000	1,635,800,000	1,822,300,000	1,792,400,000
R&D Expense						
Operating Income	76,700,000	110,600,000	93,900,000	58,300,000	102,400,000	81,300,000
Operating Margin %		6.35%	5.61%	3.56%	5.61%	4.53%
SGA Expense	763,200,000	777,800,000	777,700,000	771,100,000	812,500,000	815,000,000
Net Income	-5,000,000	52,300,000	40,500,000	294,600,000	44,400,000	31,100,000
Operating Cash Flow	141,500,000	141,400,000	-78,900,000	166,900,000	156,800,000	189,100,000
Capital Expenditure	157,600,000	92,600,000	60,800,000	59,300,000	347,000,000	128,400,000
EBITDA	44,700,000	129,400,000	110,200,000	82,000,000	120,600,000	137,700,000
Return on Assets %		3.01%	2.29%	17.58%	2.99%	1.99%
Return on Equity %		4.07%	3.28%	27.78%	4.98%	3.67%
Debt to Equity					0.13	0.06

CONTACT INFORMATION:

Phone: 212 343-6100 Fax: 212 343-6928
Toll-Free: 800-724-6527
Address: 557 Broadway, New York, NY 10012 United States

SALARIES/BONUSES:

Top Exec. Salary: $970,000 Bonus: $
Second Exec. Salary: $674,500 Bonus: $

STOCK TICKER/OTHER:

Stock Ticker: SCHL Exchange: NAS
Employees: 9,000 Fiscal Year Ends: 05/31
Parent Company:

OTHER THOUGHTS:

Estimated Female Officers or Directors: 9
Hot Spot for Advancement for Women/Minorities: Y

Sales, profits and employees may be estimates. Financial information, benefits and other data can change quickly and may vary from those stated here.

Scientific Games Corporation

NAIC Code: 511210G

www.scientificgames.com

TYPES OF BUSINESS:
Computer Software, Electronic Games, Apps & Entertainment
Pari-Mutuel Wagering Systems
Satellite Broadcasting Services
Telecommunications Products
Off-Track Betting Facilities Management
Lottery Services
Race Simulcasting

BRANDS/DIVISIONS/AFFILIATES:
Beijing Guard Libang Technology Co Ltd
Roberts Communications Network LLC
International Terminal Leasing
DEQ Systems Corp
NYX Gaming Group Limited
EM Informatica SA

CONTACTS:
Note: Officers with more than one job title may be intentionally listed here more than once.

James Kennedy, CEO, Divisional
Douglas Albregts, CEO, Divisional
Barry Cottle, CEO
Michael Quartieri, CFO
Ronald Perelman, Chairman of the Board
Michael Winterscheidt, Chief Accounting Officer
Derik Mooberry, Executive VP, Divisional
Tim Bucher, Executive VP
James Sottile, Executive VP
Patrick McHugh, Senior VP, Divisional
Larry Potts, Senior VP
Richard Haddrill, Vice Chairman of the Board
Peter Cohen, Vice Chairman of the Board

GROWTH PLANS/SPECIAL FEATURES:
Scientific Games Corporation is a leading supplier of technology-based products, systems and services to gaming markets worldwide, including 39 of the 44 U.S. jurisdictions that currently sell lottery tickets and 50 countries. Scientific Games operates in three business segments: interactive, lottery and gaming. Interactive business segment is composed of social casino-style, slot-based games through Facebook and various desktop and mobile platforms; play-for-fun and play-for-free white-label gaming for traditional land-based casinos; and provision of content and technology for land-based casino and licensed online casino operators. The lottery segment provides software, equipment and data communication services to government-sponsored and privately-operated lotteries in the U.S. and abroad. This segment includes lottery system equipment, software, data communication services and support, as well as instant game validation systems. This segment includes the company's 50% interest in Beijing Guard Libang Technology Co., Ltd., an instant game supplier to the China Sports Lottery. The gaming division sells new and used gaming machines, conversion kits and parts to commercial, tribal and governmental gaming operators; leases or otherwise provides gaming machines; and provides video lottery central monitoring and control systems for gaming regulators. This segment includes the firm's 29.4% interest in Roberts Communications Network, LLC, a provider of communications services to racing and non-racing customers; and its 50% interest in International Terminal Leasing, from which the company leases gaming machines. In January 2018, Scientific Games completed its acquisition of 38.04% of NYX Gaming Group Limited, a designer, manufacturer and distributor of digital gaming software. The following February, the firm acquired a majority stake in EM Informatica SA, a video bingo content studio in Sao Paulo, Brazil.

FINANCIAL DATA:
Note: Data for latest year may not have been available at press time.

In U.S. $	2018	2017	2016	2015	2014	2013
Revenue		3,083,600,000	2,883,400,000	2,758,800,000	1,786,400,000	1,090,900,000
R&D Expense		184,100,000	204,800,000	183,900,000	117,000,000	26,000,000
Operating Income		439,000,000	256,600,000	-100,000	-142,000,000	4,400,000
Operating Margin %		14.23%	8.89%		-7.94%	.40%
SGA Expense		613,100,000	577,000,000	567,700,000	507,700,000	266,400,000
Net Income		-242,300,000	-353,700,000	-1,394,300,000	-234,300,000	-30,200,000
Operating Cash Flow		507,100,000	419,000,000	414,200,000	203,500,000	171,200,000
Capital Expenditure		293,700,000	272,900,000	323,600,000	238,300,000	165,800,000
EBITDA		1,064,700,000	921,400,000	-126,100,000	266,600,000	179,200,000
Return on Assets %		-3.27%	-4.77%	-15.73%	-3.29%	-.93%
Return on Equity %					-123.67%	-8.16%
Debt to Equity					2170.61	8.43

CONTACT INFORMATION:
Phone: 212 754-2233 Fax:
Toll-Free:
Address: 750 Lexington Ave., New York, NY 10022 United States

SALARIES/BONUSES:
Top Exec. Salary: $1,800,000 Bonus: $
Second Exec. Salary: $725,000 Bonus: $

STOCK TICKER/OTHER:
Stock Ticker: SGMS
Employees: 8,400
Parent Company:

Exchange: NAS
Fiscal Year Ends: 12/31

OTHER THOUGHTS:
Estimated Female Officers or Directors: 1
Hot Spot for Advancement for Women/Minorities:

Plunkett Research, Ltd.

Scribd Inc

NAIC Code: 519130

www.scribd.com

TYPES OF BUSINESS:
Online Documents Platform
Online Publishing

BRANDS/DIVISIONS/AFFILIATES:
iPaper

CONTACTS: Note: Officers with more than one job title may be intentionally listed here more than once.
Trip Adler, CEO
Jared Fliesler, COO
Sabeen Minns, Sr. VP-Product & Engineering
Sabeen Minns Sabeen Minns, Head-Software Eng.
Andrew Weinstein, VP-Content Acquisition

GROWTH PLANS/SPECIAL FEATURES:
Scribd, Inc. is an online social publishing website that allows writers to share original content with the general public. Users can upload a variety of different works, including essays, presentations and puzzles that can then be shared with the community at large. Source material can come from multiple formats, ranging from Microsoft Office formats to PDF documents. The firm's proprietary iPaper reader presents content in a common form. Readers can subscribe to publishers they like and disseminate works through embedded material codes and on social media platforms like Facebook and Twitter. Once posted, readers provide feedback through comments and critiques. The website is utilized by more than 100 million unique visitors each month, and over 700,000 paying subscribers. Beyond individual users, Scribd publishes content posted by several major media companies, including the Chicago Tribune, Random House, The New York Times and Simon & Schuster. Subscribers have credits to read three books and one audiobook per month from the entire library. Unused subscriber credits roll over to the next month. Purchased content can be viewed on devices such as computers, cell phones and eBook readers. As of late-2018, readers have clocked more than 150 million hours of reading time across all genres. During 2018, Scribd launched an unlimited service, with access to books, audiobooks, news, magazines, documents and sheet music, for a monthly subscription fee; and announced a joint subscription offering between Scribd and The New York Times, for a monthly fee.

FINANCIAL DATA: Note: Data for latest year may not have been available at press time.

In U.S. $	2018	2017	2016	2015	2014	2013
Revenue						
R&D Expense						
Operating Income						
Operating Margin %						
SGA Expense						
Net Income						
Operating Cash Flow						
Capital Expenditure						
EBITDA						
Return on Assets %						
Return on Equity %						
Debt to Equity						

CONTACT INFORMATION:
Phone: 415-896-9890 Fax: 415-896-9896
Toll-Free:
Address: 539 Bryant St., Ste. 200, San Francisco, CA 94107 United States

STOCK TICKER/OTHER:
Stock Ticker: Private
Employees: 55
Parent Company:

Exchange:
Fiscal Year Ends: 12/31

SALARIES/BONUSES:
Top Exec. Salary: $ Bonus: $
Second Exec. Salary: $ Bonus: $

OTHER THOUGHTS:
Estimated Female Officers or Directors: 3
Hot Spot for Advancement for Women/Minorities: Y

Sales, profits and employees may be estimates. Financial information, benefits and other data can change quickly and may vary from those stated here.

SeaWorld Entertainment Inc

www.seaworldentertainment.com

NAIC Code: 713110

TYPES OF BUSINESS:
Theme Parks

BRANDS/DIVISIONS/AFFILIATES:
SeaWorld
Busch Gardens
Aquatica
Discovery Cove
Sesame Place
Water Country USA
Adventure Island

CONTACTS: Note: Officers with more than one job title may be intentionally listed here more than once.

Kathleen Liever, Assistant General Counsel
Marc Swanson, CFO
Elizabeth Gulacsy, Chief Accounting Officer
Yoshikazu Maruyama, Director
George Taylor, General Counsel
Christopher Dold, Other Executive Officer
John Reilly, Other Executive Officer

GROWTH PLANS/SPECIAL FEATURES:

SeaWorld Entertainment, Inc. is a leading theme park and entertainment company. The company owns or license a portfolio of brands that comprise 12 theme parks in six U.S. states. Many of the parks showcase SeaWorld Entertainment's one-of-a-kind zoological collection representing more than 800 species of animals. All the parks feature various rides, shows and attractions. In 201, the firm hosted approximately 20.8 million guests, including 2.4 million international guests. Revenue is primarily generated from selling admission to the theme parks and from purchases of food, merchandise and other spending. SeaWorld Entertainment theme parks include the following seven brands. SeaWorld, a leading marine-life theme park brand, with parks located in San Diego, California; Orlando, Florida; and San Antonio, Texas. Busch Gardens, family-oriented theme-park destinations designed to immerse guests in foreign geographic settings known for their award-winning landscaping and gardens. Busch Gardens them parks are in Tampa, Florida and Williamsburg, Virginia. Aquatica, family-oriented water park destinations designed as if in a tropical setting and located next to SeaWorld theme parks. Aquatica water parks feature high-energy rides, water attractions, white-sand beaches and marine and terrestrial animals. Discovery Cove, located next to SeaWorld Orlando, a 58-acre, reservations-only, all-inclusive marine life theme park open year-round. Its activities include dolphin swim sessions, snorkeling, wading with stingrays, hand-feeding birds in free flight, and more. Sesame Place, located between Philadelphia and New York City, is entirely dedicated to the award-winning television show, and features rides, water slides, shows and themed friends. Water Country USA is Virginia's largest family water park all set to a 1950s and 1960s surf theme. Last, Adventure Island is a water park adjacent to Busch Gardens Tampa.

FINANCIAL DATA: Note: Data for latest year may not have been available at press time.

In U.S. $	2018	2017	2016	2015	2014	2013
Revenue		1,263,324,000	1,344,292,000	1,371,004,000	1,377,812,000	1,460,250,000
R&D Expense						
Operating Income		73,169,000	68,601,000	161,704,000	172,911,000	202,613,000
Operating Margin %		5.79%	5.10%	11.79%	12.49%	17.20%
SGA Expense		228,836,000	238,557,000	214,072,000	191,943,000	237,370,000
Net Income		-202,386,000	-12,531,000	49,133,000	49,919,000	50,478,000
Operating Cash Flow		192,457,000	280,412,000	286,274,000	261,532,000	289,794,000
Capital Expenditure		172,517,000	160,518,000	157,422,000	156,541,000	166,258,000
EBITDA		-46,097,000	259,109,000	320,905,000	336,609,000	335,104,000
Return on Assets %		-9.06%	-.52%	2.03%	1.98%	1.97%
Return on Equity %		-54.06%	-2.59%	9.06%	8.09%	9.14%
Debt to Equity		5.23	3.31	3.07	2.74	2.48

CONTACT INFORMATION:
Phone: 314-577-2000 Fax: 314-613-6049
Toll-Free: 888-800-5447
Address: 9205 S. Park Center Loop, Ste. 400, Orlando, FL 32819 United States

STOCK TICKER/OTHER:
Stock Ticker: SEAS   Exchange: NYS
Employees: 13,300   Fiscal Year Ends: 12/31
Parent Company:

SALARIES/BONUSES:
Top Exec. Salary: $1,000,000   Bonus: $
Second Exec. Salary: $420,000 Bonus: $100,000

OTHER THOUGHTS:
Estimated Female Officers or Directors:
Hot Spot for Advancement for Women/Minorities:

Sega Sammy Holdings Inc

www.segasammy.co.jp

NAIC Code: 713120

TYPES OF BUSINESS:
Pachinko Arcades
Arcade Games Manufacturing
Amusement Centers
Toys
Smartphone Content
Animation Production
Karaoke Machines
Display Design & Construction Services

BRANDS/DIVISIONS/AFFILIATES:
Sega Sammy Creation Co Ltd
Paradise Sega Sammy
Sega Sammy Golf Entertainment inc
Phoenix Resort Co Ltd
Phoenix Seagaia Resort

CONTACTS: Note: Officers with more than one job title may be intentionally listed here more than once.
Hajime Satomi, CEO
Hajime Satomi, Pres.
Tomio Kazashi, Standing Corp. Auditor
Koichi Fuazawa, Sr. Exec. Officer
Hiroshi Ishikura, Exec. Officer
Koichiro Ueda, Exec. Officer
Seiichiro Kikuchi, Sr. Exec. Officer
Hajime Satomi, Chmn.

GROWTH PLANS/SPECIAL FEATURES:
Sega Sammy Holdings, Inc. (SSH) provides gaming machines, a range of entertainment content and develops and operates complexes such as facilities and hotels. The company is organized into three business segments: Pachislot and Pachinko machines, entertainment contents and resorts. The Pachislot and Pachinko machines segment derives 32.6% of annual net sales, and develops, manufactures, installs, sells and/or maintains the gaming machines through wholly-owned subsidiary, Sega Sammy Creation Co., Ltd. The gaming machines are similar to slot machines. The entertainment contents segment (64.3%) offers a variety of products and services, including: digital content planning and distribution; the development and sales of game software; the development, manufacture and sales of amusement machines; the development and operation of amusement facilities; the creation of animation and video content; and the development, manufacture and sales of toys. The resort segment (3.1%) develops and operates facilities and hotels, including: Paradise Sega Sammy, an integrated hotel and casino resort; Sega Sammy Golf Entertainment, Inc., which comprises The North Country Golf Club, comprising an 18-hole golf course and clubhouse, as well as hosted golf tournaments and events; and the Phoenix Seagaia Resort in Phoenix, Arizona, operated through Phoenix Resort Co. Ltd.

FINANCIAL DATA: Note: Data for latest year may not have been available at press time.

In U.S. $	2018	2017	2016	2015	2014	2013
Revenue	3,002,226,000	3,403,634,000	3,227,784,000	3,292,158,000	3,506,335,000	2,981,291,000
R&D Expense	214,603,700	233,962,200	226,801,300	271,733,100	243,367,800	228,090,700
Operating Income	164,412,700	273,912,900	163,457,200	163,373,800	357,450,300	176,944,200
Operating Margin %	5.47	19.49%	17.46%	17.45%	21.42%	17.80%
SGA Expense	163,800,500	170,785,100	194,354,800	215,058,300	198,315,500	156,342,800
Net Income	82,832,440	256,075,600	49,801,500	-104,426,400	284,960,300	310,366,600
Operating Cash Flow	245,686,800	548,438,000	156,815,800	343,295,500	697,545,700	172,556,800
Capital Expenditure	211,774,600	237,190,200	228,823,500	264,665,000	361,142,000	328,899,500
EBITDA	319,772,200	535,164,400	336,848,800	263,097,300	659,821,200	434,782,200
Return on Assets %	1.79%	5.23%	1.01%	-2.10%	5.73%	6.52%
Return on Equity %	2.89%	9.14%	1.74%	-3.39%	9.29%	10.95%
Debt to Equity	0.19	0.24	0.34	0.27	0.21	0.23

CONTACT INFORMATION:
Phone: 81 362159955 Fax:
Toll-Free:
Address: Shiodome Sumitomo Bldg 21F,1-9-2 Higashi Shimbashi, Tokyo, 105-0021 Japan

SALARIES/BONUSES:
Top Exec. Salary: $ Bonus: $
Second Exec. Salary: $ Bonus: $

STOCK TICKER/OTHER:
Stock Ticker: SGAMF
Employees: 15,480
Parent Company:

Exchange: PINX
Fiscal Year Ends: 03/31

OTHER THOUGHTS:
Estimated Female Officers or Directors:
Hot Spot for Advancement for Women/Minorities:

Sales, profits and employees may be estimates. Financial information, benefits and other data can change quickly and may vary from those stated here.

Seven Group Holdings Limited

NAIC Code: 515120

www.sevengroup.com.au

TYPES OF BUSINESS:
Television Broadcasting

BRANDS/DIVISIONS/AFFILIATES:
WesTrac
AllightSykes
Coates Hire
Seven West Media
Seven Network
Presto
Yahoo!7
Beach Energy Ltd

GROWTH PLANS/SPECIAL FEATURES:
Seven Group Holdings Limited is a diversified operating and investment group. The firm's core industrial operations consist of its Australian and Chinese WesTrac's Caterpillar dealerships, which are involved in the mining and construction equipment industry; AllightSykes, a supplier of lighting towers, generators and pumps; Coates Hire, an industrial and general equipment rental/hire company; and its 41% stake in Seven West Media, which is engaged in the broadcast of free television, the publishing of newspapers and magazines, and the delivery of content via the internet and radio. Seven West's brands include Seven West Media, Seven Network, West Australian Newspapers, Presto, Pacific Magazine and Yahoo!7. In addition, Seven Group owns a 25.6% share in Beach Energy Ltd., as well as other interests in oil and gas projects located in Australia and the U.S.

CONTACTS:
Note: Officers with more than one job title may be intentionally listed here more than once.

Ryan Kerry Stokes, CEO
Warren Walter Coatsworth, Company Sec.
Peter David Ritchie, Deputy Chmn.
Kerry Matthew Stokes, Chmn.

FINANCIAL DATA:
Note: Data for latest year may not have been available at press time.

In U.S. $	2018	2017	2016	2015	2014	2013
Revenue	2,241,365,000	1,599,033,000	1,988,160,000	1,947,453,000	2,163,665,000	3,329,104,000
R&D Expense						
Operating Income	194,142,800	83,864,640	88,348,630	61,444,690	108,687,700	255,226,000
Operating Margin %		5.24%	4.44%	3.15%	5.02%	7.66%
SGA Expense	510,824,700	343,515,700	389,406,600	381,769,800	353,344,800	526,729,500
Net Income	289,988,100	31,177,750	137,882,700	-252,434,700	182,964,300	340,795,200
Operating Cash Flow						
Capital Expenditure	113,360,900	22,910,390	34,470,680	76,928,470	64,060,820	38,642,190
EBITDA	505,570,000	111,399,100	244,377,500	-340,012,600	320,826,800	565,729,000
Return on Assets %		.41%	3.25%	-7.18%	4.25%	8.01%
Return on Equity %		.99%	7.49%	-15.23%	8.88%	19.36%
Debt to Equity		0.72	0.67	0.65	0.42	0.41

CONTACT INFORMATION:
Phone: 61-2-8777-7447 Fax: 61-2-8777-7192
Toll-Free:
Address: 175 Liverpool St., Level 30, Sydney, NSW 2000 Australia

STOCK TICKER/OTHER:
Stock Ticker: SVNWF Exchange: GREY
Employees: 5,708 Fiscal Year Ends: 06/30
Parent Company:

SALARIES/BONUSES:
Top Exec. Salary: $ Bonus: $
Second Exec. Salary: $ Bonus: $

OTHER THOUGHTS:
Estimated Female Officers or Directors: 1
Hot Spot for Advancement for Women/Minorities:

Seven West Media Limited

www.sevenwestmedia.com.au

NAIC Code: 515120

TYPES OF BUSINESS:
Television Broadcasting

BRANDS/DIVISIONS/AFFILIATES:
Seven
7TWO
7mate
7flix
Pacific Magazines
West Australian (The)
Yahoo!7

GROWTH PLANS/SPECIAL FEATURES:
Seven West Media Limited is a leading integrated media company in Australia. The firm is engaged in broadcast television, and in magazine/ newspaper publishing via print and online formats. Seven West is the home of many media businesses popular within the country, including Seven, 7TWO, 7mate, 7flix, Pacific Magazines, The West Australian and Yahoo!7, as well as content brands such as My Kitchen Rules, House Rules, Home and Away, Sunrise, the Australian Football League, the Olympic Games, Better Homes and Gardens, marie claire, Who, The West Australian, The Sunday Times, PerthNow, racing.com and 7plus. The company delivers its content across an array of platforms, beyond its digital broadcast channels. It is engaged in creating content and desires to expand its presence in international content production with the formation of new international production companies.

CONTACTS:
Note: Officers with more than one job title may be intentionally listed here more than once.

Tim Worner, Managing Dir.
Warwick Lynch, CFO
Katie McGrath, Group Exec.-Human Resources
Clive Dickens, Chief Digital Officer
Kerry Stokes, Chmn.

FINANCIAL DATA:
Note: Data for latest year may not have been available at press time.

In U.S. $	2018	2017	2016	2015	2014	2013
Revenue	1,114,972,000	1,148,295,000	1,164,387,000	1,219,292,000	1,175,401,000	1,197,081,000
R&D Expense						
Operating Income	223,271,900	134,497,300	206,829,000	336,000,100	188,141,300	141,427,900
Operating Margin %		11.71%	17.76%	27.55%	16.00%	11.81%
SGA Expense	321,600,900	328,296,800	339,659,500	343,630,600	346,910,200	367,040,600
Net Income	95,131,360	-521,961,700	129,117,200	-1,322,341,000	104,524,600	-48,874,100
Operating Cash Flow						
Capital Expenditure	20,367,830	22,380,020	22,354,800	28,378,760	28,356,340	20,366,430
EBITDA	262,750,700	-396,366,600	326,707,100	-1,199,663,000	347,309,600	253,604,000
Return on Assets %		-33.30%	6.99%	-52.31%	3.14%	-1.40%
Return on Equity %		-89.05%	15.05%	-92.24%	5.17%	-2.54%
Debt to Equity		1.89	0.64	0.73	0.42	0.52

CONTACT INFORMATION:
Phone: 618-9482-3111   Fax: 618-9482-9080
Toll-Free:
Address: Newspaper House, 50 Hasler Rd, Osborne Park, WA 6017 Australia

STOCK TICKER/OTHER:
Stock Ticker: WANHF
Employees: 5,041
Parent Company:

Exchange: GREY
Fiscal Year Ends: 06/30

SALARIES/BONUSES:
Top Exec. Salary: $ Bonus: $
Second Exec. Salary: $ Bonus: $

OTHER THOUGHTS:
Estimated Female Officers or Directors:
Hot Spot for Advancement for Women/Minorities:

Shanghai Media Group (SMG)
www.smg.cn/review/english_index.html

NAIC Code: 515120

TYPES OF BUSINESS:
Television Broadcasting
TV Production
Radio Production
Radio Broadcasting
Online TV Broadcasting
Cable TV Network
Newspaper Publishing
Magazine Publishing

BRANDS/DIVISIONS/AFFILIATES:
Shanghai Media & Entertainment Group
China Business Network
CBN TV
CBN Weekly
CBN Paper
CBN Radio
CBN
Oriental Pearl Company Ltd

CONTACTS:
Note: Officers with more than one job title may be intentionally listed here more than once.

Qiu Xin, Pres.
Yang Chao, Dir.-Design
Wang Jianjun, Sec.
Wu Jiaming, Dir.-Foreign Affairs

GROWTH PLANS/SPECIAL FEATURES:
Shanghai Media Group (SMG), a subsidiary of Shanghai Media & Entertainment Group, is a Chinese producer and provider of radio, TV and film entertainment. It is the holding company for China Business Network (CBN), which operates the CBN TV channel, a magazine named CBN Weekly, a newspaper called CBN Paper, a radio channel called CBN Radio and several CBN websites. In addition, SMG is engaged in the performing arts, sports and technical service sectors; and also transmits signals via airwaves, cable, satellite and IPTV (internet protocol television). Among the company's television and radio productions are news, sports, finance and entertainment programs. These programs are broadcast through SMG's 15 cable and satellite TV networks, 13 radio frequencies, 15 subscription-based digital pay TV channels, eight newspapers and magazines. SMG's film entertainment division includes features such as Kung Fu Panda 3 and Born in China (along with Disney); and Earth: One Amazing Day. SMG is a majority shareholder in Oriental Pearl Company, Ltd., a media advertising and entertainment business.

FINANCIAL DATA:
Note: Data for latest year may not have been available at press time.

In U.S. $	2018	2017	2016	2015	2014	2013
Revenue	610,000,000	593,250,000	565,000,000	590,000,000	600,000,000	589,000,000
R&D Expense						
Operating Income						
Operating Margin %						
SGA Expense						
Net Income						
Operating Cash Flow						
Capital Expenditure						
EBITDA						
Return on Assets %						
Return on Equity %						
Debt to Equity						

CONTACT INFORMATION:
Phone: 86-21-6256-5899   Fax:
Toll-Free:
Address: 298 Weihai Rd., Shanghai, Shanghai 200041 China

SALARIES/BONUSES:
Top Exec. Salary: $ Bonus: $
Second Exec. Salary: $ Bonus: $

STOCK TICKER/OTHER:
Stock Ticker: Subsidiary   Exchange:
Employees: 5,200   Fiscal Year Ends: 12/31
Parent Company: Shanghai Media & Entertainment Group

OTHER THOUGHTS:
Estimated Female Officers or Directors:
Hot Spot for Advancement for Women/Minorities:

Sales, profits and employees may be estimates. Financial information, benefits and other data can change quickly and may vary from those stated here.

Sharp Corporation

www.sharp-world.com

NAIC Code: 334310

TYPES OF BUSINESS:
Audiovisual & Communications Equipment
Electronic Components
Solar Cells & Advanced Batteries
Home Appliances
Consumer Electronics

BRANDS/DIVISIONS/AFFILIATES:
Sharp Marketing Japan Corporation
SMJ Home solutions Company
SMJ Business Solutions Company
Sharp Energy Solutions Company
Sharp Trading Corporation
ScienBiziP Japan Co Ltd
Foxconn Technology Co Ltd

GROWTH PLANS/SPECIAL FEATURES:
Sharp Corporation designs, manufactures and distributes audiovisual and communication equipment, electric and electronic application equipment, as well as electronic components. The company's products include liquid crystal display (LCD) televisions, amorphous silicon liquid crystal display modules, mobile phones, home appliances, electronic components, solar cells, sensors, modules and integrated circuits. Sharp has companies and facilities in more than 25 countries, all of which are engaged in sales, manufacturing, R&D, solar power generation or finance. A few of its domestic subsidiaries include: Sharp Marketing Japan Corporation (SMJ), SMJ Home Solutions Company, SMJ Business Solutions Company, Sharp Energy Solutions Corporation, Sharp Trading Corporation and ScienBiziP Japan Co. Ltd. Foxconn Technology Co. Ltd. owns a 66% stake in Sharp Corporation.

CONTACTS: Note: Officers with more than one job title may be intentionally listed here more than once.
Jeng-Wu Tai, CEO
Mototaka Taneya, Exec. Gen. Mgr.-Corp. R&D Group
Toshihiko Fujimoto, Exec. Gen. Mgr.-Bus. Dev. Group
Shogo Fukahori, Chief Officer-In-House Comm.
Shinichi Niihara, Exec. Officer
Fujikazu Nakayama, Sr. Exec. Managing Officer-Products Bus. Group
Akihiko Imaya, Exec. Group Gen. Mgr.-Display Device Business
Masahiro Okitsu, Exec. Group Gen. Mgr.-Health & Environment
Paul Molyneux, Exec. Gen. Mgr.-Sales & Mktg., Europe

FINANCIAL DATA: Note: Data for latest year may not have been available at press time.

In U.S. $	2018	2017	2016	2015	2014	2013
Revenue	22,514,760,000	19,021,210,000	22,833,080,000	25,844,610,000	27,151,840,000	22,990,740,000
R&D Expense						
Operating Income	835,986,200	579,307,600	-1,502,365,000	-445,838,900	1,006,975,000	-1,356,727,000
Operating Margin %	3.71	3.04%	-6.57%	-1.72%	3.70%	-5.90%
SGA Expense						
Net Income	651,389,500	-230,752,800	-2,374,332,000	-2,062,435,000	107,218,400	-5,058,502,000
Operating Cash Flow	976,458,200	1,180,163,000	-174,996,300	160,832,200	1,845,726,000	-752,031,400
Capital Expenditure	946,710,800	717,915,200	430,060,800	461,097,500	423,966,700	570,078,300
EBITDA	1,579,966,000	686,795,000	-1,258,506,000	-522,484,400	1,766,770,000	-2,553,168,000
Return on Assets %	3.81%	-1.48%	-14.49%	-10.73%	.54%	-23.19%
Return on Equity %	20.88%	-19.81%		-197.35%	7.22%	-145.31%
Debt to Equity	1.41	1.80		3.76	1.48	1.86

CONTACT INFORMATION:
Phone: 81 666211221 Fax:
Toll-Free:
Address: 1 Takumi-cho Sakai-Ku, Sakai City, Osaka, 590-8522 Japan

SALARIES/BONUSES:
Top Exec. Salary: $ Bonus: $
Second Exec. Salary: $ Bonus: $

STOCK TICKER/OTHER:
Stock Ticker: SHCAF Exchange: PINX
Employees: 50,253 Fiscal Year Ends: 03/31
Parent Company: Foxconn Technology Co Ltd

OTHER THOUGHTS:
Estimated Female Officers or Directors:
Hot Spot for Advancement for Women/Minorities:

Shaw Communications Inc

www.shaw.ca

NAIC Code: 517110

TYPES OF BUSINESS:
Cable TV Service
Internet Service Provider
Satellite Services
Digital Phone Services
Internet Infrastructure Services
Video-On-Demand
Broadcast TV

BRANDS/DIVISIONS/AFFILIATES:
Freedom Mobile
Shaw Go WiFi
BlueSky TV
Shaw Direct

CONTACTS:
Note: Officers with more than one job title may be intentionally listed here more than once.

Mcaleese Paul, CEO, Divisional
Jay Mehr, Pres.
Vito Culmone, CFO
J. Shaw, Chairman of the Board
Jim Little, Chief Marketing Officer
Zoran Stakic, Chief Technology Officer
Bradley Shaw, Director
Jim Shaw, Director
Janice Davis, Executive VP, Divisional
Trevor English, Executive VP
Peter Johnson, Executive VP
Chris Kucharski, President, Divisional
Ron McKenzie, Senior VP
Ron McKenzie, Senior VP, Divisional

GROWTH PLANS/SPECIAL FEATURES:

Shaw Communications, Inc. is a diversified Canadian communications company whose core business is providing broadband cable television, Internet, digital phone, telecommunications and satellite direct-to-home services. Shaw is organized into two business segments: Wireless and Wireline. The Wireless division, operated through Freedom Mobile, provides wireless voice and data services through an expanding and improving wireless network infrastructure. This segment now covers approximately 16 million people in some of Canada's largest urban centers, or almost half of the Canadian population. This segment currently operates in Ontario, Alberta and British Columbia, offering the leading alternative for mobile services to the three national wireless incumbent carriers. Through the Wireline segment, Shaw is one of the largest providers of residential communications services in Canada. The Wireline segment is divided into the Consumer and Business divisions. The Consumer connects consumers in their homes and on the go with broadband Internet, Shaw Go WiFi, video (including BlueSky TV) and traditional home phone services. Additionally, the Consumer division offer Satellite Services through Shaw Direct. Shaw Direct connects families across Canada with video and audio programming by satellite. Shaw Direct customers have access to over 550 digital video channels (including over 250 HD channels) and over 10,000 on-demand, pay-per-view and subscription movie and television titles. The Business division provides connectivity solutions to business customers of all sizes, from home offices to medium and large-scale enterprises. The range of services offered by Shaw Business includes: fiber internet, business internet, data connectivity, voice solutions, video and broadcast video.

FINANCIAL DATA:
Note: Data for latest year may not have been available at press time.

In U.S. $	2018	2017	2016	2015	2014	2013
Revenue	3,886,845,000	3,621,984,000	3,623,468,000	4,071,579,000	3,888,328,000	3,814,880,000
R&D Expense						
Operating Income	468,142,600	741,163,900	841,321,200	1,062,409,000	1,067,602,000	1,013,443,000
Operating Margin %		20.46%	23.21%	26.09%	27.45%	26.56%
SGA Expense						
Net Income	44,514,350	631,361,900	905,125,100	635,071,400	635,813,200	553,461,800
Operating Cash Flow	1,002,315,000	1,114,343,000	1,233,789,000	1,142,535,000	1,290,916,000	1,015,669,000
Capital Expenditure	988,218,600	1,196,694,000	888,803,100	808,677,300	827,966,900	744,131,500
EBITDA	1,096,537,000	1,449,684,000	1,403,686,000	1,749,414,000	1,657,417,000	1,658,901,000
Return on Assets %		5.69%	8.09%	6.05%	6.48%	5.75%
Return on Equity %		13.54%	20.62%	16.65%	18.97%	18.47%
Debt to Equity		0.69	0.82	0.93	0.99	0.92

CONTACT INFORMATION:
Phone: 403 750-4500   Fax: 403 750-4501
Toll-Free: 888-472-2222
Address: 630 3rd Ave. SW, Ste. 900, Calgary, AB T2P 4L4 Canada

SALARIES/BONUSES:
Top Exec. Salary: $2,500,000   Bonus: $
Second Exec. Salary: $1,750,000   Bonus: $

STOCK TICKER/OTHER:
Stock Ticker: SJR   Exchange: NYS
Employees: 14,000   Fiscal Year Ends: 08/31
Parent Company:

OTHER THOUGHTS:
Estimated Female Officers or Directors: 3
Hot Spot for Advancement for Women/Minorities: Y

Shazam Entertainment Limited

www.shazam.com

NAIC Code: 511210F

TYPES OF BUSINESS:
Computer Software, Multimedia, Graphics & Publishing
Mobile application

BRANDS/DIVISIONS/AFFILIATES:
Apple Inc
Shazam

CONTACTS:
Note: Officers with more than one job title may be intentionally listed here more than once.

Rich Riley, CEO
Todd B. Saypoff, CFO
Andrew Fisher, Chmn.

GROWTH PLANS/SPECIAL FEATURES:
Shazam Entertainment Limited operates mobile app Shazam, which enables users to discover, explore and share music and TV shows by connecting and sharing content with others. More than 1 billion people in over 190 countries connect via the Shazam app. For example, if a user is in a store and hears music that he or she likes, they can start the app, tap the Shazam button, and within seconds a digital fingerprint of the audio is created, and is then matched with Shazam's database of tracks and TV shows. Shazam provides the name of the track and the artist, as well as information such as lyrics, video, artist biography, concert tickets and recommended tracks. Shazam is a leader in audio recognition technology, which recognizes or identifies music or other media content being played on computer or in a background setting, and can then connect the user with the recognized media's information. Users can also share their favorite finds on social media platforms. The app is available on Apple, Android and Windows devices. In addition, Shazam offers a massively-scaled augmented reality (AR) platform for its brand partners, artists and users. The platform can bring any marketing materials to life via products, packaging, point of sales, advertising, events and more by utilizing the app to scan unique Shazam codes. The codes are capable of delivering AR experiences including 3D animations, product visualizations, mini-games and 360-degree videos. For example, users who visually Shazam in-store can integrate and play a co-branded AR interactive game. In September 2018, Shazam was acquired by Apple, Inc., and began operating as its wholly-owned subsidiary.

FINANCIAL DATA:
Note: Data for latest year may not have been available at press time.

In U.S. $	2018	2017	2016	2015	2014	2013
Revenue	60,000,000	55,100,200	49,557,100	44,311,595	54,747,498	47,144,997
R&D Expense						
Operating Income						
Operating Margin %						
SGA Expense						
Net Income		-23,930,900	-4,512,530	-20,811,038	-22,565,064	-3,008,323
Operating Cash Flow						
Capital Expenditure						
EBITDA						
Return on Assets %						
Return on Equity %						
Debt to Equity						

CONTACT INFORMATION:
Phone: 44-208-742-6820 Fax:
Toll-Free:
Address: 26-28 Hammersmith Grove, London, W6 7HA United Kingdom

STOCK TICKER/OTHER:
Stock Ticker: Subsidiary
Employees: 225
Parent Company: Apple Inc

Exchange:
Fiscal Year Ends: 12/31

SALARIES/BONUSES:
Top Exec. Salary: $ Bonus: $
Second Exec. Salary: $ Bonus: $

OTHER THOUGHTS:
Estimated Female Officers or Directors:
Hot Spot for Advancement for Women/Minorities:

Shenzhen Overseas Chinese Town Co Ltd (OCT Limited)

www.octholding.com
NAIC Code: 713110

TYPES OF BUSINESS:
Amusement and Theme Parks
Tourism
Real Estate
Real Estate Development
Property Management

BRANDS/DIVISIONS/AFFILIATES:
Splendid China Folk Village
Window of the World
Happy Village

GROWTH PLANS/SPECIAL FEATURES:
Shenzhen Overseas Chinese Town Co., Ltd. (OCT Limited) is engaged in the tourism and real estate sectors, primarily in regards to domestic theme parks. These properties consist of Splendid China Folk Village, Window of the World, and Happy Valley, which can include cultural tourism scenic areas, hotels, residences, commercial services and more. OCT Limited develops and manages the properties, and offers cultural industry activities and related internet services.

CONTACTS:
Note: Officers with more than one job title may be intentionally listed here more than once.

Xian Niannan Duan, Managing Dir.
Xiaowen Wang, CFO

FINANCIAL DATA:
Note: Data for latest year may not have been available at press time.

In U.S. $	2018	2017	2016	2015	2014	2013
Revenue		6,501,360,000	5,105,730,000	4,966,490,000	4,991,980,000	4,605,260,000
R&D Expense						
Operating Income						
Operating Margin %						
SGA Expense						
Net Income		1,430,820,000	1,052,040,000	807,813,000	4,991,980,000	810,627,000
Operating Cash Flow						
Capital Expenditure						
EBITDA						
Return on Assets %						
Return on Equity %						
Debt to Equity						

CONTACT INFORMATION:
Phone: 86-755-2660248   Fax: 86-755-26600936
Toll-Free:
Address: OCT Group Office Bldg., Nanshan Dist., Shenzhen, Guangdong 518053 China

STOCK TICKER/OTHER:
Stock Ticker: 69
Employees: 25,130
Parent Company:

Exchange: Shenzhen
Fiscal Year Ends: 12/31

SALARIES/BONUSES:
Top Exec. Salary: $ Bonus: $
Second Exec. Salary: $ Bonus: $

OTHER THOUGHTS:
Estimated Female Officers or Directors:
Hot Spot for Advancement for Women/Minorities:

Sales, profits and employees may be estimates. Financial information, benefits and other data can change quickly and may vary from those stated here.

Shun Tak Holdings Limited

www.shuntakgroup.com

NAIC Code: 721110

TYPES OF BUSINESS:
Investment Holding Company
High-Speed Ferry Services
Real Estate Investment
Hotel Management
Casino Management

BRANDS/DIVISIONS/AFFILIATES:
Shun Tak-China Travel Ship Management Limited
TurboJET
Shun Tak & CITS Coach (Macao) Limited
Shun Tak Real Estate Ltd
Shun Tak Property Management Ltd
Shun Tak Macau Services Ltd
Clean Living (Macau) Ltd
Macau Matters Co Ltd

CONTACTS:
Note: Officers with more than one job title may be intentionally listed here more than once.

Pansy Ho, Managing Dir.
Daisy Ho, Deputy Managing Dir.
Maisy Ho, Exec. Dir.
David Shum, Exec. Dir.
Rogier Verhoeven, Exec. Dir.
Stanley Ho, Chmn.

GROWTH PLANS/SPECIAL FEATURES:

Shun Tak Holdings Limited is a publicly-traded Hong Kong-based conglomerate with core businesses in the transportation, property, hospitality and investment sectors. The transportation segment maintains ferry and air services through the joint venture Shun Tak-China Travel Ship Management Limited, which is known under the brand name TurboJET. The company shares ownership of TurboJET with China Travel International Investment Hong Kong Limited. TurboJET operates one of the largest fleets of high-speed passenger ferries in Asia. It also maintains airport routes that connect Hong Kong International airport with Shenzhen and Macau. The segment additionally maintains bus services in Macau and the Guangdong province through joint venture Shun Tak & CITS Coach (Macao) Limited, operating 98 vehicles. Shun Tak's property division develops and invests in property in Hong Kong and Macau. Its major operations include property development and sales, developing residential, retail and commercial properties; property leasing and asset management through Shun Tak Real Estate Ltd., which markets and leases residential, retail and commercial properties; property management services through Shun Tak Property Management Ltd., which maintains the company's owned properties; cleaning services through Shun Tak Macau Services, Ltd.; and laundry services through Clean Living (Macau), Ltd. Shun Tak's hospitality segment is engaged in hotel and casino management, managing the Macau Tower Convention & Entertainment Center and owning a 70% interest in Hong Kong SkyCity Marriot Hotel. The firm's investments segment holds interests in diversified investments in Macau and Hong Kong, including a minority stake in Sociedade de Turismo e Diversoes de Macau SA; and wholly-owned Macau Matters Co. Ltd., which specializes in retail facility operations. In early-2018, the firm announced plans to establish a joint venture with a consortium of investors to invest in, acquire and develop large-scale and predominantly healthcare-integrated mixed-use developments nearby high-speed railway stations throughout China.

FINANCIAL DATA:
Note: Data for latest year may not have been available at press time.

In U.S. $	2018	2017	2016	2015	2014	2013
Revenue		815,807,200	491,888,600	562,555,000	1,218,067,000	456,617,500
R&D Expense						
Operating Income		186,759,200	26,320,860	106,174,500	376,825,700	41,392,430
Operating Margin %		22.89%	6.51%	20.04%	31.57%	21.52%
SGA Expense						
Net Income		185,184,300	-74,976,950	95,093,790	568,633,100	179,602,200
Operating Cash Flow		283,269,200	134,329,800	55,048,200	332,276,500	17,956,560
Capital Expenditure		27,992,950	145,861,500	9,716,763	7,221,903	3,480,698
EBITDA		287,208,400	20,081,600	207,035,200	759,865,700	275,338,000
Return on Assets %		2.81%	-1.25%	1.57%	10.37%	3.87%
Return on Equity %		5.46%	-2.25%	2.82%	18.72%	6.83%
Debt to Equity		0.36	0.39	0.30	0.35	0.34

CONTACT INFORMATION:
Phone: 852-2859-3111 Fax: 852-2857-7181
Toll-Free:
Address: 200 Connaught Rd., Penthouse, 39/Fl, West Tower, Hong Kong, Hong Kong

STOCK TICKER/OTHER:
Stock Ticker: SHTGF
Employees: 3,390
Parent Company:

Exchange: GREY
Fiscal Year Ends: 12/31

SALARIES/BONUSES:
Top Exec. Salary: $ Bonus: $
Second Exec. Salary: $ Bonus: $

OTHER THOUGHTS:
Estimated Female Officers or Directors: 4
Hot Spot for Advancement for Women/Minorities: Y

Sales, profits and employees may be estimates. Financial information, benefits and other data can change quickly and may vary from those stated here.

SimEx-Iwerks

NAIC Code: 512131

www.simex-iwerks.com

TYPES OF BUSINESS:
Movie Theaters-3D
Ride Simulation Theaters
Equipment & Facility Leasing
Format Conversion Services

BRANDS/DIVISIONS/AFFILIATES:
Extreme Screen Theaters

CONTACTS:
Note: Officers with more than one job title may be intentionally listed here more than once.
Michael J. Needham, CEO
Michael J. Needham, Pres.
David Needham, Sr. VP-Sales
Brian R. Peebles, Sr. VP-Oper.
Mark Cornell, Sr. VP-Attraction Dev.
Michael J. Needham, Chmn.

GROWTH PLANS/SPECIAL FEATURES:
SimEx-Iwerks is an entertainment firm that specializes in developing 3-D and 4-D cinematic experiences. The company designs, engineers, manufactures, markets and services high-tech entertainment attractions that employ a variety of projection, show control, ride simulation and software technologies. SimEx-Iwerks sells and installs ride simulation attractions in specialty theaters, large-format theaters and theaters that include special effects. It operates/supports more than 300 attractions worldwide, entertaining over 40 million guests every year. Its Extreme Screen Theaters brand of theaters feature 80x80 foot wide screens and can project 2-D, 3-D and 4-D pictures. SimEx-Iwerks also licenses and distributes the films in its library to ride simulation and large-format theaters and specialty theater attractions. The company has a catalog of over 130 titles, all of which are available in multiple languages. The firm produces and distributes films in the 5/70, 8/70 and 15/70 film formats for third parties and also invests in joint ventures by contributing its ride simulation technology, design and equipment and by participating in theater profits. In addition, SimEx-Iwerks leases camera equipment and rents post-production facilities. The primary markets for the company's attractions are theme parks; museums; movie theaters; and various types of location-based entertainment centers, destination centers and special event venues. The company produces a variety of motion-ride simulators ranging from open platforms to enclosed cabins, with seating capacities between 6 and 51 persons. Attractions developed by SimEx-Iwerks include Journey to the Center of the Earth 3-D/4-D, The Polar Express 4-D Experience, The Wizard of Oz 4-D Experience, Happy Feet 4-D Experience, Shrek 4-D, The Simpsons in 4-D, London Eye 4-D Experience and Ultimate 4-D Experience.

FINANCIAL DATA:
Note: Data for latest year may not have been available at press time.

In U.S. $	2018	2017	2016	2015	2014	2013
Revenue						
R&D Expense						
Operating Income						
Operating Margin %						
SGA Expense						
Net Income						
Operating Cash Flow						
Capital Expenditure						
EBITDA						
Return on Assets %						
Return on Equity %						
Debt to Equity						

CONTACT INFORMATION:
Phone: 416-597-1585   Fax: 416-597-0350
Toll-Free:
Address: 511 King St. W., Ste. 130, Toronto, ON M5V 1K4 Canada

STOCK TICKER/OTHER:
Stock Ticker: Private   Exchange:
Employees: Fiscal Year Ends: 06/30
Parent Company:

SALARIES/BONUSES:
Top Exec. Salary: $ Bonus: $
Second Exec. Salary: $ Bonus: $

OTHER THOUGHTS:
Estimated Female Officers or Directors:
Hot Spot for Advancement for Women/Minorities:

Simon & Schuster Inc

NAIC Code: 511130

www.simonandschuster.com

TYPES OF BUSINESS:
Book Publishing & Distribution
Online Publishing
E-Books
Children's Publishing
Audio Books

BRANDS/DIVISIONS/AFFILIATES:
CBS Corporation
Simon Pulse
Scribner
Free Press
Touchstone
Atheneum Books ofr Young Readers
Primsleur Language Programs
Simon & Schuster Australia

CONTACTS: Note: Officers with more than one job title may be intentionally listed here more than once.
Carolyn Kroll Reidy, CEO
Dennis Eulau, CFO
Liz Perl, CMO
Carolyn Connolly, Sr. VP-Human Resources
David Hillman, General Counsel
Dennis Eulau, Exec. VP-Oper.
Elinor Hirschhorn, Chief Digital Officer
Adam Rothberg, VP
Liz Perl, Sr. VP-Mktg.
Kevin Hanson, Pres., Simon & Schuster Canada
Susan Moldow, Exec. VP
Lou Johnson, Managing Dir.-Simon & Schuster Australia
Ian S. Chapman, Managing Dir.-Simon & Schuster UK

GROWTH PLANS/SPECIAL FEATURES:

Simon & Schuster, Inc. (S&S), a subsidiary of CBS Corporation, publishes and distributes books in printed, audio and digital formats in the U.S. and internationally. The company publishes under imprints such as Simon & Schuster, Scribner, Free Press, Atria, Touchstone, Gallery, Howard, Atheneum Books for Young Readers, Little Simon and Simon Pulse. S&S publishes around 2,000 titles annually and distributes physical and digital titles in more than 200 countries worldwide through four main divisions: adult publishing, children's publishing, audio publishing and international. The adult publishing group includes several publishing units in varied formats. The firm's children's publishing division offers acclaimed backlist titles, including famous characters such as Eloise, Raggedy Ann, Olivia, Henry and Mudge, The Hardy Boys, Nancy Drew, Buffy the Vampire Slayer and Shiloh. The audio division publishes audio books including fiction, nonfiction, business/finance, self-improvement and inspirational titles as well as Pimsleur Language Programs. The international group includes Simon & Schuster Australia, Simon & Schuster Canada and Simon & Schuster U.K. The company's website, SimonandSchuster.com, which includes sites based in the U.K., Australia and Canada, publishes print titles in a wide variety of genres in addition to providing users with a forum to access video and audio interviews; view national and local media and bookstore appearances; discuss books; and purchase eBooks.

FINANCIAL DATA: Note: Data for latest year may not have been available at press time.

In U.S. $	2018	2017	2016	2015	2014	2013
Revenue	835,000,000	829,000,000	800,000,000	780,000,000	778,000,000	809,000,000
R&D Expense						
Operating Income						
Operating Margin %						
SGA Expense						
Net Income						
Operating Cash Flow						
Capital Expenditure						
EBITDA						
Return on Assets %						
Return on Equity %						
Debt to Equity						

CONTACT INFORMATION:
Phone: 212-698-7000 Fax: 212-698-7099
Toll-Free:
Address: 1230 Ave. of the Americas, New York, NY 10020 United States

STOCK TICKER/OTHER:
Stock Ticker: Subsidiary
Employees: 1,400
Parent Company: CBS Corporation
Exchange:
Fiscal Year Ends: 12/31

SALARIES/BONUSES:
Top Exec. Salary: $ Bonus: $
Second Exec. Salary: $ Bonus: $

OTHER THOUGHTS:
Estimated Female Officers or Directors: 7
Hot Spot for Advancement for Women/Minorities: Y

Sales, profits and employees may be estimates. Financial information, benefits and other data can change quickly and may vary from those stated here.

Sinclair Broadcast Group Inc

NAIC Code: 515120

www.sbgi.net

TYPES OF BUSINESS:
Radio & TV Station Owner/Operator
Broadcasting & Programming Services

BRANDS/DIVISIONS/AFFILIATES:
Stadium
Tennis Channel
Ring of Honor
Comet TV
Charge!
TBD
Sinclair Original Programming
Compulse Integrated Marketing

CONTACTS:
Note: Officers with more than one job title may be intentionally listed here more than once.

Lucy Rutishauser, CFO
David Smith, Chairman of the Board
David Bochenek, Chief Accounting Officer
Steven Marks, COO
J. Smith, Director
Frederick Smith, Director
Barry Faber, Executive VP, Divisional
Steven Pruett, Executive VP
Robert Weisbord, Other Executive Officer
Christopher Ripley, President
I. Livingston, Senior VP, Divisional
Donald Thompson, Senior VP, Divisional
Rebecca Hanson, Senior VP, Divisional
Delbert Parks, Senior VP
Justin Bray, Treasurer
David Amy, Vice Chairman

GROWTH PLANS/SPECIAL FEATURES:

Sinclair Broadcast Group, Inc. is a diversified broadcasting company. The firm owns and operates, programs or provides sales services to 191 television stations in 89 markets. Sinclair's content creation department includes news operations, the Stadium multi-platform sports network, the Tennis Channel, the Ring of Honor professional wrestling company, the Comet TV channel dedicated to sci-fi entertainment, the Charge! network dedicated to action/adventure programming, the TBD digital-first content programming broadcasted on television, the KidsCLICK free over-the-air animated kids program, and the Sinclair Original Programming division that produces video content for the firm's linear and digital platforms. Sinclair's distribution platforms include television stations, digital, radio and cable; and its advertising platforms include local advertising, Compulse Integrated Marketing's web-based solutions, Sinclair Network Sales, Sinclair National Sales and Long Form's one-stop solution to paid programming across all Sinclair television stations. Technical solutions are provided by Sinclair, and comprise the following: One Media, a think tank startup focused on creating the next-generation broadcast platform for the broadcast television industry; Acrodyne, providing service and support for broadcast transmitters worldwide; and Dielectric, which offers products and solutions that equip television and radio broadcasters with antenna and signal-transmission solutions that meet the needs of low- and high-power users serving rural audiences as well as major metropolitan markets. During 2018, the Tribune merger agreement was terminated.

Sinclair employees receive life, AD&D, disability, medical, dental and vision insurance; wellness programs; flexible spending accounts; and education reimbursement.

FINANCIAL DATA:
Note: Data for latest year may not have been available at press time.

In U.S. $	2018	2017	2016	2015	2014	2013
Revenue		2,734,118,000	2,736,949,000	2,219,136,000	1,976,558,000	1,363,131,000
R&D Expense		10,000,000	4,085,000	12,436,000		
Operating Income		574,157,000	724,704,000	547,633,000	564,120,000	408,536,000
Operating Margin %		20.99%	26.47%	24.67%	28.54%	29.95%
SGA Expense		646,790,000	575,145,000	495,974,000	440,019,000	302,659,000
Net Income		576,013,000	245,301,000	171,524,000	212,279,000	73,468,000
Operating Cash Flow		431,104,000	591,766,000	400,695,000	430,454,000	160,577,000
Capital Expenditure		83,812,000	94,465,000	108,432,000	1,566,497,000	1,049,532,000
EBITDA		1,006,984,000	866,357,000	690,127,000	716,196,000	409,819,000
Return on Assets %		9.03%	4.30%	3.15%	4.42%	2.13%
Return on Equity %		53.41%	44.04%	35.97%	51.50%	52.58%
Debt to Equity		2.47	6.85	7.01	8.91	7.53

CONTACT INFORMATION:
Phone: 410 568-1500   Fax: 410 568-1533
Toll-Free:
Address: 10706 Beaver Dam Rd., Hunt Valley, MD 21030 United States

SALARIES/BONUSES:
Top Exec. Salary: $1,250,000   Bonus: $400,000
Second Exec. Salary: $1,250,000   Bonus: $

STOCK TICKER/OTHER:
Stock Ticker: SBGI   Exchange: NAS
Employees: 8,400   Fiscal Year Ends: 12/31
Parent Company:

OTHER THOUGHTS:
Estimated Female Officers or Directors: 1
Hot Spot for Advancement for Women/Minorities:

Sales, profits and employees may be estimates. Financial information, benefits and other data can change quickly and may vary from those stated here.

Singapore Press Holdings Limited

NAIC Code: 511110

www.sph.com.sg

TYPES OF BUSINESS:
Newspaper, Magazine & Multimedia Publishing
Real Estate Development
Broadcasting
Advertising

BRANDS/DIVISIONS/AFFILIATES:
Straits Times Press
SPH Data Services
ShareInvestor
SPH Radio
SPH Magazines
SPH REIT
Paragon
tabla!

CONTACTS:
Note: Officers with more than one job title may be intentionally listed here more than once.

Ng Yat chung, CEO
Anthony Mallek, CFO
Seow Choke Meng, Exec. VP-Admin. & Times Properties
Ginney Lim May Ling, General Counsel
Siew Yin Lee, Exec. VP-Corp. Dev.
Ginney Lim May Ling, Exec. VP-Corp. Comm.
Han Fook Kwang, Managing Editor-English & Malay Newspapers
Lee Boon Yang, Chmn.
Lim Jim Koon, Editor-in-Chief-Chinese Newspapers
Chua Wee Phong, Exec. VP-Circulation

GROWTH PLANS/SPECIAL FEATURES:
Singapore Press Holdings Limited (SPH) is a leading media group in Singapore with holdings in platforms such as print, digital, radio and out-of-home media. These platforms are offered in multiple languages. The company publishes newspapers in four languages. SPH's media business comprises the print and digital operations of The Straits Times, The Business Times, The New Paper, Berita Harian, Tamil Murasu and tabla!, along with their student publications. This division also includes book publishing arm Straits, Times Press; SPH Data Services, which license the use of the Straits Times Index; financial data company ShareInvestor; and radio stations, including two English stations of SPH Radio (Kiss92 and ONE FM 91.3), and SPH Golf. The Chinese media business unit publishes three Chinese newspapers in print and digital format; and SPH's other digital media initiatives include AsiaOne, Stomp, zaobao.sg and zaobao.com. Wholly-owned SPH Magazines publishes and produces more than 80 magazine titles and various online sites, covering a broad range of interests from lifestyle to information technology. The media business division also provides out-of-home advertising options where it manages large format digital screens and static billboards at key locations in the Singapore. SPH's real estate business comprises SPH REIT (real estate investment trust), established to invest in a portfolio of income-producing real estate primarily for retail purposes. Its property portfolio includes: Paragon, an upscale retail mall and medical suite/office property; The Clementi Mall, a mid-market suburban mall in the Clementi town; The Seletar Mall, a mall in Singapore; and Sky@eleven, a luxury apartment and duplex complex. Other SPH businesses include online classified ads, events and exhibitions, nursing home operations and preschool/education operations. In September 2018, SPH announced that it had acquired the PBSA Portfolio, a portfolio of operating assets for purpose-built student accommodation in the United Kingdom.

FINANCIAL DATA:
Note: Data for latest year may not have been available at press time.

In U.S. $	2018	2017	2016	2015	2014	2013
Revenue	720,295,400	756,920,300	824,242,400	862,898,700	890,832,100	908,622,500
R&D Expense						
Operating Income	195,158,000	217,955,400	267,427,600	283,791,500	281,525,500	294,122,800
Operating Margin %		42.18%	32.44%	33.73%	44.26%	32.37%
SGA Expense	51,314,420	47,689,320	51,125,280	49,814,530	47,576,420	46,393,230
Net Income	206,077,300	256,641,700	194,482,100	235,833,900	296,375,600	315,925,500
Operating Cash Flow	-14,911,660	-14,504,800	-10,127,560	29,215,600	10,212,590	-171,433,900
Capital Expenditure	16,619,750	9,368,081	11,171,470	10,048,380	13,872,880	19,018,400
EBITDA	328,019,200	370,981,600	325,640,400	380,126,800	455,035,600	427,153,400
Return on Assets %		5.81%	4.41%	5.05%	6.20%	8.26%
Return on Equity %		9.99%	7.43%	8.80%	11.19%	14.91%
Debt to Equity		0.15	0.34	0.26	0.23	0.49

CONTACT INFORMATION:
Phone: 65-6319-6319 Fax: 65-6319-8150
Toll-Free:
Address: 1000 Toa Payoh N. News Ctr., Singapore, 318994 Singapore

STOCK TICKER/OTHER:
Stock Ticker: SGPRY
Employees: 4,421
Parent Company:

Exchange: PINX
Fiscal Year Ends: 08/31

SALARIES/BONUSES:
Top Exec. Salary: $ Bonus: $
Second Exec. Salary: $ Bonus: $

OTHER THOUGHTS:
Estimated Female Officers or Directors: 7
Hot Spot for Advancement for Women/Minorities: Y

Sirius XM Holdings Inc

NAIC Code: 515111

www.siriusxm.com

TYPES OF BUSINESS:
Satellite and Online Radio
Mobile Television Content

BRANDS/DIVISIONS/AFFILIATES:
SiriusXM Radio Inc
Siriu XM Radio
SiriusXM.com
SiriusXM Travel Link
NavTraffic
Nav Weather
SiriusXM Aviation
Sirius Marine

CONTACTS:
Note: Officers with more than one job title may be intentionally listed here more than once.

David Frear, CFO
Gregory Maffei, Chairman of the Board
Thomas Barry, Chief Accounting Officer
Dara Altman, Chief Administrative Officer
Jennifer Witz, Chief Marketing Officer
James Meyer, Director
Stephen Cook, Executive VP, Divisional
Joseph Verbrugge, Executive VP, Divisional
James Cady, Executive VP, Divisional
Patrick Donnelly, Executive VP
Scott Greenstein, Other Executive Officer

GROWTH PLANS/SPECIAL FEATURES:

Sirius XM Holdings, Inc., operating as SiriusXM Radio, is a U.S.-based satellite radio provider. It offers numerous channels to its 32.7 million subscribers, including music, sports, entertainment, comedy, talk, news, traffic and weather. Many of its channels are commercial-free, including an extensive selection of music genres; live play-by-play sports from major leagues and colleges; talk and entertainment; national, international and financial news; and local traffic and weather. The company's primary source of revenue is subscription fees. Sirius radios for the car, truck, home, RV, boat, office and store are distributed through automakers and retail locations nationwide as well as online through SiriusXM.com. Sirius also has agreements with every major automaker to offer its radios as factory or dealer-installed options in their vehicles. Satellite radio services are also offered to customers of certain rental car companies. Additional services provided by the firm include SiriusXM Traffic, SiriusXM Travel Link, Nav Traffic and Nav Weather a collection of data services that provides users with information on traffic, weather, fuel prices, movie listings and sports scores and scheduling. SiriusXM delivers weather, data and information services to aircraft and boats through SiriusXM Aviation, Sirius Marine Sirius Marine Weather, XMWX Aviation and XMWX Marine. SiriusXM also holds a minority interest in SiriusXM Canada which has more than 2.7 million subscribers. Sirius XM Radio, Inc. is a subsidiary of Sirius XM Holdings, Inc. In September 2018, SiriusXM Holdings announced that it had agreed to acquire Pandora Media, Inc., the music streaming service, for $3.5 billion.

Employee benefits include medical, dental and vision coverage; employee assistance program; life and AD&D insurance; short- and long-term disability; a matching 401(k); health care spending accounts; dependent care spending accounts; and transportation an

FINANCIAL DATA:
Note: Data for latest year may not have been available at press time.

In U.S. $	2018	2017	2016	2015	2014	2013
Revenue		5,425,129,000	5,017,220,000	4,570,058,000	4,181,095,000	3,799,095,000
R&D Expense		112,427,000	82,146,000	64,403,000	62,784,000	57,969,000
Operating Income		1,640,864,000	1,432,129,000	1,178,688,000	1,119,670,000	1,044,553,000
Operating Margin %		30.24%	28.54%	25.79%	26.77%	27.49%
SGA Expense		771,762,000	727,830,000	678,990,000	630,418,000	553,159,000
Net Income		647,908,000	745,933,000	509,724,000	493,241,000	377,215,000
Operating Cash Flow		1,855,589,000	1,719,237,000	1,244,051,000	1,253,244,000	1,102,832,000
Capital Expenditure		287,970,000	205,829,000	134,892,000	121,646,000	173,617,000
EBITDA		1,908,631,000	1,691,864,000	1,463,281,000	1,366,219,000	1,095,077,000
Return on Assets %		7.93%	9.29%	6.20%	5.72%	4.17%
Return on Equity %				89.16%	24.32%	11.00%
Debt to Equity					3.43	1.12

CONTACT INFORMATION:
Phone: 212 584-5100 Fax:
Toll-Free:
Address: 1221 Ave. of the Americas, 36/Fl, New York, NY 10020 United States

STOCK TICKER/OTHER:
Stock Ticker: SIRI
Employees: 2,402
Parent Company:

Exchange: NAS
Fiscal Year Ends: 12/31

SALARIES/BONUSES:
Top Exec. Salary: $1,800,000 Bonus: $7,750,000
Second Exec. Salary: $1,500,000 Bonus: $2,600,000

OTHER THOUGHTS:
Estimated Female Officers or Directors: 3
Hot Spot for Advancement for Women/Minorities: Y

Sales, profits and employees may be estimates. Financial information, benefits and other data can change quickly and may vary from those stated here.

Six Flags Entertainment Corporation

www.sixflags.com

NAIC Code: 713110

TYPES OF BUSINESS:
Theme Parks

BRANDS/DIVISIONS/AFFILIATES:
Six Flags Over Texas
Six Flags Discovery Kingdom
Six Flags Great Adventure & Safari
Six Flags America
Six Flags Nanjing
Six Flags Membership Rewards

CONTACTS:
Note: Officers with more than one job title may be intentionally listed here more than once.

Danielle Bernthal, Assistant General Counsel
James Reid-Anderson, CEO
Marshall Barber, CFO
Taylor Brooks, Chief Accounting Officer
David Austin, Chief Information Officer
Nancy Krejsa, Director
Lance Balk, General Counsel
Kathy Aslin, Senior VP, Divisional
Bonnie Weber, Senior VP, Divisional
David McKillips, Senior VP, Divisional
Thomas Iven, Senior VP, Divisional
Brett Petit, Senior VP, Divisional
Leonard Russ, Senior VP, Divisional
Stephen Purtell, Senior VP, Divisional
Mario Centola, Vice President, Divisional

GROWTH PLANS/SPECIAL FEATURES:
Six Flags Entertainment Corporation (Six Flags) is an operator of regional theme parks, water parks and zoological parks. The company operates 25 parks, including 22 in the U.S., two in Mexico and one in Montreal. The firm's parks offer state-of-the-art and traditional thrill rides, water attractions, themed areas, concerts and shows, restaurants, game venues and retail outlets. Altogether, its parks contain over 850 rides, including over 140 roller coasters. Six Flags holds exclusive long-term licenses for theme park usage of certain Warner Bros. and DC Comics characters, including Bugs Bunny, Daffy Duck, Tweety Bird, Yosemite Sam, Superman and Batman throughout the U.S. (excluding the Las Vegas metropolitan area), Canada and Mexico. The company's operations include Six Flags Over Texas, the oldest of the parks and the original source of the company name; Six Flags Discovery Kingdom in California, featuring marine and land animal exhibits; Six Flags America in Largo, Maryland, near Washington D.C.; and Six Flags Great Adventure & Safari in New Jersey, the firm's largest location, encompassing a theme park, a water park and the adjacent a 350-acre drive-through safari attraction. In April 2018, Six Flags announced continued growth in the China market with the planned addition of three new branded parks in Nanjing. Six Flags Nanjing will offer a theme park, waterpark and an adventure park. In August of the same year, the firm unveiled a new rewards program, Six Flags Membership Rewards. The rewards program allows members to earn points towards free food, souvenirs, park tickets, and one-of-a-kind in-park experiences each time they visit the park, go on rides, see a show, or make a purchase

Six Flags offers its employees incentive bonuses, unlimited admission, free and discounted passes, health benefits and flexible scheduling.

FINANCIAL DATA:
Note: Data for latest year may not have been available at press time.

In U.S. $	2018	2017	2016	2015	2014	2013
Revenue		1,359,074,000	1,319,398,000	1,263,938,000	1,175,793,000	1,109,930,000
R&D Expense						
Operating Income		469,408,000	321,725,000	355,789,000	228,785,000	288,492,000
Operating Margin %		34.53%	24.38%	28.14%	19.45%	25.99%
SGA Expense		158,498,000	291,794,000	234,810,000	310,955,000	189,218,000
Net Income		273,816,000	118,302,000	154,690,000	76,022,000	118,552,000
Operating Cash Flow		445,067,000	463,235,000	473,761,000	392,323,000	368,682,000
Capital Expenditure		135,219,000	129,383,000	114,399,000	108,709,000	101,928,000
EBITDA		540,489,000	422,536,000	446,840,000	341,175,000	407,044,000
Return on Assets %		11.07%	4.81%	6.23%	2.95%	4.18%
Return on Equity %				124.69%	25.45%	18.73%
Debt to Equity				61.86	6.20	3.73

CONTACT INFORMATION:
Phone: 972 595-5000 Fax:
Toll-Free:
Address: 924 Avenue J East, Grand Prairie, TX 75050 United States

SALARIES/BONUSES:
Top Exec. Salary: $1,366,154 Bonus: $
Second Exec. Salary: $615,192 Bonus: $

STOCK TICKER/OTHER:
Stock Ticker: SIX
Employees: 47,000
Parent Company:

Exchange: NYS
Fiscal Year Ends: 12/31

OTHER THOUGHTS:
Estimated Female Officers or Directors: 1
Hot Spot for Advancement for Women/Minorities:

Sky Deutschland AG

NAIC Code: 515210

www.sky.de

TYPES OF BUSINESS:
Cable and Other Subscription Programming

BRANDS/DIVISIONS/AFFILIATES:
Sky plc
Sky Deutschland Fernsehen GmbH & Co KG
Sky Show
Sky Sports

CONTACTS:
Note: Officers with more than one job title may be intentionally listed here more than once.

Carsten Schmidt, CEO
Simon Robson, CFO
Euan Smith, Exec. VP-Prod.
Euan Smith, Exec. VP-Oper.
Carsten Schmidt, Chief Internet Officer
Wolfram Winter, Exec. VP-Comm.
Carsten Schmidt, Chief Officer Sports & Advertising Sales
Gary Davey, Exec. VP-Programming
Carsten Schmidt, Chmn.

GROWTH PLANS/SPECIAL FEATURES:

Sky Deutschland AG operates as a German media company providing direct broadcast satellite pay TV to its customers in Germany and Austria. The firm's offerings include subscription TV and on-demand services for private and business consumers, which are offered under the Sky trademark. Sky's network reaches nearly every household in Germany. Content includes feature films, television series, comedy, music, sports, children's programs, documentaries and racing. The company's Sky Show service is a video stream offering for films and series. Sky also offers live sports, including golf tournaments, tennis, Formula 1 racing and beach volleyball, Premier League and Bundesliga soccer, as well as HD live broadcasts of various sports matches. The firm distributes WWE's premier pay-per-view events through a multi-year agreement with World Wrestling Entertainment, Inc. Through this agreement, Sky also broadcasts Raw and SmackDown live on Sky Sports. Wholly owned subsidiary, Sky Deutschland Fernsehen GmbH & Co. KG also offers pay television services in Germany. Sky itself operates as a wholly-owned subsidiary of Sky plc, a Pan-European satellite broadcasting, on-demand internet streaming media, broadband and telephone services company headquartered in London.

FINANCIAL DATA:
Note: Data for latest year may not have been available at press time.

In U.S. $	2018	2017	2016	2015	2014	2013
Revenue						
R&D Expense						
Operating Income						
Operating Margin %						
SGA Expense						
Net Income						
Operating Cash Flow						
Capital Expenditure						
EBITDA						
Return on Assets %						
Return on Equity %						
Debt to Equity						

CONTACT INFORMATION:
Phone: 49 89995802 Fax: 49 8999587599
Toll-Free:
Address: Medienallee 26, UnterfÃ¶hring, 85774 Germany

STOCK TICKER/OTHER:
Stock Ticker: SKDTY Exchange: PINX
Employees: 2,150 Fiscal Year Ends: 12/31
Parent Company: Sky plc

SALARIES/BONUSES:
Top Exec. Salary: $ Bonus: $
Second Exec. Salary: $ Bonus: $

OTHER THOUGHTS:
Estimated Female Officers or Directors:
Hot Spot for Advancement for Women/Minorities:

Sales, profits and employees may be estimates. Financial information, benefits and other data can change quickly and may vary from those stated here.

SKY Network Television Limited

www.skytv.co.nz

NAIC Code: 517110

TYPES OF BUSINESS:
Satellite TV
Broadcast TV
Pay-Per-View TV
Online DVD Rental

BRANDS/DIVISIONS/AFFILIATES:
SKY Advertising
SKY Business
Movielink
SKY Music
Fan Pass
SKY Sport
NEON

CONTACTS: Note: Officers with more than one job title may be intentionally listed here more than once.
Martin Stewart, CEO
Martin Wrigley, Dir.-Operations
Jason Hollingworth, CFO
Rawinia Newton, Dir.-Sales & Mktg.
Cathryn Oliver, Chief of Staff
Julian Wheeler, Chief Product & Technology Officer
Jason Hollingworth, Corp. Sec.
Martin Wrigley, Dir.-Oper.
Megan King, Content Dir.-Strategy, Planning & Delivery
Kirsty Way, Head-Corp. Comm.
Rawinia Newton, Dir.-Advertising
Richard Last, Dir.-Sports Content
Martin Enright, Dir.-Content Acquisitions
Greg Drummond, Dir.-Broadcast Oper.
Peter Macourt, Chmn.

GROWTH PLANS/SPECIAL FEATURES:
SKY Network Television Limited is one of the largest providers of pay-television satellite services in New Zealand. The firm offers a range of music, movies, sports, on-demand and general content through over 100 channels on its digital satellite platform. SKY Network has a total subscriber base of more than 767,725 satellite and over-the-top (OTT) subscribers (as of mid-2018). SKY Advertising helps customers with their advertising campaigns, including general inquiries about expectations and costs, as well as complex campaign planning. This division's advertising services and solutions are sold by SKY Advertising, which has offices in Auckland, Wellington, Christchurch and Dunedin. SKY Business provides television programming and services to thousands of NZ businesses, including programming such as domestic and international sports, breaking news, documentaries, music, a quiz show and children's entertainment. SKY Business' solutions include in-room Pay Per View, hotel in-room broadband and Free to Guest Movie systems through its Movielink division. This segment can also assist clients with background and foreground music for retail and hospitality businesses through SKY Music. The company's Fan Pass is an online streaming service that viewers can purchase by the day or week in order to access SKY Sport channels, or purchase passes for individual sports such as Super Rugby, National Rugby League or Formula 1. Fan Pass is available via website or mobile app. NEON is the company's on-demand service, providing subscribers access to a vast library of TV and movies online that can be streamed or viewed through an internet browser or the NEON app for iPads and iPhones.

FINANCIAL DATA: Note: Data for latest year may not have been available at press time.

In U.S. $	2018	2017	2016	2015	2014	2013
Revenue	561,654,100	597,608,800	620,828,000	620,376,500	594,031,200	579,074,900
R&D Expense						
Operating Income	35,220,380	25,314,690	48,764,630	82,938,260	72,094,170	51,246,740
Operating Margin %		4.23%	7.85%	13.36%	12.13%	8.84%
SGA Expense	87,638,280	99,778,610	101,902,900	98,524,510	151,601,900	144,348,900
Net Income	-161,163,800	77,604,170	98,132,560	114,762,200	110,915,000	91,764,420
Operating Cash Flow						
Capital Expenditure	38,942,540	53,295,430	86,150,090	77,226,940	62,204,530	55,094,640
EBITDA	-49,446,860	195,893,200	218,012,200	247,003,500	248,428,200	235,431,700
Return on Assets %		6.05%	7.55%	9.01%	8.80%	7.10%
Return on Equity %		8.73%	11.00%	13.32%	13.73%	11.35%
Debt to Equity		0.22	0.11	0.26	0.30	0.40

CONTACT INFORMATION:
Phone: 649 579 9999   Fax: 649 579 0910
Toll-Free:
Address: 10 Panorama Rd., Auckland, 1149 New Zealand

SALARIES/BONUSES:
Top Exec. Salary: $ Bonus: $
Second Exec. Salary: $ Bonus: $

STOCK TICKER/OTHER:
Stock Ticker: SYKWF   Exchange: GREY
Employees: 1,223   Fiscal Year Ends: 06/30
Parent Company:

OTHER THOUGHTS:
Estimated Female Officers or Directors: 5
Hot Spot for Advancement for Women/Minorities: Y

Sales, profits and employees may be estimates. Financial information, benefits and other data can change quickly and may vary from those stated here.

SKY Perfect JSAT Corporation

NAIC Code: 515210

www.sptvjsat.com/en

TYPES OF BUSINESS:
Cable and Other Subscription Programming

BRANDS/DIVISIONS/AFFILIATES:
SKY Perfect JSAT Holdings Inc
SKY PerfecTV!
OceanBB plus

CONTACTS:
Note: Officers with more than one job title may be intentionally listed here more than once.

Shinji Takada, CEO
Masai Nito, CIO
Masao Nito, Sr. Exec. VP
Yutaka Nagai, Sr. Exec. VP
Osamu Inoue, Sr. Exec. VP
Hiroo Sumitomo, Sr. Managing Exec. Officer

GROWTH PLANS/SPECIAL FEATURES:
SKY Perfect JSAT Corporation provides broadcasting and communication services in Japan, Asia and Oceania. It is the core operating company of SKY Perfect JSAT Holdings, Inc. The firm offers multichannel pay-TV broadcasting and satellite communications services. SKY's operations are divided into two segments: media and space. The media segment provides SKY PerfecTV!, Japan's largest multichannel pay-TV broadcast service, serving approximately 3 million subscribers. This division also offers on-demand service for new devices, promotes 4K services and develops digital tuners. The space segment operates the company's 17 satellites, which cover all of Japan and Asia, and also provides coverage in Oceania, Russia, Middle East, Hawaii and North America. Its network is used to support program transmission through the SKY PerfecTV! service, and to provide relay circuits for terrestrial television stations. The segment's satellite communications networks also play a role in safety and security, primarily for local governments and utilities to establish disaster-response and crisis management communications infrastructures. Recently (late-2017), SKY Perfect JSAT signed agreements to deliver new-generation maritime broadband service called OceanBB plus, with KVH Industries, Inc. The maritime broadband service launched in April 2018. OceanBB plus provides data speeds up to 10Mbps from shore-to-ship and 3Mbps from ship-to-shore.

FINANCIAL DATA:
Note: Data for latest year may not have been available at press time.

In U.S. $	2018	2017	2016	2015	2014	2013
Revenue	1,349,631,000	1,789,060,000	1,511,066,000	1,514,674,000	1,592,489,000	1,480,493,000
R&D Expense						
Operating Income	145,184,000	226,643,700	224,575,200	182,064,400	201,404,400	149,831,200
Operating Margin %	10.75	12.66%	14.86%	12.02%	12.64%	10.12%
SGA Expense						
Net Income	105,307,600	161,537,200	156,454,100	125,361,800	89,594,460	89,807,800
Operating Cash Flow	209,131,000	65,199,240	230,094,200	154,283,500	309,299,800	355,929,100
Capital Expenditure	154,218,600	143,338,100	246,132,000	375,371,000	207,044,000	126,001,800
EBITDA	395,768,400	437,564,900	428,029,400	412,270,000	412,529,700	401,704,900
Return on Assets %	3.15%	5.13%	5.60%	4.74%	3.34%	3.27%
Return on Equity %	5.31%	8.55%	8.60%	7.11%	5.12%	5.13%
Debt to Equity	0.40	0.34	0.29	0.18	0.10	0.19

CONTACT INFORMATION:
Phone: 81-3-5571-7800   Fax:
Toll-Free:
Address: 14-14, Akasaka 1-chome, Minato-ku, Tokyo, 107-0052 Japan

SALARIES/BONUSES:
Top Exec. Salary: $ Bonus: $
Second Exec. Salary: $ Bonus: $

STOCK TICKER/OTHER:
Stock Ticker: SKPJF   Exchange: GREY
Employees: 1,604   Fiscal Year Ends: 03/31
Parent Company: SKY Perfect JSAT Holdings Inc

OTHER THOUGHTS:
Estimated Female Officers or Directors:
Hot Spot for Advancement for Women/Minorities:

Sales, profits and employees may be estimates. Financial information, benefits and other data can change quickly and may vary from those stated here.

Sky plc

NAIC Code: 517110

corporate.sky.com

TYPES OF BUSINESS:
Satellite TV Broadcasting
Digital TV
Broadcast TV
Mobile Phone TV
Interactive Television
Broadband Service
HD TV
Telecommunications Service

BRANDS/DIVISIONS/AFFILIATES:
Comcast Corporation
Sky UK Limited
Sky Ireland Limited
Sky Deutschland AG
Sky Italia
Amstrad Limited
The Cloud
Now TV (UK)

GROWTH PLANS/SPECIAL FEATURES:

Sky plc is a European entertainment company which serves 22.5 million customers across five countries. The firm offers a broad range of content, market-leading customer service and innovative technology in order to give customers a better TV experience. Sky provides satellite broadcasting, on-demand internet streaming media, broadband and telephone services. Subsidiaries of the firm include Sky UK Limited, Sky Ireland Limited, Sky Deutschland AG, Sky Italia, Amstrad Limited, The Cloud and Now TV (U.K.). Sky trades publicly on the London Stock Exchange, under ticker: SKY. In October 2018, U.S.-based cable and entertainment firm Comcast Corporation acquired control of Sky.

Employee benefits include a pension plan, stock options, health care coverage, retail discounts, employee discounts and free television services.

CONTACTS: Note: Officers with more than one job title may be intentionally listed here more than once.

Jeremy Darroch, CEO
Andrew Griffith, COO
Deborah Baker, Dir.-People
Didier Lebrat, CTO
Alun Webber, Managing Dir.-Prod. Design & Dev.
James Conyers, Gen. Counsel
Mai Fyfield, Group Dir.-Strategy & Bus. Dev.
Barney Francis, Managing Dir.-Sky Sports
Graham McWilliam, Group Dir.-Corp. Affairs
Chris Stylianou, Managing Dir.-Customer Service Group
Sophie Turner Laing, Managing Dir.-Content
James Murdoch, Chmn.

FINANCIAL DATA: Note: Data for latest year may not have been available at press time.

In U.S. $	2018	2017	2016	2015	2014	2013
Revenue						
R&D Expense						
Operating Income						
Operating Margin %						
SGA Expense						
Net Income						
Operating Cash Flow						
Capital Expenditure						
EBITDA						
Return on Assets %						
Return on Equity %						
Debt to Equity						

CONTACT INFORMATION:
Phone: 020 7705 3000   Fax:
Toll-Free:
Address: Grant Way, Isleworth, TW7 5QD United Kingdom

STOCK TICKER/OTHER:
Stock Ticker: BSYBF   Exchange: PINX
Employees: 31,578   Fiscal Year Ends: 06/30
Parent Company: Comcast Corporation

SALARIES/BONUSES:
Top Exec. Salary: $1,312,955   Bonus: $2,442,096
Second Exec. Salary: $826,638   Bonus: $1,153,160

OTHER THOUGHTS:
Estimated Female Officers or Directors: 4
Hot Spot for Advancement for Women/Minorities: Y

Sales, profits and employees may be estimates. Financial information, benefits and other data can change quickly and may vary from those stated here.

Societe d'Edition de Canal Plus

NAIC Code: 515120

www.canalplus.fr

TYPES OF BUSINESS:
Television Broadcasting

BRANDS/DIVISIONS/AFFILIATES:
Canal+ Africa
A+
Canal+
CanalSatellite
Canal+ Group
TELE+ Digitale
C8
Canal+Regie

CONTACTS:
Note: Officers with more than one job title may be intentionally listed here more than once.

Maxime Saada, CEO
Gregoire Castaing, CFO

GROWTH PLANS/SPECIAL FEATURES:
Societe d'Edition de Canal Plus is engaged in broadcast media. The firm provides television programming and operates direct broadcast and satellite systems, provides cable television services and distributes motion pictures, videos and digital television. Its pay TV France services offer premium and thematic channels on a pay-per-view basis. These services are available either by television set or on a smartphone or mobile device. The company also has international pay TV, which offers more than 200 channels across the globe, most of which are in French. Areas to which the company broadcasts these channels include The French Antilles, Guyana, Reunion, Mayotte, Mauritius, New Caledonia, French Polynesia, and Quebec, Canada. Canal+ Africa is broadcast in over 25 countries in Africa. The African A+ channel broadcasts to the French-speaking people in Africa in Abidjan. In Poland, the company is a key investor in the local film production of more than 150 films co-produced over the last 20 years. In Europe, Canal+, CanalSatellite and Canal+ Group are major satellite broadcasters. Operations are conducted in France, the U.K., Germany, Australia and New Zealand, and include major names in the film industry such as Joel and Ethan Coen, Joel Wright and David Lynch. Other operations include free TV channels; TELE+ Digitale, a 24/7 news channel; C8 (Canal 8), a private national French TV channel; Canal Star, a free-to-air channel that broadcasts music videos, reality shows and documentaries; and Canal News, a free-to-air 24-hour news channel. Canal+Regie is an advertising subsidiary. The firm is a subsidiary of the Canal + Group.

FINANCIAL DATA:
Note: Data for latest year may not have been available at press time.

In U.S. $	2018	2017	2016	2015	2014	2013
Revenue			2,200,000,000	2,100,000,000	2,050,948,608	2,109,227,008
R&D Expense						
Operating Income						
Operating Margin %						
SGA Expense						
Net Income					44,829,480	44,829,480
Operating Cash Flow						
Capital Expenditure						
EBITDA						
Return on Assets %						
Return on Equity %						
Debt to Equity						

CONTACT INFORMATION:
Phone: 33 171353535
Fax: 33 144251234
Toll-Free:
Address: 1 Place du Spectacle, Cedex 9, Issy-les-Moulineaux, 92863 France

STOCK TICKER/OTHER:
Stock Ticker: CNPLF
Employees:
Parent Company: Canal + Group
Exchange: GREY
Fiscal Year Ends: 12/31

SALARIES/BONUSES:
Top Exec. Salary: $
Second Exec. Salary: $
Bonus: $
Bonus: $

OTHER THOUGHTS:
Estimated Female Officers or Directors:
Hot Spot for Advancement for Women/Minorities:

Sales, profits and employees may be estimates. Financial information, benefits and other data can change quickly and may vary from those stated here.

SONIFI Solutions

www.sonifi.com

NAIC Code: 517110

TYPES OF BUSINESS:
Cable TV Service-Hospitality Industry
Satellite TV Service
Broadband Internet Access
Network-Based Video Games
Video-on-Demand

BRANDS/DIVISIONS/AFFILIATES:
Hotel Networks (The)
StayCast
SONIFI Health Solutions

CONTACTS:
Note: Officers with more than one job title may be intentionally listed here more than once.

Ahmad Ouri, CEO
Tommy Moreno, COO
John Chang, CFO
Roy Kosuge, Chief Commercial Officer
Tom Store, Pres.-Hospitality
George Rose, Chief Legal Officer

GROWTH PLANS/SPECIAL FEATURES:

SONIFI Solutions provides broadband interactive television services to the hospitality and health care industries throughout the U.S., Canada and Mexico. Through local licensing agreements, the firm delivers services to 15 other countries such as France and the UAE. It is a specialized communications company that provides on-demand digital movies, digital music and music videos, video games, high-speed internet access and other interactive television services designed to serve the needs of the lodging industry and the traveling public. Guest-pay services are purchased by guests on a per-view, hourly or daily basis and include on-demand movies, network-based video games, internet-enhanced television and high-speed internet access. Complimentary guest services include satellite-delivered premium cable television programming and other interactive entertainment and information services paid for by the hotel. SONIFI Health Solutions provides interactive patient engagement and patient/provider communications, helping to motivate active participation and healthy behavioral changes. Through subsidiary The Hotel Networks, the company provides television and place-based digital advertising and promotional marketing solutions for business-class and upscale hotels. SONIFI's StayCast, which is powered by Chromecast, enhances the hotel room experience for guests in allowing them to stream favorite movies, shows and music directly from their mobile device directly to the room's TV via the HDMI port of the television. Annually, this service benefits over 500 million travelers in approximately 1.2 million hotel rooms.

Employee benefits include medical, dental and vision insurance; life insurance and AD&D insurance; short-term disability; an employee assistance program; and a 401(k) plan.

FINANCIAL DATA:
Note: Data for latest year may not have been available at press time.

In U.S. $	2018	2017	2016	2015	2014	2013
Revenue	380,000,000	370,000,000	366,000,000	355,000,000	350,000,000	345,000,000
R&D Expense						
Operating Income						
Operating Margin %						
SGA Expense						
Net Income						
Operating Cash Flow						
Capital Expenditure						
EBITDA						
Return on Assets %						
Return on Equity %						
Debt to Equity						

CONTACT INFORMATION:
Phone: 605 988-1000 Fax: 605 330-1532
Toll-Free: 888-563-4363
Address: 3900 W. Innovation St., Sioux Falls, SD 57107 United States

SALARIES/BONUSES:
Top Exec. Salary: $ Bonus: $
Second Exec. Salary: $ Bonus: $

STOCK TICKER/OTHER:
Stock Ticker: Private
Employees: 820
Parent Company: Colony Capital LLC

Exchange:
Fiscal Year Ends: 09/30

OTHER THOUGHTS:
Estimated Female Officers or Directors: 2
Hot Spot for Advancement for Women/Minorities:

Sony Corporation

NAIC Code: 334310

www.sony.net

TYPES OF BUSINESS:
Consumer Electronics Manufacturer
Film & Television Production
Music Production
Sensors and Cameras for use in Smartphones
Semiconductors
Technology Research
Video Games
Financial Services

BRANDS/DIVISIONS/AFFILIATES:
Sony Mobile Communications Inc
Sony Pictures Entertainment
Sony Semiconductor Manufacturing Corporation
Sony Energy Devices Corporation
Sony Storage Media and Devices Corporation
Sony Financial Holdings Inc
Sony Life Insurance Co Ltd
Sony Bank Inc

CONTACTS:
Note: Officers with more than one job title may be intentionally listed here more than once.

Keninchiro Yoshida, CEO
Hiroki Totoki, CFO
Ichiro Takagi, Sr. Exec. VP
Kazushi Ambe, Exec. VP-Human Resources and General Affairs
Shiro Kambe, Exec. VP
Osamu Nagayama, Chmn.

GROWTH PLANS/SPECIAL FEATURES:

Sony Corporation develops, designs, produces, manufactures, offers and sells electronic equipment, instruments and devices for consumer, professional and industrial markets. These products and services are divided into nine primary segments, operated through Sony subsidiaries. Sony Mobile Communications, Inc. provides internet broadband network services to subscribers, as well as creates and distributes content through its portal services to various electronics product platforms such as personal computers (PCs) and mobile phones. The Game & Network Services segment provides PlayStation hardware, software, content and network services. Imaging Products & Solutions provides interchangeable lens cameras, compact digital cameras, consumer and professional video cameras, as well as display products such as projectors and medical equipment. Home Entertainment & Sound produces televisions, and video and sound products. Sony Semiconductor Solutions Corporation and its subsidiary, Sony Semiconductor Manufacturing Corporation, deliver products for complementary metal oxide semiconductor (CMOS) image sensors, charge-coupled devices (CCDs), large-scale integration systems (LSIs) and other semiconductors. Sony Energy Devices Corporation delivers products for batteries; and Sony Storage Media and Devices Corporation delivers products for audio/video/data recording media and storage media. The pictures segment is grouped into three categories: motion pictures, which includes worldwide production, acquisition and distribution of live-action and animated motion pictures; television pictures, which does the same but with television programming; and media networks, which operates television and digital networks worldwide. The music segment is grouped into three categories: recorded, comprising the distribution of physical and digital recorded music; publishing, including the management and licensing of the words and music of songs; and visual media and platform, which includes the production and distribution of animation titles, game applications and related service offerings. Last, Sony Financial Holdings, Inc. is a holding company for Sony Life Insurance Co. Ltd., Sony Assurance, Inc. and Sony Bank, Inc., providing insurance, savings and loan products and services.

FINANCIAL DATA:
Note: Data for latest year may not have been available at press time.

In U.S. $	2018	2017	2016	2015	2014	2013
Revenue	79,251,830,000	70,525,840,000	75,186,550,000	76,208,440,000	72,047,210,000	63,082,990,000
R&D Expense						
Operating Income	6,774,664,000	4,026,974,000	3,145,685,000	2,284,478,000	765,574,000	16,965,340
Operating Margin %	8.54	5.70%	4.18%	2.99%	1.06%	.02%
SGA Expense	14,685,340,000	13,968,870,000	15,693,920,000	16,802,660,000	16,033,320,000	13,520,570,000
Net Income	4,552,482,000	679,810,400	1,370,872,000	-1,168,559,000	-1,190,719,000	399,172,600
Operating Cash Flow	11,640,810,000	7,506,511,000	6,948,362,000	6,999,852,000	6,160,174,000	4,466,384,000
Capital Expenditure	2,439,420,000	3,093,546,000	3,482,218,000	2,002,783,000	2,629,276,000	3,028,439,000
EBITDA	9,962,702,000	5,502,477,000	6,742,366,000	3,876,827,000	3,950,504,000	5,592,275,000
Return on Assets %	2.67%	.42%	.90%	-.80%	-.86%	.31%
Return on Equity %	17.96%	2.95%	6.18%	-5.50%	-5.76%	2.03%
Debt to Equity	0.21	0.27	0.22	0.30	0.40	0.42

CONTACT INFORMATION:
Phone: 81 367482111   Fax: 81 367482244
Toll-Free:
Address: 1-7-1 Konan, Minato-Ku, Tokyo, 108-0075 Japan

SALARIES/BONUSES:
Top Exec. Salary: $40,000,000   Bonus: $50,000,000
Second Exec. Salary: $40,000,000   Bonus: $50,000,000

STOCK TICKER/OTHER:
Stock Ticker: SNE   Exchange: NYS
Employees: 117,300   Fiscal Year Ends: 03/31
Parent Company:

OTHER THOUGHTS:
Estimated Female Officers or Directors:

Hot Spot for Advancement for Women/Minorities:

Sony Music Entertainment Inc

www.sonymusic.com

NAIC Code: 512230

TYPES OF BUSINESS:
Recorded Music Production
Record Labels
Artist Development

BRANDS/DIVISIONS/AFFILIATES:
Orchard (The)
Arista Records
Sony Entertainment
Black Butter Records
Epic Records
Okeh
RCA Inspirational
Unties

CONTACTS:
Note: Officers with more than one job title may be intentionally listed here more than once.

Rob Stringer, CEO
Kevin Kelleher, COO
Carmine Coppola, CFO
Dasha Smith Dwin, Exec. VP
Randy Goodman, Chmn.

GROWTH PLANS/SPECIAL FEATURES:
Sony Music Entertainment, Inc. is an international record label owner and operator, and an operating subsidiary of Sony Corporation. The company's record labels include Arista Nashville, Beach Street Records, Black Butter Records, BPG Music, Bystrom Entertainment, Century Media, Columbia Nashville, Columbia Records, Day 1, Descendant Records, Disruptor Records, Epic Records, Essential Records, Essential Worship, Fo Yo Soul Recordings, House of Iona Records, Insanity Records, Kemosabe Records, Legacy Recordings, Masterworks, Masterworks Broadway, Ministry of Sound Recordings, Monument Records, OKeh, Polo Grounds Music, Portrait, RCA Inspiration, RCA Nashville, RCA Records, Relentless Records, Reunion Records, Sony Classical, Sony Music Latin, Star Time International, Syco Music and Verity Records. Artists featured under these labels include, but are not limited to, Pink, George Michael, Future, Kenny Chesney, Rachel Platten, Tim McGraw and Faith Hill, Roy Orbison and The Piano Guys. The company's music is distributed by The Orchard, Sony's media and technology distribution firm, which handles the sales, marketing operations and distributions for Sony Music's artists. Sony Music is headquartered in New York and has operations in many countries worldwide in 42 countries. In July 2018, Sony Music announced it had relaunched Arista Records, which was home to artists such as Whitney Houston, Barry Manilow and Aretha Franklin.

FINANCIAL DATA:
Note: Data for latest year may not have been available at press time.

In U.S. $	2018	2017	2016	2015	2014	2013
Revenue	6,120,000,000	6,000,000,000	5,789,005,014	4,538,000,000	4,886,000,000	4,536,199,000
R&D Expense						
Operating Income						
Operating Margin %						
SGA Expense						
Net Income						
Operating Cash Flow						
Capital Expenditure						
EBITDA						
Return on Assets %						
Return on Equity %						
Debt to Equity						

CONTACT INFORMATION:
Phone: 212-833-8000 Fax: 212-833-7416
Toll-Free:
Address: 550 Madison Ave., New York, NY 10022-3211 United States

STOCK TICKER/OTHER:
Stock Ticker: Subsidiary
Employees:
Parent Company: Sony Corporation

Exchange:
Fiscal Year Ends: 03/31

SALARIES/BONUSES:
Top Exec. Salary: $ Bonus: $
Second Exec. Salary: $ Bonus: $

OTHER THOUGHTS:
Estimated Female Officers or Directors:
Hot Spot for Advancement for Women/Minorities:

Sony Pictures Entertainment Inc

NAIC Code: 512110

www.sonypictures.com

TYPES OF BUSINESS:
Film Production & Distribution
Television Production & Distribution
Video Distribution
Film & TV Merchandising & Licensing
Digital Animation & Visual Effects
Online Games

BRANDS/DIVISIONS/AFFILIATES:
Sony Corporation
Sony Entertainment Inc
Sony Pictures Motion Picture Group
Sony Pictures Studios
Sony Pictures Television
TriStar Pictures
Columbia Pictures Producciones Mexico
SonyCrackle.com

CONTACTS: Note: Officers with more than one job title may be intentionally listed here more than once.
Tony Vinciquerra, CEO
Jon Hookstratten, Exec. VP-Oper. & Admin.
Philip Rowley, CFO
Robert Lawson, Exec. VP
Stacy Green, Chief People Officer
Chris Cookson, Pres., Sony Pictures Technologies
Bob Osher, Pres., Sony Pictures Digital Productions
Amy Pascal, Co-Chmn.
Steven N. Bersch, Pres., Sony Pictures Worldwide Acquisitions
David Bishop, Pres., Worldwide Sony Pictures Home Entertainment
Steve Mosko, Pres., Sony Pictures Television
Tony Vinciquerra, Chmn.
Jeff Blake, Chmn.-Sony Pictures Worldwide Dist.

GROWTH PLANS/SPECIAL FEATURES:
Sony Pictures Entertainment, Inc. (SPE) is the media and entertainment subsidiary of Sony Entertainment, Inc., which itself is a subsidiary of Tokyo-based Sony Corporation. SPE has three divisions: Sony Pictures Motion Picture Group, Sony Picture Studios and Sony Pictures Television (SPT). The Sony Pictures Motion Picture division encompasses Columbia Pictures, TriStar Pictures, Screen Gems, Sony Pictures Animation, Sony Pictures Classics, Sony Pictures Imageworks, Sony Pictures Home Entertainment and Sony Pictures Worldwide Acquisitions. It also includes releasing groups, Sony Pictures Releasing and Sony Pictures Releasing International. Internationally, this division's motion picture operations include Columbia Pictures Film Production Asia (Hong Kong), Columbia Films Producciones Espanolas (Madrid), Columbia Pictures Producciones Mexico, as well as operations in the U.K., Brazil and Japan. This division owns a library of more than 3,500 titles. The Sony Picture Studios division offers facilities for film and television production, including sound stages, state-of-the-art post-production facilities and world-class support. The studio also hosts a variety of private screenings and live events; and its operations include production services, post-production services, product fulfillment and asset management. The SPT division consists of the production or distribution of approximately 60 programs worldwide, spanning all formats and genres. It offers licensing rights to customers which include U.S. and international broadcast and cable networks, U.S. local television stations and digital services. The firm's network includes 150 channel feeds in 178 countries with a viewership of 1.3 billion households around the globe. SPT operates video website SonyCrackle.com, which is an online television network and entertainment portal focused on distributing original content, TV shows and films on the internet.

FINANCIAL DATA: Note: Data for latest year may not have been available at press time.

In U.S. $	2018	2017	2016	2015	2014	2013
Revenue	9,150,000,000	9,000,000,000	8,793,176,172	7,322,000,000	8,054,000,000	7,029,000,000
R&D Expense						
Operating Income						
Operating Margin %						
SGA Expense						
Net Income						
Operating Cash Flow						
Capital Expenditure						
EBITDA						
Return on Assets %						
Return on Equity %						
Debt to Equity						

CONTACT INFORMATION:
Phone: 310-244-4000 Fax: 310-244-2626
Toll-Free:
Address: 10202 W. Washington Blvd., Culver City, CA 90232 United States

STOCK TICKER/OTHER:
Stock Ticker: Subsidiary
Employees:
Parent Company: Sony Corporation

Exchange:
Fiscal Year Ends: 03/31

SALARIES/BONUSES:
Top Exec. Salary: $ Bonus: $
Second Exec. Salary: $ Bonus: $

OTHER THOUGHTS:
Estimated Female Officers or Directors: 1
Hot Spot for Advancement for Women/Minorities:

Plunkett Research, Ltd. 445

Sony Pictures Motion Picture Group www.sonypictures.com/movies
NAIC Code: 512110

TYPES OF BUSINESS:
Film Production & Distribution

BRANDS/DIVISIONS/AFFILIATES:
Sony Corporation
Sony Pictures Entertainment Inc
Columbia Pictures
TriStar Pictures
Screen Gems
Sony Pictures Animation
Sony Entertainment
Sony Pictures Imageworks

CONTACTS: Note: Officers with more than one job title may be intentionally listed here more than once.
Jon Hookstratten, Exec. VP-Admin. & Oper.
Philip Rowley-Sr. Exec. VP/CFO
Tom Rothman, Chmn.
Stacy Green-Exec. VP/Chief People Officer

GROWTH PLANS/SPECIAL FEATURES:
Sony Pictures Motion Picture Group (SPMPG) is the movie production, marketing, distribution and promotion subsidiary of Sony Pictures Entertainment, Inc., which itself is a subsidiary of Sony Entertainment (part of Sony Corporation). The group encompasses Columbia Pictures, TriStar Pictures, Screen Gems, Sony Pictures Animation, Sony Pictures Classics, Sony Pictures Imageworks, Sony Pictures Home Entertainment and Sony Pictures Worldwide Acquisitions. Its releasing groups include Sony Pictures Releasing and Sony Pictures Releasing International. SPMPG's international motion picture operations include Columbia Pictures Film Production Asia (Hong Kong), Columbia Films Producciones Espanolas (Madrid), Columbia Pictures Producciones Mexico (Mexico City) and additional operations in the U.K., Brazil and Japan. In total, SPMPG's motion picture library contains more than 3,500 titles, including 12 Best Picture Academy Award winners. In late-2018, Sony Pictures acquired all rights in North America, Australia, New Zealand, Latin America, Scandinavia, South Africa and India from Participant Media to Victor Kossakosvky's AQUARELA.

Sony Pictures Entertainment offers its employees medical, dental and vision coverage; life and accident insurance; a 401(k) plan; and flexible spending accounts. The firm also offers summer and academic year internships.

FINANCIAL DATA: Note: Data for latest year may not have been available at press time.

In U.S. $	2018	2017	2016	2015	2014	2013
Revenue						
R&D Expense						
Operating Income						
Operating Margin %						
SGA Expense						
Net Income						
Operating Cash Flow						
Capital Expenditure						
EBITDA						
Return on Assets %						
Return on Equity %						
Debt to Equity						

CONTACT INFORMATION:
Phone: 310-244-4000   Fax: 310-244-2626
Toll-Free:
Address: 10202 W. Washington Blvd., Culver City, CA 90232 United States

STOCK TICKER/OTHER:
Stock Ticker: Subsidiary
Employees:
Parent Company: Sony Corporation

Exchange:
Fiscal Year Ends: 03/31

SALARIES/BONUSES:
Top Exec. Salary: $ Bonus: $
Second Exec. Salary: $ Bonus: $

OTHER THOUGHTS:
Estimated Female Officers or Directors: 1
Hot Spot for Advancement for Women/Minorities:

Sales, profits and employees may be estimates. Financial information, benefits and other data can change quickly and may vary from those stated here.

SoundCloud Limited

NAIC Code: 519130

soundcloud.com

TYPES OF BUSINESS:
Internet Audio Broadcast Site

BRANDS/DIVISIONS/AFFILIATES:
SoundCloud Go+

GROWTH PLANS/SPECIAL FEATURES:
SoundCloud Limited is an online audio platform where people can access, create and share music and audio content. The firm is based in Berlin, Germany and the SoundCloud platform was launched in 2007 by Alexander Ljung and Eric Wahlforss. It allows users to create, upload, record, promote and share their music privately with friends or publicly through social networks, blogs and other sites. SoundCloud can be accessed anywhere via web, iOS, Android, Sonos, Chromecast and Xbox One, as well as a number of creation and sharing apps built on the SoundCloud platform. SoundCloud Go+ is a subscription music streaming service that enables access to over 190 million songs, offline playback, no ads, no previews and premium music tracks for a monthly fee.

CONTACTS:
Note: Officers with more than one job title may be intentionally listed here more than once.

Artem Fishman, Managing Dir.
Alexander Ljung, Chmn.

FINANCIAL DATA:
Note: Data for latest year may not have been available at press time.

In U.S. $	2018	2017	2016	2015	2014	2013
Revenue	119,000,000	100,000,000	61,870,900	39,463,400	21,597,500	12,098,529
R&D Expense						
Operating Income						
Operating Margin %						
SGA Expense						
Net Income			-91,616,200	-75,920,500	-48,717,600	-25,085,890
Operating Cash Flow						
Capital Expenditure						
EBITDA						
Return on Assets %						
Return on Equity %						
Debt to Equity						

CONTACT INFORMATION:
Phone: 49-30467-247600　　Fax:
Toll-Free:
Address: Rheinsberger St. 76/77, Berlin, 10115 Germany

STOCK TICKER/OTHER:
Stock Ticker: Private　　　　Exchange:
Employees: 210　　　　　　　Fiscal Year Ends:
Parent Company:

SALARIES/BONUSES:
Top Exec. Salary: $　　　Bonus: $
Second Exec. Salary: $　　Bonus: $

OTHER THOUGHTS:
Estimated Female Officers or Directors:
Hot Spot for Advancement for Women/Minorities:

Southern Cross Media Group Limited

www.southerncrossaustereo.com.au
NAIC Code: 515120

TYPES OF BUSINESS:
Television Broadcasting
Radio Broadcasting
Television Broadcasting
Digital Broadcasting
Podcasting

BRANDS/DIVISIONS/AFFILIATES:
Southern Cross Austereo Services Pty Ltd
Triple M
Hit
Nine Network
Seven Network
Network Tens
PodcastOne

GROWTH PLANS/SPECIAL FEATURES:

Southern Cross Media Group Limited is a leading entertainment company in Australia, with the ability to reach more than 95% of the country's population through its radio, television and digital assets. Led by the Triple M and Hit networks, Southern Cross owns 78 radio stations, seven digital radio stations and 34 radio stations. The firm broadcasts more than 85 free-to-air TV signals across regional Australia with its Nine Network, Seven Network and Network Tens programming. The company's premium audio and visual brands are supported by leading social media, live events, video, online and mobile assets, which deliver national and local entertainment and news content. In addition, Southern Cross has developed a new Australian podcasting network, offering listeners original on-demand audio via the PodcastOne website and app. Southern Cross Media operates as a subsidiary of Southern Cross Austereo Services Pty. Ltd.

CONTACTS:
Note: Officers with more than one job title may be intentionally listed here more than once.

Grant Blackley, CEO
John Kelly, COO
Nick McKenchnie, CFO
Brian Gallagher, Chief Sales Officer
Stephen Haddad, CTO
Peter Bush, Chmn.

FINANCIAL DATA:
Note: Data for latest year may not have been available at press time.

In U.S. $	2018	2017	2016	2015	2014	2013
Revenue	475,181,184	498,706,560	463,357,760	435,394,688	459,809,728	460,921,152
R&D Expense						
Operating Income						
Operating Margin %						
SGA Expense						
Net Income	1,040,919	79,469,296	56,542,712	-205,115,104	-214,188,128	69,544,864
Operating Cash Flow						
Capital Expenditure						
EBITDA						
Return on Assets %						
Return on Equity %						
Debt to Equity						

CONTACT INFORMATION:
Phone: 6102-9375-1041   Fax: 6102-9367-5557
Toll-Free:
Address: Level 15, 50 Goulburn St., World Square, Sydney, NSW 2000 Australia

STOCK TICKER/OTHER:
Stock Ticker: SOUTF   Exchange: GREY
Employees: 2,600   Fiscal Year Ends: 06/30
Parent Company: Southern Cross Austereo Services Pty Ltd

SALARIES/BONUSES:
Top Exec. Salary: $ Bonus: $
Second Exec. Salary: $ Bonus: $

OTHER THOUGHTS:
Estimated Female Officers or Directors:
Hot Spot for Advancement for Women/Minorities:

Spanish Broadcasting System Inc

www.spanishbroadcasting.com

NAIC Code: 515112

TYPES OF BUSINESS:
Radio Broadcasting
Spanish-Language Radio
Television Broadcasting
Online News & Entertainment

BRANDS/DIVISIONS/AFFILIATES:
AIRE Radio Networks
MegaTV
LaMusica.com

CONTACTS:
Note: Officers with more than one job title may be intentionally listed here more than once.

Raul Alarcon, CEO
Joseph Garcia, CFO
Albert Rodriguez, COO
Richard Lara, Executive VP

GROWTH PLANS/SPECIAL FEATURES:

Spanish Broadcasting System, Inc. (SBS) is one of the largest publicly-traded Hispanic-controlled media and entertainment companies in the U.S. It owns and operates radio stations in markets that reach roughly 34% of the U.S. Hispanic population and reach about 3.5 million households throughout the U.S. and Puerto Rican market. The radio stations are located in 85 of the top 100 Hispanic markets and cover 94% of the U.S. Hispanic radio market. SBS broadcasts a variety of Hispanic programs, formatting the content to include news as well as music of various genres, including Spanish Tropical, Regional Mexican, Spanish Adult Contemporary, Top 40 and Latin Rhythmic. In addition to the firm's owned and operated radio stations, it owns AIRE Radio Networks, which is comprised of approximately 250 affiliate radio stations that reach more than 17.4 million listeners in an average week. The company's television group, MegaTV, produces over 50 hours of original programming her week, which is broadcasted via the company's owned and operated stations in South Florida, Houston and Puerto Rico, as well as through distribution agreements with other stations. All of SBS' digital properties offer bilingual (Spanish-English) content related to Latin music, entertainment, news and culture. LaMusica.com and the company's network of station websites and mobile apps generate revenue primarily from advertising and sponsorships. SBS also produces live concerts and events in the U.S. and Puerto Rico. Due to the cultural diversity of the Hispanic population from region to region in the U.S., most decisions regarding day-to-day programming, sales and promotional efforts are made by local managers.

FINANCIAL DATA:
Note: Data for latest year may not have been available at press time.

In U.S. $	2018	2017	2016	2015	2014	2013
Revenue		134,709,000	144,619,000	146,899,000	146,280,000	153,774,000
R&D Expense						
Operating Income		30,660,000	42,121,000	34,300,000	33,987,000	39,220,000
Operating Margin %		22.76%	29.12%	23.34%	23.23%	25.50%
SGA Expense		99,703,000	97,806,000	107,797,000	77,259,000	78,516,000
Net Income		19,621,000	-16,342,000	-26,955,000	-19,951,000	-88,566,000
Operating Cash Flow		-5,816,000	8,797,000	-1,830,000	4,375,000	7,145,000
Capital Expenditure		1,504,000	2,202,000	2,472,000	2,216,000	2,307,000
EBITDA		35,162,000	37,140,000	28,957,000	40,474,000	-46,069,000
Return on Assets %		4.42%	-3.62%	-5.96%	-4.36%	-1.90%
Return on Equity %						
Debt to Equity						

CONTACT INFORMATION:
Phone: 305 441-6901 Fax: 305 883-3375
Toll-Free:
Address: 7007 NW 77th Ave., Miami, FL 33166 United States

SALARIES/BONUSES:
Top Exec. Salary: $1,716,346   Bonus: $
Second Exec. Salary: $514,904   Bonus: $

STOCK TICKER/OTHER:
Stock Ticker: SBSAA   Exchange: PINX
Employees: 492   Fiscal Year Ends: 12/31
Parent Company:

OTHER THOUGHTS:
Estimated Female Officers or Directors:
Hot Spot for Advancement for Women/Minorities:

Sales, profits and employees may be estimates. Financial information, benefits and other data can change quickly and may vary from those stated here.

Spotify Technology SA

NAIC Code: 515111

www.spotify.com

TYPES OF BUSINESS:
Radio Networks, Traditional, Satellite and Online
Streaming Music Service
Internet Radio
Digital Music Sales

BRANDS/DIVISIONS/AFFILIATES:
Spotify Free
Spotify Premium
Spotify Platform
Mediachain
Niland

CONTACTS: Note: Officers with more than one job title may be intentionally listed here more than once.
Daniel Ek, CEO
Barry McCarthy, CFO
Seth Farbman, CMO
Katarina Berg, Chief Human Resources Officer
Gustav Soderstrom, Chief Research and Development Officer
Gustav Soderstrom, Chief Prod. Officer
Angela Watts, VP-Global Comm.
Ken Parks, Managing Dir.-USA
Stefan Zilch, Country Mgr.-Germany, Austria & Switzerland
Steve Savoca, Head-Content
Kate Vale, Managing Dir.-Australia & New Zealand
Jeff Levick, Chief Int'l Officer

GROWTH PLANS/SPECIAL FEATURES:
Spotify Technology S.A. is a web-based subscription music service offering podcast and streaming music to registered users in most of Europe and the Americas, Australia, New Zealand and parts of Asia, the Middle East and North Africa. Spotify has more than 170 million monthly active listeners, and over 83 million paying subscribers. The firm's library of music includes approximately 40 million tracks accessed via its proprietary Spotify streaming music player program. Users can download and install the music on a variety of platforms. They can create personalized playlists and also have the option to share these playlists with other Spotify users who can then edit the playlists and make their own updates. The firm's desktop platform is available for Mac, Windows and Linux-based systems. The company maintains licensing deals with major music labels. Spotify offers two main access tiers. Spotify Free allows free access to the online music library and is supported through advertisements, while the fee-based subscription service, Spotify Premium, offers a variety of upgraded features and is ad-free. Spotify Premium can access Spotify on a variety of mobile platforms, and select artists can make new album releases exclusively available on the service for a maximum of two weeks. A discounted Premium subscription tier is available for active college students in the U.S., as well as to more than 30 other countries. Moreover, Spotify connects users to a range of music sellers, providing links to online music stores where customers can purchase albums and individual songs for download. The Spotify Platform enables third-party developers to create music-based apps.

FINANCIAL DATA: Note: Data for latest year may not have been available at press time.

In U.S. $	2018	2017	2016	2015	2014	2013
Revenue		4,658,951,000	3,362,646,000	2,209,869,000		
R&D Expense		451,086,700	235,795,300	154,918,700		
Operating Income		-430,582,800	-397,548,600	-267,690,300		
Operating Margin %		-9.24%	-11.82%	-12.11%		
SGA Expense		946,598,600	618,535,600	370,210,000		
Net Income		-1,406,798,000	-613,979,100	-261,994,800		
Operating Cash Flow		203,900,300	115,049,900	-43,286,100		
Capital Expenditure		52,398,960	34,173,240	55,816,280		
EBITDA		-1,338,452,000	-560,441,000	-220,986,900		
Return on Assets %		-47.43%	-34.21%	-21.88%		
Return on Equity %		-262.20%		-100.43%		
Debt to Equity						

CONTACT INFORMATION:
Phone: 46-70-220-4607   Fax:
Toll-Free:
Address: 42-44, Ave. de la Gare, Luxembourg City, L-1610 Luxembourg

STOCK TICKER/OTHER:
Stock Ticker: SPOT
Employees: 2,960
Parent Company:

Exchange: NYS
Fiscal Year Ends: 12/31

SALARIES/BONUSES:
Top Exec. Salary: $ Bonus: $
Second Exec. Salary: $ Bonus: $

OTHER THOUGHTS:
Estimated Female Officers or Directors: 2
Hot Spot for Advancement for Women/Minorities:

Station Casinos LLC

www.stationcasinos.com

NAIC Code: 721120

TYPES OF BUSINESS:
Casino Hotel
Casino Management
Restaurants
Movie Theaters & Entertainment Venues

BRANDS/DIVISIONS/AFFILIATES:
Red Rock Resorts inc
Palms
Red Rock
Green Valley Ranch
Palace Station
Sunset Station
Boulder Station
Santa Fe Station

GROWTH PLANS/SPECIAL FEATURES:
Station Casinos, LLC is a gaming and entertainment company concentrated in the Las Vegas area, mainly targeting locals and repeat customers. Its portfolio comprises 10 distinct hotel and casino properties, more than 4,000 hotel rooms and 24,000 casino games across the network. Gaming choices include slots, video poker, table games, live poker, keno, bingo, sports betting or horseracing. Other offerings include movie screens, bowling lanes, live entertainment venues, retail outlets, spas, restaurants and convention/meeting/banquet space. Brands of the firm include Palms, Red Rock, Green Valley Ranch, Palace Station, Sunset Station, Boulder Station, Santa Fe Station, Texas Station and Fiesta. Station Casinos operates as a wholly-owned subsidiary of Red Rock Resorts, Inc.

The firm offers employees benefits including onsite childcare, tuition reimbursement, a 401(k) and employee discounts.

CONTACTS:
Note: Officers with more than one job title may be intentionally listed here more than once.

Richard J. Haskins, Pres.
Stephen Cootey, CFO
Richard J. Haskins, General Counsel
Scott M. Nielson, Chief Dev. Officer
Wes D. Allison, Chief Acct. Officer
Thomas M. Friel, Exec. VP
Frank J. Fertitta, III, Chmn.-Red Rock

FINANCIAL DATA:
Note: Data for latest year may not have been available at press time.

In U.S. $	2018	2017	2016	2015	2014	2013
Revenue	1,000,000,000	980,000,000	960,992,000	1,352,135,000	1,291,616,000	1,261,478,000
R&D Expense						
Operating Income						
Operating Margin %						
SGA Expense						
Net Income			169,899,000	132,504,000	71,326,000	-113,493,000
Operating Cash Flow						
Capital Expenditure						
EBITDA						
Return on Assets %						
Return on Equity %						
Debt to Equity						

CONTACT INFORMATION:
Phone: 702-495-3000 Fax: 702-495-3530
Toll-Free: 800-634-3101
Address: 1505 S. Pavilion Center Dr., Las Vegas, NV 89135 United States

STOCK TICKER/OTHER:
Stock Ticker: Subsidiary
Employees: 12,000
Parent Company: Red Rock Resorts Inc
Exchange:
Fiscal Year Ends: 12/31

SALARIES/BONUSES:
Top Exec. Salary: $ Bonus: $
Second Exec. Salary: $ Bonus: $

OTHER THOUGHTS:
Estimated Female Officers or Directors:
Hot Spot for Advancement for Women/Minorities:

Sales, profits and employees may be estimates. Financial information, benefits and other data can change quickly and may vary from those stated here.

Steiner Leisure Limited

www.steinerleisure.com

NAIC Code: 812199

TYPES OF BUSINESS:
Day Spa

BRANDS/DIVISIONS/AFFILIATES:
Nemo Parent Inc
Bliss
Elemis
Jou
La Therapie
Steiner Education Group
Steiner Training Academy
Ideal Image

CONTACTS:
Note: Officers with more than one job title may be intentionally listed here more than once.

Leonard Fluxman, CEO
Glenn Fusfield, COO
Stephen Lazarus, CFO

GROWTH PLANS/SPECIAL FEATURES:
Steiner Leisure Limited is a worldwide provider of spa services, medi-spa services and personal care products. The company manufactures and distributes premium skin, body and hair care products, and provides accredited education to students, teaching the skills necessary to be a spa professional, including massage, skincare and spa management. Steiner's maritime and resort spa divisions operate in over 200 venues on land an at sea. The company's brands include Bliss, Elemis, Jou, La Therapie, Mandara and Steiner, which include skincare, wellness and haircare products. These products are distributed through Steiner-operated day spas, resorts and spas-at-sea. Elemis is also distributed to more than 1,200 third-party spas; and both Bliss and Elemis are distributed via retail outlets all over the world. The Steiner Education Group operates schools at 17 campuses located in Arizona, Colorado, Connecticut, Florida, Maryland, Nevada, Pennsylvania, Utah and Virginia. These schools are branded under the Steiner Education Group or Steiner Training Academy names. The company's Ideal Image brand of facilities comprise the largest laser hair removal spa of its kind, with more than 70 facilities throughout the U.S. Laser hair removal services are offered to both men and women. Steiner Leisure is privately-owned by Nemo Parent, Inc.

FINANCIAL DATA:
Note: Data for latest year may not have been available at press time.

In U.S. $	2018	2017	2016	2015	2014	2013
Revenue	950,000,000	924,000,000	880,000,000	860,000,000	863,454,016	855,462,016
R&D Expense						
Operating Income						
Operating Margin %						
SGA Expense						
Net Income						
Operating Cash Flow						
Capital Expenditure						
EBITDA						
Return on Assets %						
Return on Equity %						
Debt to Equity						

CONTACT INFORMATION:
Phone: 242 3560006 Fax: 242 3566260
Toll-Free:
Address: Suite 104A, Saffrey Square, Nassau, BA Bahamas

SALARIES/BONUSES:
Top Exec. Salary: $ Bonus: $
Second Exec. Salary: $ Bonus: $

STOCK TICKER/OTHER:
Stock Ticker: Private
Employees: 7,300
Parent Company: Nemo Parent Inc

Exchange:
Fiscal Year Ends: 12/31

OTHER THOUGHTS:
Estimated Female Officers or Directors:
Hot Spot for Advancement for Women/Minorities:

Sales, profits and employees may be estimates. Financial information, benefits and other data can change quickly and may vary from those stated here.

Storm8

NAIC Code: 511210G

www.storm8.com

TYPES OF BUSINESS:
Computer Software, Electronic Games, Apps & Entertainment
Social Media Gaming
Apps

BRANDS/DIVISIONS/AFFILIATES:
Candy Blast Mania
Bubble Mania
Bingo
Restaurant Story 2
Pet Shop Story
Dragon Story
Hidden Objects: Mystery Crime
CLUE Bingo

CONTACTS: Note: Officers with more than one job title may be intentionally listed here more than once.
Perry Tam, CEO
Terence Fung, Chief Strategy Officer
William Siu, Chief Product Officer
Laura Yip, Chief People Officer
Chak Ming Li, Chief Game Officer
Chack Ming Li, CTO
Jesse Wood, Lead Software Engineer
Sylvie Tongco, Contact-Public Relations
Vatsal Bhardwaj, Gen. Mgr.
Chris Kusaba, Mgr.-Recruiting
Justin Ng, Mgr.-Eng.

GROWTH PLANS/SPECIAL FEATURES:
Storm8 is a social game developer for iOS and Android with a current network of more than 50 million active monthly users worldwide. The firm has produced over 45 games that have been downloaded over a billion times by users in over 155 countries. Storm8 produces games across a variety of genres including arcade games such as Candy Blast Mania, Bubble Mania and Jewel Mania; social casino games like Bingo, Poker and Slots; social casual games like Dragon Story, Restaurant Story 2, Farm Story 2 and Pet Shop Story, which allow users to interact with and build themed worlds within the game together; and puzzle games including Hidden Objects: Mystery Crime and CLUE Bingo. Social casual games are browser based games with elements of social networking integrated into the game play, allowing users to play with one another, communicate and share objects within the game. The company offers online forums where players can interact with one another in game specific forums. Games are available for purchase through Amazon's Appstore, Google Play and iTunes.

Storm8 offers employee benefits including medical, dental, disability and life insurance; a 401(k); a discount stock purchase plan; game rooms; mobile device reimbursement; and an onsite gym.

FINANCIAL DATA: Note: Data for latest year may not have been available at press time.

In U.S. $	2018	2017	2016	2015	2014	2013
Revenue						
R&D Expense						
Operating Income						
Operating Margin %						
SGA Expense						
Net Income						
Operating Cash Flow						
Capital Expenditure						
EBITDA						
Return on Assets %						
Return on Equity %						
Debt to Equity						

CONTACT INFORMATION:
Phone: 650-596-8600　　Fax:
Toll-Free:
Address: 2000 Bridge Pkwy., Ste. 110, Redwood City, CA 94065 United States

STOCK TICKER/OTHER:
Stock Ticker: Private
Employees: 120
Parent Company:

Exchange:
Fiscal Year Ends:

SALARIES/BONUSES:
Top Exec. Salary: $　　Bonus: $
Second Exec. Salary: $　　Bonus: $

OTHER THOUGHTS:
Estimated Female Officers or Directors: 2
Hot Spot for Advancement for Women/Minorities:

Sales, profits and employees may be estimates. Financial information, benefits and other data can change quickly and may vary from those stated here.

Tabcorp Holdings Limited

NAIC Code: 713210

www.tabcorp.com.au

TYPES OF BUSINESS:
Online Gambling
Racing Television
Slot Machine Operations

BRANDS/DIVISIONS/AFFILIATES:
Keno
Luxbet
Tabcorp Gaming Solutions
Sky Racing
TAB.com.au
eBET
Sky Sports Radio
Tatts Group

CONTACTS:
Note: Officers with more than one job title may be intentionally listed here more than once.

David Attenborough, Managing Dir.
Damien Johnston, CFO
Claire Murphy, CMO
Merryl Dooley, Chief People Officer
Mandy Ross, CIO
Kerry Willcock, Exec. Gen. Mgr.-Corp., Legal & Regulatory
Doug Freeman, Exec. Gen. Mgr.-Commercial Dev.
Craig Nugent, Managing Dir.-Fixed Odds
Paula Dwyer, Chmn.
Brendan Parnell, COO-Media & Intl
Adam Rytenskild, Exec. Gen. Mgr.-Distribution

GROWTH PLANS/SPECIAL FEATURES:
Tabcorp Holdings Limited is an Australian gambling entertainment company. It brands include Keno, the Lott, TGS (Tabcorp Gaming Solutions), Sky Racing, TAB.com.au and eBET. Tabcorp also wholly owns Tatts Group, another wagering, lottery, and gaming business in Australia. Keno is a lottery-style game that gives customers a chance to win $1 million every three minutes. The game is played in over 4,000 pubs and clubs in Victoria, Queensland, and is also available online in the Australian Capital Territory (ACT). The Lott is the Australian lottery brand that encompasses all listened government lottery businesses, and is owned and run by the Tatts Group. TGS is a major gaming and venue service provider in Australia, helping club and pub venues to optimize their performance and reach potential by creating market-leading customer experiences. Its products and solutions include gaming products, venue design, marketing, loyalty programs and more. Sky Racing and Sky Sports Radio provide racing and sports analysis programs, broadcasting more than 120,000 races each year in Australia, and distributing them to over 100 countries. Its content is offered across cable, online and mobile devices. TAB.com.au is a leading multi-channel wagering brand in Australia, offering a range of betting experiences across retail and digital channels. TAB's wagering products can be found in nearly 3,000 agencies, pubs, clubs and racecourses across Victoria, New South Wales and ACT. Last, eBET is a gaming systems company that develops and markets a range of networked solutions for electronic gaming machines. It provides gaming technology solutions through its three divisions of gaming systems, gaming operations and business intelligence.

FINANCIAL DATA:
Note: Data for latest year may not have been available at press time.

In U.S. $	2018	2017	2016	2015	2014	2013
Revenue	2,682,477,000	1,565,263,000	1,533,455,000	1,510,194,000	1,427,030,000	1,400,196,000
R&D Expense						
Operating Income	1,054,579,000	933,931,200	1,008,828,000	1,058,223,000	970,433,700	958,803,300
Operating Margin %		59.66%	65.78%	70.07%	68.00%	68.47%
SGA Expense	391,158,200	247,320,100	218,944,900	164,365,600	208,575,600	198,066,300
Net Income	20,107,900	-14,572,970	118,895,800	234,358,600	91,011,000	88,698,940
Operating Cash Flow						
Capital Expenditure	204,371,900	138,303,100	128,284,200	92,202,060	139,003,700	143,067,300
EBITDA	344,706,800	200,728,700	338,050,900	359,700,100	342,955,200	333,707,000
Return on Assets %		-.59%	5.07%	10.30%	4.15%	3.96%
Return on Equity %		-1.31%	10.04%	21.09%	8.97%	8.98%
Debt to Equity		0.46	0.49	0.67	0.73	0.58

CONTACT INFORMATION:
Phone: 61 398682100   Fax: 61 398682300
Toll-Free:
Address: 5 Bowen Crescent, Melbourne, VIC 3004 Australia

STOCK TICKER/OTHER:
Stock Ticker: TACBY
Employees: 10,124
Parent Company:

Exchange: PINX
Fiscal Year Ends: 06/01

SALARIES/BONUSES:
Top Exec. Salary: $ Bonus: $
Second Exec. Salary: $ Bonus: $

OTHER THOUGHTS:
Estimated Female Officers or Directors: 5
Hot Spot for Advancement for Women/Minorities: Y

Take-Two Interactive Software Inc

www.take2games.com

NAIC Code: 511210G

TYPES OF BUSINESS:
Computer Software, Electronic Games, Apps & Entertainment
Software Distribution
Apps

BRANDS/DIVISIONS/AFFILIATES:
Rockstar Games
2K
Grand Theft Auto
Battleborn
XCOM
Private Division
Social Point
Red Dead Redemption 2

CONTACTS:
Note: Officers with more than one job title may be intentionally listed here more than once.

Strauss Zelnick, CEO
Lainie Goldstein, CFO
Daniel Emerson, Executive VP
Karl Slatoff, President

GROWTH PLANS/SPECIAL FEATURES:
Take-Two Interactive Software, Inc. is a global publisher, developer and distributor of interactive entertainment software. The firm develops, markets and publishes software titles for leading gaming and entertainment hardware platforms, including Sony's PlayStation (PS3, PS4 and PSP), Microsoft's Xbox One and Xbox 360, and the Nintendo Switch, as well as handheld gaming devices, personal computers and mobile devices. The company distributes its software through retail stores and online through digital download stores, online platforms and cloud streaming devices. Its business strategy is to capitalize on the success of popular games by creating sequels and perpetuating its consistently popular franchises while continuing to appeal to a broad range of demographics, from game enthusiasts to casual gamers and families. A majority of Take-Two's leading games are developed internally with intellectual property owned by the company, although it selectively markets and publishes externally developed titles and software based on licensed property, including sports and games based on Nick Jr. titles. The firm wholly-owns the labels Rockstar Games and 2K, and publishes titles under 2K Games, 2K Sports and 2K Play. 2K publishes owned and licensed titles across a range of genres including shooter, action, role-playing, strategy, sports and family/casual. Rockstar Games titles are primarily internally developed and include the Grand Theft Auto series. Other published franchises include Battleborn, BioShock, Borderlands, Carnival Games, Evolve, Mafia, NBA 2K, Sid Meier's Civilization, WWE 2K, Red Dead and XCOM. Take-Two's Private Division label is dedicated to bringing titles from top independent developers to market. Social Point develops and publishes free-to-play mobile games, which includes Dragon City and Monster Legends.

FINANCIAL DATA:
Note: Data for latest year may not have been available at press time.

In U.S. $	2018	2017	2016	2015	2014	2013
Revenue	1,792,892,000	1,779,748,000	1,413,698,000	1,082,938,000	2,350,568,000	1,214,483,000
R&D Expense	196,373,000	137,915,000	119,807,000	115,043,000	105,256,000	78,184,000
Operating Income	150,319,000	91,305,000	60,457,000	-258,463,000	415,256,000	5,239,000
Operating Margin %	8.38	5.13%	4.27%	-23.86%	17.66%	.43%
SGA Expense	503,920,000	496,862,000	390,761,000	410,434,000	402,370,000	404,589,000
Net Income	173,533,000	67,303,000	-8,302,000	-279,470,000	361,605,000	-29,491,000
Operating Cash Flow	393,947,000	331,429,000	261,305,000	212,814,000	700,262,000	-4,567,000
Capital Expenditure	61,557,000	21,167,000	37,280,000	49,501,000	29,813,000	16,820,000
EBITDA	295,238,000	350,661,000	223,889,000	-103,609,000	697,706,000	253,621,000
Return on Assets %	5.03%	2.34%	-.34%	-13.86%	23.50%	-2.42%
Return on Equity %	13.92%	8.49%	-1.45%	-40.95%	52.03%	-4.98%
Debt to Equity		0.25	0.85	0.84	0.56	0.57

CONTACT INFORMATION:
Phone: 646 536-2842 Fax: 646 536-2926
Toll-Free:
Address: 110 West 44th St., New York, NY 10036 United States

SALARIES/BONUSES:
Top Exec. Salary: $690,051 Bonus: $
Second Exec. Salary: $515,000 Bonus: $

STOCK TICKER/OTHER:
Stock Ticker: TTWO Exchange: NAS
Employees: 3,707 Fiscal Year Ends: 03/31
Parent Company:

OTHER THOUGHTS:
Estimated Female Officers or Directors: 1
Hot Spot for Advancement for Women/Minorities:

Sales, profits and employees may be estimates. Financial information, benefits and other data can change quickly and may vary from those stated here.

Tatts Group Limited

www.tattsgroup.com.au

NAIC Code: 713210

TYPES OF BUSINESS:
Lottery Operations
Online Gaming

BRANDS/DIVISIONS/AFFILIATES:
Tabcorp Holdings Limited
Lott (The)
UBET
MAX
George2
Tatts
NSW Lotteries
Golden Casket

CONTACTS: Note: Officers with more than one job title may be intentionally listed here more than once.
Damien Johnston, CFO
Anne Tucker, General Counsel
Barrie Fletton, COO-Wagering
Francis Catterall, Exec. Gen. Mgr.-Strategy
Dan Crane, Chief Online Officer
Carolyn Prendergast, Media Liason
Giovanni Rizzo, Gen. Mgr.-Investor Rel.
Peter Harvey, COO-Talarius
Bruce Houston, Exec. Gen. Mgr.-Govt & Industry Rel.
Kevin Szekely, COO-Bytecraft
Bill Thorburn, COO-Lotteries

GROWTH PLANS/SPECIAL FEATURES:
Tatts Group Limited is a provider of leisure and entertainment products and services to gaming and lotteries industries across all of Australia, much of New Zealand and parts of the U.K. Tatts operates four primary brands: The Lott, UBET, MAX and George2. The Lott offers lottery games, creating 232 new millionaires and delivering prize money in excess of $2 billion during 2018 alone. Its games offer Australians an opportunity to play the lottery, as well as to support Australian communities through services like hospitals and infrastructure. The Lott's licensee brands include Tatts, NSW Lotteries, Golden Casket and SA Lotteries. UBET is a premier provider of pari-mutuel and fixed-price betting. It conducts wagering on thoroughbred, harness and greyhound racing. It also conducts wagering on a variety of sports, including AFL (Australian Football League), NRL (National Rugby League), Rugby Union, soccer, Cricket and more, both domestically and internationally. MAX offers gaming machine monitoring and value-added services. George2 (George squared) is a social enterprise for raising funds for non-profits, charities and sporting clubs. It does this by providing innovative fundraising products and technology solutions such as charity-based raffles and lotteries. Tatts Group operates as a subsidiary of Australian wagering, gaming and Keno operator, Tabcorp Holdings Limited.

FINANCIAL DATA: Note: Data for latest year may not have been available at press time.

In U.S. $	2018	2017	2016	2015	2014	2013
Revenue		1,935,810,000	2,047,904,000	2,040,086,000	2,000,894,000	2,052,451,000
R&D Expense						
Operating Income		280,497,400	316,615,300	310,379,700	304,874,900	305,021,400
Operating Margin %		14.48%	15.46%	15.21%	15.23%	14.86%
SGA Expense		185,395,500	187,052,500	221,014,500	202,918,800	194,944,300
Net Income		154,498,000	163,801,600	176,531,900	140,419,700	173,289,400
Operating Cash Flow						
Capital Expenditure		73,970,430	43,636,940	71,401,950	52,839,630	48,248,440
EBITDA		304,295,500	350,365,000	360,713,200	350,552,100	346,022,600
Return on Assets %		4.18%	4.34%	4.48%	3.59%	4.76%
Return on Equity %		7.43%	7.86%	8.67%	7.16%	9.12%
Debt to Equity		0.28	0.37	0.19	0.47	0.46

CONTACT INFORMATION:
Phone: 61-7-3435-4500 Fax:
Toll-Free:
Address: 87 Ipswich Rd., Brisbane, QLD 4102 Australia

SALARIES/BONUSES:
Top Exec. Salary: $ Bonus: $
Second Exec. Salary: $ Bonus: $

STOCK TICKER/OTHER:
Stock Ticker: TTSLF   Exchange: PINX
Employees: 347   Fiscal Year Ends: 06/30
Parent Company: Tabcorp Holdings Limited

OTHER THOUGHTS:
Estimated Female Officers or Directors: 5
Hot Spot for Advancement for Women/Minorities: Y

TEGNA Inc

NAIC Code: 515120

www.tegna.com

TYPES OF BUSINESS:
Television Broadcasting
Internet Broadcasting

BRANDS/DIVISIONS/AFFILIATES:
CareerBuilder
G/O Digital
Cars.com Inc

CONTACTS:
Note: Officers with more than one job title may be intentionally listed here more than once.

David Lougee, CEO
Victoria Harker, CFO
Howard Elias, Chairman of the Board
Todd Mayman, Chief Administrative Officer
Lynn Beall, COO, Divisional

GROWTH PLANS/SPECIAL FEATURES:

TEGNA, Inc. is a media and digital media company that delivers content to consumers through broadcast television and digital media platforms. The firm's operations are divided by its four primary content delivery platforms: advertising and media services revenues, political advertising revenues, subscription revenues and other services. The advertising and media services revenues includes local and national non-political advertising, digital marketing services and advertising on stations' websites and tablet and mobile products. Advertising makes up the most significant portion of TEGNA's revenue. The segment includes 47 television stations in 39 markets. Through this segment, TEGNA is the largest independent station group of major network affiliates in the top 25 markets in the U.S., covering approximately one-third of all television households nationwide. The company's portfolio includes NBC, CBS, FOX and ABC stations operating on long-term affiliation agreements. Each of TEGNA's 47 television stations also has a digital presence across online, mobile and social media platforms. Political advertising revenues are driven by election cycles at the local and national level. These revenues are particularly prevalent in the second half of the year. The company's subscription revenues reflect fees paid by satellite, cable, OTT and telecommunications providers. Last, other services include the production of programming from third parties and production of advertising material. In June 2018, TEGNA announced the launch of DEALBOSS a commerce franchise for local stations and social platforms and in-air markets. In August of that year, TEGNA announced that it had acquired the leading television stations in Toledo, Ohio and Odessa-Midland, Texas.

FINANCIAL DATA:
Note: Data for latest year may not have been available at press time.

In U.S. $	2018	2017	2016	2015	2014	2013
Revenue		1,903,026,000	3,341,198,000	3,050,945,000	6,008,174,000	5,161,362,000
R&D Expense						
Operating Income		550,331,000	1,004,204,000	854,301,000	1,154,395,000	797,483,000
Operating Margin %		28.91%	30.05%	28.00%	19.21%	15.45%
SGA Expense		342,339,000	1,093,837,000	1,068,221,000	1,539,476,000	1,291,858,000
Net Income		273,744,000	436,697,000	459,522,000	1,062,171,000	388,680,000
Operating Cash Flow		386,211,000	683,429,000	613,106,000	821,199,000	511,488,000
Capital Expenditure		76,886,000	94,796,000	118,767,000	150,354,000	110,407,000
EBITDA		657,507,000	1,148,955,000	1,158,809,000	1,895,028,000	924,749,000
Return on Assets %		4.05%	5.11%	4.65%	10.38%	4.97%
Return on Equity %		16.76%	19.56%	16.87%	35.71%	15.41%
Debt to Equity		3.02	1.77	1.91	1.37	1.37

CONTACT INFORMATION:
Phone: 703-873-6600　Fax:
Toll-Free:
Address: 7950 Jones Branch Dr., McLean, VA 22107-0150 United States

SALARIES/BONUSES:
Top Exec. Salary: $908,333　Bonus: $1,000,000
Second Exec. Salary: $700,000　Bonus: $675,000

STOCK TICKER/OTHER:
Stock Ticker: TGNA　Exchange: NYS
Employees: 10,121　Fiscal Year Ends: 12/31
Parent Company:

OTHER THOUGHTS:
Estimated Female Officers or Directors:
Hot Spot for Advancement for Women/Minorities:

Sales, profits and employees may be estimates. Financial information, benefits and other data can change quickly and may vary from those stated here.

Tele Columbus AG

NAIC Code: 517110

www.pyur.com

TYPES OF BUSINESS:
Cable TV Service
Video-on-Demand
Internet Services
Telephony Services
Online Radio Broadcasting

BRANDS/DIVISIONS/AFFILIATES:
PYUR

GROWTH PLANS/SPECIAL FEATURES:
Tele Columbus AG operates cable networks in Germany under the name PYUR. More than 3.6 million households are connected to PYUR through the firm's nationwide network. Its architecture of fiber optic and coaxial cable complies to current transmission standards, enabling companies to benefit from PYUR's digitization advantages. PYUR means having a life path of 8, suggesting it is ambitious and goal-oriented, digitally armed to manage, organize and govern. The PYUR platform offers a variety of digital options obtainable by customers as a single product or a combined one, whichever is preferred. The products are grouped into the categories of internet, television and mobile, offering high-performance broadband cable service, internet access, telephone line connectivity and more than 250 TV programs. Package options are offered on a month-to-month basis, and can be terminated as such. Customers can receive a PYUR newsletter via email for free, which provides information on current products, promotions and new services.

CONTACTS: Note: Officers with more than one job title may be intentionally listed here more than once.

Timm Degenhardt, CEO

FINANCIAL DATA: Note: Data for latest year may not have been available at press time.

In U.S. $	2018	2017	2016	2015	2014	2013
Revenue	520,000,000	510,000,000	502,286,000	306,655,000	259,019,000	283,855,000
R&D Expense						
Operating Income						
Operating Margin %						
SGA Expense						
Net Income			-11,116,100	-71,133,100	-26,619,000	-11,838,800
Operating Cash Flow						
Capital Expenditure						
EBITDA						
Return on Assets %						
Return on Equity %						
Debt to Equity						

CONTACT INFORMATION:
Phone: 49-30-3388-3000   Fax: 49-30-3388-3330
Toll-Free:
Address: Kaiserin-Augusta-Allee 108, Berlin, 10553 Germany

STOCK TICKER/OTHER:
Stock Ticker: Private
Employees: 400
Parent Company:

Exchange:
Fiscal Year Ends: 12/31

SALARIES/BONUSES:
Top Exec. Salary: $ Bonus: $
Second Exec. Salary: $ Bonus: $

OTHER THOUGHTS:
Estimated Female Officers or Directors:
Hot Spot for Advancement for Women/Minorities:

Sales, profits and employees may be estimates. Financial information, benefits and other data can change quickly and may vary from those stated here.

Television Francaise 1 SA

NAIC Code: 515120

www.tf1.fr

TYPES OF BUSINESS:
Television Broadcasting

BRANDS/DIVISIONS/AFFILIATES:
TF1
TMC
TFX
T1 Series Films
TF1 Studio
TF1 Entertainment
Newen Studios
Teleshopping

CONTACTS: Note: Officers with more than one job title may be intentionally listed here more than once.
Gilles Pelisson, CEO
Philippe Denery, Exec. VP-Finance
Arnaud Bosom, Exec. VP-Human Resources
Gilles Maugars, Exec. VP-Tech. & Info. Systems
Jean-Michel Counillon, General Counsel
Philippe Denery, Exec. VP-Group Finance
Philippe Balland, Managing Dir.
Edouard Boccon-Gibod, Chmn.-TF1 Metro France
Jean-Francos Lancelier, Exec VP-Broadcasting, Programs & Production
Regis Ravanas, Exec. VP-Group Diversification & Development
Gilles Pelisson, Chmn.

GROWTH PLANS/SPECIAL FEATURES:
Television Francaise 1 SA, doing business as TF1 is engaged in television broadcasting and communication services. It divides its operations into three segments: broadcasting, studios and entertainment and digital. The broadcasting segment operates various TF1 channels, which provide family-oriented and events-based programming. These programs include news, light entertainment, drama, sports, feature films, youth programs, magazines and documentaries. This division also operates the TMC channel, a general interest family-oriented entertainment channel; the TFX channel, which focuses on non-scripted offerings and first-air series; T1 Series Films channel, a theme channel for French drama and storytelling programming; and LCI, an all-news French TV channel. The studios and entertainment segment comprises four primary divisions: TFI Studio, TF1 Entertainment, Newen Studios and Teleshopping. TF1 Studio produces, co-produces, develops, acquires and distributes feature films and programs, holding a portfolio of more than 2,000. Its consolidated subsidiaries include TF1 Droits AudioVisuels, TF1 Video and TF1 International. Films are distributed in theatrical, e-Cinema video, video-on-demand (VOD) and TV formats, both domestically and internationally. TF1 Entertainment is responsible for the company's publishing and distribution activities, marketing the brands of the group as well as the properties from which it acquired the rights directly. Newen Studios is engaged in audiovisual production and distribution, with a focus on fiction, magazine shows, light entertainment and animation. The digital segment focuses on brand awareness, advertising and digital conent and includes the aufeminin group, MyLittle Paris, Mariton, Livingly Media, TF1 Digital Factory, Dcotissimo, Minute Buzz, Gamned!, Studio 71 and Neweb. In 2018, TF1 acquired the aufeminin group, a digital content provider tailored to women, in April 2018; Doctimssimo, a content provider segmented for women and women's health, in October 2018; and Gamned!, a media sales platform.

FINANCIAL DATA: Note: Data for latest year may not have been available at press time.

In U.S. $	2018	2017	2016	2015	2014	2013
Revenue						
R&D Expense						
Operating Income						
Operating Margin %						
SGA Expense						
Net Income						
Operating Cash Flow						
Capital Expenditure						
EBITDA						
Return on Assets %						
Return on Equity %						
Debt to Equity						

CONTACT INFORMATION:
Phone: 33 141412732 Fax: 33 141412910
Toll-Free:
Address: 1 Quai du Point du Jour, Boulogne-Billancourt, 92656 France

STOCK TICKER/OTHER:
Stock Ticker: TVFCF Exchange: PINX
Employees: 3,057 Fiscal Year Ends: 12/31
Parent Company:

SALARIES/BONUSES:
Top Exec. Salary: $ Bonus: $
Second Exec. Salary: $ Bonus: $

OTHER THOUGHTS:
Estimated Female Officers or Directors:
Hot Spot for Advancement for Women/Minorities:

Tencent Music Entertainment Group

www.qq.com

NAIC Code: 515111

TYPES OF BUSINESS:
Radio Networks
Streaming Music Service
Internet Radio
Digital Music Sales

BRANDS/DIVISIONS/AFFILIATES:
Tencent Holdings Limited
Sony/ATV Music Publishing
QQ Music
Kugou
Kuwo

GROWTH PLANS/SPECIAL FEATURES:
Tencent Music Entertainment Group, founded in 2016, operates an online music entertainment platform that provides online music and music-centric social entertainment services in China. The firm's apps include QQ Music, Kugou and Kuwo, and have more than 700 million active users and 120 million paying subscribers. Parent Tencent Holdings Limited acquired China Music Corporation in 2016 to strengthen its music offerings, and subsequently changed China Music's name to Tencent Music Entertainment Group. In mid-2018, Sony/ATV Music Publishing acquired an equity stake in Tencent Music, and in October 2018, the firm filed for an initial public offering (IPO) of around $2 billion in the U.S. That December, Tencent Music announced that it intended to raise $1.15 billion in a U.S. IPO of American Depository Shares representing Class A ordinary shares.

CONTACTS:
Note: Officers with more than one job title may be intentionally listed here more than once.

Cussion Kar Shun Pang, CEO
Zhenyu Xie, Co-Pres.
Min Hu, CFO
Tony Cheuk Tung Yip, Chief Strategy Officer
Guomin Xie, Co-Pres.
Tong Tao Sang, Chmn.

FINANCIAL DATA:
Note: Data for latest year may not have been available at press time.

In U.S. $	2018	2017	2016	2015	2014	2013
Revenue		1,598,143,000	634,687,300			
R&D Expense						
Operating Income		204,334,100	13,534,950			
Operating Margin %						
SGA Expense		354,237,300	167,076,600			
Net Income		192,982,200	11,934,040			
Operating Cash Flow		363,842,800	127,053,900			
Capital Expenditure		11,206,360	5,967,022			
EBITDA		259,492,700	47,881,710			
Return on Assets %						
Return on Equity %						
Debt to Equity						

CONTACT INFORMATION:
Phone: 86-755-8601-3388 Fax:
Toll-Free:
Address: 17/Fl, Malata Bldg., Kejizhonegyi Rd., Midwest Dist. of Hi-tech Park, Nanshan Dist., Shenzhen, 518057 China

STOCK TICKER/OTHER:
Stock Ticker: TME
Employees: 2,459
Parent Company: Tencent Holdings Limited

Exchange: NYS
Fiscal Year Ends: 12/31

SALARIES/BONUSES:
Top Exec. Salary: $ Bonus: $
Second Exec. Salary: $ Bonus: $

OTHER THOUGHTS:
Estimated Female Officers or Directors:
Hot Spot for Advancement for Women/Minorities:

Sales, profits and employees may be estimates. Financial information, benefits and other data can change quickly and may vary from those stated here.

Texas Tribune Inc (The)

NAIC Code: 519130

www.texastribune.org

TYPES OF BUSINESS:
Online Publishing

BRANDS/DIVISIONS/AFFILIATES:

CONTACTS: Note: Officers with more than one job title may be intentionally listed here more than once.
Evan Smith, CEO
Emily Ramshaw, Editor-in-Chief
April Hinkle, Chief Revenue Officer
Rodney Gibbs, Chief Product Officer
John Jordan, Operations Mgr.
Rodney Gibbs, Chief Innovation Officer
Daniel Craigmile, Chief Technology Officer
Maggie Gilburg, Dir.-Dev.
Jacob Villanueva, Dir.-Multimedia & Art
Kara Hamann, Dir.-Finance
April Hinkle, Chief Revenue Officer
Brandi Grissom, Managing Dir.
Agnes Varnum, Dir.-Events
Tanya Erlach, Dir.-Texas Tribune Festival
John Thornton, Chmn.

GROWTH PLANS/SPECIAL FEATURES:
The Texas Tribune, Inc. is a nonprofit, nonpartisan news organization based in Austin. The company bills itself as a supplemental resource for traditional newspapers that have cut back on public interest content. The Texas Tribune focuses almost entirely on public policy, politics and government news stories to fill this void. The organization does not use advertising and runs almost entirely on donations from private citizens, corporations and endowments. It also syndicates its stories to traditional media outlets. By using an all-digital format, the company does not need to devote resources to costly printing and distribution expenses. The Texas Tribune places special attention on elections, with comprehensive candidate analyses and polling for both state and national elections. Other common topics include immigration, education, transportation, health care, the environment, law, energy and poverty. In addition to traditional written pieces, the organization also offers multimedia resources like videos, audio recordings, photo journalism, blogs and social media interaction.

FINANCIAL DATA: Note: Data for latest year may not have been available at press time.

In U.S. $	2018	2017	2016	2015	2014	2013
Revenue		7,508,251	7,522,423	7,184,902	6,188,181	7,054,908
R&D Expense						
Operating Income						
Operating Margin %						
SGA Expense						
Net Income		-791,845	26,053	46,465	-134,408	1,927,327
Operating Cash Flow						
Capital Expenditure						
EBITDA						
Return on Assets %						
Return on Equity %						
Debt to Equity						

CONTACT INFORMATION:
Phone: 512-716-8600 Fax:
Toll-Free:
Address: 919 Congress Ave., Fl. 6, Austin, TX 78701 United States

STOCK TICKER/OTHER:
Stock Ticker: Nonprofit Exchange:
Employees: 60 Fiscal Year Ends: 12/31
Parent Company:

SALARIES/BONUSES:
Top Exec. Salary: $ Bonus: $
Second Exec. Salary: $ Bonus: $

OTHER THOUGHTS:
Estimated Female Officers or Directors: 10
Hot Spot for Advancement for Women/Minorities: Y

Thomas Nelson Inc

www.thomasnelson.com

NAIC Code: 511130

TYPES OF BUSINESS:
Book Publishing
Religious Publications
Gifts & Stationery
CD-ROMs

BRANDS/DIVISIONS/AFFILIATES:
News Corporation
HarperCollins Publishers
HarperCollins Christian Publishing Inc
Thomas Nelson
Tommy Nelson
Emanate Books
Grupo Nelson
W Publishing Group

CONTACTS:
Note: Officers with more than one job title may be intentionally listed here more than once.

Mark Schoenwald, CEO

GROWTH PLANS/SPECIAL FEATURES:
Thomas Nelson, Inc. is a leading publisher, producer and distributor of books emphasizing Christian, inspirational and family value themes. The firm distributes through Christian bookstores, mass merchandisers (Barnes & Noble, Target and Walmart) and direct sales to consumers, churches and ministries. The company distributes its products internationally in South America, Europe, Australia, New Zealand, Africa, Asia and Mexico. It publishes works through its Thomas Nelson, Tommy Nelson, Emanate Books and Grupo Nelson brand names, as well as Nelson Books, W Publishing Group and NEXT Leadership Network imprint brand names. Thomas Nelson also maintains a backlist of approximately 4,000 titles, which provide the company with a stable base of recurring revenues. The firm is one of the largest commercial publishers of English and Spanish translations of the Bible, publishing more than 20 versions of the Bible based on varying translations and additional content. It holds exclusive rights to two of these versions: the New Century Version and the International Children's Bible. The New King James Version was first commissioned by Thomas Nelson in 1975 and published by the company in 1982. Other Bible-related products include commentaries, study guides, concordances, Bible software and an illustrated encyclopedia of biblical history, culture and geography. Authors and titles are supported through radio, television, cooperative advertising, author appearances and in-store promotions. Thomas Nelson also hosts conferences and themed events, such as its Women of Faith inspirational conferences, from which it derives revenues in the form of attendance fees as well as the sale of products to conference attendees. Thomas Nelson operates as a subsidiary of News Corporation via HarperCollins Publishers, through HarperCollins Christian Publishing, Inc.

FINANCIAL DATA:
Note: Data for latest year may not have been available at press time.

In U.S. $	2018	2017	2016	2015	2014	2013
Revenue						
R&D Expense						
Operating Income						
Operating Margin %						
SGA Expense						
Net Income						
Operating Cash Flow						
Capital Expenditure						
EBITDA						
Return on Assets %						
Return on Equity %						
Debt to Equity						

CONTACT INFORMATION:
Phone: Fax:
Toll-Free: 800-251-4000
Address: P.O. Box 141000, Nashville, TN 37214 United States

STOCK TICKER/OTHER:
Stock Ticker: Subsidiary
Employees: 600
Parent Company: News Corporation

Exchange:
Fiscal Year Ends: 03/31

SALARIES/BONUSES:
Top Exec. Salary: $ Bonus: $
Second Exec. Salary: $ Bonus: $

OTHER THOUGHTS:
Estimated Female Officers or Directors:
Hot Spot for Advancement for Women/Minorities:

Thomson Reuters Corporation

NAIC Code: 511120A

www.thomsonreuters.com

TYPES OF BUSINESS:
Information Services & Software
Legal & Regulatory Information Services
Financial Information & Technology
Health Care Information Tools
Scientific Data Tools

BRANDS/DIVISIONS/AFFILIATES:

CONTACTS:
Note: Officers with more than one job title may be intentionally listed here more than once.

James Smith, CEO
Stephane Bello, CFO
David Thomson, Chairman of the Board
David Binet, Deputy Chairman
Rick King, Executive VP, Divisional
Neil Masterson, Executive VP
Brian Scanlon, Executive VP
Gustav Carlson, Executive VP
Mary-Alice Vuicic, Executive VP
Deirdre Stanley, General Counsel
Carla Jones, Other Executive Officer
Brian Peccarelli, President, Divisional
David Craig, President, Divisional
Susan Martin, President, Divisional
Gonzalo Lissarrague, President, Divisional

GROWTH PLANS/SPECIAL FEATURES:

Thomson Reuters provides specialized information in digital and print formats for professional markets, with operations in more than 100 countries for more than 100 years. Thomson Reuters offers corporations end-to-end solutions pertaining to regulatory, legal and compliance challenges. For government entities, the company offers information relating to operational and policy decision making. For legal firms, Thomson Reuters provides legal products and services that combine content, deep human expertise and intuitive technology for timely guidance and answers. For news and media sectors, the firm provides award-winning global multimedia content and real-time news coverage in a partnership manner. For accounting firms, corporations, financial institutions, governments and law firms, Thomson Reuters provides tax and accounting technology, guidance and expertise. In addition, Thomson Reuters Labs engage in exploring new business opportunities for Thomson Reuters, working with customers and partners to create quick, agile and collaborative experiments and proofs-of-concept. Its artificial intelligence (AI) center encompasses a team of scientists, engineers and designers with specialized skills in cognitive technologies. During 2018, the firm sold a 55% interest in its financial and risk business to Blackstone Group; and acquired Integration Point, an international player in global trade management operations.

FINANCIAL DATA:
Note: Data for latest year may not have been available at press time.

In U.S. $	2018	2017	2016	2015	2014	2013
Revenue		11,333,000,000	11,166,000,000	12,209,000,000	12,607,000,000	12,702,000,000
R&D Expense						
Operating Income		1,755,000,000	1,390,000,000	1,734,000,000	2,545,000,000	1,516,000,000
Operating Margin %		15.48%	12.44%	14.20%	20.18%	11.93%
SGA Expense						
Net Income		1,395,000,000	3,098,000,000	1,255,000,000	1,909,000,000	137,000,000
Operating Cash Flow		2,029,000,000	2,984,000,000	2,838,000,000	2,366,000,000	2,103,000,000
Capital Expenditure		950,000,000	905,000,000	1,003,000,000	968,000,000	1,004,000,000
EBITDA		3,023,000,000	2,999,000,000	3,455,000,000	4,285,000,000	3,297,000,000
Return on Assets %		5.12%	10.87%	4.19%	6.04%	.41%
Return on Equity %		10.87%	24.60%	9.43%	12.70%	.81%
Debt to Equity		0.41	0.49	0.54	0.53	0.46

CONTACT INFORMATION:
Phone: 646 223-4000　Fax:
Toll-Free:
Address: 3 Times Square, New York, NY 10036 United States

STOCK TICKER/OTHER:
Stock Ticker: TRI　Exchange: NYS
Employees: 45,000　Fiscal Year Ends: 12/31
Parent Company:

SALARIES/BONUSES:
Top Exec. Salary: $1,591,530　Bonus: $
Second Exec. Salary: $990,820　Bonus: $

OTHER THOUGHTS:
Estimated Female Officers or Directors: 2
Hot Spot for Advancement for Women/Minorities: Y

TiVo Corporation

NAIC Code: 511210L

business.tivo.com

TYPES OF BUSINESS:
Software-Video Copyright Protection
Digital Rights Management Technologies

BRANDS/DIVISIONS/AFFILIATES:

CONTACTS:
Note: Officers with more than one job title may be intentionally listed here more than once.

Peter Halt, CFO
Wesley Gutierrez, Chief Accounting Officer
Dustin Finer, Chief Administrative Officer
Pamela Sergeeff, Chief Compliance Officer
James Meyer, Director
Raghavendra Rau, Director

GROWTH PLANS/SPECIAL FEATURES:

TiVo Corporation is an American technology company headquartered in California. The firm is engaged in licensing its intellectual property within the consumer electronics industry, including digital rights management, electronic program guide software and metadata. TiVo Corporation encompasses approximately 5,500 issued and pending patents, including about 3,300 internationally. The company also provides analytics and recommendation platforms to the TV service provider, CE manufacturer, streaming and digital media, studio, broadcaster, network and music industry sectors. TiVo's user experience solutions enable quick, seamless access to the content consumers enjoy, including live, recorded, on-demand and streaming, across all devices. These solutions incorporate search, recommendations, personalization, metadata and mobile, and offer solutions for traditional cable, IPTV and hybrid environments for the purpose of increasing engagement with consumers. Metadata services provide the foundation for intuitive search and navigation, enabling users to easily find and learn more about TV shows, movies, music, celebrities, sports, books and games. TiVo's metadata services cover television, sports, movies, digital-first, music, celebrities, books and video games, with a content library on more than 16.7 million video programs, including theatrical, digital-first, DVD and Blu-ray releases, as well as thousands of celebrities. TiVo's database also has information on 3.9 million music albums, 34 million songs, 12.1 million books, 122,000 video games, 132,000 active athletes and 123,000 sporting events. The company's products and solutions combine big data and cloud processing to retrieve behavior patterns and deliver predictive actionable insights that maximize inventory for TiVo business customers.

TiVo employees receive health, life, short- and long-term disability insurance; flexible spending accounts; employee stock purchase plan; 401(k) and 529 plans; paid vacations and holidays; employee assistance programs; and other perks.

FINANCIAL DATA:
Note: Data for latest year may not have been available at press time.

In U.S. $	2018	2017	2016	2015	2014	2013
Revenue		826,456,000	649,093,000	526,271,000	542,311,000	538,067,000
R&D Expense		194,382,000	125,172,000	100,627,000	108,746,000	112,760,000
Operating Income		23,838,000	48,757,000	73,834,000	94,149,000	89,969,000
Operating Margin %		2.88%	7.51%	14.02%	17.36%	16.72%
SGA Expense		205,024,000	192,755,000	154,448,000	136,736,000	151,325,000
Net Income		-37,956,000	32,661,000	-4,292,000	-69,744,000	-172,090,000
Operating Cash Flow		132,084,000	133,521,000	142,826,000	184,829,000	195,339,000
Capital Expenditure		39,962,000	22,847,000	11,293,000	51,392,000	19,067,000
EBITDA		183,322,000	142,932,000	150,681,000	156,398,000	175,200,000
Return on Assets %		-1.17%	1.18%	-.18%	-2.70%	-5.72%
Return on Equity %		-2.01%	2.22%	-.40%	-5.76%	-11.86%
Debt to Equity		0.52	0.50	0.93	0.72	0.90

CONTACT INFORMATION:
Phone: 408 519-9100   Fax: 408 743-8610
Toll-Free:
Address: 2160 Gold St., San Jose, CA 95002 United States

SALARIES/BONUSES:
Top Exec. Salary: $102,273   Bonus: $3,798,000
Second Exec. Salary: $625,000   Bonus: $

STOCK TICKER/OTHER:
Stock Ticker: TIVO
Employees: 1,700
Parent Company:

Exchange: NAS
Fiscal Year Ends: 12/31

OTHER THOUGHTS:
Estimated Female Officers or Directors: 1
Hot Spot for Advancement for Women/Minorities:

TNS UK Ltd

NAIC Code: 541910

www.tnsglobal.co.uk

TYPES OF BUSINESS:
Market Research
Internet Market Research
Business & Advertising Software
Consumer Tracking & Analysis

BRANDS/DIVISIONS/AFFILIATES:
Kantar Group
Kantar TNS
Connect
Matrix
Concept eValuate
ConversionModel
relationship TRI*M
Connected Life

CONTACTS: Note: Officers with more than one job title may be intentionally listed here more than once.
Amy Cashman, Managing Dir.
Martin Dewhurst, Managing Dir.-Financial Svcs & Technology
Rebecca Wynberg, CEO-TNS Qualitative
James Brooks, Dir.-Global Oper.
Matthew Froggatt, Chief Dev. Officer
Heather Payne, Chief Client Officer
Chris Riquier, CEO-Asia Pacific
Ignacio Galceran, CEO-Latin America
Kim MacIlwaine, CEO-Middle East & Africa

GROWTH PLANS/SPECIAL FEATURES:

TNS U.K. Ltd., a subsidiary of Kantar Group and branded as Kantar TNS, is one of the largest market research conglomerates in the world, with operations serving customers in more than 156 countries. The company's expertise includes the fields of automotive, brand, communication, customer strategies, innovation and product development, qualitative and shopper. The firm's business services include a number of surveys, tracking and testing instruments. Connect provides a 360-degree view of brand performance across all touchpoints and marketing tasks, helping to build brand equity by optimizing performance in relation to marketing and competition. Matrix provides a complete view of a target market, identifying and sizing incremental growth opportunities and providing a clear roadmap for action. Concept eValuate is a screening tool that provides guidance and understanding of true opportunity for individual-based investments. Its data technology significantly improves the accuracy of in-market growth predictions, even at the early stages of the innovation process. ConversionModel is a psychological measure of customer commitment. ValueManager, a choice-based simulation software, reveals the product features most valued by consumers. Brand & Communication is a brand and advertising tracking system. Locator unlocks the moments of greatest potential and displays how brands can improve performance and messaging or develop new innovations. NeedScope System measures consumer needs and motivations. Relationship TRI*M identifies and matches up what customers expect with what delivers profitable growth for businesses. Last, Connected Life is an annual study of online behavior across the world to help brands make better marketing decisions.

FINANCIAL DATA: Note: Data for latest year may not have been available at press time.

In U.S. $	2018	2017	2016	2015	2014	2013
Revenue						
R&D Expense						
Operating Income						
Operating Margin %						
SGA Expense						
Net Income						
Operating Cash Flow						
Capital Expenditure						
EBITDA						
Return on Assets %						
Return on Equity %						
Debt to Equity						

CONTACT INFORMATION:
Phone: 44-207-656-5000   Fax:
Toll-Free:
Address: 6 More London Place, London, SE1 2QY United Kingdom

STOCK TICKER/OTHER:
Stock Ticker: Subsidiary   Exchange:
Employees: 8,290   Fiscal Year Ends: 12/31
Parent Company: Kantar Group

SALARIES/BONUSES:
Top Exec. Salary: $ Bonus: $
Second Exec. Salary: $ Bonus: $

OTHER THOUGHTS:
Estimated Female Officers or Directors: 2
Hot Spot for Advancement for Women/Minorities: Y

Sales, profits and employees may be estimates. Financial information, benefits and other data can change quickly and may vary from those stated here.

Torstar Corporation

NAIC Code: 511110

www.torstar.com

TYPES OF BUSINESS:
Communications & Media-Publishing & Printing
Newspapers
Book Publishing
Internet
Television

BRANDS/DIVISIONS/AFFILIATES:
Toronto Star
thestar.com
durhamregion.com
Mississauga News (The)
Barrie Advance
HomeFinder.ca
VerticalScope Holdings Inc
eyeReturn Marketing Inc

CONTACTS: Note: Officers with more than one job title may be intentionally listed here more than once.
John Boynton, CEO
Lorenzo Demarchi, CFO
John Honderich, Director
Ian Oliver, Executive VP
Neil Oliver, Executive VP
Marie Beyette, General Counsel
Jennifer Barber, Senior VP, Divisional

GROWTH PLANS/SPECIAL FEATURES:
Torstar Corporation is a progressive media company that consists of a long history in daily and community newspapers, book publishing and digital businesses. Its current businesses include daily news brands, community brands and digital ventures. The daily news brands segment comprises a portfolio of media businesses, including: Toronto Star, Canada's largest daily print newspaper; and thestar.com, a newspaper website. This division also includes The Hamilton Spectator, the Waterloo Region Record, the St. Catharines Standard, the Niagara Falls Review, the Welland Tribune, the Peterborough Examiner, the StarMetro, the Sing Tao Daily and The Kit. The community brands segment is a community media company with operations in newspapers, digital properties, flyer distribution, consumer shows, magazines, directories and printing. This division has strong ties with the communities it serves. Community brands include durhamregion.com, The Mississauga News, Barrie Advance, gottarent.com, ideal home, Golf & Travel Show, save.ca, Mississauga.com, BusinessTimes and HomeFinder.ca. The digital ventures segment consists of digital businesses outside of the traditional newspaper operations, and includes VerticalScope Holdings, Inc., a Toronto-based vertically focused digital media company specializing in programmatic advertising. VerticalScope provides services in North America through its network of more than 600 user forums and premium content sites, which offer advertisers access to large audiences in verticals such as automotive, powersports, outdoors, home and health. This division also includes eyeReturn Marketing, Inc., a Canadian developer and provider of online advertising services. During 2018, Torstar sold its 50% interest in Workopolis; and announced plans to acquire iPolitics.ca, enhancing its coverage of the federal government.

FINANCIAL DATA: Note: Data for latest year may not have been available at press time.

In U.S. $	2018	2017	2016	2015	2014	2013
Revenue		456,780,300	508,278,900	583,606,100	636,654,600	970,999,700
R&D Expense						
Operating Income		5,312,788	-10,704,220	15,754,370	45,550,050	93,208,590
Operating Margin %		1.16%	-2.10%	2.69%	7.15%	9.59%
SGA Expense		182,439,100	222,063,500	253,601,200	268,231,600	356,335,100
Net Income		-21,642,130	-55,457,460	-299,704,700	128,116,000	-20,761,490
Operating Cash Flow		11,428,320	-7,863,460	28,229,520	47,005,670	59,895,540
Capital Expenditure		8,459,210	13,109,480	22,703,800	15,540,700	17,158,800
EBITDA		10,581,060	-24,361,220	-275,317,500	-19,564,800	27,418,610
Return on Assets %		-5.57%	-11.85%	-43.91%	13.85%	-1.98%
Return on Equity %		-10.19%	-20.09%	-62.87%	20.79%	-3.67%
Debt to Equity						0.22

CONTACT INFORMATION:
Phone: 416 869-4010 Fax: 416 869-4183
Toll-Free:
Address: 1 Yonge St., Toronto, ON M5E 1P9 Canada

SALARIES/BONUSES:
Top Exec. Salary: $ Bonus: $
Second Exec. Salary: $ Bonus: $

STOCK TICKER/OTHER:
Stock Ticker: TS.B Exchange: TSE
Employees: 3,253 Fiscal Year Ends: 12/31
Parent Company:

OTHER THOUGHTS:
Estimated Female Officers or Directors: 10
Hot Spot for Advancement for Women/Minorities: Y

Townsquare Media Inc

NAIC Code: 515112

www.townsquaremedia.com

TYPES OF BUSINESS:
Radio Broadcasting
Online Properties
Live Music Events
Online Marketing Services

BRANDS/DIVISIONS/AFFILIATES:
Oaktree Capital Management LP
Madison Square Garden Company (The)
TasteofCountry.com
Popcrush.com
Screencrush.com
Seize the Deal

CONTACTS:
Note: Officers with more than one job title may be intentionally listed here more than once.

Stuart Rosenstein, CFO
Steven Price, Chairman of the Board
Scott Schatz, Co-Founder
Erik Hellum, COO, Divisional
Dhruv Prasad, Director
Bill Wilson, Director
Claire Yenicay, Executive VP, Divisional
Michael Josephs, Executive VP, Divisional
Christopher Kitchen, Executive VP

GROWTH PLANS/SPECIAL FEATURES:
Townsquare Media, Inc. is a radio broadcasting company focused on acquiring, developing and operating radio stations in small- to mid-sized U.S. markets. It is one of the largest owners of radio stations in the U.S. (third, as of December 2018), with 321 radio stations and more than 330 companion websites in 67 U.S. markets. The company offers a variety of programming that ranges from adult contemporary music to news talk programs and country music. In addition to radio stations, the firm owns more than 200 live music and non-music events, as well as online properties such as TasteofCountry.com, Popcrush.com and Screencrush.com. Seize the Deal is Townsquare Media's proprietary deal and auction platform that offers eCommerce products which are sold by small businesses to consumers and advertisers. Townsquare's interactive division is a digital marketing and solutions business that offers a comprehensive set of products to help local businesses reach more customers, generate leads and grow their online presence across web, mobile and other channels. Townsquare's own expansion strategy is to focus on the acquisition of radio stations in mid-sized markets, where reduced competition facilitates the purchase of stations for sale. Oaktree Capital Management, LP is Townsquare Media's largest stake holder; and The Madison Square Garden Company holds a 12% minority stake. During 2018, Townsquare acquired classic rock station WOUR-FM 96.9 from Galaxy Media.

FINANCIAL DATA:
Note: Data for latest year may not have been available at press time.

In U.S. $	2018	2017	2016	2015	2014	2013
Revenue		507,434,000	516,866,000	441,222,000	373,892,000	268,578,000
R&D Expense						
Operating Income		63,384,000	77,712,000	74,382,000	40,839,000	47,051,000
Operating Margin %		12.49%	15.03%	16.85%	10.92%	17.51%
SGA Expense		33,955,000	30,467,000	31,428,000	62,735,000	21,124,000
Net Income		-11,185,000	23,059,000	9,830,000	-17,372,000	6,386,000
Operating Cash Flow		50,684,000	59,802,000	25,943,000	45,262,000	26,204,000
Capital Expenditure		22,974,000	20,937,000	15,101,000	14,041,000	9,526,000
EBITDA		89,067,000	98,381,000	71,726,000	57,299,000	61,262,000
Return on Assets %		-1.04%	2.15%	.97%	-1.84%	.82%
Return on Equity %		-2.90%	6.13%	2.78%	-6.01%	2.88%
Debt to Equity		1.46	1.44	1.62	1.56	2.78

CONTACT INFORMATION:
Phone: 203-861-0900 Fax:
Toll-Free:
Address: 240 Greenwich Ave., Greenwich, CT 06830 United States

STOCK TICKER/OTHER:
Stock Ticker: TSQ
Employees: 2,950
Parent Company:

Exchange: NYS
Fiscal Year Ends: 12/31

SALARIES/BONUSES:
Top Exec. Salary: $858,147 Bonus: $500,000
Second Exec. Salary: $710,557 Bonus: $450,000

OTHER THOUGHTS:
Estimated Female Officers or Directors:
Hot Spot for Advancement for Women/Minorities:

Sales, profits and employees may be estimates. Financial information, benefits and other data can change quickly and may vary from those stated here.

Trans World Corporation

www.transwc.com

NAIC Code: 721120

TYPES OF BUSINESS:
Casinos and Hotels

BRANDS/DIVISIONS/AFFILIATES:
Trans World Hotels Germany GmbH
American Chance Casinos
Hotel Savannah and Spa
Hotel Columbus
Hotel Auefeld
Hotel Kranichhohe
Hotel Donauwelle

CONTACTS:
Note: Officers with more than one job title may be intentionally listed here more than once.

Rami Ramadan, CEO
Malcolm Sterrett, Director

GROWTH PLANS/SPECIAL FEATURES:
Trans World Corporation owns and operates three full-service casinos and five hotels. All of the company's casinos are located in the Czech Republic: Ceska Kubice, Hate and Dolni Dvoriste. They operate under the brand name American Chance Casinos (ACC), and are situated at border locations drawing customers primarily from Germany and Austria. Each casino has a distinctive design theme, portraying historical American cultural periods: the Frank Lloyd-Wright-inspired Organic Modern in the 1930s for Ceska; the New Orleans in the 1920s for Hate; and the Miami Beach Streamline Modern in the early 1950s for Dolni Dvoriste. Trans World's hotels include: the Hotel Savannah and Spa, a 77-room deluxe hotel located in Hate, Czech Republic; the Hotel Columbus, a 117-room property in Seligenstadt, Germany; the Hotel Auefeld, a 93-room hotel in Hann Munden, Germany; the Hotel Kranichhohe, a 107-room three-star hotel located in Munich, Germany; and the Hotel Donauwelle, a 176-room hotel in Linz, Austria. Hotel Savannah and the casino in Hate comprise a gaming area, guest rooms and spa, as well as banquet halls, full-service restaurants and bars. Subsidiary Trans World Hotels Germany GmbH is the company's holding company of the Hotel Columbus, Hotel Auefeld, Hotel Kranichhohe and Hotel Donauwelle hotels. In April 2018, TWC merged with and became an indirect, wholly-owned subsidiary of Far East Consortium International Limited.

FINANCIAL DATA:
Note: Data for latest year may not have been available at press time.

In U.S. $	2018	2017	2016	2015	2014	2013
Revenue		54,108,000	53,238,000	42,386,000	38,475,000	36,487,000
R&D Expense						
Operating Income						
Operating Margin %						
SGA Expense						
Net Income		1,885,000	6,323,000	3,858,000	2,638,000	2,390,000
Operating Cash Flow						
Capital Expenditure						
EBITDA						
Return on Assets %						
Return on Equity %						
Debt to Equity						

CONTACT INFORMATION:
Phone: 212 983-3355 Fax: 212 983-8129
Toll-Free:
Address: 545 Fifth Ave., Ste. 940, New York, NY 10017 United States

STOCK TICKER/OTHER:
Stock Ticker: TWOC
Employees: 605
Parent Company:

Exchange: PINX
Fiscal Year Ends: 12/31

SALARIES/BONUSES:
Top Exec. Salary: $ Bonus: $
Second Exec. Salary: $ Bonus: $

OTHER THOUGHTS:
Estimated Female Officers or Directors: 2
Hot Spot for Advancement for Women/Minorities:

Sales, profits and employees may be estimates. Financial information, benefits and other data can change quickly and may vary from those stated here.

Trans World Entertainment Corporation

www.twec.com

NAIC Code: 443142

TYPES OF BUSINESS:
Music Stores
CDs, DVDs, Videos & Video Games
Online Sales
Digital Music Content
Used Music & Video Retail

BRANDS/DIVISIONS/AFFILIATES:
f Y e
Suncoast Motion Pictures
fye.com
secondspin.com
etailz
Record Town Inc

CONTACTS:
Note: Officers with more than one job title may be intentionally listed here more than once.

Michael Feurer, CEO
Edwin Sapienza, CFO
Michael Solow, Director
Bruce Eisenberg, Executive VP, Divisional

GROWTH PLANS/SPECIAL FEATURES:

Trans World Entertainment Corporation (TWE) is a retailer of entertainment software, including music, videos and video games and related products in the U.S. The firm operates 260 stores totaling approximately 1.4 million square feet in the U.S., Washington, D.C. and the U.S. Virgin Islands. Mall-based (231) and free-standing (23) stores operate primarily under the f.Y.e. (For Your Entertainment) brand with products including video, music, electronics, trend, video games and related products. In addition, TWE owns six video-only stores predominantly under the Suncoast Motion Pictures brand. These stores specialize in the sale of video and related products, and average about 2,500 square feet. The mall-based stores average 5,200 square feet in size, and free-standing stores average about 10,300 square feet. The company operates two retail websites: fye.com and secondspin.com, with fye.com being the company's flagship site that carries trend, video, music and electronic products; and secondspin.com, which sells CDs, DVDs, Blu-Ray and video games online. In addition, the TWE's etailz business unit operates as a third-party e-commerce market place reseller, primarily through Amazon Marketplace. etailz specializes in using a data-driven approach for market retail analytics to optimize price and inventory. TWE owns 100% of Record Town, Inc., through which it conducts most of its operations. The firm has five merchandise category groups: trend, which accounts for 37.3% of its sales; video, 30.9%; music, 19.3%; electronics, 12.5%; and video games, 0.5%. TWE's distribution center facility is in Albany, New York, through which it ships approximately 77% of its merchandise inventory. The distribution center consists of nearly 39,800 square feet of office space and 141,500 square feet of storage and distribution space.

The firm offers employees health and dental insurance, life insurance, long-term disability coverage, a 401(k) plan and a store merchandise discount.

FINANCIAL DATA:
Note: Data for latest year may not have been available at press time.

In U.S. $	2018	2017	2016	2015	2014	2013
Revenue	442,856,000	353,470,000	334,661,000	358,490,000	393,659,000	458,544,000
R&D Expense						
Operating Income	-24,081,000	-5,032,000	4,570,000	3,775,000	10,375,000	13,550,000
Operating Margin %	-5.43	-1.42%	1.36%	1.05%	2.63%	2.95%
SGA Expense	167,924,000	139,691,000	126,002,000	132,143,000	137,529,000	158,572,000
Net Income	-42,553,000	3,211,000	2,689,000	1,778,000	8,277,000	33,734,000
Operating Cash Flow	-13,000	4,436,000	7,963,000	16,808,000	7,308,000	35,633,000
Capital Expenditure	8,407,000	24,672,000	20,700,000	8,774,000	7,828,000	3,351,000
EBITDA	-28,358,000	6,495,000	9,921,000	8,233,000	14,759,000	40,803,000
Return on Assets %	-15.31%	1.10%	.97%	.60%	2.63%	10.73%
Return on Equity %	-23.89%	1.72%	1.54%	.97%	4.44%	19.69%
Debt to Equity						0.01

CONTACT INFORMATION:
Phone: 518 452-1242   Fax: 518 452-3547
Toll-Free:
Address: 38 Corporate Cir., Albany, NY 12203 United States

SALARIES/BONUSES:
Top Exec. Salary: $700,000   Bonus: $350,000
Second Exec. Salary: $350,000   Bonus: $105,000

STOCK TICKER/OTHER:
Stock Ticker: TWMC   Exchange: NAS
Employees: 3,000   Fiscal Year Ends: 01/31
Parent Company:

OTHER THOUGHTS:
Estimated Female Officers or Directors:
Hot Spot for Advancement for Women/Minorities:

Sales, profits and employees may be estimates. Financial information, benefits and other data can change quickly and may vary from those stated here.

Trans-Lux Corporation

www.trans-lux.com

NAIC Code: 334310

TYPES OF BUSINESS:
Electronic Equipment-Information Displays
LED Lighting

BRANDS/DIVISIONS/AFFILIATES:
TL Vision
Prismatronic

CONTACTS: Note: Officers with more than one job title may be intentionally listed here more than once.
J. Allain, CEO
Angela Toppi, CFO
Glenn Angiolillo, Chairman of the Board
Thomas Brandt, Co-CEO
Rihcard Brandt, Director
Al Miller, Executive VP
Matthew Brandt, Executive VP
Thomas Mahoney, Senior VP
Karl Hirschauer, Senior VP

GROWTH PLANS/SPECIAL FEATURES:
Trans-Lux Corporation designs, manufactures and services light-emitting diode (LED) display and lighting solutions for a wide range of business, sports, residential and government applications. The company's LED displays and lighting solutions have the ability to transform venues into events with the highest levels of performance and cost-efficiency. Trans-Lux operates through three main business areas: scoreboards, displays and LED lighting. The company's scoreboards are installed in thousands of locations worldwide, with a long-life that spans more than 80 years. These products are designed to engage fans and can be customized with a range of colors and enhancements to make installations unique. Trans-Lux's displays inform and advertise in both indoor and outdoor areas, offering versatile and engaging LED displays under the TL Vision and Prismatronic brand lines. TL Vision LED displays range from 1.5mm to 20mm in pitch and can be configured in virtually any size and shape for indoor/outdoor use. Prismatronic is a line of large-scale outdoor displays for billboards and similar large-format display needs. These products are used in sports arenas and stadiums; financial institutions such as brokerage firms, banks, energy companies, insurance companies and mutual fund companies; educational institutions; outdoor advertising companies; corporate and government communication centers; retail outlets; casinos, racetracks and other gaming establishments; airports, train stations, bus terminals and other transportation facilities; movie theaters; health maintenance organizations and in various other applications. LED Lighting provides energy-saving lighting solutions that feature the latest LED technologies, including green lighting solutions that emit less heat, save energy and enable creative designs. This division's LED lighting products also integrate with customer experience solutions for a seamless package delivered directly to the end customer. Trans-Lux manufactures and distributes all its lighting solutions, from single watt vanity lights to 750-watt facility lighting.

FINANCIAL DATA: Note: Data for latest year may not have been available at press time.

In U.S. $	2018	2017	2016	2015	2014	2013
Revenue						
R&D Expense						
Operating Income						
Operating Margin %						
SGA Expense						
Net Income						
Operating Cash Flow						
Capital Expenditure						
EBITDA						
Return on Assets %						
Return on Equity %						
Debt to Equity						

CONTACT INFORMATION:
Phone: Fax:
Toll-Free: 800-243-5544
Address: 135 East 57th St., 14/Fl, New York, NY 10022 United States

STOCK TICKER/OTHER:
Stock Ticker: TNLX
Employees: 80
Parent Company:

Exchange: PINX
Fiscal Year Ends: 12/31

SALARIES/BONUSES:
Top Exec. Salary: $303,590   Bonus: $
Second Exec. Salary: $300,000   Bonus: $

OTHER THOUGHTS:
Estimated Female Officers or Directors: 2
Hot Spot for Advancement for Women/Minorities:

Sales, profits and employees may be estimates. Financial information, benefits and other data can change quickly and may vary from those stated here.

Tribune Media Company

NAIC Code: 515120

www.tribunemedia.com

TYPES OF BUSINESS:
Television Broadcasting
Online News & Information
Radio Broadcasting
TV Programming Development
Media Marketing

BRANDS/DIVISIONS/AFFILIATES:
Tribune Broadcasting
WGN America
Television Food Network GP
CareerBuilder LLC
New Cubs LLC

CONTACTS:
Note: Officers with more than one job title may be intentionally listed here more than once.

Peter Kern, CEO
Chandler Bigelow, CFO
Brian Litman, Chief Accounting Officer
Edward Lazarus, Executive VP
Lawrence Wert, President, Divisional
Gavin Harvey, President, Divisional

GROWTH PLANS/SPECIAL FEATURES:
Tribune Media Company is a diversified media and entertainment business. The firm is comprised of 42 television stations either owned by Tribune Media or by others, but to which it provides certain services. The company also owns a national general entertainment cable network, a radio station, a production studio, a digital and data business, real estate assets and other related assets. Tribune Media operates its business in two segments: television and entertainment and digital and data. The television and entertainment segment provides news, entertainment and sports programming on Tribune Broadcasting-branded local television stations throughout the U.S.; high-quality television series and movies on WGN America; and news, entertainment and sports information through its websites and other digital assets. The digital and data segment provides innovative technology and services that collect, create and distribute video, music, sports and entertainment data primarily through wholesale distribution channels to consumers globally. Tribune Media holds investments in cable and digital assets, including Television Food Network GP, CareerBuilder, LLC and New Cubs, LLC. In December 2018, Tribune agreed to be acquired by Nexstar Media Group, Inc. for $4.1 billion. The combined companies would create the largest local TV company in the U.S.

FINANCIAL DATA:
Note: Data for latest year may not have been available at press time.

In U.S. $	2018	2017	2016	2015	2014	2013
Revenue		1,848,959,000	1,947,930,000	2,010,460,000	1,949,359,000	1,147,240,000
R&D Expense						
Operating Income		79,935,000	223,888,000	122,311,000	301,182,000	199,740,000
Operating Margin %		4.32%	11.49%	6.08%	15.45%	17.41%
SGA Expense		550,193,000	592,220,000	647,600,000	584,274,000	311,447,000
Net Income		197,497,000	14,246,000	-319,918,000	476,663,000	241,555,000
Operating Cash Flow		222,502,000	284,163,000	25,944,000	378,455,000	359,571,000
Capital Expenditure		66,832,000	99,659,000	89,084,000	89,438,000	70,869,000
EBITDA		264,953,000	845,467,000	136,354,000	1,188,150,000	465,238,000
Return on Assets %		2.24%	.14%	-3.02%	4.16%	2.10%
Return on Equity %		5.84%	.38%	-7.09%	9.41%	4.90%
Debt to Equity		0.90	0.95	0.90	0.67	0.76

CONTACT INFORMATION:
Phone: 312-222-9100 Fax: 312-222-1573
Toll-Free:
Address: 515 North State St., Chicago, IL 60654 United States

SALARIES/BONUSES:
Top Exec. Salary: $2,104,616 Bonus: $5,000,000
Second Exec. Salary: $750,000 Bonus: $1,500,000

STOCK TICKER/OTHER:
Stock Ticker: TRCO
Employees: 12,900
Parent Company:
Exchange: NYS
Fiscal Year Ends: 12/31

OTHER THOUGHTS:
Estimated Female Officers or Directors: 3
Hot Spot for Advancement for Women/Minorities: Y

Sales, profits and employees may be estimates. Financial information, benefits and other data can change quickly and may vary from those stated here.

Tribune Publishing Company

www.tribpub.com

NAIC Code: 511110

TYPES OF BUSINESS:
Newspaper Publishers

BRANDS/DIVISIONS/AFFILIATES:
Chicago Tribune
BestReviews
Orlando Sentinel
Sun-Sentinel
Hartford Courant
Tribune Content Agency
The Daily Meal
Baltimore Sun

CONTACTS:
Note: Officers with more than one job title may be intentionally listed here more than once.

Justin Dearborn, CEO
Terry Jimenez, CFO
Cindy Ballard, Chief Human Resources Officer
Malcolm Casselle, CTO
Julie Xanders, General Counsel
Timothy Ryan, Pres.
Tony Hunter, Pres., Divisional
Michael Ferro, Chmn.

GROWTH PLANS/SPECIAL FEATURES:
Tribune Publishing Company, formerly tronc, Inc., and its subsidiaries comprise a diversified media and marketing-solutions company that delivers innovative experiences for audiences and advertisers across all platforms. The firm operates newsrooms in eight markets with titles including the Chicago Tribune, New York Daily News, The Baltimore Sun, Orlando Sentinel, Sun-Sentinel (South Florida), Daily Press (Virginia), The Morning Call (Allentown, Pennsylvania) and the Hartford Courant. Tribune's brands have earned a combined 105 Pulitzer Prizes. Its content covers news, sports, entertainment, business, real estate, travel and more. Tribune Publishing also operates the Tribune Content Agency (TCA) and The Daily Meal. TCA is a syndication and licensing business that provides content solutions for publishers worldwide. The Daily Meal is an online publication covering topics relating to food and drink. Other prominent websites include www.tribpub.com, www.TheDailyMeal.com, www.TheActiveTimes.com and many more. In February 2018, Tribune became the majority owner of BestReviews, a product review company based in San Francisco, California and Reno, Nevada. It announced the sale of The Los Angeles Times and The San Diego Union-Tribune, along with other California properties, to Nan Capital, LLC in June 2018.

FINANCIAL DATA:
Note: Data for latest year may not have been available at press time.

In U.S. $	2018	2017	2016	2015	2014	2013
Revenue		1,524,018,000	1,606,378,000	1,672,819,968	1,707,977,984	1,795,106,944
R&D Expense						
Operating Income						
Operating Margin %						
SGA Expense						
Net Income		5,535,000	6,537,000	-2,765,000	42,288,000	94,094,000
Operating Cash Flow						
Capital Expenditure						
EBITDA						
Return on Assets %						
Return on Equity %						
Debt to Equity						

CONTACT INFORMATION:
Phone: 312-222-9100 Fax:
Toll-Free:
Address: 435 N. Michigan Ave., Chicago, IL 60611 United States

STOCK TICKER/OTHER:
Stock Ticker: TPCO
Employees: 6,581
Parent Company:

Exchange: NYS
Fiscal Year Ends:

SALARIES/BONUSES:
Top Exec. Salary: $ Bonus: $
Second Exec. Salary: $ Bonus: $

OTHER THOUGHTS:
Estimated Female Officers or Directors:
Hot Spot for Advancement for Women/Minorities:

Trusted Media Brands Inc

tmbi.com

NAIC Code: 511120

TYPES OF BUSINESS:
Magazine Publishing
Book Publishing
Television & Video Production
Music Collections
Electronic Media
Direct Marketing
Online Sales

BRANDS/DIVISIONS/AFFILIATES:
Reader's Digest Association, Inc
Reader's Digest Magazine
Taste of Home
Country Woman
Family Handyman (The)
Country
RD.com
Reader's Digest Select Editions

CONTACTS:
Note: Officers with more than one job title may be intentionally listed here more than once.

Bonnie Kintzer, CEO
Zach Friedman, Chief Revenue Officer
Dean D. Durbin, CFO
Alec Casey, CMO
Phyllis Gebhardt, Sr. VP-Human Resources
Vincent Errico, Chief Digital Officer
Andrea Newborn, General Counsel
Albert L. Perruzza, Exec. VP-Bus. Oper.
Susan Fraysse Russ, VP-Global Comm.
Susan Fraysse Russ, Pres., Reader's Digest Foundation

GROWTH PLANS/SPECIAL FEATURES:

Trusted Media Brands, Inc. (TMBI), formerly Reader's Digest Association, Inc., publishes and markets magazines, books, music collections and home videos. Reader's Digest Magazine (the company's flagship monthly) consists of original and previously published articles in condensed form and condensed versions of current full-length books. The company also publishes specialty magazines such as The Family Handyman, Taste of Home, Country and Country Woman; and produces and distributes Reader's Digest Select Editions, general books, recorded music collections and home video products. The company's general books include reference books, cookbooks and how-to and do-it-yourself (DIY) books. Other books pertain to subjects such as history, travel, religion, health, nature, home, computers and puzzles. TMBI's music collections include titles across a broad range of musical styles, released as compilations on CDs internationally. The company also sells home video products featuring travel, natural history, world history and children's animated programs. TMBI conducts marketing via direct mail, direct response television, telemarketing, catalogs, retail and online. Its branded websites include RD.com.

FINANCIAL DATA:
Note: Data for latest year may not have been available at press time.

In U.S. $	2018	2017	2016	2015	2014	2013
Revenue	1,180,000,000	1,105,000,000	1,100,000,000	1,150,000,000	1,125,000,000	1,200,000,000
R&D Expense						
Operating Income						
Operating Margin %						
SGA Expense						
Net Income						
Operating Cash Flow						
Capital Expenditure						
EBITDA						
Return on Assets %						
Return on Equity %						
Debt to Equity						

CONTACT INFORMATION:
Phone: 914-238-1000 Fax: 914-238-4559
Toll-Free: 800-310-6261
Address: Reader's Digest Rd., Pleasantville, NY 10570 United States

STOCK TICKER/OTHER:
Stock Ticker: Private
Employees: 4,700
Parent Company:

Exchange:
Fiscal Year Ends: 12/31

SALARIES/BONUSES:
Top Exec. Salary: $ Bonus: $
Second Exec. Salary: $ Bonus: $

OTHER THOUGHTS:
Estimated Female Officers or Directors: 3
Hot Spot for Advancement for Women/Minorities: Y

Sales, profits and employees may be estimates. Financial information, benefits and other data can change quickly and may vary from those stated here.

Turner Broadcasting System Inc

www.turner.com

NAIC Code: 515210

TYPES OF BUSINESS:
Cable Programming
News Programs
Sports Programs
Internet Sites
Interactive Media

BRANDS/DIVISIONS/AFFILIATES:
AT&T Inc
Warner Media LLC
Boomerang
Cartoon Network
CNN
ELEAGUE
iSreamPlanet
TNT

CONTACTS: Note: Officers with more than one job title may be intentionally listed here more than once.

David Levy, Pres.
Pascal Desroches, CFO
Molly Battin, CMO
Angela Santone, Chief Human Resources Officer
Jack Wakshlag, Chief Research Officer
Louise Sams, General Counsel
Scott Teissler, Chief Digital Tech. Strategy Officer
Kelly Regal, Exec. VP-Corp. Comm.
Stuart Snyder, Pres., Turner Animation, Young Adults & Kids Media
Steve Koonin, Pres., Turner Entertainment Networks
Jim Walton, Pres., CNN Worldwide
John Martin, Chmn.
Gerhard Zeiler, Pres., TBS Int'l

GROWTH PLANS/SPECIAL FEATURES:

Turner Broadcasting System (TBS) produces global news and entertainment programming. The firm is one of the primary subsidiaries of Warner Media LLC, itself a subsidiary of AT&T, Inc. TBS creates and programs on television and other platforms for consumers around the world. U.S. entertainment includes a blend of originals such as news, marquee sports, popular licensed series and movies, classic films and reality programming, as well as animation and kids and youth media. International programming is distributed in nearly 40 languages. Sports websites include tbs.com, NBA.com, NCAA.com and PGA.com and PGATour.com. TBS' network brands include Adult Swim, B-R, Boomerang, Cartoon Network (CN), CNN, ELEAGUE, Film Struck, Great Big Story, HLN, iStreamPlanet, tbs, NBA Digital, NBA, NBA League Pass, March Madness, Super Deluxe, Turner Classics Movies (TCM), TNT, tru TV, Turner Sports, Glitz, HTV, C-ISAT, Much, Space, TCM, TNT Series, tooncast, WB TV, GLOUD and TNT Sports. Currently, TBS and CBS have an alternating agreement through 2024, in which TBS televises the final three games of the NCAA Men's Division Final Four and the National Championship games in even-numbered years, and CBS televises them in odd-numbered years.

Employees are offered medical, vision and dental insurance; flexible spending accounts; disability coverage; transportation reimbursement accounts; a 401(k) plan; tuition reimbursement; adoption assistance; an employee assistance program; health and welln

FINANCIAL DATA: Note: Data for latest year may not have been available at press time.

In U.S. $	2018	2017	2016	2015	2014	2013
Revenue	12,200,000,000	12,081,000,000	11,364,000,000	10,596,000,000	10,396,000,000	9,983,000,000
R&D Expense						
Operating Income						
Operating Margin %						
SGA Expense						
Net Income		4,489,000,000	4,372,000,000	4,087,000,000	3,106,000,000	3,486,000,000
Operating Cash Flow						
Capital Expenditure						
EBITDA						
Return on Assets %						
Return on Equity %						
Debt to Equity						

CONTACT INFORMATION:
Phone: 404-827-1700 Fax:
Toll-Free:
Address: 1 CNN Ctr., Atlanta, GA 30303 United States

STOCK TICKER/OTHER:
Stock Ticker: Subsidiary
Employees: 7,000
Parent Company: AT&T Inc

Exchange:
Fiscal Year Ends: 12/31

SALARIES/BONUSES:
Top Exec. Salary: $ Bonus: $
Second Exec. Salary: $ Bonus: $

OTHER THOUGHTS:
Estimated Female Officers or Directors: 2
Hot Spot for Advancement for Women/Minorities:

TV Azteca SAB de CV

NAIC Code: 515120

www.tvazteca.com.mx

TYPES OF BUSINESS:
Spanish-Language Television Networks
Internet Services
Music Production

BRANDS/DIVISIONS/AFFILIATES:
Grupo Salinas
Azteca Internet
Azteca Uno
Azteca 7
adn40
a+
Monarcas Morelia
Atlast FC

CONTACTS:
Note: Officers with more than one job title may be intentionally listed here more than once.

Benjamin Francisco Salinas Sada, CEO
Esteban Galindez Aguirre, CFO
Joaquin Arrangoiz, Dir.-Strategic Svcs.
Luis. J Echarte, Chmn.-Azteca America
Ricardo Benjamin Salinas Pliego, Chmn.
Martin Breidsprecher, Pres.

GROWTH PLANS/SPECIAL FEATURES:

TV Azteca SA de CV, a subsidiary of Grupo Salinas, is one of the largest producers of Spanish-language television programming in the world and one of the largest television broadcasting companies in Mexico. The firm's programming includes a broad selection of news, sports, music, talk and entertainment programs. These include Spanish-language versions of programs from the U.S., as well as original programming such as news programs, telenovelas, reality programs, talk shows, musical variety shows and sports broadcasts, principally soccer. It operates two open television networks through more than 300 television stations in Mexico; two national channels, Azteca Uno, a channel catered toward women, and Azteca 7, a channel focused on mid- to high-income youth; free-to-air channel adn40, a national 24-hour news service; a+, a regionalized channel offering regions differentiated programs for news and sports; two first-division football teams, Monarcas Morelia and Atlas FC; and the website Azteca Internet. TV Azteca also offers telecommunication services, operates a fiber optic network in Colombia, and is engaged in selling advertising spots and airtime.

FINANCIAL DATA:
Note: Data for latest year may not have been available at press time.

In U.S. $	2018	2017	2016	2015	2014	2013
Revenue		705,419,600	724,148,600	655,945,700	659,079,000	615,069,800
R&D Expense						
Operating Income		151,952,700	116,791,900	57,527,660	136,217,200	148,673,900
Operating Margin %			16.12%	8.77%	20.66%	24.17%
SGA Expense		86,735,650	85,267,720	92,550,900	83,728,430	79,357,540
Net Income		59,345,200	161,009,400	-134,346,800	14,264,230	59,079,140
Operating Cash Flow		68,157,360	200,924,300	59,857,740	135,419,200	33,253,540
Capital Expenditure		60,582,880	51,356,830	70,424,850	91,948,230	59,140,560
EBITDA		183,537,800	6,713,459	11,970,310	134,826,800	173,600,000
Return on Assets %			-.04%	-7.23%	.78%	3.39%
Return on Equity %			-.23%	-25.60%	2.31%	9.61%
Debt to Equity			3.23	1.79	1.06	0.94

CONTACT INFORMATION:
Phone: 52-55-1720-1313 Fax: 52-55-1720-1418
Toll-Free:
Address: Periferico Sur 4121, Colonia Fuentes del Pedregal, Mexico City, DF 14140 Mexico

STOCK TICKER/OTHER:
Stock Ticker: AZTECA CPO
Employees: 6,095
Parent Company: Grupo Salinas

Exchange: MEX
Fiscal Year Ends: 12/31

SALARIES/BONUSES:
Top Exec. Salary: $ Bonus: $
Second Exec. Salary: $ Bonus: $

OTHER THOUGHTS:
Estimated Female Officers or Directors:
Hot Spot for Advancement for Women/Minorities:

Sales, profits and employees may be estimates. Financial information, benefits and other data can change quickly and may vary from those stated here.

Plunkett Research, Ltd. 475

TV Tokyo Holdings Corporation

www.tv-tokyo.co.jp.e.ck.hp.transer.com/kaisha/

NAIC Code: 515120

TYPES OF BUSINESS:
Television Broadcasting

BRANDS/DIVISIONS/AFFILIATES:
TV Tokyo Holdings Corporation
Teleto
TV TOKYO Music Inc
TV TOKYO Medianet Inc
TV TOKYO Commercial Inc
TV TOKYO Art & Lighting Inc
TV TOKYO Systems Inc
TV TOKYO Production Inc

CONTACTS:
Note: Officers with more than one job title may be intentionally listed here more than once.
Shigeru Komago, CEO
Yuji Kamiya, Managing Dir.-Financial Bureau
Naohiro Nomura, Sr. Managing Dir.
Satoshi Kikuchi, Sr. Managing Dir.
Naomichi Fujinobu, Sr. Managing Dir.
Masaaki Takashima, Managing Dir.

GROWTH PLANS/SPECIAL FEATURES:
TV TOKYO Corporation, also known as Teleto, is engaged in the production and ground-based broadcasting of television programs of various genres. In addition to terrestrial broadcasting, the company is also in the business of sales of secondary rights to broadcast programs and other broadcast-related rights. TV TOKYO manages its single digital station, Channel 7 (JOTX-DTV). It is also a leading member of the TX Network, made up of six broadcasting stations. Television programs includes news, economic programs, documentaries, information programs, sports, children's programming, variety shows, travel and gourmet, music, movie and drama and special programs. The company additionally broadcasts an abundance of anime programming. The company has branches overseas, including New York, Washington, London, Moscow, Seoul, Beijing and Shanghai. Subsidiaries of the firm include TV TOKYO Music, Inc., a music production and music channel company; TV TOKYO Medianet, Inc., a producer of programming and animation shows; and TV TOKYO Commercial, Inc., a producer of commercial and advertising media. Other subsidiaries include TV TOKYO Art & Lighting, Inc.; TV TOKYO Systems, Inc.; TV TOKYO Production, Inc.; TV TOKYO Direct, Inc.; TV TOKYO Human, Inc.; Technomax, Inc.; TV TOKYO Business Service, Inc.; AT-X, Inc.; TV TOKYO AMERICA, Inc.; BS TV TOKYO; TV TOKYO Communications Corporation; Nikkei Visual Images, Inc.; InteracTV Co. Ltd.; and Niddei CNBC Japan Inc. TV TOKYO Corporation itself is a subsidiary of broadcast holding company, TV TOKYO Holdings Corporation.

FINANCIAL DATA: *Note: Data for latest year may not have been available at press time.*

In U.S. $	2018	2017	2016	2015	2014	2013
Revenue	1,354,830,000	1,314,090,000	1,254,510,000	1,184,980,000	1,047,265,746	982,386,987
R&D Expense						
Operating Income						
Operating Margin %						
SGA Expense						
Net Income	55,792,400	39,461,000	43,328,000	28,440,000	25,158,730	22,782,040
Operating Cash Flow						
Capital Expenditure						
EBITDA						
Return on Assets %						
Return on Equity %						
Debt to Equity						

CONTACT INFORMATION:
Phone: 81-3-6632-7777 Fax:
Toll-Free:
Address: 3-2-1 Ropporgi, Minato-ku, Tokyo, 106-8007 Japan

STOCK TICKER/OTHER:
Stock Ticker: 9413   Exchange: Tokyo
Employees: 1,400   Fiscal Year Ends: 03/31
Parent Company: TV Tokyo Holdings Corporation

SALARIES/BONUSES:
Top Exec. Salary: $ Bonus: $
Second Exec. Salary: $ Bonus: $

OTHER THOUGHTS:
Estimated Female Officers or Directors:
Hot Spot for Advancement for Women/Minorities:

Sales, profits and employees may be estimates. Financial information, benefits and other data can change quickly and may vary from those stated here.

TVA Group Inc

NAIC Code: 515120

tva.canoe.com

TYPES OF BUSINESS:
Television Broadcasting
Television Production-French Language
Magazine Publishing & Editing
Media Distribution

BRANDS/DIVISIONS/AFFILIATES:
Quebecor Media Inc
TVA Nouvelles
JE

CONTACTS:
Note: Officers with more than one job title may be intentionally listed here more than once.

Sophie Riendeau, Assistant Secretary
Dominique Poulin-Gouin, Assistant Secretary
Denis Rozon, CFO
Sylvie Lalande, Chairman of the Board
A. Lavigne, Director
Michel Trudel, President, Divisional
France Lauziere, President
Marc Tremblay, Secretary
Jean-Francois Reid, Vice President, Divisional
Veronique Mercier, Vice President, Divisional
Serge Fortin, Vice President, Divisional
Daniel Boudreau, Vice President, Divisional
Donald Lizotte, Vice President, Divisional
Lyne Robitaille, Vice President, Subsidiary

GROWTH PLANS/SPECIAL FEATURES:

TVA Group, Inc., a subsidiary of Quebecor Media, Inc., is an integrated communications company with operations in broadcasting, teleshopping, multimedia, publishing, merchandising and the production and distribution of audiovisual content. The firm's broadcasting and production segment creates, produces and broadcasts entertainment (including commercial products), information and public affairs programming. It also operates a French-language television network, provides related specialty services, markets digital products associated with a variety of brands, and distributes audio/visual products and films. TVA Nouvelles is this division's news segment, offering nightly local and national (Canada) newscasts as well as a news magazine program called JE. TVA's magazine segment publishes magazines in fields such as arts, entertainment, television, fashion, sports and decor. It engages in marketing digital products that are associated with various magazine brands, provides custom publishing services, commercial print production and pre-media services. The film production and audiovisual segment offers soundstage and equipment rental, dubbing services, post-production services, visual effects and distribution services.

FINANCIAL DATA:
Note: Data for latest year may not have been available at press time.

In U.S. $	2018	2017	2016	2015	2014	2013
Revenue		437,507,000	438,366,900	437,642,800	325,948,900	330,011,600
R&D Expense						
Operating Income		23,375,230	7,003,591	10,293,940	5,432,235	29,038,190
Operating Margin %		5.34%	1.59%	2.35%	1.66%	8.79%
SGA Expense		111,228,000	119,532,900	118,218,200	93,734,610	97,012,340
Net Income		-11,834,140	-29,568,660	-40,972,490	-30,483,430	11,682,050
Operating Cash Flow		24,697,300	30,904,090	70,699,180	27,217,560	19,495,800
Capital Expenditure		17,372,470	23,270,620	19,691,660	18,285,750	14,280,200
EBITDA		13,263,790	-694,424	-14,013,120	-10,947,560	36,876,430
Return on Assets %		-2.81%	-6.52%	-8.92%	-7.31%	3.07%
Return on Equity %		-5.91%	-13.59%	-19.48%	-14.51%	5.48%
Debt to Equity		0.20	0.22	0.22	0.28	

CONTACT INFORMATION:
Phone: 514 598-2808　　Fax: 514 598-6085
Toll-Free:
Address: 1600, Boul de Maisonneuve E., Montreal, QC H2L 4P2 Canada

STOCK TICKER/OTHER:
Stock Ticker: TVA.B
Employees: 1,448
Parent Company: Quebecor Medica Inc

Exchange: TSE
Fiscal Year Ends: 12/31

SALARIES/BONUSES:
Top Exec. Salary: $　　Bonus: $
Second Exec. Salary: $　　Bonus: $

OTHER THOUGHTS:
Estimated Female Officers or Directors: 2
Hot Spot for Advancement for Women/Minorities: Y

Sales, profits and employees may be estimates. Financial information, benefits and other data can change quickly and may vary from those stated here.

Plunkett Research, Ltd.

Twentieth Century Fox Film Corporation
www.foxmovies.com

NAIC Code: 512110

TYPES OF BUSINESS:
Movie Production & Distribution
Animated Films
Television Production & Distribution
Video & DVD Distribution

BRANDS/DIVISIONS/AFFILIATES:
Walt Disney Co
Twenty-First Century Fox Inc
20th Century
Avatar
Blue Sky Studios
Fox Star Studios
Fox Studios Australia
Regency Enterprises

CONTACTS: Note: Officers with more than one job title may be intentionally listed here more than once.
Stacey Snider, CEO
Chris Petrikin, Sr. VP-Corp. Comm.

GROWTH PLANS/SPECIAL FEATURES:
Twentieth Century Fox Film Corporation (20th Century) is an American film studio that produces and distributes films in theaters. The company operates as a subsidiary of Twenty-First Century Fox, Inc., itself a subsidiary of Walt Disney Co., and has been making films for more than 75 years. 20th Century is a member of the Motion Picture Association of America, a trade association that represents the six major Hollywood studios. From the company's first Cinemascope production, The Robe, which was produced in 1953, to Avatar, its highest-grossing picture of all time, the firm has utilized innovative technology in each of its films. Currently, digital technology is at the forefront of the filmmaker's pathway. High-grossing films by the company include, but are not limited to: Titanic, Star Wars, Home Alone, X Men: Apocalypse, Dawn of the Planet of the Apes and Kung Fu Panda 3. The company also sells movies and television content DVD or Blu-ray products through its online store. 20th Century subsidiaries include: Blue Sky Studios, a computer animation film studio based in Greenwich, Connecticut; Fox Star Studios, a movie production and distribution company based in India; Fox Studios Australia, a movie studio based in Sydney; and 80%-owned Regency Enterprises, a film and television studio based in Hollywood, California.

FINANCIAL DATA: Note: Data for latest year may not have been available at press time.

In U.S. $	2018	2017	2016	2015	2014	2013
Revenue	9,010,000,000	9,000,000,000	8,650,000,000	9,525,000,000	9,679,000,000	8,642,000,000
R&D Expense						
Operating Income						
Operating Margin %						
SGA Expense						
Net Income						
Operating Cash Flow						
Capital Expenditure						
EBITDA						
Return on Assets %						
Return on Equity %						
Debt to Equity						

CONTACT INFORMATION:
Phone: 310-277-2211 Fax: 310-203-1558
Toll-Free:
Address: 10201 W. Pico Blvd., Los Angeles, CA 90035 United States

SALARIES/BONUSES:
Top Exec. Salary: $ Bonus: $
Second Exec. Salary: $ Bonus: $

STOCK TICKER/OTHER:
Stock Ticker: Subsidiary
Employees:
Parent Company: Walt Disney Co

Exchange:
Fiscal Year Ends: 06/30

OTHER THOUGHTS:
Estimated Female Officers or Directors:
Hot Spot for Advancement for Women/Minorities: Y

Sales, profits and employees may be estimates. Financial information, benefits and other data can change quickly and may vary from those stated here.

Twenty-First Century Fox Inc (21st Century Fox)
www.21cf.com

NAIC Code: 512110

TYPES OF BUSINESS:
Motion Picture and Video Production
Cable Network Programming
Satellite Direct Broadcasting
Sports Programming

BRANDS/DIVISIONS/AFFILIATES:
Fox News
Fox Television Stations Inc
FOX Broadcasting Company
FOX Affiliates
MyNetworkTV
National Geographic Partners LLC
Sky plc
21st Century Fox

CONTACTS:
Note: Officers with more than one job title may be intentionally listed here more than once.

James Murdoch, CEO
John Nallen, CFO
Keith Murdoch, Chairman of the Board, Subsidiary
Lachlan Murdoch, Co-Chairman
Charles Carey, Director
Viet Dinh, Other Executive Officer

GROWTH PLANS/SPECIAL FEATURES:
Twenty-First Century Fox, Inc. (21st Century Fox) is a global media and entertainment company. The firm divides its operations into four segments: cable network programming (CNP); television (TV); filmed entertainment (FE); and other corporate and eliminations (OCE). CNP produces and licenses news, business news, sports, general entertainment and movie programming for distribution primarily through cable television systems, direct broadcast satellite operators and telecommunications companies. This segment includes cable networks such as FOX News, FSN (Fox Sports Net, Inc.), FX, Fox Sports Racing, Fox Soccer Plus and National Geographic U.S. The TV segment is engaged in the operation of broadcast TV stations and the broadcasting of network programming. Operating in this segment are Fox Television Stations, Inc. owning and operating 28 stations; FOX Broadcasting Company, providing 15 hours of prime-time programming each week to FOX Affiliates; and MyNetworkTV, a programming distribution service. FE is engaged in the production and acquisition of live-action and animated motion pictures for distribution and licensing in all formats in all entertainment media worldwide and the production and licensing of television programming worldwide. In fiscal 2018, this division placed 19 motion pictures in general release in the U.S., with plans to release 20 in 2019, including X-Men: Dark Phoenix, The Aftermath and The Hate U Give. 21st Century Fox's joint venture with National Geographic Society (NGS), called National Geographic Partners, LLC, oversees all of NGS's media and consumer-based operations. 21st Century Fox holds a 73% stake in the company. In July 2018, The Walt Disney Company and 21st Century Fox shareholders approved the $71.3 billion acquisition of Fox's Fox Entertainment Group, FX Networks, National Geographic Partners, Star TV, Sky plc and Hulu assets; additionally, the U.S. Justice Department gave its approval contingent upon Fox's regional sports networks assets being sold to third parties.

FINANCIAL DATA:
Note: Data for latest year may not have been available at press time.

In U.S. $	2018	2017	2016	2015	2014	2013
Revenue	30,400,000,000	28,500,000,000	27,326,000,000	28,987,000,000	31,867,000,000	27,675,000,000
R&D Expense						
Operating Income	6,379,000,000	6,555,000,000	5,992,000,000	5,906,000,000	5,488,000,000	5,375,000,000
Operating Margin %		23.00%	21.92%	20.37%	17.22%	19.42%
SGA Expense	3,668,000,000	3,617,000,000	3,675,000,000	3,784,000,000	4,129,000,000	4,007,000,000
Net Income	4,464,000,000	2,952,000,000	2,755,000,000	8,306,000,000	4,514,000,000	7,097,000,000
Operating Cash Flow	4,227,000,000	3,785,000,000	3,048,000,000	3,617,000,000	2,964,000,000	3,002,000,000
Capital Expenditure	551,000,000	377,000,000	263,000,000	424,000,000	678,000,000	622,000,000
EBITDA	6,242,000,000	6,461,000,000	5,868,000,000	11,781,000,000	7,452,000,000	10,596,000,000
Return on Assets %		5.95%	5.59%	15.84%	8.53%	13.19%
Return on Equity %		20.09%	17.84%	47.95%	26.23%	34.05%
Debt to Equity		1.23	1.41	1.09	1.04	0.96

CONTACT INFORMATION:
Phone: 212-852-7000 Fax:
Toll-Free:
Address: 1211 Avenue of the Americas, New York, NY 10036 United States

STOCK TICKER/OTHER:
Stock Ticker: FOX
Employees: 22,400
Parent Company:

Exchange: NAS
Fiscal Year Ends: 06/30

SALARIES/BONUSES:
Top Exec. Salary: $7,100,000 Bonus: $
Second Exec. Salary: $3,000,000 Bonus: $

OTHER THOUGHTS:
Estimated Female Officers or Directors: 4
Hot Spot for Advancement for Women/Minorities: Y

UBM plc

NAIC Code: 511120

www.ubm.com

TYPES OF BUSINESS:
Diversified Publishing
Market Research
Press Release Distribution
Business-to-Business Publishing
Media Investments
Database Management

BRANDS/DIVISIONS/AFFILIATES:
UBM Americas
UBM Asia
UBM EMEA
Grupo CanalEnergia
Shanghai International Franchise Exhibition
ExpoMed
Live Healthcare

CONTACTS:
Note: Officers with more than one job title may be intentionally listed here more than once.

Tim Cobbold, CEO
Marina Wyatt, CFO
Eleanor Phillips, Group Dir.-Human Resources
Simon Hollins, CIO
Anne Siddell, Corp. Sec.
Andrew Crow, Dir.-Group Oper.
Peter Bancroft, Dir.-Comm.
Kate Postans, Head-Investor Rel.
James Davies, Head-Strategic Finance
Neil Mepham, Head-Mergers & Acquisitions and Taxation
Jane Risby-Rose, Exec. VP-UBM Events
Philip Chapnick, Chief Representative-UBM China
Simon Foster, CEO-UBM Live
Greg Lock, Chmn.
Jime Essink, CEO-UBM Asia

GROWTH PLANS/SPECIAL FEATURES:

UBM plc is a market research, news distribution and professional media company offering a range of market information services. The company has employees in more than 20 countries. UBM divides its business into three geographical groups: UBM Americas, UBM Asia and UBM EMEA (Europe, Middle East and Africa). UBM Americas delivers events and marketing services in the fashion, technology, licensing, advanced manufacturing, automotive/powersports, healthcare, veterinary and pharmaceutical industries, among others. This segment increases business effectiveness for customers and audiences through meaningful experiences, knowledge and connections. It includes UBM Brazil's market-leading events in construction, cargo transportation, logistics, international trade and agricultural production; and UBM Mexico's construction, advanced manufacturing and hospitality services shows. UBM Asia is the region's leading exhibition organizer, as well as a major commercial organizer in China, India and Malaysia. This division is headquartered in Hong Kong, and organizes more than 290 events across major market sectors, including trade fairs, conferences, trade publications and vertical portals. UBM EMEA connects people and creates opportunities for companies across five continents to develop new business, meet customers, launch new products, promote their brands and expand their markets. This division's exhibitions, shows, conferences, awards programs, publications, websites and training and certification programs are an integral part of the marketing plans of companies across seven industry sectors. In 2018, UBM acquired Grupo CanalEnergia, an events and media company in Brazil focusing on the energy sector, in March 2018; a 70% interest in Shanghai International Franchise Exhibition, a biannual franchising event in China with over 450 brand and more than 50,200 visitors, in June 2018; ExpoMed, an annual healthcare exhibition each June in Mexico City, in June 2018; and Live Healthcare, a platform that connects members of the healthcare industry, in June 2018.

FINANCIAL DATA:
Note: Data for latest year may not have been available at press time.

In U.S. $	2018	2017	2016	2015	2014	2013
Revenue		1,332,545,024	1,146,661,120	1,022,959,872	991,602,752	1,054,848,512
R&D Expense						
Operating Income						
Operating Margin %						
SGA Expense						
Net Income		193,989,008	653,052,032	128,351,632	199,569,520	142,834,368
Operating Cash Flow						
Capital Expenditure						
EBITDA						
Return on Assets %						
Return on Equity %						
Debt to Equity						

CONTACT INFORMATION:
Phone: 44-20-7921-5000   Fax:
Toll-Free:
Address: Ludgate House, 240 Blackfriars Rd., London, SE1 8BF United Kingdom

STOCK TICKER/OTHER:
Stock Ticker: UBMOF
Employees: 3,933
Parent Company:

Exchange: PINX
Fiscal Year Ends: 12/31

SALARIES/BONUSES:
Top Exec. Salary: $ Bonus: $
Second Exec. Salary: $ Bonus: $

OTHER THOUGHTS:
Estimated Female Officers or Directors: 4
Hot Spot for Advancement for Women/Minorities: Y

Sales, profits and employees may be estimates. Financial information, benefits and other data can change quickly and may vary from those stated here.

United Online Inc

NAIC Code: 517110

www.untd.com

TYPES OF BUSINESS:
Internet Service Provider

BRANDS/DIVISIONS/AFFILIATES:
B Riley Financial Inc
NetZero
Juno
NetZero Mobile Broadband
NetZero Home Wireless Broadband
NetZero Hotspot
Juno Turbo

CONTACTS:
Note: Officers with more than one job title may be intentionally listed here more than once.

Edward Zinser, CFO
Howard Phanstiel, Director
Mark Harrington, Executive VP
Shahir Fakiri, General Manager, Divisional
Bryant Riley, Chmn.-B. Riley Financial, Inc.

GROWTH PLANS/SPECIAL FEATURES:

United Online, Inc., a subsidiary of B. Riley Financial, Inc., provides consumer products and internet and media services over the internet. These products feature value-priced internet access through the NetZero and Juno brands. Both brands offer a variety of plans, and customers can choose the option that best meets their connection needs. NetZero Wireless offers the NetZero Mobile Broadband and NetZero Home Wireless Broadband services. NetZero Mobile Broadband provides high-speed, affordable internet access to on-the-go consumers. There are four value-priced NetZero Mobile Broadband plans to choose from. Customers are not required to sign a contract, cannot incur overage charges and can upgrade their data plan at any time. New customers can try the service free for up to one year with the purchase of a NetZero Hotspot or NetZero Stick. NetZero Home Wireless Broadband is a secure, wireless internet access service designed for home or office use. NetZero and Juno each offer four types of nationwide dial-up service. The Free service provides 10 hours of access each month free of charge and includes NetZero email. The Basic service provides unlimited access along with email and spam protection. Customers who purchase the Accelerated Dial-Up service (either NetZero HiSpeed or Juno Turbo) can surf the web at up to 5 times the speed of standard dial-up. The Toll-free service allows customers who live in hard to serve areas to connect to the internet using a toll-free 800 access number. DSL service is available in select cities and includes Norton Antivirus online and MegaMail with built-in spam and email virus protection. Additionally, United Online provides advertising solutions to marketers with brand and direct response objectives through a full suite of display, search, email, and text-link opportunities across its internet properties.

FINANCIAL DATA:
Note: Data for latest year may not have been available at press time.

In U.S. $	2018	2017	2016	2015	2014	2013
Revenue	193,000,000	191,000,000	184,400,000	151,118,000	217,244,992	233,614,000
R&D Expense						
Operating Income						
Operating Margin %						
SGA Expense						
Net Income			2,000,100	29,973,000	-5,429,000	-82,167,000
Operating Cash Flow						
Capital Expenditure						
EBITDA						
Return on Assets %						
Return on Equity %						
Debt to Equity						

CONTACT INFORMATION:
Phone: 818 287-3000   Fax: 818 287-3001
Toll-Free:
Address: 21255 Burbank Blvd, Ste 400, Woodland Hills, CA 91367 United States

STOCK TICKER/OTHER:
Stock Ticker: Subsidiary
Employees: 625
Parent Company: B Riley Financial Inc

Exchange:
Fiscal Year Ends: 12/31

SALARIES/BONUSES:
Top Exec. Salary: $ Bonus: $
Second Exec. Salary: $ Bonus: $

OTHER THOUGHTS:
Estimated Female Officers or Directors:
Hot Spot for Advancement for Women/Minorities:

United Talent Agency Inc

www.unitedtalent.com

NAIC Code: 711410

TYPES OF BUSINESS:
Talent Agency

BRANDS/DIVISIONS/AFFILIATES:
Circle Talent Agency
Civic Center Media

CONTACTS: Note: Officers with more than one job title may be intentionally listed here more than once.
Jeremy Zimmer, CEO
Christopher L. Day, Head-Corp. Comm.
Tracey Jacobs, Head-Talent
David Kramer, Head-Motion Picture Literary
Jay Sures, Head-Television
Jim Berkus, Chmn.

GROWTH PLANS/SPECIAL FEATURES:
United Talent Agency, Inc., commonly known as UTA, is a talent representation agency based in California. It is one of the largest talent agencies in the U.S., generally counted as one of the big four. UTA's business structure is designed to spread ownership among its top agents. The firm represents talent in all areas of entertainment, including music, television, movies, books, commercials, licensing, live entertainment, video games and digital media. UTA also represents behind-the-scenes personnel such as gaffers, key grips, editors, directors of photography and art directors. Among the celebrities on the firm's client roster have included Harrison Ford, Seth Rogan, Anthony Hopkins, Kirsten Dunst, January Jones, Benedict Cumberbatch, Paul Rudd, Elizabeth Banks, Daniel Radcliffe and Mark Ruffalo. Additionally, the firm searches for internet video talent through websites such as YouTube and finds work for individuals it discovers. The company operates an agent training program that trains individuals interested in becoming talent agents. After completion of the highly-competitive program, trainees may be promoted to agent status within the firm. UTA has offices in Los Angeles, New York, London, Nashville and Miami, U.S., as well as in Malmo, Sweden. During 2018, UTA acquired Circle Talent Agency, which focuses on dance and electronic music. That October, UTA announced the formation of a joint venture with Valence Media and its media rights division to develop, produce and finance TV series and partner with creative talent. The JV will be called Civic Center Media, and UTA will hold a minority stake.

FINANCIAL DATA: Note: Data for latest year may not have been available at press time.

In U.S. $	2018	2017	2016	2015	2014	2013
Revenue	237,000,000	225,000,000	216,100,000	200,000,000	180,000,000	175,000,000
R&D Expense						
Operating Income						
Operating Margin %						
SGA Expense						
Net Income						
Operating Cash Flow						
Capital Expenditure						
EBITDA						
Return on Assets %						
Return on Equity %						
Debt to Equity						

CONTACT INFORMATION:
Phone: 310-273-6700 Fax: 310-247-1111
Toll-Free:
Address: 9336 Civic Ctr. Dr., Beverly Hills, CA 90210 United States

STOCK TICKER/OTHER:
Stock Ticker: Private
Employees: 880
Parent Company:

Exchange:
Fiscal Year Ends:

SALARIES/BONUSES:
Top Exec. Salary: $ Bonus: $
Second Exec. Salary: $ Bonus: $

OTHER THOUGHTS:
Estimated Female Officers or Directors:
Hot Spot for Advancement for Women/Minorities:

Sales, profits and employees may be estimates. Financial information, benefits and other data can change quickly and may vary from those stated here.

Universal Music Group Inc

NAIC Code: 512230

www.universalmusic.com

TYPES OF BUSINESS:
Music Production & Distribution
Recorded Music Sales
Music Publishing

BRANDS/DIVISIONS/AFFILIATES:
Vivendi SA
Interscope Records
Island Records
Def Jam Recordings
Deutsche Grammophon
Decca Broadway
Universal Music Classical Management & Productions
Universal Music Publishing Group

CONTACTS:
Note: Officers with more than one job title may be intentionally listed here more than once.

Lucian Grainge, CEO
Michele Anthony, Exec. VP
Boyd Muir, CFO
Andrew Kronfeld, VP-Mktg.
Gautam Srivastava, VP-Human Resources
Michael Nash, VP-Digital Strategy
Rob Wells, Pres., Global Digital Bus.
Pascal Negre, CEO-Universal Music France
Zach Horowitz, Chmn.
Sandy Monteiro, Pres., Southeast Asia
Lucian Grainge, Chmn.
Max Hole, Chmn.

GROWTH PLANS/SPECIAL FEATURES:

Universal Music Group, Inc. (UMG), a subsidiary of Vivendi SA, is a music recording and publishing company with a catalog of over 2 million titles. The firm develops, markets, sells and distributes recorded music through a network of joint ventures, subsidiaries and licensees in over 60 countries. UMG adult contemporary music labels include Interscope Records, Geffen Records, A&M, Island Records, Def Jam Recordings, Mercury Records and Polydor Records. Additionally, the company owns classical music record labels such as Deutsche Grammophon, Decca Records and Universal Classics. The classical division also controls the firm's Broadway catalog and contemporary recordings under the Decca Broadway label, including Wicked, Les Miserables and Phantom of the Opera. The Verve Music Group is UMG's jazz recording company. Through Universal Music Classical Management and Productions, UMG manages classical artists. The company's Universal Music Publishing Group is a leading global music publishing operation, with offices in more than 35 countries. PolyGram Entertainment is UMG's film and television division.

FINANCIAL DATA:
Note: Data for latest year may not have been available at press time.

In U.S. $	2018	2017	2016	2015	2014	2013
Revenue	5,660,000,000	5,600,000,000	5,570,000,000	5,410,000,000	5,121,250,000	5,825,596,676
R&D Expense						
Operating Income						
Operating Margin %						
SGA Expense						
Net Income						
Operating Cash Flow						
Capital Expenditure						
EBITDA						
Return on Assets %						
Return on Equity %						
Debt to Equity						

CONTACT INFORMATION:
Phone: 310-865-5000   Fax:
Toll-Free:
Address: 2220 Colorado Ave., Santa Monica, CA 90404 United States

SALARIES/BONUSES:
Top Exec. Salary: $ Bonus: $
Second Exec. Salary: $ Bonus: $

STOCK TICKER/OTHER:
Stock Ticker: Subsidiary   Exchange:
Employees: 7,400   Fiscal Year Ends: 12/31
Parent Company: Vivendi SA

OTHER THOUGHTS:
Estimated Female Officers or Directors: 1
Hot Spot for Advancement for Women/Minorities:

Universal Pictures

www.universalpictures.com

NAIC Code: 512110

TYPES OF BUSINESS:
Film Production & Distribution
Online Video Distribution

BRANDS/DIVISIONS/AFFILIATES:
Comcast Corporation
NBCUniversal Inc
Focus Features LLC
Illumination
Universal Studios
Amblin Partners

CONTACTS:
Note: Officers with more than one job title may be intentionally listed here more than once.

Jimmy Horowitz, Pres.
Stephen B. Burke, CEO-NBC Universal LLC
Donna Langley, Chmn.

GROWTH PLANS/SPECIAL FEATURES:

Universal Pictures, also known as Universal Studios, creates and distributes theatrical and non-theatrical films. The company is owned by Comcast Corporation, and operates as a subsidiary of NBCUniversal, Inc. Universal Pictures produces a variety of movies, including internally-developed titles, co-productions, local acquisitions, specialty motion pictures, direct-to-video titles, specialty videos, classic titles and related consumer products. Previous films have included Academy Award-winning movies such as A Beautiful Mind, The Pianist and Lost in Translation as well as King Kong, Brokeback Mountain, Ray, The Producers and Atonement. Films scheduled for 2019 release include: Glass, Happy Death Day 2U, How to Train Your Dragon: The Hidden World and The Secret Life of Pets 2, all of which may be co-produced with other companies. Focus Features, LLC, the specialty film unit of Universal Pictures, produces, acquires, sells, internationally distributes and finances motion pictures. The company also runs Illumination, a production company dedicated to family films, which was engaged in the November 2018 release of Dr. Seuss' The Grinch. Universal Pictures has a joint venture with Syfy, also owned by NBC Universal, which produces science fiction, fantasy, supernatural and horror genre films. In addition, Universal Pictures holds a minority stake in Amblin Partners, which encompasses the DreamWorks Pictures label within DreamWorks Animation.

The firm offers employees medical, dental and vision coverage; domestic partner benefits; prescription coverage; a 401(k) and pension plans; flexible spending accounts; life insurance; and health club discounts.

FINANCIAL DATA:
Note: Data for latest year may not have been available at press time.

In U.S. $	2018	2017	2016	2015	2014	2013
Revenue	6,600,000,000	6,500,000,000	6,360,000,000	7,287,000,000	5,008,000,000	5,452,000,000
R&D Expense						
Operating Income						
Operating Margin %						
SGA Expense						
Net Income						
Operating Cash Flow						
Capital Expenditure						
EBITDA						
Return on Assets %						
Return on Equity %						
Debt to Equity						

CONTACT INFORMATION:
Phone: 818-777-1000 Fax: 818-777-6431
Toll-Free:
Address: 100 Universal City Plz., Universal City, CA 91608 United States

STOCK TICKER/OTHER:
Stock Ticker: Subsidiary
Employees:
Parent Company: Comcast Corporation
Exchange:
Fiscal Year Ends: 12/31

SALARIES/BONUSES:
Top Exec. Salary: $ Bonus: $
Second Exec. Salary: $ Bonus: $

OTHER THOUGHTS:
Estimated Female Officers or Directors: 1
Hot Spot for Advancement for Women/Minorities:

Sales, profits and employees may be estimates. Financial information, benefits and other data can change quickly and may vary from those stated here.

Univision Communications Inc

NAIC Code: 515120

www.univision.com

TYPES OF BUSINESS:
Spanish Television Broadcasting
Cable Television Programming
Online Portal
Radio Broadcasting

BRANDS/DIVISIONS/AFFILIATES:
Broadcast Media Partners Holdings Inc
Univision Network
Univision
Unimas
Univision+DN
TLNovelas Univision
Uforia
UCI Studios

CONTACTS:
Note: Officers with more than one job title may be intentionally listed here more than once.

Vincent Sadusky, CEO
Jessica Rodriguez, Pres.
Peter H. Lori, CFO
Steve Mandala, Pres.-Sales & Mktg.
Margaret Lazo, Chief Human Resources Officer
Sameer Deen, Chief Digital Officer
John W. Eck, Exec. VP-Tech., Oper. & Eng.
Jonathan Schwartz, General Counsel
Beau Ferrari, Exec. VP-Oper.
Tonia O'Connor, Pres., Content Dist. & Corp. Bus. Dev.
Monica Talan, Exec. VP-Corp. Comm. & Public Rel.
Peter H. Lori, Chief Acct. Officer
Jessica Rodriguez, Exec. VP-Program Scheduling & Promotions
Alberto Ciurana, Pres., Programming & Content
Keith Turner, Pres., Sales & Mktg.
Kevin Cuddihy, Pres., Univision Television Group
Henry Ahn, Pres.-Content Distribution

GROWTH PLANS/SPECIAL FEATURES:
Univision Communications, Inc. is a leading multimedia company serving Hispanic America. The company produces and delivers content across multiple media platforms, reaching more than 104 million unique consumers monthly. Univision's flagship network, Univision Network, is the most-watched U.S. Spanish-language broadcast network since 1992. It engages consumers through its portfolio of broadcast, cable, audio, digital, studio and brand extension platforms. Broadcast properties include: Univision and Unimas, of which the majority of their primetime content are watched live; and more than 62 other local TV stations. Cable properties include networks that serve U.S. Hispanics across Spanish- and English-language networks, including Univision+DN, Galavision, Fusion, El Rey Network, TLNovelas Univision, BandaMax, De Pelicula, DP Clasico, Foro TV, Ritmoson and TeleHit. Audio assets offer music, entertainment, news, sports updates, comedy, podcasts, games and more, and include the Uforia, Univision Audio, Uforia Music Series and Gizmodo Media Group brand names in addition to nearly 60 local radio stations. Univision's digital assets include Univision.com, Fusion, Creator Network, Earther, Splinter, Takeout, The Onion, The Root, Gizmodo, NOW, LifeHacker, DeadSpin, Jezebel, A.V. Club, Jalopnik, ClickHole and Kotaku. Studios consist of: Storyhouse, offering compelling stories that reveal unexplored worlds and sub-cultures; Onion Studios, the in-house film and TV development division of Onion, Inc.; UCI Studios, which provides marketers the means to create relevant content via analytics; and W Studios, which develops and produces edgy, action-packed primetime series. Last, Brand extensions are names or trademarks placed on new products. Univision's current brand extension properties include Univision Contigo, Copa Univision and Univision Deportes Fieston. Univision is privately-held by Broadcast Media Partners Holdings, Inc.

FINANCIAL DATA:
Note: Data for latest year may not have been available at press time.

In U.S. $	2018	2017	2016	2015	2014	2013
Revenue	3,100,000,000	3,000,000,000	2,900,000,000	2,858,400,000	2,911,400,000	2,627,400,000
R&D Expense						
Operating Income						
Operating Margin %						
SGA Expense						
Net Income				-79,600,000	900,000	216,000,000
Operating Cash Flow						
Capital Expenditure						
EBITDA						
Return on Assets %						
Return on Equity %						
Debt to Equity						

CONTACT INFORMATION:
Phone: 212-455-5200   Fax: 212-867-6710
Toll-Free:
Address: 605 Third Ave., 12/Fl, New York, NY 10158 United States

STOCK TICKER/OTHER:
Stock Ticker: Private   Exchange:
Employees: 4,200   Fiscal Year Ends: 12/31
Parent Company: Broadcast Media Partners Holdings Inc

SALARIES/BONUSES:
Top Exec. Salary: $ Bonus: $
Second Exec. Salary: $ Bonus: $

OTHER THOUGHTS:
Estimated Female Officers or Directors: 5
Hot Spot for Advancement for Women/Minorities: Y

Urban One Inc

NAIC Code: 515112

urban1.com

TYPES OF BUSINESS:
Radio Broadcasting
Television Broadcasting
Digital Broadcasting Technology
Online Publishing

BRANDS/DIVISIONS/AFFILIATES:
TV One LLC
Reach Media Inc
BlackAmericaWeb.com
Interactive One LLC (dba iONE Digital)
One Solution
BlackPlanet
TheUrbanDaily
HelloBeautiful

CONTACTS:
Note: Officers with more than one job title may be intentionally listed here more than once.

Linda Vilardo, Assistant Secretary
David Kantor, CEO, Divisional
Alfred Liggins, CEO
Peter Thompson, CFO
Catherine Hughes, Chairman of the Board

GROWTH PLANS/SPECIAL FEATURES:

Urban One, Inc. is one of the largest radio broadcasting corporations in the U.S., focusing primarily on African-American and urban audiences. The company owns and/or operates 56 stations in 15 urban markets throughout the U.S., several located in top African-American markets, including Detroit, Philadelphia, Atlanta, Houston and Washington, D.C. The firm's radio programs include a number of music genres, including adult contemporary, R&B, pop, urban, gospel and inspirational. Syndicated radio shows developed and distributed by the company include the Tom Joyner Morning Show, the Ricky Smiley Morning Show, Get Up! Mornings with Erica Campbell, the Russ Parr Morning Show, the Ed Lover Show and the DL Hughley Show. In addition to being broadcast on Urban One, syndicated radio programming is available on more than 274 non-Urban One stations throughout the country. Urban One also broadcasts news and talk radio programs in Washington, D.C.; Detroit, Michigan; Baltimore, Maryland; Cleveland, Ohio; and Richmond, Virginia. Other assets include: TV One, LLC (100%), a cable/satellite network that offers programming geared toward the African-American community; Reach Media, Inc. (80%), which operates the BlackAmericaWeb.com website; and Interactive One, LLC (100% and doing business as iONE Digital), which operates an online platform for African-American social, news, information and entertainment content. Interactive One brands include Global Grind, BlackPlanet, NewsOne, TheUrbanDaily and HelloBeautiful. The company also operates One Solution, a cross-platform/brand sales and marketing effort which allows top tier advertisers to take full advantage of the company's suite of offerings through a one-stop shop approach that has the potential to reach 80% of African-Americans. In May 2018, Urban One announced it had signed a definitive agreement to sell the assets of WPZR-FM, a radio station in Detroit, Michigan, to the Educational Media Foundation for $12.7 million.

The firm offers employees health, dental and vision coverage; life insurance; short- and long-term disability; flexible spending accounts; domestic partner coverage; and an employee assistance plan.

FINANCIAL DATA:
Note: Data for latest year may not have been available at press time.

In U.S. $	2018	2017	2016	2015	2014	2013
Revenue		460,000,000	456,219,008	450,860,992	441,387,008	448,700,000
R&D Expense						
Operating Income						
Operating Margin %						
SGA Expense						
Net Income			-423,000	-74,022,000	-62,670,000	-61,981,000
Operating Cash Flow						
Capital Expenditure						
EBITDA						
Return on Assets %						
Return on Equity %						
Debt to Equity						

CONTACT INFORMATION:
Phone: 301-429-3200   Fax: 302-636-5454
Toll-Free:
Address: 1010 Wayne Ave. 14/Fl, Silver Spring, MD 20706 United States

STOCK TICKER/OTHER:
Stock Ticker: ROIA
Employees: 1,348
Parent Company:

Exchange: NAS
Fiscal Year Ends: 12/31

SALARIES/BONUSES:
Top Exec. Salary: $ Bonus: $
Second Exec. Salary: $ Bonus: $

OTHER THOUGHTS:
Estimated Female Officers or Directors: 6
Hot Spot for Advancement for Women/Minorities: Y

Sales, profits and employees may be estimates. Financial information, benefits and other data can change quickly and may vary from those stated here.

US News and World Report LP

NAIC Code: 511120

www.usnews.com

TYPES OF BUSINESS:
Magazine Publishing
Online Media

BRANDS/DIVISIONS/AFFILIATES:
USNews.com
US News Weekly
US News Advisor Finder

CONTACTS:
Note: Officers with more than one job title may be intentionally listed here more than once.

William D. Holiber, CEO
Karen S. Chevalier, COO
William D. Holiber, Pres.
Neil Maheshwari, CFO
Kerry Dyer, Chief Advertising Officer
Chad Smolinsk, Chief Product Officer
Mark White, VP-Mfg.
Peter M. Dwoskin, General Counsel
Karen S. Chevalier, Sr. VP-Oper.
Peter M. Dwoskin, Sr. VP-Strategic Dev.
Lucy Lyons, Mgr.-Public Relations
Neil Maheshwari, VP-Finance
Kerry F. Dyer, Publisher
Brian Kelly, Editor
Margaret Mannix, Exec. Editor
Tim Smart, Exec. Editor
Eric Gertler, Exec. Chmn.

GROWTH PLANS/SPECIAL FEATURES:

U.S. News and World Report L.P. is a publisher of periodicals and internet content. Mortimer Zuckerman has owned the company since 1984, and during his ownership has overseen the development of the company's interactive arm, USNews.com, and the continued expansion of the magazine's standalone special issues. USNews.com offers news reports on general topics including health, education, money, politics/policy, science, travel and cars. The company also publishes annual reports and yearly rankings of graduate and undergraduate schools, hospitals and mutual funds. The prominence of these annual guides has greatly enhanced U.S. News' advertising profile. The firm also offers U.S. subscriptions to its weekly digital magazine, U.S. News Weekly. U.S. News and World stopped new circulation of its flagship monthly print magazine, U.S. News and World Report, which had been in print since 1933, but continues to print its annual reports and yearly rankings, though it primarily focuses on its web-based operations. The firm's U.S. News Advisor Finder is a directory of 320,000 active investment advisors and 11,000 advisory firms.

FINANCIAL DATA:
Note: Data for latest year may not have been available at press time.

In U.S. $	2018	2017	2016	2015	2014	2013
Revenue						
R&D Expense						
Operating Income						
Operating Margin %						
SGA Expense						
Net Income						
Operating Cash Flow						
Capital Expenditure						
EBITDA						
Return on Assets %						
Return on Equity %						
Debt to Equity						

CONTACT INFORMATION:
Phone: 212-716-6800 Fax: 212-643-7842
Toll-Free:
Address: 1050 Thomas Jefferson Street, NW, Washington, DC 2007-3837 United States

STOCK TICKER/OTHER:
Stock Ticker: Private
Employees:
Parent Company:

Exchange:
Fiscal Year Ends: 01/31

SALARIES/BONUSES:
Top Exec. Salary: $ Bonus: $
Second Exec. Salary: $ Bonus: $

OTHER THOUGHTS:
Estimated Female Officers or Directors: 8
Hot Spot for Advancement for Women/Minorities: Y

Sales, profits and employees may be estimates. Financial information, benefits and other data can change quickly and may vary from those stated here.

Vail Resorts Inc

NAIC Code: 713920

www.vailresorts.com

TYPES OF BUSINESS:
Ski Resorts
Luxury Hotels & Lodging
Real Estate Development
Golf Courses

BRANDS/DIVISIONS/AFFILIATES:
Vail Resorts Development Company
Perisher
Heavenly
Whistler Blackcomb
Vail
RockResorts
Grand Teton Lodge Company
Colorado Mountain Express

CONTACTS:
Note: Officers with more than one job title may be intentionally listed here more than once.

Robert Katz, CEO
Michael Barkin, CFO
Ryan Siurek, Chief Accounting Officer
Kirsten Lynch, Chief Marketing Officer
James O'Donnell, Executive VP, Divisional
David Shapiro, Executive VP
Patricia Campbell, President, Divisional

GROWTH PLANS/SPECIAL FEATURES:

Vail Resorts, Inc. (VRI), a North American resort operator, is organized as a holding company, operating through various subsidiaries. VRI currently operates in three business segments: mountain, representing 84% of revenue; lodging, 14%; and real estate, 1%. The mountain segment operates 11 mountain resort properties and three urban ski areas, as well as ancillary services, primarily including ski schools, dining operations and retail/rental operations. This segment's mountain resorts and ski areas include: Perisher, Kirkwood, Heavenly, Northstar, Whistler Blackcomb, Park City, Beaver Creek, Vail, Breckenridge, Keystone, Afton Alps, Wilmot, Mt. Brighton and Stowe. These properties are primarily located in the U.S., but also in Canada and Australia. The lodging segment: owns and/or manages luxury hotels under the RockResorts brand; owns and/or manages other strategic lodging properties; owns and/or manages condominiums located in proximity to VRI's mountain resorts; owns and operates National Park Service concessionaire properties, including Grand Teton Lodge Company, which itself operates destination resorts at Grand Teton National Park; owns and operates the Colorado Mountain Express, a resort ground transportation company; and owns and operates mountain resort golf courses. The real estate segment owns, develops and sells real estate in and around VRI's resort communities. The company has extensive real estate holdings at its mountain resorts, but primarily so throughout Summit and Eagle Counties, in Colorado. Wholly-owned Vail Resorts Development Company operates this segment.

FINANCIAL DATA:
Note: Data for latest year may not have been available at press time.

In U.S. $	2018	2017	2016	2015	2014	2013
Revenue	2,011,553,000	1,907,218,000	1,601,286,000	1,399,924,000	1,254,646,000	1,120,797,000
R&D Expense						
Operating Income	412,922,000	378,920,000	283,102,000	196,019,000	118,471,000	91,500,000
Operating Margin %		20.72%	17.94%	13.74%	9.55%	8.16%
SGA Expense	251,806,000	236,799,000				
Net Income	379,898,000	210,553,000	149,754,000	114,754,000	28,478,000	37,743,000
Operating Cash Flow	551,625,000	456,914,000	426,762,000	303,660,000	245,878,000	222,423,000
Capital Expenditure	140,611,000	144,432,000	109,237,000	123,884,000	118,305,000	94,946,000
EBITDA	617,384,000	568,077,000	444,590,000	345,142,000	259,072,000	224,188,000
Return on Assets %		6.38%	6.02%	4.92%	1.28%	1.79%
Return on Equity %		17.21%	17.20%	13.60%	3.46%	4.64%
Debt to Equity		0.78	0.78	0.93	0.76	0.96

CONTACT INFORMATION:
Phone: 303 404-1800 Fax: 303 404-6415
Toll-Free:
Address: 390 Interlocken Crescent, Broomfield, CO 80021 United States

STOCK TICKER/OTHER:
Stock Ticker: MTN Exchange: NYS
Employees: 5,900 Fiscal Year Ends: 07/31
Parent Company:

SALARIES/BONUSES:
Top Exec. Salary: $929,367 Bonus: $
Second Exec. Salary: $490,385 Bonus: $

OTHER THOUGHTS:
Estimated Female Officers or Directors: 3
Hot Spot for Advancement for Women/Minorities: Y

Value Line Inc

NAIC Code: 511120A

www.valueline.com

TYPES OF BUSINESS:
Financial Data Publishing
Investment Advisory
Financial Software
Research Services

BRANDS/DIVISIONS/AFFILIATES:
Arnold Bernhard & Company Inc
EULAV Asset Management Trust
Value Line Publishing LLC
Value Line
Value Line Investment Survey (The)
Smart Research-Smarter Investing
Timeliness
Most Trusted Name in Investment Research (The)

CONTACTS:
Note: Officers with more than one job title may be intentionally listed here more than once.

Howard Brecher, CEO
Stephen Anastasio, CFO

GROWTH PLANS/SPECIAL FEATURES:
Value Line, Inc. publishes investment-related periodicals based on research. The company provides copyright data, including certain Proprietary Ranking System and other proprietary information, to third parties under written agreements for use in third-party managed and marketed investment products as well as for other purposes. The firm's products, online information and tools impart investment education and ideas for all investors, whether a beginner or a veteran. Value Line markets under well-known brands, including Value Line, The Value Line Investment Survey, Smart Research-Smarter Investing, Timeliness and The Most Trusted Name in Investment Research. EULAV Asset Management Trust is a statutory trust, which provides the investment management services to the Value Line Funds account, which contains data on more than 20,000 no-load and low-load funds and a digital screener that offers additional fields. EULAV also provides distribution, marketing and administrative services to the Value Line Funds. Wholly-owned Value Line Publishing, LLC offers the company's investment periodicals and related publications which cover a wide range of investments including stocks, mutual funds, exchange traded funds (ETFs), options and convertible securities. Value Line Publishing's services and offerings also include investment analysis software and current/historical financial databases. Arnold Bernhard & Company, Inc. is the controlling shareholder of Value Line, owning 89.08% of its stock (as of April 2018).

FINANCIAL DATA:
Note: Data for latest year may not have been available at press time.

In U.S. $	2018	2017	2016	2015	2014	2013
Revenue	35,868,000	42,697,000	34,546,000	35,523,000	36,331,000	35,840,000
R&D Expense						
Operating Income	2,572,000	7,459,000	1,880,000	2,399,000	2,501,000	9,814,000
Operating Margin %		17.46%	5.44%	6.75%	6.88%	27.38%
SGA Expense	33,296,000	35,238,000	32,666,000	26,043,000	27,428,000	26,026,000
Net Income	14,738,000	10,367,000	7,291,000	7,292,000	6,768,000	6,619,000
Operating Cash Flow	1,071,000	-3,678,000	2,004,000	1,407,000	3,487,000	1,168,000
Capital Expenditure	408,000	1,684,000	1,962,000	2,544,000	2,687,000	2,788,000
EBITDA	3,697,000	12,082,000	5,697,000	5,114,000	4,586,000	11,366,000
Return on Assets %		11.94%	8.38%	8.36%	7.90%	7.84%
Return on Equity %		28.61%	21.12%	21.53%	20.42%	20.27%
Debt to Equity						

CONTACT INFORMATION:
Phone: 212 907-1500   Fax: 212 818-9747
Toll-Free: 800-634-3583
Address: 551 Fifth Ave., New York, NY 10176 United States

SALARIES/BONUSES:
Top Exec. Salary: $600,000   Bonus: $100,000
Second Exec. Salary: $465,000   Bonus: $160,000

STOCK TICKER/OTHER:
Stock Ticker: VALU   Exchange: NAS
Employees: 171   Fiscal Year Ends: 04/30
Parent Company:

OTHER THOUGHTS:
Estimated Female Officers or Directors:
Hot Spot for Advancement for Women/Minorities:

Sales, profits and employees may be estimates. Financial information, benefits and other data can change quickly and may vary from those stated here.

Verizon Communications Inc

NAIC Code: 517110

www.verizon.com

TYPES OF BUSINESS:
Mobile Phone and Wireless Services
Telecommunications Services
Wireless Services
Long-Distance Services
High-Speed Internet Access
Video-on-Demand Services
e-Commerce & Online Services

BRANDS/DIVISIONS/AFFILIATES:
Fios
Moment

CONTACTS:
Note: Officers with more than one job title may be intentionally listed here more than once.

Hans Vestberg, CEO
Matthew Ellis, CFO
Lowell McAdam, Chairman of the Board
Anthony Skiadas, Chief Accounting Officer
Marc Reed, Chief Administrative Officer
Craig Silliman, Executive VP, Divisional
Rima Qureshi, Executive VP
Timothy Armstrong, Executive VP

GROWTH PLANS/SPECIAL FEATURES:

Verizon Communications, Inc. is one of the world's largest providers of communications services. Its primary network technology platforms are 3G CDMA (code division multiple access), based on spread-spectrum digital radio technology, and 4G LTE (long-term evolution), which provides higher throughput performance and more improved efficiencies than 3G. Verizon operates in two segments: wireless and wireline. Wireless products and services include wireless voice, data products and other value-added services and equipment sales across the U.S. Its network provides services to a customer base of 116.3 million. The wireline segment is comprised of four units: consumer markets, enterprise solutions, partner solutions and business markets. Consumer markets provides residential fixed connectivity solutions including internet, TV and voice services. These services are provided over Verizon's 100% fiber-optic network under the Fios brand, and over a copper-based network to customers not served by Fios. The enterprise solutions unit helps customers transform their businesses to compete in the digital economy, with solutions that adapt to increasingly dynamic needs for connectivity, security and collaboration. The partner solutions unit provides communications services such as data, voice, local dial tone and broadband to local, long distance and wireless carriers that use Verizon's facilities to provide services to their own customers. Last, the business markets unit offers tailored voice and networking products, Fios services, IP networking, advanced voice solutions, security and managed IT services to U.S.-based small/medium businesses, state/local governments and educational institutions. In April 2018, Verizon acquired Moment, a New York-based design and strategy firm.

Employee benefits include 401(k); corporate discounts; health and dependent care spending accounts; life and AD&D insurance; commuter spending accounts; medical, dental and vision coverage; disability; adoption reimbursement; and tuition assistance.

FINANCIAL DATA:
Note: Data for latest year may not have been available at press time.

In U.S. $	2018	2017	2016	2015	2014	2013
Revenue		126,034,000,000	125,980,000,000	131,620,000,000	127,079,000,000	120,550,000,000
R&D Expense						
Operating Income		29,188,000,000	27,059,000,000	33,060,000,000	19,599,000,000	31,968,000,000
Operating Margin %		23.15%	21.47%	25.11%	15.42%	26.51%
SGA Expense		28,336,000,000	31,569,000,000	29,986,000,000	41,016,000,000	27,089,000,000
Net Income		30,101,000,000	13,127,000,000	17,879,000,000	9,625,000,000	11,497,000,000
Operating Cash Flow		25,305,000,000	22,715,000,000	38,930,000,000	30,631,000,000	38,818,000,000
Capital Expenditure		17,830,000,000	17,593,000,000	27,717,000,000	17,545,000,000	17,184,000,000
EBITDA		42,281,000,000	41,290,000,000	49,177,000,000	36,718,000,000	48,550,000,000
Return on Assets %		12.00%	5.37%	7.49%	3.79%	4.60%
Return on Equity %		91.74%	67.40%	124.47%	37.64%	31.93%
Debt to Equity		2.63	4.68	6.31	8.98	2.30

CONTACT INFORMATION:
Phone: 212 395-1000 Fax:
Toll-Free: 800-837-4966
Address: 1095 Avenue of the Americas, New York, NY 10036 United States

STOCK TICKER/OTHER:
Stock Ticker: VZ
Employees: 152,300
Parent Company:

Exchange: NYS
Fiscal Year Ends: 12/31

SALARIES/BONUSES:
Top Exec. Salary: $1,600,000 Bonus: $
Second Exec. Salary: $942,308 Bonus: $

OTHER THOUGHTS:
Estimated Female Officers or Directors: 5
Hot Spot for Advancement for Women/Minorities: Y

Sales, profits and employees may be estimates. Financial information, benefits and other data can change quickly and may vary from those stated here.

Verizon Media Group

NAIC Code: 519130

www.oath.com

TYPES OF BUSINESS:
Online Content Provider
Online Music Services
Online Communities
Entertainment & Information Offerings
Instant Messaging
E-Mail
Internet Service Provider

BRANDS/DIVISIONS/AFFILIATES:
Verizon Communications Inc
Yahoo!
TechCrunch
Oath: AdPlatforms
RYOT
Verizon
Aol
Oath Inc

CONTACTS: Note: Officers with more than one job title may be intentionally listed here more than once.
K. Guru Gowrappan, CEO
Julie Jacobs, Executive VP
Bob Lord, President
Susan Lyne, President, Subsidiary

GROWTH PLANS/SPECIAL FEATURES:
Verizon Media Group (formerly Oath, Inc.) is the digital content division of Verizon Communications, Inc. The firm comprises teams of creators and coders that develop content for consumers, as well as advertising solutions for brands and publishers worldwide. Brands the firm has built include Yahoo!, TechCrunch, Oath: AdPlatforms, Kanvas, Rivals, Autoblog, RYOT, Verizon, Aol. Verizon Media utilizes its expertise in media, scale and data to help advertisers build consumer connections. The company offers a publisher-driven solution that combines demand stream with insights and tools built for publishers by publishers. Its partnership strategy with clients makes full use of Verizon's media and technology assets in order to build lasting brands. In November 2018, Oath, Inc. announced a corporate-wide reorganization, with Oath being renamed as Verizon Media Group as of January 1, 2019. That same year, Oath divested Flickr, Moviefone and Polyvore, and discontinued go90.

FINANCIAL DATA: Note: Data for latest year may not have been available at press time.

In U.S. $	2018	2017	2016	2015	2014	2013
Revenue	2,100,000,000	2,050,000,000	2,000,000,000	2,225,100,000	2,527,200,000	2,319,899,904
R&D Expense						
Operating Income						
Operating Margin %						
SGA Expense						
Net Income						
Operating Cash Flow						
Capital Expenditure						
EBITDA						
Return on Assets %						
Return on Equity %						
Debt to Equity						

CONTACT INFORMATION:
Phone: 212 652-6400 Fax:
Toll-Free:
Address: 770 Broadway, New York, NY 10003 United States

SALARIES/BONUSES:
Top Exec. Salary: $ Bonus: $
Second Exec. Salary: $ Bonus: $

STOCK TICKER/OTHER:
Stock Ticker: Subsidiary Exchange:
Employees: 10,400 Fiscal Year Ends: 12/31
Parent Company: Verizon Communications Inc

OTHER THOUGHTS:
Estimated Female Officers or Directors: 7
Hot Spot for Advancement for Women/Minorities: Y

Plunkett Research, Ltd.

Viacom Inc
NAIC Code: 515210

www.viacom.com

TYPES OF BUSINESS:
Cable TV Networks
Television Production/Syndication
Film Production
Online Media
Video Distribution
Video Games

BRANDS/DIVISIONS/AFFILIATES:
National Amusements Inc
Paramount Pictures
Paramount Playes
Paramount Animation
Paramount Television
VidCon
AwesomenessTV Holdings

CONTACTS:
Note: Officers with more than one job title may be intentionally listed here more than once.

Wade Davis, CFO
Thomas May, Chairman of the Board
Katherine Gill-Charest, Chief Accounting Officer
Scott Mills, Chief Administrative Officer
Shari Redstone, Director
Doretha Lea, Executive VP, Divisional
Christa Dalimonte, Executive VP
Robert Bakish, President

GROWTH PLANS/SPECIAL FEATURES:

Viacom, Inc. is an international media conglomerate with interests in television, motion picture, internet, mobile and video game media. National Amusements, Inc., owned by the Redstone family, owns 80% of common stock and maintains a controlling interest in Viacom. The firm is composed of two segments: media networks and filmed entertainment. Media networks provides entertainment content and related branded products for consumers in targeted demographics. This division creates, acquires and distributes programming and other content for its audiences across multiple platforms such as cable, satellite, television, PCs, tablets and other mobile devices. Media networks' operations reach approximately 4.4 billion cumulative television subscribers in more than 180 countries and through 46 languages via more than 314 locally programmed and operated TV channels. These channels include Nickelodeon, Comedy Central, MTV, VH1, SPIKE, BET, CMT, TV Land, Nick Jr., Channel 5 (U.K.), Logo, Nicktoons, TeenNick and Paramount Channel, among others. The filmed entertainment segment produces, finances, acquires and distributes motion pictures, television programming and other entertainment content under the Paramount Pictures, Paramount Players, Paramount Animation, and Paramount Television brands, among others via partnerships. This division is a major global producer and distributor of filmed entertainment with a library consisting of approximately 3,500 motion pictures and a number of television programs. Distribution of motion pictures occurs theatrically and through download-to-own, DVD and Blu-ray discs; transactional video-on-demand, subscription video-on-demand, pay, basic cable and free television. In early-2018, Viacom acquired VidCon, an innovative conference and festival celebrating online video, and hosted its first Viacom-owned VidCon U.S. in June 2018, and hosted one in Australia that August, and will host one in London in February 2019. That same year, Viacom acquired AwesomenessTV Holdings, a digital-first destination for original programming serving global Gen-Z audiences (born between mid-1990s to mid-2000s).

FINANCIAL DATA:
Note: Data for latest year may not have been available at press time.

In U.S. $	2018	2017	2016	2015	2014	2013
Revenue	12,943,000,000	13,263,000,000	12,488,000,000	13,268,000,000	13,783,000,000	13,794,000,000
R&D Expense						
Operating Income	2,795,000,000	2,599,000,000	2,732,000,000	3,318,000,000	4,125,000,000	3,929,000,000
Operating Margin %		19.59%	21.87%	25.00%	29.92%	28.48%
SGA Expense	3,056,000,000	3,005,000,000	2,851,000,000	2,860,000,000	2,899,000,000	2,829,000,000
Net Income	1,719,000,000	1,874,000,000	1,438,000,000	1,922,000,000	2,391,000,000	2,395,000,000
Operating Cash Flow	1,822,000,000	1,671,000,000	1,371,000,000	2,313,000,000	2,597,000,000	3,083,000,000
Capital Expenditure	178,000,000	195,000,000	172,000,000	142,000,000	123,000,000	160,000,000
EBITDA	7,793,000,000	7,561,000,000	7,521,000,000	8,465,000,000	8,548,000,000	8,595,000,000
Return on Assets %		8.11%	6.43%	8.47%	10.18%	10.39%
Return on Equity %		36.34%	36.80%	52.96%	53.65%	37.89%
Debt to Equity		1.83	2.78	3.46	3.42	2.28

CONTACT INFORMATION:
Phone: 212 258-6000   Fax: 212 258-6100
Toll-Free:
Address: 1515 Broadway, New York, NY 10036 United States

SALARIES/BONUSES:
Top Exec. Salary: $2,769,231   Bonus: $
Second Exec. Salary: $1,750,000   Bonus: $

STOCK TICKER/OTHER:
Stock Ticker: VIA
Employees: 9,300
Parent Company: National Amusements Inc

Exchange: NAS
Fiscal Year Ends: 09/30

OTHER THOUGHTS:
Estimated Female Officers or Directors: 7
Hot Spot for Advancement for Women/Minorities: Y

Sales, profits and employees may be estimates. Financial information, benefits and other data can change quickly and may vary from those stated here.

VICE Media Inc
NAIC Code: 511120

www.vice.com

TYPES OF BUSINESS:
Book and Magazine Publishing
Film Production
Creative Services
TV Production
Music Production

BRANDS/DIVISIONS/AFFILIATES:
VICE Magazine
Vice.com
Viceland
Viceland TV
Vice Impact
VICE DVD
VICE BOOKS

CONTACTS: *Note: Officers with more than one job title may be intentionally listed here more than once.*
Nancy Dubuc, CEO
Tommy Lucente, Mgr.-Prod. & Circulation
Jon Lutzky, General Counsel
Spencer Balm, Chief Strategic Officer
Alex Detrick, Dir.-Comm.
Richard Bisson, Comptroller
Andy Capper, Global Editor
Eddy Moretti, Chief Creative Officer
Ellis Jones, Managing Editor
Shanon Kelley, Dir.-Advertising
Shane Smith, Chmn.

GROWTH PLANS/SPECIAL FEATURES:

VICE Media, Inc. is an entertainment and media company active in politicizing magazine publishing, video and film production, music production, book publishing, television production, podcasts and branding. The company's global magazine, VICE, features prepackaged political talking points on current events, fashion, music, travel, sports and technology, and targets urban men and women between the ages of 21 and 34. VICE is free of charge and available in fashion boutiques, bars, cafes, music stores and galleries around the world. VICE also runs an online site Vice.com. VICE Films produces mainly documentaries on a variety of subjects, with titles such as Lil Bub & Friendz and Reincarnated. The company's Viceland cable television network is millennial-targeted and primarily features documentary-style programs. The Viceland TV channel currently operates internationally under partnership with local cable providers in those regions. The Vice Impact digital channel focuses its content on advocacy. VICE DVD brings content from VICE Magazine to video. VICE Records is a full music publishing concern. VICE Books publishes photography collections and selected columns and articles from VICE Magazine.

FINANCIAL DATA: *Note: Data for latest year may not have been available at press time.*

In U.S. $	2018	2017	2016	2015	2014	2013
Revenue	612,000,000	608,000,000	565,000,000	525,000,000	438,000,000	195,000,000
R&D Expense						
Operating Income						
Operating Margin %						
SGA Expense						
Net Income	-50,000,000	-105,000,000				
Operating Cash Flow						
Capital Expenditure						
EBITDA						
Return on Assets %						
Return on Equity %						
Debt to Equity						

CONTACT INFORMATION:
Phone: 718-599-3101   Fax: 718-599-1769
Toll-Free:
Address: 99 N. 10th St., Ste. 204, Brooklyn, NY 11211 United States

STOCK TICKER/OTHER:
Stock Ticker: Private
Employees: 2,900
Parent Company:

Exchange:
Fiscal Year Ends:

SALARIES/BONUSES:
Top Exec. Salary: $ Bonus: $
Second Exec. Salary: $ Bonus: $

OTHER THOUGHTS:
Estimated Female Officers or Directors: 24
Hot Spot for Advancement for Women/Minorities: Y

Sales, profits and employees may be estimates. Financial information, benefits and other data can change quickly and may vary from those stated here.

Village Roadshow Limited

www.villageroadshow.com.au

NAIC Code: 713110

TYPES OF BUSINESS:
Amusement and Theme Parks

BRANDS/DIVISIONS/AFFILIATES:
Village Roadshow Theme Parks
Gold Class Cineams
Vpremium
Vmax
VJunior
Village Drive-In
Intencity
Edge

CONTACTS: Note: Officers with more than one job title may be intentionally listed here more than once.
Graham W. Burke, CEO
Simon T. Phillipson, General Counsel
Julie Raffe, Dir.-Finance
Philip S. Leggo, Group Company Sec.
Robert G. Kirby, Chmn.

GROWTH PLANS/SPECIAL FEATURES:
Village Roadshow Limited is an international entertainment and media company. The company divides its business into four segments: cinema exhibition, film distribution, theme parks, and marketing solutions. The cinema exhibition segment operates over 700 cinemas at 74 sites in Australia, and internationally. Its brands include Gold Class Cinemas, Vpremium, Vmax, VJunior, Village Drive-In and Cinema Europa. This division also operates Intencity, a chain of video arcades owned by Village Roadshow, with locations in most states of Australia. The film distribution segment distributes theatrical movies to cinema, pay television and free-to-air television in Australia and New Zealand. It also holds the exclusive distribution rights for movies produced by Los Angeles-based Village Roadshow Pictures; and has long-standing contracts to distribute movies for Warner Bros., STX, FilmNation, and other leading independent production houses. Wholly-owned Village Roadshow Theme Parks operates Warner Bros. Movie World, Sea World (Australia), Wet'n'Wild Gold Coast, Paradise Country, Australian Outback Spectacular and Sea World Resort & Water Park, all located in Australia. Last, the marketing solutions segment helps businesses find innovative, sales-focused promotions to enhance staff and customer engagement. This division has offices in Melbourne, Sydney and London; and is Australia's leading provider of digital platforms, and loyalty/reward solutions. Its products and solutions are offered under the Edge, Opia and Lifestyle Rewards brands.

FINANCIAL DATA: Note: Data for latest year may not have been available at press time.

In U.S. $	2018	2017	2016	2015	2014	2013
Revenue	666,598,500	698,142,000	726,745,600	675,093,600	655,064,800	631,270,200
R&D Expense						
Operating Income	-9,001,612	12,528,550	48,161,560	48,679,320	62,025,500	68,575,630
Operating Margin %		1.79%	6.62%	7.21%	9.46%	10.86%
SGA Expense	303,950,100	306,505,300	319,560,700	309,529,200	295,515,300	293,481,400
Net Income	153,437	-46,744,200	10,973,870	30,774,190	32,066,840	35,683,460
Operating Cash Flow						
Capital Expenditure	59,480,140	55,725,500	69,317,590	56,744,900	107,086,100	101,622,600
EBITDA	51,907,100	20,438,590	96,512,990	110,320,200	116,348,400	114,842,700
Return on Assets %		-4.42%	1.02%	3.01%	3.20%	3.66%
Return on Equity %		-15.68%	3.20%	8.63%	8.57%	9.39%
Debt to Equity		1.62	1.28	0.91	0.90	0.68

CONTACT INFORMATION:
Phone: (03) 9281 1000 Fax: (03) 9660 1764
Toll-Free:
Address: Level 1, 500 Chapel St, South Yarra, VIC 3141 Australia

STOCK TICKER/OTHER:
Stock Ticker: VLRDF
Employees: 1,249
Parent Company:

Exchange: PINX
Fiscal Year Ends: 06/30

SALARIES/BONUSES:
Top Exec. Salary: $ Bonus: $
Second Exec. Salary: $ Bonus: $

OTHER THOUGHTS:
Estimated Female Officers or Directors: 1
Hot Spot for Advancement for Women/Minorities:

Sales, profits and employees may be estimates. Financial information, benefits and other data can change quickly and may vary from those stated here.

Virgin Media Business Ltd

NAIC Code: 517110

www.virginmediabusiness.co.uk

TYPES OF BUSINESS:
Fixed-line Telecommunications
High-Speed Internet Services
Telephony Services
Voice Services
Business Telecommunications
Data Services

BRANDS/DIVISIONS/AFFILIATES:
Virgin Media Inc
Voom Fibre

CONTACTS:
Note: Officers with more than one job title may be intentionally listed here more than once.

Peter Kelly, Managing Dir.
Luke Milner, Dir.-Finance
Rob Orr, CMO
Rachel Booker, Chief People Officer
Paul Hellings, Dir.-IT
Phil Stewart, Dir.-Customer Service
Brendan Lynch, Dir.-Bus. & Partner Markets
Lee Hull, Dir.-Public Sector

GROWTH PLANS/SPECIAL FEATURES:

Virgin Media Business Ltd., a division of Virgin Media, Inc., is a leading fixed line telecommunications company in the U.K. The firm offers a national product portfolio of voice, data, internet and internet protocol (IP) services for businesses of all sizes. Virgin Media Business has invested billions of dollars in a national next-generation network which currently handles up to 86,000 calls a minute, has 38,000 breakout points, 115,575 miles of fiber-optic cabling and 330 Ethernet nodes. The company's fiber-optic network connects 17 million homes and businesses in the U.K., with plans to add another four million by 2019 through its emphasis on reaching historically under-served areas. Virgin Media Business' network also supports most of the mobile telecommunications companies in the U.K., as well as internet service providers and network operators. Products and services by the firm include broadband and internet services, customer contact services, VPN (virtual private network) solutions, LAN (local-area network) applications, site-to-site connectivity, service provider applications and telephony services. Broadband and internet services include business broadband, managed internet access and managed security services. Customer contact services include hosted call centers and call management services. VPN solutions include Ethernet VPN, IPVPN (internet protocol VPN) bandwidth options, IPSec (internet protocol security) VPN managed service and SSL (secure sockets layer) VPN for multi-site security. LAN applications include discovery services, design and assessment, installation services and maintenance and managed services. Site-to-site connectivity applications include Ethernet solutions and leased lines. Service provider applications include interconnect services, network and data services and voice services. Telephone services include business phone lines, Centrex-managed PBX (private branch exchange) services, conferencing, cordless handsets, directory inquiries and indirect access. Virgin's business broadband product, Voom Fibre, offers download speeds up to 350Mbps as a standard and 32GB of mobile data, with additional options to the package.

FINANCIAL DATA:
Note: Data for latest year may not have been available at press time.

In U.S. $	2018	2017	2016	2015	2014	2013
Revenue	1,058,000,000	1,030,000,000	1,020,432,000	960,000,000	937,151,600	915,548,430
R&D Expense						
Operating Income						
Operating Margin %						
SGA Expense						
Net Income						
Operating Cash Flow						
Capital Expenditure						
EBITDA						
Return on Assets %						
Return on Equity %						
Debt to Equity						

CONTACT INFORMATION:
Phone: 44 2072 995 000   Fax: 44 2072 996 000
Toll-Free: 800-953-0180
Address: Bartley Wood Business Park, Barley Way, Hook, RG27 9UP United Kingdom

STOCK TICKER/OTHER:
Stock Ticker: Subsidiary
Employees:
Parent Company: Virgin Media Inc

Exchange:
Fiscal Year Ends: 12/31

SALARIES/BONUSES:
Top Exec. Salary: $ Bonus: $
Second Exec. Salary: $ Bonus: $

OTHER THOUGHTS:
Estimated Female Officers or Directors:
Hot Spot for Advancement for Women/Minorities: Y

Sales, profits and employees may be estimates. Financial information, benefits and other data can change quickly and may vary from those stated here.

Vivendi SA

www.vivendi.com

NAIC Code: 512230

TYPES OF BUSINESS:
Music Production & Publishing
Cable & Satellite Television
Video Games & Software
Telecommunications Services
Cellular Telephone Service
Film Distribution
Diversified Media Operations
Digital Media

BRANDS/DIVISIONS/AFFILIATES:
Universal Music Group
Canal+ Group
Studiocanal
Havas Group
Gameloft
Vivendi Village
MyBestPro
Dailymotion

CONTACTS:
Note: Officers with more than one job title may be intentionally listed here more than once.

Stephane Roussel, COO
Herve Philippe, CFO
Frederic Crepin, Head-Legal
Simon Gillham, Sr. Exec. VP-Comm. & Public Affairs
Regis Turrini, Sr. Exec. VP-Mergers & Acquisitions
Arnaud de Puyfontaine, Chmn.

GROWTH PLANS/SPECIAL FEATURES:

Vivendi SA is an integrated media, content and communications group. The company operates businesses throughout the media value chain, from talent discovery to the creation, production and distribution of content. Vivendi's Universal Music Group engages in recorded music, music publishing and merchandising. It owns more than 50 labels covering all genres. Canal+ Group engages in pay-TV in France, as well as in Africa, Poland, Vietnam and Myanmar. Its subsidiary, Studiocanal produces, sells and distributes movies and TV series throughout Europe. Havas Group is a global communications group that creates connections between brands and audiences. It specializes in advertising, analytics, brand design, brand strategy, content production and outsourcing, digital commerce, direct marketing, engagement planning, intuitive design, healthcare communications, tailor-made solutions for premium/luxury brands, media communication across all channels, mobile marketing, corporate communications, product development and social marketing. Gameloft is a worldwide leader in mobile games, with 2.5 million games downloaded per day. Vivendi Village includes: Vivendi Ticketing, which operates in the U.K., France, Spain, Germany, Belgium, the Netherlands and the U.S.; MyBestPro, which provides counseling services; Vivendi Talents&Live, which engages in talent scouting and develops live entertainment projects; the venues L'Olympia and Theatre de l'Oeuvre in Paris, and CanalOlympia in Africa; Olympia Production, a production house for shows and concerts; and Festival Production, which develops events throughout France. Last, Dailymotion is one of the biggest video content aggregation and distribution platforms in the world, with 250 million monthly users.

FINANCIAL DATA:
Note: Data for latest year may not have been available at press time.

In U.S. $	2018	2017	2016	2015	2014	2013
Revenue						
R&D Expense						
Operating Income						
Operating Margin %						
SGA Expense						
Net Income						
Operating Cash Flow						
Capital Expenditure						
EBITDA						
Return on Assets %						
Return on Equity %						
Debt to Equity						

CONTACT INFORMATION:
Phone: 33 171711000
Fax: 33 171711001
Toll-Free:
Address: 42 Ave. de Friedland, Paris, 75380 France

SALARIES/BONUSES:
Top Exec. Salary: $
Bonus: $
Second Exec. Salary: $
Bonus: $

STOCK TICKER/OTHER:
Stock Ticker: VIVEF
Employees: 33,200
Parent Company:
Exchange: PINX
Fiscal Year Ends: 12/31

OTHER THOUGHTS:
Estimated Female Officers or Directors: 4
Hot Spot for Advancement for Women/Minorities: Y

Vodafone Kabel Deutschland GmbH

NAIC Code: 517110

kabel.vodafone.de

TYPES OF BUSINESS:
Cable TV
Internet Access

BRANDS/DIVISIONS/AFFILIATES:
Vodafone Group plc
GigaCube
HomeBox
GigaTV

GROWTH PLANS/SPECIAL FEATURES:
Vodafone Kabel Deutschland GmbH provides cable, internet and telephone services in 13 of 16 German states. The firm is a subsidiary of Vodafone Group plc, which is based in London. Vodafone Kabel offers free-to-air TV, FM and digital radio, pay TV and more. Additional products include the GigaCube Wi-Fi mobile network; the GigaTV, an internet-based television service; the HomeBox Wi-Fi home solution, offering the latest WLAN technology for enhanced bandwidth and range; and mobile products and solutions.

CONTACTS:
Note: Officers with more than one job title may be intentionally listed here more than once.

Manuel Cubero, CEO
Andreas Siemen, CFO
Insa Calsow, Sr. VP-Corp. Comm.
Elmar Baur, Head-Investor Rel.

FINANCIAL DATA:
Note: Data for latest year may not have been available at press time.

In U.S. $	2018	2017	2016	2015	2014	2013
Revenue		2,585,830,400	2,463,317,760	2,303,107,072	2,155,905,024	2,076,178,432
R&D Expense						
Operating Income						
Operating Margin %						
SGA Expense						
Net Income		301,663,072	309,481,088	272,283,712	-77,428,312	280,054,400
Operating Cash Flow						
Capital Expenditure						
EBITDA						
Return on Assets %						
Return on Equity %						
Debt to Equity						

CONTACT INFORMATION:
Phone: 49-89-960-10-888 Fax:
Toll-Free:
Address: Betastrasse 6 - 8, Unterfoehring, 85774 Germany

SALARIES/BONUSES:
Top Exec. Salary: $ Bonus: $
Second Exec. Salary: $ Bonus: $

STOCK TICKER/OTHER:
Stock Ticker: KBDHY   Exchange: PINX
Employees: 3,841   Fiscal Year Ends: 03/31
Parent Company: Vodafone Group plc

OTHER THOUGHTS:
Estimated Female Officers or Directors:
Hot Spot for Advancement for Women/Minorities:

Vox Media Inc

NAIC Code: 519130

www.voxmedia.com

TYPES OF BUSINESS:
Internet Publishing and Broadcasting and Web Search Portals
Digital Content

BRANDS/DIVISIONS/AFFILIATES:
SB Nation
Polygon
Verge (The)
Vox.com
Recode
Eater
Curbed
Vox Creative

CONTACTS:
Note: Officers with more than one job title may be intentionally listed here more than once.

Jim Bankoff, CEO
Trei Brundrett, COO
Steve Swad, CFO
Lindsay Nelson, Chief Commercial Officer
Erin Bakst, VP-Human Resources
Joe Alicata, Chief Product Officer
Marty Moe, Pres.

GROWTH PLANS/SPECIAL FEATURES:

Vox Media, Inc. is a digital company that creates and distributes content related to sports, gaming, technology, fashion, beauty, real estate and home markets. The firm has seven brands: SB Nation, Polygon, The Verge, Vox, Recode, Eater and Curbed. SB Nation focuses on creating sports sites on the web and consists of 300 individual fan-centric sports communities. Polygon primarily caters to the adult gamers offering information and stories about video games, artists and has a community based on individual consoles, titles and franchises. The Verge publishes digital content covering topics such as science, art and culture and technology. Vox is a general interest news site found at Vox.com, which covers an array of topics including business, food, sports, world affairs, politics, public policy, science and pop culture. Recode publishes news, reviews and analysis on topics pertaining to technology. Eater focuses on food, dining and drinking industry and includes information and articles on food cities, best places to eat, popular menu offerings and related services. Curbed provides content on real estate, including sale and rental price reports, new developments, neighborhood trends, interiors and architecture. Vox Media reaches 750 million people across its platforms, with 500 million minutes of video being watched every month. In addition, the firm operates the following: Vox Creative, a division that works with advertising partners to develop branded content that taps into Vox Media's editorial subject matter expertise; Vox Product, a website that features Vox Media's current projects; and Concert, a publisher-led marketplace that offers high-fidelity advertising, with a focus on brand safety and creation scale that exceeds silos.

FINANCIAL DATA:
Note: Data for latest year may not have been available at press time.

In U.S. $	2018	2017	2016	2015	2014	2013
Revenue	177,000,000	158,500,000	110,000,000	80,000,000	41,000,000	
R&D Expense						
Operating Income						
Operating Margin %						
SGA Expense						
Net Income						
Operating Cash Flow						
Capital Expenditure						
EBITDA						
Return on Assets %						
Return on Equity %						
Debt to Equity						

CONTACT INFORMATION:
Phone: 202-747-1290   Fax:
Toll-Free:
Address: 1201 Connecticut Ave. NW, Washington, DC 20036 United States

STOCK TICKER/OTHER:
Stock Ticker: Private
Employees: 950
Parent Company:

Exchange:
Fiscal Year Ends:

SALARIES/BONUSES:
Top Exec. Salary: $ Bonus: $
Second Exec. Salary: $ Bonus: $

OTHER THOUGHTS:
Estimated Female Officers or Directors:
Hot Spot for Advancement for Women/Minorities:

Vulcan Inc

NAIC Code: 523910

www.vulcan.com

TYPES OF BUSINESS:
Private Equity Investments
Film Production
Entertainment Investments
Telecommunications Investments
Sports Teams
Real Estate
Museums

BRANDS/DIVISIONS/AFFILIATES:
Vulcan Productions
Allen Institute for Artificial Intelligence
Hospital Club (The)
Seattle Seahawks
Portland Trailblazers
Allen Institute for Brain Science
Where God Left His Shoes
Vulcan Real Estate

CONTACTS:
Note: Officers with more than one job title may be intentionally listed here more than once.

Bill Hilf, CEO
David Franco, CFO
Tim Mulligan, Chief Human Resources Officer
Bill Benack, VP-Finance
Ada M. Healey, VP-Real Estate Dev.
Paul G. Allen, Chmn.

GROWTH PLANS/SPECIAL FEATURES:

Vulcan, Inc. was founded by Paul Allen, Microsoft's co-founder, to research and implement his investments. The company does everything from building museums and making original motion pictures to launching businesses and developing new technologies. It invests heavily in the Pacific Northwest and primarily focuses on projects involving education, preserving history and the arts. Though the company believes that technology can enhance these projects and deliver them to a broader audience, achieving high levels of creativity is its main objective. Its creative projects include Vulcan Productions, several museums and The Hospital Club. Vulcan Productions is an independent film studio whose recent productions include Where God Left His Shoes, Bickford Shmeckler's Cool Ideas, Ballet Now and Ghost Feet. Vulcan's museums include the EMP Museum, an interactive museum of music, popular culture and science fiction; the Living Computer Museum, a collection of vintage timesharing computers; and the Flying Heritage Collection of rare WWII airplanes. The Hospital Club is a multi-use venue for international music and film professionals created from the derelict St. Paul's Hospital in the London borough of Camden. The firm owns two major league sports teams, the Seattle Seahawks and the Portland Trail Blazers and has a partial stake in the Seattle Sounders FC. Vulcan also owns various real estate properties acquired and managed through Vulcan Real Estate, including South Lake Union, a 60-acre subdivision located near downtown Seattle. The company's technology pursuits include Allen Institute for Brain Science, to accelerate understanding of the human brain and Allen Institute for Artificial Intelligence, answering some of the critical questions in AI today, including opportunities for computers to acquire knowledge and reason.

Vulcan offers its employees medical, dental and vision coverage; a 401(k) plan; tuition reimbursement; life and AD&D insurance; short- and long-term disability; access to an athletic club; and a professional membership allowance.

FINANCIAL DATA:
Note: Data for latest year may not have been available at press time.

In U.S. $	2018	2017	2016	2015	2014	2013
Revenue						
R&D Expense						
Operating Income						
Operating Margin %						
SGA Expense						
Net Income						
Operating Cash Flow						
Capital Expenditure						
EBITDA						
Return on Assets %						
Return on Equity %						
Debt to Equity						

CONTACT INFORMATION:
Phone: 206-342-2000 Fax: 206-342-3000
Toll-Free:
Address: 505 Fifth Ave. S., Ste. 900, Seattle, WA 98104 United States

STOCK TICKER/OTHER:
Stock Ticker: Private   Exchange:
Employees: 712   Fiscal Year Ends: 12/31
Parent Company:

SALARIES/BONUSES:
Top Exec. Salary: $ Bonus: $
Second Exec. Salary: $ Bonus: $

OTHER THOUGHTS:
Estimated Female Officers or Directors: 3
Hot Spot for Advancement for Women/Minorities: Y

Sales, profits and employees may be estimates. Financial information, benefits and other data can change quickly and may vary from those stated here.

Walt Disney Company (The)

NAIC Code: 515210

corporate.disney.go.com

TYPES OF BUSINESS:
Cable TV Networks, Broadcasting & Entertainment
Filmed Entertainment
Merchandising
Television Networks
Music & Book Publishing
Online Entertainment Programs
Theme Parks, Resorts & Cruise Lines
Comic Book Publishing

BRANDS/DIVISIONS/AFFILIATES:
ESPN
Disney
Freeform
WABC
A+E
Viceland
Disneyland Resort
Marvel

CONTACTS:
Note: Officers with more than one job title may be intentionally listed here more than once.

Robert Iger, CEO
Christine Mccarthy, CFO
Brent Woodford, Executive VP, Divisional
Alan Braverman, General Counsel
Mary Parker, Other Executive Officer
Zenia Mucha, Senior Executive VP, Divisional

GROWTH PLANS/SPECIAL FEATURES:

The Walt Disney Company (Disney) is an international entertainment company operating in four primary business segments: media networks, studio entertainment, consumer products and interactive media, and parks and resorts. The media networks segment is comprised of cable and broadcast television networks, television production and distribution operations, domestic television stations and radio networks and stations. It also has investments in entities that operate programming, distribution and content management services, including television networks. This division's primary cable networks include the ESPN, Disney and Freeform brands; broadcast stations include WABC, KABC, WLS, WPVI and others; and media business brands include A+E and Viceland. The studio entertainment segment produces and acquires live-action and animated motion pictures, direct-to-video content, musical recordings and live stage plays. This division distributes films primarily under the Walt Disney Pictures, Pixar, Marvel, Lucasfilm and Touchstone banners; and distributes Dreamworks Studios-produced live-action films that were released from 2010-2016. The consumer products and interactive media segment licenses the company's trade names, characters and visual and literary properties to various manufacturers, game developers, publishers and retailers worldwide. It also develops and publishes games, primarily for mobile platforms, and books, magazines and comic books. The parks and resorts segment provides family travel and leisure experiences through its cruise line, theme parks and resorts. Brands and companies within this division include Disneyland Resort, Walt Disney World, Disneyland Paris, Tokyo Disney Resort, Hong Kong Disneyland, Disney Cruise Line, Disney Vacation Club, Aulani Disney Resort & Spa, Adventures by Disney and Walt Disney Imagineering. In July 2018, Disney and Twenty-First Century Fox, Inc. (Fox) shareholders approved the $71.3 billion acquisition of Fox's Fox Entertainment Group, FX Networks, National Geographic Partners, Star TV and Hulu assets. Additionally, the U.S. Justice Department gave its approval contingent upon Fox's regional sports networks assets being sold to third parties.

FINANCIAL DATA:
Note: Data for latest year may not have been available at press time.

In U.S. $	2018	2017	2016	2015	2014	2013
Revenue	59,434,000,000	55,137,000,000	55,632,000,000	52,465,000,000	48,813,000,000	45,041,000,000
R&D Expense						
Operating Income	14,837,000,000	13,873,000,000	14,358,000,000	13,224,000,000	11,540,000,000	9,450,000,000
Operating Margin %		25.16%	25.80%	25.20%	23.64%	20.98%
SGA Expense	8,860,000,000	8,176,000,000	8,754,000,000	8,523,000,000	8,565,000,000	
Net Income	12,598,000,000	8,980,000,000	9,391,000,000	8,382,000,000	7,501,000,000	6,136,000,000
Operating Cash Flow	14,295,000,000	12,343,000,000	13,213,000,000	10,909,000,000	9,780,000,000	9,452,000,000
Capital Expenditure	4,465,000,000	3,623,000,000	4,773,000,000	4,265,000,000	3,311,000,000	2,796,000,000
EBITDA	18,422,000,000	17,077,000,000	17,749,000,000	16,487,000,000	14,828,000,000	12,161,000,000
Return on Assets %		9.56%	10.42%	9.72%	9.06%	7.85%
Return on Equity %		21.23%	21.39%	18.73%	16.59%	14.40%
Debt to Equity		0.46	0.38	0.28	0.28	0.28

CONTACT INFORMATION:
Phone: 818 5601000 Fax:
Toll-Free:
Address: 500 S. Buena Vista St., Burbank, CA 91521 United States

STOCK TICKER/OTHER:
Stock Ticker: DIS
Employees: 201,000
Parent Company:

Exchange: NYS
Fiscal Year Ends: 09/30

SALARIES/BONUSES:
Top Exec. Salary: $2,500,000   Bonus: $
Second Exec. Salary: $1,565,000   Bonus: $

OTHER THOUGHTS:
Estimated Female Officers or Directors: 7
Hot Spot for Advancement for Women/Minorities: Y

Sales, profits and employees may be estimates. Financial information, benefits and other data can change quickly and may vary from those stated here.

Walt Disney Studios (The)

NAIC Code: 512110

studioservices.go.com

TYPES OF BUSINESS:
Movie Production & Post-Production Services
Movie Distribution
Theatrical Productions
Music Production
Music Distribution

BRANDS/DIVISIONS/AFFILIATES:
Walt Disney Company (The)
Disney Digital Studio Services
Disney
Walt Disney Animation Studios
Pixar Animation Studios
Disneynature
Walt Disney Records
Disney Music Publishing

CONTACTS:
Note: Officers with more than one job title may be intentionally listed here more than once.

Alan Horn, Chmn.

GROWTH PLANS/SPECIAL FEATURES:

The Walt Disney Studios, a division of The Walt Disney Company, acts as a central studio and production agency for its parent company's various television and cinema productions. The studio's production services include sound stages used for filming the live action sequences for films like Fantasia in 1940, and, more recently, for portions of Pearl Harbor, Pirates of the Caribbean and Armageddon. They have also been used to film TV shows such as the Mickey Mouse Club and Sports Night. The studio's business street features a 1950s facade, which has been featured in shows like Ellen, Alias, My Wife & Kids and commercials and print ads. Its backlot services include signs and graphics, a paint shop and craft services. The firm offers production services including costumes, set rentals and transportation services. Post-production services are offered through Disney Digital Studio Services and include dubbing and ADR (automated dialogue replacement) stages in the digital studio, all of which feature advanced sound editing tools and seating. Feature films are released under the following banners: Disney; Walt Disney Animation Studios; Pixar Animation Studios; Disneynature; Marvel Studios; and Touchstone Pictures, the banner under which live-action films from DreamWorks Studios are distributed. The Disney music division comprises the Walt Disney Records and Hollywood Records labels, as well as Disney Music Publishing. And the Disney theatrical division produces and licenses live events, including Disney on Broadway, Disney On Ice and Disney Live!

Employees of The Walt Disney Company receive benefits including medical, prescription, AD&D, long-term care, disability, life, dental and vision coverage; an employee assistance program; 401(k); an employee stock purchase program; education reimbursement;

FINANCIAL DATA:
Note: Data for latest year may not have been available at press time.

In U.S. $	2018	2017	2016	2015	2014	2013
Revenue	9,500,000,000	8,379,000,000	9,441,000,000	7,366,000,000	7,278,000,000	5,979,000,000
R&D Expense						
Operating Income						
Operating Margin %						
SGA Expense						
Net Income		2,355,000,000	2,703,000,000	1,973,000,000	1,549,000,000	661,000,000
Operating Cash Flow						
Capital Expenditure						
EBITDA						
Return on Assets %						
Return on Equity %						
Debt to Equity						

CONTACT INFORMATION:
Phone: 818-560-1000 Fax: 818-560-1930
Toll-Free:
Address: 500 S. Buena Vista St., Burbank, CA 91521 United States

SALARIES/BONUSES:
Top Exec. Salary: $ Bonus: $
Second Exec. Salary: $ Bonus: $

STOCK TICKER/OTHER:
Stock Ticker: Subsidiary   Exchange:
Employees: 16,000   Fiscal Year Ends: 09/30
Parent Company: Walt Disney Company (The)

OTHER THOUGHTS:
Estimated Female Officers or Directors:
Hot Spot for Advancement for Women/Minorities:

Sales, profits and employees may be estimates. Financial information, benefits and other data can change quickly and may vary from those stated here.

Plunkett Research, Ltd.   501

Warner Bros Entertainment Inc

www.warnerbros.com

NAIC Code: 512110

TYPES OF BUSINESS:

Film Production
Television Production & Broadcasting
Video Distribution
Animation
Comic Books
Brand Licensing

BRANDS/DIVISIONS/AFFILIATES:

AT&T Inc
Warner Media LLC
Warner Bros Pictures
Warner Bros Television Group
Warner Horizon Television
Warner Bros Animation
DC Entertainment Inc
Flagship Entertainment Group Limited

CONTACTS: Note: Officers with more than one job title may be intentionally listed here more than once.

Kevin Tsujihara, CEO
Kim Williams, CFO
Kiko Washington, Exec. VP-Worldwide Human Resources
John Rogovin, General Counsel
Thomas Gewechke, Exec. VP-Strategy & Bus. Dev.
Thomas Gewechke, Chief Digital Officer
Susan Nahley Fleishman, Exec. VP-Worldwide Corp. Comm. & Public Affairs
Kevin Tsujihara, Chmn.
Richard Fox, Exec. VP-Int'l

GROWTH PLANS/SPECIAL FEATURES:

Warner Bros. Entertainment, Inc. (WB), a subsidiary of AT&T, Inc.'s subsidiary Warner Media LLC, creates, produces, distributes, licenses and markets films, television shows, DVDs, animation, comic books, interactive entertainment, international cinema and television broadcasting. Films are produced under the names Warner Bros. Pictures, Warner Bros. Pictures International, Village Roadshow Pictures, Gaylord Films, Alcon Entertainment, New Line Cinema, Castle Rock, Lorimar Pictures and RKO. The firm's film library includes approximately 7,400 features. The company's film houses collectively produce and distribute between 18-22 films each year. The Warner Bros. Television Group oversees the company's television businesses, producing primetime and cable series through Warner Bros. Television and Warner Horizon Television. First-run series are produced through Telepictures, and animation series through Warner Bros. Animation. The company is also a partner with CBS within The CW Television Network. The firm's television library consists of over 100,000 hours of programming, including 5,000 television programs comprised of tens of thousands of individual episodes. Its animation library consists of animated episodes and shorts, including such brands as Looney Tunes and Hanna-Barbera. Animation programming is distributed worldwide by two category-based distribution operations: Warner Bros. Domestic Television Distribution and Warner Bros. International Television Distribution. The firm owns DC Entertainment, Inc., publisher of DC Comics, which features icons such as Superman, Batman and Wonder Woman. WB also owns the marketing rights to classic movies such as Citizen Kane, Casablanca, Gone with the Wind and Wizard of Oz. Joint venture Flagship Entertainment Group Limited develops and produces Chinese-language films, including When Larry Met Mary, Mission Milano, The Adventures, Paradox and The Meg, released in 2018. Moreover, Warner Bros. World Abu Dhabi opened mid-2018, an indoor amusement park featuring characters from Warner Bros.' franchises.

FINANCIAL DATA: Note: Data for latest year may not have been available at press time.

In U.S. $	2018	2017	2016	2015	2014	2013
Revenue	14,500,000,000	14,000,000,000	13,037,000,000	12,992,000,000	12,526,000,000	12,312,000,000
R&D Expense						
Operating Income						
Operating Margin %						
SGA Expense						
Net Income						
Operating Cash Flow						
Capital Expenditure						
EBITDA						
Return on Assets %						
Return on Equity %						
Debt to Equity						

CONTACT INFORMATION:

Phone: 818-954-6000   Fax: 212-954-7667
Toll-Free:
Address: 4000 Warner Blvd., Burbank, CA 91522 United States

SALARIES/BONUSES:

Top Exec. Salary: $ Bonus: $
Second Exec. Salary: $ Bonus: $

STOCK TICKER/OTHER:

Stock Ticker: Subsidiary
Employees: 15,000
Parent Company: AT&T Inc

Exchange:
Fiscal Year Ends: 12/31

OTHER THOUGHTS:

Estimated Female Officers or Directors: 4
Hot Spot for Advancement for Women/Minorities: Y

Sales, profits and employees may be estimates. Financial information, benefits and other data can change quickly and may vary from those stated here.

Warner Media LLC

NAIC Code: 515210

www.warnermediagroup.com

TYPES OF BUSINESS:
Cable TV Networks
Digital Entertainment
Film Production
Video Game Publishing
Entertainment Investments
Digital Media Production

BRANDS/DIVISIONS/AFFILIATES:
AT&T Inc
Turner Broadcasting System Inc
Home Box Office Inc
Warner Bros Entertainment Inc

CONTACTS:
Note: Officers with more than one job title may be intentionally listed here more than once.

John Stankey, CEO
Priya Dogra, Exec. VP-Strategy & Corp. Dev.
Jeffrey Bewkes, Chairman of the Board
Pascal Desroches, CFO
Keith Cocozza, Exec. VP-Corp. Mktg. & Communications
Jim Cummings, Chief Human Resources Officer
Gary Ginsberg, Executive VP, Divisional
Carol Melton, Executive VP, Divisional
Olaf Olafsson, Executive VP, Divisional
Paul Cappuccio, Executive VP
Karen Magee, Executive VP

GROWTH PLANS/SPECIAL FEATURES:

Warner Media, LLC is a global media and entertainment conglomerate, and a wholly-owned subsidiary of AT&T, Inc. The firm operates in three segments: Turner Broadcasting System, Inc. (Turner), consisting of cable networks and digital media; Home Box Office, Inc., a basic tier service internationally and a premium pay service internationally and domestically; and Warner Bros. Entertainment, Inc. (Warner Bros.), made up of feature film, television, home video and videogame production and distributions. The Turner segment consists principally of domestic and international networks; digital media properties, which primarily include brand-aligned websites; and basic tier and premium pay television programming. This division includes domestic and international cable networks such as TBS, TNT and CNN. Additionally, in Latin America, Turner brands include Space, I-Sat and MuchMusic. Home Box Office consists of premium pay services such as HBO and Cinemax. This segment has approximately 50 million worldwide subscribers. This segment also produces original programing via DVDs, Blu-ray and electronic sell-through. Revenue is also generated through content licensing. Internationally, HBO tailors the distribution of its programming for each territory via premium pay, basic tier television distributed by affiliates, licensing of programming to third-party providers and over the internet (OTT). The Warner Bros. segment generates revenues through production and distribution of feature films, television programming and video games. Warner Bros. produce event films such as Batman, The Hangover and Harry Potter; along with minor original films. This segment is also responsible for production of television shows both domestically and internationally. Additionally, interactive entertainment for consoles, PC/Mac and handheld platforms are created and distributed through Warner Bros. In June 2018, former parent Time Warner was acquired by AT&T, Inc. for approximately $80 billion, one of the biggest media deals in history.

FINANCIAL DATA:
Note: Data for latest year may not have been available at press time.

In U.S. $	2018	2017	2016	2015	2014	2013
Revenue	30,000,000,000	31,271,000,064	29,318,000,640	28,117,999,616	27,359,000,576	29,795,000,320
R&D Expense						
Operating Income						
Operating Margin %						
SGA Expense						
Net Income		5,247,000,064	3,926,000,128	3,832,999,936	3,827,000,064	3,691,000,064
Operating Cash Flow						
Capital Expenditure						
EBITDA						
Return on Assets %						
Return on Equity %						
Debt to Equity						

CONTACT INFORMATION:
Phone: 212 484-8000 Fax: 703 265-1000
Toll-Free:
Address: 1 Time Warner Ctr., New York, NY 10019 United States

STOCK TICKER/OTHER:
Stock Ticker: Subsidiary
Employees: 26,000
Parent Company: AT&T Inc

Exchange:
Fiscal Year Ends: 12/31

SALARIES/BONUSES:
Top Exec. Salary: $ Bonus: $
Second Exec. Salary: $ Bonus: $

OTHER THOUGHTS:
Estimated Female Officers or Directors: 3
Hot Spot for Advancement for Women/Minorities: Y

Sales, profits and employees may be estimates. Financial information, benefits and other data can change quickly and may vary from those stated here.

Warner Music Group Corp

www.wmg.com

NAIC Code: 512230

TYPES OF BUSINESS:
Recorded Music Distribution
Music Production
Music Printing
Music Publishing
Soundtracks
Compilations
Digital Music Downloads
Video Production

BRANDS/DIVISIONS/AFFILIATES:
Access Industries Inc
Atlantic Records Group
Parlophone
Warner Bros Records Inc
Warner/Chappell Music
Universal Music
Sodatone
UPROXX

CONTACTS:
Note: Officers with more than one job title may be intentionally listed here more than once.

Stephen F. Cooper, CEO
Ole Oberman, Chief Digital Officer
Eric Levin, CFO
Maria Osherova, Chief Human Resources Officer
Paul M. Robinson, General Counsel
Stephen Bryan, Exec. VP-Digital Bus. Dev. & Strategy
Cameron Strang, Chmn.

GROWTH PLANS/SPECIAL FEATURES:

Warner Music Group Corp. is a global company specializing in music content and a subsidiary of Access Industries, Inc. Warner Music Group is composed of three businesses: recorded music, music publishing and artist services. The recorded music business primarily consists of the discovery and development of artists and the related marketing, distribution and licensing of recorded music produced by such artists. This division produces revenue primarily through the marketing, sale and licensing of recorded music in various physical and digital formats, such as CDs, LPs, DVDs, downloads and ringtones. Recorded music also participates in image and brand rights associated with artists, including merchandising, sponsorships, touring and artist management. Atlantic Records Group, Parlophone and Warner Bros. Records, Inc. are among the company's most prominent music labels. Other current labels include Asylum, Big Beat, CanvasBack, EastWest, Erato, Reprise Records, Roadrunnder Records and many more. The music publishing business, which operates primarily through Warner/Chappell Music, owns and acquires rights to musical compositions and markets these compositions, receiving royalties or fees for their use. The firm's Artist Services provide artist management, merchandising, touring, fan clubs, VIP ticketing, sponsorships and brand endorsement services to help artists build their careers. Warner Music's releases in the Middle East are distributed by Universal Music as a result of its integration with EMI Group Limited. Likewise, in Turkey, the firm's releases are distributed by EMI Music Turkey. In March 2018, Warner Music Group acquired Sodatone, tech start-up whose platform identifies unsigned talent by tracking early predictors of success. In June of the same year, the firm announced that a stand-alone, fully staffed label group to be known as Elektra Music Group would be launched on October 1st. The following August, Warner Music Group acquired UPROXX, the youth culture and video production firm.

FINANCIAL DATA:
Note: Data for latest year may not have been available at press time.

In U.S. $	2018	2017	2016	2015	2014	2013
Revenue	3,660,000,000	3,576,000,000	3,246,000,000	2,966,000,000	3,027,000,000	2,871,000,000
R&D Expense						
Operating Income						
Operating Margin %						
SGA Expense						
Net Income		143,000,000	25,000,000	-91,000,000	-303,000,000	-194,000,000
Operating Cash Flow						
Capital Expenditure						
EBITDA						
Return on Assets %						
Return on Equity %						
Debt to Equity						

CONTACT INFORMATION:
Phone: 212-275-2000 Fax:
Toll-Free:
Address: 1633 Broadway, New York, NY 10019 United States

SALARIES/BONUSES:
Top Exec. Salary: $ Bonus: $
Second Exec. Salary: $ Bonus: $

STOCK TICKER/OTHER:
Stock Ticker: Subsidiary
Employees: 4,520
Parent Company: Access Industries inc

Exchange:
Fiscal Year Ends: 09/30

OTHER THOUGHTS:
Estimated Female Officers or Directors:
Hot Spot for Advancement for Women/Minorities: Y

Washington Times LLC (The)

NAIC Code: 511110

www.washingtontimes.com

TYPES OF BUSINESS:
Newspaper Publishing
Online Subscriptions

BRANDS/DIVISIONS/AFFILIATES:
WashingtonTimes.com
Inside Politics
Faith and Family
Business & Economy
National Weekly Edition
National Digital Edition

CONTACTS:
Note: Officers with more than one job title may be intentionally listed here more than once.

Christopher Dolan, Executive Editor
Thomas McDevitt, Pres.
Samantha Switzer, Mgr.-Digital Sales Oper.
Marana Moore, Dir.-Public Rel.
Mike Harris, Sports Editor
Chris Dolan, Managing Editor
Carleton Bryant, Foreign Editor

GROWTH PLANS/SPECIAL FEATURES:
The Washington Times, LLC is the publisher of The Washington Times, a newspaper based in Washington, D.C. In addition to its daily and weekly issues, the publication also offers online subscriptions from its website, WashingtonTimes.com. The firm maintains several blogs on the website, including a politics blog, Inside Politics; Faith and Family, presenting the latest news and discussions on religion, faith and family; and Business & Economy, providing economic and financial news, which are continually fresh and updated. Other topics of interest include, but are not limited to, security, culture, entertainment, technology, accountability, obituaries, opinion, sports and classified ads. The firm's website features a communities section, where readers can post their own thoughts on various topics. Additional company news providers include the National Weekly Edition, a weekly subscription offering of The Washington Times showcasing the week's biggest news and commentary; and National Digital Edition, an app designed to provide news that reads like a magazine to smartphones and tablets.

FINANCIAL DATA:
Note: Data for latest year may not have been available at press time.

In U.S. $	2018	2017	2016	2015	2014	2013
Revenue						
R&D Expense						
Operating Income						
Operating Margin %						
SGA Expense						
Net Income						
Operating Cash Flow						
Capital Expenditure						
EBITDA						
Return on Assets %						
Return on Equity %						
Debt to Equity						

CONTACT INFORMATION:
Phone: 202-636-3000 Fax:
Toll-Free: 800-277-8500
Address: 3600 New York Ave. NE, Washington, DC 20002 United States

STOCK TICKER/OTHER:
Stock Ticker: Private   Exchange:
Employees: Fiscal Year Ends:
Parent Company:

SALARIES/BONUSES:
Top Exec. Salary: $ Bonus: $
Second Exec. Salary: $ Bonus: $

OTHER THOUGHTS:
Estimated Female Officers or Directors: 4
Hot Spot for Advancement for Women/Minorities: Y

Sales, profits and employees may be estimates. Financial information, benefits and other data can change quickly and may vary from those stated here.

Wasserman Media Group LLC

NAIC Code: 711410

www.wmgllc.com

TYPES OF BUSINESS:
Sports Management Agency
Marketing and Branding Services

BRANDS/DIVISIONS/AFFILIATES:
Cycle Media

CONTACTS:
Note: Officers with more than one job title may be intentionally listed here more than once.

Casey Wasserman, CEO
Mike Watts, Pres.
Ryan Berenson, Exec. VP-Finance
Mike Mikho, CMO
Kayla Dougherty Perkins, Sr. VP-Human Resources
Bill Schechtman, VP-IT
Trista Schroeder, General Counsel
Stephanie Rudnick, VP-Corp. Comm.
Arn Tellem, Head-Team Sports Div.
Sara Munds, Co-Pres., Global Media Div.-London
Malcolm Turner, Pres., Golf Div.
Fahri Ecvet, COO-Global Football
Casey Wasserman, Chmn.
David Kogan, Co-Pres., Global Media Div.-London

GROWTH PLANS/SPECIAL FEATURES:
Wasserman Media Group, LLC is a full-service agency that serves talent, brands and properties worldwide. The company's agency expertise spans sports, entertainment, music, social, tech, style, media, content, lifestyle, art and food genres. Wasserman represents thousands of athletes, broadcasters, coaches and social media influencers, supporting their careers, business and brand opportunities. The firm provides in-house resources including branding, marketing, creative design, licensing, public relations and legal. It supports clients throughout every stage of their career, from securing an initial contract to negotiating major later contracts, introducing them to social and lifestyle brands and providing opportunities to create their own presentation. Wasserman also prepares clients for career opportunities beyond their current fields, whether it be broadcasting, coaching, owning products, producing content or other. In addition, wholly-owned subsidiary Cycle Media is a global media network made up of global creators, influencers and performers, publishing more than 50,000 pieces of original content each month. Cycle Media's services support athlete clients and social media influencers in creating and distributing original content for agency- and brand-related purposes. The firm's U.S. offices are located in Portland, Los Angeles, Carlsbad, Miami, Raleigh and New York. International offices are located in Toronto, Sao Paulo, London, The Hague, Belgium, Shanghai and Dubai.

FINANCIAL DATA:
Note: Data for latest year may not have been available at press time.

In U.S. $	2018	2017	2016	2015	2014	2013
Revenue	120,000,000	114,000,000	113,000,000	113,500,000	170,000,000	168,000,000
R&D Expense						
Operating Income						
Operating Margin %						
SGA Expense						
Net Income						
Operating Cash Flow						
Capital Expenditure						
EBITDA						
Return on Assets %						
Return on Equity %						
Debt to Equity						

CONTACT INFORMATION:
Phone: 310-407-0200 Fax:
Toll-Free:
Address: 10960 Wilshire Blvd., Ste. 2200, Los Angeles, CA 90024 United States

STOCK TICKER/OTHER:
Stock Ticker: Private
Employees: 547
Parent Company:

Exchange:
Fiscal Year Ends:

SALARIES/BONUSES:
Top Exec. Salary: $ Bonus: $
Second Exec. Salary: $ Bonus: $

OTHER THOUGHTS:
Estimated Female Officers or Directors: 5
Hot Spot for Advancement for Women/Minorities: Y

Sales, profits and employees may be estimates. Financial information, benefits and other data can change quickly and may vary from those stated here.

Webzen Inc

NAIC Code: 511210G

www.webzen.com

TYPES OF BUSINESS:
Computer Software, Electronic Games, Apps & Entertainment Apps

BRANDS/DIVISIONS/AFFILIATES:
MU
Flyff
Continent of the Ninth Seal (C9)
Age of Wulin
Chaos Castle

CONTACTS:
Note: Officers with more than one job title may be intentionally listed here more than once.

Tae Young Kim, CEO

GROWTH PLANS/SPECIAL FEATURES:
Webzen, Inc., based in Korea, is a developer and distributor of online video games. Webzen games include Age of Wulin, a massively multiplayer online role play game (MMORPG) set in ancient China; Continent of the Ninth Seal (C9), a free-to-play MORPG where users play as heroes of Glenheim taking a stand against otherworldly ruler Neper; Flyff, a MMORPG ; and MU, a fantasy RPG based on the mythical continent of the same name. MU players select a specific character with which they develop experience and enhanced game capabilities that can be carried over into sequential gaming sessions. Players can communicate with each other during the game through instant messaging and may coordinate their activities with other players to form groups, thereby coordinating their game skills to achieve various objectives. Webzen either users pay hourly or a fixed amount of time for a flat fee, usually per month. In late-2018, Webzen's MU division announced the release of Chaos Castle, a player-versus-player game designed for MMORPG MU online. In this mode, players fight against up to 50 other players until only one winner remains.

FINANCIAL DATA:
Note: Data for latest year may not have been available at press time.

In U.S. $	2018	2017	2016	2015	2014	2013
Revenue						
R&D Expense						
Operating Income						
Operating Margin %						
SGA Expense						
Net Income						
Operating Cash Flow						
Capital Expenditure						
EBITDA						
Return on Assets %						
Return on Equity %						
Debt to Equity						

CONTACT INFORMATION:
Phone: 82 1566-3003 Fax: 82 031-627-6890
Toll-Free:
Address: 242 Pangyo-ro, Bundang-gu, Seongnam-si, Gyeonggi-do, South Korea

STOCK TICKER/OTHER:
Stock Ticker: WZENY   Exchange: PINX
Employees: 414   Fiscal Year Ends: 12/31
Parent Company:

SALARIES/BONUSES:
Top Exec. Salary: $ Bonus: $
Second Exec. Salary: $ Bonus: $

OTHER THOUGHTS:
Estimated Female Officers or Directors:
Hot Spot for Advancement for Women/Minorities:

Westwood One Inc

www.westwoodone.com

NAIC Code: 515111

TYPES OF BUSINESS:
Radio Networks, Traditional, Satellite and Online

BRANDS/DIVISIONS/AFFILIATES:
Cumulus Media Inc
Westwood One Backstage
Westwood One Podcast Network

GROWTH PLANS/SPECIAL FEATURES:
Westwood One, Inc. offers nationally syndicated sports, news and entertainment content to 245 million listeners every week. A subsidiary of American broadcasting company Cumulus Media, Inc., Westwood's audio network consists of approximately 8,000 affiliated broadcast radio stations and media partners. The firm is home to premium content such as the NFL, the NCAA, the Masters, the Olympics, Westwood One Backstage, the GRAMMYs, the Academy of Country Music Awards, the Billboard Music Awards and the American Music Awards. The firm's Westwood One Podcast Network delivers popular network and industry personalities and programs. Therefore, Westwood One connects listeners via programs and platforms. During 2018, parent Cumulus emerged from bankruptcy protection.

CONTACTS:
Note: Officers with more than one job title may be intentionally listed here more than once.

Suzanne M. Grimes, Pres.
Charles Steinhauer, COO
Jean B. Clifton, CFO
Hiram Lazar, Chief Admin. Officer
Hiram Lazar, Sec.
David Landau, Co-CEO
Ken Williams, Co-CEO

FINANCIAL DATA:
Note: Data for latest year may not have been available at press time.

In U.S. $	2018	2017	2016	2015	2014	2013
Revenue	350,000,000	346,165,000	336,610,000	368,968,000	421,000,000	245,000,000
R&D Expense						
Operating Income						
Operating Margin %						
SGA Expense						
Net Income		25,635,000	-11,071,000			
Operating Cash Flow						
Capital Expenditure						
EBITDA						
Return on Assets %						
Return on Equity %						
Debt to Equity						

CONTACT INFORMATION:
Phone: 212 967-2888   Fax:
Toll-Free:
Address: 220 W. 42nd St., Candler Tower, New York, NY 10036 United States

STOCK TICKER/OTHER:
Stock Ticker: Subsidiary
Employees: 515
Parent Company: Cumulus Media Inc

Exchange:
Fiscal Year Ends: 12/31

SALARIES/BONUSES:
Top Exec. Salary: $ Bonus: $
Second Exec. Salary: $ Bonus: $

OTHER THOUGHTS:
Estimated Female Officers or Directors: 1
Hot Spot for Advancement for Women/Minorities:

Wildlife Reserves Singapore Group

www.wrs.com.sg

NAIC Code: 712130

TYPES OF BUSINESS:
Zoos and Botanical Gardens

BRANDS/DIVISIONS/AFFILIATES:
Jurong Bird Park
Night Safari
River Safari
Singapore Zoo
Waterfall Aviary

CONTACTS:
Note: Officers with more than one job title may be intentionally listed here more than once.

Mike Barclay, Board Dir.
Neo Gim Huay, Board Dir.
Suppiah Dhanabalan, Chmn.

GROWTH PLANS/SPECIAL FEATURES:

Wildlife Reserves Singapore Group (WRS) is the nonprofit holding company of the Singapore-based attractions Jurong Bird Park, Night Safari, River Safari and Singapore Zoo. A self-funded organization, WRS collaborates with various partners, organizations and institutions aimed to protect local and global biodiversity. Each year, the four attractions welcome 4.6 million visitors. Jurong Bird Park is Singapore's first wildlife park and Asia's largest bird park, offering a hillside haven for more than 3,500 birds across 400 species. The iconic Waterfall Aviary is the park's largest walk-in aviary that houses over 600 birds as well as a 99-foot-high waterfall. The park sees an annual visitor count of 850,000. Night Safari is the world's first safari park for nocturnal animals. It spans 86.5 acres of secondary forest and is home to over 900 animals of over 100 species. A large part of the park is designed to bring visitors on a 40-minute tram ride through seven geographic regions, from the Himalayan foothills to the jungles of Southeast Asia. River Safari is Asia's first and only river-themed wildlife park. Occupying 29.7 acres, it houses 400 plant species and over 7,500 animal specimens representing 240 species. River Safari is designed to profile freshwater habitats from iconic rivers of the world such as the Amazon River, Mekong River, the Mississippi River and River Nile. The Singapore Zoo has been known to have among the most beautiful settings in the world, where animals roam freely in open and natural habitats. Covering 64 acres, the park is home to over 2,400 animals representing over 300 species. The zoo is a Learning Zoo, offering a myriad of educational programs that cater to both local and overseas student groups of between 30 to 200 persons. These programs range from day and night camps, behind-the-scenes and specially guided tours and workshops to wildlife publications.

FINANCIAL DATA:
Note: Data for latest year may not have been available at press time.

In U.S. $	2018	2017	2016	2015	2014	2013
Revenue	124,542,000	110,386,000	115,815,000	111,171,000	115,126,000	94,306,900
R&D Expense						
Operating Income						
Operating Margin %						
SGA Expense						
Net Income						
Operating Cash Flow						
Capital Expenditure						
EBITDA						
Return on Assets %						
Return on Equity %						
Debt to Equity						

CONTACT INFORMATION:
Phone: 65-6269-3411 Fax:
Toll-Free:
Address: 80 Mandai Lake Rd., Singapore, 729826 Singapore

SALARIES/BONUSES:
Top Exec. Salary: $ Bonus: $
Second Exec. Salary: $ Bonus: $

STOCK TICKER/OTHER:
Stock Ticker: Non-Profit   Exchange:
Employees: Fiscal Year Ends: 03/31
Parent Company:

OTHER THOUGHTS:
Estimated Female Officers or Directors:
Hot Spot for Advancement for Women/Minorities:

William Hill plc

NAIC Code: 713210

www.williamhillplc.com

TYPES OF BUSINESS:
Gambling Operations
Online Gambling

BRANDS/DIVISIONS/AFFILIATES:
William Hill US

CONTACTS:
Note: Officers with more than one job title may be intentionally listed here more than once.

Philip Bowcock, CEO
Ruth Prior, CFO
Karen Myers, Dir.-Human Resources
Paul Durkan, CIO
Lyndsay Wright, Dir.-Investor Rel.
Neil Cooper, Group Dir.-Finance
Jurgen Reutter, Head-Mobile
Andrew Lee, Managing Dir.-Online

GROWTH PLANS/SPECIAL FEATURES:

William Hill plc operates licensed betting offices and provides telephone and internet betting and online casino and poker services. The firm divides its business into three categories: retail, online and William Hill U.S. The retail division is the U.K.'s largest bookmaker with a network of more than 2,372 licensed betting shops across the country. The retail division generates about 56% of William Hill's revenue. The online division is an online gaming and betting provider to U.K. customers, as well as a top-three online sports betting operator in Italy and Spain. This segment provides more than 1 million betting opportunities on offer every week, as well as in-play and pre-match betting and a wide range of gaming products. William Hill U.S. is America's largest legal bookmaker by outlet count, operating more than half of the sports books in Nevada, with a presence in 107 of the 190 casinos in the state. This division is also the exclusive bookmaker to the Delaware State Lottery. Additionally, the company develops and maintains its technology infrastructure that supports its sports betting platforms. In March 2018, William Hill sold its Australian division, William Hill Australia, to CrownBet Holdings Pty Ltd for around $9.5 million. William Hill greatly expanded in America during 2018, signing agreements with casinos in New Jersey, Mississippi and West Virginia.

FINANCIAL DATA:
Note: Data for latest year may not have been available at press time.

In U.S. $	2018	2017	2016	2015	2014	2013
Revenue		2,160,916,000	2,025,409,000	2,009,118,000	2,032,355,000	1,877,273,000
R&D Expense						
Operating Income		338,578,500	307,890,500	277,833,900	388,967,500	397,933,900
Operating Margin %		15.66%	15.81%	13.92%	17.44%	20.15%
SGA Expense						
Net Income		-105,071,700	207,744,000	239,821,200	260,532,400	266,720,500
Operating Cash Flow		366,361,900	335,800,200	380,001,000	464,992,900	337,947,100
Capital Expenditure		117,321,700	114,164,500	85,244,500	94,210,950	106,839,800
EBITDA		18,690,640	398,439,100	462,972,300	501,237,600	459,941,400
Return on Assets %		-3.46%	6.86%	8.03%	8.60%	9.84%
Return on Equity %		-7.27%	13.47%	15.98%	18.89%	20.64%
Debt to Equity		0.67	0.58	0.30	0.61	0.87

CONTACT INFORMATION:
Phone: 44-20-8918-3600   Fax: 44-20-8918-3775
Toll-Free:
Address: Greenside House, 50 Station Rd., Wood Green, London, N22 7TP United Kingdom

SALARIES/BONUSES:
Top Exec. Salary: $747,205   Bonus: $726,662
Second Exec. Salary: $134,181   Bonus: $101,844

STOCK TICKER/OTHER:
Stock Ticker: WIMHY
Employees: 16,425
Parent Company:

Exchange: PINX
Fiscal Year Ends: 12/31

OTHER THOUGHTS:
Estimated Female Officers or Directors: 4
Hot Spot for Advancement for Women/Minorities: Y

Sales, profits and employees may be estimates. Financial information, benefits and other data can change quickly and may vary from those stated here.

World Wrestling Entertainment Inc

NAIC Code: 512110

www.wwe.com

TYPES OF BUSINESS:
TV/Video/Theatrical, Production
Wrestling Production

BRANDS/DIVISIONS/AFFILIATES:
WWE Studios
WWE Network
WWEShop

CONTACTS:
Note: Officers with more than one job title may be intentionally listed here more than once.

Vincent Mcmahon, CEO
George Barrios, CFO
Michelle Wilson, Chief Marketing Officer
Mark Kowal, Controller
Casey Collins, Executive VP, Divisional
Paul Levesque, Executive VP, Divisional
Blake Bilstad, General Counsel
Kevin Dunn, Other Corporate Officer
Stephanie Levesque, Other Executive Officer
Michael Luisi, President, Divisional

GROWTH PLANS/SPECIAL FEATURES:

World Wrestling Entertainment, Inc. is an integrated media and entertainment company engaged in the development, production and marketing of television and pay-per-view event programming and live events and the licensing and sale of consumer products featuring its World Wrestling Entertainment brands. The company's four business segments are: live events, consumer products, media and WWE Studios. Live events represent 19% of revenue, and is comprised of a broad and talented roster of superstars that perform in numerous domestic and international markets. Live events and television programming are the division's primary content and production activities. The team develops characters and weaves them into storylines that combine physical and emotional elements. Storylines are usually played out in the ring and unfold on the company's weekly television shows and monthly marquis events distributed via pay-per-view as well as on WWE Network. Consumer products represents 14% of revenue, and is comprised of the licensing fees related to various WWE themed products (video games, toys, apparel), the sale of merchandise at live events and the sale of merchandise on the WWEShop internet site. Media represents 64% of revenue and is comprised of the subscriptions to WWE Network, fees for viewing pay-per-view and video-on-demand programming as well as advertising fees; television rights fees and advertising; the sale of WWE content via home entertainment platforms, including DVD, Blu-ray, subscription and transactional on-demand outlets; and the advertising sales on websites and third-party websites, as well as various broadband and mobile content. WWE Studios derives 2% of revenue, and oversees the company's participation in the production and global distribution of filmed entertainment content.

FINANCIAL DATA:
Note: Data for latest year may not have been available at press time.

In U.S. $	2018	2017	2016	2015	2014	2013
Revenue		800,959,000	729,216,000	658,768,000	542,620,000	507,970,000
R&D Expense						
Operating Income		75,578,000	55,641,000	38,794,000	-42,157,000	5,891,000
Operating Margin %		9.43%	7.63%	6.97%	-7.76%	1.15%
SGA Expense		240,350,000	219,132,000	192,773,000	180,457,000	154,582,000
Net Income		32,640,000	33,841,000	24,144,000	-30,072,000	2,764,000
Operating Cash Flow		96,588,000	56,621,000	49,554,000	54,687,000	23,753,000
Capital Expenditure		24,710,000	29,904,000	20,010,000	11,901,000	55,930,000
EBITDA		156,099,000	121,627,000	101,840,000	15,110,000	56,888,000
Return on Assets %		5.37%	6.70%	6.09%	-7.90%	.72%
Return on Equity %		13.24%	15.07%	11.63%	-12.74%	.98%
Debt to Equity		0.82	0.82	0.08	0.10	0.09

CONTACT INFORMATION:
Phone: 203 352-8600   Fax: 203 359-5151
Toll-Free:
Address: 1241 E. Main St., Stamford, CT 06902 United States

SALARIES/BONUSES:
Top Exec. Salary: $1,388,462   Bonus: $
Second Exec. Salary: $909,560   Bonus: $

STOCK TICKER/OTHER:
Stock Ticker: WWE   Exchange: NYS
Employees: 870   Fiscal Year Ends: 12/31
Parent Company:

OTHER THOUGHTS:
Estimated Female Officers or Directors: 3
Hot Spot for Advancement for Women/Minorities: Y

Sales, profits and employees may be estimates. Financial information, benefits and other data can change quickly and may vary from those stated here.

Wynn Resorts Limited

www.wynnresorts.com

NAIC Code: 721120

TYPES OF BUSINESS:
Hotel Casinos
Online Poker

BRANDS/DIVISIONS/AFFILIATES:
Wynn Las Vegas Resort & Country Club
Encore at Wynn Las Vegas
Wynn Macau Resort
Encore Theater
Encore at Wynn Macau
Wynn Palace
Wynn Boston Harbor

CONTACTS:
Note: Officers with more than one job title may be intentionally listed here more than once.

Craig Billings, CFO
D. Wayson, Director
Philip Satre, Director
Linda Chen, Other Corporate Officer
Ian Coughlan, Other Corporate Officer
Matt Maddox, President

GROWTH PLANS/SPECIAL FEATURES:

Wynn Resorts Limited is a developer, owner and operator of destination casino resorts. The firm owns and operates two destination casino resorts: The Wynn Las Vegas Resort & Country Club in Las Vegas, Nevada, which includes Encore at Wynn Las Vegas; and the Wynn Macau Resort in the Macau Special Administrative Region of China. The Las Vegas operations offer 4,748 rooms and suites. The 192,000-square-foot casino features 247 table games, a poker room, 1,829 slot machines and a race and sports book. The resort also features 33 food and beverage outlets; three nightclubs; two spas and salons; a Ferrari and Maserati automobile dealership; wedding chapels; an 18-hole golf course; 290,000 square feet of meeting space; and a 99,000-square-foot retail promenade featuring boutiques from Alexander McQueen, Cartier, Chanel and Louis Vuitton. At the Encore Theater, the company offers headlining entertainment acts from personalities such as Beyonce. The company's Wynn Macau resort operations, including Encore at Wynn Macau, features 1,008 rooms and suites, approximately 273,000 square feet of casino gaming space with 988 slot machines and 316 table games, eight restaurants, two health clubs, spas and 59,000 square feet of retail space. Wynn Palace, in Macau, is a resort featuring 1,706 rooms and suites, an 8-acre performance lake, sky casinos, floral sculptures, gaming space, meeting facilities, spa, salon, retail spaces and fine dining. The Wynn Boston Harbor is a new development under construction in Everett, Massachusetts (adjacent to Boston), and is scheduled to open by mid-2019.

FINANCIAL DATA:
Note: Data for latest year may not have been available at press time.

In U.S. $	2018	2017	2016	2015	2014	2013
Revenue		6,306,368,000	4,466,297,000	4,075,883,000	5,433,661,000	5,620,936,000
R&D Expense						
Operating Income		1,085,141,000	576,484,000	669,349,000	1,276,715,000	1,307,229,000
Operating Margin %		17.20%	12.90%	16.42%	23.49%	23.25%
SGA Expense		685,485,000	548,141,000	464,793,000	492,464,000	448,788,000
Net Income		747,181,000	241,975,000	195,290,000	731,554,000	728,652,000
Operating Cash Flow		1,876,577,000	970,546,000	572,813,000	1,098,317,000	1,676,642,000
Capital Expenditure		949,045,000	1,240,928,000	1,925,152,000	1,345,940,000	506,786,000
EBITDA		1,501,301,000	1,004,692,000	912,782,000	1,588,043,000	1,656,596,000
Return on Assets %		6.06%	2.15%	1.99%	8.38%	9.30%
Return on Equity %		135.13%	1052.75%			
Debt to Equity		10.09	64.10			

CONTACT INFORMATION:
Phone: 702 770-7555 Fax: 702 733-4681
Toll-Free:
Address: 3131 Las Vegas Blvd. South, Las Vegas, NV 89109 United States

STOCK TICKER/OTHER:
Stock Ticker: WYNN
Employees: 25,200
Parent Company:

Exchange: NAS
Fiscal Year Ends: 12/31

SALARIES/BONUSES:
Top Exec. Salary: $2,500,000 Bonus: $
Second Exec. Salary: $1,500,000 Bonus: $

OTHER THOUGHTS:
Estimated Female Officers or Directors: 3
Hot Spot for Advancement for Women/Minorities: Y

Sales, profits and employees may be estimates. Financial information, benefits and other data can change quickly and may vary from those stated here.

Yellow Pages Limited

NAIC Code: 511140

corporate.yp.ca/en/

TYPES OF BUSINESS:
Directories Publishing
Telephone Directories

BRANDS/DIVISIONS/AFFILIATES:
Yello Pages
YP Dine
YP Shopwise
YP NextHome
JUICE Mobile
Mediavite
411.ca
canada411.ca

CONTACTS:
Note: Officers with more than one job title may be intentionally listed here more than once.

Treena Cooper, Assistant Secretary
David Eckert, CEO
Kenneth Taylor, CFO
Franco Sciannamblo, Chief Accounting Officer
Caroline Andrews, Other Executive Officer
Ali Rahnema, President, Divisional
Paul Brousseau, President, Divisional
John Ireland, Senior VP, Divisional
Stephen Smith, Senior VP, Divisional
Dany Paradis, Senior VP, Divisional
Stephen Port, Vice President, Divisional
Nathalie d'Escrivan, Vice President, Divisional
Yan Belanger, Vice President, Divisional

GROWTH PLANS/SPECIAL FEATURES:
Yellow Pages Limited operates digital and print media in all the provinces of Canada. It also offers media and marketing solutions to small- and medium-sized businesses to enhance customer relationships. Yellow Pages' suite of digital properties help Canadian shoppers discover what is around them, locate valuable information, as well as communicate and transact with local businesses. The company also publishes both in-print and online phone number and address directories. Print, mobile app and/or online products include the Yellow Pages and YP brands of residential and business directories; the YP Dine, which provides restaurant directories; YP Shopwise, which provides a variety of shopping savings and deals; YP.app, comprising a neighborhood search engine for accessing local listings for businesses across Canada; YP NextHome, offering home listings for sale or rent; JUICE Mobile, a mobile advertising technology company whose proprietary platforms facilitate the automatic buying and selling of mobile advertising between brands and publishers; Mediavite, a digital marketing company that focuses on digital audience development and monetization, with services ranging from digital consulting and research to programmatic and native advertising; and canada411.ca and 411.ca, which offers contact information for any person or business across Canada. Yellow Pages Limited serves 229,000 Canadian businesses and attracts 644.9 million visits to its digital properties annually. In August 2018, the firm sold RedFlagDeals, a Canadian bargain hunting and coupon site, to VerticalScope, Inc. for $12 million. It announced in July 2018 that it had sold the ComFree/DuProprio Network websites for finding home, condo and chalet information to Purplebricks Group PLC for $51 million.

FINANCIAL DATA:
Note: Data for latest year may not have been available at press time.

In U.S. $	2018	2017	2016	2015	2014	2013
Revenue		553,351,900	606,863,400	615,611,900	651,043,100	720,955,100
R&D Expense						
Operating Income		58,227,740	96,677,000	133,431,800	176,499,400	264,079,900
Operating Margin %		10.52%	15.93%	21.67%	27.11%	36.62%
SGA Expense						
Net Income		-437,225,100	-299,511,100	45,297,060	139,878,900	130,842,500
Operating Cash Flow		85,574,380	117,304,900	146,575,400	116,113,500	252,752,500
Capital Expenditure		50,233,700	47,115,470	55,955,280	62,282,990	49,208,390
EBITDA		-270,257,000	-291,613,500	185,029,100	220,737,000	308,715,900
Return on Assets %		-72.31%	-28.72%	3.52%	11.05%	9.93%
Return on Equity %		-785.20%	-71.55%	8.45%	31.87%	42.48%
Debt to Equity			0.88	0.52	0.72	1.18

CONTACT INFORMATION:
Phone: 514 934-2611   Fax: 514 934-4076
Toll-Free: 877-956-2003
Address: 16 Place du Commerce, Ile des Soeurs, Verdun, QC H3E 2A5 Canada

STOCK TICKER/OTHER:
Stock Ticker: YLWDF   Exchange: GREY
Employees: 2,400   Fiscal Year Ends: 12/31
Parent Company:

SALARIES/BONUSES:
Top Exec. Salary: $ Bonus: $
Second Exec. Salary: $ Bonus: $

OTHER THOUGHTS:
Estimated Female Officers or Directors: 5
Hot Spot for Advancement for Women/Minorities: Y

Youku Tudou Inc

NAIC Code: 519130

www.youku.com/

TYPES OF BUSINESS:
Online Video Service
Mobile Broadcasting
Video Production
Advertising Services

BRANDS/DIVISIONS/AFFILIATES:
Alibaba Group Holding Limited
Youku
Tudou

GROWTH PLANS/SPECIAL FEATURES:
Youku Tudou, Inc. is a multi-screen entertainment and media company in China. The firm is China's leading internet television platform, enabling users to search, view and share high-quality video content quickly and easily across multiple devices with 580 million monthly unique visitors. Its Youku and Tudou brands are among the most recognized online video brands in the country. Youku Tudou operates as a wholly-owned subsidiary of Alibaba Group Holding Ltd.

CONTACTS: Note: Officers with more than one job title may be intentionally listed here more than once.

Victor Wing Cheung Koo, CEO
Dele Liu, Pres.
Michael Ge Xu, CFO
Yawei Dong, CMO
Leo Jian Yao, CTO
Sunny Xiangyang Zhu, Chief Content Officer
Frank Ming Wei, Sr. VP
Weidong Yang, Sr. VP
Zhou Yu, Sr. VP
Victor Wing Cheung Koo, Chmn.

FINANCIAL DATA: Note: Data for latest year may not have been available at press time.

In U.S. $	2018	2017	2016	2015	2014	2013
Revenue	1,150,000,000	1,050,000,000	900,000,000	805,000,000	652,674,880	468,015,904
R&D Expense						
Operating Income						
Operating Margin %						
SGA Expense						
Net Income						
Operating Cash Flow						
Capital Expenditure						
EBITDA						
Return on Assets %						
Return on Equity %						
Debt to Equity						

CONTACT INFORMATION:
Phone: 86 10-5885-1881 Fax: 86-10-5970-8818
Toll-Free:
Address: Sinosteel Plz., 8 Haidian St., 11/Fl, Beijing, 100080 China

STOCK TICKER/OTHER:
Stock Ticker: Subsidiary Exchange:
Employees: 2,797 Fiscal Year Ends: 12/31
Parent Company: Alibaba Group Holding Ltd

SALARIES/BONUSES:
Top Exec. Salary: $ Bonus: $
Second Exec. Salary: $ Bonus: $

OTHER THOUGHTS:
Estimated Female Officers or Directors:
Hot Spot for Advancement for Women/Minorities:

Sales, profits and employees may be estimates. Financial information, benefits and other data can change quickly and may vary from those stated here.

YouTube LLC

NAIC Code: 519130

www.youtube.com

TYPES OF BUSINESS:
Online Video Services
Video Subscriptions
Online Video Advertising Services

BRANDS/DIVISIONS/AFFILIATES:
Alphabet Inc
Google Corporation
YouTube Leanback
YouTube Partner
YouTube Insight
YouTubeToptics
YouTube Premium
YouTube Music

CONTACTS: Note: Officers with more than one job title may be intentionally listed here more than once.
Susan Wojcicki, CEO
Julie Supan, Dir.-Mktg.
Hunter Walk, Head-Product
Kevin Donahue, VP-Content
Julie Supan, Sr. Dir.-Mktg.

GROWTH PLANS/SPECIAL FEATURES:

YouTube, LLC, a subsidiary of Alphabet, Inc.'s Google, is a leading online video site, featuring significant amounts of user-generated content. It has partnered with major content providers such as WarnerMedia, ABC, CBS, Sony, National Geographic, EA and Activision. The website streams over 1 billion hours of video each day to 89 countries in 76 languages. YouTube derives most of its revenue through in-video advertising, sponsorships and brand channels. Advertisers have the option of purchasing promoted videos, which offer more visibility; 24-hour video banner ads on the website's homepage; the ability to hand-pick videos to advertise against; mobile advertisements; and the ability to advertise with content partners. The YouTube Partner program allows producers of original content that targets a wide audience to upload ad-supported videos, rentals, high quality content and live-streaming videos. Advertisers can track the impact of these advertisements with YouTube Insight, which counts page views, video popularity, demographics and audience attention. YouTube is also available through Apple TV and a variety of mobile devices. Other YouTube features and developments include: YouTube Topics search; a built-in video editor, comment searching; audience statistics; a caption editor, HTML5 video; music playlists; and low-latency pages. YouTube Premium is a monthly subscription that enables users to watch without seeing ads on most types of videos. However, YouTube channels paid for by sponsors, TV show rentals and movie rentals may still display ads. YouTube Premium also lets subscribers watch videos offline by saving them to a desktop or mobile devices for later viewing. YouTubeTV offers over 40 networks, a cloud DVR with no storage limits and six accounts per household for a monthly fee. YouTube Music was launched in 2018, a subscription music streaming service.

Alphabet offers its employees comprehensive health benefits, retirement plans and a variety of employee assistance programs.

FINANCIAL DATA: Note: Data for latest year may not have been available at press time.

In U.S. $	2018	2017	2016	2015	2014	2013
Revenue	6,600,000,000	6,250,000,000	5,000,000,000	4,354,000,000	4,000,000,000	3,125,000,000
R&D Expense						
Operating Income						
Operating Margin %						
SGA Expense						
Net Income						
Operating Cash Flow						
Capital Expenditure						
EBITDA						
Return on Assets %						
Return on Equity %						
Debt to Equity						

CONTACT INFORMATION:
Phone: 650-253-0000 Fax: 650-253-0001
Toll-Free:
Address: 901 Cherry Ave., San Bruno, CA 94066 United States

SALARIES/BONUSES:
Top Exec. Salary: $ Bonus: $
Second Exec. Salary: $ Bonus: $

STOCK TICKER/OTHER:
Stock Ticker: Subsidiary
Employees: 850
Parent Company: Alphabet Inc

Exchange:
Fiscal Year Ends: 12/31

OTHER THOUGHTS:
Estimated Female Officers or Directors: 2
Hot Spot for Advancement for Women/Minorities:

Sales, profits and employees may be estimates. Financial information, benefits and other data can change quickly and may vary from those stated here.

Zagat Survey LLC

www.zagat.com

NAIC Code: 511140

TYPES OF BUSINESS:
Consumer Based Survey Guides
Travel Guides

BRANDS/DIVISIONS/AFFILIATES:
Infatuation Inc (The)
30 Under 30
Zagat.com
Zagat.mobi
Zagat To Go
Zagat

CONTACTS: Note: Officers with more than one job title may be intentionally listed here more than once.
Tim Zagat, CEO
Nina Zagat, Co-Chmn.
Kedar Nadkarni, VP-Bus. Dev. & Strategy
Tiffany Barbalato, Dir.-Comm.
Nina Zagat, Co-Chmn.

GROWTH PLANS/SPECIAL FEATURES:
Zagat Survey, LLC provides global consumer survey-based information and ratings on restaurants and bars. The company's reviews and ratings are based on the opinion surveys of more than 400,000 people from more than 100 countries worldwide. The surveys separately rate the distinct qualities of restaurants and bars, including food, beverages, decor, service and cost. Ratings range from 1 to 5, where 5 is the most favorable; and cost estimates are based on the average cost of menu items, ranging from $ (inexpensive) to $$$$ (very expensive). Photos are displayed on the company's online and mobile channels, as well as a city's best places to try and what is simultaneously new and popular. Zagat offers printed guides to many major cities, including Atlanta, New York City, Houston, Madrid, Rome and Washington, D.C. The guides also offer ratings and reviews on family/top international travel destinations; and on America's major golf courses, shopping, theater, gourmet marketplaces and nightlife. The guides include maps to locations and venues featured in the company's reviews. Zagat's 30 Under 30 highlights thirty men and women who are up-and-coming talents in the hospitality industry, and are under 30 years of age. Talents range from chefs, mixologists and pastry makers to beekeepers. The young honorees' bios and photos can be found on the Zagat website. All of the company's products are available on several media platforms, including the printed guide books; on the web at Zagat.com; and on the mobile web with Zagat.mobi, Zagat To Go and Zagat iOS apps for smart phones. In March 2018, former parent Google sold Zagat Survey to restaurant discovery platform owner/operator, The Infatuation, Inc.

FINANCIAL DATA: Note: Data for latest year may not have been available at press time.

In U.S. $	2018	2017	2016	2015	2014	2013
Revenue						
R&D Expense						
Operating Income						
Operating Margin %						
SGA Expense						
Net Income						
Operating Cash Flow						
Capital Expenditure						
EBITDA						
Return on Assets %						
Return on Equity %						
Debt to Equity						

CONTACT INFORMATION:
Phone: 212-977-6000
Fax: 212-977-9760
Toll-Free: 800-540-9609
Address: 424 Broadway, Fl. 5, New York, NY 10013 United States

STOCK TICKER/OTHER:
Stock Ticker: Subsidiary
Employees:
Parent Company: Infatuation Inc (The)

Exchange:
Fiscal Year Ends: 12/31

SALARIES/BONUSES:
Top Exec. Salary: $
Bonus: $
Second Exec. Salary: $
Bonus: $

OTHER THOUGHTS:
Estimated Female Officers or Directors: 2
Hot Spot for Advancement for Women/Minorities:

Ziff Davis LLC

NAIC Code: 511120

www.ziffdavis.com

TYPES OF BUSINESS:
Online Content & Publishing
Conferences & Events
Advertising
Research Services
Market Intelligence

BRANDS/DIVISIONS/AFFILIATES:
j2 Global Inc
PCMag
Mashable
Speedtest
Revenu7
MarTech Advisor
HRTechnologist
ReadITQick

GROWTH PLANS/SPECIAL FEATURES:
Ziff Davis, LLC is a subsidiary of j2 Global, Inc., and a leading global digital media company. Ziff Davis provides advertising, performance marketing, data services and licensing solutions to thousands of clients worldwide. The firm operates in three core verticals: technology, gaming and shopping. Its brands produce and distribute content across multiple platforms and devices, and include PCMag, Mashable, Speedtest, ExtremeTech, Geek, Toolbox, IGN, AskMen, Offers.com, TechBargains, emedia and Salesify. Ziff Davis publishes its content in 25 languages, and partners with local publishing operators across 114 countries. In mid-2018, Ziff Davis acquired Revenu8, along with its family of brands (MarTech Advisor, HRTechnologist and ReadITQuick) which are built on a data and activation platform that provides clients with marketing, human resources and IT content.

Ziff Davis offers its employees medical, dental and vision insurance, a 401(k), disability and life insurance, paid parental leave and paid time off.

CONTACTS:
Note: Officers with more than one job title may be intentionally listed here more than once.

Steve Horowitz, Pres.
Brian Stewart, CFO
James Yaffe, Chief Strategy Officer
Stephens Hicks, General Counsel
Anurag Harsh, Sr. VP-Bus. Dev.
Will Guyatt, Head-Global Comm.
Bennet Zucker, Sr. VP
Dan Costa, Editor-In-Chief

FINANCIAL DATA:
Note: Data for latest year may not have been available at press time.

In U.S. $	2018	2017	2016	2015	2014	2013
Revenue	195,000,000	190,000,000	189,500,000	174,000,000	167,814,000	131,146,000
R&D Expense						
Operating Income						
Operating Margin %						
SGA Expense						
Net Income						
Operating Cash Flow						
Capital Expenditure						
EBITDA						
Return on Assets %						
Return on Equity %						
Debt to Equity						

CONTACT INFORMATION:
Phone: 212-503-3500   Fax:
Toll-Free:
Address: 28 E. 28th St., New York, NY 10016 United States

STOCK TICKER/OTHER:
Stock Ticker: Subsidiary   Exchange:
Employees: 700   Fiscal Year Ends: 12/31
Parent Company: j2 Global Inc

SALARIES/BONUSES:
Top Exec. Salary: $ Bonus: $
Second Exec. Salary: $ Bonus: $

OTHER THOUGHTS:
Estimated Female Officers or Directors:
Hot Spot for Advancement for Women/Minorities: Y

Zynga Inc

www.zynga.com

NAIC Code: 511210G

TYPES OF BUSINESS:
Computer Software, Electronic Games, Apps & Entertainment
Social Media Gaming
Apps

BRANDS/DIVISIONS/AFFILIATES:
FarmVille
Words with Friends
Zynga Poker
Games for Good at Zynga

GROWTH PLANS/SPECIAL FEATURES:
Zynga, Inc. is a leading developer of online social games for social media sites, online networks and mobile devices. The company's games are hosted on a variety of social networks including Facebook. Its products include casino games, word games, board games, role playing games and party games. Zynga's most successful games include FarmVille, FarmVille 2, Words with Friends and Zynga Poker. The company also administers Games for Good at Zynga, which donates money and educational goods to international nonprofits. The firm has received funding from Kleiner Perkins Caufield & Beyers, Foundry Group, Union Square Ventures, Institutional Venture Partners, Avalon Ventures, SoftBank and The Pilot Group. More than 64 million consumers play Zynga's games each month. In December 2017, the firm acquired the mobile card game studio of Peak Games, a leading global mobile gaming company.

CONTACTS:
Note: Officers with more than one job title may be intentionally listed here more than once.

Gerard Griffin, CFO
Mark Pincus, Chairman of the Board
Jeffrey Buckley, Chief Accounting Officer
Matthew Bromberg, COO
Frank Gibeau, Director
Phuong Phillips, Other Executive Officer
Jeffrey Ryan, Other Executive Officer
Bernard Kim, President, Divisional

FINANCIAL DATA:
Note: Data for latest year may not have been available at press time.

In U.S. $	2018	2017	2016	2015	2014	2013
Revenue		861,390,000	741,420,000	764,717,000	690,410,000	873,266,000
R&D Expense		256,012,000	320,300,000	361,931,000	396,553,000	413,001,000
Operating Income		25,724,000	-93,572,000	-146,056,000	-244,741,000	-55,414,000
Operating Margin %		2.98%	-12.62%	-19.09%	-35.44%	-6.34%
SGA Expense		320,683,000	276,146,000	312,857,000	325,028,000	267,321,000
Net Income		26,639,000	-108,173,000	-121,510,000	-225,900,000	-36,982,000
Operating Cash Flow		94,577,000	60,016,000	-44,447,000	-4,511,000	28,674,000
Capital Expenditure		9,971,000	10,313,000	7,832,000	9,201,000	7,813,000
EBITDA		56,018,000	-51,802,000	-91,741,000	-161,847,000	73,633,000
Return on Assets %		1.37%	-5.36%	-5.43%	-9.76%	-1.52%
Return on Equity %		1.65%	-6.42%	-6.59%	-11.97%	-1.99%
Debt to Equity						

CONTACT INFORMATION:
Phone: 800 762-2530 Fax:
Toll-Free:
Address: 699 8th St., San Francisco, CA 94103 United States

SALARIES/BONUSES:
Top Exec. Salary: $1,000,000 Bonus: $
Second Exec. Salary: $500,000 Bonus: $

STOCK TICKER/OTHER:
Stock Ticker: ZNGA
Employees: 1,681
Parent Company:

Exchange: NAS
Fiscal Year Ends: 12/31

OTHER THOUGHTS:
Estimated Female Officers or Directors: 2
Hot Spot for Advancement for Women/Minorities:

ADDITIONAL INDEXES

CONTENTS:	
Index of Firms Noted as "Hot Spots for Advancement" for Women/Minorities	**520**
Index by Subsidiaries, Brand Names and Selected Affiliations	**522**

INDEX OF FIRMS NOTED AS HOT SPOTS FOR ADVANCEMENT FOR WOMEN & MINORITIES

A H Belo Corporation
A&E Television Networks LLC
Alphabet Inc (Google)
Altice USA Inc
Amazon.com Inc
AMC Networks Inc
American Educational Products LLC
American Express Company
American Golf Corp
American Greetings Corporation LLC
Ameristar Casinos Inc
Aristocrat Leisure Limited
Ascential plc
AT&T Inc
Audible Inc
Avid Technology Inc
Barnes & Noble Inc
Beasley Broadcast Group Inc
Bertelsmann SE & Co KGaA
Best Buy Co Inc
Bloomberg LP
Boyd Gaming Corp
Brightcove Inc
British Broadcasting Corporation (BBC)
Cable News Network Inc (CNN)
Caesars Entertainment Corporation
CBS Corporation
CBS Interactive Inc
Cedar Fair LP
Central European Media Enterprises Ltd
Century Casinos Inc
Cequel Communications Holdings I LLC
Cineplex Inc
Clear Channel Outdoor Holdings Inc
CNHI LLC
Cogeco Communications Inc
Comcast Corporation
Conde Nast Publications Inc
Corus Entertainment Inc
Cox Communications Inc
Cox Enterprises Inc
Cox Media Group Inc
Crown Media Family Networks
CSS Industries Inc
Delaware North Companies Inc
Dennis Publishing Ltd
DirecTV LLC (DIRECTV)
Discovery Inc
Disney Media Networks
Dotdash
Dow Jones & Company Inc
DreamWorks Animation SKG Inc
E W Scripps Company (The)
EBSCO Industries Inc
Emmis Communications Corporation
ESPN Inc
EVINE Live Inc
Facebook Inc
Fox Broadcasting Company
Full House Resorts Inc
Galaxy Entertainment Group Limited
Gaming Partners International Corporation
Gannett Co Inc
GateHouse Media LLC
Glu Mobile Inc
GMM Grammy PCL
Graham Holdings Company
Gray Television Inc
Grupo Radio Centro SAB de CV
HarperCollins Publishers LLC
Harte-Hanks Inc
Hearst Corporation (The)
Hearst Television Inc
Hershey Company (The)
Home Box Office Inc (HBO)
Hoover's Inc
Houghton Mifflin Harcourt Company
HSN Inc (Home Shopping Network)
Hurriyet Gazetecilik ve Matbaacilik AS
IAC/InterActiveCorp
IGN Entertainment Inc
IMAX Corporation
Ink Publishing Inc
International Data Group Inc
International Game Technology PLC
ITV plc
John Wiley & Sons Inc
King Digital Entertainment plc
Leaf Group Ltd
Lee Enterprises Incorporated
Liberty Global plc
Lions Gate Entertainment Corp
LucasArts Entertainment Company LLC
Lucasfilm Ltd LLC
MarketWatch Inc
Martha Stewart Living Omnimedia Inc
McClatchy Company (The)
MDI Entertainment LLC
Meredith Corporation
Metro International SA
MGM Resorts International
Microsoft Corporation
Miramax LLC
MobiTV Inc
Modern Times Group MTG AB
Myspace LLC
Naspers Limited
National Geographic Society
NBCUniversal Media LLC
Netflix Inc
NeuLion Inc

New York Times Company (The)
News Corporation
Nexstar Media Group Inc
Nielsen Holdings plc
NPR (National Public Radio)
Oprah Winfrey Network (OWN)
Outerwall Inc
Pandora Media Inc
Paramount Pictures Corporation
Patch Media Corporation
Pearson PLC
Penguin Random House
Pinnacle Entertainment Inc
Playboy Enterprises Inc
Pro Publica Inc
Rank Group plc (The)
Raycom Media Inc
RealNetworks Inc
RELX PLC
RentPath LLC
Rogers Communications Inc
Rolling Stone LLC
Rosetta Stone Inc
Salon Media Group Inc
Sanoma Oyj
Scholastic Corporation
Scribd Inc
Shaw Communications Inc
Shun Tak Holdings Limited
Simon & Schuster Inc
Singapore Press Holdings Limited
Sirius XM Holdings Inc
SKY Network Television Limited
Sky plc
Tabcorp Holdings Limited
Tatts Group Limited
Texas Tribune Inc (The)
Thomson Reuters Corporation
TNS UK Ltd
Torstar Corporation
Tribune Media Company
Trusted Media Brands Inc
TVA Group Inc
Twentieth Century Fox Film Corporation
Twenty-First Century Fox Inc (21st Century Fox)
UBM plc
Univision Communications Inc
Urban One Inc
US News and World Report LP
Vail Resorts Inc
Verizon Communications Inc
Verizon Media Group
Viacom Inc
VICE Media Inc
Virgin Media Business Ltd
Vivendi SA
Vulcan Inc
Walt Disney Company (The)
Warner Bros Entertainment Inc
Warner Media LLC
Warner Music Group Corp
Washington Times LLC (The)
Wasserman Media Group LLC
William Hill plc
World Wrestling Entertainment Inc
Wynn Resorts Limited
Yellow Pages Limited
Ziff Davis LLC

INDEX OF SUBSIDIARIES, BRAND NAMES AND AFFILIATIONS

1010data; **Advance Publications Inc**
102.9FM-The Hog; **Saga Communications Inc**
152 Media; **EBSCO Industries Inc**
17173.com; **Changyou.com Limited**
20th Century; **Twentieth Century Fox Film Corporation**
20th Century Fox; **Fox Entertainment Group Inc**
21st Century Fox; **Sky plc**
21st Century Fox; **Hulu LLC**
21st Century Fox; **Fox Entertainment Group Inc**
21st Century Fox; **Twenty-First Century Fox Inc (21st Century Fox)**
2929 Productions; **2929 Entertainment**
2K; **Take-Two Interactive Software Inc**
3 Arena; **Live Nation Entertainment Inc**
30 Under 30; **Zagat Survey LLC**
360 Link; **ProQuest LLC**
411.ca; **Yellow Pages Limited**
5G; **Rogers Communications Inc**
7flix; **Seven West Media Limited**
7mate; **Seven West Media Limited**
7TWO; **Seven West Media Limited**
A&E; **A&E Television Networks LLC**
A&E Networks; **Hearst Corporation (The)**
A+; **Societe d'Edition de Canal Plus**
a+; **TV Azteca SAB de CV**
A+E; **Walt Disney Company (The)**
A+E Networks; **Disney Media Networks**
A20 Aviation; **Bose Corporation**
a4 Media & Data Solutions LLC; **Altice USA Inc**
ABC Entertainment; **ABC Inc (Disney-ABC)**
ABC Family Worldwide; **Disney Media Networks**
ABC Inc; **ESPN Inc**
ABC Owned Television Stations Group; **Disney Media Networks**
ABC Owned Television Stations Group; **ABC Inc (Disney-ABC)**
ABC Studios; **ABC Inc (Disney-ABC)**
ABC Television Network; **Disney Media Networks**
Aberdeen Restaurant Enterprises Limited; **Melco International Development Limited**
Academic OneFile; **Cengage Learning Holdings II Inc**
Access Industries Inc; **Warner Music Group Corp**
AccessIngram.com; **Ingram Entertainment Holdings Inc**
Aces Cribbage 2; **Concrete Software Inc**
Aces Gin Rummy; **Concrete Software Inc**
Aces Hearts; **Concrete Software Inc**
Aces Spades; **Concrete Software Inc**
Acme Building Brands; **Berkshire Hathaway Inc**
Acorn Media Enterprises; **RLJ Entertainment Inc**
Acorn TV; **RLJ Entertainment Inc**
Activision Blizzard Distribution; **Activision Blizzard Inc**
Activision Blizzard Inc; **King Digital Entertainment plc**
Activision Blizzard Studios; **Activision Blizzard Inc**
Activision Publishing Inc; **Activision Blizzard Inc**
adn40; **TV Azteca SAB de CV**
Advance Local; **Advance Publications Inc**
Advance Publications Inc; **Conde Nast Publications Inc**
Adventure Cove Waterpark; **Genting Singapore PLC**
Adventure Island; **SeaWorld Entertainment Inc**
AEG China; **Anschutz Entertainment Group Inc**
AEG Digital Media; **Anschutz Entertainment Group Inc**
AEG Global Partnerships; **Anschutz Entertainment Group Inc**
AEG Merchandising; **Anschutz Entertainment Group Inc**
AEG Presents; **Anschutz Entertainment Group Inc**
Aeon Insurance Asset Management Company; **Dalian Wanda Group Co Ltd**
Affonbladet; **Schibsted ASA**
Aftenposten; **Schibsted ASA**
AG Trucano Son and Grandsons Inc; **Nevada Gold & Casinos Inc**
Agatha Christie Limited; **RLJ Entertainment Inc**
Age of Wulin; **Webzen Inc**
AHC Proven Performance Media LLC; **A H Belo Corporation**
AION; **NCsoft Corporation**
AIRE Radio Networks; **Spanish Broadcasting System Inc**
AirPods; **Apple Inc**
AirSpeed; **Avid Technology Inc**
Alexander Street Press; **ProQuest LLC**
Aliante Casino + Hotel + Spa; **Boyd Gaming Corp**
Alibaba Group Holding Limited; **Youku Tudou Inc**
All Current; **EBSCO Industries Inc**
All Things Considered; **NPR (National Public Radio)**
All3Media; **Liberty Global plc**
Allen Institute for Artificial Intelligence; **Vulcan Inc**
Allen Institute for Brain Science; **Vulcan Inc**
AllightSykes; **Seven Group Holdings Limited**
Allrecipes; **Meredith Corporation**
Alpha Betty Saga; **King Digital Entertainment plc**
Alphabet Inc; **YouTube LLC**
Alpine Valley; **Peak Resorts Inc**
Alpoint Capital Partners LLC; **Ford Models Inc**
Altice Business; **Altice USA Inc**
Altice Europe NV; **Cequel Communications Holdings I LLC**
Altice Media Solutions; **Altice USA Inc**
Altice NV; **Altice USA Inc**
Altice USA; **Cequel Communications Holdings I LLC**
Altice USA Inc; **Altice NV**
Altira Macau; **Melco International Development Limited**
Always On; **Crackle Inc (dba SonyCrackle)**
Amazon Go; **Amazon.com Inc**
Amazon Marketplace; **Amazon.com Inc**
Amazon Prime; **Amazon.com Inc**
Amazon Web Services (AWS); **Amazon.com Inc**
Amazon.com Inc; **Audible Inc**
Amblin Partners; **DreamWorks II Holding Co LLC**
Amblin Partners; **Universal Pictures**
Amblin Partners; **Comcast Corporation**
AMC; **AMC Networks Inc**
AMC Networks Broadcasting & Technology; **AMC Networks Inc**

INDEX OF SUBSIDIARIES, BRAND NAMES AND AFFILIATIONS, CONT.

AMC Networks Inc; **RLJ Entertainment Inc**
American Angler; **Morris Communications Company LLC**
American Bandstand Express; **Dick Clark Productions Inc**
American Chance Casinos; **Trans World Corporation**
American City Business Journals; **Advance Publications Inc**
American Express Bank FSB; **American Express Company**
American Express Centurion Bank; **American Express Company**
American Express Travel Related Services Co Inc; **American Express Company**
American Golf Foundation; **American Golf Corp**
American Multi Cinema Inc; **AMC Entertainment Holdings Inc**
American Wholesale Book Company; **Books A Million Inc**
AmericanGolf.com; **American Golf Corp**
AmericanGreetings.com; **American Greetings Corporation LLC**
Ameristar Black Hawk; **Ameristar Casinos Inc**
Ameristar Casino Hotel East Chicago; **Ameristar Casinos Inc**
Ameristar Council Bluffs; **Ameristar Casinos Inc**
Ameristar Kansas City; **Ameristar Casinos Inc**
Ameristar St Charles; **Ameristar Casinos Inc**
Ameristar Vicksburg; **Ameristar Casinos Inc**
AMF; **Bowlero Corporation**
AMPED Distribution; **Alliance Entertainment LLC**
Amplify Snack Brands Inc; **Hershey Company (The)**
Amstrad Limited; **Sky plc**
Analytics on Demand; **Cengage Learning Holdings II Inc**
Andersen Press USA; **Lerner Publishing Group**
Android; **Alphabet Inc (Google)**
ANGI Homeservices Inc; **IAC/InterActiveCorp**
Angie's List; **IAC/InterActiveCorp**
Angry Birds; **LucasArts Entertainment Company LLC**
Anschutz Company (The); **Anschutz Entertainment Group Inc**
Anthem; **BioWare Corp**
Anyo Pioneer Motor Info Tech Co Ltd; **Pioneer Corporation**
Aol; **Verizon Media Group**
Apalon; **IAC/InterActiveCorp**
Apartment Guide (The); **RentPath LLC**
ApartmentGuide.com; **RentPath LLC**
Apollo Global Management LLC; **ClubCorp Holdings Inc**
Apollo Global Management LLC; **McGraw-Hill Education Inc**
Apollo Global Management LLC; **Outerwall Inc**
Apollo Global Management LLC; **Redbox Automated Retail LLC**
Apple Inc; **Shazam Entertainment Limited**
Apple TV; **Apple Inc**
Apple Watch; **Apple Inc**
Aquatica; **SeaWorld Entertainment Inc**
Architectural Digest; **Conde Nast Publications Inc**
Arctic Cat Extreme Snowmobile Racing; **Concrete Software Inc**
ArenaNet; **NCsoft Corporation**
ArenaNet; **NCsoft Corporation**
Argosy Casino Riverside; **Penn National Gaming Inc**
Arista Records; **Sony Music Entertainment Inc**
Aristocrat Technologies Inc; **Aristocrat Leisure Limited**
Aristotle Corporation (The); **American Educational Products LLC**
Arlington International Racecourse; **Churchill Downs Incorporated**
Arnold Bernhard & Company Inc; **Value Line Inc**
Arts and Exhibitions International LLC; **Premier Exhibitions Inc**
Arvato Bertelsmann; **Bertelsmann SE & Co KGaA**
AS; **Promotora de Informaciones SA**
AskMen.com; **IGN Entertainment Inc**
Associated Partners LP; **Liberty Media Corporation**
Asteroids; **Atari Interactive Inc**
ASX TV; **2929 Entertainment**
At Bat; **Major League Baseball Advanced Media LP (MLBAM)**
AT&T; **Hulu LLC**
AT&T In; **Home Box Office Inc (HBO)**
AT&T Inc; **Cable News Network Inc (CNN)**
AT&T Inc; **Central European Media Enterprises Ltd**
AT&T Inc; **DirecTV LLC (DIRECTV)**
AT&T Inc; **Turner Broadcasting System Inc**
AT&T Inc; **Warner Bros Entertainment Inc**
AT&T Inc; **Warner Media LLC**
AT&T Inc; **CW Network LLC (The)**
Atari Licensing; **Atari Interactive Inc**
Atari SA; **Atari Interactive Inc**
Atari Studios; **Atari Interactive Inc**
Atheneum Books ofr Young Readers; **Simon & Schuster Inc**
Atlantic Broadband; **Cogeco Communications Inc**
Atlantic Broadband; **Cogeco Inc**
Atlantic Records Group; **Warner Music Group Corp**
Atlantis; **Kerzner International Limited**
Atlast FC; **TV Azteca SAB de CV**
Atom Tickets; **Lions Gate Entertainment Corp**
Atypon Systems Inc; **John Wiley & Sons Inc**
Audible.com; **Audible Inc**
AudibleListener; **Audible Inc**
Auto Bild; **Axel Springer SE**
AutoExpress; **Dennis Publishing Ltd**
Autotie.fi; **Sanoma Oyj**
AutoTrader.co.za; **Naspers Limited**

INDEX OF SUBSIDIARIES, BRAND NAMES AND AFFILIATIONS, CONT.

autotrader.com; **Cox Enterprises Inc**
Avalanche Bay Indoor Waterpark; **Boyne Resorts**
Avatar; **Twentieth Century Fox Film Corporation**
Avery; **Penguin Group USA**
Aviator (The); **Miramax LLC**
Avid NEXIS; **Avid Technology Inc**
Avid VENU; **Avid Technology Inc**
Awesomeness TV; **DreamWorks Animation SKG Inc**
AwesomenessTV Holdings; **Viacom Inc**
Axel Springer Digital Classifieds; **Axel Springer SE**
Azteca 7; **TV Azteca SAB de CV**
Azteca Internet; **TV Azteca SAB de CV**
Azteca Uno; **TV Azteca SAB de CV**
Azure; **Microsoft Corporation**
B Riley Financial Inc; **United Online Inc**
Bad Genius; **GMM Grammy PCL**
Baidu Inc; **iQiyi Inc**
Balance (The); **Dotdash**
Baldur's Gate; **BioWare Corp**
Ballard Designs; **HSN Inc (Home Shopping Network)**
Baltimore Sun; **Tribune Publishing Company**
Barnes & Noble Booksellers; **Barnes & Noble Inc**
Barrie Advance; **Torstar Corporation**
Barrons; **Dow Jones & Company Inc**
Barrons.com; **MarketWatch Inc**
Battleborn; **Take-Two Interactive Software Inc**
Battlefield; **Electronic Arts Inc (EA)**
Baupost Group; **Greek Organisation of Football Prognostics SA (OPAP)**
Bay Food Service Co Ltd; **Oriental Land Co Ltd**
Bay Harbor Golf Club; **Boyne Resorts**
BBC America; **AMC Networks Inc**
BBC News; **British Broadcasting Corporation (BBC)**
BBC One; **British Broadcasting Corporation (BBC)**
BBC Radio 1; **British Broadcasting Corporation (BBC)**
BBC Radio 5 live sports extra; **British Broadcasting Corporation (BBC)**
BBC Sounds; **British Broadcasting Corporation (BBC)**
BBC Studios; **British Broadcasting Corporation (BBC)**
BBC Three; **British Broadcasting Corporation (BBC)**
BBC Two; **British Broadcasting Corporation (BBC)**
Beach Energy Ltd; **Seven Group Holdings Limited**
Beasley Media Group 2 Inc; **Beasley Broadcast Group Inc**
Beatles LOVE (The); **Cirque du Soleil Inc**
Beijing Byte Dance Telecommunications Co Ltd; **Musical.ly**
Beijing Guard Libang Technology Co Ltd; **Scientific Games Corporation**
beIN Media Group LLC; **Miramax LLC**
Bellagio; **MGM Resorts International**
Belterra Casino Resort; **Pinnacle Entertainment Inc**
Berkshire Hathaway Primary Group; **Berkshire Hathaway Inc**
Berkshire Hathaway Reinsurance Group; **Berkshire Hathaway Inc**

Bertelsmann AG; **RTL Group SA**
Bertelsmann SE & Co KGaA; **Penguin Random House**
Berwick Offray LLC; **CSS Industries Inc**
Best Buy Direct; **Best Buy Co Inc**
Best Buy Express; **Best Buy Co Inc**
Best of Car Talk; **NPR (National Public Radio)**
bestbuy.ca; **Best Buy Co Inc**
bestbuy.com; **Best Buy Co Inc**
bestbuy.com.mx; **Best Buy Co Inc**
BestReviews; **Tribune Publishing Company**
Better Homes & Gardens; **Meredith Corporation**
Beyond Yellowstone; **National Geographic Society**
BFG (The); **DreamWorks II Holding Co LLC**
Big Boulder; **Peak Resorts Inc**
Big Cats; **National Geographic Society**
Big Interview With Dan Rather (The); **2929 Entertainment**
Big Synergy; **Reliance Entertainment Pvt Ltd**
Big Ten Network; **Fox Sports Interactive Media LLC**
Biggest Little Studio; **Aristocrat Leisure Limited**
Bigpara.com; **Hurriyet Gazetecilik ve Matbaacilik AS**
Billy's Casino; **Full House Resorts Inc**
Bingo; **Storm8**
BioWare Odyssey Engine; **BioWare Corp**
Black Book; **Hearst Corporation (The)**
Black Butter Records; **Sony Music Entertainment Inc**
Black Love; **Oprah Winfrey Network (OWN)**
BlackAmericaWeb.com; **Urban One Inc**
Blackheart; **LOUD Audio LLC**
BlackPlanet; **Urban One Inc**
Blackstone Group LP (The); **Merlin Entertainments Group Plc**
Blade Online; **Changyou.com Limited**
Bliss; **Steiner Leisure Limited**
Blizzard Entertainment Inc; **Activision Blizzard Inc**
Blood & Glory; **Glu Mobile Inc**
Bloomberg BNA; **Bloomberg LP**
Bloomberg Businessweek; **Bloomberg LP**
Bloomberg Government; **Bloomberg LP**
Bloomberg Intelligence; **Bloomberg LP**
Bloomberg New Energy Finance Limited; **Bloomberg LP**
Bloomberg Terminal; **Bloomberg LP**
Bloomberg Tradebook; **Bloomberg LP**
Bloomberg Vault; **Bloomberg LP**
Blue Chip Hotel and Casino; **Boyd Gaming Corp**
Blue Man Group; **Cirque du Soleil Inc**
Blue Sky Studios; **Twentieth Century Fox Film Corporation**
BlueMountain.com; **American Greetings Corporation LLC**
BlueSky TV; **Shaw Communications Inc**
BMG; **Bertelsmann SE & Co KGaA**
Bodies Revealed; **Premier Exhibitions Inc**
Bodies; The Exhibition; **Premier Exhibitions Inc**
Boing; **Mediaset SpA**

INDEX OF SUBSIDIARIES, BRAND NAMES AND AFFILIATIONS, CONT.

Book of John Gray (The); **Oprah Winfrey Network (OWN)**
Book$mart Inc; **Books A Million Inc**
Books-A-Million; **Books A Million Inc**
booksamillion.com; **Books A Million Inc**
Boomerang; **Turner Broadcasting System Inc**
Boomers; **Palace Entertainment Holdings LLC**
Boomtown Casino Biloxi; **Penn National Gaming Inc**
Boomtown Casino Hotel; **Pinnacle Entertainment Inc**
Booth Creek Ski Group Inc; **Booth Creek Ski Holdings Inc**
Borsheim Jewelry Company Inc; **Berkshire Hathaway Inc**
Boston Mills; **Peak Resorts Inc**
Boulder Station; **Station Casinos LLC**
Bounce; **E W Scripps Company (The)**
Bourgogne et Grasset; **Gaming Partners International Corporation**
Bowlero; **Bowlero Corporation**
Bowlmor Lanes; **Bowlero Corporation**
Boyne Highlands Resort; **Boyne Resorts**
Boyne Mountain Resort; **Boyne Resorts**
Boyne Realty; **Boyne Resorts**
BrandVoice; **Forbes Media LLC**
Braves Holdings LLC; **Liberty Media Corporation**
Bravo Media; **NBCUniversal Media LLC**
Brides; **Conde Nast Publications Inc**
Brightcove Enterprise Video Suite; **Brightcove Inc**
Brightcove OTT Flow; **Brightcove Inc**
Brightcove Player; **Brightcove Inc**
Brightcove SSAI; **Brightcove Inc**
Brightcove Video Cloud; **Brightcove Inc**
Brightcove Video Marketing Suite; **Brightcove Inc**
Brightcove Zencoder; **Brightcove Inc**
Brighton Resort; **Boyne Resorts**
Bristol Renaissance Faire; **Renaissance Entertainment Corporation**
BroadbandTV; **RTL Group SA**
Broadcast Media Partners Holdings Inc; **Univision Communications Inc**
Broadview Media; **Raycom Media Inc**
Broadway Macau; **Galaxy Entertainment Group Limited**
Bronco Billy's Casino and Hotel; **Full House Resorts Inc**
Brunswick Zone; **Bowlero Corporation**
BTV; **Central European Media Enterprises Ltd**
Bubba Gump Shrimp Co; **Fertitta Entertainment Inc.**
Bubble Mania; **Storm8**
Bubble Witch Saga; **King Digital Entertainment plc**
Bud Jones; **Gaming Partners International Corporation**
Buffalo Billy's Casino; **Full House Resorts Inc**
Bug Club; **Pearson PLC**
Busch Gardens; **SeaWorld Entertainment Inc**
Business & Economy; **Washington Times LLC (The)**
Business Collection; **Cengage Learning Holdings II Inc**
Business Insider; **Axel Springer SE**
Butterick; **CSS Industries Inc**

C R Gibson LLC; **CSS Industries Inc**
C2 Design; **Nippon Columbia Co Ltd**
C8; **Societe d'Edition de Canal Plus**
Cable Guide; **I-Cable Communications Limited**
Cactus Petes and The Horseshu Jackpot; **Pinnacle Entertainment Inc**
Cactus Pete's Resort Casino; **Ameristar Casinos Inc**
Caesars Acquisition Company; **Caesars Entertainment Corporation**
Caesars Interactive Entertainment Inc; **Caesars Entertainment Corporation**
Calder Race Course; **Churchill Downs Incorporated**
California Hotel & Casino; **Boyd Gaming Corp**
Call of Duty; **Activision Blizzard Inc**
canada411.ca; **Yellow Pages Limited**
Canal+; **Societe d'Edition de Canal Plus**
Canal+ Africa; **Societe d'Edition de Canal Plus**
Canal+ Group; **Vivendi SA**
Canal+ Group; **Societe d'Edition de Canal Plus**
Canal+Regie; **Societe d'Edition de Canal Plus**
CanalSatellite; **Societe d'Edition de Canal Plus**
Candy Blast Mania; **Storm8**
Candy Crush Saga; **King Digital Entertainment plc**
Cannabis Cup (The); **Hightimes Holding Corp**
Cannes Lions; **Ascential plc**
Canterbury Park Racetrack and Card Casino; **Canterbury Park Holding Corporation**
Capital Club; **Dover Downs Gaming & Entertainment Inc**
Captain America; **Marvel Entertainment LLC**
Carbine Studios; **NCsoft Corporation**
Carbuyer; **Dennis Publishing Ltd**
CardStore.com; **American Greetings Corporation LLC**
CareerBuilder; **TEGNA Inc**
CareerBuilder LLC; **Tribune Media Company**
Carmike Cinemas Inc; **AMC Entertainment Holdings Inc**
Carowinds; **Cedar Fair LP**
Cars; **Pixar Animation Studios**
Cars.com Inc; **TEGNA Inc**
Cartoon Network; **Turner Broadcasting System Inc**
Casino Ajax; **Great Canadian Gaming Corporation**
Casino New/Nouveau Brunswick; **Great Canadian Gaming Corporation**
Casino Nova Scotia Halifax; **Great Canadian Gaming Corporation**
Casino Woodbine; **Great Canadian Gaming Corporation**
Casinos Poland Ltd; **Century Casinos Inc**
Castaway Bay Indoor Waterpark Resort; **Cedar Fair LP**
Castle Park; **Palace Entertainment Holdings LLC**
CBN; **Shanghai Media Group (SMG)**
CBN Paper; **Shanghai Media Group (SMG)**
CBN Radio; **Shanghai Media Group (SMG)**
CBN TV; **Shanghai Media Group (SMG)**
CBN Weekly; **Shanghai Media Group (SMG)**
CBS All Access; **CBS Interactive Inc**

INDEX OF SUBSIDIARIES, BRAND NAMES AND AFFILIATIONS, CONT.

CBS All Access; **CBS Corporation**
CBS Corporation; **CBS Interactive Inc**
CBS Corporation; **CW Network LLC (The)**
CBS Corporation; **Entercom Communications Corp**
CBS Corporation; **MP3.com Inc**
CBS Corporation; **Simon & Schuster Inc**
CBS Corporation; **National Amusements Inc**
CBS Films; **CBS Corporation**
CBS Interactive Inc; **MP3.com Inc**
CBS Local Digital Media; **CBS Corporation**
CBS Radio Inc; **Entercom Communications Corp**
CBS Television Network; **CBS Corporation**
CBS Television Stations; **CBS Corporation**
CBS.com; **CBS Interactive Inc**
CBSN; **CBS Interactive Inc**
CBSNews.com; **CBS Interactive Inc**
CBSSports.com; **CBS Interactive Inc**
Cedar Point; **Cedar Fair LP**
Celestial Tiger; **Lions Gate Entertainment Corp**
Cengage Gale; **Cengage Learning Holdings II Inc**
Center for News & Design; **GateHouse Media LLC**
Centipede; **Atari Interactive Inc**
Central Illinois Newspaper Group; **Lee Enterprises Incorporated**
Central Services Studios Inc; **AMC Entertainment Holdings Inc**
Century Bets! Inc; **Century Casinos Inc**
Century Casino & Hotel; **Century Casinos Inc**
Century Casino Calgary; **Century Casinos Inc**
Century Casino St. Alvert; **Century Casinos Inc**
Century Downs Racetrack and Casino; **Century Casinos Inc**
Cequel Corporation; **Cequel Communications Holdings I LLC**
Chaos Castle; **Webzen Inc**
Charge!; **Sinclair Broadcast Group Inc**
Charlotte Observer (The); **McClatchy Company (The)**
Charlotte Wedding; **Morris Communications Company LLC**
Chart House; **Fertitta Entertainment Inc.**
Charter Communications; **Advance Publications Inc**
Checked Inn; **Oprah Winfrey Network (OWN)**
Chicago; **Miramax LLC**
Chicago Tribune; **Tribune Publishing Company**
Child's Play; **MGM Holdings Inc**
Chill Online; **GMM Grammy PCL**
China Business Network; **Shanghai Media Group (SMG)**
China Oceanwide Holdings Group Co Ltd; **International Data Group Inc**
Chips Casino; **Evergreen Gaming Corporation**
Chrome; **Alphabet Inc (Google)**
Churchill Downs Racetrack; **Churchill Downs Incorporated**
Cinco Dia; **Promotora de Informaciones SA**
Cinema City; **Cineworld Group plc**
Cinema City International NV; **Cineworld Group plc**
Cinema De Lux; **National Amusements Inc**
Cinemark Holdings Inc; **Cinemark Inc**
Cinemax; **Home Box Office Inc (HBO)**
Cineplex Cinemas; **Cineplex Inc**
Cineplex Entertainment LP; **Cineplex Inc**
Cineplex Odeon; **Cineplex Inc**
Cineplex Starburst Inc; **Cineplex Inc**
Cineworld; **Cineworld Group plc**
Cineworld Group PLC; **Regal Entertainment Group**
Circle Talent Agency; **United Talent Agency Inc**
Circus Circus Las Vegas; **MGM Resorts International**
Circus Circus Reno; **Eldorado Resorts Inc**
CITV; **ITV plc**
City of Dreams; **Melco International Development Limited**
CitySpin; **Morris Communications Company LLC**
Civic Center Media; **United Talent Agency Inc**
Clark.com; **Cox Media Group Inc**
Claro SA; **Net Servicos de Comunicacao SA**
Clayton Dubilier & Rice LLC; **American Greetings Corporation LLC**
Clayton Homes Inc; **Berkshire Hathaway Inc**
Clean Living (Macau) Ltd; **Shun Tak Holdings Limited**
Clear Channel Outdoor Holdings Inc; **iHeartMedia Inc**
ClinicalKey; **Elsevier BV**
Club Fortune Casino; **Nevada Gold & Casinos Inc**
CLUE Bingo; **Storm8**
Clutch; **Cox Enterprises Inc**
CME Inc; **Nippon Columbia Co Ltd**
CNET; **MP3.com Inc**
CNET; **CBS Interactive Inc**
CNHI LLC; **Raycom Media Inc**
CNN; **Cable News Network Inc (CNN)**
CNN; **Turner Broadcasting System Inc**
CNN Aerial Imagery and Reporting (CNN AIR); **Cable News Network Inc (CNN)**
CNN International; **Cable News Network Inc (CNN)**
CNN Money; **Cable News Network Inc (CNN)**
CNN.com; **Cable News Network Inc (CNN)**
Coates Hire; **Seven Group Holdings Limited**
Coco; **Pixar Animation Studios**
Codere; **Codere SA**
Cogeco Communications Inc; **Cogeco Inc**
Cogeco Connexion; **Cogeco Communications Inc**
Cogeco Connexion; **Cogeco Inc**
Cogeco Force Radio; **Cogeco Inc**
Cogeco Inc; **Cogeco Communications Inc**
Cogeco Media; **Cogeco Inc**
Cogeco News; **Cogeco Inc**
Cogeco Nouvelles; **Cogeco Inc**
Cogeco Peer 1; **Cogeco Communications Inc**
Cogeco Peer 1; **Cogeco Inc**
Coinstar; **Outerwall Inc**
Colorado Mountain Express; **Vail Resorts Inc**

INDEX OF SUBSIDIARIES, BRAND NAMES AND AFFILIATIONS, CONT.

Columbia Marketing Co Ltd; **Nippon Columbia Co Ltd**
Columbia Pictures; **Sony Pictures Motion Picture Group**
Columbia Pictures Producciones Mexico; **Sony Pictures Entertainment Inc**
Columbia Songs Inc; **Nippon Columbia Co Ltd**
Comcast; **Hulu LLC**
Comcast Corporation; **DreamWorks Animation SKG Inc**
Comcast Corporation; **NBCUniversal Media LLC**
Comcast Corporation; **Universal Pictures**
Comcast Spectator; **Comcast Corporation**
Comet TV; **Sinclair Broadcast Group Inc**
Community Newspaper Holdings Inc; **CNHI LLC**
Compulse Integrated Marketing; **Sinclair Broadcast Group Inc**
Computer Bild; **Axel Springer SE**
Computerworld; **International Data Group Inc**
Concept eValuate; **TNS UK Ltd**
Conde Nast; **Advance Publications Inc**
Conde Nast Entertainment; **Conde Nast Publications Inc**
Condor; **MGM Holdings Inc**
Connect; **TNS UK Ltd**
Connected Life; **TNS UK Ltd**
Connected Solutions Company of North America; **Panasonic Corporation**
Continent of the Ninth Seal (C9); **Webzen Inc**
Contract Killer; **Glu Mobile Inc**
ConversionModel; **TNS UK Ltd**
Cooking Dash; **Glu Mobile Inc**
Cornerstone; **Qurate Retail Inc**
Cornerstone Brands Inc; **HSN Inc (Home Shopping Network)**
Corporation for Public Broadcasting; **NPR (National Public Radio)**
Cotai Expo; **Sands China Ltd**
Country; **Trusted Media Brands Inc**
Country Club of Boyne; **Boyne Resorts**
Country Woman; **Trusted Media Brands Inc**
Countryville; **Dick Clark Productions Inc**
Course360; **Cengage Learning Holdings II Inc**
Cox Automotive; **Cox Enterprises Inc**
Cox Business Services; **Cox Communications Inc**
Cox Business Services; **Cox Enterprises Inc**
Cox Communications Inc; **Cox Enterprises Inc**
Cox Enterprises Inc; **Cox Communications Inc**
Cox Enterprises Inc; **Cox Media Group Inc**
Cox Media; **Cox Communications Inc**
Cox Media Group; **Cox Enterprises Inc**
CoxReps; **Cox Media Group Inc**
Coyote Bob's Roadhouse; **Nevada Gold & Casinos Inc**
Cozi; **NBCUniversal Media LLC**
Crate; **LOUD Audio LLC**
Crayola LLC; **Hallmark Cards Inc**
Crazy Moose; **Nevada Gold & Casinos Inc**
Creative Solutions; **GateHouse Media LLC**
Cricket; **GameStop Corp**
Crown Media Holdings Inc; **Hallmark Cards Inc**
Crow's Blood; **Miramax LLC**
Crystal; **Cirque du Soleil Inc**
Culture Magazine; **Hightimes Holding Corp**
Cumulus Media Inc; **Westwood One Inc**
Curbed; **Vox Media Inc**
CW (The); **CW Network LLC (The)**
CW SEED; **CW Network LLC (The)**
Cycle Media; **Wasserman Media Group LLC**
Cyclist; **Dennis Publishing Ltd**
Daily Commerce; **Daily Journal Corporation**
Daily Transcript (The); **Daily Journal Corporation**
Dailymotion; **Vivendi SA**
Dakota Players Club; **Nevada Gold & Casinos Inc**
Dalian Wanda Group Co Ltd; **AMC Entertainment Holdings Inc**
Dallas Morning News (The); **A H Belo Corporation**
Dark Knight Trilogy (The); **Legendary Entertainment**
Dashfire; **Changyou.com Limited**
David C. Cook; **Integrity Music**
Dawg Nation; **Cox Media Group Inc**
DaySpring Cards Inc; **Hallmark Cards Inc**
DBI Beverage Inc; **Ingram Entertainment Holdings Inc**
DC Entertainment Inc; **Warner Bros Entertainment Inc**
Dead Rising; Endgame; **Legendary Entertainment**
Decca Broadway; **Universal Music Group Inc**
Decimal Squares; **American Educational Products LLC**
Deep Silver; **Koch Media GmbH**
Deep Silver Dambuster Studios; **Koch Media GmbH**
Deep Silver Fishlabs; **Koch Media GmbH**
Deep Silver Volition; **Koch Media GmbH**
Deer Hunter; **Glu Mobile Inc**
Def Jam Recordings; **Universal Music Group Inc**
Denton Record-Chronicle (The); **A H Belo Corporation**
Deny Designs; **Leaf Group Ltd**
DEQ Systems Corp; **Scientific Games Corporation**
Design Factory Co Ltd; **Oriental Land Co Ltd**
DesignWare; **American Greetings Corporation LLC**
Deutsche Grammophon; **Universal Music Group Inc**
Dex Media Inc; **DexYP**
Dial Books; **Penguin Group USA**
Diamond Diaries Saga; **King Digital Entertainment plc**
Dick Clark's American Bandstand Grill; **Dick Clark Productions Inc**
Dick Clark's American Bandstand Theater; **Dick Clark Productions Inc**
Digital Cinema Implementation Partners LLC; **Regal Entertainment Group**
Digital Entertainment Holdings LLC; **RLJ Entertainment Inc**
Digital Lightfield; **Magic Leap Inc**
Digonex Technologies; **Emmis Communications Corporation**
DirectNOW; **DirecTV LLC (DIRECTV)**
Discover; **Advance Publications Inc**

INDEX OF SUBSIDIARIES, BRAND NAMES AND AFFILIATIONS, CONT.

Discovery Channel; **Discovery Inc**
Discovery Cove; **SeaWorld Entertainment Inc**
Discovery Inc; **Oprah Winfrey Network (OWN)**
DISH; **DISH Network Corporation**
DISH On Demand; **DISH Network Corporation**
dishNET; **DISH Network Corporation**
Disney; **Walt Disney Company (The)**
Disney; **Walt Disney Studios (The)**
Disney Channels Worldwide; **ABC Inc (Disney-ABC)**
Disney Digital Studio Services; **Walt Disney Studios (The)**
Disney Live; **Feld Entertainment Inc**
Disney Media Networks; **ABC Inc (Disney-ABC)**
Disney Music Publishing; **Walt Disney Studios (The)**
Disney on Ice; **Feld Entertainment Inc**
Disney Village; **Euro Disney SCA**
Disney XD; **Disney Media Networks**
Disney XD; **ABC Inc (Disney-ABC)**
Disney-ABC Television Group; **ABC Inc (Disney-ABC)**
Disneyland Park; **Euro Disney SCA**
Disneyland Resort; **Walt Disney Company (The)**
Disneyland Resort Paris; **Euro Disney SCA**
Disneynature; **Walt Disney Studios (The)**
Distribion Inc; **A H Belo Corporation**
DK; **Penguin Random House**
DMAX; **Discovery Inc**
DMN CrowdSource LLC; **A H Belo Corporation**
DMV Digital Holdings Company Inc; **A H Belo Corporation**
Doctissimo; **Lagardere Active Media**
Dogan Sirketler Grubu Holding AS; **Hurriyet Gazetecilik ve Matbaacilik AS**
Dolby Atmos; **Dolby Laboratories Inc**
Dolby Digital; **Dolby Laboratories Inc**
Dolby Digital Plus; **Dolby Laboratories Inc**
Dolby TrueHD; **Dolby Laboratories Inc**
Dolby Voice; **Dolby Laboratories Inc**
Dolphin; **Gaming Partners International Corporation**
DOMA; **Central European Media Enterprises Ltd**
Donkey Kong; **Nintendo Co Ltd**
Dope Magazine; **Hightimes Holding Corp**
Dorney Park & Wildwater Kingdom; **Cedar Fair LP**
Dotdash; **IAC/InterActiveCorp**
Dover Downs Casino; **Dover Downs Gaming & Entertainment Inc**
Dover Downs Gaming Management Corp; **Dover Downs Gaming & Entertainment Inc**
Dover Downs Hotel and Conference Center; **Dover Downs Gaming & Entertainment Inc**
Dover Downs Inc; **Dover Downs Gaming & Entertainment Inc**
Dover Downs Raceway; **Dover Downs Gaming & Entertainment Inc**
Dow Jones & Company Inc; **MarketWatch Inc**
Dow Jones Curation Services; **Dow Jones & Company Inc**
Dow Jones Newswires; **Dow Jones & Company Inc**
Dow Jones Risk & Compliance; **Dow Jones & Company Inc**
Download-Free-Games.com; **IPlay**
Downtown Aquarium; **Fertitta Entertainment Inc.**
Dr WiFi; **Izzi Telecom SAB de CV**
Dragon Age; **BioWare Corp**
Dragon Story; **Storm8**
Dreamscape Immersive Inc; **AMC Entertainment Holdings Inc**
DreamWorks Animation Publishing LLC; **DreamWorks Animation SKG Inc**
DreamWorks Pictures; **DreamWorks II Holding Co LLC**
Dreamworld; **Ardent Leisure Group**
DTS Headphone; X; **DTS Inc**
DTS Play-Fi; **DTS Inc**
DTS Virtual; X; **DTS Inc**
DTS; X; **DTS Inc**
Dun & Bradstreet Corporation (D&B); **Hoover's Inc**
durhamregion.com; **Torstar Corporation**
Dutch Wonderland; **Palace Entertainment Holdings LLC**
Dutton; **Penguin Group USA**
Dynamic Beat Enhancer; **Clarion Co Ltd**
Dynamic Digitized Lightfield Signal; **Magic Leap Inc**
Dynamic Immersion; **Rosetta Stone Inc**
Dynamics; **Microsoft Corporation**
E! Entertainment; **NBCUniversal Media LLC**
Eagle Marketing; **CNHI LLC**
Eater; **Vox Media Inc**
EB Games; **GameStop Corp**
eBET; **Tabcorp Holdings Limited**
EBSCO Health; **EBSCO Industries Inc**
EBSCO Information Services; **EBSCO Industries Inc**
Echo; **Amazon.com Inc**
EchoStar 105/SES-11; **EchoStar Corporation**
EchoStar Mobile Limited; **EchoStar Corporation**
Echostar Satellite Services; **EchoStar Corporation**
EchoStar XXI; **EchoStar Corporation**
EchoStar XXIII; **EchoStar Corporation**
ecoATM; **Outerwall Inc**
Edge; **Village Roadshow Limited**
Editora Globo; **Globo Comunicacao e Participacoes SA (Grupo Globo)**
EDL Hotels SCA; **Euro Disney SCA**
Edwards; **Regal Entertainment Group**
eharmony; **ProSiebenSat.1 Media SE**
eHow; **Leaf Group Ltd**
El Huffpost; **Promotora de Informaciones SA**
El Pais; **Promotora de Informaciones SA**
Eldorado Casino; **Boyd Gaming Corp**
Eldorado Hotel and Casino Reno; **Eldorado Resorts Inc**
ELEAGUE; **Turner Broadcasting System Inc**
Electronic Arts Inc; **BioWare Corp**
Elemis; **Steiner Leisure Limited**
Elle; **Lagardere Active Media**

INDEX OF SUBSIDIARIES, BRAND NAMES AND AFFILIATIONS, CONT.

Elle; **Lagardere SCA**
EM Informatica SA; **Scientific Games Corporation**
Emanate Books; **Thomas Nelson Inc**
Emerils.com; **Martha Stewart Living Omnimedia Inc**
EMMA Delta Investment Fund; **Greek Organisation of Football Prognostics SA (OPAP)**
Emmis Digital; **Emmis Communications Corporation**
Encore at Wynn Las Vegas; **Wynn Resorts Limited**
Encore at Wynn Macau; **Wynn Resorts Limited**
Encore Theater; **Wynn Resorts Limited**
Endeavor Talent Agency; **Endeavor LLC**
English Patient (The); **Miramax LLC**
Enracha; **Rank Group plc (The)**
Entertainment Gaming Asia Inc; **Melco International Development Limited**
Epic Records; **Sony Music Entertainment Inc**
Escape; **E W Scripps Company (The)**
ESPA; **Genting Singapore PLC**
ESPN; **Walt Disney Company (The)**
ESPN; **ESPN Inc**
ESPN; **Hearst Corporation (The)**
ESPN Inc; **Disney Media Networks**
ESPN+; **ESPN Inc**
ESPNEWS; **ESPN Inc**
etailz; **Trans World Entertainment Corporation**
EULAV Asset Management Trust; **Value Line Inc**
Euro Disney Associes SCA; **Euro Disney SCA**
Europe 1; **Lagardere Active Media**
Eurosport; **Discovery Inc**
Eventful; **Entercom Communications Corp**
Everything That Rocks; **Saga Communications Inc**
Evine; **EVINE Live Inc**
Evine Too; **EVINE Live Inc**
evine.com; **EVINE Live Inc**
Evolve; **Elsevier BV**
Ex Libris; **ProQuest LLC**
Excalibur; **MGM Resorts International**
ExpoMed; **UBM plc**
Exponent Private Equity LLP; **Dennis Publishing Ltd**
Exponent Private Equity Partners IV LP; **Dennis Publishing Ltd**
Extreme Screen Theaters; **SimEx-Iwerks**
eyeReturn Marketing Inc; **Torstar Corporation**
f y e; **Trans World Entertainment Corporation**
Facebook Platform; **Facebook Inc**
Fair Grounds Race Course; **Churchill Downs Incorporated**
Fairfax Media Limited; **Nine Entertainment Co Holdings Ltd**
Faith and Family; **Washington Times LLC (The)**
Faith Inc; **Nippon Columbia Co Ltd**
Faith Talk; **Salem Media Group Inc**
Family Handyman (The); **Trusted Media Brands Inc**
Family Tree Builder; **MyHeritage Ltd**
Fan Pass; **SKY Network Television Limited**
Farm Heroes Saga; **King Digital Entertainment plc**
FarmVille; **Zynga Inc**
FastServe; **Avid Technology Inc**
Feld Entertainment Studios; **Feld Entertainment Inc**
Feng Yun; **Changyou.com Limited**
FiberTower Corp; **AT&T Inc**
Fighting with My Family; **MGM Holdings Inc**
FilePlanet.com; **IGN Entertainment Inc**
Fillmore (The); **Live Nation Entertainment Inc**
Financial News London; **MarketWatch Inc**
Finding Nemo; **Pixar Animation Studios**
Fingruppo Holding SpA; **Mediaset SpA**
Fios; **Verizon Communications Inc**
Flagship Entertainment Group Limited; **Warner Bros Entertainment Inc**
Flexdrive; **Cox Enterprises Inc**
FlightSafety International Inc; **Berkshire Hathaway Inc**
Flyff; **Webzen Inc**
Flywheel; **Ascential plc**
Focus Features LLC; **Universal Pictures**
Forbes Magazine; **Forbes Media LLC**
Forbes.com; **Forbes Media LLC**
Foreign Policy; **Graham Holdings Company**
Forest of Fear; **Renaissance Entertainment Corporation**
Forever Top (Asia) Limited; **I-Cable Communications Limited**
Formula 1; **Liberty Media Corporation**
FOX Affiliates; **Twenty-First Century Fox Inc (21st Century Fox)**
FOX Broadcasting Company; **Twenty-First Century Fox Inc (21st Century Fox)**
Fox College Sports; **Fox Sports Interactive Media LLC**
Fox Deportes; **Fox Sports Interactive Media LLC**
Fox News; **Twenty-First Century Fox Inc (21st Century Fox)**
Fox News; **Fox Entertainment Group Inc**
Fox News Channel; **Fox Broadcasting Company**
Fox Soccer Plus; **Fox Sports Interactive Media LLC**
Fox Sports; **Fox Entertainment Group Inc**
Fox Sports 1; **Fox Sports Interactive Media LLC**
Fox Sports 2; **Fox Sports Interactive Media LLC**
Fox Sports Network; **Fox Sports Interactive Media LLC**
Fox Sports Networks; **Fox Broadcasting Company**
Fox Star Studios; **Twentieth Century Fox Film Corporation**
Fox Studios Australia; **Twentieth Century Fox Film Corporation**
Fox Television Stations Inc; **Fox Broadcasting Company**
Fox Television Stations Inc; **Twenty-First Century Fox Inc (21st Century Fox)**
Fox Television Studios; **Fox Broadcasting Company**
Foxconn Technology Co Ltd; **Sharp Corporation**
Fraction Bars; **American Educational Products LLC**
Frames; **Bose Corporation**
Franklin; **Corus Entertainment Inc**

INDEX OF SUBSIDIARIES, BRAND NAMES AND AFFILIATIONS, CONT.

Free Press; **Simon & Schuster Inc**
Freedom Mobile; **Shaw Communications Inc**
Freeform; **Walt Disney Company (The)**
Frontgate; **HSN Inc (Home Shopping Network)**
FunTown World Limited; **GigaMedia Limited**
FX; **Fox Entertainment Group Inc**
FX; **Fox Broadcasting Company**
fye.com; **Trans World Entertainment Corporation**
FYI; **A&E Television Networks LLC**
G/O Digital; **TEGNA Inc**
Galaxy Macau; **Galaxy Entertainment Group Limited**
Gale Research; **Cengage Learning Holdings II Inc**
GameHouse; **RealNetworks Inc**
Gameloft; **Vivendi SA**
GamerMetrics; **IGN Entertainment Inc**
Games for Good at Zynga; **Zynga Inc**
GameSpot; **CBS Interactive Inc**
GameSpy; **IGN Entertainment Inc**
GameStop; **GameStop Corp**
Gaming and Leisure Properties Inc; **Pinnacle Entertainment Inc**
Gaming Partners International Asia Limited; **Gaming Partners International Corporation**
Gaming Partners International SAS; **Gaming Partners International Corporation**
Gaming Partners International USA Inc; **Gaming Partners International Corporation**
Gamut; **Cox Media Group Inc**
Gardaland Resort; **Merlin Entertainments Group Plc**
Garnet Hill; **HSN Inc (Home Shopping Network)**
GateHouse Live; **GateHouse Media LLC**
GateHouse Media Alaska Holdings Inc; **New Media Investment Group Inc**
Gaylord National Resort & Convention Center; **Ryman Hospitality Properties Inc**
Gaylord Opryland Resort & Convention Center; **Ryman Hospitality Properties Inc**
Gaylord Palms Resort & Convention Center; **Ryman Hospitality Properties Inc**
Gaylord Springs Golf Links; **Ryman Hospitality Properties Inc**
Gaylord Texan Resort & Convention Center; **Ryman Hospitality Properties Inc**
GDH 559 Co Ltd; **GMM Grammy PCL**
Geek Squad; **Best Buy Co Inc**
GEICO Corporation; **Berkshire Hathaway Inc**
General Jackson Showboat; **Ryman Hospitality Properties Inc**
General Re Corporation; **Berkshire Hathaway Inc**
Genie HD DVR; **DirecTV LLC (DIRECTV)**
Genting Group; **Genting Singapore PLC**
George2; **Tatts Group Limited**
Ghost in the Shell; **DreamWorks II Holding Co LLC**
GigaCloud Media; **GigaMedia Limited**
GigaCube; **Vodafone Kabel Deutschland GmbH**
GigaTV; **Vodafone Kabel Deutschland GmbH**
Ginsberg Scientific; **American Educational Products LLC**
GINSMS Inc; **Beat Holdings Limited**
Girl on the Train (The); **DreamWorks II Holding Co LLC**
GitHub; **Microsoft Corporation**
Give 5; **Patch Media Corporation**
Global Korean Network; **Korean Broadcasting System**
Global Television; **Corus Entertainment Inc**
Globo; **Globo Comunicacao e Participacoes SA (Grupo Globo)**
Globo Filmes; **Globo Comunicacao e Participacoes SA (Grupo Globo)**
Globosat; **Globo Comunicacao e Participacoes SA (Grupo Globo)**
Gmail; **Alphabet Inc (Google)**
GMM 25; **GMM Grammy PCL**
GMM CJ O Shopping Co Ltd; **GMM Grammy PCL**
GMM Z Satellite TV; **GMM Grammy PCL**
Gold Class Cineams; **Village Roadshow Limited**
Gold Coast Hotel and Casino; **Boyd Gaming Corp**
Gold Mountain Development LLC; **Nevada Gold & Casinos Inc**
Gold Town Casino; **Golden Entertainment Inc**
Golden Casket; **Tatts Group Limited**
Golden Mardi Gras Casino; **Affinity Gaming LLC**
Golden Nugget; **Fertitta Entertainment Inc.**
Goldies Shoreline Casino; **Evergreen Gaming Corporation**
Golf Disneyland; **Euro Disney SCA**
Good Night and Good Luck; **2929 Entertainment**
Google Corporation; **YouTube LLC**
Google LLC; **Alphabet Inc (Google)**
GooglePlay; **Alphabet Inc (Google)**
Gordon Ramsay DASH; **Glu Mobile Inc**
GPI Mexicana SA de CV; **Gaming Partners International Corporation**
GQ; **Conde Nast Publications Inc**
Graham Healthcare Group; **Graham Holdings Company**
Graham Media Group Inc; **Graham Holdings Company**
Grand Central Publishing; **Hachette Book Group Inc**
Grand Lodge Casino; **Full House Resorts Inc**
Grand Ole Opry (The); **Ryman Hospitality Properties Inc**
Grand Teton Lodge Company; **Vail Resorts Inc**
Grand Theft Auto; **Take-Two Interactive Software Inc**
Grand View Media Group; **EBSCO Industries Inc**
Grandin Road; **HSN Inc (Home Shopping Network)**
Great American Casino Everett; **Great Canadian Gaming Corporation**
Great Escape; **Regal Entertainment Group**
Greater Media Inc; **Beasley Broadcast Group Inc**
Green and Arts Co Ltd; **Oriental Land Co Ltd**
Green Rush Daily; **Hightimes Holding Corp**
Green Valley Ranch; **Station Casinos LLC**
Greenleaf; **Oprah Winfrey Network (OWN)**

INDEX OF SUBSIDIARIES, BRAND NAMES AND AFFILIATIONS, CONT.

Grit; **E W Scripps Company (The)**
Grosvenor Casinos; **Rank Group plc (The)**
Groundsure; **Ascential plc**
Group Nine Media; **Axel Springer SE**
Gruner + Jahr; **Bertelsmann SE & Co KGaA**
Grupo CanalEnergia; **UBM plc**
Grupo Nelson; **Thomas Nelson Inc**
Grupo Salinas; **TV Azteca SAB de CV**
Grupo Televisa SAB; **Izzi Telecom SAB de CV**
Guangzhou Wanda Puhui Microcredit Co Ltd; **Dalian Wanda Group Co Ltd**
Gulli; **Lagardere Active Media**
Gulli; **Lagardere SCA**
Hachette Book Group Canada Inc; **Hachette Book Group Inc**
Hachette Livre; **Hachette Book Group Inc**
Hale Global; **Patch Media Corporation**
Hallmark Baby; **Hallmark Cards Inc**
Hallmark Business Connections; **Hallmark Cards Inc**
Hallmark Cards Inc; **Crown Media Family Networks**
Hallmark Channel (The); **Crown Media Family Networks**
Hallmark Gold Crown; **Hallmark Cards Inc**
Hallmark Marketing Corporation; **Hallmark Cards Inc**
Hallmark Movies & Mysteries Channel (The); **Crown Media Family Networks**
Hangover (The); **Legendary Entertainment**
Happy FM; **Korean Broadcasting System**
Happy Village; **Shenzhen Overseas Chinese Town Co Ltd (OCT Limited)**
Hard Rock Casino Vancouver; **Great Canadian Gaming Corporation**
Harlequin; **HarperCollins Publishers LLC**
HarperCollins Christian Publishing Inc; **Thomas Nelson Inc**
HarperCollins Publishers; **Thomas Nelson Inc**
Harpo Productions Inc; **Oprah Winfrey Network (OWN)**
Hartford Courant; **Tribune Publishing Company**
Havas Group; **Vivendi SA**
HBO Comedy; **Home Box Office Inc (HBO)**
HBO Go; **Home Box Office Inc (HBO)**
HBO Latino; **Home Box Office Inc (HBO)**
HBO NOW; **Home Box Office Inc (HBO)**
HBO on Demand; **Home Box Office Inc (HBO)**
Hearst Communications Inc; **A&E Television Networks LLC**
Hearst Corporation (The); **Hearst Television Inc**
Hearst Corporation (The); **ESPN Inc**
Hearst News Service; **Hearst Corporation (The)**
Heartland Poker Tour; **Pinnacle Entertainment Inc**
Heartwell Golf Course; **American Golf Corp**
Heavenly; **Vail Resorts Inc**
Heide Park Resort; **Merlin Entertainments Group Plc**
HelloBeautiful; **Urban One Inc**
Helsingin Sanomat; **Sanoma Oyj**
Hershey Bars; **Hershey Company (The)**

Hershey Kisses; **Hershey Company (The)**
Hershey's Chocolate World; **Hershey Company (The)**
HGTV Canada; **Corus Entertainment Inc**
Hidden Objects; Mystery Crime; **Storm8**
Hidden Valley; **Peak Resorts Inc**
High Times; **Hightimes Holding Corp**
High Times Magazine; **Hightimes Holding Corp**
High1 C.C; **Kangwon Land Inc**
High1 Condominium; **Kangwon Land Inc**
High1 Hotel; **Kangwon Land Inc**
High1 Ski Resort; **Kangwon Land Inc**
Hintaseuranta.fi; **Sanoma Oyj**
Hipodromo de las Americas; **Codere SA**
Hipodromo de las Pidras; **Codere SA**
Hipodromo Nacional de Maronas; **Codere SA**
Hipodromo Presidente Remon; **Codere SA**
Hippodrome; **Morris Communications Company LLC**
History Channel (The); **A&E Television Networks LLC**
Hit; **Southern Cross Media Group Limited**
Hitachi Ltd; **Clarion Co Ltd**
Hollywood; **Regal Entertainment Group**
Hollywood Casino; **Penn National Gaming Inc**
Hollywood Palladium; **Live Nation Entertainment Inc**
Home Box Office Inc; **Warner Media LLC**
Home Box Office Inc (HBO); **AT&T Inc**
Home Controller; **Mediacom Communications Corporation**
Home Entertainment; **Koch Media GmbH**
HomeBox; **Vodafone Kabel Deutschland GmbH**
Homeday GmbH; **Axel Springer SE**
HomeFinder.ca; **Torstar Corporation**
HomePod; **Apple Inc**
Hong Kong Cable Enterprises Limited; **I-Cable Communications Limited**
Hong Kong Cable Television Limited; **I-Cable Communications Limited**
Hong Leong Company (Malaysia) Berhad; **Rank Group plc (The)**
Hookem.com; **Cox Media Group Inc**
Hoover's Handbooks; **Hoover's Inc**
Horizon; **Intralot SA**
Hospital Club (The); **Vulcan Inc**
Hotel Auefeld; **Trans World Corporation**
Hotel Columbus; **Trans World Corporation**
Hotel Donauwelle; **Trans World Corporation**
Hotel Kranichhohe; **Trans World Corporation**
Hotel Networks (The); **SONIFI Solutions**
Hotel Savannah and Spa; **Trans World Corporation**
House of Blues; **Live Nation Entertainment Inc**
Houston Chronicle; **Hearst Corporation (The)**
How to Train Your Dragon; **DreamWorks Animation SKG Inc**
HRG; **Aristocrat Leisure Limited**
HRTechnologist; **Ziff Davis LLC**
HSN; **HSN Inc (Home Shopping Network)**

INDEX OF SUBSIDIARIES, BRAND NAMES AND AFFILIATIONS, CONT.

HSN; **Qurate Retail Inc**
HSN Inc; **Qurate Retail Inc**
Hubbard Scientific; **American Educational Products LLC**
Hughes Communications Inc; **EchoStar Corporation**
Hulu; **NBCUniversal Media LLC**
Hulu; **Disney Media Networks**
Hulu with Live TV; **Hulu LLC**
Hurrietaile.com; **Hurriyet Gazetecilik ve Matbaacilik AS**
Hurriyet TV; **Hurriyet Gazetecilik ve Matbaacilik AS**
Hurriyet.comtr; **Hurriyet Gazetecilik ve Matbaacilik AS**
Hurriyetoto.com; **Hurriyet Gazetecilik ve Matbaacilik AS**
Hustle (The); **MGM Holdings Inc**
Hyperlink; **Aristocrat Leisure Limited**
I Am Not Your Negro; **2929 Entertainment**
IAC Films; **IAC/InterActiveCorp**
IAC/InterActiveCorp; **Dotdash**
i-Cable.com; **I-Cable Communications Limited**
ICF Films; **AMC Networks Inc**
ICM Community Partners Foundation; **ICM Partners**
Ideal Image; **Steiner Leisure Limited**
ideiasnet; **Liberty Media Corporation**
IDG Amplify; **International Data Group Inc**
IDG Connect; **International Data Group Inc**
IFC; **AMC Networks Inc**
iFound; **ProQuest LLC**
IGN.com; **IGN Entertainment Inc**
iHeartCommunications Inc; **Clear Channel Outdoor Holdings Inc**
iHeartMedia Inc; **Clear Channel Outdoor Holdings Inc**
iHeartRadio; **iHeartMedia Inc**
Ikspiari Co Ltd; **Oriental Land Co Ltd**
Illumination; **Universal Pictures**
Ilta-Sanomat; **Sanoma Oyj**
IMAGEN Brands; **EBSCO Industries Inc**
IMAX DMR; **IMAX Corporation**
IMG Live; **Endeavor LLC**
IMG Worldwide; **Endeavor LLC**
Improvements; **HSN Inc (Home Shopping Network)**
Incite; **Emmis Communications Corporation**
Incredible Hulk (The); **Marvel Entertainment LLC**
Indianapolis Monthly; **Emmis Communications Corporation**
Industrial Light & Magic; **Lucasfilm Ltd LLC**
iNEWS; **Avid Technology Inc**
Infatuation Inc (The); **Zagat Survey LLC**
Infoglobo; **Globo Comunicacao e Participacoes SA (Grupo Globo)**
inlocomedia; **Naspers Limited**
Inn at Bay Harbor (The); **Boyne Resorts**
INN Partners LC; **Lee Enterprises Incorporated**
Inside Politics; **Washington Times LLC (The)**
Instagram; **Facebook Inc**
InStyle; **Meredith Corporation**
Intelligent Tune App; **Clarion Co Ltd**

Intencity; **Village Roadshow Limited**
Interactive One LLC (dba iONE Digital); **Urban One Inc**
International Data Corporation; **International Data Group Inc**
International Terminal Leasing; **Scientific Games Corporation**
Interscope Records; **Universal Music Group Inc**
Intota; **ProQuest LLC**
Intralot Canvas; **Intralot SA**
Intralot Orion; **Intralot SA**
Investigation Discovery; **Discovery Inc**
Investment AB Kinnevik; **Metro International SA**
ION Life; **ION Media Networks**
ION Television; **ION Media Networks**
iOS; **Apple Inc**
iPad; **Apple Inc**
iPaper; **Scribd Inc**
iPhone; **Apple Inc**
Iplay.com; **IPlay**
IPO Scorecard; **Hoover's Inc**
iQiyi Motion Pictures; **iQiyi Inc**
iRadioNow; **Beasley Broadcast Group Inc**
Iron Man; **Marvel Entertainment LLC**
Iron Man Experience; **Marvel Entertainment LLC**
Island Records; **Universal Music Group Inc**
Isle Casino Hotel-Black Hawk; **Eldorado Resorts Inc**
Isle of Capri Casinos Inc; **Eldorado Resorts Inc**
iSreamPlanet; **Turner Broadcasting System Inc**
ITV; **ITV plc**
ITV; **Liberty Global plc**
ITV Encore; **ITV plc**
ITV Studios; **ITV plc**
ITV2; **ITV plc**
ITV3; **ITV plc**
ITV4; **ITV plc**
ITVBe; **ITV plc**
iWin Inc; **IPlay**
iWin.com; **IPlay**
iWorship; **Integrity Music**
j2 Global Inc; **IGN Entertainment Inc**
j2 Global Inc; **Ziff Davis LLC**
Jack Frost; **Peak Resorts Inc**
James Bond; **MGM Holdings Inc**
JE; **TVA Group Inc**
Jellyflop; **Concrete Software Inc**
JenkatGames.com; **IPlay**
Jobseeker Report; **Hoover's Inc**
Joe Muggs Café; **Books A Million Inc**
Jokers Wild Casino; **Boyd Gaming Corp**
Jou; **Steiner Leisure Limited**
JUICE Mobile; **Yellow Pages Limited**
Jumbo; **Melco International Development Limited**
Junior Scholastic; **Scholastic Corporation**
Juno; **United Online Inc**
Juno Turbo; **United Online Inc**

INDEX OF SUBSIDIARIES, BRAND NAMES AND AFFILIATIONS, CONT.

Jurong Bird Park; **Wildlife Reserves Singapore Group**
justWink.com; **American Greetings Corporation LLC**
KAIT; **Raycom Media Inc**
Kane Miller Book Publishers; **Educational Development Corporation**
Kangwon Land Casino; **Kangwon Land Inc**
Kangwon Land Convention Hotel; **Kangwon Land Inc**
Kangwon Land Hotel; **Kangwon Land Inc**
Kansas City Star; **McClatchy Company (The)**
Kantar Group; **TNS UK Ltd**
Kantar TNS; **TNS UK Ltd**
Kaplan Inc; **Graham Holdings Company**
Kaplan University; **Graham Holdings Company**
Katz Media Group; **iHeartMedia Inc**
KBS America; **Korean Broadcasting System**
KBS Arts Vision; **Korean Broadcasting System**
KBS Business; **Korean Broadcasting System**
KBS Japan; **Korean Broadcasting System**
KBS Media; **Korean Broadcasting System**
KBS N; **Korean Broadcasting System**
KCBD; **Raycom Media Inc**
Kelley Blue Book; **Cox Enterprises Inc**
Ken Ehrlich Productions; **Anschutz Entertainment Group Inc**
Keno; **Tabcorp Holdings Limited**
Kickserv; **Gannett Co Inc**
Kids Can Press; **Corus Entertainment Inc**
Kidsplace Early Education Club; **Dalian Wanda Group Co Ltd**
Kidsplace Parks; **Dalian Wanda Group Co Ltd**
Kim Kardashian; Hollywood; **Glu Mobile Inc**
King Digital Entertainment; **Activision Blizzard Inc**
Kings Dominion; **Cedar Fair LP**
Kings Island; **Cedar Fair LP**
Kinnevik AB; **Modern Times Group MTG AB**
Kinnevik Media Holding AB; **Metro International SA**
Kit Kat; **Hershey Company (The)**
Knopf Doubleday; **Penguin Random House**
Knott's Berry Farm; **Cedar Fair LP**
Knovel; **Elsevier BV**
Ko'olau Golf Club; **American Golf Corp**
Kong; Skull Island; **Legendary Entertainment**
Kovert Creative; **Endeavor LLC**
Kroenke Sports & Entertainment; **Liberty Media Corporation**
Kudzu.com; **Cox Communications Inc**
Kugou; **Tencent Music Entertainment Group**
Kung Fu Panda; **DreamWorks Animation SKG Inc**
Kuwo; **Tencent Music Entertainment Group**
Kwik Sew; **CSS Industries Inc**
La 5; **Mediaset SpA**
La Therapie; **Steiner Leisure Limited**
Lady Luck Casino-Black Hawk; **Eldorado Resorts Inc**
Laff; **E W Scripps Company (The)**
Lagadere Sports & Entertainment; **Lagardere SCA**
Lagardere Active; **Lagardere SCA**
Lagardere Publishing; **Lagardere SCA**
Lagardere SCA; **Lagardere Active Media**
Lagardere Travel Retail; **Lagardere SCA**
Lakeside Hotel and Casino; **Affinity Gaming LLC**
LaMusica.com; **Spanish Broadcasting System Inc**
Landrys; **Fertitta Entertainment Inc.**
Las Vegas Sands Corporation; **Sands China Ltd**
L'Auberge Baton Rouge; **Pinnacle Entertainment Inc**
L'Auberge Casino Resort; **Pinnacle Entertainment Inc**
L'Auberge Lake Charles; **Penn National Gaming Inc**
Lazer 103.3; **Saga Communications Inc**
Legardere SCA; **Hachette Book Group Inc**
Legend of Solgard; **King Digital Entertainment plc**
Legend of Zelda (The); **Nintendo Co Ltd**
Legendary Television & Digital Media; **Legendary Entertainment**
Lego Star Wars; **LucasArts Entertainment Company LLC**
LEGOLAND; **Merlin Entertainments Group Plc**
Lerner Digital; **Lerner Publishing Group**
Lerner eSource; **Lerner Publishing Group**
Lerner Publications; **Lerner Publishing Group**
LernerClassroom; **Lerner Publishing Group**
Let's Find Out; **Scholastic Corporation**
Levity Entertainment Group LLC; **AMC Networks Inc**
Lexia Learning; **Rosetta Stone Inc**
Liberty Interactive Corporation; **Qurate Retail Inc**
Liberty Israel Venture Fund LLC; **Liberty Media Corporation**
Liberty Mountain Resort; **Peak Resorts Inc**
Lifetime; **A&E Television Networks LLC**
Lifetime Movies; **A&E Television Networks LLC**
Lifewire; **Dotdash**
Light Between Oceans (The); **DreamWorks II Holding Co LLC**
Lightpack; **Magic Leap Inc**
Lightpath; **Altice USA Inc**
Lightwear; **Magic Leap Inc**
Lineage; **NCsoft Corporation**
Lineage; **NCsoft Corporation**
Line-Master; **American Educational Products LLC**
LINQ Promenade (The); **Caesars Entertainment Corporation**
LionsGate; **Liberty Global plc**
Lionsgate Television Group; **Lions Gate Entertainment Corp**
Literatum; **John Wiley & Sons Inc**
Little Brown and Company; **Hachette Book Group Inc**
Live Healthcare; **UBM plc**
Live Nation Entertainment; **Liberty Media Corporation**
Livelovely.com; **RentPath LLC**
LIVESTRONG.COM; **Leaf Group Ltd**
LocalEdge; **Hearst Corporation (The)**
Los Angeles Daily Journal; **Daily Journal Corporation**

INDEX OF SUBSIDIARIES, BRAND NAMES AND AFFILIATIONS, CONT.

Lotos X; **Intralot SA**
Lott (The); **Tatts Group Limited**
Love AM; **SBS (Seoul Broadcasting)**
LTE-M; **Rogers Communications Inc**
LucasArts; **Lucasfilm Ltd LLC**
Lucasfilm Animation; **Lucasfilm Ltd LLC**
Lucasfilm Ltd; **LucasArts Entertainment Company LLC**
Lucky; **2929 Entertainment**
Lumin OS; **Magic Leap Inc**
Luxbet; **Tabcorp Holdings Limited**
Luxor; **MGM Resorts International**
M6; **RTL Group SA**
Macau Matters Co Ltd; **Shun Tak Holdings Limited**
Mackie; **LOUD Audio LLC**
Macworld; **International Data Group Inc**
Madagascar; **DreamWorks Animation SKG Inc**
Madame Tussauds; **Merlin Entertainments Group Plc**
MADE; **Endeavor LLC**
Madison Newspapers Inc; **Lee Enterprises Incorporated**
Madison Paper Industries; **New York Times Company (The)**
Madison Square Garden Company (The); **Townsquare Media Inc**
Magic Leap Control; **Magic Leap Inc**
Magic Leap One; **Magic Leap Inc**
Magic Valley Group; **Lee Enterprises Incorporated**
Magnolia Home Theater; **Best Buy Co Inc**
Magnolia Pictures; **2929 Entertainment**
Mahmure.com; **Hurriyet Gazetecilik ve Matbaacilik AS**
Maihama Corporation Co Ltd; **Oriental Land Co Ltd**
Maihama Resort Line Co Ltd; **Oriental Land Co Ltd**
Main Event Entertainment; **Ardent Leisure Group**
Main Street Digital; **Morris Communications Company LLC**
MainConcept; **NeuLion Inc**
Malubu Grand Prix; **Palace Entertainment Holdings LLC**
Managed IP PBX; **Cox Communications Inc**
Mandalay Bay; **MGM Resorts International**
Mansion Global; **MarketWatch Inc**
Maps; **Alphabet Inc (Google)**
Marina Bay Sands Pte Ltd; **Las Vegas Sands Corp (The Venetian)**
Market Place; **Promotora de Informaciones SA**
MarketWatch; **Dow Jones & Company Inc**
MarketWatch Weekend; **MarketWatch Inc**
MarketWatch.com Radio Network; **MarketWatch Inc**
MarTech Advisor; **Ziff Davis LLC**
Martha Stewart Crafts; **Martha Stewart Living Omnimedia Inc**
Martha Stewart Home Office; **Martha Stewart Living Omnimedia Inc**
Martha Stewart Living; **Martha Stewart Living Omnimedia Inc**
Martha Stewart Living; **Meredith Corporation**
Martha Stewart Weddings; **Martha Stewart Living Omnimedia Inc**
MarthaStewart.com; **Martha Stewart Living Omnimedia Inc**
MarthaStewartWeddings.com; **Martha Stewart Living Omnimedia Inc**
Marvel; **Walt Disney Company (The)**
Marvel Stadium; **Marvel Entertainment LLC**
Marvel Universe Live; **Feld Entertainment Inc**
Mary & Martha; **Hallmark Cards Inc**
Mashable; **Ziff Davis LLC**
Mass Effect; **Electronic Arts Inc (EA)**
Mass Effect; Andromeda; **BioWare Corp**
Match Group Inc; **IAC/InterActiveCorp**
Matrix; **TNS UK Ltd**
Matter of Fact; **Hearst Television Inc**
MAX; **Tatts Group Limited**
maxdome; **ProSiebenSat.1 Media SE**
Mazagan; **Kerzner International Limited**
McCall Pattern Company Inc (The); **CSS Industries Inc**
McClatchy Interactive; **McClatchy Company (The)**
Meadows Casino (The); **Penn National Gaming Inc**
Mecca Bingo; **Rank Group plc (The)**
Media Composer; **Avid Technology Inc**
MediaCentral; **Avid Technology Inc**
Mediachain; **Spotify Technology SA**
Mediacom Digital Phone; **Mediacom Communications Corporation**
MediaLink; **Ascential plc**
MediaScaleX; **Concurrent Computer Corporation**
MediaScaleX Cache; **Concurrent Computer Corporation**
MediaScaleX Origin; **Concurrent Computer Corporation**
MediaScaleX Storage; **Concurrent Computer Corporation**
MediaScaleX Transcode; **Concurrent Computer Corporation**
Mediaset Extra; **Mediaset SpA**
Mediavite; **Yellow Pages Limited**
MegaTV; **Spanish Broadcasting System Inc**
Melco Resorts & Entertainment; **Melco International Development Limited**
Mendeley; **Elsevier BV**
Men's Fitness; **Dennis Publishing Ltd**
Meredith Corporation; **Myspace LLC**
Messenger; **Facebook Inc**
Mezi (www.mezi.com); **American Express Company**
MGM Grand Las Vegas; **MGM Resorts International**
Miami Herald; **McClatchy Company (The)**
Michael Jackson ONE; **Cirque du Soleil Inc**
Micromania; **GameStop Corp**
Midroll Media; **E W Scripps Company (The)**
MIH Holdings Ltd; **Naspers Limited**
Milepost (The); **Morris Communications Company LLC**
Milial Resort Hotels Co Ltd; **Oriental Land Co Ltd**
Millbrook Press; **Lerner Publishing Group**

INDEX OF SUBSIDIARIES, BRAND NAMES AND AFFILIATIONS, CONT.

MindTap; **Cengage Learning Holdings II Inc**
Mirage (The); **MGM Resorts International**
Missile Command; **Atari Interactive Inc**
Mississauga News (The); **Torstar Corporation**
Moment; **Verizon Communications Inc**
Monarcas Morelia; **TV Azteca SAB de CV**
Monarch Home Entertainment; **Ingram Entertainment Holdings Inc**
Money 20/20; **Ascential plc**
Moneyish; **MarketWatch Inc**
Monster Energy AMA Supercross; **Feld Entertainment Inc**
Monster Jam; **Feld Entertainment Inc**
Monsters Inc; **Pixar Animation Studios**
Morning Edition; **NPR (National Public Radio)**
Morris Media Network; **Morris Communications Company LLC**
Most Trusted Name in Investment Research (The); **Value Line Inc**
Mount Snow; **Peak Resorts Inc**
Move Inc; **News Corporation**
Movielink; **SKY Network Television Limited**
MPI; **Schibsted ASA**
MTG; **Modern Times Group MTG AB**
MTV Films; **Paramount Pictures Corporation**
MU; **Webzen Inc**
MultiChoice; **Naspers Limited**
Multiple Cinemas; **National Amusements Inc**
Muscle Bound; **Lerner Publishing Group**
Music Genome Project; **Pandora Media Inc**
MX1 360; **MX1 Ltd**
MyBestPro; **Vivendi SA**
MyHeritage.com; **MyHeritage Ltd**
MyLab and Mastering; **Pearson PLC**
MyNetworkTV; **Fox Broadcasting Company**
MyNetworkTV; **Twenty-First Century Fox Inc (21st Century Fox)**
Mystere; **Cirque du Soleil Inc**
MyVideoStore.com; **Ingram Entertainment Holdings Inc**
Napster; **RealNetworks Inc**
NASH; **Cumulus Media Inc**
National Amusements Inc; **CBS Corporation**
National Amusements Inc; **Viacom Inc**
National Barrel Horse Association; **Morris Communications Company LLC**
National CineMedia Inc; **Regal Entertainment Group**
National CineMedia LLC; **Cinemark Inc**
National Digital Edition; **Washington Times LLC (The)**
National Geographic Channel; **Fox Entertainment Group Inc**
National Geographic Partners LLC; **Twenty-First Century Fox Inc (21st Century Fox)**
National Teaching Aids; **American Educational Products LLC**
National Weekly Edition; **Washington Times LLC (The)**
Nav Weather; **Sirius XM Holdings Inc**
NavTraffic; **Sirius XM Holdings Inc**
NBC; **Comcast Corporation**
NBC Entertainment; **NBCUniversal Media LLC**
NBC News; **NBCUniversal Media LLC**
NBCUniversal Inc; **DreamWorks Animation SKG Inc**
NBCUniversal Inc; **Universal Pictures**
NC Interactive Inc; **NCsoft Corporation**
NCircle Entertainment; **Alliance Entertainment LLC**
NCsoft West; **NCsoft Corporation**
Need for Speed; **Electronic Arts Inc (EA)**
Nelonen; **Sanoma Oyj**
Nelvana; **Corus Entertainment Inc**
Nemo Parent Inc; **Steiner Leisure Limited**
NEON; **SKY Network Television Limited**
Nerdist.com; **Legendary Entertainment**
NET; **Net Servicos de Comunicacao SA**
NET Digital; **Net Servicos de Comunicacao SA**
NET Digital HD MAX; **Net Servicos de Comunicacao SA**
NET Fone Via Embratel; **Net Servicos de Comunicacao SA**
NET Virtua; **Net Servicos de Comunicacao SA**
NetCentral; **Books A Million Inc**
Network Tens; **Southern Cross Media Group Limited**
Network World; **International Data Group Inc**
NetZero; **United Online Inc**
NetZero Home Wireless Broadband; **United Online Inc**
NetZero Hotspot; **United Online Inc**
NetZero Mobile Broadband; **United Online Inc**
NeuLion CE SDK; **NeuLion Inc**
NeuLion Digital Platform; **NeuLion Inc**
Neverwinter Nights; **BioWare Corp**
New Cubs LLC; **Tribune Media Company**
New Foxtel; **News Corporation**
New Media Investment Group Inc; **GateHouse Media LLC**
New York Post (The); **News Corporation**
New York Renaissance Faire; **Renaissance Entertainment Corporation**
New York Times (The); **New York Times Company (The)**
New York-New York; **MGM Resorts International**
Newen Studios; **Television Francaise 1 SA**
News 12 Networks; **Altice USA Inc**
News Corp Australia; **News Corporation**
News Corporation; **HarperCollins Publishers LLC**
News Corporation; **Thomas Nelson Inc**
News Corporation; **Dow Jones & Company Inc**
News IQ; **News Corporation**
News UK; **News Corporation**
Newsquest; **Gannett Co Inc**
Newsy; **E W Scripps Company (The)**
NextRadio; **Emmis Communications Corporation**
NHL Hockey Target Smash; **Concrete Software Inc**
Nickelodeon Movies; **Paramount Pictures Corporation**

INDEX OF SUBSIDIARIES, BRAND NAMES AND AFFILIATIONS, CONT.

Night Safari; **Wildlife Reserves Singapore Group**
Niland; **Spotify Technology SA**
Nine Network; **Southern Cross Media Group Limited**
Nintendo 3DS; **Nintendo Co Ltd**
Nintendo DS; **Nintendo Co Ltd**
Nintendo DSi; **Nintendo Co Ltd**
No Country for Old Men; **Miramax LLC**
Noah's Ark; **Palace Entertainment Holdings LLC**
NOOK; **Barnes & Noble Inc**
Nordic Cinema Group Holding AB; **AMC Entertainment Holdings Inc**
Nordic Entertainment Group; **Modern Times Group MTG AB**
NOVA; **Central European Media Enterprises Ltd**
Now TV (UK); **Sky plc**
NPR Fresh Air; **NPR (National Public Radio)**
NPR Generation Listen; **NPR (National Public Radio)**
NPR.Org; **NPR (National Public Radio)**
NSW Lotteries; **Tatts Group Limited**
NuCom Group; **ProSiebenSat.1 Media SE**
NYT Live; **New York Times Company (The)**
NYTimes.com; **New York Times Company (The)**
NYX Gaming Group Limited; **Scientific Games Corporation**
O; **Cirque du Soleil Inc**
Oaktree Capital Management LP; **Townsquare Media Inc**
OASIS; **ProQuest LLC**
Oath Inc; **Verizon Media Group**
Oath; AdPlatforms; **Verizon Media Group**
Ocean Downs; **Churchill Downs Incorporated**
OceanBB plus; **SKY Perfect JSAT Corporation**
Ocesa Entretenimiento SA de CV; **Grupo Televisa SAB**
Oculus; **Facebook Inc**
Odeon and UCI Cinemas Holdings Limited; **AMC Entertainment Holdings Inc**
Office 365; **Microsoft Corporation**
Okavango Wilderness Project; **National Geographic Society**
Okeh; **Sony Music Entertainment Inc**
Omagatoko Co Ltd; **Nippon Columbia Co Ltd**
One & Only; **Kerzner International Limited**
One Solution; **Urban One Inc**
ONE31; **GMM Grammy PCL**
OnePlace.com; **Salem Media Group Inc**
Online Automotive Solutions; **New Media Investment Group Inc**
OPAP Cyprus Ltd; **Greek Organisation of Football Prognostics SA (OPAP)**
OPAP International Ltd; **Greek Organisation of Football Prognostics SA (OPAP)**
OPAP Investments Ltd; **Greek Organisation of Football Prognostics SA (OPAP)**
OPAP Services SA; **Greek Organisation of Football Prognostics SA (OPAP)**
OPAP Sports Ltd; **Greek Organisation of Football Prognostics SA (OPAP)**
Oprah Magazine (The); **Hearst Corporation (The)**
Oprah Winfrey Network (OWN, The); **Discovery Inc**
Oprah.com; **Oprah Winfrey Network (OWN)**
Opry City Stage; **Ryman Hospitality Properties Inc**
Optimum; **Altice USA Inc**
Orange County Reporter; **Daily Journal Corporation**
Orbit; **Hachette Book Group Inc**
Orchard (The); **Sony Music Entertainment Inc**
Organization Impulsora de Radio; **Grupo Radio Centro SAB de CV**
Oriental Pearl Company Ltd; **Shanghai Media Group (SMG)**
Origin; **Electronic Arts Inc (EA)**
Original Renaissance Pleasure Faire (The); **Renaissance Entertainment Corporation**
Orlando Sentinel; **Tribune Publishing Company**
Orleans Hotel and Casino (The); **Boyd Gaming Corp**
Other Art Fair (The); **Leaf Group Ltd**
Out of Eden Walk; **National Geographic Society**
Outlander; **Lions Gate Entertainment Corp**
OutTakes; **Cineplex Inc**
Overwatch; **Activision Blizzard Inc**
OVG Arena Alliance; **Oak View Group**
OVG Business Development; **Oak View Group**
OVG Facilities; **Oak View Group**
OVG Global Partnership; **Oak View Group**
OVG Media & Conferences; **Oak View Group**
OWN; Oprah Winfrey Network Canada; **Corus Entertainment Inc**
OZ Games Studio; **Aristocrat Leisure Limited**
Pacific Kitchen and Home; **Best Buy Co Inc**
Pacific Magazines; **Seven West Media Limited**
Pacific Rim; **Legendary Entertainment**
Pahrump Nugget Hotel Casino; **Golden Entertainment Inc**
Palace Casino; **Evergreen Gaming Corporation**
Palace Station; **Station Casinos LLC**
Palazzo Resort Hotel Casino (The); **Las Vegas Sands Corp (The Venetian)**
Palms; **Station Casinos LLC**
PanaHome; **Panasonic Corporation**
Panasonic Factory Solutions Company of America; **Panasonic Corporation**
Panasonic Media Entertainment Company; **Panasonic Corporation**
Panasonic System Communications Co North America; **Panasonic Corporation**
Panasonic System Solutions Co North America; **Panasonic Corporation**
Pandor API; **Pandora Media Inc**
Pandora Plus; **Pandora Media Inc**
Pandora Premium; **Pandora Media Inc**
Panoply; **Graham Holdings Company**
PANTAYA; **Lions Gate Entertainment Corp**

INDEX OF SUBSIDIARIES, BRAND NAMES AND AFFILIATIONS, CONT.

Paper Magic Group Inc; **CSS Industries Inc**
Papyrus; **American Greetings Corporation LLC**
Paradise Sega Sammy; **Sega Sammy Holdings Inc**
Paragon; **Singapore Press Holdings Limited**
Paramount Animation; **Viacom Inc**
Paramount Classics; **Paramount Pictures Corporation**
Paramount Network; **Paramount Pictures Corporation**
Paramount Pictures; **Paramount Pictures Corporation**
Paramount Pictures; **Viacom Inc**
Paramount Playes; **Viacom Inc**
Paramount Television; **Viacom Inc**
Paramount Television; **Paramount Pictures Corporation**
Paris Match; **Lagardere Active Media**
Paris Match; **Lagardere SCA**
Parisian Macao; **Las Vegas Sands Corp (The Venetian)**
Parisian Macao (The); **Sands China Ltd**
Parisian Theatre; **Sands China Ltd**
Parkifi; **DISH Network Corporation**
Parlophone; **Warner Music Group Corp**
Parques Reunidos SA; **Palace Entertainment Holdings LLC**
Patch.com; **Patch Media Corporation**
Paulson; **Gaming Partners International Corporation**
PBA Bowling Challenge; **Concrete Software Inc**
PC Pro; **Dennis Publishing Ltd**
PCMag; **Ziff Davis LLC**
Pearson plc; **Pearson North America**
Pearson plc; **Penguin Random House**
Penguin; **Penguin Random House**
Penguin Books; **Penguin Group USA**
Penguin Classics; **Penguin Group USA**
Penguin Press (The); **Penguin Group USA**
Penguin Random House; **Bertelsmann SE & Co KGaA**
Penguin Random House Inc; **Penguin Group USA**
Penske Media Corporation; **Rolling Stone LLC**
People; **Meredith Corporation**
Perisher; **Vail Resorts Inc**
Persius Books; **Hachette Book Group Inc**
Pet Shop Story; **Storm8**
Phantoms; **Reliance Entertainment Pvt Ltd**
Philadelphia Flyers; **Comcast Corporation**
Phoenix Resort Co Ltd; **Sega Sammy Holdings Inc**
Phoenix Seagaia Resort; **Sega Sammy Holdings Inc**
Photo Ark; **National Geographic Society**
Photo Works Co Ltd; **Oriental Land Co Ltd**
Picture House; **Cineworld Group plc**
Picturehouse Cinemas Ltd; **Cineworld Group plc**
Pinnacle Entertainment Inc; **Ameristar Casinos Inc**
Pinnacle Entertainment Inc; **Penn National Gaming Inc**
Pioneer Digital Design and Manufacturing Corp; **Pioneer Corporation**
Piper; **Pixar Animation Studios**
Pirate Brands; **Hershey Company (The)**
Pitchfork Media Inc; **Conde Nast Publications Inc**
Pixar Animation Studios; **Walt Disney Studios (The)**

Planet Money; **NPR (National Public Radio)**
Platinum Club; **American Golf Corp**
Playboy Magazine; **Playboy Enterprises Inc**
Playboy Radio; **Playboy Enterprises Inc**
Playboy TV; **Playboy Enterprises Inc**
Playboy.com; **Playboy Enterprises Inc**
PlayboyShop.com; **Playboy Enterprises Inc**
Player Pulse; **Intralot SA**
Plaza Macao; **Sands China Ltd**
PodcastOne; **Southern Cross Media Group Limited**
Poetica; **Conde Nast Publications Inc**
Pokemon; **Nintendo Co Ltd**
POLITICO.se; **Axel Springer SE**
PollStar; **Oak View Group**
Polygon; **Vox Media Inc**
Pompano Park; **Eldorado Resorts Inc**
Pong; **Atari Interactive Inc**
POP; **Advance Publications Inc**
Pop; **Lions Gate Entertainment Corp**
Popcrush.com; **Townsquare Media Inc**
Poptopia; **Cineplex Inc**
Portal; **Facebook Inc**
Portal+; **Facebook Inc**
Portland Trailblazers; **Vulcan Inc**
Post Oak Hotel at Uptown Houston (The); **Fertitta Entertainment Inc.**
Power; **Lions Gate Entertainment Corp**
Power FM; **SBS (Seoul Broadcasting)**
Premier Exhibition Management LLC; **Premier Exhibitions Inc**
Presto; **Seven Group Holdings Limited**
Prevent Advisors; **Oak View Group**
Primm Valley Resort and Casino; **Affinity Gaming LLC**
Primsleur Language Programs; **Simon & Schuster Inc**
PRISA; **Promotora de Informaciones SA**
Prisa Radio; **Promotora de Informaciones SA**
Prismatronic; **Trans-Lux Corporation**
Pristine Seas; **National Geographic Society**
Private Division; **Take-Two Interactive Software Inc**
Pro Tools; **Avid Technology Inc**
PRO TV; **Central European Media Enterprises Ltd**
ProPublica; **Pro Publica Inc**
ProQuest Dialog; **ProQuest LLC**
PsycEXTRA; **ProQuest LLC**
PT's Brewing Company; **Golden Entertainment Inc**
PT's Gold; **Golden Entertainment Inc**
PT's Pub; **Golden Entertainment Inc**
PureCars; **Raycom Media Inc**
Purplebricks; **Axel Springer SE**
PYUR; **Tele Columbus AG**
Qin Shi Ming Yue 2; **Changyou.com Limited**
QQ Music; **Tencent Music Entertainment Group**
QQ Reading; **China Literature Limited**
QubicaAMF Worldwide; **Bowlero Corporation**
Qubo; **ION Media Networks**

INDEX OF SUBSIDIARIES, BRAND NAMES AND AFFILIATIONS, CONT.

Quebecor Media Inc; **TVA Group Inc**
Qurate Retail Group; **HSN Inc (Home Shopping Network)**
QVC Inc; **Qurate Retail Inc**
RacelineBet Inc; **Eldorado Resorts Inc**
Racing Rivals; **Glu Mobile Inc**
Radio 101; **Mediaset SpA**
Radio Aalto; **Sanoma Oyj**
Radio Subasio; **Mediaset SpA**
Radio.com; **Entercom Communications Corp**
Raging Waters; **Palace Entertainment Holdings LLC**
Raidcall; **Changyou.com Limited**
Rail City Casino; **Affinity Gaming LLC**
Rakuten Inc; **Rakuten Commerce LLC**
Rakuten Super Points; **Rakuten Commerce LLC**
Rakuten.com; **Rakuten Commerce LLC**
Randall's Island Golf Center; **Drive Shack Inc**
Random House; **Penguin Random House**
Rare.us; **Cox Media Group Inc**
Ravenscourt; **Koch Media GmbH**
Raycom Media Inc; **CNHI LLC**
Raycom Media, Inc.; **Gray Television Inc**
Raycom Sports; **Raycom Media Inc**
RCA Inspirational; **Sony Music Entertainment Inc**
RD.com; **Trusted Media Brands Inc**
REA Group Limited; **News Corporation**
Reach Media Inc; **Urban One Inc**
ReachDisplay; **Gannett Co Inc**
ReachLocal Inc; **Gannett Co Inc**
ReachSearch; **Gannett Co Inc**
ReachSEO; **Gannett Co Inc**
ReachSite+ReachEdge; **Gannett Co Inc**
Reader's Digest Association, Inc; **Trusted Media Brands Inc**
Reader's Digest Magazine; **Trusted Media Brands Inc**
Reader's Digest Select Editions; **Trusted Media Brands Inc**
ReadITQick; **Ziff Davis LLC**
ReadMetro.com; **Metro International SA**
Ready Player One; **DreamWorks II Holding Co LLC**
Real Money; **2929 Entertainment**
RealD TrueMotion; **RealD Inc**
RealD Ultimate Screen; **RealD Inc**
RealD XL Cinema; **RealD Inc**
RealPlayer; **RealNetworks Inc**
Reaxys; **Elsevier BV**
Recode; **Vox Media Inc**
Record Reporter (The); **Daily Journal Corporation**
Record Town Inc; **Trans World Entertainment Corporation**
Recycled Paper Greetings; **American Greetings Corporation LLC**
Red Arrow Entertainment Group; **ProSiebenSat.1 Media SE**
Red Dead Redemption 2; **Take-Two Interactive Software Inc**
Red Dragon; **Nevada Gold & Casinos Inc**
Red Rock; **Station Casinos LLC**
Red Rock Resorts inc; **Station Casinos LLC**
Redbox; **Redbox Automated Retail LLC**
Redbox; **Outerwall Inc**
Reddit; **Advance Publications Inc**
Rede Globo; **Globo Comunicacao e Participacoes SA (Grupo Globo)**
REDLOC Online; **Daily Journal Corporation**
Reed Elsevier Group plc; **Elsevier BV**
Reel Power; **Aristocrat Leisure Limited**
Reese's; **Hershey Company (The)**
Regal Cinemas; **Regal Entertainment Group**
Regal Crown Club; **Regal Entertainment Group**
Regal Entertainment Group; **Cineworld Group plc**
Regency Enterprises; **Twentieth Century Fox Film Corporation**
relationship TRI*M; **TNS UK Ltd**
Relay; **Lagardere SCA**
Reliance Anil Dhirubhai Ambani Group; **Reliance Entertainment Pvt Ltd**
Reliance Animation; **Reliance Entertainment Pvt Ltd**
Reliance Education; **Reliance Entertainment Pvt Ltd**
Reliance Games; **Reliance Entertainment Pvt Ltd**
RELX Group; **RELX PLC**
RELX NV; **RELX PLC**
RenderMan; **Pixar Animation Studios**
Rent.com; **RentPath LLC**
Rentals.com; **RentPath LLC**
Resort World Sentosa; **Genting Singapore PLC**
Respawn Entertainment LLC; **Electronic Arts Inc (EA)**
Restaurant Story 2; **Storm8**
Retail Week; **Ascential plc**
Retailer Pulse; **Intralot SA**
Rete 4; **Mediaset SpA**
REVEL; **Pearson PLC**
Revenu7; **Ziff Davis LLC**
RGS; **Intralot SA**
Rhapsody International Inc; **RealNetworks Inc**
Ring of Honor; **Sinclair Broadcast Group Inc**
Risting Star Casino Resort; **Full House Resorts Inc**
River City Casino & Hotel; **Pinnacle Entertainment Inc**
River Rock Casino Resort; **Great Canadian Gaming Corporation**
River Safari; **Wildlife Reserves Singapore Group**
River Valley Newspaper Group; **Lee Enterprises Incorporated**
Riverside Business Journal; **Daily Journal Corporation**
Riverside Casino; **Evergreen Gaming Corporation**
Riverwalk Casino Hotel; **Churchill Downs Incorporated**
Rizvi Traverse Management LLC; **RealD Inc**
RMS Titanic Inc; **Premier Exhibitions Inc**

INDEX OF SUBSIDIARIES, BRAND NAMES AND AFFILIATIONS, CONT.

Roberts Communications Network LLC; **Scientific Games Corporation**
RockResorts; **Vail Resorts Inc**
Rockstar Games; **Take-Two Interactive Software Inc**
Rocky Gap Casino Resort; **Golden Entertainment Inc**
Rogers 4K TV; **Rogers Communications Inc**
Rogers Unison; **Rogers Communications Inc**
Rohit Shetty Picturez; **Reliance Entertainment Pvt Ltd**
Roku; **Roku Inc**
Roku Channel Store; **Roku Inc**
RollerCoaster Tycoon; **Atari Interactive Inc**
Rosetta Stone; **Rosetta Stone Inc**
Rosetta Stone Kids Reading; **Rosetta Stone Inc**
Roundtop Mountain; **Peak Resorts Inc**
Royal Arena; **Live Nation Entertainment Inc**
RTL; **RTL Group SA**
RTL Group; **Bertelsmann SE & Co KGaA**
RTM Productions; **Raycom Media Inc**
Rugged Events Holding LLC; **New Media Investment Group Inc**
Rugged Maniac Obstacle Race; **New Media Investment Group Inc**
RYOT; **Verizon Media Group**
Saatchi Art; **Leaf Group Ltd**
Sacramento Bee (The); **McClatchy Company (The)**
Sahara Asset Management Co Pvt Ltd; **Sahara India Pariwar Ltd**
Sahara City Homes; **Sahara India Pariwar Ltd**
Sahara Grace; **Sahara India Pariwar Ltd**
Sahara Hospital; **Sahara India Pariwar Ltd**
Sahara Housingfina Corporation Limited; **Sahara India Pariwar Ltd**
Sahara Life Insurance Company Limited; **Sahara India Pariwar Ltd**
Sahara Q Shop; **Sahara India Pariwar Ltd**
Sahara Star; **Sahara India Pariwar Ltd**
Saints Row; **Koch Media GmbH**
Salem Media Representatives; **Salem Media Group Inc**
Salem Publishing; **Salem Media Group Inc**
Salem Radio Network; **Salem Media Group Inc**
Salem Web Network; **Salem Media Group Inc**
Salon.com; **Salon Media Group Inc**
Saltgrass Steak House; **Fertitta Entertainment Inc.**
Samsung Group; **Samsung Electronics Co Ltd**
San Francisco Chronicle; **Hearst Corporation (The)**
San Francisco Daily Journal; **Daily Journal Corporation**
San Luis Resort Hotel; **Fertitta Entertainment Inc.**
Sands China Ltd; **Las Vegas Sands Corp (The Venetian)**
Sands Cotai Central; **Sands China Ltd**
Sands Expo and Convention Center (The); **Las Vegas Sands Corp (The Venetian)**
Sands Macao; **Sands China Ltd**
Sands Macao Casino (The); **Las Vegas Sands Corp (The Venetian)**
Sanoma Magazines; **Sanoma Oyj**
Santa Fe Station; **Station Casinos LLC**
Santillana; **Promotora de Informaciones SA**
Satellite TV Media; **GMM Grammy PCL**
SB Nation; **Vox Media Inc**
SBS Channel 6; **SBS (Seoul Broadcasting)**
SBS Food; **SBS (Seoul Broadcasting)**
SBS HD; **SBS (Seoul Broadcasting)**
SBS Plus; **SBS (Seoul Broadcasting)**
SBS Viceland; **SBS (Seoul Broadcasting)**
SBSu; **SBS (Seoul Broadcasting)**
Scholastic News; **Scholastic Corporation**
ScienBiziP Japan Co Ltd; **Sharp Corporation**
ScienceDiet; **Elsevier BV**
Scientific Games Corporation; **MDI Entertainment LLC**
Scope; **Scholastic Corporation**
Scopus; **Elsevier BV**
Scott Resources; **American Educational Products LLC**
Screen Gems; **Sony Pictures Motion Picture Group**
Screencrush.com; **Townsquare Media Inc**
Scribner; **Simon & Schuster Inc**
Scripps National Spelling Bee; **E W Scripps Company (The)**
Scrubby Dubby Saga; **King Digital Entertainment plc**
SEA Aquarium; **Genting Singapore PLC**
SEA LIFE; **Merlin Entertainments Group Plc**
Search; **Alphabet Inc (Google)**
Seattle Seahawks; **Vulcan Inc**
SeaWorld; **SeaWorld Entertainment Inc**
SEC Country; **Cox Media Group Inc**
secondspin.com; **Trans World Entertainment Corporation**
Secret Sauce Studio; **Aristocrat Leisure Limited**
Sega Sammy Creation Co Ltd; **Sega Sammy Holdings Inc**
Sega Sammy Golf Entertainment inc; **Sega Sammy Holdings Inc**
Seize the Deal; **Townsquare Media Inc**
Sensory Sensitive Screenings; **National Amusements Inc**
Sequential Brands Group Inc; **Martha Stewart Living Omnimedia Inc**
SES SA; **MX1 Ltd**
Sesame Place; **SeaWorld Entertainment Inc**
Sesame Street Live; **Feld Entertainment Inc**
Seven; **Seven West Media Limited**
Seven Network; **Seven Group Holdings Limited**
Seven Network; **Southern Cross Media Group Limited**
Seven West Media; **Seven Group Holdings Limited**
Shanghai International Franchise Exhibition; **UBM plc**
Shanghai Media & Entertainment Group; **Shanghai Media Group (SMG)**
Shape; **Meredith Corporation**
ShareInvestor; **Singapore Press Holdings Limited**
Sharp Energy Solutions Company; **Sharp Corporation**
Sharp Marketing Japan Corporation; **Sharp Corporation**
Sharp Trading Corporation; **Sharp Corporation**
Shaw Direct; **Shaw Communications Inc**

INDEX OF SUBSIDIARIES, BRAND NAMES AND AFFILIATIONS, CONT.

Shaw Go WiFi; **Shaw Communications Inc**
Shazam; **Shazam Entertainment Limited**
Shorelines Casino Peterborough; **Great Canadian Gaming Corporation**
Showcase Cinemas; **National Amusements Inc**
Showcase SuperLux; **National Amusements Inc**
Showmax; **Naspers Limited**
Showtime Networks; **CBS Corporation**
Shrek; **DreamWorks Animation SKG Inc**
Shrek's Adventure; **Merlin Entertainments Group Plc**
Shun Tak & CITS Coach (Macao) Limited; **Shun Tak Holdings Limited**
Shun Tak Macau Services Ltd; **Shun Tak Holdings Limited**
Shun Tak Property Management Ltd; **Shun Tak Holdings Limited**
Shun Tak Real Estate Ltd; **Shun Tak Holdings Limited**
Shun Tak-China Travel Ship Management Limited; **Shun Tak Holdings Limited**
Sierra Gold; **Golden Entertainment Inc**
Sierra-at-Tahoe Snowsports Resort; **Booth Creek Ski Holdings Inc**
Silver Dollar; **Nevada Gold & Casinos Inc**
Silver Legacy Resort Casino; **Eldorado Resorts Inc**
Silver Sevens Hotel & Casino; **Affinity Gaming LLC**
Silver Slipper Casino and Hotel; **Full House Resorts Inc**
Simon & Schuster; **CBS Corporation**
Simon & Schuster Australia; **Simon & Schuster Inc**
Simon Pulse; **Simon & Schuster Inc**
Simplicity; **CSS Industries Inc**
Simply Mac; **GameStop Corp**
Sims vs Zombies (The); **Electronic Arts Inc (EA)**
Sinclair Original Programming; **Sinclair Broadcast Group Inc**
Singapore Zoo; **Wildlife Reserves Singapore Group**
Siriu XM Radio; **Sirius XM Holdings Inc**
Sirius Marine; **Sirius XM Holdings Inc**
Sirius XM Holdings Inc; **Liberty Media Corporation**
SiriusXM Aviation; **Sirius XM Holdings Inc**
SiriusXM Radio Inc; **Sirius XM Holdings Inc**
SiriusXM Travel Link; **Sirius XM Holdings Inc**
SiriusXM.com; **Sirius XM Holdings Inc**
Six Flags America; **Six Flags Entertainment Corporation**
Six Flags Discovery Kingdom; **Six Flags Entertainment Corporation**
Six Flags Great Adventure & Safari; **Six Flags Entertainment Corporation**
Six Flags Membership Rewards; **Six Flags Entertainment Corporation**
Six Flags Nanjing; **Six Flags Entertainment Corporation**
Six Flags Over Texas; **Six Flags Entertainment Corporation**
SkinnyPop; **Hershey Company (The)**
SKY; **Grupo Televisa SAB**
SKY Advertising; **SKY Network Television Limited**
SKY Business; **SKY Network Television Limited**
Sky Deutschland AG; **Sky plc**
Sky Deutschland Fernsehen GmbH & Co KG; **Sky Deutschland AG**
Sky Ireland Limited; **Sky plc**
Sky Italia; **Sky plc**
SKY Music; **SKY Network Television Limited**
SKY Perfect JSAT Holdings Inc; **SKY Perfect JSAT Corporation**
SKY PerfecTV!; **SKY Perfect JSAT Corporation**
Sky plc; **Sky Deutschland AG**
Sky plc; **Twenty-First Century Fox Inc (21st Century Fox)**
Sky Racing; **Tabcorp Holdings Limited**
Sky Show; **Sky Deutschland AG**
SKY Sport; **SKY Network Television Limited**
Sky Sports; **Sky Deutschland AG**
Sky Sports Radio; **Tabcorp Holdings Limited**
Sky UK Limited; **Sky plc**
SkyPoint; **Ardent Leisure Group**
Skywalker Sound; **Lucasfilm Ltd LLC**
Slate Group LLC (The); **Graham Holdings Company**
SlimWare; **IAC/InterActiveCorp**
Sling Blue; **DISH Network Corporation**
Sling International; **DISH Network Corporation**
Sling Orange; **DISH Network Corporation**
Sling TV; **DISH Network Corporation**
Smadex; **Entravision Communications Corporation**
Smart Research-Smarter Investing; **Value Line Inc**
Smartbike; **Clear Channel Outdoor Holdings Inc**
SMJ Business Solutions Company; **Sharp Corporation**
SMJ Home solutions Company; **Sharp Corporation**
Social Code LLC; **Graham Holdings Company**
Social Point; **Take-Two Interactive Software Inc**
Societe Anonyme des Baines de Mer; **Galaxy Entertainment Group Limited**
Socitey 6; **Leaf Group Ltd**
Sodatone; **Warner Music Group Corp**
Som Livre; **Globo Comunicacao e Participacoes SA (Grupo Globo)**
SONIFI Health Solutions; **SONIFI Solutions**
Sony Bank Inc; **Sony Corporation**
Sony Corporation; **Sony Pictures Entertainment Inc**
Sony Corporation; **Sony Pictures Motion Picture Group**
Sony Crackle; **Crackle Inc (dba SonyCrackle)**
Sony Energy Devices Corporation; **Sony Corporation**
Sony Entertainment; **Sony Music Entertainment Inc**
Sony Entertainment; **Sony Pictures Motion Picture Group**
Sony Entertainment Inc; **Sony Pictures Entertainment Inc**
Sony Financial Holdings Inc; **Sony Corporation**
Sony Life Insurance Co Ltd; **Sony Corporation**
Sony Mobile Communications Inc; **Sony Corporation**
Sony Pictures Animation; **Sony Pictures Motion Picture Group**

INDEX OF SUBSIDIARIES, BRAND NAMES AND AFFILIATIONS, CONT.

Sony Pictures Entertainment; **Sony Corporation**
Sony Pictures Entertainment Inc; **Crackle Inc (dba SonyCrackle)**
Sony Pictures Entertainment Inc; **Sony Pictures Motion Picture Group**
Sony Pictures Imageworks; **Sony Pictures Motion Picture Group**
Sony Pictures Motion Picture Group; **Sony Pictures Entertainment Inc**
Sony Pictures Studios; **Sony Pictures Entertainment Inc**
Sony Pictures Television; **Sony Pictures Entertainment Inc**
Sony Semiconductor Manufacturing Corporation; **Sony Corporation**
Sony Storage Media and Devices Corporation; **Sony Corporation**
Sony/ATV Music Publishing; **Tencent Music Entertainment Group**
SonyCrackle.com; **Sony Pictures Entertainment Inc**
SoundCloud Go+; **SoundCloud Limited**
SoundSport; **Bose Corporation**
Southern Cross Austereo Services Pty Ltd; **Southern Cross Media Group Limited**
Southern Kitchen; **GateHouse Media LLC**
Southern Living; **Meredith Corporation**
Space Archaeology; **National Geographic Society**
Space Mountain Mission 2; **Euro Disney SCA**
Spark Arena; **Live Nation Entertainment Inc**
Spectrum; **Charter Communications Inc**
Spectrum Business; **Charter Communications Inc**
Spectrum Community Solutions; **Charter Communications Inc**
Spectrum Enterprise Solutions; **Charter Communications Inc**
Spectrum Internet; **Charter Communications Inc**
Spectrum Reach; **Charter Communications Inc**
Spectrum TV; **Charter Communications Inc**
Spectrum Voice; **Charter Communications Inc**
Speedtest; **Ziff Davis LLC**
SPH Data Services; **Singapore Press Holdings Limited**
SPH Magazines; **Singapore Press Holdings Limited**
SPH Radio; **Singapore Press Holdings Limited**
SPH REIT; **Singapore Press Holdings Limited**
Spider-Man; **Marvel Entertainment LLC**
Splendid China Folk Village; **Shenzhen Overseas Chinese Town Co Ltd (OCT Limited)**
SportsCenter; **ESPN Inc**
Spotify Free; **Spotify Technology SA**
Spotify Platform; **Spotify Technology SA**
Spotify Premium; **Spotify Technology SA**
SpotX; **RTL Group SA**
Spring Mobile; **GameStop Corp**
Spruce (The); **Dotdash**
Spy Kids; Mission Critical; **Miramax LLC**
SQL; **Microsoft Corporation**
St Jo Frontier Casino; **Affinity Gaming LLC**
St Louis Post-Dispatch LLC; **Lee Enterprises Incorporated**
Stadium; **Sinclair Broadcast Group Inc**
STAPLES Center; **Anschutz Entertainment Group Inc**
Star 102.5; **Saga Communications Inc**
Star Wars Battlefront; **LucasArts Entertainment Company LLC**
Star Wars Pinball; **LucasArts Entertainment Company LLC**
Stargate Origins; **MGM Holdings Inc**
Star-Telegram; **McClatchy Company (The)**
Starwars.com; **LucasArts Entertainment Company LLC**
StarWars; The Old Republic-Knights of the Eternal; **BioWare Corp**
StarWorld Macau; **Galaxy Entertainment Group Limited**
STARZ; **Lions Gate Entertainment Corp**
StayCast; **SONIFI Solutions**
Steel Ocean; **Changyou.com Limited**
Steiner Education Group; **Steiner Leisure Limited**
Steiner Training Academy; **Steiner Leisure Limited**
Stereo Live; **NightCulture Inc**
Stereo Live Dallas LLC; **NightCulture Inc**
Stereo Live LLC; **NightCulture Inc**
Sterling Publishing Co Inc; **Barnes & Noble Inc**
Stockman's Casino; **Full House Resorts Inc**
Storyworks; **Scholastic Corporation**
Straits Times Press; **Singapore Press Holdings Limited**
Studio City; **Melco International Development Limited**
Studio71; **ProSiebenSat.1 Media SE**
Studiocanal; **Vivendi SA**
StyleHaul; **RTL Group SA**
suddenLink; **Cequel Communications Holdings I LLC**
Suddenlink Communications; **Altice USA Inc**
Sun Is Also a Star (The); **MGM Holdings Inc**
Suncoast Hotal and Casino; **Boyd Gaming Corp**
Suncoast Motion Pictures; **Trans World Entertainment Corporation**
Sundance TV; **AMC Networks Inc**
Sunny95/94.7FM; **Saga Communications Inc**
Sun-Sentinel; **Tribune Publishing Company**
Sunset Station; **Station Casinos LLC**
Super D Inc; **Alliance Entertainment LLC**
SuperData Research; **Nielsen Holdings plc**
Supermodel of the World; **Ford Models Inc**
Svenska Dagbladet; **Schibsted ASA**
Swiggy; **Naspers Limited**
T1 Series Films; **Television Francaise 1 SA**
TAB.com.au; **Tabcorp Holdings Limited**
Tabcorp Gaming Solutions; **Tabcorp Holdings Limited**
Tabcorp Holdings Limited; **Tatts Group Limited**
tabla!; **Singapore Press Holdings Limited**
TagStation; **Emmis Communications Corporation**
Tai-Pak; **Melco International Development Limited**
Talent House; **Reliance Entertainment Pvt Ltd**

INDEX OF SUBSIDIARIES, BRAND NAMES AND AFFILIATIONS, CONT.

TAPCO; **LOUD Audio LLC**
Taste of Home; **Trusted Media Brands Inc**
TasteofCountry.com; **Townsquare Media Inc**
Tatts; **Tatts Group Limited**
Tatts Group; **Tabcorp Holdings Limited**
TBD; **Sinclair Broadcast Group Inc**
T-Bird Lounge & Restaurant; **Golden Entertainment Inc**
TechCrunch; **Verizon Media Group**
TechHive; **International Data Group Inc**
Technics; **Panasonic Corporation**
TELE+ Digitale; **Societe d'Edition de Canal Plus**
Telemundo; **Comcast Corporation**
Telenet; **Liberty Global plc**
Teleshopping; **Television Francaise 1 SA**
Teleto; **TV Tokyo Holdings Corporation**
Television Food Network GP; **Tribune Media Company**
Tencent; **Naspers Limited**
Tencent Holdings Limited; **China Literature Limited**
Tencent Holdings Limited; **Tencent Music Entertainment Group**
Tencent Holdings Limited; **Glu Mobile Inc**
Tennis Channel; **Sinclair Broadcast Group Inc**
TF1; **Television Francaise 1 SA**
TF1 Entertainment; **Television Francaise 1 SA**
TF1 Studio; **Television Francaise 1 SA**
TFX; **Television Francaise 1 SA**
Thank You for Your Service; **DreamWorks II Holding Co LLC**
THC Group; **Hightimes Holding Corp**
The Cloud; **Sky plc**
The Daily Meal; **Tribune Publishing Company**
The Game Yearbook in Spain; **Codere SA**
The National Golf Club; **American Golf Corp**
thestar.com; **Torstar Corporation**
TheUrbanDaily; **Urban One Inc**
Thomas Nelson; **Thomas Nelson Inc**
ThoughtCo; **Dotdash**
THQ Nordic AB; **Koch Media GmbH**
ThriveHive; **GateHouse Media LLC**
Thryv; **DexYP**
Tian Long Ba Bu; **Changyou.com Limited**
Tiger Island; **Ardent Leisure Group**
Time Inc; **Meredith Corporation**
Time Warner Inc; **AT&T Inc**
Timeliness; **Value Line Inc**
Times (The); **New York Times Company (The)**
Titanfall; **Electronic Arts Inc (EA)**
Titanic; The Artifact Exhibition; **Premier Exhibitions Inc**
Titanic; The Experience; **Premier Exhibitions Inc**
TKO; Total Knock Out; **MGM Holdings Inc**
TL Vision; **Trans-Lux Corporation**
TLC; **Discovery Inc**
TLNovelas Univision; **Univision Communications Inc**
TMC; **Television Francaise 1 SA**
TNI Partners; **Lee Enterprises Incorporated**

TNT; **Turner Broadcasting System Inc**
TOFF GUYS; **Miramax LLC**
Tommy Nelson; **Thomas Nelson Inc**
Toon Boom; **Corus Entertainment Inc**
Toronto Star; **Torstar Corporation**
Total Traffic & Weather Network; **iHeartMedia Inc**
Touchstone; **Simon & Schuster Inc**
Touchy-Feely; **Educational Development Corporation**
TownHall.com; **Salem Media Group Inc**
TownNews.com; **Lee Enterprises Incorporated**
Toy Story; **Pixar Animation Studios**
TPG Capital; **RCN Telecom Services LLC**
TPG Capital; **RentPath LLC**
Trans World Hotels Germany GmbH; **Trans World Corporation**
Transom Capital Group; **LOUD Audio LLC**
Tribune Broadcasting; **Tribune Media Company**
Tribune Content Agency; **Tribune Publishing Company**
Trip Savvy; **Dotdash**
Triple M; **Southern Cross Media Group Limited**
TriStar Pictures; **Sony Pictures Motion Picture Group**
TriStar Pictures; **Sony Pictures Entertainment Inc**
Triton; **E W Scripps Company (The)**
Trolls; The Experience; **Feld Entertainment Inc**
Tropicana Las Vegas; **Penn National Gaming Inc**
Tudou; **Youku Tudou Inc**
Tupelo Raycom; **Raycom Media Inc**
TurboJET; **Shun Tak Holdings Limited**
Turff Bet & Sports Bar; **Codere SA**
Turner Broadcasting System Inc; **AT&T Inc**
Turner Broadcasting System Inc; **Warner Media LLC**
Turner Broadcasting System Inc; **Cable News Network Inc (CNN)**
TV Globo; **Globo Comunicacao e Participacoes SA (Grupo Globo)**
TV Markiza; **Central European Media Enterprises Ltd**
TV NOVA; **Central European Media Enterprises Ltd**
TV One LLC; **Urban One Inc**
TV TOKYO Art & Lighting Inc; **TV Tokyo Holdings Corporation**
TV TOKYO Commercial Inc; **TV Tokyo Holdings Corporation**
TV Tokyo Holdings Corporation; **TV Tokyo Holdings Corporation**
TV TOKYO Medianet Inc; **TV Tokyo Holdings Corporation**
TV TOKYO Music Inc; **TV Tokyo Holdings Corporation**
TV TOKYO Production Inc; **TV Tokyo Holdings Corporation**
TV TOKYO Systems Inc; **TV Tokyo Holdings Corporation**
TVA Nouvelles; **TVA Group Inc**
Twentieth Century Fox Television; **Fox Broadcasting Company**

INDEX OF SUBSIDIARIES, BRAND NAMES AND AFFILIATIONS, CONT.

Twenty-First Century Fox Inc; **Fox Broadcasting Company**
Twenty-First Century Fox Inc; **Fox Entertainment Group Inc**
Twenty-First Century Fox Inc; **National Geographic Society**
Twenty-First Century Fox Inc; **Twentieth Century Fox Film Corporation**
Twenty-First Century Fox, Inc. (21st Century Fox); **Fox Sports Interactive Media LLC**
TwinSpires; **Churchill Downs Incorporated**
UBET; **Tatts Group Limited**
UBM Americas; **UBM plc**
UBM Asia; **UBM plc**
UBM EMEA; **UBM plc**
UCI Studios; **Univision Communications Inc**
UFA Film & TV Produktion; **RTL Group SA**
Uforia; **Univision Communications Inc**
UltraAVX; **Cineplex Inc**
UMC (Urban Movie Channel); **RLJ Entertainment Inc**
UniMas; **Entravision Communications Corporation**
Unimas; **Univision Communications Inc**
Unitymedia; **Liberty Global plc**
Universal; **Comcast Corporation**
Universal Music; **Warner Music Group Corp**
Universal Music Classical Management & Productions; **Universal Music Group Inc**
Universal Music Group; **Vivendi SA**
Universal Music Publishing Group; **Universal Music Group Inc**
Universal Pictures; **NBCUniversal Media LLC**
Universal Studios; **Universal Pictures**
Universal Studios Singapore; **Genting Singapore PLC**
Univision; **Entravision Communications Corporation**
Univision; **Univision Communications Inc**
Univision Communication Inc; **Grupo Televisa SAB**
Univision Network; **Univision Communications Inc**
Univision+DN; **Univision Communications Inc**
Unties; **Sony Music Entertainment Inc**
UPC; **Liberty Global plc**
UpCurve; **GateHouse Media LLC**
UpCurve Cloud; **GateHouse Media LLC**
UPROXX; **Warner Music Group Corp**
US News Advisor Finder; **US News and World Report LP**
US News Weekly; **US News and World Report LP**
USA TODAY NETWORK; **Gannett Co Inc**
Usborne Books & More; **Educational Development Corporation**
Usborne Publishing Limited; **Educational Development Corporation**
USNews.com; **US News and World Report LP**
Vail; **Vail Resorts Inc**
Vail Resorts Development Company; **Vail Resorts Inc**
Valley Joist; **EBSCO Industries Inc**
Valleyfair; **Cedar Fair LP**
Value Line; **Value Line Inc**
Value Line Investment Survey (The); **Value Line Inc**
Value Line Publishing LLC; **Value Line Inc**
Vecima Networks, Inc.; **Concurrent Computer Corporation**
Velocity; **Discovery Inc**
Venetian Macao; **Sands China Ltd**
Venetian Macao Resort Hotel (The); **Las Vegas Sands Corp (The Venetian)**
Venetian Resort Hotel Casino (The); **Las Vegas Sands Corp (The Venetian)**
Venti; **Mediaset SpA**
VEO Play; **Izzi Telecom SAB de CV**
VEO Revenue; **Izzi Telecom SAB de CV**
Verge (The); **Vox Media Inc**
Verizon; **Verizon Media Group**
Verizon Communications Inc; **Verizon Media Group**
Vertical Nerve Inc; **A H Belo Corporation**
VerticalScope Holdings Inc; **Torstar Corporation**
Very Well; **Dotdash**
VG; **Schibsted ASA**
VGSbooks.com; **Lerner Publishing Group**
Viacom; **National Amusements Inc**
Viacom Inc; **Paramount Pictures Corporation**
Viafree; **Modern Times Group MTG AB**
Viaplay; **Modern Times Group MTG AB**
VICE BOOKS; **VICE Media Inc**
VICE DVD; **VICE Media Inc**
Vice Impact; **VICE Media Inc**
VICE Magazine; **VICE Media Inc**
Vice.com; **VICE Media Inc**
Viceland; **VICE Media Inc**
VICELAND; **A&E Television Networks LLC**
Viceland; **Walt Disney Company (The)**
Viceland TV; **VICE Media Inc**
VidCon; **Viacom Inc**
Viking; **Penguin Group USA**
Village Drive-In; **Village Roadshow Limited**
Village Roadshow Theme Parks; **Village Roadshow Limited**
Vimeo; **IAC/InterActiveCorp**
Vinyl Styl; **Alliance Entertainment LLC**
Virgin Media; **Liberty Global plc**
Virgin Media Inc; **Virgin Media Business Ltd**
Visual Studio; **Microsoft Corporation**
Vivendi SA; **Universal Music Group Inc**
Vivendi Village; **Vivendi SA**
VJunior; **Village Roadshow Limited**
Vmax; **Village Roadshow Limited**
Vodafone Group plc; **Vodafone Kabel Deutschland GmbH**
Vodafone Ziggo; **Liberty Global plc**
Vogue; **Conde Nast Publications Inc**
Volta; **Cirque du Soleil Inc**

INDEX OF SUBSIDIARIES, BRAND NAMES AND AFFILIATIONS, CONT.

Voom Fibre; **Virgin Media Business Ltd**
VOX; **RTL Group SA**
Vox Creative; **Vox Media Inc**
Vox.com; **Vox Media Inc**
Vpremium; **Village Roadshow Limited**
Vulcan Industries; **EBSCO Industries Inc**
Vulcan Productions; **Vulcan Inc**
Vulcan Real Estate; **Vulcan Inc**
W Network; **Corus Entertainment Inc**
W Publishing Group; **Thomas Nelson Inc**
WABC; **Walt Disney Company (The)**
Wall Group (The); **Endeavor LLC**
Wall Street English; **Pearson PLC**
Wall Street Journal; **News Corporation**
Wall Street Journal (The); **Dow Jones & Company Inc**
Walt Disney Animation Studios; **Walt Disney Studios (The)**
Walt Disney Co; **Twentieth Century Fox Film Corporation**
Walt Disney Company (The); **ABC Inc (Disney-ABC)**
Walt Disney Company (The); **Disney Media Networks**
Walt Disney Company (The); **ESPN Inc**
Walt Disney Company (The); **Euro Disney SCA**
Walt Disney Company (The); **Hulu LLC**
Walt Disney Company (The); **LucasArts Entertainment Company LLC**
Walt Disney Company (The); **Lucasfilm Ltd LLC**
Walt Disney Company (The); **Marvel Entertainment LLC**
Walt Disney Company (The); **Pixar Animation Studios**
Walt Disney Company (The); **Walt Disney Studios (The)**
Walt Disney Company (The); **A&E Television Networks LLC**
Walt Disney Records; **Walt Disney Studios (The)**
Wanda Cities; **Dalian Wanda Group Co Ltd**
Wanda Group; **Legendary Entertainment**
Wanda Investment Company; **Dalian Wanda Group Co Ltd**
Wanda Plaza; **Dalian Wanda Group Co Ltd**
Wanda Sports; **Dalian Wanda Group Co Ltd**
WARC; **Ascential plc**
Warner Bros Animation; **Warner Bros Entertainment Inc**
Warner Bros Entertainment Inc; **AT&T Inc**
Warner Bros Entertainment Inc; **Warner Media LLC**
Warner Bros Pictures; **Warner Bros Entertainment Inc**
Warner Bros Records Inc; **Warner Music Group Corp**
Warner Bros Television Group; **Warner Bros Entertainment Inc**
Warner Horizon Television; **Warner Bros Entertainment Inc**
Warner Media LLC; **Cable News Network Inc (CNN)**
Warner Media LLC; **Home Box Office Inc (HBO)**
Warner Media LLC; **Turner Broadcasting System Inc**
Warner Media LLC; **Warner Bros Entertainment Inc**
Warner/Chappell Music; **Warner Music Group Corp**
WarnerMedia; **CW Network LLC (The)**
Warwick Castle; **Merlin Entertainments Group Plc**
WashingtonTimes.com; **Washington Times LLC (The)**
WatchESPN; **ESPN Inc**
watchOS; **Apple Inc**
WatchOWN.tv; **Oprah Winfrey Network (OWN)**
Water Country USA; **SeaWorld Entertainment Inc**
Waterfall Aviary; **Wildlife Reserves Singapore Group**
Waterview Golf Club; **American Golf Corp**
Wave; **Bose Corporation**
WE tv; **AMC Networks Inc**
WeBuyCars.co.za; **Naspers Limited**
Week (The); **Dennis Publishing Ltd**
Well+Good; **Leaf Group Ltd**
Wells Fargo Center; **Comcast Corporation**
West Australian (The); **Seven West Media Limited**
WesTrac; **Seven Group Holdings Limited**
Westwood One; **Cumulus Media Inc**
Westwood One Backstage; **Westwood One Inc**
Westwood One Podcast Network; **Westwood One Inc**
WetnWild; **Palace Entertainment Holdings LLC**
WGN America; **Tribune Media Company**
WGSN; **Ascential plc**
WhatsApp Messenger; **Facebook Inc**
Where God Left His Shoes; **Vulcan Inc**
Whistler Blackcomb; **Vail Resorts Inc**
WhiteWater World; **Ardent Leisure Group**
Whole Foods Market; **Amazon.com Inc**
Wii; **Nintendo Co Ltd**
Wii U; **Nintendo Co Ltd**
Wiley Online Library; **John Wiley & Sons Inc**
William Hill US; **William Hill plc**
William Morris Agency Inc; **Endeavor LLC**
William Morris Endeavor Entertainment LLC; **NeuLion Inc**
Window of the World; **Shenzhen Overseas Chinese Town Co Ltd (OCT Limited)**
Windows; **Microsoft Corporation**
Wirecutter (The); **New York Times Company (The)**
WME; **Endeavor LLC**
Women@Forbes; **Forbes Media LLC**
Words with Friends; **Zynga Inc**
Workplace Learning Solutions; **John Wiley & Sons Inc**
World of Warcraft; **Activision Blizzard Inc**
World Series of Poker; **Caesars Entertainment Corporation**
Wrights; **CSS Industries Inc**
WSJ Pro; **Dow Jones & Company Inc**
WWE Network; **World Wrestling Entertainment Inc**
WWE Studios; **World Wrestling Entertainment Inc**
WWEShop; **World Wrestling Entertainment Inc**
www.barnesandnoble.com; **Barnes & Noble Inc**
Wynn Boston Harbor; **Wynn Resorts Limited**
Wynn Las Vegas Resort & Country Club; **Wynn Resorts Limited**
Wynn Macau Resort; **Wynn Resorts Limited**

INDEX OF SUBSIDIARIES, BRAND NAMES AND AFFILIATIONS, CONT.

Wynn Palace; **Wynn Resorts Limited**
Xbox; **Microsoft Corporation**
XCOM; **Take-Two Interactive Software Inc**
XD Extreme Digital Cinema; **Cinemark Inc**
XFINITY; **Comcast Corporation**
Xinhua Mobile; **Beat Holdings Limited**
X-Men; **Marvel Entertainment LLC**
Xperi Corporation; **DTS Inc**
Xscape Entertainment Centre; **Cineplex Inc**
Xtream; **Mediacom Communications Corporation**
Xtreme Mystery; **Aristocrat Leisure Limited**
Yahoo!; **Verizon Media Group**
Yahoo!7; **Seven Group Holdings Limited**
Yahoo!7; **Seven West Media Limited**
Yello Pages; **Yellow Pages Limited**
Yenibiris.com; **Hurriyet Gazetecilik ve Matbaacilik AS**
Yes Planet; **Cineworld Group plc**
Youku; **Youku Tudou Inc**
Your Speakeasy LLC; **A H Belo Corporation**
Youthworker Journal; **Salem Media Group Inc**
YouTube; **Alphabet Inc (Google)**
YouTube Insight; **YouTube LLC**
YouTube Leanback; **YouTube LLC**
YouTube Music; **YouTube LLC**
YouTube Partner; **YouTube LLC**
YouTube Premium; **YouTube LLC**
YouTubeToptics; **YouTube LLC**
YP Dine; **Yellow Pages Limited**
YP Holdings; **DexYP**
YP NextHome; **Yellow Pages Limited**
YP Shopwise; **Yellow Pages Limited**
Z Capital Group LLC; **Affinity Gaming LLC**
Z Capital Partners LLC; **Affinity Gaming LLC**
Zagat; **Zagat Survey LLC**
Zagat To Go; **Zagat Survey LLC**
Zagat.com; **Zagat Survey LLC**
Zagat.mobi; **Zagat Survey LLC**
Zia Park Casino; **Penn National Gaming Inc**
Ziff Davis Inc; **IGN Entertainment Inc**
Ziggo Dome; **Live Nation Entertainment Inc**
Zulily LLC; **Qurate Retail Inc**
Zumanity; **Cirque du Soleil Inc**
Zylom; **RealNetworks Inc**
Zynga Poker; **Zynga Inc**

INDEX OF SUBSIDIARIES, BRAND NAMES AND AFFILIATIONS, CONT.

A Short Entertainment, Movie, Publishing & Media Industry Glossary

1080p: A classification for high-definition video. 1080 refers to 1,080 lines of vertical resolution; p refers to progressive scan, meaning that the lines that comprise the video picture appear on the screen sequentially. This standard is used in the production of high definition film, high definition television (HDTV) and high definition digital video disc (HD DVD). 1080p is a superior technology to 1080i (i stands for interlaced) which delivers lines of video alternatively resulting in slight distortions in picture quality.

5G Cellular: A wireless technology that is expected to produce blinding download speeds of one gigabyte per second (Gbps), and perhaps as high as 10 Gbps.

802.11a (Wi-Fi): A faster wireless network standard than 802.11b ("Wi-Fi"). 802.11a operates in the 5-GHz band at speeds of 54 Mbps. This standard may be affected by weather and is not as suitable for outdoor use. 802.11 standards are set by the IEEE (Institute of Electrical and Electronics Engineers).

802.11ac: An ultra-highspeed Wi-Fi standard. It operates on the 5 Ghz band and is backwards compatible with older 802.11 standards. 802.11 standards are set by the IEEE (Institute of Electrical and Electronics Engineers). This specfication is capable of 1 gigabit per second data transfer speeds.

802.11b (Wi-Fi): A Wi-Fi short-range wireless connection standard created by the IEEE (Institute of Electrical and Electronics Engineers). It operates at 11 Mbps and can be used to connect computer devices to each other. 802.11b competes with the Bluetooth standard. Its range is up to 380 feet, but 150 feet or so may be more practical in some installations.

802.11g (Wi-Fi): An addition to the series of 802.11 specifications for Wi-Fi wireless networks, 802.11g provides data transfer at speeds of up to 54 Mbps in the 2.4-GHz band. It can easily exchange data with 802.11b-enabled devices, but at much higher speed. 802.11g equipment, such as wireless access points, will be able to provide simultaneous WLAN connectivity for both 802.11g and 802.11b equipment. The 802.11 standards are set by the IEEE (Institute of Electrical and Electronics Engineers).

802.11n (MIMO): Multiple Input Multiple Output antenna technology. MIMO is a new standard in the series of 802.11 Wi-Fi specifications for wireless networks. It has the potential of providing data transfer speeds of 100 to perhaps as much as 500 Mbps. 802.11n also boasts better operating distances than current networks. MIMO uses spectrum more efficiently without any loss of reliability. The technology is based on several different antennas all tuned to the same channel, each transmitting a different signal.

802.15: See "Ultrawideband (UWB)." For 802.15.1, see "Bluetooth."

802.16: See "WiMAX."

Advertising-On-Demand: Television advertising that viewers can watch voluntarily, in contrast to traditional television advertising, which is shown on the air without viewer choice. See "Demand-Driven Advertising."

Affiliate: A broadcast radio or television station that is an "affiliate" of a national network, such as NBC or CBS, contracts with the national network, which provides programming to the affiliate for all or part of each day. In return, the affiliate provides the network with an agreed-upon number of minutes of advertising time, which the network then resells to advertisers.

AM: See "Amplitude Modulation (AM)."

American Research Bureau (ARB): One of several national firms that conduct audience research. ARB is the founder of Arbitron ratings.

Amplitude Modulation (AM): Radio broadcasts in the range of 535 kHz to 1705 kHz.

Analog: A form of transmitting information characterized by continuously variable quantities. Digital transmission, in contrast, is characterized by discrete bits of information in numerical steps. An analog signal responds to changes in light, sound, heat and pressure.

APAC: Asia Pacific Advisory Committee. A multi-country committee representing the Asia and Pacific region.

Applications: Computer programs and systems that allow users to interface with a computer and that collect, manipulate, summarize and report data and information. Also, see "Apps."

Apps: Short for applications, apps are small software programs designed to run primarily on mobile devices such as smartphones and tablets. Also known as "mobile apps."

Area of Dominant Influence (ADI): A market area established by Arbitron that places cities and/or parts of counties into groupings that are reached by the same local radio or television stations. It is similar to Nielsen's "Designated Market Area." For example, advertising on radio stations in Boston will reach listeners far outside of Boston within the surrounding ADI.

ARPU: See "Average Revenue Per User (ARPU)."

Asynchronous Transfer Mode (ATM): A digital switching and transmission technology based on high speed. ATM allows voice, video and data signals to be sent over a single telephone line at speeds from 25 million to 1 billion bits per second (bps). This digital ATM speed is much faster than traditional analog phone lines, which allow no more than 2 million bps. See "Broadband."

Augmented Reality: Any technology designed to enhance a user's experience by adding to the environment with computer-generated means. For example, MARA (Mobile Augmented Reality Applications) is a method of enabling detailed information about a specific geographic location to appear on a cell phone's screen, pioneered by Nokia. It relies on special tools within the cell phone, including a camera, GPS, a compass and Internet access. A MARA-equipped phone might display details about a restaurant's offerings, downloaded from the Internet, when the phone's digital camera is aimed at a restaurant's front entry. Or, the screen might display information from a service like Google Maps as an overlay on the digital camera image.

Average Revenue Per User (ARPU): A measure of the average monthly billing revenue of a wireless company on a per user basis.

Baby Boomer: Generally refers to people born from 1946 to 1964. In the U.S., the initial number of Baby Boomers totaled about 78 million. The term evolved to describe the children of soldiers and war industry workers who were involved in World War II and who began forming families after the war's end. In 2011, the oldest Baby Boomers began reaching the traditional retirement age of 65.

Bandwidth: The data transmission capacity of a network, measured in the amount of data (in bits and bauds) it can transport in one second. A full page of text is about 15,000 to 20,000 bits. Full-motion, full-screen video requires about 10 million bits per second, depending on compression.

Basic Cable: Primary level or levels of cable service offered for subscription. Basic cable offerings may include retransmitted broadcast signals as well as local and access programming. In addition, regional and national cable network programming may be provided.

Blog (Web Log): A web site consisting of a personal journal, news coverage, special-interest content or other data that is posted on the Internet, frequently updated and intended for public viewing by anyone who might be interested in the author's thoughts. Short for "web log," blog content is frequently distributed via RSS (Real Simple Syndication). Blog content has evolved to include video files (VLOGs) and audio files (Podcasting) as well as text. Also, see "Real Simple Syndication (RSS)," "Video Blog (VLOG)," "Moblog"; "Podcasting," and "User Generated Content (UGC)."

Bluetooth: An industry standard for a technology that enables wireless, short-distance infrared connections between devices such as cell phone headsets, Palm Pilots or PDAs, laptops, printers and Internet appliances.

BPO: See "Business Process Outsourcing (BPO)."

Brand: A marketing strategy that places a focus on the brand name of a product, service or firm in order to increase the brand's market share, increase sales, establish credibility, improve satisfaction, raise the profile of the firm and increase profits. Also, see "Brand."

Brand Name: See "Brand."

Branded Entertainment: Entertainment programming or content whereby a brand's message, image or positioning is built into the content in a vital and relevant manner. The benefits may include an opportunity to break through the advertising "clutter";

a chance to align the brand with relevant stars, athletes, settings or scripts; or a new opportunity to reach target audiences in a meaningful and memorable way. Also, see "Embedded Advertising."

Branding: A marketing strategy that places a focus on the brand name of a product, service or firm in order to increase the brand's market share, increase sales, establish credibility, improve satisfaction, raise the profile of the firm and increase profits. Also, see "Brand."

Broadband: The high-speed transmission range for telecommunications and computer data. Broadband generally refers to any transmission at 2 million bps (bits per second) or higher (much higher than analog speed). A broadband network can carry voice, video and data all at the same time. Internet users enjoying broadband access typically connect to the Internet via DSL line, cable modem or T1 line. Several wireless methods offer broadband as well.

Broadcast: Electronic transmission of media by radio or television; generally refers to wireless methods.

Browser: A program that allows a user to read Internet text or graphics and to navigate from one page to another. The most popular browsers are Microsoft Internet Explorer and Netscape Navigator. Firefox is an open source browser introduced in 2005 that is rapidly gaining popularity.

B-to-B, or B2B: See "Business-to-Business."

B-to-C, or B2C: See "Business-to-Consumer."

Business Process Outsourcing (BPO): The process of hiring another company to handle business activities. BPO is one of the fastest-growing segments in the offshoring sector. Services include human resources management, billing and purchasing and call centers, as well as many types of customer service or marketing activities, depending on the industry involved. Also, see "Knowledge Process Outsourcing (KPO)" and Business Transformation Outsourcing (BTO)."

Business Transformation Outsourcing (BTO): A segment within outsourcing in which the client company revamps its business processes with the goal of transforming its business by following a collaborative approach with its outsourced services provider.

Business-to-Business: An organization focused on selling products, services or data to commercial customers rather than individual consumers. Also known as B2B.

Business-to-Consumer: An organization focused on selling products, services or data to individual consumers rather than commercial customers. Also known as B2C.

Cable Modem: An interface between a cable television system and a computer or router. Most cable modems are external devices that connect to the PC through a standard 10Base-T Ethernet card and twisted-pair wiring. External Universal Serial Bus (USB) modems and internal PCI modem cards are also available.

Cable TV: A television system consisting of a local television station that is equipped with an antenna or satellite dish. The antenna or dish receives signals from distant, central network stations and retransmits those signals via TV cable to the local subscriber.

Caching: A method of storing data in a temporary location closer to the user so that it can be retrieved quickly when requested.

CAFTA-DR: See "Central American-Dominican Republic Free Trade Agreement (CAFTA-DR)."

Call Letters: Letters that identify a station, e.g., KTRU. Call letters are established by the Federal Communications Commission. Each broadcast station has unique letters. The letters may denote whether the station is in the eastern or western U.S.

Captive Offshoring: Used to describe a company-owned offshore operation. For example, Microsoft owns and operates significant captive offshore research and development centers in China and elsewhere that are offshore from Microsoft's U.S. home base. Also see "Offshoring."

CATV: Cable television.

CEM: Contract electronic manufacturing. See "Contract Manufacturing."

Central American-Dominican Republic Free Trade Agreement (CAFTA-DR): A trade agreement signed into law in 2005 that aimed to open up the Central American and Dominican Republic markets to

American goods. Member nations include Guatemala, Nicaragua, Costa Rica, El Salvador, Honduras and the Dominican Republic. Before the law was signed, products from those countries could enter the U.S. almost tariff-free, while American goods heading into those countries faced stiff tariffs. The goal of this agreement was to create U.S. jobs while at the same time offering the non-U.S. member citizens a chance for a better quality of life through access to U.S.-made goods.

Channel Definition Format (CDF): Used in Internet-based broadcasting. With this format, a channel serves as a web site that also sends an information file about that specific site. Users subscribe to a channel by downloading the file.

Circulation: The numerical distribution of print media such as magazines or newspapers. "Controlled circulation" refers to magazines that are generally sent to a defined subscriber base free-of-charge. "Audited circulation" refers to a subscription base that has been verified as to its size by an independent agency.

Click Through: In advertising on the Internet, click through refers to how often viewers respond to an ad by clicking on it. Also known as click rate.

Closed Circuit TV (CCTV): Programs or other material that limit the target audience to a specific group instead of the general public. For example, major retailers use such private TV systems, distributed via satellite, to provide training to employees at remote store locations.

Codec: Hardware or software that converts analog to digital and digital to analog (in both audio and video formats). Codecs can be found in digital telephones, set-top boxes, computers and videoconferencing equipment. The term is also used to refer to the compression of digital information into a smaller format.

Community Antenna Television: A community television system that is served through cable and is connected to a common set of antennae.

Compression: A technology in which a communications signal is squeezed so that it uses less bandwidth (or capacity) than it normally would. This saves storage space and shortens transfer time. The original data is decompressed when read back into memory.

Content Aggregator: A content aggregator collects content and distributes it to subscribers, network operators or other content companies.

Contract Manufacturing: A business arrangement whereby a company manufactures products that will be sold under the brand names of its client companies. For example, a large number of consumer electronics, such as laptop computers, are manufactured by contract manufacturers for leading brand-name computer companies such as Dell and Apple. Many other types of products, such as shoes and apparel, are made under contract manufacturing. Also see "Original Equipment Manufacturer (OEM)" and "Original Design Manufacturer (ODM)."

Controlled (Qualified) Circulation: Restricting the circulation of an advertisement to target qualified customers (e.g., sending lock-pick catalogs only to certified locksmiths, or medical equipment brochures only to doctors and hospitals).

Controlled Circulation: See "Circulation."

Cookie: A piece of information sent to a web browser from a web server that the browser software saves and then sends back to the server upon request. Cookies are used by web site operators to track the actions of users returning to the site.

Copyright: A form of protection provided to the authors of "original works of authorship," including literary, dramatic, musical, artistic, and certain other intellectual works, both published and unpublished. In the U.S., the 1976 Copyright Act generally gives the owner of copyright the exclusive right to reproduce the copyrighted work, to prepare derivative works, to distribute copies or recordings of the copyrighted work, to perform the copyrighted work publicly, or to display the copyrighted work publicly. Other nations have similar laws. In the United States, copyrights are registered by the Copyright Office of the Library of Congress. There are also cooperative, international copyright agreements and agencies.

Cord Cutting: The growing migration of consumers away from broadcast TV, cable and satellite providers to the Internet for video content.

Cost Per Click (CPC): Online advertising that is billed on a response basis. An advertiser sells a banner ad and is paid by the number of users who click on the ad.

Cost Per Thousand (CPM): A charge for advertising calculated on a fixed amount multiplied by the number of users who view an ad, computed in thousands.

CPC: See "Cost Per Click (CPC)."

CPM: See "Cost Per Thousand (CPM)."

CRM: See "Customer Relationship Management (CRM)."

Crowdsourcing: A method of gathering data that capitalizes on users of a web site or database to find and post the data. Wikipedia is a well known example.

Customer Relationship Management (CRM): Refers to the automation, via sophisticated software, of business processes involving existing and prospective customers. CRM may cover aspects such as sales (contact management and contact history), marketing (campaign management and telemarketing) and customer service (call center history and field service history). Well known providers of CRM software include Salesforce, which delivers via a Software as a Service model (see "Software as a Service (Saas)"), Microsoft and Oracle.

Cyberspace: Refers to the entire realm of information available through computer networks and the Internet.

Data Over Cable Service Interface Specification (DOCSIS): A set of standards for transferring data over cable television. DOCSIS 3.0 will enable very high-speed Internet access that may eventually reach 160 Mbps.

Decompression: See "Compression."

Demand-Driven Advertising: Allows television viewers to choose which commercials to watch, how many to watch and when to watch them.

Demographics: The breakdown of the population into statistical categories such as age, income, education and sex.

Dendrimer: A type of molecule that can be used with small molecules to give them certain desirable characteristics. Dendrimers are utilized in technologies for electronic displays. See "Organic LED (OLED)."

Designated Market Area (DMA): A television market as delineated by AC Nielsen.

Dial-Up Access: The connection of a computer or other device to a network through a modem and a public telephone network. The only difference between dial-up access and a telephone connection is that computers are at each end of the connection rather than people. Dial-up access is slower than DSL, cable modem and other advanced connections.

Digital: The transmission of a signal by reducing all of its information to ones and zeros and then regrouping them at the reception end. Digital transmission vastly improves the carrying capacity of the spectrum while reducing noise and distortion of the transmission.

Digital Millennium Copyright Act: A U.S. law created in 1998. It was written in response to the rapid growth of content on the Internet. The act contains a "safe harbor" provision that enables Internet site publishers to promptly eliminate most faults or penalties of infringement if they promptly remove online content when notified by the proper owners of that content's copyright.

Digital Multimedia Broadcasting (DMB): The practice of broadcasting television programming to cellphones and other portable devices using a designated frequency. DMB was created in Korea and is responsible for the wide use of cellphones for television viewing there.

Digital Radio Mondiale (DRM): A digital replacement for traditional long-, medium- and short-wave radio. Endorsed as the international standard, DRM was developed by a consortium of broadcasters and hardware makers such as Deutsche Welle and the BBC World Service.

Digital Rights Management (DRM): Restrictions placed on the use of digital content by copyright holders and hardware manufacturers. DRM for Apple, Inc.'s iTunes, for example, allows downloaded music to be played only on Apple's iPod player and iPhones, per agreement with music production companies Universal Music Group, SonyBMG, Warner Music and EMI.

Digital Subscriber Line (DSL): A broadband (high-speed) Internet connection provided via telecommunications systems. These lines are a cost-effective means of providing homes and small businesses with relatively fast Internet access. Common variations include ADSL and SDSL. DSL competes with cable modem access and wireless access.

Digital Video Disc (DVD): Similar to music CDs, these discs can store more than seven times as much data. (DVDs store 4.7 gigabytes of data, compared to 650 megabytes on a CD.) They are commonly used to store full-length motion pictures.

Digital Video Recorder (DVR): A device that records video files, typically television programming including movies, in digital format to be replayed at a later time. The most commonly known DVR is the TiVo. DVRs encode video as MPEG files and save them onto a hard drive. DVRs are also known as PVRs (Personal Video Recorders).

Direct Broadcast Satellite (DBS): A high-powered satellite authorized to broadcast television programming directly to homes. Home subscribers use a dish and a converter to receive and translate the TV signal. An example is the DirecTV service. DBS operates in the 11.70- to 12.40-GHz range.

Direct Marketing: A form of non-store retailing in which customers are exposed to merchandise through catalogs, direct-mail brochures, telemarketing or television. Direct marketing may be used to generate direct-response purchases, store traffic, sales leads or a combination thereof.

Direct Selling: A form of marketing which involves manufacturing and then selling merchandise or services through direct mail or through salespeople who contact consumers directly or by telephone at home or place of work (e.g., Mary Kay cosmetics).

Distributor: An individual or business involved in marketing, warehousing and/or shipping of products manufactured by others to a specific group of end users. Distributors do not sell to the general public. In order to develop a competitive advantage, distributors often focus on serving one industry or one set of niche clients. For example, within the medical industry, there are major distributors that focus on providing pharmaceuticals, surgical supplies or dental supplies to clinics and hospitals.

DS-1: A digital transmission format that transmits and receives information at a rate of 1,544,000 bits per second.

DSL: See "Digital Subscriber Line (DSL)."

Dub: A recorded copy of a TV or radio appearance on video or audiotape.

DVB-H: Digital Video Broadcasting Handheld network. This technology enables DVB-H-equipped cell phones to receive digital television broadcast signals. This means that cell phone users can watch television programs in real time, at the same time that viewers at home are watching them, with no need to download TV shows or watch them on a prerecorded basis.

DVD: See "Digital Video Disc (DVD)."

DVR: See "Digital Video Recorder (DVR)."

Dynamic Ad Insertion: A technology that allows cable TV channels to insert ads into their video on demand (VOD) services in as little at 24 hours. The practice allows advertisers to insert timely ads that viewers are unable to fast-forward through. In the past, advertisers were not so keen on VOD ads because programs often contained spots that were time sensitive and of little or no interest when viewed at a later date.

Dynamic HTML: Web content that changes with each individual viewing. For example, the same site could appear differently depending on geographic location of the reader, time of day, previous pages viewed or the user's profile.

Echo Boomers: See "Generation Y."

ECM: Electronic Contract Manufacturing. See "Contract Manufacturing."

E-Commerce: The use of online, Internet-based sales methods. The phrase is used to describe both business-to-consumer and business-to-business sales.

E-Ink: A display technology used by E-Readers, similar to printed books and newspapers. The advantage of E-Ink over typical digital displays is that it is easier to view in direct sunlight.

Electronic Book (e-Book): An electronic method of storing and accessing books online or in portable e-book viewing machines (readers), so that consumers can purchase and read a digital copy of a book instead of a traditional print copy. Advantages include the ability to search by key word and the ability to store dozens of books in digital form on one portable device.

Electronic Data Interchange (EDI): An accepted standard format for the exchange of data between various companies' networks. EDI allows for the transfer of e-mail as well as orders, invoices and other files from one company to another.

Electronic News Production System (ENPS): A content management software application designed by broadcasters for use in television newsrooms. Introduced in 1997, the application addresses nearly all newsroom activities, including scripting, messaging, archiving, news wire management and text searching of news feeds.

Electronic Paper Display (EPD): A term used to describe a recently developed type of high contrast, flexible display. The displays use low amounts of power and can be viewed in bright sunlight and at any angle. They are well suited for use as screens on mobile devices and may have broad applications in outdoor advertising.

Embedded Advertising: The practice of arranging for products and brands to be seen in use by entertainers or athletes, or in relation to a specific event or locale. For example, marketers very frequently pay substantial fees to have characters in a movie drive a certain make of car or drink a certain brand of soft drink. (Also, see "Branded Entertainment.")

EMEA: The region comprised of Europe, the Middle East and Africa.

EMS: Electronics Manufacturing Services. See "Contract Manufacturing."

Enterprise Resource Planning (ERP): An integrated information system that helps manage all aspects of a business, including accounting, ordering and human resources, typically across all locations of a major corporation or organization. ERP is considered to be a critical tool for management of large organizations. Suppliers of ERP tools include SAP and Oracle.

ePub: Short for electronic publication. ePub is an open standard for the publication of eBooks. The ePub standard was adopted by the International Digital Publishing Forum.

E-Reader: Mobile devices that specialize in text-based displays. E-Readers offer better readability and battery life than tablets at the expense of complex color displays. Examples include the Amazon Kindle and the Barnes & Noble Nook.

ERP: See "Enterprise Resource Planning (ERP)."

EU: See "European Union (EU)."

EU Competence: The jurisdiction in which the European Union (EU) can take legal action.

European Community (EC): See "European Union (EU)."

European Union (EU): A consolidation of European countries (member states) functioning as one body to facilitate trade. Previously known as the European Community (EC). The EU has a unified currency, the Euro. See europa.eu.int.

EV-DO (CDMA 2000 1xEV-DO): A 3G (third generation) cellular telephone service standard that is an improved version of 1xRTT. The EV-DO (Evolution-Data Optimized) standard introduced in 2004 allows data download speeds of as much as 2.4 Mbps. A version introduced in 2006 allows up to 14.7 Mbps data download speeds. EV-DO is also known as CDMA 2000 1xEV-DO. EV-DO's capabilities are used by the entertainment industry to enable video via cell phone.

Extensible Markup Language (XML): A programming language that enables designers to add extra functionality to documents that could not otherwise be utilized with standard HTML coding. XML was developed by the World Wide Web Consortium. It can communicate to various software programs the actual meanings contained in HTML documents. For example, it can enable the gathering and use of information from a large number of databases at once and place that information into one web site window. XML is an important protocol to web services. See "Web Services."

Extranet: A computer network that is accessible in part to authorized outside persons, as opposed to an intranet, which uses a firewall to limit accessibility.

FASB: See "Financial Accounting Standards Board (FASB)."

FCC: See "Federal Communications Commission (FCC)."

Federal Communications Commission (FCC): The U.S. Government agency that regulates broadcast television and radio, as well as satellite transmission, telephony and all uses of radio spectrum.

Femtocell: A device used to boost performance of cell phones on a local basis, such as in a consumer's home or office. It utilizes nearby licensed wireless spectrum. The femtocell, in the form of a small box, routes wireless phone calls from a cell phone handset to the central office of a cellular service provider via a consumer's high speed Internet line.

Fiber to the Home (FTTH): Refers to the extension of a fiber-optic system through the last mile so that it touches the home or office where it will be used. This can provide high speed Internet access at speeds of 15 to 100 Mbps, much faster than typical T1 or DSL line. FTTH is now commonly installed in new communities where telecom infrastructure is being built for the first time. Another phrase used to describe such installations is FTTP, or Fiber to the Premises.

Fiber to the Node (FTTN): Refers to the extension of a fiber-optic system through the last mile so that it touches a central neighborhood junction close to the home or office where it will be used. The remaining distance is covered by existing copper phone line that uses DSL (digital subscriber line) technology to speed data transfer.

Field Emission Display (FED): A self-luminescent display that can be extremely thin, draw very low power, and be very bright from all angles and in all types of light. The latest FEDs are based on carbon nanotubes. Samsung is a leader in this field. Early applications include high-end television and computer monitors.

Financial Accounting Standards Board (FASB): An independent organization that establishes the Generally Accepted Accounting Principles (GAAP).

FM: See "Frequency Modulation (FM)."

Folksonomy: A user-created taxonomy of Internet site content based on key words or concepts. This is a collaborative effort in a wiki-like environment that enables participants to organize data, such as photos, into categories. A widely known example is #hashtag system used on Twitter.

Free Video On Demand (FVOD): VOD programming offered by a network operator free of charge. FVOD programming includes on-demand advertising and on-demand programming offered as part of a basic VOD package.

Freemium: A business model in which a product or service (usually a digital game, software or web service) is offered at no charge to the user, but advanced features and services are promoted for purchase.

Frequency: The number of times that an alternating current goes through its complete cycle in one second. One cycle per second is referred to as one hertz; 1,000 cycles per second, one kilohertz; 1 million cycles per second, one megahertz; and 1 billion cycles per second, one gigahertz.

Frequency Band: A term for designating a range of frequencies in the electromagnetic spectrum.

Frequency Modulation (FM): Radio broadcasts in the range of 88 MHz to 108 MHz.

FTTC: Fiber to the curb. See "Fiber to the Home (FTTH)."

FTTP: Fiber to the premises. See "Fiber to the Home (FTTH)."

GAAP: See "Generally Accepted Accounting Principles (GAAP)."

Gamification: The use of game design and practices to enhance non-game content in order to attract users and increase engagement. For example, the use of games in online advertising and marketing, or the use of games in online education.

Gatekeeper: A person or persons controlling the flow of information. Individuals who allow information to pass through them to be disseminated to the public are referred to as gatekeepers. These include newspaper publishers, editors, reporters, television and radio producers, station owners and executives.

GDP: See "Gross Domestic Product (GDP)."

General Magazines: Consumer magazines that are not aimed at special-interest audiences.

Generally Accepted Accounting Principles (GAAP): A set of accounting standards administered by the Financial Accounting Standards Board (FASB) and enforced by the U.S. Security and Exchange Commission (SEC). GAAP is primarily used in the U.S.

Generation C: Creative consumers who are active in unpaid, consumer-generated content, such as Wikipedia, blogging, YouTube and consumer-generated advertising.

Generation M: A very loosely defined term that is sometimes used to refer to young people who have grown up in the digital age. "M" may refer to any or all of media-saturated, mobile or multi-tasking. The term was most notably used in a Kaiser Family Foundation report published in 2005, "Generation M: Media in the Lives of 8-18 year olds." Also, see "Generation Y" and "Generation Z."

Generation X: A loosely-defined and variously-used term that describes people born between approximately 1965 and 1980, but other time frames are recited. Generation X is often referred to as a group influential in defining tastes in consumer goods, entertainment and/or political and social matters.

Generation Y: Refers to people born between approximately 1982 and 2002. In the U.S., they number more than 90 million, making them the largest generation segment in the nation's history. They are also known as Echo Boomers, Millenials or the Millenial Generation. These are children of the Baby Boom generation who will be filling the work force as Baby Boomers retire.

Generation Z: Some people refer to Generation Z as people born after 1991. Others use the beginning date of 2001, or refer to the era of 1994 to 2004. Members of Generation Z are considered to be natural and rapid adopters of the latest technologies.

Geostationary: A geosynchronous satellite angle with zero inclination, making a satellite appear to hover over one spot on the earth's equator.

Global Positioning System (GPS): A satellite system, originally designed by the U.S. Department of Defense for navigation purposes. Today, GPS is in wide use for consumer and business purposes, such as navigation for drivers, boaters and hikers. It utilizes satellites orbiting the earth at 10,900 miles to enable users to pinpoint precise locations using small, electronic wireless receivers.

Globalization: The increased mobility of goods, services, labor, technology and capital throughout the world. Although globalization is not a new development, its pace has increased with the advent of new technologies.

GPS: See "Global Positioning System (GPS)."

Graphic Interchange Format (GIF): A widely used format for image files.

Gross Domestic Product (GDP): The total value of a nation's output, income and expenditures produced with a nation's physical borders.

Gross National Product (GNP): A country's total output of goods and services from all forms of economic activity measured at market prices for one calendar year. It differs from Gross Domestic Product (GDP) in that GNP includes income from investments made in foreign nations.

Gross Rating Points (GRPs): Measures the audience share of a television program's audience delivery. GRPs are the sum of individual ratings for all programs in a particular time slot. See "Ratings/Ratings Points/Ratings Share."

Haptics: A technology in which a user of electronics, wireless devices and electronic games experiences unique sensations from a video game interface or a touchscreen, such as one might find on a smartphone. Advanced touchscreens using haptics can enable the user to feel the sensation of clicks on an icon, vibrations and other types of touch sensations.

HD: High Definition.

HD Radio (High Definition Radio): A technology that enables station operators to slice existing radio spectrum into multiple, thin bands. Each band is capable of transmitting additional programming. One existing radio station's spectrum may be sliced into as many as eight channels.

HDMI: See "High-Definition Multi-Media Interface (HDMI)."

Headend: A facility that originates and distributes cable service in a given geographic area. Depending on the size of the area it serves, a cable system may be comprised of more than one headend.

Hertz: A measure of frequency equal to one cycle per second. Most radio signals operate in ranges of megahertz or gigahertz.

HFC: Hybrid Fiber Coaxial. A type of cable system.

High-Definition Multi-Media Interface (HDMI): An industry-standard interface to conduct uncompressed, all-digital audio and video signals into high definition entertainment components including HDTV. The goal is to enable consumer entertainment devices to display high quality, high-definition content. HDMI is backward-compatible with earlier DVI equipment, so that HDMI can HDMI equipment can display video received from DVI products.

High-Definition Television (HDTV): A type of television broadcasting that increases the resolution of the visual field contained by the image, making for a clearer and more movie-like viewing experience. HDTV requires advanced digital broadcasting and receiving equipment.

Homes Passed: Households that have the ability to receive cable service and may opt to subscribe.

HTML5: A specification for Internet development that represents the fifth major revision of the Hypertext Markup Language, or HTML. HTML5 is designed to better handle the types of Internet content that are rapidly growing in popularity, such as online video, audio and interactive documents and pages. For example, HTML5 enables the designer to embed images, audio and video directly into a web-based document.

ICT: See "Information and Communication Technologies (ICT)."

Idea Management: Software designed to enable employees, investors, management, customers and vendors to share ideas and opportunities for innovation in a secure environment. The goal is to foster faster development of new products and services. Idea management may be an adjunct to crowdsourcing. See "Crowdsourcing."

IFRS: See "International Financials Reporting Standards (IFRS)."

Impressions: In Internet advertising, the total number of times an ad is displayed on a web page. Impressions are not the same as "hits," which count the number of times each page or element in a page is retrieved. Since a single complicated page on a web site could consist of five or more individual elements, including graphics and text, one viewer calling up that page would register multiple hits but just a single impression.

Impulse VOD: Affords television viewers the ability to order VOD programming without having to phone in an order to the content provider.

Industry Code: A descriptive code assigned to any company in order to group it with firms that operate in similar businesses. Common industry codes include the NAICS (North American Industrial Classification System) and the SIC (Standard Industrial Classification), both of which are standards widely used in America, as well as the International Standard Industrial Classification of all Economic Activities (ISIC), the Standard International Trade Classification established by the United Nations (SITC) and the General Industrial Classification of Economic Activities within the European Communities (NACE).

Information and Communication Technologies (ICT): A term used to describe the relationship between the myriad types of goods, services and networks that make up the global information and communications system. Sectors involved in ICT include landlines, data networks, the Internet, wireless communications, (including cellular and remote wireless sensors) and satellites.

Infotainment: Programming which combines information with entertainment. It most often refers to television programming or web-based programming that informs the viewer while extolling the virtues of a product or service that is for sale.

Initial Public Offering (IPO): A company's first effort to sell its stock to investors (the public). Investors in an up-trending market eagerly seek stocks offered in many IPOs because the stocks of newly public companies that seem to have great promise may appreciate very rapidly in price, reaping great profits for those who were able to get the stock at the first offering. In the United States, IPOs are regulated by the SEC (U.S. Securities Exchange Commission) and by the state-level regulatory agencies of the states in which the IPO shares are offered.

Intellectual Property (IP): The exclusive ownership of original concepts, ideas, designs, engineering plans or other assets that are protected by law. Examples include items covered by trademarks, copyrights and patents. Items such as software, engineering plans, fashion designs and architectural designs, as well as games, books, songs and other entertainment items are among the many things that may be considered to be intellectual property. (Also, see "Patent.")

Interactive: In entertainment, advertising and communications, interactive refers to systems that enable the viewer or user to interact via a response or two-way communication. For example, interactive television advertising may enable the viewer to respond via a set-top box, immediately purchasing the item being advertised.

Interactive TV (ITV): Allows two-way data flow between a viewer and the cable TV system. A user can exchange information with the cable system—for example, by ordering a product related to a show he/she is watching or by voting in an interactive survey.

Interactive Video On Demand (IVOD): An extension of VOD that offers many of the functions typically provided by VCRs, such as pause, fast forward and fast rewind. Through a set-top box, the IVOD customer can browse, select and purchase products; avoid or select advertisements; and investigate additional details about news events.

International Financials Reporting Standards (IFRS): A set of accounting standards established by the International Accounting Standards Board (IASB) for the preparation of public financial statements. IFRS has been adopted by much of the world, including the European Union, Russia and Singapore.

Internet: A global computer network that provides an easily accessible way for hundreds of millions of users to send and receive data electronically when appropriately connected via computers or wireless devices. Access is generally through HTML-enabled sites on the World Wide Web. Also known as the Net.

Internet Appliance: A non-PC device that connects users to the Internet for specific or general purposes. A good example is an electronic game machine with a screen and Internet capabilities.

Internet of Things (IoT): A concept whereby individual objects, such as kitchen appliances, automobiles, manufacturing equipment, environmental sensors or air conditioners, are connected to the Internet. The objects must be able to identify themselves to other devices or to databases. The ultimate goals may include the collection and processing of data, the control of instruments and machinery, and eventually, a new level of synergies, artificial intelligence and operating efficiencies among the objects. The Internet of Things is often referred to as IoT. Related technologies and topics include RFID, remote wireless sensors, telecommunications and nanotechnology.

Internet Protocol Television (IPTV): Television delivered by Internet-based means such as fiber to the home (FTTH) or a very high speed DSL. Microsoft is a leading provider of advanced IPTV software. SBC and BT are two leading telecom firms that are using Microsoft's new software to offer television services over high speed Internet lines.

Internet Service Provider (ISP): A company that sells access to the Internet to individual subscribers. Leading examples are MSN and AOL.

Internet Sharing Programs: Internet networks that allow users to share files and programs, in spite of possible copyright restrictions (e.g., Napster, before the federal ruling that barred it from downloading music files free of charge).

Intranet: A network protected by a firewall for sharing data and e-mail within an organization or company. Usually, intranets are used by organizations for internal communication.

IoT: See "Internet of Things (IoT)."

IP: See "Intellectual Property (IP)."

IP Number/IP Address: A number or address with four parts that are separated by dots. Each machine on the Internet has its own IP (Internet protocol) number, which serves as an identifier.

IP VOD: See "VOD-Over-IP."

IPTV: See "Internet Protocol Television (IPTV)."

IT-Enabled Services (ITES): The portion of the Information Technology industry focused on providing business services, such as call centers, insurance claims processing and medical records transcription, by utilizing the power of IT, especially the Internet. Most ITES functions are considered to be back-office procedures. Also, see "Business Process Outsourcing (BPO)."

ITV: See "Interactive TV (ITV)."

Java: A programming language developed by Sun Microsystems that allows web pages to display interactive graphics. Any type of computer or operating systems can read Java.

Joint Photographic Experts Group (JPEG): A widely used format for digital image files.

Knowledge Process Outsourcing (KPO): The use of outsourced and/or offshore workers to perform business tasks that require judgment and analysis. Examples include such professional tasks as patent research, legal research, architecture, design, engineering, market research, scientific research, accounting and tax return preparation. Also, see "Business Process Outsourcing (BPO)."

LAC: An acronym for Latin America and the Caribbean.

LDCs: See "Least Developed Countries (LDCs)."

Least Developed Countries (LDCs): Nations determined by the U.N. Economic and Social Council to be the poorest and weakest members of the international community. There are currently 50 LDCs, of which 34 are in Africa, 15 are in Asia Pacific and the remaining one (Haiti) is in Latin America. The top 10 on the LDC list, in descending order from top to 10th, are Afghanistan, Angola, Bangladesh, Benin, Bhutan, Burkina Faso, Burundi, Cambodia, Cape Verde and the Central African Republic. Sixteen of the LDCs are also Landlocked Least Developed Countries (LLDCs) which present them with additional difficulties often due to the high cost of transporting trade goods. Eleven of the LDCs are Small Island Developing States (SIDS), which are often at risk of extreme weather phenomenon (hurricanes, typhoons, Tsunami); have fragile ecosystems; are often dependent on foreign energy sources; can have high disease rates for HIV/AIDS and malaria; and can have poor market access and trade terms.

Light Emitting Diode (LED): A small tube containing material that emits light when exposed to electricity. The color of the light depends upon the type of material. The LED was first developed in 1962 at the University of Illinois at Urbana-Champaign. LEDs are important to a wide variety of industries, from wireless telephone handsets to signage to displays for medical equipment, because they provide a very high quality of light with very low power requirements. They also have a very long useful life and produce very low heat output when. All of these characteristics are great improvements over a conventional incandescent bulb. Several advancements have been made in LED technology. See "Organic LED (OLED)," "Polymer Light Emitting Diode (PLED)," "Small Molecule Organic Light Emitting Diode (SMOLED)" and "Dendrimer."

Linear Programming: See "Linear TV."

Linear TV: A type of television programming that is (1) standard non-PVR and non-VOD television service. (2) TV programming that the producers, broadcasters, etc. do not want the viewer leaving in any way, including visiting the program advertiser's website. (3) Programming that is dependent on programming that has already been presented. (4) Non-interactive TV.

Liquid Crystal Display (LCD): A digital screen composed of liquid crystal cells that change luminosity when exposed to an electric field. The newest LCDs have a higher resolution and use less power than conventional displays.

LMDS: Local Multipoint Distribution Service. A fixed, wireless, point-to-multipoint technology designed to distribute television signals.

Local Area Network (LAN): A computer network that is generally within one office or one building. A LAN can be very inexpensive and efficient to set up when small numbers of computers are involved. It may require a network administrator and a serious investment if hundreds of computers are hooked up to the LAN. A LAN enables all computers within the office to share files and printers, to access common databases and to send e-mail to others on the network.

Location Based Advertising (LBA): The ability for advertisers and information providers to push information to mobile consumers based on their locations. For example, GPS equipped cell phones have the potential to alert consumers on the go to nearby restaurants, entertainment attractions, and special sale events at retailers.

Location-Based Entertainment: The use of entertainment themes and attractions to draw consumers to specific locations, such as shopping malls, casinos and restaurants.

LOHAS: Lifestyles of Health and Sustainability. A marketing term that refers to consumers who choose to purchase and/or live with items that are natural, organic, less polluting, etc. Such consumers may also prefer products powered by alternative energy, such as hybrid cars.

Long Form Advertisement: Usually takes the form of a lengthy television commercial with entertaining and/or educational elements. These advertisements may be offered with other commercials or as links for viewers to click on for more information about the advertised product or service.

M2M: See "Machine-to-Machine (M2M)."

Machine-to-Machine (M2M): Refers to the transmission of data from one device to another, typically through wireless means such as Wi-Fi or cellular. For example, a Wi-Fi network might be employed to control several machines in a household from a central computer. Such machines might include air conditioning and entertainment systems. Wireless sensor networks (WSNs) will be a major growth factor in M2M communications, in everything from factory automation to agriculture and transportation. In logistics and retailing, M2M can refer to the use of RFID tags to transmit information. See "Radio Frequency Identification (RFID)."

MAN: See "Metropolitan Area Network (MAN)."

Market Segmentation: The division of a consumer market into specific groups of buyers based on demographic factors.

Marketing: Includes all planning and management activities and expenses associated with the promotion of a product or service. Marketing can encompass advertising, customer surveys, public relations and many other disciplines. Marketing is distinct from selling, which is the process of sell-through to the end user.

Mass Media: Refers to all media that disseminate information throughout the world, including television, radio, film, print, photography and electronic media.

Massively Multiplayer Online Role Playing Games (MMORPG): A genre of games in which users from anywhere in the world can connect to a central server, which hosts a virtual game environment. Players can then interact with one another in cooperative or adversarial game settings. Users often pay monthly subscription fees to access the content.

Mbps (Megabits per second): One million bits transmitted per second.

M-Commerce: Mobile e-commerce over wireless devices.

Media: Used loosely to refer to the entire communications system of reporters, editors, producers, print publications, broadcast programs, magazines and online publications.

Media Literacy: Refers to an individual's ability to read, analyze and evaluate media. If one is media literate, that person can recognize the rhetorical arguments and techniques used by the media to persuade audiences.

Media Object Server (MOS): An XML-based protocol designed to transfer information between newsroom automation systems and other systems, including media servers. The MOS protocol allows various devices to be controlled from a central device or piece of software, which limits the need to have operators stationed at multiple locations throughout the news studio.

Media Oriented Systems Transport (MOST): A standard adopted in 2004 by the Consumer Electronics

Association for the integration of or interface with consumer electronics (such as iPods) into entertainment systems in automobiles.

Media Outlet: A broadcast or publication that brings news and features to the public through a distribution channel.

Mega-Theater: A movie theater with as many as 30 screens and more frequent show times. Some also offer luxury seating, with amenities such as restaurant-style food, a wait staff and reservations.

Merchandising: Any marketing method utilized to foster sales growth.

Metropolitan Area Network (MAN): A data and communications network that operates over metropolitan areas and recently has been expanded to nationwide and even worldwide connectivity of high-speed data networks. A MAN can carry video and data.

Miles of Plant: The number of cable plant miles laid or strung by a cable system; the cable miles in place.

Millenials: See "Generation Y."

MMO: See "Massively Multiplayer Online Role Playing Games (MMORPG)."

MMORPG: See "Massively Multiplayer Online Role Playing Games (MMORPG)."

Mobile Apps: See "Apps."

Mobile Internet Device (MID): A small, personal, portable device that connects wirelessly to the Internet. Intel is a leading proponent of new devices that are mobile and convenient, and that enjoy powerful chips with long battery life.

Moblog: Mobile blog. This is a blog created by cell phone or other mobile device. It often consists largely of photos taken by a cell phone's built-in camera. Also, see "Blog (Web Log)."

Modem: A device that allows a computer to be connected to a phone line, which in turn enables the computer to receive and exchange data with other machines via the Internet.

MOS: See "Media Object Server (MOS)."

MOST: See "Media Oriented Systems Transport (MOST)."

MP3: A subsystem of MPEG used to compress sound into digital files. It is the most commonly used format for downloading music and audio books. MP3 compresses music significantly while retaining CD-like quality. MP3 players are personal, portable devices used for listening to music and audio book files. See "MPEG."

MPEG, MPEG-1, MPEG-2, MPEG-3, MPEG-4: Moving Picture Experts Group. It is a digital standard for the compression of motion or still video for transmission or storage. MPEGs are used in digital cameras and for Internet-based viewing.

MSO: See "Multiple System Operator (MSO)."

Multicasting: Sending data, audio or video simultaneously to a number of clients. Also known as broadcasting.

Multimedia: Refers to a presentation using several different media at once. For example, an encyclopedia in CD-ROM format is generally multimedia because it features written text, video and sound in one package.

Multiple System Operator (MSO): An individual or company owning two or more cable systems.

Multipoint Distribution System (MDS): A common carrier licensed by the FCC to operate a broadcast-like omni-directional microwave transmission facility within a given city. MDS carriers often pick up satellite pay-TV programming and distribute it, via their local MDS transmitter, to specially installed antennas and receivers.

NAFTA: See "North American Free Trade Agreement (NAFTA)."

NAICS: North American Industrial Classification System. See "Industry Code."

NAND: An advanced type of flash memory chip. It is popular for use in consumer electronics such as MP3 players and digital cameras.

Near Video On Demand (NVOD): An alternative method of VOD television programming delivery. NVOD delivers only a small portion of the ordered programming to the customer before playback. This initial download serves as a buffer while the rest of the programming is viewed directly off the provider's server. In contrast, traditional VOD typically involves the delivery of the entire ordered programming to the customer for playback from the customer's hard drive.

Network: In computing, a network is created when two or more computers are connected. Computers may be connected by wireless methods, using such technologies as 802.11b, or by a system of cables, switches and routers.

Network Numbers: The first portion of an IP address, which identifies the network to which hosts in the rest of the address are connected.

Network Personal Video Recording (nPVR): See "Server-Based SVOD Programming."

Network Storage: See "Network-Based VOD."

Network-Based VOD: Involves a television content provider storing either all or most of its programming content at its location, usually on its servers. Network-based VOD is more typical of cable TV than satellite TV.

New Media: A wide array of digital communication technologies, including Internet development tools and services, desktop and portable personal computers, workstations, servers, audio/video compression and editing equipment, graphics hardware and software, high-density storage services and video conferencing systems.

Newspaper Syndicate: A firm selling features, photos, columns, comic strips or other special material for publication in a large number of newspapers. For example, a typical fee charged by a syndicate to a daily newspaper for a popular comic strip is $10 per day. Generally, the syndicate splits the fee with the author.

Nielsen Ratings: Ratings created by ACNielsen, a company engaged in television audience ratings and other market research.

Nielsen Station Index (NSI): An index that rates individual television stations.

Nielsen Television Index (NTI): An index that rates national television network programming.

Non-Store Retailing: A form of retailing that is not store-based. Non-store retailing can be conducted through vending machines, direct-selling, direct-marketing, party-based selling, catalogs, television programming, telemarketing and Internet-based selling.

North American Free Trade Agreement (NAFTA): A trade agreement signed in December 1992 by U.S. President George H. W. Bush, Canadian Prime Minister Brian Mulroney and Mexican President Carlos Salinas de Gortari. The agreement eliminates tariffs on most goods originating in and traveling between the three member countries. It was approved by the legislatures of the three countries and had entered into force by January 1994. When it was created, NAFTA formed one of the largest free-trade areas of its kind in the world.

nPVR: See "Network Personal Video Recording (nPVR)."

NVOD: See "Near Video On Demand (NVOD)."

ODM: See "Original Design Manufacturer (ODM)."

OECD: See "Organisation for Economic Co-operation and Development (OECD)."

OEM: See "Original Equipment Manufacturer (OEM)."

Offshoring: The rapidly growing tendency among U.S., Japanese and Western European firms to send knowledge-based and manufacturing work overseas. The intent is to take advantage of lower wages and operating costs in such nations as China, India, Hungary and Russia. The choice of a nation for offshore work may be influenced by such factors as language and education of the local workforce, transportation systems or natural resources. For example, China and India are graduating high numbers of skilled engineers and scientists from their universities. Also, some nations are noted for large numbers of workers skilled in the English language, such as the Philippines and India. Also see "Captive Offshoring" and "Outsourcing."

OLED: See "Organic LED (OLED)."

On-Demand Advertising: See "Advertising-On-Demand."

On-Demand Video Magazines: Video clips concerning a variety of subjects offered by content providers as part of a VOD programming package.

Organic LED (OLED): A type of electronic display based on the use of organic materials that produce light when stimulated by electricity. Also see "Polymer," "Polymer Light Emitting Diode (PLED)," "Small Molecule Organic Light Emitting Diode (SMOLED)" and "Dendrimer."

Organisation for Economic Co-operation and Development (OECD): A group of more than 30 nations that are strongly committed to the market economy and democracy. Some of the OECD members include Japan, the U.S., Spain, Germany, Australia, Korea, the U.K., Canada and Mexico. Although not members, Estonia, Israel and Russia are invited to member talks; and Brazil, China, India, Indonesia and South Africa have enhanced engagement policies with the OECD. The Organisation provides statistics, as well as social and economic data; and researches social changes, including patterns in evolving fiscal policy, agriculture, technology, trade, the environment and other areas. It publishes over 250 titles annually; publishes a corporate magazine, the OECD Observer; has radio and TV studios; and has centers in Tokyo, Washington, D.C., Berlin and Mexico City that distributed the Organisation's work and organizes events.

Original Design Manufacturer (ODM): A contract manufacturer that offers complete, end-to-end design, engineering and manufacturing services. ODMs design and build products, such as consumer electronics, that client companies can then brand and sell as their own. For example, a large percentage of laptop computers, cell phones and PDAs are made by ODMs. Also see "Original Equipment Manufacturer (OEM)" and "Contract Manufacturing."

Original Equipment Manufacturer (OEM): 1) A company that manufactures a component (or a completed product) for sale to a customer that will integrate the component into a final product. The OEM's customer will put its own brand name on the end product and distribute or resell it to end users. 2) A firm that buys a component and then incorporates it into a final product, or buys a completed product and then resells it under the firm's own brand name. This usage is most often found in the computer industry, where OEM is sometimes used as a verb. Also see "Original Design Manufacturer (ODM)" and "Contract Manufacturing."

Out-of-Home Advertising: Advertising in public places through billboards, signs on buses, etc. Also referred to as outdoor advertising.

Outsourcing: The hiring of an outside company to perform a task otherwise performed internally by the company, generally with the goal of lowering costs and/or streamlining work flow. Outsourcing contracts are generally several years in length. Companies that hire outsourced services providers often prefer to focus on their core strengths while sending more routine tasks outside for others to perform. Typical outsourced services include the running of human resources departments, telephone call centers and computer departments. When outsourcing is performed overseas, it may be referred to as offshoring. Also see "Offshoring."

P2P: See "Peer-to-Peer (P2P)."

Parental Guidelines: A rating system established by the television industry in 1997, which gives parents information about the content and age-appropriateness of television programming.

Passive Optical Network (PON): A telecommunications network that brings high speed fiber optic cable all the way (or most of the way) to the end user. Also, see "Fiber to the Home (FTTH)."

Patent: An intellectual property right granted by a national government to an inventor to exclude others from making, using, offering for sale, or selling the invention throughout that nation or importing the invention into the nation for a limited time in exchange for public disclosure of the invention when the patent is granted. In addition to national patenting agencies, such as the United States Patent and Trademark Office, and regional organizations such as the European Patent Office, there is a cooperative international patent organization, the World Intellectual Property Organization, or WIPO, established by the United Nations.

Pay Cable: A network or service available for an added monthly fee. Also called premium cable. Some services, called mini-pay, are marketed at an average monthly rate below that of full-priced premium.

Pay Cable Unit: Each premium service to which a household subscribes.

Pay-Per-View (PPV): A service that enables television subscribers, including cable and satellite viewers, to order and view events or movies on an individual basis. PPV programming may include sporting events.

PDA: See "Personal Digital Assistant (PDA)."

Peer-to-Peer (P2P): Refers to a connection between computers that creates equal status between the computers. P2P can be used in an office or home to create a simple computer network. However, P2P more commonly refers to networks of computers that share information online. For example, peer-to-peer music sharing networks enable one member to search the hard drives of other members to locate music files and then download those files. These systems can be used for legal purposes. Nonetheless, they became notorious as systems that enable members to collect music and videos for free, circumventing copyright and other legal restrictions. At one time Napster was widely known as a P2P music system that enabled users to circumvent copyright.

Periodical: A publication that changes on a regular publishing schedule, such as weekly or monthly. (In contrast, a book that does not change on a regular basis is referred to as a monograph.)

Personal Digital Assistant (PDA): A handheld or pocket-size device containing address and calendar information, as well as e-mail, games and other features. A Blackberry is a PDA.

Personal Television (PTV): Television programming that has been manipulated to a viewer's personal taste. For example, the TiVo service allows viewers to eliminate commercials, watch programming stored in memory or watch selected real-time moments in slow motion.

Personal Video Recorder (PVR): See "Digital Video Recorder (DVR)."

Personalized VOD Entertainment: A VOD service that automatically detects household television viewing interests by monitoring the channel-surfing behavior of residents. The system uses this viewing data to select programming relevant to the household. The service can also deliver custom VOD libraries to PVRs.

PLED: See "Polymer Light Emitting Diode (PLED)."

Podcasting: The creation of audio files as webcasts. The name comes from the ability of these files to be used on iPods and portable MP3 players. They can also be listened to on personal computers. Podcasts can be anything from unique radio-like programming to sales pitches to audio press releases. Audio RSS (Real Simple Syndication) enables the broadcast of these audio files to appropriate parties. Also see "Real Simple Syndication (RSS)," "Video Blog (VLOG)" and "Blog (Web Log)."

Polymer: An organic or inorganic substance of many parts. Most common polymers, such as polyethylene and polypropylene, are organic. Organic polymers consist of molecules from organic sources (carbon compounds). Polymer means many parts. Generally, a polymer is constructed of many structural units (smaller, simpler molecules) that are joined together by a chemical bond. Some polymers are natural. For example, rubber is a natural polymer. Scientists have developed ways to manufacture synthetic polymers from organic materials. Plastic is a synthetic polymer.

Polymer Light Emitting Diode (PLED): An advanced technology that utilizes plastics (polymers) for the creation of electronic displays (screens). It is based on the use of organic polymers which emit light when stimulated with electricity. They are solution processable, which means they can be applied to substrates via ink jet printing. Also referred to as P-OLEDs.

Portal: A comprehensive web site that is designed to be the first site seen when a computer logs on to the web. Portal sites are aimed at broad audiences with common interests and often have links to e-mail usage, a search engine and other features. Yahoo! and msn.com are portals.

Positioning: The design and implementation of a merchandising mix, price structure and style of selling to create an image of the retailer, relative to its competitors, in the customer's mind.

Powerline: A method of networking computers, peripherals and appliances together via the electrical wiring that is built in to a home or office. Powerline competes with 802.11b and other wireless networking methods.

Pre-Boomer: A term occasionally used to describe people who were born between 1935 and 1945. They are somewhat older than Baby Boomers (born between 1946 and 1962). Also see "Baby Boomer."

Programmatic Buying: An automated method of placing advertising that enables advertisers to closely define the amount of money they want to spend along with the type of audience and behavior of the audience in which they are willing to invest. While programmitic buying was initially used in online advertising, it has since migrated to TV and other types of ads.

PTV: See "Personal Television (PTV)."

Publication: A printed magazine or newspaper containing information, news or feature stories.

PVR: See "Personal Video Recorder (PVR)."

Radio Frequency Identification (RFID): A technology that applies a special microchip-enabled tag to an individual item or piece of merchandise or inventory. RFID technology enables wireless, computerized tracking of that inventory item as it moves through the supply chain from factory to transport to warehouse to retail store or end user. Also known as radio tags.

Ratings/Rating Points/Ratings Share: The rating of a medium is its audience size expressed as a percentage of the measured market, where one rating point is equivalent to 1% of the base. Ratings are often referred to as "percent coverage." A television show with a 22% share has 22 points, or 22% of the total TV audience within its market.

RDF: See "Resource Description Framework (RDF)."

Reach: The geographic area inhabited by a potential audience. Also the number of readers, listeners or viewers that are able to access a given medium. A prime time television show on a national network such as ABC has nationwide reach.

Real Simple Syndication (RSS): Uses XML programming language to let web logs and other data be broadcast to appropriate web sites and users. Formerly referred to as RDF Site Summary or Rich Site Summary, RSS also enables the publisher to create a description of the content and its location in the form of an RSS document. Also useful for distributing audio files. See "Podcasting."

Real Time: A system or software product specially designed to acquire, process, store and display large amounts of rapidly changing information almost instantaneously, with microsecond responses as changes occur.

Recommendation-Based VOD: See "Personalized VOD Entertainment."

Resource Description Framework (RDF): A software concept that integrates many different software applications using XML as a syntax for the exchange of data. It is a core concept for development of the Semantic Web, an enhanced World Wide Web envisioned by W3C, the global organization that oversees development of the web. RDF may be useful for the syndication of news or the aggregation of all types of data for specific uses.

RFID: See "Radio Frequency Identification (RFID)."

RoHS Compliant: A directive that restricts the total amount of certain dangerous substances that may be incorporated in electronic equipment, including consumer electronics. Any RoHS compliant component is tested for the presence of Lead, Cadmium, Mercury, Hexavalent chromium, Polybrominated biphenyls and Polybrominated diphenyl ethers. For Cadmium and Hexavalent chromium, there must be less than 0.01% of the substance by weight at raw homogeneous materials level. For Lead, PBB, and PBDE, there must be no more than 0.1% of the material, when calculated by weight at raw homogeneous materials. Any RoHS compliant component must have 100 ppm or less of mercury and the mercury must not have been intentionally added to the component. Certain items of military and medical equipment are exempt from RoHS compliance.

RSS: See "Real Simple Syndication (RSS)."

SaaS: See "Software as a Service (SaaS)."

SACD: See "Super Audio Compact Disc (SACD)."

Satellite Broadcasting: The use of Earth-orbiting satellites to transmit, over a wide area, TV, radio, telephony, video and other data in digitized format.

Screencast: A digital video recording of activity on a computer desktop. Usually accompanied by voice-over narration, screencasts are usually used to demonstrate software, operating systems or web site features.

Semantic Web: An initiative started by the World Wide Web Consortium (W3C) that is focused on improving the way users access databases and online content by adding semantic metadata to content that will clearly define the relationships between data. Users will get much better search results, and web site developers will be able to create pages that update results and content based on related data on-the-fly. Data will automatically be shared across applications and across organizations.

Server: A computer that performs and manages specific duties for a central network such as a LAN. It may include storage devices and other peripherals. Competition within the server manufacturing industry is intense among leaders Dell, IBM, HP and others.

Server-Based SVOD Programming: Programming that is delivered directly to the customer's TV from where it is stored on the content provider's servers. In contrast, non-server-based SVOD (satellite TV) needs a storage device at the customer's location (such as a PVR or DVR) to store and play VOD content for the viewer's TV. Server-based SVOD surpasses non-server-based SVOD in its ability to simultaneously send or receive more than one video stream to or from the customer.

Servicemark (Service Mark): Similar to a trademark, except that it identifies and distinguishes the source of a service rather than a product. The servicemark may include a logo or other identifying word or mark meant to distinguish a service from others and indicate the provider of the service. An "SM" indicates that a servicemark has been applied for (or that the owner intends to protect the servicemark) but is still pending, while ® indicates it has been processed and is legally upheld. Servicemarks must be renewed on a regular basis with the appropriate regulatory authorities. In America, trademarks are registered with the U.S. Patent and Trademark Office. There are also cooperative, international servicemark and trademark agreements and agencies. (Also, see "Trademark, (Trade Mark).")

Set-Top Box: Sits on top of a TV set and provides enhancement to cable TV or other television reception. Typically a cable modem, this box may enable interactive enhancements to television viewing. For example, a cable modem is a set-top box that enables Internet access via TV cable. See "Cable Modem."

Share: In broadcasting, the percentage of television households tuned into a particular program or category of programming. The higher the share, the larger the amount that can be charged for advertising on the program. Also, with regard to the Internet, a web site feature that allows users to share content with others through e-mail or social networks. Content can include video, images, article links or other similar media.

SIC: Standard Industrial Classification. See "Industry Code."

SMAC: See "Social, Mobile, Analytics and Cloud (SMAC)."

Small Molecule Organic Light Emitting Diode (SMOLED): A type of organic LED that relies on expensive manufacturing methods. Newer technologies are more promising. See "Polymer" and "Polymer Light Emitting Diode (PLED)."

Smartphones: Mobile devices that have the capability to perform complex tasks and run user-generated programs. Newer devices include high-speed Internet access by connecting to wireless data services. Examples include Apple's iPhone, Research in Motion's BlackBerry and various devices with Google's Android operating system.

SMOLED: See "Small Molecule Organic Light Emitting Diode (SMOLED)."

Social Media (Social Networks): Sites on the Internet that feature user generated content (UGC). Such media include wikis, blogs and specialty web sites such as MySpace.com, Facebook, YouTube, Yelp and Friendster.com. Social media are seen as powerful online tools because all or most of the content is user-generated.

Software as a Service (SaaS): Refers to the practice of providing users with software applications that are hosted on remote servers and accessed via the Internet. Excellent examples include the CRM (Customer Relationship Management) software provided in SaaS format by Salesforce. An earlier technology that operated in a similar, but less sophisticated, manner was called ASP or Application Service Provider.

Spam: A term used to refer to generally unwanted, solicitous, bulk-sent e-mail. In recent years, significant amounts of government legislation have been passed in an attempt to limit the use of spam. Also, many types of software filters have been introduced in an effort to block spam on the receiving end. In addition to use for general advertising purposes, spam may be used in an effort to spread computer viruses or to commit financial or commercial fraud.

Specialty Publication: A trade or professional magazine that is industry- or audience-specific (e.g., Shopping Center World magazine).

Spot Revenue: Revenue from advertising placed on a cable system by a local or national advertiser.

Streaming Media: One-way audio and/or video that is compressed and transmitted over a data network. The media is viewed or heard almost as soon as data is fed to the receiver; there is usually a buffer period of a few seconds.

Subscriber: A term used interchangeably with household in describing cable, Internet access or telephone customers.

Subscription Video On Demand (SVOD): Allows subscribers unlimited access to selected VOD television programming for a fixed monthly fee.

Subsidiary, Wholly-Owned: A company that is wholly controlled by another company through stock ownership.

Super Audio Compact Disc (SACD): A technology that offers high-resolution digital audio.

Superstation: A local television station with a signal that is retransmitted via satellite to distant cable systems that cannot be reached by over-the-air signals.

Superstore: A large specialty store, usually over 40,000 square feet. Many superstores focus on a particular field of merchandise. For example, BestBuy is a consumer electronics superstore.

Supply Chain: The complete set of suppliers of goods and services required for a company to operate its business. For example, a manufacturer's supply chain may include providers of raw materials, components, custom-made parts and packaging materials.

SVOD: See "Subscription Video On Demand (SVOD)."

Syndicated: A report, story, television program, radio program or graphic that is sold to multiple media outlets simultaneously. For example, popular newspaper columns are commonly syndicated to various newspapers throughout the United States, but only one newspaper per market is allowed to participate.

System (Cable): A facility that provides cable television service in a given geographic area, consisting of one or more headends.

T1: A standard for broadband digital transmission over phone lines. Generally, it can transmit at least 24 voice channels at once over copper wires, at a high speed of 1.5 Mbps. Higher speed versions include T3 and OC3 lines.

T3: Transmission over phone lines that supports data rates of 45 Mbps. T3 lines consist of 672 channels, and such lines are generally used by Internet service providers. They are also referred to as DS3 lines.

Telecommunications: Systems and networks of hardware and software used to carry voice, video and/or data within buildings and between locations around the world. This includes telephone wires, satellite signals, wireless networks, fiber networks, Internet networks and related devices.

Telescopic On-Demand PVR/VOD Advertising: A short television commercial that offers the viewer access to another longer, related commercial. The commercial is called telescopic because it can be made longer if the viewer so desires.

Third Screen: Refers to the cell phone as a viewing device that is beyond the two primary screens used by consumers--the TV and the computer monitor.

Time Shifting: Services that allow viewers to digitally record television programs for playback at a later, more convenient time. Such services include video-on-demand (VOD) and personal TV services. Time shifting will eventually make up a significant portion of all television viewing.

Time-And-Channel-Based TV: See "Linear TV."

TiVo: A digital recorder that allows customers to record television shows through a hard disk and computer schedule instead of a videotape or manual recording set-up.

Trade Book Publishing: A type of publishing in which books for mainstream consumers are sold through typical retail book channels, such as physical and online book stores. Other types of book publishers include "professional and scholarly" and "educational."

Trademark (Trade Mark): A name or phrase that has been registered by a company or organization for its exclusive use. A "TM" indicates that a trademark has been applied for (or that the owner intends to protect the trademark) but is still pending, while ® indicates it has been processed and is legally upheld. A trademark may or may not include an accompanying, distinctive design or font for the word or phrase. Trademarks must be renewed on a regular basis with the appropriate regulatory authorities. In America, trademarks are registered with the U.S. Patent and Trademark Office. There are also cooperative, international trademark agreements and agencies.

Tradename (Trade Name): A name used to distinguish a product or service. (Also, see "Trademark (Trade Mark)" and "Servicemark (Service Mark).")

Transactional VOD: Allows VOD customers to pay a single price for a single VOD program or a set of programs rather than paying a set fee for a set amount of VOD programming (as in SVOD services).

True Video On Demand (TVOD): Offers VOD customers seamless interaction with the VOD system. TVOD allows users to not only order programs, but perform VCR-like commands at VCR-like speeds on the VOD system.

TV over IP: See "Internet Protocol Television (IPTV)."

TVOD: See "True Video On Demand (TVOD)."

UGC: See "User Generated Content (UGC)."

UHF: See "Ultra High Frequency (UHF)."

Ultra High Frequency (UHF): The frequency band ranging from 300 MHz to 3,000 MHz, which includes TV channels 14 through 83.

User Generated Content (UGC): Data contributed by users of interactive web sites. Such sites can include wikis, blogs, entertainment sites, shopping sites or social networks such as Facebook. UGC data can also include such things as product reviews, photos, videos, comments on forums, and how-to advice. Also see "Social Media (Social Networks)."

Value Added Tax (VAT): A tax that imposes a levy on businesses at every stage of manufacturing based on the value it adds to a product. Each business in the supply chain pays its own VAT and is subsequently repaid by the next link down the chain; hence, a VAT is ultimately paid by the consumer, being the last link in the supply chain, making it comparable to a sales tax. Generally, VAT only applies to goods bought for consumption within a given country; export goods are exempt from VAT, and purchasers from other countries taking goods back home may apply for a VAT refund.

V-Chip: A system built into TV sets that helps parents screen out programs with questionable parental guideline ratings. Consumers can purchase a special set-top box that performs the same function.

Very High Frequency (VHF): The frequency band ranging from 30 MHz to 300 MHz, which includes TV channels 2 through 13 and FM radio.

Very Small Aperture Terminal (VSAT): A small Earth station terminal, generally 0.6 to 2.4 meters in size, that is often portable and primarily designed to handle data transmission and private-line voice and video communications.

VHF: See "Very High Frequency (VHF)."

Video Blog (VLOG): The creation of video files as webcasts. VLOGs can be viewed on personal computers and wireless devices that are Internet-enabled. They can include anything from unique TV-like programming to sales pitches to music videos, news coverage or audio press releases. Online video is one of the fastest-growing segments in Internet usage. Leading e-commerce companies such as Microsoft, through its MSN service, Google and Yahoo!, as well as mainstream media firms such as Reuters, are making significant investments in online video services. Real Simple Syndication (RSS) enables the broadcasting of these files to appropriate parties. Also see "Real Simple Syndication (RSS)," "Podcasting" and "Blog (Web Log)."

Video On Demand (VOD): A system that allows customers to request programs or movies over cable or the Internet. Generally, the customer can select from an extensive list of titles. In some cases, a set-top device can be used to digitally record a broadcast for replay at a future date.

Virtual Reality: A life-like scene, representation or world that has been generated by computers. The website secondlife.com is a well known example.

VLOG: See "Video Blog (VLOG)."

VOD: See Video On Demand (VOD)."

VOD-Over-IP: VOD (video on demand) television viewing that is distributed via the Internet.

Web 2.0: Generally refers to the evolving system of advanced services available via the Internet. These services include collaborative sites that enable multiple users to create content such as wikis, sites such as photo-sharing services that share data among large or small groups and sites such as Friendster and MySpace that enable consumers to form groups of people with similar interests. Common features of Web 2.0 are tagging, social networks and folksonomies.

Web of Things: See "Internet of Things (IoT)."

Web Services: Self-contained modular applications that can be described, published, located and invoked over the World Wide Web or another network. Web services architecture evolved from object-oriented design and is geared toward e-business solutions. Microsoft Corporation is focusing on web services with its .NET initiative. Also see "Extensible Markup Language (XML)."

Weblog: See "Blog (Web Log)."

Webmaster: Any individual who runs a web site. Webmasters generally perform maintenance and upkeep.

WiDi (Wireless Display): A technology that is primarily used to connect television sets to a computer and thus to the Internet, wirelessly. In that manner, a laptop, PC or other device can access a movie or video which will be beamed to the TV set for viewing. Intel is a major proponent of WiDi.

WiFi: See "Wi-Fi."

Wi-Fi: A popular phrase that refers to 802.11 specifications. See "802.11g (Wi-Fi)."

Wiki: A web site that enables large or small groups of users to create and co-edit data. The best known example is Wikipedia, a high traffic web site that presents a public encyclopedia that is continuously written and edited by a vast number of volunteer contributors and editors who include both experts and enthusiasts in various subjects. Also, see "User Generated Content (UGC)."

WiMAX: An advanced wireless standard with significant speed and distance capabilities, WiMAX is officially known as the 802.16 standard. Using microwave technologies, it has the theoretical potential to broadcast at distances up to 30 miles and speeds of up to 70 Mbps. The mid-term goal of the WiMAX industry is to offer 15 Mbps speed for mobile WiMAX (802.16e) users and 40 Mbps for fixed WiMAX (802.16d) users. (The 802.XX standards are set by the IEEE (Institute of Electrical and Electronics Engineers). WiMax2, or 802.16m, will offer mobile access speeds of 170 to 300 Mbps.

Wire Service: An organization that sends news stories, features and other types of information by direct line to subscribing or member newspapers, radio stations and television stations. The Associated Press (AP) is a well-known wire service.

Wireless: Transmission of voice, video or data by a cellular telephone or other wireless device, as opposed to landline, telephone line or cable. It includes Wi-Fi,

WiMAX and other local or long-distance wireless methods.

Wireless Access Protocol (WAP): A technology that enables the delivery of World Wide Web pages in a smaller format readable by screens on cellular phones.

Wireless Cable: A pay television service that delivers multiple programming services to subscribers equipped with special antennae and tuners. It is an alternative to traditional, wired cable TV systems.

World Trade Organization (WTO): One of the only globally active international organizations dealing with the trade rules between nations. Its goal is to assist the free flow of trade goods, ensuring a smooth, predictable supply of goods to help raise the quality of life of member citizens. Members form consensus decisions that are then ratified by their respective parliaments. The WTO's conflict resolution process generally emphasizes interpreting existing commitments and agreements, and discovers how to ensure trade policies to conform to those agreements, with the ultimate aim of avoiding military or political conflict.

World Wide Web: A computer system that provides enhanced access to various sites on the Internet through the use of hyperlinks. Clicking on a link displayed in one document takes you to a related document. The World Wide Web is governed by the World Wide Web Consortium, located at www.w3.org. Also known as the web.

WoT: Web of Things. See "Internet of Things."

WTO: See "World Trade Organization (WTO)."

CPSIA information can be obtained
at www.ICGtesting.com
Printed in the USA
FFHW021034160219
50573690-55902FF